Football Outsiders™ Almanac 2018

THE ESSENTIAL GUIDE TO THE 2018 NFL AND COLLEGE FOOTBALL SEASONS

Edited by Aaron Schatz

With Ben Baldwin, Ian Boyd, Bill Connelly, Brian Fremeau,

Tom Gower, Scott Kacsmar, Derrik Klassen, Bryan Knowles,

Rivers McCown, Charles McDonald, Chad Peltier, Andrew Potter,

Mike Tanier, Vincent Verhei, Robert Weintraub, and Carl Yedor

Copyright 2018 EdjSports, LLC

ISBN-10: 172344474X
ISBN-13: 978-1723444746
All rights reserved

Table of Contents

NFL Players

College Football

Further Research

Introduction

The 2017 NFL season was a season of the unexpected. The Rams enjoyed one of the greatest year-to-year turn-arounds in NFL history. They made the playoffs for the first time in 13 seasons, one of four teams that made the playoffs after an extended postseason drought. The Titans had not made the playoffs in nine years. The Jaguars had not made it in ten years. And the Buffalo Bills had not made the playoffs in 18 years, finally breaking the curse of the Music City Miracle.

It was the season of the unexpected in part because of how the unexpected happened. At Football Outsiders, we've long observed that offenses are more consistent from year to year than defenses. But 2017 was the rare year where defense was more predictable than offense. Nine of our top dozen defenses from 2016 repeated in the top dozen in 2017. The same was true for only five of the top dozen offenses.

It was also the season of the unexpected because of the type of football that led to those unexpected results. For the entire decade, the NFL had moved more and more towards spread formations, becoming more and more dependent on the passing game. Every year, there was more 11 personnel (three wide receivers) and less base defense (four defensive backs). Every year there were more plays from the shotgun, and almost every year there were more passes and fewer runs.

In 2017, all these trends suddenly reversed themselves (Table 1). Offenses spread out less than the year before, and teams depended more on the ground game. It didn't get us back to where we were at the start of the decade, but it was definitely a change after years of strategy moving solely in one direction.

Table 1. Year-By-Year NFL Strategy Trends

Year	11 Personnel	Base D	Shotgun	Pct Runs	C%	NY/P
2011	40.4%	47.7%	40.8%	42.1%	60.1%	6.32
2012	45.7%	43.9%	47.4%	39.1%	60.9%	6.25
2013	51.2%	39.8%	59.1%	38.1%	61.5%	6.24
2014	54.2%	38.0%	60.7%	38.4%	62.6%	6.35
2015	54.7%	33.2%	62.4%	37.5%	63.0%	6.36
2016	60.4%	29.7%	64.4%	37.4%	63.0%	6.37
2017	59.3%	33.1%	59.8%	38.9%	62.1%	6.15

It wasn't just strategy that changed. Offenses were less successful than they had been in previous years, especially through the air. Completion rate and net yards per pass were down after hitting all-time highs in 2016. Interceptions and sacks went up. Scoring dropped to its lowest level since 2009. Even yards per carry dipped to its lowest average since 2007.

Have we reached peak passing in the NFL? Are defenses finally learning how to counter modern offenses, after years of offenses having the upper hand? Or was this a one-year blip, possibly caused by a high number of injuries to top quarterbacks in 2017?

The analytics you'll find in *Football Outsiders Almanac 2018* address these questions and more, going past the conventional wisdom for a deeper look inside the game. With our answers, we'll try to determine what's going to happen in the NFL this season.

At its heart, the football analytics revolution is about learning more about the intricacies of the game instead of just accepting the boilerplate storylines produced by insipid pregame shows and crotchety old players from the past. It's about not accepting the idea that some guy "just wins." It's about understanding that the "skill players" aren't the only guys on the team with skills. It's about gaining insight into the complexity behind the modern offense, and that you don't just shove the ball into the line hoping to gain yardage. It's about understanding the dramatic way that strength of schedule affects the way we see a team's performance, especially at the college level. It's about figuring out which player skills translate from college to the pros, and which skills just produce meaningless scoutspeak. And it's about accepting that the pass dominates the run in the National Football League, and that it has been that way for 30 years—even though things reversed a little bit in 2017.

There's more to this analysis than just numbers. Numbers are just one way to look at what happens on the football field. Words are the meat of our analysis; numbers are just the spice. There's a rumor that stat analysts don't watch game tape. In reality, stat analysts watch more tape than most beat writers or national Internet columnists, and *a lot* more tape than the average fan. We take everything we learn off the tape, synthesize it with the statistics, and deliver it to you.

Everybody who writes about football uses both statistics (whether they be basic yardage totals or more advanced stats like ours) and scouting (whether scouting reports by professionals or just their own eyes). The same goes for us, except that the statistics portion of our analysis is far more accurate than what you normally see from football coverage. Those numbers are based on two ideas:

1) **Conventional football statistics are heavily dependent on context.** If you want to see which teams are good and which are bad, which strategies work and which do not, you first need to filter out that context. Down and distance, field position, the current score, time left on the clock, the quality of the opponent—all of these elements influence the objective of the play and/or its outcome. Yet, the official NFL stats add together all yardage gained by a specific team or player without considering the impact of that particular yardage on wins and losses.

A close football game can turn on a single bounce of the ball. In a season of only 16 games, those effects can have a huge impact on a team's win-loss record, thus obscuring the team's true talent level. If we can filter out these bits of luck and random chance, we can figure out which teams are really more likely to play better for the rest of the season, or even in the following season.

2) **On any one play, the majority of the important action is not tracked by the conventional NFL play-by-play.** That's why we started the Football Outsiders game charting project in 2005. We now partner with both ESPN Stats & Info and Sports Info Solutions to collect data on every single NFL regular-season and postseason play. We know how many pass rushers teams send on each pass, how often teams go three-wide or use two tight ends, how often teams use a play-fake or a zone blitz, and which defensive backs are in coverage, even when they don't get a tackle in the standard play-by-play.

There's also a third important precept that governs the work we do at Football Outsiders, although it's more about how to interpret numbers and not the numbers themselves. **A player's production in one year does not necessarily equal his production the next year.** This also applies to teams, of course. Even when stats are accurate, they're often extremely variable from year to year and subject to heavy forces of regression to the mean. Field goal percentage, red zone performance, third-down performance on defense, interceptions and fumble recoveries—these are but a few examples. In addition, the age curves for football players are much steeper than in other sports. Old players break down faster, and young players often improve faster. Many football analysts concentrate on looking at what players did last year. We'll talk about that as well, but we're more interested in what players are going to do *this* year. Which performances from a year ago are flukes, and which ones represent long-term improvement or decline? What will one more year of experience do to this player's production? And how will a player's role change this year, and what does it mean for the team?

As with past books, *Football Outsiders Almanac 2018* starts off with "Pregame Show" (reviewing the most important research we've done in past books) and "Statistical Toolbox" (explaining all our stats). Once again, we preserve the ridiculousness of the football season for posterity with another version of "The Year in Quotes" and we introduce you to some of the more promising (and lesser-known) young bench players with our

12th annual list of Top 25 Prospects chosen in the third round or later. This year we also have a special essay busting some of the many myths about the running game in the NFL.

Each NFL team gets a full chapter covering what happened in 2017 and our projections for the upcoming season. Are there reasons to believe that the team was inherently better or worse than its record last year? What did the team do in the offseason, and what does that mean for the team's chances to win in 2018? Each chapter also includes all kinds of advanced statistics covering 2017 performance and strategic tendencies, plus detailed commentary on each of the major units of the team: offensive line, defensive front seven, defensive secondary, and special teams.

"Skill players" (by which we mean "players who get counted in fantasy football") get their own section in the back of the book. We list the major players at each position alphabetically, along with commentary and a 2018 KUBIAK projection that will help you win your fantasy football league. We also have the most accurate projections anywhere for two fantasy football positions that people wrongly consider impossible to predict: kickers and team defense.

Next comes our preview of the college football season. We go in-depth with the top 50 projected teams in the nation. Just like with our NFL coverage, the goal of our college previews is to focus as much as possible on "why" and how," not just "which team is better." We're not just here to rank the Football Bowl Subdivision teams from 1 to 130. We break things down to look at offense and defense, pass and run, and clear passing situations compared to all plays.

We hope our book helps you raise your level of football expertise, win arguments with your friends, and win your fantasy football league. Occasionally, there are also jokes. Just don't expect it all to be right. The unexpected is part of the fun.

Aaron Schatz
Natick, Mass.
July 19, 2018

P.S. Don't forget to visit FootballOutsiders.com every day for fresh coverage of the NFL and college football, plus the most intelligent football discussion threads on the Internet.

Pregame Show

It has now been 15 years since we launched Football Outsiders. In that time, we've done a lot of primary research on the National Football League, and we reference that research in many of the articles and comments in *Football Outsiders Almanac 2018*. New readers may come across an offhand comment in a team chapter about, for example, the idea that fumble recovery is not a skill, and wonder what in the heck we are talking about. We can't repeat all our research in every new edition of *Football Outsiders Almanac*, so we start each year with a basic look at some of the most important precepts that have emerged from Football Outsiders research. You will see these issues come up again and again throughout the book.

You can also find this introduction online at http://www.footballoutsiders.com/info/FO-basics, along with links to the original research in the cases in which that research appeared online instead of (or as well as) in print.

Our various methods for projecting NFL success for college prospects are not listed below, but are referenced at times during the book. Those methods are detailed in an essay on page 440.

You run when you win, not win when you run.

If we could only share one piece of anti-conventional wisdom with you before you read the rest of our book, this would be it. The first article ever written for Football Outsiders was devoted to debunking the myth of "establishing the run." There is no correlation whatsoever between giving your running backs a lot of carries early in the game and winning the game. Just running the ball is not going to help a team score; it has to run successfully.

Why does nearly every beat writer and television analyst still repeat the tired old school mantra that "establishing the run" is the secret to winning football games? The biggest issue is confusing cause and effect. There are exceptions, but for the most part, winning teams have a lot of carries because their running backs are running out the clock at the end of wins, not because they are running wild early in games.

A sister statement to "you have to establish the run" is "team X is 8-1 when running back John Doe runs for at least 100 yards." Unless John Doe is possessed by otherworldly spirits the way Adrian Peterson was a couple years ago, the team isn't winning because of his 100-yard games. He's putting up 100-yard games because his team is winning.

At this point, it's hard to figure out why so many commentators and fans still overrate the importance of the running game. One problem has always been history. Older NFL analysts and fans came of age during the 1970s, when the rules favored the running game much more than those in the modern NFL. We used to have to explain that optimal strategies from 1974 are not optimal strategies for today. But this would seem to be a smaller problem now than it was ten years ago; most current NFL analysts played the game in the '90s or beyond, when the game was heavily pass-centric.

Another issue may be a confusion of professional football with other levels. As you go down the football pyramid, from NFL teams to FBS to FCS to Division II and so on, down to high school, at every level further down the running game becomes more important. To give an example, the New Orleans Saints led the NFL last year with 4.7 yards per carry—but that average was lower than that of half the teams in the SEC. Strategies that win on Saturday do not necessarily win on Sunday.

A great defense against the run is nothing without a good pass defense.

This is a corollary to the absurdity of "establish the run." With rare exceptions, teams win or lose with the passing game more than the running game—and by stopping the passing game more than the running game. Ron Jaworski puts it best: "The pass gives you the lead, and the run solidifies it." The reason why teams need a strong run defense in the playoffs is not to shut the run down early; it's to keep the other team from icing the clock if they get a lead. You can't mount a comeback if you can't stop the run.

Note that "good pass defense" may mean "good pass rush" rather than "good defensive backs."

Running on third-and-short is more likely to convert than passing on third-and-short.

On average, passing will always gain more yardage than running, with one very important exception: when a team is just one or two yards away from a new set of downs or the goal line. On third-and-1, a run will convert for a new set of downs 36 percent more often than a pass. Expand that to all third or fourth downs with 1-2 yards to go, and the run is successful 40 percent more often. With these percentages, the possibility of a long gain with a pass is not worth the tradeoff of an incomplete that kills a drive.

This is one reason why teams have to be able to both run and pass. The offense also has to keep some semblance of balance so they can use their play-action fakes—you can't run a play fake from an empty set—and so the defense doesn't just run their nickel and dime packages all game. Balance also means that teams do need to pass occasionally in short-yardage situations; they just need to do it less than they do now. Teams pass roughly 60 percent of the time on third-and-2 even though runs in that situation convert 20 percent more often than passes. They pass 68 percent of the time on fourth-and-2 even though runs in that situation convert twice as often as passes.

Standard team rankings based on total yardage are inherently flawed.

Check out the schedule page on NFL.com, and you will find that each game is listed with league rankings based on total yardage. That is still how the NFL "officially" ranks teams, but these rankings rarely match up with common sense. That is because total team yardage may be the most context-dependent number in football.

It starts with the basic concept that rate stats are generally more valuable than cumulative stats. Yards per carry says more about a running back's quality than total yardage, completion percentage says more than just a quarterback's total number of completions. The same thing is true for teams; in fact, it is even more important because of the way football strategy influences the number of runs and passes in the game plan. Poor teams will give up fewer passing yards and more rushing yards because opponents will stop passing once they have a late-game lead and will run out the clock instead. For winning teams, the opposite is true. For example, which team had a better pass defense last year: Chicago or Philadelphia? The answer is obviously the Eagles, yet according to the official NFL rankings, Chicago (3,376 net yards allowed on 571 pass attempts, 6.9 net yards per pass) was a better pass defense than Philadelphia (3,637 net yards allowed on 639 pass attempts, 6.5 net yards per pass).

Total yardage rankings are also skewed because some teams play at a faster pace than other teams. For example, last year Arizona (5,026) had roughly the same number of yards as Tennessee (5,024). However, the Titans were the superior offense and much more efficient; they gained those yards on only 184 drives while the Cardinals needed 195 drives.

A team will score more when playing a bad defense and will give up more points when playing a good offense.

This sounds absurdly basic, but when people consider team and player stats without looking at strength of schedule, they are ignoring this. In 2012, for example, rookie Russell Wilson had a higher DVOA rating than fellow rookie Robert Griffin III because he faced a more difficult schedule, even though Griffin had slightly better standard stats.

If their overall yards per carry are equal, a running back who consistently gains yardage on every play is more valuable than a boom-and-bust running back who is frequently stuffed at the line but occasionally breaks a long highlight-worthy run.

Our brethren at Baseball Prospectus believe that the most precious commodity in baseball is outs. Teams only get 27 of them per game, and you can't afford to give one up for very little return. So imagine if there was a new rule in baseball that gave a team a way to earn another three outs in the middle of the inning. That would be pretty useful, right?

That's the way football works. You may start a drive 80 yards away from scoring, but as long as you can earn 10 yards in four chances, you get another four chances. Long gains have plenty of value, but if those long gains are mixed with a lot of short gains, you are going to put the quarterback in a lot of difficult third-and-long situations. That means more punts and more giving the ball back to the other team rather than moving the chains and giving the offense four more plays to work with.

The running back who gains consistent yardage is also going to do a lot more for you late in the game, when the goal of running the ball is not just to gain yardage but to eat clock time. If you are a Chargers fan watching your team with a late lead, you don't want to see three straight Melvin Gordon stuffs at the line followed by a punt. You want to see a game-icing first down.

A common historical misconception is that our preference for consistent running backs means that "Football Outsiders believes that Barry Sanders was overrated." Sanders wasn't just any boom-and-bust running back, though; he was the greatest boom-and-bust runner of all time, with bigger booms and fewer busts. Sanders ranked in the top five in DYAR five times (third in 1989, first in 1990, and second in 1994, 1996, and 1997).

Rushing is more dependent on the offensive line than people realize, but pass protection is more dependent on the quarterback himself than people realize.

Some readers complain that this idea contradicts the previous one. Aren't those consistent running backs just the product of good offensive lines? The truth is somewhere in between. There are certainly good running backs who suffer because their offensive lines cannot create consistent holes, but most boom-and-bust running backs contribute to their own problems by hesitating behind the line whenever the hole is unclear, looking for the home run instead of charging forward for the four-yard gain that keeps the offense moving.

As for pass protection, some quarterbacks have better instincts for the rush than others, and are thus better at getting out of trouble by moving around in the pocket or throwing the ball away. Others will hesitate, hold onto the ball too long, and lose yardage over and over.

Note that "moving around in the pocket" does not necessarily mean "scrambling." In fact, a scrambling quarterback will often take more sacks than a pocket quarterback, because while he's running around trying to make something happen, a defensive lineman will catch up with him.

Shotgun formations are generally more efficient than formations with the quarterback under center.

Over the past five seasons, offenses have averaged roughly 5.9 yards per play from Shotgun (or Pistol), but just 5.1 yards per play with the quarterback under center. This wide split exists even if you analyze the data to try to weed out biases like teams using Shotgun more often on third-and-long, or against prevent defenses in the fourth quarter. Shotgun offense is more efficient if you only look at the first half, on every down, and even if you only look at running back carries rather than passes and scrambles.

It's hard to think of a Football Outsiders axiom that has been better assimilated by the people running NFL teams since we started doing this a decade ago. In 2001, NFL teams only used Shotgun on 14 percent of plays. Five years later, in 2006, that had increased slightly, to 20 percent of plays. By 2012, Shotgun was used on a 47.5 percent of plays (including the Pistol, but not counting the Wildcat or other direct snaps to non-quarterbacks). In 2016, the league as a whole was up to an average of 64.4

percent of plays from Shotgun or Pistol. However last season, for the first time in recent years, usage of the Shotgun dropped, down to just 59.8 percent. It remains to be seen if this is a blip or a trend, or if the league stabilizes around 60 percent.

A running back with 370 or more carries during the regular season will usually suffer either a major injury or a loss of effectiveness the following year, unless he is named Eric Dickerson.

Terrell Davis, Jamal Anderson, and Edgerrin James all blew out their knees. Larry Johnson broke his foot. Earl Campbell and Eddie George went from legendary powerhouses to plodding, replacement-level players. Shaun Alexander broke his foot *and* became a plodding, replacement-level player. This is what happens when a running back is overworked to the point of having at least 370 carries during the regular season. DeMarco Murray was the latest player to follow up a high workload with a disappointing season.

The "Curse of 370" was expanded in our book *Pro Football Prospectus 2005* and includes seasons with 390 or more carries in the regular season and postseason combined. Research also shows that receptions don't cause a problem, only workload on the ground.

Plenty of running backs get injured without hitting 370 carries in a season, but there is a clear difference. On average, running backs with 300 to 369 carries and no postseason appearance will see their total rushing yardage decline by 15 percent the following year and their yards per carry decline by two percent. The average running back with 370 or more regular-season carries, or 390 including the postseason, will see their rushing yardage decline by 35 percent, and their yards per carry decline by eight percent. However, the Curse of 370 is not a hard and fast line where running backs suddenly become injury risks. It is more of a concept where 370 carries roughly represent the point at which additional carries start to become more and more of a problem.

Wide receivers must be judged on both complete and incomplete passes.

Here's an example from last season: Tyrell Williams of the Chargers had 728 receiving yards while Josh Doctson of Washington had just 502 receiving yards, even though Doctson was targeted more often than Williams. Both receivers played with good quarterbacks, and each ran his average route roughly 14 yards downfield. But there was a big difference between them: Williams caught 62 percent of intended passes, while Doctson caught only 45 percent.

Some work has been done on splitting responsibility for incomplete passes between quarterbacks and receivers, but not enough that we can incorporate this into our advanced stats at this time. We know that wide receiver catch rates are almost as consistent from year to year as quarterback completion percentages, but it is also important to look at catch rate in the context of the types of routes each receiver runs. A few years ago, we expanded on this idea with a new plus-minus metric, which is explained in the introduction to the chapter on wide receivers and tight ends.

The total quality of an NFL team is four parts offense, three parts defense, and one part special teams.

There are three units on a football team, but they are not of equal importance. Work by Chase Stuart, Neil Paine, and Brian Burke suggests a split between offense and defense of roughly 58-42, without considering special teams. Our research suggests that special teams contributes about 13 percent to total performance; if you measure the remaining 87 percent with a 58-42 ratio, you get roughly 4:3:1. When we compare the range of offense, defense, and special teams DVOA ratings, we get the same results, with the best and worst offenses roughly 130 percent stronger than the best and worst defenses, and roughly four times stronger than the best and worst special teams.

Offense is more consistent from year to year than defense, and offensive performance is easier to project than defensive performance. Special teams is less consistent than either.

Nobody in the NFL understood this concept better than former Indianapolis Colts general manager Bill Polian. Both the Super Bowl champion Colts and the four-time AFC champion Buffalo Bills of the early 1990s were built around the idea that if you put together an offense that can dominate the league year after year, eventually you will luck into a year where good health and a few smart decisions will give you a defense good enough to win a championship. (As the Colts learned in 2006, you don't even need a year, just four weeks.) Even the New England Patriots, who are led by a defense-first head coach in Bill Belichick, have been more consistent on offense than on defense since they began their run of success in 2001.

Field goal percentage is almost entirely random from season to season, while kickoff distance is one of the most consistent statistics in football.

This theory, which originally appeared in the *New York Times* in October 2006, is one of our most controversial, but it is hard to argue against the evidence. Measuring every kicker from 1999 to 2006 who had at least ten field goal attempts in each of two consecutive years, the year-to-year correlation coefficient for field goal percentage was an insignificant .05. Mike Vanderjagt didn't miss a single field goal in 2003, but his percentage was a below-average 74 percent the year before and 80 percent the year after. Adam Vinatieri has long been considered the best kicker in the game. But even he had never enjoyed two straight seasons with accuracy better than the NFL average of 85 percent until 2010 and 2011.

On the other hand, the year-to-year correlation coefficient for kickoff distance, over the same period as our measurement of field goal percentage and with the same minimum of ten kicks per year, is .61. The same players consistently lead the league in kickoff distance. In recent years, that group includes Steven Hauschka, Graham Gano, Dustin Hopkins, and Justin Tucker.

Teams with more offensive penalties generally lose more games, but there is no correlation between defensive penalties and losses.

Specific defensive penalties of course lose games; we've all sworn at the television when the cornerback on our favorite team gets flagged for a 50-yard pass interference penalty. Yet overall, there is no correlation between losses and the total of defensive penalties or even the total yardage on defensive penalties. One reason is that defensive penalties often represent *good* play, not bad. Cornerbacks who play tight coverage may be just on the edge of a penalty on most plays, only occasionally earning a flag. Defensive ends who get a good jump on rushing the passer will gladly trade an encroachment penalty or two for ten snaps where they get off the blocks a split-second before the linemen trying to block them.

In addition, offensive penalties have a higher correlation from year to year than defensive penalties. The penalty that correlates highest with losses is the false start, and the penalty that teams will have called most consistently from year to year is also the false start.

Recovery of a fumble, despite being the product of hard work, is almost entirely random.

Stripping the ball is a skill. Holding onto the ball is a skill. Pouncing on the ball as it is bouncing all over the place is not a skill. There is no correlation whatsoever between the percentage of fumbles recovered by a team in one year and the percentage they recover in the next year. The odds of recovery are based solely on the type of play involved, not the teams or any of their players.

The New England Patriots are a good example. In 2016, the Patriots defense recovered 12 of 15 fumbles by opponents. Last year, the same defense recovered only 4 of 12 fumbles by opponents.

Fumble recovery is equally erratic on offense. In 2016, the Pittsburgh Steelers recovered only 6 of 18 fumbles on offense. In 2017, the Steelers recovered 9 of 13 fumbles.

Fumble recovery is a major reason why the general public overestimates or underestimates certain teams. Fumbles are huge, turning-point plays that dramatically impact wins and losses in the past, while fumble recovery percentage says absolutely nothing about a team's chances of winning games in the future. With this in mind, Football Outsiders stats treat all fumbles as equal, penalizing them based on the likelihood of each type of fumble (run, pass, sack, etc.) being recovered by the defense.

Other plays that qualify as "non-predictive events" include two-point conversions, blocked kicks, and touchdowns during turnover returns. These plays are not "lucky," per se, but they have no value whatsoever for predicting future performance.

Field position is fluid.

As discussed in the Statistical Toolbox, every yard line on the field has a value based on how likely a team is to score from that location on the field as opposed to from a yard further back. The change in value from one yard to the next is the same whether the team has the ball or not. The goal of a defense is not just to prevent scoring, but to hold the opposition so that the offense can get the ball back in the best possible field position. A bad offense will score as many points as a good offense if it starts each drive five yards closer to the goal line.

A corollary to this precept: The most underrated aspect of an NFL team's performance is the field position gained or lost on kickoffs and punts. This is part of why players such as Tyler Lockett and Cordarrelle Patterson can have such an impact on the game, even when they aren't taking a kickoff or punt all the way back for a touchdown.

The red zone is the most important place on the field to play well, but performance in the red zone from year to year is much less consistent than overall performance.

Although play in the red zone has a disproportionately high importance to the outcome of games relative to plays on the rest of the field, NFL teams do not exhibit a level of performance in the red zone that is consistently better or worse than their performance elsewhere, year after year. The simplest explanation why is a small(er) sample size and the inherent variance of football, with contributing factors like injuries and changes in personnel.

Injuries regress to the mean on the seasonal level, and teams that avoid injuries in a given season tend to win more games.

There are no doubt teams with streaks of good or bad health over multiple years. However, teams who were especially healthy or especially unhealthy, as measured by our adjusted games lost (AGL) metric, almost always head towards league average in the subsequent season. Furthermore, injury—or the absence thereof—has a huge correlation with wins, and a significant impact on a team's success. There's no doubt that a few high-profile teams have resisted this trend in recent years. The Patriots often deal with a high number of injuries, and the 2017 Eagles obviously overcame a number of important injuries to win the championship. Nonetheless, the overall rule still applies. Last year, six of the seven teams with the lowest AGL made the playoffs: the Los Angeles Rams, Atlanta, Tennessee, Pittsburgh, Jacksonville, and Carolina. Meanwhile, only one of the ten teams with the highest AGL made the playoffs, New Orleans at No. 24.

By and large, a team built on depth is better than a team built on stars and scrubs.

Connected to the previous statement, because teams need to go into the season expecting that they will suffer an average number of injuries no matter how healthy they were the previous year. You cannot concentrate your salaries on a handful of star players because there is no such thing as avoiding injuries in the NFL. The game is too fast and the players too strong to build a team based around the idea that "if we can avoid all injuries this year, we'll win."

Running backs usually decline after age 28, tight ends after age 29, wide receivers after age 30, and quarterbacks after age 32.

This research was originally done by Doug Drinen (editor

of pro-football-reference.com) in 2000. In recent years, a few players have had huge seasons above these general age limits, but the peak ages Drinen found a few years ago still apply to the majority of players.

As for "non-skill players," research we did in 2007 for *ESPN The Magazine* suggested that defensive ends and defensive backs generally begin to decline after age 29, linebackers and offensive linemen after age 30, and defensive tackles after age 31. However, because we still have so few statistics to use to study linemen and defensive players, this research should not be considered definitive.

The strongest indicator of how a college football team will perform in the upcoming season is their performance in recent seasons.

It may seem strange because graduation enforces constant player turnover, but college football teams are actually much more consistent from year to year than NFL teams. Thanks in large part to consistency in recruiting, teams can be expected to play within a reasonable range of their baseline program expectations each season. Our Program F/+ ratings, which represent a rolling five-year period of play-by-play and drive efficiency data, have an extremely strong (.76) correlation with the next year's F/+ rating.

Championship teams are generally defined by their ability to dominate inferior opponents, not their ability to win close games.

Football games are often decided by just one or two plays: a missed field goal, a bouncing fumble, the subjective spot of an official on fourth-and-1. One missed assignment by a cornerback or one slightly askew pass that bounces off a receiver's hands and into those of a defensive back five yards away and the game could be over. In a blowout, however, one lucky bounce isn't going to change things. Championship teams—in both professional and college football—typically beat their good opponents convincingly and destroy the cupcakes on the schedule.

Aaron Schatz

Statistical Toolbox

After 15 years of Football Outsiders, some of our readers are as comfortable with DVOA and ALY as they are with touchdowns and tackles. Yet to most fans, including our newer readers, it still looks like a lot of alphabet soup. That's what this chapter is for. The next few pages define and explain all of all the unique NFL statistics you'll find in this book: how we calculate them, what the numbers mean, and what they tell us about why teams win or lose football games. We'll go through the information in each of the tables that appear in each team chapter, pointing out whether those stats come from advanced mathematical manipulation of the standard play-by-play or tracking what we see on television with the Sports Info Solutions game charting project. This chapter covers NFL statistics only. College metrics such as Highlight Yards and F/+ are explained in the introduction to the college football section on page 384.

We've done our best to present these numbers in a way that makes them easy to understand. This explanation is long, so feel free to read some of it, flip around the rest of the book, and then come back. It will still be here.

Defense-Adjusted Value Over Average (DVOA)

One running back runs for three yards. Another running back runs for three yards. Which is the better run?

This sounds like a stupid question, but it isn't. In fact, this question is at the heart of nearly all of the analysis in this book.

Several factors can differentiate one three-yard run from another. What is the down and distance? Is it third-and-2, or second-and-15? Where on the field is the ball? Does the player get only three yards because he hits the goal line and scores? Is the player's team up by two touchdowns in the fourth quarter and thus running out the clock, or down by two touchdowns and thus facing a defense that is playing purely against the pass? Is the running back playing against the porous defense of the Chiefs, or the stalwart defense of the Vikings?

Conventional NFL statistics value plays based solely on their net yardage. The NFL determines the best players by adding up all their yards no matter what situations they came in or how many plays it took to get them. Now, why would they do that? Football has one objective—to get to the end zone—and two ways to achieve that, by gaining yards and achieving first downs. These two goals need to be balanced to determine a player's value or a team's performance. All the yards in the world won't help a team win if they all come in six-yard chunks on third-and-10.

The popularity of fantasy football only exacerbates the problem. Fans have gotten used to judging players based on how much they help fantasy teams win and lose, not how much they help *real* teams win and lose. Typical fantasy scoring further skews things by counting the yard between the one and the goal line as 61 times more important than all the other yards on the field (each yard worth 0.1 points, a touchdown worth 6.0). Let's say DeAndre Hopkins catches a pass on third-and-15 and goes 50 yards but gets tackled two yards from the goal line, and then Lamar Miller takes the ball on first-and-goal from the two-yard line and plunges in for the score. Has Miller done something special? Not really. When an offense gets the ball on first-and-goal at the two-yard line, they are going to score a touchdown five out of six times. Miller is getting credit for the work done by the passing game.

Doing a better job of distributing credit for scoring points and winning games is the goal of **DVOA**, or Defense-adjusted Value Over Average. DVOA breaks down every single play of the NFL season, assigning each play a value based on both total yards and yards towards a first down, based on work done by Pete Palmer, Bob Carroll, and John Thorn in their seminal book, *The Hidden Game of Football*. On first down, a play is considered a success if it gains 45 percent of needed yards; on second down, a play needs to gain 60 percent of needed yards; on third or fourth down, only gaining a new first down is considered success.

We then expand upon that basic idea with a more complicated system of "success points," improved over the past four years with a lot of mathematics and a bit of trial and error. A successful play is worth one point, an unsuccessful play zero points with fractional points in between (for example, eight yards on third-and-10 is worth 0.54 "success points"). Extra points are awarded for big plays, gradually increasing to three points for 10 yards (assuming those yards result in a first down), four points for 20 yards, and five points for 40 yards or more. Losing three or more yards is minus-1 point. Interceptions average minus-6 points, with an adjustment for the length of the pass and the location of the interception (since an interception tipped at the line is more likely to produce a long return than an interception on a 40-yard pass). A fumble is worth anywhere from minus-1.7 to minus-4.0 points depending on how often a fumble in that situation is lost to the defense—no matter who actually recovers the fumble. Red zone plays get a bonus: 20 percent for team offense, five percent for team defense, and 10 percent for individual players. There is a bonus given for a touchdown that acknowledges that the goal line is significantly more difficult to cross than the previous 99 yards (although this bonus is nowhere near as large as the one used in fantasy football).

(Our system is a bit more complex than the one in *Hidden Game* thanks to our subsequent research, which added larger penalty for turnovers, the fractional points, and a slightly higher baseline for success on first down. The reason why all fumbles are counted, no matter whether they are recovered by the offense or defense, is explained in the essay "Pregame Show.")

Every single play run in the NFL gets a "success value"

based on this system, and then that number gets compared to the average success values of plays in similar situations for all players, adjusted for a number of variables. These include down and distance, field location, time remaining in game, and the team's lead or deficit in the game score. Teams are always compared to the overall offensive average, as the team made its own choice whether to pass or rush. When it comes to individual players, however, rushing plays are compared to other rushing plays, passing plays to other passing plays, tight ends to tight ends, wideouts to wideouts, and so on.

Going back to our example of the three-yard rush, if Player A gains three yards under a set of circumstances in which the average NFL running back gains only one yard, then Player A has a certain amount of value above others at his position. Likewise, if Player B gains three yards on a play on which, under similar circumstances, an average NFL back gains four yards, that Player B has negative value relative to others at his position. Once we make all our adjustments, we can evaluate the difference between this player's rate of success and the expected success rate of an average running back in the same situation (or between the opposing defense and the average defense in the same situation, etc.). Add up every play by a certain team or player, divide by the total of the various baselines for success in all those situations, and you get VOA, or Value Over Average.

Of course, the biggest variable in football is the fact that each team plays a different schedule against teams of disparate quality. By adjusting each play based on the opposing defense's average success in stopping that type of play over the course of a season, we get DVOA, or Defense-adjusted Value Over Average. Rushing and passing plays are adjusted based on down and location on the field; passing plays are also adjusted based on how the defense performs against passes to running backs, tight ends, or wide receivers. Defenses are adjusted based on the average success of the *offenses* they are facing. (Yes, technically the defensive stats are "offense-adjusted." If it seems weird, think of the "D" in "DVOA" as standing for "opponent-Dependent" or something.)

The biggest advantage of DVOA is the ability to break teams and players down to find strengths and weaknesses in a variety of situations. In the aggregate, DVOA may not be quite as accurate as some of the other, similar "power ratings" formulas based on comparing drives rather than individual plays, but, unlike those other ratings, DVOA can be separated not only by player, but also by down, or by week, or by distance needed for a first down. This can give us a better idea of not just which team is better, but why, and what a team has to do in order to improve itself in the future. You will find DVOA used in this book in a lot of different ways—because it takes every single play into account, it can be used to measure a player or a team's performance in any situation. All Pittsburgh third downs can be compared to how an average team does on third down. Joe Flacco and Lamar Jackson can each be compared to how an average quarterback performs in the red zone, or with a lead, or in the second half of the game.

Since it compares each play only to plays with similar circumstances, it gives a more accurate picture of how much bet-

ter a team really is compared to the league as a whole. The list of top DVOA offenses on third down, for example, is more accurate than the conventional NFL conversion statistic because it takes into account that converting third-and-long is more difficult than converting third-and-short, and that a turnover is worse than an incomplete pass because it eliminates the opportunity to move the other team back with a punt on fourth down.

One of the hardest parts of understanding a new statistic is interpreting its scale, or what numbers represent good performance or bad performance. We've made that easy with DVOA. For each season, ratings are normalized so that 0% represents league average. A positive DVOA represents a situation that favors the offense, while a negative DVOA represents a situation that favors the defense. This is why the best offenses have positive DVOA ratings (last year, New England led the NFL at 27.3%) and the best defenses have negative DVOA ratings (with Jacksonville on top at -16.2%).

The scale of offensive ratings is wider than the scale of defensive ratings. In most years, the best and worst offenses tend to rate around +/- 30%, while the best and worst defenses tend to rate around +/- 20%. For starting players, the scale tends to reach roughly +/-40% for passing and receiving, and +/- 30% for rushing. As you might imagine, some players with fewer attempts will surpass both extremes.

Team DVOA totals combine offense and defense by subtracting the latter from the former because the better defenses will have negative DVOA ratings. (Special teams performance is also added, as described later in this essay.) Certain plays are counted in DVOA for offense and not for defense, leading to separate baselines on each side of the ball. In addition, although the league ratings for offense and defense are always 0%, the league averages for passing and rushing separately are *not* 0%. Because passing is more efficient than rushing, the average for team passing is almost always positive and the average for team rushing is almost always negative. However, ratings for individual players only compare passes to other passes and runs to other runs, so the league average for individual passing is 0%, as are the league averages for rushing and the three separate league averages for receiving by wide receivers, tight ends, and running backs.

Some other important notes about DVOA:

- Only four penalties are included in DVOA. Two penalties count as pass plays on both sides of the ball: intentional grounding and defensive pass interference. The other two penalties are included for offense only: false starts and delay of game. Because the inclusion of these penalties means a group of negative plays that don't count as either passes or runs, the league averages for pass offense and run offense are higher than the league averages for pass defense and run defense.

- Aborted snaps and incomplete backwards lateral passes are only penalized on offense, not rewarded on defense.

- Adjustments for playing from behind or with a lead in the fourth quarter are different for offense and defense, as are adjustments for the final two minutes of the first half when the offense is not near field goal range.

- Offense gets a slight penalty and defense gets a slight bonus for games indoors.

How well does DVOA work? Using correlation coefficients, we can show that only actual points scored are better than DVOA at indicating how many games a team has won (Table 1) and DVOA is a does a better job of predicting wins in the coming season than either wins or points scored in the previous season (Table 2).

(Correlation coefficient is a statistical tool that measures how two variables are related by using a number between 1 and minus-1. The closer to minus-1 or 1, the stronger the relationship, but the closer to 0, the weaker the relationship.)

Table 1. Correlation of Various Stats to Wins, 2006-2017

Stat	Offense	Defense	Total
Points Scored/Allowed	.759	-.693	.917
DVOA	.715	-.481	.864
Yards Gained/Allowed	.546	-.374	.672
Yards Gained/Allowed per Play	.543	-.353	.705

Table 2. Correlation of Various Stats to Wins Following Year, 2006-2017

Stat	Correlation
DVOA	.388
Point Differential	.385
Pythagorean Wins	.383
Yardage Differential	329
Wins	.328
Yards per Play Differential	.319

Special Teams

The problem with a system based on measuring both yardage and yardage towards a first down is what to do with plays that don't have the possibility of a first down. Special teams are an important part of football and we needed a way to add that performance to the team DVOA rankings. Our special teams metric includes five separate measurements: field goals and extra points, net punting, punt returns, net kickoffs, and kick returns.

The foundation of most of these special teams ratings is the concept that each yard line has a different value based on the likelihood of scoring from that position on the field. In *Hidden Game*, the authors suggested that the each additional yard for the offense had equal value, with a team's own goal line being worth minus-2 points, the 50-yard line 2 points, and the opposing goal line 6 points. (-2 points is not only the value of a safety, but also reflects the fact that when a team is backed up in its own territory, it is likely that its drive will stall, forcing a punt that will give the ball to the other team in good field position. Thus, the negative point value reflects the fact that the defense is more likely to score next.) Our studies have updated this concept to reflect the actual likelihood that the offense or defense will have the next score from a given position on the field based on actual results from the past few seasons. The line that represents the value of field position is not straight, but curved, with the value of each yard increasing as teams approach either goal line.

Our special teams ratings compare each kick or punt to league average based on the point value of the position of the kick, catch, and return. We've determined a league average for how far a kick goes based on the line of scrimmage for each kick (almost always the 35-yard line for kickoffs, variable for punts) and a league average for how far a return goes based on both the yard line where the ball is caught and the distance that it traveled in the air.

The kicking or punting team is rated based on net points compared to average, taking into account both the kick and the return if there is one. Because the average return is always positive, punts that are not returnable (touchbacks, out of bounds, fair catches, and punts downed by the coverage unit) will rate higher than punts of the same distance which are returnable. (This is also true of touchbacks on kickoffs.) There are also separate individual ratings for kickers and punters that are based on distance and whether the kick is returnable, assuming an average return in order to judge the kicker separate from the coverage.

For the return team, the rating is based on how many points the return is worth compared to average, based on the location of the catch and the distance the ball traveled in the air. Return teams are not judged on the distance of kicks, nor are they judged on kicks that cannot be returned. As explained below, blocked kicks are so rare as to be statistically insignificant as predictors for future performance and are thus ignored. For the kicking team they simply count as missed field goals, for the defense they are gathered with their opponents' other missed field goals in Hidden value (also explained below).

Field goal kicking is measured differently. Measuring kickers by field goal percentage is a bit absurd, as it assumes that all field goals are of equal difficulty. In our metric, each field goal is compared to the average number of points scored on all field goal attempts from that distance over the past 15 years. The value of a field goal increases as distance from the goal line increases. Kickoffs, punts, and field goals are then adjusted based on weather and altitude. It will surprise no one to learn that it is easier to kick the ball in Denver or a dome than it is to kick the ball in Buffalo in December. Because we do not yet have enough data to tailor our adjustments specifically to each stadium, each one is assigned to one of four categories: Cold, Warm, Dome, and Denver. There is also an additional adjustment dropping the value of field goals in Florida (because the warm temperatures allow the ball to carry better).

The baselines for special teams are adjusted in each year for rule changes such as the introduction of the special teams-only "k-ball" in 1999, movement of the kickoff line, and the 2016 change in kickoff touchbacks. Baselines have also been adjusted each year to make up for the gradual improvement of kickers over the last two decades, and a new baseline was set two years ago for the longer distance on extra points.

Once we've totaled how many points above or below average can be attributed to special teams, we translate those points into DVOA so the ratings can be added to offense and defense to get total team DVOA.

There are three aspects of special teams that have an impact on wins and losses, but don't show up in the standard special teams rating because a team has little or no influence on them. The first is the length of kickoffs by the opposing team, with an asterisk. Obviously, there are no defenders standing on the 35-yard line, ready to block a kickoff after the whistle blows. However, over the past few years, some teams have deliberately kicked short in order to avoid certain top return men, such as Devin Hester and Cordarrelle Patterson. The special teams formula now includes adjustments to give teams extra credit for field position on kick returns if kickers are deliberately trying to avoid a return.

The other two items that special teams have little control over are field goals against your team, and punt distance against your team. Research shows no indication that teams can influence the accuracy or strength of field goal kickers and punters, except for blocks. As mentioned above, although blocked field goals and punts are definitely skillful plays, they are so rare that they have no correlation to how well teams have played in the past or will play in the future, thus they are included here as if they were any other missed field goal or botched punt, giving the defense no additional credit for their efforts. The value of these three elements is listed separately as "Hidden" value.

Special teams ratings also do not include two-point conversions or onside kick attempts, both of which, like blocks, are so infrequent as to be statistically insignificant in judging future performance.

Defense-Adjusted Yards Above Replacement (DYAR)

DVOA is a good stat, but of course it is not a perfect one. One problem is that DVOA, by virtue of being a percentage or rate statistic, doesn't take into account the cumulative value of having a player producing at a league-average level over the course of an above-average number of plays. By definition, an average level of performance is better than that provided by half of the league and the ability to maintain that level of performance while carrying a heavy work load is very valuable indeed. In addition, a player who is involved in a high number of plays can draw the defense's attention away from other parts of the offense, and, if that player is a running back, he can take time off the clock with repeated runs.

Let's say you have a running back who carries the ball 300 times in a season. What would happen if you were to remove this player from his team's offense? What would happen to those 300 plays? Those plays don't disappear with the player, though some might be lost to the defense because of the associated loss of first downs. Rather those plays would have to be distributed among the remaining players in the offense, with

the bulk of them being given to a replacement running back. This is where we arrive at the concept of replacement level, borrowed from our friends at Baseball Prospectus. When a player is removed from an offense, he is usually not replaced by a player of similar ability. Nearly every starting player in the NFL is a starter because he is better than the alternative. Those 300 plays will typically be given to a significantly worse player, someone who is the backup because he doesn't have as much experience and/or talent. A player's true value can then be measured by the level of performance he provides above that replacement level baseline, totaled over all of his run or pass attempts.

Of course, the *real* replacement player is different for each team in the NFL. Two years ago, the player who originally was the backup running back in Chicago (Jordan Howard) ended up as the starter with a much higher DVOA than original starter Jeremy Langford. Sometimes a player such as Dion Lewis will be cut by one team and turn into a star for another. On other teams, the drop from the starter to the backup can be even greater than the general drop to replacement level. (The 2011 Indianapolis Colts will be the hallmark example of this until the end of time.) The choice to start an inferior player or to employ a sub-replacement level backup, however, falls to the team, not the starter being evaluated. Thus we generalize replacement level for the league as a whole as the ultimate goal is to evaluate players independent of the quality of their teammates.

Our estimates of replacement level are computed differently for each position. For quarterbacks, we analyzed situations where two or more quarterbacks had played meaningful snaps for a team in the same season, then compared the overall DVOA of the original starters to the overall DVOA of the replacements. We did not include situations where the backup was actually a top prospect waiting his turn on the bench, since a first-round pick is by no means a "replacement-level" player.

At other positions, there is no easy way to separate players into "starters" and "replacements," since unlike at quarterback, being the starter doesn't make you the only guy who gets in the game. Instead, we used a simpler method, ranking players at each position in each season by attempts. The players who made up the final 10 percent of passes or runs were split out as "replacement players" and then compared to the players making up the other 90 percent of plays at that position. This took care of the fact that not every non-starter is a freely available talent. (Think of Giovani Bernard or Duke Johnson, for example.)

As noted earlier, the challenge of any new stat is to present it on a scale that's meaningful to those attempting to use it. Saying that Andy Dalton's passes were worth 116 success value points over replacement in 2015 has very little value without a context to tell us if 116 is good total or a bad one. Therefore, we translate these success values into a number called "Defense-adjusted Yards Above Replacement, or DYAR. Thus, Dalton was fourth among quarterbacks with 1,135 passing DYAR. It is our estimate that a generic replacement-level quarterback, throwing in the same situations as Dalton, would have been worth 1,135 fewer yards. Note that this doesn't mean the re-placement level quarterback would have gained exactly 1,135 fewer yards. First downs, touchdowns, and turnovers all have an estimated yardage value in this system, so what we are saying is that a generic replacement-level quarterback would have fewer yards and touchdowns (and more turnovers) that would total up to be equivalent to the value of 1,135 yards.

Problems with DVOA and DYAR

Football is a game in which nearly every action requires the work of two or more teammates—in fact, usually 11 team-mates all working in unison. Unfortunately, when it comes to individual player ratings, we are still far from the point at which we can determine the value of a player independent from the performance of his teammates. That means that when we say, "In 2017, Le'Veon Bell had a DVOA of 7.9%," what we really are saying is, "In 2017, Le'Veon Bell, playing in Todd Haley's offensive system with the Pittsburgh offensive line blocking for him and Ben Roethlisberger selling the fake when necessary, had a DVOA of 7.9%."

DVOA is limited by what's included in the official NFL play-by-play or tracked by our game charting partners (ex-plained below). Because we need to have the entire play-by-play of a season in order to compute DVOA and DYAR, these metrics are not yet ready to compare players of today to play-ers throughout the league's history. As of this writing, we have processed 32 seasons, 1986 through 2017, and we add seasons at a rate of roughly two per year (the most recent season, plus one season back into history.)

In addition, because we need to turn around DVOA and DYAR quickly during the season before charting can be completed, we do not yet have charting data such as dropped passes incorporated into these advanced metrics. Eventually we will have two sets of metrics, one incorporating charting data and going back to 2005 or 2006, and another that does not incorporate charting and can be used to compare current players and teams to players and teams all the way back to 1986 or earlier.

Pythagorean Projection

The Pythagorean projection is an approximation of each team's wins based solely on their points scored and allowed. This basic concept was introduced by baseball analyst Bill James, who discovered that the record of a baseball team could be very closely approximated by taking the square of team runs scored and dividing it by the sum of the squares of team runs scored and allowed. Statistician Daryl Morey, now general manager of the Houston Rockets, later extended this theorem to professional football, refining the exponent to 2.37 rather than 2.

The problem with that exponent is the same problem we've had with DVOA in recent years: the changing offensive levels

in the NFL. 2.37 worked great based on the league 20 years ago, but in the current NFL it ends up slightly underproject-ing teams that play high-scoring games. The most accurate method is actually to adjust the exponent based on the scoring environment of each individual team. Saints games have a lot of points. Jaguars games feature fewer points.

This became known as Pythagenport when Clay Davenport of Baseball Prospectus started doing it with baseball teams. In the middle of the 2011 season, we switched our measurement of Pythagorean wins to a Pythagenport-style equation, modi-fied for the NFL. The improvement is slight, but noticeable due to the high-scoring teams that have dominated the last few years.

For a long time, Pythagorean projections did a remarkable job of predicting Super Bowl champions. From 1984 through 2004, 10 of 21 Super Bowls were won by the team that led the NFL in Pythagorean wins. Seven other Super Bowls during that time were won by the team that finished second. Super Bowl champions that led the league in Pythagorean wins but not actual wins include the 2004 Patriots, 2000 Ravens, 1999 Rams, and 1997 Broncos.

Super Bowl champions were much less predictable over the next few seasons. As of 2005, the 1980 Oakland Raiders held the mark for the fewest Pythagorean wins by a Super Bowl champion, 9.7. Then, between 2006 and 2012, four dif-ferent teams won the Super Bowl with a lower Pythagorean win total: the 2006 Colts (9.6), the 2012 Ravens (9.4), the 2007 Giants (8.6), and the 2011 Giants (7.9), the first team in the 90-year history of the National Football League to ever be outscored during the regular season and still go on to win the championship. In the past five seasons, we've returned to more standard playoff results: eight of the last ten Super Bowl teams ranked first or second in Pythagorean wins during the regular season, including both New England and Philadelphia last year.

Pythagorean wins are also useful as a predictor of year-to-year improvement. Teams that win a minimum of one full game more than their Pythagorean projection tend to regress the following year; teams that win a minimum of one full game less than their Pythagorean projection tend to improve the following year, particularly if they were at or above .500 despite their underachieving. Jacksonville, Baltimore, and the Los Angeles Chargers all qualified in 2017, although as you'll learn in their chapters, there are other reasons to believe that they may not improve this season. On the other side, there are teams that seem set for a reversion of luck. Pittsburgh went 13-3 despite just 10.5 projected wins, one of three different teams in 2017 with at least two more wins than projected wins. The others were Buffalo and Carolina.

Adjusted Line Yards

One of the most difficult goals of statistical analysis in football is isolating the degree to which each of the 22 men

---

1 The equation, for those curious, is 1.5 x log ((PF+PA)/G).

on the field is responsible for the result of a given play. Nowhere is this as significant as the running game, in which one player runs while up to nine other players—including not just linemen but also wideouts and tight ends—block in different directions. None of the statistics we use for measuring rushing—yards, touchdowns, yards per carry—differentiate between the contribution of the running back and the contribution of the offensive line. Neither do our advanced metrics DVOA and DYAR.

We do, however, have enough play-by-play data amassed that we can try to separate the effect that the running back has on a particular play from the effects of the offensive line (and other offensive blockers) and the opposing defense. A team might have two running backs in its stable: RB A, who averages 3.0 yards per carry, and RB B, who averages 3.5 yards per carry. Who is the better back? Imagine that RB A doesn't just average 3.0 yards per carry, but gets exactly 3 yards on every single carry, while RB B has a highly variable yardage output: sometimes 5 yards, sometimes minus-2 yards, sometimes 20 yards. The difference in variability between the runners can be exploited not only to determine the difference between the runners, but the effect the offensive line has on every running play.

At some point in every long running play, the running back passes all of his offensive line blocks as well as additional blocking backs or receivers. From there on, the rest of the play is dependent on the runner's own speed and elusiveness and the speed and tackling ability of the opposing defense. If David Johnson breaks through the line for 50 yards, avoiding tacklers all the way to the goal line, his offensive line has done a great job—but they aren't responsible for the majority of the yards gained. The trick is figuring out exactly how much they *are* responsible for.

For each running back carry, we calculated the probability that the back involved would run for the specific yardage on that play based on that back's average yardage per carry and the variability of their yardage from play to play. We also calculated the probability that the offense would get the yardage based on the team's rushing average and variability using all backs *other* than the one involved in the given play, and the probability that the defense would give up the specific amount of yardage based on its average rushing yards allowed per carry and variability.

A regression analysis breaks the value for rushing yardage into the following categories: losses, 0-4 yards, 5-10 yards, and 11+ yards. In general, the offensive line is 20 percent more responsible for lost yardage than it is for positive gains up to four yards, but 50 percent less responsible for additional yardage gained between five and ten yards, and not at all responsible for additional yardage past ten yards.

By applying those percentages to every running back carry, we were able to create **adjusted line yards (ALY)**, a statistic that measured offensive line performance. (We don't include carries by receivers, which are usually based on deception rather than straight blocking, or carries by quarterbacks, although we may need to reconsider that given the recent use of the read option in the NFL.) Those numbers are then adjusted based on down, distance, situation, opponent and whether or not a team is in the shotgun. (Because defenses are generally playing pass when the quarterback is in shotgun, the average running back carry from shotgun last year gained 4.52 yards, compared to just 3.94 yards on other carries.) The adjusted numbers are then normalized so that the league average for adjusted line yards per carry is the same as the league average for RB yards per carry. Adjusted line yards numbers are normalized differently in each season, so that normalization is based on that year's average for RB yards per carry rather than a historical average.

The NFL distinguishes between runs made to seven different locations on the line: left/right end, left/right tackle, left/right guard, and middle. Further research showed no statistically significant difference between how well a team performed on runs listed as having gone up the middle or past a guard, so we separated runs into just five different directions (left/right end, left/right tackle, and middle). Note that there may not be a statistically significant difference between right tackle and middle/guard either, but pending further research (and for the sake of symmetry) we still list runs behind the right tackle separately. These splits allow us to evaluate subsections of a team's offensive line, but not necessarily individual linesmen, as we can't account for blocking assignments or guards who pull towards the opposite side of the line after the snap.

Success Rate

Success rate is a statistic for running backs that measures how consistently they achieve the yardage necessary for a play to be deemed successful. Some running backs will mix a few long runs with a lot of failed runs of one or two yards, while others with similar yards-per-carry averages will consistently gain five yards on first down, or as many yards as necessary on third down. This statistic helps us differentiate between the two.

Since success rate compares rush attempts to other rush attempts, without consideration of passing, the standard for success on first down is slightly lower than those described above for DVOA. In addition, the standard for success changes slightly in the fourth quarter when running backs are used to run out the clock. A team with the lead is satisfied with a shorter run as long as it stays in bounds. Conversely, for a team down by a couple of touchdowns in the fourth quarter, four yards on first down isn't going to be a big help.

The formula for running back success rate is as follows:

- A successful play must gain 40 percent of needed yards on first down, 60 percent of needed yards on second down, and 100 percent of needed yards on third or fourth down.
- If the offense is behind by more than a touchdown in the fourth quarter, the benchmarks switch to 50 percent, 65 percent, and 100 percent.
- If the offense is ahead by any amount in the fourth quarter, the benchmarks switch to 30 percent, 50 percent, and 100 percent.

The league-average success rate in 2017 was 44.8 percent.

Success Rate is not adjusted based on defenses faced and is not calculated for quarterbacks and wide receivers who occasionally carry the ball. Note gain that our calculation of success rate for running back is different from the success rate we use as a basis for DVOA, and other success rate calculations you may find across the Internet.

Approximate Value

Approximate Value is a system created by Doug Drinen of Pro Football Reference. The goal is to put a single number on every season of every NFL player since 1950, using a very broad set of guidelines. The goal is not to make judgments on individual seasons, but rather to have a format for studying groups of seasons that is more accurate than measuring players with a very broad brush such as "games started" or "number of Pro Bowls." Skill players are rated primarily using basic stats, while offensive linemen and defensive players are rated in large part based on team performance as well as individual accolades and games started. Advanced stats from Football Outsiders play-by-play breakdown are not part of this system. It is obviously imperfect—"approximate" is right there in the name—but it's valuable for studying groups of draft picks, groups of players by age, and so on. The system is introduced and explained at https://www.pro-football-reference.com/blog/index37a8.html.

KUBIAK Projection System

Most "skill position" players whom we expect to play a role this season receive a projection of their standard 2018 NFL statistics using the KUBIAK projection system. KUBIAK takes into account a number of different factors including expected role, performance over the past two seasons, age, height, weight, historical comparables, and projected team performance on offense and defense. When we named our system KUBIAK, it was a play on the PECOTA system used by our partners at Baseball Prospectus—if they were going to name their system after a long-time eighties backup, we would name our system after a long-time eighties backup. Little did we know that Gary Kubiak would finally get a head coaching job the very next season. After some debate, we decided to keep the name, although discussing projections for Denver players was a bit awkward for a while.

To clear up a common misconception among our readers, KUBIAK projects individual player performances only, not teams.

2018 Win Projection System

In this book, each of the 32 NFL teams receives a **2018 Mean Projection** at the beginning of its chapter. These projections stem from three equations that forecast 2018 DVOA for offense, defense, and special teams based on a number of different factors. This offseason, we overhauled and improved the team projection system for the first time in a few years. The new system starts by considering the team's DVOA over the past three seasons and, on offense, a separate projection for the starting quarterback. The new system also does a much better job of measuring the value of offseason personnel changes by incorporating a measure that's based on the net personnel change in DYAR among non-quarterbacks (for offense) and the net change in Approximate Value above replacement level (for defense). Other factors include coaching experience, recent draft history, certain players returning from injury, and combined tenure on the offensive line.

These three equations produce precise numbers representing the most likely outcome, but also produce a range of possibilities, used to determine the probability of each possible offensive, defensive, and special teams DVOA for each team. This is particularly important when projecting football teams, because with only 16 games in a season, a team's performance may vary wildly from its actual talent level due to a couple of random bounces of the ball or badly timed injuries. In addition, the economic structure of the NFL allows teams to make sudden jumps or drops in overall ability more often than in other sports.

This projection system was built using the years 2003-2014. For the three years since, 2015-2017, the mean DVOA forecast by this new projection system had a correlation coefficient with actual wins of .474. By comparison, previous year's point differential had a correlation of .399, and previous year's wins had a correlation of just .265.

The next step in our forecast involves simulating the season one million times. We use the projected range of DVOA possibilities to produce 1,000 different simulated seasons with 32 sets of DVOA ratings. We then plug those season-long DVOA ratings into the same equation we use during the season to determine each team's likely remaining wins for our Playoff Odds Report. The simulation takes each season game-by-game, determining the home or road team's chance of winning each game based on the DVOA ratings of each team as well as home-field advantage. A random number between 0 and 100 determines whether the home or road team has won that game. We ran 1,000 simulations with each of the 1,000 sets of DVOA ratings, creating a million different simulations. The simulation was programmed by Mike Harris.

We use a system we call a "dynamic simulation" to better approximate the true distribution of wins in the NFL. When simulating the season, each team had 2.0% DVOA added or subtracted after a win or loss, reflecting the fact that a win or loss tends to tell us whether a team is truly better or worse than whatever their mean projection had been before the season. Using this method, a team projected with 20.0% DVOA which goes 13-3 will have a 40.0% DVOA entering the playoffs, which is much more realistic. This change gave us more projected seasons at the margins, with fewer seasons at 8-8 and more seasons at 14-2 or 2-14. The dynamic simulation also meant a slight increase in projected wins for the best teams, and a slight decrease for the worst teams. However, the conservative nature of our projection system still means the distribution of mean projected wins has a much smaller spread than the actual win-loss records we will see by the end of December. We will continue to experiment with changes to the simulation in order to produce the most accurate possible forecast of the NFL season in future years.

Football Outsiders
Game Charting Data

Each of the formulas listed above relies primarily on the play-by-play data published by the NFL. When we began to analyze the NFL, this was all that we had to work with. Just as a television broadcast has a color commentator who gives more detail to the facts related by the play-by-play announcer, so too do we need some color commentary to provide contextual information that breathes life into these plain lines of numbers and text. We added this color commentary with game charting.

Beginning in 2005, Football Outsiders began using a number of volunteers to chart every single play of every regular-season and postseason NFL game. To put it into perspective, there were over 54,000 lines of play-by-play information in each NFL season and our goal is to add several layers of detail to nearly all of them.

It gradually became clear that attempting to chart so much football with a crew of volunteers was simply not feasible, especially given our financial resources compared to those of our competitors. Over the past few years, we have partnered with larger companies to take on the responsibilities of game charting so that we can devote more time to analysis.

In 2015, Football Outsiders reached an agreement with Sports Info Solutions, formerly Baseball Info Solutions, to begin a large charting project that would replace our use of volunteers. We also have a partnership with ESPN Stats & Info, and use their data to check against the data collected by Sports Info Solutions. All charting data for the 2016 season is provided by one of these two companies.

Our partnership with Baseball Info Solutions has also resulted in the expansion of Football Outsiders Premium with a new NFL Charting Data subscription that updates some of our data such as cornerback charting and broken tackles every week during the season. We also produce the Off The Charts podcast, which explores data from game charting in a weekly discussion of the NFL season.[2]

Game charting is significantly easier now that the NFL makes coaches' film available through NFL Game Rewind. This tape, which was not publicly available when we began charting with volunteers in 2005, includes sideline and end zone perspectives for each play, and shows all 22 players at all times, making it easier to see the cause-and-effect of certain actions taken on the field. Nonetheless, all game charting is still imperfect. You often cannot tell which players did their jobs particularly well or made mistakes without knowing the play call and each player's assignment, particularly when it comes to zone coverage or pass-rushers who reach the quarterback without being blocked. Therefore, the goal of game charting from both ESPN Stats & Info and Sports Info Solutions is *not* to "grade" players, but rather to attempt to mark specific events: a pass pressure, a blown block, a dropped interception, and so on.

We emphasize that all data from game charting is unofficial. Other sources for football statistics may keep their own measurements of yards after catch or how teams perform against the blitz. Our data will not necessarily match theirs. Even ESPN Stats & Info and Sports Info Solutions have a number of disagreements, marking different events on the same play because it can be difficult to determine the definition of a "pressure" or a "dropped pass." However, any other group that is publicly tracking this data is also working off the same footage, and thus will run into the same issues of difficulty and subjectivity.

There are lots of things we would like to do with all-22 film that we simply haven't been able to do yet, such as charting coverage by cornerbacks when they aren't the target of a given pass, or even when pass pressure prevents the pass from getting into the air. Unfortunately, we are limited by what our partners are able to chart given time constraints.

In the description of data below, we have tried to designate which data from 2017 comes from ESPN Stats & Info group (ESPN S&I), which data comes from Sports Info Solutions (SIS), and where we have combined data from both companies with our own analysis.

Formation/Personnel

For each play, we have the number of running backs, wide receivers, and tight ends on the field courtesy of ESPN S&I. Players were marked based on their designation on the roster, not based on where they lined up on the field. Obviously, this could be difficult with some hybrid players or players changing positions in 2017, but we did our best to keep things as consistent as possible.

SIS also tracked this data and added the names of players who were lined up in unexpected positions. This included marking tight ends or wide receivers in the backfield, and running backs or tight ends who were lined up either wide or in the slot (often referred to as "flexing" a tight end). SIS also marked when a fullback or tight end was actually a sixth (or sometimes even seventh) offensive lineman, and they marked the backfield formation as empty back, single back, I formation, offset I, split backs, full house, or "other." These notations of backfield formation were recorded directly before the snap and do not account for positions before pre-snap motion.

SIS then marked defensive formations by listing the number of linemen, linebackers, and defensive backs. There will be mistakes—a box safety may occasionally be confused for a linebacker, for example—but for the most part the data for defensive backs will be accurate. Figuring out how to mark whether a player is a defensive end or a linebacker is a different story. The rise of hybrid defenses has led to a lot of confusion. Edge rushers in a 4-3 defense may play standing up because they used to play for a 3-4 defense and that's what they are used to. A player who is usually considered an outside linebacker for a 3-4 defense may put his hand on the ground on third down (thus looking like a 4-3 defensive end), but the tackle next to him is still two-gapping (which is generally a 3-4 principle). SIS marked personnel in a simplified fashion by designating any front seven player in a standing position as a linebacker and designating any front seven player in a crouching position as a defensive lineman.

For the last two years, we also have data from SIS on where receivers lined up before each of their pass targets (wide, slot, tight, or backfield) and what routes they ran.

Rushers and Blockers

ESPN Stats & Info provided us with two data points regarding the pass rush: the number of pass-rushers on a given play, and the number defensive backs blitzing on a given play. SIS also tracked this data for comparison purposes and then added a count of blockers. Counting blockers is an art as much as a science. Offenses base their blocking schemes on how many rushers they expect. A running back or tight end's assignment may depend on how many pass-rushers cross the line at the snap. Therefore, an offensive player was deemed to be a blocker if he engaged in an actual block, or there was some hesitation before running a route. A running back that immediately heads out into the flat is not a blocker, but one that waits to verify that the blocking scheme is working and then goes out to the flat would, in fact, be considered a blocker.

Pass Play Details

Both companies recorded the following data for all pass plays:
- Did the play begin with a play-action fake, including read-option fakes that developed into pass plays instead of being handed to a running back?
- Was the quarterback in or out of the pocket?
- Was the quarterback under pressure in making his pass?
- Was this a screen pass?

SIS game charting also marks the name of the defender who caused the pass pressure. Charters were allowed to list two names if necessary, and could also attribute a hurry to "overall pressure." No defender was given a hurry and a sack on the same play, but defenders were given hurries if they helped force a quarterback into a sack that was finished by another player. SIS also identified which defender(s) caused the pass pressure which forced a quarterback to scramble for yardage. If the quarterback wasn't under pressure but ran anyway, the play could be marked either as "coverage scramble" (if the quarterback ran because there were no open receivers) or "hole opens up" (if the quarterback ran because he knew he could gain significant yardage).

Football Outsiders (using our past game charting volunteers) reviewed a number of plays where there was disagreement between the two companies on pass pressure, and then reported those disagreements to both companies so they could decide which plays they wanted to change. All pressure data in this book is based on SIS data combined with Football Outsiders adjustments, even if ESPN S&I did not mark the play in question as a pass pressure.

Some places in this book, we divide pass yardage into two numbers: distance in the air and yards after catch. This information is tracked by the NFL, but it can be hard to find and the official scorers often make errors, so we corrected the original data based on input from both ESPN S&I and SIS. Distance in the air is based on the distance from the line of scrimmage to the place where the receiver either caught or was supposed to catch the pass. We do not count how far the quarterback was behind the line or horizontal yardage if the quarterback threw across the field. All touchdowns are counted to the goal line, so that distance in the air added to yards after catch always equals the official yardage total kept by the league.

Incomplete Passes

Quarterbacks are evaluated based on their ability to complete passes. However, not all incompletes should have the same weight. Throwing a ball away to avoid a sack is actually a valuable incomplete, and a receiver dropping an otherwise quality pass is hardly a reflection on the quarterback.

This year, our evaluation of incomplete passes began with ESPN Stats & Info, which marked passes as Overthrown, Underthrown, Thrown Away, Batted Down at the Line, Defensed, or Dropped. We then compared this data to similar data from SIS and made some changes. We also changed some plays to reflect a couple of additional categories we have kept in past years for Football Outsiders: Hit in Motion (indicating the quarterback was hit as his arm was coming forward to make a pass), Caught out of Bounds, and Hail Mary.

Our count of passes defensed will be different from the unofficial totals kept by the league for reasons explained below in the section on Defensive Secondary tables.

ESPN S&I and SIS also marked when a defender dropped an interception; Football Outsiders volunteers then analyzed plays where the two companies disagreed to come up with a final total. When a play is close, we tend to err on the side of not marking a dropped interception, as we don't want to blame a defender who, for example, jumps high for a ball and has it tip off his fingers. We also counted a few "defensed" interceptions, when a quarterback threw a pass that would have been picked off if not for the receiver playing defense on the ball. These passes counted as dropped interceptions for quarterbacks but not for the defensive players.

Defenders

The NFL play-by-play lists tackles and, occasionally, tipped balls, but it does not definitively list the defender on the play. SIS charters attempted to determine which defender was primarily responsible for covering either the receiver at the time of the throw or the location to which the pass was thrown, regardless of whether the pass was complete or not.

Every defense in the league plays zone coverage at times, some more than others, which leaves us with the question of how to handle plays without a clear man assigned to that receiver. Charters (SIS employees in 2015-2017, and FO volunteers in previous seasons) had three alternatives:
- We asked charters to mark passes that found the holes in zone coverage as Hole in Zone, rather than straining

to assign that pass to an individual defender. We asked the charter to also note the player who appeared to be responsible for that zone, and these defenders are assigned half credit for those passes. Some holes were so large that no defender could be listed along with the Hole in Zone designation.

- Charters were free to list two defenders instead of one. This could be used for actual double coverage, or for zone coverage in which the receiver was right between two close defenders rather than sitting in a gaping hole. When two defenders are listed, ratings assign each with half credit.

- Screen passes and dumpoffs are marked as Uncovered unless a defender (normally a linebacker) is obviously shadowing that specific receiver on the other side of the line of scrimmage.

Since we began the charting project in 2005, nothing has changed our analysis more than this information on pass coverage. However, even now with the ability to view all-22 film, it can be difficult to identify the responsible defender except when there is strict man-to-man coverage.

Additional Details

All draw plays were marked, whether by halfbacks or quarterbacks. Option runs and zone reads were also marked.

Both SIS and ESPN S&I when the formation was pistol as opposed to shotgun; the official play-by-play simply marks these plays all as shotgun.

Both SIS and ESPN S&I track yards after contact for each play.

SIS charters marked each quarterback sack with one of the following terms: Blown Block, Coverage Sack, QB Fault, Failed Scramble, or Blitz/Overall Pressure. Blown Blocks were listed with the name of a specific offensive player who allowed the defender to come through. (Some blown block sacks are listed with two blockers, who each get a half-sack..) Coverage Sack denotes when the quarterback has plenty of time to throw but cannot find an open receiver. QB Fault represents "self sacks" listed without a defender, such as when the quarterback drops back, only to find the ball slip out of his hands with no pass-rusher touching him. Failed Scramble represents plays where a quarterback began to run without major pass pressure because he thought he could get a positive gain, only to be tackled before he passed the line of scrimmage.

SIS tracked "broken tackles" on all runs or pass plays. We define a "broken tackle" as one of two events: Either the ballcarrier escapes from the grasp of the defender, or the defender is in good position for a tackle but the ballcarrier jukes him out of his shoes. If the ballcarrier sped by a slow defender who dived and missed, that did not count as a broken tackle. If the defender couldn't bring the ballcarrier down because he is being blocked out of the play by another offensive player, this did not count as a broken tackle. It was possible to mark multiple broken tackles on the same play. Broken tackles are not marked for special teams. Note that leaguewide broken tackle numbers have gone up roughly 10 percent each of the past two years.

Acknowledgements

Thank you to all the past game charting volunteers who helped us collect data from 2005 through 2014, and who helped us clean data from our partners in 2015 and 2016.

Thanks as well to our two game charting partners that have helped free us up to do more analysis and less data collection, including ESPN Stats & Info (particularly John McTigue, Allison Loucks, and Henry Gargiulo) and Sports Info Solutions (particularly Dan Foehrenbach and Matt Manocherian).

How to Read the Team Summary Box

Here is a rundown of all the tables and stats that appear in the 32 team chapters. Each team chapter begins with a box in the upper-right hand corner that gives a summary of our statistics for that team, as follows:

2017 Record gives each team's actual win-loss record. **Pythagorean Wins** gives the approximate number of wins expected last year based on this team's raw totals of points scored and allowed, along with their NFL rank. **Snap-Weighted Age** gives the average age of the team in 2017, weighted based on how many snaps each player was on the field and ranked from oldest (Arizona, first at 28.0) to youngest (Cleveland, 32nd at 24.6). **Average Opponent** gives a ranking of last year's schedule strength based on the average DVOA of all 16 opponents faced during the regular season. Teams are ranked from the hardest schedule of 2016 (Chicago) to the easiest (Jacksonville).

Total DVOA gives the team's total DVOA rating, with rank. **Offense**, **Defense**, and **Special Teams** list the team's DVOA rating in each category, along with NFL rank. Remember that good offenses and special teams have positive DVOA numbers, while a negative DVOA means better defense, so the lowest defensive DVOA is ranked No. 1 (last year, Denver).

2018 Mean Projection gives the average number of wins for this team based on the 2017 Win Projection System described earlier in this chapter. Please note that we do not expect any teams to win the exact number of games in their mean projection. First of all, no team can win 0.8 of a game. Second, because these projections represent a whole range of possible values, the averages naturally tend to drift towards 8-8. Obviously, we're not expecting a season where no team goes 4-12 or 12-4. For a better way to look at the projections, we offer **Postseason Odds**, which give each team's chance of making the postseason based on our simulation, and **Super Bowl Appearance** odds, which give each team's chance of representing its conference in Super Bowl XLIX. The average team will make the playoffs in 37.5 percent of simulations, and the Super Bowl in 6.3 percent of simulations.

Projected Average Opponent gives the team's strength of schedule for 2017; like the listing for last year's schedule strength in the first column of the box, this number is based not on last year's record but on the mean projected DVOA for each opponent. A positive schedule is harder, a negative schedule easier. Teams are ranked from the hardest projected schedule (Atlanta, first) to the easiest (New England, 32nd). This strength of schedule projection does not take into account which games are home or away, or the timing of the bye week.

The final column of the box gives the team's chances of finishing in four different basic categories of success:

- On the Clock (0-4 wins; NFL average 12%)
- Mediocrity (5-7 wins; NFL average 32%)
- Playoff Contender (8-10 wins; NFL average 36%)
- Super Bowl Contender (11+ wins; NFL average 20%)

The percentage given for each category is dependent not only on how good we project the team to be in 2018, but the level of variation possible in that projection, and the expected performance of the teams on the schedule.

You'll also find a table with the team's 2018 schedule placed within each chapter, along with a graph showing each team's 2017 week-to-week performance by single-game DVOA. The second, dotted line on the graph represents a five-week moving average of each team's performance, in order to show a longer-term view of when they were improving and declining. After the essays come statistical tables and comments related to that team and its specific units.

Weekly Performance

The first table gives a quick look at the team's week-to-week performance in 2017. (Table 2) This includes the play-offs for those teams that made the postseason, with the four weeks of playoffs numbered 18 (wild card) through 21 (Super Bowl). All other tables in the team chapters represent regular-season performance only unless otherwise noted.

Looking at the first week for the Carolina Panthers in 2017, the first five columns are fairly obvious: Carolina opened the season with a 23-3 win on the road in San Francisco. **YDF** and **YDA** are net yards on offense and net yards against the defense. These numbers do not include penalty yardage or special teams yardage. **TO** represents the turnover margin. Unlike other parts of the book in which we consider all fumbles as equal, this only represents actual turnovers: fumbles lost and interceptions. So, for example, the Panthers forced two more turnovers than Tampa Bay in Week 8, but committed one more turnover than Atlanta in Week 9.

Finally, you'll see DVOA ratings for this game: Total **DVOA** first, then offense (**Off**), defense (**Def**), and special teams (**ST**). Note that these are DVOA ratings, adjusted for opponent, so a loss to a good team will often be listed with a higher rating than a close win over a bad team. For example, the Cardinals have a positive DVOA for their Week 6 loss to Philadelphia, but a negative DVOA for their Week 12 win over the New York Jets.

Trends and Splits

Next to the week-to-week performance is a table giving DVOA for different portions of a team's performance, on both offense and defense. Each split is listed with the team's rank among the 32 NFL teams. These numbers represent regular season performance only.

Table 2. 2017 Panthers Stats by Week

Wk	vs.	W-L	PF	PA	YDF	YDA	TO	Total	Off	Def	ST
1	at SF	W	23	3	287	217	0	45%	-4%	-46%	3%
2	BUF	W	9	3	255	176	0	17%	-21%	-33%	5%
3	NO	L	13	34	288	362	-3	-42%	-20%	22%	0%
4	at NE	W	33	30	444	373	-2	35%	40%	6%	1%
5	at DET	W	27	24	362	242	+1	2%	1%	-7%	-6%
6	PHI	L	23	28	305	310	-2	16%	-8%	-17%	8%
7	at CHI	L	3	17	293	153	-3	-7%	-37%	-27%	2%
8	at TB	W	17	3	254	279	+2	35%	-20%	-44%	11%
9	ATL	W	20	17	330	355	-1	16%	4%	-6%	6%
10	MIA	W	45	21	548	313	+1	37%	58%	20%	-1%
11	BYE										
12	at NYJ	W	35	27	299	391	+1	-11%	-17%	25%	31%
13	at NO	L	21	31	279	400	0	5%	11%	-7%	-13%
14	MIN	W	31	24	345	356	+2	57%	25%	-32%	0%
15	GB	W	31	24	387	384	+4	43%	48%	8%	3%
16	TB	W	22	19	255	392	+2	13%	-15%	-5%	23%
17	at ATL	L	10	22	248	371	-3	-50%	-64%	-12%	1%
18	at NO	L	26	31	413	410	+1	13%	29%	12%	-5%

Total DVOA gives total offensive, and defensive DVOA in all situations. **Unadjusted VOA** represents the breakdown of play-by-play considering situation but not opponent. A team whose offensive DVOA is higher than its offensive VOA played a harder-than-average schedule of opposing defenses; a team with a lower defensive DVOA than defensive VOA player a harder-than-average schedule of opposing offenses.

Weighted Trend lowers the importance of earlier games to give a better idea of how the team was playing at the end of the regular season. The final four weeks of the season are full strength; moving backwards through the season, each week is given less and less weight until the first three weeks of the season, which are not included at all. **Variance** is the same as noted above, with a higher percentage representing less consistency. This is true for both offense and defense: Cincinnati, for example, was very consistent on defense (2.8%, third) but inconsistent on offense (16.2%, 32nd). **Average Opponent** is that the same thing that appears in the box to open each chapter, except split in half: the average DVOA of all opposing defenses (for offense) or the average DVOA of all opposing offenses (for defense).

Passing and **Rushing** are fairly self-explanatory. Note that rushing DVOA includes all rushes, not just those by running backs, including quarterback scrambles that may have begun as pass plays.

The next three lines split out DVOA on **First Down**, **Second Down**, and **Third Down**. Third Down here includes fourth downs on which a team runs a regular offensive play instead of punting or attempting a field goal. **First Half** and **Second Half** represent the first two quarters and last two quarters (plus overtime), not the first eight and last eight games of the regular season. Next comes DVOA in the **Red Zone**, which is any offensive play starting from the defense's 20-yard line through the goal line. The final split is **Late and Close**, which includes any play in the second half or overtime when the teams are within eight points of each other in either direction. (Eight points, of course, is the biggest deficit that can be made up with a single score, a touchdown and two-point conversion.)

Five-Year Performance

This table gives each team's performance over the past five seasons. (Table 3) It includes win-loss record, Pythagorean Wins, **Estimated Wins**, points scored and allowed, and turnover margin. Estimated wins are based on a formula that estimates how many games a team would have been expected to win based on 2017 performance in specific situations, normalized to eliminate luck (fumble recoveries, opponents' missed field goals, etc.) and assuming average schedule strength. The formula emphasizes consistency and overall DVOA as well as DVOA in a few specifically important situations. The next columns of this table give total DVOA along with DVOA for offense, defense, and special teams, and the rank for each among that season's 32 NFL teams.

The next four columns give the adjusted games lost (AGL) for starters on both offense and defense, along with rank. (Our total for starters here includes players who take over as starters due to another injury, such as Jay Cutler or Tyler Kroft last year, as well as important situational players who may not necessarily start, such as pass-rush specialists and slot receivers.) Adjusted games lost was introduced in *Pro Football Prospectus 2008*; it gives a weighted estimate of the probability that players would miss games based on how they are listed on the injury report. Unlike a count of "starter games missed," this accounts for the fact that a player listed as questionable who does in fact play is not playing at 100 percent capability. Teams are ranked from the fewest injuries (2017: Los Angeles Rams on offense, Minnesota on defense) to the most (2017: Arizona on offense, San Francisco on defense).

Individual Offensive Statistics

Each team chapter contains a table giving passing and receiving numbers for any player who either threw five passes or was thrown five passes, along with rushing numbers for any players who carried the ball at least five times. These numbers also appear in the player comments at the end of the book (except for runs by wide receivers). By putting them together in the team chapters we hope we make it easier to compare the performances of different players on the same team.

Players who are no longer on the team are marked with an asterisk. New players who were on a different team in 2017 are in italics. Changes should be accurate as of July 1. Rookies are not included.

All players are listed with DYAR and DVOA. Passing statistics then list total pass plays (**Plays**), net yardage (**NtYds**), and net yards per pass (**Avg**). These numbers include not just passes (and the positive yardage from them) but aborted snaps and sacks (and the negative yardage from them). Then comes average yards after catch (**YAC),** as determined by the game charting project. This average is based on charted receptions, not total pass attempts. The final three numbers are completion percentage (**C%**), passing touchdowns (**TD**), and interceptions (**Int**).

It is important to note that the tables in the team chapters contain Football Outsiders stats, while the tables in the player comments later in the book contain official NFL totals, at least when it comes to standard numbers like receptions and yardage. This results in a number of differences between the two:

- Team chapter tables list aborted snaps as passes, not runs, although aborted handoffs are still listed as runs. Net yardage for quarterbacks in the team chapter tables includes the lost yardage from aborted snaps, sacks, and intentional grounding penalties. For official NFL stats, all aborted snaps are listed as runs.
- Football Outsiders stats omit kneeldowns from run totals and clock-stopping spikes from pass totals.
- In the Football Outsiders stats, we have changed a number of lateral passes to count as passes rather than runs, under the theory that a pass play is still a pass play, even if the receiver is standing five inches behind the quarterback. This results in some small differences in totals.
- "Skill players" who played for multiple teams in 2017 are only listed in team chapters with stats from that specific team; combined stats are listed in the player comments section.

Rushing statistics start with DYAR and DVOA, then list rushing plays and net yards along with average yards per carry and rushing touchdowns. The final two columns are fumbles (**Fum**)—both those lost to the defense and those recovered by the offense—and Success Rate (**Suc**), explained earlier in this chapter. Fumbles listed in the rushing table include all quarterback fumbles on sacks and aborted snaps, as well as running back fumbles on receptions, but not wide receiver fumbles.

Receiving statistics start with DYAR and DVOA and then list the number of passes thrown to this receiver (**Plays**), the number of passes caught (**Catch**) and the total receiving yards

Table 3. Seattle Seahawks Five-Year Performance

Year	W-L	Pyth W	Est W	PF	PA	TO	Total	Rk	Off	Rk	Def	Rk	ST	Rk	Off AGL	Rk	Def AGL	Rk	Off Age	Rk	Def Age	Rk	ST Age	Rk
2013	13-3	12.8	13.0	417	231	+20	40.0%	1	9.4%	7	-25.9%	1	4.7%	5	43.8	22	16.2	7	25.7	32	26.0	27	26.1	14
2014	12-4	11.9	12.7	394	254	+10	31.9%	1	16.8%	5	-16.8%	1	-1.7%	19	39.5	24	35.3	13	25.3	31	26.3	23	25.8	24
2015	10-6	11.8	12.5	423	277	+7	38.1%	1	18.7%	1	-15.2%	4	4.2%	3	23.7	9	16.4	4	25.9	25	27.0	12	26.3	12
2016	10-5-1	9.8	9.1	354	292	+1	8.0%	11	-2.6%	16	-10.6%	5	-0.1%	15	23.8	6	17.3	4	25.7	29	27.2	7	26.4	8
2017	9-7	9.0	8.5	366	332	+8	3.8%	14	2.0%	14	-3.8%	13	-2.0%	20	45.5	23	42.7	22	26.1	29	27.0	8	25.8	20

Detroit Lions Passing

Player	DYAR	DVOA	Plays	NtYds	Avg	YAC	C%	TD	Int
M.Stafford	1004	14.9%	613	4149	6.8	5.7	65.8%	29	10
M.Cassel	-257	-96.0%	50	125	2.5	1.8	59.5%	1	2

Detroit Lions Rushing

Player	DYAR	DVOA	Plays	Yds	Avg	TD	Fum	Suc
A.Abdullah	-9	-10.0%	165	553	3.4	4	2	35%
T.Riddick	-3	-9.5%	84	286	3.4	3	1	39%
T.Green	17	0.0%	42	165	3.9	2	0	43%
D.Washington	-36	-49.1%	20	44	2.2	0	0	40%
M.Stafford	11	0.2%	19	104	5.5	0	1	-
Z.Zenner	-17	-34.5%	14	26	1.9	1	0	21%
G.Tate	14	13.2%	5	22	4.4	0	0	-
L.Blount	-9	-9.8%	173	766	4.4	2	1	43%

Detroit Lions Receiving

Player	DYAR	DVOA	Plays	Ctch	Yds	Y/C	YAC	TD	C%
G.Tate	204	9.7%	120	92	1003	10.9	6.8	5	77%
M.Jones	395	33.8%	107	61	1101	18.0	3.2	9	57%
T.J.Jones	73	6.9%	49	30	399	13.3	2.6	1	61%
K.Golladay	130	21.9%	48	28	477	17.0	6.5	3	58%
J.Abbrederis*	1	-10.1%	7	3	44	14.7	9.3	0	43%
E.Ebron*	50	2.0%	86	53	574	10.8	4.9	4	62%
D.Fells*	48	21.9%	26	17	177	10.4	7.2	3	65%
M.Roberts	-7	-21.8%	7	4	46	11.5	3.0	0	57%
L.Willson	18	4.7%	22	15	153	10.2	6.0	4	68%
L.Toilolo	38	29.6%	14	12	122	10.2	5.3	1	86%
T.Riddick	37	-4.6%	71	53	444	8.4	8.2	2	75%
A.Abdullah	33	1.7%	35	25	162	6.5	5.8	1	71%
L.Blount	25	41.4%	8	8	50	6.3	5.9	1	100%

(**Yds**). Yards per catch (**Y/C**) includes total yardage per reception, based on standard play-by-play, while yards after catch (**YAC**) is based on information from our game charting project. Finally we list total receiving touchdowns, and catch percentage (**C%**), which is the percentage of passes intended for this receiver which were caught. Wide receivers, tight ends, and running backs are separated on the table by horizontal lines.

Performance Based on Personnel

These tables provide a look at performance in 2017 based on personnel packages, as defined above in the section on marking formation/personnel as part of Sports Info Solutions charting. There are four different tables, representing:
- Offense based on personnel
- Offense based on opponent's defensive personnel
- Defense based on personnel
- Defense based on opponent's offensive personnel

Most of these tables feature the top five personnel groupings for each team. Occasionally, we will list the personnel group which ranks sixth if the sixth group is either particularly interesting or nearly as common as the fifth group. Each personnel group is listed with its frequency among 2017 plays, yards per play, and DVOA. Offensive personnel are also listed with how often the team in question called a running play instead of a pass play from given personnel. (Quarterback scrambles are included as pass plays, not runs.)

Offensive personnel are given in the standard two-digit format where the first digit is running backs and the second digit is tight ends. You can figure out wide receivers by subtracting that total from five, with a couple of exceptions. Plays with six or seven offensive linemen will have a three-digit listing such as "611" or "622." Any play with a direct snap to a non-quarterback, or with a specific running quarterback taking the snap instead of the regular quarterback, was counted as "Wildcat." No team ends up with Wildcat listed among its top five offensive personnel groups.

When defensive players come in to play offense, defensive backs are counted as wide receivers and linebackers as tight ends. Defensive linemen who come in as offensive linemen are counted as offensive linemen; if they come in as blocking fullbacks, we count them as running backs.

This year, we are not giving personnel data based on the number of defensive linemen and linebackers. This is because of the difficulty in separating between the two, especially with our simplified designation of players as defensive linemen or linebackers based simply on who has a hand on the ground. There are just too many hybrid defensive schemes in today's game: 4-3 schemes where one or both ends rush the passer from a standing position, or hybrid schemes that one-gap on one side of the nose tackle and two-gap on the other. Therefore, defensive personnel is listed in only five categories:
- Base (four defensive backs)
- Nickel (five defensive backs)
- Dime+ (six or more defensive backs)
- Big (either 4-4-3 or 3-5-3)
- Goal Line (all other personnel groups with fewer than four defensive backs)

11, or three-wide personnel, was by far the most common grouping in the NFL last year, used on 59 percent of plays, followed the standard two-tight end set 12 personnel (19 percent of plays) and the more traditional 21 personnel (8 percent). Defenses lined up in Base on 33 percent of plays, Nickel on 52 percent of plays, Dime+ on 13 percent of plays, and either Big or Goal Line on 1.7 percent of plays.

Strategic Tendencies

The Strategic Tendencies table presents a mix of information garnered from both the standard play by play and the Football Outsiders game charting project. It gives you an idea of what kind of plays teams run in what situations and with what personnel. Each category is given a league-wide **Rank** from most often (1) to least often (32) except as noted below. The sample table shown here lists the NFL average in each category for 2017.

The first column of strategic tendencies lists how often

2017 NFL Average Strategic Tendencies

Run/Pass		Rk	Formation		Rk	Pass Rush		Rk	Secondary		Rk	Strategy		Rk
Runs, first half	39%	–	Form: Single Back	77%	–	Rush 3	8.4%	–	4 DB	33%	–	Play action	22%	–
Runs, first down	50%	–	Form: Empty Back	8%	–	Rush 4	65.8%	–	5 DB	52%	–	Avg Box (Off)	6.24	–
Runs, second-long	32%	–	Pers: 3+ WR	63%	–	Rush 5	20.0%	–	6+ DB	13%	–	Avg Box (Def)	6.24	–
Runs, power sit.	56%	–	Pers: 2+ TE/6+ OL	30%	–	Rush 6+	5.8%	–	CB by Sides	78%	–	Offensive Pace	30.58	–
Runs, behind 2H	27%	–	Pers: 6+ OL	3%	–	Int DL Sacks	25.2%	–	S/CB Cover Ratio	29%	–	Defensive Pace	30.58	–
Pass, ahead 2H	46%	–	Shotgun/Pistol	60%	–	Second Level Sacks	19.5%	–	DB Blitz	9%	–	Go for it on 4th	1.00	–

teams ran in different situations. These ratios are based on the type of play, not the actual result, so quarterback scrambles count as "passes" while quarterback sneaks, draws and option plays count as "runs."

Runs, first half and **Runs, first down** should be self-evident. **Runs, second-and-long** is the percentage of runs on second down with seven or more yards to go, giving you an idea of how teams follow up a failed first down. **Runs, power situations** is the percentage of runs on third or fourth down with 1-2 yards to go, or at the goal line with 1-2 yards to go. **Runs, behind 2H** tells you how often teams ran when they were behind in the second half, generally a passing situation. **Pass, ahead 2H** tells you how often teams passed when they had the lead in the second half, generally a running situation.

In each case, you can determine the percentage of plays that were passes by subtracting the run percentage from 100 (the reverse being true for "Pass, ahead 2H," of course).

The second column gives information about offensive formations and personnel, as tracked by Sports Info Solutions.

The first two entries detail formation, i.e. where players were lined up on the field. **Form: Single Back** lists how often the team lined up with only one player in the backfield, and **Form: Empty Back** lists how often the team lined up with no players in the backfield.

The next three entries are based on personnel, no matter where players were lined up in the formation. **Pers: 3+ WR** marks how often the team plays with three or more wide receivers. **Pers: 2+ TE/6+ OL** marks how often the team plays with either more than one tight end or more than five offensive linemen. **Pers: 6+ OL** marks just plays with more than five offensive linemen. Finally, we give the percentage of plays where a team used **Shotgun or Pistol** in 2017. This does not count "Wildcat" or direct snap plays involving a non-quarterback.

The third column shows how the defensive **Pass Rush** worked in 2017.

Rush 3/Rush 4/Rush 5/Rush 6+: The percentage of pass plays (including quarterback scrambles) on which Sports Info Solutions recorded this team rushing the passer with three or fewer defenders, four defenders, five defenders, and six or more defenders. These percentages do not include goal-line plays on the one- or two-yard line.

NEW FOR 2018: Int DL Sacks/Second Level Sacks: The goal of these numbers is to split out how many sacks each team got from players who were not edge rushers. **Int DL Sacks** track the percentage of sacks from interior defensive linemen: any 3-4 lineman, or a 4-3 defensive tackle. **Second Level Sacks** track sacks that come from linebackers who are not edge rushers, plus sacks from defensive backs.

The fourth column has more data on the use of defensive backs.

4 DB/5DB/6+ DB: The percentage of plays where this defense lined up with four, five, and six or more defensive backs, according to Sports Info Solutions.

CB by Sides: One of the most important lessons from game charting is that each team's best cornerback does not necessarily match up against the opponent's best receiver. Most cornerbacks play a particular side of the field and in fact cover a wider range of receivers than we assumed before we saw the charting data. This metric looks at which teams prefer to leave their starting cornerbacks on specific sides of the field.

To figure CB by Sides, we took the top two cornerbacks from each team and looked at the percentage of passes where that cornerback was in coverage on the left or right side of the field, ignoring passes marked as "middle." For each of the two cornerbacks, we took the higher number, right or left, and then we averaged the two cornerbacks to get the final CB by Sides rating. Teams which preferred to leave their cornerbacks in the same place last season, such as Cincinnati and Tampa Bay, will have high ratings. Teams that did more to move their best cornerback around to cover the opponent's top targets, such as Arizona and Detroit, will have low ratings.

S/CB Cover Ratio: This is our attempt to track which teams like to use their safeties as hybrid safety/corners and put them in man coverage on wide receivers. This ratio takes all pass targets with a defensive back in coverage, and then gives what percentage of those targets belonged to a player who is rostered as a safety, ranging from Arizona, which used safety Tyrann Mathieu as a nickelback (49 percent) to the New York Jets, who had very defined roles for their two rookie starting safeties (21 percent).

DB Blitz: We have data on how often the defense used at least one defensive back in the pass rush courtesy of ESPN Stats & Info.

Finally, in the final column, we have some elements of game strategy.

Play action: The percentage of pass plays (including quarterback scrambles) which began with a play-action fake to the running back. This percentage does not include fake end-arounds unless there was also a fake handoff. It does include flea flickers.

Average Box: Another item added to our charting courtesy of ESPN Stats & Info Group is the number of defenders in the box before the snap. We list the average box faced by each team's offense and the average box used by this team's defense.

Offensive Pace: Situation-neutral pace represents the seconds of game clock per offensive play, with the following restrictions: no drives are included if they start in the fourth quarter or final five minutes of the first half, and drives are only included if the score is within six points or less. Teams are ranked from quickest pace (Los Angeles Rams, 27.9 seconds) to slowest pace (Kansas City, 32.6 seconds).

Defensive Pace: Situation-neutral pace based on seconds of game clock per defensive play. This is a representation of how a defense was approached by its opponents, not the strategy of the defense itself. Teams are ranked from quickest pace (Carolina, 29.0 seconds) to slowest pace (Miami, 32.1 seconds).

Go for it on fourth: This is the aggressiveness index (AI) introduced by Jim Armstrong in *Pro Football Prospectus 2006*, which measures how often a team goes for a first down in various fourth down situations compared to the league average. A coach over 1.00 is more aggressive, and one below 1.00 is less aggressive. Coaches are ranked from most aggressive to least aggressive.

Following each strategic tendencies table, you'll find a series of comments highlighting interesting data from that team's charting numbers. This includes DVOA ratings split for things like different formations, draw plays, or play-action passing. Please note that all DVOA ratings given in these comments are standard DVOA with no adjustments for the specific situation being analyzed. The average DVOA for a specific situation will not necessarily be 0%, and it won't necessarily be the same for offense and defense. For example, the average offensive DVOA on play-action passes in 2016 was 25.9%, while the average defensive DVOA was 18.9%. The average offensive DVOA when the quarterback was hurried was -54.5%; even if we remove sacks, scrambles, and intentional grounding and only look at actual passes, the average offensive DVOA was -5.3%. On average last year, there was pressure marked on 31.6 percent of pass plays.

How to Read the Offensive Line Tables

SIS charters mark blown blocks not just on sacks but also on hurries, hits, and runs stuffed at the line. However, while we have blown blocks to mark bad plays, we still don't have a metric that consistently marks good plays, so blown blocks should not be taken as the end all and be all of judging individual linemen. It's simply one measurement that goes into the conversation.

All offensive linemen who had at least 160 snaps in 2017 (not including special teams) are listed in the offensive line tables along with the position they played most often and their **Age** as of the 2018 season, listed simply as the difference between birth year and 2018. Players born in January and December of the same year will have the same listed age.

Then we list games, games started, snaps, and offensive penalties (**Pen**) for each lineman. The penalty total includes declined and offsetting penalties. Finally, there are three numbers for blown blocks in 2017.

- Blown blocks leading directly to sacks
- All blown blocks on pass plays, not only including those that lead to sacks but also those that lead to hurries, hits, or offensive holding penalties
- All blown blocks on run plays; generally, this means plays where the running back is tackled for a loss or no gain, but it also includes a handful of plays where the running back would have been tackled for a loss if not for a broken tackle, as well as offensive holding penalties on running plays

Players are given half a blown block when two offensive players are listed with blown blocks on the same play.

As with all player tables in the team chapters, players who are no longer on the team have an asterisk and those new to the team in 2018 are in italics.

The second offensive line table lists the last three years of our various line stats.

The first column gives standard yards per carry by each team's running backs (**Yds**). The next two columns give adjusted line yards (**ALY**) followed by rank among the 32 teams.

Power gives the percentage of runs in short-yardage "power situations" that achieved a first down or touchdown. Those situations include any third or fourth down with one or two yards to go, and any runs in goal-to-go situations from the two-yard line or closer. Unlike the other rushing numbers on the Offensive Line table, Power includes quarterbacks.

Stuff gives the percentage of runs that are stuffed for zero

Dallas Cowboys Offensive Line

Player	Pos	Age	GS	Snaps	Pen	Sk	Pass	Run	Player	Pos	Age	GS	Snaps	Pen	Sk	Pass	Run
Travis Frederick	C	27	16/16	1068	2	0.0	7	15	Tyron Smith	LT	28	13/13	759	8	2.0	10	9
La'el Collins	RT	25	16/16	1068	4	4.0	26	8	Chaz Green	LG/LT	26	14/4	256	3	4.0	10	0
Zack Martin	RG	26	16/16	1021	0	2.0	9	9	Byron Bell*	OT	28	12/2	245	5	5.0	13	2
Jonathan Cooper*	LG	28	13/13	838	6	0.5	13	7	*Cameron Fleming*	RT	26	12/6	369	2	2.0	6	3

Year	Yards	ALY	Rank	Power	Rank	Stuff	Rank	2nd Lev	Rank	Open Field	Rank	Sacks	ASR	Rank	Press	Rank	F-Start	Cont.
2015	4.53	4.48	6	66%	15	17%	4	1.21	12	1.01	8	33	6.6%	19	20.9%	5	26	34
2016	4.68	4.63	4	73%	3	15%	5	1.36	5	0.98	8	28	5.6%	13	28.8%	24	14	37
2017	4.26	4.66	4	77%	3	17%	4	1.16	16	0.67	19	32	6.4%	15	31.9%	21	10	30
2017 ALY by direction:			Left End: 5.61 (4)			Left Tackle: 4.88 (6)			Mid/Guard: 4.55 (4)			Right Tackle: 4.19 (12)			Right End: 4.89 (4)			

or negative gain. Since being stuffed is bad, teams are ranked from stuffed least often (1) to most often (32).

Second-Level (**2nd Lev**) Yards and **Open-Field** Yards represent yardage where the running back has the most power over the amount of the gain. Second-level yards represent the number of yards per carry that come five to ten yards past the line of scrimmage. Open-field yards represent the number of yards per carry that come 11 or more yards past the line of scrimmage. A team with a low ranking in adjusted line yards but a high ranking in open-field yards is heavily dependent on its running back breaking long runs to make the running game work, and therefore tends to have a less consistent running attack. Second-level yards fall somewhere in between.

The next five columns give information about pass protection. That starts with total sacks, followed by adjusted sack rate (**ASR**) and its rank among the 32 teams. Some teams allow a lot of sacks because they throw a lot of passes; adjusted sack rate accounts for this by dividing sacks and intentional grounding by total pass plays. It is also adjusted for situation (sacks are much more common on third down, particularly third-and-long) and opponent, all of which makes it a better measurement than raw sacks totals. Remember that quarterbacks share responsibility for sacks, and two different quarterbacks behind the same line can have very different adjusted sack rates. This year, we've also listed pressure rate: this is the percentage of pass plays where we have marked pass pressure, based on Sports Info Solutions charting. Sacks or scrambles due to coverage are not counted as passes with pressure.

F-Start gives the number of false starts, which is the offensive penalty which best correlates to both wins and wins the following season. This total includes false starts by players other than offensive linemen, but it does not include false starts on special teams. San Francisco led the league with 22, New Orleans was last with 6, and the NFL average was 14.9. Finally, Continuity score (**Cont.**) tells you how much continuity each offensive line had from game-to-game in that season. It was introduced in the Cleveland chapter of *Pro Football Prospectus 2007*. Continuity score starts with 48 and then subtracts:

- The number of players over five who started at least one game on the offensive line;
- The number of times the team started at least one dif-

ferent lineman compared to the game before; and
- The difference between 16 and that team's longest streak where the same line started consecutive games.

The perfect continuity score is 48, which no team received in 2017. Last year's highest score was 42 for the Los Angeles Rams, and last year's lowest score was 16 for Detroit.

Finally, underneath the table in italics we give 2016 adjusted line yards in each of the five directions with rank among the 32 teams. The league average was 4.03 on left end runs (**LE**), 3.96 on left tackle runs (**LT**), 4.18 on runs up the middle (**MID**), 3.81 on right tackle runs (**RT**), and 3.84 on right end runs (**RE**).

How to Read the Defensive Front Seven Tables

Defensive players make plays. Plays aren't just tackles—interceptions and pass deflections change the course of the game, and so does the act of forcing a fumble or beating the offensive players to a fumbled ball. While some plays stop a team on third down and force a punt, others merely stop a receiver after he's caught a 30-yard pass. We still cannot measure each player's opportunities to make a tackle. We can measure opportunities in pass coverage, however, thanks to the Football Outsiders game charting project.

Defensive players are listed in these tables if they made at least 20 plays during the 2017 season, or if they played at least eight games and played 25 percent of defensive snaps in those games. Defensive players who were with two teams last year are only listed with the final team they played with.

Defensive Linemen/Edge Rushers

As we've noted earlier in this toolbox: as hybrid defenses become more popular, it becomes more and more difficult to tell the difference between a defensive end and an outside linebacker. What we do know is that there are certain players whose job is to rush the passer, even if they occasionally drop into coverage. We also know that the defensive ends in a two-gapping 3-4 system have a lot more in common with run-stuffing 4-3 tackles than with smaller 4-3 defensive ends.

Therefore, we have separated front seven players into three

Jacksonville Jaguars Defensive Front Seven

						Overall						vs. Run				Pass Rush			
Defensive Line	Age	Pos	G	Snaps	Plays	TmPct	Rk	Stop	Dfts	BTkl	Runs	St%	Rk	RuYd	Rk	Sack	Hit	Hur	Dsrpt
Malik Jackson	28	DT	16	761	41	5.2%	36	32	17	6	28	71%	63	2.1	43	8.0	4	26.0	2
Abry Jones	27	DT	15	489	36	4.9%	47	27	6	5	27	70%	69	3.0	75	1.0	1	5.5	5
Marcell Dareus	29	DT	14	418	28	3.7%	68	26	6	3	24	96%	1	2.2	48	2.0	2	6.0	0
Eli Ankou	24	DT	9	174	15	3.4%	--	11	4	0	12	67%	--	3.2	--	1.5	0	3.0	0

						Overall						vs. Run				Pass Rush			
Edge Rushers	Age	Pos	G	Snaps	Plays	TmPct	Rk	Stop	Dfts	BTkl	Runs	St%	Rk	RuYd	Rk	Sack	Hit	Hur	Dsrpt
Calais Campbell	32	DE	16	807	69	8.8%	5	58	32	10	45	76%	45	2.3	47	14.5	16	37.0	4
Yannick Ngakoue	23	DE	16	772	28	3.6%	73	25	19	3	12	75%	46	3.4	80	12.0	17	33.5	2
Dante Fowler	24	DE	16	466	20	2.5%	93	17	12	7	10	70%	65	3.1	76	8.0	2	22.5	0

tables rather than two. All defensive tackles and defensive ends from 3-4 teams are listed as **Defensive Linemen**, and all ranked together. Defensive ends from 4-3 teams and outside linebackers from 3-4 teams are listed as **Edge Rushers**, and all ranked together. Most 4-3 linebackers are ranked along with 3-4 inside linebackers, and listed simply as **Linebackers**. For the most part this categorization puts players with similar roles together. Some players who have hybrid roles are ranked at the position more appropriate to their role, such as Bruce Irvin and Vic Beasley as edge rushers despite playing outside linebacker in a 4-3 scheme.

The tables for defensive linemen and edge rushers are the same, although the players are ranked in two separate categories. Players are listed with the following numbers:

Age in 2018, determined by 2018 minus birth year, plus position (**Pos**) and the number of defensive **Snaps** played in 2017.

Plays (**Plays**): The total defensive plays including tackles, pass deflections, interceptions, fumbles forced, and fumble recoveries. This number comes from the official NFL game-books and therefore does not include plays on which the player is listed by the Football Outsiders game charting project as in coverage, but does not appear in the standard play-by-play. Special teams tackles are also not included.

Percentage of team plays (**TmPct**): The percentage of total team plays involving this defender. The sum of the percentages of team plays for all defenders on a given team will exceed 100 percent, primarily due to shared tackles. This number is adjusted based on games played, so an injured player may be fifth on his team in plays but third in **TmPct**.

Stops (**Stop**): The total number of plays which prevent a "success" by the offense (45 percent of needed yards on first down, 60 percent on second down, 100 percent on third or fourth down).

Defeats (**Dfts**): The total number of plays which stop the offense from gaining first down yardage on third or fourth down, stop the offense behind the line of scrimmage, or result in a fumble (regardless of which team recovers) or interception.

Broken tackles (**BTkl**): The number of broken tackles recorded by SIS game charters.

The next five columns represent runs only, starting with the number of plays each player made on **Runs**. Stop rate (**St%**) gives the percentage of these run plays which were stops. Average yards (**AvYd**) gives the average number of yards gained by the runner when this player is credited with making the play.

Finally, we have pass rush numbers, starting with standard NFL **Sack** totals.

Hit: To qualify as a quarterback hit, the defender must knock the quarterback to the ground in the act of throwing or after the pass is thrown. We have listed hits on all plays, including those cancelled by penalties. (After all, many of the hardest hits come on plays cancelled because the hit itself draws a roughing the passer penalty.)

Hurries (**Hur**): The number of quarterback hurries recorded by Sports Info Solutions game charters. This includes both hurries on standard plays and hurries that force an offensive holding penalty that cancels the play and costs the offense yardage.

Disruptions (**Dsprt**): This stat combines two different but similar types of plays. First, plays where a pass-rusher forced an incomplete pass or interception by hitting the quarterback as he was throwing the ball. These plays are generally not counted as passes defensed, so we wanted a way to count them. Second, plays where the pass-rusher batted the ball down at the line of scrimmage or tipped it in the air. These plays are usually incomplete, but occasionally they lead to interceptions, and even more rarely they fall into the hands of offensive receivers. As with the "hit in motion" disruptions, some plays counted as tips by Football Outsiders were not counted as passes defensed by the NFL.

Defensive linemen and edge rushers are both ranked by percentage of team plays, run stop rate, and average yards per run tackle. The lowest number of average yards earns the top rank (negative numbers indicate the average play ending behind the line of scrimmage). Defensive linemen and edge rushers are ranked if they played at least 40 percent of defensive snaps in the games they were active. There are 86 defensive linemen ranked, and 95 edge rushers.

Linebackers

Most of the stats for linebackers are the same as those for defensive linemen. Linebackers are ranked in percentage of team plays, and also in stop rate and average yards for running plays specifically. Linebackers are ranked in these stats if they played at least five games and at least 35 percent of defensive snaps in the games they were active, with 86 linebackers ranked.

The final six columns in the linebacker stats come from Sports Info Solutions game charting.

Targets (**Tgts**): The number of pass players on which game

Linebackers	Age	Pos	G	Snaps	Plays	TmPct	Rk	Stop	Dfts	BTkl	Runs	St%	Rk	RuYd	Rk	Sack	Hit	Hur	Tgts	Suc%	Rk	AdjYd	Rk	PD	Int
Myles Jack	23	OLB	16	1018	93	11.8%	43	38	15	12	52	42%	85	5.1	83	2.0	3	7.0	30	34%	74	8.0	61	1	x
Telvin Smith	27	OLB	14	851	106	15.4%	18	66	27	15	62	71%	19	2.8	18	1.0	1	7.0	41	51%	32	7.6	56	6	x
Paul Posluszny*	34	MLB	16	481	62	7.9%	78	32	12	2	37	62%	45	3.7	50	1.5	1	3.0	19	50%	37	9.5	72	2	x

Year	Yards	ALY	Rank	Power	Rank	Stuff	Rank	2nd Level	Rank	Open Field	Rank	Sacks	ASR	Rank	Press	Rank
2015	3.68	3.82	8	68%	19	23%	9	1.11	15	0.58	9	36	5.8%	24	21.7%	30
2016	3.76	3.73	7	64%	18	21%	11	0.96	4	0.74	18	33	5.9%	17	27.2%	15
2017	4.27	4.37	28	59%	9	20%	19	1.16	20	0.76	19	55	9.1%	2	34.3%	3

2017 ALY by direction:	Left End: 5.20 (31)	Left Tackle: 3.24 (8)	Mid/Guard: 4.38 (25)	Right Tackle: 3.91 (19)	Right End: 4.73 (26)

charters listed this player in coverage.

Success rate (**Suc%**): The percentage plays of targeting this player on which the offense did not have a successful play. This means not only incomplete passes and interceptions, but also short completions which do not meet our baselines for success (45 percent of needed yards on first down, 60 percent on second down, 100 percent on third or fourth down). Success rate is adjusted for the quality of the receiver covered.

Adjusted yards per pass (**AdjYd**): The average number of yards gained on plays on which this defender was the listed target, adjusted for the quality of the receiver covered.

Passes defensed (**PD**): Football Outsiders' count of passes defensed. Unlike the official NFL count of passes defensed, this does not include passes batted down or tipped at the line.

These stats, including other differences between the NFL's count of passes defensed and our own, are explained in more detail in the section on secondary tables. Plays listed with two defenders or as "Hole in Zone" with this defender as the closest player count only for half credit in computing both success rate and average yards per pass. There are 76 linebackers are ranked in the charting stats, based on hitting one of two minimums: 14 charted passes with fewer than eight games started, or 11 charted passes with eight or more games started. As a result of the different thresholds, some linebackers are ranked in standard stats but not charting stats.

Further Details

Just as in the offensive tables, players who are no longer on the team are marked with asterisks, and players who were on other teams last year are in italics. Other than the game charting statistics for linebackers, defensive front seven player statistics are not adjusted for opponent.

Numbers for defensive linemen and linebackers unfortunately do not reflect all of the opportunities a player had to make a play, but they do show us which players were most active on the field. A large number of plays could mean a strong defensive performance, or it could mean that the linebacker in question plays behind a poor part of the line. In general, defensive numbers should be taken as information that tells us what happened on the field in 2017, but not as a strict, unassailable judgment of which players are better than others— particularly when the difference between two players is small (for example, players ranked 20th and 30th) instead of large (players ranked 20th and 70th).

After the individual statistics for linemen and linebackers, the Defensive Front Seven section contains a table that looks exactly like the table in the Offensive Line section. The difference is that the numbers here are for all opposing running backs against this team's defensive front. As we're on the opposite side of the ball, teams are now ranked in the opposite order, so the No. 1 defensive front seven is the one that allows the fewest adjusted line yards, the lowest percentage in Power situations, and has the highest adjusted sack rate. Directions for adjusted line yards are given from the offense's perspective, so runs left end and left tackle are aimed at the right defensive end and (assuming the tight end is on the other side) weakside linebacker.

How to Read the Secondary Tables

The first few columns in the secondary tables are based on standard play-by-play, not game charting, with the exception of broken tackles. Age, total plays, percentage of team plays, stops, and defeats are computed the same way they are for other defensive players, so that the secondary can be compared to the defensive line and linebackers. That means that total plays here includes passes defensed, sacks, tackles after receptions, tipped passes, and interceptions, but not pass plays on which this player was in coverage but was not given a tackle or passed defense by the NFL's official scorer.

The middle five columns address each defensive back's role in stopping the run. Average yardage and stop rate for running plays is computed in the same manner as for defensive linemen and linebackers.

Los Angeles Chargers Defensive Secondary

Secondary	Age	Pos	G	Snaps	Plays	Overall TmPct	Rk	Stop	Dfts	BTkl	vs. Run Runs	St%	Rk	RuYd	Rk	vs. Pass Tgts	Tgt%	Rk	Dist	Suc%	Rk	AdjYd	Rk	PD	Int
Tre Boston*	26	FS	16	1041	87	10.6%	29	20	15	13	42	12%	76	12.2	75	21	4.4%	1	15.3	58%	20	4.9	1	6	5
Jahleel Addae	28	SS	16	1032	103	12.6%	11	45	21	15	46	52%	18	4.2	9	60	12.6%	57	9.0	50%	43	7.5	30	7	0
Trevor Williams	25	CB	16	1006	67	8.2%	44	36	10	6	22	68%	9	2.8	4	68	14.7%	8	15.3	53%	33	8.0	51	14	2
Tre Boston*	26	FS	16	1041	87	10.6%	29	20	15	13	42	12%	76	12.2	75	21	4.4%	1	15.3	58%	20	4.9	1	6	5
Jahleel Addae	28	SS	16	1032	103	12.6%	11	45	21	15	46	52%	18	4.2	9	60	12.6%	57	9.0	50%	43	7.5	30	7	0
Trevor Williams	25	CB	16	1006	67	8.2%	44	36	10	6	22	68%	9	2.8	4	68	14.7%	8	15.3	53%	33	8.0	51	14	2
Casey Hayward	29	CB	16	1003	62	7.6%	54	39	15	11	10	90%	3	1.9	1	77	16.6%	16	15.2	58%	11	7.7	41	25	4
Desmond King	24	CB	16	716	76	9.3%	–	43	18	10	25	64%	–	3.8	–	34	10.2%	–	5.7	56%	–	7.7	–	4	1
Adrian Phillips	26	FS/SS	15	519	63	8.2%	64	27	11	12	23	43%	42	5.3	23	35	14.4%	66	8.2	55%	25	7.8	34	4	2

Year	Pass D Rank	vs. #1 WR	Rk	vs. #2 WR	Rk	vs. Other WR	Rk	WR Wide	Rk	WR Slot	Rk	vs. TE	Rk	vs. RB	Rk
2015	21	4.9%	20	7.6%	19	-10.5%	9	–	–	–	–	34.8%	31	14.1%	26
2016	9	-10.4%	6	5.7%	22	-25.0%	2	-20.3%	4	4.0%	16	-2.1%	15	-3.5%	17
2017	9	-11.8%	10	0.5%	17	-25.2%	3	-17.3%	5	-6.1%	10	0.9%	18	-21.3%	5

The third section of statistics represents data from Sports Info Solutions game charting. In all game charting coverage stats, passes where two defenders are listed and those listed as "Hole in Zone" with this player as the closest zone defender count for half credit. We do not count pass plays on which this player was in coverage, but the incomplete was listed as Thrown Away, Batted Down, or Hit in Motion. Hail Mary passes are also not included.

Targets (**Tgts**): The number of pass plays on which our game charters listed this player in coverage.

Target percentage (**Tgt%**): The number of plays on which this player was targeted divided by the total number of charted passes against his defense, not including plays listed as Uncovered. Like percentage of team plays, this metric is adjusted based on number of games played.

Average depth of target (**aDOT**): The average distance in the air beyond the line of scrimmage of all passes targeted at this defender. It does not include yards after catch and is useful for seeing which defenders were covering receivers deeper or shorter. This is also often referred to as "Air Yards."

Adjusted Success rate (**Suc%**): The percentage plays of targeting this player on which the offense did not have a successful play. This means not only incomplete passes and interceptions, but also short completions which do not meet our baselines for success (45 percent of needed yards on first down, 60 percent on second down, 100 percent on third or fourth down). Defensive pass interference is counted as a failure for the defensive player similar to a completion of equal yardage (and a new first down). This number is adjusted based on the quality of the receiver covered.

Adjusted Yards per Pass (**AdjYd**): The average number of yards gained on plays on which this defender was the listed target, adjusted for the quality of the receiver covered.

Passes Defensed (**PD**): This is our count of passes defensed, and will differ from the total found in NFL gamebooks. Our count includes:

- All passes listed by our charting as Defensed, based on Sports Info Solutions data.
- All interceptions, or tipped passes leading to interceptions.
- Any pass on which the defender is given a pass defensed by the official scorer, and our game charting is marked either Miscommunication or Catch Out of Bounds.

Our count of passes defensed does not include passes marked as defensed in the official gamebooks but listed by our charters as Overthrown, Underthrown, or Thrown Away. It also does not include passes tipped in the act of rushing the passer. In addition, we did a lot of work with both the NFL head office and the folks from ESPN Stats & Info and Sports Info Solutions to get the most accurate numbers possible for both drops and passes defensed. Official scorers and game charters will sometimes disagree on a drop vs. a pass defensed, or even an overthrown/underthrown ball vs. a pass defensed, and there are a number of passes where the league marked the official stats in one way and ESPN S&I or SIS marked their stats the other way.

Interceptions (**Int**) represent the standard NFL interception total.

With more and more wide receivers playing, that means more and more cornerbacks are playing, so we've had to increase our minimums so we aren't ranking a zillion cornerbacks. Cornerbacks need 50 charted passes or eight games started to be ranked in the defensive stats, with 80 cornerbacks ranked in total. Safeties require 20 charted passes or eight games started, with 76 safeties ranked in total. Strong and free safeties are ranked together. Players listed with two positions are ranked at the first position listed.

Just like the front seven, the secondary has a table of team statistics following the individual numbers. This table gives DVOA figured against different types of receivers. Each offense's wide receivers have had one receiver designated as No. 1, and another as No. 2. (Occasionally this is difficult, due to injury or a situation with "co-No. 1 receivers," but it's usually pretty obvious.) The other receivers form a third category, with tight ends and running backs as fourth and fifth categories. The defense is then judged on the performance of each receiver based on the standard DVOA method, with each rating adjusted based on strength of schedule. (Obviously, it's a lot harder to cover the No. 1 receiver of the Pittsburgh Steelers than to cover the No.1 receiver of the Tennessee Titans.) **Pass D Rank** is the total ranking of the pass defense, as seen before in the Trends and Splits table, and combines all five categories plus sacks and passes with no intended target.

The "defense vs. types of receivers" table should be used to analyze the defense as a whole rather than individual players. The ratings against types of receivers are generally based on defensive schemes, not specific cornerbacks, except for certain defenses that really do move one cornerback around to cover the opponent's top weapon (i.e., Arizona). The ratings against tight ends and running backs are in large part due to the performance of linebackers.

NEW FOR 2018: Starting in this year's book, we are also providing each team's numbers covering receivers based on where they lined up before the snap, either wide or in the slot. The "vs. Other WR" number has sometimes been misrepresented as measuring coverage of slot receivers, but in the modern NFL, the team's No. 1 or No. 2 receiver will often be working predominantly out of the slot, while other receivers will switch back and forth between the two positions. The listing of coverage of wide receivers in the slot also includes wide receivers lined up tight in a tight end position. We have this data for 2016 and 2017 but it is not listed for 2015.

How to Read the Special Teams Tables

The special teams tables list the last three years of kick, punt, and return numbers for each team.

The first two columns list total special teams DVOA and rank among the 32 teams. The next two columns list the value in actual points of field goals and extra points (**FG/XP**) when compared to how a league average kicker would do from the same distances, adjusted for weather and altitude, and rank among the 32 teams. Next, we list the estimated value in actual points of field position over or under the league average based on net kickoffs (**Net Kick**), and rank that value among the 32 teams. That is followed by the estimated point values of field position for kick returns (**Kick Ret**), net punting (**Net Punt**), and punt returns (**Punt Ret**) and their respective ranks.

The final two columns represent the value of "**Hidden**" special teams, plays which throughout the past decade have usually been based on the performance of opponents without this team being able to control the outcome. We combine the opposing team's value on field goals, kickoff distance, and punt distance, adjusted for weather and altitude, and then switch the sign to represent that good special teams by the opponent will cost the listed team points, and bad special teams will effectively hand them points. We have to give the qualifier of "usually" because, as explained above, certain returners such as Cordarrelle Patterson will affect opposing special teams strategy, and a handful of the missed field goals are blocked. Nonetheless, the "hidden" value is still "hidden" for most teams, and they are ranked from the most hidden value gained (Los Angeles Rams, 40.6 points) to the most value lost (Houston, -16.9 points).

We also have methods for measuring the gross value of kickoffs and punts. These measures assume that all kickoffs or punts will have average returns unless they are touchbacks or kicked out of bounds, then judge the kicker or punter on the value with those assumed returns. These metrics may be listed in special teams comments as **KickPts+** and **PuntPts+**. We also count special teams tackles; these include both tackles and assists, but do not include tackles on two-point conversions, tackles after onside kicks, or tackles of the player who recovers a fumble after the punt or kick returner loses the ball. The best and worst individual values for kickers, punters, returners, and kick gunners (i.e. tackle totals) are listed in the statistical appendix at the end of the book.

Administrative Minutia

Receiving statistics include all passes intended for the receiver in question, including those that are incomplete or intercepted. The word passes refers to both complete and incomplete pass attempts. When rating receivers, interceptions are treated as incomplete passes with no penalty.

For the computation of DVOA and DYAR, passing statistics include sacks as well as fumbles on aborted snaps. We do not include kneeldown plays or spikes for the purpose of stopping the clock. Some interceptions which we have determined to be "Hail Mary" plays that end the first half or game are counted as regular incomplete passes, not turnovers.

All statistics generated by ESPN Stats & Info or Sports Info Solutions game charting, or our combination of the two sources, may be different from totals compiled by other sources.

Unless we say otherwise, when we refer to third-down performance in this book we are referring to a combination of third down and the handful of rushing and passing plays that take place on fourth down (primarily fourth-and-1).

Aaron Schatz

Baltimore Ravens Special Teams

Year	DVOA	Rank	FG/XP	Rank	Net Kick	Rank	Kick Ret	Rank	Net Punt	Rank	Punt Ret	Rank	Hidden	Rank
2015	7.3%	1	4.5	7	4.5	6	4.7	6	16.0	2	7.0	6	-0.6	17
2016	4.9%	4	25.5	1	7.0	3	-2.8	23	-1.0	16	-4.1	24	11.7	3
2017	9.2%	1	19.0	1	6.6	4	12.3	1	4.1	12	3.9	5	-7.0	24

The Year In Quotes

THE GREAT WHITE NORTH: A BARREN QB WASTELAND

"I think they had me pretty good, outnumbered three-to-one, with the coaches. Definitely different, being a little ghost town out there. I missed Tyrod and T.J. both. We have a good time out there. So hopefully they'll get back quick."

—Buffalo Bills rookie quarterback Nathan Peterman, equating the quarterback situation in Buffalo to a "ghost town" after Tyrod Taylor and T.J. Yates were absent from practice for concussion protocol. (Buffalo Bills)

THIS MAN LOVES FOOTBALL TO A FAULT

"We're focused on the team we play and the teams that we cross over with. In this case, Kansas City, the teams that they've played, obviously, we'll see them. But two teams that aren't on our schedule that played each other last week, generally, we wouldn't be poring over that film unless there was some particular reason."

—New England Patriots head coach Bill Belichick, stating in an interview with Boston-area radio station WEEI that he has watched every 2017 preseason game. That's FORTY-NINE games. And it's not even a good product. (WEEI, Boston.com)

A UNIQUE RELATIONSHIP

"We go way back to when I was little. I think he babysat me some times."

—Carolina Panthers running back Christian McCaffrey reveals that San Francisco 49ers head coach Kyle Shanahan may have babysat McCaffrey at a young age. During the late 1990s, Kyle's father Mike Shanahan coached McCaffrey's dad, wideout Ed McCaffrey, on the Denver Broncos. (Cam Inman, Bay Area News Group)

"If I did [babysit him], I probably left my sister to do it very quickly and moved on. His dad was my hero growing up. I was close with Ed and his wife Lisa—that's really why I wore 87 in college. Ed was the man. I knew all his sons, they were a lot younger when I knew them, but they've all turned out be pretty good athletes and real good people."

—Kyle Shanahan responding to the alleged babysitting incident. (NFL.com)

TEAMMATES JUST HELPING EACH OTHER OUT

"We were just trying to get Johnny [Hekker] in the Pro Bowl again."

—Los Angeles Rams running back Todd Gurley said that his team's slow start against the Houston Texans helped punter Johnny Hekker's Pro Bowl campaign. (The Checkdown, Instagram)

SUNDAY NIGHT FOOTBALL GETS ... SEXUAL?

"[Dallas Cowboys quarterback Dak Prescott] told us the other day that he weighed 240 [pounds]. And I knew kinda what the weight was, and he said 'I'm 240, and about 220 of it are in my legs.' And you could see it in a pair of shorts, this is a really thickly built guy, and when you lean into him, he doesn't always go down."

—NBC Sunday Night Football commentator Cris Collinsworth gets down and dirty and talks about just how thick Dallas Cowboys quarterback Dak Prescott's legs are. (NBC Sports via Sports GIFs & Videos)

"Dak is oddly already dripping wet. Did nice job of NOT throwing 1st two. Looked like Brice Butler should've caught his ball."

—FS1 personality Skip Bayless also gets into "That's What She Said" territory. (Skip Bayless, Twitter)

THE STENCH OF DEFEAT

"Dont'a Hightower. Every time I go by, he stinks. He's putting in work. To tell you the truth, our whole team needs these pods after practice. I'm pretty sure we use them—I'll have to ask whoever does the laundry after practice. I definitely think they need these pods after practice; our whole team is stinky after practice."

—New England Patriots tight end Rob Gronkowski answers the question that has captivated the nation: which Patriots player smells the worst? Gronkowski is a spokesman for Tide Sport PODS, so maybe he can score some free samples for Patriots linebacker Dont'a Hightower. (Sporting News)

JOSH NORMAN, INVENTOR OF THE 'TRASH TALK MONOLOGUE'

"First off, you don't come in here and say what you gon' put up on somebody. 200 yards ... did he even catch two balls? He only caught one, huh? So please, whatever you do, do not run your mouth if you a wide receiver and expect to show up on Sunday, cuz I'm telling you. We are here, and we are waitin'. Don't come out here and tell me what you gonna do, show me. You 'gonna have to run through me to get that, and we ain't gonna let that happen. Whatever that young cat said, Coop, go on and take it back. Crabtree? I have nothing to say to you. I may be Cover-2. I'm Cover-1, Cover-2, Cover-3, and Cover-4. All of 'em. All of them ingredients in making a perfect attack."

—Washington Redskins cornerback Josh Norman goes scorched earth on the Oakland Raiders receiving corps. Amari Cooper and Michael Crabtree, touted as one of the best wide-receiving pairs in the NFL coming into the season, combined for 13 total yards against the Washington secondary. (CBS Sports)

NOT VERY SCIENTIFIC

"Somebody please explain how asparagus does it. And you know what I mean by 'it.'"

—Minnesota Vikings quarterback Case Keenum asks a pretty innocent question on Twitter...

*"I'll tell you how if you explain how you're a soft ass bitch and cry about opponent teams fan base after you get your ass handed to you by 31 you Charmin ass b****"*

... which was met with some Twitter-esqe responses.

"Doesn't seem to be much science behind that one."

—We're with Case on this one. Wonder if he ever found out about that asparagus thing? (Case Keenum/Twitter)

BREAKING: BUFFALO THUMB WRESTLING TOURNAMENT GOES AWRY

"Ramon Humber (thumb) & Jordan Matthews (thumb) DNP. Kyle Williams (thumb) full practice. Jerel Worthy (thumb) & Mike Tolbert (thumb) removed."

—Mike Rodak notes that the Buffalo Bills' injury report is pretty thumb-centric this week. (Mike Rodak, Twitter)

...I AWARD YOU NO POINTS AND MAY GOD HAVE MERCY ON YOUR SOUL

"The score was in the teens for most of the game. Is that a style of play your team is comfortable playing?"

—A question asked of New England Patriots head coach Bill Belichick at the press conference following a win over the Los Angeles Chargers.

"What are you talking about?"

—Belichick, in response.

"Do you prefer the low-scoring, grind-it-out type of games?"

The reporter, trying to clarify.

"We prefer to win."

—Belichick, stating the obvious. (Doug Kyed, Twitter)

NOTHIN' LIKE A NEW YORK SLICE

"Pizza Hut & Dominos better anyways"

—New York Giants nose tackle Damon "Snacks" Harrison had this to say following the news from Papa John's that earnings were down, and that then-CEO John Schnatter was blaming the decline on NFL players who were kneeling for the national anthem. Snacks, you live in New York, arguably the Mecca of American pizza. Why are you even eating Pizza Hut and Dominos? C'mon, man! (Damon Harrison, Twitter)

'MIKE ZIMMER THE SCIENCE GUY' DOESN'T FLOW AS WELL

"We're going to try something a little bit different than most of the other teams, and I'll either look smart or I'll look dumb ... morning practice on Wednesday, and then we'll leave that night and then get there Thursday and have a Thursday practice when we get [to London]. We've had sleep people come talk to us; you know, we're getting the whole gamut. I was looking into all the scientific things for this."

—Minnesota Vikings head coach Mike Zimmer pulled out all the stops for his team's trip to London to face off against the Cleveland Browns. It seemed to work, as the Vikings won 33-16. (Vikings.com)

TAKE THE JETS OFF HIS SHORT LIST

"I speak on behalf of the New York Jets, we'll give you $60 million in cash if you come play for us."

—An avid Jets fan reaches out to Pittsburgh Steelers running back Le'Veon Bell to see if he'll come to the Big Apple.

"That ain't enough to come run with the Jets..."

—Bell's response. (Le'Veon Bell/Twitter)

AND LE'VEON BELL, UNLIKE WINTER, IS NOT COMING

"Life for a Jets fan is an unending torment."

—Game of Thrones author and die-hard New York Jets fan George R.R. Martin lets us all know what true pain and suffering is. (George R.R. Martin, Twitter)

THE ONLY SPRINTING HE'S DOING IS TOWARD THE BEER AISLE

"T.J. what was your 40?"

—Detroit Lions guard T.J. Lang was asked this question after talking about the NFL combine on Twitter.

"Was Steel Reserve for a while until I switched to Coors."

—Huh. We pinned Lang for an Olde English kind of guy. (T.J. Lang/Twitter)

WADE PHILLIPS: KING OF DAD JOKES

"It's expensive agency, not free agency."

—Los Angeles Rams defensive coordinator Wade Phillips was blessing Twitter timelines with his dad jokes in March. (Wade Phillips/Twitter)

"I have to do 1 more—By Signing Aqib and Marcus, looks like we (the Rams) have Cornered the market. Sorry but it had [to] be said."

—More Wade. (Wade Phillips/Twitter)

"I think the defensive coordinator has more swag than all of them, so we'll be in good shape."

—Los Angeles Rams head coach Sean McVay, when asked about how he's going to handle all these new personalities, notes that the coolest cat in the locker room doesn't even suit up for games. (Gary Klein/Twitter)

SOME RIVALRIES TAKE PRIORITY OVER EVERYTHING—EVEN FAMILY

"All my family is from Texas and a lot of them say they're Eagles fans, but I think deep down they root. Like even last year, the Cowboys go to the playoffs, and I heard my grandma in there rooting for Dallas. And I said to her 'If you want to live to see 75 you better shut your ass up.' Just messin' with her, but it is what it is."

—Philadelphia Eagles offensive tackle Lane Johnson had to set the record straight with his Texas-native grandma during last year's playoffs. (NBC Sports Philadelphia, Twitter)

URINE HAS OFFICIALLY BEEN RENAMED DING-DING SAUCE; ALL OTHER NAMES ARE INCORRECT

"I'm sorry, though, look. It's either this, or that, and I can't afford that. I apologize. But if you do not understand what this is, it's when you put your ding-ding sauce out and give them a sample."

—Oakland Raiders running back Marshawn Lynch announces to the media he won't be speaking to them due to a drug test. In the process, he renames what we commonfolk call "urine." (CBS Sports)

THE FAMILY THAT BROUGHT YOU BUBBA RAY, D-VON, SPIKE, AND SIGN GUY NOW HAS A NEW BROTHER: GRONK DUDLEY

"Did you ever go through any tables?"

—Unnamed reporter asking New England Patriots tight end Rob Gronkowski a rather strange question.

"Not at a tailgate, but I've been through tables before. For sure."

—Gronkowski's even stranger reply.

"What setting?"

—The reporter doing what good reporters do and pressing for more information.

"Family get-togethers, growing up, I've definitely been through tables."

—Gronkowski's explanation. The Gronkowski family, natives of the Rochester, New York, area, are no strangers to the beer-guzzling, table-breaking fans colloquially known as "Bills Mafia." (Casey Baker, Twitter)

THE FOUNTAIN OF YOUTH LIES SOMEWHERE IN BALTIMORE

"I don't know, I never get tired of them, I can tell you that. He has an amazing ability. Terrell Suggs, I mean, he's Ponce de León—you should put that on the back of his jersey—he has found the Fountain of Youth. He's playing as well, or better, than I've seen him ever play since I have been here."

—Baltimore Ravens head coach John Harbaugh fawns over edge rusher Terrell Suggs' ability to stay elite late into his career. (ProFootballTalk)

THE MUSINGS OF MIKE LEACH

"Well first of all, there should be more sharks [as mascots] if you're by an ocean. That tiger at LSU, that's a live real tiger sitting in there, in some metal structure that he could rip his way out of if he wanted to, if he half-wanted to, that's an awesome one. The buffalo in Colorado, that's an awesome one. There's a place in Kansas called Pitt State. I used to see them on film, we didn't play them. Called Pitt State and they're the Gorillas. And there should be a lot more gorillas for mascots."

—Washington State head coach Mike Leach breaks down some of the best mascots in the country, and addresses the need for more sharks and gorillas in college football. (Lindsay Joy, Twitter)

"Tracked a raccoon one time in the snow because I was in the neighborhood and was just curious where this raccoon lived, you know? There's fresh raccoon tracks and he had been digging through someone's garbage so I followed the tracks. I don't even know if these people know it but he lives right in the back of their house in a bunch brush and trees. Because you can follow it approximately right where he's at. ... "It was like on a cartoon or something, blatant tracks. It was residential enough, so I was curious where this sucker lived. I walked about a half-mile out of my way to sort that out."

—Washington State head coach Mike Leach is apparently an especially good tracker when he isn't coaching football. During one of Leach's walks to work, he allegedly tracked a raccoon for three and a half miles just to see where he lives. (Pardon My Take/Instagram)

ADDRESSING THE ELEPHANT IN THE STADIUM

"The 49ers sent out a questionnaire to fans asking 'In terms of game day experience, how important is it that your team wins?'"

—San Francisco Chronicle columnist Ann Killion shed some light on how the 49ers are attempting to gauge the fans' emotional reaction to the team's 0-7 start. (Ann Killion, Twitter)

SO ... WHO WANTS TO SPOIL IT FOR HIM?

"Yeah, we just lost a great player, but, nevertheless, you know ... the Titanic still has to go."

—Carolina Panthers quarterback Cam Newton relates his team to the unsinkable and definitely-not-at-the-bottom-of-the-ocean Titanic after his team traded away wide receiver Kelvin Benjamin. (Independent NFL reporter Dov Kleiman, Twitter)

"Absolutely, you know we did. We had to get on him about that. We are not sinking."

—Carolina linebacker Thomas Davis confirms that Newton has been told about the Titanic's fate, and that the Panthers' hearts will go on. (Pro Football Talk, Twitter)

WHEN THERE'S SOMETHING STRANGE IN YOUR URINE SAMPLE ... WHO YOU GONNA CALL?

"I don't know. There's a lot of ghosts around here. Maybe a ghost put it in me. You know like the Ghost of Christmas Past? A ghost might have put it in me. I don't know."

—New York Jets wide receiver Jeremy Kerley comes up with an unorthodox response when asked how a banned substance ended up in his urine sample. (New York Post)

LARRY WRITING CHECKS THAT J.P. CAN'T CASH

"I need @LarryFitzgerald to convince my GF to drive with me to the game today"

—Arizona Cardinals fan J.P. Walther reached out to wide receiver Larry Fitzgerald for some help convincing his girlfriend to go to the team's game in Washington in December. (J.P. Walther, Twitter)

"Dear J.P.'s girlfriend,
Come with him to the game and he will propose for Christmas!!
Love,
Fitz"

—Larry Fitzgerald lays out a pretty big ultimatum for J.P.'s girlfriend. (Larry Fitzgerald, Twitter)

WHEN YOUR EX IS HANDLING THE BREAKUP WAY BETTER THAN YOU ARE

"I am a huge fan of the Rams players. They're basically— I don't want to say my players—but I had a lot to do with that roster. Left them in pretty good shape, and Sean, as he has shown in a short period of time, is an outstanding young coach."

—Former Los Angeles Rams head coach Jeff Fisher thinks he deserves some of the credit for the Rams' success this season. Fisher was 31-45 during his tenure with the Rams, including a 4-9 record last year. (Rich Hammond, Twitter)

BRUCE ARIANS PLANTING HIS FLAG AT MIDFIELD

"Thank you for coming to my house. I hope you get home safe."

—Arizona Cardinals head coach Bruce Arians led off his press conference after a victory at the Seahawks' CenturyLink Field with this gem. Arians retired with a 4-1 record at CenturyLink. (ESPN)

MARCUS PETERS WON'T TAKE YOUR SYMPATHIES

"Let's go Marcus!"

—A Chiefs fan in the tunnel gives some genuine cheers for Kansas City Chiefs cornerback Marcus Peters after the Chiefs lost to the Tennessee Titans 22-21.

*"Shi*t, where we going, home?"*

—Peters' response as he runs into the locker room. (NFL Update, Twitter)

BILL BELICHICK: NOT A FAN OF DVOA

"You know how I feel about stats. Stats are for losers. Final scores are for winners."

—New England Patriots head coach Bill Belichick wages war on stats nerds and analytics with this quote. Maybe we should send him a copy of this Almanac to sway him to the Dark Side. (Pardon My Take, Instagram)

DO I STILL HAVE NCAA ELIGIBILITY LEFT? BECAUSE I WANNA PLAY FOR THIS GUY

"I am not trying to recruit Swag masters, dancers, fashion experts, professional trash talkers, 'grown ass men!' or stand up comedians ... I am trying to recruit Football Players. Hard-nosed, team first, coach-able, dirty, nasty, gritty, Football Players. Give me those guys."

—State University of New York College at Buffalo defensive backs coach Jordan Hoolihan lays out the agenda for the kind of players he wants to recruit. (Jordan Hoolihan, Twitter)

THE HAMSTER RUNNING ON THE WHEEL INSIDE GRONK'S HEAD IS WORKING OVERTIME

"We got yelled at. We're not allowed to talk about celebrations. That's what we got told. But, I kind of want to talk about it, but I kind of don't because I'll get in trouble, so I don't know what to do. So, it just happened on the spot. It wasn't planned. We'll just keep it there."

—New England Patriots tight end Rob Gronkowski goes to war in his own head as to whether or not he should talk about a celebration he and wide receiver Brandin Cooks performed during a 35-17 win over the Miami Dolphins. (Patriots Wire, which had the video of Cooks riding Gronkowski like a horse)

BLAKE BORTLES: THE LeBRON JAMES OF THE NFL

"It'll probably never stop. There's people that think LeBron James sucks. So if that happens, I'm sure there are a lot of people who will always think I suck."

—Jacksonville Jaguars quarterback Blake Bortles compares himself to NBA All-Star LeBron James when asked how much more Bortles has to do to silence his critics. (Alyssa Lang, Twitter)

QUOTE OF THE YEAR

"Everybody play naked. Butt naked. Everybody play butt-ass naked!"

—Washington Redskins defensive line coach Jim Tomsula dropped this gem while mic'd up talking to his players this against the Philadelphia Eagles. (NFL Network, as captured by Twitter user Dov Kleiman)

Compiled by Cale Clinton

Full 2018 Projections

The following table lists the mean DVOA projections for all 32 NFL teams. We also list the average number of wins for each team in our one million simulations, along with how often each team made the playoffs, reached the Super Bowl, and won the NFL Championship.

Full 2018 Projections

| Team | Avg Wins | Postseason Odds | | | Mean DVOA Projections | | | | | | | | | Schedule | |
		Make Playoffs	Reach Super Bowl	Win Super Bowl	Total DVOA	Rk	Off DVOA	Rk	Def DVOA	Rk	ST DVOA	Rk	Average Opponent	Rk
NE	10.5	78.5%	24.3%	13.4%	17.8%	2	13.2%	2	-0.6%	14	3.9%	2	-4.5%	32
PIT	10.2	70.8%	23.8%	13.8%	18.5%	1	15.6%	1	-3.6%	8	-0.7%	17	0.0%	17
LAR	9.5	58.9%	13.5%	7.2%	13.1%	4	2.5%	11	-7.2%	1	3.4%	3	0.2%	13
NO	9.4	58.9%	14.3%	7.9%	15.4%	3	12.5%	3	-3.1%	9	-0.2%	11	2.2%	4
GB	9.3	55.1%	10.9%	5.6%	10.4%	7	11.1%	4	0.1%	17	-0.6%	15	-1.8%	27
MIN	9.2	53.0%	10.1%	5.2%	10.6%	6	4.6%	7	-6.3%	2	-0.3%	12	-0.4%	22
PHI	9.1	52.9%	10.9%	5.7%	11.0%	5	3.9%	8	-4.8%	3	2.2%	5	0.9%	11
DAL	9.1	52.1%	10.0%	5.1%	10.3%	8	9.3%	5	0.2%	18	1.2%	7	0.0%	18
BAL	8.4	42.2%	6.6%	3.1%	3.4%	10	-6.0%	26	-4.0%	7	5.4%	1	0.1%	14
HOU	8.3	42.6%	5.7%	2.6%	0.5%	12	-2.7%	21	-4.4%	5	-1.3%	27	-2.7%	31
SEA	8.3	38.7%	5.4%	2.5%	2.7%	11	1.5%	14	-1.3%	13	-0.2%	10	0.4%	12
IND	8.1	39.5%	5.1%	2.3%	-1.0%	15	1.6%	13	4.2%	29	1.6%	6	-2.0%	28
ATL	8.1	37.3%	5.4%	2.6%	4.3%	9	7.6%	6	2.7%	24	-0.6%	16	3.0%	2
TEN	8.0	37.8%	4.6%	2.0%	-1.5%	17	0.5%	15	1.4%	19	-0.6%	14	-1.7%	26
LAC	7.9	38.9%	4.4%	1.9%	-2.2%	18	0.4%	16	1.6%	21	-1.0%	23	-1.5%	25
OAK	7.9	38.6%	4.5%	2.0%	-0.8%	14	2.4%	12	2.4%	23	-0.9%	20	-0.7%	24
Team	Avg Wins	Postseason Odds			Mean DVOA Projections									Schedule	
		Make Playoffs	Reach Super Bowl	Win Super Bowl	Total DVOA	Rk	Off DVOA	Rk	Def DVOA	Rk	ST DVOA	Rk	Average Opponent	Rk
WAS	7.8	32.1%	3.9%	1.8%	0.0%	13	3.4%	10	1.6%	20	-1.8%	32	1.7%	8
DET	7.8	30.4%	3.3%	1.5%	-2.3%	19	3.4%	9	6.6%	30	0.9%	8	0.1%	15
JAX	7.7	33.0%	3.8%	1.7%	-4.1%	24	-4.9%	23	-1.7%	10	-0.9%	21	-0.4%	21
KC	7.6	33.9%	3.8%	1.6%	-2.8%	21	-1.7%	19	3.9%	28	2.7%	4	1.0%	9
ARI	7.6	28.0%	3.0%	1.4%	-3.2%	23	-3.6%	22	-1.4%	12	-1.0%	24	0.9%	10
CAR	7.5	28.7%	3.4%	1.5%	-1.3%	16	-6.1%	27	-4.6%	4	0.2%	9	3.3%	1
CLE	7.5	28.8%	3.3%	1.4%	-2.8%	22	-5.4%	25	-4.3%	6	-1.7%	31	1.7%	7
MIA	7.5	29.9%	2.8%	1.1%	-7.2%	27	-5.0%	24	1.9%	22	-0.3%	13	-2.7%	30
CIN	7.4	28.1%	3.1%	1.3%	-2.6%	20	-1.2%	18	-0.2%	16	-1.5%	29	1.9%	5
SF	7.4	25.9%	2.4%	1.0%	-5.1%	25	-0.7%	17	3.4%	25	-1.0%	25	-0.4%	23
TB	7.0	22.3%	2.0%	0.8%	-6.8%	26	-2.5%	20	3.5%	26	-0.8%	19	2.5%	3
DEN	7.0	26.2%	2.2%	0.9%	-8.6%	28	-9.3%	29	-1.7%	11	-1.0%	22	0.1%	16
NYJ	6.9	22.3%	1.6%	0.6%	-12.5%	29	-11.5%	31	-0.4%	15	-1.4%	28	-2.5%	29
CHI	6.2	13.3%	0.7%	0.3%	-15.7%	31	-10.8%	30	3.8%	27	-1.2%	26	-0.1%	19
NYG	6.1	12.4%	0.7%	0.3%	-14.9%	30	-6.4%	28	6.9%	32	-1.6%	30	1.8%	6
BUF	5.4	8.9%	0.4%	0.1%	-23.3%	32	-15.8%	32	6.8%	31	-0.8%	18	-0.4%	20

Arizona Cardinals

2017 Record: 8-8	**Total DVOA:** -11.2% (22nd)	**2018 Mean Projection:** 7.6 wins	**On the Clock (0-4):** 12%
Pythagorean Wins: 6.1 (24th)	**Offense:** -18.4% (30th)	**Postseason Odds:** 28.0%	**Mediocrity (5-7):** 37%
Snap-Weighted Age: 28.0 (1st)	**Defense:** -12.6% (4th)	**Super Bowl Odds:** 3.0%	**Playoff Contender (8-10):** 38%
Average Opponent: 0.6% (13th)	**Special Teams:** -5.5% (28th)	**Proj. Avg. Opponent:** 0.9% (10th)	**Super Bowl Contender (11+):** 13%

2017: Palmer's final ride is doomed from the start.

2018: The Cardinals really take that offensive rebuild thing to heart.

A disappointing 2016 season left Arizona with question marks throughout the roster. After looking like Super Bowl contenders at the start of the season, the Cardinals had sputtered to a 7-8-1 record. The offense, led by Carson Palmer and Larry Fitzgerald, was mediocre and old, and only stood to get older. The defense ranked third in DVOA but had to replace over 5,000 snaps on that side of the ball. Arizona decided to give it one final go with the offensive core that had earned a first-round bye in the 2015 playoffs, in the hopes that the underwhelming 2016 season was just an aberration. With stud dual threat running back David Johnson still in the fold, it seemed reasonable that he would be able to compensate (at least somewhat) for the likely age-related decline of Palmer and Fitzgerald.

Well, that was a nice idea. Johnson suffered a dislocated wrist against the Lions in Week 1, and his season ended after logging only 11 carries and six receptions. Coming off a 2016 season in which he accounted for 2,118 yards from scrimmage and 20 touchdowns, Johnson's absence left a gaping hole in the Arizona backfield. The Cardinals scuffled along for a few weeks while relying on the likes of Chris Johnson, Kerwynn Williams, and Andre Ellington to try to fill in for the former Northern Iowa product, topping out at 83 yards rushing in an overtime win against the Colts in Week 2.

After a blowout at the hands of the eventual Super Bowl champion Eagles, the Cardinals pulled the trigger on a trade that would have been incredibly exciting five years ago, acquiring Adrian Peterson from New Orleans. Peterson rewarded their faith in his first game with the team, rushing for 134 yards and leading the Cardinals to a win over Tampa Bay. However, over the course of the season, Peterson proved why he had been buried on the Saints' depth chart, finishing 46th out of 47 qualifying running backs in both rushing DYAR and DVOA. Peterson's poor performance and the lack of better options surrounding him played a large part in Arizona's rushing offense coming in dead last in DVOA.

The hope for Arizona was that the ground game would be able to offset any additional decline in performance from Palmer after a mediocre 2016 season from the former MVP candidate. Palmer actually managed a slight improvement from -7.8% to -3.3% in passing DVOA, but his season ended on injured reserve after breaking his left arm against the Rams. While Arizona attempted to replace their starting running back with a former MVP, their replacement quarterbacks were not nearly as decorated, with head coach Bruce Arians turning first to Blaine Gabbert and then to Drew Stanton in Palmer's stead. Rather than listing out exactly how poorly that ended for those two passers, let's move on from them, much like Arizona did. Arians headed out the door as well, retiring from coaching at season's end.

Normally, a bottom-dwelling offense is reason for widespread changes throughout the unit. Arizona is taking that approach to the extreme entering the 2018 season. In most cases, that would be hyperbole, but for new head coach Steve Wilks and offensive coordinator Mike McCoy, it is absolutely accurate. After years of employing an aggressive downfield aerial assault under Arians, the Cardinals will be moving to a less balls-to-the-wall approach on offense. McCoy is installing a scheme designed to feature the running game while making use of a fullback and focusing on short to intermediate passes. The emphasis on shorter throws represents a departure from the old Arians ways, where the mantra of "no risk-it, no biscuit" defined how the Cardinals attacked defenses with Palmer at the helm. In 2017, Arizona rarely lined up with more than one running back, so incorporating a fullback will be another big stylistic change in the desert. In another stark contrast, Arizona led the league by using an empty backfield 17 percent of the time; McCoy's Denver unit finished 25th in that metric.

With such a massive stylistic change, you would expect some significant turnover on offense, and that is clearly what is happening with the Cardinals as they replace nearly all of their passes and carries from the 2017 season. Thanks to Palmer's retirement and Gabbert's and Stanton's departures in free agency, the only player to attempt a pass for the 2017 Cardinals who will be on the roster in 2018 is Larry Fitzgerald. He completed one pass for 21 yards and is a wide receiver. Arizona logged 410 total carries in 2017 and is only bringing back players responsible for 54 of them. All told, Wilks will need to replace 94.5 percent of the team's carries and pass attempts for the 2018 season in his first season replacing the retired Arians (Table 1).

Excluding situations caused by preseason injuries, the 2018 Cardinals will have the second-most offensive turnover in terms of carries and pass attempts in the last 20 years, coming in behind the 2002 Ravens. That was a similar situation: a franchise undergoing changes at quarterback while losing a star running back (Jamal Lewis) for the entirety of the preceding season. Because of Lewis' injury and then subsequent

2018 Cardinals Schedule

Week	Opp.	Week	Opp.	Week	Opp.
1	WAS	7	DEN (Thu.)	13	at GB
2	at LAR	8	SF	14	DET
3	CHI	9	BYE	15	at ATL
4	SEA	10	at KC	16	LAR
5	at SF	11	OAK	17	at SEA
6	at MIN	12	at LAC		

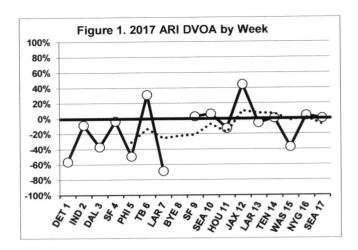

Figure 1. 2017 ARI DVOA by Week

return, the Ravens ended up replacing 99.4 percent of the previous season's carries and pass attempts year over year. Baltimore's quarterbacks in 2001 were Elvis Grbac and Randall Cunningham, who both retired following the season. The only other player to attempt a pass for the 2001 Ravens was their punter, who left for Minnesota in 2002.

At quarterback, the Cardinals will initially be moving forward with Sam Bradford, but there is no guarantee that his knees will be able to hold up in the future. Bradford's contract is technically a two-year deal, though the second year is a team option that Arizona seems unlikely to exercise given their first-round draft selection of UCLA quarterback Josh Rosen. After watching Baker Mayfield, Sam Darnold, and Josh Allen all come off the board in the first seven picks, the Cardinals moved up five spots to get their long-term quarterback of the future.

Rosen projects as a roughly average first-round quarterback prospect and rated third out of the five first-round quarterbacks from 2018 in our QBASE projection system, behind Mayfield and Lamar Jackson. There were reasonable concerns about Rosen's mobility and his risk-taking tendencies coming from a college program where he often needed to make a ton of plays to keep his team in games thanks to a defense that ranked 120th in S&P+ and 93rd in FEI. However, a sizable chunk of the discussion surrounding Rosen's future success as a prospect related to concerns some evaluators had about his off-field interests and perceived lack of desire to focus on football.

With that in mind, Cardinals fans can likely be happy with how Rosen reacted to falling all the way to the 10th pick in the draft, saying that the teams ahead of Arizona made a mistake by not selecting him. If that moment is indicative of Rosen's

competitive drive, it probably bodes well for maintaining his motivation to develop into a top-flight quarterback.

Regardless of whether Arizona's primary starting quarterback for 2018 is Bradford, Rosen, or Mike Glennon (please, no), they should at least have some support on the offensive side of the ball thanks to the return of David Johnson in the backfield. Barring another serious injury, Johnson poses a major threat to defenses due to his ability to impact the game as both a runner and a receiver. Two years ago, he finished ninth in rushing DYAR and first in receiving DYAR among running backs. His receiving total of 274 DYAR would have ranked eighth among wide receivers. Not bad for a third-round pick from a small school.

Johnson's return combined with the possibility that Bradford could play well before eventually turning over the quarterbacking duties to Rosen are a big part of why Arizona's offense is projected to bounce back to merely below average as opposed to one of the worst units in the league. Throughout his career, Bradford's biggest problem has been his inability to stay healthy, but there is reason to believe that he could play well enough to keep Rosen out of the lineup until at least 2019.

In 2016, Bradford ranked 16th in passing DYAR despite playing behind one of the worst offensive lines in the league. Minnesota's line may have finished 17th in adjusted sack rate

Table 1: A Fresh Start: Top 10 Offenses with the Fewest Returning Pass Attempts and Carries, 1999-2018

Team	Year	Passes Y-1	Runs Y-1	Returning Passes	Returning Runs	Percent Returning	Off DVOA Y-1	Off DVOA	DVOA Change
BAL	2002	557	483	0	8	0.8%	-7.0%	-6.1%	+0.9%
ARI	2018	598	410	1	54	5.5%	-18.0%	--	--
CLE	2018	574	384	0	89	9.3%	-20.1%	--	--
DAL	2004	510	515	2	94	9.4%	-6.8%	-4.6%	+2.2%
DEN	2009	620	387	1	97	9.7%	19.2%	1.3%	-17.9%
CLE	2014	681	348	97	12	10.6%	-14.4%	-10.2%	+4.2%
DEN	2018	566	457	45	98	14.0%	-19.0%	--	--
WAS	2010	533	391	3	130	14.4%	-8.3%	-11.3%	-3.0%
SD	2001	578	351	0	134	14.4%	-26.2%	0.0%	+26.2%
MIA	2008	558	389	0	144	15.2%	-6.1%	12.0%	+18.1%

that year, but that was largely due to how quickly Bradford was getting the ball out of his hands in setting what was then the record for highest completion percentage in a season (Drew Brees subsequently eclipsed that mark in 2017). In Bradford's two games played in 2017, with a much-improved unit protecting him, he ended up with 169 DYAR. For context, Palmer needed seven starts to reach 143 DYAR, and Gabbert and Stanton gave all of that positive DYAR back and then some.

Arizona's lackluster performance on offense dragged down a defense that, in spite of losing key contributors such as stud defensive end Calais Campbell and safety Tony Jefferson, only fell from third to fourth in DVOA. Spearheaded by their top-ranked run defense and edge rusher Chandler Jones' 17 sacks, the Arizona defense kept the Cardinals in enough games to finish the season at 8-8. By DVOA, Arizona had the league's worst rushing offense but best rushing defense, leading to some nicely symmetric futility on the ground in games involving the 2017 Cardinals.

Arizona's outstanding defense definitely helped them eke out a few low-scoring slugfests against the Titans, Colts, and 49ers, the latter two of which came in overtime. Arizona actually performed quite well in close games, finishing with a record of 6-2 in games decided by a touchdown or less. This led to the Cardinals outperforming their expected win-loss record (by point differential) by 1.9 wins. Given how bad the offense was, it was a minor miracle that Arizona managed to finish the season at .500.

In addition to Jones' production getting after the passer, he also led the team in stops and defeats by a wide margin, with 54 and 33, respectively. That level of production was certainly what Arizona had in mind when they traded for him in 2016 and then subsequently signed him to a five-year deal worth up to $82.5 million.

As impressive as Jones was, he certainly had some help throughout the defense. Perennial Pro Bowl cornerback Patrick Peterson finished the season with an adjusted success rate of 63 percent, ranking fourth in the league among qualifying cornerbacks. Inside linebacker Karlos Dansby staved off Father Time for one more year to nearly match Jones with 53 stops of his own in his age-36 season. In spite of forcing a below average number of turnovers per drive, Arizona was still one of the best defensive units in the league, which generally bodes well for sustained success on that side of the ball.

Looking forward, there is reason for optimism from some young defensive players as well. Outside linebacker Haason Reddick and safety Budda Baker should take on larger roles in their second seasons. Former first-round defensive lineman Robert Nkemdiche could potentially make good on the upside that originally made him a top national recruit coming out of high school now that he no longer has to worry about staying on Bruce Arians' good side.

Unfortunately, there are several reasons to be concerned about whether the defense will be able to maintain the standards it has set in recent years. Since 2012, the Cardinals have never finished lower than seventh in defensive DVOA, which is quite the feat. The potential growth from the young defensive players already on the team is a source of optimism, but the new coaching staff is changing the defensive scheme, causing some uncertainty on that side of the ball. Additionally, Arizona only used one of their six draft picks on a defensive player, cornerback Chris Campbell of Penn State in the sixth round.

But the biggest cause for concern is that the defense lost 16 Approximate Value (AV) above replacement and added zero over the course of the offseason. This was the largest net loss for any defense in the league, with Chicago second at -10. The losses of Dansby, defensive ends Frostee Rucker and Josh Mauro, and defensive backs Tyrann Mathieu and Tramon Williams (among others) will surely be felt in 2018 as the Cardinals attempt to match their defensive excellence from recent years. Arizona is clearly banking on a lot of internal growth to fill those roles, as the only free-agent defenders from other teams who signed with the Cardinals were former Cowboys defensive end Benson Mayowa and cornerbacks Marcus Williams and Bené Benwikere of the Texans and Cowboys, respectively (Williams was cut before we even got to June).

Wilks and defensive coordinator Al Holcomb will have their work cut out for them as Arizona transitions from a base defense of 3-4 to 4-3. In his first season as Panthers defensive coordinator, Wilks cranked up the heat in the passing game by calling the most blitzes in the league. Arizona was one of the heaviest-blitzing teams in the league during Arians' tenure, so the familiarity of that aggressive style should help. Wilks relied on a heavy diet of zone defense to complement his blitz-happy play calling, while former defensive coordinator James Bettcher used more of a mix of man and zone coverage. Wilks' scheme is a simpler one than Bettcher's, and it should give the stud athletes in the Arizona front the opportunity to think less and play faster.

While Holcomb and Wilks had a sustained run of success on the defensive side of the ball during their time coaching the Panthers, it will likely take time for the team to effectively transition between schemes on that side of the ball. The simplicity of the new scheme should help shorten the adjustment period, but with players (particularly young ones like Reddick) changing roles and responsibilities, there could be some speed bumps along the way. Add up all that uncertainty, and it will be hard for Arizona to reach its previous heights in 2018.

Looking forward, it isn't all doom and gloom in the desert. There is undeniably talent on the roster, and they are bound to have some positive regression on offense with the return of David Johnson. If Johnson and Bradford can approach their previous level of performance, it would come as no surprise if Arizona does end up competing for a playoff spot.

However, it is more likely that with all the changes taking place, the 2018 season will be more of a placeholder year as Arizona aims for bigger and better things in subsequent seasons. The NFC currently projects to hold eight of the 11 best teams in the league by DVOA, including two of Arizona's division rivals in the Rams and the Seahawks. So while Arizona's offense will almost certainly see some improvement over its disappointing 2017 season, that improvement will probably not be enough to fuel a playoff push in 2018.

Carl Yedor

2017 Cardinals Stats by Week

Wk	vs.	W-L	PF	PA	YDF	YDA	TO	Total	Off	Def	ST
1	at DET	L	23	35	308	367	-3	-56%	-39%	4%	-13%
2	at IND	W	16	13	389	266	0	-9%	-27%	-23%	-5%
3	DAL	L	17	28	332	273	0	-37%	-6%	18%	-13%
4	SF	W	18	15	368	305	0	-4%	-22%	-23%	-4%
5	at PHI	L	7	34	307	419	0	-49%	-5%	19%	-25%
6	TB	W	38	33	432	412	0	31%	35%	2%	-2%
7	at LAR	L	0	33	193	425	-1	-69%	-53%	0%	-15%
8	BYE										
9	at SF	W	20	10	368	329	0	3%	-14%	-25%	-8%
10	SEA	L	16	22	290	287	-1	6%	-7%	-7%	6%
11	at HOU	L	21	31	292	357	0	-13%	-25%	-9%	3%
12	JAX	W	27	24	344	219	+1	45%	-11%	-47%	9%
13	LAR	L	16	32	312	303	-1	-6%	-6%	-20%	-20%
14	TEN	W	12	7	261	204	+2	0%	-27%	-36%	-8%
15	at WAS	L	15	20	286	218	-1	-37%	-45%	1%	9%
16	NYG	W	23	0	289	293	+1	4%	-28%	-30%	2%
17	at SEA	W	26	24	259	296	-1	0%	-9%	-12%	-3%

Trends and Splits

	Offense	Rank	Defense	Rank
Total DVOA	-18.0%	30	-12.7%	4
Unadjusted VOA	-15.6%	29	-8.7%	5
Weighted Trend	-17.7%	31	-17.1%	3
Variance	4.2%	4	3.5%	5
Average Opponent	0.2%	19	0.2%	16
Passing	-6.7%	27	-3.9%	10
Rushing	-25.6%	32	-24.4%	1
First Down	-11.8%	26	-11.8%	5
Second Down	-19.4%	28	-11.7%	3
Third Down	-27.8%	31	-15.6%	9
First Half	-17.5%	29	-20.8%	2
Second Half	-18.5%	28	-4.9%	11
Red Zone	-37.8%	31	9.3%	24
Late and Close	-18.3%	28	-2.6%	17

Five-Year Performance

Year	W-L	Pyth W	Est W	PF	PA	TO	Total	Rk	Off	Rk	Def	Rk	ST	Rk	Off AGL	Rk	Def AGL	Rk	Off Age	Rk	Def Age	Rk	ST Age	Rk
2013	10-6	9.5	10.4	379	324	-1	10.0%	10	-2.4%	20	-16.4%	2	-4.1%	27	26.8	11	36.1	22	27.9	4	28.0	2	27.0	3
2014	11-5	8.3	7.4	310	299	+8	-6.4%	22	-9.3%	23	-5.0%	7	-2.2%	21	24.0	8	48.8	24	27.3	10	27.1	9	26.4	5
2015	13-3	12.1	11.6	489	313	+9	27.4%	3	15.7%	4	-15.6%	3	-4.0%	29	21.2	4	41.3	25	28.2	3	26.0	26	25.8	21
2016	7-8-1	9.4	7.7	418	362	0	1.3%	16	-6.0%	21	-13.6%	3	-6.3%	30	35.4	17	42.4	21	28.3	1	25.9	29	25.5	27
2017	8-8	6.1	5.6	295	361	-4	-10.8%	22	-18.0%	30	-12.7%	4	-5.5%	28	74.8	32	30.8	13	28.6	1	28.1	2	26.5	6

2017 Performance Based on Most Common Personnel Groups

ARI Offense					ARI Offense vs. Opponents					ARI Defense					ARI Defense vs. Opponents			
Pers	Freq	Yds	DVOA	Run%	Pers	Freq	Yds	DVOA	Run%	Pers	Freq	Yds	DVOA	Pers	Freq	Yds	DVOA
11	52%	4.8	-21.5%	30%	Base	35%	4.3	-21.1%	57%	Base	27%	4.4	-24.8%	11	70%	5.3	-4.5%
12	25%	5.2	2.1%	55%	Nickel	49%	5.3	-5.7%	26%	Nickel	65%	5.3	-4.6%	12	17%	4.7	-27.1%
10	14%	6.1	12.3%	6%	Dime+	13%	5.6	-28.9%	4%	Dime+	7%	4.4	-42.9%	21	5%	4.6	-33.7%
13	4%	2.9	-67.0%	64%	Goal Line	0%	0.0	-5.4%	100%	Goal Line	1%	0.6	0.9%	13	4%	3.3	-47.7%
20	1%	2.7	-70.8%	10%	Big	3%	5.2	-17.9%	70%	Big	1%	6.5	-15.8%	611	1%	3.1	-37.2%
611	1%	1.6	-71.9%	90%										01	1%	3.1	-24.9%

Strategic Tendencies

Run/Pass		Rk	Formation		Rk	Pass Rush		Rk	Secondary		Rk	Strategy		Rk
Runs, first half	38%	21	Form: Single Back	81%	9	Rush 3	7.0%	15	4 DB	27%	24	Play action	17%	28
Runs, first down	48%	22	Form: Empty Back	17%	1	Rush 4	60.5%	21	5 DB	65%	7	Avg Box (Off)	6.21	22
Runs, second-long	29%	22	Pers: 3+ WR	69%	9	Rush 5	23.7%	9	6+ DB	7%	18	Avg Box (Def)	6.23	18
Runs, power sit.	39%	32	Pers: 2+ TE/6+ OL	32%	12	Rush 6+	8.7%	6	CB by Sides	58%	31	Offensive Pace	30.72	16
Runs, behind 2H	25%	24	Pers: 6+ OL	2%	26	Int DL Sacks	28.4%	13	S/CB Cover Ratio	49%	1	Defensive Pace	30.42	15
Pass, ahead 2H	46%	17	Shotgun/Pistol	45%	30	Second Level Sacks	16.2%	18	DB Blitz	13%	6	Go for it on 4th	1.13	11

The Cardinals ranked first or second in the league in usage of an empty backfield for all five years of the Bruce Arians regime.
🖝 For the second straight year, the Cardinals ran the ball less than any other team when the quarterback was in shotgun. Only

5.4 percent of shotgun plays were handoffs to a back. This is, of course, connected to the fact that the Cardinals had a lot of empty backfields when they went shotgun. ☜ Arizona also used four or five wide receivers on 14.5 percent of plays. No other team was above 7.5 percent. ☜ Without David Johnson around, the Cardinals dropped from ninth (61 percent) to dead last (39 percent) in frequency of runs in short-yardage, "power" situations. ☜ Arizona had -98.2% DVOA in goal-to-go situations, the worst we've ever recorded. The 2011 St. Louis Rams previously held that record. ☜ The Cardinals benefited from a league-high 160 penalties and 1,128 penalty yards. This marks the fifth straight year Arizona ranked in the top five, which makes them an exception to the usually low year-to-year correlation of opponent penalties (correlation coefficient of roughly 0.15). ☜ Lest you think that a new administration and a new 4-3 scheme means an end to Arizona's heavy pass-rushing ways, know that Steve Wilks took over in Carolina last season and doubled the frequency of rushing five guys so that the Panthers went from 25th in the league to first.

Passing

Player	DYAR	DVOA	Plays	NtYds	Avg	YAC	C%	TD	Int
C.Palmer*	145	-3.2%	289	1828	6.3	4.6	61.4%	10	7
B.Gabbert*	-189	-26.4%	194	944	4.9	4.3	55.9%	6	6
D.Stanton*	-75	-18.3%	166	850	5.1	3.8	49.7%	6	5
M.Glennon	-231	-37.1%	150	756	5.0	3.6	66.4%	4	5
S.Bradford	169	44.2%	48	342	7.1	4.8	74.4%	3	0

Rushing

Player	DYAR	DVOA	Plays	Yds	Avg	TD	Fum	Suc
A.Peterson*	-81	-24.5%	129	453	3.5	3	3	39%
K.Williams*	10	-6.6%	120	426	3.6	1	0	43%
C.Johnson*	-19	-19.6%	45	114	2.5	0	0	31%
E.Penny	33	15.8%	31	124	4.0	2	0	61%
B.Gabbert*	-21	-36.0%	18	82	4.6	0	2	-
A.Ellington*	8	5.5%	15	53	3.5	1	0	47%
D.Johnson	-40	-100.3%	11	23	2.1	0	1	18%
C.Palmer*	-18	-45.0%	8	16	2.0	0	2	-
D.Foster	-6	-44.0%	6	19	3.2	0	0	17%

Receiving

Player	DYAR	DVOA	Plays	Ctch	Yds	Y/C	YAC	TD	C%
L.Fitzgerald	147	-1.3%	161	109	1156	10.6	3.7	6	68%
Ja.Brown*	6	-11.5%	69	31	477	15.4	2.8	4	45%
J.Nelson	48	-1.9%	61	29	508	17.5	2.0	2	48%
Jo.Brown*	-51	-24.4%	55	21	299	14.2	2.8	3	38%
B.Golden*	6	-2.8%	9	5	70	14.0	9.8	0	56%
C.Williams	7	-0.4%	7	3	31	10.3	2.0	0	43%
B.Butler	135	61.6%	23	15	319	21.3	1.9	3	65%
C.Hamilton	-30	-63.2%	6	1	8	8.0	4.0	0	17%
J.Gresham	22	-0.1%	46	33	322	9.8	4.1	2	72%
R.Seals-Jones	5	-4.6%	28	12	201	16.8	6.2	3	43%
T.Niklas*	-7	-11.8%	23	11	132	12.0	5.1	1	48%
A.Ellington*	42	2.3%	50	33	297	9.0	6.3	1	66%
D.J.Foster	-1	-14.3%	28	17	133	7.8	4.8	0	61%
A.Peterson*	-11	-26.0%	16	9	66	7.3	5.7	0	56%
K.Williams*	21	11.6%	15	10	93	9.3	4.6	0	67%
D.Johnson	-9	-33.0%	9	6	67	11.2	7.7	0	67%
C.Johnson*	16	28.9%	6	5	43	8.6	6.0	0	83%
E.Penny	6	6.3%	6	4	38	9.5	10.3	0	67%

Offensive Line

Player	Pos	Age	GS	Snaps	Pen	Sk	Pass	Run	Player	Pos	Age	GS	Snaps	Pen	Sk	Pass	Run
A.Q. Shipley	C	32	16/16	1124	5	5.0	9	16	Evan Boehm	RG	25	15/8	592	5	3.5	18	3
John Wetzel	RT/LT	27	16/11	920	1	8.0	33	5	Will Holden	LT/LG	25	7/5	331	1	2.5	12	5
Jared Veldheer*	RT/LT	31	13/13	895	8	5.5	20	5	D.J. Humphries	LT	25	5/5	204	0	0.5	3	3
Alex Boone*	LG	31	14/13	878	2	4.5	17	19	Andre Smith	RT	31	13/8	541	8	3.0	16	3
Earl Watford*	RG	28	10/9	611	3	4.0	12	5	Justin Pugh	RT/LG	28	8/8	435	1	2.0	6	4

Year	Yards	ALY	Rank	Power	Rank	Stuff	Rank	2nd Lev	Rank	Open Field	Rank	Sacks	ASR	Rank	Press	Rank	F-Start	Cont.
2015	4.59	4.56	3	51%	29	20%	16	1.22	6	1.15	4	27	5.0%	5	28.1%	23	16	32
2016	4.28	4.54	7	72%	5	21%	20	1.23	12	0.82	11	41	6.3%	21	30.9%	29	13	22
2017	3.38	4.02	17	68%	9	20%	13	0.90	32	0.30	32	52	8.1%	26	29.7%	11	17	26
2017 ALY by direction:			Left End: 3.48 (24)			Left Tackle: 4.11 (16)			Mid/Guard: 4.05 (21)			Right Tackle: 3.69 (20)			Right End: 4.53 (9)			

2015 first-round pick D.J. Humphries' third season was unfortunately cut short due to a torn MCL and dislocated kneecap suffered against the Seahawks in Week 10. Humphries also missed time early in the season with an MCL sprain. This didn't stop the Cardinals from picking up his fifth-year option in the offseason, but at this point Humphries has only been healthy for 18 of 48 regular season games in his career. ☜ When Humphries was initially on the shelf, Arizona went with John Wetzel instead of sliding Jared Veldheer over to the blind side. After Humphries went on injured reserve, Arizona moved Veldheer to left tackle in light of Wetzel's poor performance. Wetzel allowed 8.0 sacks on the season, which was a half-sack shy of the most in the league. Veldheer, to his credit, was Arizona's only average lineman in terms of snaps per blown block, finishing 19th out of 37 right tackles with enough snaps to qualify. ☜ Evan Boehm started the season as the right guard before losing his job to

Earl Watford. Watford had signed a two-year deal with the Jaguars in the offseason, but they let him go prior to Week 1, and he signed with Arizona a month later. Now he has left Arizona as well, signing a one-year deal with the Bears. ✎ Alex Boone has had a long career and played on some strong rushing offenses with the 49ers, but his 2017 campaign was a season to forget. Boone had 19 blown blocks on running plays, the most in the NFL, and had the third-fewest snaps per blown run block overall. ✎ A.Q. Shipley also struggled in run blocking, finishing with the third-fewest snaps per blown run block among centers. Shipley is holding onto the starting center job for now, but if he struggles, he could lose his job to rookie third-rounder Mason Cole out of Michigan. Cole brings both positional flexibility and durability to Arizona after playing both left tackle and center in college and tying the school record with 51 career starts. ✎ Arizona is hoping that free agents Justin Pugh and Andre Smith will solidify a line that struggled in pass protection. Pugh ranked 11th among right tackles in snaps per blown block, but Smith played badly in last year's return to the Bengals, particularly in pass protection.

Defensive Front Seven

Defensive Line	Age	Pos	G	Snaps	Plays	TmPct	Rk	Stop	Dfts	BTkl	Runs	St%	Rk	RuYd	Rk	Sack	Hit	Hur	Dsrpt
				Overall							**vs. Run**					**Pass Rush**			
Frostee Rucker*	35	DE	16	607	29	3.6%	72	23	11	7	25	76%	53	1.5	19	1.5	9	16.5	2
Corey Peters	30	DT	12	440	22	3.6%	70	21	7	2	20	95%	3	1.1	3	1.0	4	7.0	1
Olsen Pierre	27	DE	14	352	31	4.4%	--	30	16	1	21	100%	--	0.5	--	5.5	3	7.0	3
Josh Mauro*	27	DE	13	334	23	3.5%	--	15	3	1	21	62%	--	2.7	--	1.0	4	4.0	1
Rodney Gunter	26	DT	16	294	16	2.0%	--	11	2	2	14	64%	--	3.9	--	1.0	2	8.5	1
Robert Nkemdiche	24	DE	12	256	11	1.8%	--	10	3	3	11	91%	--	0.5	--	0.0	2	9.5	0
Xavier Williams*	26	DE	11	252	20	3.6%	--	18	2	2	19	89%	--	2.1	--	0.5	1	4.0	0
Benson Mayowa	*27*	*DT*	*14*	*383*	*21*	*3.0%*	*85*	*15*	*6*	*1*	*15*	*73%*	*52*	*1.4*	*19*	*1.0*	*5*	*11.0*	*0*

Edge Rushers	Age	Pos	G	Snaps	Plays	TmPct	Rk	Stop	Dfts	BTkl	Runs	St%	Rk	RuYd	Rk	Sack	Hit	Hur	Dsrpt
				Overall							**vs. Run**					**Pass Rush**			
Chandler Jones	28	OLB	16	1046	60	7.5%	13	54	33	8	37	89%	8	1.3	18	17.0	21	36.5	3
Kareem Martin	26	OLB	16	458	25	3.1%	82	21	7	3	17	88%	11	0.7	6	1.0	4	13.0	3
Haason Reddick	24	OLB	16	445	32	4.0%	64	18	11	1	16	69%	74	2.7	66	2.5	4	14.0	1

Linebackers	Age	Pos	G	Snaps	Plays	TmPct	Rk	Stop	Dfts	BTkl	Runs	St%	Rk	RuYd	Rk	Sack	Hit	Hur	Tgts	Suc%	Rk	AdjYd	Rk	PD	Int
				Overall							**vs. Run**					**Pass Rush**			**vs. Pass**						
Karlos Dansby	37	ILB	16	923	98	12.2%	42	53	13	13	53	60%	55	3.2	27	1.0	4	9.5	41	58%	14	5.9	24	4	1
Deone Bucannon	26	ILB	12	707	85	14.1%	26	39	13	7	42	60%	58	4.0	62	1.0	1	2.5	40	49%	38	5.6	17	2	1
Josh Bynes	29	ILB	14	236	30	4.3%	--	16	8	6	12	67%	--	2.7	--	1.0	0	1.0	15	59%	--	4.4	--	4	1

Year	Yards	ALY	Rank	Power	Rank	Stuff	Rank	2nd Level	Rank	Open Field	Rank	Sacks	ASR	Rank	Press	Rank
2015	3.71	3.32	2	62%	13	27%	2	1.05	8	0.87	21	36	5.7%	27	29.3%	3
2016	3.30	3.58	3	61%	13	23%	6	0.95	3	0.31	2	48	7.5%	3	32.1%	2
2017	3.36	3.34	3	62%	12	23%	6	0.96	6	0.56	6	37	5.9%	24	30.2%	17
2017 ALY by direction:		Left End: 3.80 (15)			Left Tackle: 2.59 (3)			Mid/Guard: 3.81 (8)			Right Tackle: 2.76 (3)			Right End: 2.38 (4)		

Casual fans likely are not familiar with Corey Peters, but the defensive lineman ranked third in the league in run stop rate at 95 percent. Peters signed a three-year extension towards the end of the 2017 season. ✎ Olsen Pierre was another highly productive player for the Cardinals in 2017 despite not being a household name. His 5.5 sacks as a 3-4 defensive end may have drawn some attention, but the fact that he amassed those sacks on just 352 snaps should be even more reason to keep an eye on the 27-year-old moving forward. ✎ Arizona ranked in the top ten in adjusted line yards for each direction except for runs off left end, where they fell to a more average 15th. But when one average-ranked split represents a big drop compared to every other direction, that's a good sign for your run defense. ✎ The Cardinals used a pretty heavy rotation among their interior defensive linemen in 2017, with only two players across the three-man front playing enough snaps to qualify for the league-wide rankings. ✎ Robert Nkemdiche has not lived up to the potential that made him such a tantalizing prospect, but he started to show flashes in his second season. Nkemdiche registered 10 run stops and 10 hurries on 256 snaps. After running with the starters in OTAs, Nkemdiche will have every opportunity to finally break out while replacing the departed Frostee Rucker. ✎ Deone Bucannon is slated to play in 2018 on his fifth-year option at weakside linebacker after spending his first four seasons inside in Arizona's old 3-4. ✎ 2017 first-rounder Haason Reddick will be lining up opposite Bucannon on the strong side after spending his rookie year as an edge rusher, while Josh Bynes is taking over for the departed Karlos Dansby in the middle.

Defensive Secondary

Secondary	Age	Pos	G	Snaps	Plays	Overall TmPct	Rk	Stop	Dfts	BTkl	Runs	vs. Run St%	Rk	RuYd	Rk	Tgts	vs. Pass Tgt%	Rk	Dist	Suc%	Rk	AdjYd	Rk	PD	Int
Tyrann Mathieu*	26	FS/CB	16	1056	80	9.9%	40	34	19	15	23	52%	18	8.2	56	65	13.4%	64	12.1	52%	37	8.0	35	6	2
Patrick Peterson	28	CB	16	1015	42	5.2%	79	18	6	7	6	33%	61	13.8	77	57	12.2%	2	11.9	63%	4	6.0	9	9	1
Antoine Bethea	34	FS	15	743	66	8.7%	56	28	13	6	28	43%	44	6.5	41	24	7.0%	14	15.9	53%	30	8.1	37	9	5
Tramon Williams*	35	CB	13	670	52	8.0%	49	24	9	2	5	40%	47	5.4	25	56	18.0%	24	10.4	55%	19	6.8	23	13	2
Tyvon Branch*	32	SS	9	578	72	15.9%	2	36	10	5	38	55%	14	4.7	16	25	9.2%	34	9.1	57%	21	5.3	6	3	0
Budda Baker	22	SS	16	517	65	8.1%	66	24	14	11	22	55%	16	3.8	5	39	16.2%	72	11.1	41%	68	9.4	53	7	0
Justin Bethel*	28	CB	16	452	34	4.2%	--	13	6	3	10	50%	--	4.9	--	45	21.4%	--	16.2	47%	--	9.1	--	4	1
Jamar Taylor	28	CB	16	967	72	8.4%	41	31	10	12	18	39%	51	5.8	36	73	17.0%	19	11.2	48%	58	9.8	78	12	0

Year	Pass D Rank	vs. #1 WR	Rk	vs. #2 WR	Rk	vs. Other WR	Rk	WR Wide	Rk	WR Slot	Rk	vs. TE	Rk	vs. RB	Rk
2015	4	-12.4%	6	-24.8%	3	-20.5%	5	--	--	--	--	-13.1%	7	9.7%	23
2016	3	-5.0%	10	17.2%	27	-1.2%	13	5.5%	23	1.4%	13	-19.7%	6	-43.5%	1
2017	10	11.4%	23	-19.8%	6	-9.9%	9	-4.7%	15	-8.4%	9	-14.6%	7	-0.5%	17

Patrick Peterson has spent most of his decorated career locking down opposing teams' top wide receivers. The Cardinals "only" finished 10th in DVOA against No. 1 receivers, but they also faced the lowest rate of passes thrown to No. 1 receivers at just 16 percent. Peterson ranked fourth in success rate at 63 percent, but opposing teams did find success if they could spot their top receiver without Peterson lurking. Passes to No. 1 receivers were the only ones where Arizona allowed positive DVOA. ☞ The flip side of shutting down No. 1 receivers: for the third straight year, Arizona led the league in the percentage of opposing passes that went to No. 3 or "other" receivers, although the rate (22.5 percent) was significantly lower than in 2015 or 2016. ☞ Antoine Bethea and Tramon Williams turned back the clock in logging a combined 22 passes defensed and seven interceptions. Williams parlayed that success into a two-year deal with the Packers that will take him through his age-36 season. ☞ Former Pro Bowler Tyrann Mathieu was released during the offseason after leading the team's defensive backs in defeats with 19. Mathieu's contract and injury history played a large role in his release, as the team had to eat more than $9 million in dead money when they let him go. ☞ Balancing out the 34-year-old Bethea will be 2017 second-round pick Budda Baker, who started seven games as a 21-year-old rookie in place of the injured Tyvon Branch at strong safety. Despite Baker's lack of size, he was not afraid to stick his nose in there and help against the run, ranking fifth among safeties in average yards on rushing tackles at 3.8. Part of that stems from how he was used in Arizona's old 3-4 defense, but his willingness as a tackler will likely help mitigate the loss of Mathieu and Branch. However, he'll have to improve in coverage, as his adjusted success rate of 41 percent ranked 68th in the league. ☞ Jamar Taylor signed a three-year contract extension with Cleveland at the end of 2016, but he only lasted one season with the Browns before being traded to Arizona for a future sixth-round pick in May. Taylor led Browns cornerbacks in snaps in 2017, but the defensive backfield makeover in Cleveland left Taylor without a spot in their secondary moving forward

Special Teams

Year	DVOA	Rank	FG/XP	Rank	Net Kick	Rank	Kick Ret	Rank	Net Punt	Rank	Punt Ret	Rank	Hidden	Rank
2015	-4.0%	29	-1.8	24	0.4	17	0.5	11	-12.7	30	-6.3	29	-11.4	31
2016	-6.3%	30	-8.9	30	-4.9	27	1.7	10	-14.7	31	-4.6	26	-2.8	20
2017	-5.5%	28	-8.9	28	-5.5	27	-2.1	20	-10.0	27	-0.9	20	-7.5	27

The Cardinals continued their trend of fielding one of the worst special teams units in the league in 2017. During Bruce Arians' tenure with the team, the Cardinals special teams never finished higher than 21st. New special teams coordinator Jeff Rodgers will hopefully be able to get things turned around, but he has not coached a special teams unit that finished in the top half of the league in DVOA since his Denver unit finished 13th in 2012. ☞ Rookie wide receiver Christian Kirk and second-year running back T.J. Logan could add some juice to the kickoff return unit. Kirk returned seven kicks for touchdowns (six punts, one kickoff) in college, and Logan set the school record at North Carolina with five kickoff return touchdowns. Logan missed the 2017 season with a wrist injury suffered during the preseason. ☞ Arizona finished 27th in net punting despite the fact Andy Lee was in the top five in points of field position from punts alone, which suggests there were big problems with their coverage unit downfield. ☞ Rookie safety Budda Baker finished third in the league in special teams tackles with 16.

Atlanta Falcons

2017 Record: 10-6	**Total DVOA:** 1.5% (15th)	**2018 Mean Projection:** 8.1 wins	**On the Clock (0-4):** 8%
Pythagorean Wins: 9.1 (11th)	**Offense:** 8.2% (9th)	**Postseason Odds:** 37.3%	**Mediocrity (5-7):** 32%
Snap-Weighted Age: 26.5 (13th)	**Defense:** 5.6% (22nd)	**Super Bowl Odds:** 5.4%	**Playoff Contender (8-10):** 42%
Average Opponent: 3.7% (4th)	**Special Teams:** -1.2% (19th)	**Proj. Avg. Opponent:** 3.0% (2nd)	**Super Bowl Contender (11+):** 18%

2017: Atlanta comes up smallest in the biggest moments.

2018: Too much talent to be bad, but can all the moving parts click?

Unharnessed potential is one of the most frustrating issues an organization can deal with. It's difficult to put together and *keep* together a world-class team under modern free agency and salary cap rules, so every missed opportunity hurts. For the second year in a row, the Falcons gave the eventual Super Bowl champions their best shot in the postseason, only to come up short in heartbreaking fashion.

The odds that the Falcons would be able to maintain their historic 2016 level of offensive production, despite the departure of former offensive coordinator Kyle Shanahan, were always low. The hope was that the transition to Steve Sarkisian would be a smooth one, allowing enough of that offensive success to carry over, propelling them back to the Super Bowl and allowing them to take that final step towards a championship in 2017.

That didn't happen.

The Falcons dropped from first in offensive DVOA in 2016 to ninth last year, as the offense struggled in its transition. The good news is that transitions are temporary. With a star-studded offense featuring former MVP Matt Ryan, Julio Jones, Devonta Freeman, and one of the better offensive lines in the league, there's every reason to believe that Atlanta's offense will rebound some in 2018.

Atlanta's problem wasn't really efficiency last season. They ranked second in yards per drive, and seventh in points per drive. That's not quite as good as they were in 2016, when they led the league in both categories, but the situation was not quite as dire as some of the media would have you believe.

The problem, however, is that the Falcons had very few opportunities with the ball. They had just 157 drives last season, last in the NFL. In 2016, they had the fourth-fewest drives, so it's not like there was a massive drop-off from year-to-year. But when you have fewer opportunities, you have to make each and every one count.

The Falcons' otherworldly efficiency in 2016 was absolutely critical to their success. They scored 3.06 points per drive in their Super Bowl year, one of only three teams to average more than a field goal per drive since the start of our drive data in 1993. That was never going to be replicable, but dropping all the way to 2.17 points per drive was a larger fall than most people would have predicted.

The culprit? It was confluence of issues. You had poor offensive situational strategy gumming up the offense in the most crucial situations. You had the combination of a lack of turnovers on defense and some special teams regression resulting in worse field position to start with, forcing the offense to travel further drive after drive. And then you top it all off with a helping of good old-fashioned bad luck. That's how you drop by 11.7 points per game.

Let's talk about luck, first. The Falcons had some problems with turnovers in 2017 on both sides of the ball. They fell from a +11 differential to -2, dropping from fourth in the league to 19th. Offensive turnovers kill drives, while a lack of defensive turnovers means a lack of short fields to capitalize on. Both will have a massive impact in the scoreboard.

But this drop wasn't because Matt Ryan suddenly forgot how to pass. Ryan saw his interception total rise from seven to 12 last season, but five of those interceptions bounced off the hands of his intended targets into the hands of defenders. That's the most tipped interceptions for any quarterback in a season since Eli Manning also had five in 2010. Even when you take into account a pair of dropped interceptions, Ryan's adjusted interception rate falls from 2.2 percent to 1.6 percent. That's actually better than his adjusted rate from his MVP season. He threw three fewer adjusted interceptions (nine) than actual interceptions (12) last year, the first quarterback to do so since Tom Brady in 2013. In other words, Ryan's on-field performance in many ways improved last season, but he ended up with worse results. That's bad luck for you.

Of course, we can't use bad luck to explain away everyone's 2017, and Ryan was far from alone in sliding back to the pack. Julio Jones only scored three touchdowns in 2017, his lowest total since 2013 when he only played five games. Devonta Freeman's production took a bit of a nosedive, dropping from 148 DYAR in 2016 to 90 DYAR in 2017. Tevin Coleman's receiving DVOA dropped from first to fourth among running backs. The only skill position player to improve on his efficiency from 2016 to 2017 was Mohamed Sanu, whose DVOA increased from 6.5% to 10.7%.

Some of that is expected regression. By DVOA, the Falcons had the top quarterback, top two wide receivers, top tight end, and top receiving running back in football in 2016. That wasn't going to happen again. At the same time, when you have all the same ingredients but your meal tastes funny, it's reasonable to put some of the blame on the new chef. The issue the Falcons had on offense last season wasn't a lack of tal-

2018 Falcons Schedule

Week	Opp.	Week	Opp.	Week	Opp.
1	at PHI (Thu.)	7	NYG (Mon.)	13	BAL
2	CAR	8	BYE	14	at GB
3	NO	9	at WAS	15	ARI
4	CIN	10	at CLE	16	at CAR
5	at PIT	11	DAL	17	at TB
6	TB	12	at NO (Thu.)		

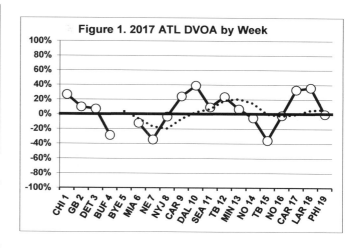

Figure 1. 2017 ATL DVOA by Week

ent. They were just a bit out of sync with their new offensive coordinator.

Calling plays in the NFL is a difficult job, but it's not uniformly difficult. There's less pressure dialing up plays on first-and-10 from midfield than there is on third-and-goal. A tied game is a lot less stressful in the first quarter than it is in the last two minutes. With very few exceptions, Sarkisian's offense was much, much better in less pressure-packed situations than it was in the most crucial moments.

Take red zone offense, for example. Atlanta ranked 19th in red zone passing DVOA, 26th in red zone running DVOA, and 23rd in total red zone DVOA. An offense with the overwhelming amount of firepower and talent Atlanta brings to bear shouldn't be among the worst red zone offenses in the league.

What's even more confusing about Atlanta sputtering in the red zone is the fact that they were a legitimately good offense in every area other area of the field. When we split the field by 20-yard sections, the Falcons ranked 11th or better on each portion of the field *except* the red zone. So they often cruised right down the field, only to struggle when it was time to turn that yardage into seven instead of three. Remove all red zone plays, and Atlanta's offensive DVOA rises to 12.6%, sixth in the league.

Red zone scoring often requires a bit of creativity from offensive coordinators; it wasn't surprising that a first-time NFL offensive coordinator struggled to draw up plays that would fool longtime NFL coaches in difficult situations. While it's worth noting that Atlanta's red zone offense in 2016 ranked just 14th, the minor issues they had when running out of real estate two years ago were exacerbated by repetitive and questionable play calling last season. And, indeed, that's where the Falcons' season ended, with Atlanta getting four cracks inside the Eagles' 10-yard-line to win their divisional round matchup, only to fall just short.

Those four season-ending attempts against Philadelphia ended up as a microcosm of Sarkisian's issues. To wit:

- On first-and-goal from the 9-yard line, Atlanta ran an incomplete fade to Julio Jones. Jones does a great many things well, but fades aren't one of them; he had a -5.8% DVOA on fades in 2017. In addition, Jones started far outside the numbers and took an immediate outside release, meaning an experienced corner like Ronald Darby could diagnose it as a fade essentially from the snap. Uncreative play call, poor use of specific player's strengths, and poor execution.

- On second-and-goal, Atlanta tried a shovel pass to Terron Ward. Asking Ryan to underhand a ball is probably not using his talents for the best; it nearly resulted in a fumble. Even if it had been completed, there were four unblocked Philadelphia defenders ready to pounce instantly. No pre-snap motion or any other trickery was attempted to open up the middle of the field; the play only would have worked if Ward had suddenly become intangible.

- On third-and-goal, Atlanta ran its one successful play, a seven-yard dig to Jones. It was the best play call of the bunch, using the threat of the fade from first down to force Darby to stick to the outside. If there's any quibble here, it's that Jones ran a route parallel to the end zone rather than towards it; had he been running a slant, his momentum might have taken him across the goal line when he was tackled. Still, small quibbles.

- On fourth-and-goal—fourth-and-season, really—with all the talent Atlanta's offensive weapons bring to bear, Sarkisian split fullback Derrick Coleman out wide, alone on the left side of the offense, essentially broadcasting that the play would not be going in that direction. Strike one. He had Tevin Coleman and Levine Toilolo stay in to block, meaning there were only two viable receiving options on the play. Strike two. He had Jones and Sanu run routes that ended up with them standing within 2 yards of one another in the end zone, meaning three Eagles defenders were in the only area into which Ryan could throw. Strike three, you're out. Ryan and Jones nearly bailed him out with some tremendous effort, but had they scored, it would have been despite the play calling and not because of it.

There are plenty of other examples of poor red zone play calling we could point out—the Taylor Gabriel jet sweep (with an empty backfield) that they tried on fourth-and-goal at the 1-yard line against the Patriots is an all-timer—but you get the general point. Sarkisian's play calling in key situations left plenty to be desired.

This isn't just a red zone issue, either. Atlanta had the fifth-best offense on first downs; it fell to 23rd on third-and-longs.

They had the third-best offense in the first quarter; that fell to 23rd in late-and-close situations. When the situation called for the Falcons to dig deep and bring out their best plays, they came up the smallest. That's fair to blame on the first-year coordinator.

So, what did Sarkisian do or not do that ended up working out so poorly? What changes do the Falcons need to make going forward?

One thing that might help would be restoring the play-action pass. Kyle Shanahan's offenses love the play-action pass; few coordinators in football dial it up as frequently or as effectively. In 2016 the Falcons used play-action 27 percent of the time, more than any other offense, and were second with 10.3 yards per play. Last season, Atlanta once again had one of the elite play-action offenses in the league, ranking in the top five with 8.7 yards per pass, but they only ranked 13th in percentage of play-action plays called with 23 percent. It's a small difference, but it has an effect, and Sarkisian would be well advised to use play-action more frequently in 2018.

Another problem Sarkisian had was poorly using the assets Shanahan left him, and there's no better example than Gabriel. At 5-foot-8, 165 pounds, Gabriel has a very unusual body type for an NFL receiver; Stephen Baker of the late '80s Giants is the only other receiver to top 600 yards at that size. Gabriel is not someone you just plug into any old offensive system and get good results. He's someone you have to scheme carefully to put into mismatch situations. Shanahan schemed to get Gabriel as many open looks as possible, allowing him to create big plays after the catch. Sarkisian's scheme is more conservative, with less pre-snap motion, and that meant Gabriel was asked to beat one-on-one coverage more, which is not his strong suit. Route selection was odd, as well; Gabriel was ninth in the league on post routes in 2016 (min. eight targets) with a 57.7% DVOA; last year, he only had two targets on post routes.

In Sarkisian's defense, he didn't have a lot of time to get comfortable with his new weapons before the season began. Including both training camp and preseason, Ryan, Jones, Gabriel, and Freeman were on the field together for a grand total of eight plays, thanks to a variety of injuries That's not sufficient time for anyone to install a new system or to get comfortable with players they have never worked with before.

Sarkisian now has had a full offseason to work with his stars. He has also been able to bring in players he may be more comfortable working with—some of his own guys, rather than Shanahan's leftovers. The Falcons drafted Alabama wide receiver Calvin Ridley with the 26th overall pick to immediately fill the third receiver role and sustain a strong receiving corps as Sanu potentially moves on after the 2018 season. Ridley is a much more traditionally built receiver than Gabriel; he ran a full route tree at Alabama and should be fairly plug-and-play into whatever role Sarkisian feels is best for him right off the bat. It's a great fit for player, team, and coordinator.

The Falcons offense saw a gargantuan statistical leap from 2015 to 2016 in Kyle Shanahan's second year with the team; with the addition of Ridley and free-agent guard Brandon Fusco, this year's offense is arguably more talented than the offense that ripped the NFC apart en route to a Super Bowl appearance. If Sarkisian can clean up his situational play-calling efforts, it's an offense that could really shine.

It would help, of course, if that offense was placed in positive situations in 2018 as it was in 2016. The Super Bowl Falcons' ranked 13th in starting field position, with their average drive starting on the 28.52-yard line. Last year's edition started back at the 25.96, second-worst in the league. This isn't exactly a groundbreaking statement, but it's difficult to score when you're further away from the end zone.

Poor field position is, in part, a direct consequence of the shoddy special teams play from which the Falcons suffered last year. The Falcons finished with the No. 19 special teams unit according to DVOA. That's actually understating the effect of special teams on field position, because part of that score belongs to Matt Bryant's consistency at field goals and extra points, which ranked ninth in the league. At every aspect of special teams dealing with field position—coverage and returns, both on kickoffs and punts—Atlanta was below average. They were in the bottom 10 in three of those four categories, with only punter Matthew Bosher saving a little bit of face.

They have tried to patch up holes there with the addition of former Pro Bowl special-teamer Justin Bethel from the Cardinals and the draft acquisitions of LSU wide receiver Russell Gage and Yale linebacker Foye Oluokun. If the Falcons are able to improve their special teams performance, their offense will gain a boost in terms of field position. While it will still be up to the offense to make the most of those situations, a bad offense will score as many points as a good offense if it gets to start each drive 5 yards closer to the goal line. Every little bit of yardage helps.

Of course, the other way Atlanta can improve their field position is if the defense actually stops someone for once.

The Falcons' defense ranked 20th in yards per drive, 18th in points per drive, and 26th in turnovers per drive. The Falcons had horrible turnover luck throughout the season, with several interceptions being negated due to penalties. Atlanta ranked 30th in defensive interception rate at a staggeringly low 1.4 percent. With a defensive backfield that has had a fair amount of draft picks and cap space invested into it, Atlanta should be much higher on this list than 30th.

Atlanta's inability to create turnovers or get off the field meant all those offensive stars were more often cooling their heels on the bench than actually seeing action. And perhaps the single biggest reason Atlanta had issues getting off the field was their abysmal third-down defense. The Falcons "boasted" DVOA's No. 29 third-down defense last season. They were 27th in DVOA on third-down passing plays. This is not something that can continue if the Falcons want to remain a perennial playoff team.

Atlanta's front seven is an up-and-coming group of dynamic, young playmakers. The problem is, they have been "up-and-coming" for two years now, and the end result has been less than the sum of its parts. The potential is still here, but the Falcons have to hope that it all finally gels together in a way it hasn't over the past few seasons.

Since 2015, the Falcons have drafted Vic Beasley, Grady Jarrett, Keanu Neal, Deion Jones, De'Vondre Campbell, Brian Poole, and Takk McKinley, all major contributors on the defense. They have struggled with consistency, but when they hit their peak they can play like a top-10 defense. In the second half of the season the Falcons defense ranked 11th in total defensive DVOA. They flashed their true potential in the playoffs when they shut down the Los Angeles Rams, then slowed down Philadelphia's explosive offense in their playoff loss. Their speed and playmaking ability in the back seven can make them a tough pass defense. Jones has developed into one of the premier coverage linebackers in the league; his presence was crucial as the Falcons defense improved over the second half of the season.

It's worth noting, of course, that this is the second straight year that the Falcons defense improved in the second half of the season, especially against the pass. In 2016, the Falcons went from 10.3% DVOA in Weeks 1-9 to 3.0% in Weeks 10-17, and then were even better in their playoff run (up until about midway through the third quarter of the Super Bowl). In 2017, they went from 13.0% DVOA in Weeks 1-9 to -2.1% in Weeks 10-17. Finishing strong is certainly not a bad attribute to have, but it isn't predictive. That improvement from the second half of 2016 didn't roll over to 2017 at all. We can't necessarily expect the improvement Atlanta saw on the field late in 2017 to stick in 2018, either.

That improvement didn't really show itself in Atlanta's pass rush, either, which was a major contributor to the Falcons' poor third-down performance. When Atlanta's pass rush gets hot, they have the top-end athletes along the defensive line to really create chaos in the backfield. However, they only finished 22nd in pressure rate and 16th in adjusted sack rate last season.

Atlanta certainly has the talent to become a more dangerous pass-rushing team, but they're going to need some of their younger players to play up to their potential. Rookie defensive end Takk McKinley had a strong inaugural season with six sacks in the regular season and two more in the playoffs; he'll see a significant boost to his playing time with Adrian Clayborn moving on to the Patriots in free agency. Joining McKinley at defensive end is Vic Beasley, who is coming back to the position full-time after splitting time at linebacker each of the past two seasons. Beasley led the league in sacks in 2016 with 15.5. Due to injury, a bit more time in coverage, and normal regression, he was only able to post 5.0 sacks in 2017.

Atlanta's returning leader in pass-rush pressures is defensive tackle Grady Jarrett, a fifth-round pick in 2015 who has established himself as one of the best defensive tackles in the league. To replace Jarrett's running mate Dontari Poe, who signed with the Carolina Panthers, Atlanta drafted South Florida defensive tackle Deadrin Senat and signed Terrell McClain in free agency. Beasley, McKinley, Jarrett, and Senat have a ton of potential, and they're going to play a crucial role in Atlanta's pass defense.

The theme of unharnessed potential kept rearing its head throughout the 2017 season. Atlanta's offense is too talented to have the drastic drop-off they did offensively. Their defense has too many potential playmakers to continue to rank among the lower third of the league. They do have some reason to believe they'll improve. The Falcons' instant-impact 2016 draft class (Keanu Neal, Deion Jones, Austin Hooper, and De'Vondre Campbell) is about to start its third season. The offense will bring back the vast majority of its players, Steve Sarkisian enters his second year with the team, and they still have the steady guidance of Dan Quinn and Thomas Dimitroff.

On the other hand, the core pieces of this offense—most notably Matt Ryan, Julio Jones, and Alex Mack—aren't getting any younger. The Falcons barely scraped into the playoffs last season, needing last-second victories over Detroit and Seattle to keep their wild-card slot. They're faced with the second-toughest projected schedule this season. A team is only going to have so many chances to turn talent into results, and you have to wonder how many more chances these Falcons are going to get.

With the Falcons' postseason success ending in heartbreaking fashion each of the past two years, the pressure is mounting to finally bring a Lombardi Trophy to a city that hasn't had a major pro championship since 1995. The clock is ticking for this Falcons team to truly maximize its Super Bowl window. They certainly have the personnel to be one of the elite, marquee NFL teams. For Atlanta, the age-old question remains the same: will they be able to execute in the most critical situations? Unless they find better answers than they had a year ago, they're going to remain a rung or two below the truly top teams in the league.

Charles McDonald and Bryan Knowles

2017 Falcons Stats by Week

Wk	vs.	W-L	PF	PA	YDF	YDA	TO	Total	Off	Def	ST
1	at CHI	W	23	17	372	301	0	27%	36%	12%	2%
2	GB	W	34	23	364	367	+2	10%	30%	27%	7%
3	at DET	W	30	26	428	324	-3	7%	-8%	-4%	11%
4	BUF	L	17	23	389	281	-3	-29%	-11%	16%	-2%
5	BYE										
6	MIA	L	17	20	339	289	0	-12%	14%	16%	-10%
7	at NE	L	7	23	343	403	0	-35%	8%	22%	-20%
8	at NYJ	W	25	20	386	279	-1	-3%	9%	15%	3%
9	at CAR	L	17	20	355	330	+1	24%	23%	0%	1%
10	DAL	W	27	7	336	233	+1	39%	11%	-28%	1%
11	at SEA	W	34	31	279	360	+1	9%	14%	-4%	-9%
12	TB	W	34	20	516	373	-1	24%	45%	26%	4%
13	MIN	L	9	14	275	312	0	7%	18%	8%	-3%
14	NO	W	20	17	343	306	-2	-5%	-24%	-16%	2%
15	at TB	W	24	21	410	373	+1	-36%	6%	33%	-9%
16	at NO	L	13	23	331	315	-1	-2%	-14%	-17%	-5%
17	CAR	W	22	10	371	248	+3	33%	-3%	-29%	7%
18	at LAR	W	26	13	322	361	+2	36%	17%	-4%	14%
19	at PHI	L	10	15	281	334	+2	0%	15%	16%	1%

Trends and Splits

	Offense	Rank	Defense	Rank
Total DVOA	8.1%	9	5.6%	22
Unadjusted VOA	8.4%	9	6.7%	22
Weighted Trend	6.9%	10	2.1%	19
Variance	3.5%	2	3.8%	7
Average Opponent	0.7%	21	3.5%	3
Passing	27.8%	10	13.3%	20
Rushing	-6.2%	16	-4.3%	20
First Down	13.9%	5	6.0%	24
Second Down	-1.2%	15	-3.7%	14
Third Down	11.7%	9	20.0%	29
First Half	18.4%	3	0.4%	14
Second Half	-3.1%	17	10.5%	25
Red Zone	-11.8%	23	-17.6%	6
Late and Close	-9.0%	23	-14.0%	8

Five-Year Performance

Year	W-L	Pyth W	Est W	PF	PA	TO	Total	Rk	Off	Rk	Def	Rk	ST	Rk	Off AGL	Rk	Def AGL	Rk	Off Age	Rk	Def Age	Rk	ST Age	Rk
2013	4-12	5.9	6.5	353	443	-7	-10.4%	25	3.2%	14	13.5%	29	-0.1%	17	53.9	27	36.1	23	27.6	7	26.7	15	25.9	21
2014	6-10	7.1	7.2	381	417	+5	-5.4%	20	7.2%	10	15.7%	32	3.0%	9	60.6	30	33.2	12	26.8	16	26.6	21	26.4	7
2015	8-8	7.8	5.8	339	345	-7	-16.3%	26	-7.3%	23	6.9%	22	-2.1%	22	10.9	2	17.8	5	27.5	8	26.9	14	26.7	5
2016	11-5	10.9	11.8	540	406	+11	19.8%	3	24.6%	1	7.3%	26	2.5%	7	19.3	2	32.9	16	27.8	5	26.0	25	27.3	2
2017	10-6	9.1	8.5	353	315	-2	1.4%	15	8.1%	9	5.6%	22	-1.2%	19	11.2	3	5.1	3	27.4	8	25.7	25	26.5	5

2017 Performance Based on Most Common Personnel Groups

ATL Offense					ATL Offense vs. Opponents					ATL Defense				ATL Defense vs. Opponents			
Pers	Freq	Yds	DVOA	Run%	Pers	Freq	Yds	DVOA	Run%	Pers	Freq	Yds	DVOA	Pers	Freq	Yds	DVOA
11	50%	6.1	14.0%	31%	Base	39%	5.9	9.5%	55%	Base	24%	4.7	-11.8%	11	59%	5.4	10.3%
12	20%	7.0	20.9%	52%	Nickel	49%	6.2	12.6%	34%	Nickel	72%	5.6	12.3%	12	16%	5.2	2.8%
21	16%	5.5	-0.4%	51%	Dime+	11%	6.3	25.8%	16%	Dime+	2%	5.4	9.6%	21	9%	5.7	0.3%
20	4%	5.8	14.4%	46%	Goal Line	1%	-0.1	-56.5%	75%	Goal Line	2%	2.6	10.7%	22	5%	4.6	-3.1%
10	3%	5.3	48.8%	0%										13	4%	5.9	2.3%
22	2%	3.8	-24.8%	86%										621	2%	2.9	-47.9%

Strategic Tendencies

Run/Pass		Rk	Formation		Rk	Pass Rush		Rk	Secondary		Rk	Strategy		Rk
Runs, first half	39%	15	Form: Single Back	70%	27	Rush 3	6.7%	18	4 DB	24%	28	Play action	22%	13
Runs, first down	49%	19	Form: Empty Back	8%	14	Rush 4	73.1%	10	5 DB	72%	2	Avg Box (Off)	6.26	13
Runs, second-long	37%	9	Pers: 3+ WR	57%	22	Rush 5	18.1%	20	6+ DB	2%	22	Avg Box (Def)	6.06	29
Runs, power sit.	70%	4	Pers: 2+ TE/6+ OL	27%	22	Rush 6+	2.1%	32	CB by Sides	92%	4	Offensive Pace	31.14	21
Runs, behind 2H	33%	4	Pers: 6+ OL	4%	10	Int DL Sacks	19.2%	21	S/CB Cover Ratio	32%	10	Defensive Pace	32.35	32
Pass, ahead 2H	50%	11	Shotgun/Pistol	43%	32	Second Level Sacks	15.4%	19	DB Blitz	2%	32	Go for it on 4th	0.64	28

One significant change from Kyle Shanahan to Steve Sarkisian is that Sarkisian mixed plays in the second half in a more standard fashion. The Falcons passed less than the year before when winning (dropping from 11th to 17th) and ran less than the year before when losing (dropping from fifth to 24th). ☞ This was the second straight year the Falcons used less shotgun/pistol than any other offense. Their difference between DVOA in the shotgun and DVOA under center is average. ☞ In 2016, Matt Ryan averaged just 4.9 yards against a DB blitz. Real strategy to stop Ryan, or just a statistical fluke? Well, last year's data says it was clearly "fluke." In 2017, Ryan averaged 9.4 yards per pass against a DB blitz, second in the league behind only Jared Goff. ☞ Atlanta opponents threw short a lot: 85 percent of passes were less than 16 yards in the air, second in the league behind only Cleveland. And Atlanta opponents threw to their running backs on a league-leading 25 percent of passes.

Passing

Player	DYAR	DVOA	Plays	NtYds	Avg	YAC	C%	TD	Int
M.Ryan	1084	19.1%	552	3917	7.1	5.4	65.1%	20	12

Rushing

Player	DYAR	DVOA	Plays	Yds	Avg	TD	Fum	Suc
D.Freeman	89	1.5%	195	862	4.4	7	4	51%
T.Coleman	14	-6.5%	156	628	4.0	5	1	40%
T.Ward*	10	-0.3%	30	129	4.3	0	1	47%
M.Ryan	54	43.4%	20	153	7.7	0	1	-
T.Gabriel*	36	39.5%	8	49	6.1	0	0	-
M.Sanu	29	48.3%	5	18	3.6	0	0	-

Receiving

Player	DYAR	DVOA	Plays	Ctch	Yds	Y/C	YAC	TD	C%
J.Jones	313	13.7%	148	88	1444	16.4	5.5	3	59%
M.Sanu	179	10.7%	96	67	703	10.5	3.7	5	70%
T.Gabriel*	18	-8.0%	51	33	378	11.5	6.6	1	65%
J.Hardy	59	12.5%	29	20	221	11.1	3.8	3	69%
M.Hall	-6	-20.9%	9	2	60	30.0	0.0	1	22%
A.Hooper	71	9.4%	65	49	526	10.7	5.3	3	75%
L.Toilolo*	38	29.6%	14	12	122	10.2	5.3	1	86%
D.Freeman	102	23.6%	47	36	317	8.8	6.8	1	77%
T.Coleman	121	41.2%	39	27	299	11.1	8.1	3	69%
D.Coleman*	-14	-48.6%	7	2	20	10.0	8.5	0	29%

Offensive Line

Player	Pos	Age	GS	Snaps	Pen	Sk	Pass	Run	Player	Pos	Age	GS	Snaps	Pen	Sk	Pass	Run
Jake Matthews	LT	26	16/16	1025	4	2.3	20	9	Andy Levitre	LG	32	13/13	699	5	0.0	12	10
Alex Mack	C	33	16/16	1025	2	1.0	5	6	Ben Garland	G	30	16/3	343	4	1.0	8	2
Wes Schweitzer	RG	25	16/16	1016	6	4.0	10	15	Ty Sambrailo	OT	26	15/2	209	1	2.3	10	5
Ryan Schraeder	RT	30	14/14	834	3	2.0	6	10	Brandon Fusco	RG	29	16/16	1085	6	5.5	12	8

Year	Yards	ALY	Rank	Power	Rank	Stuff	Rank	2nd Lev	Rank	Open Field	Rank	Sacks	ASR	Rank	Press	Rank	F-Start	Cont.
2015	4.07	4.17	15	61%	21	22%	22	1.33	1	0.67	19	32	5.4%	9	24.3%	13	12	36
2016	4.66	4.40	10	61%	17	22%	23	1.30	7	1.20	3	37	6.5%	23	29.5%	25	19	48
2017	4.25	4.35	8	64%	17	21%	20	1.25	6	0.85	10	24	4.8%	8	31.5%	19	17	34

2017 ALY by direction: Left End: 4.37 (12)   Left Tackle: 5.14 (3)   Mid/Guard: 4.52 (5)   Right Tackle: 3.80 (17)   Right End: 3.65 (21)

This is a mostly solid offensive line, though the Falcons keep trying to close a rotating door at right guard. ☞ Prior to Alex Mack's arrival in 2016, Atlanta's offensive line was largely a mess. Over the past two years, Mack may have been the best center in the league. Mack and right tackle Ryan Schraeder both ranked sixth at their positions in snaps per blown block, and their presence has allowed the Falcons to get away with some inconsistent play from their right guard spot. ☞ Barring injury, Atlanta will have its third starting right guard in as many years with Brandon Fusco (ex-49ers and Vikings) joining the team via free agency. His arrival knocks Wes Schweitzer to the bench, and Schweitzer and Ben Garland make for a good depth duo at guard. ☞ The Falcons also have a few interesting depth pieces at offensive tackle. As far as backup offensive tackles go, Austin Pasztor was a fairly sought-after commodity in free agency before last season. Daniel Brunskill was a tight end for most of his career at San Diego State and held his own against Miami first-round pick Charles Harris in the preseason. Less intriguing is Denver castoff Ty Sambrailo, who started two early games and showed why the Broncos were willing to give up on a former second-round pick so quickly. Before Atlanta acquired him for a fifth-round pick, most Falcons fans probably knew Sambrailo as the poor offensive tackle Vic Beasley beat for four sacks in Denver during the 2016 season.

Defensive Front Seven

Defensive Line	Age	Pos	G	Snaps	Plays	TmPct	Rk	Stop	Dfts	BTkl	Runs	St%	Rk	RuYd	Rk	Sack	Hit	Hur	Dsrpt
						Overall						vs. Run				Pass Rush			
Grady Jarrett	25	DT	16	794	52	6.4%	18	43	18	4	42	81%	29	1.1	6	4.0	10	23.0	0
Dontari Poe*	28	DT	16	786	41	5.1%	41	32	8	5	34	76%	48	2.4	59	2.5	8	21.5	3

Edge Rushers	Age	Pos	G	Snaps	Plays	TmPct	Rk	Stop	Dfts	BTkl	Runs	St%	Rk	RuYd	Rk	Sack	Hit	Hur	Dsrpt
						Overall						vs. Run				Pass Rush			
Adrian Clayborn*	30	DE	16	567	21	2.6%	92	18	13	6	6	83%	21	3.3	77	9.5	10	27.5	3
Vic Beasley	26	OLB	14	485	31	4.4%	57	21	10	7	16	75%	46	0.8	8	5.0	1	19.0	3
Brooks Reed	31	DE	16	412	39	4.8%	--	34	7	4	34	85%	--	2.3	--	4.0	3	10.5	0
Takkarist McKinley	23	DE	16	401	21	2.6%	--	19	12	4	13	85%	--	1.3	--	6.0	4	22.0	1
Derrick Shelby	29	DE	16	397	30	3.7%	--	26	6	6	27	93%	--	1.8	--	1.0	1	9.0	0

Linebackers	Age	Pos	G	Snaps	Plays	TmPct	Rk	Stop	Dfts	BTkl	Runs	St%	Rk	RuYd	Rk	Sack	Hit	Hur	Tgts	Suc%	Rk	AdjYd	Rk	PD	Int
						Overall						vs. Run				Pass Rush				vs. Pass					
Deion Jones	24	MLB	16	1021	148	18.3%	4	68	28	15	78	45%	83	4.8	81	1.0	0	2.5	61	56%	21	4.4	3	10	3
De'Vondre Campbell	25	OLB	16	948	94	11.6%	47	42	13	8	50	48%	80	4.6	78	2.0	4	9.5	42	53%	28	5.7	19	3	0
Duke Riley	24	OLB	12	223	24	4.0%	--	12	0	10	16	69%	--	2.9	--	0.0	0	0.0	9	36%	--	10.7	--	0	0

Year	Yards	ALY	Rank	Power	Rank	Stuff	Rank	2nd Level	Rank	Open Field	Rank	Sacks	ASR	Rank	Press	Rank
2015	4.06	4.14	19	73%	27	18%	22	1.15	20	0.80	17	19	3.7%	32	21.5%	31
2016	4.28	4.47	25	63%	16	19%	18	1.29	26	0.64	13	34	5.4%	24	26.4%	20
2017	3.84	4.15	19	76%	29	20%	17	1.09	13	0.51	4	39	6.6%	16	29.5%	22

2017 ALY by direction: Left End: 4.73 (26)   Left Tackle: 3.85 (14)   Mid/Guard: 4.08 (13)   Right Tackle: 4.22 (24)   Right End: 3.85 (14)

Deion Jones and De'Vondre Campbell were both added to revamp Atlanta's group of linebackers during the 2016 draft. Jones has turned into one of the NFL's premier coverage linebackers. His interior run defense can be a bit shaky at times, but he's elite in space and has even shown the ability to cover wide receivers. Jones is the prototype when analysts talk about the "new age" NFL linebacker, and his six interceptions in the past two seasons are tied for first among all linebackers in that span. ☞ Campbell doesn't have the consistency that Jones does, but his athleticism paired with his frame (6-foot-4, 232 pounds) has turned him into a jack-of-all-trades linebacker for the Falcons. He has made an impact as a run defender, as a coverage piece against tight ends and running backs, and even as a pass-rusher, where he logged two sacks and 9.5 hurries during the regular season. Campbell looks primed to start again next to Jones for the 2018 season, unless 2017 third-round pick Duke Riley makes major strides. Coming out of LSU, Riley's calling card was his speed, which let him recover from mental mistakes in coverage or run defense. While that's a fine plan for a college linebacker, it doesn't work so well in the NFL where everyone is fast. ☞ Grady Jarrett is one of the rare Day 3 draft picks who turned into a legitimate star player. His athleticism and natural leverage have helped him develop into one of the best penetrating tackles in the NFL. Jarrett tied for fourth in the league last year with 18 run tackles for a loss or no gain. ☞ Joining Grady Jarrett at defensive tackle will be Terrell McClain (the likely starter), Jack Crawford, Justin Zimmer, Garrison Smith, and third-round rookie Deadrin Senat. Senat's athletic testing won't blow anyone away, but he was a source of explosive plays for the University of South Florida, with 10.5 tackles for a loss and six sacks in his senior season. ☞ Much of the success of this front seven hinges on the development and growth of Vic Beasley and Takk McKinley. Beasley was the league-leading sack artist with 15.5 in 2016, but his production dropped off after shaking off an ankle injury and splitting some time at linebacker throughout the season. He also cut his hurries in half from 38 to 19. Beasley's impact has been inconsistent throughout his tenure with the Falcons. The natural talent he has is otherworldly, but Beasley needs to figure out how to be a more dangerous pass-rusher and edge defender than he is right now. The Falcons picked up Beasley's fifth-year option right before the 2018 draft, but he's going to need to significantly increase his production to secure a lucrative long-term deal with the team. ☞ McKinley exploded onto the scene as a rookie. He collected 6.0 sacks in the regular season and added 2.0 more in the playoffs. With Adrian Clayborn moving on to New England, McKinley will see a huge increase to his snap count, from 38 percent of snaps last year to something close to (or more than) the 53 percent Clayborn played last year. Brooks Reed and Derrick Shelby spell Beasley and McKinley at defensive end.

Defensive Secondary

Secondary	Age	Pos	G	Snaps	Overall						vs. Run					vs. Pass									
					Plays	TmPct	Rk	Stop	Dfts	BTkl	Runs	St%	Rk	RuYd	Rk	Tgts	Tgt%	Rk	Dist	Suc%	Rk	AdjYd	Rk	PD	Int
Keanu Neal	23	SS	16	1045	118	14.6%	3	48	18	13	53	49%	25	5.2	21	67	15.4%	70	9.0	45%	63	8.2	38	7	1
Robert Alford	30	CB	16	1043	85	10.5%	9	38	13	9	13	62%	14	5.4	24	92	21.1%	44	11.0	52%	39	6.4	14	19	1
Ricardo Allen	27	FS	15	957	56	7.4%	69	13	9	8	25	16%	74	10.5	72	26	6.4%	10	12.4	51%	40	10.1	63	1	1
Desmond Trufant	28	CB	15	902	51	6.7%	65	24	14	2	11	45%	39	9.0	68	56	14.9%	9	13.0	49%	49	8.1	52	13	2
Brian Poole	26	CB	15	635	67	8.9%	37	30	11	13	13	38%	52	9.2	69	55	20.7%	42	8.5	46%	70	7.3	35	4	0
Kemal Ishmael	27	SS	16	114	23	2.9%	--	10	2	2	18	44%	--	3.9	--	5	10.5%	--	8.8	22%	--	9.0	--	0	0
Ron Parker*	31	FS	15	1034	71	9.3%	49	18	8	18	37	24%	69	9.5	59	32	8.2%	27	17.5	47%	52	9.9	59	4	2

Year	Pass D Rank	vs. #1 WR	Rk	vs. #2 WR	Rk	vs. Other WR	Rk	WR Wide	Rk	WR Slot	Rk	vs. TE	Rk	vs. RB	Rk
2015	22	-11.1%	7	8.0%	20	-11.7%	7	--	--	--	--	-14.0%	6	31.9%	32
2016	18	-3.4%	11	-5.6%	8	14.5%	27	-20.5%	3	14.5%	24	-5.6%	12	16.5%	25
2017	20	14.6%	25	19.3%	25	-7.9%	12	-2.3%	16	17.8%	23	-2.3%	14	8.4%	21

This underrated unit is where Dan Quinn has really transformed the Falcons defense. ☞ Desmond Trufant and Robert Alford were added in the first and second round of the 2013 NFL draft, respectively. Alford struggled prior to Quinn's arrival, but now he's legitimately one of the better starting cornerbacks in the league. He was targeted much more than Trufant last season but had a higher success rate and allowed fewer yards per pass. Alford used to be an enemy of the Falcons' fan base with his tendency for ill-timed pass interference penalties, but has become far more consistent. Even with Trufant healthy, the Falcons showed a lot of faith in Alford by not using Trufant to specifically track the opponent's top receiver. They ranked fourth in "CB by Sides" after ranking 30th in 2016. ☞ Mike Smith's coaching staff didn't have much use for Ricardo Allen. Allen was a practice squad candidate throughout the entirety of his rookie year in 2014, even though he was a fifth-round draft pick. He struggled at cornerback, but then Quinn arrived and changed his position to free safety. Since then, Allen has turned into one of the Falcons' defensive leaders and has a chance to earn a second contract with the team as its free safety of the future. He has 2017 fifth-round pick Damontae Kazee giving him a push, but Allen has dealt with competition before. ☞ The Falcons added two Florida Gators in 2016, first-round safety Keanu Neal and undrafted cornerback Brian Poole. Neal has started every game he has played and has become Dan Quinn's new version of Kam Chancellor with his extremely physical style of play. Poole has been the team's primary slot cornerback, and he has greatly exceeded expectations as an undrafted free agent, but he ranked 70th in adjusted success rate out of 80 qualifying corners last year, so the Falcons do have room to improve. It won't be surprising if second-round rookie Isaiah Oliver (Colorado) pushes him for playing time this year. Oliver fits the prototype of what heavy Cover-3 and man-coverage teams, like the Falcons, look for. He has the height and length to be a force on the exterior of Atlanta's defense. He probably wouldn't be a great fit as a slot defender, but Alford and Trufant have both shown the ability to play inside. Meanwhile, Poole has experience playing some safety in college; he'll have a big role in Atlanta's defense even if Oliver takes some of his snaps.

Special Teams

Year	DVOA	Rank	FG/XP	Rank	Net Kick	Rank	Kick Ret	Rank	Net Punt	Rank	Punt Ret	Rank	Hidden	Rank
2015	-2.1%	22	-4.3	28	-3.9	26	0.2	13	-4.6	21	2.1	12	7.8	5
2016	2.5%	7	11.1	2	-3.0	25	-1.7	19	2.1	12	3.8	9	-4.3	22
2017	-1.2%	19	6.4	9	-4.5	25	-3.6	25	-1.0	19	-3.1	25	-3.0	16

Matt Bryant has become a consistent weapon for the Falcons, earning the nickname "Money Matt." Bryant has ranked in the top ten in field goal value in three of the past four seasons. But he was the only positive part of Atlanta's special teams last season. ☞ Matt Bosher was fairly average at both punts and kickoffs, while Atlanta struggled with kickoff coverage and both kickoff and punt returns. ☞ With Andre Roberts gone, the Falcons have a handful of options to use as return men. Justin Hardy looks to be the guy right now, but he could see competition from both Calvin Ridley and rookie running back Ito Smith.

Baltimore Ravens

2017 Record: 9-7	**Total DVOA:** 18.5% (7th)	**2018 Mean Projection:** 8.4 wins	**On the Clock (0-4):** 7%
Pythagorean Wins: 10.5 (8th)	**Offense:** -4.5% (21st)	**Postseason Odds:** 42.2%	**Mediocrity (5-7):** 29%
Snap-Weighted Age: 26.9 (9th)	**Defense:** -13.8% (3rd)	**Super Bowl Odds:** 6.6%	**Playoff Contender (8-10):** 43%
Average Opponent: -4.7% (31st)	**Special Teams:** 9.2% (1st)	**Proj. Avg. Opponent:** 0.1% (14th)	**Super Bowl Contender (11+):** 22%

2017: Other than that last play, how was the season Mrs. Harbaugh?

2018: An offensive overhaul to get fans dreaming of 2019.

Before the season, Baltimore would surely have signed up for the following situation: just get a stop on fourth-and-12 near midfield, in the friendly confines of a frigid, windy M&T Bank Stadium, against Andy Dalton, in the season finale, and the team would make the playoffs.

Of course, the Ravens didn't make that stop. Dalton hit Tyler Boyd with a stunning 49-yard touchdown pass with 44 seconds left to cap a 90-yard drive that eliminated Baltimore from the postseason. It was the third consecutive season the Ravens missed out on the tournament.

In the long run, it was probably the best thing that could have happened to the franchise.

Slipping into the playoffs, and even winning a game or more, would have been illusory progress that may have convinced outgoing general manager Ozzie Newsome and head coach John Harbaugh that the team was closer to its old form than it actually is. They may have even been witness to another postseason roll from Joe Flacco that would have obscured a season's worth of poor play. The 2017 Ravens were similar to past incarnations, in that they used a patented blend of excellent special teams and very good defense to overcome a blah offense. It's just that this particular defense wasn't nearly as nasty as the Lewis/Reed/Ngata versions, and the offense was even more lackluster, though it did become sporadically more effective by season's end.

That the Purple Birds turned this recipe into nine wins was mainly a mixture of turnovers and circumstance. The Ravens turned opponents over on 18 percent of drives, the top rate in football, while also leading in total takeaways and turnover margin. Add that to special teams domination and the team had the league's best average field position as well, starting at the 32.3-yard line. The short fields allowed the 21st-ranked offense to squeeze out enough points to win more than they lost.

Then there was the nature of the opposition. The Ravens banked two wins right off the top by shutting out a much different Cincinnati squad, which at the time was so offensively inept they canned their coordinator five days later, then squashing the hapless Browns in a game in which shaky rookie quarterback DeShone Kizer was forced to sit due to migraines and give way to shakier backup (and Bobby Douglass reincarnate) Kevin Hogan. Baltimore was gifted an amazing ten turnovers in the two games, nearly a third of its season total.

The Ravens also got to play Miami with Matt Moore at quarterback, and Green Bay with Brett Hundley, and Houston with Tom Savage, and Oakland with EJ Manuel. The opponent adjustments in their excellent defensive DVOA were somewhat artificially inflated due to playing ordinarily strong offenses that were missing their ringleaders. Indeed, that final game might well have been about Baltimore trying to deny the Bengals a playoff spot rather than the other way around, had Cincy played against Hundley and Savage rather than Aaron Rodgers and Deshaun Watson.

The Ravens project to be a mid-major team once again, carried along by kicker Justin Tucker more than Flacco. They will have to overcome a likely rebound in those turnover margins, not just on defense but on offense too, where Baltimore posted the fewest fumbles per drive in the league (and sixth-fewest turnovers overall). Indeed, their fumble luck was extraordinary—the Ravens fell on 11 of their 15 fumbles on offense, the best rate in the NFL, and pounced on 11 of 18 fumbles on defense. They were also penalized the fewest yards of any offense, a stat that surely will be tough to replicate.

While opposing quarterback luck is a floating crap game, the 2018 Ravens are slated to face Matt Ryan, Drew Brees, Cam Newton, Jameis Winston, Derek Carr, Philip Rivers, and Marcus Mariota, in addition to the twice-annual duel with Ben Roethlisberger (plus a host of unknowns—Pat Mahomes, Josh Allen/AJ McCarron, whoever plays for the Browns, and of course, the DaltonCoaster). If Baltimore is as fortunate in this area as they were a year ago, then the old Colts horseshoe must remain hidden somewhere under that Ravens logo on the team's helmets.

Despite the almost certain regression, there are a few factors working to Baltimore's advantage. First and foremost, the AFC projects to be incredibly weak once again, so even another mediocre edition of the Ravens should be cusp-of-playoffs stuff. The defense, which we've just chopped down to size a bit, is still pretty darn good, while the special teams should again be excellent. Baltimore underperformed its Pythagorean prediction of 10.5 wins, which usually suggests more victories the following season. And the schedule, though festooned with good quarterbacks, projects as average in difficulty, and finishes with five of the final eight games at home (there is a three-game roadie before that to compensate).

Much about Baltimore's 2018 season will be determined by this offseason's offensive remodel. Newsome went out with

2018 Ravens Schedule

Week	Opp.	Week	Opp.	Week	Opp.
1	BUF	7	NO	13	at ATL
2	at CIN (Thu.)	8	at CAR	14	at KC
3	DEN	9	PIT	15	TB
4	at PIT	10	BYE	16	at LAC
5	at CLE	11	CIN	17	CLE
6	at TEN	12	OAK		

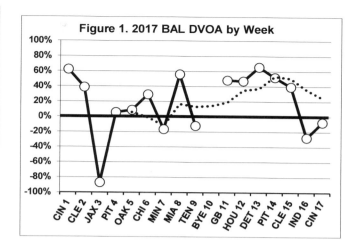

Figure 1. 2017 BAL DVOA by Week

a bang in his last draft before stepping aside to an emeritus role with the Ravens. After four drafts that saw ten front-seven players picked in the first three rounds (and an apparent bust of a wide receiver in Breshad Perriman), Newsome attacked the offense, adding a pair of pass-catching tight ends and a potential future franchise quarterback. He also brought in an entirely new set of wide receivers via free agency. While the cupboard isn't stocked so much that new general manager Eric DeCosta can put his feet up and chillax, the Ravens figure to be at least a little better on offense in the present tense, and possibly a lot better in the near future.

The Ravens new quarterback, Lamar Jackson, has been the subject of all kinds of analysis since demolishing any number of school records at Louisville (not to mention winning the 2016 Heisman Trophy) and entering the draft process—the pigskin version of the scene from *Lovely and Amazing* where Durmot Mulroney ruthlessly picks apart Emily Mortimer's body. Most of the chatter around Jackson had disturbing racial undertones. Some saw him as the next Michael Vick; others wanted him to convert to wide receiver. Few were inclined to see him for what he is—a very good, if mechanically flawed, prospect who operated from the pocket perfectly well in Bobby Petrino's pro-style attack. Clearly, Newsome saw him that way, which is all that matters in the end.

Our QBASE projection system found Jackson to be as good as any passer in the draft except Baker Mayfield, and that didn't even factor in Jackson's electrifying abilities as a runner. Jackson's low completion rate (59.1 percent) was used against him, but his adjusted yards per attempt figure was just fine (8.7) and the Cardinals were 11th in the country in passing S&P+, particularly good given the lack of talent on Louisville's offense in 2017. He profiled in our methodology to be a late first-round pick, which is exactly where Newsome traded up with Philly to grab Jackson.

It's entirely possible that Jackson's biggest contribution to the 2018 Ravens is as a motivational tool for Flacco. Since memorably winning the Super Bowl and parlaying his spectacular playoff run into a monster contract, the 33-year-old Flacco has seldom lived up to his paycheck (which simultaneously has hampered roster construction). He was brutal in 2017, finishing 32nd in DYAR, just behind Savage and just ahead of Trevor Siemian, horrifying company given Delaware Joe's enormous cap hit. Yes, a lack of viable targets hurt Flacco's cause, as did a preseason back injury and lingering effects from his torn ACL suffered in 2016. But clearly Newsome and the Ravens brain trust have seen enough.

The plan in Baltimore figures to be the Kansas City model, with Flacco as Alex Smith and Jackson as Mahomes. Flacco's 2016 contract restructuring reduced Baltimore's liability if they cut Flacco after the 2018 season from an impossible $26.5 million to a more palatable, if hardly tasty, $16 million. Obviously, the team would love it if Flacco sees this year as a "prove it" challenge similar to the one he responded to so well back in 2012. Regardless, quarterbacks drafted in the first round in this day and age play sooner rather than later. Assuming Jackson is anywhere close to being ready, it's hard to see him manning the backup spot beyond this year.

Meanwhile, offensive coordinator Marty Mornhinweg, who coached Steve Young and Vick among other upwardly mobile quarterbacks, and assistant head coach Greg Roman, who worked (under the other Harbaugh brother) with Colin Kaepernick during his heyday in San Francisco, are tasked with designing packages to get Jackson on the field even while Flacco remains the starter. Also on hand: Robert Griffin III, who not so long ago was the hot new dual-threat. Griffin is a longshot to be active on game days, barring injury, but as an in-house cautionary tale he's aces.

Baltimore has never been a particularly progressive or imaginative franchise when it comes to offense, certainly not compared to its rivals in Pittsburgh and Cincinnati. But they are certainly among the smartest and most adaptable teams, and it isn't hard to imagine the Purple slashing its way into a new era of regular postseason appearances behind Jackson's running and gunning. If nothing else, they won't be such a grinding, soulless offense to watch—and perhaps might even become Must See (Red Zone) TV.

In the meantime, Newsome's attempt to rebuild on the fly meant importing a host of new weapons for his incumbent quarterback, while shedding a sizable number of the old ones. The team totalled 567 pass targets a year ago; only 223 of those went to players who remain on the roster. The top three receivers by number of targets (Mike Wallace, Ben Watson, and Jeremy Maclin) are gone. The new receivers include Michael Crabtree, who came over from Oakland for $11 million guaranteed; Willie Snead, a restricted free agent to whom the Ravens gave an offer the Saints could refuse; and former

Arizona slot man John Brown, signed to a one-year deal after injuries halted a promising start to his career in the desert. At a glance it appears to be an upgrade, if a modest one. Certainly the Ravens have had success with veteran receivers such as Anquan Boldin and Steve Smith in the recent past.

The Ravens also went hard at tight end in the draft, using their first pick (all but forgotten after the later Jackson selection) on South Carolina's Hayden Hurst and a third-round selection on Mark Andrews of Oklahoma. Hurst has excellent hands, though he is 25, having washed out of his first sport, baseball, after developing Steve Blass disease, unable to find home plate with a GPS. Andrews is a similar player, a sure-handed seam threat who racked up the receptions while playing with Baker Mayfield. Neither player can block his way out of a paper bag, which would seem to limit their usefulness, certainly their simultaneous usefulness. (Hurst at least gives an effort, so perhaps he can improve in the NFL.) Baltimore was the only team to use two-tight end sets on more than half of its plays, and much of that came with using a tight end in the backfield. The addition of two playmaking tight ends who are essentially slot receivers with Workout Anytime memberships figures to change this basic tenet of the scheme—unless Hurst is so adept at running routes from the H-back position that his lack of conviction in lead blocking becomes a moot point.

Newsome loves to double-dip at his former position—back in 2010 he picked both Dennis Pitta and Ed Dickson. Neither had the desired impact; Pitta had ceaseless hip injuries and Dickson only found himself once he left Baltimore. Watching the development of Hurst and Andrews won't be as fascinating as following Jackson, perhaps, but it will be a huge part of the legacy of Newsome's last draft.

Fortunately, there is far more consistency on the defensive side of the ball—indeed, every defender who took a snap in 2017 is back in purple except Lardarius Webb. There is one significant change however. Dean Pees re-retired as defensive coordinator (then re-un-retired and joined Tennessee), replaced by linebackers coach Don "Wink" Martindale (sorry, Don, there's no escaping that nickname). No less an authority on the Ravens defense than Terrell Suggs said in the spring that Martindale was "taking the handcuffs off" the unit. What that means in practical terms remains to be seen, but it's fair to say that the less experienced coordinator will be leaning on his veterans, like T-Sizzle and safety Eric Weddle, to have both game-plan and in-game adjustment input.

The vets were frustrated with the team's inability to make stops at the end of big games. While Baltimore's defense was first in the league in fourth-quarter/overtime DVOA (-31.0%), a closer look shows that a lot of that was bully ball during blowouts. In late-and-close situations—second half, score within eight points—that ranking fell to 11th (-10.9%). In addition to the Bengals disaster, Pittsburgh put up 19 fourth-quarter points to steal a crucial December win. Tennessee put together a 75-yard clock-killing drive to ice a close game. The Bears marched down the field in overtime to stun the Ravens in Baltimore. No team is perfect at money time, but given how close the team came to the postseason, those relatively few moments stood out.

So while we all spend 2018 Waiting For Lamar, the Ravens figure to be in much the same situation as a year ago—a clear step behind Pittsburgh, roughly equal with Cincinnati, and a clear step (or two) ahead of Cleveland. And speaking of the Browns, they're coming to M&T Bank Stadium to finish out the season on December 30. Deep in his or her heart, any Ravens fan would probably sign up right now for the following: final game of the season, playoff spot on the line, at home, defense on the field, fourth-and-long for the opponent. Surely they can't give it up twice in a row, right?

Robert Weintraub

2017 Ravens Stats by Week

Wk	vs.	W-L	PF	PA	YDF	YDA	TO	Total	Off	Def	ST
1	at CIN	W	20	0	268	221	+4	62%	-28%	-90%	0%
2	CLE	W	24	10	337	386	+3	39%	14%	-26%	-2%
3	at JAX	L	7	44	186	410	-3	-87%	-53%	35%	2%
4	PIT	L	9	26	288	381	-2	6%	-11%	-16%	1%
5	at OAK	W	30	17	365	245	+1	8%	10%	2%	0%
6	CHI	L	24	27	291	342	-1	29%	-40%	-16%	53%
7	at MIN	L	16	24	208	357	+1	-17%	-18%	-6%	-5%
8	MIA	W	40	0	295	196	+2	56%	-2%	-52%	6%
9	at TEN	L	20	23	341	257	-1	-12%	-9%	2%	-1%
10	BYE										
11	at GB	W	23	0	219	265	+4	48%	-37%	-67%	19%
12	HOU	W	23	16	294	303	+3	47%	-2%	-26%	24%
13	DET	W	44	20	370	372	+3	66%	45%	-10%	11%
14	at PIT	L	38	39	413	545	-1	52%	50%	14%	16%
15	at CLE	W	27	10	376	266	+4	39%	9%	-21%	10%
16	IND	W	23	16	323	296	0	-28%	-4%	12%	-12%
17	CIN	L	27	31	312	359	0	-7%	-16%	17%	26%

Trends and Splits

	Offense	Rank	Defense	Rank
Total DVOA	-4.5%	21	-13.9%	3
Unadjusted VOA	-0.6%	17	-17.8%	2
Weighted Trend	0.5%	16	-11.5%	5
Variance	7.8%	17	10.5%	32
Average Opponent	0.9%	23	-3.5%	28
Passing	-4.9%	26	-15.4%	2
Rushing	2.4%	7	-12.0%	9
First Down	-7.5%	22	-15.4%	2
Second Down	-1.4%	16	-5.1%	10
Third Down	-3.9%	19	-25.1%	4
First Half	-3.6%	18	-6.2%	10
Second Half	-5.5%	21	-21.9%	1
Red Zone	17.7%	8	-28.9%	3
Late and Close	1.4%	14	-10.9%	11

Five-Year Performance

Year	W-L	Pyth W	Est W	PF	PA	TO	Total	Rk	Off	Rk	Def	Rk	ST	Rk	Off AGL	Rk	Def AGL	Rk	Off Age	Rk	Def Age	Rk	ST Age	Rk
2013	8-8	7.1	6.8	320	352	-5	-6.7%	23	-21.7%	30	-8.7%	7	6.3%	3	34.0	16	13.4	5	26.6	18	27.5	6	25.9	22
2014	10-6	10.9	11.5	409	302	+2	21.9%	5	9.4%	9	-4.6%	8	8.0%	2	25.0	10	27.6	8	27.4	8	26.8	15	25.4	31
2015	5-11	6.0	7.5	328	401	-14	-3.0%	17	-5.2%	20	5.1%	20	7.3%	1	70.1	32	26.0	12	26.5	18	27.1	10	25.6	27
2016	8-8	8.6	9.1	343	321	+5	7.4%	12	-7.5%	24	-9.9%	6	4.9%	4	29.4	12	30.9	14	28.0	3	27.2	5	26.1	18
2017	9-7	10.5	10.4	395	303	+17	18.6%	7	-4.5%	21	-13.9%	3	9.2%	1	58.7	27	42.9	23	27.3	10	27.0	6	25.7	22

2017 Performance Based on Most Common Personnel Groups

BAL Offense					BAL Offense vs. Opponents					BAL Defense				BAL Defense vs. Opponents			
Pers	Freq	Yds	DVOA	Run%	Pers	Freq	Yds	DVOA	Run%	Pers	Freq	Yds	DVOA	Pers	Freq	Yds	DVOA
11	40%	4.2	-16.9%	27%	Base	51%	4.9	1.2%	57%	Base	30%	5.0	-9.1%	12	15%	5.1	-14.5%
12	36%	5.4	-6.6%	45%	Nickel	38%	4.6	-11.8%	25%	Nickel	40%	5.3	-8.6%	21	5%	4.9	-7.8%
22	10%	4.8	29.2%	83%	Dime+	8%	4.3	-17.5%	8%	Dime+	28%	4.9	-37.6%	22	4%	5.8	26.0%
13	6%	5.0	6.9%	50%	Goal Line	1%	4.2	31.4%	71%	Goal Line	1%	0.9	69.9%	13	2%	5.2	9.5%
21	3%	6.1	66.9%	52%	Big	2%	5.6	76.8%	86%					621	2%	5.8	-35.4%
10	1%	7.1	46.5%	13%													

Strategic Tendencies

Run/Pass		Rk	Formation		Rk	Pass Rush		Rk	Secondary		Rk	Strategy		Rk
Runs, first half	38%	20	Form: Single Back	64%	30	Rush 3	6.8%	17	4 DB	30%	16	Play action	25%	6
Runs, first down	52%	16	Form: Empty Back	8%	15	Rush 4	66.8%	14	5 DB	40%	24	Avg Box (Off)	6.34	7
Runs, second-long	34%	15	Pers: 3+ WR	43%	32	Rush 5	21.9%	13	6+ DB	28%	6	Avg Box (Def)	6.32	10
Runs, power sit.	63%	10	Pers: 2+ TE/6+ OL	55%	1	Rush 6+	4.5%	22	CB by Sides	87%	9	Offensive Pace	29.42	6
Runs, behind 2H	30%	7	Pers: 6+ OL	4%	14	Int DL Sacks	12.2%	29	S/CB Cover Ratio	35%	7	Defensive Pace	29.56	2
Pass, ahead 2H	41%	27	Shotgun/Pistol	50%	26	Second Level Sacks	25.6%	9	DB Blitz	14%	4	Go for it on 4th	0.91	21

Though you wouldn't think of the Ravens as a "fast" team, they've ranked in the top ten in situation-neutral pace for every year of Joe Flacco's career. Last year, only Buffalo went at a faster pace when trailing. ☞ Baltimore ran twice as many two-tight end sets as it did the year before; those tight ends often were lined up in the backfield, and the Ravens got 50 percent of their running back carries out of two-back sets. The 49ers were the only other team at 50 percent or higher, with the Patriots right below. Baltimore had a similar DVOA running with one back as it did with two backs but gained 1.4 yards per carry more from one-back sets, which was a change from recent years when the Ravens were clearly better running from two-back sets. ☞ Baltimore's offense ranked 10th with the quarterback under center, and 28th with the quarterback in shotgun. ☞ The Ravens made a dramatic change in the usage of dime coverage instead of nickel, with roughly 20 percent of defensive plays switching from nickel in 2016 to dime in 2017. ☞ The Ravens defense was No. 1 against the pass in the red zone, but 26th against the run. ☞ Although the Ravens brought pressure at a below-average rate, they had the best pass defense DVOA in the league when they brought pressure. ☞ Baltimore was exceptional when it blitzed a defensive back, which it did more than almost any other defense. On these plays, the Ravens allowed just 3.5 net yards per pass and a league-best -99.5% DVOA. ☞ Baltimore had one of the league's biggest gaps between pass defense against play-action (7.2 yards, 31.0% DVOA) and defense against other passes (5.4 yards, -25.5% DVOA).

Passing

Player	DYAR	DVOA	Plays	NtYds	Avg	YAC	C%	TD	Int
J.Flacco	-301	-19.3%	574	2924	5.1	4.1	64.6%	18	13
R.Mallett*	42	28.3%	16	56	3.5	3.3	56.3%	2	0

Rushing

Player	DYAR	DVOA	Plays	Yds	Avg	TD	Fum	Suc
A.Collins	205	15.1%	212	980	4.6	6	2	51%
J.Allen	96	6.2%	153	591	3.9	4	0	47%
T.West*	14	0.2%	39	139	3.6	2	1	51%
D.Woodhead*	-1	-9.8%	14	56	4.0	0	0	36%
J.Flacco	24	37.0%	10	68	6.8	1	0	-
M.Campanaro*	29	57.7%	5	42	8.4	0	0	-

Receiving

Player	DYAR	DVOA	Plays	Ctch	Yds	Y/C	YAC	TD	C%
M.Wallace*	96	0.4%	92	52	748	14.4	2.9	4	57%
J.Maclin*	-36	-19.1%	72	40	440	11.0	2.7	3	56%
C.Moore	-4	-14.1%	38	18	248	13.8	2.3	3	47%
B.Perriman	-158	-71.8%	35	10	77	7.7	0.5	0	29%
M.Campanaro*	34	3.4%	27	19	173	9.1	4.3	1	70%
C.Matthews*	-8	-29.1%	6	3	25	8.3	1.7	0	50%
G.Whalen*	-15	-46.3%	6	4	23	5.8	0.5	0	67%
M.Crabtree	52	-6.5%	101	58	618	10.7	3.3	8	57%
J.Brown	-51	-24.4%	55	21	299	14.2	2.8	3	38%
W.Snead	-23	-31.0%	16	8	92	11.5	4.0	0	50%
B.Watson*	-1	-7.5%	79	61	522	8.6	4.1	4	77%
N.Boyle	-32	-19.3%	37	28	203	7.3	5.5	0	76%
M.Williams	-43	-43.3%	18	15	86	5.7	6.7	1	83%
J.Allen	-10	-16.7%	60	46	250	5.4	4.7	2	77%
D.Woodhead*	-9	-18.0%	39	33	200	6.1	3.6	0	85%
A.Collins	-92	-55.6%	36	23	187	8.1	8.4	0	64%
B.Rainey*	-30	-90.8%	7	5	18	3.6	6.8	0	71%

Offensive Line

Player	Pos	Age	GS	Snaps	Pen	Sk	Pass	Run	Player	Pos	Age	GS	Snaps	Pen	Sk	Pass	Run
James Hurst	LG	27	16/16	1086	6	1.0	9	11	Ronnie Stanley	LT	24	15/15	1010	5	2.3	11	5
Ryan Jensen*	C	27	16/16	1086	3	2.0	7	7	Matt Skura	RG	25	12/12	739	1	1.0	9	12
Austin Howard*	RT	31	16/16	1082	4	4.3	16	1	Jermaine Eluemunor	G	24	8/2	198	2	1.3	4	2

Year	Yards	ALY	Rank	Power	Rank	Stuff	Rank	2nd Lev	Rank	Open Field	Rank	Sacks	ASR	Rank	Press	Rank	F-Start	Cont.
2015	3.97	4.22	14	54%	28	23%	25	1.21	11	0.62	21	24	3.8%	2	23.5%	12	18	25
2016	4.02	4.07	20	70%	9	20%	14	1.11	20	0.66	18	33	5.3%	8	26.9%	19	13	27
2017	4.22	4.36	6	69%	7	20%	14	1.27	5	0.70	17	27	4.3%	4	26.1%	6	11	30

2017 ALY by direction:	Left End: 5.87 (2)	Left Tackle: 3.61 (20)	Mid/Guard: 4.43 (6)	Right Tackle: 3.74 (19)	Right End: 4.11 (14)

Is one Marshal Yanda worth two starters? The Ravens line lost a pair of starters to free agency, center Ryan Jensen and right tackle Austin Howard, while the stalwart Yanda returns after losing his season to an ankle injury. When healthy, the right guard is one of the best linemen in the game, so having him as an anchor (along with left tackle Ronnie Stanley) aids in the transition that is coming in 2018. ☙ The Ravens can be optimistic about withstanding the changes, given how the line handled Yanda's loss—it was top-ten in both pass- and run-blocking metrics across the board. ☙ With Jensen and Howard departing, the re-signing of utility lineman James Hurst became a priority. The Ravens gave him a large contract to stay, and to justify it are moving him from left guard, where he was steady if unspectacular, to right tackle, a key spot in the modern NFL. Hurst has played (left) tackle in the pros before, to withering effect—he was awful as an injury replacement back in 2015. ☙ Taking over for Hurst at left guard is Alex Lewis, who missed all of 2017 with a torn labrum. Lewis was penciled in as a starter before getting hurt, so the Ravens are confident he can handle the gig—so long as he stays healthy (he's also had an ankle ailment and a concussion in his three years as a pro). ☙ The new center is third-year man Matt Skura, who came off the practice squad and held his own in relief of Yanda, though he was the only Ravens lineman to come out below average in snaps per blown block. Skura will seek to emulate Jensen, another journeyman who stepped up when asked to take over in the middle of the Ravens line. It paid off for Jensen with gobs of free-agent money. Skura was a four-year starting center at Duke, so he's actually "transitioning" back to his natural position. Skura is said to have bulked up to 315 pounds, bigger than Jensen, but doesn't have the latter's willingness to scrap at the drop of a hat. Skura is also a Pittsburgh native and confessed Steelers fan, so there is always the outside possibility he's a traitor from within. ☙ To shore up the tackle depth, the team drafted legacy lineman Orlando Brown, son of the fabled Zeus, the late Ravens tackle (who tragically passed at age 40), though no relation to the Orlando Brown who starred in *That's So Raven*. Brown Jr. was considered first-round material at Oklahoma but was so weak and non-athletic at the combine and in subsequent testing that many teams shied away entirely. Brown went in the third round, and if that proves a steal, Hurst isn't likely to be long for tackle. If it proves an overdraft, the team may have issues with opponents stacking their left side with pass-rushers. ☞ The Ravens also drafted tackle Greg Senat, the pride of Wagner College on Staten Island, in the sixth round for depth. Senat played hoops as well as football for the Seahawks, and has intriguing athleticism, though he's quite raw and awfully slender for an NFL tackle.

Defensive Front Seven

Defensive Line	Age	Pos	G	Snaps	Plays	TmPct	Rk	Stop	Dfts	BTkl	Runs	St%	Rk	RuYd	Rk	Sack	Hit	Hur	Dsrpt
						Overall						**vs. Run**					**Pass Rush**		
Willie Henry	24	DE	14	598	37	5.0%	44	29	8	1	24	75%	57	2.5	63	3.5	9	15.5	5
Michael Pierce	26	DT	16	595	49	5.8%	27	45	4	5	47	91%	5	2.2	44	1.0	2	11.5	0
Brandon Williams	29	DE	12	475	32	5.1%	40	27	6	1	30	83%	22	1.5	16	0.0	2	7.5	2
Carl Davis	26	DE	15	302	20	2.5%	--	17	5	2	18	83%	--	1.9	--	0.5	0	4.5	1

Edge Rushers	Age	Pos	G	Snaps	Plays	TmPct	Rk	Stop	Dfts	BTkl	Runs	St%	Rk	RuYd	Rk	Sack	Hit	Hur	Dsrpt
						Overall						**vs. Run**					**Pass Rush**		
Terrell Suggs	36	OLB	16	845	52	6.2%	25	39	20	11	32	72%	59	1.5	21	11.0	11	47.5	6
Matt Judon	26	OLB	16	789	61	7.3%	17	46	22	6	33	73%	55	2.6	65	8.0	12	14.5	3
Za'Darius Smith	26	OLB	14	531	24	3.3%	80	16	6	3	18	61%	88	3.7	88	3.5	13	29.0	1

Linebackers	Age	Pos	G	Snaps	Plays	TmPct	Rk	Stop	Dfts	BTkl	Runs	St%	Rk	RuYd	Rk	Sack	Hit	Hur	Tgts	Suc%	Rk	AdjYd	Rk	PD	Int
						Overall						**vs. Run**				**Pass Rush**				**vs. Pass**					
C.J. Mosley	26	ILB	16	1078	139	16.6%	12	68	25	8	74	58%	62	3.5	38	1.0	3	5.0	53	43%	57	8.0	62	6	2
Patrick Onwuasor	26	ILB	16	648	90	10.7%	57	42	9	7	57	58%	63	3.9	60	1.0	0	0.0	30	21%	76	9.0	69	0	0

Year	Yards	ALY	Rank	Power	Rank	Stuff	Rank	2nd Level	Rank	Open Field	Rank	Sacks	ASR	Rank	Press	Rank
2015	3.96	4.26	20	68%	21	18%	24	0.94	2	0.67	12	37	6.1%	19	23.9%	26
2016	3.82	3.95	10	50%	3	21%	12	1.05	8	0.59	11	31	5.7%	22	26.7%	19
2017	4.12	3.85	7	62%	14	21%	15	1.10	14	0.87	26	41	6.8%	13	29.6%	20
2017 ALY by direction:			Left End: 1.08 (1)			Left Tackle: 4.50 (25)			Mid/Guard: 3.79 (6)			Right Tackle: 4.21 (23)			Right End: 4.36 (21)	

Thanks to a pair of elite run-stuffers, Michael Pierce and Brandon Williams, and all-purpose linebacker C.J. Mosley, the Ravens were even tougher to run against than the year before. When Williams missed four games his absence was felt—the run defense had a -14.8% DVOA in the 12 games Williams clogged the middle, and a -6.7% DVOA without him, as well as allowing a full half-yard more per carry. ☞ End Brent Urban also missed time with lower leg injuries; he is back and will contribute. ☞ Running at the Ravens' right (offensive left) was an adventure in extremes—the team was the best in the league at stopping runs charted as going around end, but 25th against runs charted as going off-tackle. ☞ Mosley may be the standout player, but the emotional heart of the defense remains Terrell Suggs, still playing good ball at age 35. (Suggs and ageless corner Terence Newman are the last remaining players from the draft class of 2003.) Suggs not only led the team in sacks (11, plus 59 hits/hurries and six disruptions) but was an underrated run defender. T-Sizzle is a borderline Hall of Famer, though he could use a deep playoff run where he (not Ray Lewis) is the standard-bearer of the defense to clinch his candidacy. Every eligible candidate above Suggs on the all-time sacks list is in Canton except Leslie O'Neal. Meanwhile, there's no reason to assume that season No. 17 in purple will be any less effective than the 16 that came before it. ☞ While the sack numbers were good, Baltimore's overall pressure rate was stagnant. The team needs a pair of highly-drafted second-year players, outside linebackers Tyus Bowser and Tim Williams, to step up and provide more pressure. These players also need to get better in helping to cover tight ends, the lone area of pass defense where the Ravens weren't excellent last season (29th in DVOA).

Defensive Secondary

Secondary	Age	Pos	G	Snaps	Plays	Overall TmPct	Rk	Stop	Dfts	BTkl	vs. Run Runs	St%	Rk	RuYd	Rk	vs. Pass Tgts	Tgt%	Rk	aDOT	Suc%	Rk	AdjYd	Rk	PD	Int
Tony Jefferson	26	SS	16	1085	81	9.7%	45	34	13	9	42	48%	30	5.3	22	29	6.3%	9	9.7	50%	46	7.4	28	1	1
Eric Weddle	33	FS	16	1085	71	8.5%	62	25	12	11	37	32%	60	9.9	65	27	6.0%	7	13.4	57%	23	8.0	36	9	6
Brandon Carr	32	CB	16	1024	68	8.1%	45	26	11	13	16	38%	53	11.7	73	85	19.9%	38	14.9	46%	68	8.9	66	11	4
Jimmy Smith	30	CB	12	599	37	5.9%	72	16	9	1	6	17%	78	8.3	66	39	15.5%	13	10.7	59%	9	8.0	48	9	3
Marlon Humphrey	22	CB	16	596	45	5.4%	74	22	10	7	5	20%	75	5.4	25	63	25.3%	69	14.1	63%	3	6.7	18	10	2
Lardarius Webb*	33	FS	16	377	41	4.9%	74	19	10	8	12	75%	1	5.3	25	35	22.1%	76	11.8	45%	61	9.7	58	4	2
Maurice Canady	24	CB	8	319	25	6.0%	--	11	5	2	4	75%	--	2.8	--	24	18.2%	--	8.9	54%	--	7.6	--	2	0
Anthony Levine	31	SS	16	262	23	2.7%	--	16	7	1	5	80%	--	4.8	--	19	17.5%	--	6.4	65%	--	4.6	--	2	1

Year	Pass D Rank	vs. #1 WR	Rk	vs. #2 WR	Rk	vs. Other WR	Rk	WR Wide	Rk	WR Slot	Rk	vs. TE	Rk	vs. RB	Rk
2015	25	-5.4%	10	18.3%	26	21.5%	29	--	--	--	--	10.7%	23	-0.4%	16
2016	10	-5.9%	7	-6.3%	7	9.9%	22	-10.5%	8	7.9%	18	-28.8%	3	12.7%	24
2017	2	-24.7%	4	-39.7%	2	-1.0%	16	-26.7%	4	-17.4%	5	19.6%	29	-16.8%	6

Marlon Humphrey improved as his rookie season went along, and by season's end was well along in his progress to becoming a shutdown corner (as it was, he finished third in the league in adjusted success rate). Humphrey joins elite but injury-prone Jimmy Smith and Brandon Carr, whose main ability is availability. Carr has started every game of his 10-year career, though he has ranked 50th or lower in both success rate and yards per pass for the last three years. ☞ Lardarius Webb was released in training camp but resurfaced and played well at slot corner in place of the injured Maurice Canady. He has been let go again, this time, it appears, for good, clearing the way for Canady or Tavon Young (coming off a torn Achilles after an excellent rookie season in 2016) to move up the depth chart. ☞ Tony Jefferson was signed to allow Eric Weddle more room to roam, but he wasn't quite the impact defender Baltimore thought it was getting, especially in run defense. ☞ Jefferson reportedly chafed under former defensive coordinator Dean Pees, and the hope is that Wink Martindale keeps Jefferson in his box-safety comfort zone—Jefferson didn't exactly play up to his rich free-agent contract, regardless of usage. ☞ The Ravens struggled in allowing open-field yards, which was a surprise given their veteran safeties. Weddle was very strong against the pass, which can in part be chalked up to having Jefferson around. ☞ The Ravens are thin behind the starters at safety, though sixth-rounder DeShon Elliott of Texas has athletic upside.

Special Teams

Year	DVOA	Rank	FG/XP	Rank	Net Kick	Rank	Kick Ret	Rank	Net Punt	Rank	Punt Ret	Rank	Hidden	Rank
2015	7.3%	1	4.5	7	4.5	6	4.7	6	16.0	2	7.0	6	-0.6	17
2016	4.9%	4	25.5	1	7.0	3	-2.8	23	-1.0	16	-4.1	24	11.7	3
2017	9.2%	1	19.0	1	6.6	4	12.3	1	4.1	12	3.9	5	-7.0	24

The Ravens topped our special teams ratings for the second time in three years. The incredible Justin Tucker is the main reason why, of course—he was once again best in the league at placekicking, and second in gross kickoff value. ☞ Punter Sam Koch was closer to the middle of the pack than usual, but he and Tucker both benefitted from better-than-average gunner units. ☞ Less well-known was the three-headed monster that returned kicks in Charm City. Bobby Rainey, Chris Moore, and Michael Campanaro combined to be the best returner in the game and helped the Ravens to enjoy the best average starting line of scrimmage in the NFL. Alas, only Moore remains with the team, so if he handles return duties alone (Campanaro was the punt returner, so Moore may pull double duty), expect his efficiency to drop with more attempts.

Buffalo Bills

The year 2017 represented a fresh start for the long-suffering Buffalo Bills. As is often the way with a new management tandem, general manager Brandon Beane and head coach Sean McDermott came in last offseason and decided to completely change the way the Bills did things on both sides of the ball.

Over the better part of the past decade, the Buffalo Bills have had an inability to field both a good offense and defense at the same time. (Table 1). The upside of this is that usually one unit is working pretty well. The Bills quietly had a pretty good offense under the floundering Rex Ryan. They were 10th in offensive DVOA in 2016 and ninth in offensive DVOA in 2015. To be certain, anchoring your offense to Tyrod Taylor is not the convenient way for coaches to do football. As critics have pointed out, he does miss throws, and he is a little passive with the ball. However, the offense that Ryan's underlings created around Taylor worked out well—and would have been lauded as a cost-efficient ingenuity had the Bills ever been able to put a good defense on the field with it. Think about this: they fielded a top-10 NFL offense with a quarterback they pulled out of nowhere. Coaches often talk about how they just need to create a good system for their quarterback and it's OK if they don't have an elite signal-caller. Rarely does this talk lead to an offense anywhere near as good as the one the Bills had with Taylor.

Ryan was building off the shattered ashes of the Doug Marrone Bills, who built an amazing defense under the direction of Jim Schwartz and paired it with Kyle Orton, EJ Manuel, and trace amounts of Jeff Tuel. The Bills under Terry Pegula continuously dial up new regimes that have good solutions to their problems, but completely neglect what the team already did well. The result has been like watching a political swing district go back and forth, with each new incumbent blaming the problems on his predecessor.

When McDermott and Beane arrived, they ignored the offense that was already working and instead set out to rebuild it in the spirit of the Carolina Panthers team they had success with. In theory, that means building a power-run team that operates off play-action and emphasizes the vertical passing game. In practice, it meant bringing in fullbacks by the bushel and publicly haranguing Taylor's warts until they turned to Nathan Peterman against the Chargers and realized they had no backup plan. It meant trading Sammy Watkins before the season and then trading for Kelvin Benjamin a few weeks later once they realized that they actually did need wide receivers.

The question never asked was: why? What about the Carolina Panthers offense was seen as worthy of replicating? The Panthers have had two top-10 DVOA offensive teams under former offensive coordinator Mike Shula in five seasons, both barely cracking that threshold and not showing much in the way of staying power. (Shula was replaced this past offseason by the oldest of old school coordinators, Norv Turner.) They also have 2015 NFL Most Valuable Player Cam Newton, a quarterback who changes the dynamic of any offense and, when healthy and firing correctly, one of the few quarterbacks who can stress defenses vertically and horizontally. The numbers haven't always matched Newton's skill level, but how much of that is Newton, and how much of that is the offenses he has played in? And if it's the offenses he's played in, why on earth would you want to emulate them?

After a year under caretaker offensive coordinator Rick Dennison, the Bills have now hired Brian Daboll away from Alabama to run their offense. A long-time Bill Belichick wide receivers coach, Daboll has four years of offensive coordinator experience in the NFL and the best he could do was 20th in offensive DVOA with the 2011 Dolphins. The last taste of Daboll's NFL experience involved having Jamaal Charles at his peak and still being unable to design a semi-functional passing game around an in-his-prime yards per carry leader. That Kansas City team ended up starting Matt Cassel and Brady Quinn for 16 games in Yet Another Failed Patriots Regime. Daboll and McDermott know each other because McDermott played at William & Mary when Daboll was a graduate assistant. We're not saying that Daboll has learned nothing from his time at Alabama, or that he hasn't grown as a coach.

Table 1: The Teeter-Totter Bills, 2011-2017

Year	Off DVOA	Rank	Def DVOA	Rank
2011	0.3%	16	8.3%	24
2012	-4.2%	20	10.6%	27
2013	-11.5%	25	-13.8%	4
2014	-11.2%	26	-15.5%	2
2015	9.8%	9	8.6%	24
2016	10.7%	10	7.8%	27
2017	-11.1%	26	1.7%	15

2018 Bills Schedule

Week	Opp.	Week	Opp.	Week	Opp.
1	at BAL	7	at IND	13	at MIA
2	LAC	8	NE (Mon.)	14	NYJ
3	at MIN	9	CHI	15	DET
4	at GB	10	at NYJ	16	at NE
5	TEN	11	BYE	17	MIA
6	at HOU	12	JAX		

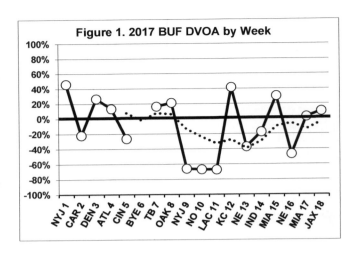

Figure 1. 2017 BUF DVOA by Week

But even a carefully optimistic reading of his last 10 years of coaching would say that his offenses have struggled without a reliable quarterback to build around.

Here's where we get to pin the tail on the donkey. Buffalo made a major move at quarterback, trading up in the draft to land Wyoming's Josh Allen. Allen is a player who was custom-built in a laboratory for our QBASE projection system to hate. He completed 56.3 percent of his passes in his final season at Wyoming, and the Cowboys finished 119th in passing S&P+ out of the 130 FBS teams.

Allen's 2017 season was an exercise in watching the national football commentariat refuse to be wrong about a player. Before the season, NFL.com profiled him as perhaps the "most talented" quarterback prospect since Newton ("talented" appeared to mean "does his arm make us ooh and ahh" in this context). In the season opener against Iowa, Allen completed 23 of 40 passes for 174 yards and two picks as the Cowboys lost 24-3. Two weeks later, he completed just 9 of 24 passes for a grand total of 64 yards in a 49-13 loss to Oregon. Things didn't get much better once Allen started his Western Athletic Conference schedule, where he only topped 150 passing yards three times. Every week was a new attempt to justify the poor play, and every time he happened to run up against a real FBS opponent, he'd play even worse. Most of the media draftniks we trust to grind the tape graded Allen as no better than a developmental prospect. Noted exception Mel Kiper could only offer the tepid "stats are for losers" defense against Allen's critics.

In the post-truth era of news coverage, Allen was essentially a litmus test for suckers, and the team that drafted him based on his rocket arm and ability to pull a few stupid-good plays out of his ass is no different than the team which would wire money to a needy Nigerian prince. The irony inherent in the fact that no college coach wanted anything to do with him until he had a late growth spurt to get to 6-foot-5 is precious and telling. Josh Allen looks like he should be a great quarterback, but he isn't.

Negative-QBASE passers chosen in the first round include Mark Sanchez, Josh Freeman, Kyle Boller, Rex Grossman, J.P. Losman, and Patrick Ramsey. Even Carson Wentz, the player that most optimistic Allen backers point to as a scout-friendly, lower-level quarterback with mediocre numbers, made it to a mean projection of 274 DYAR. Beane wouldn't get into how his quarterback board looked in a post-draft press conference—a glaring tell that Allen wasn't the No. 1 player at the position for him—but offered the boilerplate "he can make all the throws" nonsense that you'd have to believe to invest this pick in a player like Allen. The problem is that Allen isn't even an accurate deep arm right now. He can throw a deep ball like Grandma can quit smoking any time she wants to. And, as Cian Fahey offered in his analysis of Allen in his *Pre-Snap Reads Quarterback Catalogue* this year, remember that two of the biggest-armed passers in the NFL last year were Joe Flacco and Derek Carr. Neither of them finished in the top 20 in deep ball accuracy per his charting.

Now that we've cemented our future selection as a Freezing Cold Takes photo essay, let's pull back and look at this as optimistically as we can. Allen has the raw tools to be a successful quarterback. The Bills have surrounded Allen with the following:

- A supporting cast that's not much better than what he had at Wyoming. The Bills didn't spend a pick on any skill-position player before the sixth round. (A lot of their picks went to trading up for Allen and linebacker Tremaine Edmunds.) What they return in the receiving corps is solid third banana Charles Clay and Kelvin Benjamin, who hasn't been fast since 2014. Zay Jones, the nominal No. 2 receiver, would kill to have a catch rate as high as Allen's college completion percentage.
- A star running back who turns 30 before the season, running behind an offensive line which lost its best two players and traded a tackle who could have returned to health and benefitted them outside.
- A coordinator who played the wrong quarterback at Alabama all season, and who will make Allen's life easier by virtue of having had a few conversations with Tom Brady.
- A quarterback coach, David Culley, with zero experience at the position in the NFL; he last coached quarterbacks at Southwestern Louisiana in 1988.
- A placeholder quarterback, AJ McCarron, who only managed a positive DVOA because Cincinnati surrounded him with a dynamic offense for a handful of 2015 starts, and couldn't even find a Mike Glennon-level contract in the era of the rising salary cap.

This is the blind leading the blind. The Bills have set their raw quarterback the task to develop without much in the way of actual help. Wentz had Doug Pederson's no-huddle and a dominant offensive line, throwing to tight end Zach Ertz over the middle. And, you know what? Wentz still was not good in his first season. He needed some time.

Optimistic Bills fans who embrace the Wentz comparison should take heed that 2018 is not the year that Allen will prove us all wrong. All the money that would have gone into fixing the offense is instead dead cap space. Beane talked with Peter King on the MMQB after trading Taylor and offered this quote: "Getting the 65th pick was huge. Patience was the key. I am very happy how it worked out for the Bills and for Tyrod, and the financial part was a part of it. When it's all said and done, we're going to have about $45 million in dead money this year. That was part of my plan—to eat all of it, or as much as we could, this year." That's what it looks like when your general manager all but admits he's not trying his best this year and is playing for the future. A more close-to-the-vest general manager could have extended Taylor while given Allen time to grow, then traded Taylor next year. Instead, all Allen will have to do to get into the starting lineup is have his coaching staff watch McCarron for three or four weeks.

It's a shame that this offensive blueprint is so irresponsible because it's erasing the good work that the Bills have done on defense and special teams. Carolina's defensive system has a track record of achievement and the Bills had instant success creating a good pass defense despite a lack of non-Jerry Hughes pressure. Tre'Davious White had one of the best years of any rookie in 2017. Jordan Poyer and Micah Hyde shored up a leaky Bills back end. Their play of replacing Ronald Darby with E.J. Gaines was a short-term win for the franchise.

Edmunds looks like their first stab at a Luke Kuechly-/Thomas Davis-type player. The signing of Star Lotulelei (wonder what team he played for?) should help fix a run defense that was a sieve last season, finishing 31st in run defense DVOA. In an attempt to improve the pass rush, the Bills also took a chance on Trent Murphy, who finished second on Washington with nine sacks in 2016 before missing 2017 to an ACL tear.

The depth isn't strong yet, another problem when you trade up in the first round as frequently as the Bills, but they do have all of their 2019 picks intact as well as an extra fourth-rounder from Kansas City. Meanwhile, after a couple of struggling years under Ryan, McDermott and Beane (and holdover coordinator Danny Crossman) had the special teams unit right back in the top 10. Create a world in which good offensive free agents are available and willing to come to Buffalo, and that cap space that Beane worked for—as of June 1, the Bills were third in available 2019 cap space, according to Overthe-Cap.com—might even help out.

The Bills marketing department this year has gone with the slogan "One Heart, Beat Louder." Our projections predict what the slogan literally tries to tell you: they're going to get beat louder this year. The moderately easy schedule will help soften the blow, and there are subjective reasons to believe that the defense can outplay its projection, perhaps even by a lot. Run defense tends to be more predictive of the following season than pass defense, but McDermott should be a good bulwark against the Bills regressing to where their defense was two and three years ago.

Nonetheless, this team looked the gift horse in the mouth with the Taylor-McCoy offense and cemented the problems by creating a unit that will need to add an all-world wideout from a high draft slot to save 2019. And that's taking the radically optimistic leap that Allen is not a complete NFL washout and that the offensive line is competent. A lot of belief has to be invested to get to the point where the Bills have a good offense *two seasons from now*.

The Bills spent the middle of the summer filing a patent for the phrase "Respect the Process." But they are asking us to respect their process when it's conclusively not a good process, and barring something unexpected, these Bills are on course to launch another one after 2019. Hopefully, for the sake of Buffalo fans, they'll find someone who can amplify the good defense that McDermott and Beane are creating while also erasing an offense that seems likely to be as unoriginal and insipid as the slogan they want to patent. This process is just following conventional quarterback scouting wisdom and building to win in the 1980s. It's the kind of offense you'd create after listening to nothing but Phil Simms broadcasts on a loop. And it is likely to go over about as successfully as Simms' broadcasting career in the post-Twitter world.

Rivers McCown

2017 Bills Stats by Week

Wk	vs.	W-L	PF	PA	YDF	YDA	TO	Total	Off	Def	ST
1	NYJ	W	21	12	408	214	+1	46%	21%	-33%	-7%
2	at CAR	L	3	9	176	255	0	-22%	-32%	-16%	-6%
3	DEN	W	26	16	272	366	+2	27%	13%	-1%	13%
4	at ATL	W	23	17	281	389	+3	13%	-11%	-16%	8%
5	at CIN	L	16	20	221	388	+2	-26%	-39%	-4%	9%
6	BYE										
7	TB	W	30	27	434	447	+2	16%	23%	9%	2%
8	OAK	W	34	14	331	367	+4	21%	15%	5%	12%
9	at NYJ	L	21	34	307	331	-3	-66%	-40%	34%	7%
10	NO	L	10	47	198	482	0	-67%	-30%	35%	-2%
11	at LAC	L	24	54	393	429	-6	-67%	-36%	30%	-1%
12	at KC	W	16	10	268	236	+1	42%	-17%	-43%	16%
13	NE	L	3	23	268	435	0	-37%	-34%	6%	3%
14	IND	W	13	7	319	227	-2	-17%	-33%	-17%	-1%
15	MIA	W	24	16	328	349	+3	30%	21%	-11%	-2%
16	at NE	L	16	37	326	411	+1	-47%	-20%	27%	0%
17	at MIA	W	22	16	312	356	+1	3%	13%	11%	0%
18	at JAX	L	3	10	263	230	-2	10%	-27%	-30%	7%

Trends and Splits

	Offense	Rank	Defense	Rank
Total DVOA	-11.1%	26	1.6%	15
Unadjusted VOA	-7.3%	22	3.1%	18
Weighted Trend	-13.6%	28	7.2%	26
Variance	6.1%	13	5.4%	14
Average Opponent	4.5%	32	1.8%	10
Passing	-9.5%	28	0.6%	12
Rushing	-7.9%	19	2.7%	30
First Down	-12.3%	27	12.1%	30
Second Down	-16.2%	25	0.8%	17
Third Down	-2.0%	18	-18.6%	6
First Half	-4.4%	19	0.7%	15
Second Half	-18.5%	29	2.4%	19
Red Zone	-17.3%	24	0.6%	19
Late and Close	-22.4%	29	-15.7%	7

Five-Year Performance

Year	W-L	Pyth W	Est W	PF	PA	TO	Total	Rk	Off	Rk	Def	Rk	ST	Rk	Off AGL	Rk	Def AGL	Rk	Off Age	Rk	Def Age	Rk	ST Age	Rk
2013	6-10	6.7	7.1	339	388	+3	-3.3%	18	-11.5%	25	-13.8%	4	-5.6%	30	17.9	6	26.4	12	26.4	24	26.0	26	26.1	12
2014	9-7	9.6	9.0	343	289	+7	10.5%	9	-11.2%	26	-15.5%	2	6.2%	4	27.2	14	31.9	11	26.6	21	26.1	26	26.1	15
2015	8-8	8.5	8.8	379	359	+6	2.7%	12	9.8%	9	8.6%	24	1.5%	12	37.2	19	43.3	28	26.2	21	26.4	21	26.5	9
2016	7-9	8.5	7.4	399	378	+6	1.0%	17	10.7%	10	7.8%	27	-1.9%	22	37.0	19	60.8	28	26.6	19	27.2	6	27.3	1
2017	9-7	6.3	6.8	302	359	+9	-9.8%	21	-11.1%	26	1.6%	15	2.9%	10	29.0	13	15.5	8	27.8	2	26.8	11	27.5	1

2017 Performance Based on Most Common Personnel Groups

BUF Offense

Pers	Freq	Yds	DVOA	Run%
11	56%	5.3	0.0%	27%
12	17%	4.3	-26.2%	50%
21	16%	4.8	-8.9%	66%
22	5%	4.2	-43.1%	82%
621	2%	6.1	19.7%	90%
611	2%	5.8	10.9%	50%

BUF Offense vs. Opponents

Pers	Freq	Yds	DVOA	Run%
Base	42%	4.5	-14.8%	63%
Nickel	42%	5.4	0.6%	30%
Dime+	14%	5.3	-15.6%	15%
Goal Line	1%	3.1	-6.8%	70%
Big	1%	0.0	-17.2%	80%

BUF Defense

Pers	Freq	Yds	DVOA
Base	33%	5.2	4.6%
Nickel	66%	5.7	0.3%
Goal Line	1%	0.4	0.4%

BUF Defense vs. Opponents

Pers	Freq	Yds	DVOA
11	59%	5.7	4.2%
12	22%	5.3	-0.3%
21	7%	6.9	20.8%
13	3%	5.3	-3.5%
22	2%	4.3	8.7%
611	2%	4.4	1.7%

Strategic Tendencies

Run/Pass		Rk	Formation		Rk	Pass Rush		Rk	Secondary		Rk	Strategy		Rk
Runs, first half	39%	16	Form: Single Back	73%	24	Rush 3	2.7%	27	4 DB	33%	15	Play action	22%	17
Runs, first down	52%	15	Form: Empty Back	7%	19	Rush 4	74.1%	6	5 DB	66%	5	Avg Box (Off)	6.43	2
Runs, second-long	41%	4	Pers: 3+ WR	56%	24	Rush 5	18.2%	19	6+ DB	0%	31	Avg Box (Def)	6.28	12
Runs, power sit.	57%	14	Pers: 2+ TE/6+ OL	28%	20	Rush 6+	5.0%	21	CB by Sides	88%	8	Offensive Pace	29.63	9
Runs, behind 2H	25%	25	Pers: 6+ OL	4%	9	Int DL Sacks	29.6%	12	S/CB Cover Ratio	27%	16	Defensive Pace	30.32	13
Pass, ahead 2H	38%	29	Shotgun/Pistol	52%	24	Second Level Sacks	25.9%	8	DB Blitz	9%	16	Go for it on 4th	0.91	22

The Bills threw in the middle of the field about 50 percent more often than they did in 2016, and it continued to be effective. On short passes (up to 15 yards through the air), Buffalo ranked 12th on passes up the middle compared to 23rd on passes to the left and 31st in passes to the right. ☞ Sean McDermott didn't have Luke Kuechly and Thomas Davis in Buffalo, but he still kept two linebackers on the field all the time, just as he did in Carolina. Buffalo had gone dime on 11 percent of plays in 2016 but used it only in extreme situations last year. Buffalo and Carolina were 31st and 32nd in use of dime defense. ☞ The Bills defense continued to struggle with tackling, tied for 29th with 144 broken tackles after ranking 27th in 2016. ☞ The Buffalo defense was No. 5 against the pass in the red zone, but 31st against the run. ☞ Buffalo brought a league-low 28 percent pressure rate when it blitzed at least one defensive back. The NFL average was 48 percent. Buffalo was also 31st in this metric in 2016, at 29 percent.

Passing

Player	DYAR	DVOA	Plays	NtYds	Avg	YAC	C%	TD	Int
T.Taylor*	121	-7.0%	467	2540	5.4	4.8	62.7%	14	4
N.Peterman	-194	-73.8%	50	244	4.9	2.9	50.0%	2	5
J.Webb*	-71	-167.5%	7	35	5.0	1.5	28.6%	0	1
AJ McCarron	0	-11.1%	15	57	3.8	8.1	50.0%	0	0

Rushing

Player	DYAR	DVOA	Plays	Yds	Avg	TD	Fum	Suc
L.McCoy	-26	-10.8%	286	1138	4.0	6	3	43%
T.Taylor*	110	20.8%	69	436	6.3	4	1	-
M.Tolbert*	-9	-12.1%	66	248	3.8	1	2	39%
T.Cadet	-1	-9.9%	22	93	4.2	0	0	45%
M.Murphy	6	11.7%	7	41	5.9	0	0	43%
J.Webb*	14	28.3%	7	55	7.9	0	0	-
N.Peterman	-18	-84.2%	6	20	3.3	0	1	-
C.Ivory	-38	-17.0%	112	386	3.4	1	2	38%

Receiving

Player	DYAR	DVOA	Plays	Ctch	Yds	Y/C	YAC	TD	C%
Z.Jones	-131	-35.2%	74	27	316	11.7	2.3	2	36%
D.Thompson*	57	1.4%	51	27	430	15.9	3.0	1	53%
J.Matthews*	33	-0.6%	36	25	282	11.3	5.0	1	69%
K.Benjamin	25	-0.3%	27	16	217	13.6	2.4	1	59%
A.Holmes	43	9.8%	23	13	120	9.2	0.8	3	57%
B.Tate*	1	-12.1%	14	6	81	13.5	6.2	1	43%
K.Clay	-39	-47.5%	15	5	57	11.4	3.4	0	33%
C.Clay	22	-2.8%	74	49	558	11.4	5.3	2	66%
N.O'Leary	73	29.9%	32	22	322	14.6	5.8	2	69%
L.Thomas	4	-0.2%	9	7	67	9.6	1.6	1	78%
L.McCoy	48	-1.8%	78	60	448	7.5	6.9	2	77%
M.Tolbert*	-24	-44.2%	17	14	78	5.6	3.4	0	82%
T.Cadet	0	-14.2%	16	13	93	7.2	5.9	0	81%
P.DiMarco	-25	-49.0%	10	7	28	4.0	1.4	0	70%
C.Ivory	27	4.4%	28	21	175	8.3	9.0	1	75%

Offensive Line

Player	Pos	Age	GS	Snaps	Pen	Sk	Pass	Run	Player	Pos	Age	GS	Snaps	Pen	Sk	Pass	Run
Eric Wood*	C	32	16/16	1055	4	0.5	5	11	Cordy Glenn*	LT	29	6/5	275	1	2.0	5	3
Richie Incognito*	LG	35	16/16	1043	6	1.5	9	12	John Miller	RG	25	4/4	256	3	0.0	0	4
Jordan Mills	RT	28	16/16	1026	8	5.5	17	10	Russell Bodine	C	26	16/16	966	2	0.0	3	8
Vladimir Ducasse	RG	31	12/12	799	3	2.5	11	12	Marshall Newhouse	RT	30	14/14	847	5	4.0	9	6
Dion Dawkins	LT	24	16/11	784	4	4.0	13	8									

Year	Yards	ALY	Rank	Power	Rank	Stuff	Rank	2nd Lev	Rank	Open Field	Rank	Sacks	ASR	Rank	Press	Rank	F-Start	Cont.
2015	4.68	3.92	23	71%	10	21%	17	1.28	2	1.18	2	42	8.4%	27	26.8%	19	15	26
2016	5.12	4.16	16	60%	20	22%	22	1.41	1	1.32	2	46	9.3%	31	31.8%	30	6	32
2017	3.96	3.67	27	61%	22	26%	27	1.17	15	0.90	8	47	9.3%	31	32.7%	23	10	34
2017 ALY by direction:			Left End: 2.13 (29)			Left Tackle: 2.21 (31)			Mid/Guard: 3.98 (24)			Right Tackle: 3.77 (18)			Right End: 5.56 (1)			

The main item of interest is how this unit will deal with the retirement of center Eric Wood. The initial solution in free agency was to go out and sign ex-Bengals center Russell Bodine. Bodine was rightfully viewed as part of the problem in Cincinnati, and just doesn't anchor well enough to use his plus athleticism. ☞ Cordy Glenn's trade to the Bengals (he can rent Bodine's house) leaves the left tackle spot open for Dion Dawkins. Dawkins struggled a bit early but was one of the most improved Bills in the second half of the season. Dawkins has more of a guard athletic profile but got away with it last year. With Jordan Mills back at right tackle, Buffalo will return both its bookends. Mills struggles with top-tier speed rushers but is capable otherwise. ☞ Guard Richie Incognito was still the best player on the line, even at 35. But his sudden retirement/trip off the reservation in April was just about the last thing the Bills needed, especially after they convinced him to take a pay cut. Vlad Ducasse has been solid after a shaky beginning to his career, but nothing exceptional. John Miller was the guy who Ducasse beat out last year. Taking away the two stellar players on this line with no real replacement talent infusion will put the Bills in a bind. Fifth-rounder Wyatt Teller (Virginia Tech) had bad 2017 tape, but the tools are there for him to start at guard eventually.

Defensive Front Seven

Defensive Line	Age	Pos	G	Snaps	Plays	TmPct	Overall Rk	Stop	Dfts	BTkl	Runs	vs. Run St%	Rk	RuYd	Rk	Pass Rush Sack	Hit	Hur	Dsrpt
Kyle Williams	35	DT	16	758	42	4.8%	48	32	10	6	35	77%	45	2.5	65	3.0	7	16.0	2
Adolphus Washington	24	DT	15	510	35	4.3%	59	24	8	3	30	70%	70	3.4	83	1.0	1	4.0	2
Cedric Thornton*	30	DT	15	389	27	3.3%	--	21	6	1	21	81%	--	3.0	--	2.0	2	4.5	0
Star Lotulelei	29	DT	16	590	26	3.4%	74	21	10	3	20	85%	13	0.5	2	1.5	3	10.0	3

Edge Rushers	Age	Pos	G	Snaps	Plays	TmPct	Overall Rk	Stop	Dfts	BTkl	Runs	vs. Run St%	Rk	RuYd	Rk	Pass Rush Sack	Hit	Hur	Dsrpt
Jerry Hughes	30	DE	16	735	44	5.0%	45	38	17	13	38	84%	18	0.8	10	4.0	9	33.5	0
Eddie Yarbrough	25	DE	16	464	36	4.1%	63	27	5	2	30	77%	40	2.2	41	1.0	7	14.5	1
Ryan Davis*	29	DE	16	456	24	2.7%	89	17	6	4	16	69%	74	2.6	58	3.0	6	19.0	0
Shaq Lawson	24	DE	11	435	34	5.7%	35	28	10	1	26	81%	30	2.1	38	4.0	4	13.0	2
Tenny Palepoi	28	DE	15	270	23	3.0%	--	18	8	2	21	76%	--	2.0	--	1.0	0	3.0	0

Linebackers	Age	Pos	G	Snaps	Plays	TmPct	Overall Rk	Stop	Dfts	BTkl	Runs	vs. Run St%	Rk	RuYd	Rk	Pass Rush Sack	Hit	Hur	vs. Pass Tgts	Suc%	Rk	AdjYd	Rk	PD	Int
Preston Brown*	26	MLB	16	1098	147	16.8%	9	72	16	7	81	67%	22	3.2	26	0.0	2	6.5	49	51%	31	6.9	42	3	0
Lorenzo Alexander	35	OLB	16	671	65	7.4%	83	33	17	19	38	58%	63	3.7	48	4.0	13	24.0	20	38%	67	7.6	54	1	0
Ramon Humber	31	OLB	13	568	84	11.8%	44	45	14	11	47	55%	72	4.1	64	1.0	3	4.5	32	57%	17	4.9	8	1	0
Matt Milano	24	OLB	16	452	45	5.1%	86	28	13	13	26	73%	14	2.5	11	0.0	2	6.0	21	52%	29	6.7	38	2	1

Year	Yards	ALY	Rank	Power	Rank	Stuff	Rank	2nd Level	Rank	Open Field	Rank	Sacks	ASR	Rank	Press	Rank
2015	4.52	4.71	29	72%	25	16%	31	1.24	26	0.77	16	21	3.8%	31	21.8%	29
2016	4.50	4.41	22	57%	6	19%	16	1.30	28	0.88	25	39	7.1%	7	29.0%	9
2017	4.48	4.18	21	76%	28	22%	10	1.36	32	1.00	29	27	5.4%	28	27.0%	31

2017 ALY by direction:	Left End: 3.87 (17)	Left Tackle: 4.36 (23)	Mid/Guard: 4.36 (23)	Right Tackle: 3.93 (20)	Right End: 3.41 (13)

The Bills struck big in free agency, guaranteeing former Panthers nose Star Lotulelei $18.5 million, a top-six amount among 4-3 defensive tackles. The run defense definitely needed the upgrade, but it seems like a bit much to pay one player given the weaknesses up and down this unit. ☞ On the edge, Jerry Hughes continues to pay dividends after being swindled from the Colts. He has been by far the most consistent edge player the Bills have against the pass, but he's turning 30 this year and the Bills haven't shown any interest in extending him past 2019, where his contract ends. ☞ The battle for the other edge spot will be between ex-Washington linebacker Trent Murphy and incumbent disappointment Shaq Lawson, who has spent his entire career hurt. Murphy received a PED suspension and a torn ACL wiped out his 2017, but he sets a good edge and proved he could be a fine second banana to Ryan Kerrigan. This could be a nice blossoming spot for him assuming the light doesn't come on for Lawson. ☞ Only 22 players from the 2006 class played in the NFL in 2017, and Kyle Williams will be one of a handful of those 22 to make it back in 2018. Obviously, he's winning more on guile and technique than speed at this point, but Williams is still a load. ☞ Buffalo traded up for Tremaine Edmunds, a 20-year-old Hokies linebacker who oozes potential. As you'd expect from a 20-year-old, though, his instincts were dinged as average to poor depending on which scouts you listened to. He should one day fill the Thomas Davis/Shaq Thompson role for the PantherBills, but the rawness indicates we may be in for a rollercoaster rookie year. ☞ Lorenzo Alexander is versatile, you've got to give him that much. He's a core special teams player, he racked up the second-most hurries on the team after a Rex Ryan breakout year in 2016, and he's a heady linebacker if not the most physically imposing. At 35, though, sudden decline would not be a surprise. ☞ Third-round rookie Harrison Phillips (Stanford) showed some promise as an interior disruptor and will probably be broken in on passing downs. Depth is lacking up and down this unit. Third-year tackle Adolphus Washington hasn't shown much yet but would be the likely first man up on the interior line, and Ramon Humber is the closest thing to a known quantity on a linebacker depth chart filled mostly with recent late-round picks and UDFAs.

Defensive Secondary

Secondary	Age	Pos	G	Snaps	Plays	Overall					vs. Run					vs. Pass									
						TmPct	Rk	Stop	Dfts	BTkl	Runs	St%	Rk	RuYd	Rk	Tgts	Tgt%	Rk	Dist	Suc%	Rk	AdjYd	Rk	PD	Int
Tre'Davious White	23	CB	16	1092	88	10.1%	18	43	15	8	25	52%	31	6.3	48	77	19.7%	37	13.9	54%	23	8.1	53	18	4
Micah Hyde	28	SS	16	1065	94	10.7%	25	31	19	7	38	21%	71	12.8	76	44	11.5%	54	13.9	61%	10	5.8	9	13	5
Jordan Poyer	27	FS	15	1038	108	13.2%	7	46	19	14	48	48%	28	6.2	38	39	10.4%	48	10.0	65%	5	5.1	4	12	5
Leonard Johnson*	28	CB	15	673	58	7.1%	61	27	13	13	10	50%	32	4.9	18	59	24.4%	67	7.8	45%	74	8.2	54	9	0
E.J. Gaines*	26	CB	11	654	68	11.3%	4	32	12	5	15	47%	38	6.9	55	52	22.1%	52	8.9	53%	30	5.3	2	8	1
Shareece Wright*	31	CB	12	455	47	7.2%	--	18	5	7	14	43%	--	4.7	--	37	22.8%	--	9.9	50%	--	7.2	--	5	1
Phillip Gaines	27	CB	14	419	34	4.8%	--	7	6	4	12	25%	--	9.8	--	42	27.0%	--	14.7	45%	--	8.8	--	3	0
Vontae Davis	30	CB	5	330	23	8.9%	--	6	1	1	6	33%	--	4.8	--	27	23.6%	--	12.5	40%	--	10.4	--	3	0
Rafael Bush	31	FS	14	184	23	3.2%	--	12	8	3	12	50%	--	7.4	--	12	17.4%	--	8.8	70%	--	3.7	--	0	0

Year	Pass D Rank	vs. #1 WR	Rk	vs. #2 WR	Rk	vs. Other WR	Rk	WR Wide	Rk	WR Slot	Rk	vs. TE	Rk	vs. RB	Rk
2015	18	-13.3%	5	-12.9%	8	6.0%	18	--	--	--	--	-9.0%	13	16.5%	29
2016	21	3.1%	19	-0.4%	16	12.0%	25	-1.4%	17	11.8%	21	-5.9%	11	7.9%	21
2017	12	-0.1%	14	-29.7%	3	-28.0%	1	-10.0%	11	-22.7%	3	-3.9%	13	5.9%	20

Buffalo's big move in free agency was a gamble on former star corner Vontae Davis, one of Ryan Grigson's rare good acquisitions in Indianapolis who has run into problems staying on the field of late. Davis had finished in the top 20 of adjusted success rate by our numbers four years in a row prior to 2017, and if he is healthy, the Bills have a steal. ☞ Tre'davious White had a phenomenal rookie year that was overshadowed by fellow rookie corner Marshon Lattimore, and Buffalo's glee at his development is probably a big reason they didn't rush to re-sign E.J. Gaines. He could be a bit better in off-man, but that's picking the nits. ☞ The third-corner battle looks to be a fight between Kansas City washout Phillip Gaines and fourth-rounder Taron Johnson (Weber State), a smaller slot corner who plays bigger than his size. Either player will have a hard time filling the value that Gaines provided last year, though they could replace Leonard Johnson pretty easily. ☞ Micah Hyde responded with a big season after being freed from Green Bay, following in the footsteps of fellow ex-Packers defensive back Casey Hayward. We criticized Buffalo's front office plenty earlier in the chapter, but one thing they're good at is identifying fits for Sean McDermott's defense. Hyde was one they nailed. ☞ Fellow safety Jordan Poyer, pilfered from the Browns after they gave him just six starts in four seasons, launched his own breakout campaign. While he wasn't targeted often, he was a big play machine when it happened. Just don't ask him to make an open-field tackle. ☞ The primary backup at both safety spots is probably ex-Saints safety Rafael Bush, a priority target for the Bills in free agency.

Special Teams

Year	DVOA	Rank	FG/XP	Rank	Net Kick	Rank	Kick Ret	Rank	Net Punt	Rank	Punt Ret	Rank	Hidden	Rank
2015	1.5%	12	-1.7	23	18.2	1	-6.1	30	4.0	10	-6.9	31	-5.2	22
2016	-1.9%	22	-7.7	28	-2.6	21	-3.7	25	-2.9	21	7.6	5	-4.9	23
2017	2.9%	10	11.5	4	2.0	15	-4.9	29	4.3	11	1.8	11	-9.0	29

Beefed up and emphasized in the early days of Buffalo's regime change, this unit also delivered. Kicker Steven Hauschka had an excellent season. Joe Webb, Andre Holmes, and Patrick DiMarco were also regulars brought in last offseason who contributed to turning the unit around. Punter Colton Schmidt has been fairly inconsistent, but not necessarily a problem. ☞ Return man Brandon Tate is gone in free agency. Micah Hyde is penciled in to replace him on punt returns barring a late acquisition. Kick returns are likely to be handled by a depth receiver, possibly Kaelin Clay or sixth-round pick Ray-Ray McCloud.

Carolina Panthers

In preparing for his first playoff start since Super Bowl 50, Cam Newton told reporters in January what his edge is. "I'm comfortable running the football," Newton said. "I feel like I help the team when I'm running the football, and as long as I'm playing this game, I'm going to run the football."

Newton finished the 2017 season with career-highs in rushes (139) and rushing yards (754). But when he brings his A game as a passer, Carolina is almost unbeatable. Since becoming a near-annual playoff team in 2013, the Panthers are 25-2 when Newton has a passer rating above 100.0. The only other quarterbacks in that stretch to win more than 90 percent of their games when doing that is the gold standard trio of Peyton Manning (21-0), Tom Brady (38-3), and Aaron Rodgers (31-3).

The 2017 season really showcased Newton at his best at times. In back-to-back road wins over the Patriots and Lions in Weeks 4 and 5, Newton completed at least 75 percent of his passes with over 300 yards and three touchdowns in each game, becoming only the eighth quarterback in NFL history to do so in consecutive games. He has never done that in any of his other 114 games. Newton also threw four touchdowns against both the Dolphins and Packers, which is something he had only done four other times in his career.

However, one hallmark of Newton's career has been his erraticism. We also saw some of his worst moments last season. In Week 17, he had a career-low 31.5 passer rating with three interceptions in Atlanta. Those stellar passing games against the Patriots and Lions were bookended by three-interception games against the Saints and Eagles. Even between the wins, Newton managed to lose his yogurt sponsorship with Dannon after another rough moment at an October press conference. Jourdan Rodrigue, a female sportswriter for *The Charlotte Observer*, asked Newton a question regarding passing routes. Newton smirked and responded "It's funny to hear a female talk about routes." No one would have batted an eye at that in 1977, but these are different times, and more is expected of Newton in the spotlight.

Carolina's offense finished a middling 17th in DVOA last year but was also 26th in variance, proof of the inconsistency. Newton headlined several of the team's best wins last year, but it was really the No. 7 defense and No. 6 special teams that paved the way for Carolina's return to the playoffs. With wins over the Patriots and Vikings and a close loss to the Eagles,

Carolina was able to hang with anyone in 2017—well, anyone except for the Saints, the Panthers' rivals who swept all three meetings, including the season-ending 31-26 loss in the wild-card round. The Saints were the only team to score more than 30 points on Carolina last year, doing so in all three match-ups. The Saints were the only team to compile 400 yards of offense on Carolina, doing so in both regular-season games in New Orleans. We mentioned Newton's 25-2 record since 2013 when he has a passer rating over 100.0. You may have guessed it—both of the losses were the games in New Orleans last season. While there is no escaping the Saints in 2018, the good news is that these NFC South rivalries tend to even out over time. Before the three-game sweep, the Saints had lost four of the previous five games to the Panthers.

Oddly enough, the Saints are the type of offense the Panthers should strive to emulate more. While Carolina used the eighth overall pick on running back Christian McCaffrey last year, New Orleans only used a third-round pick on Alvin Kamara. But it was the Saints who got an Offensive Rookie of the Year performance from their rookie scatback. The Saints even got a career year out of ex-Carolina wideout Ted Ginn, a testament to the team's plug-and-play approach under Sean Payton and Drew Brees. No matter which non-quarterback parts change in New Orleans, the offense remains consistently efficient. Carolina has not come close to matching that, but 2018 has a chance to be different.

For starters, Mike Shula is out after five seasons as offensive coordinator. He is replaced by Norv Turner, whom we last saw resigning from his coordinator post in Minnesota during the 2016 season. Turner hasn't coached an offense that has ranked higher than 16th in DVOA since the 2011 Chargers, and his last three teams all immediately improved on offense after he left them. So it's not the most exciting hire the team could have made in 2018. However, Turner now has the best quarterback he has had since Philip Rivers in San Diego.

There are also reasons to think this is the deepest set of skill players that Newton has had in his eight seasons in Carolina. Tight end Greg Olsen should be healthy after a broken foot cost him nine games last year and left him ineffective in several others. He led the team in catches and receiving yards in each season from 2013 to 2016. The Panthers also should not be trading away their No. 1 wide receiver halfway through the season like they did last year with Kelvin Benjamin. That

2018 Panthers Schedule

Week	Opp.	Week	Opp.	Week	Opp.
1	DAL	7	at PHI	13	at TB
2	at ATL	8	BAL	14	at CLE
3	CIN	9	TB	15	NO (Mon.)
4	BYE	10	at PIT (Thu.)	16	ATL
5	NYG	11	at DET	17	at NO
6	at WAS	12	SEA		

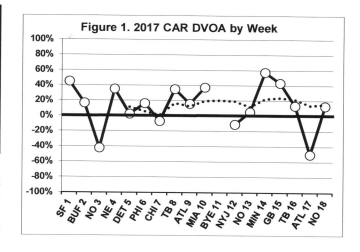

Figure 1. 2017 CAR DVOA by Week

move at least helped Devin Funchess break out in his third year with career-highs in catches (63), yards (840), and touchdowns (eight). Carolina also used a first-round pick on Maryland wideout D.J. Moore, who had the best Playmaker Score projection in this draft class.

The development of Funchess, McCaffrey, and Moore should provide three receiving threats that all flourish with different styles of play. This is a far cry from Benjamin and an inexperienced Funchess standing tall like Ents from Tolkien's *Lord of the Rings*. McCaffrey and Moore have the ability to eat up yards after the catch. McCaffrey had a slow start to his rookie season, but started to get into a bit of a groove later. Moore's strengths as a receiver closely align with McCaffrey's, so it will be interesting to see how the Panthers utilize the two and how Moore develops as a route-runner.

Carolina could easily go six deep at wide receiver this season. Beyond Funchess and Moore, the team signed veteran deep threat Torrey Smith from the Eagles, and added Jarius Wright from Minnesota, where he had his best years under Turner in 2014 and 2015. Curtis Samuel was a second-round pick in 2017, and Damiere Byrd created a handful of explosive plays towards the end of the season, including two touchdowns in the Week 15 win over Green Bay.

The biggest amount of pressure will be on the Panthers' offensive line. Losing All-Pro guard Andrew Norwell in free agency is a massive deficit for the Panthers, especially considering their backup situation. Carolina drafted Taylor Moton with the last pick in the second round in 2016, but has been reluctant to play him. He would likely be an upgrade over Amini Silatolu, who has been a disaster just about every time he has stepped on a professional football field. Outside of the left guard situation, the Panthers have an intriguing offensive tackle duo. Matt Kalil was signed in free agency last year to man the left tackle spot, where he unsurprisingly had an up-and-down season. Right tackle Daryl Williams was an All-Pro, but his selection was a bit shocking. Williams had a lot of help from tight ends and backs in pass protection; he really struggled when isolated against athletic edge rushers 1-on-1. Their fit with a prototypical Turner offense looks troubling, and Kalil has already struggled with Turner in Minnesota. The deep drops in the passing game ask for tackles to hold their blocks a bit longer than most offenses and that's not something that Kalil and Williams have shown they can do to this point.

One can question whether Turner has the right personnel to run the type of offense that he had his most success with, namely in Dallas (1991-1993) and San Diego (2007-2012).

Those offenses were not big on spreading the field horizontally, but instead relied heavily on one great wide receiver doing damage down the field à la Michael Irvin or Vincent Jackson. Newton obviously loves the deep ball, so that's right in his wheelhouse. However, those are big shoes for Funchess to step into, even if he finally showed the potential last season. Free-agent addition Smith should serve in the Alvin Harper or Malcom Floyd role. Turner's also big on tight ends—think Jay Novacek and Antonio Gates—and that should be no problem with Olsen back.

The dilemma may come at running back, where Turner's offenses have largely been dependent on workhorse backs, including Emmitt Smith, LaDainian Tomlinson, and Adrian Peterson. The Panthers let Jonathan Stewart go after 10 seasons, but signed C.J. Anderson from Denver. Anderson usually looks the part of a quality starter until an inevitable injury, but he did play all 16 games last year and had his first 1,000-yard rushing season. Anderson should still see the bulk of carries, but McCaffrey has to get his share too. After all, the Panthers didn't just draft him so high to catch passes. It's not clear that McCaffrey would have reached 80 receptions had Olsen been healthy and if Benjamin wasn't traded, but the offense did turn into a "checkdown or bomb" approach last season. There's always the idea of playing Anderson in the backfield and splitting McCaffrey out in the slot, but that's not something most NFL offenses experiment with, let alone one led by a traditionalist like Turner.

McCaffrey had 30 targets on screen passes last year, and surprisingly had negative DYAR (-3) on those plays. The 19 running back screens weren't as bad (20 DYAR), but McCaffrey did not gain more than 9 yards on any of his 11 screens where he lined up as a wide receiver. In fact, McCaffrey lined up in the slot or out wide on 34 percent of his targets last year, which ranked seventh among running backs and barely trailed Kamara's usage (35 percent). However, it was just not effective. McCaffrey had -28.3% DVOA from the slot and 5.6% DVOA out wide compared to a much more respectable 15.5% DVOA when lined up as a traditional running back. In moving to the slot, McCaffrey's catch rate dropped from 75 percent to 58 percent. It's easy to say the Panthers should use McCaffrey in the slot more often, but if he performs like he did as a rookie, then it will actually hurt the offense more than it will help. Getting a talent like Moore involved heavily from the slot while Funchess and Smith play outside could be the best strategy for Carolina this year, although that is putting high expectations on a rookie.

Speaking of expectations, with Newton entering his eighth season, it may be time to accept that he's likely to be a quarterback who always struggles with passing consistency. No matter which receivers, offensive linemen, running backs, or coordinators the Panthers bring in, there will be those passes that sail well over an open target's head and leave us scratching our heads a bit too frequently. According to ESPN Stats & Info, Newton has the fifth-highest rate of off-target passes since 2011 at 22.0 percent. Newton's passing plus-minus—which adjusts throws for down, distance, and depth of target—is -64.9, which ranks as the third lowest since 2011; only Blaine Gabbert (-65.7) and Blake Bortles (-69.3) are lower. We can say Newton needs better pass protection to stay healthy, but his career DVOA when not pressured is 43.4%, which puts him right between Ryan Tannehill (43.1%) and Derek Carr (44.8%) among quarterbacks drafted since 2011. Newton's average ranking in DVOA without pressure is 18.6, peaking at No. 8 in his 2015 MVP season.

It's not realistic to expect dramatic improvement from Newton as he enters his eighth season. Really, no quarterback short of John Elway (look up what he did from 1983 till 1992, then compare it what he did from 1993 onwards) has ever shown a massive, sustained increase in passing efficiency so late in his career. At least that sets a precedent, but it was a situation that included adding several Hall of Famers and some great coaching.

Newton's shortcomings in the passing game obviously have not prevented Carolina from consistently making the playoffs or even getting to a Super Bowl, but this is a team that must be strong on defense and special teams to help out the inconsistent offense. In the three seasons that Carolina has had a winning record under head coach Ron Rivera, the offense ranked sixth (2013), second (2015), and sixth (2017) in average starting field position. In the four seasons with losing records, the offense ranked 18th (2011), 28th (2012), 18th (2014), and third (2016) in average starting field position. Adding to the Newton puzzle is that those monster games against the Patriots and Lions happened without Olsen even active, so it's not always about the players around Newton. If the Panthers can ever find a way to bring out his A game more often, then this team will have one of the deadliest offenses in the league.

The other side of the ball has some question marks as well. Carolina only has two returning defensive backs who played at least 40 percent of the team's defensive snaps in 2017: 37-year-old safety Mike Adams and cornerback James Bradberry. Former first-round linebacker Shaq Thompson had a higher percentage of the snaps than the team's third cornerback, which is certainly not the norm in today's pass-happy league. Carolina used third-round picks on cornerback Donte Jackson (LSU) and do-it-all defensive back Rashaan Gaulden (Tennessee). Those two players are big unknowns, but as wide

open as the secondary is, they'll likely be asked to play substantial roles as rookies.

Carolina's front seven is really the strength of the team. The unit is loaded with stud talent as it returns Kawann Short, Luke Kuechly, Thomas Davis, and Julius Peppers while adding Dontari Poe in free agency. Short, Poe, and former first-rounder Vernon Butler have a chance to be a deadly trio at defensive tackle. Short by himself is enough to cause headaches for opposing offensive lines, but with the athletic presence of Poe, Carolina has two defensive tackles who can penetrate up the field while holding firm against double-teams in the run game. If Butler can regain the flashes he had early in his rookie season, he'll make Carolina's defensive trio among the best in the league. At edge rusher they have an older duo with Peppers and Mario Addison, but each of them had 11 sacks despite being on the wrong side of 30 (and in Peppers' case, approaching 40). Older players can fall off at any second, so that is a concern with the pass rush this season.

Veteran leadership will be crucial again as Carolina moves onto its third defensive coordinator in as many seasons. Rivera's defensive background will help smooth the transition for first-time coordinator Eric Washington, but the team will need a grace period as they adjust to Washington's calls. Washington had previously served as the team's defensive line coach for the past seven seasons.

The new-look secondary presents an interesting challenge for Washington, who really has only specialized in defensive line at the pro level. Steve Wilks, the 2017 coordinator and new head coach of the Arizona Cardinals, was the defensive back guru in Carolina. In 2017, Wilks blitzed on a league-high 43 percent of pass plays, but the Panthers had mediocre results, ranking 16th in pressure rate and 15th in DVOA. That was a big change from 2016 when Sean McDermott was the defensive coordinator and the Panthers only rushed five or more defenders 23 percent of the time. We'll have to see how aggressive Washington can be while risking his secondary against what figures to be a tough slate of receivers, including Julio Jones, A.J. Green, Odell Beckham, Mike Evans, Antonio Brown, Marvin Jones, Doug Baldwin, Michael Thomas, and Josh Gordon. The patchwork secondary will be put to the fire early and often this season, so Carolina will know quickly if the new coaching hires are equipped for the job.

The margins should be ultra-thin in a deep NFC this year where even a minor slippage to 9-7 or 10-6 could keep the Panthers at home in January. Last year, the Panthers did a great job walking the tightrope in crunch time. Carolina had the NFL's best record (8-1) in close games in 2017, defined as games involving a fourth-quarter comeback or game-winning drive opportunity on either side of the ball. The offense was 3-1 at game-winning drive opportunities while the defense led the league with seven holds of a one-score lead while not blowing any leads in the fourth quarter. While the playoff loss ended up being a close one, things just tended to go Carolina's way last year for all three units. Graham Gano finally hit a clutch 48-yard field goal to beat the Patriots. If Tyrod Taylor had been throwing to a real NFL wide receiver instead of Zay Jones, the Panthers would have blown a late lead against

Buffalo in Week 2. The Panthers needed two return touchdowns to put away the lowly Jets in Week 12. Green Bay's final rally effort ended after Geronimo Allison lost a fumble in the final two minutes in Week 15. A week later against Tampa Bay, Newton fumbled a snap, but luckily recovered to score a game-winning touchdown with 35 seconds left. For the season, Carolina recovered nine of 14 fumbles on offense and 11 of 14 fumbles on defense. It was just that kind of year.

Such seasons practically never repeat themselves, so you should expect the Panthers to lose out on more fumbles and struggle to win all the close games they won a year ago. Maybe some of that can be offset by playing more consistently so that disasters like a 17-3 defeat to Chicago (when the offense allowed two return touchdowns) don't happen again, but the Panthers are still stuck in a tough division with one of the league's hardest projected schedules in 2018. The Panthers have to make two trips to Pennsylvania in the middle of the season, and won't get a chance for revenge against those Saints until December,

with a battle against Atlanta coming in between.

Consistency is the name of the game for the 2018 Carolina Panthers. They bring in new coaches, new personnel, and a new offensive scheme to break in. Perhaps the change will be good if the veteran leadership can perform and hold strong through the ups and downs created by having a younger team. The quarterback is still young too, but this is Newton's swan song for his twenties. If Newton can become a more refined passer under Turner, then Carolina's window should be open for many more years, giving the Panthers a strong long-term outlook in a division where Drew Brees is in a battle with Father Time, the Buccaneers are dysfunctional, and the Falcons are eternal underachievers. But there's still a good chance that Newton won't become a more refined passer under Turner, or that it will take more than one year together. That makes our short-term outlook a bit more pessimistic.

Scott Kacsmar and Charles McDonald

2017 Panthers Stats by Week

Wk	vs.	W-L	PF	PA	YDF	YDA	TO	Total	Off	Def	ST
1	at SF	W	23	3	287	217	0	45%	-4%	-46%	3%
2	BUF	W	9	3	255	176	0	17%	-21%	-33%	5%
3	NO	L	13	34	288	362	-3	-42%	-20%	22%	0%
4	at NE	W	33	30	444	373	-2	35%	40%	6%	1%
5	at DET	W	27	24	362	242	+1	2%	1%	-7%	-6%
6	PHI	L	23	28	305	310	-2	16%	-8%	-17%	8%
7	at CHI	L	3	17	293	153	-3	-7%	-37%	-27%	2%
8	at TB	W	17	3	254	279	+2	35%	-20%	-44%	11%
9	ATL	W	20	17	330	355	-1	16%	4%	-6%	6%
10	MIA	W	45	21	548	313	+1	37%	58%	20%	-1%
11	BYE										
12	at NYJ	W	35	27	299	391	+1	-11%	-17%	25%	31%
13	at NO	L	21	31	279	400	0	5%	11%	-7%	-13%
14	MIN	W	31	24	345	356	+2	57%	25%	-32%	0%
15	GB	W	31	24	387	384	+4	43%	48%	8%	3%
16	TB	W	22	19	255	392	+2	13%	-15%	-5%	23%
17	at ATL	L	10	22	248	371	-3	-50%	-64%	-12%	1%
18	at NO	L	26	31	413	410	+1	13%	29%	12%	-5%

Trends and Splits

	Offense	Rank	Defense	Rank
Total DVOA	-0.5%	17	-8.8%	7
Unadjusted VOA	0.9%	16	-5.5%	9
Weighted Trend	2.2%	15	-6.5%	9
Variance	10.1%	26	5.1%	10
Average Opponent	2.1%	26	4.5%	1
Passing	6.9%	17	-3.6%	11
Rushing	-2.2%	11	-16.9%	5
First Down	-2.0%	18	-8.7%	8
Second Down	1.3%	12	-8.6%	5
Third Down	-0.6%	16	-9.4%	11
First Half	3.9%	15	-7.3%	7
Second Half	-5.2%	19	-10.4%	4
Red Zone	-0.6%	16	-11.6%	8
Late and Close	-0.8%	16	-23.3%	3

Five-Year Performance

Year	W-L	Pyth W	Est W	PF	PA	TO	Total	Rk	Off	Rk	Def	Rk	ST	Rk	Off AGL	Rk	Def AGL	Rk	Off Age	Rk	Def Age	Rk	ST Age	Rk
2013	12-4	11.7	11.0	366	241	+11	24.6%	3	7.9%	10	-15.7%	3	1.0%	13	42.4	21	28.4	17	28.2	2	26.6	16	26.6	7
2014	7-8-1	7.0	7.4	339	374	+3	-8.5%	24	-4.7%	20	-1.7%	15	-5.5%	30	39.7	25	11.7	1	26.4	26	27.2	8	26.4	6
2015	15-1	12.4	11.1	500	308	+20	26.0%	4	10.1%	8	-18.4%	2	-2.4%	23	28.2	14	22.7	8	27.0	14	28.1	3	26.8	3
2016	6-10	7.1	6.7	369	402	-2	-5.5%	24	-8.4%	25	-5.3%	10	-2.5%	25	36.9	18	19.6	7	27.0	12	26.2	23	26.6	6
2017	11-5	9.0	10.3	363	327	-1	13.0%	9	-0.5%	17	-8.8%	7	4.7%	6	31.9	14	11.0	5	26.3	25	28.4	1	26.6	4

2017 Performance Based on Most Common Personnel Groups

CAR Offense					CAR Offense vs. Opponents					CAR Defense					CAR Defense vs. Opponents			
Pers	Freq	Yds	DVOA	Run%	Pers	Freq	Yds	DVOA	Run%	Pers	Freq	Yds	DVOA		Pers	Freq	Yds	DVOA
11	50%	5.6	5.1%	30%	Base	30%	4.9	2.9%	68%	Base	50%	5.3	-5.6%		11	58%	5.9	-0.5%
12	22%	5.0	-2.6%	45%	Nickel	63%	5.2	-6.7%	33%	Nickel	49%	5.8	-9.5%		12	14%	5.3	-12.7%
21	12%	5.0	-3.9%	47%	Dime+	5%	8.8	93.3%	10%	Goal Line	1%	0.0	-85.8%		21	11%	5.6	-16.9%
22	4%	6.3	8.3%	74%	Goal Line	2%	1.7	21.0%	84%						612	4%	5.6	7.2%
612	4%	4.7	-11.3%	95%	Big	1%	9.4	47.4%	75%						13	3%	5.0	-13.3%
13	4%	5.3	24.1%	83%											22	2%	3.5	-30.1%

Strategic Tendencies

Run/Pass		Rk	Formation		Rk	Pass Rush		Rk	Secondary		Rk	Strategy		Rk
Runs, first half	42%	4	Form: Single Back	68%	29	Rush 3	1.9%	31	4 DB	50%	3	Play action	19%	26
Runs, first down	52%	13	Form: Empty Back	10%	8	Rush 4	55.4%	27	5 DB	49%	20	Avg Box (Off)	6.33	8
Runs, second-long	39%	7	Pers: 3+ WR	51%	27	Rush 5	35.6%	1	6+ DB	0%	32	Avg Box (Def)	6.33	9
Runs, power sit.	65%	6	Pers: 2+ TE/6+ OL	37%	4	Rush 6+	7.1%	10	CB by Sides	79%	15	Offensive Pace	30.98	20
Runs, behind 2H	29%	9	Pers: 6+ OL	6%	2	Int DL Sacks	25.0%	14	S/CB Cover Ratio	29%	13	Defensive Pace	28.98	1
Pass, ahead 2H	46%	19	Shotgun/Pistol	73%	4	Second Level Sacks	20.0%	11	DB Blitz	13%	5	Go for it on 4th	1.02	15

For years, the strategy against the Panthers has been to send blitzes at Cam Newton. Last year, teams suddenly started blitzing Newton much less. He faced an extra pass-rusher on 29 percent of plays, still seventh in the league but much lower than what it had been in 2015 (39 percent) and 2016 (38 percent). This change came even though blitzes still worked well. Carolina's offensive DVOA dropped from 18.1% with four pass-rushers to -0.4% with five pass-rushers to a dismal -45.3% (at just 3.8 net yards per pass) with six or more pass-rushers. ☞ Carolina's offense ranked second in DVOA running on third down, but 29th passing on third down. ☞ Most of the time, play-action passes are going to be more successful than other passes. But Carolina's defense was phenomenal against play-action passing, allowing an absurdly low 4.9 yards per pass and -42.7% DVOA on play-action passes. By comparison, the Panthers allowed 6.6 yards per pass and 8.3% DVOA on other passes. That gap in yards per pass was three times larger than the gap for any other team, and by "any other team" we mean Cincinnati, because the Bengals were the only other team to allow more yards per pass on regular passes than on play-action passes. ☞ The Panthers were assigned a particularly quiet slate of officials last year, as they finished dead last in total penalties but also tied for 29th in penalties by opponents.

Passing

Player	DYAR	DVOA	Plays	NtYds	Avg	YAC	C%	TD	Int
C.Newton	141	-6.9%	525	3059	5.8	5.5	59.5%	22	15
D.Anderson*	-18	-41.5%	8	17	2.1	3.0	25.0%	0	0

Rushing

Player	DYAR	DVOA	Plays	Yds	Avg	TD	Fum	Suc
J.Stewart*	-54	-14.8%	198	681	3.4	6	3	45%
C.Newton	120	6.5%	122	760	6.2	6	5	-
C.McCaffrey	11	-6.2%	117	435	3.7	2	1	45%
C.Artis-Payne	11	4.1%	18	95	5.3	1	0	44%
F.Whittaker	4	2.8%	7	18	2.6	0	0	57%
C.J.Anderson	16	-6.9%	245	1007	4.1	3	1	42%

Receiving

Player	DYAR	DVOA	Plays	Ctch	Yds	Y/C	YAC	TD	C%
D.Funchess	168	6.8%	112	63	840	13.3	4.5	8	56%
K.Benjamin*	100	12.4%	51	32	475	14.8	3.2	2	63%
R.Shepard	-38	-27.9%	32	17	202	11.9	6.2	1	53%
C.Samuel	-12	-18.3%	26	15	115	7.7	3.4	0	58%
D.Byrd	0	-13.0%	17	10	105	10.5	6.1	2	59%
K.Clay*	-39	-47.5%	15	5	57	11.4	3.4	0	33%
B.Bersin*	19	5.6%	14	8	128	16.0	1.6	0	57%
T.Smith	-29	-18.2%	69	37	427	11.5	3.3	2	54%
J.Wright	84	29.0%	25	18	198	11.0	4.9	2	72%
E.Dickson*	83	18.1%	48	30	437	14.6	6.7	1	63%
G.Olsen	-44	-24.5%	38	17	191	11.2	2.8	1	45%
C.McCaffrey	128	5.7%	113	80	651	8.1	7.4	5	71%
J.Stewart*	-20	-38.8%	15	8	52	6.5	8.6	1	53%
F.Whittaker	17	30.4%	6	5	47	9.4	11.8	1	83%
C.J.Anderson	1	-13.2%	40	28	224	8.0	7.7	1	70%

Offensive Line

Player	Pos	Age	GS	Snaps	Pen	Sk	Pass	Run	Player	Pos	Age	GS	Snaps	Pen	Sk	Pass	Run
Andrew Norwell*	LG	27	16/16	1079	2	0.5	7	2	Tyler Larsen	C	27	14/10	724	0	0.5	3	3
Daryl Williams	RT	26	16/16	1079	2	4.0	20	2	Ryan Kalil	C	33	6/6	347	0	2.0	4	2
Matt Kalil	LT	29	16/16	1076	11	4.5	23	6	Amini Silatolu*	G/T	29	14/3	256	2	3.0	8	3
Trai Turner	RG	25	13/13	848	5	0.0	7	4	Jeremiah Sirles	LG	27	14/4	344	3	0.0	8	1

Year	Yards	ALY	Rank	Power	Rank	Stuff	Rank	2nd Lev	Rank	Open Field	Rank	Sacks	ASR	Rank	Press	Rank	F-Start	Cont.
2015	4.10	4.24	12	76%	2	18%	8	1.23	5	0.61	22	33	6.9%	21	25.7%	17	12	34
2016	3.90	3.83	25	73%	3	22%	24	1.10	23	0.63	19	36	6.2%	19	26.8%	17	14	27
2017	3.61	3.78	25	72%	5	19%	12	0.94	30	0.53	22	35	7.1%	19	29.3%	9	9	30

2017 ALY by direction:	Left End: 3.95 (17)	Left Tackle: 3.13 (27)	Mid/Guard: 4.16 (15)	Right Tackle: 2.89 (29)	Right End: 2.80 (28)

Andrew Norwell led left guards in snaps per blown block and helped left tackle Matt Kalil clean up some of his mistakes, but unfortunately Norwell signed a massive contract with Jacksonville at the start of free agency. It's unclear who is going to replace Norwell at this moment. The team has Amini Silatolu currently slated to be the starting left guard, which is bad news for the Panthers. Based on the production that Silatolu has given Carolina in the past, they would be better served rolling the dice on 2016 second-round pick Taylor Moton. The Western Michigan product looked good in the preseason against backups and didn't have a blown block in 60 snaps as a sixth offensive lineman last year. ☞ The rest of Carolina's interior is set. Ryan Kalil (brother of Matt) has played his entire career at center for the Panthers. Since 2007, he has been to the Pro Bowl five times and has made three All-Pro teams. His recent struggles with injuries have sapped some of his effectiveness, but he's still a decent option at center for the team. He has announced his retirement at the end of the coming season. ☞ Trai Turner, who had a bit of a down year, flanks him at right guard. Turner has the talent to be an elite guard in the league, but he needs to stay healthy and maintain his consistency to regain the performance that secured him a lucrative contract extension from Carolina last summer. Runs on the right side behind Turner and right tackle Daryl Williams were a significant problem for last year's Panthers. ☞ The backup situation in Carolina isn't great either. Tyler Larsen wasn't charted with a lot of blown blocks in place of the injured Ryan Kalil but was consistently subpar at a level above "egregious blown block." Free-agent signing Jeremiah Sirles was borderline nonexistent in pass protection when he got playing time in Minnesota. ☞ With the loss of Norwell, Carolina really can't afford to suffer an injury on the offensive line. Their backups just haven't proven to be NFL-caliber players yet.

Defensive Front Seven

Defensive Line	Age	Pos	G	Snaps	Plays	Overall TmPct	Rk	Stop	Dfts	BTkl	Runs	vs. Run St%	Rk	RuYd	Rk	Pass Rush Sack	Hit	Hur	Dsrpt
Kawann Short	29	DT	16	704	50	6.6%	15	43	19	7	40	85%	13	1.1	5	7.5	10	26.0	2
Star Lotulelei*	29	DT	16	590	26	3.4%	74	21	10	3	20	85%	13	0.5	2	1.5	3	10.0	3
Kyle Love	32	DT	16	379	16	2.1%	--	10	4	1	11	55%	--	2.1	--	3.5	5	12.0	0
Vernon Butler	24	DT	14	297	14	2.1%	--	12	3	1	12	83%	--	1.7	--	0.0	3	10.5	1
Dontari Poe	28	DT	16	786	41	5.1%	41	32	8	5	34	76%	48	2.4	59	2.5	8	21.5	3

Edge Rushers	Age	Pos	G	Snaps	Plays	Overall TmPct	Rk	Stop	Dfts	BTkl	Runs	vs. Run St%	Rk	RuYd	Rk	Pass Rush Sack	Hit	Hur	Dsrpt
Mario Addison	31	DE	16	654	45	5.9%	31	33	18	3	28	64%	78	3.0	73	11.0	4	34.5	2
Julius Peppers	38	DE	16	500	33	4.4%	59	30	17	3	18	83%	21	1.6	24	11.0	6	11.5	0
Charles Johnson*	32	DE	12	390	17	3.0%	84	14	5	5	15	80%	31	0.9	11	0.0	2	10.0	1
Wes Horton	28	DE	16	360	16	2.1%	--	11	9	1	9	56%	--	2.8	--	5.5	4	13.0	0

Linebackers	Age	Pos	G	Snaps	Plays	Overall TmPct	Rk	Stop	Dfts	BTkl	Runs	vs. Run St%	Rk	RuYd	Rk	Pass Rush Sack	Hit	Hur	vs. Pass Tgts	Suc%	Rk	AdjYd	Rk	PD	Int
Luke Kuechly	27	MLB	15	920	131	18.5%	2	70	30	12	71	66%	26	3.3	28	1.5	3	8.0	42	53%	27	7.0	44	8	3
Thomas Davis	35	OLB	15	793	76	10.7%	58	43	15	9	40	63%	42	3.4	35	2.5	5	13.5	44	56%	23	5.0	10	2	0
Shaq Thompson	24	OLB	14	644	58	8.8%	72	34	13	5	31	81%	4	2.1	5	2.0	5	11.0	28	42%	60	8.4	67	0	0

Year	Yards	ALY	Rank	Power	Rank	Stuff	Rank	2nd Level	Rank	Open Field	Rank	Sacks	ASR	Rank	Press	Rank
2015	3.78	3.50	4	87%	32	24%	6	1.02	6	0.76	15	44	7.1%	11	26.3%	12
2016	3.83	3.61	4	78%	32	24%	5	1.10	10	0.73	17	47	7.3%	5	30.2%	7
2017	3.89	3.51	5	47%	2	26%	4	1.12	18	0.94	27	50	9.1%	3	32.9%	6

2017 ALY by direction:	Left End: 2.77 (3)	Left Tackle: 2.35 (2)	Mid/Guard: 3.92 (10)	Right Tackle: 4.15 (21)	Right End: 3.31 (11)

The case can be made that Carolina has an elite front seven. Luke Kuechly, Thomas Davis, Kawann Short, and Dontari Poe are an imposing foursome in the middle of Carolina's defense. Poe is arguably an upgrade over Star Lotulelei and comes with the bonus of stealing talent away from the division-rival Falcons. ☞ The Panthers do a lot of rotation on their defensive line. Eight different defensive linemen played at least one-third of snaps in games they were active, and Short played the most at just 70.3 percent of snaps. ☞ Carolina still has an intriguing prospect on their defensive line in 2016 first-round pick Vernon Butler, who has yet to really get his career going. He has battled injuries, but if he can live up to his former draft status Carolina will have a deadly defensive tackle trio with Short, Poe, and Butler. They would also like to get production from 2017 third-rounder Daeshon Hall, a defensive end who only played nine snaps in his rookie season. ☞ Behind their defensive line sits arguably the best linebacker duo in the league. Luke Kuechly and Thomas Davis are both elite talents who dominate the run and pass. Davis has battled through *three* ACL tears and is still on top of his game, though he will be suspended for the first four games after testing positive for a banned supplement. Shaq Thompson is the "other" name who fills out their trio of linebackers, a decent coverage weapon who Carolina uses to cover slot receivers from time to time. ☞ Carolina doesn't have much behind those three (not that they need to), but they added an intriguing option in the draft with the fourth-round selection of Marquis Haynes. At the beginning of Haynes' Ole Miss career, he looked like he was going to be a future first-round pick as a pass-rusher. He never really progressed past that point, but he has value as a blitzer and can give Carolina a bit more flexibility with the fronts they use in obvious passing situations.

Defensive Secondary

Secondary	Age	Pos	G	Snaps	Plays	TmPct	Rk	Stop	Dfts	BTkl	Runs	St%	Rk	RuYd	Rk	Tgts	Tgt%	Rk	Dist	Suc%	Rk	AdjYd	Rk	PD	Int
James Bradberry	25	CB	16	990	95	12.5%	1	32	15	10	25	40%	47	5.7	33	99	24.7%	68	12.4	51%	42	8.2	57	10	2
Mike Adams	37	SS	16	967	78	10.3%	33	37	7	8	38	50%	21	6.2	39	41	10.4%	47	11.3	59%	17	5.9	12	10	2
Daryl Worley*	23	CB	15	729	73	10.3%	14	33	9	9	15	53%	27	7.8	63	76	25.8%	70	10.9	52%	37	6.8	25	10	2
Kurt Coleman*	30	FS	12	721	79	13.9%	4	25	12	9	29	45%	39	8.3	57	34	11.5%	55	14.3	47%	53	9.6	56	2	0
Captain Munnerlyn	30	CB	14	388	32	4.8%	--	15	8	4	3	0%	--	9.3	--	22	14.0%	--	8.6	57%	--	7.1	--	3	0
Kevon Seymour	25	CB	16	319	23	3.0%	--	7	2	4	5	40%	--	4.4	--	28	21.3%	--	15.6	57%	--	11.2	--	4	0
Colin Jones	31	SS	16	214	22	2.9%	--	8	2	2	13	38%	--	4.8	--	8	8.7%	--	6.6	34%	--	8.7	--	2	1
Ross Cockrell	27	CB	16	681	60	7.2%	59	37	15	7	21	52%	30	5.0	19	54	17.6%	22	13.0	71%	1	5.8	6	12	3
Da'Norris Searcy	30	SS	16	363	25	3.1%	--	7	4	7	12	25%	--	5.2	--	9	6.9%	--	14.1	59%	--	11.6	--	2	1

Year	Pass D Rank	vs. #1 WR	Rk	vs. #2 WR	Rk	vs. Other WR	Rk	WR Wide	Rk	WR Slot	Rk	vs. TE	Rk	vs. RB	Rk
2015	2	-24.7%	3	-9.5%	12	-30.4%	3	--	--	--	--	-40.4%	1	-10.5%	8
2016	11	6.1%	24	-1.1%	15	10.1%	23	-3.6%	14	9.4%	19	-7.9%	9	-8.4%	12
2017	11	9.5%	19	5.4%	20	3.4%	19	1.6%	19	11.7%	20	-22.2%	4	-3.0%	14

Outside of James Bradberry and Mike Adams, Carolina's secondary is wide open for playing time. The Panthers have a lot of options to fill out their secondary, most of them unknowns. ☞ Carolina drafted Donte Jackson from LSU in the second round to compete for a starting cornerback spot. Jackson's frame (5-foot-10, 178 pounds) fits the profile of a slot cornerback, but he was primarily an outside corner for LSU. ☞ Free-agent addition Ross Cockrell's No. 1 rank in adjusted success rate for the Giants screams "fluky nickelback season," but Cockrell was mostly covering receivers lined up wide and by the end of the season he was covering the opponent's No. 1 option. In Week 16 against Arizona, he played every defensive snap and his only target was an end zone interception covering Larry Fitzgerald. In Week 17, he held Josh Doctson to two catches for 16 yards in seven targets. But his charting stats were poor in 2015 and middle-of-the-pack in 2016. ☞ Kevon Seymour struggles with shifty, agile receivers, giving up his biggest plays of the year to Tarik Cohen, Randall Cobb, and Taylor Gabriel. ☞ Joining Mike Adams at safety will be Colin Jones and Da'Norris Searcy. That's a position that looks like it could be an issue for Carolina this season. Adams is 37 years old and is no longer playing at his Pro Bowl level of 2014 and 2015. Jones spent his whole career as a backup until the second half of last year. Searcy is better playing in the box than in deep centerfield, a problem considering the Panthers look for versatility at the position. Losing Kurt Coleman to the Saints could prove to be an underrated transaction that rears its ugly head during the season. ☞ Another possible body at safety is third-round rookie Rashaan Gaulden, who played both nickelback and safety for the Tennessee Vols. He's lauded for strong tackling and sifting through traffic to get to the ballcarrier, but he's relatively slow and disappointed scouts with a poor combine performance.

Special Teams

Year	DVOA	Rank	FG/XP	Rank	Net Kick	Rank	Kick Ret	Rank	Net Punt	Rank	Punt Ret	Rank	Hidden	Rank
2015	-2.4%	23	-1.5	21	-5.1	28	-1.8	19	-6.3	24	2.8	11	5.5	10
2016	-2.5%	25	-3.8	21	5.2	7	1.0	12	-10.4	29	-4.3	25	4.2	12
2017	4.7%	6	6.3	10	2.2	14	5.3	6	7.8	5	1.9	10	-0.2	13

The Panthers will bring back kicker Graham Gano after signing him to a very lucrative four-year, $17 million extension in March. Gano is coming off his best season as a placekicker, hitting 29-of-30 field goals, but he's susceptible to the same inconsistency as most other kickers: he hadn't hit over 90 percent of field goals since he went 4-of-4 his rookie year, and he hit only 79 percent of attempts in 2016. Gano is consistently one of the top kickoff men in the league, but it's more likely the Panthers paid him big money based on a one-year field goal percentage that is unlikely to be repeated. Rookie Matt Palardy was below-average in gross punt value but got great coverage; punt returns against the Panthers were worth a league-best 8.7 points of estimated field position below average. Christian McCaffrey struggled on punt returns averaging, just 7.4 yards per attempt. That ranked 19th out of 25 among all players with at least 20 punt returns on the season. Carolina's positive value on punt returns came from the departed Kaelin Clay instead. Curtis Samuel will likely resume his role as the primary kickoff returner, although it was Damiere Byrd who was responsible for a 103-yard touchdown return late in the season. Rookies D.J. Moore (10.2 yards per punt return in college) and Donte Jackson have the speed and explosiveness to see potential time as return men as well.

Chicago Bears

2017 Record: 5-11	**Total DVOA:** -15.9% (25th)	**2018 Mean Projection:** 6.2 wins	**On the Clock (0-4):** 25%
Pythagorean Wins: 6.2 (23rd)	**Offense:** -14.9% (28th)	**Postseason Odds:** 13.3%	**Mediocrity (5-7):** 45%
Snap-Weighted Age: 26.3 (19th)	**Defense:** -1.5% (14th)	**Super Bowl Odds:** 0.7%	**Playoff Contender (8-10):** 24%
Average Opponent: 6.8% (1st)	**Special Teams:** -2.4% (23rd)	**Proj. Avg. Opponent:** -0.1% (19th)	**Super Bowl Contender (11+):** 5%

2017: By the time John Fox realized the Bears drafted a quarterback, he was fired.

2018: However, not everyone can be Sean McVay.

Every franchise is bound to hit a rough patch, but seven seasons without a playoff appearance is especially rough for the Bears. The only other time that's happened to Chicago was a 13-year period from 1964 to 1976, a time when the wild card didn't exist and the forward pass was still considered risqué (doubly risqué if Bobby Douglass was asked to throw it). It probably would have been a better time for John Fox, who finished his three-year tenure by coaching the Bears as if they were a dead-ball team last year.

Fox historically has been very conservative—he ranks 98th out of 104 coaches since 1986 in Aggressiveness Index (minimum 20 fourth-down decisions). However, even by his standards, 2017 was taking things back to the Stone Age. No offense last season averaged fewer yards per drive or went three-and-out as often as the Bears did. Chicago managed two overtime wins where they didn't even crack 120 net yards passing, something that had only happened twice in overtime games in the NFL's previous 12 seasons. Chicago had a 17-3 win over Carolina in which the offense only ran 37 offensive plays, the fewest plays in a win since the Colts had 35 in Miami in 2009. The 2017 Bears are the only NFL team since 1960 to have two games in a season where the offense ran fewer than 38 plays. Fantasy football fans will cry foul, but it was also a bad situation for the team's young offensive players to develop.

Fox was the wrong man for the job, but the 2017 plan by general manager Ryan Pace never made sense either. The Bears ended up paying backup quarterback Mike Glennon $18.5 million, and he only started four games while barely throwing the ball. He was benched for rookie Mitchell Trubisky, who cost the Bears significant draft value in a trade to move one spot up, which Fox reportedly had no idea was the plan. We did not get to see much from the rookie in an offense that only had 473 throws, the fewest in the league.

That pairing of a conservative coach with a highly-drafted rookie quarterback had some drawing comparisons to Jeff Fisher's rough time with Jared Goff in Los Angeles in 2016. After the Bears fired Fox and hired Kansas City offensive coordinator Matt Nagy, then added talent in the offseason, the comparison shifted to Nagy having a Sean McVay type of impact on Chicago in 2018. That playoff drought? Well, it seemed certain to be a thing of the past.

Skip this paragraph if you want to continue living the dream, because we're about to rain on Chicago's parade. The problem with expecting a repeat of McVay's success is that his debut was one of the biggest turnarounds in NFL history, and it's exceedingly rare for everything to fall one way like it did for the Rams. So we really need to slow down the hype train for the Bears in what is still a very deep and competitive NFC. Green Bay gets Aaron Rodgers back. Seattle has always had winning seasons in the Russell Wilson era. The Cowboys shouldn't have to deal with a six-game suspension to Ezekiel Elliott this time. Kyle Shanahan expects to get a full season out of Jimmy Garoppolo at quarterback for the 49ers. Oh yeah, none of those four teams made the playoffs last year, and Chicago still has to deal with the defending champion Eagles, the aforementioned (and fully reloaded) Rams, a very talented Vikings team, and an NFC South still stocked with franchise quarterbacks and three teams coming off postseason appearances. The Bears could finish 8-8 and still be lucky to finish 10th in the conference. That's what happened to Arizona last year, and the Cardinals are now one of the few NFC teams you can reasonably conclude are behind the Bears going into 2018.

The good news is that the Bears appear to be moving in the right direction again. Nagy is the latest branch from the Andy Reid coaching tree, which has had some considerable successes in Super Bowl winners John Harbaugh (Ravens) and Doug Pederson (Eagles). Nagy has spent the last decade with Reid, starting as an intern in Philadelphia before following him to Kansas City to coach Alex Smith and the quarterbacks. He was promoted to offensive coordinator in 2017 and helped Smith to the first 4,000-yard passing season of his career. Reid usually calls the plays on game day, but he handed that duty over to Nagy in Week 13. The offense responded with a hot finish until things fizzled out in the second half of that playoff loss to the Titans.

The 40-year-old Nagy has his work cut out for him. If he is to improve Chicago's offensive DVOA from its 2017 mark of -15.1% to the levels his Chiefs (15.9%) or McVay's Rams (11.1%) reached last year, then we are talking about an increase of more than 25 percentage points. Since 1990, only six rookie head coaches were able to make that kind of improvement right away. Table 1 shows the top 12 offensive DVOA improvements by a rookie head coach since 1990. We made note of whether that coach's style leaned towards offense or

2018 Bears Schedule

Week	Opp.	Week	Opp.	Week	Opp.
1	at GB	7	NE	13	at NYG
2	SEA (Mon.)	8	NYJ	14	LAR
3	at ARI	9	at BUF	15	GB
4	TB	10	DET	16	at SF
5	BYE	11	MIN	17	at MIN
6	at MIA	12	at DET (Thu.)		

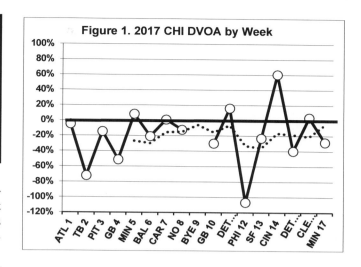

Figure 1. 2017 CHI DVOA by Week

defense (half the names in the table are actually defensive-minded coaches). We also included the quarterback and what his level of experience was. After all, the assumption here is that Trubisky, like Goff, is entering his second year and an offensive mind like Nagy's should be great for him.

We said McVay's turnaround was historic, and his increase of 48.9% in offensive DVOA was only bested by Ron Rivera in Carolina (54.0%). However, Rivera came into the league with No. 1 overall pick Cam Newton as his starter. He wasn't fixing the mess that, fittingly enough, John Fox left with Jimmy Clausen in 2010. McVay helped Goff improve to very respectable levels after a historically bad rookie season. That's more in line with what Nagy will try to do with Trubisky, though you can see a lot of coaches here inherited a very good player who was already in the prime of his career, such as when Drew Brees and Sean Payton got together in New Orleans or Mike McCoy's debut with Philip Rivers in San Diego.

In fact, there are only two situations even remotely comparable to McVay/Goff and Nagy/Trubisky. In 2000, Jim Haslett took the New Orleans job and pegged veteran Jeff Blake as his starter, but an injured Blake gave way to second-year player Aaron Brooks, who helped the Saints win their first-ever playoff game. The other similar situation involved Nick Foles, who took advantage of Chip Kelly's early success with the Eagles to have one wild season in 2013 where he threw 27 touchdowns with only two interceptions. We still might call

it the greatest one-year wonder season by any quarterback in NFL history, but at least Foles put together a Super Bowl run for the Eagles to forever cement a weird but notable legacy.

We only found 12 examples of an offensive guru hooking up with a franchise quarterback in his second or third year. Things did not work out well in most cases, which are listed in chronological order in Table 2. The best duo was Mike Holmgren and Brett Favre in Green Bay, but that's a little misleading since Favre was a rookie with the Falcons and came to the Packers in a trade in 1992. He only came off the bench after Don Majkowski was injured, and the rest is history.

More realistically, you get situations like the one where Dennis Erickson's arrival in Seattle did not get better play out of notable bust Rick Mirer. The Browns twice tried with Pat Shurmur/Colt McCoy (2011) and Rob Chudzinski/Brandon Weeden (2013), but no luck there. Timm Rosenbach and Robert Griffin III saw their careers impacted by injury, but sometimes the quarterback was just never going to be a hit, like Danny Kanell or Ryan Leaf. Leaf actually didn't play in 1999 (training camp injury), but Mike Riley never stood a chance with him. The Buccaneers are also going through this right

Table 1. Largest Improvements in Offensive DVOA by Rookie Head Coach, 1990-2017

Rk	Head Coach	Style	Debut	Team	Quarterback	Exp	Off DVOA	Rk	Prev Yr Off DVOA	Rk	Off DVOA Diff
1	Ron Rivera	DEF	2011	CAR	Cam Newton	1	18.2%	4	-35.8%	32	+54.0%
2	Sean McVay	OFF	2017	LAR	Jared Goff	2	11.1%	6	-37.8%	32	+48.9%
3	Chip Kelly	OFF	2013	PHI	Nick Foles	2	22.9%	3	-10.8%	25	+33.7%
4	Mike McCoy	OFF	2013	SD	Philip Rivers	10	23.1%	2	-10.0%	24	+33.1%
5	Bruce Arians	OFF	2013	ARI	Carson Palmer	11	-2.4%	20	-30.9%	32	+28.5%
6	Eric Mangini	DEF	2006	NYJ	Chad Pennington	7	5.6%	12	-19.8%	31	+25.3%
7	Mike Smith	DEF	2008	ATL	Matt Ryan	1	8.5%	9	-16.2%	27	+24.7%
8	Marc Trestman	OFF	2013	CHI	Jay Cutler	8	13.3%	6	-10.9%	26	+24.2%
9	Bill Belichick	DEF	1991	CLE	Bernie Kosar	7	3.7%	13	-20.3%	26	+24.0%
10	Jim Haslett	DEF	2000	NO	J.Blake/A.Brooks*	9/2	-1.3%	19	-24.3%	31	+23.0%
11	Nick Saban	DEF	2005	MIA	Gus Frerotte	12	-7.3%	18	-29.5%	31	+22.2%
12	Sean Payton	OFF	2006	NO	Drew Brees	6	10.0%	8	-12.0%	25	+22.0%

*Jeff Blake started 11 games, but Aaron Brooks finished the season into the playoffs.

Table 2. When the Offensive-Minded Coach Meets the Young Franchise QB (Since 1990)

Head Coach	Debut	Team	Quarterback	Exp	Outcome	Starts Together
Joe Bugel	1990	PHX	Timm Rosenbach	2	Rosenbach's 1991 injury led to 3 more career starts	19
Mike Holmgren	1992	GB	Brett Favre	2	Seven winning seasons together; 1-1 in Super Bowl	109
Dennis Erickson	1995	SEA	Rick Mirer	3	Mirer traded to CHI in 1997	22
Jim Fassel	1997	NYG	Danny Kanell	2	Kanell cut after 1998	20
Mike Riley	1999	SD	Ryan Leaf	2	Leaf on IR (1999) and cut after 2000	9
Ken Whisenhunt	2007	ARI	Matt Leinart	2	Leinart benched in 2007	6
Pat Shurmur	2011	CLE	Colt McCoy	2	McCoy demoted to backup in 2012	13
Chip Kelly	2013	PHI	Nick Foles	2	2015: Foles traded to STL, Kelly fired on 12/29	18
Rob Chudzinski	2013	CLE	Brandon Weeden	2	Browns released both after 2013	5
Jay Gruden	2014	WAS	Robert Griffin	3	Griffin demoted to QB3 in 2015; cut 3/7/2016	7
Dirk Koetter	2016	TB	Jameis Winston	2	Entering third year as QB-HC duo	29 (active)
Sean McVay	2017	LAR	Jared Goff	2	Entering second year after 11-5 debut	15 (active)
Matt Nagy	**2018**	**CHI**	**Mitchell Trubisky**	**2**	**Entering first season together**	**TBD**

now with Dirk Koetter and Jameis Winston, though Koetter got the job through promotion after he coordinated the offense in Winston's rookie season. Their next game will make them the second duo on the list to have 30 regular-season starts together, which is not even a high bar.

Most teams end up bringing a coach and quarterback in together to help with the development process. Trubisky, however, may have picked up some bad habits last year, including some that Nagy and his staff may not be best suited to coach out of him. For instance, Trubisky had the seventh-highest rate of failed completions (36.2 percent) in a season since 1989.[1] One of the main issues was failed screen passes to running back Tarik Cohen, who led the league with 35 failed receptions. Even in his best season last year, Alex Smith ranked 29th in failed completion rate (29.0 percent) playing for Nagy in Kansas City. This is part of what keeps turnovers down in a safe offense, but players have to make great efforts after the catch to make this offense work. Chicago did not have that last year.

Trubisky also ranked dead last in ALEX on third downs, throwing his average pass 2.4 yards short of the sticks. That's an area where Nagy has helped Smith improve (he finished 22nd last year at +0.7), but it's still not a strength. Chicago's lack of throwing last year hurt Trubisky with staying ahead in the down-and-distance battle. He was actually an aggressive passer on first down, throwing his average pass 10.4 yards down the field (third behind only Carson Palmer and Jameis Winston). But on second down, Trubisky's average depth of target dropped to 5.9 yards and he averaged a league-worst 4.4 net yards per pass. To make matters worse, Trubisky faced the longest second-down situations on average at 11.0 yards to go. He was up against the longest third-down plays as well, at 8.5 yards to go.

Further, Trubisky did not handle pressure well last season. His DVOA under pressure (-99.9%) was the third-lowest in the league. He was basically league average (46.9%) when kept clean, but suffered the second-biggest drop in DVOA when pressure was added in 2017. This is something that should be correctable with more experience, and playing in a higher-volume passing offense should help Trubisky a lot this season.

Perhaps we just buried the lede, but it actually is understandable why Chicago was indifferent towards the forward pass last season. The leaders in targets were slot receiver Kendall Wright, rookie RB2 Tarik Cohen, Josh "Not Bill" Bellamy, and midseason Chargers castoff Dontrelle Inman. When the options break down to Jordan Howard and Cohen in the backfield behind a solid offensive line, and this group of receivers, the choice to run looks more attractive than usual.

While this offensive cast absolutely needed to get better this offseason, injuries were a big part of the problem last year. In defense of Fox's tenure, the Bears suffered an alarming number of injuries over his three years. Chicago leads all teams with 366 adjusted games lost to injury since 2015 (NFL average is 214.4 AGL). That's not entirely all Kevin White, but Chicago's wide receivers have been hit the hardest, and the effects of some of those injuries will carry over into 2018. White may be more folklore than anything real at this point as injuries have led to him playing five games in three years. He's still on the roster, but expectations should be kept super low. Cameron Meredith was poised to be the team's No. 1 wide receiver in 2017 before he tore his ACL in the preseason. The Saints signed him to an offer sheet this April, and the Bears declined to match. Even tight end Zach Miller failed to escape 2017 without suffering a gruesome knee injury that almost cost him his leg. The Bears did a nice thing for Miller by re-signing him to a one-year deal worth the veteran-minimum $458,000 even though he will not play this season.

So which players will actually be catching Trubisky's passes this fall? The Bears made a splash signing, handing $42 million over three years to Jacksonville's Allen Robinson. He looked to be on a star path in 2015 when he had 1,400 receiving yards and 14 touchdowns from Blake Bortles, but he saw a huge drop in production (883 yards and six scores on the

---

[1] Failed completions are complete passes that do not meet the FO metric for success given the down and distance.

same number of targets) in 2016, then tore his ACL in Week 1 of last season. He can be the No. 1 target in this passing game, but expectations of him repeating his 2015 success should be tempered. The Bears also added slot receiver Taylor Gabriel from Atlanta. He can fill the role of Wright (or Kansas City's Albert Wilson) for this offense, which means he's there to catch bubble screens, slants, and curls.

Chicago traded up in the second round to acquire Memphis receiver Anthony Miller. Miller has actually drawn comparisons to Wright with his production inside and ability to produce YAC, and should be heavily involved this season. The Bears also needed to upgrade at tight end. Philadelphia's Trey Burton didn't have eye-popping numbers with the Eagles (629 yards in four seasons), but he was always playing behind Zach Ertz and Brent Celek. He caught five touchdowns last year and *threw* a pretty memorable one to Foles in the Super Bowl. (It was about the only play of 2017 that could compete with the beautiful design the Bears showed on a two-point conversion against the Vikings in Week 5, when tight end Zach Miller made an option pitch to Trubisky for the score.) For $32 million over four years, the Bears better also hope they see a career season from Burton, and they should.

Chicago's injuries were far-reaching throughout the roster, spreading beyond the offense. Bears linebackers were among the most injured units in the last two years. The injury numbers don't even account for the multiple suspensions of Jerrell Freeman. He only started one game in 2017 before suffering a pectoral injury and concussion. His season was over either way after getting a 10-game suspension for violating the league's performance-enhancing drug policy a second time.

Freeman retired in May, but the Bears already found their next inside linebacker by taking Georgia's Roquan Smith with the eighth pick in the draft. Many scouts have pegged Smith as the best linebacker in this class, an exciting prospect for a team that has led the way in star power at inside linebacker throughout history. Some have said Smith is a bit undersized for the position, but he was listed at the combine as 6-foot-1 and 236 pounds. Patrick Willis, a sure-fire Hall of Famer who played for defensive coordinator Vic Fangio in San Francisco, was 6-foot-1 and 240 pounds. Lance Briggs, a seven-time Pro Bowler with the Bears, was 6-foot-1 and 238 pounds. This is not a red flag at all. With Smith's elite athleticism, he should be a building block for years to come alongside fellow first-round linebacker Leonard Floyd, who has missed 10 games

to injury in his first two seasons. If they can keep these players on the field with veteran Danny Trevathan, then the Bears should field one of the best linebacker corps in the league.

Much attention will be on Smith since he is the shiny, new puzzle piece to this defense, which returns nine starters from a year ago and has retained Fangio as the coordinator for a fourth season. One big criticism of Fangio's defense is the lack of takeaways. Chicago's 50 takeaways since 2015 only beat the Browns (47) in that time. Nagy's Chiefs lead the way with 88 takeaways since 2015, but his specialty is offense, and unfortunately he won't be able to bring Marcus Peters with him to Chicago. Peters has 19 interceptions since 2015 while the Chicago defense only has 24, the fewest in the NFL.

It was surprising to see the Bears not seek any help in the secondary. The Bears haven't had a player intercept more than two passes in any of the last three seasons. Yet if the pass rush can improve—and it hasn't seen a player with double-digit sacks since 2014—then that should help the secondary out. The Bears still ranked 10th in DVOA without pressure last season, but were only 22nd in pressure rate (30.6 percent). One key takeaway can often make the difference in those close games that Chicago kept losing under Fox. The Bears have gone 0-for-their-last-13 in fourth-quarter comeback opportunities.

As much as we've groaned about Chicago's heavy prime-time placement in past seasons, it should be interesting to see this team get tested right away by opening in Green Bay on Sunday Night Football and hosting the Seahawks on Monday Night Football in Week 2. A win in either contest gives Nagy some early credibility. The six division games and home games against the Patriots and Rams give the Bears plenty of challenges this season. One could argue that even with a strong sophomore season from Trubisky, the Bears could still have the least impressive quarterback in the division, and a defense that is unlikely to topple the one in Minnesota this year. If there is a considerable offensive improvement and better luck with injuries and turnovers, the Bears can expect to be right in that wild-card mix in the NFC this year. They would have a great shot at being a playoff team if they were in the AFC. But in the NFC, that playoff drought is likely to continue one more year before we talk more glowingly about this team going into 2019.

Scott Kacsmar

2017 Bears Stats by Week

Wk	vs.	W-L	PF	PA	YDF	YDA	TO	Total	Off	Def	ST
1	ATL	L	17	23	301	372	0	-5%	9%	14%	0%
2	at TB	L	7	29	310	311	-3	-72%	-63%	2%	-7%
3	PIT	W	23	17	306	282	0	-15%	-23%	-10%	-1%
4	at GB	L	14	35	308	260	-4	-51%	-30%	18%	-3%
5	MIN	L	17	20	274	300	-2	8%	-9%	-20%	-2%
6	at BAL	W	27	24	342	291	+1	-21%	-9%	-34%	-46%
7	CAR	W	17	3	153	293	+3	1%	-27%	-29%	-1%
8	at NO	L	12	20	307	387	+1	-12%	-12%	-7%	-7%
9	BYE										
10	GB	L	16	23	323	342	-1	-30%	-22%	11%	3%
11	DET	L	24	27	398	352	0	16%	46%	27%	-3%
12	at PHI	L	3	31	140	420	+1	-107%	-97%	10%	1%
13	SF	L	14	15	147	388	+1	-23%	-36%	6%	19%
14	at CIN	W	33	7	482	234	+2	60%	44%	-17%	-1%
15	at DET	L	10	20	349	293	-2	-40%	-31%	1%	-7%
16	CLE	W	20	3	258	254	+3	4%	-8%	-11%	1%
17	at MIN	L	10	23	201	327	0	-28%	-31%	13%	15%

Trends and Splits

	Offense	Rank	Defense	Rank
Total DVOA	-15.1%	28	-1.5%	14
Unadjusted VOA	-15.9%	30	-0.4%	15
Weighted Trend	-10.8%	24	-0.5%	14
Variance	12.1%	31	3.1%	4
Average Opponent	-1.8%	9	3.8%	2
Passing	-13.0%	29	4.7%	14
Rushing	-6.8%	17	-9.1%	13
First Down	-18.3%	29	8.2%	28
Second Down	-17.3%	26	-8.0%	7
Third Down	-4.9%	20	-10.1%	10
First Half	-17.4%	28	3.9%	21
Second Half	-12.9%	25	-7.6%	9
Red Zone	14.7%	10	4.2%	20
Late and Close	-9.6%	24	-3.1%	15

Five-Year Performance

Year	W-L	Pyth W	Est W	PF	PA	TO	Total	Rk	Off	Rk	Def	Rk	ST	Rk	Off AGL	Rk	Def AGL	Rk	Off Age	Rk	Def Age	Rk	ST Age	Rk
2013	8-8	7.3	9.2	445	478	+5	6.6%	11	13.3%	6	8.7%	25	2.0%	11	6.9	1	55.6	30	27.5	8	27.3	10	27.5	1
2014	5-11	4.9	6.4	319	442	-5	-13.8%	26	-0.1%	14	10.6%	28	-3.1%	25	41.0	27	60.6	26	27.9	3	27.0	12	26.3	9
2015	6-10	6.3	6.8	335	397	-4	-5.7%	19	6.9%	10	11.3%	31	-1.2%	21	64.7	30	28.2	16	27.4	10	25.8	31	26.2	13
2016	3-13	4.7	6.2	279	399	-20	-8.3%	25	-2.6%	17	5.0%	23	-0.6%	18	84.0	31	71.1	32	26.7	16	26.0	24	26.2	11
2017	5-11	6.2	5.9	264	320	0	-16.0%	25	-15.1%	28	-1.5%	14	-2.4%	23	57.5	26	60.6	30	26.6	20	26.1	17	26.0	10

2017 Performance Based on Most Common Personnel Groups

CHI Offense					CHI Offense vs. Opponents					CHI Defense					CHI Defense vs. Opponents			
Pers	Freq	Yds	DVOA	Run%	Pers	Freq	Yds	DVOA	Run%	Pers	Freq	Yds	DVOA		Pers	Freq	Yds	DVOA
11	46%	5.3	-6.1%	22%	Base	42%	4.7	-11.8%	65%	Base	30%	5.0	-0.2%		11	63%	5.8	1.8%
12	22%	4.2	-33.5%	56%	Nickel	45%	5.2	-8.3%	28%	Nickel	64%	5.3	-2.9%		12	16%	4.3	-13.7%
21	19%	5.3	3.7%	52%	Dime+	11%	5.5	-13.2%	7%	Dime+	5%	7.8	0.9%		21	8%	5.2	2.6%
13	5%	6.1	11.0%	80%	Goal Line	1%	0.4	2.7%	50%	Goal Line	1%	0.5	35.0%		22	3%	3.4	-19.7%
22	5%	3.9	-32.5%	83%	Big	1%	1.2	-142.3%	100%						13	2%	6.1	10.5%

Strategic Tendencies

Run/Pass		Rk	Formation		Rk	Pass Rush		Rk	Secondary		Rk	Strategy		Rk
Runs, first half	46%	1	Form: Single Back	76%	19	Rush 3	15.0%	6	4 DB	30%	17	Play action	20%	25
Runs, first down	55%	6	Form: Empty Back	5%	24	Rush 4	61.6%	17	5 DB	64%	9	Avg Box (Off)	6.29	11
Runs, second-long	36%	10	Pers: 3+ WR	47%	30	Rush 5	19.9%	15	6+ DB	5%	20	Avg Box (Def)	6.09	27
Runs, power sit.	53%	18	Pers: 2+ TE/6+ OL	33%	11	Rush 6+	3.5%	25	CB by Sides	93%	3	Offensive Pace	33.31	32
Runs, behind 2H	24%	26	Pers: 6+ OL	4%	11	Int DL Sacks	34.5%	7	S/CB Cover Ratio	25%	23	Defensive Pace	31.60	29
Pass, ahead 2H	38%	29	Shotgun/Pistol	53%	22	Second Level Sacks	19.0%	13	DB Blitz	6%	26	Go for it on 4th	0.93	20

A change is gonna come: Chicago ranked No. 1 in run/pass ratio in the first half of games, while Matt Nagy's Kansas City Chiefs ranked No. 32, running on just 32 percent of first-half plays. ☞ Less likely to change: Chicago and Kansas City were the two slowest offenses in the league based on situation-neutral pace. ☞ Mitchell Trubisky gained only 3.7 net yards per pass with -30.6% DVOA when he faced a defensive back blitz. ☜ The Bears ranked No. 1 in rushing in the red zone, even though they were just 17th rushing overall. ☜ Chicago had the league's lowest defensive pressure rate on first downs but ranked in the top ten on both second and third downs. ☜ Chicago's defense recovered 12 of 14 fumbles, a rate which will assuredly regress towards the mean. ☜ Chicago's defense ranked 23rd on third downs with 1 to 6 yards to go, but second on third downs with 7-plus yards to go.

Passing

Player	DYAR	DVOA	Plays	NtYds	Avg	YAC	C%	TD	Int
M.Trubisky	-119	-16.8%	362	1981	5.5	5.1	59.8%	7	7
M.Glennon*	-231	-37.1%	150	756	5.0	3.6	66.4%	4	5

Rushing

Player	DYAR	DVOA	Plays	Yds	Avg	TD	Fum	Suc
J.Howard	160	5.8%	276	1124	4.1	9	1	42%
T.Cohen	6	-6.8%	87	372	4.3	2	2	46%
M.Trubisky	32	9.7%	34	251	7.4	2	3	-
B.Cunningham	-3	-16.1%	9	29	3.2	0	0	22%
M.Burton	-9	-35.9%	4	9	2.3	0	0	50%
T.Gabriel	36	39.5%	8	49	6.1	0	0	-

Receiving

Player	DYAR	DVOA	Plays	Ctch	Yds	Y/C	YAC	TD	C%
K.Wright*	53	-4.8%	91	59	614	10.4	3.1	1	65%
J.Bellamy	20	-6.8%	46	24	376	15.7	4.8	1	52%
D.Inman*	70	10.7%	40	23	334	14.5	1.2	1	58%
D.Thompson*	7	-7.4%	18	11	125	11.4	1.8	1	61%
M.Wheaton*	-66	-66.2%	17	3	51	17.0	1.0	0	18%
T.McBride*	27	10.6%	15	8	144	18.0	6.3	0	53%
T.Gentry	-2	-17.8%	6	3	35	11.7	0.3	0	50%
T.Gabriel	18	-8.0%	51	33	378	11.5	6.6	1	65%
Z.Miller*	24	4.4%	35	20	236	11.8	3.6	2	57%
D.Sims	-12	-14.3%	29	15	180	12.0	4.5	1	52%
D.Brown	11	2.1%	20	13	129	9.9	3.5	0	65%
A.Shaheen	40	26.0%	14	12	127	10.6	4.1	3	86%
T.Burton	85	35.0%	31	23	248	10.8	1.5	5	74%
T.Cohen	-64	-30.6%	71	53	356	6.7	5.9	1	75%
J.Howard	-60	-53.3%	32	23	125	5.4	6.7	0	72%
B.Cunningham	72	39.6%	26	20	240	12.0	12.4	2	77%

Offensive Line

Player	Pos	Age	GS	Snaps	Pen	Sk	Pass	Run	Player	Pos	Age	GS	Snaps	Pen	Sk	Pass	Run
Charles Leno	LT	27	16/16	990	13	4.3	14	6	Kyle Long	RG	30	10/9	447	5	2.0	6	8
Cody Whitehair	C	26	16/16	966	9	0.0	6	8	Tom Compton*	LG/RG	29	11/5	342	1	0.0	6	2
Bobby Massie	RT	29	15/15	913	4	5.5	15	11	Bradley Sowell	G/T	29	16/2	299	5	0.8	6	3
Josh Sitton*	LG	32	13/13	712	4	2.0	2	8	Hroniss Grasu	C	27	6/4	261	2	2.0	5	7

Year	Yards	ALY	Rank	Power	Rank	Stuff	Rank	2nd Lev	Rank	Open Field	Rank	Sacks	ASR	Rank	Press	Rank	F-Start	Cont.
2015	3.89	4.46	7	74%	4	16%	2	1.05	23	0.30	32	34	5.6%	12	30.1%	27	19	26
2016	4.69	4.48	8	75%	1	18%	11	1.27	10	1.06	5	28	4.9%	7	23.4%	9	18	29
2017	4.08	3.65	28	58%	26	26%	28	1.20	11	0.97	6	39	7.7%	23	30.3%	13	18	27
2017 ALY by direction:		Left End: 4.23 (14)			Left Tackle: 2.47 (30)			Mid/Guard: 4.05 (20)			Right Tackle: 4.21 (10)			Right End: 2.43 (29)				

New offensive line coach Harry Hiestand held this same position with the Bears from 2005 to 2009. He inherits a solid group that will see one major change from last year. ☜ The Bears declined to pick up left guard Josh Sitton's option after two seasons with the team, which led to his departure in free agency to Miami. He was Chicago's best lineman last season, but it is not a crushing blow. Sitton even missed Chicago's Week 3 triumph over Pittsburgh when the ground game piled up 222 yards. Thanks in part to injuries, the Bears have a few versatile linemen with experience at guard and tackle, and on both sides of the line. Veteran Bradley Sowell is one option to replace Sitton after he inked a two-year extension, but the Bears also drafted Iowa's James Daniels in the second round. Daniels was a college center, but the Bears made it clear right away that left guard is where his career will start, and it makes a lot of sense given the potential for him to step into Sitton's spot. ☜ Left tackle Charles Leno had his best season yet in our charting as a third-year starter. ☜ Center Cody Whitehair seemed to take a step back at times with some shoddy snaps, but he improved with Trubisky under center and actually finished 13th in snaps per blown block after ranking 29th as a rookie. He also got some experience at guard, but should be able to stick to center this season barring any injury situations. ☜ Right guard Kyle Long had another season marred by injury, and it likely contributed to his rank of 30th in snaps per blown block. He's an asset when healthy, but Long has missed 14 games since 2016. ☜ Right tackle Bobby Massie is far past the "total liability" phase of his career in Arizona, but he has likely hit his ceiling already in Chicago. This will be his third year as the team's right tackle.

Defensive Front Seven

Defensive Line	Age	Pos	G	Snaps	Plays	TmPct	Rk	Stop	Dfts	BTkl	Runs	St%	Rk	RuYd	Rk	Sack	Hit	Hur	Dsrpt
						Overall						vs. Run				Pass Rush			
Akiem Hicks	29	DE	16	899	54	6.6%	16	47	19	6	45	84%	17	1.5	18	8.5	13	26.0	1
Eddie Goldman	24	DT	15	608	44	5.7%	30	30	6	5	38	68%	74	2.9	74	1.5	5	15.0	0
Jonathan Bullard	25	DE	16	437	27	3.3%	78	23	3	2	22	82%	27	2.2	45	1.0	1	6.0	2
Mitch Unrein*	31	DE	12	389	31	5.1%	43	25	5	3	27	85%	12	2.0	37	1.5	3	4.5	0

Edge Rushers	Age	Pos	G	Snaps	Plays	TmPct	Rk	Stop	Dfts	BTkl	Runs	St%	Rk	RuYd	Rk	Sack	Hit	Hur	Dsrpt
						Overall						vs. Run				Pass Rush			
Sam Acho	30	OLB	16	640	41	5.0%	46	27	9	6	26	69%	70	3.7	89	3.0	15	18.5	2
Leonard Floyd	26	OLB	10	582	37	7.2%	18	25	12	6	21	62%	84	2.5	56	5.5	7	26.5	1
Pernell McPhee*	29	OLB	13	386	24	3.6%	71	18	8	3	13	69%	70	4.1	92	4.0	7	14.0	3
Lamarr Houston*	31	OLB	10	378	18	3.5%	75	17	8	4	9	100%	1	0.8	7	5.0	6	13.0	1

Linebackers	Age	Pos	G	Snaps	Plays	TmPct	Rk	Stop	Dfts	BTkl	Runs	St%	Rk	RuYd	Rk	Sack	Hit	Hur	Tgts	Suc%	Rk	AdjYd	Rk	PD	Int
						Overall						vs. Run				Pass Rush				vs. Pass				
Danny Trevathan	28	ILB	12	714	93	15.2%	19	54	12	7	56	57%	67	4.4	72	2.0	3	8.0	28	48%	45	5.8	21	3	1
Christian Jones*	27	ILB	16	624	86	10.5%	60	38	13	5	44	48%	81	4.4	71	2.0	1	4.5	33	47%	50	6.4	33	1	0
Nick Kwiatkoski	25	ILB	11	382	47	8.4%	75	25	8	3	23	57%	69	4.4	73	2.0	1	5.5	20	58%	16	4.9	7	1	0

Year	Yards	ALY	Rank	Power	Rank	Stuff	Rank	2nd Level	Rank	Open Field	Rank	Sacks	ASR	Rank	Press	Rank
2015	4.33	5.01	32	68%	21	15%	32	1.27	27	0.44	5	35	6.2%	18	24.7%	20
2016	4.41	4.33	20	60%	10	17%	24	1.13	14	0.84	24	37	7.3%	4	28.1%	13
2017	4.16	4.50	30	79%	30	14%	32	1.06	9	0.62	11	42	7.6%	8	29.9%	19

2017 ALY by direction:	Left End: 4.70 (25)	Left Tackle: 5.18 (30)	Mid/Guard: 4.35 (21)	Right Tackle: 3.77 (15)	Right End: 4.93 (28)

Here is another area where better health could really benefit the Bears. ☞ Leonard Floyd has shown pass-rushing potential, but not everything is rosy with the 2016 first-round pick. Floyd has missed 10 games in two seasons, and he hasn't been beneficial to the run defense yet. If he can put together his first 16-game season, then double-digit sacks should be doable after Floyd had 48 hurries in 22 games. ☞ Danny Trevathan plays next to Floyd inside, but he has missed 11 games since coming over from Denver in 2016. Trevathan can do a little bit of everything for Chicago—except for staying on the field consistently. The Bears drafted Joel Iyiegbuniwe (Western Kentucky) in the fourth round, a wake-up call to Trevathan that he could be cheaply replaced in 2019 if things don't get better this season. ☞ Chicago also added linebacker Roquan Smith with the No. 8 pick, one of this year's most obvious no-brainer selections. Smith was often considered the best linebacker in this draft, and defensive coordinator Vic Fangio can only hope that Smith serves his role as well as Patrick Willis or NaVorro Bowman did for him in San Francisco. ☞ Fangio also coached Aaron Lynch when he was a rookie in 2014, and Lynch has a good shot to start as the edge rusher opposite of Floyd this season. Off-field issues and durability problems have followed Lynch throughout his career, but he once looked like a young, promising pass-rusher for the 49ers. ☞ The defensive line is less heralded, but Akiem Hicks has enjoyed the two best seasons of his career since joining Chicago in 2016. Hicks has racked up 56 hurries in that time, and he was the unit's best run defender last season. ☞ Nose tackle Eddie Goldman has not lived up to his status as the 39th pick in the 2015 draft yet; he'll be backed up by John Jenkins again. ☞ Jonathan Bullard, a 2016 third-round pick, should take over as full-time starter at the other end spot. Like Mitch Unrein before him, Bullard's job is to help make life easier for the talented linebackers behind him in Fangio's 3-4 defense.

Defensive Secondary

Secondary	Age	Pos	G	Snaps	Plays	TmPct	Rk	Stop	Dfts	BTkl	Runs	St%	Rk	RuYd	Rk	Tgts	Tgt%	Rk	Dist	Suc%	Rk	AdjYd	Rk	PD	Int
						Overall						vs. Run					vs. Pass							
Eddie Jackson	24	SS	16	1055	76	9.3%	50	25	10	10	33	39%	52	7.8	51	38	10.1%	45	11.7	49%	48	8.2	39	6	2
Kyle Fuller	26	CB	16	1015	90	11.0%	5	45	15	18	19	53%	29	5.8	37	106	29.6%	76	12.5	61%	6	6.1	11	22	2
Prince Amukamara	29	CB	14	848	53	7.4%	57	20	3	1	13	54%	26	5.5	28	50	16.6%	17	13.7	47%	63	7.8	43	7	0
Adrian Amos	25	FS	13	670	70	10.5%	32	32	15	8	28	46%	33	5.9	32	28	11.7%	56	6.7	63%	7	5.1	2	2	1
Bryce Callahan	27	CB	12	512	31	5.1%	--	18	10	9	5	80%	--	1.4	--	34	18.9%	--	8.4	57%	--	7.5	--	5	2

Year	Pass D Rank	vs. #1 WR	Rk	vs. #2 WR	Rk	vs. Other WR	Rk	WR Wide	Rk	WR Slot	Rk	vs. TE	Rk	vs. RB	Rk
2015	23	20.7%	31	-12.7%	9	0.8%	15	--	--	--	--	26.5%	30	-1.8%	14
2016	17	12.3%	27	-1.7%	14	0.2%	15	10.2%	28	-2.2%	12	18.2%	28	-10.5%	11
2017	14	10.4%	20	-16.5%	7	19.4%	26	4.2%	23	5.6%	15	-6.2%	11	-3.4%	13

The Bears had seven defensive backs play at least 200 defensive snaps in 2017 (the five listed above, plus cornerbacks Marcus Cooper and Cre'von LeBlanc), and all seven are returning this season. Chicago did not draft any defensive backs, nor did it sign anyone noteworthy unless you are a CFL fan hoping for Jonathon Mincy to make the team. ☞ Chicago made sure to sign cornerback Kyle Fuller to a long-term deal. He had arguably his best season in 2017, easily outperforming the metrics of teammate Prince Amukamara, who also signed on for a three-year extension worth $27 million. The Bears may have locked up their top corner duo, but the track record of both players suggests this is far from a sure thing as a long-term solution. ☞ Bryce Callahan was effective as a slot corner and could be someone who cashes in elsewhere in 2019 should this season go well. ☞ Safety Eddie Jackson proved to be good value right away from the fourth round. He was one of nine drafted rookies to start all 16 games last year, but the only one drafted after the third round. He should be able to build on that rookie experience, which included returning a fumble and an interception for touchdowns. The last rookie to accomplish that was Janoris Jenkins in 2012. ☞ Adrian Amos, who was born eight weeks after *Amos & Andrew* (1993) hit theaters, was not the starting safety to begin 2017. He only regained the job after Quintin Demps was injured, but he made sure to justify keeping it this time. Amos' career year saw him rank seventh in adjusted success rate and second in adjusted yards per pass. That is a major improvement from his 2015 rookie season when he ranked 70th in those categories. His first career interception (a 90-yard pick-six vs. Baltimore) was a fluky bounce, but it was an incredible return on his behalf.

Special Teams

Year	DVOA	Rank	FG/XP	Rank	Net Kick	Rank	Kick Ret	Rank	Net Punt	Rank	Punt Ret	Rank	Hidden	Rank
2015	-1.2%	21	3.5	9	-15.0	32	3.3	9	3.0	15	-0.9	18	-8.2	27
2016	-0.6%	18	-4.8	24	2.9	10	-1.5	17	-1.4	17	1.5	11	-12.9	32
2017	-2.4%	23	-6.0	25	-2.2	23	-1.2	17	-12.3	30	9.7	2	-12.3	31

Chicago ranked below average in special teams DVOA for the fourth year in a row. ☞ The post-Robbie Gould kicking situation actually got worse. The Bears released Connor Barth in November after he missed a game-tying 46-yard field goal attempt. Instead of continuing to deal with quick rentals such as Cairo Santos and Mike Nugent, the Bears signed Cody Parkey to a four-year deal in March. In a way, Parkey is just as much of a retread as those other kickers. Chicago will be his fourth team in four years after he peaked as a rookie with the Eagles in 2014. For Miami last year, Parkey made 21 of his 23 field goals, but he finished just 15th in gross kickoff value. ☞ Punter Pat O'Donnell only landed 31.0 percent of his punts inside the opponent 20, the fourth-lowest rate in the league. ☞ Chicago's kick return unit was middling last season, but rookie Tarik Cohen had some success with his opportunities. The Bears finished No. 2 in punt returns where Cohen was much more valuable, including a 61-yard touchdown against San Francisco. Cohen's value also showed up in Week 17 against the Vikings when the Bears pulled off one of the more unique trick plays you'll see. As Cohen lined up to return the punt, teammate Bryce Callahan knelt near the team's sideline. When the ball was kicked, Cohen and the rest of the Bears flocked to his right, but that's not where the ball was headed. Instead it came down on the other side of the field, where Callahan caught it and raced 59 yards for an easy touchdown. (The Rams used this play in 2014 against Seattle, which used it in 2015 against Chicago, which used it last year against Minnesota, which will no doubt spring it on some unsuspecting opponent in the next year or two.) The Bears also hit the Vikings for a touchdown pass on a fake punt in the first meeting last season. It certainly seems useful for teams to get more creative in the kicking game—at least until rule changes are made to prohibit these types of tricks.

Cincinnati Bengals

2017 Record: 7-9	**Total DVOA:** -12.5% (24th)	**2018 Mean Projection:** 7.4 wins	**On the Clock (0-4):** 13%
Pythagorean Wins: 6.2 (21st)	**Offense:** -6.4% (22nd)	**Postseason Odds:** 28.1%	**Mediocrity (5-7):** 39%
Snap-Weighted Age: 26.2 (22nd)	**Defense:** 3.7% (17th)	**Super Bowl Odds:** 3.1%	**Playoff Contender (8-10):** 36%
Average Opponent: -1.1% (21st)	**Special Teams:** -2.4% (21st)	**Proj. Avg. Opponent:** 1.9% (5th)	**Super Bowl Contender (11+):** 12%

2017: The song that never ends is a song that never ends.

2018: If all goes well, they just perhaps could be a little bit above average. Maybe.

The only games that meant anything for the 2017 Cincinnati Bengals were the pair at the beginning of the season and the pair at the end of the season. Cincy was effectively out of the playoff race after five days, thanks to two ugly losses at home on opening Sunday and the ensuing Thursday night. The offense mustered a grand total of nine points (and no touchdowns) in the two contests, which ended the Cincinnati tenure of offensive coordinator Ken Zampese, let go after the normally reticent A.J. Green voiced his frustration with Zamp's work.

Agonizing as that damp squib of a start was for Bengals fans, it was the final two games that, long-term, cut deeper. Ironically, they were both victories, wins over Detroit and Baltimore that separated those teams from their playoff dreams (and got the Bills into the postseason, making Andy Dalton an unlikely folk hero in Buffalo for his game-winning, fourth-down touchdown bomb in the dying seconds to best the Ravens).

Alas, somehow those two wins convinced owner Mike Brown that head coach Marvin Lewis, who was all but fired when his team was 5-9, remained the man to lead the franchise forward, despite his 15-year track record of mediocrity (his winning percentage is .512, including an 0-7 playoff blot). Incredibly, the coaching cockroach will man the striped sideline for at least two more seasons after signing an extension just after New Year's Day. If Cleveland is the "Factory of Sadness," than rehiring Lewis proves Cincinnati, as the local T-shirts say, is the "Factory of Sameness."

Lewis supporters, and there are some, point to the days after the 2010 season, when it appeared certain Lewis would be fired. Instead, he pulled concessions from his tightwad owner that included modernizing many aspects of the football operation (and taking some decision-making power from Brown), moves that in part led to the mini-renaissance in Cincy during the first part of this decade. Lewis hinted that similar internal restructuring was part and parcel of his new deal, but public proof of that has been hard to determine thus far.

Retaining Lewis meant that Andy Dalton would remain at quarterback, mainly since those two meaningless victories at season's end pushed Cincinnati out of range for drafting any of the top prospects to replace the Ginger Gunslinger. There were rumors floating around draft day that the Bengals were considering taking Lamar Jackson, the Heisman-winning

Mike Vick-alike from Louisville. If nothing else, that would have made the Bengals interesting to watch. But of course, not only did that not happen, Jackson was picked by Baltimore instead, so now Cincy will have to defend the mercurial quarterback twice a year.

Running it back with Lewis and Dalton means the Bengals enter 2018 with a concrete ceiling, one that maxes out at wild-card weekend if all goes well. The odds (and our projection) suggest they will fall shy of that modest aim for the third straight year.

But hey, knocking the Ravens out of the playoffs sure felt good.

It's not that the Bengals are bad. Indeed, that is the problem with Lewis and Dalton; if they have proven anything in their years together it's that they are just good enough to remain stuck in the NFL's Middle Earth. Most Bengals fans would welcome being outright bad at this point, which is what they were after 14 games in 2017. Instead, they project to be average, as they mostly have been since Dalton took over (with the exception of 2015). Everything about their projection screams mediocrity, from the mean win total of 7.1 to their mean projected DVOA, all three phases of which hover around 0.0%. Indeed, the season-long chase to finish at that magically mundane mark across the board might provide some drama in what otherwise could be an unmemorable campaign. Unfortunately, the one number that stands out is schedule strength. Only five teams face a harder projected schedule than Cincinnati, thanks in part to games against the potent NFC South and tricky AFC West. The first and final quartet of games feature three road contests apiece, so opening pace and closing kick will be tricky to manufacture as well.

So whither optimism? For one, the coaching staff underneath Lewis was subjected to a major overhaul. Another reason is that for such a seemingly bland outfit, there is a ton of unpredictable volatility on the roster. If most of these "ifs" and "maybes" have positive outcomes, the Bengals may be able to regain some of the strength that briefly placed them among the league's elite just three seasons ago.

The unknowns start up front, on the offensive line, where much of the team's dysfunction began. Cincy is still reeling from the decision tree that took root in 2016, when the team decided to let its stalwart offensive linemen, Andrew Whitworth and Kevin Zeitler, depart in free agency. They were meant to be replaced by top 2015 draftees Cedric Ogbuehi

2018 Bengals Schedule

Week	Opp.	Week	Opp.	Week	Opp.
1	at IND	7	at KC	13	DEN
2	BAL (Thu.)	8	TB	14	at LAC
3	at CAR	9	BYE	15	OAK
4	at ATL	10	NO	16	at CLE
5	MIA	11	at BAL	17	at PIT
6	PIT	12	CLE		

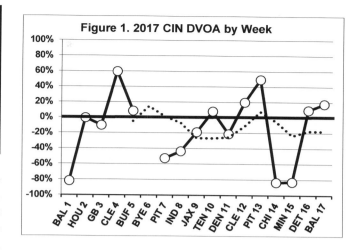

Figure 1. 2017 CIN DVOA by Week

and Jake Fisher, but Ogbuehi has been terrible, unable to play either tackle position with any semblance of power or consistency. Fisher has been moderately better, but he missed most of 2017 with a heart-related ailment. Those misfires and the continued employment of center Russell Bodine, who played every game for four seasons in underwhelming fashion, contributed to a stuck-in-the-muck offense that has been bottom-third in most categories the last two seasons.

To their credit, the team at last acknowledged the colossal bollixing this offseason. O-line coach Paul Alexander, another lifetime Bengal and the progenitor of the "let the All-Pros walk, I can turn my grandmother into a superb lineman" strategy, was canned. He was replaced by Frank Pollack, who coached the Cowboys linemen into a dominant unit the last few years. (Alexander, ironically, was subsequently hired by Dallas, so comparing the fortunes of the two lines in the near future will be a rare opportunity to test the isolated value of position coaches.)

Alexander has long taught an unusual style with methods that marked him as an outsider in league circles. That didn't matter so long as the Bengals churned out excellent linemen, from Willie Anderson and Bobbie Williams and Rich Braham to the dearly departed Whitworth and Zeitler. Pollack has reportedly had to bring in tons of new equipment for training, materials considered *de rigeur* elsewhere in the NFL but foreign to the Bengals practice grounds. As is the case with all new coaches, at every position, Pollack promises new aggressiveness and attacking mindsets for his charges. Whether he can make that happen without the high-end talent he had to work with in Dallas remains to be seen. The pressure is on Pollack to emulate another former Cowboys assistant who came to Cincinnati and had great success—Mike Zimmer, who parlayed his work with the Bengals defense into the head coaching gig in Minnesota.

Cincinnati did begin to overhaul that feeble line. They turned the No. 12 pick into a pair of immediate starters: left tackle Cordy Glenn, who came via a trade with Buffalo, and center Billy Price out of Ohio State, whom the team drafted after dealing down. Both are excellent talents, though both have concerning injury histories. (This will be a common thread as we explore the possibilities of the Bengals season.) Glenn is a top-third left tackle when healthy, but he has missed 16 games over the last two seasons with foot problems, which often recur when unnatural amounts of weight are placed upon them (Glenn is listed at 345 pounds). If he can play, Glenn represents a massive upgrade at left tackle. He's not quite

Whitworth, but he certainly won't be the sieve on the edge that Ogbuehi was, either.

Price was an ironman in Columbus, starting 55 consecutive games for the Buckeyes and winning the Rimington Trophy as the nation's top center. Then he freakishly tore a pectoral muscle while bench pressing during the combine. It wasn't a devastating tear, fortunately, and Price's doctor gave him a clean bill of health prior to the draft. Still, this marked the third time in four drafts the Bengals' top choice was infirm (and the fourth, corner William Jackson, was lost to injury for his rookie season). For a franchise that historically finishes closer to the bottom of our adjusted games lost standings than the top, they sure don't mind taking risks on less-than-fully healthy prospects.

Aside from the pierced pec, Price is a fine prospect—tough, strong, smart, lauded far and wide as a great leader. But he also is somewhat limited athletically, with a tendency to lunge into blocks, and many draft analysts didn't regard him as well as Frank Ragnow of Arkansas, whom the Lions picked just in front of the Bengals. Nor does Price possess the incredible athleticism of James Daniels, the Iowa center/guard who went in the second round to Chicago. Price is undoubtedly an upgrade over Bodine, and if he becomes another Braham and steadies the interior of the Bengals line for the next decade, no one will complain. But if Ragnow is Trevor Frederick 2.0, and Daniels becomes Dwight Stephenson, the Bengals might rue this lost opportunity to be elite at the position, rather than fine.

Pollack's immediate boss, offensive coordinator Bill Lazor, will also be under the microscope. The offense improved after he replaced Zampese in Week 3, although it had nowhere to go but up. There were still some offensive duds with the Lazor Beam at the helm, and the tendency was for a fast (scripted) start to dissolve into nothingness once the defense adjusted. From Week 3 onwards, the Bengals had 16.7% offensive DVOA in the first half of games (fourth in the league) but dropped to -18.1% DVOA (28th) after halftime. The season would have looked quite different if Cincy had not blown large leads against both Green Bay and Pittsburgh.

In fairness, Lazor could only tweak what was put in place by Zampese. Lazor has been outspoken about rebuilding the unit in his own image now that he can install his schemes during the offseason. He has also talked about the need to make Dalton "uncomfortable," which didn't extend to bringing in any competition—though the team did hire respected quarterbacks coach Alex Van Pelt away from Green Bay, a move that set off Aaron Rodgers' touchy temper. What the changes do for Dalton remains to be seen, but expecting him to suddenly become the player he hasn't been in his seven seasons is folly, regardless of who is in his ear.

Lazor has been on both sides of the midseason coordinator shuffle; he was canned five games into the 2015 season while with the Dolphins. His 2017 offense put up a 1.4% DVOA in 14 games, not great but 2007 Pats-esque compared to the -94.0% (!) and -27.0% ratings the offense managed in the first two weeks. Lazor likes to use screens (only the Saints ran more running back screens in 2017) and run/pass options, which play into the strengths of the Bengals backs and Dalton, respectively. Expect a wide array of them in the scheme this season.

Cincy's offensive numbers have declined for two straight seasons, so the pendulum is likely to return them upward in 2018. Lazor's cause would be helped greatly should another "maybe" tilt the Bengals way. Tight end Tyler Eifert showed the world what the Cincinnati offense looks like with him dominating in the red zone when he caught 13 touchdowns back in 2015. But Eifert only has 33 receptions over the last two injury-beset seasons. Re-signed to a one-year prove-it contract, Eifert needs to get on the field and justify the team's investment in him.

Yet another "let's hope" player is last year's ninth overall draft pick, wide receiver John Ross, last seen recording exactly zero catches as a rookie while sleeping atop Marvin Lewis' doghouse and pretending to be a WWI flying ace. The Bengals and Lazor never got to deploy the scorching deep speed and excellent ball-tracking ability Ross showed in college, thanks to (*beep*—"this is a recording") injuries. Ross also earned Lewis' ire for fumbling on his first touch in the pros, for stopping short on a deep route later in the year, and for hiding a left shoulder injury (not to be confused with the right shoulder injury that kept him out of training camp, or the knee injury that kept him out early in the year, or the knee injuries that plagued him in college). Ross was a "healthy scratch" for several games during the campaign, though he likely was not actually healthy during that stretch. This seems to be the classic case of a player with an "injury-prone" label trying to play when he shouldn't have, thus making matters worse.

Fans dream of Ross taking off the top of the defense while Eifert flies down the seam and Green does what Green does, all while running backs Joe Mixon and Gio Bernard take full advantage of the space caused by those threats. Last year, none of that came to fruition. If Ross and Eifert can actually play, and if Glenn and Price stay healthy as well, and if the line coheres around them, and if Dalton can elevate his game, and if Lazor can implement an Eagles-like scheme that spreads the wealth around a number of playmakers, well, the Bengals could have something here.

"If."

Quietly, the defense has an air of mystery as well, starting with the coordinator position. Paul Guenther left to join Jon Gruden's initial staff in Oakland, replaced by Teryl Austin. Austin is fresh off the Lions job, where his units declined from third in the NFL in DVOA in 2014 to dead last by 2016, before rebounding last year to 19th. Austin and Lewis both are Ravens alums (Austin coached the defensive backs when Baltimore won the Super Bowl in 2012), and Austin has been a head coaching candidate with several interviews under his belt. If he can return the Bengals defense to snarling, it's not impossible to see him as the next branch in the Lewis coaching tree (which includes Hue Jackson, Jay Gruden, Vance Joseph, and Zimmer).

There are fewer ifs for Austin to worry about on this side of the ball, save outside linebacker Vontaze Burfict's annual September Sitdown. This year the Tazmanian Devil will miss the first four games with a PED suspension, marking the third consecutive season the league has forced him to sit out at least the opener for cause. When he finally hits the field, Burfict will have missed 33 of the last 70 games due to suspension or injury, making him the defensive version of Eifert—hugely productive when he plays, but so unreliable as to wonder whether he is worth keeping on the roster.

The key area for improvement is that great year-to-year mystery—turnovers. The Bengals mustered just 14 takeaways in 2017, just above Cleveland for fewest in the league, and were 30th in the league with just 7.7 percent of enemy drives ending in turnovers. That is almost certain to bounce back through regression. Not taking any chances, Lewis & Co. are making takeaways their new priority. The accent is on safety, where Shaun Williams and George Iloka are solid positionally but aren't ballhawks. The team tried to sign Kurt Coleman and flirted with Eric Reid, but they were outbid for the former and not woke enough for the latter. Instead, they used their second-round pick on Jessie Bates of Wake Forest, who had a modest six picks in two seasons with the Deacs but possesses excellent range and route diagnostic ability. Getting a good cover safety out there would help alleviate Cincy's perennial problems covering tight ends and extra wideouts (they were 28th in DVOA against No. 3/4 wide receivers, 31st vs. tight ends, and 21st against slot receivers in 2017—but ninth in covering perimeter wideouts), while also allowing the team to deploy a box safety. Cincinnati also selected an intriguing corner from Western Michigan, Darius Phillips, in the fifth round. Phillips set an FBS record last year in Kalamazoo with a dozen return touchdowns, including six turnover returns (five picks, one fumble), and six more on kicks and punts. He could be an electrifying sleeper if he can translate that speed and knack for stealin' and scorin' to the pros.

There's that word again—If. You can't spell "terrific" without it, after all. But the sheer tonnage of Queen City question marks means that for stability, the team will rely upon its head coach and its quarterback. Which means that come midseason, the dominant emotion of Bengals fans is likely to be indifference. Which also requires an "i" and an "f."

Robert Weintraub

2017 Bengals Stats by Week

Wk	vs.	W-L	PF	PA	YDF	YDA	TO	Total	Off	Def	ST
1	BAL	L	0	20	221	268	-4	-82%	-94%	-14%	-2%
2	HOU	L	9	13	295	266	-1	-1%	-27%	-1%	25%
3	at GB	L	24	27	301	344	0	-10%	12%	1%	-22%
4	at CLE	W	31	7	350	215	0	60%	31%	-17%	12%
5	BUF	W	20	16	388	221	-2	8%	-3%	-19%	-8%
6	BYE										
7	at PIT	L	14	29	179	420	-2	-53%	-50%	14%	11%
8	IND	W	24	23	276	331	-1	-44%	-24%	7%	-12%
9	at JAX	L	7	23	148	408	+1	-19%	8%	10%	-17%
10	at TEN	L	20	24	308	416	0	8%	9%	3%	2%
11	at DEN	W	20	17	190	341	+2	-21%	-8%	-1%	-13%
12	CLE	W	30	16	361	405	0	20%	35%	26%	11%
13	PIT	L	20	23	353	374	+1	49%	50%	6%	5%
14	CHI	L	7	33	234	482	-2	-83%	-41%	50%	7%
15	at MIN	L	7	34	161	346	-1	-83%	-70%	2%	-11%
16	DET	W	26	17	364	276	0	10%	7%	-4%	-2%
17	at BAL	W	31	27	359	312	0	18%	34%	-8%	-24%

Trends and Splits

	Offense	Rank	Defense	Rank
Total DVOA	-6.5%	22	3.7%	17
Unadjusted VOA	-9.6%	25	-0.8%	14
Weighted Trend	-0.3%	18	8.4%	27
Variance	16.3%	32	2.9%	3
Average Opponent	-2.7%	3	-4.5%	29
Passing	1.3%	21	10.1%	17
Rushing	-10.3%	20	-3.4%	24
First Down	1.1%	16	1.8%	17
Second Down	-13.5%	24	-3.9%	13
Third Down	-11.0%	25	18.2%	26
First Half	7.2%	10	5.9%	27
Second Half	-23.2%	30	1.6%	17
Red Zone	13.1%	11	-4.3%	12
Late and Close	-2.8%	18	-0.6%	19

Five-Year Performance

Year	W-L	Pyth W	Est W	PF	PA	TO	Total	Rk	Off	Rk	Def	Rk	ST	Rk	Off AGL	Rk	Def AGL	Rk	Off Age	Rk	Def Age	Rk	ST Age	Rk
2013	11-5	11.1	10.1	430	305	+1	14.2%	9	0.4%	17	-12.6%	5	1.2%	12	11.2	2	30.5	19	26.0	29	27.4	8	26.3	9
2014	10-5-1	8.6	9.0	365	344	0	5.0%	12	-1.4%	18	-2.3%	14	4.2%	6	48.5	28	23.2	5	25.9	29	28.1	2	26.1	14
2015	12-4	11.7	12.3	419	279	+11	27.9%	2	18.6%	2	-7.1%	10	2.2%	8	10.0	1	18.2	6	26.2	23	28.1	2	26.5	10
2016	6-9-1	8.3	8.0	325	315	+3	4.0%	13	7.5%	11	0.8%	17	-2.7%	28	24.7	7	10.4	2	26.7	17	28.2	1	26.4	7
2017	7-9	6.2	6.7	290	349	-9	-12.6%	24	-6.5%	22	3.7%	17	-2.4%	21	43.4	22	37.5	19	26.6	19	26.4	14	25.1	29

2017 Performance Based on Most Common Personnel Groups

CIN Offense					CIN Offense vs. Opponents					CIN Defense					CIN Defense vs. Opponents			
Pers	Freq	Yds	DVOA	Run%	Pers	Freq	Yds	DVOA	Run%	Pers	Freq	Yds	DVOA		Pers	Freq	Yds	DVOA
11	71%	5.2	-1.5%	30%	Base	30%	4.6	-12.4%	50%	Base	30%	4.6	-1.5%		11	54%	5.4	3.2%
12	20%	5.0	-7.1%	54%	Nickel	49%	5.2	-10.2%	36%	Nickel	67%	5.4	5.4%		12	20%	4.8	-0.9%
13	4%	2.6	-28.9%	79%	Dime+	19%	5.4	19.8%	21%	Dime+	1%	5.8	24.9%		21	9%	5.2	14.9%
613	1%	2.2	86.5%	50%	Goal Line	1%	2.1	76.2%	58%	Goal Line	2%	1.1	5.8%		22	6%	5.2	13.7%
10	1%	4.8	57.3%	30%											20	2%	8.3	78.9%
611	1%	3.1	-70.0%	78%											13	2%	3.2	-28.1%

Strategic Tendencies

Run/Pass		Rk	Formation		Rk	Pass Rush		Rk	Secondary		Rk	Strategy		Rk
Runs, first half	40%	11	Form: Single Back	79%	16	Rush 3	1.7%	32	4 DB	30%	18	Play action	27%	5
Runs, first down	50%	18	Form: Empty Back	4%	28	Rush 4	83.1%	2	5 DB	67%	4	Avg Box (Off)	6.14	24
Runs, second-long	34%	14	Pers: 3+ WR	73%	6	Rush 5	11.2%	30	6+ DB	1%	26	Avg Box (Def)	6.21	21
Runs, power sit.	47%	26	Pers: 2+ TE/6+ OL	26%	23	Rush 6+	4.0%	23	CB by Sides	94%	1	Offensive Pace	29.23	4
Runs, behind 2H	27%	16	Pers: 6+ OL	5%	5	Int DL Sacks	23.2%	19	S/CB Cover Ratio	16%	32	Defensive Pace	30.46	16
Pass, ahead 2H	54%	2	Shotgun/Pistol	66%	12	Second Level Sacks	17.1%	16	DB Blitz	7%	23	Go for it on 4th	0.97	18

One big change Bill Lazor made was keeping his foot on the pedal when the Bengals had a lead. In 2016, the Bengals ranked 30th in passing when ahead in the second half; last year, that zoomed up to second. Unfortunately, as noted earlier in the chapter, the offense after halftime wasn't particularly successful despite staying aggressive. ☞ Cincinnati not only used a lot of running back screens, they were great at them: 10.4 yards per pass with 52.5% DVOA. But they were lousy at wide receiver screens, with just 3.8 yards per pass and -30.0% DVOA. ☞ The Bengals were dead last with just 75 broken tackles on offense. Joe Mixon and Giovani Bernard each had only 22, tied for 51st in the NFL, and there were only four broken tackles total from wide receivers who were not named A.J. Green. ☞ On defense, the Bengals cleaned up their tackling, with average broken tackle rates after they led the NFL in broken tackles in 2016. ☞ Cincinnati was the beneficiary of a league-leading 44 dropped passes by opponents.

Passing

Player	DYAR	DVOA	Plays	NtYds	Avg	YAC	C%	TD	Int
A.Dalton	87	-8.6%	536	3061	5.7	5.8	60.3%	25	12
AJ McCarron*	0	-11.1%	15	57	3.8	8.1	50.0%	0	0

Rushing

Player	DYAR	DVOA	Plays	Yds	Avg	TD	Fum	Suc
J.Mixon	68	1.0%	177	606	3.4	4	1	41%
G.Bernard	48	3.4%	105	458	4.4	2	0	40%
J.Hill*	-9	-14.2%	37	121	3.3	0	1	41%
A.Dalton	24	11.3%	19	117	6.2	0	0	-
B.Hill	6	6.7%	11	37	3.4	0	0	36%
A.Erickson	5	-21.2%	5	16	3.2	0	0	-

Receiving

Player	DYAR	DVOA	Plays	Ctch	Yds	Y/C	YAC	TD	C%
A.Green	73	-6.4%	143	75	1086	14.5	4.0	8	52%
B.LaFell	-30	-16.9%	89	52	548	10.5	4.6	3	58%
T.Boyd	76	19.5%	32	22	225	10.2	4.1	2	69%
J.Malone	-30	-36.9%	17	6	63	10.5	2.3	1	35%
A.Erickson	54	31.1%	16	12	180	15.0	3.3	1	75%
T.Kroft	35	1.3%	62	42	404	9.6	4.6	7	68%
C.J.Uzomah	7	-1.1%	15	10	92	9.2	5.0	1	67%
G.Bernard	11	-10.3%	60	43	381	8.9	10.0	2	72%
J.Mixon	13	-6.8%	35	31	307	9.9	10.9	0	89%

Offensive Line

Player	Pos	Age	GS	Snaps	Pen	Sk	Pass	Run	Player	Pos	Age	GS	Snaps	Pen	Sk	Pass	Run
Clint Boling	LG	29	16/16	967	1	2.0	7	12	Jake Fisher	RT	25	8/7	360	4	2.0	9	2
Russell Bodine*	C	26	16/16	966	2	0.0	3	8	T.J. Johnson	G	28	13/4	236	1	2.0	3	0
Trey Hopkins	RG	26	13/12	712	3	0.0	2	16	Eric Winston*	RT	35	8/2	204	0	0.0	4	0
Cedric Ogbuehi	LT	26	14/13	669	2	7.0	15	10	Bobby Hart	RT	24	10/7	525	4	4.0	13	6
Andre Smith*	RT	31	13/8	541	8	3.0	16	3	Cordy Glenn	LT	29	6/5	275	1	2.0	5	3

Year	Yards	ALY	Rank	Power	Rank	Stuff	Rank	2nd Lev	Rank	Open Field	Rank	Sacks	ASR	Rank	Press	Rank	F-Start	Cont.
2015	4.00	4.59	1	68%	13	17%	3	1.20	14	0.42	31	32	5.9%	15	21.2%	6	18	36
2016	3.91	4.20	14	60%	19	20%	15	1.04	26	0.55	23	41	7.3%	26	22.5%	8	15	38
2017	3.70	3.79	24	59%	24	18%	9	1.17	12	0.41	31	40	7.2%	20	28.9%	8	10	28

2017 ALY by direction:	Left End: 1.97 (30)	Left Tackle: 4.15 (15)	Mid/Guard: 4.23 (13)	Right Tackle: 3.10 (28)	Right End: 3.87 (17)

The unit wasn't as bad as it was in 2008, when we dubbed the Bengals O-line "the worst position group in the NFL." But it was pretty poor and a far cry from just two years ago, when the 2015 line ranked first in adjusted line yards. Only mainstay left guard Clint Boling remains from that front five. ☞ It was in the run game that this offensive line was particularly poor, especially in blown blocks—Cincy was actually top-ten in passing blown blocks per snap (and pressure rate allowed), but 24th in the same metric when rushing. ☞ As Joe Mixon and Gio Bernard can attest, too often runners had to avoid tacklers before they ever reached the line of scrimmage—though the No. 31 finish in open-field yards proves the backs didn't take up the slack when they got loose. ☞ Cordy Glenn takes over at left tackle for the horrid Cedric Ogbuehi, who gave up seven sacks and blew 25 blocks, yet was actually better than he had been in 2016. ☞ One significant improvement in 2017 was in false starts, usually a problem area—the Bengals line had just ten, good for third-fewest in the NFL. ☞ Jake Fisher is likely to start at right tackle, another big question mark given his health and performance history. Fisher gets unfairly lumped in with Ogbuehi at times—he has been mediocre, rather than atrocious, and it's fair to assume his illness affected his play last year. With decrepit Bobby Hart and ancient Eric Winston behind him, Fisher will be secure in his job this year, but the Bengals will be in the market for another tackle unless he steps it up. ☞ Right guard will be a competition between guys who haven't made anyone forget Kevin Zeitler, though Christian Westerman, Trey Hopkins and Alex Redmond all played well in short bursts last year.

Defensive Front Seven

Defensive Line	Age	Pos	G	Snaps	Plays	TmPct	Rk	Stop	Dfts	BTkl	Runs	St%	Rk	RuYd	Rk	Sack	Hit	Hur	Dsrpt
						Overall						vs. Run				Pass Rush			
Geno Atkins	30	DT	16	755	46	5.2%	37	35	15	3	36	69%	72	2.4	61	9.0	11	33.5	1
Ryan Glasgow	25	DT	16	412	23	2.6%	--	16	5	1	23	70%	--	2.2	--	0.0	1	4.0	0
Andrew Billings	23	DT	15	336	13	1.6%	--	9	5	7	13	69%	--	0.8	--	0.0	1	2.0	0
Pat Sims*	33	DT	14	307	25	3.2%	--	14	4	0	24	54%	--	2.9	--	0.5	2	3.0	0
Chris Baker	31	DT	15	457	34	4.4%	55	25	4	2	29	69%	73	2.4	62	0.5	4	7.5	3

Edge Rushers	Age	Pos	G	Snaps	Plays	TmPct	Rk	Stop	Dfts	BTkl	Runs	St%	Rk	RuYd	Rk	Sack	Hit	Hur	Dsrpt
						Overall						vs. Run				Pass Rush			
Carlos Dunlap	29	DE	16	877	50	5.6%	36	39	18	6	29	72%	57	2.3	48	7.5	18	49.5	9
Michael Johnson	31	DE	15	690	50	6.0%	29	39	14	6	38	71%	62	2.6	61	5.0	3	15.5	1
Carl Lawson	24	OLB	16	482	15	1.7%	95	13	11	3	5	80%	31	0.6	4	8.0	13	30.5	2
Chris Smith*	26	DE	16	403	28	3.2%	--	20	13	3	16	69%	--	2.9	--	3.0	6	12.0	3
Jordan Willis	23	DE	16	361	25	2.8%	--	22	6	2	23	87%	--	1.7	--	1.0	1	12.5	0

Linebackers	Age	Pos	G	Snaps	Plays	TmPct	Rk	Stop	Dfts	BTkl	Runs	St%	Rk	RuYd	Rk	Sack	Hit	Hur	Tgts	Suc%	Rk	AdjYd	Rk	PD	Int
						Overall						vs. Run				Pass Rush				vs. Pass				
Nick Vigil	25	OLB	11	757	82	13.5%	33	44	17	11	41	56%	71	4.6	79	1.0	1	11.0	37	53%	26	6.4	31	3	1
Vincent Rey	31	OLB	14	611	85	11.0%	53	47	11	6	52	60%	57	3.8	54	0.0	0	5.0	26	42%	62	10.0	73	1	1
Vontaze Burfict	28	OLB	10	587	70	12.7%	39	45	19	7	37	65%	31	3.9	58	2.0	4	4.0	22	68%	3	6.7	36	2	0
Jordan Evans	23	OLB	15	314	35	4.2%	--	16	10	5	15	47%	--	3.9	--	0.0	1	2.0	18	53%	--	9.9	--	2	0
Kevin Minter*	28	MLB	9	199	32	6.4%	--	18	1	1	28	64%	--	3.6	--	0.0	0	0.0	6	0%	--	7.9	--	0	0
Preston Brown	26	MLB	16	1098	147	16.8%	9	72	16	7	81	67%	22	3.2	26	0.0	2	6.5	49	51%	31	6.9	42	3	0

Year	Yards	ALY	Rank	Power	Rank	Stuff	Rank	2nd Level	Rank	Open Field	Rank	Sacks	ASR	Rank	Press	Rank
2015	4.20	3.97	14	60%	10	22%	11	1.11	16	0.94	26	42	7.0%	12	26.6%	9
2016	4.44	4.33	19	66%	23	17%	22	1.28	24	0.80	20	33	5.9%	16	30.8%	6
2017	4.06	4.38	29	70%	25	19%	25	1.26	26	0.49	3	41	6.3%	19	33.8%	5

2017 ALY by direction:	Left End: 4.37 (21)	Left Tackle: 3.27 (9)	Mid/Guard: 4.61 (28)	Right Tackle: 4.72 (28)	Right End: 4.17 (19)

The Bengals prioritized pass rush in the 2017 offseason after their raw sack total fell in 2016, though their pressure rate had actually improved over 2015. By drafting Carl Lawson and Jordan Willis and trading for Chris Smith to go with vaunted rushers Carlos Dunlap (sixth in the league in hurries, second in disruptions) and Geno Atkins (you know about him), Cincinnati boosted its sacks back up to 41 and was even better at overall pressure, finishing fifth in the NFL. ☞ Lawson in particular had a strong rookie season, finishing with 8.0 sacks and a combined 44 hits and hurries, though he wilted a bit down the stretch. ☞ Ends Smith and Michael Johnson found new life as inside pass-rushers in nickel packages; with Smith gone to free agency, that role could be filled by Willis and third-round draft choice Sam Hubbard of Ohio State, who lacks refined pass-rush moves that would work on tackles but possesses strength and drive that should abet inside work. ☞ If Hubbard can help stop the run, that would be even better. The Bengals were grim in run defense, leading to the import of nose tackle Chris Baker and linebacker Preston Brown, both of whom are good run-stoppers, if limited elsewhere. How much impact they make when teams spread Cincy's defense out is questionable. ☞ Fifth-round pick Andrew Brown (Virginia) is an explosive one-gap penetrator who could see playing time if he shows up like he did in the Senior Bowl. ☞ A another key rookie could be third-rounder Malik Jefferson of Texas. Think of him as a defensive version of Lamar Jackson—wildly athletic and capable of game-tilting plays when he attacks the line of scrimmage. But in Austin, Jefferson was too often caught out of position and displayed poor instincts. If that can be coached out of him, Jefferson could provide the splash linebacker Cincy desperately needs, especially with unit leader/loose cannon Vontaze Burfict suspended for the first four games.

Defensive Secondary

Secondary	Age	Pos	G	Snaps	Plays	TmPct	Rk	Stop	Dfts	BTkl	Runs	St%	Rk	RuYd	Rk	Tgts	Tgt%	Rk	Dist	Suc%	Rk	AdjYd	Rk	PD	Int
George Iloka	28	FS	16	992	84	9.5%	48	30	8	9	52	44%	40	5.5	29	24	7.3%	15	11.4	53%	36	5.6	8	5	1
Darqueze Dennard	27	CB	16	901	89	10.1%	19	41	12	4	25	56%	22	6.1	44	69	22.9%	59	8.1	51%	41	6.1	10	8	2
Dre Kirkpatrick	29	CB	14	871	69	8.9%	36	33	17	10	17	47%	37	4.9	17	78	27.0%	72	13.1	47%	61	7.5	39	12	1
William Jackson	25	CB	15	702	39	4.7%	--	27	8	8	9	56%	--	6.2	--	41	17.6%	--	15.8	73%	--	4.1	--	15	1
Shawn Williams	27	SS	11	580	52	8.5%	58	26	8	7	30	60%	9	4.5	13	16	8.0%	26	7.9	52%	38	7.0	22	3	1
Josh Shaw	26	CB	16	554	37	4.2%	--	10	4	5	17	24%	--	5.5	--	22	11.7%	--	11.4	55%	--	7.2	--	3	0
Clayton Fejedelem	25	SS	16	378	44	5.0%	--	7	4	3	35	9%	--	9.2	--	9	6.8%	--	9.1	67%	--	4.0	--	2	1
Adam Jones*	35	CB	9	298	27	5.4%	73	7	3	4	8	25%	71	9.9	71	36	35.9%	79	11.4	46%	69	8.4	60	4	1

Year	Pass D Rank	vs. #1 WR	Rk	vs. #2 WR	Rk	vs. Other WR	Rk	WR Wide	Rk	WR Slot	Rk	vs. TE	Rk	vs. RB	Rk
2015	10	-4.5%	13	2.7%	17	-11.4%	8	--	--	--	--	-9.5%	12	10.0%	24
2016	14	-0.4%	13	8.1%	25	-2.2%	12	-14.9%	6	16.2%	29	-1.8%	17	-7.7%	14
2017	17	-14.4%	8	-4.4%	15	22.2%	28	-10.5%	9	11.9%	21	19.6%	30	-5.6%	11

Lost amid all the players who haven't lived up to expectations in Cincinnati is one who has—William Jackson III, who rebounded from an injury redshirt in his rookie year to establish himself as the team's top corner in 2017. Whether it was turning in a pick-six off Aaron Rodgers (just the second thrown by the almighty A-Rod in his career) or blanketing Antonio Brown (zero catches allowed in two games), Jackson displayed elite skills. His adjusted success rate of 73 percent would have led the league had he started enough games to qualify. Opposing quarterbacks learned quickly that the going was easier elsewhere—Jackson was only targeted on 17.6 percent of passes (41 total), yet still managed more pass breakups (15) than anyone on the team. ☞ It will be interesting to see if new defensive coordinator Teryl Austin has Jackson follow top wideouts more than Paul Guenther did. No team kept its corners to predetermined sides more than Cincinnati in 2017, and no team saw opposing No. 2 targets thrown to fewer times, percentage-wise, which indicates teams merely put their best wideout away from Jackson. ☞ You could do worse for a No. 2 corner than Dre Kirkpatrick, who is solid despite too many big penalties (his 155 penalty yards were the most in the NFL), but a little scheme diversity couldn't hurt. ☞ While the Bengals struggled up front against the run, they were third in preventing open-field yards, which speaks to the good secondary tackling. Slot corner Darqueze Dennard was particularly good in this overlooked area, partially making up for lapses in coverage.

Special Teams

Year	DVOA	Rank	FG/XP	Rank	Net Kick	Rank	Kick Ret	Rank	Net Punt	Rank	Punt Ret	Rank	Hidden	Rank
2015	2.2%	8	1.5	13	7.2	3	-2.0	20	3.4	13	1.1	15	0.9	15
2016	-2.7%	28	-12.1	31	0.9	14	9.0	3	-2.7	20	-8.7	30	-11.4	29
2017	-2.4%	21	2.7	14	-2.9	24	-5.3	31	-6.0	22	-0.2	17	4.8	11

Cincy's decline in special teams can be summed up by the saga of Jake Elliott. The Bengals spent a fifth-round draft pick on the Memphis kicker, only to cut him after he flubbed training camp and the preseason. Elliott wound up in Philly, of course, where he made several big kicks, including three field goals in Super Bowl LII. The Bengals are sticking with the decent enough Randy Bullock, because to get rid of him now would be a humiliating cherry on top of a sundae of embarrassment. ☞ Kevin Huber was good at killing punts inside the 20 (32, tied for fifth in the NFL). It was when his punts were returnable that problems ensued. Only Shane Lechler and Andy Lee suffered from worse gunner units. ☞ Bengals kickoff coverage wasn't great either. Free-agent defections have withered these units along with the offensive line and receiving corps in recent years. ☞ When there are fewer kickoff returns in the game, there's going to be smaller sample size and thus more variance in performance. That's the best explanation for Alex Erickson going from No. 3 in kick return value in 2016 to dead last in 2017. Erickson is not particularly strong on punt returns either, leaving both gigs open to potential replacements, such as rookie cornerback Darius Phillips or wideout Tyler Boyd.

Cleveland Browns

2017 Record: 0-16	Total DVOA: -27.2% (32nd)	2018 Mean Projection: 7.5 wins	On the Clock (0-4): 13%
Pythagorean Wins: 3.3 (32nd)	Offense: -20.1% (32nd)	Postseason Odds: 28.8%	Mediocrity (5-7): 37%
Snap-Weighted Age: 24.6 (32nd)	Defense: 2.0% (16th)	Super Bowl Odds: 3.3%	Playoff Contender (8-10): 37%
Average Opponent: 2.1% (9th)	Special Teams: -5.1% (27th)	Proj. Avg. Opponent: 1.7% (7th)	Super Bowl Contender (11+): 13%

2017: Easily the best team to ever go 0-16.

2018: There's a lot of promise for the future, especially if the analytics are right about Baker Mayfield.

Bailiff: NFL court is now in session, in the case of the People vs. Sashi Brown. The honorable Ed Hochuli and his beautiful arms presiding.

Judge Hochuli: Please wind the game clock and move the chains. Mr. Tanier, you will give an opening statement.

Mike Tanier, for the prosecution: Ladies and gentlemen of the jury,

Time is the most important variable in almost every equation and the most precious commodity in the NFL.

The average length of an NFL career is 3.3 years, according to Statista. Most rookies sign four-year contracts. The average length of a head coaching tenure, as tabulated by Donovan Rose for The Cauldron in 2016, was 3.13 years.[1] Three years is practically an NFL lifetime.

I will prove in the pages to come that the defendant is guilty of two counts of malicious season-slaughter, with intent to commit a third. The defendant was, in fact, stopped just short of killing not just an organization, but the entire analytic movement.

Counsel for the defense will try to sell you on the defendant's so-called "three-year rebuilding plan," backing it up with fancy-shmancy stats and claims of improvement. Well, I am here to tell you what you already know: there is no such thing as a three-year rebuilding plan in the NFL.

Three years is the span in which star players grow old, affordable youngsters become expensive, rank-and-file players come and go, coaches make or destroy reputations. Three years must represent the culmination of a worst-to-first rebuilding plan, not the first phase of one. And anyone with even a cursory understanding of the analytics the defendants claim to cherish knows it.

Sashi Brown and his so-called "Moneyballers" used analytics as an excuse to stall, procrastinate, and conduct thought experiments while other teams drafted franchise quarterbacks and won Super Bowls with the resources the Browns frittered away. It was gross negligence with a pseudoscientific sheen, and the results are both obvious and damning: the worst two-year stretch in modern football history, and an organization that would have been far better off if this "Moneyball" era had never taken place.

Judge Hochuli: Thank you, Mr. Tanier. Mr. Schatz, for the defense?

Aaron Schatz, for the defense: When you are hired for a job, you are hired with an action plan and a goal. And you are a success at that job if you achieve your goal.

Sashi Brown was not hired with the goal of turning the Cleveland Browns around immediately. He was hired with a long-term goal of building talent in the organization. Yes, I will talk about a "three-year rebuilding plan," but not to try to sell you on it. Jimmy Haslam was already sold on it when he hired Sashi Brown in the first place.

The three-year plan was obvious to anybody looking at the organization's moves during the Brown era. What, do you really think DeShone Kizer was meant to be the long-term answer at quarterback?

The Cleveland organization is filled with far more talent and far better set up to compete than it was before Sashi Brown is hired. In the long run, the plan to accumulate draft capital worked, and John Dorsey will get to reap the benefits.

So, what about that 0-16 record? Clearly, that was a mark of failure, but whose failure? No, the Browns were not supposed to be this bad during the rebuilding process. I'll present to you an alternate theory of the case: that the worst two-year stretch in modern football history is more a product of bad coaching with a side of bad luck.

And if the coaches can get their act together, and luck evens out, the Cleveland Browns could even be wild-card contenders during the 2018 season.

Court explodes in "rabble rabble" noises.

Hochuli: Order, please. Order in the court. Don't make me come out there. Mr. Tanier, you may proceed with your main argument.

Tanier: Early in the 2016 offseason, the Browns traded the second overall pick in that year's draft to the Eagles in exchange for the eighth overall pick that year, a first-round pick in 2017 and a host of other assets. In doing so, the Browns passed up the chance to select Carson Wentz, who led the Eagles to the Super Bowl and was an MVP candidate last season. So history has already proven that this trade was a comically, catastrophically bad decision by the Browns.

---

1 https://bit.ly/2LnLsa9

2018 Browns Schedule

Week	Opp.	Week	Opp.	Week	Opp.
1	PIT	7	at TB	13	at HOU
2	at NO	8	at PIT	14	CAR
3	NYJ (Thu.)	9	KC	15	at DEN (Sat.)
4	at OAK	10	ATL	16	CIN
5	BAL	11	BYE	17	at BAL
6	LAC	12	at CIN		

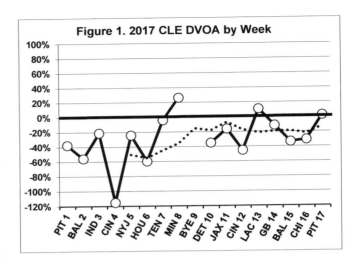

Figure 1. 2017 CLE DVOA by Week

Schatz: Objection! The Carson Wentz trade made perfect sense at the time. Analytics weren't up or down on Wentz; they were non-existent. An FCS quarterback with the No. 2 overall pick was far from a sure thing.

Tanier: Withdrawn. The prosecution graciously allows that this Wentz trade was logical and justifiable at the time. The Browns were rebuilding, after all, so a trade to amass extra draft picks made sense. And Wentz's status as an FCS quarterback made him a high-risk statistical outlier as a second overall pick.

Prosecution now offers into evidence Exhibit A: the sum total compensation that the Browns received in exchange for trading the right to draft Wentz:

Corey Coleman, Shon Coleman, Cody Kessler, Derrick Kindred, Spencer Drango, Ricardo Louis, Jordan Payton, Jabril Peppers, DeShone Kizer, Denzel Ward.

You will notice two quarterbacks on the Exhibit A list: Kessler and Kizer. Neither is currently on the Browns roster. The defense argued in its opening statement that neither Kizer nor (presumably) Kessler were "meant to be the long-term answer at quarterback." Yet they represent a significant amount of the precious draft capital the Browns received in exchange for Wentz. The defense is trying to have it both ways, claiming that Brown was cannily acquiring future resources while hand-waving away the haphazard squandering of a major chunk of those resources.

Prosecution now offers Exhibit B: The Brock Osweiler trade. The Browns acquired Osweiler and a 2018 second-round pick from the Texans in March of 2017 in exchange for eating millions of dollars in cap space and cash from Osweiler's exorbitant Texans contract. Osweiler not only failed to make the Browns 2017 roster but, as evidenced by the stories from minicamp and training camp that year, was useless as a veteran mentor to Kizer and Kessler. Still, the defendant's supporters hailed the wisdom of the trade because it provided even more future draft capital. The value of a second-round pick to our defendant seems to vary according to whether the Browns are wasting one (on Kizer) or wasting other resources to get one.

So the Browns entered 2017 training camp with a quarterback depth chart of Osweiler, young journeymen Kessler and Kevin Hogan, and Kizer, whom the defense has already stated was never meant to be a long-term answer at quarterback. Oh, and the team passed on drafting Deshaun Watson as well, for reasons that are not as easily justified by analytics.

If we accept the defense's argument about Kizer and the pre-vailing wisdom about the Osweiler trade, then Sashi Brown willfully, maliciously used exotic and unusual means to create a purposely bad quarterback situation. And yet the defense has the audacity to blame the coaching staff for an 0-16 season.

But let's get real: the defendant wasn't going all *Major League* with the Browns roster. He was just buying "lottery tickets" with quarterbacks Osweiler, Kessler, and Kizer. If any panned out, he was a genius. If not, he believed he could hide behind the cover of his so-called "three-year plan," which no one in their right minds believes meant "spend three years waiting for the perfect quarterback before you do anything."

Note that two of the players in Exhibit A were wide receivers: Coleman and Louis. Neither has developed. Why would Brown invest precious draft essence in receivers without creating at least a temporary workable solution at quarterback? This was a scattershot approach to team building, the old analytics adage about the draft being a crapshoot (so just keep rolling the dice) taken to an illogical extreme but hidden beneath a veneer of science.

There are several other exhibits the prosecution could offer, like the release of Joe Haden (who mysteriously went from "washed up" to a valuable contributor to the 13-win Steelers) or the signing of Kenny Britt (who sure looked and sounded like he thought the 2017 season didn't matter). But the prosecution will save time by offering the most damning evidence of all as Exhibit C: Joe Thomas.

The defendant inherited an incalculably precious commodity with a rapidly approaching expiration date: a Hall of Fame left tackle in the late peak of his career. Thomas should have been the blindside protector for young Wentz or Watson and a veteran leader to a rising core of young players.

But the defendant squandered Thomas' final seasons because of his obsession with draft picks and three-year plans. Worse, for all of his talk about analytics and value, he made no contingency plan for the aging of his most valuable asset. The only tackle Brown drafted was Shon Coleman, a third-round pick who belongs on the right side, not the left.

No one with even a cursory old-school *or* analytical understanding of football would let the career of Joe Thomas whittle away while twiddling his thumbs waiting for a quarterback better than Wentz and Watson to fall into his lap. That's the strategy of someone who is more obsessed with testing theories he read in some old research journals—and preserving his own job security—than giving his employers, fans, or players what they deserve.

The prosecution confidently rests.

Hochuli: Clock will stop on change of possession. Mr. Schatz, please make your argument.

Schatz: The problem with the prosecution's line of reasoning is that we are arguing about two different things. He is arguing about the past, and I'm arguing about the future. Because the Sashi Brown administration was about building for the future. And the future is arriving this season.

But first, let's talk about just how bad the Cleveland Browns have been, and why it's not as bad as it looks on the surface. The defense is happy to stipulate that the Cleveland Browns have not been a good team for the last two years. But they were not 0-16 bad. Cleveland's winless season was the product of a perfect storm of bad play, bad coaching, and bad luck.

Cleveland finished dead last in DVOA last season. There's no getting around it: that's the sign of a bad team. But Cleveland's -27.2% DVOA gave them the best rating of any team to finish in last place since the 1988 Detroit Lions finished 28th in a 28-team league at 26.6% DVOA. By comparison, the winless Detroit Lions of 2008 had a last-place DVOA of -48.4%.

The Browns went an astonishing 1-11 over the last two years in games decided by less than a touchdown. Four of those losses came in overtime. Check points scored and allowed, and the Pythagorean projection suggests the Browns were good enough to win 3.3 games, not zero. That ties them with the 2001 San Diego Chargers (5-11, projection of 8.3 wins) for the worst luck of any team since the NFL started playing a 16-game schedule.

The bad luck goes even deeper than just comparing wins and losses to points scored and allowed. As we know, fumble recovery is essentially random, and the Browns had a horrid record of recovering fumbles: they recovered only six of 17 fumbles on offense and only six of 20 fumbles on defense.

It's reasonable to criticize the Browns front office for depending solely on "lottery ticket" quarterbacks such as Kessler and Kizer, instead of adding a veteran passer who might help stabilize the quarterback room. But it's more reasonable to criticize the Browns front office for depending on Hue Jackson to develop the youngsters, given that historically he has shown a preference for veteran passers. Jackson does not have a history of developing young quarterbacks, other than Joe Flacco back in 2008 and 2009. And it's not the front office's fault that Jackson continuously spent the last two years dicking around with his quarterbacks, pulling them in and out of the lineup and never building an offensive scheme that focused on ways they could succeed.

But the bigger problem last year wasn't the head coach, it was defensive coordinator Gregg Williams. The Browns last year took all their young defensive talent and built a scheme designed for the 1980s instead of the 2010s.

As you might expect from a winless team that faced a lot of opponents running out the clock, the Browns led the league in using base defense, which they had on the field for 66 percent of plays. Except it turns out this has nothing to do with opponents running out the clock. In the first half of games, the Browns were in base defense 66 percent of the time. When the score was tied or even when the Browns had a lead, the Browns were in base defense 66 percent of the time. Cleveland ranked fourth in run defense DVOA thanks in part to their talented young front seven. But they also ranked 26th in pass defense DVOA because if you never go into nickel or dime packages, you're going to have trouble stopping receivers in the modern NFL.

The scheme is even stranger when you add to this the way Jabrill Peppers at the free safety position was constantly placed in the deepest possible centerfield. All throughout the season, commentators would watch the Browns and remark on how far away Peppers was from the line of scrimmage. But this scheme is particularly strange given that the Browns were usually behind and faced a league-low 14 percent of passes going deep (16 or more yards in the air).

Peppers is an important part of any discussion of the Browns because he's one of their three first-round draft picks from 2017. The goal of accumulating all that draft capital was not just to accumulate draft capital. It was to pick players. Sashi Brown was never allowed to finish the job. And so, instead, John Dorsey was given the ability to build a talented young roster with all the cap space and draft capital he was handed when Sashi got sacked.

The prosecution accuses Cleveland of having a plan to "spend three years waiting for the perfect quarterback before you do anything." But, in fact, Cleveland has not spent the last three years doing nothing. The Browns were not only building draft value, but also using that draft value to build a lineup they could eventually plug a top quarterback into.

Now that top quarterback should be here. Baker Mayfield was by far the top projected quarterback in this year's draft according to our QBASE forecast system. He had the fourth-highest QBASE projection of any quarterback going back to 1998. If you believe that college production translates at all into NFL performance, Mayfield comes out as a top prospect. Mayfield owns the top two NCAA seasons of all-time in adjusted net yards per attempt. And before you say "Colt Brennan," well, Mayfield is far from a system quarterback. Cleveland certainly wasn't the only team ready to select him on draft day. He was roundly accepted as a first-round talent.

Tanier: Objection! The defense is giving Sashi Brown credit for drafting a quarterback he did not select, with a draft pick he did not acquire, with a first overall pick the defense asserts was not part of his design!

Schatz: Sorry, I'll rephrase. It's true that Brown did not draft Baker Mayfield. But everything in the organizational plan pointed towards the idea that the Browns would select a quarterback in the first round of the 2018 draft unless the lottery ticket on Kizer or Kessler unexpectedly hit. Even if the Browns had won five or six games, the organization would have had both its own pick and the Houston pick. At some point, they would have had an opportunity to take a top prospect at the same level as Watson, be it Mayfield, Josh Rosen, or Sam Darnold.

The attorney for the prosecution is one of many critics who have lambasted the Browns for their decisions to trade down rather than draft either Wentz or Watson. But these criticisms ignore two important points.

First, the development of a quarterback is about more than just letting him loose in the NFL and telling him to do his thing. It matters how good the coaching is, how beneficial the scheme that young quarterback enters, how good his teammates are. The idea that the Browns made a huge mistake passing on Wentz assumes that Wentz would have become "Carson Wentz, 2017 MVP candidate" playing under Hue Jackson instead of Doug Pederson, with the inexperienced Cleveland receivers instead of the quality veterans Philadelphia signed last year, sharing a locker room and field position with the still-maturing Cleveland defense instead of the stellar Philadelphia defense.

Second, we don't know for sure that Baker Mayfield will be as good as Wentz and Watson were last year. But let's be honest; we don't know over the long term if Wentz and Watson themselves will be as good as they were last year. Given Mayfield's college performance and QBASE forecast, it's certainly reasonable to believe that Mayfield has even odds to become an above-average NFL starting quarterback. Instead of just trying to develop Wentz surrounded by a bunch of other rookies, Cleveland will have Mayfield with a more mature team around him *and* all the picks they've gotten in that trade and the other trades that fed off it. The same goes for Watson vs. Mayfield plus the other picks Cleveland has made over the last two years.

I think that even the attorney for the prosecution would agree with the general analytical sentiment that the NFL draft is more of a random crapshoot than scouts and general managers wish to believe. The best way to beat the draft is to make the most draft picks, preferably high draft picks since those players will succeed more often. And by moving down

Exhibit D. Most Draft Capital in Common Draft Era

Rk	Team	Year	Value
1	DAL	1991	132.2
2	CIN	1968	121.4
3	NE	1982	118.6
4	BUF	1979	115.7
5	LAR	1975	114.2
6	BUF	1985	113.9
7	SEA	1976	107.7
8	BALC	1982	107.3
9	TB	1987	106.0
10	CIN	1977	105.7
11	MIN	1967	104.7
12	**CLE**	**2018**	**101.5**
13	BALC	1974	100.7
14	IND	1992	100.3

Source: FootballPerspective.com, https://bit.ly/2L8JjSN

throughout his two drafts, that's the legacy Sashi Brown was able to leave for the Cleveland Browns. According to the Chase Stuart draft value chart, Cleveland entered the offseason with 119.9 points of draft capital, which would have been the most of any team since the 1991 Dallas Cowboys after the Herschel Walker trade. Exhibit D shows the all-time leaders in draft capital after the Browns made a couple of predraft trades. They dropped out of the top ten, but those trades brought them a bridge quarterback (Tyrod Taylor) to play until Mayfield is ready and a new free safety (Damarious Randall) who himself is also a former first-round pick.

DVOA projects that the defense is going to be very good as soon as this year. The Browns were 16th in defensive DVOA last year and have a top-10 defensive projection this year. Besides the addition of more talent such as fourth overall pick Denzel Ward and a number of veteran defensive backs, two trends point strongly to Cleveland's defense improving even further in 2018.

First, turnovers. I already mentioned Cleveland's awful fumble luck. Overall, the Browns were 31st in the league with turnovers on just 7.3 percent of opposing drives. That's a stat that tends to regress heavily towards the mean.

The second trend has to do with that phenomenal run defense. One thing Football Outsiders has discovered is that run defense is more consistent and easier to predict than pass defense. That means teams with very strong run defense but poor pass defense are strongly likely to improve the following year.

Cleveland was one of only three teams to ever have a gap of over 40 percentage points between run defense DVOA and pass defense DVOA, and the first since the 1991 Patriots. In Exhibit E, we look only at the teams with the biggest gaps between run and pass defense since 2002. On average, these teams improved another four percentage points of DVOA the following year. And this isn't a question of normal regression, since these defenses were generally average during the first year in question.

As for the offense, it is bound to improve even if Taylor is a below-average quarterback, because run-of-the-mill below-average is much better than what the Browns put out there last year. And Taylor is not just a below-average quarterback, no matter what they say on Buffalo sports radio. Over the last three seasons, Taylor's average rank in passing DVOA has been 16th. But his average rank in ESPN QBR, which accounts for his rushing value, has been 11th.

There's also going to be a dramatic improvement in the red zone. As Football Outsiders has shown many times, extremely good or bad red zone performance tends to regress towards the mean the following year. And there, I introduce Exhibit F. The 2017 Cleveland Browns were completely horrifying in the red zone, with the fifth-worst passing DVOA inside the 20 we've ever measured. That's bound to improve in 2018.

The problem with all this promise, of course, is that Cleveland still has the same coaching staff. That may mean the same problems that the Browns have had the last two years. We still don't know whether Hue Jackson will be able to develop Mayfield. The Browns defense may not be able to close that gap between run defense and pass defense if they're still running base defense out there against 11 personnel all the time.

But the coaching staff was hired by the owner, not the former general manager (or, for that matter, the current one). Failures by Jackson and Williams are not crimes against the football analytics community. They're just crimes against the people of Cleveland.

Hochuli: Thank you, Mr. Schatz. And now, Mr. Tanier, you have time for a brief concluding statement.

Tanier: The prosecution concedes that the Browns have the potential to be an exciting young team in 2018 and grow quickly into contenders after that. Of course, that's exactly where they should have been two solid years ago, or last year.

The prosecution also concedes that Hue Jackson and Gregg Williams severely exacerbated the Browns situation, turning 3-13 type seasons into historical failures. A cynic would accuse the defense of convenient scapegoating: of course the analytics community blames the "Old School Football Guys" for the failure of the Browns experiment, and Jackson and Williams can be accused of further sabotage if the optimistic Baker Mayfield future never materializes! But I won't challenge the defense on that point, because Jackson and Williams clearly stink. Instead, I ask a more damning question:

What caliber of coach would EVER agree to a rebuilding plan that produces no results for three full years?

Top coaching candidates will never agree to take part in such a prolonged rebuilding experiment: they don't want to risk the potential stain on their resumes, they don't want to spend two full years trying not to lose the locker room, and so on. Frank Reich or Josh McDaniels would hear a pitch like this and laugh their way to the airport; for top college coaches, three years is an entire recruiting cycle! The only coaches who would ever agree to be as bad as the Browns were for two full years are newbies with no track record, has-beens with bad reputations (Williams), and backroom politicians seeking

a potential power vacuum when things go sideways (Jackson). If the Browns experiment was reliant on great coaching to win a handful of games or spin draft straw into gold, then it was doomed by design.

Sashi Brown's version of "Moneyball" required laboratory conditions to succeed: unlimited patience from ownership and fans, 100 percent buy-in from players and coaches, analytics-approved rookie quarterbacks arriving in the nick of time. It put the worst possible face on analytics: unrealistic, over-optimistic, unwilling to compromise, obsessed with "draft capital" spreadsheets but disinterested in what really happens on hot August afternoons, blithely assuming that humans will behave like economic units. It was like a bad parody of real analytics, and it reinforced the worst stereotypes about analytics in NFL circles.

Maybe the operation will eventually turn out to be a success. But analytics need to be about finding treatments that don't leave the patient on a deathbed for two years.

Hochuli: Thank you, Mr. Tanier. Mr. Schatz, your concluding statement.

Schatz: There's a difference between a deathbed and a convalescence. Sometimes, it takes a lot of rest for the body to recover from a sickness. And make no mistake, the Cleveland Browns were a very sick franchise when Sashi Brown was hired in 2016. Eight straight losing seasons. Seven of those seasons at 5-11 or worse. Very little young talent thanks to draft failures both unpredictable (Justin Gilbert) and predictable (using a first-round pick on a 29-year-old Brandon Weeden).

Jimmy Haslam brought in Sashi Brown and his analytics crew to perform some experimental surgery. It's surgery that has worked in other sports. The Houston Astros and Chicago Cubs won the World Series. After all those jokes about "the process," the Philadelphia 76ers went 52-30 last year. We don't know if this kind of experimental surgery will work in the NFL. But we can't write it off when the first attempt isn't

Exhibit E. Largest Gap Between Pass Defense and Run Defense DVOA, 2002-2017

Year	Team	Defense DVOA	Rank	Pass D DVOA	Rank	Run D DVOA	Rank	Gap	Total Defense Y+1	Rank	DVOA Change
2017	**CLE**	**2.0%**	**16**	**21.8%**	**27**	**-21.0%**	**4**	**42.8%**	---	---	---
2015	TB	3.3%	18	20.6%	26	-16.6%	9	37.1%	-2.9%	13	-6.2%
2012	TB	2.9%	20	16.9%	26	-19.6%	3	36.6%	-6.8%	8	-9.7%
2016	NE	-1.8%	16	13.1%	22	-23.3%	5	36.4%	10.9%	31	12.8%
2007	MIN	-0.1%	17	13.6%	24	-22.1%	2	35.7%	-19.3%	4	-19.1%
2017	**GB**	**4.9%**	**20**	**21.6%**	**26**	**-13.0%**	**8**	**34.6%**	---	---	---
2015	BAL	5.1%	20	19.9%	25	-14.4%	12	34.3%	-9.9%	6	-15.0%
2016	LAR	-2.0%	15	11.6%	20	-20.3%	6	31.9%	-9.7%	6	-7.7%
2009	MIN	-1.0%	15	11.5%	23	-19.3%	1	30.8%	-2.5%	12	-1.6%
2013	NYJ	-5.6%	12	7.5%	18	-23.0%	2	30.5%	3.5%	21	9.0%
2012	NE	1.4%	15	14.0%	23	-16.0%	6	30.0%	4.2%	20	2.8%
2014	TB	1.1%	18	14.9%	23	-14.5%	8	29.3%	3.3%	18	2.1%
2017	**NYJ**	**4.0%**	**18**	**17.0%**	**22**	**-11.0%**	**11**	**27.9%**	---	---	---
2016	DAL	1.1%	18	11.0%	19	-15.8%	8	26.9%	5.9%	25	4.8%
2010	SF	-1.4%	15	10.9%	25	-15.9%	6	26.8%	-14.6%	3	-13.3%
AVERAGE (2002-2016)		*0.3%*	*16.6*	*13.8%*	*22.8*	*-18.4%*	*5.7*	*32.2%*	*-3.2%*	*13.9*	*-3.4%*

even over yet.

The goal of the Sashi Brown administration was to fill the Cleveland Browns organization with young, top-notch talent. And that's exactly what it did. This year's projected starting lineup on defense features five different first-round picks. Another three starters will be second- or third-round picks. On offense, the Browns will soon have high draft picks at all the skill positions and a No. 1 overall pick at quarterback. That leaves the offensive line, which is where the Browns have spent the most money investing their free-agent dollars.

Obviously, there's no guarantee that all these draft picks will hit. We know the Browns have already missed on some of their recent picks, especially at wide receiver. But the more high picks you have, the better shot you have at developing star players.

Cleveland is not just a run-of-the-mill young and developing team. Last year, they were *extremely* young. Cleveland ranked last in snap-weighted age for all three units. Their overall snap-weighted age of 24.6 made them the youngest team in the NFL since 2006. There is a lot of opportunity for growth here.

The prosecution accuses me of giving Sashi Brown credit for things that happened after he was fired. But while Brown was fired, the rest of the analytics department is still there:

Paul DePodesta, Kevin Meers, Ken Kovash, and others. And the drafting of Baker Mayfield first overall suggests that Dorsey hasn't completely shut them out of the decision-making process. This experiment is still ongoing.

We don't know yet if all this young talent is going to work out for the Browns. And yes, the three-year plan seems to have turned into more of a four-year plan. But it is far too early to call the Sashi Brown administration a failure. We have to see what happens over the next couple seasons first, and this roster is quite promising. Brown planted the seeds. Now Dorsey gets to tend the garden.

Hochuli: Thank you, both of you, for your arguments this afternoon.

(Turns to you reading the book.)

Jury, you will now discuss the case and render a verdict. Did the Sashi Brown administration ruin the Browns? Would a more conventional rebuild have been more successful? How badly have the last two years of Cleveland besmirched the cause of analytics in the NFL?

You are the people in the case of The People vs. Sashi Brown, and it is up for you to decide.

Now if you excuse me, I'm late for my workout.

Aaron Schatz and Mike Tanier

Exhibit F. Worst Red Zone Passing DVOA, 1986-2017

Year	Team	Red Pass DVOA	Rank	Red Rush DVOA	Rank	All Offense DVOA	Rank	Y+1 Offense DVOA	Rank
1991	PHX	-215.2%	28	-19.8%	24	-20.4%	24	-0.2%	15
1992	IND	-157.9%	28	8.5%	14	-26.9%	26	-20.3%	27
1997	SD	-141.1%	30	-16.8%	26	-28.3%	29	-25.4%	30
2004	CHI	-138.4%	32	6.1%	13	-36.5%	32	-17.1%	28
2017	**CLE**	**-126.9%**	**32**	**8.6%**	**12**	**-20.1%**	**32**	**--**	**--**
2002	HOU	-112.4%	32	-1.6%	24	-43.3%	32	-14.7%	28
2008	STL	-111.7%	32	-42.8%	31	-28.2%	32	-29.5%	32
1995	NYG	-111.3%	30	22.4%	7	-5.9%	21	-21.3%	29
2000	ARI	-110.2%	31	-43.5%	30	-19.6%	27	5.2%	9
1987	GB	-107.3%	28	5.9%	10	-11.9%	24	-20.8%	27
1990	DAL	-106.5%	28	22.3%	4	-23.6%	28	17.6%	4
1994	HOIL	-103.7%	28	34.5%	1	-21.9%	28	-12.9%	26
1992	DEN	-102.9%	27	8.4%	15	-15.7%	25	14.8%	3
2011	STL	-101.8%	32	-5.6%	21	-27.2%	32	-4.2%	21
AVERAGE (w/o CLE)		-124.6%		-1.7%		-23.8%		-9.9%	

2017 Browns Stats by Week

Wk	vs.	W-L	PF	PA	YDF	YDA	TO	Total	Off	Def	ST
1	PIT	L	18	21	237	290	0	-38%	-15%	0%	-23%
2	at BAL	L	10	24	386	337	-3	-56%	-45%	13%	1%
3	at IND	L	28	31	346	335	-2	-21%	-16%	10%	5%
4	CIN	L	7	31	215	350	0	-115%	-66%	28%	-21%
5	NYJ	L	14	17	419	212	-2	-24%	-10%	-3%	-18%
6	at HOU	L	17	33	247	340	-2	-60%	-60%	3%	4%
7	TEN	L	9	12	284	269	-2	-4%	-41%	-35%	3%
8	MIN	L	16	33	276	375	-1	26%	18%	-11%	-2%
9	BYE										
10	at DET	L	24	38	413	345	-1	-35%	-2%	26%	-7%
11	JAX	L	7	19	184	284	-4	-16%	-58%	-39%	2%
12	at CIN	L	16	30	405	361	0	-45%	5%	39%	-11%
13	at LAC	L	10	19	291	429	-2	11%	10%	1%	1%
14	GB	L	21	27	345	341	-2	-12%	7%	9%	-9%
15	BAL	L	10	27	266	376	-4	-34%	-28%	15%	10%
16	at CHI	L	3	20	254	258	-3	-31%	-23%	7%	-1%
17	at PIT	L	24	28	374	348	0	2%	0%	-16%	-14%

Trends and Splits

	Offense	Rank	Defense	Rank
Total DVOA	-20.1%	32	2.0%	16
Unadjusted VOA	-22.9%	32	3.7%	19
Weighted Trend	-15.0%	29	0.5%	16
Variance	7.2%	15	4.4%	9
Average Opponent	-2.3%	6	-0.9%	19
Passing	-30.5%	32	21.6%	26
Rushing	0.8%	9	-20.8%	4
First Down	-23.6%	31	2.3%	20
Second Down	-4.2%	19	1.7%	18
Third Down	-38.1%	32	1.9%	16
First Half	-15.9%	27	4.2%	22
Second Half	-24.2%	31	-0.4%	16
Red Zone	-53.9%	32	13.1%	27
Late and Close	-23.4%	30	9.6%	26

Five-Year Performance

Year	W-L	Pyth W	Est W	PF	PA	TO	Total	Rk	Off	Rk	Def	Rk	ST	Rk	Off AGL	Rk	Def AGL	Rk	Off Age	Rk	Def Age	Rk	ST Age	Rk
2013	4-12	5.5	4.4	308	406	-8	-21.8%	28	-14.4%	26	8.2%	24	0.9%	14	24.8	9	16.3	8	26.6	21	25.4	30	24.9	31
2014	7-9	6.9	7.2	299	337	+6	-6.7%	23	-10.2%	24	-3.0%	11	0.4%	14	30.5	16	36.6	14	26.6	18	26.4	22	25.8	23
2015	3-13	4.0	4.5	278	432	-9	-23.0%	30	-13.2%	27	10.5%	29	0.7%	15	37.1	18	33.7	21	27.4	9	27.1	8	25.6	25
2016	1-15	3.3	1.5	264	452	-12	-30.4%	31	-13.4%	29	14.5%	30	-2.5%	26	46.2	23	50.2	23	26.7	15	25.1	32	24.5	32
2017	0-16	3.3	3.3	234	410	-28	-27.2%	32	-20.1%	32	2.0%	16	-5.1%	27	21.3	7	31.3	14	24.9	32	24.5	32	24.1	32

2017 Performance Based on Most Common Personnel Groups

CLE Offense					CLE Offense vs. Opponents					CLE Defense					CLE Defense vs. Opponents			
Pers	Freq	Yds	DVOA	Run%	Pers	Freq	Yds	DVOA	Run%	Pers	Freq	Yds	DVOA	Pers	Freq	Yds	DVOA
11	64%	5.2	-19.8%	23%	Base	26%	5.5	-3.5%	55%	Base	66%	5.1	-0.2%	11	51%	6.0	13.0%
21	15%	4.5	-9.5%	49%	Nickel	54%	4.9	-18.1%	28%	Nickel	31%	6.2	12.3%	12	24%	5.1	-9.2%
12	13%	5.2	-7.7%	38%	Dime+	19%	5.0	-40.6%	9%	Dime+	1%	2.0	-28.4%	22	8%	4.7	0.6%
13	4%	4.0	-72.4%	44%	Goal Line	1%	0.4	-13.7%	62%	Goal Line	1%	0.2	-34.5%	13	4%	4.8	34.7%
22	3%	4.7	0.2%	73%						Big	1%	3.0	-4.9%	21	4%	2.2	-55.1%

Strategic Tendencies

Run/Pass		Rk	Formation		Rk	Pass Rush		Rk	Secondary		Rk	Strategy		Rk
Runs, first half	37%	24	Form: Single Back	81%	10	Rush 3	7.9%	13	4 DB	66%	1	Play action	16%	29
Runs, first down	45%	27	Form: Empty Back	4%	29	Rush 4	54.1%	31	5 DB	31%	29	Avg Box (Off)	6.25	15
Runs, second-long	23%	28	Pers: 3+ WR	64%	16	Rush 5	28.8%	2	6+ DB	1%	27	Avg Box (Def)	6.53	2
Runs, power sit.	57%	16	Pers: 2+ TE/6+ OL	21%	29	Rush 6+	9.2%	4	CB by Sides	76%	21	Offensive Pace	31.19	22
Runs, behind 2H	24%	27	Pers: 6+ OL	5%	4	Int DL Sacks	14.7%	26	S/CB Cover Ratio	25%	22	Defensive Pace	30.71	21
Pass, ahead 2H	35%	31	Shotgun/Pistol	73%	3	Second Level Sacks	38.2%	3	DB Blitz	16%	1	Go for it on 4th	1.64	4

Continuing the discussion of Cleveland's base defense tendency from earlier in the chapter: Cleveland had 245 snaps where their base defense was matched up against 11 personnel. Only the Panthers and Rams joined them above 100. To put it another way, roughly one-sixth of all 11-versus-base snaps in the NFL were played by the Browns defense. ☞ In a case of Gregg

Williams doing his Gregg Williams thing, the Browns blitzed much more often than in 2016, going from average to near the top of the league. They sent a defensive back blitz twice as often as the year before, a big reason why so many of their sacks came from second-level defenders. ☜ In 2016, the Browns led the league with 25 percent of passes going to running backs. This went up to 26 percent in 2017, but the Browns dropped to seventh, because seven different teams threw to running backs more than the No. 1 team of 2016. ☜ Cleveland threw to the right side on a league-leading 47 percent of passes and threw deep (16-plus yards) on a league-leading 26 percent of passes. ☜ The young Browns defense had problems tackling, tied for 29th with 144 broken tackles.

Passing

Player	DYAR	DVOA	Plays	NtYds	Avg	YAC	C%	TD	Int
D.Kizer*	-756	-34.5%	514	2679	5.2	5.5	53.8%	11	20
K.Hogan*	-120	-32.4%	82	484	5.9	4.8	62.7%	4	5
C.Kessler*	-98	-66.4%	30	82	2.7	6.4	50.0%	0	1
T.Taylor	121	-7.0%	467	2540	5.4	4.8	62.7%	14	4
D.Stanton	-75	-18.3%	166	850	5.1	3.8	49.7%	6	5

Rushing

Player	DYAR	DVOA	Plays	Yds	Avg	TD	Fum	Suc
I.Crowell*	46	-2.9%	205	851	4.2	2	1	40%
D.Johnson	90	15.7%	81	344	4.2	4	1	53%
D.Kizer*	32	-3.7%	74	408	5.5	5	3	-
K.Hogan*	27	45.5%	10	71	7.1	0	0	-
M.Dayes	-4	-24.7%	5	13	2.6	0	0	20%
C.Hyde	12	-7.4%	239	940	3.9	8	2	44%
T.Taylor	110	20.8%	69	436	6.3	4	1	-

Receiving

Player	DYAR	DVOA	Plays	Ctch	Yds	Y/C	YAC	TD	C%
R.Louis	-50	-23.0%	61	27	357	13.2	3.0	0	44%
C.Coleman	-41	-21.5%	58	23	305	13.3	1.1	2	40%
R.Higgins	-41	-23.1%	51	28	316	11.3	5.3	2	55%
J.Gordon	16	-7.8%	42	18	335	18.6	6.8	1	43%
K.Britt*	-11	-16.6%	38	18	233	12.9	4.7	2	47%
K.Williams*	-21	-25.1%	18	9	84	9.3	1.7	0	50%
B.Treggs*	-36	-40.3%	18	5	79	15.8	0.6	0	28%
S.Coates*	-16	-32.5%	11	6	70	11.7	2.7	0	55%
J.Landry	98	-4.9%	161	112	987	8.8	4.4	9	70%
D.Njoku	-10	-9.7%	60	32	386	12.1	4.7	4	53%
S.DeValve	-15	-11.5%	58	33	395	12.0	5.2	1	57%
D.Fells	48	21.9%	26	17	177	10.4	7.2	3	65%
D.Johnson	110	6.7%	94	75	697	9.3	8.6	3	80%
I.Crowell*	-52	-35.9%	43	29	184	6.3	6.9	0	67%
C.Hyde	-43	-22.4%	89	60	350	5.8	5.4	0	67%

Offensive Line

Player	Pos	Age	GS	Snaps	Pen	Sk	Pass	Run	Player	Pos	Age	GS	Snaps	Pen	Sk	Pass	Run
Kevin Zeitler	RG	28	16/16	1069	3	3.5	16	8	Spencer Drango	LT	26	16/10	607	0	8.5	33	6
Joel Bitonio	LG	27	16/16	1069	0	4.0	15	10	Joe Thomas*	LT	34	7/7	465	1	1.0	1	1
JC Tretter	C	27	16/16	1069	2	1.0	8	8	Chris Hubbard	RT	27	16/10	781	3	4.5	17	7
Shon Coleman	RT	27	16/16	1045	14	6.5	26	10	Greg Robinson	LT	26	6/6	394	5	2.0	6	2

Year	Yards	ALY	Rank	Power	Rank	Stuff	Rank	2nd Lev	Rank	Open Field	Rank	Sacks	ASR	Rank	Press	Rank	F-Start	Cont.
2015	3.75	3.61	29	65%	17	26%	31	0.98	30	0.78	14	53	8.1%	26	33.7%	31	23	35
2016	4.82	3.73	28	71%	7	22%	27	1.40	2	1.36	1	66	10.6%	32	30.5%	28	20	23
2017	4.15	4.09	14	74%	4	19%	11	1.23	8	0.75	15	50	7.6%	22	32.9%	24	11	39

2017 ALY by direction:	Left End: 4.86 (7)	Left Tackle: 5.14 (4)	Mid/Guard: 4.43 (7)	Right Tackle: 2.24 (31)	Right End: 1.75 (32)

Joe Thomas' ruptured triceps was the end of an era in Cleveland, ending a streak of 10,363 snaps that is believed to be the longest in NFL history ("believed" because snap data doesn't exist for most of the 20th century). The change at the left tackle position without Thomas was pretty obvious. Among the 33 left tackles with at least 400 snaps last year, Joe Thomas had the most snaps per blown block, and replacement Spencer Drango had the fewest. Drango also tied for the league lead by giving up 8.5 sacks. ☜ When John Dorsey made a number of moves for offensive linemen this offseason, the most important had to be replacing Thomas, right? Wrong. The biggest free-agent contract was a five-year, $37.5 million deal ($18 million guaranteed) for ex-Steelers utility lineman Chris Hubbard, who has started 14 games over the last two seasons. He's penciled in at right tackle. ☜ So if Dorsey didn't replace Thomas in free agency, did he do it on draft day? It's hard to tell. The Browns selected Austin Corbett with the first pick of the second round. Corbett was a four-year starter at Nevada who mostly played left tackle, but he shines with toughness and technique over athleticism and most scouts saw him as a guard in the NFL. He had an impressive Senior Bowl week, where he was lining up in practices at every position *except* left tackle. But left tackle would seem to be where he fits here, because the three interior linemen (Joel Bitonio, JC Tretter, and Kevin Zeitler) are all signed to big contracts. ☜ Nonetheless, the expected starter at left tackle for Opening Day is last year's right tackle, Shon Coleman. This doesn't augur well for the Browns offense. Scouting reports on Coleman call him a far more accomplished run-blocker than pass-blocker but notice that the Browns were horrible running to the right side of the field. Coleman was also 26th among right tackles in snaps per blown block and ranked third in the league with 14 penalties (including declined).

Defensive Front Seven

Defensive Line	Age	Pos	G	Snaps	Plays	TmPct	Rk	Stop	Dfts	BTkl	Runs	St%	Rk	RuYd	Rk	Sack	Hit	Hur	Dsrpt
						Overall						**vs. Run**				**Pass Rush**			
Trevon Coley	24	DT	15	659	42	5.2%	35	31	14	5	34	71%	68	2.2	47	2.0	2	8.0	2
Danny Shelton*	25	DT	14	471	34	4.6%	53	30	6	8	33	88%	8	1.6	23	0.0	1	6.5	1
Larry Ogunjobi	24	DT	14	303	32	4.3%	--	25	11	0	29	79%	--	0.8	--	1.0	3	4.5	0
Jamie Meder	27	DT	10	179	13	2.4%	--	11	2	0	12	83%	--	1.5	--	0.0	1	2.0	0

Edge Rushers	Age	Pos	G	Snaps	Plays	TmPct	Rk	Stop	Dfts	BTkl	Runs	St%	Rk	RuYd	Rk	Sack	Hit	Hur	Dsrpt
						Overall						**vs. Run**				**Pass Rush**			
Carl Nassib	25	DE	16	646	36	4.2%	62	33	13	4	26	88%	9	1.7	25	3.0	5	18.0	4
Myles Garrett	23	DE	11	520	30	5.1%	44	25	13	3	21	76%	43	1.2	15	7.0	13	28.5	1
Emmanuel Ogbah	25	DE	10	462	35	6.6%	23	32	12	4	24	88%	13	0.8	9	4.0	3	14.0	6
Nate Orchard	25	DE	16	433	24	2.8%	88	17	5	5	17	76%	42	1.9	33	2.0	5	10.5	0
Chris Smith	26	DE	16	403	28	3.2%	--	20	13	3	16	69%	--	2.9	--	3.0	6	12.0	3

Linebackers	Age	Pos	G	Snaps	Plays	TmPct	Rk	Stop	Dfts	BTkl	Runs	St%	Rk	RuYd	Rk	Sack	Hit	Hur	Tgts	Suc%	Rk	AdjYd	Rk	PD	Int
						Overall						**vs. Run**				**Pass Rush**			**vs. Pass**					
Christian Kirksey	26	OLB	16	1072	143	16.7%	10	82	31	16	65	68%	21	3.4	30	3.5	3	15.0	54	47%	47	6.8	40	3	0
Joe Schobert	25	MLB	16	1072	146	17.1%	7	81	22	26	99	63%	41	4.1	65	3.0	4	11.0	31	49%	40	7.7	60	2	1
James Burgess	24	OLB	14	650	73	9.8%	66	38	21	9	39	64%	38	2.2	6	4.0	4	11.5	16	36%	72	7.4	52	2	0
Jamie Collins	28	OLB	6	330	34	10.6%	59	24	9	9	19	89%	1	0.9	1	1.0	2	2.0	17	45%	--	7.7	--	2	1
Mychal Kendricks	28	OLB	15	612	78	10.9%	55	48	15	8	38	74%	11	2.3	7	2.0	4	6.5	31	65%	4	5.2	12	6	0

Year	Yards	ALY	Rank	Power	Rank	Stuff	Rank	2nd Level	Rank	Open Field	Rank	Sacks	ASR	Rank	Press	Rank
2015	4.57	4.73	30	70%	24	17%	28	1.27	28	0.86	20	29	5.8%	25	23.6%	27
2016	4.50	4.85	32	61%	12	15%	30	1.25	22	0.69	14	26	5.7%	21	23.7%	28
2017	3.35	3.27	2	56%	8	30%	1	1.08	12	0.60	8	34	6.5%	17	29.6%	21
2017 ALY by direction:		Left End: 3.05 (4)			Left Tackle: 3.14 (7)			Mid/Guard: 3.49 (2)			Right Tackle: 3.04 (7)			Right End: 2.08 (3)		

Myles Garrett's 28.5 hurries in 11 games work out to 41.5 in a full season, which would have put Garrett 13th in the league. Not bad for a rookie. ☞ Emmanuel Ogbah was supposed to be a one-dimensional pass-rusher coming out of Oklahoma State, but in the NFL he has really developed his ability to set the edge on running plays. ☞ Gregg Williams ran a lot of stunts and slants to get Garrett and/or Ogbah into the backfield. He also moved Garrett inside on some plays. ☞ Third-round rookie Chad Thomas (Miami) is another athletic and versatile defensive lineman who can play on the edge or be moved inside on passing downs. He's going to need a lot of work on his technique, especially his hands, to be successful in the NFL. Thomas is also a talented musician who plays nine instruments and produced beats for the last Rick Ross album under the name "Major Nine." ☞ Second-year tackle Larry Ogunjobi has an explosive first step; his breakout rookie season was one of the reasons the Browns felt they could deal nose tackle Danny Shelton to the Patriots. ☞ Only two players in the NFL last season played 100 percent of their team's defensive snaps, and both were in Cleveland: middle linebacker Joe Schobert and weakside linebacker Christian Kirksey. ☞ Kirksey has developed into one of the league's unsung playmakers. He tied for third in the NFL with 31 defeats last year, and those were not mostly plays rung up when opponents were running out the clock late in games. Seventeen of his defeats were tackles or tipped passes to prevent third-down conversions. ☞ The Eagles cut Mychal Kendricks for cap relief, but he certainly didn't look like he was in decline last year. For a guy considered limited as a two-down run-stuffer, Kendricks was pretty good against the pass in 2017. ☞ A concussion followed by an MCL tear limited Jamie Collins to just six games last season, and his play in those six games was somewhat disappointing. There's some thought that signing Kendricks will allow the Browns to use Collins more as a pass-rusher, where hopefully he can create the same kind of havoc he specialized in when he was in New England.

Defensive Secondary

Secondary	Age	Pos	G	Snaps	Plays	TmPct	Rk	Stop	Dfts	BTkl	Runs	St%	Rk	RuYd	Rk	Tgts	Tgt%	Rk	Dist	Suc%	Rk	AdjYd	Rk	PD	Int
						Overall						vs. Run					vs. Pass								
Jamar Taylor*	28	CB	16	967	72	8.4%	41	31	10	12	18	39%	51	5.8	36	73	17.0%	19	11.2	48%	58	9.8	78	12	0
Jason McCourty*	31	CB	14	903	78	10.4%	10	39	15	3	9	56%	23	8.3	66	71	17.7%	23	11.6	52%	38	7.2	33	14	3
Jabrill Peppers	23	FS	13	809	59	8.5%	60	13	4	9	28	25%	66	10.4	71	22	6.2%	8	11.7	36%	75	13.0	74	3	1
Derrick Kindred	25	SS	14	691	61	8.2%	65	31	22	10	31	61%	8	3.5	2	23	7.5%	17	11.3	41%	69	9.4	54	4	1
Briean Boddy-Calhoun	25	CB	13	535	42	6.1%	--	16	7	8	11	27%	--	8.0	--	27	11.2%	--	9.4	42%	--	6.6	--	5	0
Michael Jordan	26	CB	15	211	20	2.5%	--	7	4	5	5	0%	--	6.0	--	17	18.2%	--	10.5	59%	--	6.3	--	3	0
T.J. Carrie	28	CB	16	1024	93	11.4%	3	40	18	8	22	41%	46	5.8	35	69	15.3%	12	10.7	49%	52	8.0	49	9	0
Damarious Randall	26	CB	14	721	56	7.6%	56	29	14	5	19	58%	17	5.0	20	45	16.2%	14	12.2	53%	31	6.9	29	9	4
Terrance Mitchell	26	CB	15	706	70	9.2%	29	24	13	2	16	19%	77	7.7	62	93	35.4%	78	15.0	49%	48	9.3	73	19	4
E.J. Gaines	26	CB	11	654	68	11.3%	4	32	12	5	15	47%	38	6.9	55	52	22.1%	52	8.9	53%	30	5.3	2	8	1

Year	Pass D Rank	vs. #1 WR	Rk	vs. #2 WR	Rk	vs. Other WR	Rk	WR Wide	Rk	WR Slot	Rk	vs. TE	Rk	vs. RB	Rk
2015	27	4.2%	19	8.7%	21	28.9%	31	--	--	--	--	-1.7%	17	16.1%	28
2016	29	14.9%	30	6.0%	23	-4.5%	10	5.1%	22	10.6%	20	39.7%	32	3.5%	20
2017	26	22.0%	29	-7.5%	12	-6.4%	13	10.8%	27	1.4%	14	27.8%	32	24.9%	30

There are so many new bodies here that everyone's going to have to wear name tags. Jabrill Peppers is wearing one too, but you'll need to use binoculars to read it. ☞ Actually, it looks like we can retire our "Jabrill Peppers is far away" jokes thanks to the trade for former Green Bay first-round pick Damarious Randall. Randall will be moving from cornerback back to his college position of free safety, which in turn moves Peppers closer to the line of scrimmage as the strong safety and theoretically moves Derrick Kindred to the bench. ☞ Or, perhaps the Browns will take this opportunity to develop a three-safety package, getting away from all that base defense they played last year by using Kindred in a "moneybacker" role. Kindred had an excellent second season, leading all safeties with 22 defeats. Fifteen of those were run defeats and 13 of the 15 were on tackles at or behind the line of scrimmage, so Kindred certainly was spending plenty of time down as an extra defender in the box last year. ☞ With Jamar Taylor traded to Arizona and Jason McCourty to New England, it's possible that the top Browns' four cornerbacks will all be new to the team in 2018. The No. 1 will be the No. 4 overall selection in the draft, Denzel Ward out of Ohio State. Ward is almost everything you want out of a No. 1 cornerback—physical, athletic, aggressive, with strong ball skills and a 4.32 40. At 5-foot-11, 183 pounds, the only thing he doesn't have is the size to take on big receivers such as 6-foot-4 division rival A.J. Green. Good thing Antonio Brown is only 5-foot-10. ☞ Based on contract size, the starting cornerback opposite Ward should be T.J. Carrie, signed away from Oakland on a four-year, $31 million deal. But Carrie has never really been a regular outside corner, playing some safety early in his career and mostly lining up in the slot last season. Opponents avoided Carrie last year, but mostly because Sean Smith and David Amerson were so combustible. ☞ A more likely scenario might have Carrie starting and then moving inside for E.J. Gaines in nickel. Gaines signed a one-year, $4 million deal. Gaines had a very strong rookie season under Gregg Williams for the 2014 Rams and was quietly strong for the Bills last year as well. ☞ The fourth cornerback is either holdover Briean Boddy-Calhoun or free-agent signing Terrance Mitchell, who was often tested deep as a fill-in for Steven Nelson with last year's Chiefs.

Special Teams

Year	DVOA	Rank	FG/XP	Rank	Net Kick	Rank	Kick Ret	Rank	Net Punt	Rank	Punt Ret	Rank	Hidden	Rank
2015	0.7%	15	-0.3	16	1.4	11	-4.0	25	-2.4	20	8.7	3	-2.6	18
2016	-2.5%	26	-4.5	23	3.3	9	-6.6	28	-1.4	18	-3.6	23	4.5	9
2017	-5.1%	27	-3.5	21	-6.0	28	2.1	9	-11.5	29	-6.8	30	-4.8	21

Rookie kicker Zane Gonzalez was a bit of a disappointment, connecting on just 15 of his 20 field goal attempts. He was better on kickoffs, where he had positive gross kickoff value but was let down by Cleveland's coverage. The Browns allowed 7.5 estimated points of field position on kick returns; only Tampa Bay was worse. ☞ Brandon Colquitt was in the same boat, to a lesser degree. After three years below average, he improved to rank sixth in gross punt value. Yet Cleveland's net value on punts was near the bottom of the league. ☞ Matt Dayes is the best all-around special-teamer on the Browns, responsible for their good rating on kick returns and second on the team in special teams tackles. ☞ Jabrill Peppers' poor rating returning punts (he had 30 of Cleveland's 38 returns) comes in large part from the fact that he couldn't hold onto the ball. Peppers muffed three punts and fumbled two others in the middle of a return. The other problem was his propensity to go nowhere, or worse, backwards. He tied for the league lead with 11 returns that had zero (seven) or negative (four) yardage.

Dallas Cowboys

2017 Record: 9-7	Total DVOA: 5.4% (13th)	2018 Mean Projection: 9.1 wins	On the Clock (0-4): 4%
Pythagorean Wins: 8.6 (15th)	Offense: 6.7% (10th)	Postseason Odds: 52.1%	Mediocrity (5-7): 22%
Snap-Weighted Age: 25.9 (30th)	Defense: 5.9% (25th)	Super Bowl Odds: 10.0%	Playoff Contender (8-10): 43%
Average Opponent: 0.1% (15th)	Special Teams: 4.6% (7th)	Proj. Avg. Opponent: 0.0% (18th)	Super Bowl Contender (11+): 30%

2017: The suspended running back got the headlines, but the injured tackle torpedoed the season.

2018: The talent is undeniable, but the cap management is horrendous.

For many, many years, the Dallas Cowboys lived life like a college kid signing up for every credit card that would take them. They asked themselves what was in their wallet, never left home without it, and found it was everywhere they wanted to be. They were so enamored with their cashback bonuses and airline points, they never asked what this spending spree would lead to down the road. Which brings us to the present day, when they should be investing in their future, and instead have to deal with massive annual fees and a twenty percent APR.

Yes, it's austerity time in Dallas. After a half-decade of answering every financial question with "we'll worry about this later," the bills have come due. That's not going to torpedo their entire season—we actually rate them as slight favorites to win the NFC East—but it could mean the difference between a short playoff run and a championship parade.

How did we get to this point? The steps on this journey began in March of 2013 when the Cowboys signed quarterback Tony Romo to a massive contract extension, one that would theoretically last through the 2019 NFL season. The deal offered Dallas some short-term financial relief, lowering Romo's cap hit by about $5 million that season, but it included enormous payouts down the line—up to $108 million, with $55 million guaranteed. Just two years later, the Cowboys had to restructure that deal to cut Romo's $27 million 2015 cap hit nearly in half. In the process, however, they raised his cap hit in each of the next four years. The Cowboys made similar moves with the contracts of Tyron Smith in 2016 and 2017, and Travis Frederick in 2017, shuffling debts around from one year to the next.

The Cowboys also paid heavily for some personnel moves that simply didn't work out. They signed Cedric Thornton to a four-year, $18 million deal in 2016, then cut him after one year and zero starts. Nolan Carroll signed a three-year, $10 million deal in free agency last year, played in two games, then was cut in October. Most recently, Dez Bryant was released three years after signing a five-year contract with $45 million guaranteed in the summer of 2015. (In a vacuum, the Bryant release made sense. He had produced only four 100-yard games since signing his extension and was no longer worth the financial or emotional turmoil he was causing to the franchise. The timing of the move, however, was bizarre. Bryant wasn't released until April 14, long after free agency had begun, so any potential replacement would have signed elsewhere. Some speculated that Bryant was cut so Dallas could use his cap space to trade for Earl Thomas during the draft, but obviously that never happened.)

As a result of all this can-kicking and roster-purging, the Cowboys go into 2018 with more than $24 million in dead money, second-most in the league behind the Buffalo Bills. That includes a charge of nearly $9 million for Romo, who last won a start for Dallas in Week 11 of 2015. The two biggest cap hits among Dallas fantasy position players this year belong to Romo and Bryant, neither of whom wear the star anymore.

This would all be bad news for any club, but it's particularly bad news for Dallas because it means they are letting the NFL's most precious commodity—a good quarterback on a rookie deal—go to waste. A year ago, the Eagles had Carson Wentz on a cap hit of barely $6 million, so they went on a spending spree. They added LeGarrette Blount, Alshon Jeffery, Timmy Jernigan, Chris Long, and even a backup to Wentz in Nick Foles, each of whom made major contributions to a Super Bowl championship team. Jared Goff's cap numbers have been similar to Wentz's, and so the Rams have been stockpiling talent for two years now, acquiring Robert Woods and Andrew Whitworth in 2017 and Brandin Cooks, Ndamukong Suh, Marcus Peters, and Aqib Talib this year.

The Cowboys? Even though Dak Prescott's cap hit is less than $800,000—not even 15 percent that of Goff or Wentz—they couldn't make nearly as big a splash because of all that dead money. Oh, they added some veterans here and there this year. A journeyman pass-rusher on his third-team in three seasons. A utility lineman who couldn't nail down a starting spot in four years in New England. A trio of wide receivers, none of whom made the top 100 players in catches last year. And that's about it. These are not the kind of moves that typically lead to postseason glory. Aside from rookie linebacker Leighton Vander Esch, a first-round draft pick out of Boise State, it's hard to find a starter in Dallas who is more talented than the man he replaced in last year's lineup.

Right about now, you're probably looking back to the table at the top of this page and wondering how we can be so negative about Dallas' roster management, yet so positive about their chances to return to the playoffs this season. There's a simple explanation: for most of the past two years, the Cow-

2018 Cowboys Schedule

Week	Opp.	Week	Opp.	Week	Opp.
1	at CAR	7	at WAS	13	NO (Thu.)
2	NYG	8	BYE	14	PHI
3	at SEA	9	TEN (Mon.)	15	at IND
4	DET	10	at PHI	16	TB
5	at HOU	11	at ATL	17	at NYG
6	JAX	12	WAS (Thu.)		

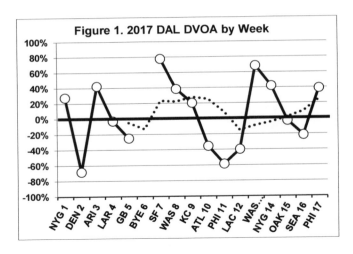

Figure 1. 2017 DAL DVOA by Week

boys' roster has been *really* good. From Week 1 in 2017 through Week 9 last year, they went 18-6. They were second overall in DVOA in 2016, and eighth through Week 9 in 2017. And then things went south. Starting with a three-game losing streak in which they were outscored 92-22, they went 4-4 down the stretch, ranking 19th in DVOA after Week 10. The biggest decline was on offense, where their DVOA fell from 17.5% in the first half of the year to -5.4% in the second. That decline can largely be explained by the absence of two players, both of whom should be available for 16 games this year.

After exploding on the scene as a rookie in 2016, Ezekiel Elliott spent most of his sophomore season battling an on-again, off-again suspension concerning domestic violence accusations. We don't have the time or space to get into details here but suffice to say that after a lot of lawyers made a lot of money, Elliott was suspended for six games starting in Week 10. That coincided with Dallas' three-game skid, and there's no question that the Cowboys offense played worse when Elliott was away from the team. They averaged 24.4 points with Elliott in the lineup, but just 18.3 without him. Their offensive DVOA was 13.2% with Elliott, -5.5% without him. However, most of that decline was due to a bevy of mistakes in the passing game. Dallas' rushing attack was nearly as effective in the games Elliott missed (10.6% DVOA, 121.3 yards per game) as in the games he played (12.5% DVOA, 144.2 yards per game).

The bigger issue for Dallas was the absence of left tackle Tyron Smith. Watching Smith play football can be a surreal experience—it's hard to believe what you're seeing is real and not computer-generated. All NFL linemen are big and powerful, but Smith's frame is abnormally lean, almost wiry compared to his peers. It's hard to comprehend a man with so much mass and none of it wasted. He has the power to drive defenders into the turf or swat them out of his path. He's somehow nimble enough to deal with any speed rusher. And when he gets moving and obliterates defenders downfield, his own running backs sometimes struggle to keep up with his 320-pound frame. "I don't think he's a person," Tampa Bay defensive tackle Gerald McCoy once said about Smith to NFL Network. "He might be some sort of mutant or metahuman or demigod or something."

Unfortunately for Dallas, Smith has missed plenty of time with knee, back, and groin injuries in the past two seasons. (At least, that's what the Cowboys would have you believe; it's just as plausible that he has been off fighting Thanos with the rest of the Avengers.) And when he has been gone, Dallas has

been a completely different football team. Smith missed three games entirely last year, and only played three offensive snaps against Seattle before leaving with an injury. Dallas won just one of those four games, never scoring more than 12 points, with a total offensive DVOA of -22.0%. In the 12 games when Smith saw significant snaps, Dallas went 8-4, averaged 26.7 points per game, and had an offensive DVOA of 15.4%. In particular, when Smith left, so did Prescott's pass protection. The Cowboys surrendered 15 sacks in 12 games with Smith, but 17 in four games without him. The Smith effect was less dramatic in 2016, but still notable. With their star tackle, Dallas went 11-2 with an offensive DVOA of 22.0%; without him, 2-1 and 11.4%.

Hopefully for Dallas, Smith will be on the field more often in 2018—he told the team's website in April that he was "feeling great" and "in the best shape I've been in a while," and that he had been visiting a rehab facility in California to work on his stretching. Should he go down again, though, the Cowboys at least have better options than they did last year, when Chaz Green and Byron Bell were forced into action and looked in no way capable of playing in the NFL. Cameron Fleming wasn't able to stick in New England, but he has started at least five games in each of the past three seasons. Second-round draft pick Connor Williams could also be an option if Smith is unavailable.

So there's reason to believe that the Cowboys will rebound on offense this fall, and there's plenty to like on defense too, especially in the front seven. The star, obviously, is fifth-year edge rusher Demarcus Lawrence. He had 14.5 sacks last season, most by any Cowboys player since 2011, and most ever by anyone not named DeMarcus Ware. According to Sports Info Solutions, he led the league with 57.0 pass pressures. And he's only 26 this year. On the other side, Taco Charlton only had 3.0 sacks as a part-timer in his rookie season. There's plenty of reason to expect more playing time and more production in Year 2.

The Cowboys also boast one of the NFL's best linebacker corps. It remains to be seen just how they'll all fit on the field together, but Sean Lee is just one year removed from an All-Pro season, while Jaylon Smith should develop in his second year after a torn ACL. Vander Esch could start his career as a third linebacker behind those two, but he's got the skills and versatility to play all three downs and can fill any role that is needed.

That's enough to make Dallas a slight division favorite despite some obvious weaknesses at other positions. The Cowboys had no choice but to release Bryant, but that left them with a massive void at wide receiver—the quintet of Allen Hurns, Deonte Thompson, Terrance Williams, Cole Beasley, and third-round draftee Michael Gallup isn't going to scare anyone. Things are even more dire at tight end, where Jason Witten's surprise retirement left the Cowboys with a trio of veterans with a combined total of nine NFL catches, plus rookie fourth-rounder Dalton Schultz. The secondary also has plenty of questions, with Byron Jones' move back to corner being the solitary, unsatisfying answer. And this is where all that dead money really hurts the Cowboys. With more cash, they could have been the ones to sign an Allen Robinson or Sammy Watkins, or trade for someone like Marcus Peters or Aqib Talib.

It would be nice to say that Dallas has learned its lesson and will be more fiscally responsible going forward, but there's little sign that that is the case. The Cowboys once again restructured contracts this year to add debt down the road, redoing deals for Travis Frederick and La'el Collins. Even Witten agreed to restructure his deal before choosing to retire. In doing so, Witten actually takes up *more* of Dallas' cap this year than he would have otherwise, but then will come off the books in 2019. So in the long run, he might have done Dallas a favor. Then news broke during minicamp that four-time Pro Bowl guard Zack Martin had signed a six-year extension worth up to $84 million with $40 million guaranteed. The deal makes Martin the highest-paid guard in the league, and deservedly so. It also—you'll never guess—saves Dallas some cap space in the short term while eating up massive cap space in the future. Expect to read stories about Martin restructuring his deal in 2021.

Technically, Dallas has a lot of cap space in 2019—roughly $50.7 million after the Martin deal—but they are going to need a lot of that to re-sign their own players. That includes Lawrence, who will play in 2018 on a one-year franchise deal for more than $17 million. More pressing, Prescott will be eligible for a new deal after this season, and odds seem slim that he would be willing to play for a (relatively) paltry six-digit salary when he should have the leverage to force Dallas into a deal that averages $20-some million per year. And a few years down the line, Elliott will be eligible for his own mega-deal—it's not too early to start planning for that signing.

Amidst all this bean-counting, it's fair to question what the future holds for Jason Garrett. The team has basically been in win-now mode since Garrett was hired in 2010, and in that time he has won 67 games, but made the playoffs just twice. Since the AFL merger, only two other coaches had so many wins but so few playoff appearances: Forrest Gregg and Sam Wyche. Dallas coaches had their share of strategic missteps in 2017, notably failing to get Chaz Green any help as Adrian Clayborn abused him for 6.0 sacks in Week 10. There was also the remarkable sequence against Seattle in Elliott's return to the lineup when Dallas managed to turn first-and-goal at the 3 into a short run, a pass and a holding penalty, a sack, a short completion, and finally a missed field goal. The play calling was so bad that fans in Arlington started to boo as soon as Prescott lined up in shotgun on second down from the 2, not even waiting for the ball to be snapped. Technically, offensive coordinator Scott Linehan called those plays, but Garrett must ultimately take responsibility for a game plan that took the ball out of Elliott's hands in a spot where he could have been most effective.

While Garrett, Linehan, and defensive coordinator Rod Marinelli all remain with the team, there is a critical new face on the coaching staff: Kris Richard, whose formal title is "Passing Game Coordinator/Defensive Backs." Richard played cornerback for Pete Carroll at USC around the turn of the century, then played 39 games for the Seahawks and 49ers before beginning his coaching career. He started working with Seattle's defensive backs in 2010 and was the Seahawks' defensive coordinator from 2015 until he was fired this offseason. In short, he had a front-row seat to the rise and fall of the Legion of Boom. It's highly unlikely that he'll get similar results out of this secondary, but if he can, then there's no limit to what this team can accomplish.

In the end, it will be the players on the field who determine the Cowboys' fate, and we're not sure they have the right players in the right places to win a championship. The Cowboys have largely squandered the money they've saved by getting Prescott on his rookie deal, and the championship window that created will shut after this year. If they don't learn some budget management in a hurry, they could squander the rest of his career as well.

Vincent Verhei

2017 Cowboys Stats by Week

Wk	vs.	W-L	PF	PA	YDF	YDA	TO	Total	Off	Def	ST
1	NYG	W	19	3	392	233	+1	28%	10%	-9%	9%
2	at DEN	L	17	42	268	380	0	-68%	-36%	42%	10%
3	at ARI	W	28	17	273	332	0	43%	42%	9%	10%
4	LAR	L	30	35	440	412	-2	-3%	27%	15%	-14%
5	GB	L	31	35	408	342	-2	-25%	11%	37%	1%
6	BYE										
7	at SF	W	40	10	501	290	+3	78%	58%	-17%	4%
8	at WAS	W	33	19	307	285	+2	39%	7%	-19%	13%
9	KC	W	28	17	375	323	+1	20%	30%	9%	0%
10	at ATL	L	7	27	233	336	-1	-35%	-27%	5%	-4%
11	PHI	L	9	37	225	383	-4	-58%	-53%	29%	24%
12	LAC	L	6	28	247	515	-2	-40%	-1%	46%	8%
13	WAS	W	38	14	275	280	+4	68%	8%	-31%	29%
14	at NYG	W	30	10	454	330	+2	42%	45%	-2%	-5%
15	at OAK	W	20	17	330	293	-1	-3%	-9%	-1%	4%
16	SEA	L	12	21	282	136	-3	-21%	-22%	-11%	-10%
17	at PHI	W	6	0	301	219	+1	39%	17%	-27%	-5%

Trends and Splits

	Offense	Rank	Defense	Rank
Total DVOA	6.5%	10	5.8%	25
Unadjusted VOA	5.6%	10	6.0%	21
Weighted Trend	3.9%	12	0.1%	15
Variance	9.4%	23	5.8%	19
Average Opponent	-1.2%	11	0.5%	14
Passing	5.4%	18	12.9%	18
Rushing	11.8%	2	-4.1%	22
First Down	4.1%	12	-7.3%	9
Second Down	3.4%	11	15.6%	32
Third Down	16.3%	6	14.7%	24
First Half	5.9%	14	-3.2%	11
Second Half	7.2%	11	14.1%	30
Red Zone	16.2%	9	14.4%	29
Late and Close	18.0%	3	8.7%	24

Five-Year Performance

Year	W-L	Pyth W	Est W	PF	PA	TO	Total	Rk	Off	Rk	Def	Rk	ST	Rk	Off AGL	Rk	Def AGL	Rk	Off Age	Rk	Def Age	Rk	ST Age	Rk
2013	8-8	8.2	8.2	439	432	+8	-2.8%	17	7.5%	11	13.8%	30	3.4%	8	16.4	5	50.2	29	26.5	22	26.1	24	25.3	28
2014	12-4	10.8	10.3	467	352	+6	13.7%	6	16.8%	4	4.0%	22	0.9%	13	9.3	2	66.8	28	26.4	25	26.1	25	25.6	29
2015	4-12	5.2	4.4	275	374	-22	-18.0%	27	-15.6%	31	4.1%	19	1.8%	11	24.1	11	27.6	15	26.9	15	25.9	29	25.7	23
2016	13-3	11	11.8	421	306	+5	20.3%	2	19.9%	3	1.1%	18	1.6%	9	37.5	20	33.1	17	26.6	20	26.3	20	26.1	16
2017	9-7	8.6	8.9	354	332	-1	5.3%	13	6.5%	10	5.8%	25	4.6%	7	7.8	2	29.4	12	26.8	18	25.1	30	25.9	15

2017 Performance Based on Most Common Personnel Groups

DAL Offense					DAL Offense vs. Opponents					DAL Defense					DAL Defense vs. Opponents			
Pers	Freq	Yds	DVOA	Run%	Pers	Freq	Yds	DVOA	Run%	Pers	Freq	Yds	DVOA		Pers	Freq	Yds	DVOA
11	61%	5.5	6.5%	33%	Base	34%	5.6	10.5%	64%	Base	25%	4.7	4.6%		11	69%	5.4	3.9%
12	15%	6.3	15.3%	52%	Nickel	44%	4.7	-2.3%	35%	Nickel	55%	5.3	5.8%		12	18%	5.6	25.0%
13	9%	4.5	4.6%	78%	Dime+	19%	7.2	27.8%	21%	Dime+	20%	5.9	6.0%		13	3%	4.6	-0.3%
22	6%	5.7	13.7%	89%	Goal Line	1%	0.7	28.6%	100%						21	3%	4.7	-33.5%
21	4%	4.3	-25.4%	53%	Big	2%	3.5	13.2%	76%						10	2%	4.6	14.8%
01	3%	6.8	48.2%	4%											22	2%	3.8	16.8%

Strategic Tendencies

Run/Pass		Rk	Formation		Rk	Pass Rush		Rk	Secondary		Rk	Strategy		Rk
Runs, first half	41%	7	Form: Single Back	79%	15	Rush 3	9.6%	9	4 DB	25%	27	Play action	22%	19
Runs, first down	58%	2	Form: Empty Back	9%	9	Rush 4	69.6%	12	5 DB	55%	17	Avg Box (Off)	6.32	9
Runs, second-long	33%	17	Pers: 3+ WR	64%	15	Rush 5	18.2%	18	6+ DB	20%	9	Avg Box (Def)	5.98	31
Runs, power sit.	73%	2	Pers: 2+ TE/6+ OL	32%	13	Rush 6+	2.5%	28	CB by Sides	76%	20	Offensive Pace	30.98	19
Runs, behind 2H	32%	5	Pers: 6+ OL	2%	31	Int DL Sacks	25.0%	14	S/CB Cover Ratio	34%	8	Defensive Pace	31.34	27
Pass, ahead 2H	38%	28	Shotgun/Pistol	53%	21	Second Level Sacks	7.9%	31	DB Blitz	11%	12	Go for it on 4th	1.25	8

One big change for the Cowboys' offense last season: they dropped from an otherworldly 8.2-yard average on passes thrown behind the line of scrimmage to a much more mundane 5.8 yards. ☜ The Cowboys ranked 30th in offensive DVOA if they were losing by more than a touchdown, but seventh in offensive DVOA in all other situations. ☞ Dak Prescott was one of four quarterbacks last year big-blitzed (six or more pass-rushers) more than 8.0 percent of the time, along with Jacoby Brissett, Carson Wentz, and Brian Hoyer. The Dallas offense was excellent against the blitz last year, with 6.2 yards per play and 2.0% team DVOA against a regular pass rush but 7.2 yards per play and 36.1% DVOA against five or more pass-rushers. ☞ Dallas recovered only two of eight fumbles on offense. ☞ The Dallas defense was seventh against the run in the red zone but 30th against the pass in the red zone. ☞ The Dallas defense had the highest pressure rate in the league on first and third downs but ranked 25th on second downs.

Passing

Player	DYAR	DVOA	Plays	NtYds	Avg	YAC	C%	TD	Int
D.Prescott	375	-0.2%	520	3139	6.0	4.4	63.1%	22	13

Receiving

Player	DYAR	DVOA	Plays	Ctch	Yds	Y/C	YAC	TD	C%
D.Bryant*	-9	-13.5%	132	69	838	12.1	3.9	6	52%
T.Williams	67	-1.9%	78	53	568	10.7	4.4	0	68%
C.Beasley	-22	-16.9%	63	36	314	8.7	3.4	4	57%
B.Butler*	135	61.6%	23	15	319	21.3	1.9	3	65%
N.Brown	-14	-29.9%	9	4	33	8.3	5.5	0	44%
R.Switzer*	11	7.1%	7	6	41	6.8	3.0	0	86%
A.Hurns	149	20.6%	56	39	484	12.4	4.5	2	70%
D.Thompson	57	1.4%	51	27	430	15.9	3.0	1	53%
T.Austin	-99	-68.2%	24	15	56	3.7	6.4	0	63%
J.Witten*	40	-0.4%	87	63	560	8.9	1.7	5	72%
J.Hanna*	18	23.5%	9	4	88	22.0	7.3	1	44%
E.Elliott	5	-11.2%	38	26	249	9.6	10.0	2	68%
R.Smith	50	26.9%	23	19	202	10.6	9.3	1	83%
A.Morris*	-2	-18.4%	9	7	45	6.4	6.3	0	78%
J.Olawale	5	-2.3%	7	6	33	5.5	4.0	0	86%

Rushing

Player	DYAR	DVOA	Plays	Yds	Avg	TD	Fum	Suc
E.Elliott	205	11.1%	242	983	4.1	7	1	57%
A.Morris*	79	8.4%	115	547	4.8	1	0	51%
R.Smith	81	23.9%	55	232	4.2	4	0	60%
D.Prescott	167	46.9%	51	363	7.1	6	0	-
T.Austin	97	-6.0%	59	270	4.6	1	0	-
J.Olawale	27	47.9%	9	43	4.8	1	1	78%

Offensive Line

Player	Pos	Age	GS	Snaps	Pen	Sk	Pass	Run	Player	Pos	Age	GS	Snaps	Pen	Sk	Pass	Run
Travis Frederick	C	27	16/16	1068	2	0.0	7	15	Tyron Smith	LT	28	13/13	759	8	2.0	10	9
La'el Collins	RT	25	16/16	1068	4	4.0	26	8	Chaz Green	LG/LT	26	14/4	256	3	4.0	10	0
Zack Martin	RG	26	16/16	1021	0	2.0	9	9	Byron Bell*	OT	28	12/2	245	5	5.0	13	2
Jonathan Cooper*	LG	28	13/13	838	6	0.5	13	7	Cameron Fleming	RT	26	12/6	369	2	2.0	6	3

Year	Yards	ALY	Rank	Power	Rank	Stuff	Rank	2nd Lev	Rank	Open Field	Rank	Sacks	ASR	Rank	Press	Rank	F-Start	Cont.
2015	4.53	4.48	6	66%	15	17%	4	1.21	12	1.01	8	33	6.6%	19	20.9%	5	26	34
2016	4.68	4.63	4	73%	3	15%	5	1.36	5	0.98	8	28	5.6%	13	28.8%	24	14	37
2017	4.26	4.66	4	77%	3	17%	4	1.16	16	0.67	19	32	6.4%	15	31.9%	21	10	30

2017 ALY by direction: Left End: 5.61 (4)   Left Tackle: 4.88 (6)   Mid/Guard: 4.55 (4)   Right Tackle: 4.19 (12)   Right End: 4.89 (4)

Tyron Smith wasn't the only Cowboys lineman to miss time in 2017. While center Travis Frederick and right tackle La'el Collins each played every offensive snap of the season, Jonathan Cooper spent three weeks on the bench before taking over for Chaz Green at left guard, while right guard Zack Martin was knocked out of the Thanksgiving game against the Chargers with a concussion. In the eight games when Smith, Cooper, and Martin each played at least half of the offense's snaps, Dallas' line was dominant, right up there with the best lines in the league.

Dallas Offensive Line with Five Healthy Starters, 2017

Weeks	Yards	ALY	Rank	Power	Rank	Stuff	Rank	2nd Lev	Rank	Open Field	Rank	Sacks	ASR	Rank	Press	Rank
4-9, 13-15	4.94	4.99	2	74%	5	15%	2	1.27	8	0.78	14	9	4.0%	2	30.9%	12

At least one position will have a new starter in 2018, perhaps two. Cooper signed with San Francisco in free agency, and Dallas opened OTAs with second-round draftee Connor Williams in Cooper's old spot at left guard. Williams was a first-team All-America left tackle for the Texas Longhorns as a sophomore in 2016 but suffered multiple knee injuries and a drop in production in 2017. His arms measured only 33 inches at the combine, so many projected him as a guard in the NFL, and that appears to be where he will begin his career in Dallas. ✆ Should Williams struggle at guard, the Cowboys could move Collins back to that spot, where he played in his first two seasons. Collins has said he would prefer to stay at tackle, but also says he could play anywhere except center. ✆ Two veteran free agents could also see the starting lineup. Cam Fleming never started more than seven games in any of his four seasons in New England, but he has experience at both tackle spots and would likely step in at right tackle should Collins move to guard. Interior lineman Marcus Martin was a healthy scratch in all 16 games for Cleveland last year, but he's still only 25 and was a third-round pick four years ago. ✆ One more new face along the Cowboys line: Paul Alexander, who will coach the unit after holding the same position for the Cincinnati Bengals for the past 23 seasons. Alexander helped turn Willie Anderson and Andrew Whitworth into All-Pros and coached 11 other linemen who started at least 60 games over that timeframe. In his 2011 book *Perform*, Alexander talked about training with a concert pianist and how there are 437,514 possible ways for 11 defenders to fill eight gaps in an offensive front. This suggests a disciplined, systematic approach to the game, signs of a deep thinker. He also wrote about evaluating linemen by the way they pour ketchup out of the bottle, so he may be insane as well.

Defensive Front Seven

Defensive Line	Age	Pos	G	Snaps	Plays	TmPct	Rk	Stop	Dfts	BTkl	Runs	St%	Rk	RuYd	Rk	Sack	Hit	Hur	Dsrpt
						Overall						**vs. Run**				**Pass Rush**			
Maliek Collins	23	DT	16	688	22	2.7%	84	15	8	3	16	75%	57	1.9	33	2.5	8	22.5	0
David Irving	25	DT	8	337	28	7.0%	11	25	15	1	14	79%	38	1.7	28	7.0	3	11.5	5
Richard Ash	26	DT	10	234	16	3.2%	--	13	3	0	14	86%	--	1.6	--	0.0	2	4.0	2
Brian Price	24	DT	8	149	9	2.2%	--	4	0	1	8	38%	--	3.6	--	0.0	1	4.0	1

Edge Rushers	Age	Pos	G	Snaps	Plays	TmPct	Rk	Stop	Dfts	BTkl	Runs	St%	Rk	RuYd	Rk	Sack	Hit	Hur	Dsrpt
						Overall						**vs. Run**				**Pass Rush**			
Demarcus Lawrence	26	DE	16	704	59	7.3%	15	48	23	14	37	76%	44	2.1	39	14.5	14	55.0	5
Tyrone Crawford	29	DE	16	630	29	3.6%	72	26	9	4	21	86%	14	2.1	40	4.0	8	28.0	2
Taco Charlton	24	DE	16	401	19	2.4%	--	12	6	1	12	50%	--	4.1	--	3.0	4	12.0	1
Benson Mayowa*	27	DE	14	383	21	3.0%	85	15	6	1	15	73%	52	1.4	19	1.0	5	11.0	0
Kony Ealy	27	OLB	15	452	23	3.0%	83	21	8	4	12	83%	21	2.3	49	1.0	3	23.5	9

Linebackers	Age	Pos	G	Snaps	Plays	TmPct	Rk	Stop	Dfts	BTkl	Runs	St%	Rk	RuYd	Rk	Sack	Hit	Hur	Tgts	Suc%	Rk	AdjYd	Rk	PD	Int
						Overall						**vs. Run**				**Pass Rush**				**vs. Pass**					
Sean Lee	32	OLB	11	625	102	18.4%	3	50	20	8	51	59%	59	2.5	10	0.0	2	3.5	37	47%	52	6.2	26	1	1
Jaylon Smith	23	MLB	16	578	83	10.3%	62	39	7	9	52	52%	77	4.5	76	1.0	2	4.5	30	55%	24	5.6	18	2	0
Anthony Hitchens*	26	MLB	12	547	85	14.1%	26	43	13	5	50	66%	29	3.0	22	0.0	2	5.0	27	23%	75	7.3	50	1	0
Damien Wilson	25	OLB	16	325	30	3.7%	--	15	4	3	16	63%	--	3.5	--	1.0	3	6.0	11	21%	--	16.1	--	1	0

Year	Yards	ALY	Rank	Power	Rank	Stuff	Rank	2nd Level	Rank	Open Field	Rank	Sacks	ASR	Rank	Press	Rank
2015	4.31	4.26	21	76%	30	21%	17	1.35	29	0.74	14	31	6.5%	16	24.6%	22
2016	4.02	4.01	13	69%	25	22%	8	1.28	25	0.58	10	36	6.5%	12	23.1%	29
2017	4.12	3.95	11	83%	32	22%	11	1.25	25	0.76	20	38	6.7%	14	35.5%	2

2017 ALY by direction: Left End: 3.13 (8)   Left Tackle: 4.01 (17)   Mid/Guard: 3.99 (11)   Right Tackle: 4.73 (29)   Right End: 3.89 (15)

Linebacker was the position that saw the most turmoil in 2017 and that will see the most turnover in 2018. A nagging hamstring injury knocked Sean Lee out of several games, but when healthy, he was going to start and play most of the contest, usually 90 percent or more of the team's defensive snaps. A tibial plateau fracture suffered in the preseason knocked Anthony Hitchens out for the first four games, but he started every game from that point forward. Jaylon Smith, coming off a redshirt rookie year in 2016, started each of the season's first five games but just once after that. He was far from benched, however, often playing more than half the team's snaps and almost always getting more playing time than Damien Wilson. Wilson played in every game and started nine times but was on the field more than half the time in just one game. ✆ With Hitchens now in Kansas City, look for Lee and Smith to be constants in 2018, with rookie first-rounder Leighton Vander Esch making frequent cameos too. One would think the long-term plan is for Vander Esch to eventually replace Lee, who has two more years left on his deal. ✆ The rest of the front seven is pretty straightforward, as there were few significant departures or arrivals at end or tackle over the offseason. Kony Ealy replaces Benson Mayowa as the fourth edge rusher in the rotation. That should be an upgrade—Ealy has 15.0 sacks in four NFL seasons, while Mayowa has 9.0 in five—but it's not likely to make a significant impact. ✆ Dallas only had three stops on "power" (i.e. short-yardage) runs all season, a trio of first-and-goal plays against the Falcons, Giants, and Seahawks. On the one hand, Dallas' last-place ranking in power downs is something of a small-sample size fluke—they only faced 22 power runs all season, fewer than anyone except Minnesota (also 22) and Philadelphia (20). On the other hand, the Cowboys have ranked 20th or worse against power runs every year since 2012, and nine times in the past 11 seasons, so this has been a weakness for Dallas for a long time.

Defensive Secondary

Secondary	Age	Pos	G	Snaps	Plays	TmPct	Rk	Stop	Dfts	BTkl	Runs	St%	Rk	RuYd	Rk	Tgts	Tgt%	Rk	Dist	Suc%	Rk	AdjYd	Rk	PD	Int
						Overall						vs. Run					vs. Pass								
Byron Jones	26	FS/CB	16	910	74	9.2%	53	33	20	7	34	41%	47	10.1	67	49	13.4%	63	8.9	59%	18	5.8	11	6	1
Jeff Heath	27	SS	15	881	66	8.7%	56	12	6	11	29	17%	73	10.1	66	28	8.0%	24	9.6	36%	74	9.9	60	5	3
Anthony Brown	25	CB	16	845	65	8.1%	46	24	9	8	15	27%	68	6.0	42	77	22.8%	57	12.8	46%	72	7.9	45	13	2
Jourdan Lewis	23	CB	15	748	64	8.5%	40	27	12	6	15	40%	47	6.1	45	64	21.5%	47	11.5	46%	67	6.7	21	9	1
Orlando Scandrick*	31	CB	11	614	39	7.0%	62	19	7	8	13	69%	8	3.6	6	45	18.4%	27	10.1	50%	47	8.7	64	4	0
Xavier Woods	23	FS/SS	16	550	43	5.3%	71	12	6	8	12	25%	66	10.3	70	28	12.8%	60	10.1	43%	65	8.3	40	3	1
Chidobe Awuzie	23	CB	10	312	32	6.4%	--	17	6	2	7	43%	--	6.1	--	26	20.9%	--	9.5	46%	--	5.1	--	6	1
Kavon Frazier	25	SS	15	221	26	3.4%	--	12	2	5	13	69%	--	2.7	--	10	10.8%	--	6.7	26%	--	8.7	--	0	0

Year	Pass D Rank	vs. #1 WR	Rk	vs. #2 WR	Rk	vs. Other WR	Rk	WR Wide	Rk	WR Slot	Rk	vs. TE	Rk	vs. RB	Rk
2015	17	19.6%	30	-11.5%	10	9.0%	21	--	--	--	--	-25.0%	3	8.2%	20
2016	19	-5.0%	9	3.1%	18	-11.9%	8	-19.0%	5	13.2%	22	31.2%	30	-2.2%	18
2017	18	10.7%	21	13.5%	23	-14.9%	8	-15.2%	6	18.8%	25	12.5%	25	14.5%	28

Hey, kids! Did you like the 2017 Dallas secondary? The one that blew second-half leads against Derek Carr, Carson Palmer, Jared Goff, Alex Smith, and Aaron Rodgers (twice!)? The squad that gave up four touchdowns to *Trevor Siemian?* The unit whose defining moment came when they missed a bevy of tackles and gave up a 56-yard touchdown to Tyreek Hill on a screen pass on the last play of the first half? Well, good, because by and large it'll be the same group defending opposing receivers in 2018. Orlando Scandrick left for Washington, Byron Jones is moving back to corner to replace him, and Xavier Woods is becoming a full-time starter in his second season. That's it for changes. ☞ It's kind of stunning that the Cowboys failed to sign a veteran defensive back or find one in the draft, but they did employ the crap-against-the-wall methodology afterwards, signing five undrafted free agent corners and safeties. Kris Richard favored big defensive backs in Seattle, and likely had a say in those signings—all five stand at least 6-foot-1. (One is even named Kam, though Mr. Kelly from San Diego State isn't likely to make the same kind of impact in Big D that Mr. Chancellor did in the Pacific Northwest.) It's a marked change from last year, when the Cowboys' biggest defensive back, Jeff Heath, stood just 6-foot-1 himself.

Special Teams

Year	DVOA	Rank	FG/XP	Rank	Net Kick	Rank	Kick Ret	Rank	Net Punt	Rank	Punt Ret	Rank	Hidden	Rank
2015	1.8%	11	8.6	3	-6.2	29	-0.1	14	13.3	4	-6.7	30	5.8	8
2016	1.6%	9	4.5	7	1.0	13	-2.0	20	6.1	7	-1.8	19	10.2	5
2017	4.6%	7	-7.0	26	4.5	8	2.3	8	16.9	2	6.2	3	14.8	2

Dan Bailey has converted a higher percentage of his field goal attempts than any kicker in league history outside Justin Tucker, but he had his worst year in 2017. Through six games, he was a perfect 7-of-7 of field goals and 16-of-16 on extra points. He injured his groin against San Francisco and missed four weeks, with Mike Nugent going a respectable 7-of-9 on field goals in his absence. Bailey returned in Week 13 against the Giants, but maybe he shouldn't have—he went just 8-of-13 on field goals and 10-of-12 on extra points to finish the year. Presumably a healthy Bailey will return to form in 2018. He's average at best on kickoffs, but you'll take that when he's nailing close to 90 percent of his place kicks. ☞ At punter, Chris Jones is not historically great like Bailey, but he's more than adequate; after finishing seventh in gross punt value in 2015, he dipped to 16th in 2016, but rebounded last year to eighth. Jones is excellent at denying opponents a chance to return his punts. ☞ Dallas was better than average in both punt and kickoff coverage. You'd hope so, considering that starting defensive backs Byron Jones and Jeff Heath were among their leaders in coverage tackles. ☞ It's not clear who's going to return kickoffs and punts for the Cowboys this year. Ryan Switzer did a fine job of both last season, but he was traded to the Raiders. Presumably the punt return job will fall to Tavon Austin, who had a few highlights and a lot of follies in that role with the Rams—he's as fast as a racehorse, but not nearly as good at catching footballs. Deonte Thompson, signed away from the Bills in free agency, has averaged 24.8 yards on 82 kickoff returns in his career, and led the league with 35 kickoff returns with the Bears in 2016. Cornerback Jourdan Lewis did not return a kickoff as a rookie last season, but he was second in the Big Ten with a 25.2-yard average with the Michigan Wolverines in 2015.

Denver Broncos

2017 Record: 5-11	**Total DVOA:** -20.9% (29th)	**2018 Mean Projection:** 7.0 wins	**On the Clock (0-4):** 17%
Pythagorean Wins: 5.4 (28th)	**Offense:** -18.9% (31st)	**Postseason Odds:** 26.2%	**Mediocrity (5-7):** 42%
Snap-Weighted Age: 26.6 (11th)	**Defense:** -5.5% (10th)	**Super Bowl Odds:** 2.2%	**Playoff Contender (8-10):** 32%
Average Opponent: -1.9% (22nd)	**Special Teams:** -7.4% (30th)	**Proj. Avg. Opponent:** 0.1% (16th)	**Super Bowl Contender (11+):** 10%

2017: The best quarterback on the payroll was the overmatched team president.

2018: The best quarterback on the payroll is the journeyman being overpaid by the overmatched team president.

The Broncos have a John Elway problem. The public at large doesn't realize it, because Elway's Broncos reached Super Bowl XLVIII and won Super Bowl 50, granting Elway at least five years of residual genius cred on top of his All-Time Champion cred. It's not talked about much in Denver, where criticizing Elway aloud can get you burned as a heretic (and worse, your team media credential revoked). But it only takes a little bit of careful Broncos observation to discover that Elway's draft record over the last five years has been miserable, he meddles too imperiously and impetuously with the team's coaching staff, and he's prone to wishful thinking at the quarterback position.

The underlying cause of the Elway problem is unclear. Some observers feel that Elway himself is a shrewd, aggressive decision-maker who is too easily swayed by the ever-changing cast of courtiers in his inner circle. That theory sounds iffy; shrewd, aggressive decision-makers, by definition, are not easily swayed. Others paint Elway as a Jerry Jones who happened to have once been a Hall of Fame quarterback: a go-with-the-gut type who is always looking to hit the next Peyton Manning/Von Miller grand slam. In this scenario, trusted advisors like Tom Heckert, Matt Russell, and Gary Kubiak are always jostling to grab the helm whenever Elway gets distracted.

No matter what goes on behind closed doors in team headquarters, it's clear that the Broncos began collapsing the moment Peyton Manning retired. They masked the issues with great defense and some good luck in 2016 (just as they did when Manning aged from 38 to 68 in the course of 2014 and 2015), but they were reduced to dust during last season's eight-game losing streak, when the bottom fell out of the quarterback situation and the defense proved that it was no longer capable of generating wins all by itself.

The Elway problem remains the underlying cause of the team's many, problems: the president of the Broncos still doesn't realize just how bad things really are, which only makes things worse. Elway's team entered the offseason with one of the weakest offensive depth charts in the NFL and a still-strong but transitioning defense. But the Broncos convinced themselves that they were just a quarterback away from returning to the Super Bowl. Then they compromised on the quarterback.

You know the brushstrokes of the Case Keenum Saga: undrafted 2012 rookie turned career third-stringer for the Texans and Rams; signed for peanuts by the Vikings to back up Sam Bradford last offseason; became the Vikings starter in Week 2 after the traditional Bradford injury; got hot for a stacked team and threw for 22 touchdowns in 11 regular-season victories; hit the free-agent market and the jackpot at age 30 as a probationary Franchise-Caliber Quarterback.

Keenum led the NFL in passing DVOA last year, so he's not just your typical Ryan Fitzpatrick-type journeyman getting rich off a very temporary sugar rush. And there are enough Brad Johnson/Rich Gannon success stories scattered around NFL history to make it plausible that Keenum's late-career ascendency is more than just a one-year, situation-assisted fluke.

That said, Vikings coach Mike Zimmer spent almost every press conference last year throwing ice water on Keenum expectations and talking about his lucky "horseshoe." The Vikings then spent $80 million upgrading to Kirk Cousins when they could have retained Keenum for far less money. So the coaches and execs who worked with Keenum every day in practice last year decided that he wasn't the quarterback to lead their well-constructed roster over that last hurdle. But Elway decided that Keenum was just the man to bring the Broncos back to contention, or at least Elway convinced himself of that after comparing Cousins' contract expectations to the Broncos' cap situation.

Charting data and research for Football Outsiders by John Kinsley[1] provide some clues about why the Vikings were so lukewarm about Keenum. Kinsley graded Keenum with the worst deep-ball efficiency score in the NFL, based on Keenum's completion rates and the catchability of his passes at various distances beyond the 15-yard range. Most strikingly, Kinsley found that Keenum benefited from 15 "inaccurate completions," off-target long throws that became big gains thanks to great catches by Vikings receivers. Most quarterbacks only enjoyed a handful of inaccurate completions. Keenum's success, including his high DVOA, was probably the product of accurate short passing, the great situation the

---

1 https://bit.ly/2k69tpP

70

2018 Broncos Schedule

Week	Opp.	Week	Opp.	Week	Opp.
1	SEA	7	at ARI (Thu.)	13	at CIN
2	OAK	8	at KC	14	at SF
3	at BAL	9	HOU	15	CLE (Sat.)
4	KC (Mon.)	10	BYE	16	at OAK (Mon.)
5	at NYJ	11	at LAC	17	LAC
6	LAR	12	PIT		

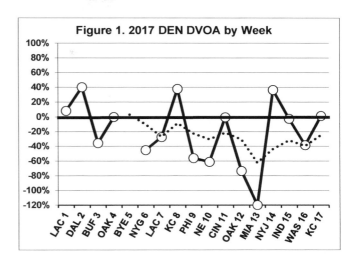

Figure 1. 2017 DEN DVOA by Week

Vikings put him in, and about one big boost per game from Adam Thielen or Stefon Diggs.

Keenum's two-year, $36 million contract at least positioned the Broncos to hedge their bets by drafting a potential challenger/quarterback of the future, but they didn't do so. Elway, echoing a sentiment that was stated by many of the team's veterans, wanted both an experienced quarterback and an off-season without uncertainty or controversies at the position. What team doesn't want both of those things? But handing an unchallenged starting job to a 30-year-old third-stringer coming off a career year may not be the wisest way to ensure peace and prosperity at the position.

Keenum's backups happen to be a pair of Elway pet projects on semi-permanent scholarships: future e-gaming superstar Paxton Lynch and Jim Kelly's couchsurfer nephew Chad. Choosing not to draft another quarterback may have had as much to do with Elway face-saving (demoting Lynch to third string or cutting him would confirm his bust status) as with the team's confidence in Keenum.

Instead of insulating the quarterback position, the Broncos selected Bradley Chubb with the fifth overall pick. Elway then spent a surprising amount of additional draft capital on defense, taking cornerback Isaac Yiadom in the third round and linebacker Josey Jewell in the fourth. The investments were necessary because the Broncos defense slipped from first to 10th in DVOA last year, and the team traded Aqib Talib in the offseason after losing a host of key defensive starters (Demarcus Ware, Malik Jackson, T.J. Ward, Danny Trevathan, Sylvester Williams) since the Super Bowl run, with scant reinforcements.

If you are scoring at home: Elway convinced himself that the Broncos were a second-tier quarterback away from contention because of their great defense, then spent his first-round pick and other resources to make the Broncos defense great again. It's an impressive floor display of mental gymnastics. Even if Chubb and Von Miller prove to be as formidable as Miller and Ware, this is not the Broncos defense you remember from Super Bowl 50, and Elway tacitly acknowledges as such while simultaneously building an offense designed to complement a championship-caliber defense.

With their leftover mid-round picks, the Broncos tried to address a potentially critical problem: lack of depth and playmaking ability at the skill positions. The Broncos ranked dead last in the NFL last season with just three pass plays of 40-plus yards and tied for 20th in the league with just eight runs of 20-plus yards.

Terrible quarterbacking was part of the problem, but the quarterbacks weren't helped by the fact that the Broncos were still trying to make Virgil Green (another Elway project) a thing at tight end, sinking costs in Bennie Fowler and Cody Latimer (have we mentioned how hard it is for the Broncos to part with Elway's high draft picks?) as third and fourth receivers, and convincing themselves that Jamaal Charles was still a spry third-down scatback. Opponents could double-cover Demaryius Thomas and Emmanuel Sanders (when he was healthy) and dare the Broncos quarterbacks to beat them with secondary weapons, knowing full well that the Broncos quarterbacks weren't good enough to beat them with primary weapons.

Rookie arrivals on offense include: polarizing receiver Courtland Sutton, who looked like an improved version of Demaryius Thomas against weaker opposition but vanished whenever SMU played anyone good; Royce Freeman, Oregon's all-time leading running back who spent his final two seasons coping with nagging injuries and the Ducks' scheme change; DaeSean Hamilton, a fine prospect as a slot receiver; and tight end Tony Fumagalli, who will back up Jake Butt if everything went according to plan during Butt's medical redshirt year.

The draft class looks solid enough on both sides of the ball, at least on paper: Chubb was a low-risk selection, Freeman was a BackCAST darling, and there are no wacky reaches. But it is hard to get enthusiastic about a Broncos draft class, given Elway's recent track record. Recent drafts have been full of major busts: Lynch (almost certainly), Latimer, Ty Sambrailo, Shane Ray (whom Chubb will replace), Brock Osweiler, Ronnie Hillman, Montee Ball, Michael Schofield. The Broncos haven't truly hit on a late-round pick since Jackson and Trevathan in 2012. There's even a sameness to the pedigrees of this year's class—Oregon's all-time leading rusher, Penn State's all-time leading receiver, the award-laden Jewell—that suggests the Broncos are just grabbing guys with big names and numbers without thinking too hard about deep scouting details.

At least Green, Fowler, Latimer, and Charles are no longer cluttering up the depth chart. But yeoman running back C.J.

Anderson is also gone after carrying the Broncos offense in a handful of victories. Freeman, Butt, and others will be thrust into immediate roles, ready or not. Meanwhile, the offensive line that allowed 52 sacks last year returns more or less as is; the Broncos hope to solve the line's problem by solving other problems, even though they aren't coming up with great solutions for the other problems.

The Broncos' draft record would look better if the coaching staff did a better job of developing what talent was available. Elway addressed the development problem in January by firing a brace of Broncos-lifer assistants that head coach Vance Joseph chose (read: was required) to retain when he came aboard. New arrivals include some offensive assistants scooped up from John Fox's Bears staff, including running backs coach Curtis Modkins and receivers coach Zach Azzani, and longtime Giants assistant Mike Sullivan as quarterbacks coach. Old-school West Coast Offense guru Bill Musgrave remains the offensive coordinator after replacing Mike McCoy in the middle of last season.

The names are unimportant and the pedigrees unspectacular: all that matters is the muddled sense of who is hiring whom. Joseph has not yet put his stamp on the roster or his staff, which is not surprising when Kubiak, his predecessor, is one of Elway's closest confidantes and high draft picks are granted eternal redshirt status. And there's a stench of egomania to the coaching changes: Elway's draft acumen simply cannot be the problem, so it must be the position coaches.

Ultimately, none of Elway's offseason moves are compatible with any of the other moves. Keenum isn't capable of elevating a team without a strong supporting cast. The defense is no longer stout enough to overcome a mediocre offense. The Broncos did little to prepare for the future but didn't do enough to serve the present. Their roster looks like it was assembled by a committee trying to compromise on a set of conflicting goals, or by a distracted executive flitting from idea to idea.

The 2018 Broncos will be a better team than the 2017 Broncos, because Keenum is better than last year's three-headed monstrosity, Chubb will reinvigorate the pass rush, and the skill-position rookies are an almost certain upgrade over Elway's Wonder Pets. But Elway sunk a ton of effort and resources into making the Broncos very good on defense and non-embarrassing on offense. They are an expensive, veteran .500 team.

But here's the kicker: they think they're contenders.

Elway's greatest strength as a top exec—perhaps his only strength—is that he's John Freakin' Elway. His reputation helped the Broncos recruit Peyton Manning. It insulates him from unpopular decisions, like parting ways with Tim Tebow. Elway's name recognition and stature can help the Broncos lure the best coaches and free agents if he chooses to do so. Right now, his status as NFL royalty and a local demigod is buying him time to correct several years of bad decisions.

If he doesn't turn things around, even Elway's name won't be able to save him. In fact, the NFL could catch on quickly to his shortcomings. Then he'll be the one with an Elway problem, one that can't be solved with coach firings, scattershot drafts, or journeyman quarterback signings.

Mike Tanier

2017 Broncos Stats by Week

Wk	vs.	W-L	PF	PA	YDF	YDA	TO	Total	Off	Def	ST
1	LAC	W	24	21	321	249	-1	8%	-2%	-9%	1%
2	DAL	W	42	17	380	268	0	40%	34%	-28%	-22%
3	at BUF	L	16	26	366	272	-2	-36%	-28%	10%	2%
4	OAK	W	16	10	298	254	+1	0%	-7%	-27%	-20%
5	BYE										
6	NYG	L	10	23	412	266	-3	-45%	-23%	4%	-19%
7	at LAC	L	0	21	251	242	-3	-27%	-35%	-23%	-16%
8	at KC	L	19	29	364	276	-3	38%	-4%	-49%	-7%
9	at PHI	L	23	51	226	419	-1	-56%	-46%	25%	15%
10	NE	L	16	41	339	396	-2	-61%	-6%	21%	-34%
11	CIN	L	17	20	341	190	-2	0%	-20%	-16%	3%
12	at OAK	L	14	21	216	348	0	-74%	-61%	13%	0%
13	at MIA	L	9	35	270	367	0	-124%	-94%	5%	-25%
14	NYJ	W	23	0	273	100	+2	36%	-21%	-57%	1%
15	at IND	W	25	13	462	228	-1	-3%	4%	-3%	-10%
16	at WAS	L	11	27	330	386	-1	-38%	-23%	18%	3%
17	KC	L	24	27	336	379	-1	2%	-4%	2%	7%

Trends and Splits

	Offense	Rank	Defense	Rank
Total DVOA	-19.0%	31	-5.3%	10
Unadjusted VOA	-15.3%	28	-5.2%	11
Weighted Trend	-25.4%	32	-2.3%	11
Variance	8.5%	21	5.9%	20
Average Opponent	4.1%	31	2.1%	7
Passing	-18.0%	31	8.2%	15
Rushing	-11.9%	22	-21.0%	3
First Down	-21.8%	30	3.4%	21
Second Down	-20.2%	30	-8.0%	6
Third Down	-12.2%	27	-16.4%	8
First Half	-20.9%	30	1.3%	16
Second Half	-16.7%	26	-12.1%	3
Red Zone	-37.4%	30	-2.8%	15
Late and Close	-17.2%	26	-21.0%	5

Five-Year Performance

Year	W-L	Pyth W	Est W	PF	PA	TO	Total	Rk	Off	Rk	Def	Rk	ST	Rk	Off AGL	Rk	Def AGL	Rk	Off Age	Rk	Def Age	Rk	ST Age	Rk
2013	13-3	11.7	14.1	606	399	0	32.7%	2	33.5%	1	-0.2%	15	-1.0%	21	37.8	19	45.8	26	27.9	3	26.3	18	26.8	5
2014	12-4	11.0	13.3	482	354	+5	29.5%	2	20.0%	3	-13.2%	4	-3.7%	27	11.7	4	25.2	6	28.6	2	25.7	31	25.6	27
2015	12-4	9.7	10.7	355	296	-4	17.7%	8	-8.7%	25	-25.8%	1	0.7%	14	42.9	22	13.8	2	28.3	2	26.5	19	25.6	26
2016	9-7	9.1	8.5	333	297	+2	3.7%	14	-12.3%	28	-18.3%	1	-2.3%	24	26.0	8	34.2	18	26.6	18	26.7	12	25.1	30
2017	5-11	5.4	5.6	289	382	-17	-21.1%	29	-19.0%	31	-5.3%	10	-7.4%	30	28.1	11	37.8	20	27.1	14	26.7	12	25.0	30

2017 Performance Based on Most Common Personnel Groups

DEN Offense					DEN Offense vs. Opponents					DEN Defense				DEN Defense vs. Opponents			
Pers	Freq	Yds	DVOA	Run%	Pers	Freq	Yds	DVOA	Run%	Pers	Freq	Yds	DVOA	Pers	Freq	Yds	DVOA
11	66%	5.1	-9.2%	28%	Base	29%	4.8	-17.6%	58%	Base	41%	4.4	-12.1%	11	54%	5.7	5.4%
12	15%	5.4	-10.5%	48%	Nickel	58%	4.9	-11.9%	31%	Nickel	27%	5.6	2.6%	12	29%	4.8	-4.5%
21	7%	5.5	-5.7%	66%	Dime+	12%	6.1	3.6%	18%	Dime+	30%	5.6	1.7%	21	7%	4.8	-4.9%
22	5%	3.5	-16.2%	82%	Goal Line	1%	0.7	-130.6%	83%	Goal Line	1%	0.2	-70.6%	13	4%	3.0	-54.5%
13	3%	2.8	-65.0%	62%	Big	0%	1.8	-72.9%	100%	Big	1%	1.8	94.1%	22	2%	0.8	-79.7%

Strategic Tendencies

Run/Pass		Rk	Formation		Rk	Pass Rush		Rk	Secondary		Rk	Strategy		Rk
Runs, first half	39%	17	Form: Single Back	79%	13	Rush 3	4.4%	24	4 DB	41%	5	Play action	24%	8
Runs, first down	48%	21	Form: Empty Back	5%	25	Rush 4	59.5%	23	5 DB	27%	32	Avg Box (Off)	6.14	25
Runs, second-long	35%	13	Pers: 3+ WR	68%	11	Rush 5	24.9%	8	6+ DB	30%	5	Avg Box (Def)	6.39	4
Runs, power sit.	56%	17	Pers: 2+ TE/6+ OL	25%	25	Rush 6+	11.2%	2	CB by Sides	86%	10	Offensive Pace	29.64	10
Runs, behind 2H	28%	15	Pers: 6+ OL	2%	27	Int DL Sacks	36.4%	5	S/CB Cover Ratio	36%	5	Defensive Pace	30.69	20
Pass, ahead 2H	42%	26	Shotgun/Pistol	65%	13	Second Level Sacks	18.2%	14	DB Blitz	7%	24	Go for it on 4th	1.01	16

The Broncos used five defensive backs nearly four times as often as they did the year before ... and still ranked dead last in frequency of nickel personnel. ☞ Denver opponents continue to eschew use of play-action fakes despite Denver's heavy pass rush. After finishing dead last in the NFL in 2015 and 2016, the Broncos were 31st in 2017, with opponents only using play-action on 18 percent of pass plays. Broncos opponents avoided play-action even though the Broncos ranked 31st in DVOA (51.4%) and 26th in yards per pass (8.1) allowed against play-action. It was the second straight year the Broncos were much worse against play-action than they were against passes without play-action. ☞ Denver continued to be a strong tackling defense. After leading the league with broken tackles on just 7.4 percent of plays in 2016, they ranked fifth with broken tackles on just 9.0 percent of plays in 2017. ☞ The Broncos were much better running from one-back sets (4.3 yards, -5.7% DVOA) than from two-back sets (3.3 yards, -36.1% DVOA). ☞ Denver benefited from a league-low 107 opponent penalties.

Passing

Player	DYAR	DVOA	Plays	NtYds	Avg	YAC	C%	TD	Int
T.Siemian*	-327	-24.6%	382	2063	5.4	4.9	59.0%	12	14
B.Osweiler*	-56	-16.2%	180	1018	5.7	5.3	56.5%	5	5
P.Lynch	-224	-76.3%	54	242	4.5	4.0	66.7%	2	3
C.Keenum	1293	28.1%	503	3403	6.8	5.6	67.6%	22	7

Rushing

Player	DYAR	DVOA	Plays	Yds	Avg	TD	Fum	Suc
C.J.Anderson*	16	-6.9%	245	1007	4.1	3	1	42%
D.Booker	-2	-9.2%	79	299	3.8	1	1	47%
J.Charles*	2	-7.9%	69	305	4.4	1	2	51%
T.Siemian*	1	-11.4%	24	133	5.5	1	1	-
B.Osweiler*	2	-8.5%	11	70	6.4	1	0	-
D.Henderson	-15	-50.6%	7	13	1.9	0	0	29%
A.Janovich	4	1.0%	6	12	2.0	1	0	67%
P.Lynch	5	16.5%	5	30	6.0	0	0	-
C.Keenum	76	58.3%	22	180	8.2	1	0	-

Receiving

Player	DYAR	DVOA	Plays	Ctch	Yds	Y/C	YAC	TD	C%
D.Thomas	146	0.2%	140	83	949	11.4	3.6	5	59%
E.Sanders	-40	-18.2%	91	46	565	12.3	3.6	2	51%
B.Fowler*	12	-9.8%	56	29	350	12.1	3.7	3	52%
C.Latimer*	88	21.9%	31	19	287	15.1	3.4	2	61%
J.Taylor	3	-10.9%	20	13	142	10.9	3.5	0	65%
I.McKenzie	-50	-66.8%	13	4	29	7.3	2.5	0	31%
A.J.Derby*	-16	-15.0%	31	19	224	11.8	3.9	2	61%
V.Green*	12	0.8%	22	14	191	13.6	6.6	1	64%
J.Heuerman	20	11.6%	18	9	142	15.8	7.0	2	50%
A.Traylor	17	9.6%	13	8	100	12.5	5.3	0	62%
C.J.Anderson*	1	-13.2%	40	28	224	8.0	7.7	1	70%
D.Booker	45	7.7%	38	30	277	9.2	7.8	0	79%
J.Charles*	-6	-18.5%	28	23	129	5.6	6.9	0	82%
A.Janovich	9	13.1%	6	4	35	8.8	6.0	0	67%

Offensive Line

Player	Pos	Age	GS	Snaps	Pen	Sk	Pass	Run	Player	Pos	Age	GS	Snaps	Pen	Sk	Pass	Run
Matt Paradis	C	29	16/16	1125	1	1.0	10	14	Allen Barbre*	LG/RT	34	16/4	550	7	3.0	11	5
Garett Bolles	LT	26	16/16	1104	15	7.0	28	6	Menelik Watson	RT	30	7/7	446	4	8.5	17	4
Max Garcia	LG	27	16/16	868	1	3.0	13	10	Connor McGovern	RG	25	15/5	418	2	1.5	8	7
Ronald Leary	RG	29	11/11	709	6	2.5	5	2	Donald Stephenson*	RT	30	7/4	303	2	3.0	18	6

Year	Yards	ALY	Rank	Power	Rank	Stuff	Rank	2nd Lev	Rank	Open Field	Rank	Sacks	ASR	Rank	Press	Rank	F-Start	Cont.
2015	4.33	4.07	17	61%	23	23%	23	1.24	3	0.93	9	39	5.8%	13	27.5%	22	11	32
2016	3.78	4.09	18	51%	29	21%	21	1.19	13	0.50	26	40	7.4%	27	24.6%	12	20	32
2017	4.03	4.31	9	65%	15	18%	7	1.11	18	0.51	26	52	9.1%	29	31.1%	16	17	28

2017 ALY by direction:	Left End: 3.32 (25)	Left Tackle: 4.77 (9)	Mid/Guard: 4.28 (10)	Right Tackle: 4.64 (6)	Right End: 4.03 (15)

The Broncos terrible quarterback play made evaluating their offensive line tricky last season. Paxton Lynch was a sack waiting to happen when he wasn't throwing a designed screen. Trevor Siemian grew more indecisive the more he played. Brock Osweiler was capable of getting rid of the ball to avoid sacks, but his inability to complete passes stagnated the whole offense. Lack of even replacement-level depth and playmaking ability at running back compounded the issue. Here's what can be said for certain: center Matt Paradis and guard Ron Leary were good, everyone else needs to get better. ☞ Garrett Bolles committed ten holding penalties in addition to his sacks allowed. John Elway stated at the start of OTAs that Bolles' priority for this season was to clean up his play, which presumably means fewer penalties; hopefully Bolles does not interpret that to mean that he should give up when beaten and allow Joey Bosa or Khalil Mack to hammer Case Keenum. Jared Veldheer was acquired in a trade with the Cardinals to solve the right tackle problem. Veldheer has suffered several injuries over the last two seasons and had some holding problems of his own (five fouls) last year. Manelik Watson, the previous oft-injured former Raiders tackle the Broncos signed, returns to compete for a backup role after a miserable 2017 season. ☞ Ronald Leary was excellent when healthy last year, ranking third at his position in snaps per blown block, but he missed the final five games of the season with a back injury. Leary also has a concussion history and dealt with knee inflammation early in the offseason. Leary played right guard last year so Max Garcia could allow pressure up the middle for 16 full games; as you may have noticed if you are reading carefully, recent Broncos draft picks get seventh chances, but even more recent draft picks like Connor McGovern and Sam Jones are in the pipeline, so Garcia's scholarship may be in jeopardy. Leary was a limited participant through most of the offseason, and it was unclear whether the Broncos planned to return him to left guard or keep moving him around to accommodate a less effective player.

Defensive Front Seven

Defensive Line	Age	Pos	G	Snaps	Plays	Overall TmPct	Rk	Stop	Dfts	BTkl	vs. Run Runs	St%	Rk	RuYd	Rk	Pass Rush Sack	Hit	Hur	Dsrpt
Adam Gotsis	26	DE	16	558	45	6.1%	22	39	7	4	36	83%	22	1.5	20	2.0	3	6.0	4
Shelby Harris	27	DE	16	516	37	5.0%	45	27	11	1	28	64%	78	2.6	69	5.5	5	9.0	2
Domata Peko	34	DT	14	461	37	5.7%	29	33	10	2	33	88%	8	1.7	26	1.0	1	3.5	0
Derek Wolfe	28	DE	11	459	31	6.1%	21	25	9	2	26	81%	30	1.8	31	2.0	4	8.5	0
Zach Kerr	28	DE	11	250	20	4.0%	--	17	4	2	18	83%	--	1.8	--	0.5	2	3.0	1
Clinton McDonald	31	DT	14	467	30	4.1%	61	20	8	3	19	53%	84	3.9	85	5.0	5	7.5	1

Edge Rushers	Age	Pos	G	Snaps	Plays	Overall TmPct	Rk	Stop	Dfts	BTkl	vs. Run Runs	St%	Rk	RuYd	Rk	Pass Rush Sack	Hit	Hur	Dsrpt
Von Miller	29	OLB	16	850	59	8.0%	11	49	25	4	42	81%	29	1.3	17	10.0	13	53.0	5
Shaquil Barrett	26	OLB	16	667	36	4.9%	51	27	10	7	25	84%	19	1.8	29	4.0	8	31.5	1
Shane Ray	25	OLB	8	354	16	4.3%	60	10	5	3	13	62%	86	1.5	20	1.0	3	10.0	0

Linebackers	Age	Pos	G	Snaps	Plays	Overall TmPct	Rk	Stop	Dfts	BTkl	vs. Run Runs	St%	Rk	RuYd	Rk	Pass Rush Sack	Hit	Hur	vs. Pass Tgts	Suc%	Rk	AdjYd	Rk	PD	Int
Brandon Marshall	29	ILB	16	912	110	14.9%	21	55	18	16	54	65%	32	3.9	56	3.0	2	7.5	51	41%	63	7.2	47	4	0
Todd Davis	26	ILB	14	522	82	12.7%	37	46	9	6	61	62%	44	3.5	37	1.0	0	3.5	23	45%	56	8.1	63	1	0

Year	Yards	ALY	Rank	Power	Rank	Stuff	Rank	2nd Level	Rank	Open Field	Rank	Sacks	ASR	Rank	Press	Rank
2015	3.07	3.35	3	83%	31	24%	5	0.73	1	0.37	2	52	8.1%	1	32.7%	1
2016	4.03	4.60	28	65%	20	11%	32	0.91	1	0.52	7	42	7.6%	2	32.2%	1
2017	3.44	3.37	4	45%	1	26%	3	0.91	3	0.60	9	33	6.9%	11	32.7%	7
2017 ALY by direction:		Left End: 3.19 (9)			Left Tackle: 3.30 (10)			Mid/Guard: 3.54 (3)			Right Tackle: 1.90 (1)			Right End: 3.94 (17)	

Finally, we get to say some good things about the Broncos! ☞ Von Miller finished second to Tank Lawrence in the NFL with 53 pass pressures last season. Our SackSEER projection system is lukewarm about Bradley Chubb—his sack-per-game rates and combine measurables were low for a top-five selection in the draft—but Chubb looks much better as a complementary pass-rusher to Miller than he would look on some team desperate to generate sacks. Chubb and Shaquil Barrett will share the field on obvious passing downs and compete for playing time in other situations; Barrett was more effective last year when he played more snaps, which could impact the rotation. ☞ Shane Ray suffered a wrist injury in OTAs and is likely to go the way of most Broncos high draft picks of the last five years. Ray started over Barrett when healthy late in the season, even though Barrett outplayed him. Again, you have read far enough into this chapter to figure out why. Oh wait, sorry, this is the *positive* Broncos section! ☞ The rest of the front seven is stout. Derek Wolfe is reportedly healthy after a scary-looking neck injury late last season. Domata Peko remains an excellent run-stuffer in a 40-snap role. Brandon Marshall is an effective three-down linebacker, though he was asked to do too much in coverage last year. Todd Davis is an excellent gap-plugger between the tackles. There's even depth: undrafted rookie Shelby Harris was a revelation last season, and fourth-round rookie Josey Jewell (Iowa) possesses a similar skillset to Davis.

Defensive Secondary

Secondary	Age	Pos	G	Snaps	Plays	Overall TmPct	Rk	Stop	Dfts	BTkl	vs. Run Runs	St%	Rk	RuYd	Rk	vs. Pass Tgts	Tgt%	Rk	Dist	Suc%	Rk	AdjYd	Rk	PD	Int
Darian Stewart	30	FS	16	891	68	9.2%	52	30	12	12	35	57%	12	4.9	20	33	7.8%	22	13.3	46%	59	10.4	67	5	3
Chris Harris	29	CB	16	872	47	6.4%	68	24	10	3	10	80%	5	4.1	11	60	14.4%	7	11.2	56%	16	7.7	40	7	2
Aqib Talib*	32	CB	15	752	37	5.4%	75	14	6	2	8	38%	53	7.5	61	45	12.5%	3	8.8	55%	21	5.4	3	8	1
Justin Simmons	25	SS	13	737	68	11.4%	20	28	17	7	35	46%	36	7.3	48	24	6.7%	12	11.0	53%	31	6.7	21	6	2
Bradley Roby	26	CB	16	677	59	8.0%	47	30	17	7	8	38%	53	5.9	39	67	20.7%	41	13.0	58%	10	5.7	4	17	1
Will Parks	24	SS	16	597	51	6.9%	70	30	13	9	23	74%	2	1.6	1	45	15.9%	71	8.5	46%	58	7.1	23	4	1

Year	Pass D Rank	vs. #1 WR	Rk	vs. #2 WR	Rk	vs. Other WR	Rk	WR Wide	Rk	WR Slot	Rk	vs. TE	Rk	vs. RB	Rk
2015	1	-20.7%	4	-22.1%	4	-28.0%	4	--	--	--	--	-12.0%	8	-33.4%	2
2016	1	-29.6%	2	-58.5%	1	-24.0%	4	-9.1%	11	-54.4%	1	-20.7%	5	-7.1%	15
2017	15	-33.6%	2	-13.3%	9	28.5%	30	-28.6%	3	-2.1%	12	19.8%	31	5.6%	19

The No Fly Zone enjoyed enviable health last season. Chris Harris, Darian Stewart, Bradley Roby, and the now-departed Aqib Talib were all available for nearly every worthwhile snap. Justin Simmons missed the final three games of the season with a high ankle sprain (suffered while celebrating a strip-sack) but was healthy when the Broncos were relevant and showed no lingering effects in OTAs. That good health creates a minor depth dilemma, however, now that Talib is gone. Broncos backups in the secondary rarely played last year (counting Roby as a starter, because that's what third cornerbacks are). The team added two well-known role players to improve their depth and flexibility, but one saw very limited action last year, and the other was out of the league. ☞ Harris is at his best when working out of the slot. Roby, one of the few recent Broncos draft picks to not take the midnight train to Bustville, has replaced Harris on the outside for 40 to 50 plays per game for four years and is ready for a slightly expanded role. Tramaine Brock, who was only active for a handful of Vikings games last year after bouncing between multiple training camps in the offseason, was reportedly pushing hard for the third cornerback role in the offseason. In the previous two seasons, Brock ranked 10th and 24th among cornerbacks in adjusted success rate, so he could be a vital addition if there's anything left in the tank. ☞ William Parks was a liability as a nickel safety and Simmons' late-season replacement last year. Su'a Cravens left USC as an ideal nickel safety specimen and could be the solution to one of the Broncos' few real defensive problems: a tendency to get burned underneath by slot receivers, tight ends, and backs. But Cravens, acquired from Washington in the offseason, is returning from an early retirement due to concussion issues. Cravens is healthy and hungry to return this year, by all accounts, which is great to hear. But his health status bears constant monitoring.

Special Teams

Year	DVOA	Rank	FG/XP	Rank	Net Kick	Rank	Kick Ret	Rank	Net Punt	Rank	Punt Ret	Rank	Hidden	Rank
2015	0.7%	14	-0.6	17	0.1	18	-2.2	22	4.9	7	1.3	14	-2.8	19
2016	-2.3%	24	1.6	12	-8.6	29	-0.9	14	3.3	11	-6.8	28	4.3	11
2017	-7.4%	30	-10.3	29	-9.8	31	-3.6	24	-8.8	26	-4.5	27	-2.6	15

Marquette King in five career games at Mile High: 39 punts, 50.0 gross yards per punt, 44.0 average net yards, and 16 kicks inside the 20. The 50-gross yards per punt mark for a single season has only been reached seven times: twice by Shane Lechler, once by Andy Lee, once each by Brandon Fields and Thomas Morstead in 2012, and the all-time record of 51.4 by Sammy Baugh in an era when early-down punting still happened and balls often rolled far away from the safeties tasked with returning them. King may not threaten any records this year in Denver, but he will be fun to watch. ☞ The Broncos are overloaded with return men, because the Broncos thought they were a Super Bowl contender for the last two years and kept drafting luxury items. Isaiah McKenzie is a 5-foot-7 junebug who was ineffective last year but will get another shot. Devontae Booker and De'Angelo Henderson are young players with return-man skills who did nothing with their trials last year. Undrafted rookie Philip Lindsay is a tiny all-purpose back with an ornery streak who could push for a roster spot as a returner. If Emmanuel Sanders is sent out to field punts again for the Broncos this year, something has gone very wrong. ☞ Kicker Brandon McManus has performed well under a variety of conditions, so there is no reason to panic over some missed chip shots last year. McManus' biggest issue, for fantasy gamers at least, is the fact that you cannot kick field goals if your offense can't get past midfield.

Detroit Lions

2017 Record: 9-7	**Total DVOA:** 5.6% (12th)	**2018 Mean Projection:** 7.8 wins	**On the Clock (0-4):** 11%
Pythagorean Wins: 8.9 (14th)	**Offense:** 4.5% (12th)	**Postseason Odds:** 30.4%	**Mediocrity (5-7):** 35%
Snap-Weighted Age: 26.2 (23rd)	**Defense:** 4.0% (19th)	**Super Bowl Odds:** 3.3%	**Playoff Contender (8-10):** 39%
Average Opponent: 1.1% (12th)	**Special Teams:** 5.1% (5th)	**Proj. Avg. Opponent:** 0.1% (15th)	**Super Bowl Contender (11+):** 15%

2017: Missed the playoffs by a few inches.

2018: From *Weekend at Bernie's* to Silent Bob with a pencil.

Whether things were good or bad, happy or sad, Jim Caldwell always kept his poker face together. Despite posting a winning record in three of his four seasons, Caldwell was fired by the Lions in January. His 36-28 record is the best by any Detroit head coach since Buddy Parker (1951-1956). Caldwell's tenure saw the team sustain a consistent competitiveness, but straddling the line between near-playoff team and wild-card loser was his downfall. Consistency is good, but Detroit had higher aspirations that Caldwell never seemed likely to fulfill.

General manager Bob Quinn was blunt about this after Caldwell was fired. "We didn't beat the real good teams," Quinn said. "Our record was above average. We're 9-7 the last two years, but our record against the better teams in the league has not been that good." That was exactly the point we made to end last year's essay. Since 2009, Detroit's 8-61 (.116) mark in games against teams with a winning record for the season is the second-worst record in the NFL. No team falters as much from its usual performance against winning teams like the Lions. Quarterback Matthew Stafford's record as a starter in games against winning teams is now 6-52 (.103). That includes a 4-25 record under Caldwell and a 2-27 record in road games. Hey, at least Detroit beat the Vikings in Minnesota last year.

Otherwise, 2017 was par for the course in Detroit. The Lions finished 1-6 in games against winning teams, matching the record they had in such contests in 2016. Detroit actually improved its scoring differential from last year, and each unit had a higher DVOA than the 2016 playoff team, but the end result was 9-7 again, a record not usually good enough for a trip to the NFL playoffs (Table 1). It was enough for the 2016 Lions, but 9-7 teams historically make the playoffs 45.9 percent of the time. That increases to 80.6 percent for 10-6 teams—a record of which the Lions were well within striking distance in 2017, but the late-game magic that carried them through the previous season did not return. After setting an NFL record with eight fourth-quarter comeback wins in 2016, the Lions were just 1-5 in 2017 when faced with a fourth-quarter comeback opportunity. Comeback regression is very real.

Detroit just could not close against the good teams. In Week 8, against Pittsburgh in prime time, Detroit gained the third-most yards (482) in NFL history for a team that did not score a touchdown and lost 20-15. The Lions also tried to stage a wild 35-point comeback in New Orleans in Week 6, but after getting to within a touchdown, a deflected pass in the end zone was caught by Cameron Jordan for an unorthodox pick-six in a 52-38 loss. The real kicker was in Week 3 against Atlanta. Golden Tate appeared to score a go-ahead touchdown in the final seconds, but replay showed that he was down just inches short of the end zone, which led to the clock expiring in a 30-26 loss. The Falcons went on to finish 10-6 and claimed the No. 6 seed that likely would have gone to Detroit if Tate kept his body off the ground for a few more inches.

So the Lions have been close to doing greater things, but those final adjustments to get past the NFL's best have eluded them. Detroit's solution was not to spend crazy money in free agency or make risky decisions on draft night. Instead, the Lions are banking on rookie head coach Matt Patricia to develop a winning culture like he learned in his past 14 seasons from Bill Belichick in New England.

The main problem with replicating Belichick's success is that we don't know exactly how much influence his coordinators had when Belichick loves to be in control of every facet of the team. There's no grooming a Darth Vader to assist Belichick's Emperor Palpatine. It's not like the Rams where we literally can see Sean McVay coaching up the offense while Wade Phillips is running the defense on game day. Various coordinators have enjoyed success with Belichick, but they have found very little success after leaving him to branch out on their own.

Patricia had to build his way up in New England. An offensive lineman in college, Patricia started on that side of the

Table 1. A Different Type of 9-7 (2016 Lions vs. 2017 Lions)

Metric	2016	2017
Record	9-7	9-7
Scoring differential	-12	+34
DVOA	-15.6% (27)	5.5% (12)
Offense DVOA	-0.6% (15)	4.4% (12)
Defense DVOA	18.5% (32)	4.0% (19)
Special Teams DVOA	3.5% (6)	5.1% (5)
4QC record	8-4	1-5
Record vs. winning teams	1-6	1-6

Regular season only

2018 Lions Schedule

Week	Opp.	Week	Opp.	Week	Opp.
1	NYJ (Mon.)	7	at MIA	13	LAR
2	at SF	8	SEA	14	at ARI
3	NE	9	at MIN	15	at BUF
4	at DAL	10	at CHI	16	MIN
5	GB	11	CAR	17	at GB
6	BYE	12	CHI (Thu.)		

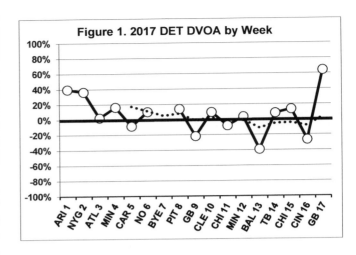

Figure 1. 2017 DET DVOA by Week

ball in 2004 before moving over to coach linebackers in 2006. After a brief stint with the safeties in 2011, Patricia finally moved up to defensive coordinator in 2012. It was then that Patricia started to have a visible presence during New England games. He was hard to miss with his bright red hoodie, backwards baseball cap, and pencil always tucked above his ear. He'd make a great *Family Guy* character if they ever wanted to give the defensive coordinator some lines in one of the episodes that feature the Patriots.

But make no mistake about Patricia. While Caldwell could have been confused for the title character of *Weekend at Bernie's*, Patricia is no Silent Bob, despite the resemblance. New England safety Devin McCourty spoke highly of Patricia last December. "When he's pissed, everyone knows, and when he's happy, everyone sees that, too," McCourty said. Patricia is engaging and can warrant the "wicked smaht" approval from New England fans given his degree in aeronautical engineering. Yes, Patricia is a rocket scientist, and that might soon join "Ryan Fitzpatrick went to Harvard" and "Antonio Gates played college basketball" in the NFL commentator lexicon.

While he grew up in New York, Patricia reportedly turned down the Giants job so that he could cut his teeth in a smaller market for his first head coaching gig. Patricia was very familiar with Quinn due to their time together in New England, where Quinn was in charge of scouting before taking the Lions' general manager position in 2016. With a ringing endorsement from Belichick and the connection with Quinn, Patricia's arrival in Detroit makes plenty of sense.

However, that close bond may have created some bad PR after the hire. In May, a report in the *Detroit News* revealed that Patricia had been indicted by a grand jury on one count of aggravated sexual assault in 1996. There was never a trial and the case was dismissed in January 1997. The Lions said they were unaware of this indictment, as their background check only covered criminal convictions. Deadspin reported that it found Patricia's indictment online in 30 seconds, which makes this look like a simple type of vetting that one may not do if hiring a close friend.

The Lions released a statement in May where Patricia categorically denied the allegation. "As someone who was falsely accused of this very serious charge over 22 years ago, and never given the opportunity to defend myself and clear my name, I find it incredibly unfair, disappointing, and frustrating that this story would resurface now with the only purpose being to damage my character and reputation. I firmly maintain my innocence, as I have always done."

The NFL looked into the matter and is not issuing any discipline to Patricia or the Lions. It was determined that the Lions handled the interview process properly, Patricia did not mislead the team about his past, and it is not subject to the personal conduct policy since the allegations happened prior to Patricia's NFL employment. That's the best news for Patricia and the team, but this was not a good way to start his tenure.

Patricia is trying to break the pattern of Belichick's assistants not being able to stand on their own. Romeo Crennel (28-55), Eric Mangini (33-48), Josh McDaniels (11-17), and Bill O'Brien (32-35) all have losing records as NFL head coaches. No one said it was an easy job. You can even ask Belichick, who was 37-45 after five seasons with Cleveland. He only managed one winning season with the Browns, which is just as many as Crennel had with the inferior 2.0 version of the Browns. Belichick was even 5-13 in New England until Tom Brady took over at quarterback in 2001, and the rest is history.

This just goes to show the importance of the quarterback position and why we spend so much time on it. Crennel was stuck with Charlie Frye and Brady Quinn (a failed Charlie Weis-coached prospect who even followed him to Kansas City), but did at least manage a 10-win season with Derek Anderson in 2007. Before Mangini shared that Cleveland quarterback pain, he had one playoff season with Chad Pennington (2006), who was always hurt or ineffective in odd-numbered years. Mangini had the Jets at 8-3 in 2008 with Brett Favre before injury to the old gunslinger led to a 9-7 finish and his firing. Josh McDaniels jettisoned Jay Cutler from Denver and tried to win with Kyle Orton. That worked … for six games before everything fell apart and he was fired during the season in 2010. O'Brien has pulled off some 9-7 seasons in Houston with various quarterbacks thanks to playing in the lean AFC South. We'll see if he can do anything with a healthy Deshaun Watson in 2018, but if the quarterback isn't in place, then most coaches would be fortunate to pull off one winning season.

This is why Patricia has a chance for both instant and sustained success. Quarterback is already figured out with Matthew Stafford. Sure, he has his flaws, but Stafford averages the second-most passing yards per game (278.0) in NFL history. He has the most fourth-quarter comeback wins (26) through a quarterback's first nine seasons. Stafford can carry a team, but without more help his ceiling appears to be wild-card weekend.

That's where Patricia has to make his mark. This is Year 10 of trying to find a running game and defense for Stafford. The passing game should still be the best aspect of the team. The wide receivers have well-defined responsibilities: Golden Tate is the slot and YAC receiver, Marvin Jones does a great job of winning 50/50 balls, and Kenny Golladay can be a deep threat if he stays healthy in his second year. The Lions spent heavily on the right side of the offensive line last year, and it worked from a pass protection standpoint with T.J. Lang and Ricky Wagner excelling there. Taylor Decker should be healthier for his third season at left tackle.

What about that running game? Try as they might, the Lions just never seem to get the ground game to work. Detroit has averaged just 83.3 yards per game of rushing support (non-quarterback carries only) in Stafford's starts. Among 38 quarterbacks with at least 80 starts since 2001, only Stafford gets less than 90.0 yards, and he is one of only three passers with a running game that averages less than 4.0 yards per carry (3.91 to be exact). The average quarterback in that sample receives an average of 104.7 rushing yards per game and 4.3 yards per carry. This may not sound like a huge difference, but when so many Detroit games come down to the wire, a few extra first downs or big runs could be significant.

Detroit hasn't had a 100-yard rusher since Reggie Bush did it on Thanksgiving in 2013. The Lions have played 68 regular-season games since then. According to research by Chase Stuart, the NFL record for the longest streak without a 100-yard rusher is 72 games by the Redskins in the 1960s. Detroit has a good shot to break that record, but individual 100-yard rushers are a bit overrated. Stafford would gladly take a 150-yard effort from his backfield even if it meant two or three players contributing to that. Patricia comes from New England, where the committee approach with specialized roles has been very successful. He looks to continue that here, even bringing in veteran ex-Patriot LeGarrette Blount to complement receiving back Theo Riddick.

The Lions also could give Ameer Abdullah one more shot, but second-round rookie Kerryon Johnson figures to be a significant part of the running game this year. He had a big rushing year (1,391 yards and 18 touchdowns) for Auburn as a junior and expects to be a three-down player. Whether he becomes the workhorse or just part of a committee, the Lions can keep him fresh with their options in the backfield.

None of these backs will have a successful year if the blocking doesn't improve. Detroit finished last in adjusted line yards (3.16) last season while also allowing the second-highest rate of stuffed runs and ranking 32nd in power situations. Detroit had five backs with at least 14 carries last season and none of them were able to average 4.0 yards per carry behind this line. It's another area where the coaching needs to make a difference. Patricia brought in Jeff Davidson, another old buddy from the Patriots (they worked together in 2004), to coach the offensive line. Since leaving New England, Davidson has bounced around with some unimpressive results, coaching the lines of the 2005 Browns, 2011-2015 Vikings, 2016 Chargers,

and 2017 Broncos. At least in Denver last year, the Broncos ranked ninth in adjusted line yards, but they struggled more in pass protection. Stafford and the quick passing game from (holdover) offensive coordinator Jim Bob Cooter can help negate a lot of the pressure. The improvement must come in the run blocking.

However, no one is expecting Patricia to stir this running back cocktail into the return of Barry Sanders. Defense is what he's known for, and he certainly coached some interesting defenses under Belichick. The Patriots shed a lot of their talent in the front seven in recent years, but that hasn't prevented them from keeping the score down most weeks. In 2016, the Patriots allowed the fewest points in the league despite only ranking 16th in DVOA, the lowest DVOA ranking for any No. 1 scoring defense since 1986. In 2017, the Patriots finished 31st in DVOA and 32nd in yards per drive allowed, but still ranked sixth in points per drive allowed. That too is the biggest disconnect in our database, and part of that was a great advantage on special teams—New England's defense had the best starting field position in both 2016 and 2017. Detroit has been solid in that regard too, so that could be an advantage that Patricia could carry over, in addition to defending well in the red zone and getting timely turnovers.

The "bend but don't break" style that Belichick loves to employ could very well follow Patricia to Detroit. He's not known for calling many blitzes, and the Patriots were often content to drop eight defenders off the line and pick up a lot of coverage sacks. Since 2015, the Patriots have used fewer than four pass-rushers on 445 plays, 205 more times than the next closest team (Colts). The rest of the NFL has averaged 127.4 such plays since 2015; Detroit ranks 26th with 67 three-man rushes. A lot of this is due to New England playing conservatively with big leads, but there is still a strategic preference for it.

Simply hiring a defensive coach hasn't always led to instant improvement on that side of the ball. Detroit fans will recall that Jim Schwartz was hired in 2009, and the team finished 32nd in DVOA for the second year in a row. However, Patricia is not inheriting an 0-16 team. He's getting the solid core of a 9-7 team that finished 19th in defensive DVOA. We looked at the biggest increases in defensive DVOA for rookie head coaches since 1990. Seven of the top 10 were produced by offensive-minded coaches. The only defensive-minded coaches in the top 10 were Butch Davis (2001 Browns), John Harbaugh (2008 Ravens), and Rex Ryan (2009 Jets). Davis took over a rough situation in Cleveland's third year back in the league. Harbaugh and Ryan had instant success in reaching AFC Championship Games, but had a really solid foundation of defenders to work with too. There's really not a 2009 Darrelle Revis or a core like Ray Lewis, Ed Reed, Terrell Suggs, and Haloti Ngata in Detroit. In fact, the Lions let an aging Ngata go this offseason.

Detroit already improved from 32nd in defensive DVOA in 2016 to 19th last year, so another big jump without any major talent additions could be difficult. If it does happen though, Patricia will certainly earn a lot of the credit. As for the players to make it happen, it has to be Ziggy Ansah and Darius Slay leading the way again. Ansah was given the franchise tag ($17.5 million) and could break the bank in Detroit or elsewhere with a big season. He's an inconsistent pass-rusher (nine of his 12 sacks came in three games last year), but he is the type of edge rusher that Patricia didn't have in New England after Chandler Jones was traded. The Patriots didn't have anyone with more than 7.0 sacks in each of the last two seasons; hopefully Ansah can surpass that production and allow the Lions to dial back on the blitzes that were more common in Teryl Austin's scheme.

As for "Big Play Slay," he certainly earned that nickname in 2017 with a career-high eight interceptions. However, Slay had just six interceptions in his first four seasons combined, so there should be some regression here. In fact, Detroit's defense was second in the league with 16.8 percent of drives ending with takeaways, a part of the game that usually regresses to the mean. Since 2011, the year-to-year correlation for takeaways per drive is just 0.11. Super Bowl LII benching weirdness aside, Patricia was fine with using cornerback Malcolm Butler to shadow top receivers in New England. Slay has already proven he can do the same thing. In fact, Detroit's 2017 defense was very reliant on his coverage. The Lions finished third in DVOA against No. 1 wide receivers (often Slay's assignment), but were 22nd against No. 2 wide receivers, 20th against other wideouts, and 26th against tight ends.

Ansah and Slay can be great again, but expecting career years from players entering their sixth season—or in back-to-back-seasons in Slay's case—is a tall order. Detroit is unlikely to take that next step up on defense unless some of the young starters acquired in recent drafts improve. They first have to adjust to Patricia's scheme change, and sometimes that simply takes a couple of seasons to pay off.

The schedule looks to give us a good idea early if the Lions are ready for that next step. They host the Patriots and Packers before their Week 6 bye, and later host the Seahawks, Panthers, and Rams. One would expect the six division games to be tougher this year. The Vikings are still going to be very talented with Kirk Cousins taking over at quarterback. Mitchell Trubisky is no longer a rookie and has a new receiving corps to go along with an offensive-minded head coach in Matt Nagy. It's hard to imagine the Lions can get two games against the Packers without Aaron Rodgers again. Detroit outscored the Rodgers-less Packers 65-28 in a sweep last year, meaning the Lions were outscored by three points in their other 14 games.

We have grown accustomed to the Lions losing to teams they simply weren't better than. Football isn't rocket science, but we'll see if the Lions can create an edge by being smarter and better prepared than the opponent. That's assuming Belichick hasn't programmed Patricia to say "Doesn't look like anything to me" the first time he has to make an in-game adjustment this season.

Scott Kacsmar

2017 Lions Stats by Week

Wk	vs.	W-L	PF	PA	YDF	YDA	TO	Total	Off	Def	ST
1	ARI	W	35	23	367	308	+3	40%	19%	-22%	-2%
2	at NYG	W	24	10	257	270	0	36%	-5%	-15%	27%
3	ATL	L	26	30	324	428	+3	3%	-3%	0%	6%
4	at MIN	W	14	7	251	284	+3	16%	1%	-17%	-1%
5	CAR	L	24	27	242	362	-1	-8%	5%	12%	-2%
6	at NO	L	38	52	347	379	-2	10%	-39%	-25%	24%
7	BYE										
8	PIT	L	15	20	482	392	+1	14%	-1%	-9%	5%
9	at GB	W	30	17	417	311	-1	-22%	9%	28%	-3%
10	CLE	W	38	24	345	413	+1	10%	23%	20%	6%
11	at CHI	W	27	24	352	398	0	-8%	39%	50%	2%
12	MIN	L	23	30	289	408	-2	4%	10%	16%	10%
13	at BAL	L	20	44	372	370	-3	-39%	4%	36%	-7%
14	at TB	W	24	21	434	400	+2	9%	13%	1%	-3%
15	CHI	W	20	10	293	349	+2	13%	5%	1%	10%
16	at CIN	L	17	26	276	364	0	-27%	-13%	16%	3%
17	GB	W	35	11	356	256	+4	64%	23%	-35%	7%

Trends and Splits

	Offense	Rank	Defense	Rank
Total DVOA	4.4%	12	4.0%	19
Unadjusted VOA	0.9%	15	1.7%	16
Weighted Trend	6.1%	11	9.4%	28
Variance	3.1%	1	5.5%	15
Average Opponent	-2.6%	4	-0.7%	18
Passing	23.1%	11	8.7%	16
Rushing	-20.2%	30	-1.8%	28
First Down	-6.7%	21	1.9%	18
Second Down	22.1%	4	7.4%	26
Third Down	-1.3%	17	3.2%	18
First Half	6.5%	13	5.5%	24
Second Half	2.3%	15	2.4%	18
Red Zone	8.6%	14	20.0%	32
Late and Close	3.5%	13	10.5%	29

Five-Year Performance

Year	W-L	Pyth W	Est W	PF	PA	TO	Total	Rk	Off	Rk	Def	Rk	ST	Rk	Off AGL	Rk	Def AGL	Rk	Off Age	Rk	Def Age	Rk	ST Age	Rk
2013	7-9	8.5	7.7	395	376	-12	-1.5%	16	-1.9%	19	-0.8%	14	-0.4%	20	31.9	14	30.7	20	27.0	14	27.0	13	26.8	6
2014	11-5	9.2	8.7	321	282	+7	4.4%	14	-3.8%	19	-13.9%	3	-5.7%	31	26.4	13	41.1	21	27.0	15	27.5	6	25.9	20
2015	7-9	6.9	7.4	358	400	-6	1.2%	13	1.8%	13	1.6%	16	1.0%	13	21.7	5	55.0	30	26.2	24	27.3	6	26.2	15
2016	9-7	7.7	5.3	346	358	-1	-15.6%	27	-0.6%	15	18.5%	32	3.5%	6	40.0	22	29.4	13	26.2	25	26.4	18	25.9	21
2017	9-7	8.9	8.4	410	376	+10	5.5%	12	4.4%	12	4.0%	19	5.1%	5	27.9	10	44.8	24	26.6	21	26.0	21	26.0	9

2017 Performance Based on Most Common Personnel Groups

DET Offense					DET Offense vs. Opponents					DET Defense				DET Defense vs. Opponents			
Pers	Freq	Yds	DVOA	Run%	Pers	Freq	Yds	DVOA	Run%	Pers	Freq	Yds	DVOA	Pers	Freq	Yds	DVOA
11	75%	5.8	10.3%	27%	Base	23%	5.6	11.2%	56%	Base	29%	5.5	0.9%	11	56%	5.8	2.0%
12	18%	5.6	-0.7%	56%	Nickel	63%	5.7	5.6%	30%	Nickel	52%	5.9	1.3%	12	20%	6.4	13.1%
13	3%	3.3	-32.6%	73%	Dime+	13%	5.8	3.5%	17%	Dime+	15%	5.9	4.1%	21	10%	6.4	11.0%
22	1%	5.3	8.5%	77%	Goal Line	0%	0.3	-39.9%	100%	Goal Line	1%	2.0	82.8%	22	4%	3.2	-34.0%
21	1%	7.3	48.6%	30%						Big	3%	4.8	9.6%	10	2%	4.9	32.8%
10	1%	5.2	-9.3%	0%										20	2%	4.8	-5.7%

Strategic Tendencies

Run/Pass		Rk	Formation		Rk	Pass Rush		Rk	Secondary		Rk	Strategy		Rk
Runs, first half	33%	31	Form: Single Back	90%	3	Rush 3	5.5%	19	4 DB	29%	20	Play action	20%	24
Runs, first down	50%	17	Form: Empty Back	6%	21	Rush 4	69.6%	13	5 DB	52%	19	Avg Box (Off)	6.10	28
Runs, second-long	24%	27	Pers: 3+ WR	76%	5	Rush 5	17.8%	22	6+ DB	15%	11	Avg Box (Def)	6.15	24
Runs, power sit.	39%	31	Pers: 2+ TE/6+ OL	23%	26	Rush 6+	7.0%	11	CB by Sides	59%	30	Offensive Pace	31.70	27
Runs, behind 2H	26%	18	Pers: 6+ OL	3%	16	Int DL Sacks	17.1%	25	S/CB Cover Ratio	22%	30	Defensive Pace	30.23	11
Pass, ahead 2H	49%	12	Shotgun/Pistol	77%	1	Second Level Sacks	20.0%	11	DB Blitz	11%	11	Go for it on 4th	0.58	29

Detroit had a league-leading 9.4 net yards per pass with play-action and ranked second with 60.6% DVOA. They only averaged 6.3 yards and 15.6% DVOA without play-action. ➾ Detroit only ran the ball on 28 percent of second downs, the lowest figure in the league. ➾ Matthew Stafford averaged the same 7.2 yards per pass against blitzes as he did on other passes, but Detroit's offensive DVOA dropped from 35.9% to 9.9% on blitzes. ➾ Here's an odd offensive split: Detroit was the worst offense in the league on third-and-short (1 or 2 yards to go), but the best offense on third-and-medium (3 to 6 yards), and then average on third-and-long (7-plus yards). ➾ Hopefully, Patricia has some new defensive back blitzes in his playbook, because the ones the Lions have been using don't work. The Lions allowed 49.3% DVOA when blitzing a defensive back, 29th in the league. In 2016, they had ranked 32nd at 64.2% DVOA.

Passing

Player	DYAR	DVOA	Plays	NtYds	Avg	YAC	C%	TD	Int
M.Stafford	1004	14.9%	613	4149	6.8	5.7	65.8%	29	10
M.Cassel	-257	-96.0%	50	125	2.5	1.8	59.5%	1	2

Rushing

Player	DYAR	DVOA	Plays	Yds	Avg	TD	Fum	Suc
A.Abdullah	-9	-10.0%	165	553	3.4	4	2	35%
T.Riddick	-3	-9.5%	84	286	3.4	3	1	39%
T.Green	17	0.0%	42	165	3.9	2	0	43%
D.Washington	-36	-49.1%	20	44	2.2	0	0	40%
M.Stafford	11	0.2%	19	104	5.5	0	1	-
Z.Zenner	-17	-34.5%	14	26	1.9	1	0	21%
G.Tate	14	13.2%	5	22	4.4	0	0	-
L.Blount	-9	-9.8%	173	766	4.4	2	1	43%

Receiving

Player	DYAR	DVOA	Plays	Ctch	Yds	Y/C	YAC	TD	C%
G.Tate	204	9.7%	120	92	1003	10.9	6.8	5	77%
M.Jones	395	33.8%	107	61	1101	18.0	3.2	9	57%
T.J.Jones	73	6.9%	49	30	399	13.3	2.6	1	61%
K.Golladay	130	21.9%	48	28	477	17.0	6.5	3	58%
J.Abbrederis*	1	-10.1%	7	3	44	14.7	9.3	0	43%
E.Ebron*	50	2.0%	86	53	574	10.8	4.9	4	62%
D.Fells*	48	21.9%	26	17	177	10.4	7.2	3	65%
M.Roberts	-7	-21.8%	7	4	46	11.5	3.0	0	57%
L.Willson	18	4.7%	22	15	153	10.2	6.0	4	68%
L.Toilolo	38	29.6%	14	12	122	10.2	5.3	1	86%
T.Riddick	37	-4.6%	71	53	444	8.4	8.2	2	75%
A.Abdullah	33	1.7%	35	25	162	6.5	5.8	1	71%
L.Blount	25	41.4%	8	8	50	6.3	5.9	1	100%

Offensive Line

Player	Pos	Age	GS	Snaps	Pen	Sk	Pass	Run	Player	Pos	Age	GS	Snaps	Pen	Sk	Pass	Run
Graham Glasgow	LG	26	16/16	1044	4	3.5	7	7	Corey Robinson	RT/G	26	8/5	327	3	2.5	9	9
T.J. Lang	RG	31	13/13	808	7	1.0	1	3	Brian Mihalik	LT	26	15/2	190	1	2.0	7	2
Ricky Wagner	RT	29	13/13	792	3	4.5	8	7	Joe Dahl	G	25	6/3	185	0	1.5	5	1
Travis Swanson*	C	27	11/11	709	3	0.0	4	11	Kenny Wiggins	RG	30	16/16	1042	3	3.0	20	13
Taylor Decker	LT	24	8/8	474	6	3.0	15	3	Wesley Johnson	C	27	15/15	940	5	5.0	14	12
Greg Robinson*	LT	26	6/6	394	5	2.0	6	2									

Year	Yards	ALY	Rank	Power	Rank	Stuff	Rank	2nd Lev	Rank	Open Field	Rank	Sacks	ASR	Rank	Press	Rank	F-Start	Cont.
2015	3.76	3.93	22	69%	12	24%	29	1.11	20	0.59	24	44	6.9%	22	21.6%	9	12	26
2016	3.64	3.49	31	56%	26	23%	29	1.10	21	0.47	27	37	6.1%	18	27.1%	20	16	30
2017	3.31	3.16	32	45%	32	27%	31	0.94	29	0.52	23	47	7.5%	21	30.6%	15	10	16

2017 ALY by direction: Left End: 3.01 (26) Left Tackle: 3.58 (21) Mid/Guard: 3.45 (32) Right Tackle: 1.94 (32) Right End: 3.51 (22)

Detroit's expensive solution to fixing the right side of the line almost worked. Guard T.J. Lang and tackle Ricky Wagner both relied on their pass-protection prowess to rank in the top seven at their positions in snaps per blown block, and Lang actually had the league's best average in a Pro Bowl season. However, both players missed three games and made up 40 percent of the worst run-blocking line in the NFL. The Lions ranked dead last in adjusted line yards for runs marked middle/guard and for runs off right tackle. Pass protection is very important, but that remains an area where a quarterback like Matthew Stafford can really help out. Detroit needs to see more out of Lang and Wagner when running the ball too. ☞ Shoulder surgery set back left tackle Taylor Decker's development in his second season. He started the final eight games after the Lions had to flirt with noted bust Greg Robinson for a stretch. Decker hasn't charted well in his first two seasons, ranking 24th and 28th in snaps per blown block. We'll see if a full offseason with a new coaching staff brings out the best in him. ☞ As for left guard and center, don't ask Graham Glasgow to choose a side. "I'm an interior offensive lineman," Glasgow told reporters in May. Glasgow has played both center and guard in his first two seasons, and his charting numbers were greatly improved from his rookie season. He jumped from 39th to fourth in snaps per blown block, albeit while splitting time at two positions. Most of that time has been at guard, but don't count out Glasgow taking over center for the (not dearly) departed Travis Swanson. The other player in this mix is first-round rookie Frank Ragnow (Arkansas), who some scouts believed was the best center in the draft. Ragnow won't wow anyone with his athleticism, but he brings physicality and should keep Stafford happy with his pass protection. While he would seem like a natural fit to take over for Swanson, he could actually make the move to left guard this season. ☞ Veteran guard Kenny Wiggins was signed in March for depth. He did not chart well (29th in snaps per blown block) in his lone starter season as the Chargers' right guard last year.

Defensive Front Seven

Defensive Line	Age	Pos	G	Snaps	Plays	Overall TmPct	Rk	Stop	Dfts	BTkl	vs. Run Runs	St%	Rk	RuYd	Rk	Pass Rush Sack	Hit	Hur	Dsrpt
A'Shawn Robinson	23	DT	16	737	59	7.0%	10	45	10	4	47	77%	47	2.8	71	0.5	6	17.0	5
Akeem Spence*	27	DT	16	661	39	4.6%	52	31	10	4	33	76%	54	1.7	30	3.0	7	13.0	0
Jeremiah Ledbetter	24	DT	16	348	14	1.7%	--	10	1	2	12	67%	--	3.6	--	0.5	3	6.5	0
Sylvester Williams	30	DT	15	351	19	2.5%	--	17	3	0	19	89%	--	1.6	--	0.0	0	0.5	0

Edge Rushers	Age	Pos	G	Snaps	Plays	Overall TmPct	Rk	Stop	Dfts	BTkl	vs. Run Runs	St%	Rk	RuYd	Rk	Pass Rush Sack	Hit	Hur	Dsrpt
Anthony Zettel	26	DE	16	753	42	5.0%	47	27	14	3	30	57%	92	2.5	53	6.5	10	27.0	0
Ezekiel Ansah	29	DE	14	516	43	5.9%	32	33	17	1	26	69%	70	3.0	72	12.0	7	20.5	1
Cornelius Washington	29	DE	15	453	27	3.4%	77	21	10	4	20	75%	46	3.4	79	2.5	8	15.5	0
Dwight Freeney*	38	DE	9	227	4	0.9%	--	4	3	1	0	0%	--	0.0	--	3.0	2	8.0	1
Jeremiah Valoaga	24	DE	9	153	6	1.3%	--	5	2	2	5	80%	--	2.4	--	1.0	5	3.0	0

Linebackers	Age	Pos	G	Snaps	Plays	Overall TmPct	Rk	Stop	Dfts	BTkl	vs. Run Runs	St%	Rk	RuYd	Rk	Pass Rush Sack	Hit	Hur	vs. Pass Tgts	Suc%	Rk	AdjYd	Rk	PD	Int
Tahir Whitehead*	28	OLB	16	950	112	13.3%	35	60	14	17	73	60%	56	3.5	39	1.0	6	9.0	45	49%	39	5.9	22	2	1
Jarrad Davis	23	MLB	14	830	99	13.5%	32	55	13	20	53	64%	37	3.7	52	2.0	3	8.0	33	37%	70	9.1	70	2	1
Paul Worrilow*	28	OLB	13	277	31	4.5%	--	19	3	3	22	82%	--	2.1	--	0.0	1	2.0	11	29%	--	9.8	--	1	0
Jalen Reeves-Maybin	23	OLB	14	239	26	3.5%	--	14	4	3	9	56%	--	3.0	--	0.5	0	0.0	14	71%	--	5.9	--	1	0
Christian Jones	27	MLB	16	624	86	10.5%	60	38	13	5	44	48%	81	4.4	71	2.0	1	4.5	33	47%	50	6.4	33	1	0
Devon Kennard	27	OLB	15	545	43	5.5%	85	29	13	5	28	61%	50	3.6	43	4.0	5	11.5	8	76%	--	5.2	--	1	0

Year	Yards	ALY	Rank	Power	Rank	Stuff	Rank	2nd Level	Rank	Open Field	Rank	Sacks	ASR	Rank	Press	Rank
2015	4.08	3.60	5	56%	7	24%	4	1.06	11	1.02	28	43	7.3%	8	24.9%	18
2016	4.35	4.40	21	73%	31	15%	29	1.20	20	0.73	15	26	5.4%	25	23.1%	30
2017	4.18	4.32	25	61%	11	17%	29	1.23	24	0.66	13	35	6.1%	22	28.1%	27

2017 ALY by direction: Left End: 4.64 (24)   Left Tackle: 4.07 (18)   Mid/Guard: 4.75 (30)   Right Tackle: 3.16 (8)   Right End: 3.93 (16)

Defensive end Ziggy Ansah will play on the franchise tag for $17.5 million this season, but Anthony Zettel actually led the team with 27 hurries last year. Kerry Hyder was a pleasant surprise for the team in 2016 with 25 hurries, but he tore his Achilles in the first preseason game last year. That opened the door for Zettel, who did his best Hyder impersonation and will likely start this season at left defensive end. Hyder is back on a one-year deal and could provide great depth for the edge rushers. ☞ The Lions also used a fourth-round pick on Alabama's Da'Shawn Hand, who always has had the physical traits, but never the production to match. SackSEER projected Hand with 10.3 sacks through his first five years, so he's likely more of a rotational player than future starter. ☞ Defensive tackle A'Shawn Robinson made the type of progression a team wants to see from a second-year player. He notched just one hurry in 2016, but that number jumped to 17 and he scored his first touchdown on a rare 2-yard pick-six thrown by Drew Brees in a wild game. Robinson has also been good for at least five pass disruptions in each of his two seasons. ☞ The Lions chose not to bring back Haloti Ngata after an injury-shortened season. Veteran Akeem Spence is also not returning, so 2017 sixth-round pick Jeremiah Ledbetter could start next to Robinson. The Lions also signed former first-round pick Sylvester Williams, who only spent one year with the Titans after leaving Denver. ☞ At linebacker, all eyes are on Jarrad Davis to lead the way. His rookie season was marred by 20 broken tackles (fifth most in the league) and some terrible metrics in pass coverage. Fortunately, first-round rookies tend to get better, and linebacker is an area where new coach Matt Patricia has plenty of experience at grooming. ☞ For outside linebacker, the Lions said goodbye to Tahir Whitehead and used free agency to add Christian Jones (Bears) and Devon Kennard (Giants). Both players turned 27 this year and have starting experience, but no one is expecting them to become stars of this defense. Serviceable will do, especially when the prices were right.

Defensive Secondary

Secondary	Age	Pos	G	Snaps	Plays	TmPct	Rk	Stop	Dfts	BTkl	Runs	St%	Rk	RuYd	Rk	Tgts	Tgt%	Rk	Dist	Suc%	Rk	AdjYd	Rk	PD	Int
Darius Slay	27	CB	16	1065	87	10.4%	13	42	18	10	9	56%	23	14.7	78	104	23.4%	64	14.4	53%	27	6.4	13	26	8
Glover Quin	32	FS	16	1055	90	10.7%	26	40	21	12	42	45%	37	7.9	52	22	5.0%	2	16.0	66%	3	11.3	72	5	3
Quandre Diggs	25	CB	16	788	64	7.6%	53	27	19	8	17	35%	59	8.2	64	39	11.9%	1	9.4	51%	40	8.8	65	7	3
Nevin Lawson	27	CB	15	556	47	6.0%	70	13	3	6	15	27%	68	6.1	43	46	19.6%	36	12.1	47%	66	9.0	67	5	0
Tavon Wilson	28	SS	10	545	57	10.9%	24	29	15	12	30	47%	32	6.7	44	23	9.9%	42	11.9	70%	1	8.7	44	2	1
D.J. Hayden*	28	CB	16	488	51	6.1%	--	21	5	6	8	25%	--	8.6	--	48	23.4%	--	13.0	53%	--	6.8	--	10	0
Miles Killebrew	25	SS	16	352	36	4.3%	75	18	6	4	16	50%	21	5.5	27	22	14.7%	67	11.7	60%	15	9.3	52	5	1
Teez Tabor	23	CB	10	190	11	2.1%	--	2	0	2	2	50%	--	3.0	--	15	18.3%	--	7.9	56%	--	6.1	--	2	0

Year	Pass D Rank	vs. #1 WR	Rk	vs. #2 WR	Rk	vs. Other WR	Rk	WR Wide	Rk	WR Slot	Rk	vs. TE	Rk	vs. RB	Rk
2015	19	9.5%	24	5.5%	18	-5.0%	14	--	--	--	--	26.0%	29	-10.7%	7
2016	32	11.5%	26	5.0%	21	27.4%	32	13.9%	29	14.7%	26	21.7%	29	34.4%	29
2017	16	-25.6%	3	11.3%	22	5.8%	20	-5.0%	12	-2.5%	11	12.9%	26	-12.7%	8

The Lions are returning essentially every defensive back that played for them on defense last season except for D.J. Hayden, who had respectable coverage metrics in his one-year stop. ✎ Darius Slay's fifth season was the best of the cornerback's career, resulting in his first Pro Bowl and All-Pro selection. He provided tight coverage and had a league-high eight interceptions and 26 passes defensed. He also did not allow many big plays again, ranking in the top 16 in adjusted yards per pass allowed for the second year in a row. It was extra important for Slay to be great given the rest of the secondary all ranked 44th or worse in that category. ✎ To their credit, starting safeties Glover Quin and Tavon Wilson had excellent rankings in adjusted success rate, so they may have allowed a few big plays, but not a consistent amount of successful plays. Even young Miles Killebrew saw the same split in his stats last year. ✎ Detroit was one of three teams (Cleveland and Cincinnati the others) to not have a safety with at least 25 targets faced. Offenses greatly favored targeting the cornerbacks in coverage, and it was another down year for Nevin Lawson and Quandre Diggs in that regard. ✎ Third-round rookie safety Tracy Walker (Louisana-Lafayette) actually expected to go in the fifth round, but he could be a future starter in Detroit. He's noted for his 6-foot-10 wingspan, and he can play center field while also being a willing tackler (97 stops as a senior). ✎ Teez Tabor, a second-round pick in 2017, is someone from whom the Lions need to see more this season. In a limited role as a rookie, he was successful at defending short passes. He is likely the team's best option to form a strong duo with Slay.

Special Teams

Year	DVOA	Rank	FG/XP	Rank	Net Kick	Rank	Kick Ret	Rank	Net Punt	Rank	Punt Ret	Rank	Hidden	Rank
2015	1.0%	13	6.0	5	-2.6	21	3.3	8	3.2	14	-4.7	24	-4.4	20
2016	3.5%	6	2.5	11	-2.9	24	-1.5	16	10.7	5	8.5	3	2.4	14
2017	5.1%	5	7.3	8	5.8	5	-4.0	27	-1.5	20	17.9	1	6.4	6

Detroit is coming off its highest special teams DVOA since the 2003 season. Despite the coaching changes, the Lions retained special teams coordinator Joe Marciano and his assistant Devin Fitzsimmons. ✎ Matt Prater continues to be one of the best kickers in the NFL, and the Lions showed an impressive amount of faith in his ability to hit from long distance. Prater had 11 field goal attempts of 50-plus yards in 2017, which has only been done three other times in a season since 2001. Prater missed three field goals from 55-plus yards away, but missed just twice on distances shorter than that. ✎ Punter and kickoff specialist Sam Martin flipped his 2016 script in 2017. He had his best year yet on kickoffs, but declined from third in gross punt value to 29th in the league. A most unusual ankle injury kept Martin out of action until Week 8. According to Justin Rogers from *The Detroit News*, Martin suffered a freak accident last summer while on vacation in the Bahamas when he either stepped on or dropped a conch shell on his foot. So perhaps that had an impact on his punting performance. ✎ Fifth-round rookie Jamal Agnew was named a first-team All-Pro for his league-best excellence on punt returns, including two touchdown returns. However, Detroit's kick return value ranked 27th, the biggest weakness for its special teams last year. Agnew was rarely used on kick returns, and he had the sixth-lowest return value when doing so. He'll try to sustain his punt success and improve on kickoffs (under new league rules, of course) in 2018.

Green Bay Packers

2017 Record: 7-9	Total DVOA: -3.3% (17th)	2018 Mean Projection: 9.3 wins	On the Clock (0-4): 4%
Pythagorean Wins: 6.2 (22nd)	Offense: 0.4% (15th)	Postseason Odds: 55.1%	Mediocrity (5-7): 20%
Snap-Weighted Age: 26.1 (25th)	Defense: 4.9% (20th)	Super Bowl Odds: 10.9%	Playoff Contender (8-10): 43%
Average Opponent: 4.8% (2nd)	Special Teams: 1.3% (14th)	Proj. Avg. Opponent: -1.8% (27th)	Super Bowl Contender (11+): 33%

2017: Kissing the curve in your clavicle.

2018: Gutekunst is a type of cheese, right?

Green Bay's attempt to match an NFL record with a ninth consecutive playoff appearance was always tied to the health of quarterback Aaron Rodgers. After thrilling comeback wins over the Bengals (Week 3) and Cowboys (Week 5)—not something Green Bay fans were particularly used to—Rodgers looked to be in MVP form again for the 4-1 Packers.

Everything changed in the first quarter of Week 6. A hit by Minnesota's Anthony Barr broke Rodgers' collarbone for the second time in five seasons. When that happened in 2013, Rodgers missed seven games and returned just in time for the season finale in Chicago to lead the Packers to the playoffs again. To give history a chance to repeat itself, the 2017 club needed some wild overtime wins against a bad Tampa Bay team and a winless Cleveland team. (Yes, the closest 0-16 Cleveland came to a win was its 21-7 lead over Green Bay in the fourth quarter.) Brett Hundley was largely ineffective in place of Rodgers, but those comebacks kept the scrappy Packers afloat at 7-6 when Rodgers returned in Week 15 against Carolina. Running the table was really the only option for the Packers to keep the playoff streak alive. However, there were obvious signs of rust as Rodgers threw three uncharacteristic interceptions and Green Bay fell 31-24.

With their playoff hopes dashed, the Packers shut Rodgers down and finished 7-9, the team's first losing record since 2008 when they were 6-10 in Rodgers' first year as a starter. That effectively closed the book on an era of football in Green Bay. Sure, Rodgers is returning for his age-35 season and head coach Mike McCarthy is still at the helm, but there has been a major organizational change that should shape the final years of Rodgers' career.

Brian Gutekunst has taken over for Ted Thompson as general manager. Gutekunst has been with Green Bay in some capacity since 1998, so this was an in-house promotion. While Thompson is staying on as senior advisor to football operations, the 44-year-old Gutekunst is calling the shots now and has already made his mark by making trades, parting ways with long-time veterans, and signing a few big names in free agency. Are you not entertained, Cheeseheads? Your team was finally active in March. Gutekunst's first draft has also received rave reviews, especially for the way he acquired New Orleans' first-round pick in 2019.

To understand where Gutekunst can take the team moving forward, we first have to acknowledge where Thompson held the Packers back.

Thompson was more stubbornly dedicated to building a team through the draft than any general manager in the league. We can debate his draft success, but it should be pointed out that Thompson's first ever draft pick as GM was Rodgers in 2005. We have to give him some credit for that because ending Rodgers' memorable slide to No. 24 was a gamble with Brett Favre still in town. However, Rodgers is that rare type of quarterback who can cover up so many flaws that he undoubtedly provided Thompson with extra years of job security. With a quarterback like that, the win-loss results won't reflect all the high draft picks that turned out to be disappointments or outright busts, including Justin Harrell, Brandon Jackson, Brian Brohm, Derek Sherrod, Jerel Worthy, and Datone Jones. The sting of both Eddie Lacy and Casey Hayward (now a Pro Bowler for the Chargers) leaving without a second contract in Green Bay is softened thanks to the playoff streak, even though the team has been struggling to find running backs and cornerbacks ever since.

The Thompson era will be viewed as a success because it did ultimately deliver the goal of a Super Bowl championship in 2010. However, that *singular* Super Bowl is also the reason why many will view his tenure as a disappointment. Given the caliber of quarterback in place, there was potential for more accomplishment.

Take away Rodgers, and the cupboards are rather bare—as we saw in 2013 and 2017, when the Packers were 5-12-1 in the games where Rodgers either broke his collarbone or was out entirely. Even the 2017 Cardinals were 5-4 in games where Blaine Gabbert or Drew Stanton started for Carson Palmer, and that's not even to mention the main competition in the NFC for Green Bay. The Eagles just won the Super Bowl with backup Nick Foles going 5-1 as a starter down the stretch. Minnesota took the NFC North last year and won a playoff game with third-stringer Case Keenum behind center. Foles and Keenum may be special cases, but neither likely would have achieved those heights if they had to work with Rodgers' supporting cast in Green Bay.

You can only pull so much magic out of a quarterback before everyone catches on to your one-man show. From the 2015 wins that required miraculous Hail Marys to the 4-6 start in 2016 that required a "run the table" finish, the Packers have

2018 Packers Schedule

Week	Opp.	Week	Opp.	Week	Opp.
1	CHI	7	BYE	13	ARI
2	MIN	8	at LAR	14	ATL
3	at WAS	9	at NE	15	at CHI
4	BUF	10	MIA	16	at NYJ
5	at DET	11	at SEA (Thu.)	17	DET
6	SF (Mon.)	12	at MIN		

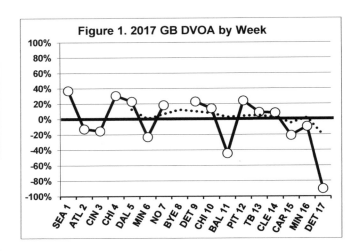

Figure 1. 2017 GB DVOA by Week

been slipping for a few years now. Their last season with more than 10 wins was in 2014. Even if Rodgers did not injure his collarbone last year, the Packers still had to navigate a tough schedule (No. 2 by DVOA) in a deep conference. Maybe the Packers would have snuck in as a wild-card team again, but a deep run was unlikely.

In a way, this losing season was *good* for Green Bay. It showed that resting on laurels and just making the playoffs was no longer good enough. Something has to change, and that's hopefully what Gutekunst can do for the team. One of his first big moves was to sign defensive end Muhammad Wilkerson in free agency in March. It's just a one-year deal for $5 million, but this is the type of gamble that Thompson rarely ever tried during his tenure. Just two summers ago Wilkerson signed a mega-deal worth up to $85 million with the Jets, but after building a reputation for missing team meetings, he was released. He only had 8.0 sacks in the last two seasons combined after a career-high 12.0 sacks in 2015, his contract year. This all sounds worrisome, but Wilkerson will only be 29 this year and could be rejuvenated by switching to a team expected to be a contender. Either way, the Packers finally used free agency to acquire a starter who isn't just a tight end.

Over the last few offseasons, Thompson's biggest free-agent signings were really just two tight ends: Jared Cook and Martellus Bennett. The latter was a major disappointment last year, and Bennett actually was waived by the team in November after a squabble over the handling of his health. (For what it's worth, Bennett played very little for New England after he returned there and later announced his retirement in March.) Green Bay has struggled to fill the tight end position ever since Jermichael Finley departed. Enter Jimmy Graham, one of the more productive pass-catching tight ends in NFL history and certainly the most talented tight end that Rodgers has ever had. This would have been a bigger deal a few years ago, but Graham is now going on 32 and averaged a career-low 9.1 yards per catch in 2017. He had 10 touchdown catches in Seattle despite an injury-plagued season, so Graham should still have a considerable impact in the red zone.

A new favorite target in the red zone is necessary after the Packers said goodbye to Jordy Nelson, ending a decade of service. Rodgers-to-Nelson will go down as one of the most efficient connections in NFL history, posting a stat line of 469 completions on 682 attempts (68.8 percent) for 6,919 yards, 10.2 yards per attempt, and a 127.9 passer rating. Just think of all the times Rodgers made that play-action fake before find-

ing Nelson open for a touchdown bomb. Those memories are growing more distant as Nelson missed all of the 2015 season with a torn ACL and then was not the same player physically in 2016. Last year he still caught six touchdowns from Rodgers but struggled in Rodgers' absence and averaged a career-low 9.1 yards per reception at age 32. It was time to move on.

What's left is a receiving corps that may be the weakest yet in the Rodgers era. Joining Nelson in past years were productive veterans such as Donald Driver, Greg Jennings, and James Jones. Now things are stretched thin with starters Davante Adams and Randall Cobb, who have combined for one 1,000-yard receiving season in their careers. Adams' improvement is offset a bit by Cobb's recent decline in the offense. The backups have great names, but Geronimo Allison and rookie Equanimeous St. Brown have made bigger splashes on Twitter than on NFL fields so far. Graham can help, but at his age he is not the vertical threat he used to be. Rodgers has always been more in favor of throwing to his wideouts than his tight ends anyway. In the 13 seasons since Rodgers was drafted, the Packers have had a tight end break 700 receiving yards once, when Jermichael Finley had 767 yards in 2011.

It should come as no surprise that the statistical peak of Rodgers' career (2009-2014) came when the Packers had what was considered the deepest receiving corps in the NFL. Now that it's been so diminished, we have seen an understandable drop in efficiency since 2015, but the drop has been so significant that one has to wonder if we'll ever see Peak Rodgers again. Sure, he's still one of the best ever at managing his touchdown-to-interception ratio, but yards per attempt (YPA) is a key stat where Rodgers used to dominate. From 2009 to 2014, Rodgers' YPA was 8.41, a mark that would rank higher than anyone born after World War II. Since 2015, his YPA has dropped to 6.99, which ranks 25th over the last three seasons and is below the NFL average of 7.24. We gathered some YPA splits on Rodgers' peak versus his last three years and the results are fairly shocking (Table 1).

Remember when the Packers were the best front-running team in the NFL? Those days are over. In first quarters, Rodgers' YPA has dropped from a dazzling 8.81 to a dismal 6.71. Rodgers only trailed by multiple scores in the second half 23

Table 1. Peak Aaron Rodgers vs. Recent Aaron Rodgers

Split	2009-2014			2015-2017		
	YPA	Rk	AVG	YPA	Rk	AVG
All Passes	8.41	1	7.26	6.99	25	7.24
First Down	8.30	3	7.58	6.53	38	7.51
Third Down	9.15	1	7.21	7.91	4	7.15
First Quarter	8.81	1	7.28	6.71	31	7.27
Fourth Quarter/OT	8.39	1	7.05	7.71	9	7.12
Deep Balls (16+ Air Yards)	14.56	3	11.81	12.31	18	11.99
QB Pressured	5.36	11	5.02	5.82	17	5.59
Vs. Blitz	8.58	2	7.40	6.76	29	7.44
Play-Action Passing	10.80	1	8.68	6.41	40	8.75

Source: ESPN Stats & Information Group

times in his first 121 games (19.0 percent). He has done so 16 times in his last 37 games (43.2 percent), often playing catch-up after slow starts.

Maybe the most shocking split is on first down, where Rodgers' 6.53 YPA is 38th in the NFL since 2015. He only ranks ahead of Joe Flacco (6.35), DeShone Kizer (6.19), and Brock Osweiler (6.10). Coaching may explain some of the first-down issues in 2017. Rodgers' first-down ALEX was -4.6, the lowest in the NFL, and backup Brett Hundley ranked 31st at -3.3. The Packers were very conservative with short throws on first downs last season.

Some may argue that a lack of a running game is the cause for this dip for Rodgers. However, Green Bay has ranked in the top 10 in rushing DVOA in each of the last three years. Rodgers' scrambling has a lot to do with that, but ESPN also has the Packers ranked 10th in expected points added by rushing on carries only by running backs. Also, have we forgotten just how little of a running game the Packers had in the past? The 2010 Super Bowl team was led in rushing by Brandon Jackson's 703 yards. The 2011 Packers (when Rodgers was in terrific MVP form) barely got 1,100 rushing yards from James Starks and Ryan Grant. 2012 may have been the nadir of the running game with Alex Green, Cedric Benson, and Starks each failing to crack 3.7 yards per carry or 500 yards on the ground. Rodgers was still fantastic that year, albeit with a deep receiving corps.

That's also what gets us back to Nelson, and namely that play-action bomb that was once so successful. With that element lacking in this offense the last three years, we have seen Green Bay's play-action game completely fall apart. At his peak, Rodgers averaged 10.8 YPA on play-action, the best in the game. Since 2015, he is down to 6.4 YPA, which is only above Kizer (5.39), his new backup. (One of Gutekunst's first transactions involved trading disappointing cornerback Damarious Randall to Cleveland in exchange for Kizer. Granted, Kizer is merely an upgraded version of Hundley, and we know the Packers aren't winning a Super Bowl if Rodgers is hurt again. However, it is the type of move that shows Gutekunst's Packers are open for business year-round.) We have never found a link between rushing success and play-action success, so Rodgers' struggles can't simply be blamed on an anemic

rushing attack. McCarthy has taken some heat in recent years for the design of the offense. We can also see this in Rodgers' YPA against the blitz, which has dropped from 8.58 to 6.76. Where are the quick-hitting plays with YAC? Nelson used to be a great "early blocker" on those plays as someone like Cobb got easy yardage. Rodgers' passes have still earned an above-average amount of YAC since 2015, but this offense no longer makes anything look easy.

The only area where Rodgers' YPA hasn't significantly decreased has been under pressure, which speaks to his increased reliance on scrambling around to make things happen. It doesn't help that Rodgers has had his three highest pressure rates since 2009 in the last three years. If the Packers want to get back to the glory days of offensive efficiency and more on-time plays, it could help that Joe Philbin has returned as offensive coordinator to replace a fired Edgar Bennett, who served in the role since 2015. Bennett was not the playcaller, and Philbin's goal, according to himself in January, is to do what he did from 2007 to 2011: "[Make] Mike McCarthy look like the smartest playcaller in the NFL." While Philbin failed as a head coach in Miami, he can simply focus on retooling the offense in Green Bay. McCarthy spoke highly of Philbin back in January: "We've taken a little bit of a back-to-basics approach on offense. We're going back and building a playbook like you would if it was your first year as a staff. Joe's such a great teacher. So, it's been a lot of fun so far."

We'll see just how much of the offense changes, but the general theme in Green Bay has always been that as long as Rodgers is healthy, the Packers have a shot to be very productive on that side of the ball. The defense has been the bigger problem in Green Bay for quite some time. Save for that 2010 Super Bowl unit that ranked No. 2 in DVOA and created huge takeaways in the postseason, the Packers have continuously been let down by Dom Capers' defense. Green Bay has finished 20th in defensive DVOA in each of the last three seasons.

After nine years, Capers is finally out, and former Browns coach Mike Pettine has taken over as defensive coordinator. While Pettine was just 10-22 in Cleveland, doesn't that sound respectable considering the Browns have gone 1-31 since he was fired? The 2014 Browns even finished 11th in defensive DVOA, the team's highest ranking in the last 15 seasons. Pettine has had defensive success in multiple cities, but he also can bring a stylistic change that may suit the Packers better this year. Along with Dick LeBeau, Capers was known for being one of the forefathers of the zone blitz, but in recent years the Packers have taken a passive approach and played more zone coverage. Pettine's history is rooted deep in the Rex Ryan coaching tree. With the Jets in 2009-2012, Pettine oversaw a 3-4 defense that was very aggressive in blitzing while playing press-man coverage with great cornerback play from the likes of Darrelle Revis and Antonio Cromartie.

Pettine probably doesn't have a Revis, but he should like what he has up front with Wilkerson joining Kenny Clark and Mike Daniels along the defensive line. That could even be the strength of the pass rush as Clay Matthews' production has dropped off in recent years. Outside linebacker Nick Perry has struggled to stay healthy throughout his career, but there has always been potential there. Pettine will hope to get out of him what he got out of Jerry Hughes in Buffalo in 2013. Hughes was considered a bust in Indianapolis, but after going to Buffalo to be a situational pass-rusher in Pettine's defense, Hughes stepped up with 10.0 sacks. Perry could be in for a career year under Pettine.

The secondary, especially at cornerback, has been the bugaboo for this defense. Injuries did not help last season as only the Dolphins (29.9) accumulated more adjusted games lost in the secondary than the Packers (28.3). Fortunately, Gutekunst has been addressing this problem in every way he can. He signed Chicago cornerback Kyle Fuller to an offer sheet for $56 million over four years, but the Bears matched to keep him on their side of the rivalry. Safety Morgan Burnett is out after eight years, but cornerback Tramon Williams has returned to add a veteran presence besides Ha Ha Clinton-Dix. Otherwise, the secondary is loaded with youngsters. Kevin King and Josh Jones were second-round picks in 2017, and both should be competing for starting jobs in 2018. Gutekunst continued the upgrades at cornerback by drafting Jaire Alexander (Louisville) and Josh Jackson (Iowa) with his first two picks.

With perhaps two second-year starters and a rookie (Alexander) in the slot, this is likely to be another very young secondary for Green Bay. Is it too young to go all the way? Since 2010, none of the 25 defenses with a secondary that had a snap-weighted age of 25.0 or less won a Super Bowl. Table 2 shows the last eight Super Bowl winners and their secondary's rank in snap-weighted age that season.

Table 2. Snap-Weighted Age of Super Bowl Winning Secondaries, 2010-2017

Team	Year	DB SWA	Rk
GB	2010	27.6	4
NYG	2011	28.5	4
BAL	2012	28.3	2
SEA	2013	25.2	27
NE	2014	26.9	13
DEN	2015	27.0	15
NE	2016	26.2	17
PHI	2017	26.9	9

The 2013 Seahawks did win with the sixth-youngest secondary, but that came during the prime years of the Legion of Boom with Richard Sherman, Earl Thomas, and Kam Chancellor. It doesn't seem likely that the Packers have acquired players of that caliber, but there is some hope to draw from here. The 2016 Packers had the league's youngest secondary and still reached the NFC Championship Game. The 2017 Saints had the league's youngest secondary in eight years and were a play away from advancing to the NFC title game as well. It doesn't help that New Orleans rookie safety Marcus Williams ducked on the Stefon Diggs game-winning touchdown, but as Packers fans know well, the playoffs can often come down to one snap. What the Packers cannot afford is to get shredded again as they did in Atlanta two years ago, when even Rodgers couldn't keep up with the pace. Gutekunst has rebuilt this secondary with enough veterans and high draft stock to where the lack of experience should not be a hindrance this year.

The return of Rodgers and new optimism for the defense are two major reasons to really like Green Bay this year, but the schedule also looks favorable. Green Bay very well could be the favorite in each of the first six games before the bye week. The bottom of the NFC West is rebuilding, and most of the AFC East is a mess. By finishing in third place in the division last year, the Packers get a road trip to Washington, which should be an advantage over the Vikings visiting Philadelphia. The middle portion of the schedule should really test the Packers when they have four road games in Los Angeles (Rams), New England, Seattle, and Minnesota. However, the final five games could set up the Packers on another good run going into the postseason.

Green Bay was never going to have the most exciting offseason in an improving NFC North. Detroit and Chicago added new head coaches. Minnesota briefly made Kirk Cousins the highest-paid player in NFL history, which is something Rodgers will reclaim very soon. He could even be the NFL's first $200 million man, but to really maximize that contract, the Packers have to take more chances on acquiring talent and making the team stronger. Gutekunst has started that process, but now it's up to McCarthy, his new coordinators, and Rodgers' health to finish the job.

Scott Kacsmar

2017 Packers Stats by Week

Wk	vs.	W-L	PF	PA	YDF	YDA	TO	Total	Off	Def	ST
1	SEA	W	17	9	370	225	0	37%	12%	-28%	-3%
2	at ATL	L	23	34	367	364	-2	-13%	9%	23%	1%
3	CIN	W	27	24	344	301	0	-15%	-5%	15%	5%
4	CHI	W	35	14	260	308	+4	31%	25%	-2%	3%
5	at DAL	W	35	31	342	408	+2	23%	36%	7%	-5%
6	at MIN	L	10	23	227	351	-1	-23%	-45%	-20%	2%
7	NO	L	17	26	260	485	+1	18%	17%	3%	5%
8	BYE										
9	DET	L	17	30	311	417	+1	23%	37%	5%	-9%
10	at CHI	W	23	16	342	323	+1	14%	18%	4%	0%
11	BAL	L	0	23	265	219	-4	-44%	-59%	-20%	-6%
12	at PIT	L	28	31	307	462	+3	24%	24%	-1%	-1%
13	TB	W	26	20	276	395	0	9%	7%	6%	8%
14	at CLE	W	27	21	341	345	+2	8%	7%	17%	17%
15	at CAR	L	24	31	384	387	-4	-21%	20%	44%	3%
16	MIN	L	0	16	239	236	-2	-9%	-30%	-16%	5%
17	at DET	L	11	35	256	356	-4	-90%	-54%	32%	-4%

Trends and Splits

	Offense	Rank	Defense	Rank
Total DVOA	0.3%	15	4.9%	20
Unadjusted VOA	-2.8%	18	7.2%	26
Weighted Trend	-5.5%	20	6.0%	24
Variance	9.6%	25	3.7%	6
Average Opponent	-2.2%	7	2.0%	8
Passing	-1.9%	25	22.0%	27
Rushing	10.6%	3	-13.5%	8
First Down	11.1%	7	1.2%	15
Second Down	-4.1%	18	6.2%	23
Third Down	-11.3%	26	10.3%	23
First Half	-7.9%	22	5.8%	26
Second Half	6.8%	13	4.0%	20
Red Zone	18.4%	7	11.0%	26
Late and Close	11.2%	7	9.6%	27

Five-Year Performance

Year	W-L	Pyth W	Est W	PF	PA	TO	Total	Rk	Off	Rk	Def	Rk	ST	Rk	Off AGL	Rk	Def AGL	Rk	Off Age	Rk	Def Age	Rk	ST Age	Rk
2013	8-7-1	7.8	7.3	417	428	-3	-6.0%	20	8.6%	9	14.4%	31	-0.3%	19	59.1	29	43.9	24	26.0	30	26.3	19	25.2	29
2014	12-4	11.2	10.8	486	348	+14	23.3%	3	24.7%	1	-1.0%	16	-2.3%	22	11.0	3	31.0	9	25.7	30	26.7	18	25.9	19
2015	10-6	9.3	9.9	368	323	+5	9.9%	10	2.2%	11	-7.3%	9	0.4%	17	29.7	15	26.5	14	26.7	16	26.3	23	25.5	28
2016	10-6	9.1	9.8	432	388	+8	12.3%	7	16.6%	4	2.5%	20	-1.9%	21	35.2	16	35.3	19	26.8	14	25.8	30	25.4	28
2017	7-9	6.2	7.7	320	384	-3	-3.3%	17	0.3%	15	4.9%	20	1.3%	14	46.0	24	38.8	21	27.0	16	25.5	28	25.2	28

2017 Performance Based on Most Common Personnel Groups

GB Offense					GB Offense vs. Opponents					GB Defense					GB Defense vs. Opponents			
Pers	Freq	Yds	DVOA	Run%	Pers	Freq	Yds	DVOA	Run%	Pers	Freq	Yds	DVOA		Pers	Freq	Yds	DVOA
11	64%	5.3	11.2%	28%	Base	26%	5.2	9.4%	43%	Base	23%	4.6	-13.1%		11	57%	6.1	12.6%
12	11%	6.1	21.9%	49%	Nickel	65%	4.9	-1.0%	32%	Nickel	34%	5.8	3.0%		12	21%	6.0	13.7%
21	7%	5.0	-23.2%	41%	Dime+	8%	5.6	10.9%	12%	Dime+	42%	6.0	16.9%		21	9%	5.1	-3.4%
01	4%	4.4	-15.6%	7%	Goal Line	1%	1.1	29.2%	80%	Goal Line	0%	-1.3	42.7%		13	5%	3.7	-4.2%
20	3%	3.5	-40.1%	53%						Big	0%	4.6	41.6%		22	4%	4.3	-30.5%
22	3%	4.1	-6.4%	77%											612	2%	2.6	-66.5%

Strategic Tendencies

Run/Pass		Rk	Formation		Rk	Pass Rush		Rk	Secondary		Rk	Strategy		Rk
Runs, first half	37%	25	Form: Single Back	69%	28	Rush 3	5.4%	20	4 DB	23%	30	Play action	22%	16
Runs, first down	41%	31	Form: Empty Back	14%	3	Rush 4	61.4%	18	5 DB	34%	27	Avg Box (Off)	6.07	29
Runs, second-long	31%	20	Pers: 3+ WR	76%	4	Rush 5	27.2%	5	6+ DB	42%	2	Avg Box (Def)	6.26	14
Runs, power sit.	48%	25	Pers: 2+ TE/6+ OL	17%	31	Rush 6+	6.0%	15	CB by Sides	59%	29	Offensive Pace	31.54	25
Runs, behind 2H	27%	17	Pers: 6+ OL	3%	18	Int DL Sacks	31.1%	8	S/CB Cover Ratio	39%	3	Defensive Pace	31.04	25
Pass, ahead 2H	54%	1	Shotgun/Pistol	66%	11	Second Level Sacks	17.6%	15	DB Blitz	10%	14	Go for it on 4th	1.62	5

The Packers went without a tight end on 6.7 percent of plays, which was tied for second in the NFL. But this was not a good idea. The Packers averaged a miserable 2.7 yards with -53.5% DVOA on these plays. ☞ The Packers had a league-low 29 penalties on offense. ☞ Green Bay opponents dropped only 17 passes, the lowest figure in the league. ☞ Green Bay allowed 4.1 yards per carry and -2.7% DVOA to running backs out of two-back sets, but 3.7 yards per carry and -23.5% DVOA to running backs out of one-back sets. ☞ Green Bay's defense was sixth against the run in the red zone but 29th against the pass in the red zone. ☞ The Packers and Oakland were tied with the worst DVOA in the league when the defense didn't get pass pressure.

Passing

Player	DYAR	DVOA	Plays	NtYds	Avg	YAC	C%	TD	Int
B.Hundley	-396	-28.3%	347	1607	4.6	5.3	61.1%	9	12
A.Rodgers	334	7.8%	259	1513	5.8	5.6	65.0%	16	6
J.Callahan*	-26	-72.3%	7	11	1.6	1.8	71.4%	0	0
D.Kizer	-756	-34.5%	514	2679	5.2	5.5	53.8%	11	20

Rushing

Player	DYAR	DVOA	Plays	Yds	Avg	TD	Fum	Suc
J.Williams	108	7.4%	153	556	3.6	4	0	48%
A.Jones	143	31.3%	81	448	5.5	4	0	53%
T.Montgomery	37	2.8%	71	273	3.8	3	0	49%
B.Hundley	100	40.3%	33	273	8.3	2	1	-
A.Rodgers	55	48.7%	17	133	7.8	0	0	-
R.Cobb	1	-34.8%	8	23	2.9	0	0	-
A.Ripkowski	-8	-55.1%	5	13	2.6	0	0	0%
D.Mays	-42	-276.9%	4	3	0.8	0	2	0%
D.Kizer	32	-3.7%	74	408	5.5	5	3	-

Receiving

Player	DYAR	DVOA	Plays	Ctch	Yds	Y/C	YAC	TD	C%
D.Adams	215	10.3%	117	74	885	12.0	4.5	10	63%
R.Cobb	48	-6.0%	93	67	647	9.7	6.2	4	72%
J.Nelson*	58	-5.0%	89	53	482	9.1	2.4	6	60%
G.Allison	-8	-15.0%	39	23	253	11.0	5.2	0	59%
M.Clark	-37	-46.6%	14	4	41	10.3	2.8	0	29%
T.Davis	9	4.6%	7	5	70	14.0	6.8	0	71%
M.Bennett*	-13	-11.9%	38	24	233	9.7	5.0	0	63%
L.Kendricks	-40	-22.7%	35	18	203	11.3	4.9	1	51%
R.Rodgers*	28	18.8%	19	12	160	13.3	7.4	1	63%
J.Graham	9	-6.0%	96	57	520	9.1	3.7	10	59%
J.Williams	84	29.9%	34	25	262	10.5	10.2	2	74%
T.Montgomery	19	-3.7%	31	23	173	7.5	9.3	1	74%
A.Jones	-60	-75.4%	18	9	22	2.4	3.3	0	50%
A.Ripkowski	-6	-23.6%	10	7	39	5.6	3.1	0	70%

Offensive Line

Player	Pos	Age	GS	Snaps	Pen	Sk	Pass	Run	Player	Pos	Age	GS	Snaps	Pen	Sk	Pass	Run
Corey Linsley	C	27	16/16	1047	5	2.0	5	9	Jason Spriggs	RT	24	7/5	279	0	2.5	8	3
Lane Taylor	LG	29	15/15	939	0	2.0	7	6	Bryan Bulaga	RT	29	5/5	232	1	0.0	7	0
Jahri Evans*	RG	35	14/14	912	3	2.0	12	7	Kyle Murphy	LT/RT	25	3/3	228	1	4.0	6	2
David Bakhtiari	LT	27	12/12	754	2	3.5	9	2	Lucas Patrick	G	25	12/2	227	1	1.5	5	1
Justin McCray	RT/G	26	13/8	594	3	5.5	19	8									

Year	Yards	ALY	Rank	Power	Rank	Stuff	Rank	2nd Lev	Rank	Open Field	Rank	Sacks	ASR	Rank	Press	Rank	F-Start	Cont.
2015	4.00	3.88	25	61%	21	23%	27	1.11	19	0.73	16	47	7.4%	23	30.2%	29	10	28
2016	4.36	4.08	19	49%	30	20%	17	1.15	15	0.94	9	35	5.5%	11	26.3%	16	13	33
2017	4.13	4.60	5	66%	11	16%	2	1.10	19	0.51	24	51	8.6%	28	35.1%	28	11	21

2017 ALY by direction: Left End: 4.79 (9)   Left Tackle: 5.32 (2)   Mid/Guard: 4.37 (8)   Right Tackle: 5.00 (3)   Right End: 3.81 (19)

Health was not kind to this unit last season. In fact, center Corey Linsley was the only offensive player to start all 16 games for the Packers in 2017. Linsley improved from a rank of 38th in snaps per blown block in 2016 to 12th last season. ☞ Right tackle was hit hardest where Bryan Bulaga missed 11 games. We would say this should improve in 2018, but Bulaga has missed 43 games in his eight-year career, including two ACL tears. He is serviceable when available, but that is hardly a lock. Bulaga needs to stay healthy to keep Jason Spriggs off the field. The 2016 second-round pick has gained some experience thanks to injuries to others, but he has not impressed in those games, especially when he moved to right tackle last year. ☞ Green Bay's best offensive lineman is still left tackle David Bakhtiari, who ranked second at his position in snaps per blown block last year. He may have notched a consecutive Pro Bowl if he didn't miss a quarter of the season. ☞ Lane Taylor should keep his job at left guard where he finished fifth in snaps per blown block last year, improving on his charting from 2016 when he ranked 14th. ☞ Right guard is the wild-card spot. The Packers got 14 starts out of a 34-year-old Jahri Evans last year, but that was a one-year rental. Former Arena Football League player Justin McCray could win the job, but he didn't exactly inspire much confidence in his first NFL starts last season. McCray was the only qualified Green Bay lineman to rank outside the top 16 in snaps per blown block. He was 35th while juggling starts at both guard positions and right tackle. Perhaps a focus on just one position can do wonders for him. ☞ The Packers also drafted Cole Madison (Washington State) in the fifth round. Madison didn't learn a playbook in college due to playing in Mike Leach's Air Raid offense. Green Bay might want to make sure he knows what he's doing before he lines up a few feet away from Aaron Rodgers.

Defensive Front Seven

Defensive Line	Age	Pos	G	Snaps	Plays	Overall TmPct	Rk	Stop	Dfts	BTkl	Runs	vs. Run St%	Rk	RuYd	Rk	Pass Rush Sack	Hit	Hur	Dsrpt
Kenny Clark	23	DT	15	688	56	7.1%	9	45	12	4	48	79%	35	2.4	60	4.5	2	14.5	2
Mike Daniels	29	DE	14	630	49	6.6%	14	39	14	2	42	76%	51	2.3	52	5.0	6	14.5	0
Dean Lowry	24	DE	16	496	33	3.9%	64	30	10	1	27	89%	6	2.0	37	2.0	2	14.5	1
Quinton Dial*	28	DT	13	309	20	2.9%	--	13	2	3	16	69%	--	3.2	--	0.0	1	1.5	1
Muhammad Wilkerson	29	DE	13	699	50	7.6%	4	42	10	3	38	84%	18	2.3	55	3.5	3	15.5	4

Edge Rushers	Age	Pos	G	Snaps	Plays	Overall TmPct	Rk	Stop	Dfts	BTkl	Runs	vs. Run St%	Rk	RuYd	Rk	Pass Rush Sack	Hit	Hur	Dsrpt
Clay Matthews	32	OLB	14	659	45	6.1%	28	31	16	4	28	71%	60	2.6	59	7.5	14	23.5	2
Nick Perry	28	OLB	12	545	38	6.0%	30	26	11	4	28	61%	90	3.6	85	7.0	9	23.5	1
Kyler Fackrell	27	OLB	16	448	23	2.7%	91	16	10	5	13	69%	70	2.1	37	3.0	4	19.0	1
Ahmad Brooks*	34	OLB	12	346	21	3.3%	79	20	7	2	15	100%	1	0.6	4	1.5	4	6.0	3

Linebackers	Age	Pos	G	Snaps	Plays	Overall TmPct	Rk	Stop	Dfts	BTkl	Runs	vs. Run St%	Rk	RuYd	Rk	Pass Rush Sack	Hit	Hur	vs. Pass Tgts	Suc%	Rk	AdjYd	Rk	PD	Int
Blake Martinez	24	ILB	16	982	150	17.7%	5	84	24	16	90	61%	49	3.6	46	1.0	1	3.5	50	48%	42	6.3	29	7	1
Jake Ryan	26	ILB	15	507	79	9.9%	64	48	6	7	62	66%	27	3.6	44	1.0	0	1.0	8	68%	--	11.4	--	0	0

Year	Yards	ALY	Rank	Power	Rank	Stuff	Rank	2nd Level	Rank	Open Field	Rank	Sacks	ASR	Rank	Press	Rank
2015	4.15	3.87	11	67%	17	25%	3	1.21	24	0.92	25	43	6.7%	15	26.5%	10
2016	4.12	3.84	9	72%	30	20%	13	1.16	17	0.82	22	40	7.0%	8	27.0%	16
2017	3.81	3.93	9	56%	7	20%	21	1.08	10	0.57	7	37	7.3%	9	29.0%	26

| 2017 ALY by direction: | Left End: 3.34 (12) | Left Tackle: 5.02 (28) | Mid/Guard: 4.62 (29) | Right Tackle: 3.40 (12) | Right End: 1.53 (2) |

The addition of Muhammad Wilkerson has somewhat gone under the radar this offseason. It was just in 2015 when he was New York's prized defender, earning a contract worth $17 million per season. Always a staunch run defender, Wilkerson saw his pass-rush production slip to its lowest level since his rookie season last year. He also was basically a healthy scratch for the final three games after the Jets were not happy with his tardiness to a team meeting. This has been pegged as a "rebirth" year for Wilkerson, and he should be a natural fit at defensive end after working with Mike Pettine for his first two seasons with the Jets. If Wilkerson is a huge success, then the Packers will have to decide whether he can be trusted to produce after another huge contract or to let someone else roll those dice as he'll be 30 years old in 2019. The one-year "prove it" deal definitely looks like the smart move for Green Bay here. ⬤ Nose tackle Kenny Clark progressed as a team would hope from a second-year player and late first-round pick. It did take him 30 games (including playoffs) to notch his first sack, but that's not his main purpose in this defense. Clark notched just as many hurries as defensive end Mike Daniels, who saw his hurries drop from 23 to 15 despite only playing 34 fewer snaps than he did in 2016. ⬤ As for the outside linebackers, the depth is not great behind Clay Matthews and Nick Perry. Don't just take it from us—Matthews basically said as much to reporters in May: "But obviously, you look at the depth at the outside linebacker position, and it's not that great." Matthews and Perry tied for the team lead with 23.5 hurries each, but 57 defenders across the league had more hurries than that in 2017. ⬤ Green Bay drafted Vanderbilt's Oren Burks in the third round, but he projects to play inside. Perhaps he could give Blake Martinez a few more breathers after a busy 2017. Martinez's 84 stops led the league, and only three inside linebackers were involved in more pass plays. However, Martinez also saw his broken tackles double to 16 from just eight in his rookie year.

Defensive Secondary

Secondary	Age	Pos	G	Snaps	Plays	TmPct	Rk	Stop	Dfts	BTkl	Runs	St%	Rk	RuYd	Rk	Tgts	Tgt%	Rk	Dist	Suc%	Rk	AdjYd	Rk	PD	Int
Ha Ha Clinton-Dix	26	FS	16	1048	85	10.0%	37	23	8	6	32	41%	49	7.8	49	35	8.5%	30	12.2	39%	72	9.6	57	7	3
Josh Jones	24	SS	16	735	72	8.5%	61	33	14	6	26	50%	21	4.7	17	39	13.7%	65	8.3	38%	73	8.9	46	4	1
Morgan Burnett*	29	SS	12	729	71	11.2%	21	31	13	3	35	51%	20	5.3	24	27	9.6%	38	8.5	46%	57	6.3	16	3	0
Damarious Randall*	26	CB	14	721	56	7.6%	56	29	14	5	19	58%	17	5.0	20	45	16.2%	14	12.2	53%	31	6.9	29	9	4
Davon House	29	CB	12	659	50	7.9%	50	18	8	8	12	42%	44	5.3	22	51	20.0%	39	15.6	48%	56	9.2	71	5	1
Josh Hawkins	25	CB	15	407	43	5.4%	--	13	6	7	14	21%	--	10.5	--	41	25.8%	--	11.4	40%	--	8.1	--	6	0
Kevin King	23	CB	9	382	32	6.7%	--	15	5	8	7	86%	--	1.4	--	39	26.4%	--	11.0	46%	--	7.8	--	5	0
Kentrell Brice	24	FS	6	289	24	7.6%	--	8	3	5	11	27%	--	10.9	--	15	13.0%	--	10.9	64%	--	11.3	--	2	1
Tramon Williams	35	CB	13	670	52	8.0%	49	24	9	2	5	40%	47	5.4	25	56	18.0%	24	10.4	55%	19	6.8	23	13	2

Year	Pass D Rank	vs. #1 WR	Rk	vs. #2 WR	Rk	vs. Other WR	Rk	WR Wide	Rk	WR Slot	Rk	vs. TE	Rk	vs. RB	Rk
2015	6	7.5%	21	-31.7%	2	6.4%	19	--	--	--	--	-20.8%	4	-24.7%	4
2016	23	12.3%	28	18.0%	28	13.7%	26	7.7%	26	19.1%	31	-17.4%	7	-7.9%	13
2017	27	31.9%	32	22.1%	26	-9.4%	10	8.3%	26	28.1%	31	4.1%	21	17.3%	29

This sounds odd, but the cornerback with the best charting metrics on the Packers last year was Damarious Randall, the player they traded away to Cleveland. He even led the team in interceptions (four) and passes defensed (nine) in what was arguably his best season yet. However, inconsistency was always an issue with Randall. If he wasn't giving up a gross amount of touchdowns, he was getting beat for big plays. He didn't start last season well either, and a good finish for a team that finished poorly may not have resonated with Gutekunst. ☞ Kevin King's rookie season was far from a smashing success, but there's hope that he'll get more comfortable as an every-week starter in 2018. ☞ The team's top two draft picks join him in the competition: Jaire Alexander (Louisville) and Josh Jackson (not to be confused with the kid from *The Mighty Ducks*). Alexander has a shot to start right away in a nickel/slot role. Jackson displayed great ball skills at Iowa with eight interceptions and 26 passes defensed in 2017 but will have to prove he's more than a one-year wonder. ☞ It's not all about youth in the secondary. Tramon Williams, 35, returns to the Packers after stops in Cleveland and Arizona. He charted well with the Cardinals last year and can still give this defense starter-caliber play while serving as a mentor to the young draft picks. ☞ Ha Ha Clinton-Dix no longer has Morgan Burnett as his partner in crime at safety, but Josh Jones showed enough as a rookie to make that move for 2018. Jones led the secondary with 33 stops last year and fits the mold of the modern "dollar" safety/linebacker hybrid.

Special Teams

Year	DVOA	Rank	FG/XP	Rank	Net Kick	Rank	Kick Ret	Rank	Net Punt	Rank	Punt Ret	Rank	Hidden	Rank
2015	0.4%	17	5.0	6	-7.8	31	5.4	5	4.7	9	-5.6	25	-4.9	21
2016	-1.9%	21	0.7	13	-8.7	30	-2.5	22	0.1	14	1.1	13	-8.4	26
2017	1.3%	14	-2.8	19	0.1	17	0.2	13	5.1	9	4.0	4	-12.0	30

The start of Mason Crosby's second decade as Green Bay's kicker was unusual for how little we saw of him. With the quarterback situation being what it was, Crosby set career lows for field goal attempts (19) and extra point attempts (35). It was the first time we didn't see Crosby attempt at least 28 field goals in his 11-year career. A better offense should fix that problem, and Crosby was still good enough on kickoffs. ☞ Punter has been a struggle for the Packers. Justin Vogel got the boot after one year on the job that saw him rank 20th in gross punting value. Vogel only dropped 26.8 percent of his punts inside the opponent's 20, the second-lowest rate in 2017. Alabama punter JK Scott is the first punter the Packers have drafted since they errantly took B.J. Sander in the third round in 2004. At least Scott only cost a fifth-round pick, but that's still more than what most teams spend to get their punter. ☞ Trevor Davis handled both return jobs but was far more successful on punt returns than he was on kickoff returns. ☞ Backup safety Marwin Evans led the team with nine tackles on special teams and was one of six players in the league with multiple punt saves to prevent touchdowns on long returns.

Houston Texans

2017 Record: 4-12	Total DVOA: -20.3% (28th)	2018 Mean Projection: 8.3 wins	On the Clock (0-4): 7%
Pythagorean Wins: 5.5 (27th)	Offense: -10.2% (25th)	Postseason Odds: 42.6%	Mediocrity (5-7): 30%
Snap-Weighted Age: 26.1 (26th)	Defense: 5.6% (23rd)	Super Bowl Odds: 5.7%	Playoff Contender (8-10): 42%
Average Opponent: 1.3% (11th)	Special Teams: -4.5% (26th)	Proj. Avg. Opponent: -2.7% (31st)	Super Bowl Contender (11+): 21%

2017: Après Deshaun le déluge.

2018: With the return of Deshaun and a rebound on defense, serious contenders.

The Houston Texans were a great offense but also a terrible one in 2017. The greatness came with Deshaun Watson in the lineup. In the six games he played, the Texans had an offensive DVOA of 13.8%, which would have ranked fifth in the league had they sustained that level of play over the course of a full season. Without Watson, the Texans had an offensive DVOA of -24.8%, which would have comfortably ranked last in the league. It is a cliché to say that as the quarterback goes, so an NFL team goes, but for the 2017 Texans it was also the truth.

What about the Texans offense worked and did not work with Watson? What, if anything, still worked well without Watson, and what did not work without him? Are the things that worked in 2017 likely to work as well in 2018? Is there anything comparable players can tell us to expect from Watson in his second season? In light of this, what can we reasonably expect from the Texans in 2018?

One thing that didn't get worse when Watson left the lineup was how well Texans running backs ran the ball. Houston backs actually had a worse rushing DVOA in Watson's six starts than they did in their other ten games, -9.7% with him as opposed to -1.1% without him. Watson himself was an efficient and effective runner, both as a scrambler and otherwise, but his success as a runner and passer did not appear to redound to the benefit of the Texans' run game as a whole.

The value of Watson thus came largely through his ability to throw the ball effectively. But even here, he did not stand out in all areas. Watson was exceptional on short passes of 5 yards or less, leading the league in DVOA on such throws (Table 1). He was excellent in the screen game, but also on other short throws. But he was also an exceptionally efficient passer on the deepest ("bomb") throws, ranking fourth in DVOA among the 29 quarterbacks with at least ten such throws.

Table 1. Watson vs. Other Texans QBs by Pass Distance, Passing DVOA

Watson	Distance	Other QBs
55.6%	Short (5 Yards or Less)	-27.8%
16.0%	Medium (6-15 Yards)	23.5%
34.5%	Deep (16-25 Yards)	24.6%
149.8%	Bomb (26+ Yards)	35.7%

What happens on those bomb passes will help determine just how effective Watson will be in 2018. With a small sample size, these tend to regress toward the mean from one season to the next. But some quarterbacks are truly good deep throwers, and some are not. Watson's profile out of college suggested he was a good downfield passer, and DeAndre Hopkins and Will Fuller present him exactly the kind of targets he might be able to efficiently exploit on an annual basis. Many of Watson's misses on deep balls came when he did not have his feet set and tried to throw off-balance. As far as quarterbacking sins go, that is an easier one to fix. It seems reasonable to continue to expect him to be above average there, which puts increased importance on improving those mid-range throws where he was no more effective than Tom Savage.

As to what comparable players can tell us about Watson, the answer is not very much at all, because the precise details of Watson's season are *sui generis*. Highly drafted rookies who are good tend to play the entire season. Highly drafted rookies who only start for part of the season tend to be pretty bad. Watson started for part of the season, but was quite good. His 23.2% passing DVOA was seventh among qualifying passers. The only other quarterback drafted in the first or second round in the past 20 years to make between five and eight starts in his first or second season and play at an above-average level was Colin Kaepernick with the 2012 49ers. But Kaepernick is not a perfect comparison, for a couple of reasons. He started three more games in the playoffs, putting him by attempts closer to the company of Ben Roethlisberger, who started nearly the entire season as a rookie. It was his second season in the NFL and second in the playbook. Further, Kaepernick was, by passing DVOA, almost exactly as good as Alex Smith had been before he took over—in contrast to the huge gap between Watson and Houston's other quarterbacks.

A couple of other quarterbacks comparable to Watson emerge if we loosen our playing time restrictions a little bit. One of them is completely unhelpful in divining Watson's fate: the excellent play of Jimmy Garoppolo, whose own future is yet to be determined, with the 49ers last year. Going back in time, a more helpful comparable might be a player with Houston connections, Jim Everett. The Oilers made him the third overall pick in 1986, and he ended up starting five games for the Rams as a rookie after a holdout and trade. By conventional statistics, his performance was average. DVOA

2018 Texans Schedule

Week	Opp.	Week	Opp.	Week	Opp.
1	at NE	7	at JAX	13	CLE
2	at TEN	8	MIA (Thu.)	14	IND
3	NYG	9	at DEN	15	at NYJ (Sat.)
4	at IND	10	BYE	16	at PHI
5	DAL	11	at WAS	17	JAX
6	BUF	12	TEN (Mon.)		

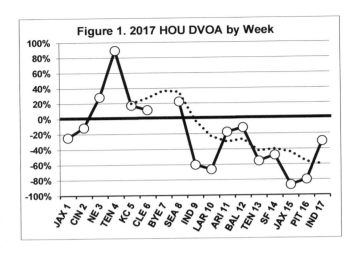

Figure 1. 2017 HOU DVOA by Week

rates him more highly, 10.9%, while the Rams' other quarterbacks were closer to replacement level. Like Watson, a lot of his success was driven by high yards per completion and throwing touchdowns at an above-average rate.

Everett may now be mostly known for his fight/publicity stunt with Jim Rome ("Chris") but after an average second season where he failed to sustain that high touchdown rate, he was one of the most effective quarterbacks in the NFL. He ranked in the top 11 in passing DYAR six times from 1988 to 1995, including top-three finishes in 1988, 1989, and 1994. This suggests a note of caution for the upcoming season, but the future could be bright.

One thing Everett did do that Watson as a rookie did not was avoid getting sacked. Part of what made Watson's season so unusual was he was an above-average quarterback despite throwing interceptions at a high rate and getting sacked at a high rate. Since 1970, only veterans Lynn Dickey in 1982 and Steve Beuerlein in 2002 were average passers by adjusted net yards per attempt while getting sacked and throwing interceptions at a rate at least one standard deviation worse than the NFL average. The likely next step in Watson's development will be to follow the curve NFL passing games as a whole have followed, by throwing shorter passes more successfully,

Table 2. First-Round Picks, 1998-2017, With High Interceptions Rates as Rookies, First and Second Seasons

Player	Rookie Year	Rookie Int%+[1]	Year 2 Int%+[1]
Ryan Leaf	1998	60	64
Peyton Manning	1998	77	107
Kyle Boller	2003	85	114
Eli Manning	2004	76	102
Alex Smith	2005	40	92
Josh Freeman	2009	53	123
Mark Sanchez	2009	63	105
Christian Ponder	2011	73	105
Blake Bortles	2014	82	89
Jared Goff	2016	81	115
Deshaun Watson	2017	73	--

Minimum 100 pass attempts each season.

[1]*Int%+, as calculated by Pro Football Reference. 100 represents the league average for that season. Numbers under 100 are worse than average, while numbers greater than 100 are better than average. The league average interception rate has declined so much over time that comparisons by straight interception percentage are much less useful.*

likely bringing down his yards per completion and interception rate while increasing his completion percentage.

One piece of good news is that that high picks who throw a lot of interceptions as a rookie tend not to throw interceptions nearly as frequently in their second season. Table 2 shows the first-round picks in the past 20 years who as rookies threw interceptions at a rate at least one standard deviation worse than the league average. All threw interceptions at a lower rate in their second season, and most of them were even better than average.

His sack rate, though, may be a trickier thing to manage. Disentangling the effects between a quarterback, offensive scheme, and the quality of the blocking is a tricky proposition, and we've only seen Watson in one scheme and with one offensive line. One split where Watson excelled was DVOA without pass pressure, leading the league with a 99.3% DVOA. He was significantly worse when pressured, with the sixth-largest gap between DVOA when pressured and DVOA without pressure. That Tom Savage had the fifth-largest gap suggests this might be a Bill O'Brien-related issue. That Brock Osweiler had the ninth-largest such gap in 2016 and Brian Hoyer the league's biggest in 2015 reinforces that impression.

Keeping Watson clean looks imperative. This is especially problematic because Watson had the highest rate of being pressured last year at 41.9 percent. Part of that might be being a rookie; Jared Goff went from an extraordinarily high pressure rate as a rookie to the middle of the pack in his second season. That Savage had the fourth-highest pressure rate, at 38.5 percent, suggests it might also be a problem with the Texans' offensive line. Watson's personal adjusted sack rate of 8.9 percent ranked ninth among passers with at least 100 pass plays. Tom Savage was sixth at 9.0 percent, and T.J. Yates, who started the final three games, had the highest at 11.2 percent.

Our game charting confirms the perception that Houston's line was a significant problem. The Texans had 31.0 sacks coming from blown blocks, as opposed to sacks from unblocked rushers or coverage sacks. That was tied for the second-highest total in the league, behind only Arizona. And it was not just sacks—they also had the fourth-highest rate of blown blocks on pass plays.

Unlike the Rams last offseason, Houston could not add a quality left tackle in free agency. The top available tackle was Nate Solder, but he signed with the Giants. Without picks in the first or second rounds after the Watson and Osweiler trades last year, Houston could not find a sure plug-and-play starter in the draft. Last year's fourth-round pick Julie'n Davenport is the favorite to start at left tackle. This year's third-round pick Martinas Rankin looked like the favorite at right tackle until he had foot surgery following an injury in rookie mini-camp. He should be ready for the start of the regular season, but training camp availability is an open question. This group will probably not be worse than last year's line, because it would be hard to be worse than last year's line, but it is also no guarantee of an upgrade.

The good news for the Texans is that even if the offense is just average, they should still be a playoff contender. The defense has ranked in the top nine by DVOA five of the past seven seasons, including 2014-2016, before slumping to 23rd last year, so our projections suggest what Bill James dubbed the Plexiglass Principle is likely to come into play. The Principle is simple: teams that dramatically improve from one season to the next are likely to decline the next season, and vice versa. (It's explored further from the other side in the Los Angeles Rams chapter.)

Just how much the Texans defense does rebound will depend on a couple of things. Most prominent may be the play of J.J. Watt. The Watt we saw from 2012 to 2015 posted one of the greatest stretches of defensive play in NFL history, tallying an incredible 69.0 sacks and winning three Defensive Player of the Year Awards. He has played just eight games the past two seasons, and did not have a sack in the five games he played in 2017. Bill O'Brien has been customarily cagey about Watt's return from injury, describing him in May as being "on schedule" while not specifying a projected actual return date—for example, "the start of training camp," the return date O'Brien gave for the also "on schedule" Watson.

One key reason to expect the Texans defense to rebound regardless of Watt's fate is turnovers. Just 8.0 percent of opposing drives last year ended in a turnover, the fourth-lowest rate in the league. This generally regresses toward the mean from one season to the next. The return from injury not just potentially of Watt but also of leading 2016 sacker Whitney Mercilus, lost for the season after five games, suggests the Texans should improve here. Red zone performance is another reason to expect Houston's defense to improve. They ranked 30th in points allowed per red zone possession last year. Outside of New England, red zone defense tends to be inconsistent from year to year, so Houston is likely to improve somewhat here. Houston's defensive decline was also exclusively a pass defense decline; their run defense actually improved slightly. Pass defense is more inconsistent than run defense from year to year, so this is another reason to expect improvement.

Put an offense that could easily be around average together with a defense likely to rebound to average or above, and as long as the special teams are once again just bad and not disastrous, 2018 could easily be the best Texans team we have seen since the 2012 AFC South champions. This does not guarantee them the good fortune that ushered the 2015 and 2016 squads into the postseason. But despite the improvement of the AFC South, we still project the Texans to face one of the easiest schedules in the league. The conference as a whole still lacks solid teams outside of New England and Pittsburgh, and Houston looks like as good a bet for the third-best team in the AFC as any. The key may be successfully navigating what we project to be the NFL's tightest division, where luck in a couple close games could be the difference between first and last place.

Tom Gower

2017 Texans Stats by Week

Wk	vs.	W-L	PF	PA	YDF	YDA	TO	Total	Off	Def	ST
1	JAX	L	7	29	203	280	-4	-24%	-23%	3%	2%
2	at CIN	W	13	9	266	295	+1	-11%	-13%	-14%	-12%
3	at NE	L	33	36	417	396	-1	28%	6%	-18%	4%
4	TEN	W	57	14	445	195	+4	89%	23%	-59%	7%
5	KC	L	34	42	392	450	-1	17%	41%	11%	-13%
6	CLE	W	33	17	340	247	+2	11%	-5%	-19%	-3%
7	BYE										
8	at SEA	L	38	41	509	479	-2	22%	31%	11%	3%
9	IND	L	14	20	288	371	0	-60%	-33%	23%	-4%
10	at LAR	L	7	33	283	443	-4	-66%	-45%	13%	-9%
11	ARI	W	31	21	357	292	0	-18%	-2%	10%	-5%
12	at BAL	L	16	23	303	294	-3	-12%	-21%	-3%	6%
13	at TEN	L	13	24	384	344	0	-56%	-8%	30%	-18%
14	SF	L	16	26	311	416	0	-48%	-19%	19%	-11%
15	at JAX	L	7	45	186	464	-1	-87%	-42%	41%	-3%
16	PIT	L	6	34	227	330	-2	-80%	-50%	20%	-10%
17	at IND	L	13	22	209	250	-1	-30%	-18%	5%	-6%

Trends and Splits

	Offense	Rank	Defense	Rank
Total DVOA	-9.9%	24	5.6%	23
Unadjusted VOA	-9.8%	27	7.5%	27
Weighted Trend	-17.3%	30	13.4%	31
Variance	7.0%	14	5.7%	17
Average Opponent	-1.0%	13	-1.2%	21
Passing	-0.4%	24	19.1%	25
Rushing	-11.2%	21	-9.9%	12
First Down	-7.6%	23	5.4%	23
Second Down	-2.9%	17	5.6%	22
Third Down	-26.2%	29	6.0%	21
First Half	-12.5%	24	5.7%	25
Second Half	-7.1%	23	5.5%	21
Red Zone	-21.4%	27	19.3%	31
Late and Close	-4.2%	19	13.7%	31

Five-Year Performance

Year	W-L	Pyth W	Est W	PF	PA	TO	Total	Rk	Off	Rk	Def	Rk	ST	Rk	Off AGL	Rk	Def AGL	Rk	Off Age	Rk	Def Age	Rk	ST Age	Rk
2013	2-14	4.2	3.9	276	428	-20	-26.5%	30	-18.9%	29	2.5%	18	-5.1%	29	35.1	18	28.6	18	27.5	9	26.2	22	25.7	26
2014	9-7	9.8	6.7	372	307	+12	-4.5%	19	-6.8%	21	-6.2%	6	-3.9%	28	18.8	6	41.1	20	27.2	12	26.0	28	26.1	17
2015	9-7	8.8	7.8	339	313	+5	-4.8%	18	-8.5%	24	-9.3%	8	-5.7%	32	49.8	26	15.0	3	26.5	17	26.2	24	25.8	20
2016	9-7	6.5	4.6	279	328	-7	-21.9%	29	-21.2%	30	-5.8%	9	-6.5%	31	51.8	27	40.0	20	25.7	30	26.5	17	26.2	12
2017	4-12	5.5	5.1	338	436	-12	-20.0%	28	-9.9%	24	5.6%	23	-4.5%	26	62.2	30	45.1	26	26.1	30	26.0	18	26.1	8

2017 Performance Based on Most Common Personnel Groups

HOU Offense					HOU Offense vs. Opponents						HOU Defense					HOU Defense vs. Opponents			
Pers	Freq	Yds	DVOA	Run%	Pers	Freq	Yds	DVOA	Run%		Pers	Freq	Yds	DVOA		Pers	Freq	Yds	DVOA
11	52%	6.1	2.4%	30%	Base	32%	4.7	-15.8%	59%		Base	38%	5.9	3.8%		11	52%	5.8	2.2%
21	13%	4.4	-3.1%	36%	Nickel	55%	5.3	-2.1%	35%		Nickel	34%	5.4	-8.5%		12	21%	6.2	13.6%
12	11%	4.4	-35.4%	42%	Dime+	13%	6.5	9.7%	13%		Dime+	24%	6.9	23.9%		21	12%	7.5	15.1%
611	5%	5.0	13.9%	69%	Goal Line	0%	0.0	-115.8%	100%		Goal Line	2%	3.5	24.4%		22	4%	4.8	-4.7%
20	5%	5.6	19.7%	38%							Big	2%	8.4	33.8%		13	4%	4.0	-22.9%
710	4%	3.9	-9.7%	64%															
620	3%	5.1	-21.5%	69%															
610	3%	2.8	-36.6%	78%															

Strategic Tendencies

Run/Pass		Rk	Formation		Rk	Pass Rush		Rk	Secondary		Rk	Strategy		Rk
Runs, first half	41%	8	Form: Single Back	74%	21	Rush 3	9.0%	11	4 DB	38%	7	Play action	22%	18
Runs, first down	58%	3	Form: Empty Back	9%	13	Rush 4	58.1%	25	5 DB	34%	28	Avg Box (Off)	6.24	17
Runs, second-long	22%	31	Pers: 3+ WR	60%	19	Rush 5	22.5%	11	6+ DB	24%	8	Avg Box (Def)	6.37	5
Runs, power sit.	51%	22	Pers: 2+ TE/6+ OL	29%	17	Rush 6+	10.5%	3	CB by Sides	78%	18	Offensive Pace	29.57	8
Runs, behind 2H	34%	3	Pers: 6+ OL	5%	7	Int DL Sacks	17.2%	24	S/CB Cover Ratio	34%	9	Defensive Pace	30.88	23
Pass, ahead 2H	44%	21	Shotgun/Pistol	70%	7	Second Level Sacks	37.5%	4	DB Blitz	13%	7	Go for it on 4th	0.80	24

Houston threw 35 percent of passes to its No. 1 receiver, DeAndre Hopkins. It was the highest percentage of passes thrown to a No. 1 receiver since the 2012 Chicago Bears threw 41 percent of passes to Brandon Marshall. ☞ Perhaps the Texans got the memo about running on second-and-long. In 2016, they did it more than almost any other team even though they had a horrible -58.9% DVOA. In 2017, they did it roughly half as often, dropping to 31st. (They were still bad, with -38.3% DVOA.) ☞ Houston used more six-lineman sets than any other offense but they weren't particularly good from those formations, with 4.1 yards per play (compared to NFL average of 3.9) and -12.1% DVOA (compared to NFL average of -3.8%). The Texans used eight different personnel groups on at least 2.5 percent of plays, but four of these were groupings with six or seven offensive linemen. ☞ Houston continues to do a terrible job of breaking tackles on offense. They ranked 31st in broken tackles for the second straight season, with just 95 in 2016 and 84 in 2017. Lamar Miller only had a broken tackle on 12.4 percent of touches, the worst figure of any starting running back except Orleans Darkwa, and no Houston receiver or tight end had double-digit broken tackles. ☞ Houston nearly doubled its use of big blitzes (six or more pass-rushers) compared to the year before. In 2016, the Texans were phenomenal with just 3.3 yards per pass allowed on big blitzes. That reversed in 2017: the Texans sent more big blitzes but allowed 8.8 yards per pass on those plays, 30th in the NFL. That was particularly slanted towards a handful of big plays—four passes of more than 50 yards but only two passes between 20 and 50 yards—so their DVOA was better at 17.7% (ranked 21st).

Passing

Player	DYAR	DVOA	Plays	NtYds	Avg	YAC	C%	TD	Int
T.Savage*	-249	-27.5%	243	1255	5.2	4.1	56.6%	5	6
D.Watson	497	23.1%	221	1583	7.2	5.3	62.4%	19	6
T.J.Yates*	-235	-45.0%	110	447	4.1	4.0	48.5%	4	2
J.Webb	-71	-167.5%	7	35	5.0	1.5	28.6%	0	1

Rushing

Player	DYAR	DVOA	Plays	Yds	Avg	TD	Fum	Suc
L.Miller	57	-2.8%	238	892	3.7	3	1	45%
D.Foreman	10	-5.5%	78	327	4.2	2	2	42%
A.Blue	14	-4.0%	71	262	3.7	1	0	42%
D.Watson	70	29.3%	35	270	7.7	2	1	-
A.Ellington*	-14	-75.9%	5	2	0.4	0	0	20%
T.J.Yates*	12	32.8%	5	51	10.2	0	0	-
T.Ervin	-2	-17.1%	4	12	3.0	0	0	75%
J.Webb	14	28.3%	7	55	7.9	0	0	-

Receiving

Player	DYAR	DVOA	Plays	Ctch	Yds	Y/C	YAC	TD	C%
D.Hopkins	367	13.3%	174	96	1378	14.4	3.7	13	55%
B.Ellington	-53	-24.5%	57	29	329	11.3	4.7	2	51%
W.Fuller	126	17.6%	50	28	423	15.1	3.5	7	56%
B.Miller	-31	-26.9%	29	19	162	8.5	3.7	1	66%
D.White	-33	-79.9%	7	1	24	24.0	1.0	0	14%
C.Thompson	42	76.0%	6	5	84	16.8	6.0	0	83%
C.Hamilton*	-30	-63.2%	6	1	8	8.0	4.0	0	17%
S.Coates	-16	-32.5%	11	6	70	11.7	2.7	0	55%
S.Anderson	-22	-14.0%	52	25	342	13.7	3.8	1	48%
R.Griffin	-6	-11.0%	26	13	158	12.2	5.6	1	50%
C.J.Fiedorowicz*	-2	-8.6%	22	14	127	9.1	2.6	0	64%
L.Miller	134	42.7%	45	36	327	9.1	8.2	3	80%
T.Ervin	-10	-32.0%	11	8	38	4.8	1.6	0	73%
A.Ellington*	17	20.9%	9	6	72	12.0	5.0	0	67%
A.Blue	15	15.8%	9	7	54	7.7	6.0	0	78%
D.Foreman	25	39.8%	8	6	83	13.8	11.0	0	75%

Offensive Line

Player	Pos	Age	GS	Snaps	Pen	Sk	Pass	Run	Player	Pos	Age	GS	Snaps	Pen	Sk	Pass	Run
Breno Giacomini*	RT	33	16/16	1102	9	8.0	33	14	Julie'n Davenport	LT	23	11/4	241	4	1.5	2	2
Xavier Su'a-Filo*	LG	27	16/16	1082	4	8.5	19	8	Chad Slade	G	26	5/3	167	1	1.5	3	2
Nick Martin	C	25	14/14	975	3	1.0	9	12	Kendall Lamm	OT	26	10/4	160	0	3.0	5	0
Jeff Allen	RG/LT	28	12/12	732	9	3.5	13	3	Zach Fulton	C/G	27	15/12	794	2	1.5	3	4
Greg Mancz	RG/C	26	10/7	565	0	1.5	12	10	Senio Kelemete	G/T	28	16/8	634	4	1.0	3	6
Chris Clark*	LT	23	11/4	241	9	2.5	15	4									

Year	Yards	ALY	Rank	Power	Rank	Stuff	Rank	2nd Lev	Rank	Open Field	Rank	Sacks	ASR	Rank	Press	Rank	F-Start	Cont.
2015	3.79	4.06	18	65%	16	19%	9	1.02	25	0.47	29	36	6.3%	17	21.3%	8	18	24
2016	4.14	4.16	15	61%	18	16%	6	1.14	16	0.61	20	32	5.6%	12	30.2%	27	7	29
2017	3.78	3.89	20	63%	18	21%	18	0.99	26	0.51	25	54	9.2%	30	36.9%	31	20	23

2017 ALY by direction: Left End: 1.30 (32)   Left Tackle: 3.89 (17)   Mid/Guard: 4.23 (12)   Right Tackle: 3.60 (22)   Right End: 3.48 (24)

A season entered with question marks proved a season of failure for the Texans offensive line. Right tackle Derek Newton missed the entire season after his double patellar tear and was released in April. Duane Brown's offseason holdout over dissatisfaction with his contract extended in to the regular season, leading to his eventual trade to Seattle. The second-round pick was good compensation, even though it cannot be used until next year. ☞ Left tackle was a mess, with Brown, Chris Clark, Julie'n Davenport, Kendall Lamm, and normal right guard Jeff Allen all making starts. If Davenport can hold down the job all year, the continuity alone should provide an upgrade. ☞ Senio Kelemete (ex-Saints utility lineman) and Seantrel Henderson (ex-Bills starter) provide non-disastrous options should rookie Martinas Rankins' foot injury linger into the regular season or one of the youngsters prove inadequate at right tackle. ☞ The departed Breno Giacomini led the league in blown blocks. ☞ Allen's tackle tenure was most notable for back-to-back-to-back false starts on fourth down in a comeback drive against the Titans. Houston converted the ensuing fourth-and-19, but Tom Savage was intercepted on the next play. ☞ Both starting guards could be ex-Chiefs, as the Texans gave Zach Fulton a surprising four-year, $28 million contract to fill the vacancy created by the disappointing Xavier Su'a-Filo's departure. ☞ The concussion that ended Allen's season was still an issue in May, as were ankle injuries. If Allen cannot go, Kelemete looks like the favorite to fill the other guard spot. ☞ At least Nick Martin at center is locked in and should be fine.

Defensive Front Seven

Defensive Line	Age	Pos	G	Snaps	Plays	TmPct	Rk	Stop	Dfts	BTkl	Runs	St%	Rk	RuYd	Rk	Sack	Hit	Hur	Dsrpt
						Overall					vs. Run					Pass Rush			
D.J. Reader	24	DT	14	526	48	7.1%	7	34	8	0	42	71%	63	2.2	49	1.0	4	10.0	0
Brandon Dunn	26	DT	16	419	26	3.4%	76	18	4	0	22	82%	27	2.0	40	0.0	2	4.5	0
Carlos Watkins	25	DE	12	330	22	3.8%	65	19	5	2	19	84%	18	1.2	7	0.0	0	6.5	1
Joel Heath	25	DE	13	325	24	3.8%	--	16	3	3	22	68%	--	2.4	--	1.0	0	3.0	0
Angelo Blackson	26	DE	9	195	10	2.3%	--	8	0	3	9	78%	--	2.1	--	0.0	2	5.0	0
Ufomba Kamalu	26	DE	9	183	6	1.4%	--	5	3	0	4	75%	--	1.8	--	2.0	1	4.0	0

Edge Rushers	Age	Pos	G	Snaps	Plays	TmPct	Rk	Stop	Dfts	BTkl	Runs	St%	Rk	RuYd	Rk	Sack	Hit	Hur	Dsrpt
						Overall					vs. Run					Pass Rush			
Jadeveon Clowney	25	OLB	16	898	60	7.8%	12	47	31	9	42	74%	51	1.5	23	9.5	13	45.0	2
Brennan Scarlett	25	OLB	11	302	27	5.1%	43	21	7	6	18	83%	21	2.0	36	2.0	1	6.5	1

Linebackers	Age	Pos	G	Snaps	Plays	TmPct	Rk	Stop	Dfts	BTkl	Runs	St%	Rk	RuYd	Rk	Sack	Hit	Hur	Tgts	Suc%	Rk	AdjYd	Rk	PD	Int
						Overall					vs. Run					Pass Rush				vs. Pass				
Benardrick McKinney	26	ILB	16	963	96	12.5%	40	49	15	7	68	57%	66	3.7	51	3.0	6	13.0	17	56%	22	5.6	16	0	0
Zach Cunningham	24	ILB	16	816	87	11.3%	50	65	22	10	46	89%	2	1.9	2	1.5	1	4.0	30	59%	12	7.7	59	3	0
Dylan Cole	24	ILB	12	205	28	4.9%	--	22	9	5	17	76%	--	2.9	--	1.0	1	1.0	7	83%	--	3.2	--	3	2

Year	Yards	ALY	Rank	Power	Rank	Stuff	Rank	2nd Level	Rank	Open Field	Rank	Sacks	ASR	Rank	Press	Rank
2015	4.17	3.83	9	59%	8	21%	13	1.14	19	0.88	23	45	7.5%	6	27.0%	8
2016	3.86	4.16	17	60%	10	17%	23	1.10	12	0.48	6	31	5.8%	18	26.2%	22
2017	3.93	3.86	8	70%	25	22%	7	1.11	17	0.75	17	32	6.2%	21	29.0%	24

2017 ALY by direction: Left End: 3.10 (6) | Left Tackle: 3.06 (5) | Mid/Guard: 3.79 (7) | Right Tackle: 3.85 (18) | Right End: 6.05 (32)

Having three outstanding players is the key to the Texans defensive success. Having all three of them on the field at the same time approaches a miracle. ☛ Whitney Mercilus was working out in May after his season-ending pectoral tear and should be ready for the season. Jadeveon Clowney was not practicing in the offseason after January knee surgery but should be ready for training camp. J.J. Watt at anything like his old self at any point in the season is approaching a special treat rather than a reasonable expectation. ☛ Highlighted by Watt's injury, the Texans ranked 31st in adjusted games lost on the defensive line. ☛ D.J. Reader is not an up-the-field player, but he had a fine season for a primarily run-stuffing nose tackle. The other non-Watt options at defensive line are unproven and unheralded. ☛ Whether Clowney is a down lineman or a stand-up rusher, he showcases rare ability to flat-out dominate NFL players. His 17 defeats on run plays were second in the NFL to Luke Kuechly, and his 31 total defeats tied for third, while 45 hurries were good for tenth. ☛ For the first time since the glory days of Brian Cushing and DeMeco Ryans, inside linebacker is a strength for the Texans. Bernardrick McKinney is a thumper and effective pass-rusher. Zach Cunningham had a fine rookie season and gives them a much-needed coverage option. Dylan Cole flashed as an undrafted rookie and could give the Texans an intriguing three-linebacker package.

Defensive Secondary

Secondary	Age	Pos	G	Snaps	Plays	TmPct	Rk	Stop	Dfts	BTkl	Runs	St%	Rk	RuYd	Rk	Tgts	Tgt%	Rk	Dist	Suc%	Rk	AdjYd	Rk	PD	Int
						Overall					vs. Run					vs. Pass								
Andre Hal	26	FS	16	943	75	9.8%	44	29	12	12	42	40%	50	6.8	45	33	7.6%	20	12.6	48%	51	10.6	69	6	3
Kareem Jackson	30	CB	16	872	82	10.7%	7	41	15	9	22	68%	9	4.0	10	75	19.0%	31	11.0	48%	53	8.2	55	8	1
Marcus Gilchrist*	30	SS	16	817	62	8.1%	67	21	9	8	23	30%	61	8.6	58	42	11.2%	52	12.2	46%	55	10.1	62	6	1
Johnathan Joseph	34	CB	16	748	56	7.3%	58	25	8	3	14	29%	67	7.1	58	66	19.4%	34	13.2	56%	13	10.3	79	8	2
Kevin Johnson	26	CB	12	581	47	8.2%	--	24	9	13	15	60%	--	6.6	--	48	18.1%	--	9.9	39%	--	10.2	--	2	0
Eddie Pleasant*	30	SS	16	307	30	3.9%	76	15	11	3	8	38%	54	5.5	27	24	17.3%	74	7.2	46%	56	9.2	49	3	1
Corey Moore	25	SS	14	240	22	3.3%	--	11	3	4	15	40%	--	6.9	--	9	7.8%	--	14.7	69%	--	5.2	--	2	0
Ibraheim Campbell	26	SS	9	196	16	3.3%	--	6	3	1	8	50%	--	6.0	--	7	8.1%	--	14.6	33%	--	10.7	--	1	0
Marcus Williams*	27	CB	15	185	20	2.8%	--	8	3	3	3	0%	--	13.7	--	30	38.0%	--	18.5	51%	--	8.9	--	4	1
Tyrann Mathieu	26	FS/CB	16	1056	80	9.9%	40	34	19	15	23	52%	18	8.2	56	65	13.4%	64	12.1	52%	37	8.0	35	6	2
Aaron Colvin	27	CB	16	705	49	6.2%	--	25	13	9	13	62%	--	6.7	--	44	15.7%	--	6.6	52%	--	5.4	--	4	0
Johnson Bademosi	28	CB	16	215	21	2.6%	--	4	1	2	4	25%	--	6.5	--	18	18.1%	--	13.4	33%	--	9.8	--	1	0

Year	Pass D Rank	vs. #1 WR	Rk	vs. #2 WR	Rk	vs. Other WR	Rk	WR Wide	Rk	WR Slot	Rk	vs. TE	Rk	vs. RB	Rk
2015	7	-7.6%	8	10.7%	23	-39.3%	1	--	--	--	--	-11.6%	9	2.2%	18
2016	5	1.8%	17	-38.1%	2	1.8%	17	-8.6%	12	-10.9%	6	-40.6%	2	23.3%	28
2017	25	12.4%	24	37.8%	30	16.6%	24	6.3%	24	33.6%	32	15.2%	27	-16.7%	7

The days when the Texans had outstanding depth at corner feel like a long time ago. Maybe Romeo Crennel in his return to the defensive coordinator job can find some of the solutions Mike Vrabel in his interregnum year did not. ☞ Age is definitely catching up to Johnathan Joseph. His deep speed has fallen off, and only Janoris Jenkins allowed more adjusted yards per play. It's a significant contrast to his strong rank in adjusted success rate, where technique and savvy still help. Two post-pattern touchdowns allowed in consecutive weeks stand out: 45 yards by T.Y. Hilton (43 in the air) in Week 9 and 94 yards by Robert Woods (44 yards in the air) in Week 10. ☞ Beyond the injuries to the front seven, the player who stood out the most in Houston's defensive decline was Kevin Johnson. The former first-round pick had an abysmal third season following an injury-plagued sophomore campaign. He would have ranked third-worst in success rate and adjusted yards per pass had he not just missed our qualifying thresholds. He also had the sixth-highest broken tackle rate among the 184 defensive backs with at least 20 tackles. ☞ Aaron Colvin arrives from Jacksonville as a necessary upgrade. A fine player in a pure slot role for the division champs, the possibility of winning one of the outside jobs enticed him to sign with Houston. We'll see. ☞ Free safety Andre Hal was diagnosed with cancer, specifically Hodgkin's lymphoma, in June, and is out indefinitely. Veteran corner Kareem Jackson worked extensively at safety in Hal's absence. The position switch has been long speculated outside Reliant Stadium. ☞ Tyrann Mathieu was signed to a one-year deal in free agency. He did a bit of everything in Arizona, but Houston has been working him as a pure safety. Strong safety was a position in dire need of an upgrade, but you don't see any strong safeties these days at 185 pounds and just 5-foot-9. Hal's absence may allow Mathieu to play a more familiar free safety role. ☞ If Jackson is not the other starter at safety, third-round pick Justin Reid (Stanford) will be. He is probably a better fit as a strong safety and projected to replace Mathieu next year before Hal's diagnosis. Even if not a starter, he may be asked to play in dime packages.

Special Teams

Year	DVOA	Rank	FG/XP	Rank	Net Kick	Rank	Kick Ret	Rank	Net Punt	Rank	Punt Ret	Rank	Hidden	Rank
2015	-5.7%	32	-3.7	27	1.0	12	-2.6	24	-15.1	31	-8.1	32	5.6	9
2016	-6.5%	31	-5.9	26	-12.9	32	-7.5	30	-13.0	30	6.7	6	1.4	15
2017	-4.5%	26	-5.8	24	0.1	18	-5.3	30	-10.7	28	-1.1	21	-16.9	32

By rank, 2017 was the best year for Houston special teams since they were 13th in 2011. It has been more than half a decade of very special teams. ☞ Not helping the cause: the Texans had the league's worst luck regarding opponent field goal kickers, as they missed just two field goal attempts and one extra point all season. ☞ Also not helping the cause: Houston opponents also led the league in gross punt value, with a league-high 24 punts landing inside the 10. ☞ Shane Lechler led the league in gross punting value, but the Texans were a bottom-five punting unit anyway because they finished last in punt coverage. Cue the classic complaint about Lechler "outkicking the coverage." ☞ Kai Fairbairn was slightly below average on kickoff value, while kick return coverage was fine. ☞ Fairbairn was not fine when it came to scoring points. Only one kicker missed more than his three extra points, and his field goals were also spotty. ☞ Will Fuller had 3.9 points worth of estimated field position on nine punt returns. He is too valuable to be used regularly but provides evidence the position is not irretrievably cursed. Chris Thompson, Bruce Ellington, and, if healthy, Tyler Ervin could all figure into a typically unattractive mix on returns.

Indianapolis Colts

2017 Record: 4-12	**Total DVOA:** -22.4% (31st)	**2018 Mean Projection:** 8.1 wins	**On the Clock (0-4):** 9%
Pythagorean Wins: 4.2 (30th)	**Offense:** -17.7% (29th)	**Postseason Odds:** 39.5%	**Mediocrity (5-7):** 32%
Snap-Weighted Age: 25.9 (29th)	**Defense:** 8.4% (27th)	**Super Bowl Odds:** 5.1%	**Playoff Contender (8-10):** 41%
Average Opponent: -2.4% (25th)	**Special Teams:** 3.7% (8th)	**Proj. Avg. Opponent:** -2.0% (28th)	**Super Bowl Contender (11+):** 19%

2017: No Luck + no answers = no more Chuck Pagano to kick around.

2018: Luck returns to find Frank Reich now looking for answers.

Football Outsiders has been writing a preseason annual since the 2005 NFL season. And in the previous 13 books, the Indianapolis Colts chapters all read pretty much the same. We say a few things about the heralded quarterback and then talk about whether the rest of the team is good enough for them to ride the play of that quarterback deep into the postseason. This does not mean the previews have always been the same. Some years have been Peyton Manning chapters or Andrew Luck chapters, while others have been about other aspects of the franchise's operation. Even in 2011 and 2017, when the quarterback missed the entire season and the Colts ended up with a top-three pick because of it, the chapters looked very similar, because we still went into the season thinking the quarterback was going to play.

But this year has a few new twists.

For one, we do not know just what to expect from Andrew Luck. On June 13, he did what he did not do in a game in 2017 and had not done at all since October: he threw a football before a member of the media. His rehab from the shoulder injury first suffered in 2015 and played through in 2016 had turned especially mysterious, dating at least to owner Jim Irsay's suggestion on last year's preseason telecast that Luck's injury was at least as much mental as physical. Still, Irsay sounded optimistic that Luck would be ready for the regular season. And then we waited. And waited. Luck was close to returning. Luck was throwing. Luck was not throwing. Luck was out for the year (and, at that point, the Colts were too, so why not). Luck was gone, maybe in Europe for treatment of some sort. Luck was not throwing. Luck was still not throwing. Chris Ballard accepted the Jets' offer of three second-round picks to move back in the draft and out of prime quarterback range, an excellent sign the team was pretty confident in Luck's long-term future (or maybe just that Ballard didn't like the signal-callers who might be available then). Finally, Luck threw.

We have no more specific insight into what Luck will be able to do, and when, and how successfully, and whether he will be able to keep doing it, than anybody else does. What we do know is that good quarterbacks (and a healthy Luck is at least a good quarterback, even if not a great one, as we covered two years ago) can get injured and end up having fine careers. Tom Brady tore his ACL in 2008 and was a great quarterback in 2009 and for many years thereafter. The shoul-

der injury that ended Drew Brees' 2005 season depressed his free-agent market, but it did not prevent him from being one of the league's best quarterbacks for the next decade and counting. On the odd occasion he was actually healthy, even Chad Pennington was very good.

If Luck is not completely healthy, the place it might show up is in his deep ball. He was lousy on deep passes in 2015 when he missed half the season and very good there in 2016. Jacoby Brissett in his stead tried to throw deep as much as he could, sometimes succeeding when he made or got the chance to do so. Exit, with head coach Chuck Pagano, offensive coordinator Rob Chudzinski and his vertical orientation. Enter the guru to the league's best passer, notwithstanding his spotty deep ball, Josh Mc… *Wait, Josh, come back!* Oh, never mind, Mr. McDaniels spurned Indianapolis and chose to remain in Foxborough following the Patriots' playoff run. Instead, enter assistant guru to the team that beat the Patriots in the Super Bowl, former Eagles offensive coordinator Frank Reich, and his right-hand man, new offensive coordinator Nick Sirianni.

Reich has yet to run purely his own offense, with his stints as coordinator coming under offense-minded head coaches Mike McCoy in San Diego and Doug Pederson in Philadelphia. Sirianni's history as a position coach, including under Reich in San Diego, suggests his primary role will be as adjutant to Reich and facilitator of his interests as he has to deal with the aspects of head coaching that go beyond directing the players who try to gain yards. Though Reich is a bit of a wild card, it seems safe to assume the Colts will do more to spread the ball horizontally rather than vertically, and to look to short passes to create big gains. Sirianni said as much in June, noting that "[as] you emphasize the quicker throws, the deep ones come," and that chunk plays need not come from deep passes. Sirianni saw that first-hand last year, as the Chargers ranked second in DVOA on passes 1 to 10 yards past the line of scrimmage and led the league in yards after catch on such throws.

Helping Luck gain those yards will be a pair of familiar faces, who were also the apple of Jacoby Brissett's eye last year. The former Patriot who ended up playing almost all of the season after a preseason trade had a process that seemingly went like this: look deep for T.Y. Hilton, look short for tight end Jack Doyle, check it down to a back, then take a sack if you cannot throw the ball away. Hilton and Doyle were each targeted on at

2018 Colts Schedule

Week	Opp.	Week	Opp.	Week	Opp.
1	CIN	7	BUF	13	at JAX
2	at WAS	8	at OAK	14	at HOU
3	at PHI	9	BYE	15	DAL
4	HOU	10	JAX	16	NYG
5	at NE (Thu.)	11	TEN	17	at TEN
6	at NYJ	12	MIA		

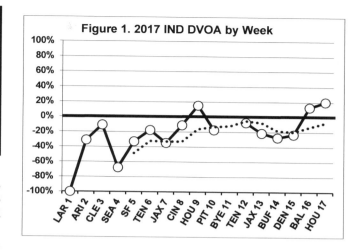

Figure 1. 2017 IND DVOA by Week

least 22 percent of Brissett's plays with an intended receiver, more than twice that of any other Colts player. The next players on the most-targeted list—Donte Moncrief, Kamar Aiken, and Frank Gore—have all departed this offseason.

Enter, to fill the void, former Detroit top-ten pick Eric Ebron and Ryan Grant, after Baltimore flunked him on his physical so they could sign Michael Crabtree instead. Ebron has the potential to fill a vertical receiving tight end role akin to the role Zach Ertz played for Reich in Philadelphia. Grant, well, somebody has to play receiver opposite Hilton. The other candidates are former UDFA Chester Rogers and a pair of Day 3 picks in Deon Cain (Clemson) and Daurice Fountain (Northern Iowa). Enter, as well, a couple of Day 3 running backs—North Carolina State all-purpose offensive weapon Nyheim Hines and Ole Miss bellcow Jordan Wilkins—to let Reich replicate the Eagles' committee approach.

The Colts could, if they choose, go with the seven-offensive linemen sets Luck saw with Jim Harbaugh at Stanford. After all, they used two of the four picks they got from the Jets, including No. 6 overall, on offensive guards Quenton Nelson (Notre Dame) and Braden Smith (Auburn). Golden Domer Nelson was by some accounts the draft's best prospect regardless of position, the latest and greatest "best guard prospect since Steve Hutchinson," the best puller anybody had seen, and well-schooled by new Bears offensive line coach Harry Hiestand. He slots in immediately at the left guard spot filled a year ago by Jeremy Vujnovich. Smith will be the right guard sooner rather than later, though his 6-foot-6 frame will always leave him vulnerable to squatty interior rushers.

Table 1. Colts Opening Day Defense, 2016-2018

2016		2017		Projected 2018	
Pos	Player	Pos	Player	Pos	Player
DE	Zach Kerr	DE	Henry Anderson	DE	Tarell Basham
DT	David Parry	DT	Al Woods	DT	Al Woods
DE	Kendall Langford	DE	Jonathan Hankins	DT	Denico Autry
OLB	Robert Mathis	OLB	Jabaal Sheard	DE	Jabaal Sheard
OLB	Erik Walden	OLB	John Simon	WLB	Darius Leonard
ILB	Sio Moore	ILB	Antonio Morrison	MLB	Anthony Walker
ILB	D'Qwell Jackson	ILB	Jon Bostic	SLB	Tyrell Adams
CB	Patrick Robinson	CB	Rashaan Melvin	CB	Pierre Desir
CB	Antonio Cromartie	CB	T.J. Green	CB	Quincy Wilson
SS	T.J. Green	SS	Matthias Farley	SS	Clayton Geathers
FS	Mike Adams	FS	Malik Hooker	FS	Malik Hooker

On defense, Chris Ballard's rebuilding project continues into its second season, and the changes in the defensive lineup each of the last two offseasons have been substantial (Table 1). The man overseeing that changeover, which includes not just personnel but scheme, is Matt Eberflus. He comes from Dallas and was McDaniels' hand-picked selec... oh, yeah, the Cowboys missed the playoffs so Eberflus could sign his contract to become the new defensive coordinator well before McDaniels could put pen to paper, and he was among those left in the lurch when McDaniels backed out. But Reich fits the same mold of an offensive-minded head coach who will likely be content with leaving the defense mostly in somebody else's hands, so the job remained his. Eberflus was influenced by Rod Marinelli, and the defense will change back to a 4-3 scheme with some Tampa roots, much more along the lines of what the Colts ran back in the Dungy era than what Chuck Pagano tried to do.

Eberflus' task is complicated by a defensive depth chart that has few sure answers anywhere. A number of starting spots are subject to training camp battles. At No. 36, South Carolina State star Darius Leonard was the first of the draft picks devoted to the defense; he has missed the offseason due to a hamstring injury, a potentially significant setback for his early prospects coming from a lower level of college football. The entire linebacker corps is steeped in uncertainty, with Eberflus commenting in June, "One through 10, we have no idea who is one and we have no idea who is 10." Leonard may be the only mortal lock for the roster.

The most promising member of the secondary, or the defense as a whole, was another member of the offseason injury brigade. Early last season, Malik Hooker improved weekly and showed clear flashes of the ball-hawking ability at Ohio State that made him look like a steal with the 15th pick in last year's draft. A torn ACL in October leaves his status for the start of the season uncertain, while a recurrence of Clayton Geathers' perennial injury issues cost him much of the offseason as well. Cornerback Quincy Wilson, last year's second-rounder who struggled to find the field as a rookie under Chuck Pagano for mysterious reasons, also missed some time in the offseason. The scheme change to more zone coverage should help him.

If Eberflus can find players who get on the field and stay there, we do have some good news for the Colts defense: they were gobsmackingly awful on third downs last year. This seems like an exceptionally odd piece of good news, but it actually bodes well for the Colts' prospects next year. Table 2 shows the worst teams of the DVOA era by third-down defensive DVOA and how they performed the next year, both on third downs and overall. Not one was gobsmackingly awful on third downs the next season. All improved on third downs, from anywhere between "run-of-the-mill bad" to actually good, and ten of the 12 improved overall.

We also drilled down and looked only at recent teams with a similar performance. For a long time, one of the most important precepts at Football Outsiders was what we called "the third-down rebound effect." Teams that were better on third down than on first and second down tended to decline the following year, and teams that were worse on third down than on first and second down tended to improve the following year. Over the past decade, we've noticed this effect becoming smaller. Since 2007, in fact, there's really been no difference between "the third-down rebound effect" and simple regression towards the mean—except with teams at the extremes. And the Colts were so horrendous on third down that they definitely qualify as an extreme.

The Colts were tenth in the league on first down with -6.0% DVOA, and they were 16th in the league with a very average -0.1% DVOA on second down. No defense since 2007 has had a larger gap between third-down and overall performance. We looked at other teams with extreme gaps, and for each team we compared a simple forecast based only on regression towards the mean to that team's actual defensive DVOA in the following season (Table 3). These teams with horrific third-down defenses tended to improve much more than we would have expected otherwise.

No, this doesn't mean we're projecting the Colts to suddenly field one of the best defenses in the league in 2018. There is too much uncertainty, not enough history, and not enough investment for us to project the Colts to be anything other than a below-average defense. Nonetheless, an improvement from last year appears very likely. The offense should also greatly improve with a full season of Luck, even if he is not quite the same Luck we have seen at his best in the past. This story of potentially significant improvement on both offense and defense sounds like the one currently being told in Houston and Tennessee, while Jacksonville tries to hold off our projected defensive regression. That should make the AFC South the most competitive division in football, where a break or two could make any of the four teams division champ. If Luck misses significant time or plays but is severely hampered, all bets are off, but if Luck plays all 16 games at his previous level of performance, a return to the postseason would not be too much of a surprise. True contender status, though, will take at least one more offseason of work.

Tom Gower

Table 2. Worst Third Down Defenses of the DVOA Era (1986-2017)

Year	Team	3rd Down DVOA	All Downs DVOA	Rank	3rd Down Y+1	All Downs Y+1	Rank Y+1
1990	CLE	60.8%	12.2%	23	24.9%	1.1%	14
1987*	TB	58.6%	16.9%	26	24.2%	2.5%	17
2017	**IND**	**50.0%**	**8.7%**	**27**	--	--	--
2001	ATL	47.5%	11.8%	26	2.9%	-4.1%	12
2011	SD	47.0%	10.8%	29	4.9%	2.0%	18
1987*	DAL	45.9%	0.5%	17	4.9%	9.0%	24
2003	SD	43.7%	12.0%	30	-17.6%	-4.2%	13
2015	JAX	43.7%	9.7%	26	4.1%	-3.1%	12
1987*	ATL	43.0%	17.6%	27	-11.3%	2.6%	18
1989	HOIL	42.5%	10.6%	22	-9.8%	1.6%	15
2006	WAS	41.0%	15.0%	32	7.5%	-7.9%	7
2012	BUF	40.8%	10.6%	27	-22.9%	-13.8%	4
2009	JAX	40.6%	11.3%	28	24.1%	17.7%	32
AVERAGE (w/o 2017 IND)		46.6%	11.4%		3.0%	0.3%	

*Not including strike games.

Table 3. Biggest Gap between Third-Down and Overall Defensive DVOA Since 2007

Year	Team	3rd Down DVOA	Rank	All Downs DVOA	Rank	Gap	Simple Forecast Y+1	Actual DVOA Y+1
2017	**IND**	**50.0%**	**32**	**8.7%**	**27**	**41.3%**	**3.3%**	--
2010	NYJ	28.1%	32	-10.9%	5	39.0%	-4.5%	-16.1%
2011	SD	47.0%	32	10.8%	29	36.2%	4.1%	2.0%
2015	JAX	43.7%	32	9.7%	26	34.0%	3.7%	-3.1%
2016	WAS	37.5%	32	6.8%	25	30.7%	2.6%	-4.9%
2014	NYJ	33.9%	32	3.5%	21	30.5%	1.2%	-13.8%
2012	BUF	40.8%	32	10.6%	27	30.2%	4.1%	-13.8%
2009	JAX	40.6%	32	11.3%	28	29.3%	4.3%	17.7%
2009	PIT	21.7%	30	-4.6%	9	26.3%	-2.0%	-20.7%
2013	DEN	25.5%	29	-0.2%	15	25.8%	-0.2%	-13.2%
2013	MIN	36.1%	32	10.5%	27	25.6%	4.0%	4.3%
2013	CLE	33.9%	31	8.2%	24	25.6%	3.1%	-3.0%
AVERAGE (w/o 2017 IND)		35.3%		5.1%		30.3%	1.9%	-5.9%

2017 Colts Stats by Week

Wk	vs.	W-L	PF	PA	YDF	YDA	TO	Total	Off	Def	ST
1	at LAR	L	9	46	225	373	-2	-102%	-77%	11%	-14%
2	ARI	L	13	16	266	389	0	-31%	-32%	0%	1%
3	CLE	W	31	28	335	346	+2	-11%	-2%	15%	6%
4	at SEA	L	18	46	237	477	0	-68%	-31%	39%	3%
5	SF	W	26	23	447	402	-1	-33%	-29%	14%	10%
6	at TEN	L	22	36	297	473	0	-18%	-4%	22%	9%
7	JAX	L	0	27	232	518	+2	-35%	-30%	13%	8%
8	at CIN	L	23	24	331	276	+1	-11%	-13%	-3%	-1%
9	at HOU	W	20	14	371	288	0	15%	3%	-6%	6%
10	PIT	L	17	20	267	316	0	-17%	-31%	-9%	4%
11	BYE										
12	TEN	L	16	20	254	276	+1	-7%	-27%	-11%	9%
13	at JAX	L	10	30	290	426	-2	-21%	5%	29%	3%
14	at BUF	L	7	13	227	319	+2	-27%	-26%	-13%	-14%
15	DEN	L	13	25	228	462	+1	-23%	-4%	28%	9%
16	at BAL	L	16	23	296	323	0	13%	16%	8%	5%
17	HOU	W	22	13	250	209	+1	20%	-7%	-12%	15%

Trends and Splits

	Offense	Rank	Defense	Rank
Total DVOA	-17.8%	29	8.7%	27
Unadjusted VOA	-18.7%	31	7.1%	24
Weighted Trend	-11.4%	27	5.9%	23
Variance	4.9%	9	2.7%	2
Average Opponent	-3.0%	2	-4.8%	30
Passing	-14.8%	30	28.5%	32
Rushing	-12.3%	24	-11.9%	10
First Down	-27.5%	32	-6.0%	10
Second Down	-19.2%	27	-0.1%	16
Third Down	1.0%	15	50.0%	32
First Half	-5.5%	20	2.5%	19
Second Half	-30.6%	32	14.9%	31
Red Zone	-29.0%	29	-2.9%	14
Late and Close	-30.8%	31	4.3%	22

Five-Year Performance

Year	W-L	Pyth W	Est W	PF	PA	TO	Total	Rk	Off	Rk	Def	Rk	ST	Rk	Off AGL	Rk	Def AGL	Rk	Off Age	Rk	Def Age	Rk	ST Age	Rk
2013	11-5	9.4	9.5	391	336	+13	3.2%	13	4.3%	13	0.9%	16	-0.1%	18	75.5	30	25.2	11	25.8	31	27.7	4	26.0	20
2014	11-5	10.2	8.8	458	369	-5	4.5%	13	-1.1%	17	-2.3%	13	3.3%	8	56.6	29	48.2	23	26.2	28	28.3	1	26.1	12
2015	8-8	6.0	5.5	333	408	-5	-12.9%	23	-15.6%	30	-2.2%	13	0.5%	16	22.0	6	43.1	26	27.1	13	28.6	1	26.3	11
2016	8-8	8.5	7.0	411	392	-5	-4.6%	23	3.7%	12	12.5%	29	4.1%	5	27.3	9	51.1	24	25.8	27	28.0	2	25.9	20
2017	4-12	4.2	4.3	263	404	+5	-22.8%	31	-17.8%	29	8.7%	27	3.7%	8	56.4	25	44.8	25	26.4	24	25.7	24	25.3	27

2017 Performance Based on Most Common Personnel Groups

IND Offense

Pers	Freq	Yds	DVOA	Run%
11	65%	4.9	-10.0%	29%
12	28%	4.7	-22.7%	61%
13	4%	3.3	-24.5%	76%
02	1%	2.9	87.2%	11%
612	1%	1.0	5.4%	83%
WC	1%	2.3	-82.6%	100%

IND Offense vs. Opponents

Pers	Freq	Yds	DVOA	Run%
Base	35%	4.3	-25.8%	64%
Nickel	54%	4.9	-5.5%	30%
Dime+	10%	5.0	-16.1%	10%
Goal Line	1%	1.5	32.6%	100%

IND Defense

Pers	Freq	Yds	DVOA
Base	42%	5.4	-4.5%
Nickel	44%	5.9	14.6%
Dime+	11%	8.0	42.1%
Goal Line	1%	0.8	34.4%
Big	2%	6.3	1.1%

IND Defense vs. Opponents

Pers	Freq	Yds	DVOA
11	50%	6.2	16.1%
12	19%	6.3	7.8%
21	9%	6.0	5.9%
13	4%	4.3	-62.6%
22	3%	4.7	0.0%
10	2%	8.3	31.4%

Strategic Tendencies

Run/Pass		Rk	Formation		Rk	Pass Rush		Rk	Secondary		Rk	Strategy		Rk
Runs, first half	42%	5	Form: Single Back	80%	12	Rush 3	20.4%	3	4 DB	42%	4	Play action	22%	15
Runs, first down	53%	10	Form: Empty Back	7%	20	Rush 4	58.5%	24	5 DB	44%	23	Avg Box (Off)	6.23	20
Runs, second-long	32%	19	Pers: 3+ WR	66%	12	Rush 5	16.1%	25	6+ DB	11%	14	Avg Box (Def)	6.36	6
Runs, power sit.	50%	23	Pers: 2+ TE/6+ OL	34%	8	Rush 6+	5.0%	20	CB by Sides	75%	23	Offensive Pace	31.21	23
Runs, behind 2H	34%	2	Pers: 6+ OL	9%	1	Int DL Sacks	36.0%	6	S/CB Cover Ratio	24%	24	Defensive Pace	30.41	14
Pass, ahead 2H	52%	5	Shotgun/Pistol	57%	18	Second Level Sacks	14.0%	23	DB Blitz	7%	21	Go for it on 4th	0.98	17

Jacoby Brissett gained just 4.0 yards per pass with -48.2% DVOA against five-man blitzes but rebounded to 7.8 yards per pass with -1.7% DVOA against six-man blitzes. ☞ The Colts were the worst offense when running the ball on second-and-long with an absolutely brutal -70.1% DVOA and just 2.8 yards per carry. ☞ The Colts offense ranked in the bottom six for broken tackles for the third straight season. ☞ For the fourth straight year, the Colts had one of the league's largest gaps between defense against multi-back runs (3.0 yards per carry, -30.1% DVOA) and defense against single-back runs (4.4 yards per carry, -10.3% DVOA). ☞ Possibly connected: somehow the Colts were the No. 1 defense against the run on first downs but ranked 26th against the run on second downs and dead last against the run on third downs. ☞ The Colts allowed a brutal 71.9% DVOA when they blitzed a defensive back. ☞ Overall, the Colts allowed fewer yards per play the more pass-rushers they sent, but also allowed a higher DVOA the more pass-rushers they sent:

Indianapolis Defense by Number of Pass-Rushers, 2017

Pass-Rushers	Frequency	Yd/Pass	DVOA
2-3	20%	6.9	14.8%
4	59%	8.1	27.8%
5	16%	7.3	52.3%
6+	5%	6.0	65.0%

Passing

Player	DYAR	DVOA	Plays	NtYds	Avg	YAC	C%	TD	Int
J.Brissett	-105	-14.4%	518	2774	5.4	5.7	59.5%	13	7
S.Tolzien*	-110	-91.6%	22	99	4.5	8.0	50.0%	0	2

Rushing

Player	DYAR	DVOA	Plays	Yds	Avg	TD	Fum	Suc
F.Gore*	66	-2.3%	261	955	3.7	3	3	44%
M.Mack	6	-6.9%	93	365	3.9	4	1	41%
J.Brissett	-4	-13.7%	53	263	5.0	4	3	-
R.Turbin	7	-2.4%	23	53	2.3	1	0	52%
M.Jones*	9	36.8%	5	14	2.8	0	0	40%

Receiving

Player	DYAR	DVOA	Plays	Ctch	Yds	Y/C	YAC	TD	C%
T.Y.Hilton	75	-3.8%	109	57	966	16.9	5.3	4	52%
D.Moncrief*	94	11.4%	47	26	391	15.0	3.0	2	55%
K.Aiken*	-144	-55.8%	44	15	133	8.9	3.1	0	34%
C.Rogers	28	-3.1%	37	23	284	12.3	4.5	1	62%
R.Grant	146	16.7%	65	45	573	12.7	5.2	4	69%
J.Doyle	-2	-7.5%	108	80	690	8.6	4.2	4	74%
B.Williams*	5	-2.6%	17	13	121	9.3	6.0	0	76%
D.Daniels	-55	-65.3%	13	3	26	8.7	5.3	0	23%
E.Ebron	50	2.0%	86	53	574	10.8	4.9	4	62%
R.Travis	-46	-69.6%	12	5	43	8.6	3.2	0	42%
F.Gore*	35	4.1%	38	29	245	8.4	9.5	1	76%
M.Mack	38	9.2%	33	21	225	10.7	13.5	1	64%
R.Turbin	-1	-16.9%	11	9	56	6.2	7.7	0	82%

Offensive Line

Player	Pos	Age	GS	Snaps	Pen	Sk	Pass	Run	Player	Pos	Age	GS	Snaps	Pen	Sk	Pass	Run
Jeremy Vujnovich	LG	28	16/16	1030	3	4.5	16	18	Jack Mewhort	RG	27	5/5	313	2	0.5	4	3
Anthony Castonzo	LT	30	16/16	1030	5	6.0	21	7	Denzelle Good	RG	27	6/5	293	1	0.0	5	4
Joe Haeg	RT	25	16/15	987	4	8.0	19	10	Deyshawn Bond	C	24	4/4	189	1	0.0	1	2
Ryan Kelly	C	25	7/7	394	0	0.5	7	6	Austin Howard	RT	31	16/16	1082	4	4.3	16	1
Le'Raven Clark	RG/T	25	15/5	323	2	2.0	10	2	Matt Slauson	LG	32	7/7	425	2	0.0	6	5
Mike Person*	C	30	12/4	317	1	1.0	3	1	Mark Glowinski	LG	26	10/2	198	1	1.0	5	1

Year	Yards	ALY	Rank	Power	Rank	Stuff	Rank	2nd Lev	Rank	Open Field	Rank	Sacks	ASR	Rank	Press	Rank	F-Start	Cont.
2015	3.52	3.78	27	60%	24	23%	24	0.99	29	0.48	28	37	6.1%	16	25.8%	18	12	26
2016	3.83	4.69	2	63%	15	13%	1	1.01	28	0.26	32	44	7.6%	28	33.3%	31	18	24
2017	3.63	3.98	18	81%	2	20%	16	1.00	25	0.44	29	56	10.0%	32	37.0%	32	20	20

2017 ALY by direction:	Left End: 4.64 (10)	Left Tackle: 3.64 (19)	Mid/Guard: 4.11 (18)	Right Tackle: 3.35 (24)	Right End: 4.54 (8)

Jacoby Brissett was knocked down 116 times, which was third in the league (sacks and QB hits, including nullified plays). This was the fifth time in six years that the Colts' starting quarterback ranked in the top three. So poor pass protection is an Indianapolis tradition at this point. ☞ Just three Colts offensive linemen played the 400 snaps necessary to be ranked on our blown block tables, undoubtedly part of what led Ballard to spend those high picks on Quenton Nelson and Braden Smith. Only the Saints have a lower three-year continuity score. The fact that New Orleans has maintained consistently low sack and pressure rates suggests that quarterback and scheme are more important for those stats than the men up front. ☞ A team with a more settled offensive line might think about whether Anthony Castonzo is worth good left tackle money. Here, being a capable starter means he gets ignored so you can just worry about everybody else. ☞ Ryan Kelly injured his foot in August, wasn't good when he returned, and had his season ended prematurely by concussion. Six more snaps, and he would have had the second-highest blown block rate among qualifying centers. ☞ Matt Slauson looks like the favorite to start at right guard until Smith is ready; he was average last year for the Chargers. ☞ New offensive line coach Dave DeGuglielmo, last seen as a line coach during the Dante Scarnecchia interregnum in New England, would probably like Denzelle Good to be the starter at right tackle. Austin Howard, signed in May, looks like the favorite to start Week 1; he is an outstanding run blocker and an average at best pass blocker. Another season of Joe Haeg would not be a problem if the rest of the line was solid. ☞ Jack Mewhort, a good guard on the too-infrequent occasions he has been healthy, was also re-signed. ☞ DeGuglielmo should have plenty of options, even if injury strikes.

Defensive Front Seven

Defensive Line	Age	Pos	G	Snaps	Plays	TmPct	Rk	Stop	Dfts	BTkl	Runs	St%	Rk	RuYd	Rk	Sack	Hit	Hur	Dsrpt
								Overall					**vs. Run**				**Pass Rush**		
Johnathan Hankins*	26	DT	15	685	46	5.9%	24	44	13	2	40	95%	3	1.4	12	2.0	3	8.5	3
Margus Hunt	31	DE	16	578	30	3.6%	71	23	11	3	26	77%	46	1.3	10	1.0	7	28.0	3
Al Woods	31	DT	16	566	43	5.2%	39	36	8	3	39	85%	16	1.6	25	1.0	2	5.0	0
Henry Anderson*	27	DE	9	382	20	4.3%	58	14	4	3	15	73%	60	2.6	66	2.0	6	10.5	0
Grover Stewart	25	DT	15	256	23	3.0%	--	16	2	1	22	68%	--	3.2	--	0.0	0	1.5	0
Denico Autry	28	DT	16	592	41	5.0%	46	34	17	3	20	85%	13	1.6	21	5.0	6	18.5	6

Edge Rushers	Age	Pos	G	Snaps	Plays	TmPct	Rk	Stop	Dfts	BTkl	Runs	St%	Rk	RuYd	Rk	Sack	Hit	Hur	Dsrpt
								Overall					**vs. Run**				**Pass Rush**		
Jabaal Sheard	29	OLB	16	898	54	6.5%	24	47	16	14	42	88%	12	1.9	32	5.5	9	50.5	4
Barkevious Mingo*	28	OLB	16	501	46	5.5%	38	28	9	9	28	64%	78	3.6	87	2.0	6	16.5	2
John Simon	28	OLB	9	469	41	8.8%	4	25	14	5	30	63%	81	2.9	71	3.0	9	14.0	2

Linebackers	Age	Pos	G	Snaps	Plays	TmPct	Rk	Stop	Dfts	BTkl	Runs	St%	Rk	RuYd	Rk	Sack	Hit	Hur	Tgts	Suc%	Rk	AdjYd	Rk	PD	Int
								Overall					**vs. Run**				**Pass Rush**				**vs. Pass**				
Jon Bostic*	27	ILB	14	915	99	13.6%	31	58	17	5	64	72%	17	3.0	21	1.0	2	7.0	28	47%	49	6.9	43	2	0
Antonio Morrison	24	ILB	15	812	109	14.0%	28	62	10	9	79	65%	35	3.8	55	0.0	0	1.0	27	48%	43	6.2	28	0	0

Year	Yards	ALY	Rank	Power	Rank	Stuff	Rank	2nd Level	Rank	Open Field	Rank	Sacks	ASR	Rank	Press	Rank
2015	4.16	4.08	17	59%	9	20%	18	1.05	9	1.00	27	35	5.7%	28	26.5%	11
2016	4.81	4.83	31	48%	2	16%	28	1.42	31	0.82	21	33	6.3%	13	19.0%	32
2017	3.96	4.09	16	64%	18	20%	20	1.11	16	0.69	15	25	4.5%	31	31.7%	10
2017 ALY by direction:		Left End: 3.82 (16)			Left Tackle: 4.10 (19)			Mid/Guard: 4.25 (16)			Right Tackle: 2.84 (4)			Right End: 4.95 (29)	

Jabaal Sheard was tied for fourth in the league in hurries. Now the Colts just need to find a second pass-rusher. ☞ Robert Mathis, chosen in 2003, was the last Colts draft pick to have as many as 8.0 sacks in Indianapolis. That's for a career, not just in a season. Ballard and Eberflus are hoping second-round pick Kemoko Turay (Rutgers) ends that streak. A one-year starter held back by injuries, he is an explosive prospect who could easily be a better NFL than college player. He will likely be eased into the lineup as a pass-rush specialist. ☞ John Simon is a man on the spot. Neck and shoulder injuries cost him time in 2017, and he is undersized for a 4-3 defensive end, part of why his entire career to date has been as a 3-4 outside linebacker. ☞ Last year's third-round pick Tarell Basham spent his Ohio tenure lined up with his hand down and has the size and length Simon does not, so he should benefit from the scheme change. He had seven hurries in 222 snaps. ☞ Denico Autry (ex-Raiders) is the big free-agency addition. He is a solid interior pass-rusher but at only 270 pounds might be best served as a defensive end on base downs. Tyquan Lewis (Ohio State), the last of Indy's four second-round picks, has a similar profile. ☞ The release of Johnathan Hankins, not as valuable in the new scheme, offers the chance for rotational defensive linemen—including Al Woods, Margus Hunt, and Hassan Ridgeway—to earn more playing time. Or not. ☞ Colts linebacker may be the most wide open position group in the league. Once he's healthy, second-round pick Darius Leonard (South Carolina State) should start on the weak side. Other positions, or all of them if Leonard is not healthy and ready, are up for grabs. Najee Goode is the cheap veteran import; Antonio Morrison the two-down thumper; Anthony Walker the special-teamer looking for a bigger role on defense; Matthew Adams (Houston) and Zaire Franklin (Syracuse) the late-round rookies; and Skai Moore (South Carolina) the heralded undrafted free agent.

Defensive Secondary

Secondary	Age	Pos	G	Snaps	Plays	Overall TmPct	Rk	Stop	Dfts	BTkl	vs. Run Runs	St%	Rk	RuYd	Rk	vs. Pass Tgts	Tgt%	Rk	Dist	Suc%	Rk	AdjYd	Rk	PD	Int
Matthias Farley	26	SS	16	928	100	12.0%	17	42	12	15	65	48%	29	6.0	35	37	11.4%	53	11.1	53%	33	9.5	55	6	2
Rashaan Melvin*	29	CB	10	552	49	9.4%	25	26	13	1	9	78%	7	2.4	2	54	28.0%	74	11.7	53%	26	6.5	15	14	3
Nate Hairston	24	CB	14	536	40	5.5%	--	20	14	5	6	17%	--	7.7	--	43	23.2%	--	9.5	52%	--	7.5	--	5	1
Darius Butler*	32	FS	15	504	33	4.2%	--	9	5	6	8	13%	--	12.9	--	16	8.9%	--	14.4	47%	--	8.7	--	4	0
Malik Hooker	22	FS	7	410	24	6.6%	--	5	3	3	7	14%	--	11.3	--	12	8.5%	--	18.3	39%	--	13.8	--	5	3
Quincy Wilson	22	CB	7	402	28	7.7%	--	16	6	2	8	63%	--	6.0	--	31	21.9%	--	13.1	60%	--	8.6	--	6	1
Kenny Moore	23	CB	16	383	37	4.5%	--	12	5	7	9	22%	--	8.0	--	29	21.5%	--	13.9	33%	--	12.0	--	6	1
T.J. Green	23	FS	16	378	42	5.1%	--	19	6	5	30	53%	--	4.1	--	8	6.1%	--	11.8	55%	--	9.0	--	1	0
Pierre Desir	28	CB	9	375	39	8.3%	--	15	3	3	6	17%	--	6.5	--	36	27.3%	--	15.1	48%	--	9.6	--	7	1
Vontae Davis*	30	CB	5	330	23	8.9%	--	6	1	1	6	33%	--	4.8	--	27	23.6%	--	12.5	40%	--	10.4	--	3	0
Kenneth Acker	26	CB	16	209	20	2.5%	--	5	2	2	7	43%	--	8.3	--	19	23.8%	--	11.4	30%	--	10.5	--	3	1

Year	Pass D Rank	vs. #1 WR	Rk	vs. #2 WR	Rk	vs. Other WR	Rk	WR Wide	Rk	WR Slot	Rk	vs. TE	Rk	vs. RB	Rk
2015	12	-4.8%	11	-10.5%	11	23.4%	30	--	--	--	--	6.5%	20	-7.9%	11
2016	26	13.7%	29	-3.3%	12	-1.1%	14	8.3%	27	1.7%	15	33.1%	31	38.5%	31
2017	32	7.6%	18	22.7%	27	28.5%	31	22.3%	32	18.4%	24	9.9%	23	27.9%	31

Rashaan Melvin was the best player in the secondary last year, but he was not nearly as good a fit for a scheme built more on zone and off coverage than press and man, so the Colts let him walk in free agency. ☞ Vontae Davis was once one of the best corners in the league, but his Colts career thudded to a close with a lingering groin injury and poor play leading to a November release. ☞ Quincy Wilson's solid charting numbers make his occasional healthy scratch status all the more puzzling. ☞ Waiver-wire addition Pierre Desir was fine when healthy and was re-signed in the offseason. ☞ The Colts seem high on Nate Hairston, a fifth-round pick who had a decent rookie season primarily as a slot corner, and Kenny Moore, an undrafted player who was primarily a special teams player. ☞ With Malik Hooker still recovering from last year's ACL tear and questionable for the start of the regular season, safety is filled with more potential than answers. Can Clayton Geathers (112 snaps) stay healthy long enough to get a starting job back from Matthias Farley, and can he match the discipline and consistency that made Farley the one constant in last year's secondary? ☞ For a team so short on big investments outside of Hooker and rated so lousy by DVOA, the Colts secondary was not that bad. More pass rush and quick adaptation to the new scheme could help lead to the defensive improvement we project.

Special Teams

Year	DVOA	Rank	FG/XP	Rank	Net Kick	Rank	Kick Ret	Rank	Net Punt	Rank	Punt Ret	Rank	Hidden	Rank
2015	0.5%	16	4.5	8	4.8	5	-1.2	18	-0.1	19	-5.6	26	6.9	6
2016	4.1%	5	8.9	4	1.6	12	9.0	4	3.5	10	-2.3	21	4.4	10
2017	3.7%	8	0.4	16	1.6	16	-1.2	18	20.2	1	-2.6	23	5.0	9

Adam Vinatieri continued his late career resurgence from distance, hitting five of six kicks from longer than 50 yards, but he uncharacteristically missed three attempts from 30 to 39 yards. Only Phil Dawson missed more kicks in that range. In Vinatieri's defense, one did come in the blizzard in Buffalo, in which he also hit an incredible 43-yard extra point. ☞ Rigoberto Sanchez had an excellent season replacing Pat McAfee at punter, combining above-average punt distance with excellent coverage. He was also average on kickoffs. ☞ All told, the Colts ranked fifth on punt coverage and eighth on kickoff coverage—though no Colts gunner had more than five special teams tackles. ☞ The departure of Quan Bray leaves the kickoff and punt return jobs open. Chester Rogers was average on punt returns when he got the chance but might be needed more on offense. Kick returner should be wide open; rookie Nyheim Hines was getting some looks there during OTAs.

Jacksonville Jaguars

2017 Record: 10-6	**Total DVOA:** 13.1% (8th)	**2018 Mean Projection:** 7.7 wins	**On the Clock (0-4):** 12%
Pythagorean Wins: 11.9 (3rd)	**Offense:** -0.2% (16th)	**Postseason Odds:** 33.0%	**Mediocrity (5-7):** 36%
Snap-Weighted Age: 26.0 (28th)	**Defense:** -16.1% (1st)	**Super Bowl Odds:** 3.8%	**Playoff Contender (8-10):** 38%
Average Opponent: -5.6% (32nd)	**Special Teams:** -2.8% (24th)	**Proj. Avg. Opponent:** -0.4% (21st)	**Super Bowl Contender (11+):** 15%

2017: Can the Jaguars overcome their own recent historical trends?

2018: Can the Jaguars overcome recent league-wide historical trends?

If branding is an essential element of notoriety, then the Jaguars social media team hit the high note of 2017 when it debuted the #Sacksonville Twitter tag after the defense recorded 10 sacks in a season-opening win over the Texans. Those 10 sacks became 55 by the end of the regular season, second-most in the league behind Pittsburgh, and the Jaguars had two players finish in the top ten for individual sacks (Calais Campbell with 14.5, and Yannick Ngakoue with 12.0). More broadly, the Jaguars were the runaway leader in pass defense DVOA, with a bigger difference between their efficiency and that of No. 2 Baltimore than between the Ravens and No. 11 Arizona. Unhindered by an offensive approach that focused mostly on staying out of their own way, this outstanding pass defense was enough to propel the Jaguars not only into the playoffs as the winner of the AFC South, but all the way to the AFC Championship Game.

In the end, the Jaguars were one quarter of play—and one Tom Brady fourth-quarter comeback—away from the Super Bowl. A team that had not eclipsed 12 wins in any three-year period since 2010 won 12 games in the 2017 season alone. The secondary is young and dynamic. All of the pass-rushers remain in place. Offensive workhorse Leonard Fournette isn't going anywhere, and the losses on offense are a pair of receivers who missed large chunks of the season due to injury (Allen Robinson, Allen Hurns) and a tight end who turned 34 in May (Marcedes Lewis). On the defense, the only departures are nickelback Aaron Colvin and retired two-down linebacker Paul Posluszny. Posluszny was a beloved veteran on the downside of his career, while Colvin has been directly replaced by former Raiders first-round pick D.J. Hayden. One season removed from a money line of only 6.0 wins and odds of 80-1 against them winning the AFC, the Jaguars enter the 2018 season as a trendy pick to win their division at the very least, and a top-five pick to win the conference.

Our projections are less enthused. While there is little doubt that the Jaguars had a very good season last time out, we have learned to be skeptical of teams that show a very sudden massive improvement in one single facet of the game—especially a facet as volatile as pass defense. The Jaguars are the first team since the 2009 Jets to finish No. 1 in defensive DVOA after ranking outside the top ten the previous year. The 2010 Jets ranked seventh—good, yes, but not the level expected of the Jaguars this coming season. The 2010 Steelers leapt from ninth to first, then also fell back to seventh. The 2007 Titans leapt from 20th to first, then fell back to fifth the following year. It is tempting to give coaching and roster additions full credit for the team's improvement, but a lot of external factors must also break right for a team to make that big a leap in a single season. Generally, those factors are not sustained: defenses that make a big leap forward should be expected to land somewhere between the two extremes during the following campaign.

That is doubly true for teams that have a top-five pass defense but a mediocre or worse run defense. Since 1988, 15 teams have ranked in the top five for overall defense DVOA but 15th or lower against the run (Table 1). Only four of those teams had a top-five overall defense the following year; on average, they fell to 11th. The numbers are slightly better for the smaller sample of No. 1 pass defenses, but only slightly. If a roughly sixth-ranked finish from general regression would be a disappointment, a ninth- or tenth-ranked finish would be alarming for a team so dependent on its defense for success.

Table 1. Top-Five Total Defense, 15th or Lower in Run Defense, 1986-2017

Year	Team	Pass D	Rank	Run D	Rank	Total D	Rank	All Y+1	Rank Y+1
1988	LAR	-13.0%	3	-4.6%	15	-9.3%	5	-2.0%	13
1995	CAR	-19.0%	2	-4.6%	17	-12.5%	5	-12.2%	6
1996	DAL	-21.2%	2	-4.8%	17	-13.1%	5	2.4%	17
1997	GB	-19.7%	2	-0.4%	20	-10.6%	3	-7.7%	6
1999	TB	-32.2%	1	-0.4%	23	-19.4%	2	-13.6%	5
2000	MIA	-29.7%	1	-2.7%	16	-17.4%	3	-6.7%	10
2000	TB	-21.7%	3	-2.1%	17	-13.6%	5	-15.4%	2
2001	CLE	-25.7%	1	0.0%	21	-13.1%	3	-5.1%	10
2005	IND	-15.0%	2	-4.6%	17	-10.2%	5	8.5%	25
2007	TEN	-20.4%	1	-5.3%	16	-14.4%	1	-18.6%	5
2010	GB	-21.2%	1	-4.7%	16	-13.9%	2	8.6%	25
2010	NYG	-15.8%	2	-5.1%	15	-11.2%	3	2.4%	19
2013	BUF	-22.8%	2	-3.1%	19	-13.8%	4	-15.5%	2
2016	DEN	-31.1%	1	-3.8%	21	-18.3%	1	-5.5%	10
2017	**JAX**	**-27.5%**	**1**	**-2.8%**	**26**	**-16.1%**	**1**	**--**	**--**
AVERAGE (w/o 2017 JAX)						-13.6%	3.4	-5.7%	11.1
AVERAGE FOR NO. 1 PASS DEFENSES						-16.1%	2.0	-6.8%	10.8

2018 Jaguars Schedule

Week	Opp.	Week	Opp.	Week	Opp.
1	at NYG	7	HOU	13	IND
2	NE	8	PHI (U.K.)	14	at TEN (Thu.)
3	TEN	9	BYE	15	WAS
4	NYJ	10	at IND	16	at MIA
5	at KC	11	PIT	17	at HOU
6	at DAL	12	at BUF		

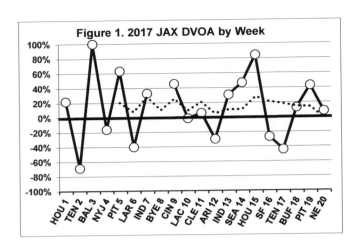

Figure 1. 2017 JAX DVOA by Week

History can be subject to interpretation, of course, and there are good reasons to believe that the Jaguars have the capacity to buck those trends. There are, however, three very specific areas in which we expect the Jaguars pass defense to regress beyond simply their overall DVOA rank.

Firstly, and perhaps most importantly, the Jaguars defense was exceptionally healthy in 2017. They had the third-fewest adjusted games lost at every level (line, linebackers, secondary) and the second-fewest games lost overall. Every single starter on defense played at least 14 games; only linebacker Telvin Smith (14) and nose tackle Abry Jones (15) missed an appearance. Even Jones only missed the meaningless season finale against Tennessee, in which he would most likely have played had the stakes been higher. The entire secondary and the top three pass-rushers had a flawless appearance record. That is a remarkable level of good fortune with injuries; the average team lost two seasons' worth (32.9) of adjusted games from its defense. The Jaguars themselves lost 25.0 AGL to injury on defense in 2016, and they should expect to see a regression on that front next season.[1]

Secondly, the Jaguars are likely to claim turnovers at a lower rate in 2018. Last season, 16.2 percent of drives against the Jaguars defense ended in a turnover, which was the third-highest rate behind Baltimore and Detroit. Over the past decade, defenses that ranked in the top three by this measure had an average rank of 12th the following year, with the average per-drive turnover rate among those teams falling by approximately 5.0 percent year-on-year. (Those numbers hold up over the shorter five-year period, too; since 2011, the average rank the following season is 14th and the average falloff is 4.9 percent.) Whether per drive or per play, turnover rate simply is not consistent from one season to the next. Since 2007, only two franchises have finished in the top three in consecutive seasons—the 2015-16 Kansas City Chiefs and the 2010-12 New England Patriots—and those teams had an average DVOA rank of just 17th. Turnover rate often tells us more about the opponent and the game situation than it does about the pure ability of the defense.

Similarly, we should expect the Jaguars to have fewer sacks next year. The #Sacksonville Jaguars finished second by adjusted sack rate, but that metric is surprisingly inconsistent from one year to the next. Since 2010, teams that finished in the top three in ASR have an average rank of 14th in the following season. For every 2012-13 Rams (third to first in

consecutive seasons), or 2015-16 Broncos (first to second), there is an equivalent 2014-15 Bills (first to 31st) or 2015-16 Patriots (second to 27th). The Jaguars also finished in the top three in pressure rate, which is usually more consistent than sack rate, so it is reasonable to expect that they will remain an elite pass rush in the season to come; however it is also plausible that their 2017 numbers were artificially inflated by games against Texans and Colts backups (24 of those sacks, or more than 40 percent of their total, were inflicted on Tom Savage, T.J. Yates, and Jacoby Brissett) who probably won't even see the field against them in 2018.

The players who *do* see the field against them in 2018 should present a greater challenge. Last season's Jaguars faced the second-easiest schedule of opposing offenses, ahead of only division rivals Tennessee. The Jaguars were already up 19-0 before they faced Deshaun Watson in Week 1, when Bill O'Brien inexplicably opened the season with Tom Savage under center. Watson and Savage were both out for the year by the time the teams met again in Week 15. Andrew Luck has not thrown a pass in a real game for 18 months and counting, but he is finally expected to return to the field this September. Instead of Joe Flacco, Blaine Gabbert, and DeShone Kizer, this season's non-divisional opponents include the Super Bowl Champion Eagles, one of the league's most dangerous rushing attacks in the Dallas Cowboys, and a rematch against Tom Brady and the Patriots. Even a slight regression against a more difficult slate of opponents could easily be enough to keep the Jaguars away from the playoff hunt, especially if those divisional opponents do improve with the return of their franchise quarterbacks.

On the topic of franchise quarterbacks, the Jaguars offense is highly unlikely to make up for any defensive drop-off. Blake Bortles is now entering his fifth season as a professional, and to this point has been a first-round quarterback bust. A competent 2017 season was achieved mostly by protecting Bortles from himself: his 547 pass attempts were the fewest since his rookie year (in which Chad Henne started the first three games of the season) and Bortles only threw more than 38 passes twice. That

---

1 For a table showing some of the effects of regression on defensive injuries, see the Minnesota chapter.

was not just a function of winning, as he averaged slightly fewer attempts in defeats (37) than in victories (39). Most teams pay lip service to the idea of "establishing the run," but the Jaguars really did focus their offense around a bruising, tackle-breaking running back and a mauling offensive line. For most of the year, Bortles played the part of Jets-era Mark Sanchez: hand the ball off, don't do anything stupid, and don't put the defense in a hole. Even then, he still tied for the seventh-most interceptions thrown, and his 2.49 percent interception rate was almost exactly league average among quarterbacks with at least 100 pass attempts—which marks another year-on-year improvement for Bortles, but only in the most favorable circumstances the team could possibly manufacture.

Those favorable circumstances can hardly be overstated. The Jaguars scored first in 12 of their 19 games last season, going 10-2 in those contests. They were 2-5 when they allowed the first score. They led the NFL in first-quarter offensive DVOA but ranked just 21st the rest of the time. Those leads were critical to the success of the defense, too: Jacksonville's defensive DVOA when losing by more than a touchdown ranked 31st in the NFL, ahead of only the Buffalo Bills. The Jaguars won only one game in which they were not already ahead by halftime: a 20-17 overtime win against the Chargers, in which the halftime score was 7-6 to Los Angeles and Bortles threw a season-high 51 passes. The team went to great lengths to hide their quarterback in their regular offense, but no modern team can hide that position indefinitely.

This came to a head during the AFC playoffs. The wild-card victory over the Bills maintained the recent AFC tradition of at least one first-round game featuring a barely watchable clinic of terrible quarterback play. (For one reason or another, the AFC has seen some remarkably dreadful playoff quarterback matchups in recent seasons.) Against Pittsburgh, the 45-42 score disguised another mediocre passing performance, as Leonard Fournette and T.J. Yeldon ran wild against a defense that had collapsed without star linebacker Ryan Shazier. Against the Patriots, the Jaguars built a 20-10 lead on their foundation of running and outstanding defense, but whe the Patriots adjusted their strategy, the Jaguars could not. They gained only two first downs on their final four drives while allowing two touchdowns on defense, and eventually succumbed 24-20. With a better quarterback, the Jaguars would

be a prohibitive favorite in the AFC. Sadly for non-Patriots (and perhaps, non-Steelers) fans, the Jaguars do not have an obviously better quarterback.

Given the opportunity to perhaps rectify that in the draft, Tom Coughlin's front office instead chose to augment the already formidable pass rush with Florida 3-technique tackle Taven Bryan, add depth at safety with Alabama's Ronnie Harrison, and help restock the wide receiver room with LSU's DJ Chark. The team did draft Nebraska's Tanner Lee on Day 3 but, despite the one often-cited exception, rare is the sixth-round quarterback who goes on to have a productive professional career. For better or worse, the offense the Jaguars will have in 2018 is by and large the same as the offense they had in 2017: run the ball, keep Blake Bortles from having to do too much, hope for the occasional explosive play, but above all don't dig the defense into a hole.

That leaves the 2018 Jaguars in much the same boat as their 2017 squad. As with most talent-rich running-and-defense outfits, the Jaguars are a formidable opponent when they can control the game script. When they cannot, they are likely to struggle. Against what is likely to be a much tougher schedule, they will probably need to find a way to win when their preferred option falters. The very best teams can beat you in multiple ways; we have seen very little evidence that the Jaguars are yet among those sides.

If this outlook seems overly pessimistic, it still represents significant progress for a team that had been mired in the league basement alongside the Browns for half a decade. Last season's Jaguars took a huge leap forward, eventually ripening into a legitimate Super Bowl contender as several years of strategic planning finally paid off. The core of the team is intact, but they are unlikely to reach such a giddy height this year. This is a still a team that requires favorable game scripts, careful management, and a lot of hard-to-control factors to go right to be successful. They demonstrated in 2017 that they can ride those factors a long way, but sustained success has to come from more than just surfing a favorable wind. We certainly do not expect the Jaguars to be *bad* this year, but we do expect them to take a half-step backward before they have a chance to go forward.

Andrew Potter

2017 Jaguars Stats by Week

Wk	vs.	W-L	PF	PA	YDF	YDA	TO	Total	Off	Def	ST
1	at HOU	W	29	7	280	203	+4	22%	0%	-38%	-15%
2	TEN	L	16	37	310	390	-2	-69%	-26%	35%	-7%
3	BAL	W	44	7	410	186	+3	100%	52%	-44%	4%
4	at NYJ	L	20	23	311	471	+1	-16%	-13%	3%	0%
5	at PIT	W	30	9	313	371	+4	63%	-3%	-60%	6%
6	LAR	L	17	27	389	249	0	-40%	-2%	-18%	-56%
7	at IND	W	27	0	518	232	-2	33%	5%	-26%	2%
8	BYE										
9	CIN	W	23	7	408	148	-1	46%	10%	-11%	24%
10	LAC	W	20	17	398	322	0	-1%	-9%	-8%	0%
11	at CLE	W	19	7	284	184	+4	6%	-43%	-60%	-11%
12	at ARI	L	24	27	219	344	-1	-30%	-33%	0%	3%
13	IND	W	30	10	426	290	+2	31%	21%	-8%	2%
14	SEA	W	30	24	424	401	+2	47%	43%	14%	18%
15	HOU	W	45	7	464	186	+1	84%	32%	-37%	15%
16	at SF	L	33	44	472	369	-2	-27%	2%	22%	-7%
17	at TEN	L	10	15	229	232	-3	-44%	-47%	-23%	-20%
18	BUF	W	10	3	230	263	+2	13%	-28%	-35%	5%
19	at PIT	W	45	42	378	545	+2	43%	53%	10%	1%
20	at NE	L	20	24	374	344	+1	8%	6%	5%	7%

Trends and Splits

	Offense	Rank	Defense	Rank
Total DVOA	-0.3%	16	-16.2%	1
Unadjusted VOA	3.7%	11	-19.1%	1
Weighted Trend	-2.0%	19	-13.1%	4
Variance	8.1%	19	7.6%	29
Average Opponent	0.3%	20	-5.1%	31
Passing	13.3%	15	-27.6%	1
Rushing	-5.0%	12	-2.8%	27
First Down	11.8%	6	-3.1%	12
Second Down	-8.7%	23	-21.8%	1
Third Down	-10.5%	24	-30.8%	2
First Half	7.1%	11	-23.4%	1
Second Half	-9.1%	24	-10.0%	6
Red Zone	9.3%	13	-18.0%	5
Late and Close	-40.6%	32	-25.7%	2

Five-Year Performance

Year	W-L	Pyth W	Est W	PF	PA	TO	Total	Rk	Off	Rk	Def	Rk	ST	Rk	Off AGL	Rk	Def AGL	Rk	Off Age	Rk	Def Age	Rk	ST Age	Rk
2013	4-12	3.1	3.2	247	449	-6	-38.2%	32	-29.8%	32	10.9%	28	2.5%	9	47.3	24	26.8	14	26.6	20	26.2	23	24.7	32
2014	3-13	3.6	3.3	249	412	-6	-29.5%	32	-24.3%	31	1.5%	20	-3.6%	26	33.5	19	44.3	22	24.7	32	26.1	27	25.5	30
2015	5-11	6.2	5.8	376	448	-10	-16.0%	25	-5.4%	21	9.7%	26	-0.9%	20	25.7	12	43.2	27	25.6	30	26.4	22	25.4	29
2016	3-13	5.8	5.4	318	400	-16	-10.4%	26	-11.3%	27	-3.1%	12	-2.3%	23	47.6	26	25.0	10	25.6	31	25.9	28	25.5	26
2017	10-6	11.9	9.0	417	268	+10	13.2%	8	-0.3%	16	-16.2%	1	-2.7%	24	33.3	15	5.0	2	26.1	28	25.9	22	26.0	11

2017 Performance Based on Most Common Personnel Groups

JAX Offense					JAX Offense vs. Opponents					JAX Defense					JAX Defense vs. Opponents			
Pers	Freq	Yds	DVOA	Run%	Pers	Freq	Yds	DVOA	Run%	Pers	Freq	Yds	DVOA	Pers	Freq	Yds	DVOA	
11	54%	5.7	-4.4%	26%	Base	46%	5.4	9.2%	65%	Base	33%	5.5	-1.2%	11	61%	4.4	-26.0%	
12	16%	5.8	18.9%	59%	Nickel	37%	5.7	-3.9%	29%	Nickel	66%	4.3	-26.1%	12	16%	6.0	9.7%	
21	14%	5.7	15.9%	63%	Dime+	12%	6.4	8.9%	6%	Dime+	0%	8.0	8.1%	21	8%	5.2	-6.6%	
22	7%	4.2	-15.5%	92%	Goal Line	2%	1.0	6.4%	86%	Goal Line	0%	0.5	65.3%	13	4%	4.3	-31.7%	
13	5%	2.9	-29.9%	79%	Big	2%	4.0	-53.6%	79%					22	3%	5.7	8.5%	
622	2%	5.2	12.0%	86%														

Strategic Tendencies

Run/Pass		Rk	Formation		Rk	Pass Rush		Rk	Secondary		Rk	Strategy		Rk
Runs, first half	43%	3	Form: Single Back	74%	23	Rush 3	2.0%	30	4 DB	33%	14	Play action	23%	12
Runs, first down	57%	4	Form: Empty Back	3%	31	Rush 4	83.7%	1	5 DB	66%	6	Avg Box (Off)	6.56	1
Runs, second-long	44%	2	Pers: 3+ WR	55%	25	Rush 5	8.4%	32	6+ DB	0%	29	Avg Box (Def)	6.25	17
Runs, power sit.	72%	3	Pers: 2+ TE/6+ OL	31%	16	Rush 6+	5.9%	16	CB by Sides	78%	16	Offensive Pace	30.11	13
Runs, behind 2H	26%	19	Pers: 6+ OL	4%	8	Int DL Sacks	24.5%	18	S/CB Cover Ratio	23%	29	Defensive Pace	30.50	17
Pass, ahead 2H	32%	32	Shotgun/Pistol	57%	17	Second Level Sacks	14.5%	21	DB Blitz	9%	17	Go for it on 4th	1.13	10

With Leonard Fournette in town, boy oh boy did the Jaguars re-discover the run. In 2016, the Jaguars had been below average in run/pass ratio in the first half, on first down, in second-and-long, and in short yardage. They went from second to 32nd in how often they passed with a lead in the second half. They also went from 30th to 12th in how often they used a play-fake on passes, and from 26th to first in the average box faced on offense. ☞ Jacksonville's offense jumped from 108 broken tackles (26th in 2016) to 150 broken tackles (third in 2017). ☞ The Jacksonville offense ranked sixth in DVOA at home, but 24th on the road. Well, in the regular season, anyway. As the Steelers know, the playoffs were a different story. ☞ The Jaguars allowed just 3.4 yards per pass when blitzing a defensive back. It's the second year out of three where the Jaguars allowed less than 3.5 yards per pass on DB blitzes, but what's odd is that in the year in between, 2016, the Jaguars allowed a league-high 10.5 yards per pass on DB blitzes. ☞ The Jaguars' huge dichotomy between run and pass defense meant that the Jaguars actually allowed an average yard more with the quarterback under center (5.3) than with the quarterback in shotgun (4.3).

Passing

Player	DYAR	DVOA	Plays	NtYds	Avg	YAC	C%	TD	Int
B.Bortles	408	0.3%	547	3552	6.5	6.1	60.3%	21	13
C.Kessler	-98	-66.4%	30	82	2.7	6.4	50.0%	0	1

Receiving

Player	DYAR	DVOA	Plays	Ctch	Yds	Y/C	YAC	TD	C%
M.Lee	119	3.0%	96	56	702	12.5	5.2	3	58%
K.Cole	35	-7.4%	83	42	752	17.9	7.0	3	51%
A.Hurns*	149	20.6%	56	39	484	12.4	4.5	2	70%
D.Westbrook	-35	-21.5%	51	27	339	12.6	3.7	1	53%
J.Mickens	22	10.1%	11	6	77	12.8	6.5	2	55%
D.Moncrief	94	11.4%	47	26	391	15.0	3.0	2	55%
M.Lewis*	27	1.0%	48	24	318	13.3	6.8	5	50%
J.O'Shaughnessy	5	-4.1%	24	14	149	10.6	5.9	1	58%
B.Koyack	-14	-38.6%	7	5	38	7.6	2.8	0	71%
A.Seferian-Jenkins	-83	-23.4%	74	50	357	7.1	2.3	3	68%
N.Paul	-16	-20.1%	19	13	94	7.2	2.4	0	68%
L.Fournette	58	7.2%	48	36	302	8.4	8.5	1	75%
T.J.Yeldon	8	-9.9%	41	30	224	7.5	6.3	0	73%
C.Ivory*	27	4.4%	28	21	175	8.3	9.0	1	75%
T.Bohanon	0	-13.2%	11	6	43	7.2	4.7	1	55%

Rushing

Player	DYAR	DVOA	Plays	Yds	Avg	TD	Fum	Suc
L.Fournette	115	2.1%	268	1040	3.9	9	2	44%
C.Ivory*	-38	-17.0%	112	386	3.4	1	2	38%
T.J.Yeldon	4	-6.7%	49	253	5.2	2	2	43%
B.Bortles	84	25.1%	44	328	7.5	2	2	-
C.Grant	79	53.6%	30	248	8.3	2	0	63%
T.Bohanon	1	-4.7%	5	5	1.0	2	0	40%

Offensive Line

Player	Pos	Age	GS	Snaps	Pen	Sk	Pass	Run	Player	Pos	Age	GS	Snaps	Pen	Sk	Pass	Run
A.J. Cann	RG	27	15/15	1040	3	1.0	15	17	Josh Wells	RT/LT	27	15/4	468	1	2.0	22	2
Brandon Linder	C	26	13/13	932	2	0.0	3	12	Tyler Shatley	C	27	16/4	380	0	1.0	5	9
Cam Robinson	LT	23	15/15	893	12	4.0	21	17	Chris Reed	LG	26	6/3	213	2	2.0	6	1
Jermey Parnell	RT	32	13/13	892	4	1.0	18	12	Andrew Norwell	LG	27	16/16	1079	2	0.5	7	2
Patrick Omameh	LG	29	13/13	865	3	4.0	12	16									

Year	Yards	ALY	Rank	Power	Rank	Stuff	Rank	2nd Lev	Rank	Open Field	Rank	Sacks	ASR	Rank	Press	Rank	F-Start	Cont.
2015	3.80	4.11	16	39%	31	22%	21	1.01	28	0.63	20	51	7.9%	25	27.4%	21	8	41
2016	3.80	3.73	27	58%	24	20%	18	1.06	24	0.55	24	34	5.3%	9	22.2%	7	18	28
2017	4.16	4.12	13	62%	19	19%	10	0.98	27	0.96	7	24	4.4%	5	33.2%	25	17	26

2017 ALY by direction: Left End: 4.32 (13) Left Tackle: 4.34 (14) Mid/Guard: 4.01 (22) Right Tackle: 4.31 (7) Right End: 4.36 (10)

Rookie left tackle Cam Robinson battled injuries during his debut season, but the only game he missed was the meaningless season finale against Tennessee. Robinson occasionally struggled in pass protection, frequently overplaying the outside rush in particular, but already looks to be one of the game's best run-blocking tackles. ☞ However, Robinson had his good plays and his bad: he had the third-worst rate of snaps per blown block among left tackles even on running plays. Furthermore, the Jaguars line as a whole had the worst rate of snaps per blown block and was the only line to rank in the bottom three in both pass and run snaps per blown block (they ranked 30th in each category). Only center Brandon Linder ranked better than 27th at his position in snaps per blown block. ☞ Another point of emphasis for Robinson in 2018: he needs to cut down on penalties. Only two left tackles had more penalties than his 12: Charles Leno (Chicago, 13) and Garrett Bolles (Denver, 15). Robinson was flagged six times for false starts, four times for offensive holding, and once each for a facemask and illegal use of hands. ☞ Overall, the Jaguars tied at 22 for the second-most false starts in the league, though four of the those occurred on special teams and a fifth during a kneeldown at the end of the Cincinnati game. False starts were their only major issue with penalties on offense; the team ranked in the middle of the pack for total penalties. ☞ The right side of the line frequently struggled with games on the defensive line. The majority of sacks on that side came as a result of a stunt or twist, most commonly with both players blocking the outside rusher and allowing the inside rusher to get free. A.J. Cann and Jermey Parnell both return, so they have something to work on together during the offseason. ☞ Fourth-round pick Will Richardson (North Carolina State) projects as a backup and possible swing tackle initially, but he will have the chance to compete with Parnell at right tackle in the medium to long term. Richardson is a talented player who probably fell in the draft due to a history of drug and alcohol violations. Dave Caldwell has also stated his belief that Richardson has the skill set to play guard, though Richardson never played that position in college. If A.J. Cann struggles, Richardson may be at the front of the queue for a chance on the interior line.

Defensive Front Seven

Defensive Line	Age	Pos	G	Snaps	Plays	TmPct	Rk	Stop	Dfts	BTkl	Runs	St%	Rk	RuYd	Rk	Sack	Hit	Hur	Dsrpt
						Overall						vs. Run				Pass Rush			
Malik Jackson	28	DT	16	761	41	5.2%	36	32	17	6	28	71%	63	2.1	43	8.0	4	26.0	2
Abry Jones	27	DT	15	489	36	4.9%	47	27	6	5	27	70%	69	3.0	75	1.0	1	5.5	5
Marcell Dareus	29	DT	14	418	28	3.7%	68	26	6	3	24	96%	1	2.2	48	2.0	2	6.0	0
Eli Ankou	24	DT	9	174	15	3.4%	--	11	4	0	12	67%	--	3.2	--	1.5	0	3.0	0

Edge Rushers	Age	Pos	G	Snaps	Plays	TmPct	Rk	Stop	Dfts	BTkl	Runs	St%	Rk	RuYd	Rk	Sack	Hit	Hur	Dsrpt
						Overall						vs. Run				Pass Rush			
Calais Campbell	32	DE	16	807	69	8.8%	5	58	32	10	45	76%	45	2.3	47	14.5	16	37.0	4
Yannick Ngakoue	23	DE	16	772	28	3.6%	73	25	19	3	12	75%	46	3.4	80	12.0	17	33.5	2
Dante Fowler	24	DE	16	466	20	2.5%	93	17	12	7	10	70%	65	3.1	76	8.0	2	22.5	0

Linebackers	Age	Pos	G	Snaps	Plays	TmPct	Rk	Stop	Dfts	BTkl	Runs	St%	Rk	RuYd	Rk	Sack	Hit	Hur	Tgts	Suc%	Rk	AdjYd	Rk	PD	Int
						Overall						vs. Run				Pass Rush				vs. Pass					
Myles Jack	23	OLB	16	1018	93	11.8%	43	38	15	12	52	42%	85	5.1	83	2.0	3	7.0	30	34%	74	8.0	61	1	x
Telvin Smith	27	OLB	14	851	106	15.4%	18	66	27	15	62	71%	19	2.8	18	1.0	1	7.0	41	51%	32	7.6	56	6	x
Paul Posluszny*	34	MLB	16	481	62	7.9%	78	32	12	2	37	62%	45	3.7	50	1.5	1	3.0	19	50%	37	9.5	72	2	x

Year	Yards	ALY	Rank	Power	Rank	Stuff	Rank	2nd Level	Rank	Open Field	Rank	Sacks	ASR	Rank	Press	Rank
2015	3.68	3.82	8	68%	19	23%	9	1.11	15	0.58	9	36	5.8%	24	21.7%	30
2016	3.76	3.73	7	64%	18	21%	11	0.96	4	0.74	18	33	5.9%	17	27.2%	15
2017	4.27	4.37	28	59%	9	20%	19	1.16	20	0.76	19	55	9.1%	2	34.3%	3

2017 ALY by direction:	Left End: 5.20 (31)	Left Tackle: 3.24 (8)	Mid/Guard: 4.38 (25)	Right Tackle: 3.91 (19)	Right End: 4.73 (26)

Prior to Calais Campbell and Yannick Ngakoue both eclipsing ten sacks last year, no Jaguars player had posted a double-digit sack total since Bobby McCray in 2006—the second-longest drought in the league behind only Tampa Bay (Simeon Rice, 2005). The last time Jacksonville had two players reach double figures in the same season was 1999, when they had three: Tony Brackens, Kevin Hardy, and Gary Walker. That team also lost in the AFC Championship Game. ☞ In addition to his franchise sack record, Campbell had the second-most defeats in the league behind only overall sack leader Chandler Jones. Campbell had more pass defeats (22) than any other player, closely tailed by teammate Jalen Ramsey (21). ☞ After acquiring Marcell Dareus ahead of the team's Week 8 bye, the team's run defense posted three of its five best DVOA performances from Weeks 9 to 11. After that, however, it reverted to type: the Week 14 performance against Seattle was their second-worst of the season, and the five-week stretch from Weeks 11 to 16 saw a worse average DVOA—both mean and median—than Weeks 1 to 7. ☞ Myles Jack made his average run tackle after a gain of 5.1 yards, the fifth-worst figure among front seven defenders. Telvin Smith made *his* average run tackle after a gain of 2.8 yards, which is slightly better than average for a linebacker. Smith's 15 run defeats were second among off-ball linebackers, tied with Bobby Wagner behind Luke Kuechly, and he ranked eighth in total defeats among all linebackers. ☞ First-round draft pick Taven Bryan (Florida) projects as a 3-technique defensive tackle but could see some time as a 5-technique end in a similar role to Calais Campbell. He is likely to begin as a situational and rotational interior rusher behind Malik Jackson and Marcell Dareus. ☞ Seventh-round pick Leon Jacobs (Wisconsin) will compete with 2016 fifth-rounder Blair Brown for third linebacker duties after the retirement of Paul Posluszny. Former Ravens undrafted free agent Donald Payne is also in the mix after impressing the coaching staff during the early offseason. At least two, and quite likely all three will probably be retained for depth and special teams.

Defensive Secondary

Secondary	Age	Pos	G	Snaps	Plays	TmPct	Rk	Stop	Dfts	BTkl	Runs	St%	Rk	RuYd	Rk	Tgts	Tgt%	Rk	Dist	Suc%	Rk	AdjYd	Rk	PD	Int
Tashaun Gipson	28	FS	16	1020	71	9.0%	54	32	13	6	36	56%	13	4.0	7	31	7.7%	21	12.9	63%	8	6.5	17	7	4
A.J. Bouye	27	CB	16	1015	74	9.4%	26	28	14	5	17	12%	79	7.2	60	83	20.8%	43	16.1	55%	20	6.3	12	20	6
Jalen Ramsey	24	CB	16	998	80	10.2%	16	36	23	5	15	20%	75	6.6	51	88	22.3%	55	13.7	61%	7	5.3	1	17	4
Barry Church	30	SS	16	990	80	10.2%	35	34	9	14	48	44%	41	5.6	30	30	7.6%	19	14.4	47%	54	10.8	70	6	4
Aaron Colvin*	27	CB	16	705	49	6.2%	--	25	13	9	13	62%	--	6.7	--	44	15.7%	--	6.6	52%	--	5.4	--	4	0
D.J. Hayden	28	CB	16	488	51	6.1%	--	21	5	6	8	25%	--	8.6	--	48	23.4%	--	13.0	53%	--	6.8	--	10	0
Cody Davis	29	FS/SS	7	281	23	6.4%	--	9	3	3	12	25%	--	7.7	--	5	4.8%	--	12.3	93%	--	1.1	--	3	1

Year	Pass D Rank	vs. #1 WR	Rk	vs. #2 WR	Rk	vs. Other WR	Rk	WR Wide	Rk	WR Slot	Rk	vs. TE	Rk	vs. RB	Rk
2015	31	9.9%	25	13.4%	24	17.7%	26	--	--	--	--	23.8%	28	14.2%	27
2016	15	0.9%	15	4.4%	19	16.1%	29	23.6%	32	-10.1%	7	-1.9%	16	-28.5%	2
2017	1	-58.4%	1	-14.1%	8	-8.5%	11	-36.4%	1	-23.9%	2	2.3%	20	-1.6%	16

In addition to his first-place rank in adjusted yards per pass, as already mentioned above Jalen Ramsey's 21 pass defeats were the most of any defensive back in 2017, three ahead of Washington's Kyle Fuller. ☞ If he had faced enough targets to qualify for our leaderboards, nickelback Aaron Colvin's 5.4 adjusted yards per target would have ranked fourth behind Ramsey, E.J. Gaines, and Aqib Talib. Colvin left for Houston in free agency but should be directly replaced by incoming free agent D.J. Hayden. ☞ Hayden was Oakland's first-round pick in 2013, but he left the Raiders at the end of his rookie contract. He spent 2017 in Detroit, where he was expected to replace Quandre Diggs at nickelback but ended up splitting snaps with Nevin Lawson at outside corner. ☞ Despite a reputation for physical man coverage, the Jaguars conceded the joint second-fewest defensive pass interference penalties in 2017, and they lost the third-fewest yards to those penalties. They also had the fewest defensive holding penalties, losing only 9 yards on a mere three defensive holding calls in the regular season. ☞ Jacksonville lists Tashaun Gipson as free safety and Barry Church as strong safety, but Gipson is often the player closer to the line of scrimmage. Gipson made his average run tackle after a gain of 4.0 yards, tenth among starting safeties with at least ten run tackles. He also tied for ninth in run defeats among safeties. ☞ Church is generally considered the weakest link in the Jaguars secondary. Church had the most broken tackles, fewest defeats, and the worst success rate of the team's five-man starting secondary. His 10.8 adjusted yards allowed per pass was the seventh-worst figure among not only safeties but all qualifying defensive backs. His spot is probably secure for 2018, but he is the player most likely to be threatened by a rookie, in this case third-rounder Ronnie Harrison (Alabama). Harrison is an archetypal strong safety: a powerful hitter in the mold of Kam Chancellor who is at his best playing close to the line of scrimmage but is also capable of taking on responsibilities in coverage against backs and tight ends. He has experience in the slot and is a proficient blitzer, so he could also make an impact in a situational moneybacker role.

Special Teams

Year	DVOA	Rank	FG/XP	Rank	Net Kick	Rank	Kick Ret	Rank	Net Punt	Rank	Punt Ret	Rank	Hidden	Rank
2015	-0.9%	20	-4.6	29	2.4	10	-0.9	17	-9.3	27	7.8	5	6.0	7
2016	-2.3%	23	0.5	14	0.0	16	8.9	5	-8.9	28	-11.8	32	-3.7	21
2017	-2.7%	24	-3.6	22	-8.8	30	-0.5	15	-4.4	21	3.8	6	-7.0	23

Veteran punter Brad Nortman was released this offseason after posting his lowest gross average per punt since his rookie season. Nortman's gross and net averages both ranked 25th in the league. Nortman's expected replacement, seventh-round rookie Logan Cooke, averaged 41.7 yards per punt across four years at Mississippi State. ☞ Cooke was also a kickoff specialist in college, averaging 63.6 yards per kickoff with a touchback rate of 59 percent. The Jaguars had the third-worst kickoff unit in the league in 2017; Josh Lambo's 64.7-yard average was the shortest kickoff distance of any player with at least 40 kicks, and his touchback rate was a mere 53 percent. (Those are our numbers; the official NFL figures include squib and onside kicks and count all kickoffs into the end zone at the same length. So officially, Lambo's touchback rate was 39 percent, ahead of only Tampa's Patrick Murray.) Cooke's figures are not directly comparable to Lambo's due to differences in methodology and the size of the balls used at each level, but Cooke is expected to double as a kickoff specialist in Jacksonville. ☞ Jaydon Mickens averaged 10.6 yards per punt return, the fifth-highest figure among players with at least 10 attempts. His average return was a full yard longer than the team's average of 9.6. ☞ Kick coverage was a clear weakness in 2017, but that should be improved by rookies Ronnie Harrison and Leon Jacobs. Harrison in particular excelled on special teams at Alabama, leading the team in special teams tackles in 2016 before earning the starting strong safety job for 2017. He is exactly the type of quick and powerful downhill tackler who should make a top-tier punt gunner.

Kansas City Chiefs

2017 Record: 10-6	**Total DVOA:** 10.5% (10th)	**2018 Mean Projection:** 7.6 wins	**On the Clock (0-4):** 12%
Pythagorean Wins: 10.0 (10th)	**Offense:** 15.7% (4th)	**Postseason Odds:** 33.9%	**Mediocrity (5-7):** 37%
Snap-Weighted Age: 26.5 (12th)	**Defense:** 10.6% (30th)	**Super Bowl Odds:** 3.8%	**Playoff Contender (8-10):** 38%
Average Opponent: -3.2% (27th)	**Special Teams:** 5.3% (4th)	**Proj. Avg. Opponent:** 1.0% (9th)	**Super Bowl Contender (11+):** 13%

2017: Different Alex Smith, same first-round playoff exit.

2018: Gun-shy to gunslinger; how far can Patrick Mahomes carry the Chiefs?

Since being traded to the Kansas City Chiefs in 2013, Alex Smith had been chastised for being too cautious and lackluster as the team's starting quarterback. Smith developed and solidified a character as the league's most milquetoast passer; a quarterback who would not sink the ship, but would not be able to guide it where it needed to go either. Smith's skill set had always come with an explanation via asterisk: Smith had a strong enough arm, said his supporters, but he had never been aggressive enough to show it. Smith appeared to turn a new leaf in 2017, however. A newfound aggression and a surprising sense of confidence propelled Smith to heights he had never reached before.

Smith was aided in his ascension by a near-perfect situation, surrounded by unique, dynamic skill players. Head coach Andy Reid and offensive coordinator Matt Nagy concocted an offense that catered perfectly to Smith and his supporting cast. For example, the Chiefs were one of the handful of teams to regularly use the pistol formation. The pistol formation allows the quarterback to align as if he were in the shotgun, but the primary running back stands a few feet behind the quarterback rather than by his side,. It is the best of both worlds in that the quarterback has the ease of vision that comes from the shotgun, while the running back has smoother and more flexible rushing lanes similar to an under-center formation. From the pistol formation, the Chiefs could more smoothly run speed-option, read-option, and run-pass option concepts than they may have been able to in other, more traditional formations.

Creativity was a staple for the Chiefs offense, as well. The shovel-option play has taken over college football over the past half-decade, and the Chiefs were at the forefront in establishing it in the NFL. They were not the first team to do it, but with an elite athlete at tight end in Travis Kelce and other sneaky weapons such as Albert Wilson, the Chiefs were able to execute the shovel-option at a high level, especially early in the season. In their Week 1 domination of the then-reigning champion New England Patriots, the pistol formation and shovel-option both showed up in full force. That game, in particular, established Kansas City's early-season creativity and offensive success.

Additionally, the skill position cupboard was loaded for Smith. Wide receiver Tyreek Hill became a staple deep threat and a legitimate receiver, rather than a speedy gadget player. Hill's yards per reception skyrocketed from 9.7 in 2016 to 15.8 in 2017, helping Hill secure the eighth-best DYAR for wide receivers in the league, sandwiched between Julio Jones and Stefon Diggs. To no surprise, tight end Travis Kelce erupted once again as a dominant force across the middle, asserting himself as second only to Rob Gronkowski at his position.

Reid and Nagy did well to use Hill and Kelce in harmony, often creating route combinations in which the stress one of them put on the defense would create space for the other. Even rookie running back Kareem Hunt became a key part of the passing game. The Chiefs used Hunt regularly as a vertical seam threat, making them one of the few progressive teams to do so, alongside Sean McVay's Rams and Kyle Shanahan's 2016 Falcons. With quality role players such as the speedy De'Anthony Thomas or the ever-reliable Wilson serving as accents, Kansas City's offense was bolstered both with star talent and depth.

Smith was able to flourish on the stat sheet. From accumulating a career-best 26-to-5 touchdown-to-interception ratio, to posting career-highs in DYAR and DVOA, Smith was statistically the best version of himself. However, Smith's Cinderella season at 33 years old was more of a half-season of unsustainable dominance, as opposed to a full season of success.

Of the Chiefs' 11 best games in offensive passing DVOA, eight came during the first nine games of the season. More specifically, four of the top six performances happened during Kansas City's 5-0 start. Smith threw 11 touchdowns through those first five games, with no interceptions. Then he threw 15 touchdowns and all five of his interceptions on the year over the following ten games before rookie Patrick Mahomes started the final game of the season. Kansas City also posted just four games with a negative offensive passing DVOA—three of those four games were in Weeks 11, 12, and 14.

Granted, the devolution of the offense was not all on Smith. For one, some of the fresh, innovative concepts Reid and Nagy implemented just were not sustainable at the rate they were using them early on. Option football was central to the offense through the first handful of games, but as teams got better at defending them, option concepts of all sorts had to become secondary. They were still plenty effective in smaller doses, but needing to use those concepts in smaller doses hurt the offense because those plays did not require a lot from Smith. In addition, the offensive line overachieved with the talent on hand early on. As soon as minor injuries began to roll in, as they often do along any offensive line, the entire unit

2018 Chiefs Schedule

Week	Opp.	Week	Opp.	Week	Opp.
1	at LAC	7	CIN	13	at OAK
2	at PIT	8	DEN	14	BAL
3	SF	9	at CLE	15	LAC (Thu.)
4	at DEN (Mon.)	10	ARI	16	at SEA
5	JAX	11	at LAR (Mon./Mex.)	17	OAK
6	at NE	12	BYE		

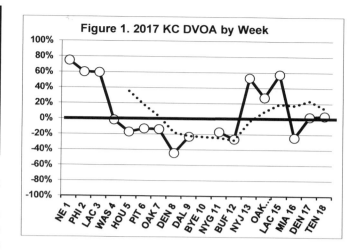

Figure 1. 2017 KC DVOA by Week

declined and returned to mediocrity during the middle portion of the season.

The Chiefs could not count on their defense down the stretch either. Much like the offense declined over the course of the year, the defense became a shell of itself after Week 3. The Chiefs' defense appeared fairly solid through the first few weeks, holding opponents to an average of fewer than 20 points per game. A combination of injuries and old age catching up to key players ravaged the unit shortly thereafter. The loss of Eric Berry, who tore his Achilles in Week 1, was eventually exposed by opponents. Tamba Hali was not able to play until late in the season and did not return at full strength, which became especially problematic given Dee Ford's season-ending injury in Week 6. On top of the injuries, 35-year-old Derrick Johnson finally lost his juice and no longer looked like the All-Pro linebacker he once was. The Chiefs had above-average defensive DVOA in the first three games of the season. The concentration of injuries and subpar play at every level of the defense led the Chiefs to have only three more above-average defensive DVOA games in the final 13.

Despite the second-half fade, the Chiefs finished the year with a 10-6 record and the fourth seed in the AFC playoffs, which earned them a date with the Tennessee Titans. In any NFL season, one or two teams sneak into the playoffs without deserving to do so, and the Titans were one of those teams in 2017. Given the Titans' overachievement and the Chiefs' potential for dominance, there was not much room for the Chiefs to botch the opportunity.

But, of course, they did. The Chiefs opened the game strong with three touchdowns in the first half, matched only by a field goal from the Titans. In peak Chiefs fashion, the tables turned entirely in the second half. The Titans scored 19 unanswered points as running back Derrick Henry ran rampant against a crippled Chiefs' front seven. In response, the Chiefs' offense had nothing. Reid, Nagy, and Smith opted for a safe approach to close out the game, and it came back to haunt them. Through the Chiefs' first three possessions of the second half, the team ran the ball or scrambled on six plays, while also throwing the ball four times within 5 yards of the line of scrimmage. Smith threw just one pass beyond 5 yards during that stretch, an incompletion on third-and-2 that ended the drive. It was not until the team's fourth and final drive of the second half that Smith let loose, but it was too late and to no avail. Smith and Co. were unable to get anything going and turned the ball over on downs, while the Titans had suffocated the clock and scored on each of their first three second-half

possessions, bringing the game to a close with their fourth and final possession.

The Alex Smith Era in Kansas City came to an end in poetic fashion. It is almost too perfect for Smith to have had the season he did, yet have the Chiefs find themselves with the same result they always do: a first-round playoff exit. Even more fitting, Smith's borderline MVP campaign was, in many ways, more representative of a poor quarterback landscape for the 2017 season, rather than Smith himself being fantastic.

Smith's 104.7 passer rating was the best in the league, but it was the lowest league-leading mark since Peyton Manning's 2005 and 2006 seasons at 104.1 and 101.0, respectively. Smith's 26 passing touchdowns were also the fewest of any league-leader in passer rating since Steve McNair's 2003 season. As the cherry on top, Smith's DYAR of 1,022 yards was only good for ninth in the league last season, barely edging out Matthew Stafford and leaving him below names such as Carson Wentz, Jared Goff, and Case Keenum. Smith's best season, though still plenty impressive, came with too many caveats and qualifiers for it to have kept Smith in Kansas City any longer.

Smith's entire 2017 season came with a countdown clock, because he already had an heir apparent waiting in the wings: Patrick Mahomes Jr., the gunslinging Air Raid prodigy for whom the Chiefs traded up in the 2017 NFL draft. Mahomes is as different from Smith as any two quarterbacks can be. Whereas Smith is reserved and by the books, Mahomes is daring and free-flowing. Mahomes is willing to test the limits of his mesmerizing arm strength and dare defenses to run him down as he scrambles around.

Mahomes' origin as an Air Raid quarterback from the Big 12 concerned the masses during the draft process. The track record for that brand of quarterback is admittedly poor, though it looks a lot better after the seasons Jared Goff and Case Keenum put up in 2017. By and large, the concern with Air Raid quarterbacks is that the Air Raid produces exaggerated numbers but does not challenge and prepare young passers for the NFL the way other offenses would. That is not the case with Mahomes. Mahomes played at Texas Tech under Kliff Kingsbury, whose system was crafted for Mahomes as a blend between a true Mike Leach Air Raid and an NFL-style offense. Kingsbury has served under a number of Air Raid coaching legends and played in the system himself in college, but also spent time as a backup quarterback in the NFL. His unique experience allowed him to give Mahomes the best of both worlds. By Mahomes' sophomore season, he was given the full-time starting job and an escalating level of control at the line of scrimmage as time went on.

Between exceptional arm strength and a deep understanding of Kingsbury's complex system, Mahomes was able to dominate the Big 12 as best as Texas Tech's talent enabled him to. Mahomes cemented himself in the conference record books with just two seasons as a full-time starter. More important than collegiate accolades, however, is how well Mahomes' college career projected him to the pros. Despite adjustments for a Big 12 schedule, Mahomes came out on top of the Class of 2017 quarterbacks in Football Outsiders' QBASE projection system, ahead of three other top-60 picks at the position.

The exciting part for Chiefs fans is not just having a young strong-armed quarterback, or having a young quarterback with a good statistical projection. It is having any promising young quarterback to root for whatsoever. Before Mahomes, the Chiefs had not drafted a quarterback in the first round since drafting Todd Blackledge in 1983. Furthermore, the team only drafted two quarterbacks in the top 50 between 1983 and 2017. Mike Elkins (1989) and Matt Blundin (1992) were the Chiefs' previous two experiments with quarterbacks in the top 50, and neither made it past his second year with the team or ever started a game. Over that span, the Chiefs relied on stretches of quality play from veterans via free agency and trades, including Steve DeBerg, Trent Green, and most recently Smith. Mahomes, an in-house first-round pick heading into his age-23 season, will be the first of his kind in Kansas City in roughly three decades.

Starting a new, young quarterback is enough of a signal of a paradigm shift on its own. Considering the context of Smith vs. Mahomes, as well as the Chiefs' draft history, that signal is amplified. Sprinkle on top the signing of Sammy Watkins as another deep threat across from Tyreek Hill, and it becomes clear how much Reid and the front office yearned for a new era on offense. Chiefs fans do not have to worry about experiencing another season without a single touchdown reception by a wide receiver any time soon.

Change is afoot on the other side of the ball as well. Hali and Johnson were the core of the Kansas City defense for a dozen years, but neither will return in 2018. And the trade of 2016 All-Pro cornerback Marcus Peters to the Rams continues the gradual departure of the other defensive stars of the Reid era.

Defensive renovations have been on the horizon for a couple years. The Chiefs' defense steadily declined since their 2015 campaign, which was to be expected of a defense with so many aging stars. In 2015, the Chiefs' defense ranked sixth in the NFL in defensive DVOA, but fell to 15th in 2016 and plummeted further to 30th in 2017.

Sean Smith was the first domino to fall. Following the 2015 season, Smith was allowed to walk in free agency, but was not replaced appropriately. Kansas City took a chance on Kavarie Russell in the third round in the following draft, but did not make any notable free agents signing at the position to fill Smith's immediate vacancy. The departure of Dontari Poe following the 2016 season was the next move. Though Poe had lost a step in 2016, he still could have provided value for Kansas City moving forward; instead, he ended up doing so for the Atlanta Falcons. Poe was replaced by Bennie Logan in free agency, but Logan's odd fit in Kansas City's defense made the move questionable despite Logan being a better player on paper. Logan was not retained by the Chiefs this offseason.

In 2017, the culmination of losing cornerstone pieces from the 2015 season, suffering key injuries, and older stars hitting their walls resulted in disaster. Berry's injury entirely derailed the secondary. Injuries to Hali and Ford rendered the team to rely only on Justin Houston for pass-rushing presence. Johnson devolving into a shell of his former self was the icing on the cake.

The immediate future does not appear any brighter, either. Berry will return and may be able to shore up the secondary, but injuries have piled up through his career and it is tough to assume he will return to elite form. Further regarding the secondary, Peters being traded away and being (partially) replaced by Kendall Fuller is likely a downgrade for the unit. Fuller was an elite slot cornerback for the Washington Redskins, but will be playing more outside to replace a top-notch outside cornerback in Peters. Swapping Peters for Fuller maxes out as a move that breaks even. Hali's replacement is Breeland Speaks, a second-round draft pick from Ole Miss who is generally considered an overdraft. Johnson departed as well, leaving the team to spend big in free agency for Anthony Hitchens. The Chiefs gave Hitchens a five-year, $45 million contract that allows the team to cut him following the second year of the contract. Given that Hitchens never proved to be more than serviceable in Dallas, signing him to an expensive deal feels like a desperation signing more than anything.

Key players returning from injury, as well as minor additions through the offseason, will help the Chiefs' defense, but there is still a long road ahead. We're projecting the Chiefs defense to rank somewhere in the mid-20s. Though that would be a small step in the right direction, there is little reason to believe the Chiefs defense will be what propels the team in 2018.

Looking ahead is a more exciting approach for Kansas City than prepping for immediate success with a new quarterback and a rebuilding defense. With a slew of explosive skill players and a daring signal-caller in Mahomes, the offense will be fun to experience, but it is rare that a first-year starting quarterback finds great success. Likewise, the defense may have intriguing young players such as Fuller and Chris Jones, as well as a handful of rookies, but the unit is not primed for consistent success in the short term.

A first-round quarterback is the beacon of hope any team and fanbase can rally behind, and Mahomes is a fantastic candidate to deliver on that hope. Bringing Mahomes along and seeing him deliver on his potential would be as important as anything else the Chiefs could realistically accomplish this season. Though the record may not reflect it right away, the Chiefs are bringing on a better, more exciting identity.

Derrik Klassen

2017 Chiefs Stats by Week

Wk	vs.	W-L	PF	PA	YDF	YDA	TO	Total	Off	Def	ST
1	at NE	W	42	27	537	371	-1	75%	63%	-17%	-5%
2	PHI	W	27	20	344	406	+2	60%	48%	-5%	7%
3	at LAC	W	24	10	311	330	+3	60%	18%	-35%	6%
4	WAS	W	29	20	429	331	+1	-1%	36%	26%	-12%
5	at HOU	W	42	34	450	392	+1	-17%	19%	54%	18%
6	PIT	L	13	19	251	439	+1	-13%	-16%	16%	20%
7	at OAK	L	30	31	425	505	0	-13%	26%	47%	7%
8	DEN	W	29	19	276	364	+3	-44%	-41%	16%	12%
9	at DAL	L	17	28	323	375	-1	-23%	6%	30%	1%
10	BYE										
11	at NYG	L	9	12	363	317	-2	-17%	-19%	4%	6%
12	BUF	L	10	16	236	268	-1	-26%	-28%	-3%	-1%
13	at NYJ	L	31	38	474	488	0	53%	76%	27%	3%
14	OAK	W	26	15	408	268	+2	28%	7%	-8%	13%
15	LAC	W	30	13	397	307	+4	57%	36%	-20%	1%
16	MIA	W	29	13	404	345	+2	-24%	7%	37%	6%
17	at DEN	W	27	24	379	336	+1	3%	14%	15%	3%
18	TEN	L	21	22	325	397	+2	4%	33%	25%	-3%

Trends and Splits

	Offense	Rank	Defense	Rank
Total DVOA	15.9%	4	10.7%	30
Unadjusted VOA	18.0%	4	9.1%	28
Weighted Trend	8.3%	7	14.0%	32
Variance	10.3%	28	6.2%	21
Average Opponent	1.2%	24	-0.2%	17
Passing	30.6%	8	17.2%	23
Rushing	8.8%	5	3.0%	32
First Down	19.6%	3	17.5%	31
Second Down	13.9%	8	7.4%	27
Third Down	11.3%	10	1.9%	15
First Half	13.5%	7	6.4%	28
Second Half	18.2%	4	15.3%	32
Red Zone	-8.6%	21	7.2%	21
Late and Close	26.6%	1	3.6%	21

Five-Year Performance

Year	W-L	Pyth W	Est W	PF	PA	TO	Total	Rk	Off	Rk	Def	Rk	ST	Rk	Off AGL	Rk	Def AGL	Rk	Off Age	Rk	Def Age	Rk	ST Age	Rk
2013	11-5	11.1	10.0	430	305	+18	17.5%	6	3.0%	15	-6.7%	9	7.8%	1	29.4	13	10.6	3	26.1	27	26.4	17	25.8	23
2014	9-7	10.1	9.4	353	281	-3	10.4%	10	5.0%	12	1.3%	19	6.7%	3	36.0	20	62.8	27	26.6	19	26.6	20	25.7	26
2015	11-5	11.2	11.4	405	287	+14	25.2%	5	11.7%	6	-11.6%	6	2.0%	9	26.3	13	28.6	18	25.8	28	27.4	5	25.8	19
2016	12-4	10.1	9.7	389	311	+16	13.5%	6	2.9%	13	-2.8%	14	7.8%	1	33.2	14	66.1	30	25.9	26	26.5	16	25.1	31
2017	10-6	10.0	10.0	415	339	+15	10.6%	10	15.9%	4	10.7%	30	5.3%	4	43.1	21	36.9	18	26.3	26	27.1	5	25.9	16

2017 Performance Based on Most Common Personnel Groups

KC Offense					KC Offense vs. Opponents					KC Defense				KC Defense vs. Opponents			
Pers	Freq	Yds	DVOA	Run%	Pers	Freq	Yds	DVOA	Run%	Pers	Freq	Yds	DVOA	Pers	Freq	Yds	DVOA
11	52%	6.5	32.4%	31%	Base	24%	5.4	1.6%	54%	Base	27%	4.7	-8.1%	11	67%	6.3	15.8%
12	26%	6.0	21.2%	34%	Nickel	51%	6.1	21.6%	33%	Nickel	29%	6.8	28.1%	12	15%	6.1	6.1%
21	6%	5.6	-7.8%	48%	Dime+	24%	7.3	46.6%	24%	Dime+	42%	6.2	13.6%	21	5%	3.7	-22.8%
13	6%	6.3	15.8%	36%	Goal Line	0%	1.3	-92.8%	33%	Goal Line	1%	0.5	-6.1%	22	5%	3.7	-26.9%
22	4%	5.8	10.3%	85%	Big	1%	4.1	15.4%	100%	Big	1%	3.4	7.4%	13	2%	4.4	-7.7%

Strategic Tendencies

Run/Pass		Rk	Formation		Rk	Pass Rush		Rk	Secondary		Rk	Strategy		Rk
Runs, first half	32%	32	Form: Single Back	81%	8	Rush 3	21.8%	2	4 DB	28%	23	Play action	22%	14
Runs, first down	46%	25	Form: Empty Back	6%	23	Rush 4	60.5%	22	5 DB	29%	30	Avg Box (Off)	6.04	30
Runs, second-long	30%	21	Pers: 3+ WR	55%	26	Rush 5	14.2%	28	6+ DB	42%	3	Avg Box (Def)	6.19	23
Runs, power sit.	74%	1	Pers: 2+ TE/6+ OL	39%	3	Rush 6+	3.5%	26	CB by Sides	82%	13	Offensive Pace	32.57	31
Runs, behind 2H	29%	11	Pers: 6+ OL	4%	12	Int DL Sacks	43.5%	3	S/CB Cover Ratio	27%	18	Defensive Pace	30.20	9
Pass, ahead 2H	52%	8	Shotgun/Pistol	74%	2	Second Level Sacks	14.5%	22	DB Blitz	6%	27	Go for it on 4th	0.83	23

Kansas City led the league with 166 broken tackles. Not only did Kareem Hunt lead the NFL with 89, but Tyreek Hill was fifth among wide receivers with 19 and Travis Kelce led all tight ends with 19. Even Albert Wilson added another 13. ☜ Alex Smith was blitzed on just 18 percent of passes, the lowest figure of any quarterback, but the Chiefs also allowed pressure on 54 percent of those blitzes, the highest figure of any offense. ☜ Once again, the Chiefs led the league by throwing 26 percent of passes at or behind the line of scrimmage. ☜ Kansas City threw a league-high 32 percent of passes to tight ends, and a league-low 10 percent of passes to No. 3 or "other" receivers. ☜ The Chiefs offense slowed down as it gradually got closer to the goal line. The Chiefs were No. 1 in DVOA from their own 20 to the 40, then No. 8 between the 40s, No. 18 between the opposing 40 and 20, and No. 21 in the red zone. This was the second straight year the Chiefs struggled in the red zone after they had been one of the top red zone offenses from 2013 to 2015. ☜ Kansas City's offense also hit a wall once it got a big lead. With a lead of more than a touchdown, the Chiefs offense ranked 28th in DVOA. The rest of the time, the Chiefs ranked third, and they were No. 1 in "late and close" situations. ☜ The Chiefs allowed a league-worst 9.2 yards per pass and 61.6% DVOA when blitzing, compared to just 6.5 yards per pass and 11.5% DVOA otherwise. ☜ Kansas City had very good fumble recovery luck last season, recovering 7 of 10 fumbles on offense and 8 of 13 fumbles on defense.

Passing

Player	DYAR	DVOA	Plays	NtYds	Avg	YAC	C%	TD	Int
A.Smith*	1026	18.3%	541	3840	7.1	5.7	67.7%	26	5
P.Mahomes	54	11.7%	37	269	7.3	7.9	62.9%	0	1

Rushing

Player	DYAR	DVOA	Plays	Yds	Avg	TD	Fum	Suc
K.Hunt	222	11.9%	272	1327	4.9	8	1	47%
A.Smith*	85	20.3%	50	366	7.3	1	0	-
C.West	-2	-11.4%	18	72	4.0	2	0	33%
T.Hill	-2	-41.3%	16	50	3.1	0	0	-
A.Sherman	31	35.3%	14	40	2.9	1	0	43%
A.Hunt	-1	-11.6%	8	23	2.9	0	0	25%
D.Williams	-25	-22.7%	46	181	3.9	0	0	28%

Receiving

Player	DYAR	DVOA	Plays	Ctch	Yds	Y/C	YAC	TD	C%
T.Hill	304	23.6%	106	76	1192	15.7	6.1	7	72%
A.Wilson*	167	21.4%	62	42	554	13.2	7.5	3	68%
D.Robinson	-14	-16.9%	39	21	212	10.1	2.0	0	54%
C.Conley	50	27.2%	16	11	175	15.9	4.1	0	69%
D.Thomas	20	4.7%	16	14	143	10.2	5.2	2	88%
S.Watkins	216	24.1%	70	39	593	15.2	4.7	8	56%
T.Kelce	197	17.0%	122	83	1038	12.5	4.9	8	68%
D.Harris	-37	-23.3%	35	18	224	12.4	7.2	1	51%
R.Travis*	-46	-69.6%	12	5	43	8.6	3.2	0	42%
K.Hunt	102	15.6%	63	53	455	8.6	7.8	3	84%
C.West	-31	-31.6%	34	27	150	5.6	4.9	2	79%
A.Sherman	11	11.2%	8	6	47	7.8	6.8	0	75%
A.Hunt	-10	-40.9%	7	4	31	7.8	11.3	0	57%
D.Williams	44	12.2%	28	20	155	7.8	7.7	1	71%

Offensive Line

Player	Pos	Age	GS	Snaps	Pen	Sk	Pass	Run	Player	Pos	Age	GS	Snaps	Pen	Sk	Pass	Run
Mitchell Schwartz	RT	29	16/16	1033	4	6.0	23	2	Laurent Duvernay-Tardif	RG	27	11/11	637	6	1.0	4	3
Eric Fisher	LT	27	16/15	966	5	6.0	14	10	Mitch Morse	C	26	7/7	384	1	0.0	2	4
Bryan Witzmann	LG	28	16/13	883	9	1.0	4	6	Cameron Erving	RG	26	13/4	277	3	0.0	5	3
Zach Fulton*	C/G	27	15/12	794	2	1.5	3	4									

Year	Yards	ALY	Rank	Power	Rank	Stuff	Rank	2nd Lev	Rank	Open Field	Rank	Sacks	ASR	Rank	Press	Rank	F-Start	Cont.
2015	4.43	4.53	5	70%	11	18%	6	1.22	8	0.84	11	46	8.7%	28	25.0%	15	15	22
2016	3.91	4.10	17	59%	21	18%	10	1.04	27	0.57	22	32	5.7%	14	21.0%	5	23	32
2017	4.66	4.14	12	82%	1	18%	8	1.23	9	1.17	2	37	6.7%	17	31.4%	18	18	24

2017 ALY by direction:	Left End: 3.78 (19)	Left Tackle: 4.77 (8)	Mid/Guard: 4.15 (17)	Right Tackle: 3.97 (16)	Right End: 4.14 (13)

Through the early portion of the season, left guard Bryan Witzmann executed Kansas City's various zone and counter concepts at a high level. He proved to have the lateral agility and second-level coordination to work on zone concepts reasonably well. However, as the middle of the season approached, Witzmann started to play more like the career backup that he is. Though Witzmann recorded just six blown blocks on 319 run blocking snaps, he had too many plays in which he struggled to maintain his block or provided nothing more than the bare minimum. Those more minor failures do not get counted as blown blocks but can still be plenty damaging to the overall functionality of an offensive line. ☜ Right guard Laurent Duvernay-Tardif had a rollercoaster of a year as well. Duvernay-Tardif was clicking with the teammates around him and performing well through the first three weeks, but a sprained knee in Week 4 left him sidelined until Week 9. Upon return, it took Duvernay-Tardif a few weeks to get back to form, finally picking up full steam toward the last month of the season. The offensive line as a whole stepped up its play once he was clicking again. ☞ Center Mitch Morse also suffered a foot injury in Week 2. Once Duvernay-Tardif went down a couple weeks later, the interior of the offensive line lost its consistency for a few weeks. The downhill stylings of Cameron Erving and Zach Fulton helped maintain success in short-yardage situations, but Erving was far too inconsistent a player to keep the offensive line gelled. Erving racked up eight blown blocks on just 260 total snaps. From Week 5 through Week 12, stretching from Erving's first start through the first few weeks after Duvernay-Tardif's return, the Chiefs posted six of their seven negative rushing DVOA performances, as well as their "worst" positive performance in a game against the New York Giants who finished the year 26th in run defense DVOA. ☞ Kansas City's offensive line got more help from their running backs than most other offensive lines did. Kansas City and New Orleans were the only two teams in the top 12 in adjusted line yards whose running back yards per carry were higher than their adjusted line yards, suggesting that running back Kareem Hunt was able to take advantage of the Chiefs' adequate offensive line play better than many other backs could have. ☞ If anything, last year proved that Kansas City's offensive line has untapped potential. A myriad of injuries stripped the team of its best possible offensive line, even if backups such as Fulton played reasonably well when forced onto the field. Morse and Duvernay-Tardif can anchor an effective interior when healthy, but the duo hardly got to play together last season. With Eric Fisher and Mitchell Schwartz as bookends, the Chiefs' offensive line can assert itself as a top-10 unit next season, if health permits.

Defensive Front Seven

Defensive Line	Age	Pos	G	Snaps	Plays	TmPct	Rk	Stop	Dfts	BTkl	Runs	St%	Rk	RuYd	Rk	Sack	Hit	Hur	Dsrpt
						Overall						vs. Run				Pass Rush			
Chris Jones	24	DE	16	680	39	4.8%	50	35	16	5	23	83%	25	1.3	9	6.5	9	23.5	5
Allen Bailey	29	DE	14	626	38	5.3%	34	32	11	5	34	82%	26	1.7	27	2.0	2	20.0	0
Bennie Logan*	29	DT	15	574	53	6.9%	12	42	14	0	47	79%	37	1.3	11	1.5	1	7.5	1
Rakeem Nunez-Roches	25	DE	16	392	24	2.9%	--	15	4	9	22	59%	--	3.1	--	0.5	1	8.0	0
Jarvis Jenkins	30	DE	11	220	9	1.6%	--	6	1	5	7	57%	--	2.3	--	1.0	2	5.0	0
Xavier Williams	26	DE	11	252	20	3.6%	--	18	2	2	19	89%	--	2.1	--	0.5	1	4.0	0

Edge Rushers	Age	Pos	G	Snaps	Plays	TmPct	Rk	Stop	Dfts	BTkl	Runs	St%	Rk	RuYd	Rk	Sack	Hit	Hur	Dsrpt
						Overall						vs. Run				Pass Rush			
Justin Houston	29	OLB	15	952	62	8.1%	10	50	18	7	39	85%	17	1.8	28	9.5	11	38.5	5
Frank Zombo	31	OLB	16	588	39	4.8%	52	25	10	4	32	66%	76	4.9	94	1.5	4	17.5	1

Linebackers	Age	Pos	G	Snaps	Plays	TmPct	Rk	Stop	Dfts	BTkl	Runs	St%	Rk	RuYd	Rk	Sack	Hit	Hur	Tgts	Suc%	Rk	AdjYd	Rk	PD	Int
						Overall						vs. Run				Pass Rush				vs. Pass					
Derrick Johnson*	36	ILB	15	848	78	10.2%	63	42	16	16	47	62%	47	3.4	31	0.0	0	5.0	33	60%	9	4.5	5	6	0
Reggie Ragland	25	ILB	12	323	44	7.2%	--	24	4	7	35	60%	--	4.4	--	0.0	0	1.0	8	69%	--	3.0	--	0	0
Kevin Pierre-Louis*	27	ILB	14	251	37	5.2%	--	18	3	5	25	52%	--	3.7	--	0.0	1	4.0	13	55%	--	8.5	--	2	0
Anthony Hitchens	26	ILB	12	547	85	14.1%	26	43	13	5	50	66%	29	3.0	22	0.0	2	5.0	27	23%	75	7.3	50	1	0

Year	Yards	ALY	Rank	Power	Rank	Stuff	Rank	2nd Level	Rank	Open Field	Rank	Sacks	ASR	Rank	Press	Rank
2015	3.83	3.82	7	50%	2	22%	10	1.06	10	0.58	8	47	7.7%	4	28.1%	5
2016	4.43	4.72	30	65%	22	18%	19	1.39	30	0.47	5	28	5.1%	26	24.4%	27
2017	4.23	4.35	26	60%	10	20%	23	1.35	31	0.55	5	31	5.8%	26	30.3%	16

2017 ALY by direction:	Left End: 5.15 (30)	Left Tackle: 4.21 (21)	Mid/Guard: 4.57 (27)	Right Tackle: 2.66 (2)	Right End: 4.42 (23)

For as solid a player as Bennie Logan is, his fit in the Chiefs' defense was not ideal. Logan was an explosive, yet inconsistent presence in the run game. Logan too often either ripped through to the backfield immediately or found himself blown off the ball. While a player such as Logan can be a good starter, those types of players work best with fast linebackers who can slip through behind them and clean up the tackle for loss. For example, a linebacker such as Telvin Smith is perfect for Jacksonville's explosive front. Kansas City did not have any linebackers like that in 2017. Additionally, Logan provided close to nothing as a pass-rusher, leaving him to be a two-down player whose explosiveness could not be appropriately taken advantage of by the rest of the defense. ☞ Justin Houston could have been the Defensive Player of the Year if the team around him gave him an ounce of help. Houston was dominant when the defense was healthier early in the season, getting off to a hot start with four total sacks through the first three games of the season and furthering that total to 7.5 sacks by the midway point in the year. Unfortunately, due to injuries and lackluster play from others, offenses were able to game-plan around him down the stretch, either by running away from him or allocating extra help to his side in pass protection. Houston recorded just two sacks through his final seven starts on the season. ☞ After a down year from Dontari Poe in 2016 and a complete absence of him in 2017, it became clear that an anchor at nose tackle is critical to the team's defensive structure. The team tried to shake things up with a more independent force in Logan, but it did not work out. Drafting Derrick Nnadi (Florida State) is a signal that Bob Sutton wants to return to the old structure. Nnadi is not near the same caliber of athlete as Logan, but he can provide consistent run support from the middle in a way that Logan could not. Nnadi is more inclined to feel a play out and maintain run fits, as opposed to Logan's boom-or-bust approach. Any step to improve a defensive line that has been bottom-eight in opponent adjusted line yards for two straight years is a step in the right direction. ☞ Off-ball linebacker is still a question mark. The Chiefs did well to move on from an aging Derrick Johnson, but the team's best replacement plan was to sign Anthony Hitchens, who spent the past four seasons rotating in and out of the Dallas Cowboys' starting lineup. Hitchens was a fine role player in Dallas, primarily versus the run, but was not trusted to be a three-down player and full-time starter. Reggie Ragland and Hitchens may make for a decent run-oriented duo, but the lack of pass coverage skill will put stress on other areas of the defense to step up. Additionally, though Hitchens is better versus the run than the pass, Hitchens' run defense is nothing to boast over his predecessor. Hitchens' stop rate (66 percent) and average gain on run tackles (3.0) are only slight improvements over Johnson's numbers (62 percent, 3.4). Only the Buffalo Bills posted allowed more second-level yardage than the Chiefs' defense in 2017, and the signing of Hitchens does not explicitly suggest that Kansas City is going to make a significant turnaround from that type of poor performance in 2018. With a five-year, $45 million contract, Hitchens is a relatively expensive gamble on a player who is likely just a minor upgrade over Johnson versus the run and a weaker link in coverage. ☞ Trying to make sense of second-round pick Breeland Speaks is tricky. Speaks was not expected by media outlets to be drafted as high as the second round, and furthermore, the Chiefs needed more traditional pass-rush help than what Speaks can provide. Speaks is a hybrid player who can line up as a 5-tech or as a stand-up outside linebacker, similar to Pernell McPhee or Courtney Upshaw near the end of his stint with the Baltimore Ravens. On top of a unique role in college, Speaks participated as a defensive tackle at the NFL combine and weighed in at 6-foot-2 and 283 pounds at the event. Though he tested fairly well for a defensive tackle, Speaks' 4.87-second 40-yard dash time and 7.86 3-cone drill time are not good marks for an edge rusher. Football Outsiders' SackSEER system gives Speaks a 30.7% rating and projects him with just 4.1 sacks through his fifth year, putting him in the same tier as seventh-round pick Leon Jacobs and undrafted free agent Hercules Mata'afa. On the other hand, Speaks' size profile and path from college defensive tackle to NFL outside linebacker matches that of one of SackSEER's biggest misses: none other than the man he's nominally replacing, Tamba Hali.

Defensive Secondary

Secondary	Age	Pos	G	Snaps	Plays	TmPct	Rk	Stop	Dfts	BTkl	Runs	St%	Rk	RuYd	Rk	Tgts	Tgt%	Rk	Dist	Suc%	Rk	AdjYd	Rk	PD	Int
Ron Parker*	31	FS	15	1034	71	9.3%	49	18	8	18	37	24%	69	9.5	59	32	8.2%	27	17.5	47%	52	9.9	59	4	2
Daniel Sorensen	28	SS	15	993	94	12.3%	14	37	17	18	45	42%	45	6.0	37	37	10.0%	43	10.5	57%	22	7.4	29	5	1
Marcus Peters*	25	CB	14	967	55	7.7%	52	24	16	11	11	55%	25	5.9	41	73	20.2%	40	14.9	48%	59	7.9	44	9	5
Terrance Mitchell*	26	CB	15	706	70	9.2%	29	24	13	2	16	19%	77	7.7	62	93	35.4%	78	15.0	49%	48	9.3	73	19	4
Steven Nelson	25	CB	9	514	45	9.8%	--	17	7	6	9	56%	--	5.1	--	46	24.1%	--	9.8	46%	--	8.4	--	4	0
Eric Murray	24	FS	14	439	35	4.9%	73	10	5	3	8	25%	66	10.6	73	33	20.2%	75	9.0	41%	66	6.6	20	3	0
Phillip Gaines*	27	CB	14	419	34	4.8%	--	7	6	4	12	25%	--	9.8	--	42	27.0%	--	14.7	45%	--	8.8	--	3	0
Kenneth Acker*	26	CB	16	209	20	2.5%	--	5	2	2	7	43%	--	8.3	--	19	23.8%	--	11.4	30%	--	10.5	--	3	1
Kendall Fuller	23	CB	16	725	64	7.6%	55	36	19	7	19	37%	56	7.0	57	54	18.5%	29	10.2	65%	2	6.8	27	10	4
David Amerson	27	CB	6	287	22	7.2%	--	8	2	2	2	50%	--	4.5	--	23	17.8%	--	13.6	37%	--	12.3	--	4	0

Year	Pass D Rank	vs. #1 WR	Rk	vs. #2 WR	Rk	vs. Other WR	Rk	WR Wide	Rk	WR Slot	Rk	vs. TE	Rk	vs. RB	Rk
2015	5	7.6%	22	-15.7%	7	9.0%	20	--	--	--	--	-36.4%	2	-28.9%	3
2016	7	0.2%	14	-10.0%	6	-24.9%	3	-9.4%	10	-13.4%	4	3.4%	20	-20.5%	4
2017	23	29.5%	31	-6.0%	14	0.8%	18	2.3%	20	19.6%	26	-5.9%	12	-23.1%	3

To offset the decision to trade Marcus Peters, the Chiefs acquired a third-round pick (which turned into Nnadi) and Kendall Fuller as part of the Alex Smith deal with Washington. Fuller dominated in the slot for Washington. Fuller had one of the best success rates in the league, as well as the third-most passes defended, trailing only Darius Slay and Casey Hayward. By most every measure, Fuller proved himself to be one of the best slot cornerbacks around. However, Fuller is not a direct Peters replacement. Peters was a true No.1 outside cornerback. Fuller's accomplishments in the slot do not necessarily correlate to success outside, and he will not always play outside the way Peters did. That is not to say Fuller will struggle outside, but it may be lofty to expect a converted slot cornerback to replace one of the NFL's few true No.1 cornerbacks. ☞ Fuller is expected to play outside in base packages, but often slide inside to the slot in nickel packages, similar to how the Atlanta Falcons have used Robert Alford in previous seasons. ☞ Peters and Fuller are not the only players to shuffle in or out of the Chiefs' secondary.

Out of the top eight secondary players last year, with 5,281 combined snaps, five players who accounted for a total of 3,335 snaps are no longer on the roster. Losing just over 60 percent of the team's secondary snaps could suggest the secondary will go through growing pains, even with the understanding that Fuller is a top-tier talent and that Eric Berry will be returning from injury. ☞ To that note, the state of the Chiefs' secondary hinges significantly on how well Berry returns to form. In his lone performance last season, Berry erased New England's Rob Gronkowski from the game, holding the Patriots tight end to fewer receptions and yards than he had in any game for the rest of the season. Berry was matching up tightly with Gronkowski in the red zone, as well as capping him vertically between the 20s. Without Berry, the Chiefs did not have anyone who could fulfill that role, and the defense suffered for it. Berry posted adjusted success rates of 59 percent and 53 percent in 2015 and 2016, respectively; both were among the best in the league for a safety with his volume of snaps. If Berry can return playing at that level, the transition of having so many new faces in the secondary will be made smoother.

Special Teams

Year	DVOA	Rank	FG/XP	Rank	Net Kick	Rank	Kick Ret	Rank	Net Punt	Rank	Punt Ret	Rank	Hidden	Rank
2015	2.0%	9	-2.9	25	0.6	16	-0.8	16	16.2	1	-3.1	20	2.8	12
2016	7.8%	1	0.5	15	0.5	15	5.7	7	11.3	4	20.8	1	3.2	13
2017	5.3%	4	11.8	3	7.1	2	0.0	14	6.2	8	1.7	12	5.0	8

A preseason castoff by the Carolina Panthers, kicker Harrison Butker revitalized Kansas City's placekicking as a rookie in 2017. Prior to Butker, the team relied on Cairo Santos, who hovered around league average at the position. Butker immediately excelled beyond Santos' past two seasons, placing himself alongside Justin Tucker as one of the league's top field goal kickers and kickoff specialists. ☞ Butker's presence was not enough to maintain the Chiefs' place atop the special teams rankings. The team's return quality took a step back in 2017 due in part to Tyreek Hill's reduced role. In 2016, Hill was responsible for 14 kickoff returns and all but one of the team's 40 punt returns. Hill scored a combined three times and was particularly devastating on punt returns. However, in 2017, Hill became too important to the offense. He was removed from kickoff duty altogether; he also fielded fewer punts and was significantly less effective as a punt returner. Akeem Hunt and De'Anthony Thomas did fine in relief of Hill, but neither quite matched Hill's explosive potential. ☞ The Chiefs did not have a definitive special teams tackling ace the way many teams do, yet the unit still did well to limit both kick and punt returns. Eighteen unique teams had at least one player with ten or more special teams tackles, including a handful of teams with multiple such players. Eric Murray and Kevin Pierre-Louis led the Chiefs with six special teams tackles apiece.

Los Angeles Chargers

2017 Record: 9-7	**Total DVOA:** 7.9% (11th)	**2018 Mean Projection:** 7.9 wins	**On the Clock (0-4):** 10%
Pythagorean Wins: 10.5 (9th)	**Offense:** 10.7% (7th)	**Postseason Odds:** 38.9%	**Mediocrity (5-7):** 33%
Snap-Weighted Age: 26.4 (16th)	**Defense:** -4.7% (12th)	**Super Bowl Odds:** 4.4%	**Playoff Contender (8-10):** 40%
Average Opponent: -4.1% (29th)	**Special Teams:** -7.5% (31st)	**Proj. Avg. Opponent:** -1.5% (25th)	**Super Bowl Contender (11+):** 16%

2017: Los Angelenos all come from somewhere / To live in sunshine, their funky exile.

2018: Laying low in the canyons / Making up for all the time gone by.

Tackling and field goal kicking are rarely major themes of a *Football Outsiders Almanac* chapter.

Neither is a hot analytics subject. Tackling is a presupposed football skill, like blocking, running, and breathing: everyone who reaches the NFL is assumed to be relatively good at it. Teams may lose games here and there because of missed tackles, and some teams may be better at tackling than others, but it's very unusual for terrible tackling to be the primary reason a team missed the playoffs.

Placekicking is a similar topic. We talk about field goals when a team is particularly dependent on them (the Ravens, for about the last 20 years) or when a team does something dumbfounding at the kicker position (the Buccaneers' Roberto Aguayo selection will resonate across decades). But there is a reason special teams get their own subsection: kickers, for better or worse, are supposed to only be a tiny part of a team's story.

But the 2017 Chargers were unique. They missed the playoffs because they could not tackle or kick field goals.

The Chargers defense allowed 147 broken tackles last year, the second-highest total in the league. Their defense allowed broken tackles on 13.3 percent of opponent's plays, the second-highest rate in the NFL. The Steelers topped the Chargers in both categories; the Steelers and Chargers were the only teams to allow broken tackles on more than 12 percent of opponent's plays, and their rates were the highest in the three years that Football Outsiders and Sports Info Solutions have jointly collected data. But Pittsburgh's tackling woes were largely a two-man issue: linebacker Ryan Shazier and defensive back Sean Davis finished third and fourth in the NFL with 23 and 21 tackles broken, respectively. The Chargers' tackling issues were not nearly as localized. Eight of their defenders surrendered ten or more missed tackles (Table 1). No other team had more than six such defenders. The Chargers could not bench a defender for bad tackling or schematically hide a weak link. Their entire defense was the weak link when it came to bringing down ballcarriers.

The tackling issues were particularly acute against the run. The Chargers allowed 101 broken tackles on running plays, missing a tackle on 23.5 percent of carries, both the worst figures in the NFL. Their defense finished 28th in the NFL in second-level yards and worst in open-field yards. Opponents enjoyed 18 running plays of 20-plus yards (highest in the league) and six 50-plus yard runs (tied with the Jets for highest).

The Chargers excelled at preventing big plays in the passing game (37 pass plays of 20-plus yards, third-best in the league, and just four 40-plus yard passes, tied with three teams for second-best), thanks to their pass rush and coverage. But teams could avoid Joey Bosa and Melvin Ingram just by running between them. Gash runs played large roles in both losses to the Chiefs, the Eagles loss, and (on a fake punt) the Jaguars loss.

Despite the porous run defense and miserable tackling, the Chargers could have avoided the 0-4 start that doomed their season if they had not tried to cut financial corners at kicker.

Undrafted rookie Younghoe Koo won the kicking job from veteran Josh Lambo in last year's training camp. Koo kicked just one 27-yard field goal in the preseason, while Lambo hit a 53-yarder and a 37-yarder, so Lambo was probably competing against his own salary more than he was competing with Koo. (Koo was just 1-of-6 on preseason touchbacks, so kickoffs were not the deciding factor.) Once the season started, Koo had a potential game-tying 44-yarder blocked in the final seconds against the Broncos and missed 43- and 44-yarders (the second a potential last-second game winner) in the two-point loss to the Dolphins.

Nick Novak replaced Koo a few games later and stabilized the kicking situation, though Novak also had a kick blocked in the Patriots loss. Then the 36-year-old Novak suffered a back injury, so Travis Coons and Nick Rose mopped up the season; both were terrible, though they didn't cost the Chargers any games. In total, the Chargers suffered three blocked field goals, missed five extra points (one blocked), and were just 3-of-11 on kicks beyond 40 yards. Their field goal statistics would not look out of place in the 1960s, when some teams still used backup running backs as kickers.

Table 1. Chargers Missed Tackles

Player	Pos	Missed Tackles
Jahleel Addae	SS	15
Melvin Ingram	DE	13
Tre Boston	FS	13
Hayes Pullard	MLB	12
Adrian Phillips	FS/SS	12
Casey Hayward	CB	11
Denzel Perryman	MLB	10
Desmond King	CB	10

2018 Chargers Schedule

Week	Opp.	Week	Opp.	Week	Opp.
1	KC	7	TEN (U.K.)	13	at PIT
2	at BUF	8	BYE	14	CIN
3	at LAR	9	at SEA	15	at KC (Thu.)
4	SF	10	at OAK	16	BAL
5	OAK	11	DEN	17	at DEN
6	at CLE	12	ARI		

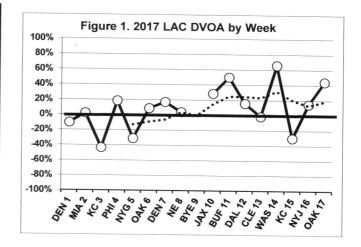

Figure 1. 2017 LAC DVOA by Week

Between the missed tackles and the missed field goals, the Chargers missed a playoff opportunity, squandered another terrific late-career Philip Rivers season, had nothing to show for Joey Bosa and Melvin Ingram's 23 combined sacks, wasted a 102-catch Comeback Player of the Year season by Keenan Allen, and squandered a chance to generate some enthusiasm in a new market. While the Rams were winning back the love of Angelenos, the Chargers played in a converted soccer stadium in Carson that opponents' fans used as an Airbnb. Starting the season 0-4 and then 3-6 did nothing to create a smidge of home-field advantage or further Los Angeles Chargers brand penetration.

The good news for the Chargers entering Year 2 of the Anthony Lynn era is that it's easier to rebuild the middle of the defense and find a kicker than it is to acquire a new quarterback, edge rushers, cornerbacks, or any of the other hard-to-find pieces that the Chargers already possess.

First-round safety Derwin James will immediately cut down on the amount of 25-yard runs the Chargers allow. James has Kam Chancellor-level upside and should become a high-impact starter immediately, though one of the knocks on him is (uh-oh) a tendency to take bad angles in pursuit and miss some tackles.

Fourth-round pick Kyzir White is a box safety or safety/linebacker hybrid who gets high marks for his instincts and effort. The Chargers also added no-nonsense North Carolina State run-stuffer Justin Jones to bolster a thin interior defensive line. Uchenna Nwosu is a 250-pound thumper at outside linebacker who will add even more juice to the pass rush. All four rookies are likely to contribute in 2018.

Former Eagles kicker Caleb Sturgis, who was reliable in 2015 and 2016 before suffering an early-season injury and losing his job to Jake Elliott last year, arrives in Carson to quell the field goal emergency. Roberto Aguayo is also in camp to provide competition and a cautionary tale.

The rookie crop and kicker investment will help. But the Chargers should have done more. It's neither difficult nor expensive to upgrade the interior defense in free agency. Any of the affordable linebackers or safeties on the market would have provided plenty of worry-free bang for the buck. But the Chargers opted to do most of their offseason spending on offense, signing Mike Pouncey at center and reclamation projects Virgil Green (who may play a major offensive role in the wake of Hunter Henry's injury) and Geno Smith at the skill positions. If rookies like James blow a few assignments while ramping up to the NFL, the Chargers defense will be right back where it was last season.

The Chargers cap management strategy, it should be noted, is a little strange. According to OverTheCap.com, no team in the NFL pays more veterans middle- to elite-level salaries than the Chargers. Much of that money is tied up in what Over The Cap calls "middle" salaries: the $4.8 million to $8.5 million range. That's the tax bracket for Jahleel Addae, Joe Barksdale, Travis Benjamin, Casey Hayward, Corey Liuget, Brandon Mebane, Pouncey, and Jason Verrett. There are some fine players on that list (Hayward), at least one over-the-hill blocking sled (Mebane), and a lot of ordinary players fetching premium-level salaries.

The bloat in the middle of the budget keeps the Chargers from making the kind of bold moves teams like their Los Angeles neighbors made to try to get off the perpetual also-ran treadmill. It also forces the team to economize, not just at kicker but across their bench. Between the overpaid underachievers and talented-but-mistake-plagued youngsters with major roles such as Austin Ekeler and Tyrell Williams, it's no surprise that the Chargers often lose games in the most maddening ways imaginable.

The Chargers needed to be aggressive this offseason because Philip Rivers is 36 years old and deep into a late-career Renaissance that could end at any time. Melvin Gordon will enter his expensive option year in 2019, and Joey Bosa will be angling to be the NFL's highest-paid player by 2020. Their division rivals are also in various states of rebuilding or upheaval, creating the type of wide-open field the Chargers never had when Peyton Manning was in Denver or Andy Reid's veteran-heavy Chiefs were an annual lock for double-digit wins.

The Chargers squandered a string of good-to-outstanding Rivers seasons since 2013, with nothing to show for it except one forgotten playoff run. They are running out of time with their current nucleus. This was the offseason to go all-in, but instead they will hope that James and some other youngsters can plug that big leak between Ingram and Bosa, which would be a more prudent strategy if Rivers was seven years younger and the franchise had more time to slow-cook a contender.

Perhaps the team is saving its big splurge for 2019, when it moves into the new L.A. pleasure palace to help the Rams with the rent. The Chargers organization has been in a stadium-related holding pattern for years, which has created a kind of paradox: they enjoyed one of the NFL's stable quarterback situations, yet they chose to live surrounded by their own suitcases and packing crates and make roster management a year-to-year afterthought. Their mediocrity has escaped national attention because they alienated their original fanbase and have barely caught the attention of a new one. They're the NFL's most forgettable team, the one relegated to playing late-night season openers, contributing to a Cowboys-centric narrative on Thanksgiving, and (this year) traveling to London for a game which will start at 6:30 a.m. West Coast time.

The Chargers can make a strong bid to win the AFC West. Perhaps they can even win the 11 games they might have won last season if not for a missed tackle here and missed field goal there. But their lack of urgency is puzzling and discouraging. The Chargers appear too content to be pretty good at too many positions, and they don't seem too concerned to be expensive-

ly ordinary at some positions (interior defensive line) and razor-thin at others (the backup quarterback situation is … mysterious). Lynn made little impression as a first-year coach, in part because Ken Whisenhunt still directs the offense (though Lynn made the Chargers more run-oriented early in games last year, which was as ineffective as you would expect) and in part because it's hard to set a head-coaching tone when your team is losing due to terrible fundamentals.

The Chargers won't lose due to dramatic shortcomings next year. They'll lose—or at least fall short of true Super Bowl contention—because they remain ordinary by design. This is the team that's built by being more concerned about stadium stuff than the win-loss column. It's frustrating because they should be so much better. For the Chargers' sake, let's hope future season-ticket holders aren't paying close attention.

Mike Tanier

2017 Chargers Stats by Week

Wk	vs.	W-L	PF	PA	YDF	YDA	TO	Total	Off	Def	ST
1	at DEN	L	21	24	249	321	+1	-10%	12%	2%	-21%
2	MIA	L	17	19	367	336	0	2%	41%	16%	-22%
3	KC	L	10	24	330	311	-3	-43%	-36%	-1%	-8%
4	PHI	L	24	26	400	454	-1	18%	37%	10%	-8%
5	at NYG	W	27	22	382	335	+1	-31%	-26%	9%	4%
6	at OAK	W	17	16	343	274	+1	9%	3%	-20%	-15%
7	DEN	W	21	0	242	251	+3	17%	-19%	-20%	16%
8	at NE	L	13	21	349	414	-1	4%	30%	-7%	-32%
9	BYE										
10	at JAX	L	17	20	322	398	0	28%	17%	-19%	-8%
11	BUF	W	54	24	429	393	+6	50%	36%	-17%	-3%
12	at DAL	W	28	6	515	247	+2	16%	25%	-12%	-22%
13	CLE	W	19	10	429	291	+2	-2%	14%	11%	-4%
14	WAS	W	30	13	488	201	0	66%	22%	-36%	8%
15	at KC	L	13	30	307	397	-4	-30%	-15%	16%	1%
16	at NYJ	W	14	7	379	295	+3	15%	5%	-13%	-3%
17	OAK	W	30	10	495	336	+2	44%	36%	-10%	-2%

Trends and Splits

	Offense	Rank	Defense	Rank
Total DVOA	10.6%	7	-4.7%	12
Unadjusted VOA	15.6%	5	-8.0%	7
Weighted Trend	14.4%	4	-9.6%	7
Variance	5.8%	12	2.4%	1
Average Opponent	2.3%	28	-1.3%	22
Passing	40.8%	2	-6.2%	9
Rushing	-15.8%	27	-3.0%	25
First Down	5.0%	11	-2.4%	13
Second Down	20.4%	6	-7.1%	8
Third Down	7.5%	13	-5.2%	13
First Half	10.2%	9	-8.3%	6
Second Half	11.1%	7	-1.4%	14
Red Zone	-27.3%	28	-43.5%	1
Late and Close	7.5%	11	-1.8%	18

Five-Year Performance

Year	W-L	Pyth W	Est W	PF	PA	TO	Total	Rk	Off	Rk	Def	Rk	ST	Rk	Off AGL	Rk	Def AGL	Rk	Off Age	Rk	Def Age	Rk	ST Age	Rk
2013	9-7	9.2	8.8	396	348	-4	6.4%	12	23.1%	2	17.5%	32	0.8%	15	46.3	23	44.8	25	27.5	10	25.8	28	26.0	17
2014	9-7	8.0	8.0	348	348	-5	-0.6%	16	7.0%	11	4.9%	25	-2.7%	23	82.1	32	37.0	15	27.9	4	26.7	17	26.6	4
2015	4-12	5.9	6.0	320	398	-4	-14.8%	24	0.9%	15	10.4%	28	-5.3%	31	55.7	27	25.7	10	27.6	7	25.9	30	26.5	7
2016	5-11	7.7	6.9	410	423	-7	-1.1%	19	-3.2%	18	-6.8%	7	-4.8%	29	61.7	29	66.0	29	27.9	4	25.7	31	25.7	24
2017	9-7	10.5	8.4	355	272	+12	7.9%	11	10.6%	7	-4.7%	12	-7.5%	31	35.9	17	31.7	15	27.6	5	25.7	26	25.4	25

2017 Performance Based on Most Common Personnel Groups

LAC Offense					LAC Offense vs. Opponents					LAC Defense					LAC Defense vs. Opponents			
Pers	Freq	Yds	DVOA	Run%	Pers	Freq	Yds	DVOA	Run%	Pers	Freq	Yds	DVOA		Pers	Freq	Yds	DVOA
11	57%	6.7	30.9%	26%	Base	38%	5.6	1.7%	59%	Base	26%	5.4	-5.2%		11	65%	5.3	-5.6%
12	22%	6.0	12.7%	45%	Nickel	43%	6.5	27.9%	29%	Nickel	27%	4.9	0.3%		12	17%	5.8	3.0%
21	7%	5.7	0.7%	64%	Dime+	18%	6.8	27.5%	19%	Dime+	46%	5.7	-6.4%		21	7%	6.3	17.2%
13	5%	5.6	8.0%	60%	Goal Line	1%	0.1	-47.7%	89%	Goal Line	1%	-0.7	-56.8%		13	5%	2.7	-48.5%
22	5%	2.6	-52.3%	81%											22	2%	8.1	11.3%

Strategic Tendencies

Run/Pass		Rk	Formation		Rk	Pass Rush		Rk	Secondary		Rk	Strategy		Rk
Runs, first half	38%	22	Form: Single Back	77%	17	Rush 3	9.6%	10	4 DB	26%	26	Play action	18%	27
Runs, first down	52%	14	Form: Empty Back	9%	10	Rush 4	73.6%	8	5 DB	27%	31	Avg Box (Off)	6.15	23
Runs, second-long	28%	25	Pers: 3+ WR	58%	21	Rush 5	14.7%	27	6+ DB	46%	1	Avg Box (Def)	6.05	30
Runs, power sit.	59%	13	Pers: 2+ TE/6+ OL	35%	7	Rush 6+	2.1%	31	CB by Sides	63%	26	Offensive Pace	30.43	14
Runs, behind 2H	28%	13	Pers: 6+ OL	2%	25	Int DL Sacks	3.5%	32	S/CB Cover Ratio	40%	2	Defensive Pace	31.03	24
Pass, ahead 2H	48%	15	Shotgun/Pistol	67%	10	Second Level Sacks	16.3%	17	DB Blitz	7%	25	Go for it on 4th	1.06	13

For the first time in a few years, the Chargers were not significantly better when they used play-action. Instead, they were excellent passing both with play-action (40.5% DVOA) and without (45.5% DVOA). ☞ The Chargers were much better running from one-back sets (4.3 yards, -8.6% DVOA) than from two-back sets (2.9 yards, -41.7% DVOA). ☞ Los Angeles ranked second with 64.0% DVOA with an empty backfield, trailing only Minnesota. ☞ The Chargers offense started slow (23rd in DVOA in the first quarter), then put things together and ranked fifth in DVOA from the second quarter onward. ☞ The Chargers got a league-leading 80 percent of sacks from edge rushers. ☞ The Chargers tripled their use of dime personnel, going from 15 percent to 46 percent to lead the league. The shift came after the first month of the season, and from Week 5 onward the Chargers had dime personnel on the field 60 percent of the time.

Passing

Player	DYAR	DVOA	Plays	NtYds	Avg	YAC	C%	TD	Int
P.Rivers	1412	26.1%	594	4342	7.3	5.9	63.3%	28	9
K.Clemens*	-32	-67.3%	8	36	4.5	1.0	75.0%	0	1
G.Smith	-83	-41.4%	39	195	5.0	5.1	58.3%	1	0

Rushing

Player	DYAR	DVOA	Plays	Yds	Avg	TD	Fum	Suc
M.Gordon	21	-6.8%	284	1105	3.9	8	1	40%
A.Ekeler	59	22.7%	47	260	5.5	2	1	55%
B.Oliver*	-32	-31.4%	35	83	2.4	0	0	34%
T.Benjamin	54	43.5%	12	89	7.4	0	0	-
A.Williams	-17	-61.6%	9	25	2.8	0	0	44%
D.Watt	-3	-19.4%	6	24	4.0	0	0	33%

Receiving

Player	DYAR	DVOA	Plays	Ctch	Yds	Y/C	YAC	TD	C%
K.Allen	378	16.5%	159	102	1395	13.7	4.9	6	64%
T.Williams	150	15.4%	69	43	728	16.9	7.7	4	62%
T.Benjamin	65	0.5%	66	35	574	16.4	6.6	4	53%
M.Williams	-10	-18.0%	23	11	95	8.6	1.0	0	48%
H.Henry	165	32.3%	62	45	579	12.9	4.2	4	73%
A.Gates*	13	-3.2%	52	30	316	10.5	2.2	3	58%
V.Green	12	0.8%	22	14	191	13.6	6.6	1	64%
M.Gordon	76	3.0%	83	58	476	8.2	8.5	4	70%
A.Ekeler	84	27.1%	35	27	279	10.3	9.3	3	77%
B.Oliver*	-29	-56.3%	11	6	26	4.3	5.2	0	55%

Offensive Line

Player	Pos	Age	GS	Snaps	Pen	Sk	Pass	Run	Player	Pos	Age	GS	Snaps	Pen	Sk	Pass	Run
Spencer Pulley	C	25	16/16	1056	2	1.0	14	18	Joe Barksdale	RT	29	11/11	659	6	0.0	10	10
Kenny Wiggins*	RG	30	16/16	1042	3	3.0	20	13	Matt Slauson*	LG	32	7/7	425	2	0.0	6	5
Russell Okung	LT	31	15/15	927	6	2.0	19	15	Michael Schofield	RT/G	28	15/5	406	2	1.0	8	2
Dan Feeney	LG	24	15/9	666	3	1.0	15	10	Mike Pouncey	C	29	16/16	974	9	2.5	9	8

Year	Yards	ALY	Rank	Power	Rank	Stuff	Rank	2nd Lev	Rank	Open Field	Rank	Sacks	ASR	Rank	Press	Rank	F-Start	Cont.
2015	3.53	3.47	31	73%	6	20%	15	0.85	32	0.53	27	40	5.4%	11	24.3%	14	20	22
2016	3.92	3.97	23	66%	13	21%	19	1.01	30	0.76	12	36	6.6%	24	28.7%	23	19	37
2017	3.93	3.71	26	58%	25	24%	26	1.17	13	0.78	12	18	4.2%	3	31.8%	20	17	26

2017 ALY by direction:	Left End: 4.12 (15)	Left Tackle: 3.14 (26)	Mid/Guard: 3.60 (30)	Right Tackle: 3.62 (21)	Right End: 4.62 (5)

Mike Pouncey solves the revolving-door issue the Chargers have faced since Nick Hardwick's career ended. Like many solutions to Chargers problems, Pouncey is a little too expensive—two years, $15 million—for the level of upgrade he provides. Pouncey played all 16 games last year for the first time in four seasons and has performed at roughly Just Another Guy levels throughout that span, which is one reason the Dolphins let him go. (The other is that they are the Dolphins and lack both cap management skills and object permanence.) Still, he's an improvement over other recent Chargers center solutions, like playing Matt Slauson out of position or throwing former UDFA Spencer Pulley onto the field and crossing their fingers. ☞ Forrest Lamp, a victim of last offseason's Chargers spring injury plague, is penciled in at right guard. He's a mauler, and he and Pouncey should upgrade the interior run blocking, especially if left guard Dan Feeney steps up after fading at the end of his rookie season. Unfortunately, Lamp also got sucked up by *this* offseason's Chargers spring injury plague and needed a procedure on his knee in May. He's expected to be ready for training camp, but you know how things go for this team. ☞ Russell Okung will cost the Chargers $15 million in cap space and is worth it. Veteran right tackle Joe Barksdale will cost the team $6 million, is a liability as a run blocker and can be beaten by speed. There is no depth at the tackle positions because of the top-heavy nature of the Chargers' salary structure.

Defensive Front Seven

Defensive Line	Age	Pos	G	Snaps	Plays	TmPct	Rk	Stop	Dfts	BTkl	Runs	St%	Rk	RuYd	Rk	Sack	Hit	Hur	Dsrpt
						Overall						vs. Run				Pass Rush			
Brandon Mebane	33	DT	16	535	30	3.7%	67	19	4	6	28	64%	78	3.1	78	0.0	2	3.0	0
Corey Liuget	28	DT	12	413	21	3.4%	75	15	8	4	14	57%	82	2.5	64	1.5	2	18.5	2
Damion Square	29	DT	16	364	21	2.6%	--	17	3	3	16	81%	--	2.4	--	0.0	2	5.5	3

Edge Rushers	Age	Pos	G	Snaps	Plays	TmPct	Rk	Stop	Dfts	BTkl	Runs	St%	Rk	RuYd	Rk	Sack	Hit	Hur	Dsrpt
						Overall						vs. Run				Pass Rush			
Melvin Ingram	29	DE	16	891	56	6.9%	20	40	22	13	39	64%	80	2.6	63	10.5	14	50.5	2
Joey Bosa	23	DE	16	852	71	8.7%	6	54	22	7	56	70%	66	3.4	78	12.5	13	42.0	2
Darius Philon	24	DE	16	510	31	3.8%	68	23	10	3	23	70%	67	3.0	75	4.5	5	5.0	2
Tenny Palepoi*	28	DE	15	270	23	3.0%	--	18	8	2	21	76%	--	2.0	--	1.0	0	3.0	0

Linebackers	Age	Pos	G	Snaps	Plays	TmPct	Rk	Stop	Dfts	BTkl	Runs	St%	Rk	RuYd	Rk	Sack	Hit	Hur	Tgts	Suc%	Rk	AdjYd	Rk	PD	Int
						Overall						vs. Run				Pass Rush				vs. Pass				
Jatavis Brown	24	OLB	16	506	77	9.4%	67	34	11	7	39	54%	74	4.5	74	0.0	4	5.0	23	35%	73	7.6	55	1	0
Hayes Pullard	26	MLB	13	476	73	11.0%	52	33	8	12	40	58%	65	5.5	85	0.0	0	3.5	27	39%	65	7.2	48	1	1
Kyle Emanuel	27	OLB	16	303	34	4.2%	--	21	6	2	20	60%	--	5.0	--	1.5	0	1.0	11	51%	--	7.4	--	3	1
Denzel Perryman	25	MLB	7	274	37	10.4%	61	17	3	10	19	74%	11	2.1	4	0.0	0	2.0	16	26%	--	5.4	--	1	0
Korey Toomer*	30	MLB	15	266	50	6.5%	--	31	5	5	35	71%	--	4.2	--	1.0	1	1.0	14	72%	1	4.3	2	2	1

Year	Yards	ALY	Rank	Power	Rank	Stuff	Rank	2nd Level	Rank	Open Field	Rank	Sacks	ASR	Rank	Press	Rank
2015	4.95	4.60	28	73%	27	18%	25	1.38	31	1.21	32	32	5.8%	26	25.2%	16
2016	3.85	3.65	6	71%	28	24%	4	1.18	18	0.73	16	35	5.9%	15	26.8%	18
2017	4.82	4.31	24	64%	18	20%	16	1.27	28	1.26	32	43	7.8%	7	30.6%	15

2017 ALY by direction:	Left End: 3.33 (11)	Left Tackle: 4.47 (24)	Mid/Guard: 4.26 (17)	Right Tackle: 5.24 (31)	Right End: 4.3 (20)

Year	Yards	ALY	Rank	Power	Rank	Stuff	Rank	2nd Level	Rank	Open Field	Rank	Sacks	ASR	Rank	Press	Rank
2015	4.95	4.60	28	73%	27	18%	25	1.38	31	1.21	32	32	5.8%	26	25.2%	16
2016	3.85	3.65	6	71%	28	24%	4	1.18	18	0.73	16	35	5.9%	15	26.8%	18
2017	4.82	4.31	24	64%	18	20%	16	1.27	28	1.26	32	43	7.8%	7	30.6%	15

2017 ALY by direction:	Left End: 3.33 (11)	Left Tackle: 4.47 (24)	Mid/Guard: 4.26 (17)	Right Tackle: 5.24 (31)	Right End: 4.3 (20)

Joey Bosa and Melvin Ingram are awesome. Denzel Perryman and Corey Liuget are good when healthy. Brandon Mebane is an overpaid big-name blocking sled, and everyone else is roster fodder. That concludes the Chargers front seven segment.

OK, you want a little more elaboration.

Gus Bradley used a lot of heavy dime 4-1-6 groupings as his base defense, with Bosa and Ingram classified as two of the four linemen. It looked as much like John Pagano's old system as anything Bradley ran in Seattle or Jacksonville. Bosa and Ingram delivered (Ingram's missed tackles are a by-product of a borderline-reckless style that also leads to sacks and pressures), but the middle of the run defense was porous when Liuget was healthy and a big play waiting to happen when Damion Square or Darius Philon was getting meaningful snaps next to Mebane. Perryman's absence for the first nine games of the season exacerbated the problem, as Jatavis Brown regressed after a strong rookie season in 2016 and journeyman Hayes Pullard, a Bradley carryover from Jacksonville, ended up playing far too large a role in the defense. ☞ Second-round linebacker Uchenna Nwosu (USC) is a high-effort pass-rusher who can make the Chargers' pass rush more three-dimensional. Bosa and Ingram provide a ton of pressure, but the rest of the Chargers front seven offered little last season. Nwosu is likely to play a role similar to Bruce Irvin in Seattle: outside linebacker on early downs, edge rusher in passing situations. ☞ Third-round pick Justin Jones (North Carolina State) is a pure lane-clogger who should make Mebane expendable, though the organization has a blind spot when it comes to Mebane (who was one of Bradley's Seahawks long ago). ☞ Perryman has never played a full 16-game season in three years in the NFL. If the Chargers are counting on his return to full health to upgrade the front seven, they must have forgotten their own history when they left San Diego.

Defensive Secondary

Secondary	Age	Pos	G	Snaps	Plays	TmPct	Rk	Stop	Dfts	BTkl	Runs	St%	Rk	RuYd	Rk	Tgts	Tgt%	Rk	Dist	Suc%	Rk	AdjYd	Rk	PD	Int
Tre Boston*	26	FS	16	1041	87	10.6%	29	20	15	13	42	12%	76	12.2	75	21	4.4%	1	15.3	58%	20	4.9	1	6	5
Jahleel Addae	28	SS	16	1032	103	12.6%	11	45	21	15	46	52%	18	4.2	9	60	12.6%	57	9.0	50%	43	7.5	30	7	0
Trevor Williams	25	CB	16	1006	67	8.2%	44	36	10	6	22	68%	9	2.8	4	68	14.7%	8	15.3	53%	33	8.0	51	14	2
Tre Boston*	26	FS	16	1041	87	10.6%	29	20	15	13	42	12%	76	12.2	75	21	4.4%	1	15.3	58%	20	4.9	1	6	5
Jahleel Addae	28	SS	16	1032	103	12.6%	11	45	21	15	46	52%	18	4.2	9	60	12.6%	57	9.0	50%	43	7.5	30	7	0
Trevor Williams	25	CB	16	1006	67	8.2%	44	36	10	6	22	68%	9	2.8	4	68	14.7%	8	15.3	53%	33	8.0	51	14	2
Casey Hayward	29	CB	16	1003	62	7.6%	54	39	15	11	10	90%	3	1.9	1	77	16.6%	16	15.2	58%	11	7.7	41	25	4
Desmond King	24	CB	16	716	76	9.3%	--	43	18	10	25	64%	--	3.8	--	34	10.2%	--	5.7	56%	--	7.7	--	4	1
Adrian Phillips	26	FS/SS	15	519	63	8.2%	64	27	11	12	23	43%	42	5.3	23	35	14.4%	66	8.2	55%	25	7.8	34	4	2

Year	Pass D Rank	vs. #1 WR	Rk	vs. #2 WR	Rk	vs. Other WR	Rk	WR Wide	Rk	WR Slot	Rk	vs. TE	Rk	vs. RB	Rk
2015	21	4.9%	20	7.6%	19	-10.5%	9	--	--	--	--	34.8%	31	14.1%	26
2016	9	-10.4%	6	5.7%	22	-25.0%	2	-20.3%	4	4.0%	16	-2.1%	15	-3.5%	17
2017	9	-11.8%	10	0.5%	17	-25.2%	3	-17.3%	5	-6.1%	10	0.9%	18	-21.3%	5

The Chargers are set at cornerback. Casey Hayward shouldn't be asked to play bump-and-run with no safety help against Tyreek Hill ever again (no one except 1994 Deion Sanders should) and will whiff on some tackles, but he can shut down most receivers and will make quarterbacks pay for bad decisions and sloppy throws. Trevor Williams was solid in a full season of relief of Jason Verrett. Rookie Desmond King was too hands-on in coverage but performed well in an all-purpose slot-hybrid role. ☞ Verrett was a full participant in June minicamp after suffering the second ACL tear of his career in Week 1 last year. Verrett was a Pro Bowler in his one healthy pro season (2015). He can provide a major boost if he pulls a Keenan Allen and finally gets healthy again. ☞ First-round pick Derwin James took snaps all over the field during OTAs and minicamp. The most likely scenario is for James to start at strong safety, with Jahleel Addae moving to free safety to replace Tre Boston, who was unsigned at press time despite a solid 2017 season. Addae, who lined up at free safety often in minicamp, has excellent range and is fast enough to handle some man coverage duties but is a disastrous open-field tackler. Adrian Phillips, a fly-around hustle guy who has slowly bubbled up from the practice squad over four seasons, could also end up at free safety, with James inheriting Phillips' role as an often-used hybrid safety/linebacker.

Special Teams

Year	DVOA	Rank	FG/XP	Rank	Net Kick	Rank	Kick Ret	Rank	Net Punt	Rank	Punt Ret	Rank	Hidden	Rank
2015	-5.3%	31	-1.2	19	-2.7	22	-4.3	26	-12.3	29	-6.1	28	-7.8	25
2016	-4.8%	29	-8.7	29	-2.6	20	-4.7	26	-5.8	25	-2.2	20	-12.3	31
2017	-7.5%	31	-22.2	32	-7.4	29	-3.9	26	-6.1	24	2.3	9	-4.7	20

Special teams coordinator George Stewart described the battle between Caleb Sturgis and Roberto Aguayo as "even" at the end of OTAs. "They both were high draft picks in terms of specialists," he said. "Caleb, when he came out, he was a fifth-round pick," continued Stewart. "Roberto is a second-round pick. Obviously, those guys have some quality to them in terms of where they were drafted."

(Shuffling papers. Adjusting glasses. Sighing heavily.)

OK, Stewart has to say *something* about the kickers during press conferences. And announcing kickers' stats from May practices is a bad idea for multiple reasons. He's probably not sitting in his office thinking, "Oooh, I have two kickers who were *drafted*. What could possibly go wrong?" But some coaching staffs forget when players were drafted the moment they come to camp and instead base competition solely on what they see on the field, while others keep receipts from the long-ago mistakes of other general managers. ☞ It's hard to imagine the Chargers choosing Aguayo after the 2016 fiasco. A mythology has grown around the former Bucs' second-round mistake, that he was a can't-miss Next Adam Vinatieri before suffering some sort of mental block. In fact, he was a major-program kicker who set accuracy records with strings of 30-yarders and was insanely overvalued. Sturgis makes his living providing ordinary professionalism, which is what the Chargers sorely need on field goals. ☞ Travis Benjamin will earn a ton of money to combine huge plays with crippling mistakes as a punt returner. He hasn't returned a kickoff since 2014, but the Chargers may want to give him a try under the new rules, as neither Desmond King nor Austin Ekeler did much in the role last year. ☞ Somehow, the Chargers' mediocre coverage units had three of the league's top ten players in special teams tackles. Linebacker Nick Dzubnar led the league with 21, Ekeler was second with 17, and Michael Davis had another 14. It was a bit of a fluke, as official scorers gave tackle credit to two Chargers instead of one on an extremely abnormal number of special teams plays. Seven of those 21 Dzubnar plays, for example, had him as the second tackler listed. And only 52 percent of Dzubnar's special teams tackles led to a better than average result for the Chargers; the NFL average for all special teams tackles is 61 percent.

Los Angeles Rams

2017 Record: 11-5	**Total DVOA:** 27.7% (2nd)	**2018 Mean Projection:** 9.5 wins	**On the Clock (0-4):** 3%
Pythagorean Wins: 11.6 (5th)	**Offense:** 11.1% (6th)	**Postseason Odds:** 58.9%	**Mediocrity (5-7):** 18%
Snap-Weighted Age: 25.8 (31st)	**Defense:** -9.7% (6th)	**Super Bowl Odds:** 13.5%	**Playoff Contender (8-10):** 42%
Average Opponent: -0.4% (18th)	**Special Teams:** 6.8% (2nd)	**Proj. Avg. Opponent:** 0.2% (13th)	**Super Bowl Contender (11+):** 37%

2017: The greatest year-over-year improvement in modern NFL history.

2018: Beware the Plexiglass my son: the jaws that bite, the claws that catch.

It was the story of a young *wunderkind* and his wise old mentor, riding out west to earn their fortune. It was the story of a rag-tag group, beaten into despondency after years of obeying the whims of a cruel, mustachioed dictator. Together, they managed to silence all the doubters and haters out there, and ride into the sunset of … uh, a wild-card playoff loss. OK, they may need to work on their feel-good endings a tad, but the best story to come out of Hollywood in 2017 was the Los Angeles Rams.

Our final projections last season had the Rams 13th in DVOA, raising some skeptical eyebrows (even among the Football Outsiders staff, if we're being honest). We predicted a significant step forward on defense with Wade Phillips working his typical first-year magic, and we knew that their special teams would remain special. On offense, however, we were more skeptical that Sean McVay could dig the Rams out of their massive offensive hole in his first year as head coach.

The Rams' chapter from *Football Outsiders Almanac 2017* was filled with hedges—phrases like "if [Jared] Goff can just be a normal level of bad" and "it would be nearly impossible for the offense to be worse in 2017 than it was in 2016." Talk about damning with faint praise. This was a team that hadn't seen a winning season in 14 years; one that hadn't put together a competent offense since Marc Bulger was throwing to Torry Holt half a continent away. The Rams couldn't live up to our fancy-schmancy model's projections, right?

To be fair, they didn't live up to them. They blew right past them.

The Rams jumped 56.3% in DVOA and 48.9% in offensive DVOA. Those are both the second-highest increases in DVOA history, going back to 1986—and both would have been first if the Rams had not rested their starters in a meaningless Week 17 game (Table 1). They scored an additional 15.9 points per game, the biggest year-over-year increase since the 1950 New York Yanks. They were the only team to go from last to first in points scored in a single season in the Super Bowl era. There aren't enough superlatives to describe that turnaround.

Jared Goff's turnaround—his 98.8% improvement in passing DVOA nearly doubles the previous season-over-season record—was equally astounding. Part of that was Goff's natural talent showing through; the Rams traded up to get him in 2016 because of his potential, and there were reasonable expectations that he'd do better than his baseline of "literally the worst passing DVOA we've ever recorded." A larger part likely comes from having a functioning offensive line in front of him, as the Rams rose from 29th to ninth in adjusted sack rate.

But the largest part of his improvement came from being placed in McVay's scheme. He helped simplify Goff's reads by having the team hurry to the line, using the extra time before the mandatory helmet radio cutoff to help communicate what the defense was doing and take some of the pre-snap computational load off of Goff's shoulders. McVay's system also places great emphasis on pre-snap motion, tight spacing of receivers and effective route combinations, forcing defenders to tip their hands early and providing natural bumps, picks, and screens to make the quarterback's life that much easier.

This revitalized passing game forced opposing defenses to put more defenders in pass coverage; the Rams saw an average of just 6.12 defenders in the box (26th in the NFL) despite sitting on some heavy leads. Combined with the aforementioned improved offensive line, that helped produce a bounce-back season from running back Todd Gurley. After sputtering as a sophomore in 2016, Gurley had more than 2,000 yards from scrimmage and earned MVP consideration.

With all that success, expectations in Los Angeles are high—which brings us to this year's forecast. Their overall projection is still high, but their mean offensive projection lin-

Table 1. Biggest Year-to-Year Improvement in Total DVOA, 1986-2017

Year	Team	DVOA	Improve	W-L	DVOA Y+1	W-L Y+1
2013	KC	17.5%	57.6%	11-5	10.4%	9-7
2017	LAR	27.7%	56.3%	11-5	--	--
2010	DET	-1.1%	50.5%	6-10	10.1%	10-6
2012	DEN	36.5%	48.3%	13-3	32.7%	13-3
1999	STL	34.0%	43.8%	13-3	11.2%	10-6
2012	SEA	38.7%	40.2%	11-5	40.0%	13-3
1987	IND	9.5%*	39.9%	7-5*	1.1%	9-7
1999	OAK	21.2%	39.5%	8-8	20.8%	12-4
2000	NO	-0.9%	39.4%	10-6	-8.7%	7-9
2004	PIT	37.6%	39.1%	15-1	27.2%	11-5
2004	BUF	31.3%	38.7%	9-7	-17.8%	5-11
2008	CAR	18.0%	38.6%	12-4	7.1%	8-8

Not including strike games.

2018 Rams Schedule

Week	Opp.	Week	Opp.	Week	Opp.
1	at OAK (Mon.)	7	at SF	13	at DET
2	ARI	8	GB	14	at CHI
3	LAC	9	at NO	15	PHI
4	MIN (Thu.)	10	SEA	16	at ARI
5	at SEA	11	KC (Mon./Mex.)	17	SF
6	at DEN	12	BYE		

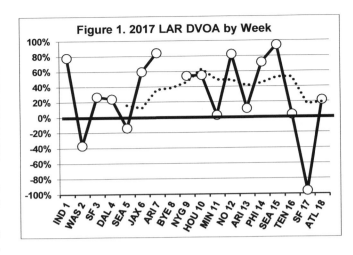

Figure 1. 2017 LAR DVOA by Week

gers down near the league average, despite all that progress from last season. To explain why, we need to talk about the Plexiglass Principle.

First coined by famed baseball stats guru Bill James, the Plexiglass Principle states that teams which significantly improve (or decline) in one season have a tendency to relapse or bounce back in the next. It's counterintuitive at first glance. Isn't a team that took big strides in one year on a path to continue moving forward? The data, however, shows a clear and statistically significant trend (Table 2).

Table 2. Plexiglass Bounces, 1987-2016

DVOA Change	Teams	DVOA Change Y+1	Win Change Y+1	Pct of Teams Improving	Pct of Teams Declining
+30% or better	42	-9.1%	-1.2	26.2%	73.8%
+20% to +30%	81	-9.9%	-1.8	27.2%	72.8%
+10% to +20%	166	-5.9%	-1.0	36.1%	63.9%
0% to +10%	164	-0.5%	+0.2	46.3%	53.7%
-10% to 0%	199	+0.9%	+0.4	50.8%	49.2%
-20% to -10%	133	+4.1%	+0.2	60.9%	39.1%
-30% to -20%	81	+10.9%	+2.3	76.5%	23.5%
-30% or worse	47	+14.3%	+2.2	83.0%	17.0%

This shouldn't be conflated with simple regression to the mean, either. It's not a case of teams just being unable to reproduce a great season due to teams tending to drift towards .500. Teams in the "20/20 club"—with at least a 20.0% DVOA and a 20-point improvement from the year before—drop an average of 5.2 points more than your average over-20.0% DVOA squad. When teams smack into that Plexiglass ceiling, they suffer something of a hangover the next season.

So, what's going on here? The important thing to remember is that progress is generally slow and gradual—personnel changes and standard player development tend to not produce large season-to-season fluctuations. All things being equal, you should not expect a team's talent to suddenly change drastically in one direction or the other—and such a one-season jump likely indicates that a significant chunk of luck was involved, on top of any sustainable on-field gains. That doesn't mean that the underlying talent level *didn't* improve, just that at least some of the huge gains made can generally be chalked up to the randomness present in a 16-game sample size.

2017 saw quite a few teams make significant jumps and bump into Plexiglass territory. Five teams saw their DVOA jump at least 20 points between 2016 and 2017, and three of them join the 20/20 club, including the Vikings and Saints. The Rams' massive jump laps the field and then some, however, making them the Plexiglass poster boys for 2018.

The 2018 Rams will be treading on rarely-traveled ground. They had a DVOA above 20.0%, a feat matched by just 137 (out of 918) teams from 1987 to 2016. They got there despite having a negative DVOA the year prior, which shrinks that pool to just 25 teams. And they're trying to improve yet *again* this season. Only four teams in our database have managed to do that: the 2003 Chiefs, 2004 Colts, 2009 Ravens and 2013 Seahawks. For every success story, there are five or six teams that ended up backsliding the next year, and about 40 percent fell right back to where they started, erasing essentially all of their gains from the year prior (most recently, the 2016 Panthers).

This is usually the point where fans go "well, *our* team is different, because of *reasons*," and we smile and nod and mark them down for an 8-8 season anyway, tsking about rose-colored glasses and confirmation bias and things of that nature. Yet the Rams actually have good, serious reasons to believe they can avoid regression, or at least limit its effects, so it's worth looking at them more seriously.

Go back to the four teams that the Rams are trying to emulate, and you'll find some commonalities. Three of the four had new head coaches—John Harbaugh was in his first year with the Ravens, while Dick Vermeil and Tony Dungy were entering their sophomore years in Kansas City and Indianapolis when they had their big turnarounds. The odd one out is Pete Carroll, who didn't see his huge turnaround until his third season in Seattle. Extend your list to look at teams that stayed within 10.0% DVOA of their big turnaround years, and you can add Jon Gruden coming to Oakland (uh, the first time) and John Fox taking over in Denver.

It makes a lot of sense on paper. A team's struggles often are caused by previous administrations doing a poor job in both talent acquisition and optimization, bringing bad players onto the team and not getting the most out of the talent available once it's there. The gap in quality between Jeff Fisher and Sean McVay cannot be overstated. We mentioned earlier that

Goff had the greatest single-season turnaround for any quarterback we've ever measured. Well, the sixth-greatest turnaround ever belongs to Goff's colleague on the 2016 Rams, Case Keenum, who blew up with Minnesota last year. Add in Nick Foles' career rejuvenation since leaving the Rams, and Sam Bradford's performance (when healthy) with the Eagles and Vikings, and it becomes pretty clear—the best career move a young quarterback can make is getting as far away from Fisher as physically possible.

It's not only issues of play calling or strategy that improve when you bid farewell to the all-time leader in losses as a head coach. Bringing in a new regime usually brings with it a spring cleaning of the roster. Failed projects, draft picks who never quite clicked, and players optimized for a scheme that wasn't working are swept aside, replaced with players who better fit the new coach's plans. The Rams were no exception. As Chase Stuart at Football Perspective first noted, 35 percent of their starts last season came from players who were not on the active roster in 2016.

So, it's not that the Rams' offensive line suddenly started playing better; it's the additions of Andrew Whitworth and John Sullivan that improved Los Angeles' blocking. It's not that Rams receivers suddenly learned how to catch; it's Cooper Kupp, Sammy Watkins, and Robert Woods replacing less successful and less talented players. It makes sense that an improvement caused by replacing bad players with better ones is more sustainable than bad players suddenly taking an uncharacteristic step forward.

It also would seem to make sense that upgrading at the most important position would produce the largest gains. Once again, three of our four examples had recent changes at quarterback. Russell Wilson and Joe Flacco were rookie starters when their teams took huge jumps, and Trent Green was in his second season replacing Elvis Grbac when the Chiefs rapidly improved. Again, it seems logical that offenses that have recently replaced their quarterbacks would achieve more "real" gains than an offense that stuck with the same personnel.

Do these logical inferences hold up? Are Sean McVay and Jared Goff reason enough to believe the Rams will buck Plexiglass history? To find out, we took every team that saw at least a 20.0% DVOA increase and checked if they had a coach or quarterback in their first or second year with the team (Table 3). While all sets of teams declined, the franchises who had made major personnel changes were more likely to hold on to more of their gains.

It's important to remember, of course, that a lot of coaches have been hailed as saviors in one season before their special sauce wore off. Mike Mularkey in Tennessee, Jack Del Rio in Oakland, and Chip Kelly in Philadelphia all had great debuts, only to have their luster wear off quickly. None are still employed. Quarterbacks such as Christian Ponder, Josh Freeman, and Matt Cassel have looked like players around whom a team could build, only to quickly fall off. That being said, the fact that the Rams' sudden boost coincided with a significant regime change increases their odds of keeping that momentum going into 2018.

Also on their side going forward are their offseason moves.

Table 3. 20.0%+ DVOA Increases, 1986-2016, With or Without Major Changes

Set	Teams	DVOA Change Y+1	Win Change Y+1	Pct of Teams Improving	Pct of Teams Declining
All Teams	123	-9.6%	-1.5	26.8%	73.2%
New Coach	65	-5.2%	-0.7	38.5%	61.5%
No New Coach	58	-14.5%	-2.5	13.8%	86.2%
New QB	68	-6.8%	-1.2	29.4%	70.6%
No New QB	55	-13.0%	-2.0	23.6%	76.4%
Both	46	-4.8%	-0.8	34.8%	65.2%
Neither	36	-16.6%	-2.7	11.1%	88.9%

It's easy to imagine a franchise being satisfied with their first winning season in more than a decade and looking to simply consolidate their gains and limit turnover as they try to repeat. Not the Rams, however, whose offseason is the most remarkable we've seen in nearly a generation.

Having a quality quarterback on a rookie deal is a humongous advantage under the current CBA. Just in the division alone, Jimmy Garoppolo counts $37 million against the 49ers' cap, while Russell Wilson will cost the Seahawks nearly $24 million. Jared Goff ranks 27th in cap hit among quarterbacks this season, at a mere $7.6 million. That frees up gobs of extra cap space to work with, allowing the Rams to bring in more expensive veterans. We've seen other teams take advantage of this in the past, but the Rams have taken it to a whole other level.

With the extra space provided in part by rookie contracts for Goff, Todd Gurley, and Aaron Donald, the Rams were able to bring in four All-Pro-caliber players this offseason. They traded for defensive backs Marcus Peters and Aqib Talib, two of the top corners in the league. They signed Ndamukong Suh in free agency, pairing him with Donald to create an interior line duo that had 68.5 pass pressures in 2017. This defensive trio will help compensate for a less impressive collection of edge rushers, as you don't need top-flight talent there if nobody can get open and the interior offensive line is buckling. The Rams also traded for Brandin Cooks, who has put up three seasons with at least 1,000 receiving yards and seven receiving touchdowns all before turning 25. He fits better in McVay's offense than Sammy Watkins did, with greater speed forcing safeties to stay deep to prevent the home run ball. Put it all together, and you have one heck of a haul.

All four players have put up an Approximate Value (Pro Football Reference's metric that puts all players on a single scale) of 12 or higher in one of the last two seasons. The last team to bring in four such players was the 1994 San Francisco 49ers, who essentially rented a defense with Deion Sanders, Richard Dent, Rickey Jackson, and Ken Norton Jr. They went on to win Super Bowl XXIX, and while most of those players were gone after a season or two and the team eventually collapsed under the weight of its salary cap obligations, banners fly forever.

What won't fly forever, however, is keeping this much talent under the salary cap. Cooks and Suh are free agents in

2019, as are LaMarcus Joyner, Rodger Saffold, Rob Havenstein, and Jamon Brown. Aaron Donald will join them assuming his 2018 holdout doesn't last as long as his 2017 holdout (he must report by August 11 to be an unrestricted free agent in 2019). Todd Gurley has a major payday coming up in the not too distant future. Eventually, the lack of high draft picks and cheap players on rookie contracts will come back to hurt Los Angeles; various trades have meant they have had no first-round picks in either 2017 or 2018, and just one second-round pick between 2016 and 2019. Tough decisions will need to be made, even with significant cap room to work with in 2019 and 2020.

That, however, sounds like a problem for *future* Los Angeles to handle. The Rams have gone all-in on maximizing their available talent in this brief window of salary-cap flexibility to an extent we haven't seen before. They're essentially choosing to bypass the developmental process and plug in established veterans at their most important positions, in exchange for a more difficult roster picture in the future. This is exciting! If this works, this could be the model for future teams to follow, trading away gobs of picks to surround promising rookie quarterbacks with a veritable who's who of established veterans.

It could also backfire horrendously, which is exciting in and of itself. Not every free-agency splurge gives you championship gold like the 1994 49ers. We've seen teams go around collecting established veterans before, with less than stellar results. The 2011 Eagles "Dream Team" is the canonical example, with the additions of Jason Babin, Dominique Rodgers-Cromartie, Nnamdi Asomugha, and "the other" Steve Smith helping turn a 10-6 team into an 8-8 team, and then a 4-12 team the year after. There are always questions about fits in new schemes and whether or not past success will translate into future success. The NFL isn't a game of *Madden*, where you can plug in superstars willy-nilly and have everything just sort of work out; that's what the NBA is for. When you bring in a new player, no matter how good they are, there are issues of scheme, fit, and chemistry that need to be addressed in order for these superstar acquisitions to continue to perform at a high level. For as good as Los Angeles' new foursome have been, there's every chance that they'll fail to live up to those expectations in blue and white (and random splotches of gold).

Take Suh, for example. Suh is almost assuredly going to be an upgrade over the likes of Morgan Fox, Ethan Westbrooks, and Tyrunn Walker; you just have to watch film for ten minutes to realize that. On passing downs, having Suh and Donald at the 3-tech charging at quarterbacks is going to be an interior pass rush that no other team in the league can match. But the Rams' defensive weakness last year was in their *rush* defense, where they ranked 22nd in DVOA, and that gets a little more interesting.

Suh is switching fronts, becoming a nose tackle in Los Angeles' 3-4. Wade Phillips' 3-4 front isn't your typical 3-4 front; it's a one-gap scheme that shares many similarities with a standard 4-3 front. Suh also does have experience as a 1- and 0-tech, as both the Lions and Dolphins frequently shifted their lines around, so it's not like Phillips is asking Suh to something entirely unfamiliar and new. However, the fact remains that the majority of both Suh's snaps and production in terms of sacks, hurries and, yes, run defeats throughout his career have come in the B-gap as a 3- or 4-tech player. Suh is not a double-team expert, and while Phillips' scheme won't be asking him to two-gap as if he were Damon Harrison, it is a different role than he has been asked to play throughout his career.

Phillips is going to put Suh into positions where he can be as explosive as possible, shading him off to one side and using twists and stunts to give him more direct paths to the ball carrier. Because Suh won't be two-gapping all that much, the Rams are going to be relying on their linebackers to step up and make a lot of plays, filling in the other gap that the nose tackle would be responsible for in a more traditional 3-4 front. The linebacking corps didn't exactly excel at that last season, and things may be even worse now with Alec Ogletree traded out of town.

Good players and good coaches can make these transitions work. We're not trying to say that Suh will not be an overall net gain in run defense—and, if for some reason he isn't, the Rams have options to shift players around to cover for some of those issues. We're just saying that sometimes, transitions look a little cleaner on paper than they end up looking on the field.

This isn't a Suh-specific argument either. You could raise concerns about Talib's age, as he turned 32 in February. You could raise concerns about Peters' history of wearing out his welcome at both the University of Washington and in Kansas City. You could raise concerns about Cooks' history as something of a boom-or-bust receiver and acknowledge that as improved as Goff was last season, Cooks is downgrading from Tom Brady and Drew Brees. Again, none of these acquisitions are bad and all will more likely than not be improvements over what the Rams had last year. It's just that there are complexities when integrating new players—even new superstars—into new roles on a new team. This is one significant reason why the offseason champs don't always look the best when everyone gets on the field.

And that's assuming that everyone *stays* on the field. If there's one big red flashing warning light pointing to regression for the Rams, it's with their injury luck.

For the second year in a row, the Rams finished tops in adjusted games lost, with just 15.6 AGL. This included just 3.6 AGL on offense, a ridiculously small number. It's a lot easier to run a complicated offensive scheme when you don't have to worry about giving extra help to backup linemen!

There is very little year-to-year correlation in AGL, particularly when it comes to keeping AGL low. The last team to rank in the top five in AGL for three straight years was the 2007-2009 Tennessee Titans. No team has demonstrated a consistent ability to avoid injuries, and there's no reason to believe that the Rams will continue to lead the league in health just because they did so the last two seasons. After all, Kayvon Webster's Achilles could have ruptured just as easily in Week 2 as in Week 14, and neither Michael Brockers' postseason MCL tear nor Dominique Easley's preseason ACL tear counted against Los Angeles in terms of AGL. They were fortunate that their most significant injuries either happened early enough that they were able to plan for them in preseason, or late enough that they didn't impact the majority of the 2017 season.

We're not saying the Rams are due for a wave of injuries, because that's not how statistics work. It's likely, however, that the Rams' injury luck will not continue. We don't know how McVay will react to being required to replace injured players, because he has never really had to do it. It's possible the next man up will step in and everything will keep running smoothly, but it's those kinds of shifts in luck that help push Plexiglass teams down in their next seasons. You can't count on everything going perfectly two years in a row.

You can find plenty of other areas for potential regression as well, especially on offense. The Rams had 27 drives start in opposing territory, the most in the league last season. Fifteen of those resulted in touchdowns. Their average starting field position was the 32.2, second-best in the league. While those numbers are certainly helped by a strong defense and great special teams, it's likely that both numbers will fall back to the pack some in 2018, resulting in longer fields for the offense. That field position was helped by the fact they were ninth in turnover differential, a stat that's markedly inconsistent from year to year. Goff's 1.5 percent interception rate from a year ago is almost certainly unsustainable, and the Rams were fortunate enough to recover roughly 60 percent of the fumbles they forced on defense a year ago. That turnover differential

is likely coming down. They're projected to face a tougher schedule in 2018, and everyone will have a full year of film of McVay's offense to break down. The road will be tougher in 2018, and it remains to be seen how the Rams will respond.

The Rams will likely be up to the task. The Rams will likely not be as good this season. These aren't contradictory statements.

Expecting a repeat of 2017, especially on offense, is probably too much to ask. It was a season where nearly everything that could have gone well did, in terms of injuries and turnovers and player development. Some of that is bound to come crashing down to Earth. Goff isn't the same quarterback who explored new levels of terribleness as a rookie, but it remains to be seen if he can stick in the top 10 in DVOA, especially if other teams start to figure out McVay's offense. Los Angeles is likely to face more adversity going forward, and that's going to take its toll on their offensive production.

But we still have the Rams with the top defensive projection in the league. We have them with top-three special teams. They have the Coach of the Year ready to make tweaks and adjustments and get his team to rise to the task. With all that in mind, we basically come to the same conclusion as last year— if Goff and the offense can be above average, the Rams will be a Super Bowl contender.

Given what 2017 looked like, there's every reason for optimism. But then again, Hollywood sequels are always a little bit rougher than the originals, aren't they?

Bryan Knowles

2017 Rams Stats by Week

Wk	vs.	W-L	PF	PA	YDF	YDA	TO	Total	Off	Def	ST
1	IND	W	46	9	373	225	+2	78%	9%	-58%	11%
2	WAS	L	20	27	332	385	-2	-37%	-15%	19%	-3%
3	at SF	W	41	39	418	421	0	27%	31%	-3%	-7%
4	at DAL	W	35	30	412	440	+2	24%	18%	13%	18%
5	SEA	L	10	16	375	241	-3	-14%	-35%	-36%	-16%
6	at JAX	W	27	17	249	389	0	60%	11%	-23%	26%
7	ARI	W	33	0	425	193	+1	84%	23%	-50%	11%
8	BYE										
9	at NYG	W	51	17	473	319	+3	54%	41%	1%	14%
10	HOU	W	33	7	443	283	+4	55%	8%	-40%	8%
11	at MIN	L	7	24	254	451	-1	2%	16%	17%	3%
12	NO	W	26	20	415	346	-1	82%	54%	-10%	19%
13	at ARI	W	32	16	303	312	+1	11%	-4%	1%	16%
14	PHI	L	35	43	307	455	-1	72%	65%	-3%	4%
15	at SEA	W	42	7	352	149	+1	94%	3%	-64%	27%
16	at TEN	W	27	23	402	366	0	3%	20%	-8%	-25%
17	SF	L	13	34	251	461	+1	-96%	-65%	35%	4%
18	ATL	L	13	26	361	322	-2	22%	16%	-4%	2%

Trends and Splits

	Offense	Rank	Defense	Rank
Total DVOA	11.1%	6	-9.8%	6
Unadjusted VOA	9.7%	8	-8.7%	6
Weighted Trend	12.7%	5	-9.0%	8
Variance	10.1%	27	8.5%	30
Average Opponent	-2.6%	5	-1.9%	24
Passing	31.4%	7	-14.3%	3
Rushing	0.3%	10	-4.1%	21
First Down	6.4%	9	-15.4%	3
Second Down	7.9%	10	-11.5%	4
Third Down	25.6%	2	3.2%	17
First Half	15.8%	5	-10.8%	5
Second Half	6.1%	14	-8.5%	8
Red Zone	28.5%	2	-3.1%	13
Late and Close	1.3%	15	-13.2%	9

Five-Year Performance

Year	W-L	Pyth W	Est W	PF	PA	TO	Total	Rk	Off	Rk	Def	Rk	ST	Rk	Off AGL	Rk	Def AGL	Rk	Off Age	Rk	Def Age	Rk	ST Age	Rk
2013	7-9	7.6	7.8	348	364	+8	2.4%	14	-9.5%	22	-5.7%	11	6.3%	4	26.1	10	21.4	10	26.1	28	25.0	31	25.0	30
2014	6-10	7.1	6.1	324	354	-2	-3.8%	18	-11.1%	25	-3.8%	9	3.5%	7	37.6	21	26.5	7	26.5	23	25.0	32	25.2	32
2015	7-9	6.5	7.9	280	330	+5	-2.2%	16	-15.0%	29	-10.5%	7	2.4%	7	32.3	16	48.0	29	25.2	32	26.1	25	24.9	32
2016	4-12	3.3	4.6	224	394	-11	-28.6%	30	-37.8%	32	-2.0%	15	7.1%	3	7.7	1	21.3	8	25.5	32	26.0	26	25.4	29
2017	11-5	11.6	11.3	478	329	+7	27.7%	2	11.1%	6	-9.8%	6	6.8%	2	3.6	1	12.0	6	26.0	31	26.0	19	25.0	31

2017 Performance Based on Most Common Personnel Groups

LAR Offense					LAR Offense vs. Opponents					LAR Defense				LAR Defense vs. Opponents			
Pers	Freq	Yds	DVOA	Run%	Pers	Freq	Yds	DVOA	Run%	Pers	Freq	Yds	DVOA	Pers	Freq	Yds	DVOA
11	81%	6.3	25.5%	38%	Base	15%	6.0	14.5%	61%	Base	58%	5.4	-9.3%	11	45%	5.5	-8.6%
12	12%	6.1	-1.2%	65%	Nickel	77%	5.9	15.1%	43%	Nickel	37%	5.5	-12.5%	12	28%	5.5	-15.1%
01	5%	3.3	-48.0%	75%	Dime+	8%	7.3	48.5%	10%	Dime+	2%	4.8	-10.2%	21	10%	6.0	-10.7%
13	1%	1.8	-78.0%	75%	Big	1%	4.0	-22.4%	80%	Big	2%	5.5	0.1%	10	6%	6.3	-2.7%
10	1%	0.9	-87.1%	0%										13	5%	3.5	-13.5%

Strategic Tendencies

Run/Pass		Rk	Formation		Rk	Pass Rush		Rk	Secondary		Rk	Strategy		Rk
Runs, first half	36%	28	Form: Single Back	92%	2	Rush 3	4.9%	22	4 DB	58%	2	Play action	29%	2
Runs, first down	53%	11	Form: Empty Back	4%	30	Rush 4	61.1%	19	5 DB	37%	25	Avg Box (Off)	6.12	26
Runs, second-long	40%	6	Pers: 3+ WR	87%	1	Rush 5	27.4%	4	6+ DB	2%	23	Avg Box (Def)	6.41	3
Runs, power sit.	69%	5	Pers: 2+ TE/6+ OL	13%	32	Rush 6+	6.6%	13	CB by Sides	63%	27	Offensive Pace	27.90	1
Runs, behind 2H	38%	1	Pers: 6+ OL	2%	24	Int DL Sacks	46.9%	2	S/CB Cover Ratio	28%	15	Defensive Pace	30.22	10
Pass, ahead 2H	42%	25	Shotgun/Pistol	43%	31	Second Level Sacks	6.3%	32	DB Blitz	5%	28	Go for it on 4th	1.14	9

Although the Vikings used play-action slightly more often overall, the Rams were the only team to use play-action fakes on more than half of first-down passes: 57 percent, to be exact. ☞ The Rams ran 40 percent of the time when they had three or more wide receivers on the field, the highest figure in the league. ☞ Los Angeles led the NFL with 11.4 average yards after the catch on passes behind the line of scrimmage and 6.6 average YAC overall. They were one of only two teams to have a higher DVOA on passes behind the line of scrimmage (70.0%) than beyond it (64.1%). Indianapolis was the other. (FYI, these DVOA ratings are ridiculously high in part because sacks and a number of incompletes such as throwaways are not included.) ☞ A big part of that first number comes from a red-hot screen game. On wide receiver screens, the Rams led the NFL with 133.0% DVOA and were fifth with 7.3 yards per pass. On running back screens, the Rams led the NFL with 11.8 yards per pass and were tied for seventh with 64.9% DVOA. ☞ The Rams picked up Wade Phillips' love of good old-fashioned base defense, using just four defensive backs roughly three times as often as they did in 2016. The Rams were one of only three teams to use base defense more often than they used nickel or dime. (The others were Cleveland and, just barely, Carolina.) The Rams also followed Phillips' philosophy of rarely blitzing defensive backs after the Rams had ranked first or second in DB blitzes from 2014 to 2016. ☞ Despite having one of the top defenses in the league, Los Angeles was near the bottom (30th) by forcing a three-and-out on just 18.9 percent of drives. ☞ Demonstrating the effect of running out a lead, the Rams had the fastest pace in the league in the first half of games (one play each 25.4 seconds) and the next-to-slowest pace in the second half (one play each 30.0 seconds). ☞ The Rams led the NFL with 34 penalties on special teams, with 25 of those coming on punts.

Passing

Player	DYAR	DVOA	Plays	NtYds	Avg	YAC	C%	TD	Int
J.Goff	1125	24.0%	500	3619	7.2	6.8	62.6%	28	7
S.Mannion	-141	-66.6%	40	162	4.1	3.3	59.5%	0	0

Rushing

Player	DYAR	DVOA	Plays	Yds	Avg	TD	Fum	Suc
T.Gurley	268	13.9%	279	1305	4.7	13	5	53%
M.Brown	4	-6.9%	63	246	3.9	1	1	33%
T.Austin*	97	-6.0%	59	270	4.6	1	0	–
J.Goff	-6	-20.6%	14	68	4.9	1	1	–
L.Dunbar*	24	43.6%	11	51	4.6	1	0	55%
B.Cooks	6	-28.1%	9	40	4.4	0	0	–

Receiving

Player	DYAR	DVOA	Plays	Ctch	Yds	Y/C	YAC	TD	C%
C.Kupp	272	24.8%	92	60	869	14.5	6.0	5	65%
R.Woods	172	13.4%	85	56	781	13.9	5.2	5	66%
S.Watkins*	216	24.1%	70	39	593	15.2	4.7	8	56%
T.Austin*	-99	-68.2%	24	15	56	3.7	6.4	0	63%
J.Reynolds	-35	-31.0%	24	11	104	9.5	3.1	1	46%
P.Cooper	-53	-49.2%	19	11	84	7.6	4.9	0	58%
M.Thomas	10	4.5%	7	5	93	18.6	4.4	0	71%
B.Cooks	258	14.9%	114	65	1082	16.6	3.5	7	57%
T.Higbee	-9	-10.4%	45	25	295	11.8	3.4	1	56%
G.Everett	-20	-17.0%	32	16	244	15.3	6.8	2	50%
D.Carrier*	5	-0.8%	11	8	71	8.9	6.3	0	73%
T.Gurley	236	35.9%	87	64	788	12.3	12.3	6	74%
M.Brown	-7	-24.6%	11	9	53	5.9	6.6	0	82%

Offensive Line

Player	Pos	Age	GS	Snaps	Pen	Sk	Pass	Run	Player	Pos	Age	GS	Snaps	Pen	Sk	Pass	Run
Jamon Brown	RG	25	16/16	1037	6	1.0	10	8	Andrew Whitworth	LT	37	15/15	922	5	5.0	16	9
Rob Havenstein	RT	26	15/15	972	8	5.0	18	7	John Sullivan	C	33	15/15	866	2	1.0	6	5
Rodger Saffold	LG	30	15/15	950	2	2.0	10	9	Austin Blythe	C	26	16/1	197	1	0.5	4	9

Year	Yards	ALY	Rank	Power	Rank	Stuff	Rank	2nd Lev	Rank	Open Field	Rank	Sacks	ASR	Rank	Press	Rank	F-Start	Cont.
2015	4.24	3.88	24	64%	20	23%	28	1.03	24	1.17	3	18	3.5%	1	27.0%	20	16	25
2016	3.23	3.66	29	61%	16	22%	28	0.89	31	0.30	30	49	8.1%	29	28.0%	21	20	29
2017	4.53	4.70	3	50%	29	22%	23	1.42	1	0.82	11	28	5.6%	9	29.8%	12	20	42

2017 ALY by direction: Left End: 3.58 (23)   Left Tackle: 6.18 (1)   Mid/Guard: 4.80 (3)   Right Tackle: 4.11 (13)   Right End: 4.61 (6)

The Rams had a perfect offensive line continuity score through Week 16—the same five starters week in and week out. That goes a long way to explaining the consistency and chemistry the line was able to develop. We already know it won't happen again in 2018, with right guard Jamon Brown earning a substance-abuse suspension for the first two games of the year. ☞ It's difficult to overstate how important adding Andrew Whitworth was to the Rams' line. The Rams jumped from 4.42 to 6.18 adjusted line yards running off left tackle, tops in the league. Whitworth only allowed 1.5 fewer sacks than Greg Robinson had the year before and ranked roughly the same in blown blocks, but it was the quality of his *successes* that really stood out. Whitworth didn't just stop people; he took them out of the play. Whitworth also only drew five penalty flags last season. Robinson had twice as many holding calls alone in 2016. ☞ Whitworth got all the press but adding veteran John Sullivan in the center of the line was nearly as important. Sullivan had just 11 blown blocks all year, and helped the Rams rank third in Adjusted Line Yards up the middle (4.80). ☞ Rodger Saffold looked like an entirely different player compared to the year before. He had the most blown blocks of any left guard two years ago but was middle-of-the-pack in 2017. ☞ There was talk of swapping Brown and right tackle Rob Havenstein during training camp last season, but Brown proved just too slow to handle speedy edge rushers. Havenstein actually had a slightly better snaps-per-blown-block rate than Whitworth (35.6 to 34.0), so leaving him at tackle worked out all right. ☞ Whitworth and Sullivan are both on the wrong side of 30, while the other three starters are all free agents after 2018. That's why the Rams' first two draft picks were tackle Joseph Noteboom (TCU) and center Brian Allen (Michigan State). Noteboom's an athletic project; Allen's a high-effort grinder. Both will hopefully spend most of 2018 on the bench.

Defensive Front Seven

Defensive Line	Age	Pos	G	Snaps	Plays	TmPct	Rk	Stop	Dfts	BTkl	Runs	St%	Rk	RuYd	Rk	Sack	Hit	Hur	Dsrpt
						Overall						vs. Run				Pass Rush			
Aaron Donald	27	DT	14	789	41	5.7%	31	37	19	4	29	86%	11	1.2	8	11.0	21	48.5	2
Michael Brockers	28	DT	16	729	58	7.1%	8	48	13	5	46	80%	31	2.0	39	2.5	0	6.0	1
Morgan Fox	24	DE	16	334	18	2.2%	--	14	3	3	14	71%	--	2.9	--	4.0	2	2.5	1
Ethan Westbrooks	28	DE	16	333	24	2.9%	--	21	8	2	18	83%	--	1.7	--	1.0	0	4.5	4
Tyrunn Walker*	28	DT	16	308	26	3.2%	--	21	5	3	18	83%	--	2.4	--	1.0	0	4.5	4
Tanzel Smart	24	DT	16	308	14	1.7%	--	12	0	2	11	91%	--	1.7	--	0.0	2	3.5	1
Ndamukong Suh	31	DT	16	883	50	6.5%	17	40	18	2	40	78%	44	1.6	22	4.5	10	20.5	3

Edge Rushers	Age	Pos	G	Snaps	Plays	TmPct	Rk	Stop	Dfts	BTkl	Runs	St%	Rk	RuYd	Rk	Sack	Hit	Hur	Dsrpt
						Overall						vs. Run				Pass Rush			
Connor Barwin*	32	OLB	14	658	33	4.6%	54	24	8	4	23	70%	67	3.4	83	5.0	8	18.5	0
Robert Quinn*	28	OLB	15	634	33	4.3%	61	24	17	5	16	56%	93	5.4	95	9.0	5	19.0	0
Matt Longacre	27	OLB	14	377	21	2.9%	87	18	8	1	14	86%	14	3.0	73	5.5	9	15.5	1
Samson Ebukam	23	OLB	16	351	22	2.7%	--	13	2	4	16	63%	--	4.2	--	2.0	2	7.0	0
Cory Littleton	25	OLB	16	279	35	4.3%	--	24	6	5	20	75%	--	4.0	--	1.0	2	2.5	1

Linebackers	Age	Pos	G	Snaps	Plays	TmPct	Rk	Stop	Dfts	BTkl	Runs	St%	Rk	RuYd	Rk	Sack	Hit	Hur	Tgts	Suc%	Rk	AdjYd	Rk	PD	Int
						Overall						vs. Run				Pass Rush				vs. Pass				
Alec Ogletree*	27	ILB	15	923	105	13.6%	30	63	15	19	58	59%	61	4.6	80	2.0	5	17.5	42	59%	13	7.0	45	5	1
Mark Barron	29	ILB	14	823	89	12.4%	41	49	18	12	51	67%	22	3.1	25	1.0	1	3.0	55	54%	25	7.3	49	5	3

Year	Yards	ALY	Rank	Power	Rank	Stuff	Rank	2nd Level	Rank	Open Field	Rank	Sacks	ASR	Rank	Press	Rank
2015	3.97	3.70	6	63%	14	24%	7	1.13	17	0.90	24	41	6.3%	17	28.3%	4
2016	3.99	3.43	1	64%	19	29%	1	1.10	11	1.04	30	31	5.0%	29	28.4%	11
2017	4.65	4.36	27	63%	16	18%	28	1.14	19	1.19	31	48	7.9%	5	31.5%	11

2017 ALY by direction:	Left End: 4.29 (20)	Left Tackle: 5.10 (29)	Mid/Guard: 4.36 (22)	Right Tackle: 4.22 (25)	Right End: 3.25 (9)

In *FOA 2017*, we mentioned that Aaron Donald and Ndamukong Suh tied for the most defeats among interior linemen. They nearly pulled off the feat again in 2017—Suh was one defeat short. It remains to be seen how opposing guards and centers handle these two together; our best guess is "not well." They won't even get a break with the two rotating out; they were first and second in percentage of team snaps among defensive tackles last season. ☞ Donald also led all interior linemen in sacks, knockdowns, QB hits, and yards per play. If there's anything he does "poorly," it's stop the run, where his 86 percent stop rate was only 10th in the league. So, you know, don't bother giving him a massive extension or anything. ☞ Suh has more snaps in the past eight years than any other defensive lineman, but only three percent of them have come at nose tackle. Wade Phillips' scheme is more similar to 4-3 fronts than most 3-4 defenses, and Suh should have plenty of one-gap opportunities. ☞ The shift to a 3-4 helped Michael Brockers, who recorded a career high in tackles. He tore his MCL in the wild-card loss to Atlanta but is expected back for the regular season. ☞ The projected starters at edge rusher, Matt Longacre and Samson Ebukam, have just 7.5 career sacks, all recorded last season. They each played about 350 snaps a year ago; they'll be asked to handle double the workload in 2018. ☞ The lack of experience at the edge is a great opportunity for fifth-round pick Ogbonnia Okoronkwo (Oklahoma). An offseason broken foot will slow his early development, but he's an explosive, athletic pass-rusher who should see heavy sub-package work fairly early on in his career. ☞ Mark Barron was the third-most targeted linebacker in pass coverage in 2017. His speed makes him a useful coverage player, which is why the Rams ask him to do it so often. However, you'd expect a former safety to have a higher success rate than Barron did; he was firmly middle-of-the-pack. ☞ With Alec Ogletree gone, the second inside linebacker slot is an open battle. So far, Cory Littleton has taken the most advantage of the vacancy, immediately stepping in during OTAs and impressing the coaching staff. He was the first man up last year when Barron or Ogletree went down, and Sean McVay singled him out for praise on his communication abilities. He stopped short of saying Littleton has the job, however. Keep an eye on fifth-round pick Micah Kiser, a tackling machine with great run defense instincts. In three years as a starter at Virginia, Kiser had 397 combined tackles (including assists) and 33.5 tackles for loss. Bryce Hager or Ramik Wilson will also get consideration during training camp., This may be the most wide-open battle on the team. ☞ The Rams went heavy on the front seven with their limited draft picks. In addition to Okoronkwo and Kiser, they also took defensive end John Franklin-Myers from the FCS-level Stephen F. Austin Lumberjacks. The Rams will try him out at the 5-tech, where his 82-inch wingspan should be great for getting into passing lanes.

Defensive Secondary

Secondary	Age	Pos	G	Snaps	Plays	Overall TmPct	Rk	Stop	Dfts	BTkl	vs. Run Runs	St%	Rk	RuYd	Rk	vs. Pass Tgts	Tgt%	Rk	Dist	Suc%	Rk	AdjYd	Rk	PD	Int
Trumaine Johnson*	28	CB	16	935	79	9.6%	23	32	18	7	14	36%	58	6.7	53	84	23.9%	66	13.6	45%	73	9.3	72	13	2
John Johnson	23	SS	16	718	82	10.0%	39	36	9	6	42	52%	17	5.9	34	41	15.3%	69	12.9	51%	41	6.0	15	11	1
Lamarcus Joyner	28	FS	12	688	57	9.3%	51	18	9	6	22	27%	63	10.6	74	25	9.5%	37	17.8	63%	6	5.8	10	9	3
Nickell Robey-Coleman	26	CB	15	655	54	7.0%	64	35	15	8	10	60%	15	5.5	29	55	22.3%	56	6.7	56%	14	6.7	20	10	2
Kayvon Webster*	27	CB	11	550	45	8.0%	48	19	7	3	7	57%	18	12.9	76	46	22.2%	54	12.1	53%	25	6.7	22	7	1
Cody Davis*	29	FS/SS	7	281	23	6.4%	--	9	3	3	12	25%	--	7.7	--	5	4.8%	--	12.3	93%	--	1.1	--	3	1
Troy Hill	27	CB	12	267	21	3.4%	--	12	4	7	4	50%	--	5.0	--	37	37.1%	--	12.1	61%	--	7.2	--	4	0
Marcus Peters	25	CB	14	967	55	7.7%	52	24	16	11	11	55%	25	5.9	41	73	20.2%	40	14.9	48%	59	7.9	44	9	5
Aqib Talib	32	CB	15	752	37	5.4%	75	14	6	2	8	38%	53	7.5	61	45	12.5%	3	8.8	55%	21	5.4	3	8	1

Year	Pass D Rank	vs. #1 WR	Rk	vs. #2 WR	Rk	vs. Other WR	Rk	WR Wide	Rk	WR Slot	Rk	vs. TE	Rk	vs. RB	Rk
2015	8	-26.4%	2	-19.1%	6	4.1%	16	--	--	--	--	-4.0%	16	-3.0%	13
2016	20	3.7%	21	-3.8%	11	17.8%	30	20.5%	31	-3.3%	11	-6.0%	10	-20.1%	6
2017	3	-5.4%	12	-24.8%	4	-16.8%	7	-10.4%	10	-16.0%	6	1.2%	19	-9.8%	9

Marcus Peters posted a 57 percent adjusted success rate as a rookie in 2015, followed by 54 percent in 2016. In 2017, Peters' adjusted success rate dipped to 48 percent and he recorded the fewest passes defended in his career. Peters is still a dominant player, but Kansas City's defensive devolution did not allow him to show it as often. When he is enabled to shine, few cornerbacks in recent history can rival Peters' knack for finding the ball. Since 2000, only three defensive backs have recorded at least 19 interceptions through their first three seasons: Ed Reed (21), Richard Sherman (20), and Peters (19). Just this past season, quality passers such as Phillip Rivers and Marcus Mariota fell victim to Peters' savvy for jumping routes on the far side of the field that most cornerbacks would not even dare attempt. Additionally, Peters has a combined 10 forced fumbles and fumble recoveries since 2015, a feat matched only by Josh Norman. ☞ Aqib Talib's average depth of target dropped from the mid 11s to 8.8 last season, possibly a result of him playing off the ball more. Reuniting with Wade Phillips, expect Talib to go back to pressing at the line like he did in Denver in 2015 and 2016. ☞ Amidst all the love for Talib and Peters, Nickell Robey-Coleman gets lost somewhat in the shuffle, but his 60 percent success rate was the third-highest among slot defenders in 2017. He benefitted enormously in the move from Buffalo's zone scheme to Los Angeles' man-to-man coverage. ☞ It's safe to call LaMarcus Joyner's move from slot corner to moveable safety an unqualified success. He posted the best charting numbers of his career in a great example of how the proper scheme fit can allow players to blossom. ☞ As a rookie, John Johnson took over the starting strong safety job in October and never looked back. He had the fifth-most passes defended among safeties despite playing about 300 fewer snaps than the rest of the top of the leaderboard. The Rams moved him all around the field, showing a surprising amount of versatility for a first-year player. When he's the weak link in your secondary, you have a special group.

Special Teams

Year	DVOA	Rank	FG/XP	Rank	Net Kick	Rank	Kick Ret	Rank	Net Punt	Rank	Punt Ret	Rank	Hidden	Rank
2015	2.4%	7	-6.7	30	2.5	9	4.0	7	10.4	5	1.6	13	1.0	14
2016	7.1%	3	3.8	9	4.0	8	1.3	11	29.2	1	-2.6	22	0.7	16
2017	6.8%	2	11.3	5	-0.3	19	9.2	2	10.3	3	3.7	7	40.6	1

The Rams lapped the rest of the league in our "hidden" special teams rating—40 points of value, when no one else was above 15. Some of this value wasn't actually all that hidden: three blocked punts, a blocked field goal, and a blocked extra point. Even without considering the blocked punts, however, the Rams finished in the bottom five in both gross punt value and gross kickoff value by opponents. And opponents were just 23-for-34 on field goals, with four misses on field goals of less than 40 yards and another two missed extra points on top of the block. ☞ It's better to be lucky than good, but it's best to be both lucky *and* good. All four of Los Angeles' specialists—kicker Greg Zuerlein, punter Johnny Hekker, returner Pharoh Cooper, and long snapper Jake McQuaide—made the Pro Bowl. That's the first time in NFL history that has ever occurred. ☞ Cooper averaged 12.5 yards per punt return after taking the role over in October. Tavon Austin's best year had him at just 11.4, plummeting all the way down to 4.4 last season. And the Rams got a pick for him! By Football Outsiders metrics, Cooper ranked second in punt return value (behind Detroit's Jamal Agnew) and third in kick return value (trailing Tyler Lockett and Alvin Kamara).

Miami Dolphins

2017 Record: 6-10	**Total DVOA:** -19.8% (27th)	**2018 Mean Projection:** 7.5 wins	**On the Clock (0-4):** 13%
Pythagorean Wins: 4.9 (29th)	**Offense:** -13.0% (27th)	**Postseason Odds:** 29.9%	**Mediocrity (5-7):** 38%
Snap-Weighted Age: 26.9 (6th)	**Defense:** 9.4% (28th)	**Super Bowl Odds:** 2.8%	**Playoff Contender (8-10):** 37%
Average Opponent: 1.7% (10th)	**Special Teams:** 2.6% (12th)	**Proj. Avg. Opponent:** -2.7% (30th)	**Super Bowl Contender (11+):** 13%

2017: Jay Cutler's retirement party went about how everyone thought Jay Cutler's retirement party would go.

2018: The team that will need eight different dominoes to fall in Week 16 just to make Week 17 mean something.

The three most important people in a football organization, the saying goes, are the owner, the head coach, and the quarterback. Last season in Miami, the bloom quickly came off the rose for all three of these people. The 2016 season, when the Dolphins were the sixth-best team in a three-team AFC, now feels like forever ago. It would surprise nobody if the Dolphins dispatched their head coach and quarterback after this year, and it would also surprise nobody if Stephen Ross looked at the available replacements and shrugged.

Ross bought the Miami Dolphins in 2008. Since then, the Dolphins' owner has mostly been hands-off in a world where doing that can haunt you if the right people aren't in place. He left Jeff Ireland enough rope to hang himself multiple times and created a muddled front office full of other people he wanted to promote. He stood behind Joe Philbin for an eternity even before the Richie Incognito saga shook the Dolphins. And while resisting the urge to fully clean house in the organization, he's always had someone in his ear to keep him from hiring the best.

Former Jets general manager Mike Tannenbaum, who gave us hits such as "trading up for Mark Sanchez in the 2009 NFL Draft," and "then also trading for Tim Tebow," was a consultant for the Dolphins and had enough sway on Ross to become de facto general manager. Tannenbaum, fresh off being named the second-least trusted executive in an anonymous poll of agents by *USA Today*, is now in Year 4 of a rebuild that has looked completely indistinguishable from Ireland's. The only other thing Ross has done of recent public note is leave his players utterly confused on where he stands on national anthem standing, earning himself a mention as what "embod[ies] everything wrong with the NFL" by the *New York Daily News*.

After a blessed 2016 season, head coach Adam Gase's genius tag wore off in a hurry. In 2017, he was applauded for improving quarterback Ryan Tannehill and then getting a 2-1 record out of journeyman Matt Moore when Tannehill tore his left ACL. "Despite talent limitations on both sides of the ball," wrote Rotoworld's Patrick Daugherty, "Gase displayed an innate ability to put his players in the best position to succeed." CBS' Pete Prisco declared him "a star in the making." The 2016 season also involved the Dolphins winning 10 games despite a negative point differential, which is a situation that is tailor-made to make the head coach look good. In 2017, the team had the same flat start they had in 2016, made an example

of Jay Ajayi by trading him, and then left enough hope at the end of the season with the unearthing of Kenyan Drake and an upset of the Patriots to make you question what happened for the first two months. The major difference was that Jay Cutler, reunited with Gase, was a turnover waiting to happen to the methodical, slow offense that Gase has built in Miami. Those long drives that made things a little closer in 2016 would now sometimes end with Cutler's trademark bizarre decisions. The legacy to apathy that was Cutler in London, split out wide in a Wildcat formation with his hands on his hips, will outlive anything else the Dolphins did in 2017.

This makes for a favorable comparison for Tannehill, a quarterback who is too good to get rid of and not good enough to carry a team anywhere on his own. Having missed the last year due to an ACL he re-injured in training camp, Tannehill surely needs a healthy year to maintain his reputation. As he showed down the stretch of 2016, when he accumulated 321 DYAR from Week 6 to Week 14, Tannehill has the talent to be a good NFL quarterback. He was accurate in Gase's system without being turnover-prone, and he has the hose to stick tight-window throws as long as he's being kept clean in structure. That was Tannehill's best NFL work to date, and there's no telling what effect the injury will have on his play. He was on pace to at least become a late bloomer in the Steve Beuerlein mold before he missed his last 20 potential appearances. Now? It's all up in the air.

With so much on the line, you might think that the Dolphins would consider creating a stable environment to perform their litmus test against Y-1 and Y-2. Instead, they got rid of the two players they had who were most well-regarded by other organizations, Ndamukong Suh and Jarvis Landry.

Landry is a statistical anomaly. Older Dolphins fans will remember Chris Chambers, a speedy outside wideout who generated awful DYAR totals by having an obscenely low catch rate. Landry was the exact opposite of Chambers for the Dolphins: a terrific catch rate with an obscenely high usage rate and little in the way of broken tackles or extra yardage after the catch. Landry had a positive DVOA as a receiver once in four seasons. The Browns will have to be the ones to find out if Landry has another gear, after trading a third-round pick for him and giving him a five-year, $75 million contract with $47 million in guarantees. On a purely statistical level, the Dolphins dodged a bullet by not paying for the inefficient pro-

2018 Dolphins Schedule

Week	Opp.	Week	Opp.	Week	Opp.
1	TEN	7	DET	13	BUF
2	at NYJ	8	at HOU (Thu.)	14	NE
3	OAK	9	NYJ	15	at MIN
4	at NE	10	at GB	16	JAX
5	at CIN	11	BYE	17	at BUF
6	CHI	12	at IND		

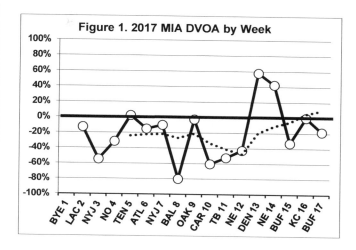

Figure 1. 2017 MIA DVOA by Week

duction Landry provided. They got a pick for their troubles, and they couldn't afford to give Landry that contract anyway given where they were with the salary cap.

The problem was that the Dolphins still valued Landry's production highly enough to go get not one, but two slot receivers in free agency to replace him. Danny Amendola has been a quality slot receiver for the Patriots for years, but he is injury-prone and 32 years old. His cap hit this season, on a team with almost no salary cap space, is $6 million. Albert Wilson showed some promise for the Chiefs and was given a three-year deal with $14.45 million in guarantees that locks him on to the roster for two seasons. His cap hit this season is $4.85 million. Both are among the 12 highest-paid Dolphins, on a team that is severely lacking in star power outside Cameron Wake.

And a reason they're lacking star power is because the cascade effect of signing those two receivers was releasing Suh, their all-world defensive tackle who went on to get a one-year deal worth $14 million despite not being available at the start of free agency. Suh had a down 2017 season compared to his absolute peak and is rightfully regarded as a bit of a pariah for what we'll call poor sportsmanship. He still finished second on the Dolphins in pressures and is an impact inside passrusher—a brand of player not often available. And by releasing him now, the Dolphins locked in to a $13.1 million charge on next year's cap.

The problem with the Dolphins as currently constructed isn't that they don't have replacements for Landry and Suh. It's that by subtracting the only two players they have regarded as stars, they don't have much left that qualifies. They have built a team of good-to-solid football players with few elite talents to take them up that notch. When you go that route in

the current AFC, you can make the playoffs if every one of your contracts is successful and you draft well, but you can't create a stable playoff team. Of the players currently under contract in Miami, only Wake, Josh Sitton, and Robert Quinn have had a year approaching dominance in their last five seasons. Wake and Sitton are both into their mid-thirties. Quinn hasn't been the same player since injuries struck in 2015 and was seen as expendable by a Rams team without another established edge rusher.

Kiko Alonso and Andre Branch signed contracts in 2017 that were detriments on the bottom line for 2018 the minute the ink dried (Table 1). Branch had 4.5 sacks and 17 hurries on the edge last year and has a $10 million cap figure. Alonso has been unable to stay with tight ends and middle-of-the-field receivers to the point where the Dolphins had to draft coverage linebackers Raekwon McMillian and Jerome Baker with early picks in each of the last two years. Alonso's rate of 52 solo tackles to 16 broken tackles was among the ten worst in the NFL for linebackers as well. His cap figure this year is $9.63 million. Neither Branch nor Alonso had even so much as a pay-cut blurb written about them in the local papers.

A lot of the criticism around Miami is about the lack of a consistent plan. To be certain, the Dolphins have been poster children for the idea that even signing the very top of a free-agent class can't turn around an organization without true depth of talent. If you want to take a glass-half-full approach

Table 1: Top Ten Dolphins Cap Hits, 2018

Player	Cap Hit	Comments
Robert Quinn	$11.44 mil	Had 19 hurries last year, tying him with Demario Davis.
Andre Branch	$10.00 mil	Had 17 hurries last year, half a hurry less than Barkevious Mingo.
Kenny Stills	$9.75 mil	55% catch rate last year was his best in three Dolphins seasons.
Kiko Alonso	$9.63 mil	Guaranteed money in his contract ranks fourth among 4-3 OLB; performance does not rank fourth among 4-3 OLB.
Cameron Wake	$9.63 mil	Became one of just four edge rushers to notch 10+ sacks after 35 since 2010, joining John Abraham, Terrell Suggs, and Julius Peppers.
Ja'Waun James	$9.34 mil	An average right tackle.
Ryan Tannehill	$8.67 mil	An enigmatic quarterback.
Josh Sitton	$6.50 mil	A terrific guard who is now 32.
Danny Amendola	$6.00 mil	A solid slot receiver who is now 32.
Daniel Kilgore	$5.38 mil	Was awful last season and before that hadn't played a full season since 2013.

to this, a healthy Tannehill still gives them as good a chance as any of the middle-tier AFC teams of making the playoffs in 2018. A full season of Kenyan Drake that plays like he did in 2017 gives them the makings of a new version of the 2016 Dolphins—a team that can eat clock on leads and manage to be effective enough on offense to compensate for some talent shortcomings on both sides of the ball.

But the Dolphins are where they are today not because of a lack of an organizational plan so much as poor player evaluation. When your top 10 cap hits include players such as Branch, Alonso, Amendola, and Daniel Kilgore—passable pieces if healthy but no one worth breaking the bank for—your team is at a big disadvantage no matter how much goes right for you. It's hard to say that Kenny Stills is a bad contract on pure talent, but if he can't elevate beyond a single-digit DVOA when Tannehill is healthy, is he even worth a $9.75 million cap charge?

The sum up of the Dolphins is that we expect them to be a mediocre team in a mediocre conference. Neither the offense or defense is especially good, but they should be functional in a conference where some teams don't have that luxury. The Dolphins project to have one of the easiest schedules in the AFC, and boosted by games against the Bills and Jets, could easily find their way into the playoff talk in November and December.

But one thing we can almost certainly say is that they won't be is a real contender. Barring Tannehill's layoff leading to him suddenly playing like Tom Brady, this team lacks star power. The best-case scenario for them, regardless of what happens in the aggregate, will be that the quarterback and head coach prove conclusively one way or another that they are objectively good or bad. Such a scenario would allow this team to take a leap off of the pseudo-contention cycle and declare a proper rebuild or win-now phase.

And if someone caught Ross' ear and told him that finding a better personnel czar would help get this franchise out of the mud, that would go a long way as well. Hands-off ownership is extremely beneficial when the right people are in place. But if ownership can't tell if the right people are in place, or mistakes the wrong people for the right people, it creates a void in the story of a football team. That's where we have been in Miami since Dan Marino hung it up and the Jay Fiedler/Jason Taylor/Zach Thomas Dolphins ceased to be. This team is the filler material waiting for the next plot line to emerge.

Rivers McCown

2017 Dolphins Stats by Week

Wk	vs.	W-L	PF	PA	YDF	YDA	TO	Total	Off	Def	ST
1	BYE										
2	at LAC	W	19	17	336	367	0	-13%	11%	26%	2%
3	at NYJ	L	6	20	225	336	-1	-55%	-36%	10%	-8%
4	NO	L	0	20	186	347	-1	-31%	-27%	1%	-4%
5	TEN	W	16	10	178	188	0	2%	-39%	-34%	8%
6	at ATL	W	20	17	289	339	0	-15%	-4%	13%	3%
7	NYJ	W	31	28	357	272	0	-10%	-1%	14%	5%
8	at BAL	L	0	40	196	295	-2	-80%	-62%	10%	-9%
9	OAK	L	24	27	395	379	+1	-2%	43%	41%	-4%
10	at CAR	L	21	45	313	548	-1	-60%	11%	73%	1%
11	TB	L	20	30	448	321	-5	-52%	-58%	-4%	2%
12	at NE	L	17	35	221	417	-1	-43%	-43%	6%	7%
13	DEN	W	35	9	367	270	0	58%	-1%	-35%	24%
14	NE	W	27	20	362	248	+2	43%	18%	-23%	2%
15	at BUF	L	16	24	349	328	-3	-33%	-24%	24%	14%
16	at KC	L	13	29	345	404	-2	0%	0%	-5%	-5%
17	BUF	L	16	22	356	312	-1	-18%	1%	24%	4%

Trends and Splits

	Offense	Rank	Defense	Rank
Total DVOA	-13.1%	27	9.4%	28
Unadjusted VOA	-9.6%	26	10.8%	31
Weighted Trend	-11.3%	26	10.3%	29
Variance	8.5%	20	7.4%	27
Average Opponent	2.2%	27	3.2%	5
Passing	-0.3%	23	24.6%	29
Rushing	-20.5%	31	-9.0%	15
First Down	-3.8%	19	7.1%	27
Second Down	-19.8%	29	7.1%	25
Third Down	-21.3%	28	18.5%	28
First Half	-22.8%	32	18.9%	32
Second Half	-4.4%	18	-1.4%	13
Red Zone	-1.8%	17	9.6%	25
Late and Close	-8.2%	21	-0.6%	20

Five-Year Performance

Year	W-L	Pyth W	Est W	PF	PA	TO	Total	Rk	Off	Rk	Def	Rk	ST	Rk	Off AGL	Rk	Def AGL	Rk	Off Age	Rk	Def Age	Rk	ST Age	Rk
2013	8-8	7.5	6.8	317	335	-2	-6.5%	22	-1.8%	18	2.4%	17	-2.4%	23	41.3	20	18.6	9	26.5	23	27.3	11	26.0	18
2014	8-8	8.4	8.8	388	373	+2	3.5%	15	10.1%	8	0.5%	17	-6.1%	32	40.3	26	39.1	18	26.2	27	27.3	7	25.7	25
2015	6-10	5.8	5.8	310	389	-3	-19.0%	29	-7.3%	22	9.0%	25	-2.7%	24	23.0	7	40.5	24	25.5	31	26.6	16	25.3	30
2016	10-6	7.5	8.9	363	380	+2	1.0%	18	1.8%	14	1.6%	19	0.8%	12	46.3	24	52.8	25	26.3	23	26.9	10	25.6	25
2017	6-10	4.9	5.6	281	393	-14	-19.8%	27	-13.1%	27	9.4%	28	2.6%	12	61.8	29	53.6	29	27.3	11	27.1	4	25.8	19

2017 Performance Based on Most Common Personnel Groups

MIA Offense					MIA Offense vs. Opponents					MIA Defense				MIA Defense vs. Opponents			
Pers	Freq	Yds	DVOA	Run%	Pers	Freq	Yds	DVOA	Run%	Pers	Freq	Yds	DVOA	Pers	Freq	Yds	DVOA
11	75%	5.2	-11.2%	27%	Base	23%	4.8	-5.3%	59%	Base	36%	5.6	8.4%	11	52%	5.8	8.6%
12	15%	5.6	7.2%	55%	Nickel	63%	5.6	-0.8%	30%	Nickel	60%	5.8	11.3%	12	23%	6.0	25.0%
13	6%	3.1	-33.6%	81%	Dime+	13%	3.8	-55.6%	9%	Dime+	1%	5.0	13.8%	21	11%	5.7	7.6%
01	2%	3.9	33.6%	5%	Goal Line	0%	0.3	-42.0%	67%	Goal Line	2%	0.9	-9.4%	22	3%	4.9	-9.5%
10	1%	5.0	41.6%	33%						Big	1%	6.0	33.3%	13	3%	6.4	5.9%

Strategic Tendencies

Run/Pass		Rk	Formation		Rk	Pass Rush		Rk	Secondary		Rk	Strategy		Rk
Runs, first half	40%	13	Form: Single Back	88%	6	Rush 3	5.4%	21	4 DB	36%	9	Play action	23%	10
Runs, first down	40%	32	Form: Empty Back	7%	17	Rush 4	65.8%	15	5 DB	60%	14	Avg Box (Off)	6.11	27
Runs, second-long	34%	16	Pers: 3+ WR	79%	2	Rush 5	23.1%	10	6+ DB	1%	25	Avg Box (Def)	6.22	19
Runs, power sit.	52%	19	Pers: 2+ TE/6+ OL	21%	28	Rush 6+	5.7%	17	CB by Sides	82%	12	Offensive Pace	32.02	29
Runs, behind 2H	23%	29	Pers: 6+ OL	6%	3	Int DL Sacks	21.7%	20	S/CB Cover Ratio	30%	11	Defensive Pace	32.14	31
Pass, ahead 2H	51%	9	Shotgun/Pistol	70%	8	Second Level Sacks	15.0%	20	DB Blitz	11%	10	Go for it on 4th	1.72	1

Same offensive scheme, worse quarterback, so how on earth did the Dolphins drop from third to dead last in run/pass ratio on first downs? ☞ Miami had the league's biggest gap in offensive DVOA between passes with play-action (45.6%) and passes without (-13.7%). ☞ Miami was second in the league with 163 penalties; Seattle was the only other team with more than 150. However, the Dolphins also ranked second in the league with 152 penalties by opponents. ☞ One oddity: the Dolphins had seven different penalties during turnover returns, while no other team had more than four. ☞ Miami was only leading for an average of 9:47 in each game. Every other team except Cleveland (6:11) led for an average of 15 minutes or more each game. ☞ Miami's defense faced a league-high 26 percent of passes to tight ends and ranked No. 2 with 25 percent of opponent passes going to running backs. ☞ Gase's No. 1 rank in Aggressiveness Index requires a bit of explanation. It's based heavily on the meaningless Week 17 game where Gase basically just told David Fales to go out and sling it no matter the down-and-distance. Without that game, Gase still has an above-average Aggressiveness Index, but it's 1.14, which would rank tied for ninth.

Passing

Player	DYAR	DVOA	Plays	NtYds	Avg	YAC	C%	TD	Int
J.Cutler*	35	-9.9%	451	2533	5.6	4.6	62.1%	19	14
M.Moore*	-41	-16.1%	138	766	5.6	4.1	61.9%	4	5
D.Fales	45	3.7%	44	244	5.5	5.6	69.0%	1	1
B.Osweiler	-56	-16.2%	180	1018	5.7	5.3	56.5%	5	5

Rushing

Player	DYAR	DVOA	Plays	Yds	Avg	TD	Fum	Suc
J.Ajayi*	3	-8.1%	138	477	3.5	0	1	43%
K.Drake	-14	-11.3%	133	648	4.9	3	2	44%
D.Williams*	-25	-22.7%	46	181	3.9	0	0	28%
J.Cutler*	5	1.4%	9	39	4.3	0	1	-
S.Perry	7	14.7%	8	30	3.8	0	0	50%
M.Gray	9	21.9%	5	14	2.8	0	0	80%
F.Gore	66	-2.3%	261	955	3.7	3	3	44%
B.Osweiler	2	-8.5%	11	70	6.4	1	0	-

Receiving

Player	DYAR	DVOA	Plays	Ctch	Yds	Y/C	YAC	TD	C%
J.Landry*	98	-4.9%	161	112	987	8.8	4.4	9	70%
K.Stills	107	0.4%	105	58	854	14.7	2.7	6	55%
D.Parker	12	-11.0%	96	57	670	11.8	3.7	1	59%
J.Grant	60	22.1%	23	14	210	15.0	11.4	2	61%
L.Carroo	-14	-26.3%	14	7	69	9.9	1.6	0	50%
D.Amendola	138	8.4%	86	61	659	10.8	3.4	2	71%
A.Wilson	167	21.4%	62	42	554	13.2	7.5	3	68%
J.Thomas*	-30	-14.6%	62	41	388	9.5	3.6	3	66%
A.Fasano*	-21	-27.6%	16	12	110	9.2	3.3	1	75%
A.J.Derby	-37	-67.8%	9	2	20	10.0	9.0	0	22%
K.Drake	-13	-19.1%	48	32	239	7.5	6.7	1	67%
D.Williams*	44	12.2%	28	20	155	7.8	7.7	1	71%
J.Ajayi*	-44	-55.7%	20	14	67	4.8	4.8	0	70%
F.Gore	35	4.1%	38	29	245	8.4	9.5	1	76%

Offensive Line

Player	Pos	Age	GS	Snaps	Pen	Sk	Pass	Run	Player	Pos	Age	GS	Snaps	Pen	Sk	Pass	Run
Mike Pouncey*	C	29	16/16	974	9	2.5	9	8	Ja'Wuan James	RT	26	8/8	494	5	1.0	5	0
Laremy Tunsil	LT	24	15/15	937	12	5.5	14	4	Sam Young	RT	31	10/6	453	4	0.5	8	6
Jesse Davis	RG	27	16/10	750	3	2.0	13	8	Anthony Steen*	LG	28	6/6	327	0	0.0	3	5
Jermon Bushrod*	RG	34	10/10	605	7	2.0	7	3	Daniel Kilgore	C	31	16/16	1100	7	4.0	10	12
Ted Larsen	LG	31	8/8	524	4	1.5	8	14	Josh Sitton	LG	32	13/13	712	4	2.0	2	8

Year	Yards	ALY	Rank	Power	Rank	Stuff	Rank	2nd Lev	Rank	Open Field	Rank	Sacks	ASR	Rank	Press	Rank	F-Start	Cont.
2015	4.28	3.76	28	58%	27	24%	30	1.22	7	1.01	7	45	7.6%	24	28.2%	25	19	33
2016	4.59	3.97	22	52%	28	24%	31	1.40	3	1.13	4	30	6.3%	21	26.8%	18	14	25
2017	4.09	3.26	30	71%	6	27%	30	1.09	20	1.07	4	33	5.8%	11	29.6%	10	21	30

2017 ALY by direction:	Left End: 1.82 (31)	Left Tackle: 3.44 (22)	Mid/Guard: 3.51 (31)	Right Tackle: 2.47 (30)	Right End: 3.86 (18)

The Dolphins decided to pay two players over one in releasing longtime center Mike Pouncey to bring in Bears cap casualty Josh Sitton at right guard and make a trade for ex-49ers center Daniel Kilgore. Sitton still plays at a high level, but Kilgore has been a disappointment in terms of both ability and availability. On talent, Miami made a slight improvement in this trade if you include "not having to play Jermon Bushrod again," but it's hardly a masterstroke. ☞ The first year at left tackle for Laremy Tunsil was a bit of an adventure. The pass-blocking was adequate but didn't live up to franchise blind side standards. The run blocking was average. Ja'Waun James is on his fifth-year option on the right side and has been about what you would expect from a late first-round right tackle project. ☞ The left guard spot will be won by either third-year UDFA Jesse Davis or journeyman Ted Larsen. Davis likely has more upside than Larsen and started games at three different line positions last season. Larsen was dead last among 102 interior linemen in snaps per blown block last year (minimum 400 blocking snaps).

Defensive Front Seven

Defensive Line	Age	Pos	Overall							vs. Run					Pass Rush			
			G	Snaps	Plays	TmPct	Rk	Stop	Dfts	BTkl	Runs	St%	Rk	RuYd	Rk	Sack	Hit	Hur	Dsrpt
Ndamukong Suh*	31	DT	16	883	50	6.5%	17	40	18	2	40	78%	44	1.6	22	4.5	10	20.5	3
Davon Godchaux	24	DT	15	504	41	5.7%	32	33	6	1	38	79%	36	2.0	36	0.0	3	7.0	0
Jordan Phillips	26	DT	13	404	19	3.0%	82	14	7	2	10	80%	32	2.2	46	2.0	4	11.5	3
Akeem Spence	27	DT	16	661	39	4.6%	52	31	10	4	33	76%	54	1.7	30	3.0	7	13.0	0

Edge Rushers	Age	Pos	Overall							vs. Run					Pass Rush			
			G	Snaps	Plays	TmPct	Rk	Stop	Dfts	BTkl	Runs	St%	Rk	RuYd	Rk	Sack	Hit	Hur	Dsrpt
Cameron Wake	36	DE	16	615	34	4.4%	56	23	14	2	18	61%	88	4.4	93	10.5	16	29.5	1
Andre Branch	29	DE	14	565	24	3.6%	74	19	11	2	16	81%	28	1.9	31	4.5	4	17.0	1
Charles Harris	23	DE	16	500	21	2.7%	90	16	8	1	15	73%	52	2.2	43	2.0	10	19.0	2
William Hayes	33	DE	10	274	19	3.9%	67	18	5	0	18	94%	4	1.1	12	1.0	4	8.0	0
Robert Quinn	28	OLB	15	634	33	4.3%	61	24	17	5	16	56%	93	5.4	95	9.0	5	19.0	0

Linebackers	Age	Pos	Overall							vs. Run					Pass Rush			vs. Pass					
			G	Snaps	Plays	TmPct	Rk	Stop	Dfts	BTkl	Runs	St%	Rk	RuYd	Rk	Sack	Hit	Hur	Tgts	Suc%	Rk	AdjYd	Rk	PD	Int
Kiko Alonso	28	OLB	16	1016	115	14.9%	23	50	20	13	48	65%	34	4.1	63	1.0	5	7.5	67	42%	58	8.1	64	1	0
Lawrence Timmons*	32	OLB	14	801	87	12.9%	36	59	13	16	49	73%	13	3.4	33	0.0	5	10.0	34	59%	11	4.7	6	1	0
Chase Allen	25	OLB	16	225	33	4.3%	--	23	2	6	28	75%	--	2.9	--	0.0	0	0.0	6	68%	--	3.6	--	0	0
Mike Hull	27	MLB	16	183	26	3.4%	--	15	4	4	14	57%	--	4.3	--	0.0	1	1.0	10	65%	--	6.6	--	0	0
Rey Maualuga*	31	MLB	6	177	23	7.9%	76	12	2	6	16	63%	42	4.4	70	0.0	0	0.0	7	43%	--	5.9	--	0	0

Year	Yards	ALY	Rank	Power	Rank	Stuff	Rank	2nd Level	Rank	Open Field	Rank	Sacks	ASR	Rank	Press	Rank
2015	4.08	3.85	10	66%	16	24%	8	1.21	23	0.84	19	31	5.9%	22	25.3%	15
2016	4.54	4.32	18	57%	6	22%	10	1.45	32	0.82	23	33	4.7%	31	31.4%	4
2017	4.13	3.94	10	50%	3	24%	5	1.26	27	0.85	25	30	5.7%	27	27.7%	29

2017 ALY by direction:	Left End: 4.85 (27)	Left Tackle: 4.68 (26)	Mid/Guard: 3.61 (4)	Right Tackle: 3.23 (9)	Right End: 5.89 (31)

The post-Ndamukong Suh Dolphins don't have much in the way of front-end talent in the defensive front seven, but they have a lot of solid players. 2017 first-round end Charles Harris looks poised to step in for Suh's production somewhere on the line. Harris racked up a ton of hurries in limited snaps last year and would likely deserve an expanded role even if Suh were still around. More than a few draftniks noted he might be a good fit as an interior rusher, something that the Dolphins may want to test in their nickel packages. ☞ Cameron Wake continues to be impossible to block even well into his mid-thirties. The star edge rusher has notched 10 sacks in three of his last four seasons and recorded seven in just seven games in the other. ☞ Miami dealt for Rams edge rusher Robert Quinn, a move that would have really piqued eyebrows in 2014. Quinn missed a bunch of time in 2015 and 2016, then was somewhat of a disappointment in 2017 as a stand-up rusher for Wade Phillips. Perhaps moving back to 4-3 end will rejuvenate him—many other teams were interested in trading for Quinn. ☞ The direct replacement for Suh will likely be Davon Godchaux or flyer Akeem Spence, who was re-united with former Lions defensive line coach Kris Kocurek in a trade for a conditional seventh-round pick in April. Godchaux would seem to have the upper hand. ☞ Andre Branch is a fine third end, though wildly overpaid at a $10 million cap number for the last real year of his deal. Jordan Phillips is a candidate to be that overpaid next year after he hits the market as the rare nose who can add a little pressure. ☞ Kiko Alonso has a cap figure of $9.6 million and can't cover whatever you're sitting in as you read this. ☞ The awesomely named Raekwon McMillan tore his ACL in the first preseason game of his rookie season, but his second-round status and the lack of alternatives should make him a shoe-in to start at middle linebacker. He had good speed coming out of Ohio State and, paired with his instincts in zone, a healthy return should see him as a three-down linebacker. ☞ Third-rounder Jerome Baker (Ohio State) offers premium speed and coverage ability but was dinged for his lack of physicality and tackling ability. ☞ Primary special-teamers Chase Allen and Mike Hull round out the depth chart, though it's worth saying a word about former New Orleans first-round pick Stephone Anthony. He definitely had NFL-level speed and physicality coming out of college. Given the lack of players ahead of him on the depth chart, we may see him resurface here.

Defensive Secondary

Secondary	Age	Pos	G	Snaps	Plays	Overall TmPct	Rk	Stop	Dfts	BTkl	vs. Run Runs	St%	Rk	RuYd	Rk	vs. Pass Tgts	Tgt%	Rk	Dist	Suc%	Rk	AdjYd	Rk	PD	Int
Xavien Howard	25	CB	16	1024	60	7.8%	51	27	14	8	15	40%	47	4.5	13	75	16.5%	15	12.7	55%	17	5.7	5	13	4
Reshad Jones	30	SS	16	1022	125	16.2%	1	50	20	10	68	47%	31	7.2	47	43	9.4%	35	12.6	53%	35	9.2	51	7	2
Bobby McCain	25	CB	16	668	52	6.7%	--	20	13	6	6	50%	--	7.3	--	43	14.3%	--	10.5	57%	--	6.6	--	8	2
Cordrea Tankersley	25	CB	11	641	38	7.2%	60	14	5	3	9	11%	80	19.9	79	38	13.2%	5	13.0	46%	71	8.5	62	6	0
T.J. McDonald	27	FS	8	547	48	12.4%	13	18	7	7	25	48%	27	6.9	46	21	8.6%	31	16.0	40%	70	14.4	75	2	1
Nate Allen*	31	FS	7	362	21	6.2%	--	5	2	4	8	25%	--	6.6	--	10	5.9%	--	16.8	37%	--	12.3	--	1	0

Year	Pass D Rank	vs. #1 WR	Rk	vs. #2 WR	Rk	vs. Other WR	Rk	WR Wide	Rk	WR Slot	Rk	vs. TE	Rk	vs. RB	Rk
2015	29	29.4%	32	21.5%	27	9.2%	22	--	--	--	--	-10.5%	11	6.3%	19
2016	16	-15.1%	5	-15.6%	4	22.9%	31	-20.5%	2	13.2%	23	4.7%	21	-11.1%	10
2017	29	11.2%	22	-8.2%	11	15.4%	23	0.0%	17	9.7%	19	17.1%	28	1.8%	18

Cordrea Tankersley had a fairly solid rookie season, only missing a few games to concussion. The Dolphins mainly played press-man coverage last season, and Tankersley's biggest strength was that opposing receivers rarely found any yardage after the catch against him (2.2 YAC average, seventh of 80 qualifying corners). Hard outside fakes were a bugaboo, though, and he'll have to learn to play balls in the middle of the field better. ☞ Despite an excellent yards-per-pass number, Howard was incredibly up and down in his second year. Howard has the size, speed, and fluidity to be a great press-man corner but was feinted out of his position often and gave up quite a few touchdowns in coverage. 2017 was a step up in his development, but he's capable of more. ☞ Depth is also a strength. Bobby McCain had a terrific year in the slot, and 2015 fifth-rounder Tony Lippett also showed some flashes before missing all of last year with a torn Achilles. ☞ Signed to a huge extension with $35 million guaranteed before the 2017 season, Reshad Jones is a nice front-seven safety with a lot of versatility. He restructured to help the Dolphins this offseason, and his contract terms will look more onerous later. For now, though, he should continue to be a plus. ☞ With the ninth overall pick, the Dolphins found a franchise safety in Alabama's Minkah Fitzpatrick, a rare four-year Crimson Tide starter. Fitzpatrick offers a lot of flexibility to the Dolphins defense and could even transition them into some dime looks as a Deone Bucannon-esque linebacker. ☞ T.J. McDonald joined as a Jeff Fisher refugee and immediately parlayed that into a four-year deal with $10 million in guarantees. He missed eight games last season after a DUI led to a suspension. As long as he can stay out of trouble with John Law, McDonald's a decent role player.

Special Teams

Year	DVOA	Rank	FG/XP	Rank	Net Kick	Rank	Kick Ret	Rank	Net Punt	Rank	Punt Ret	Rank	Hidden	Rank
2015	-2.7%	24	-1.7	22	0.8	14	-9.1	31	-11.2	28	7.9	4	18.8	1
2016	0.8%	12	-6.2	27	6.0	5	6.6	6	-3.5	22	1.2	12	21.0	1
2017	2.6%	12	3.4	12	5.3	6	-1.5	19	6.6	6	-0.6	19	6.4	5

Rookie punter Matt Haack was average, but the Dolphins had excellent punt coverage. Most of the core special-teamers are still here, but Miami will miss Mike Thomas, who has ranked first or second on the team in special teams tackles for three years. He signed with the Giants. ☞ With kicker Cody Parkey walking, the Dolphins will have a training camp battle between UDFA Greg Joseph (Florida Atlantic) and seventh-rounder Jason Sanders (New Mexico). Or, you know, they'll sign someone later if those don't work out. ☞ Jakeem Grant is likely ticketed for another year of returns, with occasional appearances by Senorise Perry to back him up.

Minnesota Vikings

2017 Record: 13-3	**Total DVOA:** 25.1% (4th)	**2018 Mean Projection:** 9.2 wins	**On the Clock (0-4):** 4%
Pythagorean Wins: 11.7 (4th)	**Offense:** 12.0% (5th)	**Postseason Odds:** 53.0%	**Mediocrity (5-7):** 21%
Snap-Weighted Age: 27.1 (4th)	**Defense:** -13.9% (2nd)	**Super Bowl Odds:** 10.1%	**Playoff Contender (8-10):** 44%
Average Opponent: 2.4% (8th)	**Special Teams:** -0.9% (18th)	**Proj. Avg. Opponent:** -0.4% (22nd)	**Super Bowl Contender (11+):** 31%

2017: The home Super Bowl that just wasn't meant to be.

2018: Captain Kirk looks to lead where no Minnesota team has gone before.

Since the advent of 16-game schedules in 1978, the Vikings have had three seasons with at least 12 wins, and each one gave fans dreams about that elusive Super Bowl victory. 1998 was an incredible 15-1 campaign where a senior Randall Cunningham and a rookie Randy Moss led a record-setting scoring attack that came a field goal short of getting to the Super Bowl. In 2009, a 40-year-old Brett Favre put on a virtuoso performance that ended just short of the big one after The Gunslinger misfired in game-winning field goal range against the Saints, who won in overtime. In 2017, Case Keenum shocked everyone by breaking out in his sixth season to lead the league in passing DVOA and guide the Vikings to another NFC Championship Game. However, the clock struck midnight on Keenum in Philadelphia, where the Eagles stomped the favored Vikings 38-7.

The problem with these dream seasons for Minnesota fans: they always awaken *before* the team gets to the Super Bowl, to the cold reality of another Championship Sunday disappointment. This latest loss was especially tough since the Vikings would have played Super Bowl LII in their home at U.S. Bank Stadium. Things seemed to be falling their way all year, starting with major quarterback injuries in the NFC to rival Aaron Rodgers (caused by a hit from Minnesota linebacker Anthony Barr) and Carson Wentz on the top-seeded Eagles. Of course, there was also the Minneapolis Miracle when New Orleans' rookie Marcus Williams ducked in coverage on Stefon Diggs, who raced 61 yards for the first ever fourth-quarter walk-off touchdown in NFL playoff history.

Lest we forget, Minnesota had a 7-0 lead in Philadelphia in the NFC Championship Game, but everything snowballed after Keenum threw a pick-six. That's not to make Keenum the scapegoat for the loss, because the whole Minnesota team played very poorly that day. It was uncharacteristic of head coach Mike Zimmer, who has quietly built an impressive record over the last four seasons in Minnesota. Zimmer is 44-23 (.657) against the point spread, the best record among active head coaches (Table 1).

Zimmer's 31-point loss in Philadelphia is the third-worst loss by a favorite in the playoffs since 1990. The worst still belongs to the 2000 Vikings, who fell 41-0 to the Giants in the NFC Championship Game. (We promise not to bring up many more nightmares from Minnesota's past.)

The successors to those past dream seasons fell apart when the quarterbacks showed a need for Medicaid, which is what happened to Cunningham at age 36 in 1999 and Favre at age 41 in 2010. That shouldn't have been the case this time with Keenum entering his age-30 season, but the Vikings pulled a plot twist worthy of *The Bachelor*. Zimmer had been enjoying casual flings and getting the best out of Teddy Bridgewater (2015), Sam Bradford (2016), and Keenum the last three years, but all three were free to see other people in 2018. Instead of making a long-term commitment to any of these guys with shaky histories, the Vikings decided to present Kirk Cousins with the final rose that Washington never gave him. Of course Cousins accepted the offer when the Vikings offered a fully guaranteed contract for three years and $84 million, the first contract of its kind in the NFL. Cousins' $28 million per year salary briefly set a new benchmark until Atlanta's Matt Ryan surpassed it in May. Still, this is major money for a quarterback with just three years as a full-time starter, someone who has never thrown for 30 touchdowns in a season or won a playoff game.

Yet this is a marriage that needed to happen. Quarterbacks of Cousins' caliber and age (he'll turn 30 in August) almost never hit the market in good health. Cousins passed for at least 4,000 yards and 25 touchdowns in three consecutive seasons for Washington. Minnesota has had three such seasons by a quarterback in team history, and the Vikings have not had the same passing leader for more than two years in a row since Daunte Culpepper's five-year run from 2000 to 2004.

Table 1. Best Active Coach Records vs. Point Spread

Rk	Head Coach	Games	Record	Pct
1	Mike Zimmer	67	44-23	.657
2	Sean McDermott	17	10-6-1	.618
3	Doug Pederson	35	21-14	.600
4	Mike McCarthy	210	118-86-6	.576
5	Bill Belichick	407	229-168-10	.575
6	Doug Marrone	53	30-23	.566
7	Kyle Shanahan	16	9-7	.563
8	Ron Rivera	119	64-51-4	.555
9	Pat Shurmur	33	17-14-2	.545
10	Andy Reid	328	176-147-5	.544
11	Sean Payton	188	100-85-3	.540
12	Todd Bowles	51	26-22-3	.539

Spread data source: Pro Football Reference

2018 Vikings Schedule

Week	Opp.	Week	Opp.	Week	Opp.
1	SF	7	at NYJ	13	at NE
2	at GB	8	NO	14	at SEA (Mon.)
3	BUF	9	DET	15	MIA
4	at LAR (Thu.)	10	BYE	16	at DET
5	at PHI	11	at CHI	17	CHI
6	ARI	12	GB		

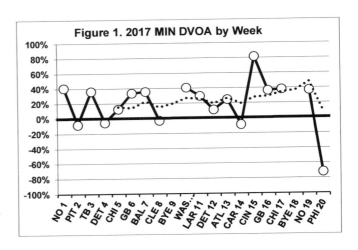

Figure 1. 2017 MIN DVOA by Week

The Vikings needed stability at quarterback, but what exactly are they getting with Cousins? He can be a polarizing figure for analysts. Some see a top-10 passer with his best years ahead of him, while others see a system quarterback who will never lead a team anywhere. The truth may be somewhere in the middle. The passer-friendly era into which Cousins was drafted in 2012 has a lot to do with the impressive numbers he has compiled over the last three years. Cousins is a pocket passer with good accuracy. He has the fourth-highest completion rate (65.5 percent) in NFL history, but he only ranks sixth in that category since 2012.[1] Cousins is also in the top 25 in lowest interception rate (2.6 percent) in NFL history, but he ranks just 30th since 2012. He consistently throws a dozen picks a season as a full-time starter, though some of the uglier ones would lead you to believe he has bigger problems with taking care of the ball. Cousins also ranks seventh in NFL history with 261.4 passing yards per game, but he is sixth among active quarterbacks, and four more active players are within 6 yards of his average.

Basically, Cousins is the Matt Schaub (circa 2008-2012) of this era. While Atlanta fans were spellbound by Michael Vick's scrambles, Schaub was actually the steadier pro passer between the two. Cousins had a similar role in Washington as a fourth-round pick while Robert Griffin III was receiving all the accolades in their rookie season in 2012. Since becoming the full-time starter in 2015, Cousins shows up in great company on many statistical leaderboards. For example, Cousins takes a sack on 4.81 percent of his dropbacks, which puts him right between Matt Ryan (4.75 percent) and Tom Brady (4.88 percent) for their careers.

But like Schaub, Cousins tends to stick out like a sore thumb at times. Since 2001, these are the leaders in passing yards per attempt (always a key stat) on first down: Peyton Manning (8.70), Trent Green (8.51), Kirk Cousins (8.39), and Matt Schaub (8.24). Griffin (8.17) is actually fifth, and it should be noted that Cousins, Schaub, and Griffin all excelled under Kyle Shanahan as a playcaller. Shanahan is also credited for helping Matt Ryan in his 2016 MVP season, and now for what he's doing with Jimmy Garoppolo in San Francisco as a head coach. This lends some credence to the system quarterback theory, but Shanahan was out of Washington after 2013. Cousins was then stuck with offensive coordinator Sean McVay for three years, which … actually strengthens the system quarterback argument. Look at the incredible turnaround job that McVay did with the Rams and Jared Goff last year.

Alas, 2017 really showed that Cousins deserves more credit for his success. McVay was gone, as were Cousins' top wideouts in Pierre Garcon and DeSean Jackson. The Redskins had the second-most adjusted games lost to injury (70.6) on offense, and were hit especially hard along the offensive line. Cousins was still statistically respectable despite all the inefficiencies around him. Some will put Cousins down for having a 26-31-1 record as a starter, but Washington has been battered by injuries for the last three years. The defense has never ranked higher than 16th in points per drive allowed, yet Cousins has continued to keep this team competitive in the deeper conference.

In 2016, Washington missed the playoffs with an 8-7-1 record. Cousins took a lot of heat for a poor showing in Week 17 against the Giants. However, earlier that season he led a go-ahead touchdown drive in Detroit with 1:05 left, only to see the defense give up a 75-yard touchdown drive in a 20-17 loss that ultimately decided the No. 6 seed. In overtime against the Bengals, Cousins set Washington up for a 34-yard field goal to win the game, but Dustin Hopkins missed and the game ended in a tie. That's a thin margin between 8-7-1 and 10-6, and Cousins did his job both times.

Those who view Cousins as a stat compiler will also point out that Washington was just 3-13 against playoff teams in the last three seasons. Where are the signature wins for Cousins? How can he be expected to win three or four games in the playoffs when he has three such wins spread out over three years? Those questions may be fair for the $28 Million Man, but just last year he led game-winning drives on the road against the Rams and Seahawks. A signature win looked to be in sight in Kansas City on Monday Night Football in Week 4, but Josh Doctson dropped a go-ahead touchdown in the final minute before the Chiefs won. In New Orleans, Cousins was excellent in building a 31-16 lead for his team with six minutes to play, but the defense again failed to hold on, allowing Drew Brees to lead the Saints back for a stunning 34-31 overtime win. Brees only got

---

1 Yes, you read that correctly. Peyton Manning, Tony Romo, and Alex Smith rank ahead of Cousins since 2012, but rank behind him in career completion rate because of their numbers prior to 2012. The interception rate numbers are similar.

the ball back in regulation to tie after the Redskins failed to convert a third-and-1 run. Failed runs were a staple during Cousins' tenure in Washington—the team's rushing offense ranked 32nd in DVOA in 2015 and 28th in 2017.

Like with Schaub—at least before Richard Sherman shattered his confidence forever with a pick-six in 2013—we probably have not been giving Cousins enough credit for functioning at the level he has for multiple seasons. Even if these players are not as great as their numbers suggest, they're also better than the reputation they carry.

Now for the burning question: how much of an upgrade is Cousins over Keenum? This is a tricky one since Cousins has given us three quality seasons to analyze while Keenum's 2017 is one of the most unlikely breakout years by a quarterback on record. One defining quality of Keenum's success was his ability to handle pressure. Thanks to escaping countless sacks and making throws on the move, Keenum pulled off the rare feat of having positive DVOA (6.8%) while under pressure. Cousins had his usual so-so performance under pressure, ranking 18th in DVOA (-55.8%). Table 2 shows how Cousins and the Minnesota starting quarterback have fared with and without pressure since 2014.

Table 2. Kirk Cousins vs. Minnesota QBs Under Pressure Since 2014

Year	Player	DVOA with Pressure	Rk	DVOA w/o Pressure	Rk	Pressure Pct.	Rk
2014	K.Cousins	-75.2%	20	35.6%	25	17.6%	3
	T.Bridgewater	-102.8%	32	45.3%	18	28.3%	28
2015	K.Cousins	-110.1%	35	69.0%	4	20.5%	5
	T.Bridgewater	-62.9%	14	53.8%	12	36.0%	37
2016	K.Cousins	-54.5%	15	65.5%	4	24.9%	13
	S.Bradford	-72.2%	21	36.7%	24	24.5%	11
2017	K.Cousins	-55.8%	18	60.0%	13	35.6%	27
	C.Keenum	6.8%	2	59.0%	15	39.0%	33

Minnesota quarterbacks have often faced more pressure than Cousins, which in part is a testament to his ability to get rid of the ball quickly. However, Cousins has never been anything special under pressure, and he lacks the scrambling ability to make things happen that way. As Keenum's brutal 2016 with the Rams and his shaky postseason last year show, performance under pressure is difficult to sustain or repeat. Still, it's a nice area in which to excel at times, and it is the one area where the Vikings may actually be taking a step backwards with this move. Cousins will need better protection than what Keenum had last year for this to be a big success.

Helping Cousins acclimate to his new surroundings will be new offensive coordinator John DeFilippo, who is taking over for Pat Shurmur, now the Giants' head coach. This is a big task for the quarterback-centric DeFilippo, who has a spotty resume, including stops as the position coach for troubled rookies JaMarcus Russell (2007 Raiders), Mark Sanchez (2009 Jets), and Derek Carr (2014 Raiders). However, DeFilippo was in Philadelphia the last two years where he helped Carson Wentz along and got Nick Foles ready for the biggest games

of his life. Now he has a chance to create something new with Cousins and a very talented roster. DeFilippo said in February that "the three most important attributes of playing the quarterback position are decision-making, timing and accuracy."

Is instant success likely? As much as building chemistry is associated with offense, these things usually work right away if they're going to work at all. Even Chad Pennington received MVP votes in 2008 after signing with the Dolphins in August. A 31-year-old Brad Johnson once pulled off the Reverse Cousins (going from Minnesota to Washington) in 1999 and led that offense to great heights right away in a playoff season.

We said before that quarterbacks like Cousins rarely hit the market. In fact, we dug up every example we could find, but some constraints needed to be applied. This wasn't like adding Ryan Fitzpatrick or Josh McCown to a bad team. This also wasn't like Shaun Hill getting starts for the 2010 Lions and 2014 Rams just because Matthew Stafford and Sam Bradford were injured again. We wanted to find free-agent quarterbacks who were actually intended to be new starters for contenders.

We found 28 instances since 1970 where a playoff team added a quarterback age 28 or older, and that player threw at least 200 passes in his debut season with his new team. Eight of those 28 cases were Minnesota teams, so Vikings fans are more used to this than anyone. However, not all of these examples are similar to Cousins, because 12 times the team was only starting this player because the intended starter was injured or benched. That includes Jay Cutler coming out of retirement last August to replace an injured Ryan Tannehill in Miami, as well as four Minnesota examples. Jeff George wasn't supposed to lead the 1999 Vikings, but Cunningham was benched after an ineffective start. Brad Johnson's second Minnesota stint in 2005 happened after Daunte Culpepper tore his ACL. Matt Cassel wasn't acquired to lead the 2013 Vikings, but Christian Ponder was in and out of the lineup with injuries. Teddy Bridgewater suffered that gruesome knee injury in the 2016 preseason, prompting the team to trade for Sam Bradford just before Week 1.

In the end we were left with 15 examples, which are listed in Table 3. Peyton Manning (2012 Broncos) and Favre (2009 Vikings) were two of the most recent, but also two of the most successful. None of these 15 players got to a Super Bowl in his debut season, but Manning (2013 Broncos) and Brad Johnson (2002 Buccaneers) got there in their second seasons with their new teams. Johnson won his ring behind a great defense, and Manning finally got his second in 2015 behind another great defense. Most of these players did not last more than a season or two with their new team, but Cousins is also one of the youngest players listed.

Is Cousins as good as a Manning or Brees? No, but he doesn't have to be to win a Super Bowl. Manning clearly wasn't himself in 2015 when he won behind Denver's great defense. Does Minnesota's defense have to be 2015 Denver quality to win a Super Bowl? No, because the offense should be stronger than Manning's Broncos were that season, providing a better balance. Remember, this is a league where Nick Foles is the reigning Super Bowl MVP after he got the job done with a great supporting cast in Philadelphia. Eli Manning (twice) and Joe Flacco were great enough for one month to win Super Bowls. If Cousins can always keep a flawed team around .500 in Washington, then why can't he excel with one of the most talented rosters in the NFL and win the whole damn thing with Minnesota?

Expectations are understandably high right away with Cousins added to a 13-3 team. We tend to avoid position-by-position rundowns in these essays, but Minnesota's roster deserves some respect. Cousins has arguably the best wide receiver duo in the league in Diggs and Adam Thielen. Kyle Rudolph has been a Pro Bowl tight end, while Dalvin Cook returns to the backfield with Latavius Murray. The offensive line is not a strength, but it also should not be an issue like it was in 2016 to prevent this team from winning a championship—especially not with a defense that is stacked with so much talent at each level. The defensive line already had superb edge rushers in Danielle Hunter and Everson Griffen and a run-stopper in Linval Joseph, and now the Vikings welcome Sheldon Richardson to the starting lineup. Anthony Barr and Eric Kendricks are two very good linebackers. Safety Harrison Smith and cornerback Xavier Rhodes are both All-Pro selections in the secondary. Maybe Kai Forbath will be the latest kicker to ruin things for Cousins, but he's serviceable.

Where can things go wrong? Injuries, of course, but we can say that for every team. However, while Minnesota's starting 22 can match up with any team, there are several positions where the Vikings are notably thin or top-heavy. An injury to Diggs or Thielen would leave a pretty pedestrian receiving corps as neither Kendall Wright nor Laquon Treadwell can get open against man coverage the way those players can. When Cousins lost Jordan Reed in Washington, he still had Vernon Davis to throw to. The Vikings have no such answer at tight end behind Rudolph. Even with Cook's return, the Vikings lost a versatile back in Jerick McKinnon, who filled in admirably last year.

The defensive side of the ball is where things could especially get interesting, or ugly depending on your perspective. The backups at defensive tackle, linebacker, and safety are filled with inexperienced players, late-round picks, and undrafted free agents. Last year, Minnesota had the healthiest defense with just 4.9 adjusted games lost (AGL) on its way to a No. 2 ranking in DVOA. That type of injury luck is unlikely to repeat itself in 2018. We looked at every team since 2002 which had the lowest AGL on defense and how it fared the following year in defensive AGL and DVOA (Table 4). These teams went from first in AGL to an average rank of 15.3, so very close to the middle of the pack. Only the 2006-07 Chiefs were able to have the healthiest defense two years in a row. These defenses also slipped an average of roughly seven spots in the DVOA rankings in the following year.

Injuries are an unpredictable part of the game, but the Vikings are returning 10 of 11 defensive starters from last year (everyone but defensive tackle Tom Johnson). That's also 10 starters from the playoff loss in Philadelphia where the Eagles embarrassed Minnesota on third down by converting 10 of their first 13 opportunities before a meaningless kneeldown to end the game. That was especially hard to see after Minnesota was historically great on third down in the regular season. Minnesota allowed opponents to only convert 25.2 percent of third downs, the lowest rate since at least 1991. They were in the top four in conversion rate and DVOA for all third-down splits, so some regression is expected there. Between expectations for more injuries and fewer third-down successes in 2018, there are reasons to be down on this defense living up to its 2017 reputation.

One counterpoint for how things could get better: takeaways. Minnesota only ranked 22nd in takeaways per drive, and the defense managed just one takeaway in the four losses last season. As championship teams have shown us time and time again, you have to take the ball away in big moments in the postseason.

Best-case scenario: Cousins keeps the offense hot and leads the Vikings over the hump in the playoffs to win their first Super Bowl. If the Eagles can do it with Foles, then all bets are off, right? More realistically, the Vikings are a definite playoff contender, but it's a deep NFC that should especially be stronger in the division. Minnesota cannot count on Aaron Rodgers to be injured for both matchups this year, and the Lions and Bears have new head coaches who may not be the cardboard cutouts

Table 3. Notable Debuts of Age-28+ Quarterbacks on Playoff Teams

Team	Year	QB1	TmRec	Result	Y N+1	New QB	Age	TmRec	Result	Quarterback Note
HOIL	1969	Pete Beathard	6-6-2	Lost AFL-DIV	1970	Charley Johnson	32	3-10-1	No playoffs	3-11 as HOIL starter (1970-71)
MIN	1971	Gary Cuozzo	11-3	Lost NFC-DIV	1972	Fran Tarkenton	32	7-7	No playoffs	Started 3 Super Bowls (0-3)
HOIL	1979	Dan Pastorini	11-5	Lost AFC-CG	1980	Ken Stabler	35	11-5	Lost AFC-WC	1980: Last career playoff game
LAR	1984	Jeff Kemp	10-6	Lost NFC-WC	1985	Dieter Brock	34	11-5	Lost NFC-CG	Only played one NFL season
KC	1992	Dave Krieg	10-6	Lost AFC-WC	1993	Joe Montana	37	11-5	Lost AFC-CG	Retired after 1994
MIN	1992	Rich Gannon	11-5	Lost NFC-WC	1993	Jim McMahon	34	9-7	Lost NFC-WC	Went to ARI in 1994
NO	1992	Bobby Hebert	12-4	Lost NFC-WC	1993	Wade Wilson	34	8-8	No playoffs	Backed up Jim Everett in 1994
MIN	1993	Jim McMahon	9-7	Lost NFC-WC	1994	Warren Moon	38	10-6	Lost NFC-WC	1994: Last career playoff game
MIA	1999	Dan Marino	9-7	Lost AFC-DIV	2000	Jay Fiedler	29	11-5	Lost AFC-DIV	Five-year starter in Miami
BAL	2000	Trent Dilfer	12-4	Won SB	2001	Elvis Grbac	31	10-6	Lost AFC-DIV	Retired after season
TB	2000	Shaun King	10-6	Lost NFC-WC	2001	Brad Johnson	33	9-7	Lost NFC-WC	2002: Won SB XXXVII
DAL	2003	Quincy Carter	10-6	Lost NFC-WC	2004	Vinny Testaverde	41	6-10	No playoffs	Back to NYJ in 2005
MIN	2008	Gus Frerotte	10-6	Lost NFC-WC	2009	Brett Favre	40	12-4	Lost NFC-CG	Retired after 2010
SEA	2010	Matt Hasselbeck	7-9	Lost NFC-DIV	2011	Tarvaris Jackson	28	7-9	No playoffs	Russell Wilson's backup 2013-15
DEN	2011	Tim Tebow	8-8	Lost AFC-DIV	2012	Peyton Manning	36	13-3	Lost AFC-DIV	Retired after SB 50 win

Jim Caldwell and John Fox were. The schedule also could be particularly grueling this season. In the first five weeks, Minnesota has to travel to Green Bay, Los Angeles (Rams), and Philadelphia. After Thanksgiving, there is a three-game stretch where the Vikings host Green Bay before traveling to New England and Seattle, two of the toughest venues in the NFL.

The window for Minnesota to win is now. Keeping this core together for the long haul is not very feasible, but that's the price of acquiring so many good players in the salary-cap era. In April, Minnesota extended Kendricks to a five-year deal worth $50 million, and in late June it was Hunter's turn for a five-year extension worth $72 million with $40 million guaranteed. When Cousins' cap number balloons to $29 million in 2019, the Vikings will still have two key free agents in Diggs and Barr. When you sign a quarterback to such a big contract, you have to believe he is the type of player who will help save money at other positions. It's not clear that Cousins is that kind of quarterback, but he is worth the gamble if the Vikings are ever going to turn the long-awaited dream of a championship into a reality.

Scott Kacsmar

Table 4. The Healthiest Defense and Regression

Year	Team	AGL	Rk	DEF DVOA	Rk	Year N+1	AGL	Rk	DEF DVOA	Rk
2002	DEN	1.0	1	-0.4%	17	2003	20.5	20	-4.2%	12
2003	DAL	0.0	1	-12.7%	5	2004	31.5	21	10.8%	25
2004	HOU	5.3	1	1.9%	18	2005	12.1	13	20.1%	32
2005	ATL	4.6	1	11.9%	28	2006	22.0	21	2.8%	18
2006	KC	3.5	1	2.3%	17	2007	4.1	1	-3.8%	14
2007	KC	4.1	1	-3.8%	14	2008	19.3	14	13.3%	28
2008	MIA	1.6	1	-0.1%	16	2009	21.2	13	1.5%	18
2009	DEN	3.3	1	-9.8%	7	2010	40.7	28	16.6%	30
2010	KC	4.2	1	2.1%	20	2011	21.7	13	-3.2%	13
2011	NO	7.2	1	10.2%	28	2012	23.6	14	14.8%	32
2012	SF	4.5	1	-14.4%	3	2013	46.8	27	-4.6%	13
2013	NYJ	9.1	1	-5.6%	12	2014	22.8	4	3.5%	21
2014	CAR	11.7	1	-1.7%	15	2015	22.7	8	-18.4%	2
2015	NYJ	13.2	1	-13.8%	5	2016	43.7	22	3.7%	21
2016	NE	8.1	1	-1.8%	16	2017	24.6	10	10.9%	31
2017	MIN	4.9	1	-13.9%	2	2018	-	-	-	-
Average		*5.4*	*1.0*	*-3.1%*	*13.9*	-	*25.1*	*15.3*	*4.3%*	*20.7*

2017 Vikings Stats by Week

Wk	vs.	W-L	PF	PA	YDF	YDA	TO	Total	Off	Def	ST
1	NO	W	29	19	470	344	0	41%	42%	-1%	-3%
2	at PIT	L	9	26	237	335	-1	-8%	-3%	9%	3%
3	TB	W	34	17	494	342	+3	36%	39%	0%	-3%
4	DET	L	7	14	284	251	-3	-6%	-16%	-14%	-3%
5	at CHI	W	20	17	300	274	+2	12%	4%	-13%	-5%
6	GB	W	23	10	351	227	+1	34%	-19%	-53%	0%
7	BAL	W	24	16	357	208	-1	36%	6%	-14%	15%
8	at CLE	W	33	16	375	276	+1	-3%	8%	11%	0%
9	BYE										
10	at WAS	W	38	30	406	394	-1	41%	38%	4%	7%
11	LAR	W	24	7	451	254	+1	29%	32%	-11%	-14%
12	at DET	W	30	23	408	289	+2	11%	17%	-6%	-13%
13	at ATL	W	14	9	312	275	0	25%	20%	-1%	3%
14	at CAR	L	24	31	356	345	-2	-9%	-2%	3%	-3%
15	CIN	W	34	7	346	161	+1	82%	0%	-67%	14%
16	at GB	W	16	0	236	239	+2	36%	-6%	-43%	-1%
17	CHI	W	23	10	327	201	0	38%	23%	-28%	-13%
18	BYE										
19	NO	W	29	24	403	358	+1	37%	23%	-20%	-6%
20	at PHI	L	7	38	333	456	-3	-72%	-21%	51%	1%

Trends and Splits

	Offense	Rank	Defense	Rank
Total DVOA	12.0%	5	-13.9%	2
Unadjusted VOA	11.5%	6	-12.7%	4
Weighted Trend	11.2%	6	-18.5%	1
Variance	3.8%	3	5.2%	11
Average Opponent	-0.9%	15	0.5%	13
Passing	36.4%	3	-11.8%	4
Rushing	-7.7%	18	-16.9%	6
First Down	0.9%	17	-5.6%	11
Second Down	22.7%	3	-4.7%	11
Third Down	17.2%	5	-43.1%	1
First Half	14.0%	6	-18.5%	4
Second Half	9.8%	8	-9.7%	7
Red Zone	24.2%	4	-35.1%	2
Late and Close	13.6%	6	-20.8%	6

Five-Year Performance

Year	W-L	Pyth W	Est W	PF	PA	TO	Total	Rk	Off	Rk	Def	Rk	ST	Rk	Off AGL	Rk	Def AGL	Rk	Off Age	Rk	Def Age	Rk	ST Age	Rk
2013	5-10-1	6.1	6.5	391	480	-12	-11.4%	26	-4.7%	21	10.5%	27	3.8%	6	21.4	8	32.5	21	26.6	19	27.1	12	25.8	24
2014	7-9	7.5	7.2	325	343	-1	-8.7%	25	-7.4%	22	4.3%	23	3.0%	10	39.0	23	17.1	3	26.7	17	25.9	29	25.6	28
2015	11-5	9.8	9.5	365	302	+5	5.7%	11	0.0%	16	-1.8%	14	3.9%	4	36.5	17	22.5	7	26.4	19	27.5	4	25.7	22
2016	8-8	8.6	8.6	327	307	+11	-1.7%	20	-9.8%	26	-6.6%	8	1.5%	10	92.1	32	28.6	12	27.1	10	27.8	3	26.3	10
2017	13-3	11.7	12.0	382	252	+5	25.0%	4	12.0%	5	-13.9%	2	-0.9%	18	42.8	20	4.9	1	26.9	17	27.9	3	25.7	23

2017 Performance Based on Most Common Personnel Groups

MIN Offense					MIN Offense vs. Opponents					MIN Defense				MIN Defense vs. Opponents			
Pers	Freq	Yds	DVOA	Run%	Pers	Freq	Yds	DVOA	Run%	Pers	Freq	Yds	DVOA	Pers	Freq	Yds	DVOA
11	56%	6.1	16.8%	30%	Base	34%	5.9	19.7%	62%	Base	21%	4.6	-11.3%	11	63%	5.0	-12.0%
12	21%	5.3	7.0%	60%	Nickel	54%	5.8	9.6%	36%	Nickel	77%	4.9	-16.1%	12	18%	4.9	-1.0%
22	8%	5.1	-1.5%	80%	Dime+	10%	5.3	7.6%	17%	Dime+	0%	5.3	38.8%	21	8%	3.7	-35.5%
21	5%	7.4	31.0%	51%	Goal Line	2%	2.7	81.6%	76%	Goal Line	1%	0.6	-5.7%	13	4%	4.1	-31.3%
13	2%	5.5	14.3%	58%	Big	1%	5.0	6.6%	67%					20	1%	3.6	-50.2%

Strategic Tendencies

Run/Pass		Rk	Formation		Rk	Pass Rush		Rk	Secondary		Rk	Strategy		Rk
Runs, first half	40%	12	Form: Single Back	80%	11	Rush 3	2.3%	28	4 DB	21%	31	Play action	30%	1
Runs, first down	59%	1	Form: Empty Back	6%	22	Rush 4	73.3%	9	5 DB	77%	1	Avg Box (Off)	6.37	6
Runs, second-long	36%	10	Pers: 3+ WR	60%	20	Rush 5	17.9%	21	6+ DB	0%	28	Avg Box (Def)	6.21	20
Runs, power sit.	46%	28	Pers: 2+ TE/6+ OL	36%	6	Rush 6+	6.4%	14	CB by Sides	68%	25	Offensive Pace	29.50	7
Runs, behind 2H	30%	8	Pers: 6+ OL	2%	29	Int DL Sacks	17.6%	23	S/CB Cover Ratio	23%	28	Defensive Pace	31.98	30
Pass, ahead 2H	45%	20	Shotgun/Pistol	53%	23	Second Level Sacks	12.2%	26	DB Blitz	7%	22	Go for it on 4th	0.34	32

Play-action was a hugely important part of the Minnesota offense. The Vikings went play-action more than any other team and had a league-leading 69.0% DVOA on play-action passes. ☞ Of course, it's hard to use play-action from an empty backfield, but the Vikings also had the best offense in the league from those formations, with 75.1% DVOA. ☞ Mike Zimmer's defense, as always, was phenomenal when bringing a big blitz. The Vikings allowed just 5.8 yards per pass with three or four pass-rushers, which improved to 5.2 yards with five pass-rushers and then 2.8 yards with six or more. ☞ Running back screens are a popular strategy against the Minnesota defense, but the Vikings dramatically improved their ability to stop them, going from 8.4 yards per play and 58.7% DVOA in 2016 to 2.3 yards per play and -68.8% DVOA in 2017. ☞ The Vikings continued to be one of the top tackling teams in the league, finishing second in the league with only 85 broken tackles after they had finished sixth in 2016. They also allowed a league-low 4.4 average yards after the catch, including just 6.8 average YAC on passes behind the line of scrimmage. ☞ Minnesota recovered only three of nine fumbles on offense and only four of 12 fumbles on defense.

Passing

Player	DYAR	DVOA	Plays	NtYds	Avg	YAC	C%	TD	Int
C.Keenum*	1293	28.1%	503	3403	6.8	5.6	67.6%	22	7
S.Bradford*	169	44.2%	48	342	7.1	4.8	74.4%	3	0
K.Cousins	395	-0.6%	586	3709	6.3	6.1	64.6%	27	13
T.Siemian	-327	-24.6%	382	2063	5.4	4.9	59.0%	12	14

Rushing

Player	DYAR	DVOA	Plays	Yds	Avg	TD	Fum	Suc
L.Murray	59	-2.3%	216	842	3.9	8	1	44%
J.McKinnon*	-24	-12.7%	150	570	3.8	3	2	43%
D.Cook	48	7.4%	74	354	4.8	2	1	55%
C.Keenum*	76	58.3%	22	180	8.2	1	0	-
S.Diggs	-4	-48.3%	8	13	1.6	0	0	-
C.J.Ham	11	16.2%	7	13	1.9	1	0	71%
K.Cousins	21	-2.3%	36	168	4.7	4	3	-
T.Siemian	1	-11.4%	24	133	5.5	1	1	-
M.Brown*	-9	-30.1%	8	29	3.6	0	0	38%

Receiving

Player	DYAR	DVOA	Plays	Ctch	Yds	Y/C	YAC	TD	C%
A.Thielen	261	10.1%	142	91	1276	14.0	4.9	4	64%
S.Diggs	295	24.7%	95	64	849	13.3	4.7	8	67%
L.Treadwell	-15	-18.2%	35	20	200	10.0	2.9	0	57%
J.Wright*	84	29.0%	25	18	198	11.0	4.9	2	72%
M.Floyd*	-30	-36.4%	17	10	78	7.8	3.4	0	59%
K.Wright	53	-4.8%	91	59	614	10.4	3.1	1	65%
T.King	16	-7.5%	37	18	240	13.3	4.3	3	49%
K.Rudolph	88	8.8%	81	57	532	9.3	4.0	8	70%
D.Morgan	24	20.3%	12	10	95	9.5	5.7	1	83%
J.McKinnon*	48	-0.4%	68	51	421	8.3	9.0	2	75%
L.Murray	2	-11.6%	17	15	103	6.9	8.3	0	88%
D.Cook	-5	-19.0%	16	11	90	8.2	9.5	0	69%
C.J.Ham	34	92.0%	8	7	68	9.7	12.0	0	88%

Offensive Line

Player	Pos	Age	GS	Snaps	Pen	Sk	Pass	Run	Player	Pos	Age	GS	Snaps	Pen	Sk	Pass	Run
Joe Berger*	RG	36	16/16	1116	3	2.5	10	10	Mike Remmers	RT	29	11/11	678	5	1.0	8	7
Riley Reiff	LT	30	15/15	1007	6	3.5	22	18	Rashod Hill	RT	26	11/7	592	4	2.0	16	14
Pat Elflein	C	24	14/14	960	3	3.0	15	17	Jeremiah Sirles*	LG	27	14/4	344	3	0.0	8	1
Nick Easton	LG	26	12/12	750	7	0.0	12	12	Tom Compton	LG/RG	29	11/5	342	1	0.0	6	2

Year	Yards	ALY	Rank	Power	Rank	Stuff	Rank	2nd Lev	Rank	Open Field	Rank	Sacks	ASR	Rank	Press	Rank	F-Start	Cont.
2015	4.55	4.31	10	76%	2	20%	12	1.24	4	1.12	5	45	8.8%	29	36.0%	32	13	48
2016	3.15	3.64	30	47%	31	22%	26	0.81	32	0.28	31	38	6.0%	17	23.6%	10	18	23
2017	3.98	3.96	19	67%	10	21%	19	1.11	17	0.77	13	27	4.4%	6	36.1%	29	11	27

2017 ALY by direction:	Left End: 2.15 (28)	Left Tackle: 4.58 (11)	Mid/Guard: 4.00 (23)	Right Tackle: 4.22 (9)	Right End: 4.34 (11)

There are so many parts of this Minnesota roster upon which we could heap praise, but the offensive line is not one of them. It looked like a huge improvement because the 2016 unit was destroyed by injury, but objects in the mirror may be more mediocre than they appear. General manager Rick Spielman has at least tried to improve this unit, but the results have not been great so far. ☞ Let's start with the tackles. Conventional wisdom said that Riley Reiff would at least be serviceable at left tackle in a quick-passing attack, but had more concerns over Mike Remmers taking over at right tackle where, as a member of the Panthers, he infamously fell apart against Von Miller in Super Bowl 50. The fact is, Reiff actually had worse numbers in blown blocks than Remmers. Reiff ranked 29th among left tackles in snaps per blown block while Remmers was 10th among right tackles. If both could just play at a league-average level in 2018, then that should suit Kirk Cousins well enough. He dealt with a lot of injured offensive linemen in Washington. ☞ Right guard Joe Berger was arguably the most consistent of Minnesota's linemen last year, but he retired in the offseason. Tom Compton, who has 11 career starts and was taken in the same Washington draft as Cousins in 2012, could take over that position. ☞ Left guard Nick Easton struggled last year and ranked 31st in snaps per blown block, but he was new to the position. A fractured ankle also kept Easton out of the postseason. ☞ Rookie center Pat Elflein showed some flashes, but also ranked 31st in snaps per blown block. ☞ Seeking a future replacement? Enter second-round rookie tackle Brian O'Neill from Pittsburgh. He has been praised for his athleticism, but the most common knocks are on his lack of strength and composure. "O'Neill needs to get thicker and stronger or swing tackle could be his ceiling," wrote NFL draft analyst Lance Zierlein. Ouch.

Defensive Front Seven

Defensive Line	Age	Pos	G	Snaps	Plays	TmPct	Rk	Stop	Dfts	BTkl	Runs	St%	Rk	RuYd	Rk	Sack	Hit	Hur	Dsrpt
						Overall						**vs. Run**				**Pass Rush**			
Tom Johnson*	34	DT	16	675	32	4.3%	57	24	8	4	27	74%	59	2.2	50	2.0	11	22.0	1
Linval Joseph	30	DT	16	664	68	9.1%	2	46	8	3	58	71%	67	3.2	80	3.5	8	14.0	0
Shamar Stephen*	27	DT	15	384	28	4.0%	63	21	2	2	26	73%	61	2.8	72	1.0	2	7.0	0
Sheldon Richardson	28	DT	15	655	45	5.8%	28	32	8	6	38	71%	66	3.1	76	1.0	10	15.0	1

Edge Rushers	Age	Pos	G	Snaps	Plays	TmPct	Rk	Stop	Dfts	BTkl	Runs	St%	Rk	RuYd	Rk	Sack	Hit	Hur	Dsrpt
						Overall						**vs. Run**				**Pass Rush**			
Everson Griffen	31	DE	15	795	46	6.6%	22	37	20	4	29	72%	57	2.9	70	13.0	15	36.5	3
Danielle Hunter	24	DE	16	775	46	6.2%	26	38	16	3	33	79%	35	2.8	68	7.0	5	39.5	1
Brian Robison	35	DE	15	563	22	3.1%	81	20	9	2	13	92%	6	2.7	67	4.0	4	21.5	3

Linebackers	Age	Pos	G	Snaps	Plays	TmPct	Rk	Stop	Dfts	BTkl	Runs	St%	Rk	RuYd	Rk	Sack	Hit	Hur	Tgts	Suc%	Rk	AdjYd	Rk	PD	Int
						Overall						**vs. Run**				**Pass Rush**				**vs. Pass**					
Eric Kendricks	26	ILB	16	970	117	15.7%	15	63	25	16	63	54%	73	4.0	61	1.0	5	6.5	55	61%	6	4.9	9	5	1
Anthony Barr	26	OLB	16	925	81	10.9%	56	49	22	4	33	61%	51	3.3	29	1.0	5	9.0	41	61%	8	4.4	4	2	0
Ben Gedeon	24	OLB	16	244	25	3.4%	--	19	2	4	22	82%	--	2.6	--	0.0	0	0.0	5	65%	--	7.0	--	0	0

Year	Yards	ALY	Rank	Power	Rank	Stuff	Rank	2nd Level	Rank	Open Field	Rank	Sacks	ASR	Rank	Press	Rank
2015	4.23	4.37	25	53%	3	18%	23	1.22	25	0.63	10	43	7.1%	10	28.0%	7
2016	4.17	4.46	24	59%	9	15%	31	1.08	9	0.56	8	41	7.8%	1	31.2%	5
2017	3.56	3.99	13	55%	5	19%	26	0.91	2	0.33	2	37	6.3%	18	31.1%	13

2017 ALY by direction:	Left End: 3.89 (18)	Left Tackle: 2.32 (1)	Mid/Guard: 4.35 (20)	Right Tackle: 4.39 (26)	Right End: 3.37 (12)

Minnesota's front seven is as good as any in the league right now, and there is a chance that the best for this unit has yet to come. ☞ The major personnel change is Sheldon Richardson replacing Tom Johnson at defensive tackle. It's hard not to see that as an upgrade even though Johnson played well last season. It was only three years ago when Richardson had more than 25 hurries for the Jets, and the Vikings get six years younger at the position. Richardson will be paired up with devoted run-stopper Linval Joseph. ☞ Depth in the front seven has helped win a few championships in recent years, most notably with the 2013 Seahawks and 2017 Eagles, and the Vikings have strong depth on the edge. Danielle Hunter and Everson Griffen were one of two duos last year (along with Chargers' Joey Bosa and Melvin Ingram) to rank in the top 20 in quarterback hurries. The Vikings also still have Brian Robison, whom Hunter replaced in the starting lineup last year to great success. Robison still picked up 22 hurries in a limited role, and the Vikings need that kind of pass-rush production to carry over into the playoffs. ☞ Minnesota also drafted Ohio State lineman Jalyn Holmes with the 102nd pick in April. General manager Rick Spielman gushed about Holmes' physical skills on draft night: "You can't teach that length, you can't teach that athleticism." Holmes played end in Columbus but will move to tackle in Minneapolis. ☞ Eric Kendricks got his extension, and fellow linebacker Anthony Barr could get one any day now. They probably should have had better metrics against the run given the talent that plays in front of them, but both had excellent coverage numbers in 2017, ranking in the top 10 in both success rate and yards per pass. ☞ Ben Gedeon did not see a ton of action as a fourth-round rookie, but he's technically a starter. Just don't expect him to be part of many third-down packages—he only played 16 snaps on third down last year according to ESPN Stats & Info. Gedeon was also Minnesota's top tackler on special teams with 12 tackles.

Defensive Secondary

Secondary	Age	Pos	G	Snaps	Plays	TmPct	Rk	Stop	Dfts	BTkl	Runs	St%	Rk	RuYd	Rk	Tgts	Tgt%	Rk	Dist	Suc%	Rk	AdjYd	Rk	PD	Int
Harrison Smith	29	FS	16	973	90	12.1%	16	44	19	7	35	63%	6	4.4	12	43	10.3%	46	11.6	53%	32	6.6	19	9	5
Trae Waynes	26	CB	16	918	76	10.2%	15	40	15	11	21	95%	2	4.6	15	93	23.8%	65	14.4	53%	28	8.4	61	10	2
Xavier Rhodes	28	CB	16	906	67	9.0%	30	22	10	3	9	33%	61	5.9	40	85	22.1%	53	13.5	53%	32	6.7	19	10	2
Andrew Sendejo	31	SS	13	780	84	13.9%	5	30	13	6	38	39%	51	5.9	33	28	8.3%	28	12.5	55%	27	7.2	25	7	2
Terence Newman	40	CB	16	560	40	5.4%	--	23	6	3	13	69%	--	2.5	--	40	16.6%	--	9.7	65%	--	5.2	--	6	1
Mackensie Alexander	25	CB	14	323	21	3.2%	--	11	8	8	2	50%	--	4.5	--	33	24.1%	--	12.6	47%	--	7.4	--	6	1

Year	Pass D Rank	vs. #1 WR	Rk	vs. #2 WR	Rk	vs. Other WR	Rk	WR Wide	Rk	WR Slot	Rk	vs. TE	Rk	vs. RB	Rk
2015	11	-6.1%	9	17.0%	25	-30.4%	2	--	--	--	--	16.1%	25	8.7%	22
2016	8	-1.9%	12	-4.2%	10	-23.9%	5	-3.2%	15	-19.1%	3	12.3%	24	-12.1%	8
2017	4	-13.1%	9	-22.2%	5	-3.5%	15	-4.9%	13	-15.3%	7	-24.2%	2	-37.6%	1

We get so used to writing about annual roster changes, but the Vikings are returning their top seven defensive backs from 2017. Yes, even when Terence Newman looked to have finally moved on, the Vikings brought him back at the end of April for his age-40 season. Oh, that move was also right after they added a first-round corner to the mix in Mike Hughes. Hughes is a raw prospect, but the Vikings can afford to ease him into one of their deepest positions. ☞ Trae Waynes had his best season yet, so it was no surprise to see the team pick up his fifth-year option for 2019. He'll still give up the big play from time to time, but he's growing into a competent No. 2 corner behind Xavier Rhodes, who made his first All-Pro team in 2017. With the Vikings able to use Newman and Mackensie Alexander in the slot, not much should really change from last year's setup. ☞ Safety Harrison Smith also notched his first All-Pro season and tied his career high with five interceptions. Smith and Andrew Sendejo continue to make for a good safety tandem. Sendejo even had a slightly higher coverage success rate in 2017 than Smith. Now this unit just has to stay healthy again, or not bite so hard on those pesky flea-flicker passes in Philadelphia.

Special Teams

Year	DVOA	Rank	FG/XP	Rank	Net Kick	Rank	Kick Ret	Rank	Net Punt	Rank	Punt Ret	Rank	Hidden	Rank
2015	3.9%	4	2.0	11	-3.7	25	16.1	1	1.1	16	4.0	7	-8.7	28
2016	1.5%	10	-5.5	25	-10.7	31	9.4	2	5.9	8	8.3	4	-6.4	25
2017	-0.9%	18	-3.1	20	-5.0	26	-2.6	21	2.9	17	3.1	8	-4.2	19

When Kai Forbath missed a 49-yard field goal before halftime of the team's playoff game against New Orleans, you can tell there was some nervousness in the building given Minnesota's playoff history with kickers. But fear not, because Forbath delivered with kicks from 49 and 53 yards in the fourth quarter of a tight win. If not for that 53-yard kick with 1:29 left, the game likely would have never reached its Minneapolis Miracle conclusion. While Forbath has been reliable on field goals, he has missed eight extra points since 2016, tied with Mike Nugent for the most in that time. His kickoffs were also a weakness last season. The Vikings' fifth-round selection of Auburn kicker Daniel Carlson could signal the end for Forbath in Minnesota. ☞ The punting game was middling for Minnesota last year, but Ryan Quigley was the league's only full-time punter who did not have a single touchback. He also led all punters with 33 fair catches on his punts. ☞ Marcus Sherels led all punt returners with 39 returns, but he did not score a touchdown as he had done in four of the previous five seasons. He's still one of the more valuable punt returners in the league. Sherels wasn't going to outdo what Cordarrelle Patterson is capable of on kick returns, but he's still an option there. The Vikings could also give that job to second-year wideout Stacy Coley.

New England Patriots

2017 Record: 13-3	**Total DVOA:** 22.6% (6th)	**2018 Mean Projection:** 10.5 wins	**On the Clock (0-4):** 1%
Pythagorean Wins: 12.0 (2nd)	**Offense:** 27.3% (1st)	**Postseason Odds:** 78.5%	**Mediocrity (5-7):** 10%
Snap-Weighted Age: 27.0 (5th)	**Defense:** 10.9% (31st)	**Super Bowl Odds:** 24.3%	**Playoff Contender (8-10):** 35%
Average Opponent: -3.9% (28th)	**Special Teams:** 6.3% (3rd)	**Proj. Avg. Opponent:** -4.5% (32nd)	**Super Bowl Contender (11+):** 54%

2017: One stop too few.

2018: One more runback of the Brady/Belichick Era that just won't end … or will it?

Tom Brady. Bill Belichick. Robert Kraft. The league's premier franchise since the turn of the millennium. What new ground is there to cover with this team? Brady was given Brandin Cooks and instantly adapted to a deep ball-focused passing game. The Patriots were their usual superior selves on offense, and rode that to the Super Bowl, where they lost on account of a strip sack and one of the best coaching performances in NFL history.

The media has been trying to find something new to say about the Patriots for a while now, and they immediately played up reported fractures between Brady, fitness coach Alex Guerrero, Belichick, and Kraft this season. Seth Wickersham's bombshell story for ESPN focused on a team torn about the future of its quarterback spot and the impact of Brady's harsh competitiveness on Jimmy Garoppolo. The clash of egos in the building resulted in Garoppolo being sent to San Francisco for only a second-round pick, a price that was far below what the Cleveland Browns were rumored to be offering.

The collateral damage of this is that the Patriots don't have a real backup plan at quarterback for the post-Brady future. Left unsaid in any of this discussion was that Brady never really gave them a reason to have one. Brady is anywhere from an inner-circle Hall of Famer to the best quarterback of all-time depending on what metrics and accomplishments you want to weight. He missed four games in 2016 due to suspension, but otherwise has played through pain and been available for every single game since his 2008 ACL tear. It was one thing to be cautious about it as Brady got older, and to be prepared to pull that trigger if there was a point where he fell off, à la Brett Favre. But it hasn't happened yet, and coming off a 503-yard performance in the Super Bowl, there's not much reason to believe it will happen in the near future outside of chanting "he's old" and praying that it comes to fruition. As much as what Brady does with Guerrero smells of pseudo-science, there's no denying that Brady keeps himself in fantastic shape and meets every challenge thrown at him.

Having a good backup quarterback when you have Tom Brady is a little like the proverbial mule with the spinning wheel: danged if he knows what to do with it. You could argue that the Pats didn't get the best deal they could have because of the egos involved, but other than that, they returned the value they invested, and that's about all you can ask for when it comes to a draft pick that almost never played.

As for the ego stuff, what can the Patriots do to fight any perception of their interior disagreements? Brady is a loud, type-A guy. Belichick doesn't come off that way in public but is a demanding taskmaster. Kraft wants them both to be happy but can't breach a gap where both sides have different incentives. As much as Wickersham's story played on the idea of a breakup, there was never a reason for the trio to separate as long as Brady continued to be one of the best quarterbacks in the NFL. Belichick has infinite job security and leaving would have to be considered something he'd do only if he were bored and looking for a new challenge. Brady blows up at Josh McDaniels on the sideline, but has he seen the league's other coaching staffs? Both of them, leaving one of the easiest divisions in the NFL, with an owner who happily spends to keep them both happy? That just sounds ridiculous on its face.

New England did not pick a quarterback early in this year's draft despite rampant speculation they would be interested in Lamar Jackson. Seventh-rounder Danny Etling is on the roster as Brian Hoyer's understudy, and they're now all-in on Brady once again. As weird as it is to say this about a quarterback in his forties, Brady is still one of the safest bets in the NFL.

In a broad-picture sense, the Patriots are still the Patriots. We introduced a more conservative win projection system in 2012. In five of the seven preseasons since then, including this year, the Patriots have had a mean projection of 10.5 wins or more (Table 1). Every other team in the NFL has combined for a mean projection 10.5 wins or more only six times. Last year's Patriots had the easiest schedule in the NFL. This year's Patriots have the easiest projected schedule in the NFL. Last year's Patriots had defensive question marks that they hoped would be solved with bold moves. This year's Patriots defense is unsettled for different reasons, but the overall situation is similar.

Last year's plan to have the cornerbacks handle things hit some snags as the Patriots discovered that Stephon Gilmore was much less effective outside of press coverage, and the whole enterprise sunk early on as miscommunication was rampant. New England didn't hold an opponent under a 25.0% single-game passing DVOA until Week 6. They didn't have a negative passing DVOA allowed in a game until Week 11. They clearly soured on Malcolm Butler, to the point where he was surprisingly benched in the Super Bowl and then al-

2018 Patriots Schedule

Week	Opp.	Week	Opp.	Week	Opp.
1	HOU	7	at CHI	13	MIN
2	at JAX	8	at BUF (Mon.)	14	at MIA
3	at DET	9	GB	15	at PIT
4	MIA	10	at TEN	16	BUF
5	IND (Thu.)	11	BYE	17	NYJ
6	KC	12	at NYJ		

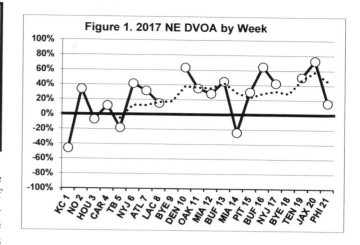

Figure 1. 2017 NE DVOA by Week

lowed to depart in free agency. Their attempt to fill the hole Butler left was finagling Devin McCourty's brother Jason, off a good year in Cleveland, for a sixth-round pick. Jason has experience with a number of different coverages and should be a player more apt to fit into Belichick's wrinkles. Last year's defensive coordinator, Matt Patricia, now coaches the Detroit Lions, and Bill Belichick found his replacement in ... Bill Belichick. Linebackers coach Brian Flores will call the signals, but with no formal title elevation.

In two of the last three seasons, the Patriots have managed to have high adjusted sack rates despite poor pressure ratings. Last year, they ranked 10th with 7.1 percent ASR but only 30th with a pressure rate of 27.0 percent. The discrepancy in 2017 sacks can be attributed in large part to sacks that were caused less by pass rush and more by forcing the opposing quarterback to extend the play. The Patriots led the league with 16 of what we might call "non-pressure sacks," those marked "Coverage Sack," "QB Fault," or "Failed Scramble" (Table 2).

One player, however, was bringing the heat even when he didn't take down the quarterback. Trey Flowers' 42.5 hurries last year is the most we have recorded in any of the last three years for the Patriots. Yes, even more than Chandler Jones' 2015 season.

Flowers' 2017 season can be the start to the plan to creating a non-designed pass rush for the Patriots. The Pats are still lacking the true five-star edge rusher that every defense has to design around, but the hope is that third-round redshirt Derek

Rivers can provide some additional rush. Free-agent signee Adrian Clayborn should be a steadying force if neither Rivers nor Flowers can develop into a star, but the Patriots are again facing the prospect of lacking a top-tier edge rusher and having to generate sacks with schemes rather than talent.

New England's biggest 2017 problem, though, was their run defense. A 2.8% DVOA allowed doesn't seem too bad, but that's only because passing is more efficient than rushing, so nearly all NFL defenses end up with a run defense DVOA below zero. That 2.8% rating put the Patriots 31st in the NFL, just ahead of the Chiefs. The good news there for the Patriots is that A) they're traditionally very stout against the run and the failure wasn't schematic, and B) reinforcements are here. The Pats traded for Browns nose tackle Danny Shelton, a big reason Cleveland had the fourth-best rush defense in the NFL last year, and will plug him right into the starting lineup. If you expect improvement in this area, and improvement in that the Patriots won't be asking Gilmore to play outside of his comfort zone, the defense can rebound quite a bit.

But perhaps the most interesting move of the offseason was when the Patriots went against the analytical code and dropped a first-round pick on Georgia running back Sony Michel. This

Table 1. Top Team Projections in Football Outsiders Almanac, 2012-2018

Team	Year	Mean Wins	Final W-L	Playoffs
NE	2012	12.0	12-4	Lost AFC-CG
NE	2017	11.6	13-3	Lost Super Bowl
GB	2012	11.1	11-5	Lost NFC-Div
PIT	2017	10.7	13-3	Lost AFC-Div
SEA	2015	10.7	10-6	Lost NFC-Div
DEN	2014	10.7	12-4	Lost AFC-Div
NE	2013	10.6	12-4	Lost AFC-CG
NE	**2018**	**10.5**	--	--
SEA	2016	10.5	10-5-1	Lost NFC-Div
NE	2015	10.5	12-4	Lost AFC-CG
GB	2013	10.4	8-7-1	Lost NFC-WC
ARI	2016	10.4	7-8-1	Missed playoffs
PIT	**2018**	**10.2**	--	--

Table 2. Highest Rate of 'Non-Pressure' Sacks, 2017

Team	Non-Pressure Sacks	Total Sacks	Rate
TB	9	22	41%
NE	16	42	38%
HOU	11	32	34%
NYG	9	27	33%
LAC	13	43	30%
KC	9	31	29%
NYJ	8	28	29%
GB	10	37	27%
MIN	10	37	27%
NO	11	42	26%
CAR	13	50	26%
OAK	8	31	26%

Includes sacks marked QB Fault, Coverage Sack, or Failed Scramble.

was a deep running back class, but most outside analysts put Michel a tier below obvious No. 1 back Saquon Barkley and Browns second-rounder (and Michel's teammate at Georgia) Nick Chubb. Most even put him behind LSU's Derrius Guice. It was a pick that was jarring not only because the player was not seen as a consensus best talent, but because it just felt entirely out of sync with New England's philosophy. This is a team that started heaving four backs around every year to combat injuries. This is a team that gave us Jonas Gray's 200-yard game. One that already had Rex Burkhead, James White, and Mike Gillislee on the roster, and could have spent the 31st overall pick on a crack at a real edge rusher like Boston College product Harold Landry.

Michel's three-down ability could give the Patriots their finest runner since Corey Dillon, but overcoming the fumble issues that plagued him in college will be the major test. Moreover, the Patriots lost the No. 1 finisher in rushing DVOA last year, Dion Lewis. So barring Michel having some sort of breakout, Alvin Kamara-esque rookie season, the Patriots will only be trying to stay level as far as production at the position. They do have plenty of depth at the position in the event that Michel is suddenly banished to the land of fumbles by Belichick.

The other major change to the offense was the offseason exchange that sent Brandin Cooks to the Rams. The Patriots coaxed the highest DVOA of Cooks' career out of him, but also his lowest catch rate. They got to see first-hand the flaws that made the Saints think of him as expendable—issues getting off press coverage, mainly—and decided to move on before Cooks got expensive. With Julian Edelman coming back, and coming off an ACL tear, this is actually a bit of a dangerous move. At the very least, it will change New England's offense back to what it was pre-Cooks: a more short toss-focused, less explosive scheme. The Patriots still have plenty of seemingly good receivers waiting in the wings if Edelman's comeback stalls out. It would not be at all surprising to see Jordan Matthews resurface in his Philadelphia form here, or for Malcolm Mitchell to shine brightly in a lead outside role if he can possibly shake off the injuries that cost him the 2017 season. It's just a situation that leads with some uncertainty, rather than the sure thing it might feel like if Cooks were on the team.

For what it's worth, New England's passing offense in 2016 was marginally better than it was in 2017: 49.6% DVOA to 47.0% DVOA. And getting Brady out of the habit of holding the ball will also help an offensive line that is thin on the outside and asking Georgia's Isaiah Wynn to step in at tackle even when most draftniks regarded him as a better fit at guard.

Regardless, it's hard to project anything but dominance from this team. It bears repeating that they are just so far ahead of the rest of the AFC at this point that it's mind-boggling. Our projection system, a thing that more often than not generates a mean projection between seven and nine wins for most teams, are giving them the third-highest projection by wins since we started having a projection system. Our projection system, a thing that more often than not generates a mean projection between seven and nine wins for most teams, is once again giving them a projection for double-digit wins. In our other team chapters, we're talking about things like "does this team have a good offensive line?" or "what part of this team was bad, and why is there no hope for the near future?" In the Patriots chapter, we talk about whether the offense will be able to push the ball downfield quite as much as they did last season.

And given just how down the AFC has been over the past few seasons, it's even harder to project a real tumble for the Patriots when there are no other real contenders. This is a nominal juggernaut team in a division with three rebuilding projects and in a conference where only the Steelers really qualify as finished products. These Pats not only have a good team, they have the security of being one of the rare good teams in a bad conference.

As long as Brady, Belichick, and Kraft are on the same page, no sane projection system is ever going to predict the fall. Could this be the year that Brady falters, loses a little bit of his quick-twitch ability on his throws, and tumbles down from being an elite quarterback? Maybe! Eventually the Patriots are going to crash and burn. No team can defy regression forever.

But it might not happen until Tom Brady is 47.

Rivers McCown

2017 Patriots Stats by Week

Wk	vs.	W-L	PF	PA	YDF	YDA	TO	Total	Off	Def	ST
1	KC	L	27	42	371	537	+1	-46%	-2%	48%	4%
2	at NO	W	36	20	555	429	0	34%	61%	15%	-12%
3	HOU	W	36	33	396	417	+1	-7%	5%	15%	3%
4	CAR	L	30	33	373	444	+2	12%	44%	39%	7%
5	at TB	W	19	14	402	409	-2	-18%	-3%	22%	7%
6	at NYJ	W	24	17	375	408	+1	42%	38%	-4%	0%
7	ATL	W	23	7	403	343	0	32%	40%	11%	4%
8	LAC	W	21	13	414	349	+1	15%	26%	21%	11%
9	BYE										
10	at DEN	W	41	16	396	339	+2	63%	52%	13%	25%
11	at OAK	W	33	8	421	344	+2	35%	24%	3%	14%
12	MIA	W	35	17	417	221	+1	28%	13%	-23%	-8%
13	at BUF	W	23	3	435	268	0	45%	22%	-14%	8%
14	at MIA	L	20	27	248	362	-2	-24%	-3%	31%	10%
15	at PIT	W	27	24	360	413	0	31%	36%	11%	6%
16	BUF	W	37	16	411	326	-1	65%	52%	-2%	10%
17	NYJ	W	26	6	330	247	0	43%	17%	-15%	11%
18	BYE										
19	TEN	W	35	14	438	267	0	51%	45%	-3%	4%
20	JAX	W	24	20	344	374	-1	73%	64%	8%	17%
21	PHI	L	33	41	613	538	0	16%	63%	29%	-18%

Trends and Splits

	Offense	Rank	Defense	Rank
Total DVOA	27.3%	1	10.9%	31
Unadjusted VOA	29.4%	1	10.7%	30
Weighted Trend	28.7%	1	3.9%	22
Variance	4.3%	5	3.9%	8
Average Opponent	2.5%	29	-1.0%	20
Passing	47.0%	1	16.6%	21
Rushing	10.4%	4	2.8%	31
First Down	31.8%	1	21.9%	32
Second Down	32.5%	1	9.8%	28
Third Down	7.5%	12	-7.3%	12
First Half	30.4%	1	11.1%	30
Second Half	23.5%	2	10.8%	26
Red Zone	27.2%	3	-18.7%	4
Late and Close	22.1%	2	20.2%	32

Five-Year Performance

Year	W-L	Pyth W	Est W	PF	PA	TO	Total	Rk	Off	Rk	Def	Rk	ST	Rk	Off AGL	Rk	Def AGL	Rk	Off Age	Rk	Def Age	Rk	ST Age	Rk
2013	12-4	10.5	11.0	444	338	+9	18.9%	5	16.4%	4	4.2%	20	6.7%	2	47.8	25	49.8	28	27.6	6	25.8	29	25.6	27
2014	12-4	11.8	10.8	468	313	+12	22.1%	4	13.5%	6	-3.0%	12	5.7%	5	24.4	9	37.6	16	27.7	5	26.6	19	26.1	16
2015	12-4	11.7	10.9	465	315	+7	22.6%	6	15.4%	5	-3.3%	12	3.9%	5	60.6	29	32.7	19	27.2	12	25.9	27	25.9	18
2016	14-2	12.8	11.9	441	250	+12	24.9%	1	20.8%	2	-1.8%	16	2.3%	8	47.2	25	7.3	1	27.3	7	26.6	14	26.3	9
2017	13-3	12.0	11.0	458	296	+6	22.6%	6	27.3%	1	10.9%	31	6.3%	3	36.7	18	24.6	10	27.7	3	26.3	15	26.7	3

2017 Performance Based on Most Common Personnel Groups

NE Offense					NE Offense vs. Opponents					NE Defense					NE Defense vs. Opponents			
Pers	Freq	Yds	DVOA	Run%	Pers	Freq	Yds	DVOA	Run%	Pers	Freq	Yds	DVOA	Pers	Freq	Yds	DVOA	
11	44%	6.4	28.8%	25%	Base	36%	5.6	18.0%	55%	Base	15%	5.0	-14.2%	11	68%	6.1	15.9%	
21	25%	6.6	50.5%	48%	Nickel	47%	6.6	37.3%	33%	Nickel	48%	6.1	20.1%	12	14%	6.3	15.2%	
12	17%	6.3	45.3%	48%	Dime+	16%	6.6	46.9%	23%	Dime+	37%	6.3	11.0%	21	8%	5.1	-5.0%	
22	6%	4.3	-7.6%	87%	Goal Line	2%	0.7	10.4%	75%	Goal Line	1%	-0.5	-42.0%	13	2%	6.2	-7.7%	
13	3%	5.8	-35.9%	33%										01	1%	4.7	-30.2%	

Strategic Tendencies

Run/Pass		Rk	Formation		Rk	Pass Rush		Rk	Secondary		Rk	Strategy		Rk
Runs, first half	37%	23	Form: Single Back	61%	31	Rush 3	23.7%	1	4 DB	15%	32	Play action	28%	3
Runs, first down	52%	12	Form: Empty Back	12%	5	Rush 4	55.0%	28	5 DB	48%	21	Avg Box (Off)	6.42	3
Runs, second-long	22%	30	Pers: 3+ WR	46%	31	Rush 5	18.6%	17	6+ DB	37%	4	Avg Box (Def)	5.97	32
Runs, power sit.	57%	15	Pers: 2+ TE/6+ OL	28%	19	Rush 6+	2.7%	27	CB by Sides	61%	28	Offensive Pace	27.92	2
Runs, behind 2H	25%	23	Pers: 6+ OL	2%	23	Int DL Sacks	10.7%	30	S/CB Cover Ratio	39%	4	Defensive Pace	30.55	19
Pass, ahead 2H	50%	10	Shotgun/Pistol	51%	25	Second Level Sacks	41.7%	1	DB Blitz	7%	20	Go for it on 4th	1.09	12

While run/pass ratios went up around the NFL last year, they went down for the Patriots in pretty much every situation. And yet, the Patriots used play-action more often than the year before, despite running less, going from 20 percent (11th) to 28 percent (third). ☙ This was the second straight year the Patriots ranked third in average opposition men in the box. That's likely a lack of respect for Brady's deep ball more than it is any fear that the Patriots are going to ground-and-pound. ☙ If it feels like the Patriots never take their foot off the gas, well, you're right: they had the league's fastest pace when leading and ranked No. 2 in pace (behind Tampa Bay) when leading by a touchdown or more. ☙ The Patriots offense is usually slanted towards the left side of the field, but never quite to the extent it was in 2017. Tom Brady threw a league-leading 46 percent of passes to the left side, and just 27 percent of passes to the right side—where every other offense was at 34 percent or higher. The Patriots, by the way, had the highest DVOA in the league on passes to both the left and right sides. ☙ The Patriots had a 47.9% DVOA between the 40s, the third highest figure we've ever recorded after the 2007 Patriots and the 1995 Cowboys. ☙ After an off year in 2016, where they finished 21st in broken tackles, the Patriots defense was back to having tackling as a strength in 2017. They ranked fifth with 86 broken tackles, the fourth year out of five where they ranked in the top five. ☙ New England was one of only two defenses, along with Arizona, where opponents threw to No. 2 receivers (20 percent) more often than No. 1 receivers (19 percent). ☙ New England had the worst run defense DVOA (10.6%) against runs from formations with three or more wide receivers, allowing 5.2 yards per carry. ☙ The Patriots finished 30th in penalties, the third straight year they have ranked in the bottom five.

Passing

Player	DYAR	DVOA	Plays	NtYds	Avg	YAC	C%	TD	Int
T.Brady	1595	27.8%	617	4366	7.1	5.0	66.4%	32	8
B.Hoyer	8	12.2%	6	42	7.0	10.0	66.7%	0	0

Rushing

Player	DYAR	DVOA	Plays	Yds	Avg	TD	Fum	Suc
D.Lewis*	273	27.6%	180	896	5.0	6	0	56%
M.Gillislee	39	-0.8%	104	383	3.7	5	1	58%
R.Burkhead	56	10.5%	64	264	4.1	5	1	53%
J.White	-1	-9.3%	43	171	4.0	0	0	51%
B.Bolden	22	31.8%	13	67	5.2	0	0	54%
T.Brady	0	-12.2%	13	39	3.0	0	0	-
B.Cooks*	6	-28.1%	9	40	4.4	0	0	-
J.Hill	-9	-14.2%	37	121	3.3	0	1	41%
C.Patterson	60	47.3%	13	121	9.3	2	0	-

Receiving

Player	DYAR	DVOA	Plays	Ctch	Yds	Y/C	YAC	TD	C%
B.Cooks*	258	14.9%	114	65	1082	16.6	3.5	7	57%
D.Amendola*	138	8.4%	86	61	659	10.8	3.4	2	71%
C.Hogan	71	2.5%	59	34	439	12.9	5.0	5	58%
P.Dorsett	45	21.6%	18	12	194	16.2	5.7	0	67%
C.Patterson	17	-7.4%	42	31	305	9.8	6.3	0	74%
K.Britt	-11	-16.6%	38	18	233	12.9	4.7	2	47%
J.Matthews	33	-0.6%	36	25	282	11.3	5.0	1	69%
R.Gronkowski	339	40.4%	105	69	1084	15.7	5.0	8	66%
D.Allen	-57	-42.6%	22	10	86	8.6	6.4	1	45%
J.Hollister	-40	-58.0%	11	4	42	10.5	1.3	0	36%
M.Bennett*	12	25.1%	6	6	53	8.8	8.2	0	100%
T.Niklas	-7	-11.8%	23	11	132	12.0	5.1	1	48%
W.Tye	-7	-21.9%	6	4	38	9.5	4.8	0	67%
J.White	86	6.4%	72	56	429	7.7	6.1	3	78%
R.Burkhead	102	33.7%	36	30	254	8.5	6.1	3	83%
D.Lewis*	90	32.0%	35	32	214	6.7	7.0	3	91%
J.Develin	-2	-16.9%	10	6	38	6.3	4.3	0	60%

Offensive Line

Player	Pos	Age	GS	Snaps	Pen	Sk	Pass	Run	Player	Pos	Age	GS	Snaps	Pen	Sk	Pass	Run
Shaq Mason	RG	25	16/16	1138	1	1.5	10	9	Marcus Cannon	RT	30	7/7	478	2	5.5	11	1
Joe Thuney	LG	26	16/16	1136	3	4.0	13	9	Cameron Fleming*	RT	26	12/6	369	2	2.0	6	3
Nate Solder*	LT	30	16/16	1116	10	5.0	24	5	LaAdrian Waddle	RT	27	12/4	336	1	0.0	7	4
David Andrews	C	26	14/14	992	2	4.0	14	6	Trenton Brown	RT	25	10/10	668	7	1.5	7	7

Year	Yards	ALY	Rank	Power	Rank	Stuff	Rank	2nd Lev	Rank	Open Field	Rank	Sacks	ASR	Rank	Press	Rank	F-Start	Cont.
2015	3.88	4.56	2	64%	19	16%	1	1.17	16	0.42	30	38	6.5%	18	25.5%	16	13	15
2016	3.99	4.46	9	59%	22	20%	16	1.10	22	0.60	21	24	4.6%	6	25.6%	14	14	38
2017	4.43	5.05	1	65%	14	16%	3	1.35	2	0.60	20	35	6.4%	13	27.0%	7	13	29

2017 ALY by direction:	Left End: 4.82 (8)	Left Tackle: 4.88 (7)	Mid/Guard: 5.08 (1)	Right Tackle: 5.36 (1)	Right End: 4.92 (3)

After letting left tackle Nate Solder walk for an obscene amount of guaranteed money, the Patriots spent a first-round pick on Georgia's Isaiah Wynn, announcing him as a tackle where most of the draft community thought he was a guard. Wynn was one of the most highly regarded interior linemen in the draft, so he should add talent somewhere. The Pats also brought back

LaAdrian Waddle and inked Matt Tobin in free agency, though the idea of protecting Tom Brady with an ex-Seattle interior lineman might make you vomit in your mouth just a little. ☞ What all that talk will mask is one of the best interior lines in the league. Joe Thuney had a solid second season, and Shaq Mason and David Andrews took massive steps forward in helping Dion Lewis lead the NFL in rushing DVOA. There are still little nits to pick about Mason in pass protection, but he was the only Patriots lineman to finish in the top ten at his position in snaps per blown block. This part of the line will give Brady plenty of opportunity to step up and buy time. ☞ Marcus Cannon is the sole survivor among last season's tackles; after a breakout 2016 campaign, the inconsistent Cannon took a step back and then finished 2017 on IR. Cannon's highs are worth the technical flaws he sometimes has, but the squeeze may be on: the Patriots traded for 49ers tackle Trent Brown, another high-upside blocker who plays up-and-down but is younger than Cannon. Or Brown could play left tackle, as he was doing in OTAs, with Wynn replacing Thuney at left guard. Wynn on the inside would make this the deepest interior line in the NFL.

Defensive Front Seven

Defensive Line	Age	Pos	G	Snaps	Plays	Overall TmPct	Rk	Stop	Dfts	BTkl	vs. Run Runs	St%	Rk	RuYd	Rk	Pass Rush Sack	Hit	Hur	Dsrpt
Malcom Brown	24	DT	13	539	48	7.4%	5	37	8	0	42	79%	38	2.4	57	2.5	2	10.5	0
Adam Butler	24	DT	16	475	19	2.4%	85	10	3	0	15	53%	83	3.9	84	2.0	0	15.5	0
Alan Branch*	34	DT	12	273	12	2.0%	--	7	2	2	12	58%	--	1.9	--	0.0	1	3.0	0
Danny Shelton	25	DT	14	471	34	4.6%	53	30	6	8	33	88%	8	1.6	23	0.0	1	6.5	1

Edge Rushers	Age	Pos	G	Snaps	Plays	Overall TmPct	Rk	Stop	Dfts	BTkl	vs. Run Runs	St%	Rk	RuYd	Rk	Pass Rush Sack	Hit	Hur	Dsrpt
Trey Flowers	25	DE	14	804	64	9.2%	2	41	16	8	45	60%	91	2.6	64	6.5	18	42.5	3
Lawrence Guy	28	DE	16	582	58	7.3%	16	40	11	5	51	73%	56	2.4	52	1.0	4	11.5	1
Deatrich Wise	24	DE	16	545	27	3.4%	78	19	8	2	16	63%	83	3.6	86	5.0	14	23.0	1
Eric Lee	24	DE	6	282	21	7.0%	19	17	9	4	12	75%	46	3.4	80	3.5	1	11.0	2
Adrian Clayborn	30	DE	16	567	21	2.6%	92	18	13	6	6	83%	21	3.3	77	9.5	10	27.5	3

Linebackers	Age	Pos	G	Snaps	Plays	Overall TmPct	Rk	Stop	Dfts	BTkl	vs. Run Runs	St%	Rk	RuYd	Rk	Pass Rush Sack	Hit	Hur	vs. Pass Tgts	Suc%	Rk	AdjYd	Rk	PD	Int
Kyle Van Noy	27	OLB	13	711	75	11.6%	48	36	16	12	41	49%	78	4.3	67	5.5	2	10.0	20	47%	51	8.6	68	1	0
Elandon Roberts	24	OLB	15	560	67	9.0%	70	34	8	7	46	57%	69	3.7	47	2.0	1	3.5	19	37%	68	12.4	76	1	0
Marquis Flowers	26	OLB	16	283	31	3.9%	--	17	11	2	15	53%	--	4.7	--	3.5	0	4.0	9	51%	--	4.0	--	0	0
David Harris*	34	MLB	10	182	23	4.6%	--	7	1	5	17	24%	--	6.3	--	1.5	1	2.0	3	61%	--	2.5	--	1	0

Year	Yards	ALY	Rank	Power	Rank	Stuff	Rank	2nd Level	Rank	Open Field	Rank	Sacks	ASR	Rank	Press	Rank
2015	3.92	3.95	13	60%	10	19%	21	1.02	7	0.66	11	49	7.8%	2	24.7%	21
2016	3.61	3.96	11	63%	14	17%	21	1.03	7	0.27	1	34	5.0%	27	24.7%	26
2017	4.69	4.51	31	62%	15	16%	30	1.28	29	0.95	28	42	7.1%	10	27.5%	30

2017 ALY by direction: Left End: 3.74 (14) — Left Tackle: 3.13 (6) — Mid/Guard: 5.06 (32) — Right Tackle: 4.19 (22) — Right End: 4.87 (27)

The Pats moved to solidify the defensive line early in the league year by reeling in nose tackle Danny Shelton in a trade with the Browns. Shelton's health was a big part of the Cleveland run defense resurgence in 2017, and though he's a two-down player, the Pats needed this kind of upgrade after finishing 30th in run defense DVOA. However, the defensive tackle position will be in flux after the season because the Patriots declined the fifth-year options on both Shelton and incumbent Malcom Brown. ☞ Adrian Clayborn is a solid second/third edge rusher the Pats brought in during free agency, just so long as everyone understands that his baptism by fire of Cowboys tackle Chaz Green was an outlier of historic proportions. ☞ 2015 fourth-round pick Trey Flowers was the best edge on passing downs the Pats had to offer—he's not necessarily a speedy end, but he's able to win with technique and hand placement and enters his contract year as the clear No. 1. ☞ 2017 third-rounder Derek Rivers, who missed his entire rookie season with a torn ACL, had an intriguing profile coming out of Youngstown State and should be monitored. Rivers broke the Youngstown State career sack record before he even reached his senior year, and was a force at the Senior Bowl. Then, he put on a show at the combine. Deatrich Wise played in Rivers' stead last year and posted a respectable hurry total. The addition of Clayborn and Rivers takes a depth chart problem and turns it into a possible strength. ☞ The most important factor in New England's defensive prospects will be the healthy return of Dont'a Hightower. The last real star in the front seven after the Chandler Jones and Jamie Collins trades, Hightower missed the last 11 games of the regular season. ☞ The other linebacker spot could still use some reinforcement. Elandon Roberts struggles in pass coverage, and the Patriots essentially drafted a younger version of him in fifth-rounder Ja'Whuan Bentley (Purdue). Kyle Van Noy has a killer athletic profile but doesn't play up to it, though he's been a bigger part of the defense in New England than he ever was in Detroit.

Defensive Secondary

Secondary	Age	Pos	G	Snaps	Plays	Overall TmPct	Rk	Stop	Dfts	BTkl	vs. Run Runs	St%	Rk	RuYd	Rk	vs. Pass Tgts	Tgt%	Rk	Dist	Suc%	Rk	AdjYd	Rk	PD	Int
Malcolm Butler*	28	CB	16	1040	71	8.9%	33	30	10	8	15	33%	61	7.2	59	90	18.7%	30	12.7	50%	44	9.1	69	15	2
Devin McCourty	31	FS	16	1032	99	12.5%	12	32	11	6	44	36%	55	9.8	62	61	12.7%	58	11.5	54%	29	7.6	32	8	1
Patrick Chung	31	SS	16	930	87	10.9%	22	36	14	8	28	46%	33	4.5	14	65	15.1%	68	9.7	61%	11	5.4	7	9	1
Stephon Gilmore	28	CB	13	819	58	9.0%	31	20	8	3	11	36%	57	6.8	54	67	17.5%	20	10.8	48%	55	7.4	38	9	2
Duron Harmon	27	FS	16	705	30	3.8%	--	8	4	7	5	20%	--	10.4	--	15	4.6%	--	19.3	67%	--	5.1	--	7	4
Jonathan Jones	25	CB	16	439	44	5.5%	--	23	11	5	8	38%	--	10.9	--	49	23.9%	--	11.7	57%	--	8.5	--	9	1
Jordan Richards	25	SS	16	276	23	2.9%	--	8	6	6	9	33%	--	5.0	--	17	13.3%	--	7.1	50%	--	5.5	--	1	0
Eric Rowe	26	CB	8	260	16	4.0%	--	4	4	2	3	0%	--	9.0	--	25	20.4%	--	9.0	48%	--	9.2	--	2	0
Johnson Bademosi*	28	CB	16	215	21	2.6%	--	4	1	2	4	25%	--	6.5	--	18	18.1%	--	13.4	33%	--	9.8	--	1	0
Jason McCourty	31	CB	14	903	78	10.4%	10	39	15	3	9	56%	23	8.3	66	71	17.7%	23	11.6	52%	38	7.2	33	14	3

Year	Pass D Rank	vs. #1 WR	Rk	vs. #2 WR	Rk	vs. Other WR	Rk	WR Wide	Rk	WR Slot	Rk	vs. TE	Rk	vs. RB	Rk
2015	15	-1.2%	17	1.1%	15	21.4%	28	--	--	--	--	-8.3%	15	1.7%	17
2016	22	3.6%	20	-5.6%	9	4.0%	19	2.2%	20	1.4%	14	-3.4%	14	9.2%	22
2017	21	18.9%	26	4.9%	19	6.8%	22	-4.9%	14	24.2%	29	-11.6%	8	10.1%	22

Singled out as a problem by Jon Robinson in Tennessee, Jason McCourty had a good year in Cleveland despite playing through injuries and Gregg Williams' scheme. He was more effective in off coverage but was decent playing press-man when asked to do so. The Browns left him on an island all year by playing their deep safety in rural Canada. ☞ On the other hand, you have Stephon Gilmore. New England's early season torchings were largely keyed by miscommunication around Gilmore, and he's just not worth his $12.5 million cap number if he's trying to be an off-man corner instead of what's more natural for him, playing press-man. Gilmore did improve in the second half of the season, allowing 8.9 adjusted yards per pass from Weeks 5 to 10 but 6.8 adjusted yards per pass after returning from a concussion in Week 10. ☞ The Pats tried Eric Rowe in the slot and it was a bit of an awkward fit. Rowe's size and lack of fluidity lead to him playing a bit better outside as a boundary corner, and Jonathan Jones started cutting into his time. That may happen again this season. ☞ Second-rounder Duke Dawson (Florida) profiles as a slot corner and will push the Rowe/Jones winner for early playing time. He's not much of a physical specimen but plays with good technique and blanked Arizona second-rounder Christian Kirk in their high-profile matchup last season. ☞ A sneaky player to watch is undrafted rookie J.C. Jackson, who was a four-star recruit out of high school and ran a 4.46 40 at the combine. Jackson ran into legal trouble with robbery charges at the University of Florida, then transferred to Maryland after acquittal and showed speed and athleticism worthy of a Day 2 draft pick. He was running with the first-string defense at OTAs, ahead of Rowe and Jones. ☞ Devin McCourty, as close to a non-Brady stalwart as you can find on this roster, has been around since 2010. Reuniting with his twin brother is a fun story, though you have to imagine the Pats won't be keeping him too much longer. A dominant cover safety even at 30, McCourty's contract is up in 2019. ☞ From punch line to player, Patrick Chung has been a nice box safety for the Patriots, able to handle most tight ends without too much trouble. Duron Harmon has blossomed into a capable dime safety, which is basically a starter in New England's defense, but his missed tackle rate of 30 percent was obscene for a defensive back.

Special Teams

Year	DVOA	Rank	FG/XP	Rank	Net Kick	Rank	Kick Ret	Rank	Net Punt	Rank	Punt Ret	Rank	Hidden	Rank
2015	3.9%	5	14.1	1	8.2	2	0.7	10	-6.7	25	3.1	10	0.1	16
2016	2.3%	8	0.2	17	10.4	2	-3.6	24	12.1	3	-7.7	29	11.6	4
2017	6.3%	3	8.9	6	8.4	1	6.4	4	8.2	4	-0.6	18	13.1	3

Despite missing ace Matthew Slater for half the season, Patriots special teams continued to be a soulless killing machine. The Patriots have now ranked in the top eight in special teams DVOA for eight straight years and have been above-average every single year since 1996. ☞ For the latest wrinkle, Bill Belichick's boys have mastered the art of the short kickoff to gain themselves an edge. New England's defense had the second-best average starting field position after kickoffs. A league-leading 35 Patriots kickoffs were caught between the 1 and the 10. (By percentage, the Patriots tied the Bengals for the league lead at 36 percent). Thirteen of these 35 kickoffs had returns tackled at or behind the 20, while none were advanced past the 31. The Patriots have essentially broken our method for splitting out gross kickoff distance from return value, which is why Stephen Gostkowski isn't on the top of the ratings in the appendix at the back of the book. ☞ Gostkowski's weird accuracy problems on field goals have gone into their second season. Yes, he hit 92.5 percent of his regular-season field goals, but he missed two extra points plus a field goal in three playoff games. Is this just the new normal? The Pats will live with it as long as the kickoffs are great and the leg strength is there. ☞ Punter Ryan Allen is consistently average, helped significantly by the Patriots' great coverage units. He'll have a training camp battle for his job against New Mexico UDFA Corey Bojorquez. ☞ The one area where New England had some issues last year was punt returns. So, naturally, they went and brought in one of the most successful returners in modern NFL history in Cordarrelle Patterson. Nominally a kickoff guy only, he might get some looks on punts as well. Otherwise punt returns will probably belong to sixth-round slot receiver Braxton Berrios (Miami).

New Orleans Saints

2017 Record: 11-5	Total DVOA: 30.7% (1st)	2018 Mean Projection: 9.4 wins	On the Clock (0-4): 3%
Pythagorean Wins: 11.1 (6th)	Offense: 21.6% (2nd)	Postseason Odds: 58.9%	Mediocrity (5-7): 19%
Snap-Weighted Age: 26.1 (27th)	Defense: -7.9% (8th)	Super Bowl Odds: 14.3%	Playoff Contender (8-10): 43%
Average Opponent: -0.3% (17th)	Special Teams: 1.2% (15th)	Proj. Avg. Opponent: 2.2% (4th)	Super Bowl Contender (11+): 35%

2017: Who dat got a running game and defense? Who dat just ducked Stefon Diggs!?

2018: Can the next all-time passing leader get a happy ending too?

The Saints won the competitive NFC South for the first time since 2011, in large part because they also won the 2017 draft. Rarely does a team select so many high-impact rookies, but the Saints nailed their first four picks. First-round cornerback Marshon Lattimore won the Defensive Rookie of the Year award after intercepting five passes in 13 games. Third-round running back Alvin Kamara had a fascinating all-purpose season and was named the Offensive Rookie of the Year, making the Saints the only team since the merger to sweep the top rookie awards. Right tackle Ryan Ramczyk and safety Marcus Williams were also full-time starters who helped the Saints return to prominence.

This history-making draft class will always be the defining story of the 2017 Saints, and Williams made sure of that after he made one of the all-time blunders to seal his team's fate in the divisional round. Saints fans are probably trying to forget the Minneapolis Miracle, but there is no forgetting the first walk-off touchdown in the fourth quarter in NFL play-off history. With the Saints clinging to a 24-23 lead, Williams ducked under wide receiver Stefon Diggs and ended up taking out his teammate Ken Crawley, the last line of defense, in the process. Diggs was off to the races for a 61-yard touchdown that truly felt like a miracle. Williams owned up to his mistake, telling reporters in January that "I'm going to take it upon myself to do all I can to never let that happen again, and if it happens again, then I shouldn't be playing." Incredibly, New Orleans had the No. 1 ranked defense in late-and-close situations (-32.1% DVOA) and the lowest rate of plays with a missed tackle (7.7 percent), and Williams did not surrender a touchdown in coverage in the regular season. Whoops.

Williams is young and should be able to overcome that moment. So should the Saints, as NFL history is filled with examples of teams bouncing back gracefully from a devastating playoff defeat. The 1975 Vikings lost at home in the playoffs to Dallas on Roger Staubach's famous Hail Mary to Drew Pearson, but Minnesota was in the Super Bowl the very next season. The recent play that best resembles Williams' gaffe was when Denver safety Rahim Moore badly misjudged a deep ball from Joe Flacco to Jacoby Jones for a shocking 70-yard touchdown in the 2012 AFC divisional round. Denver still rebounded to make the Super Bowl the following year, though Moore's career did not last much longer.

There were too many positives from New Orleans' season to dwell too much on that one play. It should also be noted that Williams had a big interception off Case Keenum in the third quarter that helped the Saints get their comeback started in the first place. Had Brees chosen to retire after that game, it would have been an awful ending to an era of football in New Orleans. Fortunately, he is still the quarterback, and these young players have another chance to make things right in 2018.

New Orleans desperately needed a great draft going into the 2017 season. Three straight 7-9 campaigns left us wondering if head coach Sean Payton had more in common with Jeff Fisher than surprise onside kicks and a platonic love for Gregg Williams. Year after year we used this space to write about how New Orleans' terrible defense, which ranked 31st or 32nd in DVOA in four of the previous five seasons, was wasting the final years of Brees' golden arm.

Before the start of the 2017 season, Football Outsiders was considering an article showing just how many superb seasons by Brees had resulted in no postseason due to his defense. That research was never put into words, but after the Saints got off to a bad 0-2 start, we figured we would hold it to use in this chapter. Granted, the Patriots and Vikings made for two tough initial opponents, but this team did not look capable of making the playoffs. The defense allowed 1,025 yards in those first two games, which is just 10 yards shy of the NFL record for the first two games of a season. Meanwhile, the experiment (which never made any sense) with Adrian Peterson at running back never proved successful, and the passing game was lacking big plays after the Saints had traded wideout Brandin Cooks to the Patriots.

So how did the Saints get from that 0-2 start to a No. 1 finish in overall DVOA and one unfathomable play away from going to Philadelphia for the NFC Championship Game?

This is what makes New Orleans one of the toughest projections for 2018, because you really have to view last season in three parts. The first part is the 0-2 start where the Saints were clearly outclassed by two of 2017's best teams. The second part was the eight-game winning streak, mostly against soft competition, where the Saints were dominant and discovered both a defense and running game for Brees. New Orleans won each of the first seven of those games by at least eight points, only the 13th team since the merger to have such a winning streak. Ten of those 12 previous teams reached the Super Bowl, and the other two (1998 Vikings and 2005 Colts)

2018 Saints Schedule

Week	Opp.	Week	Opp.	Week	Opp.
1	TB	7	at BAL	13	at DAL (Thu.)
2	CLE	8	at MIN	14	at TB
3	at ATL	9	LAR	15	at CAR (Mon.)
4	at NYG	10	at CIN	16	PIT
5	WAS (Mon.)	11	PHI	17	CAR
6	BYE	12	ATL (Thu.)		

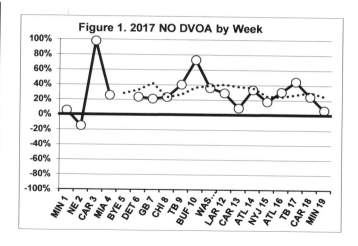

Figure 1. 2017 NO DVOA by Week

were regular-season juggernauts. The final part of the Saints' season, which included the playoffs, saw New Orleans finish 4-4 with a perfect home record and winless road record. That team largely resembled the Saints of recent years, where the offense wasn't nearly as potent on the road and the defense coughed up three fourth-quarter leads.

Who were the real Saints? We compiled DVOA ratings for New Orleans on both sides of the ball, including run and pass splits, during those three parts of the season (Table 1). The true Saints are probably somewhere between the last two parts, but it is interesting how the defense and running game went from outstanding in Weeks 3 to 11 to almost middle-of-the-pack down the stretch. As you may have predicted, Brees and the passing game remained the most consistent part of the team from start to finish.

Thanks to Peyton Manning and Tom Brady, we know that with just enough help you can win a Super Bowl with a 39-year-old quarterback. Brees does not need the best defense or running game in the league to win again, but he needs a little more help than what the Saints were providing late in the season when things like home-field advantage or the next round of the playoffs were within reach.

There are some concerns that the Saints' fast rise last year could fall victim to some regression in 2018. Let's start with the defense, which had the team's highest finish in DVOA (eighth) since 1997. Acquiring a shutdown corner like Lattimore certainly helped with that turnaround. He deserves a lot of credit for this transformation, because it's not like the Saints made a sexy hire at defensive coordinator or a big splash in free agency. Dennis Allen returned as coordinator, a position he had taken over from Rob Ryan in 2015. Defensive end Cameron Jordan is still the unit's star, and he was as good as ever in 2017. But after Jordan and Lattimore, there aren't many household names (yet) on this defense.

It also was not a good year health-wise for the Saints, who ranked 31st in defensive AGL. This is something we normally expect to see regress to the mean the following year. However, that was mostly thanks to three players: cornerback Delvin

Breaux (16 AGL), defensive tackle Nick Fairley (16 AGL), and linebacker Alex Anzalone (12 AGL). Breaux and Fairley are no longer on the roster, so it's not like the Saints are returning those players in good health. Breaux had impressive charting numbers in 2015 when he ranked 16th in adjusted success rate, but he missed 10 games in 2016 and had another serious injury in 2017 that was misdiagnosed by two team doctors, who ended up being fired over the snafu. Breaux remains a free agent and would be a depth piece if the Saints decide to bring him back. Fairley's serious heart condition was only discovered after he had signed a four-year deal worth roughly $30 million in 2017. He never saw the field last year, and the Saints released him in February.

When the Saints were putrid on defense to start the season, rookie linebacker Anzalone was part of the problem. The Patriots toyed with him in coverage for a few touchdowns in Week 2. He projects to start this season at weakside linebacker, though Craig Robertson filled in admirably for him after a shoulder injury cost Anzalone the final 12 games of the season.

If health luck isn't going to improve for the Saints, maybe fumble luck will. The Saints only recovered 33 percent of all fumbles last season, including just four of 16 fumbles on defense. They offset that a bit by ranking second in interceptions per drive (11.4 percent). New Orleans even lost two games after intercepting Matt Ryan and Jameis Winston three times each. Prior to that, quarterbacks were 0-19 against the Saints since 2000 when throwing at least three picks.

Experience should help. Seven of the Saints' 11 projected starters on defense are entering their second or third seasons. Last year, New Orleans had the second-youngest defense in the league as measured by snap-weighted age (24.9 years old).

Table 1. 2017 Saints: A Tale of Three Seasons

Weeks	Offense						Defense					
	DVOA	Rk	Pass DVOA	Rk	Rush DVOA	Rk	DVOA	Rk	Pass DVOA	Rk	Rush DVOA	Rk
Weeks 1-2	22.9%	8	46.7%	9	-18.5%	23	30.0%	30	74.0%	32	-20.8%	13
Weeks 3-11	28.2%	2	38.4%	5	24.0%	1	-18.2%	2	-36.7%	2	4.6%	29
Weeks 12-19	15.0%	5	27.6%	9	-1.4%	13	-3.2%	13	1.0%	12	-8.4%	13

The secondary (23.4 years old) was the youngest of any team since 2010. The Saints saw their 2016 rookies improve in their second seasons, including Sheldon Rankins, Ken Crawley, Vonn Bell, and David Onyemata. They'll hope to see Lattimore, Williams, and Anzalone make similar leaps in 2018.

Developing home-grown talent is a fine strategy, but one has to wonder if the Saints would have been better off trying to acquire All-Pro cornerback Marcus Peters, who was traded to the Rams, or a pass-rusher like Michael Bennett, who was traded to the Eagles. That's the type of move to make when you want to maximize your championship window with an old quarterback.

The Saints operated with a confusing philosophy this offseason. When they traded up from No. 27 to No. 14 in April's draft, it was thought to be for quarterback Lamar Jackson as a successor to Brees. That was the only pick for which it would make sense to give up a first-round pick in 2019. However, the Saints surprised many by taking edge rusher Marcus Davenport. Davenport will be part of the rotation this year, but it's not necessarily a pick that will immediately give the Saints a big-impact pair of pass-rushing bookends. Teams almost never stack great drafts in succession, so don't expect a lot of immediate return from this draft class like last year's provided. New Orleans' only other picks in the first four rounds were wide receiver Tre'Quan Smith and offensive tackle Rick Leonard. A WR4 (at best) and backup tackle aren't getting the Saints past any team in 2018, so from the perspective of improving the roster, the offseason was a bit disappointing.

There's just not likely going to be a surprise stud in the way that Kamara was last year as a third-round pick. Kamara and Mark Ingram each surpassed 1,500 yards from scrimmage, a first for any running back tandem in a season in NFL history. It was special to watch last year, but we already know they're not going to repeat that performance in 2018. In May, Ingram was hit with a four-game suspension for violating the league's performance-enhancing drug policy. The Saints should be just fine in his absence with Kamara taking on a bigger workload, though Ingram will miss the Week 3 showdown with Atlanta.

More Kamara sounds like a great thing, because he was a treat to watch last year and led the NFL by averaging 6.07 yards per carry. However, only one running back in NFL history has ever had multiple seasons with 6.00 yards per carry on at least 100 rushes: Joe Perry for the San Francisco 49ers in 1954 and 1958. (Michael Vick did it four times, but he was a quarterback.) Kamara was never given more than 12 carries in any game last season, and it's possible we'll see that trend continue this year even when Ingram is suspended. Kamara has a ton of value as a receiver. He led all backs with 278 receiving DYAR last year. New Orleans ran a fairly unique running back-centric offense last year with Kamara and Ingram. The Saints threw to their running backs on a league-high 34 percent of their targets. It was the first time an offense was over 30 percent since the 2013 Saints, and the highest rate in our Strategic Tendencies database going back to 2007. That had a lot to do with Brees resetting the single-season record for completion rate at 72.0 percent.

Between Ingram's suspension and Kamara's limited touches, the Saints hope to keep the backs healthy for the stretch run. Their production really dipped late last season, and the playoffs were especially disappointing. Against the Panthers and Vikings, Kamara and Ingram averaged 100.5 yards from scrimmage per game, barely half their regular-season average of 193.4 yards per game. So while this is everyone's favorite new running back duo, the fact is they did a lot of their damage during the team's eight-game winning streak, and they weren't nearly as effective over the last eight games. New Orleans even beat Carolina in the wild-card round despite the duo producing just 68 yards on 21 touches. Carolina's rookie back Christian McCaffrey almost equaled that on one 56-yard touchdown catch, which made the ending a lot closer than it should have been.

In fact, the last three games of the season had a *Groundhog Day* feel for New Orleans. Brees played well and put the team in position with a late lead even though the running game was bottled up. The defense had its moments, but each time had to watch a quarterback loft a potential game-winning touchdown pass in the final seconds. Jameis Winston hit Chris Godwin for 39 yards and a 31-24 victory in Week 17. Cam Newton just missed a throw to Devin Funchess in the end zone in New Orleans' 31-26 wild-card win. And in the divisional round, Case Keenum … well, you know.

It's practically impossible to win a Super Bowl without surviving a few of those coin-flip endings in the playoffs, but the Saints haven't had the desired outcome since Tracy Porter intercepted Brett Favre and Peyton Manning way back in the 2009 season. Someone else has to step up for the Saints like that again, because we know that Brees will deliver. His 34.5% passing DVOA in the playoffs is the highest among active players (minimum 150 passes).

Of course, the elephant in the room is that Brees is 39 this season. Brees needs only 1,496 yards to surpass Manning as the NFL's all-time passing leader, but Father Time is gaining ground. Brees signed a two-year extension in March worth $50 million, but there's no guarantee that 2018 is not the last hurrah.

Has age already begun to set in? Last year, Brees threw 23 touchdowns, his lowest total since 2003. His 4,334 passing yards were the lowest in a season since he joined the Saints in 2006. He did not have a completion gain more than 54 yards until the playoffs. Brees still led the NFL with 8.09 yards per attempt, and the success of the running game did limit some of his usual counting statistics. However, the Saints really shifted to a dink-and-dunk approach in 2017. Brees threw the shortest passes in the NFL at just 6.44 air yards per attempt. His ALEX on all downs was the lowest in the league at -2.3, and Brees ranked 14th in third-down pass conversion rate. Brees had ranked in the top eight in that stat in every season from 2006 to 2016. The story was the same on every down. On first downs, Brees' average throw was 4.5 yards short of the sticks, the second-lowest average in 2017. This offense just did not attack deep as much as it used to, and that led to some struggles in scoring points against tougher competition. The Saints added Cameron Meredith from Chicago and returned Benjamin Watson at tight end, trying to give Brees a full arsenal again in 2018.

This isn't to say that Brees was not stellar last year. He helped Ted Ginn (of all people) to a No. 2 finish in receiving DVOA (34.8%). The way he led a 15-point comeback in the final six minutes against Washington was vintage Brees. He also did basically anything he wanted to against Carolina's defense in a three-game sweep, and he still put the team ahead late in Minnesota before Diggs added to his record number of lost comebacks.

Brees' legacy is going to be that he's the greatest player in NFL history to never be considered the best at his position. He lived in the shadow of Manning and Brady, and when we thought it was his time to make that a trio in 2010, Aaron Rodgers jumped him in line. With the all-time passing records in sight and arguably the best playoff metrics of this era, future generations are going to be confused as to how Brees was considered the *fourth-best* quarterback of his time. Alas, it is a legacy that has at least one more chapter to be written.

The NFC South is arguably the toughest division in which to repeat as champions. The Saints have never been able to do that in the Brees-Payton era. New Orleans could get a boost from the schedule, where five of the first six games are against non-playoff teams from last year. That leads into a rematch with the Vikings in Minnesota in Week 8, and the Saints are fortunate to get marquee late-season matchups with the Rams, Eagles, and Steelers at home.

New Orleans did not have the type of offseason that makes us optimistic that the team is ready to improve on its 2017 performance, which was already such a big improvement over recent years. Most of the other NFC contenders took a more aggressive approach to getting better this offseason, although that's never a sure thing either. The Saints are sticking with homegrown talent and development, but success still hinges on Brees not hitting a sudden age-related decline. With the running game expected to be less efficient this year, Brees cannot let the passing game falter. This is still a team that's going to be identified by its offense. As for the young defenders, should the season come down to another stop in the playoffs, hopefully they'll make a play that looks more like 2009 Tracy Porter rather than 2017 Marcus Williams.

Scott Kacsmar

2017 Saints Stats by Week

Wk	vs.	W-L	PF	PA	YDF	YDA	TO	Total	Off	Def	ST
1	at MIN	L	19	29	344	470	0	6%	27%	27%	6%
2	NE	L	20	36	429	555	0	-15%	19%	32%	-1%
3	at CAR	W	34	13	362	288	+3	98%	68%	-34%	-4%
4	at MIA	W	20	0	347	186	+1	26%	3%	-25%	-2%
5	BYE										
6	DET	W	52	38	379	347	+2	24%	-9%	-58%	-25%
7	at GB	W	26	17	485	260	-1	22%	21%	1%	2%
8	CHI	W	20	12	387	307	-1	24%	10%	-11%	3%
9	TB	W	30	10	407	200	-1	41%	31%	-31%	-22%
10	at BUF	W	47	10	482	198	0	73%	49%	-18%	6%
11	WAS	W	34	31	535	456	-1	36%	61%	33%	9%
12	at LAR	L	20	26	346	415	+1	30%	34%	10%	5%
13	CAR	W	31	21	400	279	0	9%	21%	5%	-7%
14	at ATL	L	17	20	306	343	+2	34%	-1%	-32%	3%
15	NYJ	W	31	19	412	294	-1	18%	9%	2%	11%
16	ATL	W	23	13	315	331	+1	31%	-9%	-29%	12%
17	at TB	L	24	31	323	455	+2	45%	15%	-6%	24%
18	CAR	W	31	26	410	413	-1	25%	42%	23%	6%
19	at MIN	L	24	29	358	403	-1	7%	10%	0%	-2%

Trends and Splits

	Offense	Rank	Defense	Rank
Total DVOA	21.6%	2	-7.9%	8
Unadjusted VOA	21.3%	2	-2.6%	12
Weighted Trend	20.0%	2	-10.0%	6
Variance	5.2%	10	6.9%	25
Average Opponent	1.3%	25	1.8%	11
Passing	33.3%	5	-11.3%	5
Rushing	12.0%	1	-3.7%	23
First Down	27.4%	2	-12.1%	4
Second Down	20.8%	5	-11.9%	2
Third Down	10.5%	11	6.4%	22
First Half	20.4%	2	3.1%	20
Second Half	22.9%	3	-20.2%	2
Red Zone	20.4%	6	-14.9%	7
Late and Close	17.2%	5	-32.1%	1

Five-Year Performance

Year	W-L	Pyth W	Est W	PF	PA	TO	Total	Rk	Off	Rk	Def	Rk	ST	Rk	Off AGL	Rk	Def AGL	Rk	Off Age	Rk	Def Age	Rk	ST Age	Rk
2013	11-5	10.8	10.0	414	304	0	19.3%	4	16.0%	5	-5.8%	10	-2.5%	24	12.3	3	59.0	31	28.4	1	26.0	25	26.2	10
2014	7-9	7.4	7.6	401	424	-13	-0.9%	17	10.6%	7	13.1%	31	1.6%	11	26.4	12	31.6	10	29.0	1	26.2	24	25.9	22
2015	7-9	6.4	5.2	408	476	+2	-18.7%	28	10.5%	7	26.1%	32	-3.2%	26	19.7	3	36.3	23	28.2	4	26.5	20	26.7	4
2016	7-9	8.3	8.6	469	454	-3	-1.9%	21	15.4%	6	14.6%	31	-2.6%	27	22.4	5	58.9	27	28.3	2	26.8	11	27.0	4
2017	11-5	11.1	13.4	448	326	+7	30.7%	1	21.6%	2	-7.9%	8	1.2%	15	33.6	16	62.3	31	27.5	6	24.9	31	25.7	21

2017 Performance Based on Most Common Personnel Groups

NO Offense					NO Offense vs. Opponents					NO Defense				NO Defense vs. Opponents			
Pers	Freq	Yds	DVOA	Run%	Pers	Freq	Yds	DVOA	Run%	Pers	Freq	Yds	DVOA	Pers	Freq	Yds	DVOA
11	49%	6.7	34.3%	33%	Base	38%	5.5	15.0%	61%	Base	23%	5.4	-7.3%	11	62%	5.9	-8.3%
12	16%	7.3	32.7%	46%	Nickel	52%	6.9	27.4%	33%	Nickel	61%	5.6	-14.8%	12	15%	5.6	-20.7%
21	13%	7.1	25.1%	53%	Dime+	9%	7.6	38.7%	18%	Dime+	13%	6.5	15.8%	21	9%	5.3	-2.2%
612	6%	3.6	-12.2%	86%	Goal Line	1%	0.9	16.5%	60%	Goal Line	3%	3.0	18.2%	13	4%	4.8	13.3%
13	3%	6.0	15.7%	73%										22	3%	4.7	-5.6%
20	3%	5.8	-15.2%	0%										612	2%	4.1	21.4%
22	3%	6.2	17.9%	57%													
10	3%	7.4	0.4%	14%													

Strategic Tendencies

Run/Pass		Rk	Formation		Rk	Pass Rush		Rk	Secondary		Rk	Strategy		Rk
Runs, first half	41%	10	Form: Single Back	71%	26	Rush 3	7.4%	14	4 DB	23%	29	Play action	20%	23
Runs, first down	54%	8	Form: Empty Back	11%	7	Rush 4	54.6%	30	5 DB	61%	12	Avg Box (Off)	6.24	16
Runs, second-long	32%	18	Pers: 3+ WR	56%	23	Rush 5	26.1%	7	6+ DB	13%	12	Avg Box (Def)	6.28	11
Runs, power sit.	60%	12	Pers: 2+ TE/6+ OL	31%	14	Rush 6+	11.8%	1	CB by Sides	72%	24	Offensive Pace	30.53	15
Runs, behind 2H	28%	14	Pers: 6+ OL	5%	6	Int DL Sacks	9.5%	31	S/CB Cover Ratio	35%	6	Defensive Pace	31.47	28
Pass, ahead 2H	47%	16	Shotgun/Pistol	49%	27	Second Level Sacks	28.6%	5	DB Blitz	11%	12	Go for it on 4th	1.43	6

A big part of the Saints' big season was broken tackles: forcing them on offense and avoiding them on defense. New Orleans led the league with broken tackles on 14.2 percent of plays and was second behind Kansas City with 161 total broken tackles. The Saints were the only team where two players had at least 50 broken tackles: Alvin Kamara with 66 and Mark Ingram with 56. ☞ On defense, the Saints had the fewest broken tackles (82) and their rate of plays with broken tackles (7.7 percent) was nearly a percentage point lower than any other defense. Out of 105 defenders with double-digit broken tackles in 2017, only one played for the Saints: cornerback Ken Crawley, who had 11. ☞ New Orleans' offense was exceptionally multiple, as the Saints had eight different personnel groups that they used on at least 3.0 percent of plays. Particularly remarkable was how they used the 20 personnel group that put Kamara and Ingram on the field at the same time. There were 32 plays from this personnel group, and all 32 were passing plays. This is part of a general trend where the Saints didn't run the ball much from shotgun formations: only 9.1 percent of their plays from shotgun were runs, although they had a league-leading 29.1% DVOA on shotgun runs. The Saints did run with both Kamara and Ingram on the field, but only if they also had six offensive linemen and a tight end in an under-center formation. ☞ Bringing in that extra offensive lineman generally didn't work well for the Saints, though. New Orleans had 5.2 yards per play and 11.7% DVOA from six-lineman sets in 2016, but that dropped to 2.8 and -13.9% DVOA in 2017. ☞ On the other hand, the Saints had a league-leading 8.9 yards per play and 59.6% DVOA from empty backfields in 2017. ☞ The Saints led the league in fewest dropped passes (18) and lowest rate of dropped passes (3.4 percent). ☞ Although the Saints brought more big blitzes than any other defense, this wasn't necessarily a wise strategy. The Saints defense was down to 5.3 yards per pass (-47.8% DVOA) with five pass-rushers, but then allowed 7.0 yards per pass (34.1% DVOA) with six or more pass-rushers. ☞ The Saints defense was No. 20 before halftime but only Baltimore had a better defense after halftime.

Passing

Player	DYAR	DVOA	Plays	NtYds	Avg	YAC	C%	TD	Int
D.Brees	1390	27.4%	555	4171	7.5	6.1	72.6%	23	8
T.Savage	-249	-27.5%	243	1255	5.2	4.1	56.6%	5	6

Rushing

Player	DYAR	DVOA	Plays	Yds	Avg	TD	Fum	Suc
M.Ingram	193	11.2%	230	1127	4.9	12	2	49%
M.Ingram	193	11.2%	230	1127	4.9	12	2	49%
A.Kamara	255	44.5%	120	728	6.1	8	1	53%
A.Peterson*	-4	-11.4%	27	81	3.0	0	0	44%
D.Brees	6	-5.6%	13	28	2.2	2	1	-
T.Ginn	20	-0.8%	10	39	3.9	0	0	-
T.Edmunds	-8	-31.2%	9	48	5.3	1	0	33%
Z.Line	20	33.4%	7	28	4.0	0	0	100%

Receiving

Player	DYAR	DVOA	Plays	Ctch	Yds	Y/C	YAC	TD	C%
M.Thomas	330	15.0%	149	104	1245	12.0	4.1	5	70%
T.Ginn	259	34.8%	70	53	787	14.8	5.4	4	76%
B.Coleman	53	6.0%	37	23	374	16.3	6.7	3	62%
W.Snead*	-23	-31.0%	16	8	92	11.5	4.0	0	50%
T.Lewis	-12	-22.8%	15	10	116	11.6	5.2	1	67%
C.Fleener*	107	50.1%	30	22	295	13.4	5.0	2	73%
J.Hill	-56	-45.1%	23	17	117	6.9	5.2	1	74%
M.Hoomanawanui	-13	-23.8%	10	6	52	8.7	4.5	1	60%
B.Watson	-1	-7.5%	79	61	522	8.6	4.1	4	77%
A.Kamara	278	36.4%	100	81	826	10.2	8.5	5	81%
M.Ingram	13	-10.7%	71	58	418	7.2	8.7	0	82%

Offensive Line

Player	Pos	Age	GS	Snaps	Pen	Sk	Pass	Run	Player	Pos	Age	GS	Snaps	Pen	Sk	Pass	Run
Ryan Ramczyk	RT	24	16/16	1039	6	2.0	8	8	Senio Kelemete*	G/T	28	16/8	634	4	1.0	3	6
Max Unger	C	32	16/16	1039	0	2.5	6	5	Terron Armstead	LT	27	10/10	543	2	3.0	9	2
Andrus Peat	LG	25	15/14	920	6	3.0	11	5	Josh LeRibeus	C	28	16/0	207	1	0.0	0	2
Larry Warford	RG	27	14/14	825	4	1.0	6	4	Jermon Bushrod	RG	34	10/10	605	7	2.0	7	3

Year	Yards	ALY	Rank	Power	Rank	Stuff	Rank	2nd Lev	Rank	Open Field	Rank	Sacks	ASR	Rank	Press	Rank	F-Start	Cont.
2015	4.00	4.23	13	74%	5	20%	14	1.17	17	0.68	18	32	5.1%	7	21.3%	7	19	25
2016	4.53	4.93	1	70%	9	14%	2	1.11	19	0.85	10	27	4.5%	5	18.9%	3	19	21
2017	5.11	4.93	2	69%	7	15%	1	1.30	3	1.37	1	20	4.0%	2	20.9%	1	6	23

2017 ALY by direction:	Left End: 5.69 (3)	Left Tackle: 4.54 (12)	Mid/Guard: 4.94 (2)	Right Tackle: 4.65 (5)	Right End: 5.15 (2)

All five offensive line starters are returning for 2018. All of those players ranked in the top 10 at their respective position in snaps per blown block except for left guard Andrus Peat, who ranked 11th. *What a slacker.* Peat unfortunately broke his fibula in the wild-card win over Carolina, but he should be ready to go this summer. ☞ Left tackle Terron Armstead has missed multiple games in every season of his career, but he's otherwise been a reliable starter to protect Drew Brees' blindside. ☞ Max Unger is already entering his fourth season as New Orleans' center. He hasn't notched a Pro Bowl since Seattle's rise to prominence in 2012 and 2013, but he has more or less been the same player from those years since New Orleans made him part of the Jimmy Graham trade in 2015. ☞ Speaking of Pro Bowls, right guard Larry Warford made his first one last year. He was a replacement for Super Bowl-bound Brandon Brooks, but that's still impressive from a player with little fanfare going into the season. Warford had an uneven career in Detroit. His 2013 rookie season was often considered his high point, and he had big shoes to fill in replacing Jahri Evans last year for the Saints. The first year of his four-year, $34 million deal went about as well as it possibly could. ☞ Warford replacing Evans wasn't the only big replacement the Saints had to make on the right side of their line last year. First-round rookie Ryan Ramczyk had to take over for an injured Zach Strief, who has been with the team since 2006 and announced his retirement this past March. Ramczyk actually started the year at left tackle when Armstead was injured, so he has the experience on both sides and was already a standout in his first season.

Defensive Front Seven

Defensive Line	Age	Pos	G	Snaps	Plays	Overall TmPct	Rk	Stop	Dfts	BTkl	Runs	vs. Run St%	Rk	RuYd	Rk	Pass Rush Sack	Hit	Hur	Dsrpt
Sheldon Rankins	24	DT	16	812	27	3.3%	79	20	8	0	23	70%	71	3.3	81	2.0	12	27.0	0
David Onyemata	26	DT	16	598	39	4.7%	51	28	8	2	33	67%	76	2.6	68	2.0	4	16.5	1
Tyeler Davison	26	DT	16	589	31	3.7%	66	25	6	0	30	80%	32	2.2	51	0.0	2	6.0	1
John Hughes*	30	DT	8	162	10	2.4%	--	5	0	0	10	50%	--	3.5	--	0.0	1	4.5	0

Edge Rushers	Age	Pos	G	Snaps	Plays	Overall TmPct	Rk	Stop	Dfts	BTkl	Runs	vs. Run St%	Rk	RuYd	Rk	Pass Rush Sack	Hit	Hur	Dsrpt
Cameron Jordan	29	DE	16	990	70	8.4%	8	56	23	7	41	71%	63	2.4	50	13.0	18	49.0	13
Alex Okafor	27	DE	10	486	46	8.9%	3	37	17	4	31	77%	39	1.5	22	4.5	6	13.5	5
Trey Hendrickson	24	DE	12	282	15	2.4%	--	7	4	3	11	27%	--	3.1	--	2.0	2	13.0	2
Hau'oli Kikaha	26	OLB	12	211	11	1.8%	--	9	5	0	6	67%	--	2.3	--	4.0	0	3.5	0

Linebackers	Age	Pos	G	Snaps	Plays	Overall TmPct	Rk	Stop	Dfts	BTkl	Runs	vs. Run St%	Rk	RuYd	Rk	Pass Rush Sack	Hit	Hur	Tgts	vs. Pass Suc%	Rk	AdjYd	Rk	PD	Int
Craig Robertson	30	OLB	16	793	82	9.9%	65	48	17	5	43	70%	20	2.7	15	2.0	0	7.5	33	71%	2	4.2	1	5	2
A.J. Klein	27	OLB	12	664	58	9.3%	68	29	10	7	30	47%	82	5.9	86	2.0	4	8.5	22	58%	15	7.6	57	2	0
Manti Te'o	27	MLB	16	503	64	7.7%	79	35	12	3	43	60%	54	2.7	16	0.0	0	3.5	13	57%	19	8.4	66	3	0
Demario Davis	29	ILB	16	1118	138	17.1%	8	83	25	13	85	64%	40	3.9	59	5.0	9	19.0	52	64%	5	5.4	14	2	0

Year	Yards	ALY	Rank	Power	Rank	Stuff	Rank	2nd Level	Rank	Open Field	Rank	Sacks	ASR	Rank	Press	Rank
2015	5.06	4.74	31	68%	20	16%	30	1.46	32	1.20	31	31	6.0%	20	21.3%	32
2016	4.21	4.09	15	65%	20	20%	14	1.13	13	0.94	27	30	5.0%	28	27.3%	14
2017	4.11	4.10	17	66%	21	21%	13	1.08	11	0.80	22	42	7.8%	6	32.3%	8

2017 ALY by direction:	Left End: 4.44 (22)	Left Tackle: 3.71 (13)	Mid/Guard: 4.30 (18)	Right Tackle: 2.98 (6)	Right End: 4.65 (25)

Cameron Jordan has long been the best defender in New Orleans, and 2017 was his best season yet. Not only did a career-high 13.0 sacks lead to his first All-Pro selection, but he had a league-high 13 disruptions, four more than any other defender. These are plays where the defender batted or tipped a pass at the line of scrimmage, or when he hit a quarterback in motion to cause an incompletion. Jordan's disruptive ways last year were on display to clinch the playoff win against the Panthers. His pressure on Cam Newton led to an intentional grounding penalty that set the Panthers back into a third-and-23 situation. The penalty was suspect, but Jordan's pass-rush attack was no joke in 2017. ☞ Jordan now has plenty of help at edge rusher. Sheldon Rankins made major strides in his second season. Forget the fact that his sacks were cut in half despite a lot more snaps, because he increased his hurries from six to 27 and could see a big increase in sacks in 2018. Rankins moved from defensive tackle to edge rusher after Alex Okafor tore his Achilles. The Saints can keep Rankins outside with Okafor as his backup, or use both together with Rankins using his speed inside. ☞ If that wasn't enough, then the Saints traded up to draft Marcus Davenport with the 14th pick. SackSEER had Davenport with the second-highest projection of sacks through five seasons of any pass-rusher in this draft class. He didn't post huge sack numbers in college (21.5 in four years), but Davenport's combine was physically impressive. He should be a big part of the rotation this year. ☞ Tyeler Davison was the team's top run-stopper up front, and David Onyemata was another young defensive tackle who showed improvement in his second season with the team. ☞ The linebackers are the bland unit in this defense, but A.J. Klein and Manti Te'o had respectable free-agent debuts. Then the Saints used free agency to bring in Demario Davis from the Jets. Davis' 83 stops ranked second in the league in 2017, and he had excellent coverage metrics. The latter is not consistent with his career, but the Saints are getting a 29-year-old coming off a career year and ready to step up to the MIKE. ☞ Alex Anzalone will have a good shot to win the weakside spot again should he stay healthy. The good news: he's no longer a rookie, and there is no Rob Gronkowski on this regular-season schedule.

Defensive Secondary

Secondary	Age	Pos	G	Snaps	Plays	Overall TmPct	Rk	Stop	Dfts	BTkl	Runs	vs. Run St%	Rk	RuYd	Rk	Tgts	vs. Pass Tgt%	Rk	Dist	Suc%	Rk	AdjYd	Rk	PD	Int
Marcus Williams	22	FS	15	960	78	10.0%	36	17	7	7	27	26%	65	10.1	68	27	7.5%	16	18.4	60%	14	10.4	66	7	4
Ken Crawley	25	CB	13	822	70	10.4%	11	31	8	11	14	21%	74	9.3	70	82	26.7%	71	14.2	59%	8	6.7	17	18	1
Vonn Bell	24	FS	16	787	80	9.7%	47	30	15	8	40	45%	38	5.4	26	33	11.2%	51	9.3	41%	67	8.8	45	2	0
Marshon Lattimore	22	CB	13	754	70	10.4%	11	32	17	2	16	31%	65	10.8	72	66	23.2%	63	12.6	53%	34	6.8	26	17	5
Kenny Vaccaro*	27	SS	12	692	66	10.6%	30	37	18	7	27	59%	10	4.0	6	43	16.4%	73	8.8	49%	49	9.0	48	4	3
P.J. Williams	25	CB	16	633	56	6.8%	--	30	14	5	19	53%	--	5.4	--	34	14.1%	--	12.3	46%	--	9.6	--	9	2
Rafael Bush*	31	FS	14	184	23	3.2%	--	12	8	3	12	50%	--	7.4	--	12	17.4%	--	8.8	70%	--	3.7	--	0	0
Kurt Coleman	30	FS	12	721	79	13.9%	4	25	12	9	29	45%	39	8.3	57	34	11.5%	55	14.3	47%	53	9.6	56	2	0
Patrick Robinson	31	CB	16	710	63	8.2%	43	39	20	10	11	64%	13	3.7	8	70	21.5%	48	10.4	62%	5	7.3	37	19	4

Year	Pass D Rank	vs. #1 WR	Rk	vs. #2 WR	Rk	vs. Other WR	Rk	WR Wide	Rk	WR Slot	Rk	vs. TE	Rk	vs. RB	Rk
2015	32	14.9%	29	23.0%	29	18.9%	27	--	--	--	--	46.0%	32	28.7%	31
2016	30	5.5%	23	11.3%	26	15.3%	28	16.0%	30	4.4%	17	4.8%	22	43.4%	32
2017	5	-19.1%	6	0.6%	18	-21.8%	5	-31.6%	2	7.9%	16	-17.0%	6	-5.5%	12

We just want to reiterate that this was the youngest NFL secondary by snap-weighted age (23.4 years) in the last eight years. ☞ The best is yet to come for many of these players, but cornerback Marshon Lattimore had a transformative effect on the defense that we rarely see from a rookie. His charting numbers won't blow you away, but he made plays on the ball and drew the toughest assignments on a weekly basis. ☞ How about that other rookie in the secondary? Despite the postseason catastrophe, Marcus Williams had a solid rookie season at safety. Offenses did like to test him deep. His 18.4 aDOT was the third-highest among qualified safeties, and about double that of teammates Vonn Bell (9.3) and Kenny Vaccaro (8.8), who played much closer to the box. Vaccaro remains a free agent after multiple surgeries this offseason. ☞ Similar to Williams, Ken Crawley was involved in some of the defense's more egregious late-game touchdowns allowed, but he made huge strides over his rookie season. The Saints have an intriguing young duo starting at cornerback for the first time in many years. ☞ Speaking of passes defensed, Patrick Robinson (19) had more of those for the Eagles last year than either Crawley (18) or Lattimore (17) in New Orleans. His big pick-six in the NFC Championship Game sparked a Philadelphia blowout. Robinson was an underwhelming first-round pick by the Saints in 2010 and has bounced around three different teams since 2015. He seems to have found his niche in the slot corner role, and he should see plenty of action this season in his second stint with New Orleans. At the very least, the 31-year-old will raise the unit's snap-weighted age.

Special Teams

Year	DVOA	Rank	FG/XP	Rank	Net Kick	Rank	Kick Ret	Rank	Net Punt	Rank	Punt Ret	Rank	Hidden	Rank
2015	-3.2%	26	-15.4	31	-2.4	20	-2.1	21	3.8	11	0.2	16	14.0	3
2016	-2.6%	27	0.0	18	-5.1	28	-8.0	31	0.8	13	-1.0	15	-6.3	24
2017	1.2%	15	-0.9	17	-0.3	20	5.6	5	6.5	7	-5.0	28	10.3	4

The Saints have not ranked in the top 10 in special teams DVOA since they were third in 2004. Last year was the first for special teams coordinator Bradford Banta, who replaced longtime coordinator Greg McMahon (2008-2016). The result was an improvement to mediocrity (No. 15), but there were some high points. ☞ Punter Thomas Morstead ranked third in gross punt value, improving his mark for the third year in a row. ☞ In his attempt to prove he can do everything well, rookie running back Alvin Kamara had a 106-yard kick return touchdown. Overall, he added 8.3 points of value on 10 kick returns. That was second in the league between Seattle's Tyler Lockett (8.4 points on 37 returns) and Los Angeles' Pharoh Cooper (8.3 points on 34 returns), a very impressive figure on such limited work. That work will likely have to remain limited with his duties on offense, but if the Saints are ever going to set up a return in a big moment, then Kamara has to be involved. ☞ While Ted Ginn's Big Easy debut on offense was a successful one, he did not bring the value the team had hoped for as a punt returner. Ginn averaged a career-low 5.4 yards per punt return and ranked 46th in punt return value. ☞ Kicker Wil Lutz is reliable enough on field goals and extra points. He improved his kickoffs in 2017 after a poor rookie season, but still had negative value in that area.

New York Giants

2017 Record: 3-13	Total DVOA: -22.2% (30th)	2018 Mean Projection: 6.1 wins	On the Clock (0-4): 27%
Pythagorean Wins: 4.0 (31st)	Offense: -9.0% (23rd)	Postseason Odds: 12.4%	Mediocrity (5-7): 46%
Snap-Weighted Age: 26.1 (24th)	Defense: 5.7% (24th)	Super Bowl Odds: 0.7%	Playoff Contender (8-10): 23%
Average Opponent: 3.3% (5th)	Special Teams: -7.5% (32nd)	Proj. Avg. Opponent: 1.8% (6th)	Super Bowl Contender (11+): 5%

2017: After a successful 2016 season, the Giants could not McAdoo it again.

2018: When will they quit Eli Manning?

The 2016 season feels like an eternity ago for the New York Giants. By the end of that campaign, the Giants had amassed an 11-5 record and a top-10 spot in overall DVOA. Though they were swiftly knocked out of the playoffs, the ensuing 2017 season appeared to be a fresh opportunity. Per Football Outsiders' projections, the Giants were looking at a mean projection of 8.4 wins and a measly 7.5 percent chance of ending up "on the clock" (meaning they would have a top-four pick in the draft) by season's end,. By and large, both sides of the ball remained intact. The Giants were again set to be carried by stars such as Landon Collins, Janoris Jenkins, and Odell Beckham Jr. Our projections expected the team to regress, but there were still plenty of signs the Giants would be a competitive team in 2017. Instead, the Giants were slain, and they crawled into the offseason with a 3-13 record and the second overall pick in the draft, suddenly yearning for a change of direction.

In large part, the devolution of the Giants' defense became the team's downfall. After finishing a dismal 30th in defensive DVOA in 2015, the unit was entirely overhauled, primarily through the additions of Janoris Jenkins and Olivier Vernon. The new and improved defense skyrocketed to a second-place DVOA finish in 2016 through a high pressure rate and outstanding secondary play. Given the volatility of going from 30th to second in a single offseason, some regression was to be expected. That was the largest jump in defensive DVOA rank in history, after all. However, with the slew of new faces leading the charge, there was plenty of reason to believe that it was not good fortune that propelled the unit, but rather legitimate progress and talent upgrades.

As it turned out, the same players who thrived in 2016 could not repeat their feats again. Aside from defensive tackle Johnathan Hankins leaving in free agency and some shuffling around at linebacker, the defensive roster was largely the same as the dominant squad from the year before, and the team had even gotten back Darian Thompson from injury after he missed almost his entire rookie season in 2016. And with mostly the same players, New York's defense plummeted back down to 24th in defensive DVOA in 2017, sandwiched between Houston and Dallas.

Jenkins, the team's lockdown cornerback, was still a force early on in 2017, but as a nagging ankle injury grew worse, Jenkins' play fell off. The ankle injury initially sidelined Jenkins in Week 2, but he continued to play through it, and did so fairly well for a good stretch to open the year. However, after the cornerback showed up late to team facilities during New York's bye in Week 8, head coach Ben McAdoo suspended Jenkins for Week 9. In the wake of his suspension, Jenkins became even more volatile than before; his frustrations with coaching did not make it any easier for him to continue playing through injury. From Week 10 through Week 12, he allowed more than 16 yards per pass. Jenkins ultimately opted to undergo surgery prior to Week 13, allowing him to end a lost season before the injury grew any worse.

Compounding Jenkins' absence and volatile play was a lack of development from second-year cornerback Eli Apple. There was hope that Apple could turn some of his rookie flashes into something more reliable, but he was instead used by opposing teams as an expressway to free passing yards.

Rounding out the starting unit was the veteran Dominique Rodgers-Cromartie, who often played from the slot. Rodgers-Cromartie took a noticeable step back, due in part to losing some of the aggression and twitch that had carried him in 2016. Like Jenkins, Rodgers-Cromartie did not get along with McAdoo particularly well. Rodgers-Cromartie was suspended for Week 6 after confronting McAdoo about his playing time from the previous week. From that point on, Rodgers-Cromartie's performance and snap totals became less predictable than they were during his 2016 season. As the unit collectively struggled to find stable ground, the secondary's troubles trickled down to the rest of the defense, leaving linebackers exposed in coverage and stressing a pass rush that had no depth. Only eight defensive linemen in the league played at least 85 percent of snaps when active; Vernon and Jason Pierre-Paul were two of the eight, and the only pair of teammates.

Meanwhile, the Giants offense was eroded by injuries. Star wide receiver Odell Beckham Jr. suffered a season-ending ankle fracture just five games into the season, immediately stripping the offense of any star talent. During the same game, wide receivers Brandon Marshall and Dwayne Harris also suffered lower body injuries that sidelined them for the remainder of the year. Granted, Marshall had been disappointing in his first few games with the Giants and Harris was more of a return specialist than a receiving threat, but losing three of your top four wide receivers in the same game is not ideal. Sterling

2018 Giants Schedule

Week	Opp.	Week	Opp.	Week	Opp.
1	JAX	7	at ATL (Mon.)	13	CHI
2	at DAL	8	WAS	14	at WAS
3	at HOU	9	BYE	15	TEN
4	NO	10	at SF (Mon.)	16	at IND
5	at CAR	11	TB	17	DAL
6	PHI (Thu.)	12	at PHI		

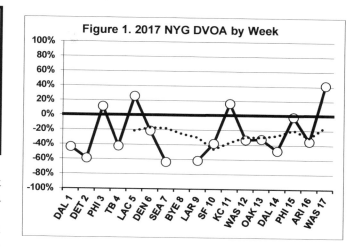

Figure 1. 2017 NYG DVOA by Week

Shepard, the only prominent wideout to make it through that game without going on IR, missed five other games with a variety of minor injuries.

Given McAdoo's scheme was more isolation-centric than most other offenses, losing two of the team's top three receivers and intermittently being without the third put the offense in a bind. Backup and practice-squad players were asked to straight-up beat starting-caliber cornerbacks. In turn, the passing game became constipated. Eli Manning, already a middling passer at this point in his career, was forced into an impossible situation and ultimately struggled.

McAdoo could not use injuries as an excuse for Manning's disappointing play, though. As the head coach and former offensive coordinator, McAdoo was expected to make the offense work no matter what. Sitting with a 2-9 record heading into Week 13, panic set in for McAdoo. The decision to bench Manning was not as strange as who McAdoo benched him for: he decided in favor of Geno Smith, a cast-off from the team across the Meadowlands and a player who had generally been considered a bust, rather than giving rookie Davis Webb a chance. This strange move was the final straw for the Giants organization. McAdoo did not survive the following week with his job.

The McAdoo era didn't even last two full seasons, but it left the Giants' fans and front office yearning for a new era on offense. In an effort to remove themselves from McAdoo's isolation offense, the Giants sought after Pat Shurmur, who had previously served as Chip Kelly's offensive coordinator in Philadelphia and as a position coach and offensive coordinator for Mike Zimmer in Minnesota. In 2017, Shurmur's Vikings offense, quarterbacked by journeyman Case Keenum, finished fifth in offensive DVOA and third in passing offense DVOA.

Shurmur approaches an offensive scheme as an interconnected collection of concepts and a means to dictate the pace of the game, as opposed to McAdoo's propensity to call plays separate of each other and hope for a cohesive product. Shurmur also does more within each play concept to work players open, rather than banking on isolation routes and simply using checkdowns to get the ball to the running back. For example, Shurmur makes it a point to create conflicts for the defense. Be it a physical conflict such as forcing the defense to pass off or follow a wheel route, or a mental conflict such as stretching the field via slot fade and various high-low concepts, Shurmur focuses on mitigating individual defensive talent to create opportunities for his players.

After bringing in Shurmur, the Giants organization has made it a point to load the offense with talent for him to work with. Health permitting, Shurmur will have two high-quality receivers again in Beckham and Shepard, in addition to explosive second-year tight end Evan Engram. Many of the Giants' offseason resources were spent on filling out the roster around those three young pass-catchers.

Leading the charge in revamping the roster is new general manager Dave Gettleman, who spent four years as the Carolina Panthers' general manager before being fired in July of 2017. Gettleman subscribes to the philosophy that an offense should be rooted in a strong running game, particularly one led by brawling offensive linemen. In Carolina, Cam Newton's dynamism gave life to Gettleman's otherwise outdated, slow-paced concept of football, but the personnel Gettleman surrounded Newton with still resulted in an offense that was often looking to grind games out. Gettleman's solution to the escalating issue of an obstructed offense was to draft a running back who could run precise routes out of the backfield, Christian McCaffrey. To his misfortune, Gettleman never got to experience the fruition of the McCaffrey pick first-hand in Carolina, but he has already set out to recreate the McCaffrey selection in New York.

A handful of talented players in recent years have sparked the conversation about the value of running backs in the first round of the draft, but none did so to the level of Saquon Barkley, the star runner from Penn State. To Gettleman, the perceived value of the second overall pick did not matter—he simply wanted the best player available. Barkley was the easy answer in Gettleman's mind.

Measured at 6-foot-0 and 233 pounds at the NFL combine, Barkley ran a 4.40-second 40-yard dash and recorded a 41-inch vertical jump, both of which scored above the 90th percentile. As a runner, pass-catcher, and return specialist, Barkley regularly stunted on opposing defenses with highlight plays. Be it hurdling over defenders (sorry, Iowa fans) or breaking away from defenders with blazing speed on his way to the end zone, Barkley was always good for a handful of special plays that other running backs in recent years could not match.

However, Barkley's boom was accompanied by plenty of bust while at Penn State. Bill Connelly uses a stat called marginal efficiency rating to measure how often a runner picks up the required amount of yards for a "success" on a given play. Barkley scored a 0.6 rating, which placed 16th among 27 qualifying running back prospects. In fairness to Barkley, Penn State's offensive line was mostly a disaster and did not stack up against bruising gangs at other Big Ten programs such as Michigan State and Ohio State. Barkley often took it upon himself to clean up the mess by bouncing outside too early or dancing in the backfield to try to make something happen. Regardless, Barkley's efficiency is still disappointing, even with that context in mind.

Luckily for Barkley, investments were made along the Giants' offensive line to ensure he will get more help than he did at Penn State. Free-agent left tackle Nate Solder was brought in to kill two birds with one stone: Solder is an upgrade over Ereck Flowers at left tackle, while Flowers, who played right tackle as a freshman at Miami in 2012, should be better than the dismal right tackle combination of Bobby Hart and Chad Wheeler that New York used last year. Via the draft, offensive guard Will Hernandez (UTEP) was brought in to steer the offensive line toward a meaner, more downhill style of rushing. Hernandez, akin to names such as Andrew Norwell and Richie Incognito, is an excellent pull player who meshes well with Barkley's boxer-like running style and can be used by Barkley as an obstacle with which to manipulate defenders.

Barkley also had to carry a massive workload in college, which will not necessarily be the case during his rookie season. As the team's token veteran skill-player signing, running back Jonathan Stewart will serve as the thunder to Barkley's lightning. Stewart struggled last season, but he has familiarity with the downhill rushing attack that New York is setting up for. At the very least, he can provide Barkley with a veteran presence that will hopefully take some of the pressure off him.

The significance of the rookie and veteran pairing stretches beyond their production, though. On top of whatever their on-field values may be, Barkley and Stewart serve as a sort of symbol for what the Dave Gettleman era in New York will be like. Stewart is a remnant from Gettleman's four-year tenure as the general manager of the Panthers. Though Gettleman did not draft Stewart, he held onto an archaic brand of offense that favored Stewart: a commitment to a power-run ground game. Barkley, on the other hand, is effectively Gettleman's second chance at what he wanted in McCaffrey, albeit with more natural talent and a higher ceiling.

Gettleman's recreation of his Carolina teams bleeds through into his decisions regarding the defense as well. He traded fourth- and sixth-round picks for Rams linebacker Alec Ogletree, who he likely believes can be somewhat reminiscent of the hyper-athletic, coverage-savvy player that Luke Kuechly is in Carolina. Taking on his four-year, $42.75 million contract feels a bit rich, but Ogletree did post a quietly impressive 59 percent success rate in coverage last year. Ogletree also racked up 17.5 quarterback hurries.

Likewise, Gettleman sought out to replicate the defensive line prowess and depth featured in Carolina. Due to investments in Barkley and Hernandez in the first two rounds, Gettleman could not commit premium resources to the defensive line like he did with Carolina in 2013, when he doubled down on defensive tackles with Star Lotulelei and Kawann Short. The Giants did select defensive end B.J. Hill (North Carolina State) and defensive tackle R.J. McIntosh (Miami) in the third and fifth round, respectively. Veterans Kareem Martin and Josh Mauro were also added to fill out the depth chart, though neither should stop Gettleman from investing in the defensive line in upcoming drafts.

In some ways, Gettleman's direct mirror of his time in Carolina is worrisome. It may be early in his tenure, but after so many moves to parallel his Carolina teams, there has to be concern that Gettleman did not learn anything from his firing and is instead set in his ways, believing that he was wronged in Carolina and that his methods can be successful in the modern NFL. Gettleman certainly deserves a grace period with his new team, and his old tactics did have some success in Carolina, but the same issues persisted throughout his Panthers teams for years and regularly had to be patched up by Newton.

What remains constant through Gettleman's early reign in New York is that what is new is actually old. For one, the hiring of Shurmur and the drafting of Barkley are supposed to signal a new era on offense, but 37-year-old Manning is still the starting quarterback. Gettleman pushed off drafting a potential heir to Manning at quarterback until the fourth round, where he selected Kyle Lauletta out of Richmond. Though taking a shot on a quarterback is generally not a bad idea, the Giants had already drafted Webb in the third round a year ago. Gettleman was not really "adding" a quarterback to groom behind Manning; he just wanted his own.

Furthermore, drafting a running back second overall is Gettleman's way to immediately restructure his new team around the principle that an offense ought to live and die through the running game. Drafting a running back in the top 10 immediately after having done so in Carolina clearly signals Gettleman's approach. The problem is that it is hard to make the argument for this kind of investment in a running back given the pass-heavy focus of today's National Football League. Both pass offense and pass defense correlate to winning more than run offense and run defense. Of course, less correlation doesn't make running the ball completely worthless, but then we have to ask the question: who is most responsible for a strong, consistent running game? NFL teams have clearly voted here with their wallets. Forty-two offensive linemen are under contract for a higher average salary than every running back with one exception (Le'Veon Bell, who will be playing under the franchise tag in 2018). Every year, teams make it clear in their free-agency decisions that running backs are simply more replaceable than quality offensive linemen.

Additionally, part of the NFL draft's value is that teams can get discounts on players because contracts are based on draft slot under the current CBA. For example, a quarterback earning $8 million or so as the first overall pick is dramatically cheap relative to the market of the position. However, the same cannot be said of running backs taken with premium picks. Barkley will earn nearly $7.9 million per year under his rookie contract, giving him the fourth-highest annual earnings among all running backs. That is not any sort of bargain; it is a top-dollar investment in a player who has yet to play professional football. To contextualize that investment, keep in mind that 2018 second-round running backs Kerryon Johnson and Ronald Jones will make less than $2 million per year through their rookie contracts, and both are slated to contribute plenty for their respective teams. Even Rashaad Penny, the 27th pick in the draft, will make less than half of Barkley's annual salary. Money aside, many of the league's top running backs are not former first-round picks. The likes of LeSean McCoy, Jordan Howard, David Johnson, Devonta Freeman, and Bell were selected outside the first round.

The Giants are in a unique position. They give off inklings of potential as weapons such as Beckham and Jenkins recover from injury, in addition to bringing in Barkley to add another playmaker to the offense, but they are still banking on too many fragile variables to be considered a competitive team. Manning's arm is rapidly approaching the condition of his brother Peyton's during his final days in Denver. The defense, though headlined by a few star players, still does not look good enough to stop the offenses of the NFC East. Lastly, Gettleman's old-school philosophy of run-oriented football seldom succeeds in today's NFL, and it requires highly efficient quarterback play even when it does—think of the 2012-2014 Seahawks or the 2016 Cowboys, for example. Manning is not going to provide that.

As the team stands now, the best the Giants should hope for is that Shurmur showcases the creativity and coordination that earned him the head coaching job. The offense is loaded with skill players and Shurmur could be the one to finally get something out of it. That being said, Gettleman is going to need time to fix the defense, which tended to be where he had more success in Carolina, and Shurmur is going to need a quarterback who is not Manning. This is Year Zero for the new Giants regime. The franchise as a whole is in for an overhaul over the next few years. With that in mind, keep expectations to a minimum as the Giants head into the 2018 season.

Derrik Klassen

2017 Giants Stats by Week

Wk	vs.	W-L	PF	PA	YDF	YDA	TO	Total	Off	Def	ST
1	at DAL	L	3	19	233	392	-1	-44%	-26%	17%	-1%
2	DET	L	10	24	270	257	0	-59%	-29%	1%	-28%
3	at PHI	L	24	27	415	354	-1	12%	22%	8%	-2%
4	at TB	L	23	25	379	434	0	-42%	0%	28%	-14%
5	LAC	L	22	27	335	382	-1	26%	6%	-15%	5%
6	at DEN	W	23	10	266	412	+3	-21%	-10%	6%	-6%
7	SEA	L	7	24	177	425	0	-64%	-37%	15%	-11%
8	BYE										
9	LAR	L	17	51	319	473	-3	-62%	-6%	35%	-20%
10	at SF	L	21	31	374	474	+1	-38%	17%	45%	-10%
11	KC	W	12	9	317	363	+2	16%	-12%	-29%	-1%
12	at WAS	L	10	20	170	323	0	-33%	-45%	-9%	3%
13	at OAK	L	17	24	265	401	-1	-32%	-23%	17%	8%
14	DAL	L	10	30	330	454	-2	-48%	-9%	32%	-7%
15	PHI	L	29	34	504	341	-1	-2%	29%	11%	-20%
16	at ARI	L	0	23	293	289	-1	-35%	-38%	-10%	-7%
17	WAS	W	18	10	381	197	+2	41%	-16%	-67%	-9%

Trends and Splits

	Offense	Rank	Defense	Rank
Total DVOA	-9.1%	23	5.7%	24
Unadjusted VOA	-9.4%	24	7.2%	25
Weighted Trend	-11.0%	25	3.2%	21
Variance	4.8%	8	7.6%	28
Average Opponent	-0.9%	14	2.5%	6
Passing	2.1%	20	13.0%	19
Rushing	-16.5%	29	-2.9%	26
First Down	-6.4%	20	0.2%	14
Second Down	-0.2%	14	13.0%	30
Third Down	-26.7%	30	4.3%	20
First Half	-12.9%	25	-1.3%	13
Second Half	-5.3%	20	13.3%	28
Red Zone	2.3%	15	-0.5%	18
Late and Close	-8.3%	22	10.6%	30

Five-Year Performance

Year	W-L	Pyth W	Est W	PF	PA	TO	Total	Rk	Off	Rk	Def	Rk	ST	Rk	Off AGL	Rk	Def AGL	Rk	Off Age	Rk	Def Age	Rk	ST Age	Rk
2013	7-9	5.6	5.5	294	383	-15	-15.7%	27	-22.0%	31	-11.4%	6	-5.1%	28	80.9	32	60.3	32	27.4	12	27.4	7	26.1	15
2014	6-10	7.5	7.0	380	400	-2	-5.8%	21	-0.3%	15	4.9%	24	-0.6%	15	65.9	31	71.3	30	26.6	20	27.6	5	26.7	3
2015	6-10	7.5	7.4	420	442	+7	-7.1%	20	-1.8%	19	10.7%	30	5.4%	2	66.9	31	71.8	31	26.2	22	27.0	13	26.5	8
2016	11-5	8.8	9.8	310	284	-2	9.6%	8	-6.0%	22	-14.5%	2	1.2%	11	27.7	11	24.7	9	26.3	22	25.9	27	26.2	13
2017	3-13	4.0	4.4	246	388	-3	-22.3%	30	-9.1%	23	5.7%	24	-7.5%	32	59.9	28	36.4	17	26.5	23	26.0	20	25.6	24

2017 Performance Based on Most Common Personnel Groups

NYG Offense					NYG Offense vs. Opponents					NYG Defense				NYG Defense vs. Opponents			
Pers	Freq	Yds	DVOA	Run%	Pers	Freq	Yds	DVOA	Run%	Pers	Freq	Yds	DVOA	Pers	Freq	Yds	DVOA
11	61%	5.2	-2.8%	28%	Base	30%	4.5	-14.0%	57%	Base	29%	4.9	2.0%	11	57%	6.5	9.3%
12	27%	5.1	-2.5%	45%	Nickel	55%	5.0	-6.7%	30%	Nickel	60%	6.4	10.8%	12	20%	5.7	8.1%
13	5%	3.2	-12.9%	57%	Dime+	14%	5.7	14.9%	15%	Dime+	11%	7.1	-1.1%	13	11%	4.0	-5.4%
21	2%	3.8	-57.6%	60%	Goal Line	1%	1.2	81.9%	67%	Goal Line	1%	-0.6	-80.2%	21	6%	6.6	8.2%
22	2%	4.0	-18.4%	83%										22	2%	4.5	7.7%
														612	2%	4.7	17.3%

Strategic Tendencies

Run/Pass		Rk	Formation		Rk	Pass Rush		Rk	Secondary		Rk	Strategy		Rk
Runs, first half	40%	14	Form: Single Back	90%	4	Rush 3	15.5%	5	4 DB	29%	21	Play action	21%	21
Runs, first down	53%	9	Form: Empty Back	2%	32	Rush 4	57.8%	26	5 DB	60%	15	Avg Box (Off)	6.25	14
Runs, second-long	27%	26	Pers: 3+ WR	62%	18	Rush 5	18.7%	16	6+ DB	11%	13	Avg Box (Def)	6.27	13
Runs, power sit.	43%	30	Pers: 2+ TE/6+ OL	36%	5	Rush 6+	8.0%	7	CB by Sides	76%	22	Offensive Pace	29.10	3
Runs, behind 2H	26%	20	Pers: 6+ OL	3%	22	Int DL Sacks	13.0%	28	S/CB Cover Ratio	29%	14	Defensive Pace	30.76	22
Pass, ahead 2H	43%	23	Shotgun/Pistol	64%	14	Second Level Sacks	27.8%	7	DB Blitz	15%	3	Go for it on 4th	1.28	7

With the arrival of Evan Engram and Rhett Ellison, the Giants used two or more tight ends four times as often as they did in 2016. Their rank in two-TE sets zoomed from dead last to fifth. ☞ New York's offense led the league in both dropped passes (46) and rate of dropped passes (7.3 percent). ☞ You can expect to see Saquon Barkley getting the ball for a lot of screen passes, as both the Giants and Pat Shurmur's Vikings were near the top of the league in using running back screens. The Giants had a below-average 10.1% DVOA on these plays in 2017 after they had an excellent 43.6% DVOA the year before. ☞ As always, Eli Manning was blitzed less often than almost any other quarterback. Usually he has the lowest rate in the league; last year, it was fourth-lowest, with opponents sending extra pass-rushers just 21 percent of the time. ☞ The Giants threw deep (16-plus yards) on a league-low 14 percent of passes. ☞ Where did the Giants defense collapse between 2016 and 2017? In the blitz. Big Blue's 7.0 net yards per pass allowed with three or four pass-rushers wasn't much different from the 6.8 net yards per pass they allowed in 2016. But in 2016, they got much better with a blitz. In 2017, they got much worse, allowing 7.7 net yards per pass with five pass-rushers and 8.4 net yards per pass with six or more.

Passing

Player	DYAR	DVOA	Plays	NtYds	Avg	YAC	C%	TD	Int
E.Manning	117	-8.2%	602	3270	5.4	4.6	61.6%	19	13
G.Smith*	-83	-41.4%	39	195	5.0	5.1	58.3%	1	0

Rushing

Player	DYAR	DVOA	Plays	Yds	Avg	TD	Fum	Suc
O.Darkwa*	53	-1.3%	171	751	4.4	5	1	46%
W.Gallman	15	-5.2%	111	476	4.3	0	3	50%
S.Vereen*	-22	-22.6%	45	164	3.6	0	0	42%
P.Perkins	-29	-27.1%	41	90	2.2	0	0	20%
E.Manning	-1	-15.1%	6	32	5.3	1	1	–
J.Stewart	-54	-14.8%	198	681	3.4	6	3	45%
T.Watson	-4	-21.1%	5	8	1.6	0	0	60%

Receiving

Player	DYAR	DVOA	Plays	Ctch	Yds	Y/C	YAC	TD	C%
S.Shepard	120	4.9%	84	59	733	12.4	5.0	2	70%
R.Lewis	-35	-18.7%	72	36	416	11.6	2.1	2	50%
O.Beckham	57	3.5%	41	25	302	12.1	2.6	3	61%
T.King*	16	-7.5%	37	18	240	13.3	4.3	3	49%
B.Marshall*	-33	-24.9%	33	18	154	8.6	2.2	0	55%
T.Rudolph	-49	-43.2%	21	8	101	12.6	5.4	0	38%
H.Sharp	14	10.7%	8	5	54	10.8	4.6	1	63%
C.Latimer	88	21.9%	31	19	287	15.1	3.4	2	61%
E.Engram	-5	-8.0%	115	64	722	11.3	4.7	6	56%
R.Ellison	56	17.7%	32	24	235	9.8	5.5	2	75%
J.Adams	18	17.0%	11	8	92	11.5	3.5	0	73%
S.Vereen*	-26	-22.7%	53	44	253	5.8	5.6	0	83%
W.Gallman	-2	-14.6%	48	34	193	5.7	5.9	1	71%
O.Darkwa*	10	-7.3%	28	19	116	6.1	6.2	0	68%
P.Perkins	-7	-26.5%	10	8	46	5.8	7.4	0	80%
J.Stewart	-20	-38.8%	15	8	52	6.5	8.6	1	53%

Offensive Line

Player	Pos	Age	GS	Snaps	Pen	Sk	Pass	Run	Player	Pos	Age	GS	Snaps	Pen	Sk	Pass	Run
Ereck Flowers	LT	24	15/15	1002	9	6.0	21	10	Justin Pugh*	RT/LG	28	8/8	435	1	2.0	6	4
Brett Jones	C	27	16/13	968	2	2.0	6	13	Jon Halapio	RG	27	10/6	404	2	0.0	0	3
John Jerry	LG/RG	32	16/16	958	3	0.0	4	10	Chad Wheeler	OT	24	11/5	261	0	2.0	7	4
Bobby Hart*	RT	24	10/7	525	4	4.0	13	6	Weston Richburg*	C	27	4/4	239	1	0.0	4	0
D.J. Fluker*	RG	27	9/6	447	4	2.0	13	4	Nate Solder	LT	30	16/16	1116	10	5.0	24	5

Year	Yards	ALY	Rank	Power	Rank	Stuff	Rank	2nd Lev	Rank	Open Field	Rank	Sacks	ASR	Rank	Press	Rank	F-Start	Cont.
2015	4.02	4.31	11	47%	30	19%	11	1.10	21	0.59	23	27	5.1%	6	23.3%	11	13	28
2016	3.70	3.89	24	63%	14	17%	9	1.01	29	0.40	29	22	3.9%	2	21.6%	6	11	30
2017	4.02	4.06	15	50%	29	17%	6	1.02	24	0.68	18	34	5.8%	10	25.5%	5	13	20

| 2017 ALY by direction: | Left End: 3.62 (22) | Left Tackle: 3.87 (18) | Mid/Guard: 3.97 (25) | Right Tackle: 5.07 (2) | Right End: 3.78 (20) |

It hardly mattered that Ereck Flowers was noticeably improved in 2017. The bar for Flowers' play was set so slow through the first two years of his career that even major improvement left him a below-average left tackle. Flowers showed more consistency in 2017, but the major blunders remained too frequent and damaging. ✏ Though not obvious on paper, Nate Solder will be an upgrade over Flowers at left tackle. Solder averaged 26.3 snaps per blown block in pass protection compared to Flowers' 28.9 snap average in 2017. However, New England's passing offense more regularly used deeper dropbacks and took longer to get rid of the ball then New York's offense, thus making Solder's job more difficult overall. Pat Shurmur's offense will be slower developing than Ben McAdoo's was, which would put Flowers at more of a disadvantage than Solder. ✏ The Giants' offensive line ranked 15th in adjusted line yards and sixth in stuff rate, yet placed just 29th in power rate and 24th in second-level yardage. This combination suggests the offensive line was able to provide the bare minimum and prevent negative plays in the run game, but failed to generate anything extra or win in obvious short-yardage run situations. When paired with lackluster running backs who could not generate more than the bare minimum themselves, the run game was left to be a low-ceiling endeavor. ✏ Pairing Saquon Barkley with offensive guard Will Hernandez through the draft is reminiscent of what the Buffalo Bills had with LeSean McCoy and Richie Incognito. Barkley mimics McCoy's athletic, jumpy style of running, while Hernandez does his best work as a downhill force and pull player. The Giants certainly hope their new duo has similar success.

Defensive Front Seven

Defensive Line	Age	Pos	G	Snaps	Plays	TmPct	Rk	Stop	Dfts	BTkl	Runs	St%	Rk	RuYd	Rk	Sack	Hit	Hur	Dsrpt
Damon Harrison	30	DT	16	645	79	9.5%	1	69	17	3	69	88%	7	1.6	24	1.5	1	15.5	2
Dalvin Tomlinson	24	DT	16	589	52	6.3%	19	39	8	1	49	76%	56	2.1	42	1.0	1	6.0	2
Jay Bromley*	26	DT	16	427	20	2.4%	--	18	5	4	14	93%	--	2.2	--	1.0	5	10.5	0
Josh Mauro	27	DE	13	334	23	3.5%	--	15	3	1	21	62%	--	2.7	--	1.0	4	4.0	1

Edge Rushers	Age	Pos	G	Snaps	Plays	TmPct	Rk	Stop	Dfts	BTkl	Runs	St%	Rk	RuYd	Rk	Sack	Hit	Hur	Dsrpt
Jason Pierre-Paul*	29	DE	16	1011	71	8.6%	7	53	20	5	52	71%	61	2.5	55	8.5	5	40.0	4
Olivier Vernon	28	DE	12	701	38	6.1%	27	27	11	11	27	63%	82	3.6	84	6.5	8	27.0	0
Avery Moss	24	DE	11	248	15	2.6%	--	13	2	2	13	85%	--	3.3	--	0.0	5	8.5	4

Linebackers	Age	Pos	G	Snaps	Plays	TmPct	Rk	Stop	Dfts	BTkl	Runs	St%	Rk	RuYd	Rk	Sack	Hit	Hur	Tgts	Suc%	Rk	AdjYd	Rk	PD	Int
Devon Kennard*	27	OLB	15	545	43	5.5%	85	29	13	5	28	61%	50	3.6	43	4.0	5	11.5	8	76%	--	5.2	--	1	0
Ray-Ray Armstrong	27	OLB	15	476	62	7.9%	77	36	6	7	42	67%	22	3.8	53	1.0	0	0.0	24	50%	35	6.6	35	2	2
Jonathan Casillas*	31	OLB	8	457	35	8.5%	73	19	6	7	21	62%	46	4.2	66	0.0	2	6.0	14	36%	71	8.3	65	1	0
Kelvin Sheppard*	30	OLB	7	388	53	14.6%	24	25	9	3	28	54%	75	3.6	41	0.0	1	3.0	16	57%	--	8.8	--	5	2
Calvin Munson	24	MLB	14	388	55	7.6%	80	30	10	4	33	76%	9	2.5	9	2.0	0	2.0	13	28%	--	7.1	--	1	0
B.J. Goodson	25	MLB	7	374	54	14.9%	22	25	6	4	30	53%	76	5.1	84	0.0	0	0.5	23	45%	54	10.5	74	2	0
Keenan Robinson*	29	MLB	6	292	34	11.0%	54	13	4	3	16	44%	84	4.3	69	0.0	1	0.0	18	42%	--	6.9	--	2	0
Alec Ogletree	27	ILB	15	923	105	13.6%	30	63	15	19	58	59%	61	4.6	80	2.0	5	17.5	42	59%	13	7.0	45	5	1

Year	Yards	ALY	Rank	Power	Rank	Stuff	Rank	2nd Level	Rank	Open Field	Rank	Sacks	ASR	Rank	Press	Rank
2015	4.35	4.33	22	67%	17	20%	19	1.18	21	0.88	22	23	4.1%	30	25.9%	13
2016	3.64	4.12	16	63%	14	17%	20	0.91	2	0.45	4	35	5.5%	23	29.2%	8
2017	4.22	4.30	23	53%	4	22%	12	1.23	22	0.79	21	27	4.9%	30	29.0%	25

2017 ALY by direction:	Left End: 5.00 (29)	Left Tackle: 3.96 (15)	Mid/Guard: 4.07 (12)	Right Tackle: 3.45 (13)	Right End: 5.35 (30)

The only reliable run defenders on the Giants last season played defensive tackle. Damon Harrison's 69 stops lead all interior defensive linemen. Rookie Dalvin Tomlinson came on strong as well, providing the versatility to allow him and Harrison to rotate between 1-technique and 3-technique. With occasional relief by Jay Bromley, The duo held together the interior to help the Giants maintain league-average adjusted line numbers up the middle despite poor linebacker play. ☞ In 2016, the Giants' pass rush created pressure at a high rate relative to the rest of the league but got rather unlucky in terms of converting that pressure into sacks. It was thought that if they could maintain the same relative pressure rate, they would generate more sacks in 2017. Instead the Giants fell from eighth in pressure rate to 25th. Their adjusted sack rate also dropped from 23rd to 30th. Granted, their raw pressure rate remained roughly the same, but relative to the league, they took a major step back. ☞ New defensive coordinator James Bettcher could be the one to get the team's pass rush back into shape. Following a sting as a 3-4 outside linebackers coach, Bettcher was Arizona's defensive coordinator from 2015 to 2017. Bettcher's defenses earned top-three finishes in pressure rate in 2015 and 2016, and the team's 17th-place finish in 2017 can be credited in part to losing Calais Campbell in free agency and Markus Golden to injury. ☞ Along with an aggressive coordinator in Bettcher, the Giants added outside linebacker Lorenzo Carter in the third round of the draft. Carter burst onto the scene as a freshman at Georgia in 2014, recording 4.5 sacks and seven tackles for loss. Unfortunately, Carter did little to build on his freshman success and produced an inconsistent college career. Like many other former five-star recruit pass-rushers, Carter coasted by with superb quickness and closing speed, but never properly grasped how to beat offensive linemen head-on or develop countermoves. Either Carter beat the offensive tackle off the snap around the edge or did not beat him at all. However, with an athletic profile such as his, the Giants are hopeful they can mold him into a legitimate edge rusher opposite Olivier Vernon. ☞ Giants linebackers accrued a total of 2,920 snaps for the Giants last season. Four of those players, who accounted for nearly 60 percent of those snaps, are no longer with the team. ☞ Recently acquired Alec Ogletree will assume one of the starting inside linebacker positions in Bettcher's 3-4 defense. B.J. Goodson's seniority on the team may earn him the best chance to start alongside Ogletree, but Ray-Ray Armstrong produced better both as a run defender and pass defender in 2017. Even if Goodson starts Week 1, it may not be long before Armstrong is playing more frequently. ☞ The addition of Ogletree may help the unit's coverage issues from a year ago, but Ogletree does not make the team's run defense any better. Ogletree's average run tackle came after a gain of 4.6 yards, which would have ranked second-worst on the team last season. Ogletree also missed a whopping 19 tackles on the year. He may flash with impressive ability to dart through open holes when the offensive line breaks down, but on the whole, Ogletree is not a reliable run defender.

Defensive Secondary

Secondary	Age	Pos	G	Snaps	Plays	TmPct	Rk	Stop	Dfts	BTkl	Runs	St%	Rk	RuYd	Rk	Tgts	Tgt%	Rk	Dist	Suc%	Rk	AdjYd	Rk	PD	Int
Darian Thompson	25	FS	16	1065	81	9.8%	43	18	9	15	44	20%	72	10.2	69	31	6.4%	11	12.4	52%	39	8.5	42	4	1
Landon Collins	24	SS	15	908	105	13.5%	6	50	18	15	54	48%	26	4.8	18	44	10.7%	49	14.0	53%	34	10.5	68	6	2
Ross Cockrell*	27	CB	16	681	60	7.2%	59	37	15	7	21	52%	30	5.0	19	54	17.6%	22	13.0	71%	1	5.8	6	12	3
Eli Apple	23	CB	11	649	57	10.0%	20	26	10	1	17	53%	28	6.6	52	58	19.6%	35	11.4	45%	75	8.2	56	8	0
Janoris Jenkins	30	CB	9	618	40	8.6%	38	23	12	12	7	57%	18	6.1	46	54	19.3%	33	13.0	54%	24	10.4	80	9	3
Dominique Rodgers-Cromartie*	32	CB	15	607	49	6.3%	--	27	7	10	24	67%	--	5.0	--	23	8.4%	--	7.3	48%	--	7.5	--	1	0
Andrew Adams	26	FS	16	276	30	3.6%	--	17	5	1	12	50%	--	3.9	--	17	13.6%	--	10.9	65%	--	5.6	--	2	0
Brandon Dixon	28	CB	5	257	25	9.7%	--	9	4	3	8	38%	--	5.4	--	23	19.4%	--	10.2	38%	--	11.3	--	2	0
William Gay	33	CB	16	268	22	2.9%	--	12	10	5	5	60%	--	7.0	--	15	11.7%	--	11.3	45%	--	6.4	--	3	1

Year	Pass D Rank	vs. #1 WR	Rk	vs. #2 WR	Rk	vs. Other WR	Rk	WR Wide	Rk	WR Slot	Rk	vs. TE	Rk	vs. RB	Rk
2015	28	-1.7%	15	1.1%	16	-6.0%	12	--	--	--	--	20.5%	27	8.5%	21
2016	4	-29.7%	1	-12.8%	5	-14.2%	7	-37.4%	1	-4.8%	8	15.7%	26	-25.8%	3
2017	19	-2.8%	13	42.4%	32	-17.3%	6	2.8%	22	8.9%	17	-0.4%	15	-2.8%	15

It was a rollercoaster year for Janoris Jenkins. Though he was able to maintain a decent success rate, Jenkins' yards per pass plummeted as he allowed more big plays. Jenkins has always played an all-or-nothing style of football, but a nagging ankle injury made it more difficult for him to keep up down the field and recover from some of the aggressive mistakes he made early on in some plays. Jenkins' San Francisco performance in Week 10 was particularly damning as he allowed an 83-yard touchdown to Marquise Goodwin (complete with a blown tackle) and a handful of other 10-plus-yard gains. ☞ The lack of development from Eli Apple was disheartening. Apple had a rough rookie season in 2016 but showed moments of potential through his athleticism. In 2017, however, Apple was again the team's most exploitable cornerback. Apple was particularly poor in press coverage, which did not blend well with Steve Spagnuolo's affinity for press. ☞ Dominique Rodgers-Cromartie took a major step back after a fantastic 2016 campaign. Rodgers-Cromartie finished the 2016 season with a league-high 71 percent adjusted success rate but saw that plummet to 48 percent in 2017. Being forced to play more on the outside in lieu of an injured Janoris Jenkins certainly affected Rodgers-Cromartie, but he underperformed regardless of alignment. ☞ Preseason pickup Ross Cockrell was the secondary's only real beacon of hope. Cockrell took surprisingly well to Spagnuolo's press system, which became necessary in Jenkins' absence. Though not one to dazzle with playmaking like Jenkins, Cockrell provided reliable coverage on a snap-to-snap basis, especially versus short to intermediate concepts. Releasing Cockrell may prove to be a costly mistake. ☞ The difference between free safety Darian Thompson and his understudy Andrew Adams is marginal. Adams played well in place of an injured Thompson in 2016 and was plenty serviceable when on the field in 2017. It is unlikely that Adams unseats Thompson at any point, but Adams being on the field in favor of Thompson does not really hurt the defense. In fact, Adams has the advantage as a slot defender. ☞ Landon Collins wasn't quite the Defensive Player of the Year candidate he had been in 2016, but he remains one of the game's best box safeties. ☞ To make up for the team's lack of quality linebackers, Bettcher may see fit to swap out Goodson or Armstrong with a defensive back such as Collins on clear passing downs. In effect, Collins would move to linebacker next to Ogletree, and Adams would fill in at his safety position alongside Thompson. Bettcher's Cardinals teams were known to be creative with defensive backs in this way, be it converting safety Deone Bucannon to inside linebacker or moving Tyrann Mathieu around from the slot to free safety and anywhere in between.

Special Teams

Year	DVOA	Rank	FG/XP	Rank	Net Kick	Rank	Kick Ret	Rank	Net Punt	Rank	Punt Ret	Rank	Hidden	Rank
2015	5.4%	2	9.5	2	-3.1	24	9.1	2	7.4	6	4.0	8	-6.4	24
2016	1.2%	11	4.6	6	-3.0	26	2.5	9	10.6	6	-8.7	31	-11.3	27
2017	-7.5%	32	-12.2	30	-0.8	22	-3.5	23	-16.5	32	-4.5	26	-3.5	17

Giants special teams suffered the biggest year-to-year drop-off in the league, tumbling 21 spots from 11th in 2016 to 32nd in 2017. It was the biggest drop in our special teams rankings since the Bills dropped from ninth in 2012 to 30th in 2013. ☞ Kicker Aldrick Rosas had a baffling season as a placekicker. Rosas nailed all three of his attempts beyond 50 yards but hit just 7-of-14 attempts between 30 and 50 yards. On kickoffs, however, Rosas' degree of success was less vague, as he posted the third-lowest gross value in the league. ☞ Punting is normally the most consistent part of special teams from year to year, so you have to wonder if there was something physically wrong with Brad Wing in 2017. In 2016, Wing finished fourth in the league in gross punt value. In 2017, he was dead last in both gross and net value. The Giants moved on after the season, and there will be a camp battle between former Denver punter Riley Dixon (who has had negative gross punt value the last two seasons) and former Texas Tech punter Taylor Symmank. ☞ Punt returns are a lost art in New York, with the Giants ranking in the bottom eight for the last two seasons. Backup wide receiver Kalif Raymond was the primary returner on both kicks and punts for most of 2017, but everyone who tried returns for the Giants had a negative value, so it's time to take a close look at the blocking schemes. Raymond will probably be on returns again this year, possibly with some participation from Sterling Shepard.

New York Jets

2017 Record: 5-11	Total DVOA: -17.3% (26th)	2018 Mean Projection: 6.9 wins	On the Clock (0-4): 18%
Pythagorean Wins: 5.6 (26th)	Offense: -10.2% (24th)	Postseason Odds: 22.3%	Mediocrity (5-7): 43%
Snap-Weighted Age: 26.3 (21st)	Defense: 4.0% (18th)	Super Bowl Odds: 1.6%	Playoff Contender (8-10): 31%
Average Opponent: -0.2% (16th)	Special Teams: -3.2% (25th)	Proj. Avg. Opponent: -2.5% (29th)	Super Bowl Contender (11+): 9%

2017: Somehow overachieved to five wins, got their franchise quarterback anyway, and all their fans are still unhappy.

2018: Andrew Luck's rookie season or everybody gets fired.

The New York Jets never came up with a real quarterback solution after giving up on Mark Sanchez. They spent a second-round pick on Geno Smith and quickly determined he wasn't the answer. They got two mildly successful veteran stopgap seasons out of Ryan Fitzpatrick and, last year, Josh McCown. They drafted Christian Hackenberg and were deservingly laughed out of the metaphorical room that is Draft Twitter. Hackenberg has as many regular-season NFL passes in two seasons as you do. When he got on the field in the preseason, he embarrassed himself with a completion rate below 50 percent.

But this history is actually instructive given how New York's quest for a quarterback would end. Hackenberg and Bryce Petty, the two quarterbacks drafted under Mike Maccagnan, were prototypical-sized passers with arm talent and questions about how they could actually play the position. The Jets were not the team that was going to take a chance on the outliers, and they also were never in a position to draft the scouting prototypes such as Jameis Winston, Marcus Mariota, and Carson Wentz.

And so the lesson they learned is that you must strike early. In a draft with four legitimate top-10 quarterback prospects, three of whom fit ideal scout body specifications and had arm strength to spare, the Jets paid a ransom to the Colts in giving up three second-round picks to move up three spots.

By giving up that many picks to make a short move up, the Jets cemented themselves among the biggest recent overpayers in NFL draft history. In the last 10 years, the only two teams that spent more on draft pick value than the Jets for this No. 3 pick were Washington to move up to get Robert Griffin III, and Houston to move up to get Deshaun Watson. (Table 1)

The Jets also famously didn't even consult with the owners of the No. 2 overall pick, the Giants, in their search for a trade. So they took a stand before the draft, paid heavily for it to secure the third overall pick in advance, but clearly weren't trying to shop the deal around all that much once they found it. "We felt good about the third spot, in terms of compensation for it," Maccagnan said to NJ Advance Media. "You spend a lot of time looking at previous draft compensations for movement. The idea of keeping our [first-rounder] going forward was an important thing to us."

However, the Jets lucked out in a way. The Browns decided to select Baker Mayfield at No. 1, and then the Giants decided not to take a quarterback to serve as heir apparent to Eli Manning. And so USC's Sam Darnold, the presumed No. 1 overall pick for most of the draft process, fell into the franchise's lap at No. 3. Some observers suggest that they traded up for the best quarterback prospect in the draft with the third pick. We … are not quite there. But we do think Darnold is at least an average top-10 quarterback prospect.

Had the Jets stayed at six, they would have had, at the very least, their pick of Josh Allen or Josh Rosen. The glass half-full view would be that Darnold falling to the Jets kept them from drafting Allen, giving them a scouting prototype who wasn't a total Hackenberg. The glass half-empty view would be that the Jets gave up three second-round picks to take someone roughly equivalent to Rosen, the quarterback Arizona selected at No. 10.

QBASE gives Darnold the fourth-highest score of the passers in this year's draft (Table 2), but the difference between second and fourth is fairly negligible. Darnold was dinged by QBASE for playing just two seasons as a starter, putting him in a grouping with several of the biggest quarterback busts of the last 20 years. And while he played against the hardest defensive slate of any quarterback this season, he also failed

Table 1: Recent Early Quarterback Trade-Ups by Football Perspective Draft Value Returned

Moving Up	Moving Down	Year	Quarterback	Pick	Return
HOU	CLE	2017	Deshaun Watson	12th	212%
WAS	STL	2012	Robert Griffin	2nd	209%
NYJ*	**IND**	**2018**	**Sam Darnold**	**3rd**	**198%**
KC	BUF	2017	Patrick Mahomes	10th	172%
BUF	**TB**	**2018**	**Josh Allen**	**7th**	**167%**
PHI	CLE	2016	Carson Wentz	2nd	165%
LAR	TEN	2016	Jared Goff	1st	164%
CHI	SF	2017	Mitch Trubisky	2nd	152%
ARI	OAK	2018	Josh Rosen	10th	135%
JAX	WAS	2011	Blaine Gabbert	10th	134%
NYJ	CLE	2009	Mark Sanchez	5th	129%

Second-round pick assumed value, not final.
Value of return from http://www.footballperspective.com/draft-value-chart/

2018 Jets Schedule

Week	Opp.	Week	Opp.	Week	Opp.
1	at DET (Mon.)	7	MIN	13	at TEN
2	MIA	8	at CHI	14	at BUF
3	at CLE (Thu.)	9	at MIA	15	HOU (Sat.)
4	at JAX	10	BUF	16	GB
5	DEN	11	BYE	17	at NE
6	IND	12	NE		

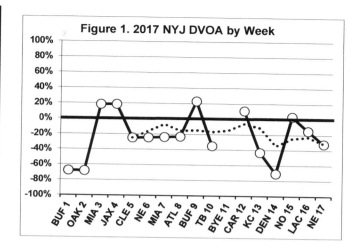

Figure 1. 2017 NYJ DVOA by Week

to live up to the lofty standards of his 2016 season. Further, he doesn't statistically separate himself in any way from Mayfield, Rosen, or Lamar Jackson.

While Darnold has the prototype size and arm talent to tempt scouting-heavy front offices, he also flashes a lot of talent under pressure. Darnold was credited by draftniks like Matt Waldman for his pump fakes, which generated little slivers of extra time when plays were breaking down. He's a decent scrambler, and he can occasionally pull a rabbit out of a hat when the play seems entirely dead. This will help immensely with the offensive line the Jets are planning to run out in 2018.

The issue with Darnold, and something that helped wreck his 2017 season for the Trojans, is that his pre-snap work was spotty at best. His questionable decision-making led to 13 picks in 14 starts, and he may have a lengthy learning process figuring out on what throws his arm can cash in in the NFL. There were a lot of pass breakups on his college film that told the story of a quarterback who never believed a zone defender could recover.

Nonetheless, Darnold is the composed CEO of a leader that NFL general managers want out of their quarterback. He's got the arm talent and some funky mechanics that people get worried about. He's also got happy feet under pressure if he's delivering as soon as he can rather than resetting. But the arm strength, accuracy from a composed pocket, and ability to scramble should at least keep him from being a Jared Goff-esque mess in his rookie season.

The Jets are, unfortunately, in a position where they might have to call on Darnold very early. They re-signed Josh McCown to a one-year, $10 million deal, but McCown is a mentor masquerading as a starting quarterback who gets hurt every time they try to put him out there. Teddy Bridgewater will be a great gamble if he's healthy, but nobody is actually sure if he is. Hackenberg was traded to the Raiders in late May for couch crumbs. So the depth chart is constructed in such a

Table 2: QBASE 2018

Quarterback	Mean DYAR Projection Years 3-5	College	NFL Team
Baker Mayfield	1,549	Oklahoma	CLE
Lamar Jackson	621	Louisville	BAL
Josh Rosen	425	UCLA	ARI
Sam Darnold	**398**	**USC**	**NYJ**
Mason Rudolph	363	Oklahoma State	PIT
Josh Allen	-90	Wyoming	BUF

way that it would be a major surprise if Darnold didn't play at some point this season. If only the rest of the roster looked better, that might not be a problem.

Maccagnan has spent his Jets tenure making safe, NFL-scout approved picks with his early selections. Leonard Williams was advertised as a beast and has been one. Jamal Adams was the heady safety everyone with an eye for defensive back talent wanted. So why haven't the Jets been more successful? Well, it's mostly about the turnover.

The 2015 Jets had 15 players with 300 or more offensive snaps. Five of them were on the roster in 2017: the starting guard tandem of James Carpenter and Brian Winters, third-down back Bilal Powell, injured Quincy Enunwa, and W(I)R Devin Smith. The 2015 Jets had 12 players with 300 or more defensive snaps. Four of them were on the roster in 2017: Williams, Buster Skrine, the now departed Muhammad Wilkerson, and their on-and-off affair Demario Davis (who was in Cleveland for the year between). We admit that Rex Ryan did not exactly leave the cupboard overflowing with talent, but Maccagnan has let a lot of players walk who garnered interest around the league. Sheldon Richardson at least got the Jets a receiver and a draft pick. Damon Harrison got a huge deal from the Giants. Wilkerson and Davis had free-agent markets. Eric Decker got money from the Titans, as did Chris Ivory from the Jags. Brandon Marshall caught on with the Giants. Somehow, Ryan Fitzpatrick keeps getting work.

The Jets set dollar amounts they weren't willing to exceed, but at the same time never actually came up with a new plan for that money besides carrying it as dead cap. They entered the 2018 offseason with more cap space than anyone but the Browns.

Now, to Maccagnan's credit, the Jets this year were aggressive with their money in free agency. Trumaine Johnson is as close to a true No. 1 corner as hit the market, and the Jets pounced all over him. They made a heavily competitive offer to Kirk Cousins, who took less money to go to Minnesota instead. But the Jets also frittered a lot of money away. Avery Williamson wasn't even a three-down linebacker in Tennessee last year, and the Titans offered him four years and $12 million. The Jets gave him $16 million *guaranteed*. Spencer

Long never had a particularly remarkable season with Washington and now has a three-year deal with a cap figure of at least $6.5 million each year. New York is spending about $16 million on salary cap space on two quarterbacks who aren't Darnold. They spent $5 million more to add Terrelle Pryor and Andre Roberts to a wideout depth chart where roughly 800 promising young receivers were already waiting for a chance.

But the reason the 2015 roster was able to win 10 games, outside of the massive fluke year from Fitzpatrick, was that Maccagnan was supplementing the existing core with veterans like Marshall and Darrelle Revis. As he gets deeper into his tenure, Maccagnan is building a team of His Guys, and even if His Guys need some work, they're getting more of the benefit of the doubt than Rex's Guys, who are now scattered to the four divisions of the NFL. This is the traditional approach, echoed a million times over NFL history: you build through the draft. The Jets just took a slightly longer approach to get there because they were worried about their ability to compete in the short-term.

The problem with that roster strategy is that it's great if you have the 2012 Seahawks draft. When you have spent three drafts in control of the front office and the only non-first-round picks who are getting any burn are Brandon Shell, Marcus Maye, and Jordan Jenkins, it's suddenly less fun. Especially when Darron Lee looks completely lost and two of your second-rounders were Hackenberg and Smith. And now you've emptied the cupboard of second-round picks for Darnold and suddenly there's even less hope that the Jets might hit the jackpot at another position.

Given the massive shortfalls in talent the Jets have accumulated both in the draft under Maccagnan and through attrition of aging players and injuries, what they're asking Darnold to be is an instant hit. He needs to cover for their offensive line maladies, he has to win shootouts because there is no pass rush, and he has to do it not only without a true No. 1 wideout, but with no real tight end of note.

The Jets also pushed out the architect of their unlikely offensive success last season, John Morton, and replaced him with NFL nepotism all-star Jeremy Bates, who has one season of coordinating to his name. Morton clashed with other minds in the locker room that wanted more on the plate of the run offense and less on the plate of Robby Anderson, per the *New York Post*. But Morton was getting praise from our Charles McDonald for opening up the Jets offense with concepts he learned as Saints wide receivers coach.[1] Bates, on the other hand, coordinated the 2010 Seahawks to a 29th-place finish in offensive DVOA. In a world of Patriots coaches wandering the landscape with their resumes filled with success with Tom Brady, the best Bates can point to is his work as Jay Cutler's quarterback coach. Until he took the Jets quarterback coaching job last year, he was completely out of the league for the three years.

Our projection for the Jets is about as unkind as you'd expect. A statistical system that takes the long view on rookies and didn't much care for Darnold's college profile isn't going to predict instant success from him, and without him being special, it's a Josh McCown-led offense in 2018. We like the defense to improve with their new additions in the secondary and another year of maturity for the young players, but there are still holes up and down the front seven.

When you pay far above the retail price for a quarterback, the only way he can redeem you is by playing as well as Deshaun Watson played for the Texans in 2017. If Darnold is that guy, the Jets will have the beginning rumblings of something that could knock off the Patriots. If not, the 2018 Jets could be the laughingstock everyone predicted they would be last season, with all the front office and coaching staff turnover that usually implies.

Rivers McCown

---

1 https://bit.ly/2LsFowF

2017 Jets Stats by Week

Wk	vs.	W-L	PF	PA	YDF	YDA	TO	Total	Off	Def	ST
1	at BUF	L	12	21	214	408	-1	-68%	-38%	27%	-2%
2	at OAK	L	20	45	271	410	-2	-68%	-12%	55%	-2%
3	MIA	W	20	6	336	225	+1	18%	-2%	-17%	3%
4	JAX	W	23	20	471	311	-1	19%	-5%	-22%	1%
5	at CLE	W	17	14	212	419	+2	-25%	-24%	10%	10%
6	NE	L	17	24	408	375	-1	-24%	-15%	6%	-3%
7	at MIA	L	28	31	272	357	0	-24%	-7%	9%	-8%
8	ATL	L	20	25	279	386	+1	-23%	-7%	11%	-6%
9	BUF	W	34	21	331	307	+3	23%	18%	-1%	4%
10	at TB	L	10	15	275	271	-1	-35%	-46%	-13%	-3%
11	BYE										
12	CAR	L	27	35	391	299	-1	11%	31%	-4%	-24%
13	KC	W	38	31	488	474	0	-43%	11%	59%	5%
14	at DEN	L	0	23	100	273	-2	-71%	-60%	0%	-10%
15	at NO	L	19	31	294	412	+1	4%	-1%	-12%	-7%
16	LAC	L	7	14	295	379	-3	-15%	-16%	-1%	0%
17	at NE	L	6	26	247	330	0	-32%	-39%	-13%	-6%

Trends and Splits

	Offense	Rank	Defense	Rank
Total DVOA	-10.3%	25	3.9%	18
Unadjusted VOA	-9.1%	23	4.2%	20
Weighted Trend	-9.2%	23	0.7%	17
Variance	5.8%	11	5.5%	16
Average Opponent	2.6%	30	2.0%	9
Passing	0.0%	22	16.9%	22
Rushing	-14.4%	26	-11.0%	11
First Down	-13.5%	28	6.3%	25
Second Down	-21.0%	31	-6.1%	9
Third Down	12.1%	8	15.6%	25
First Half	-1.6%	17	1.4%	17
Second Half	-17.9%	27	6.7%	22
Red Zone	-20.3%	25	-1.4%	17
Late and Close	-18.2%	27	6.4%	23

Five-Year Performance

Year	W-L	Pyth W	Est W	PF	PA	TO	Total	Rk	Off	Rk	Def	Rk	ST	Rk	Off AGL	Rk	Def AGL	Rk	Off Age	Rk	Def Age	Rk	ST Age	Rk
2013	8-8	5.4	7.5	290	387	-14	-7.7%	24	-15.3%	27	-5.6%	12	2.1%	10	33.9	15	9.1	1	26.2	26	26.7	14	26.1	13
2014	4-12	4.8	5.9	283	401	-11	-15.5%	27	-11.2%	27	3.5%	21	-0.8%	16	18.7	5	22.8	4	27.3	9	27.0	11	26.1	13
2015	10-6	10.0	9.7	387	314	+6	12.4%	9	1.6%	14	-13.8%	5	-2.9%	25	48.7	25	13.2	1	28.5	1	27.1	9	26.6	6
2016	5-11	4.4	4.6	275	409	-20	-32.4%	32	-21.9%	31	3.7%	21	-6.8%	32	67.6	30	42.9	22	27.5	6	26.4	19	26.0	19
2017	5-11	5.6	5.2	298	382	-4	-17.2%	26	-10.3%	25	3.9%	18	-3.0%	25	39.0	19	8.4	4	27.1	13	25.6	27	25.9	13

2017 Performance Based on Most Common Personnel Groups

NYJ Offense					NYJ Offense vs. Opponents					NYJ Defense				NYJ Defense vs. Opponents			
Pers	Freq	Yds	DVOA	Run%	Pers	Freq	Yds	DVOA	Run%	Pers	Freq	Yds	DVOA	Pers	Freq	Yds	DVOA
11	62%	5.5	3.9%	30%	Base	35%	4.3	-24.2%	55%	Base	37%	5.1	-6.6%	11	57%	5.8	11.5%
12	13%	5.5	-2.6%	43%	Nickel	52%	5.7	5.3%	34%	Nickel	53%	5.9	11.6%	12	19%	5.7	5.9%
21	7%	4.8	-17.3%	58%	Dime+	11%	5.4	4.7%	12%	Dime+	8%	6.9	32.6%	21	12%	6.0	10.7%
611	4%	4.8	-11.4%	71%	Goal Line	2%	1.3	-16.2%	72%	Goal Line	2%	0.9	-1.6%	13	5%	4.1	-32.6%
22	4%	4.6	-47.9%	65%						Big	2%	0.7	-73.1%	22	2%	1.5	-36.8%

Strategic Tendencies

Run/Pass		Rk	Formation		Rk	Pass Rush		Rk	Secondary		Rk	Strategy		Rk
Runs, first half	41%	9	Form: Single Back	75%	20	Rush 3	11.3%	8	4 DB	37%	8	Play action	14%	31
Runs, first down	55%	7	Form: Empty Back	9%	11	Rush 4	53.7%	32	5 DB	53%	18	Avg Box (Off)	6.23	19
Runs, second-long	35%	12	Pers: 3+ WR	65%	14	Rush 5	27.8%	3	6+ DB	8%	16	Avg Box (Def)	6.53	1
Runs, power sit.	49%	24	Pers: 2+ TE/6+ OL	29%	18	Rush 6+	7.2%	9	CB by Sides	57%	32	Offensive Pace	31.39	24
Runs, behind 2H	31%	6	Pers: 6+ OL	3%	19	Int DL Sacks	30.4%	10	S/CB Cover Ratio	21%	31	Defensive Pace	29.67	4
Pass, ahead 2H	46%	18	Shotgun/Pistol	56%	19	Second Level Sacks	39.3%	2	DB Blitz	13%	8	Go for it on 4th	0.58	30

The Jets were the worst offense in the league throwing to the left side of the field, but ranked fifth on passes up the middle and ninth on passes to the right side. ☞ A good example of splits that are completely unsustainable: the Jets were 26th in run offense DVOA on first downs, dead last on second downs, and first in the league on third downs. ☞ New York finally found some tight ends! For years, the Jets led the league in plays without a tight end on the field. It peaked at 37.5 percent of plays in 2016. But last year, the Jets went without a tight end on just 2.0 percent of plays. ☞ The Jets' offense ranked seventh in DVOA in the first quarter but 27th from the second quarter onward. ☞ Gang Green led the NFL in the frequency of going max protect, defined as seven or more blockers with at least two more blockers than pass-rushers. ☞ The Jets tied Pittsburgh with a league-low 30 percent of sacks coming from edge rushers. ☞ The Jets defense ranked 27th in DVOA when opponents were in shotgun, compared to sixth when the opposing quarterback was under center. ☞ The Jets allowed a league-high 10.8 yards after catch on passes at or behind the line of scrimmage. No other team was above 10.2 YAC. But the Jets allowed a below-average 3.5 YAC on passes beyond the line of scrimmage. ☞ The Jets benefited from opposing field goal kickers going just 21-for-29, including three misses from less than 40 yards.

Passing

Player	DYAR	DVOA	Plays	NtYds	Avg	YAC	C%	TD	Int
J.McCown	62	-8.9%	437	2659	6.1	4.7	68.4%	18	9
B.Petty*	-122	-26.8%	121	492	4.1	4.5	50.4%	1	1

Rushing

Player	DYAR	DVOA	Plays	Yds	Avg	TD	Fum	Suc
B.Powell	-43	-14.8%	178	772	4.3	5	0	35%
M.Forte*	-20	-13.9%	103	382	3.7	2	1	41%
E.McGuire	-56	-25.8%	88	315	3.6	1	1	34%
J.McCown	50	24.3%	20	138	6.9	5	1	-
B.Petty*	20	53.7%	6	56	9.3	0	0	-
A.Stewart	18	39.2%	5	24	4.8	0	0	-
I.Crowell	46	-2.9%	205	851	4.2	2	1	40%
T.Rawls	-83	-40.9%	58	157	2.7	0	1	33%

Receiving

Player	DYAR	DVOA	Plays	Ctch	Yds	Y/C	YAC	TD	C%
R.Anderson	113	-0.1%	116	65	949	14.6	4.4	7	56%
J.Kearse	146	5.2%	102	65	810	12.5	4.4	5	64%
J.Kerley*	64	19.0%	27	22	225	10.2	3.0	1	81%
C.Hansen	-17	-26.3%	17	9	94	10.4	2.0	0	53%
A.Stewart	-37	-45.4%	15	8	85	10.6	3.8	0	53%
T.Pryor	23	-5.3%	37	20	240	12.0	2.9	1	54%
T.McBride	27	10.6%	15	8	144	18.0	6.3	0	53%
A.Seferian-Jenkins*	-83	-23.4%	74	50	357	7.1	2.3	3	68%
E.Tomlinson	38	44.1%	11	8	121	15.1	8.5	1	73%
N.Sterling	8	4.5%	11	6	82	13.7	7.0	0	55%
W.Tye*	-7	-21.9%	6	4	38	9.5	4.8	0	67%
C.Walford	-11	-22.2%	13	9	80	8.9	2.4	0	69%
M.Forte*	44	5.6%	45	37	293	7.9	6.8	1	82%
B.Powell	-30	-30.4%	33	23	170	7.4	7.0	0	70%
E.McGuire	18	-1.4%	26	17	177	10.4	8.4	1	65%
L.Thomas	17	25.3%	7	6	43	7.2	5.5	0	86%
I.Crowell	-52	-35.9%	43	29	184	6.3	6.9	0	67%
T.Rawls	28	26.8%	13	9	94	10.4	9.2	0	69%

Offensive Line

Player	Pos	Age	GS	Snaps	Pen	Sk	Pass	Run	Player	Pos	Age	GS	Snaps	Pen	Sk	Pass	Run
James Carpenter	LG	29	16/16	1038	5	3.5	11	8	Brent Qvale	RT	27	16/6	395	6	3.5	8	5
Kelvin Beachum	LT	29	16/16	1037	6	4.5	10	9	Dakota Dozier	G	27	14/3	249	1	0.0	3	2
Wesley Johnson*	C	27	15/15	940	5	5.0	14	12	Travis Swanson	C	27	11/11	709	3	0.0	4	11
Brian Winters	RG	27	13/13	809	9	2.5	10	18	Spencer Long	C	28	7/6	397	0	1.0	5	7
Brandon Shell	RT	26	12/12	699	2	6.0	9	9									

Year	Yards	ALY	Rank	Power	Rank	Stuff	Rank	2nd Lev	Rank	Open Field	Rank	Sacks	ASR	Rank	Press	Rank	F-Start	Cont.
2015	4.06	3.87	26	59%	26	23%	26	1.14	18	0.90	10	22	4.1%	3	22.4%	10	21	35
2016	4.25	4.30	12	74%	2	16%	7	1.24	11	0.66	17	35	6.3%	20	24.9%	13	16	20
2017	3.96	3.40	29	48%	31	26%	29	1.03	23	1.04	5	47	8.6%	27	32.2%	22	14	27

2017 ALY by direction:	Left End: 3.76 (20)	Left Tackle: 2.77 (29)	Mid/Guard: 3.74 (29)	Right Tackle: 3.17 (25)	Right End: 2.83 (27)

There was a time not too long ago where the Jets had one of the best offensive lines in the NFL. D'Brickashaw Ferguson and Nick Mangold were long-term difference-makers, and players like Matt Slauson would pop up every now and then. That time is over. ☞ The Jets have built the entire left side of the line in retread free agency. Kelvin Beachum was a decent find at left tackle but has a lengthy injury history and is going to win on technique rather than pure physicality. James Carpenter is a solid run blocker who has problems dealing with stunts and fell off after a big 2016. ☞ New center Spencer Long (ex-Washington) will be taking over for Wesley Johnson at the pivot and hasn't been much better than Johnson. ☞ On the other side of the line, Brandon Shell, great-nephew of Art Shell, looks nothing like his great-uncle in pass protection. Well, no, he looks like him, but the technique is sorely lacking. Ben Ijalana is the swing tackle and guy who earns the distinction "a little extra depth" from news-breaking reporters who have nothing good to say about his play. ☞ Brian Winters is the closest thing this unit had to a building block—a right guard who has yet to be more than an average starter and struggled with anchoring. Winters has no guaranteed money remaining on his contract after this year's age-27 season.

Defensive Front Seven

Defensive Line	Age	Pos	G	Snaps	Plays	TmPct	Rk	Stop	Dfts	BTkl	Runs	St%	Rk	RuYd	Rk	Sack	Hit	Hur	Dsrpt
						Overall						vs. Run					Pass Rush		
Leonard Williams	24	DE	16	878	48	5.9%	23	38	8	5	41	76%	55	2.0	35	2.0	23	29.5	2
Muhammad Wilkerson*	29	DE	13	699	50	7.6%	4	42	10	3	38	84%	18	2.3	55	3.5	3	15.5	4
Steve McLendon	32	DT	16	488	45	5.6%	33	42	12	1	41	95%	2	1.4	14	1.5	1	11.5	0
Mike Pennel	27	DT	16	305	35	4.3%	--	29	1	1	35	83%	--	1.9	--	0.0	2	2.0	1
Xavier Cooper	27	DT	13	305	18	2.6%	--	13	6	3	13	77%	--	2.4	--	1.5	4	7.5	2
Henry Anderson	27	DE	9	382	20	4.3%	58	14	4	3	15	73%	60	2.6	66	2.0	6	10.5	0

Edge Rushers	Age	Pos	G	Snaps	Plays	TmPct	Rk	Stop	Dfts	BTkl	Runs	St%	Rk	RuYd	Rk	Sack	Hit	Hur	Dsrpt
						Overall						vs. Run					Pass Rush		
Jordan Jenkins	24	OLB	16	717	47	5.8%	34	35	9	6	33	82%	27	2.6	60	3.0	8	21.0	5
Josh Martin	27	OLB	14	491	31	4.4%	58	25	14	1	21	95%	3	0.4	1	1.5	8	15.0	0
Kony Ealy*	27	OLB	15	452	23	3.0%	83	21	8	4	12	83%	21	2.3	49	1.0	3	23.5	9
David Bass	28	DE	15	351	24	3.1%	--	14	5	2	18	56%	--	3.8	--	3.5	4	10.0	0

Linebackers	Age	Pos	G	Snaps	Plays	TmPct	Rk	Stop	Dfts	BTkl	Runs	St%	Rk	RuYd	Rk	Sack	Hit	Hur	Tgts	Suc%	Rk	AdjYd	Rk	PD	Int
						Overall						vs. Run				Pass Rush				vs. Pass					
Demario Davis*	29	ILB	16	1118	138	17.1%	8	83	25	13	85	64%	40	3.9	59	5.0	9	19.0	52	64%	5	5.4	14	2	0
Darron Lee	24	ILB	15	1028	96	12.7%	38	54	16	12	53	66%	28	2.8	17	3.0	4	7.0	49	47%	48	6.9	41	2	0
Avery Williamson	26	ILB	16	654	94	11.5%	49	48	9	6	70	57%	67	3.6	45	3.0	1	9.5	15	52%	30	5.9	23	0	0
Kevin Pierre-Louis	27	ILB	14	251	37	5.2%	--	18	3	5	25	52%	--	3.7	--	0.0	1	4.0	13	55%	--	8.5	--	2	0
Kevin Minter	28	ILB	9	199	32	6.4%	--	18	1	1	28	64%	--	3.6	--	0.0	0	0.0	6	0%	--	7.9	--	0	0

Year	Yards	ALY	Rank	Power	Rank	Stuff	Rank	2nd Level	Rank	Open Field	Rank	Sacks	ASR	Rank	Press	Rank
2015	3.35	3.19	1	62%	12	28%	1	0.96	4	0.55	6	39	6.0%	21	28.0%	6
2016	3.99	3.62	5	51%	4	27%	2	1.16	16	0.91	26	27	4.3%	32	26.3%	21
2017	3.67	3.77	6	70%	24	22%	8	0.93	4	0.66	12	28	5.8%	25	30.0%	18
2017 ALY by direction:		Left End: 3.62 (13)			Left Tackle: 3.99 (16)			Mid/Guard: 4.11 (15)			Right Tackle: 2.87 (5)			Right End: 3.17 (8)		

This was once a strength under Rex Ryan, but Muhammad Wilkerson and Sheldon Richardson aren't walking through that door. ☞ Leonard Williams was the safest selection in his draft class and has been a difference-maker on the defensive line since he was drafted in 2015. He's now very lonely. ☞ Out of the Jets' four leading players in hurries after Williams, Jordan Jenkins is the sole returner—and even he could only turn in 3.5 sacks. The Jets traded up for a quarterback, but in doing so left themselves with no real way to address their edge rusher need. Lorenzo Mauldin may be in line for a starting spot despite missing the entire 2017 season. There aren't many reasons for optimism here. ☞ Darron Lee has been a disappointment as an every-down linebacker, enough so that the Jets prioritized bringing in Avery Williamson to help him out. Williamson will take over for Demario Davis at about double the price. Williamson was a plus for the Titans, and the Jets had money to burn, but he's probably not a humongous upgrade on Davis' 2017 season. ☞ The Jets traded a seventh-round pick for Colts end Henry Anderson. Anderson is a good player, but one who never seems to stay healthy—he missed part of last year with a laryngeal fracture and hasn't played 12 games in a season yet. ☞ While Anderson will be the short-term solution at 5-technique, third-rounder Nathan Shepherd (Division II Fort Hays State) has enormous potential. The Canadian prospect, looking to follow in Akiem Hicks' footsteps, notched 12.5 tackles for loss and 3.0 sacks last season and didn't look lost at the Senior Bowl. ☞ Steve McClendon has been a perfectly functional nose since coming over from Pittsburgh, and Xavier Cooper had an interesting 204 snaps and could be something. We're trying to find nice things to say, we really are.

Defensive Secondary

Secondary	Age	Pos	G	Snaps	Plays	TmPct	Rk	Stop	Dfts	BTkl	Runs	St%	Rk	RuYd	Rk	Tgts	Tgt%	Rk	Dist	Suc%	Rk	AdjYd	Rk	PD	Int
												vs. Run						**vs. Pass**							
Jamal Adams	23	SS	16	1103	88	10.9%	23	46	21	13	50	62%	7	4.3	10	39	9.5%	36	12.1	45%	60	8.7	43	5	0
Marcus Maye	25	FS	16	1066	80	9.9%	41	23	6	11	45	33%	58	8.2	54	23	5.7%	6	21.7	50%	47	10.2	64	2	2
Buster Skrine	29	CB	15	1013	71	9.4%	27	30	13	11	16	44%	40	6.5	50	82	21.8%	51	12.3	50%	43	6.8	24	11	1
Morris Claiborne	28	CB	15	921	51	6.7%	66	19	10	7	12	42%	44	5.7	31	73	21.4%	46	12.9	48%	54	7.9	46	7	1
Rashard Robinson	23	CB	14	499	36	4.9%	80	13	6	4	9	33%	61	4.8	16	47	37.0%	80	14.8	49%	50	8.6	63	9	1
Darryl Roberts	28	CB	15	468	45	5.9%	71	18	6	7	10	50%	32	12.6	75	53	30.3%	77	15.6	48%	57	9.1	68	9	1
Juston Burris	25	CB	14	336	20	2.8%	--	6	6	9	5	20%	--	9.0	--	30	24.1%	--	10.9	42%	--	8.1	--	2	1
Trumaine Johnson	28	*CB*	16	935	79	9.6%	23	32	18	7	14	36%	58	6.7	53	84	23.9%	66	13.6	45%	73	9.3	72	13	2

Year	Pass D Rank	vs. #1 WR	Rk	vs. #2 WR	Rk	vs. Other WR	Rk	WR Wide	Rk	WR Slot	Rk	vs. TE	Rk	vs. RB	Rk
2015	9	-2.1%	14	-51.8%	1	10.6%	24	--	--	--	--	-8.8%	14	-3.0%	12
2016	31	11.5%	25	25.1%	32	7.7%	21	7.5%	25	24.1%	32	0.9%	19	-5.9%	16
2017	22	21.1%	28	-7.0%	13	-26.7%	2	13.7%	28	-15.0%	8	-7.4%	9	13.3%	26

After striking out on Kirk Cousins, the Jets spent heavily to bring in former Rams franchise player Trumaine Johnson. Per Ian Wharton's film study at Bleacher Report, Johnson was the best press cornerback in the NFL in 2017. That makes him a perfect fit for Todd Bowles, who wants to match his best corner against the opposition's top receiver. In Los Angeles, Johnson had 63 targets covering the opposition's No. 1 receiver, tied for second in the league behind Xavier Rhodes. ☞ Last year's top Jets cornerback, Morris Claiborne, was fifth on that list with 54 targets. Brought over from Dallas on a one-year "prove it" deal, Claiborne proved it. He's a capable starting corner with the body to play press coverage and he has learned enough at the line of scrimmage to be effective with it. The Jets let Claiborne test the market, but with a glut of corners he settled for proving it again. ☞ Buster Skrine was a bust as an outside corner, but with Johnson in the fold, he could return to the slot where he has had more success in his career. Daryl Roberts is functional depth, capable of holding his own but also rather mistake-prone. Rashard Robinson, who started some with the 49ers and came over in a midseason trade, might also get a look. ☞ Of the Jets' two rookie safeties, Marcus Maye had the more inconsistent year at free safety—he has a head-scratching tendency to create extra yards for the offense by leaving his feet on tackle attempts. ☞ Meanwhile, Jamal Adams proved worthy of a top-10 selection, showing ridiculous range and playing capably as a run defender despite his stature. No interceptions, but he showcased star upside in his rookie season.

Special Teams

Year	DVOA	Rank	FG/XP	Rank	Net Kick	Rank	Kick Ret	Rank	Net Punt	Rank	Punt Ret	Rank	Hidden	Rank
2015	-2.9%	25	0.8	14	4.4	7	-5.6	29	-17.9	32	3.6	9	-7.9	26
2016	-6.8%	32	0.3	16	-0.4	17	-6.2	27	-21.1	32	-6.6	27	-11.8	30
2017	-3.0%	25	2.8	13	3.9	9	-3.4	22	-6.0	23	-12.2	32	5.8	7

Jets special teams were sneaky killers last year. Hand-picked 23-year-old returner JoJo Natson struggled mightily, gaining just 38 yards on 16 punt returns. Four different players handled a punt return, and four players handled a kick return. Three of them return to the Jets in 2018! Hooray mediocrity aspirations! ☞ Chandler "Settlers of" Catanzaro moved on for a free-agent deal in Tampa Bay (eight wheat over three years) so the Jets are going with Kansas City cast-off Cairo Santos, which probably isn't a downgrade given Santos only lost his job to injury. Santos was average on both kickoffs and field goals in 2016. ☞ Lachlan Edwards, an Aussie-rules footballer-turned-punter who wound up at Sam Houston State, showed some improvement in his sophomore season. That didn't stop the Jets from signing Ben Turk, Matt Turk's nephew, who had not been in an NFL mini-camp since 2013. To put that in perspective, Chad Ochocinco got looks more recently than the young Turk.

Oakland Raiders

2017 Record: 6-10	**Total DVOA:** -6.6% (19th)	**2018 Mean Projection:** 7.9 wins	**On the Clock (0-4):** 10%
Pythagorean Wins: 6.0 (25th)	**Offense:** 3.9% (13th)	**Postseason Odds:** 38.6%	**Mediocrity (5-7):** 34%
Snap-Weighted Age: 26.9 (8th)	**Defense:** 10.3% (29th)	**Super Bowl Odds:** 4.5%	**Playoff Contender (8-10):** 40%
Average Opponent: -0.6% (19th)	**Special Teams:** -0.2% (17th)	**Proj. Avg. Opponent:** -0.7% (24th)	**Super Bowl Contender (11+):** 16%

2017: The one with Jack Del Rio getting fired.

2018: The one where an old flame returns.

Millennials find the old TV show *Friends* "problematic." If you are part of the original Football Outsiders writer demographic, you probably watched *Friends* every week, laughed and loved along with the gang, and didn't think too much about how white and straight the entire cast was. Or perhaps you *did* notice and avoided/ignored the show for its lack of inclusivity, but you didn't have a generational groundswell at your back. In the late '90s and early 2000s, popular shows like *Friends, Seinfeld, Frasier*, and others typically had all-white casts. There were also shows with mostly black casts, occupying what amounted to a subgenre. Diversity (especially on sitcoms) was relatively rare and tended to call attention to itself when it did occur, and most viewers thought nothing of a mostly segregated television dial.

It wasn't just the representation that was backward as recently as 15 years ago, though sitcom segregation provides the most graphic example of how one generation's normal is the next generation's unacceptable. In the early 2000s, prestige cable programming was in its infancy and Netflix still sent DVDs of movies through the mail. Even cutting-edge comedies still usually had three cameras, laugh tracks, and no overarching mythologies or arcs beyond some will-they-or-won't-they romance. *Seinfeld's* self-referential humor, *Frasier's* intellectualism and *Friends'* "frank" sexiness all feel quaint by today's standards, even after you push past the all-white New Yorks and Seattles they took place in.

As you have surely gathered, *Friends* and the trendsetting sitcoms of the late 1990s and early 2000s are being used as a metaphor for Jon Gruden's era of relevancy, which spanned roughly the same era. In Gruden's heyday, a coach could still reconfigure the original West Coast Offense slightly and dazzle defenses. Gruden won a Super Bowl before Tom Brady and Peyton Manning redefined offensive possibilities and expectations (think of Brady-Manning as HBO programming of the 2000s if you want to strain the metaphor); before the modern versions of spread and up-tempo offenses; before nickel defense became base; before the read-option, RPO, and dozens of less publicized offensive and defensive wrinkles; before the modern CBA changed everything from salary structures to practice schedules.

None of which precludes Gruden from being forward thinking or successful. But Gruden made it clear at the 2018 NFL scouting combine that he doesn't want to be forward thinking.

Particularly when it comes to the topics we love and support here at Football Outsiders.

Here are Gruden's now-legendary comments when asked a vaguely-worded sports science question at the combine:

"Are you talking about the analytics, the GPS, all the modern technology?. Man, I'm trying to throw the game back to 1998. You know, really as a broadcaster, I went around and observed every team, asked a lot of questions, took a look at the facilities, how they're doing business, there's a stack of analytic data—or DAY-tuh, however you want to say that word—people don't even know how to read it. It's one thing to have the data—or DAY-tuh—it's another thing to know how to read the damn thing.

"So, I'm not going to rely on GPSs and all the modern technology. I will certainly have some people that are professional that can help me from that regard. But I still thing doing things the old-fashioned way is a good way, and we're going to try to lean the needle that way a little bit."

Those of us in the room when Gruden made those statements began sharpening our skewers almost immediately. Before we roast Gruden on a rotisserie spit, fairness requires us to point out that:

- Gruden had a point. Teams are indeed swimming in new GPS data that no one has figured out how to apply in any meaningful way;
- He walked back these comments, a little bit, in follow-up interviews minutes after his combine press conference; and
- He's hardly the first coach to publicly play the "throwback" card, which is popular with every fan base, but resonates most deeply with Raiders fans who want to relive the bicentennial forever.

Fair enough. Gruden did not spend the offseason running around screaming STATS ARE FOR LOSERS. He also spoke highly of spread offenses and no-huddle concepts as a broadcaster, sometimes musing aloud that he would love to run an NFL offense full of the new ideas that have taken hold in the college ranks.

Gruden's actions, however, do not suggest that he's spouting old-school rhetoric to throw opponents off the scent while secretly pioneering a new era of data-driven offensive innovation. His coaching hires, free-agent signings and draft selections suggest a weird mix of comfort-zone thinking and out-

2018 Raiders Schedule

Week	Opp.	Week	Opp.	Week	Opp.
1	LAR (Mon.)	7	BYE	13	KC
2	at DEN	8	IND	14	PIT
3	at MIA	9	at SF (Thu.)	15	at CIN
4	CLE	10	LAC	16	DEN (Mon.)
5	at LAC	11	at ARI	17	at KC
6	SEA (U.K.)	12	at BAL		

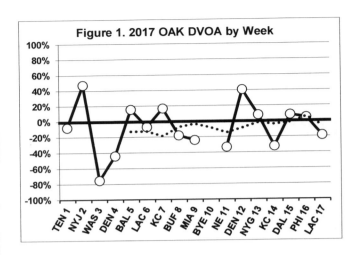

Figure 1. 2017 OAK DVOA by Week

of-touch decision-making—the kind you might expect from, say, a guy who has only had to think deeply enough about the NFL for the last ten years to sound informed during a telecast.

Let's start with the most notorious of Gruden's coaching hires: former Seahawks offensive line coach, assistant head coach, and perennial saboteur Tom Cable. Table 1 shows how well Cable's units ranked in our offensive line stats over the past five years. The adjusted line yards were strong until two seasons ago, but Cable had Max Unger under center through 2014 and Russell Okung at left tackle through 2015. He then spent two seasons coaching the available Seahawks linemen downward into one of the NFL's most comically inept units. And if you think Russell Wilson scrambled his way into some of the sacks, you never watched a Seahawks game; a less mobile quarterback than Wilson would have gotten crippled by Cable's negligence. If anything, Wilson's rushing threat kept the Seahawks' adjusted line yards higher than they should have been for a few years.

Table 1. Tom Cable's Seattle Offensive Lines, 2013-2017

Year	ALY	Rank	ASR	Rank	Pressure	Rank
2013	4.30	9	9.6%	32	35.9%	32
2014	4.52	4	8.7%	24	39.3%	32
2015	4.56	4	9.0%	30	31.8%	30
2016	3.77	26	6.9%	25	33.7%	32
2017	3.18	31	8.1%	25	36.9%	30

Cable is also a former Raiders head coach who was accused of punching one of his assistants in the jaw after a training camp disagreement in 2009. Oh, and three different women accused Cable of domestic assault, including two ex-wives. It's not an exaggeration to call Cable one of the NFL's worst humans: incompetent coach, dangerous coworker, unrepentant of a shameful past. The Seahawks considered him an organizational leader, which tells you a lot about the NFL's culture. And Cable now gets to coach the men who will protect Derek Carr.

Cable's direct supervisor will be Greg Olson, who has served as offensive coordinator for five teams (including the Raiders in 2013 and 2014) over ten seasons, finishing in the top half of the NFL in yards just once with the elderly Greatest Show Rams in 2006. Most recently, Olson coached Jaguars offenses that finished 21st in the league in DVOA in 2015 and 27th in 2016; his previous Raiders offenses finished 28th and

30th. Olson spent 2017 as Jared Goff's quarterback coach for the Rams; maybe Sean McVay introduced Olson to avocado toast and now he's a whole new man.

Also on Gruden's Old Boy's Club Dream Team: special teams coordinator Rich Bisaccia, a trusted lieutenant from Gruden's Tampa years; quarterback coach Brian Callahan, son of former Gruden assistant/replacement Bill Callahan; and strength and conditioning assistant Deuce Gruden, whose previous coaching experience was under his Uncle Jay in Washington.

It's not all old buddies and favorite sons. Defensive coordinator Paul Guenther has a strong track record after moving through Marvin Lewis' ranks in Cincinnati. Receivers coach Edgar Bennett was a well-regarded Packers assistant for 13 years before this offseason's coaching reboot in Wisconsin. Through strength and conditioning coach Tom Shaw (who comes from the performance academy ranks, which could be good or bad but is at least different) the Raiders hired Kelsey Martinez, the NFL's first full-time female strength coach.

But if the Raiders thought the $100 million they have invested in Gruden would buy them forward-thinking football ideas, they should be a little disappointed to see Olson and Cable back, plus a defensive staff any new head coach should be able to cobble together and some young dudes with familiar last names. If Gruden was serious about adding all the fresh ideas he raved about during episodes of his QB School, he could have sought someone from the Chip Kelly family or an Air Raid disciple. Instead, he filled the staff with a mix of safe, predictable, and bad choices.

Then free agency arrived and things got really crazy.

The 2017 Raiders, one year removed from a near-MVP season by Carr and lots of Next Big Thing notice in 2016, needed a new offensive scheme—Todd Downing proved bland and predictable in his rookie season as an NFL coordinator—along with some adjustments at the skill positions and a significant overhaul on the back end of the defense. Gruden decided to address these well-defined needs by going totally HAM across the entire roster. He gobbled up fading big names at the skill positions (Jordy Nelson, Doug Martin), so-so veteran defenders (Tahir Whitehead, Emmanuel Lamur, Shareece Wright), and some last-legs old-timers on defense (Leon Hall, Derrick Johnson). He then added some receivers in draft-day trades (Martavis Bryant, Ryan Switzer), all the while filling his shopping cart with all the Breno Giacomini, Dwayne Harris, and Marcus Gilchrist types he could cheaply acquire.

It would take about four pages to analyze all of these selections. Wright will be a useful slot corner. Bryant, Martin, and Nelson might each be worth a die roll to see if they bounce back, though signing three of them is a little like spending the mortgage money at the race track. What players like Giacomini and Hall offer that the Raiders couldn't get in rookie free agency is anyone's guess.

Many of the acquisitions were the types of players your brother-in-law selects for his fantasy team because he recognizes their names. Gruden probably wasn't merely pounding the table for players who impressed him in telecasts over the years, but some of the selections look like they were made by someone who hadn't looked too closely at recent tape, scouting reports, news bulletins or (heaven forbid) stat profiles of the players being signed.

The draft added yet another layer of mystery. Top pick Kolton Miller is a youthful reinforcement for an aging offensive line; draftniks are divided on him, but that's the best thing that can be said about any tackle in this year's draft class. Then the Raiders spent the rest of the draft adding small-program heroes (defensive lineman P.J. Hall, left tackle Brandon Hall), extreme character risks (Arden Key), extreme injury risks (Maurice Hurst) and a fifth-round punter (Johnny Townsend), because Gruden didn't like the cut of Marquette King's jib.

Nearly every draft pick was a swing for the upper decks, so the chance of the whole class going bust is frighteningly high, especially since Miller and Hall will be entrusted to Cable, who has destroyed more offensive line prospects in the last five years than the zero he developed.

The Raiders' offseason 90-man roster is a groaning hodgepodge of iffy veterans, risky rookies, and lots of last-regime holdovers who shouldn't get too comfortable if they aren't named Carr, Mack, or Cooper. The one certainty in camp competitions is that Gruden will prefer "his guys;" it's practically his catchphrase. The Raiders will end up old on both offense and defense, yet they won't have the veteran chemistry that comes from players coming up though the same system together, and many of their backups will be the long-range projects from this draft class. Positions like linebacker and wide receiver may have gotten short-term upgrades from all the free-agent moves, and the Raiders (who still have the nucleus of a team that won 12 games two years ago) should compete for a wild card or even squeak out an AFC West title with so much of the division in transition. But it doesn't take a $100 million coaching mastermind to craft a .500 roster out of 28- to 36-year-olds.

Building old, expensive, and ordinary rosters is a Raiders tradition, however: one the franchise had finally moved away from in recent years, but one which Gruden—despite his success in the early 2000s—has always fallen squarely into. Gruden's best Raiders teams were teeming with 30-somethings: Rich Gannon, Tim Brown, Andre Rison, Eric Allen, William Thomas, Greg Biekert, Steve Wisniewski, and so on (plus Jerry Rice in his 40s). His Super Bowl Bucs were also a veteran team: Brad Johnson, Keyshawn Johnson, John Lynch and Warren Sapp were all 30-plus the year Gruden took them all the way; Derrick Brooks and Mike Alstott were 29. The hope in Oakland is that Gruden can coach up his new over-the-hill gang the way he managed those teams.

But it's easy to forget that Gruden remained a head coach through the 2008 season. He spent those final years relying on old-timers like Jeff Garcia, Joey Galloway, and Ike Hilliard on offense, dragging Brooks and Ronde Barber onto the field with dwindling reinforcements, even bringing Warrick Dunn back at age 33. The drafts of the Gruden Bucs years were mostly horrendous, his track record with younger players (see: Chris Simms) often disgraceful. The teams often cleared .500 but were prone to late-season slumps and playoff letdowns.

Gruden's coaching career, like a creaky sitcom, ran a few years too long and became predictable and disappointing at the end of its run.

The old-fashioned three-camera sitcom may be making a comeback. *Full House* and *One Day at a Time* were rebooted with varying degrees of success; *Rosanne* got competitive ratings before all sociopolitical hell broke loose. *The Big Bang Theory* chugs along while quirkier, funnier shows like *Brooklyn Nine-Nine* are forced to change networks to make room for Tim Allen vehicles. Success in network television is not about maximizing quality, but about getting millions of our parents to watch something familiar while younger, more engaged viewers watch YouTube video game livestreams or write thinkpieces about *Atlanta*.

Success for the Jon Gruden Raiders may mean convincing Las Vegas high-rollers to invest in luxury boxes and PSLs while placating fans in Oakland until the move. It may mean giving Mark Davis a chance to relive an era he thinks of as glory years or letting him make the kind of coaching hire his father made.

But you don't win the Super Bowl by selling the most hats or making the most headlines. You do it by being innovative, forward-thinking and a little scientific; and by using every available resource, even the ones that weren't there 15 years ago. Gruden may truly have some new tricks up his sleeve, and there may even be some merit to reintroducing one or two of the NFL's forgotten ideas. But the pilot episode of *Gruden: The Next Generation* looks really, really rocky.

Mike Tanier

2017 Raiders Stats by Week

Wk	vs.	W-L	PF	PA	YDF	YDA	TO	Total	Off	Def	ST
1	at TEN	W	26	16	359	350	0	-8%	19%	31%	4%
2	NYJ	W	45	20	410	271	+2	47%	62%	18%	4%
3	at WAS	L	10	27	128	472	-1	-75%	-59%	24%	8%
4	at DEN	L	10	16	254	298	-1	-44%	-27%	26%	9%
5	BAL	L	17	30	245	365	-1	15%	29%	13%	0%
6	LAC	L	16	17	274	343	-1	-7%	-19%	-5%	8%
7	KC	W	31	30	505	425	0	17%	55%	22%	-16%
8	at BUF	L	14	34	367	331	-4	-18%	19%	26%	-10%
9	at MIA	W	27	24	379	395	-1	-24%	32%	65%	9%
10	BYE										
11	NE	L	8	33	344	421	-2	-33%	-17%	12%	-4%
12	DEN	W	21	14	348	216	0	41%	19%	-21%	1%
13	NYG	W	24	17	401	265	+1	8%	14%	-5%	-11%
14	at KC	L	15	26	268	408	-2	-32%	-29%	1%	-2%
15	DAL	L	17	20	293	330	+1	8%	-3%	-17%	-6%
16	at PHI	L	10	19	274	216	-3	5%	-49%	-54%	0%
17	at LAC	L	10	30	336	495	-2	-19%	5%	29%	5%

Trends and Splits

	Offense	Rank	Defense	Rank
Total DVOA	4.0%	13	10.3%	29
Unadjusted VOA	3.4%	12	9.8%	29
Weighted Trend	-0.2%	17	3.1%	20
Variance	12.0%	30	7.3%	26
Average Opponent	0.8%	22	0.3%	15
Passing	20.7%	13	26.1%	30
Rushing	-5.5%	14	-8.3%	16
First Down	5.2%	10	2.1%	19
Second Down	0.2%	13	15.1%	31
Third Down	7.3%	14	18.2%	27
First Half	6.7%	12	13.3%	31
Second Half	1.3%	16	6.9%	23
Red Zone	-6.4%	20	-5.8%	11
Late and Close	-4.7%	20	-21.8%	4

Five-Year Performance

Year	W-L	Pyth W	Est W	PF	PA	TO	Total	Rk	Off	Rk	Def	Rk	ST	Rk	Off AGL	Rk	Def AGL	Rk	Off Age	Rk	Def Age	Rk	ST Age	Rk
2013	4-12	4.9	2.1	322	453	-9	-34.1%	31	-16.7%	28	10.3%	26	-7.1%	31	49.7	26	27.2	15	26.7	17	27.6	5	26.1	16
2014	3-13	3.1	4.8	253	452	-15	-27.4%	29	-19.4%	30	6.3%	26	-1.7%	18	26.1	11	77.5	32	26.5	22	27.7	4	26.2	11
2015	7-9	6.9	7.4	359	399	+1	0.1%	14	-1.3%	18	-1.5%	15	-0.1%	19	23.7	8	33.9	22	26.2	20	26.6	17	27.2	1
2016	12-4	8.8	8.9	416	385	+16	8.2%	10	12.2%	8	4.3%	22	0.3%	14	32.5	13	32.4	15	26.5	21	26.6	13	26.9	5
2017	6-10	6.0	7.7	301	373	-14	-6.6%	19	4.0%	13	10.3%	29	-0.2%	17	12.1	5	32.0	16	27.6	4	26.6	13	25.8	17

2017 Performance Based on Most Common Personnel Groups

OAK Offense					OAK Offense vs. Opponents					OAK Defense				OAK Defense vs. Opponents			
Pers	Freq	Yds	DVOA	Run%	Pers	Freq	Yds	DVOA	Run%	Pers	Freq	Yds	DVOA	Pers	Freq	Yds	DVOA
11	73%	5.9	13.2%	30%	Base	22%	5.2	0.0%	58%	Base	35%	5.8	6.3%	11	57%	6.0	17.9%
12	12%	6.0	3.9%	49%	Nickel	53%	5.9	13.5%	37%	Nickel	57%	5.7	13.7%	12	18%	5.9	9.5%
13	6%	3.6	-33.7%	82%	Dime+	23%	6.0	17.5%	11%	Dime+	7%	7.6	21.1%	21	7%	6.0	-3.0%
01	4%	4.3	1.7%	17%	Goal Line	1%	0.3	-6.2%	83%	Goal Line	1%	0.5	-41.4%	13	6%	4.9	-6.6%
612	1%	2.3	-60.6%	77%	Big	1%	1.4	-87.9%	90%					22	5%	4.6	-17.3%

Strategic Tendencies

Run/Pass		Rk	Formation		Rk	Pass Rush		Rk	Secondary		Rk	Strategy		Rk
Runs, first half	42%	6	Form: Single Back	85%	7	Rush 3	8.1%	12	4 DB	35%	12	Play action	14%	30
Runs, first down	44%	28	Form: Empty Back	13%	4	Rush 4	72.7%	11	5 DB	57%	16	Avg Box (Off)	5.98	32
Runs, second-long	37%	8	Pers: 3+ WR	78%	3	Rush 5	17.0%	24	6+ DB	7%	17	Avg Box (Def)	6.14	25
Runs, power sit.	64%	7	Pers: 2+ TE/6+ OL	23%	27	Rush 6+	2.2%	30	CB by Sides	77%	19	Offensive Pace	32.50	30
Runs, behind 2H	21%	32	Pers: 6+ OL	4%	13	Int DL Sacks	17.7%	22	S/CB Cover Ratio	27%	17	Defensive Pace	30.55	18
Pass, ahead 2H	53%	4	Shotgun/Pistol	70%	9	Second Level Sacks	8.1%	30	DB Blitz	8%	18	Go for it on 4th	1.67	2

Despite the arrival of Marshawn Lynch, the average box faced by the Raiders went down, from 6.40 defenders in 2016 (fourth) to 6.14 defenders in 2017 (25th). ☛ The Raiders allowed a league-low 27 percent pressure rate when opponents blitzed. ☛ Once again, the Raiders were one of the most frequent employers of an empty backfield. Oakland had just 5.3 yards per play and -13.7%

DVOA on empty-backfield plays after gaining 7.1 yards per play with 46.7% DVOA the year before. ☞ The Raiders defense may have declined but it did a few things better than the year before, and one of those was preventing yards after the catch. The Raiders allowed 5.0 average YAC (14th) after being league-worst with 5.7 average YAC in 2016. ☞ Oakland is also a strong tackling defense; they ranked fifth with just 83 broken tackles in 2016 and ranked fourth with just 94 broken tackles in 2017. ☞ Oakland got 74 percent of sacks from edge rushers, second behind the Chargers. ☞ The Raiders were tied with Green Bay with the worst DVOA in the league when the defense didn't get pass pressure. ☞ The Raiders fumbled or muffed the ball a league-leading 11 times on kick/punt returns and only lost the ball once.

Passing

Player	DYAR	DVOA	Plays	NtYds	Avg	YAC	C%	TD	Int
D.Carr	709	9.7%	534	3399	6.4	5.0	62.8%	22	11
EJ Manuel	56	9.6%	47	236	5.0	3.5	55.8%	1	1

Rushing

Player	DYAR	DVOA	Plays	Yds	Avg	TD	Fum	Suc
M.Lynch	165	10.1%	207	891	4.3	7	1	49%
D.Washington	-55	-33.1%	57	153	2.7	2	1	40%
J.Richard	15	-1.4%	56	275	4.9	1	1	38%
C.Patterson*	60	47.3%	13	121	9.3	2	0	-
D.Carr	-35	-66.5%	12	75	6.3	0	4	-
J.Olawale*	27	47.9%	9	43	4.8	1	1	78%
D.Martin	-77	-22.5%	138	405	2.9	3	1	35%
M.Bryant	10	9.5%	6	22	3.7	0	0	-

Receiving

Player	DYAR	DVOA	Plays	Ctch	Yds	Y/C	YAC	TD	C%
M.Crabtree*	52	-6.5%	101	58	618	10.7	3.3	8	57%
A.Cooper	27	-9.1%	95	48	680	14.2	6.0	7	51%
S.Roberts	34	-5.8%	65	43	459	10.7	2.5	1	66%
C.Patterson*	17	-7.4%	42	31	305	9.8	6.3	0	74%
J.Holton	21	3.0%	18	9	218	24.2	4.4	3	50%
J.Nelson	58	-5.0%	89	53	482	9.1	2.4	6	60%
M.Bryant	118	4.9%	84	50	603	12.1	3.4	3	60%
R.Switzer	11	7.1%	7	6	41	6.8	3.0	0	86%
G.Whalen	-15	-46.3%	6	4	23	5.8	0.5	0	67%
J.Cook	53	2.1%	86	54	688	12.7	3.9	2	63%
C.Walford*	-11	-22.2%	13	9	80	8.9	2.4	0	69%
L.Smith	9	4.6%	11	8	76	9.5	4.0	0	73%
D.Carrier	5	-0.8%	11	8	71	8.9	6.3	0	73%
D.Washington	1	-13.6%	45	34	197	5.8	4.9	1	76%
J.Richard	86	33.3%	36	27	266	9.9	9.0	1	75%
M.Lynch	-23	-27.2%	31	20	151	7.6	8.2	0	65%
J.Olawale*	5	-2.3%	7	6	33	5.5	4.0	0	86%
D.Martin	-18	-30.4%	18	9	84	9.3	6.7	0	50%

Offensive Line

Player	Pos	Age	GS	Snaps	Pen	Sk	Pass	Run	Player	Pos	Age	GS	Snaps	Pen	Sk	Pass	Run
Rodney Hudson	C	29	16/16	1013	3	0.5	2	5	Donald Penn	LT	35	14/14	820	8	2.5	8	7
Kelechi Osemele	LG	29	16/16	1012	4	2.5	10	7	Vadal Alexander	G/T	24	15/4	260	1	1.0	14	3
Gabe Jackson	RG	27	15/15	893	7	0.0	2	8	Breno Giacomini	RT	33	16/16	1102	9	8.0	33	14
Marshall Newhouse*	RT	30	14/14	847	5	4.0	9	6									

Year	Yards	ALY	Rank	Power	Rank	Stuff	Rank	2nd Lev	Rank	Open Field	Rank	Sacks	ASR	Rank	Press	Rank	F-Start	Cont.
2015	3.98	4.02	19	72%	7	18%	6	1.02	26	0.74	15	33	4.6%	4	20.7%	3	28	33
2016	4.66	4.39	11	59%	23	17%	8	1.28	8	1.00	7	18	3.4%	1	17.7%	1	24	31
2017	4.14	4.17	11	62%	21	22%	22	1.17	14	0.73	16	24	4.6%	7	23.1%	3	18	26

2017 ALY by direction:	Left End: 5.32 (5)	Left Tackle: 3.40 (23)	Mid/Guard: 4.25 (11)	Right Tackle: 4.04 (15)	Right End: 4.24 (12)

Donald Penn, Kelechi Osemele, and Rodney Hudson are all veterans still playing at a relatively high level, so the left side of the Raiders line appears set. Gabe Jackson gets the job done at right guard, and newcomers Kolton Miller (Josh Rosen's BFF at UCLA, which may not make him old-school enough for Jon Gruden) and Breno Giacomini (a 32-year-old journeyman who led the NFL in blown blocks with Houston last season) are expected to battle to replace Marshall Newhouse at right tackle. ☞ Rather than going into some deep dive about Hudson's footwork or adjusted line yards or something, let's round this comment out with some vignettes from the Raiders offseason.

Vignette 1: Levi Damien of SBNation reported that Raiders linemen are responding to well Tom Cable's tough-guy approach, in contrast to former line coach Mike Tice's relatively warm-'n'-fuzzy style. "With Cable it's definitely one of those things where it's a challenge and a strain mentally, he kinda wants to try and 'dick with you,' as he would say," Osemele said. "With Tice it was just kind of, you know, straightforward, coaching guys. Maybe a little bit of babying here and there, but … just tough coaching from Cable."

Vignette 2: Vic Tafur of The Athletic reported that several unnamed Raiders linemen showed up for OTAs considerably overweight.

"We had five offensive linemen who were between 30 and 40 pounds heavier than when they left the facility last season," strength and conditioning coach Tom Shaw told Tafur. "They were eating whatever they wanted and were doing nothing." Gruden assigned the linemen to conditioning work with Shaw in lieu of instructional drills, and Shaw said the organization would fine the overweight linemen $665 per day, twice per week. "That's 12 grand if you're ten pounds over," Shaw said. "I could buy a new truck."

Vignette 3: Penn admitted on a podcast that he got so mad when the Raiders drafted Miller that he rage-dialed Gruden. "I'm not going to lie, as soon as I saw the draft pick, I called Gruden immediately. Like 'man, what the f---?,'" Penn said. "He didn't answer, but when I saw him the next Monday, he was joking with me saying, 'You were ready to kick my ass, huh, Donald?! You were mad as a mother------!'" Penn, it should be noted, turned 35 the day after the draft.

This sounds like it's going to be one harmonious, focused family by midseason, doesn't it?

Defensive Front Seven

Defensive Line	Age	Pos	G	Snaps	Plays	Overall TmPct	Rk	Stop	Dfts	BTkl	Runs	vs. Run St%	Rk	RuYd	Rk	Sack	Pass Rush Hit	Hur	Dsrpt
Denico Autry*	28	DT	16	592	41	5.0%	46	34	17	3	20	85%	13	1.6	21	5.0	6	18.5	6
Eddie Vanderdoes	24	DT	16	465	18	2.2%	86	14	2	2	17	76%	48	1.5	17	0.0	2	8.0	0
Justin Ellis	28	DT	16	462	48	5.9%	26	36	5	2	46	76%	52	2.6	67	0.5	0	1.5	0
Treyvon Hester	26	DT	14	346	19	2.7%	--	13	1	1	18	72%	--	2.7	--	0.0	4	7.0	0

Edge Rushers	Age	Pos	G	Snaps	Plays	Overall TmPct	Rk	Stop	Dfts	BTkl	Runs	vs. Run St%	Rk	RuYd	Rk	Sack	Pass Rush Hit	Hur	Dsrpt
Khalil Mack	27	DE	16	931	80	9.8%	1	66	21	5	61	82%	26	2.9	69	10.5	12	52.0	2
Bruce Irvin	31	OLB	16	880	60	7.3%	14	44	23	3	30	77%	40	1.8	27	8.0	7	20.5	2
Mario Edwards	24	DE	14	475	27	3.8%	69	24	7	2	21	90%	7	2.2	44	3.5	4	8.5	0
Tank Carradine	28	DE	8	214	18	4.3%	--	12	2	1	16	63%	--	4.0	--	1.5	2	4.0	0

Linebackers	Age	Pos	G	Snaps	Plays	Overall TmPct	Rk	Stop	Dfts	BTkl	Runs	vs. Run St%	Rk	RuYd	Rk	Sack	Pass Rush Hit	Hur	Tgts	vs. Pass Suc%	Rk	AdjYd	Rk	PD	Int
NaVorro Bowman*	30	MLB	15	997	127	16.2%	14	71	20	17	78	65%	30	3.7	49	1.5	4	4.0	41	48%	41	5.2	13	3	1
Nicholas Morrow	23	OLB	16	554	61	7.5%	82	34	12	6	34	59%	59	4.6	77	0.0	2	4.5	23	50%	36	6.3	30	4	0
Cory James	25	OLB	10	455	57	11.2%	51	34	12	3	29	72%	16	2.0	3	0.0	0	1.5	24	51%	33	6.2	27	1	0
Marquel Lee	23	MLB	13	171	22	3.3%	--	15	3	3	17	71%	--	2.8	--	0.0	0	1.0	5	54%	--	10.1	--	0	0
Tahir Whitehead	28	OLB	16	950	112	13.3%	35	60	14	17	73	60%	56	3.5	39	1.0	6	9.0	45	49%	39	5.9	22	2	1
Derrick Johnson	36	ILB	15	848	78	10.2%	63	42	16	16	47	62%	47	3.4	31	0.0	0	5.0	33	60%	9	4.5	5	6	0

Year	Yards	ALY	Rank	Power	Rank	Stuff	Rank	2nd Level	Rank	Open Field	Rank	Sacks	ASR	Rank	Press	Rank
2015	3.93	4.09	18	53%	4	22%	12	1.07	12	0.72	13	38	5.9%	23	24.1%	25
2016	4.52	4.43	23	63%	17	16%	26	1.13	15	0.98	28	25	4.9%	30	26.9%	17
2017	4.10	4.26	22	67%	22	19%	24	1.11	15	0.68	14	31	6.1%	23	27.8%	28

2017 ALY by direction:	Left End: 3.07 (5)	Left Tackle: 3.67 (12)	Mid/Guard: 4.53 (26)	Right Tackle: 4.64 (27)	Right End: 2.89 (6)

One of the great mysteries of the Jack Del Rio era in Oakland is that Del Rio, general manager Reggie McKenzie, and defensive coordinator Ken Norton were all outstanding linebackers, but the organization could not find or develop an inside linebacker if their jobs depended on it. Which, in Del Rio's and Norton's cases, it did. ☻ The Raiders signed NaVorro Bowman at midseason in a desperate effort to rescue them from the undrafted rookies and late-round experiments manning the position. Bowman provided some thud in run defense but had to be carefully protected in pass coverage. The 30-year-old Bowman was not old or worn down enough for the Gruden regime, however, so the Raiders signed 36-year-old Derrick Johnson in the offseason. Johnson is getting by on guile at this point in his career. ☻ The Raiders also added Tahir Whitehead, a stout run defender from Detroit, and Emmanuel Lamur, a 29-year-old former Paul Guenther experiment from the Bengals who played mostly special teams for the Vikings last year. The trio of veterans provide a modest upgrade, but they are a trio of veterans: none will get appreciably better or provide much long-term value, but they will soak up cap space and reps better spent on developing players. ☻ The Raiders took a pair of low-risk flyers on the defensive line in the draft. Fifth-round pick Maurice Hurst (Michigan) was a first-round value as a 3-tech penetrator, but a heart condition scared other teams off. Arden Key had a checkered LSU career: he entered rehab for a marijuana habit, and his conditioning lapsed early in his college career, resulting in a hot-and-cold athletic profile that leaves SackSEER unimpressed. As always, we root for everyone's physical/mental/emotional health here at Football Outsiders while pointing out that there is a very slim chance that the Raiders unearthed a pair of

All-Pros that other teams had taken off their draft boards. ☞ Khalil Mack, in the final year of his rookie contract, held out of minicamp. That situation obviously bears monitoring. ☞ As for the rest of the front seven … look, 34-year-old Frostee Rucker and 32-year-old Ahtyba Rubin were competing for defensive line jobs in minicamp. This is not normal.

Defensive Secondary

Secondary	Age	Pos	G	Snaps	Plays	TmPct	Rk	Stop	Dfts	BTkl	Runs	St%	Rk	RuYd	Rk	Tgts	Tgt%	Rk	Dist	Suc%	Rk	AdjYd	Rk	PD	Int
						Overall						vs. Run							vs. Pass						
Reggie Nelson	35	FS	16	1027	94	11.5%	18	33	8	10	50	36%	57	8.0	53	24	5.3%	4	15.5	67%	2	10.0	61	4	1
T.J. Carrie*	28	CB	16	1024	93	11.4%	3	40	18	8	22	41%	46	5.8	35	69	15.3%	12	10.7	49%	52	8.0	49	9	0
Karl Joseph	24	SS	15	867	82	10.7%	27	34	13	12	41	39%	53	6.6	43	30	7.9%	23	12.1	61%	12	7.3	27	3	1
Sean Smith*	31	CB	14	702	38	5.3%	--	12	6	7	7	14%	--	8.7	--	46	14.7%	--	14.1	46%	--	10.6	--	3	2
Dexter McDonald	27	CB	15	534	50	6.5%	67	20	6	7	8	25%	71	12.0	74	50	21.3%	45	9.7	47%	64	6.9	28	7	0
David Amerson*	27	CB	6	287	22	7.2%	--	8	2	2	2	50%	--	4.5	--	23	17.8%	--	13.6	37%	--	12.3	--	4	0
Marcus Gilchrist	30	SS	16	817	62	8.1%	67	21	9	8	23	30%	61	8.6	58	42	11.2%	52	12.2	46%	55	10.1	62	6	1
Daryl Worley	23	CB	15	729	73	10.3%	14	33	9	9	15	53%	27	7.8	63	76	25.8%	70	10.9	52%	37	6.8	25	10	2
Rashaan Melvin	29	CB	10	552	49	9.4%	25	26	13	1	9	78%	7	2.4	2	54	28.0%	74	11.7	53%	26	6.5	15	14	3
Shareece Wright	31	CB	12	455	47	7.2%	--	18	5	7	14	43%	--	4.7	--	37	22.8%	--	9.9	50%	--	7.2	--	5	1
Leon Hall	34	CB	9	209	17	3.6%	--	5	2	6	8	38%	--	8.3	--	11	11.8%	--	10.8	49%	--	9.0	--	1	0

Year	Pass D Rank	vs. #1 WR	Rk	vs. #2 WR	Rk	vs. Other WR	Rk	WR Wide	Rk	WR Slot	Rk	vs. TE	Rk	vs. RB	Rk
2015	16	-4.6%	12	-1.1%	14	4.8%	17	--	--	--	--	-11.0%	10	17.0%	30
2016	25	-17.0%	4	5.0%	20	6.0%	20	-0.8%	18	-4.1%	10	7.7%	23	9.8%	23
2017	30	22.3%	30	14.9%	24	25.8%	29	15.2%	29	28.0%	30	0.1%	16	13.9%	27

Gareon Conley, who missed most of last season with a shin injury, was a full participant in the offseason and drew praise from Raiders coaches. The 2017 first-round pick is penciled in at one cornerback spot. ☞ Rashaan Melvin was the other starter in minicamp. Melvin is a veteran career nickel defender who started for the Colts last year and recorded some great charting numbers, albeit with his best work coming against the likes of DeShone Kizer and Tom Savage. Leon Hall also ran with the starters in minicamp, because Hall is 33 years old and has a history with the coaching staff, making him the quintessential 2018 Raider. Shareece Wright should supplant Hall as the nickel by the start of the season. ☞ Wait, Daryl Worley surfaced in Oakland too, after the Eagles released him just days after trading for him in March because of a substance-related arrest? This is bananas. At least Worley is only 23 this season. ☞ Strong safety Karl Joseph is one of the few Raiders defenders who qualifies as young, good, and relatively content with his contract. Reggie Nelson is 34 years old and has started to become a liability in coverage but played for coordinator Paul Guenther for several years in Cincinnati. Obi Melifonwu, a second-round size/speed project who missed most of last offseason and season with a variety of injuries, was still limited in OTAs and minicamp and could be squeezed to make way for this this regime's projects. ☞ Hmm, there don't seem to be any totally superfluous 30-ish free-agent acquisitions gumming up the safety depth charts. Oops, almost missed Marcus Gilchrist. OK, we're good.

Special Teams

Year	DVOA	Rank	FG/XP	Rank	Net Kick	Rank	Kick Ret	Rank	Net Punt	Rank	Punt Ret	Rank	Hidden	Rank
2015	-0.1%	19	-1.4	20	-6.2	30	-2.3	23	14.0	3	-4.6	23	16.4	2
2016	0.3%	14	-1.6	19	5.3	6	-1.4	15	-5.5	24	4.9	7	13.2	2
2017	-0.2%	17	-4.3	23	2.2	13	4.7	7	4.8	10	-8.6	31	-3.8	18

A team that's three-deep with pricey veterans at every position has to be young and cheap somewhere. The Raiders let Sebastian Janikowski quietly fade away last year, and Jon Gruden took umbrage with Marquette King's attention-seeking personality and set the punter loose in free agency. ☞ Fifth-round pick Johnny Townsend punted for Florida for four years and has a clean delivery. And really, who needs a fifth-round pick to develop at a non-specialist position when you can sign Frostee Rucker, Leon Hall, Emmanuel Lamur, and the rest of the 2013 Bengals? ☞ Kicker Giorgio Tavecchio had an uneventful rookie season. The Raiders didn't ask him to do much. He'll compete in camp with UDFA (and Townsend's college teammate) Eddy Pineiro, Florida's career leader in field goal accuracy at 88.4 percent. ☞ Ryan Switzer arrived in a draft-day trade to compete for return duties. Switzer generated a few highlights as the Cowboys punt and kick returner last year (8.0 combined points of estimated field position) but offered no real value as a slot receiver and Cole Beasley impersonator. If Switzer doesn't impress, Gruden will probably trade for Darren Sproles or something.

Philadelphia Eagles

2017 Record: 13-3	**Total DVOA:** 23.5% (5th)	**2018 Mean Projection:** 9.1 wins	**On the Clock (0-4):** 4%
Pythagorean Wins: 12.0 (1st)	**Offense:** 10.0% (8th)	**Postseason Odds:** 52.9%	**Mediocrity (5-7):** 22%
Snap-Weighted Age: 26.9 (7th)	**Defense:** -12.6% (5th)	**Super Bowl Odds:** 10.9%	**Playoff Contender (8-10):** 43%
Average Opponent: -2.2% (24th)	**Special Teams:** 0.9% (16th)	**Proj. Avg. Opponent:** 0.9% (11th)	**Super Bowl Contender (11+):** 31%

2017: I could never lose, went and bought some better jewels / Mansion on the hills, with the better views.

2018: Wins and losses. It come with being bosses.

The Eagles won the Super Bowl, and nothing will ever be the same again.

Fourth-down conversions and goal-line decisions will never be the same again. Expectations for new coaches and young quarterbacks will never be the same again. The conversations around "Moneyball" and the wisdom of treating the acquisition of draft capital as an end in itself will never be the same again. The debates about player protest and social justice, at least among those who are being honest instead of grandstanding for political gain (whoever they are), will never be the same again.

The Eagles redefined aggressiveness, both on fourth downs and in roster construction. Yet they did it with the most unassuming group of dad jeans-wearing coaches and executives you could hope to assemble. Doug Pederson exerted his authority and individuality by embracing compromise and adapting the ideas of his predecessor. Howie Roseman returned from GM in the Iron Mask exile behind the Eagles weight room to rebuild the Eagles by trading **away** draft picks and a starting quarterback. The most politically outspoken locker room in the NFL remained unified and nearly drama-free, even with the international media pressing down on them during Super Bowl week.

It all felt backwards. Yet the Eagles out-Moneyballed the Moneyballers, then outperformed and outcoached Bill Belichick and the Patriots, violating just about every other NFL dictate—even the one about needing an elite quarterback to win in the playoffs—along the way.

Some of what the Eagles did last year, namely the political stuff, falls well beyond the parameters of *Football Outsiders Almanac*. But most of it is right in our wheelhouse and provides a case study in how analytics are a living, breathing, and ever-changing field of study, not a set of commandments handed down from a mountaintop.

Fourth-Down Aggressiveness

Pederson was the most aggressive fourth-down coach in the NFL last year, and one of the most aggressive we have ever measured (Table 1). Granted, he did not rank first in our Aggressiveness Index, due to the design of that system: Adam Gase passed him in the final lap by shrugging his shoulders in a meaningless Week 17 game and going for a bunch of fourth-and-mediums. But Pederson went for it 22 times on 117 quali-

fying fourth-down opportunities in the regular season. In the postseason, he added another three fourth-and-1s and another two fourth-down tries in the red zone. Keep in mind that these were just "discretionary" go-for-it situations, not desperate fourth-quarter attempts when trailing; the Eagles only faced a few of those all year. Philadelphia's regular-season success rate on fourth downs of 65.4 percent was high but not shocking. What was shocking was the sheer number of attempts.

Table 1. Most Fourth-Down 'Go For It' Decisions, 1986-2017

Year	Team	Head Coach	No.
1996	NE	Bill Parcells	27
2007	JAX	Jack Del Rio	26
2017	**PHI**	**Doug Pederson**	**22**
1989	NYG	Bill Parcells	20
2007	NE	Bill Belichick	19
1995	NE	Bill Parcells	19
2009	NE	Bill Belichick	18
1996	CHI	Dave Wannstedt	18
1991	SD	Dave Henning	18
1987	CHI	Mike Ditka	18
2006	NE	Bill Belichick	17
2005	TEN	Jeff Fisher	17
1998	KC	Marty Schottenheimer	17

Regular season only. Includes 1987 strike games. Excludes obvious catch-up situations: third quarter, trailing by 15 or more points; fourth quarter, trailing by nine or more points; and the last five minutes of the game, trailing by any amount.

The Eagles went for it on fourth-and-short in part because they faced fourth-and-short far more often than most teams. The Eagles found themselves in a qualifying fourth-and-1 23 times last year; no other team faced more than 17 such situations. The Eagles had the best third-down DVOA (41.9%) in the NFL and were even better on third-and-long (89.2% DVOA). But even the team's failed efforts on third-and-long often created fourth-and-short opportunities which the Eagles then converted. Aggressiveness was built into the game plans; see the Bears and Rams games, when third-and-long attempts around midfield that came up a yard short were quickly followed by fourth-down conversions.

The Philly Special, the Trey Burton-to-Nick Foles trick play

2018 Eagles Schedule

Week	Opp.	Week	Opp.	Week	Opp.
1	ATL (Thu.)	7	CAR	13	WAS (Mon.)
2	at TB	8	at JAX (U.K.)	14	at DAL
3	IND	9	BYE	15	at LAR
4	at TEN	10	DAL	16	HOU
5	MIN	11	at NO	17	at WAS
6	at NYG (Thu.)	12	NYG		

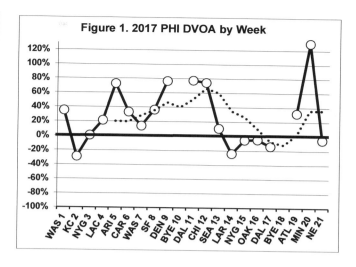

Figure 1. 2017 PHI DVOA by Week

on fourth-and-goal before halftime in the Super Bowl, is the Pederson decision that will be immortalized for all time. But Pederson also "gambled" on fourth-and-goal for a touchdown in the Falcons playoff game. And the fourth-and-1 conversion from Nick Foles to Zach Ertz with five minutes left in the fourth quarter of the Super Bowl, trailing by one point and just shy of midfield, may have been the most daring decision of all. Conventional wisdom screams to punt and "trust your defense," even against Tom Brady. Pederson trusted the percentages instead. According to EdjSports' model, Philadelphia's Game Winning Chance was 46.6 percent in going for it compared to 34.6 percent with a punt.

Eagles copycats will make the whole NFL much more aggressive on fourth downs and at the goal line for years to come. Coaches who "play it safe" on fourth-and-inches near midfield will be the ones who endure all the second-guessing.

Roster Construction

The entire Eagles organization, from front office to roster, was in disarray in the wake of Chip Kelly's Colonel Kurtz season in 2015. The Eagles responded with a series of potentially disastrous moves in an attempt to restore order in the winter of 2016. They retrieved Roseman, who lost a power struggle with Kelly, from the bowels of team headquarters. They hired Pederson as what appeared to be a consolation prize on the head coaching market, then defensive coordinator Jim Schwartz as a built-in replacement if things went wrong. With Pederson's long history under Andy Reid, both the coaching and front office moves looked like desperate attempts to get back to normal instead of getting better.

Roseman then tried to use the time stone on the Infinity Gauntlet to undo everything Kelly did, trading away players such as DeMarco Murray and Byron Maxwell for whatever he could get while spending large amounts of future draft capital to work his way up the draft board to select Carson Wentz, an FCS standout whose lack of a useable analytics profile was a major caution flag. Roseman also signed veterans Fletcher Cox and Lane Johnson to hefty extensions early in his revival tour, eating a lot of cap space that the Eagles didn't appear to have after Kelly's 2015 binge.

Meanwhile, Pederson assembled a staff of none-too-heralded assistants like career second-fiddle Frank Reich and John "Flip" DiFilippo, a would-be quarterback guru who kept getting stuck with substance-abusing quarterbacks (JaMarcus Russell, Johnny Manziel).

Based on the bullet-point analytics that even we are some-

times guilty of at Football Outsiders, most of the Eagles' early 2016 moves were terrible. A rebuilding team with a bloated roster of expensive veterans is supposed to purge-purge-purge, acquire more future draft picks instead of trading them away, and seek mathematically justifiable solutions in the draft instead of tall, strong-armed small-school wonders. Also: innovative new ideas from outside the NFL hivemind like Kelly's are good, retread coaches and executives are bad. Last year, after Wentz's lukewarm rookie season and the Eagles' 7-9 finish, it was hard to find analytics-based justifications for claiming the Eagles were building toward anything particularly special, let alone being months away from their first championship in over 50 years.

We could write an entire book fine-combing through all of the surprises, secret successes and "Umm, actually" moments of the Eagles' relationship with mainstream analytics over the last two seasons, from the Sam Bradford trade to last year's midseason deals (acquiring Ronald Darby and Jay Ajayi for Jordan Matthews and picks) to the whole brouhaha about Wentz's "Air Yards" in his rookie year.

But to paint with a broad brush: the Eagles found an undertow of market inefficiency working against the prevailing tide of inefficiencies that we have written about for years. It's not much of an oversimplification to say that they rode a market correction into the Super Bowl.

When organizations fetishize draft capital like you win some kind of trophy for acquiring the most of it (the Browns), you can sometimes give them a bundle of it in exchange for a commodity you might need much more than extra picks, like a Carson Wentz. When organizations like the Bills and Dolphins are eager to make the "smart" move to deal disgruntled veterans like Darby and Ajayi so they can rebuild their culture, you can acquire young veteran talent inexpensively. And in an era when too many teams operate as if the draft was the final stage in a player's developmental journey, the Eagles protected their investment in Wentz, first by surrounding him by a trio of quarterback-friendly coaches, then by stabilizing the offensive line (extending Lane Johnson) and clarifying his role (trading Sam Bradford), then finally by signing Alshon Jeffery and Torrey Smith and upgrading the running game.

As an added bonus, Pederson's staff and the overall Eagles culture was welcoming to Darby, Ajayi, LeGarrette Blount, the politically minded Torrey Smith and Chris Long and other players whom other coaches might have branded as trouble-makers or (ugh) distractions. If political leanings have become an NFL market force (and they have), the Eagles have created an inviting environment for players who other teams might make excuses to get rid of.

The Eagles Super Bowl roster was a triumph of scientific method over scientific dogma. It debunked bad theories about how to build a team. It made some of us in the analytics field think a little harder and dig a little deeper about our cherished precepts. By proving how quickly a team can turn things around by using analytics more like a chef's knife than a sledgehammer, the Eagles made it harder both for Moneyball gurus to declare five-year rebuilding cycles and for old skool football guyz to cry poor while swapping out the old regime's players for "system fits."

The System (and Its Origins)

The most famous—and overrated—contribution by the 2017 Eagles to the evolution of NFL football may be the run-pass option (RPO), a concept born of the marriage of read-option philosophy and play-action pass design. With television announcers repeating the letters "RPO" like meth-addled auctioneers whenever Nick Foles play-faked throughout the playoffs, you may be stunned to discover that the Eagles were not a very good play-action passing team. They used play-action on 27 percent of snaps, the fifth highest rate in the NFL, but averaged just 6.4 yards per attempt, 26th in the NFL. With Wentz at quarterback, the Eagles actually averaged more yards per pass (7.0) without a play-action fake.

Our play-action data probably does not accurately reflect the success or impact of the RPO. The "option" in RPO means that it's often a running play, so some of the tactic's success may be hidden within our rushing data. It also became a bigger part of game plans when Foles replaced Wentz, so most of the play-action in our regular-season data may just be plain old play-action. Finally, it's more of a situational strategy used to exploit tendencies and weaknesses than some overarching philosophy.

What's most interesting about the RPO is that it isn't a Pederson or Reich idea. It was a Chip Kelly holdover that position coaches and Foles were more comfortable with and prevailed upon their head coach and offensive coordinator to adopt.

Pederson retained other Kelly concepts besides the RPO, combining them with Reich's ideas, Andy Reid-flavored West Coast offense principles, a few of Flip's concepts, and even plays that worked for Wentz at North Dakota State. In a league where coaches treat their playbooks like sacred texts and all the ideas of outgoing administrations as blasphemy, Pederson merged and adapted his system to preexisting systems. He then tailored game plans to make both his second-year quarterback and veteran backup more comfortable, not by scaling things back but by expanding them.

After watching Pederson build a Super Bowl offense through collaboration and tailor it to both a guy two years removed from Nowhere State and a backup who almost left

football for the ministry, it will be hard to listen when future coaches insist that results must wait until the perfect players are found to fit their precious systems.

Aggressiveness, adaptivity, and insight into a deeper level of analytics resulted in one of the most dramatic, unexpected Super Bowl victories in history. But that was last year. This year, forces threaten to pull the Eagles back to the pack, including:

Statistical regression: As mentioned earlier, the Eagles were tremendously successful on third-and-long. Third-and-long sample sizes are small and a handful of conversions can lead to significant swings in the win-loss column.

The Eagles were the league's best offense on third down despite ranking just 13th on first down and 20th on second down. That's one of the biggest gaps of the last few years between third-down and overall performance. Back in the Indianapolis chapter (p. 100), we looked at teams over the last decade with extreme gaps between third-down defense and overall defense. Table 2 does the same thing for the difference between third-down offense and overall offense. Once again, for each team, we're going to compare a simple forecast based only on regression towards the mean to the team's actual offensive DVOA in the following season. You'll notice that these offenses seem to regress towards the mean more than would normally be expected for above-average offenses—although this isn't true of three of the top five teams on the table.

Table 2. Biggest Gap between Third-Down and Overall Offensive DVOA Since 2007

Year	Team	3rd Down DVOA	Rank	All Downs DVOA	Rank	Gap	Simple Forecast Y+1	Actual DVOA Y+1
2009	GB	63.6%	1	18.8%	5	44.7%	10.4%	11.5%
2010	NE	84.3%	1	42.2%	1	42.1%	27.2%	31.9%
2007	PIT	50.6%	1	8.5%	9	42.1%	4.1%	-1.5%
2009	TEN	42.3%	2	4.2%	15	38.0%	1.6%	-4.5%
2016	NE	57.8%	1	20.8%	2	37.0%	11.7%	27.3%
2011	SD	45.0%	4	13.0%	5	32.0%	6.8%	-10.0%
2017	**PHI**	**41.9%**	**1**	**10.1%**	**8**	**31.8%**	**5.0%**	**--**
2011	TEN	29.5%	6	0.6%	15	29.0%	-0.3%	-20.5%
2016	TEN	39.7%	2	10.8%	9	28.9%	5.4%	-2.1%
2010	TB	36.8%	2	8.0%	8	28.9%	3.8%	-11.5%
2009	ATL	34.4%	4	5.9%	14	28.6%	2.6%	8.0%
2013	TEN	30.0%	4	1.4%	16	28.6%	0.1%	-16.4%
AVERAGE (w/o 2017 PHI)		*46.7%*		*12.2%*		*34.5%*	*6.7%*	*1.1%*

Even more impressive than Philadelphia's passing performance on third downs was their passing performance in the red zone. Philadelphia's red zone passing DVOA of 110.8% was the third highest of any offense since 1986 (Table 3). We've written numerous times about the fact that red zone performance does not correlate from year to year as well as overall performance. A little regression in a small, volatile sample turns touchdowns into field goals, quickly shaving a win or two off the standings. The good news here for the Eagles is that while their passing performance in the red zone was exceptional, their rushing performance in the red zone was pretty bad, 28th in the league. Just as their red zone passing is likely to regress towards the mean, so is their ground game near the goal line.

Coaching brain drain: Pederson lost Reich and Flip to the Colts and Vikings hours after the Super Bowl. The collaborative nature of the Eagles coaching staff cuts two ways in this case: Pederson loses more input from two excellent assistants than most other head coaches would, but a management philosophy that rewards creative thinking could also result in more fresh ideas from returnees like Duce Staley (now assistant head coach), Mike Groh (now offensive coordinator), and other assistants. The few veteran additions to the staff, such as receivers coach Gunter Brewer, have a chance to do more in Philly than line the guys up for drills. Still, for a team that got so much mileage from situational gameplanning and the ability to prepare quarterbacks, the losses of an offensive coordinator and quarterback coach are likely to be significant.

Carson Wentz's injury: At press time, Wentz's ACL recovery did not look like a matter of serious concern. Wentz was a limited participant in May OTAs—even running and throwing in some drills—and Foles is still around despite the media's best efforts to trade him. But the possibility does remain that the Eagles may be without Wentz in Week 1 or that he is rusty or at less than peak capacity when he does return.

General post-Super Bowl attrition: The Eagles roster didn't suffer major post-championship erosion. Contributors such as Blount and Mychael Kendricks left, but the core of the roster remains intact. Large chunks of the defensive line underwent offseason surgery, but Haloti Ngata and Michael Bennett arrived as potential reinforcements. Cornerback Syd-

ney Jones, last year's first-round pick, is back after a medical redshirt year, as are old-timers Jason Peters and Darren Sproles, who each missed most of the Super Bowl run. The Eagles fit all of this under the cap and more (like a bonus for Foles to stick around one more year) because Roseman's budget philosophy isn't "save for a rainy day" but "spend wisely and you can polish the Lombardi trophy when it's raining."

Most Super Bowl teams lose coaches and free agents, and most enjoyed an unsustainable hot streak or two on something like third-down performance, injury rate, or fumble luck on their way to a championship. The same forces tugging the Eagles down pull on all great teams; even the Patriots have to flap their wings extra hard to stay in flight these days. They drag the Eagles down into the wild-card morass in our playoff projections, with an improved NFC East and a first-place schedule further pulling them down toward the NFC's deep-and-talented chase group.

But that doesn't matter, because the Eagles won the Super Bowl and changed the conversation forever.

Reich and Flip are already spreading Eagles Incorporated to other franchises. The copycats will start running trick plays at the goal line and going for more fourth-and-1 situations. Versions of the RPO will be everywhere.

Not all the lessons will be the correct lessons: some coaches will panic after the first fourth-down failure, and yet another crop of tall, strong-armed quarterbacks with iffy college resumes will get tossed into the lineup too early faster than you can say "Josh Allen." But some organizations will realize that the Eagles were built on a method and mentality, not just on trades, some new Xs and Os, or a lucky break in the draft.

It's not easy to do as many things right as the Eagles did over the last two years. But the NFL will be a better place if more teams are at least trying.

Mike Tanier

Table 3. Best Red Zone Passing DVOA, 1986-2017

Year	Team	Red Zone Pass	Rk	Red Zone Run	Rk	Total Offense	Rank	Red Zone Pass Y+1	Rk	Total Offense Y+1	Rk Y+1
1999	KC	135.9%	1	26.8%	6	14.0%	6	22.7%	9	12.9%	7
1993	PHI	124.3%	1	14.0%	8	6.3%	8	-51.3%	27	-1.6%	15
2017	**PHI**	**110.8%**	**1**	**-27.6%**	**28**	**10.1%**	**8**	--	--	--	--
1991	NYG	103.7%	1	9.4%	9	12.5%	6	37.9%	2	9.3%	7
1995	GB	101.9%	1	1.3%	12	20.9%	2	62.3%	1	15.2%	3
2005	SD	96.3%	1	51.5%	2	22.1%	6	81.6%	1	25.7%	2
2016	TEN	94.9%	1	27.6%	5	10.8%	9	-14.7%	25	-2.2%	18
1987	MIA	93.8%	1	12.3%	7	23.1%	2	12.9%	8	18.1%	2
2002	NYJ	93.7%	1	8.0%	19	18.0%	4	12.2%	14	12.0%	7
1990	LARD	88.2%	1	17.1%	7	20.0%	2	-29.5%	19	-0.9%	16
1988	CIN	85.6%	1	52.5%	1	30.8%	1	82.1%	1	17.5%	2
2004	SD	84.7%	1	6.8%	12	16.7%	7	96.3%	1	22.1%	6
1994	SF	84.6%	1	2.8%	8	18.9%	1	3.5%	8	18.6%	5
AVERAGE (w/o 2017 PHI)		99.0%	1.0	19.2%	8.0	17.8%	4.5	26.3%	9.7	12.2%	7.5

2017 Eagles Stats by Week

Wk	vs.	W-L	PF	PA	YDF	YDA	TO	Total	Off	Def	ST
1	at WAS	W	30	17	356	264	+2	35%	3%	-26%	7%
2	at KC	L	20	27	406	344	-2	-29%	-2%	15%	-12%
3	NYG	W	27	24	354	415	+1	1%	11%	18%	8%
4	at LAC	W	26	24	454	400	+1	21%	17%	5%	10%
5	ARI	W	34	7	419	307	0	73%	52%	1%	22%
6	at CAR	W	28	23	310	305	+2	33%	5%	-26%	3%
7	WAS	W	34	24	371	344	0	14%	18%	8%	4%
8	SF	W	33	10	304	238	+1	36%	-11%	-43%	4%
9	DEN	W	51	23	419	226	+1	77%	53%	-27%	-4%
10	BYE										
11	at DAL	W	37	9	383	225	+4	78%	32%	-62%	-16%
12	CHI	W	31	3	420	140	-1	75%	8%	-63%	3%
13	at SEA	L	10	24	425	310	-2	11%	13%	10%	8%
14	at LAR	W	43	35	455	307	+1	-24%	17%	25%	-16%
15	at NYG	W	34	29	341	504	+1	-5%	13%	21%	3%
16	OAK	W	19	10	216	274	+3	-5%	-57%	-63%	-10%
17	DAL	L	0	6	219	301	-1	-14%	-30%	-14%	2%
18	BYE										
19	ATL	W	15	10	334	281	-2	32%	12%	-19%	0%
20	MIN	W	38	7	456	333	+3	130%	83%	-38%	10%
21	NE	W	41	33	538	613	0	-5%	23%	34%	6%

Trends and Splits

	Offense	Rank	Defense	Rank
Total DVOA	10.1%	8	-12.3%	5
Unadjusted VOA	10.5%	7	-14.1%	3
Weighted Trend	7.4%	8	-17.7%	2
Variance	7.3%	16	9.8%	31
Average Opponent	-0.3%	17	-1.5%	23
Passing	33.0%	6	-6.9%	8
Rushing	-5.9%	15	-21.6%	2
First Down	4.1%	13	-19.3%	1
Second Down	-5.1%	20	4.6%	21
Third Down	41.9%	1	-26.1%	3
First Half	10.7%	8	-18.9%	3
Second Half	9.4%	9	-6.1%	10
Red Zone	29.0%	1	-2.0%	16
Late and Close	6.5%	12	-12.9%	10

Five-Year Performance

Year	W-L	Pyth W	Est W	PF	PA	TO	Total	Rk	Off	Rk	Def	Rk	ST	Rk	Off AGL	Rk	Def AGL	Rk	Off Age	Rk	Def Age	Rk	ST Age	Rk
2013	10-6	9.4	10.2	442	382	+12	15.2%	8	22.9%	3	4.9%	23	-2.8%	25	21.2	7	11.0	4	27.5	11	26.2	21	26.0	19
2014	10-6	9.7	9.7	474	400	-8	12.8%	7	1.1%	13	-3.3%	10	8.3%	1	32.2	18	16.4	2	27.2	11	26.9	13	26.9	1
2015	7-9	6.7	6.8	377	430	-5	-11.2%	22	-10.1%	26	3.0%	17	1.9%	10	23.7	10	28.3	17	27.2	11	26.7	15	26.9	2
2016	7-9	9	9.9	367	331	+6	14.4%	5	-5.5%	20	-12.4%	4	7.5%	2	20.6	3	17.8	5	27.0	11	26.9	9	27.0	3
2017	13-3	12.0	11.1	457	295	+11	23.4%	5	10.1%	8	-12.3%	5	0.9%	16	28.5	12	25.0	11	27.1	12	26.9	9	26.4	7

2017 Performance Based on Most Common Personnel Groups

PHI Offense					PHI Offense vs. Opponents					PHI Defense					PHI Defense vs. Opponents			
Pers	Freq	Yds	DVOA	Run%	Pers	Freq	Yds	DVOA	Run%	Pers	Freq	Yds	DVOA	Pers	Freq	Yds	DVOA
11	67%	6.1	19.7%	37%	Base	31%	5.0	2.5%	48%	Base	27%	5.1	-16.4%	11	62%	5.4	-8.2%
12	22%	5.2	14.5%	36%	Nickel	56%	5.9	19.0%	39%	Nickel	60%	5.4	-4.0%	12	20%	5.0	-16.8%
13	5%	3.5	0.1%	57%	Dime+	12%	6.6	35.7%	19%	Dime+	10%	5.4	-34.6%	13	6%	4.9	-25.1%
612	2%	4.0	9.3%	92%	Goal Line	1%	-0.8	-11.3%	67%	Goal Line	1%	0.7	-14.8%	21	5%	3.6	-54.1%
611	2%	3.5	-28.9%	47%						Big	2%	1.8	-78.5%	10	2%	8.8	76.1%
10	2%	5.3	19.2%	37%										22	2%	4.4	3.4%

Strategic Tendencies

Run/Pass		Rk	Formation		Rk	Pass Rush		Rk	Secondary		Rk	Strategy		Rk
Runs, first half	38%	19	Form: Single Back	95%	1	Rush 3	2.1%	29	4 DB	27%	25	Play action	27%	4
Runs, first down	44%	29	Form: Empty Back	4%	27	Rush 4	78.9%	3	5 DB	60%	13	Avg Box (Off)	6.28	12
Runs, second-long	41%	5	Pers: 3+ WR	69%	10	Rush 5	10.0%	31	6+ DB	10%	15	Avg Box (Def)	6.25	16
Runs, power sit.	63%	9	Pers: 2+ TE/6+ OL	31%	15	Rush 6+	9.0%	5	CB by Sides	89%	7	Offensive Pace	30.75	17
Runs, behind 2H	23%	30	Pers: 6+ OL	2%	30	Int DL Sacks	25.0%	14	S/CB Cover Ratio	27%	19	Defensive Pace	29.98	8
Pass, ahead 2H	49%	14	Shotgun/Pistol	71%	6	Second Level Sacks	13.2%	24	DB Blitz	9%	15	Go for it on 4th	1.64	3

One problem that continued for the Eagles defense in 2017 was tackling. The Eagles ranked 25th with 128 broken tackles last season, after they were 30th with 131 broken tackles the year before. ☞ Philadelphia's defense had the best DVOA (-18.0%) against runs from formations with three or more wide receivers as well as the best DVOA (-25.7%) against runs from shotgun. (There's a lot of overlap between these categories, obviously.) ☞ When Philadelphia blitzed, it was frequently a big blitz with six or more pass-rushers. Only Jacksonville sent five less often, but only four teams sent six more often. The Eagles allowed just 4.6 yards per pass with a big blitz (-46.0% DVOA) compared to 6.0 yards with four pass-rushers and 7.0 yards with five. ☞ The Eagles really struggled against screen passes, allowing 5.9 yards per pass and 24.3% DVOA on wide receiver screens and 8.1 yards per pass with a league-worst 82.2% DVOA on running back screens. ☞ A league-high 27 percent of Eagles plays from the shotgun were runs.

Passing

Player	DYAR	DVOA	Plays	NtYds	Avg	YAC	C%	TD	Int
C.Wentz	1047	23.8%	471	3100	6.6	4.6	60.5%	33	7
N.Foles	-114	-28.5%	107	486	4.5	4.2	56.4%	5	2
N.Sudfeld	-22	-24.5%	26	110	4.2	4.3	82.6%	0	0

Rushing

Player	DYAR	DVOA	Plays	Yds	Avg	TD	Fum	Suc
L.Blount*	-9	-9.8%	173	766	4.4	2	1	43%
C.Clement	71	14.5%	74	321	4.3	4	0	50%
J.Ajayi	25	0.9%	70	408	5.8	1	2	43%
C.Wentz	52	6.7%	50	306	6.1	0	3	-
W.Smallwood	-20	-19.5%	47	174	3.7	1	0	36%
K.Barner*	7	3.1%	16	57	3.6	1	0	31%
D.Sproles	2	-5.5%	15	61	4.1	0	0	40%

Receiving

Player	DYAR	DVOA	Plays	Ctch	Yds	Y/C	YAC	TD	C%
A.Jeffery	108	-1.2%	120	57	789	13.8	3.4	9	48%
N.Agholor	141	6.7%	95	62	768	12.4	4.9	8	65%
T.Smith*	-29	-18.2%	69	37	427	11.5	3.3	2	54%
M.Hollins	59	25.0%	22	16	226	14.1	2.7	1	73%
M.Johnson*	-7	-22.4%	8	5	45	9.0	1.4	0	63%
M.Wallace	96	0.4%	92	52	748	14.4	2.9	4	57%
B.Treggs	-36	-40.3%	18	5	79	15.8	0.6	0	28%
M.Wheaton	-66	-66.2%	17	3	51	17.0	1.0	0	18%
Z.Ertz	154	14.2%	110	74	829	11.2	3.4	8	67%
T.Burton*	85	35.0%	31	23	248	10.8	1.5	5	74%
B.Celek*	-14	-15.6%	24	13	130	10.0	6.5	1	54%
R.Rodgers	28	18.8%	19	12	160	13.3	7.4	1	63%
W.Smallwood	30	14.2%	18	13	103	7.9	6.7	0	72%
C.Clement	50	41.7%	15	10	123	12.3	12.8	2	67%
J.Ajayi	26	20.6%	14	10	91	9.1	10.9	1	71%
D.Sproles	16	12.7%	12	7	73	10.4	11.9	0	58%
L.Blount*	25	41.4%	8	8	50	6.3	5.9	1	100%
K.Barner*	6	-0.5%	8	5	56	11.2	10.4	0	63%

Offensive Line

Player	Pos	Age	GS	Snaps	Pen	Sk	Pass	Run	Player	Pos	Age	GS	Snaps	Pen	Sk	Pass	Run
Jason Kelce	C	31	16/16	1079	5	0.5	8	4	Stefen Wisniewski	LG	29	14/11	696	1	1.0	16	7
Brandon Brooks	RG	29	16/16	1077	2	0.0	3	5	Jason Peters	LT	36	7/7	422	1	2.0	5	3
Lane Johnson	RT	28	15/15	964	10	0.5	13	9	Chance Warmack	LG	27	11/3	318	2	0.0	0	1
Halapoulivaati Vaitai	LT	25	16/10	829	6	8.5	25	5	Isaac Seumalo	LG	25	14/2	284	3	5.5	12	4

Year	Yards	ALY	Rank	Power	Rank	Stuff	Rank	2nd Lev	Rank	Open Field	Rank	Sacks	ASR	Rank	Press	Rank	F-Start	Cont.
2015	4.09	3.54	30	84%	1	21%	18	1.21	10	0.81	13	37	6.6%	20	20.8%	4	20	34
2016	4.28	4.28	13	57%	25	18%	12	1.36	6	0.67	16	33	5.4%	10	25.7%	15	26	26
2017	4.52	3.85	22	64%	16	21%	21	1.30	4	1.14	3	36	6.2%	12	34.4%	26	16	28

2017 ALY by direction:	Left End: 3.85 (18)	Left Tackle: 3.32 (24)	Mid/Guard: 4.17 (14)	Right Tackle: 3.40 (23)	Right End: 3.49 (23)

Jason Peters lumbered around the practice field throughout OTAs and minicamp, taking occasional ceremonial reps with the first team but mostly watching the proceedings like some battered old gladiator. Peters was still playing at a high level before getting hurt last year. Assuming he is healthy, he will push Halapoulivaati Vaitai back to the bench. Big V is like the Nick Foles of left tackles: late in the season, he looked like a big reason why the Eagles would go one-and-done in the playoffs, but he then played well enough through the offseason to suggest he might be a future solution at one of the tackle positions. ☞ There may someday be a statue of Jason Kelce in a Mummer's costume next to Rocky outside the Philadelphia Museum of Art. But Kelce isn't posing for any sculptures just yet: he's back after a bounce-back season in 2017. Under Chip Kelly, Kelce was known for delivering flashy open-field blocks on screens but was an inconsistent pass protector who drew too many penalties. He was more steady and reliable last year. Barrett Brooks and Lane Johnson are also back, giving the Eagles line a rock-solid right side as long as Johnson avoids suspensions and doesn't get too caught up in the extracurriculars. Doug Pederson made a point of telling players (Johnson) to "put the dog masks away" at minicamp. ☞ Left guard was last year's weakness, with three different players earning starts. Stefen Wisniewski somewhat stabilized the position once he took over, but he also ranked 34th out of 37 left guards in snaps per blown block. ☞ Chance Warmack, Isaac Seumalo, and Big V provide depth. None of them are spectacular, but all three are experienced, and the Eagles know what they are getting when they step in. ☞ Former defensive tackle Taylor Hart is in camp trying to complete a conversion to left tackle. Hulking (6-foot-8, 346-pound) Australian rugby star Jordan Mailata combines Peters-level size and athleticism with an accent rarely heard in South Philly, a pleasant demeanor, and absolutely no idea what he is doing.

Defensive Front Seven

Defensive Line	Age	Pos	G	Snaps	Plays	Overall TmPct	Rk	Stop	Dfts	BTkl	Runs	St%	vs. Run Rk	RuYd	Rk	Sack	Pass Rush Hit	Hur	Dsrpt
Fletcher Cox	28	DT	14	608	28	4.2%	60	24	9	1	18	83%	22	1.7	29	5.5	13	28.5	3
Timmy Jernigan	26	DT	15	492	29	4.0%	62	24	14	1	23	87%	10	1.1	4	2.5	7	10.0	0
Beau Allen*	27	DT	15	422	20	2.8%	83	17	6	1	19	84%	18	1.4	13	1.0	2	9.0	0
Destiny Vaeao	24	DT	11	230	11	2.1%	--	7	1	1	9	67%	--	4.0	--	0.0	0	2.0	1

Edge Rushers	Age	Pos	G	Snaps	Plays	Overall TmPct	Rk	Stop	Dfts	BTkl	Runs	St%	vs. Run Rk	RuYd	Rk	Sack	Pass Rush Hit	Hur	Dsrpt
Brandon Graham	30	DE	15	666	48	6.7%	21	40	24	6	33	79%	35	2.2	45	9.5	4	26.0	1
Vinny Curry*	30	DE	16	578	42	5.5%	39	36	14	5	37	84%	20	1.1	14	3.0	20	27.5	2
Chris Long	33	DE	16	496	28	3.7%	70	23	11	5	20	80%	31	2.3	46	5.0	15	34.5	2
Derek Barnett	22	DE	15	424	21	2.9%	86	19	12	2	14	93%	5	0.6	3	5.0	11	19.5	0
Michael Bennett	33	DE	16	934	41	4.9%	50	35	21	10	30	80%	31	1.3	16	8.5	17	38.5	2

Linebackers	Age	Pos	G	Snaps	Plays	Overall TmPct	Rk	Stop	Dfts	BTkl	Runs	St%	vs. Run Rk	RuYd	Rk	Sack	Pass Rush Hit	Hur	Tgts	vs. Pass Suc%	Rk	AdjYd	Rk	PD	Int
Nigel Bradham	29	OLB	15	923	96	13.4%	34	57	20	17	44	77%	7	3.0	20	1.0	2	8.5	28	60%	10	5.7	20	6	0
Mychal Kendricks*	28	OLB	15	612	78	10.9%	55	48	15	8	38	74%	11	2.3	7	2.0	4	6.5	31	65%	4	5.2	12	6	0
Jordan Hicks	26	MLB	7	268	28	8.4%	74	14	8	3	7	71%	18	2.6	12	0.0	2	3.0	18	43%	--	5.2	--	0	0
Paul Worrilow	28	OLB	13	277	31	4.5%	--	19	3	3	22	82%	--	2.1	--	0.0	1	2.0	11	29%	--	9.8	--	1	0

Year	Yards	ALY	Rank	Power	Rank	Stuff	Rank	2nd Level	Rank	Open Field	Rank	Sacks	ASR	Rank	Press	Rank
2015	4.57	4.36	23	74%	29	17%	27	1.18	22	1.04	29	37	6.8%	13	24.9%	19
2016	4.20	3.44	2	70%	27	24%	3	1.20	19	1.13	31	34	6.6%	11	31.6%	3
2017	3.35	2.99	1	55%	6	29%	2	0.88	1	0.83	23	38	6.3%	19	32.2%	9
2017 ALY by direction:		Left End: 2.43 (2)			Left Tackle: 2.82 (4)			Mid/Guard: 3.04 (1)			Right Tackle: 3.24 (10)			Right End: 3.28 (10)	

Everyone on the defensive line was either recovering from surgery, excused from the bulk of OTA sessions, or wrapped up in some sociopolitical drama this offseason, making it hard to glean too many specifics about the Eagles defensive line. It was among the deepest and best lines in the NFL last season, and it promises to be just as strong this year assuming most of the key figures are healthy and rested and have not been deported or anything. ☞ First, the surgeries. Brandon Graham underwent an ankle procedure in May. Timmy Jernigan underwent herniated disc surgery at around the same time. Both were among the Eagles' best defensive linemen last season. Both are expected to be full speed at the start of the season. ☞ Next, the excused absences. Fletcher Cox doesn't practice much in spring. Offseason pickup Haloti Ngata, still on the mend from an October torn bicep, was a limited participant in most offseason work. Cox remains the anchor of the Eagles defense. Ngata, when healthy, is still effective as a 20- to 25-snap run plugger. ☞ Finally, politics and stuff. Michael Bennett stands accused of assaulting a security guard after Super Bowl LI and is one of the NFL's most polarizing individuals. He was absent for all of OTAs but participated in minicamp. Chris Long was around for everything, and good thing, too: he's as important when the Eagles are battling political opponents as he is when battling football opponents. Bennett (assuming there are no legal issues) is likely to platoon with second-year edge rusher and Super Bowl hero Derek Barnett, with Bennett playing more on run downs and moving inside on passing downs. Long plays mostly in waves and packages. ☞ The cap-driven release of Mychal Kendricks leaves the Eagles relatively thin at linebacker. Nigel Bradham excels in coverage and is the three-down guy; coaches raved during minicamp about his ability to call the defense and make quick on-field assignment adjustments. Jordan Hicks, on the mend from an Achilles injury, is penciled in beside Bradham. Free-agent addition Paul Worrilow suffered an ACL tear at the start of OTAs, leaving special teams ace Kamu Grugier-Hill and converted college safety Nate Geary as the frontrunners for the weakside spot. If the Eagles get all of their bodies back on the defensive line, it won't matter much who the third linebacker is, especially since Philadelphia played nickel or dime on 70 percent of snaps last season.

Defensive Secondary

Secondary	Age	Pos	G	Snaps	Plays	TmPct	Rk	Stop	Dfts	BTkl	Runs	St%	Rk	RuYd	Rk	Tgts	Tgt%	Rk	Dist	Suc%	Rk	AdjYd	Rk	PD	Int
													vs. Run					**vs. Pass**							
Malcolm Jenkins	31	SS	16	948	75	9.8%	42	35	17	7	27	59%	10	5.7	31	55	12.7%	59	6.8	55%	26	5.9	13	7	2
Jalen Mills	24	CB	15	932	78	10.9%	6	37	11	12	14	79%	6	3.6	7	93	21.7%	50	11.4	49%	51	7.3	34	14	3
Rodney McLeod	28	FS	14	846	56	8.4%	63	18	10	13	23	30%	61	9.5	60	22	5.7%	5	12.1	56%	24	11.3	71	4	3
Patrick Robinson*	31	CB	16	710	63	8.2%	43	39	20	10	11	64%	13	3.7	8	70	21.5%	48	10.4	62%	5	7.3	37	19	4
Rasul Douglas	23	CB	14	420	35	5.2%	78	21	7	10	3	100%	1	3.0	5	52	27.0%	73	11.9	54%	22	8.0	50	11	2
Ronald Darby	24	CB	8	382	43	11.2%	--	18	7	0	11	27%	--	10.9	--	45	25.7%	--	11.6	60%	--	7.8	--	9	3
Corey Graham*	33	FS	14	370	36	5.4%	--	14	10	3	11	45%	--	6.9	--	11	6.5%	--	10.1	61%	--	8.6	--	4	2

Year	Pass D Rank	vs. #1 WR	Rk	vs. #2 WR	Rk	vs. Other WR	Rk	WR Wide	Rk	WR Slot	Rk	vs. TE	Rk	vs. RB	Rk
2015	14	7.8%	23	-5.1%	13	-12.4%	6	--	--	--	--	4.7%	19	-0.8%	15
2016	2	-18.5%	3	1.6%	17	2.3%	18	-2.3%	16	-12.0%	5	-52.8%	1	-11.9%	9
2017	8	-15.8%	7	-48.5%	1	5.9%	21	-12.1%	7	-25.4%	1	0.7%	17	-6.1%	10

Sydney Jones, last year's first-round pick who slipped in the draft due to a pre-combine foot injury, looked great early in OTAs before missing several sessions with an unelaborated-upon "soreness." The Eagles are bringing him along slowly. Jones and gamble-and-guess type Ronald Darby are the projected starters, with Jalen Mills—who played well until opponents figured out that he fell for every double-move in the playbook—likely to move to the slot to replace Patrick Robinson. ☜ Rasul Douglas, a Richard Sherman-sized second-round pick who was forced to play a lot of snaps last year, came around late in the year after a very shaky early season. Douglas had a strong offseason, giving the Eagles enviable depth on the corners if Jones gets healthy. ☜ Malcolm Jenkins has spent his career slowly and gracefully transitioning from cornerback to safety to box safety to congressman/lobbyist/news-channel personality/something. He can be exposed in man coverage but makes up for it with his capabilities in zone and run support. Free safety Rodney McLeod is the quiet, unsung hero of the defense. Tre Sullivan, an undrafted training camp star in 2017, has the inside track to be the third safety when Jenkins plays slot in the heavy nickel.

Special Teams

Year	DVOA	Rank	FG/XP	Rank	Net Kick	Rank	Kick Ret	Rank	Net Punt	Rank	Punt Ret	Rank	Hidden	Rank
2015	1.9%	10	-2.9	26	0.7	15	-0.2	15	1.0	18	11.1	2	-13.8	32
2016	7.5%	2	3.5	10	14.3	1	15.1	1	0.1	15	4.8	8	-11.3	28
2017	0.9%	16	3.9	11	-0.8	21	0.6	12	3.4	14	-2.5	22	0.8	12

Jake Elliott represents everything we talk about when we talk about kickers here at Football Outsiders. The Bengals drafted him, which was a mistake, then soured on him in training camp, which compounded that mistake. (Elliott was 2-of-5 beyond 40 yards in Bengals preseason games, so you can't blame them, but imagine evaluating a quarterback on five passes). The Eagles signed him when Caleb Sturgis got hurt, and Elliott became a folk hero after his 62-yard game-winner against the Giants. Elliott went 5-of-5 from 50-plus yards but 4-of-7 inside 40 yards, plus three missed extra points in the regular season and one in the Super Bowl. That stat line screams BEWARE, because 50-yard field goal rates fluctuate wildly while shorter kicks and extra points should hover much closer to 100 percent. But the Eagles let Sturgis walk and brought in no competitors for Elliott. ☜ Australian-born former Ohio State punter Cameron Johnston replaces Donnie Jones. Johnston spent all of last offseason in Eagles camp but did not survive the final round of cuts. Johnston led the Big Ten in punting in 2016 and is the Buckeyes' all-time record holder on punts inside the 20. ☜ Darren Sproles is expected back to return punts, with Donnell Pumphrey and Mack Hollins also capable of return chores if the Sproles comeback doesn't happen. The Eagles also need a new kickoff returner with Kenjon Barner moving on; Corey Clement had a 35-yard kick return last year, and Shelton Gibson returned kicks at West Virginia.

Pittsburgh Steelers

2017 Record: 13-3	Total DVOA: 27.1% (3rd)	2018 Mean Projection: 10.2 wins	On the Clock (0-4): 2%
Pythagorean Wins: 10.6 (7th)	Offense: 17.6% (3rd)	Postseason Odds: 70.8%	Mediocrity (5-7): 12%
Snap-Weighted Age: 26.5 (14th)	Defense: -6.4% (9th)	Super Bowl Odds: 23.8%	Playoff Contender (8-10): 37%
Average Opponent: -2.1% (23rd)	Special Teams: 3.1% (9th)	Proj. Avg. Opponent: 0.0% (17th)	Super Bowl Contender (11+): 48%

2017: Best chance for a Super Bowl trip yet, but it all comes crashing down in a very familiar fashion.

2018: Best chance for a Super Bowl trip yet. If not now, then when?

For the third straight year, our projections have the Steelers in the NFL's top five. For the fourth straight year, we've put them in the top ten. There are at least 25 teams that would love to be in Pittsburgh's shoes—the second longest playoff appearance streak, division crowns in three of the past four seasons, arguably the best skill position group in the NFL, a near-guaranteed championship opportunity every season. And yet...

Predicting a Steelers season is fairly simple, as the past few years have all ended up going the same way:

- Pencil in wins over all quality opponents at home. The Steelers are 12-5 at home against teams with a winning record over the past four seasons, the second-highest mark in the league.
- Flip any Patriots games to a loss. Two of those five home losses were against the Patriots, and Pittsburgh is 1-6 against New England in the past decade. Make sure that bumps the Steelers down at least one playoff seed, preferably out of home field advantage (à la 2017) or a first-round bye (à la 2016).
- Add in at least one loss to a struggling team, usually on the road, in a game where it appears everyone in a black and yellow uniform has forgotten how to play football. See the loss to the 0-2 Bears last year, the 1-4 Dolphins the year before, the 4-10 Ravens the year before that, or the 1-8 Jets the year before *that*. Bonus points if it comes the week before a crucial matchup against a huge rival; the last couple of upset losses have come before rivalry games with Baltimore and New England.
- Fill in any remaining games with wins over bad teams and a .500 record on the road against good teams, and you've got your regular season results; typically, a 12ish-win season.
- Top it off with a loss in a playoff game, normally coupled with a "what could have been"-level excuse. Typically, that's been one of the Killer B's being injured, either before or early during the game in question, though last season they mixed it up by having the ninth-rated defense get ripped to shreds by Blake Bortles.

That's not a bad season at all, in a vacuum. No team can expect to win the Super Bowl every year, and making regular playoff appearances is the best way to eventually get there. It's just the *Groundhog Day* level of having the same season happen over and over and over again that eventually drives you mad.

It is somewhat rare for a team to make the playoffs this consistently and never even make it to the big game. Forty-two teams since the merger, including these Steelers, have had playoff streaks of four seasons or longer; 71.4 percent of them reached the Super Bowl. If the Steelers have another Steelers season and make it five in a row without a trip to Atlanta, they would be one of just seven teams to have a streak that long without reaching the summit.

Sometimes, however, the fifth time is the charm. It took Tony Dungy and Peyton Manning's Colts five attempts to get past Tom Brady and make it to a Super Bowl. The Harbaugh/Flacco Ravens took five tries as well, as did the Reid/McNabb Eagles, John Madden's Raiders and Tom Landry's Cowboys. When you spend most of your time playing second banana to a dynasty in your own conference—be it the current Patriots, the '70s Steelers or the '60s Packers—it sometimes takes a little longer to break through. Perhaps the fifth time will be the charm for the Steelers, as well.

It had better be. Only one franchise in NFL history made more than five consecutive playoff appearances before reaching a Super Bowl: the 1973-1980 Rams, who took seven tries before they finally earned the opportunity to lose to the Steelers in Super Bowl XIV. They had to make changes at head coach and quarterback before they made it, too. If you have the same corps coming back year after year, but can't get over the hump in more than half a decade of close calls, it's unrealistic to expect to ever take that final step.

So, this is year number five in Pittsburgh. It might be their best chance yet. It also might be their *last* chance, at least as they currently stand.

The Steelers' 2018 projection isn't quite as high as last year's projection—but this time, it's the best in the league. New England has the higher win projection due to a much easier schedule, but the Steelers' are projected to be the better team by DVOA. Their offensive projection is, as normal, spectacular. This is the third straight year we've had Pittsburgh projected as the top offense in the league. It's also, perhaps surprisingly, the strongest *defensive* projection they've had during this playoff run. Once again, the Steelers should count themselves as one of the NFL's top teams, and anyone who has Super Bowl aspirations in the AFC will have to go through them.

It also may be the last time the Killer B's are all togeth-

2018 Steelers Schedule

Week	Opp.	Week	Opp.	Week	Opp.
1	at CLE	7	BYE	13	LAC
2	KC	8	CLE	14	at OAK
3	at TB (Mon.)	9	at BAL	15	NE
4	BAL	10	CAR (Thu.)	16	at NO
5	ATL	11	at JAX	17	CIN
6	at CIN	12	at DEN		

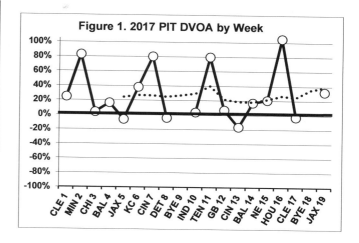

Figure 1. 2017 PIT DVOA by Week

er. Le'Veon Bell has been franchised for the second straight season, with talks for a long-term extension sputtering and stalling. Franchising him for a third straight year in 2019 is not realistic, and unless a deal is done by July 16, Bell will have many suitors next offseason. Ben Roethlisberger has flirted with retirement for multiple offseasons now, and was not pleased that Pittsburgh drafted an heir apparent in Mason Rudolph. Antonio Brown doesn't seem to be going anywhere, having signed an extension just last year, but the end of the era for these triplets looms in the not-too-distant future.

All the more reason to strike while the iron's hot and win a Super Bowl this season, right? All Pittsburgh really needs is a couple of tweaks to help them clear those final hurdles.

Pittsburgh's offense comes back mostly intact, and arguably improved by replacing Martavis Bryant with second-round pick James Washington, a big-play threat with the speed to stretch defenses deep downfield. From a personnel standpoint, then, this should be much of the same as we've seen in past seasons.

The major change comes on the sidelines. Pittsburgh fired offensive coordinator Todd Haley, a decision which brought with it much rejoicing throughout the Steel City. Haley was able to constantly put together some of the best offenses in the league and deserves credit for helping lower Roethlisberger's sack rate and improving his completion percentage. Roethlisberger's numbers were better under Haley than under previous coordinator Bruce Arians (Table 1). If you're looking for someone to design an offensive scheme from the ground up, Haley is a very good choice. On game days, however, Haley became much less valuable. His game plans and situational play calling were sketchy, at best.

In short-yardage and third-down situations, especially, Haley had a habit of being too cute for his own good, often finding excuses to throw bubble screens or take deep shots or run slow-developing pitches rather than having the best running back in football or the biggest quarterback in football plow forward for 6 inches. Roethlisberger hasn't run a quarterback sneak since 2015, which is nearly coaching malpractice. Pitts-

burgh ranked sixth in rushing DVOA in 2017, but 27th when rushing on third downs. That's not "Le'Veon Bell forgot how to run on third downs," that's a product of trying to over-complicate things and push the envelope, running jet sweeps and misdirection rather than simply letting the best collection of offensive talent in the league overpower people.

In addition, Haley had a long-running and much-publicized feud with Big Ben. While it's not necessary for a coordinator and his quarterback to be BFFs and go to ice-cream socials and spend the offseason riding dirt bikes together or anything in order to have success, it's also not ideal for the two to be in a Hatfield-McCoy level feud, having fired shots at one another ever since they were brought together in 2012. By the end of last season, Roethlisberger had reportedly recruited other members of the coaching staff to serve as a buffer between him and Haley, and convinced Mike Tomlin to move quarterbacks coach Randy Fichtner from the press box to the sidelines. This relationship between the two had pretty much deteriorated beyond repair.

So Haley's out and Fichtner is in at offensive coordinator, which should improve sideline friction and provide Roethlisberger with play calling that better fits his personal preferences at the very least. Fichtner's not just a surrogate for Roethlisberger on the sidelines, however. Before joining the Steelers in 2007, Fichtner was the offensive coordinator first at Arkansas State and then at Memphis, so we have some ideas of what his offensive philosophy might be.

Fichtner's Memphis teams were noted for their use of no-huddle and an up-tempo, high-paced offense in the years before it had spread throughout college football. In his peak years in 2003 and 2004, Memphis had more than 5,000 yards of offense and around 400 points, comfortably ranking among

Table 1: Ben Roethlisberger's Stats by Offensive Coordinator

Coordinator	Years	G	W-L	Cmp/G	Att/G	C%	Yds/G	TD/G	INT/G	Sk/G	ANY/A	Rtg	DYAR	DVOA
Ken Whisenhunt	2004-06	47	34-12	15.6	25.1	62.2%	207.0	1.3	1.1	2.3	7.4	87.8	2416	22.3%
Bruce Arians	2007-11	81	56-25	19.8	31.5	62.9%	246.9	1.5	0.8	3.0	7.6	92.4	3921	13.5%
Todd Haley	2012-17	93	58-34	24.2	37.1	65.2%	285.9	1.9	0.9	1.9	7.7	95.6	6248	17.1%

Includes both regular season and playoffs

the national leaders. At both Memphis and Arkansas State, Fichtner's scheme set school records, as the up-tempo offense kept opposing defenses tired and unable to stop players such as DeAngelo Williams and Cleo Lemon. Notably, Fichtner was praised at the time for both his in-game adjustments and his willingness to listen to his players; pretty much the polar opposite of Haley.

Roethlisberger has been calling for more no-huddle for years. Haley was reluctant to do so, in part because he loved his shifts and his motions and his sub personnel, which seemed to occasionally end up with the genius idea of throwing eight thousand quick screens as he tried to play four-dimensional chess. It's a story that popped up in every preseason for years now, with the two firing not-so-subtle shots at one another through the media about their conflicting offensive philosophies.

There's no conflict now. While Fitchner is unlikely to re-invent the wheel and make massive changes to a successful offense, you can expect the Steelers to pick up the pace dramatically in 2018. They were 26th in situation-neutral seconds per play, taking 31.69 seconds per snap on offense. Expect that number to decrease dramatically going forward, as the no-huddle and other up-tempo concepts spice up the offense. It will mean a cutback in shifts and motions for Pittsburgh, but it also means defenses will be unable to substitute freely and will have to rely on more vanilla schemes. Simplicity is a good thing here; the Steelers can line up and dare opponents to find a way to somehow cover Bell and Brown and JuJu Smith-Schuster and the rest of Pittsburgh's potent offense. With that kind of talent at their disposal, simple might work really, really well for the Steelers.

Expecting the offense to play at a high level is one thing. In the past few seasons, it has been the defense that has ultimately let the Steelers down, especially in the playoffs. They ended last season ranked ninth with a -6.4% DVOA, but there's a sad asterisk to that. The Steelers were fourth in defensive DVOA up through Week 12, with a -14.3% mark, but the Ryan Shazier injury coincided with a December swoon that eventually saw the Steelers unable to slow down the juggernaut that was Blake Bortles and the 16th-ranked Jacksonville Jaguars in the playoffs (Table 2).

Table 2: Pittsburgh's Defensive Decline Post-Shazier

Weeks	Total	Rk	vs. Pass	Rk	vs. Run	Rk
Weeks 1-12	-14.3%	4	-11.3%	5	-18.0%	8
Weeks 13-17	9.8%	29	1.6%	16	20.5%	32
Week 19	40.8%	—	46.7%	—	36.1%	—

Our projection system thinks that's less likely to happen this year. To be perfectly honest, it's one of the more surprising projections, but it's not like Pittsburgh's defense wasn't fairly good last season. It was actually very good until Shazier went down. It's just what Pittsburgh was bad at, they were *really* bad at.

Try tackling, for example—heaven knows, Pittsburgh's defense didn't. The Steelers defense allowed 150 broken tackles on 123 plays. That's a 14.1 percent broken tackle rate on all defensive snaps, the worst in the league. It's not even close, either—the Chargers were just ahead of them with a 13.3 percent rate. This goes a long way to explaining their No. 18 rushing defense; it's easy to pick up extra yards when defenders are sliding off you left and right. Pittsburgh ranked 30th in both second-level and open-field yards, and that's due in large part to these tackling woes.

There are two reasons to believe this might get better in 2018. First, while Pittsburgh also had an above-average amount of broken tackles in 2016, they weren't nearly as bad then as they were a season ago. Some simple regression to the mean should help here; it's unlikely that Pittsburgh will be as unlucky in 2018 as they were the year before.

The other big reason for hope here is the *breadth* of the problem. On most teams that had a lot of broken tackles, a lot of different players were missing a few tackles each. Not so much the case for the Steelers. Only five players had 20 or more broken tackles in 2017, and the Steelers employed two of them—Ryan Shazier had 23 and Sean Davis had 21. If you combined Shazier and his main replacement, Sean Spence, into one player, their combined 27 broken tackles would have led the league. In addition, you had Mike Hilton in third place, with 14 broken tackles of his own.

That's more than 40 percent of Pittsburgh's broken tackles problem in just three positions, which was the worst total in the league. It's not "Pittsburgh had a problem tackling," it's "those three specific guys had a problem tackling." That's a lot easier problem to deal with than a team-wide tackling epidemic.

First-round pick Terrell Edmunds will either send Davis to the bench or move him to a more of a free safety role, either of which would reduce Davis' tackle opportunities. Edmunds is a hard hitter who covers a lot of ground. He only missed a handful of tackles last year at Virginia Tech, although he was better in run support than chasing people in the open field. His tackling skills will be an instant upgrade over Davis. The Steelers can also hope that a little more experience helps Hilton's tackling skills; last year was his first season on an active NFL roster. Assuming Hilton and Davis take a step forward this season, that will be a nice boost for Pittsburgh's defense.

Replacing Shazier didn't go well last season, but that's partly because the Steelers had to come up with a way to replace an exceptionally crucial piece of their defense in just a week. They have now had a full offseason to plan around his absence, and while they don't have a second Shazier waiting in the wings, they have a couple solid options. Jon Bostic arrives from the Colts as a free agent; while he's a step down from Shazier in most respects, he did allow only five broken tackles in all of 2017 and would be an improvement over Spence regardless. Third-year player Tyler Matakevich received first-team OTA snaps while Bostic was learning the terminology and is in the mix for the spot as well. No matter who lines up next to Vince Williams, it will be the weakest part of Pittsburgh's defense. That can be mitigated somewhat with scheme and careful planning, and the missed tackle epidemic should be at least somewhat improved in 2018.

The other major problem Pittsburgh had in run defense was power situations—runs on third or fourth down with 2 yards or less to go, or right up against their own goal line. The Steelers ranked 31st in those situations, with opponents getting a first down or touchdown on 82 percent of their opportunities. Unlike tackling, however, this was a team effort.

With the exceptions of Bud Dupree and Stephon Tuitt, everyone in the front seven was, at best, average when asked to stop the run. Vince Williams was the worst of the bunch, with just a 39 percent stop rate in the run game, but both Shazier and rookie T.J. Watt had more than their fair share of struggles throughout the season. Communication was also a real problem, with missed assignments and open gaps being rife throughout the year. As a result, there was nearly always somewhere open for running backs to go, and plenty of broken tackles to turn those 2-yard gains into 6-yard gains. Something had to be done.

Part of the repair plan is new personnel, as both Edmunds and fifth-round rookie safety Marcus Allen could have roles as thumpers in the box, at least in sub packages. More interesting, however, is the way the Steelers might address their run issues schematically. During OTAs, they were experimenting with four-man fronts while using the same 3-4 personnel, with Dupree serving as the fourth lineman. The Steelers already use plenty of four-man fronts in sub-package passing situations, but this looks more like a commitment to experimenting with it on base downs in order to stop the run. They're also looking at flipping Dupree and Watt's positions on a regular basis, rather than keeping them to their specific sides—presumably to keep Watt as an off-the-ball player regardless of where opposing tight ends line up.

This makes a lot of sense with the Steelers' current personnel. Without Shazier, the inside linebacking corps is weaker, so having an extra inside linebacker to split the load at the second level will help prevent Watt or Williams from being isolated as much. Allowing Watt and Dupree to swap back and forth, depending on the offensive alignment, will allow Watt's superior coverage skills and Dupree's explosiveness to be used to their fullest extent. The quickness of Hargrave, Tuitt, and Heyward would work well in a more aggressive front, crashing down to collapse gaps. It still feels somewhat blasphemous to see the Steelers using four-man fronts, but that might be exactly what they need to get the most out of their front seven's strengths and hide their biggest weaknesses.

If these schematic tweaks work, and Pittsburgh's pass defense remains as good as it was last season, that high defensive projection seems readily attainable. Couple that with that up-tempo, no-huddle attack from the uber-talented offense and you might just have the best team in football.

We've seen all this before. All the high expectations, all the glowing preseason predictions, all the promises that this year things will be different. And every year, we get a variation of the same old story.

A 12-4 season and a playoff exit would be another good season in a string of good seasons. If that's all the 2018 Steelers can do, however, maybe it's time to admit that good isn't good enough. For Mike Tomlin and his coaching staff, this year may be a choice between going to the Super Bowl and finding a new place to work.

Bryan Knowles

2017 Steelers Stats by Week

Wk	vs.	W-L	PF	PA	YDF	YDA	TO	Total	Off	Def	ST
1	at CLE	W	21	18	290	237	0	25%	15%	-6%	4%
2	MIN	W	26	9	335	237	+1	83%	44%	-34%	4%
3	at CHI	L	17	23	282	306	0	4%	12%	-9%	-17%
4	at BAL	W	26	9	381	288	+2	17%	8%	-14%	-5%
5	JAX	L	9	30	371	313	-4	-6%	-19%	-8%	4%
6	at KC	W	19	13	439	251	-1	38%	30%	-24%	-16%
7	CIN	W	29	14	420	179	+2	80%	27%	-49%	4%
8	BYE							-4%	0%	6%	2%
9	at DET	W	20	15	392	482	-1				
10	at IND	W	20	17	316	267	0	4%	-4%	-15%	-7%
11	TEN	W	40	17	349	316	+4	80%	35%	-29%	15%
12	GB	W	31	28	462	307	-3	7%	11%	12%	8%
13	at CIN	W	23	20	374	353	-1	-17%	18%	41%	6%
14	BAL	W	39	38	545	413	+1	17%	51%	39%	5%
15	NE	L	24	27	413	360	0	21%	21%	4%	4%
16	at HOU	W	34	6	330	227	+2	105%	42%	-47%	16%
17	CLE	W	28	24	348	374	0	-3%	-17%	6%	21%
18	BYE										
19	JAX	L	42	45	545	378	-2	32%	69%	41%	4%

Trends and Splits

	Offense	Rank	Defense	Rank
Total DVOA	17.6%	3	-6.4%	9
Unadjusted VOA	19.6%	3	-7.5%	8
Weighted Trend	19.5%	3	-1.9%	12
Variance	4.3%	6	6.8%	24
Average Opponent	0.1%	18	-3.0%	26
Passing	34.0%	4	-7.1%	7
Rushing	3.0%	6	-5.6%	18
First Down	15.4%	4	-9.5%	6
Second Down	19.1%	7	6.5%	24
Third Down	19.6%	4	-20.2%	5
First Half	17.4%	4	-2.3%	12
Second Half	17.8%	5	-10.3%	5
Red Zone	20.7%	5	9.0%	23
Late and Close	10.9%	8	-5.2%	13

Five-Year Performance

Year	W-L	Pyth W	Est W	PF	PA	TO	Total	Rk	Off	Rk	Def	Rk	ST	Rk	Off AGL	Rk	Def AGL	Rk	Off Age	Rk	Def Age	Rk	ST Age	Rk
2013	8-8	8.2	8.3	379	370	-4	0.9%	15	4.4%	12	4.0%	19	0.5%	16	55.3	28	27.5	16	26.4	25	28.4	1	25.7	25
2014	11-5	9.7	9.4	436	368	0	12.1%	8	22.5%	2	11.3%	30	0.9%	12	4.1	1	38.7	17	26.5	24	27.8	3	26.2	10
2015	10-6	10.7	10.8	423	319	+2	21.3%	7	17.3%	3	-3.8%	11	0.1%	18	43.2	23	23.9	9	28.2	5	27.0	11	26.2	14
2016	11-5	9.9	10.2	399	327	+5	17.1%	4	12.5%	7	-4.7%	11	-0.1%	16	35.2	15	26.7	11	27.1	9	26.5	15	25.7	23
2017	13-3	10.6	11.3	406	308	+2	27.1%	3	17.6%	3	-6.4%	9	3.1%	9	15.2	6	15.3	7	27.4	7	25.7	23	25.9	14

2017 Performance Based on Most Common Personnel Groups

PIT Offense					PIT Offense vs. Opponents					PIT Defense				PIT Defense vs. Opponents			
Pers	Freq	Yds	DVOA	Run%	Pers	Freq	Yds	DVOA	Run%	Pers	Freq	Yds	DVOA	Pers	Freq	Yds	DVOA
11	70%	6.4	28.6%	27%	Base	28%	5.5	-3.5%	64%	Base	38%	5.9	0.1%	11	51%	5.6	-7.5%
12	11%	6.2	16.4%	55%	Nickel	55%	6.1	28.0%	32%	Nickel	36%	4.9	-14.8%	12	19%	5.4	-12.6%
22	6%	4.8	-9.0%	83%	Dime+	15%	8.1	47.2%	10%	Dime+	24%	5.4	-8.0%	21	13%	4.6	-4.8%
621	5%	5.0	1.7%	81%	Goal Line	1%	0.5	38.8%	75%	Goal Line	1%	1.0	53.3%	13	5%	5.1	-11.5%
21	3%	4.1	-17.8%	46%	Big	2%	3.7	-22.8%	78%					22	3%	5.0	8.9%

Strategic Tendencies

Run/Pass		Rk	Formation		Rk	Pass Rush		Rk	Secondary		Rk	Strategy		Rk
Runs, first half	36%	27	Form: Single Back	74%	22	Rush 3	16.6%	4	4 DB	38%	6	Play action	11%	32
Runs, first down	46%	24	Form: Empty Back	11%	6	Rush 4	60.9%	20	5 DB	36%	26	Avg Box (Off)	6.24	18
Runs, second-long	41%	3	Pers: 3+ WR	71%	7	Rush 5	20.3%	14	6+ DB	24%	7	Avg Box (Def)	6.10	26
Runs, power sit.	45%	29	Pers: 2+ TE/6+ OL	26%	24	Rush 6+	2.2%	29	CB by Sides	93%	2	Offensive Pace	31.69	26
Runs, behind 2H	26%	21	Pers: 6+ OL	3%	21	Int DL Sacks	41.1%	4	S/CB Cover Ratio	26%	20	Defensive Pace	31.32	26
Pass, ahead 2H	49%	13	Shotgun/Pistol	71%	5	Second Level Sacks	28.6%	5	DB Blitz	15%	2	Go for it on 4th	0.49	31

Pittsburgh's offense ranked third in lowest pressure rate on first downs, then first on second downs, but declined to 16th on third downs. ☞ Once again, the Steelers were near the top of the league in use of wide receiver screens. In 2017 they ranked fourth with 43 screens, although they gained just 4.4 yards per play with 10.6% DVOA (close to the NFL average of 13.1%). ☞ For the second year in a row, the Steelers were the only team to use play-action more often on second down (15 percent) than first down (12 percent). This was true even though that 15 percent ranked them 31st in play-action frequency for second downs. At least the Steelers can argue that they used play-action less than any other team because they weren't any better with a play fake: the Steelers had a slightly higher DVOA without play-action, and they gained 7.6 yards per play without play-action compared to just 6.6 yards per play with it. ☞ The Steelers did run a lot on second down, though, and they were the best offense in the league on second-and-long (5.5 yards per carry, 20.3% DVOA). Only five offenses had a positive DVOA when running the ball on second-and-long: Pittsburgh, Kansas City, New Orleans, Oakland, and Baltimore. ☞ The Pittsburgh defense got killed by play-action, with the league's biggest yardage difference between play-action (9.1 yards, 33.3% DVOA) and other passes (5.1 yards, -16.8% DVOA). ☞ The Steelers tied the Jets with a league-low 30 percent of sacks coming from edge rushers. ☞ Pittsburgh had a clear split in responsibilities between safeties, with Sean Davis making his average play at 7.4 yards and Mike Mitchell at 14.7 yards. Only New Orleans had a larger gap.

Passing

Player	DYAR	DVOA	Plays	NtYds	Avg	YAC	C%	TD	Int
B.Roethlisberger	1270	21.8%	580	4112	7.1	5.7	64.6%	28	14
L.Jones	-52	-36.5%	31	220	7.1	3.4	82.1%	1	1

Rushing

Player	DYAR	DVOA	Plays	Yds	Avg	TD	Fum	Suc
L.Bell	214	7.9%	321	1315	4.1	9	2	49%
J.Conner	20	10.2%	32	144	4.5	0	0	53%
S.Ridley	34	27.1%	26	108	4.2	1	0	38%
B.Roethlisberger	6	-2.1%	11	66	6.0	0	0	-
F.Toussaint	13	40.4%	6	25	4.2	0	0	67%
M.Bryant*	10	9.5%	6	22	3.7	0	0	-
T.Watson*	-4	-21.1%	5	8	1.6	0	0	60%

Receiving

Player	DYAR	DVOA	Plays	Ctch	Yds	Y/C	YAC	TD	C%
A.Brown	430	20.1%	163	101	1533	15.2	4.8	9	62%
M.Bryant*	118	4.9%	84	50	603	12.1	3.4	3	60%
J.Smith-Schuster	317	37.3%	79	58	917	15.8	6.7	7	73%
E.Rogers*	-28	-22.3%	36	18	154	8.6	4.5	1	50%
J.Hunter	-12	-29.6%	10	4	23	5.8	3.5	1	40%
J.James	-23	-12.8%	63	43	372	8.7	4.5	3	68%
V.McDonald	7	-2.4%	24	14	188	13.4	6.3	1	58%
X.Grimble	-27	-46.5%	9	5	32	6.4	3.2	1	56%
L.Bell	101	2.5%	106	85	655	7.7	8.0	2	80%

Offensive Line

Player	Pos	Age	GS	Snaps	Pen	Sk	Pass	Run	Player	Pos	Age	GS	Snaps	Pen	Sk	Pass	Run
Alejandro Villanueva	LT	30	16/16	1079	6	6.5	25	10	Chris Hubbard*	RT	27	16/10	781	3	4.5	17	7
David DeCastro	RG	28	15/15	1049	7	0.5	7	12	Marcus Gilbert	RT	30	7/7	399	1	0.0	7	4
Maurkice Pouncey	C	29	15/15	1038	5	0.5	6	12	B.J. Finney	C/G	27	14/4	236	1	1.0	2	1
Ramon Foster	LG	32	14/14	929	0	2.0	13	4									

Year	Yards	ALY	Rank	Power	Rank	Stuff	Rank	2nd Lev	Rank	Open Field	Rank	Sacks	ASR	Rank	Press	Rank	F-Start	Cont.
2015	4.53	4.45	8	60%	24	19%	10	1.22	9	1.01	6	33	5.4%	8	19.2%	1	17	39
2016	4.47	4.68	3	71%	7	15%	4	1.40	4	0.52	25	21	4.1%	4	18.6%	2	21	31
2017	4.07	4.36	7	65%	12	17%	5	1.22	10	0.48	27	24	3.9%	1	22.7%	2	14	26
2017 ALY by direction:			Left End: 4.52 (11)			Left Tackle: 4.43 (13)			Mid/Guard: 4.33 (9)			Right Tackle: 4.20 (11)			Right End: 4.60 (7)			

Pittsburgh has managed to keep the same starting five together for three years in a row. That level of year-to-year continuity goes a long way to explaining how effective they have been. ☞ Pittsburgh's top spot in adjusted sack rate is all the more impressive thanks to Alejandro Villanueva's issues in pass protection. Only three left tackles had more than Villanueva's 25 blown pass blocks, and all three of their teams finished 16th or lower in ASR. ☞ The Steelers averaged an extra 6.8 points per game when Marcus Gilbert was in the lineup, as opposed to dealing with a hamstring injury or serving a PED suspension. ☞ David DeCastro does everything well, but his work as a pass protector last season really stood out. He has only given up 0.5 sacks in the past two seasons combined. Paired with Maurkice Pouncey, that A-gap might as well be a brick wall. ☞ Ramon Foster had an odd split in 2017—he had three times as many blown blocks in pass protection as he did in the running game. That was not the case earlier in his career; it may well just be a random spike. ☞ Third-round pick Chukwuma Okorafor (Western Michigan) is likely a multi-year project. You can't teach body type, and his 6-foot-6, 320-pound frame is pretty much what you would make if you were creating a tackle in Madden, but he has only been playing football since he was a junior in high school, and his technique needs some work.

Defensive Front Seven

Defensive Line	Age	Pos	Overall								vs. Run					Pass Rush			
			G	Snaps	Plays	TmPct	Rk	Stop	Dfts	BTkl	Runs	St%	Rk	RuYd	Rk	Sack	Hit	Hur	Dsrpt
Cameron Heyward	29	DE	15	787	47	6.7%	13	37	23	5	28	71%	63	2.3	53	12.0	11	28.0	5
Stephon Tuitt	25	DE	12	571	27	4.8%	49	22	13	3	20	80%	32	0.2	1	3.0	14	20.0	1
Javon Hargrave	25	DT	16	454	33	4.4%	54	25	6	6	27	78%	42	2.0	34	2.0	2	13.5	1
Tyson Alualu	31	DE	16	436	39	5.2%	38	31	12	2	32	78%	41	2.3	56	4.0	2	7.5	1

Edge Rushers	Age	Pos	G	Snaps	Plays	TmPct	Rk	Stop	Dfts	BTkl	Runs	St%	Rk	RuYd	Rk	Sack	Hit	Hur	Dsrpt
					Overall							vs. Run				Pass Rush			
Bud Dupree	25	OLB	15	799	41	5.8%	33	31	16	9	26	88%	9	0.5	2	6.0	2	26.5	1
T.J. Watt	24	OLB	15	752	58	8.2%	9	44	18	10	35	74%	50	1.9	34	7.0	7	19.5	2
Anthony Chickillo	26	OLB	16	270	15	2.0%	--	10	4	7	7	71%	--	3.9	--	3.0	0	6.0	0

Linebackers	Age	Pos	G	Snaps	Plays	TmPct	Rk	Stop	Dfts	BTkl	Runs	St%	Rk	RuYd	Rk	Sack	Hit	Hur	Tgts	Suc%	Rk	AdjYd	Rk	PD	Int
					Overall							vs. Run				Pass Rush				vs. Pass					
Vince Williams	29	ILB	16	738	88	11.7%	46	38	12	6	59	39%	86	5.0	82	8.0	6	8.0	19	48%	46	9.2	71	1	1
Ryan Shazier*	26	ILB	12	672	99	17.6%	6	57	28	23	47	62%	47	3.6	42	0.0	2	10.0	37	42%	59	6.7	37	11	3
Jon Bostic	27	ILB	14	915	99	13.6%	31	58	17	5	64	72%	17	3.0	21	1.0	2	7.0	28	47%	49	6.9	43	2	0

Year	Yards	ALY	Rank	Power	Rank	Stuff	Rank	2nd Level	Rank	Open Field	Rank	Sacks	ASR	Rank	Press	Rank
2015	3.80	4.06	16	55%	5	21%	14	1.13	18	0.56	7	48	7.4%	7	24.2%	24
2016	4.39	4.07	14	67%	24	22%	9	1.24	21	0.99	29	38	5.8%	19	24.7%	24
2017	4.47	3.96	12	82%	31	20%	18	1.31	30	1.04	30	56	9.8%	1	34.3%	4
2017 ALY by direction:		Left End: 6.27 (32)			Left Tackle: 4.25 (22)			Mid/Guard: 3.82 (9)			Right Tackle: 3.28 (11)			Right End: 4.02 (18)		

It's difficult to find a defensive end duo better than Cameron Heyward and Stephon Tuitt. Heyward's 23 quarterback knock-downs (sacks plus hits) were second among 3-4 ends last season; any discussion of the best pass disrupters in the league has to include him from the very start. ☞ Tuitt was just behind Heyward with 17 quarterback knockdowns, and also led the league in lowest average yards on run tackles, regardless of position. ☞ T.J. Watt showed tremendous coverage skills as a rookie. He managed a 71 percent success rate, and only two other edge rushers were listed in coverage on more passes than Watt last season. ☞ There's a loud minority opinion among some Pittsburgh fans that Bud Dupree has underperformed in some way, usually pointing to his 14.5 career sacks and wondering why he doesn't have more. That ignores his tremendous contributions to run defense, where he is an absolute terror—Dupree ranked second among edge rushers and third among all players in aver-age yards on run tackles. His QB hurries also jumped from eight to 26.5 last season; even with his increase in snaps, that's a significant increase in his pressure rate. ☞ Ryan Shazier leaves some massive shoes to fill. Vince Williams proved a more than capable replacement for Lawrence Timmons at two-thirds the cost, but it meant the Steelers were an inside linebacker down when it came time to replace Shazier, and Sean Spence really wasn't up to the task. The top replacement option might be Jon Bostic, who was really more of a rotational player thrust into a starting role in Indianapolis because of a lack of talent around him. Tyler Matakevich, last year's seventh-round pick, is another option.

Defensive Secondary

Secondary	Age	Pos	G	Snaps	Plays	TmPct	Rk	Stop	Dfts	BTkl	Runs	St%	Rk	RuYd	Rk	Tgts	Tgt%	Rk	Dist	Suc%	Rk	AdjYd	Rk	PD	Int
					Overall							vs. Run					vs. Pass								
Artie Burns	23	CB	16	976	67	8.9%	34	26	10	8	13	23%	73	6.2	47	70	15.0%	10	13.9	53%	29	7.1	31	13	1
Sean Davis	25	SS	16	950	98	13.0%	8	41	18	21	48	46%	35	4.8	19	45	9.9%	41	10.7	43%	64	10.3	65	8	3
Mike Mitchell*	31	FS	13	682	55	9.0%	55	10	3	8	27	15%	75	9.9	64	17	5.2%	3	22.6	40%	71	19.8	76	1	0
Joe Haden	29	CB	11	614	27	5.2%	77	11	4	4	4	50%	32	26.3	80	40	13.6%	6	15.0	52%	35	7.9	47	7	1
Mike Hilton	24	CB	16	579	59	7.9%	--	39	22	14	21	76%	--	2.2	--	39	14.0%	--	9.2	67%	--	5.1	--	7	2
William Gay*	33	CB	16	268	22	2.9%	--	12	10	5	5	60%	--	7.0	--	15	11.7%	--	11.3	45%	--	6.4	--	3	1
Coty Sensabaugh	30	CB	14	241	20	3.0%	--	9	2	2	6	50%	--	3.2	--	26	22.1%	--	13.2	45%	--	11.1	--	3	1
Morgan Burnett	29	SS	12	729	71	11.2%	21	31	13	3	35	51%	20	5.3	24	27	9.6%	38	8.5	46%	57	6.3	16	3	0

Year	Pass D Rank	vs. #1 WR	Rk	vs. #2 WR	Rk	vs. Other WR	Rk	WR Wide	Rk	WR Slot	Rk	vs. TE	Rk	vs. RB	Rk
2015	13	12.2%	26	10.2%	22	-9.2%	11	--	--	--	--	-16.1%	5	-8.6%	9
2016	12	19.8%	32	-18.9%	3	-30.4%	1	7.0%	24	-21.0%	2	-4.4%	13	3.3%	19
2017	7	4.3%	17	-10.9%	10	17.5%	25	-10.7%	8	21.7%	28	-34.6%	1	12.5%	23

There's no doubting first-round pick Terrell Edmunds' athleticism; you don't run a 4.47-second 40 or dominate the vertical and broad jumps without turning a few heads. He has the talent to play any spot in the secondary, as well as inside as a linebacker. His ideal spot is probably still strong safety, but it will be very interesting to see where Edmunds lines up when Pittsburgh goes into their nickel and dime packages. ☞ The Steelers have a hole at free safety with Mike Mitchell out of town. First up will be ex-Packer Morgan Burnett, but he may not stick. If Edmunds develops fast enough to be the starting strong safety from

Day 1, don't be surprised to see Sean Davis get some chances at free safety. That's probably a better fit for his skill set, at any rate. ➾ Mike Hilton is not your average slot corner. Hilton's more of a blitzer than a coverage guy; his 9.5 quarterback hurries were second among defensive backs last season and no cornerback managed more than his eight quarterback knockdowns. He also had the highest adjusted success rate of any cornerback in Pittsburgh last season, albeit in a limited sample size. ➾ Joe Haden was only targeted 40 times in 2017, the lowest number for any cornerback who started at least eight games. It wasn't quite the lowest target rate, thanks to missing five games with a leg injury, but opponents went out of their way to pick on Artie Burns or Coty Sensabaugh rather than Haden. ➾ Burns took some positive steps between his rookie and sophomore seasons. His success rate rose from 50 percent to 54 percent and he allowed nearly 2 yards less after the catch on average. There's still room for improvement, though; Burns too often takes chances and guesses at routes, which sometimes comes back to burn him. ➾ Fifth-round pick Marcus Allen (Penn State) is a tackling machine and should have an immediate impact on special teams. His speed is an issue, and his coverage skills aren't what you would want out of a future starting safety, but he could find success as a sub package linebacker/safety hybrid, as is all the rage these days.

Special Teams

Year	DVOA	Rank	FG/XP	Rank	Net Kick	Rank	Kick Ret	Rank	Net Punt	Rank	Punt Ret	Rank	Hidden	Rank
2015	0.1%	18	-1.0	18	3.7	8	-4.8	27	3.4	12	-0.6	17	-11.1	30
2016	-0.1%	16	9.1	3	-2.2	19	-1.6	18	-4.4	23	-1.3	17	-0.2	17
2017	3.1%	9	8.4	7	5.2	7	1.3	10	3.3	15	-2.9	24	-8.0	28

Pittsburgh was above average in every aspect of special teams except for punt returns. For the second time in two years, Eli Rogers won the job out of training camp—and for the second time, he was demoted midway through the season. ➾ With Rogers no longer on the team, the Steelers would have Antonio Brown and JuJu Smith-Schuster as their primary returners. Having your starting receivers as returners is not exactly the safest strategy, so another option might be UDFA Quadree Henderson, who had seven return touchdowns at Pitt. ➾ Chris Boswell made his first Pro Bowl last season, had his highest-ever field goal percentage, and was 4-for-4 from beyond 50 yards. Even so, Pittsburgh's FG/XP value dropped a tad, as Boswell missed a pair of extra points and a couple more field goals shorter than 40 yards. Even with those short misses, Boswell has the fifth-highest field goal percentage over the past three seasons (minimum 50 field goal attempts). He has missed just 10 field goals in his career. He's a real weapon. ➾ Jordan Berry will return as Pittsburgh's punter, though there was a brief immigration scare for the Aussie. As a restricted free agent, technically Berry was unemployed after the season ended, which caused issues with his expiring U.S. work visa. Pittsburgh had to quickly get a deal done to make sure their punter would be in Latrobe and not Victoria come training camp.

San Francisco 49ers

2017 Record: 6-10	Total DVOA: 3.2% (20th)	2018 Mean Projection: 7.4 wins	On the Clock (0-4): 13%
Pythagorean Wins: 6.6 (19th)	Offense: -2.8% (19th)	Postseason Odds: 25.9%	Mediocrity (5-7): 39%
Snap-Weighted Age: 26.3 (20th)	Defense: 8.3% (26th)	Super Bowl Odds: 2.4%	Playoff Contender (8-10): 35%
Average Opponent: 0.5% (14th)	Special Teams: 2.9% (11th)	Proj. Avg. Opponent: -0.4% (23rd)	Super Bowl Contender (11+): 12%

2017: A ray of hope shines in from the northeast.

2018: An up-and-coming squad is not quite ready for the beast.

"I learned the way to get people to feel good about 6-10 is just to start 0-9." Head coach Kyle Shanahan may have had his tongue firmly planted in his cheek when he said that, but it is hard to blame the 49ers faithful for their optimism after several frustrating seasons in the post-Jim Harbaugh era. After two underwhelming years under former head coaches Jim Tomsula and Chip Kelly, the 49ers finally developed a real vision for the future under the leadership of Shanahan and general manager John Lynch in 2017.

The roster the two of them inherited was pretty bare, particularly at quarterback, but there was reason to believe that Shanahan would be able to turn the team around in light of his massive success as the Falcons' offensive coordinator in 2016. The 49ers already had some young talent in place on the defensive line in former first-round picks Arik Armstead and DeForest Buckner, so the outlook was not purely doom and gloom. However, the 2017 season was always going to be a rebuilding year, with the hope that the 49ers would take a step forward in 2018.

One of the keys for San Francisco was going to be upgrading at quarterback, and it certainly looked like the 49ers would have their pick of a deep draft class of quarterbacks after they started the season 0-8 with the combination of Brian Hoyer and C.J. Beathard under center. In six starts, the veteran Hoyer finished 28th in passing DVOA out of 35 qualifying quarterbacks. Beathard, a third-round rookie out of Iowa, was even worse: 31st in passing DVOA. Coming out of college, Beathard was not regarded as much of a prospect, but after how poorly Hoyer had performed, it made sense for the 49ers to at least give the rookie a chance to play to see if there was some potential there. There wasn't. It became clear that the 49ers would have to look outside the organization for their quarterback of the future.

Rather than wait until March or April to address their need in free agency or the draft, San Francisco took advantage of the quarterback logjam in New England, trading a second-round pick for Patriots backup Jimmy Garoppolo. All of a sudden, the 49ers had someone around whom they could build. They gave Beathard three more starts to allow Garoppolo time to learn the playbook, but after Beathard got injured late in Week 12 against the Seahawks, it was Garoppolo's time to shine.

Garoppolo had shown great promise in limited playing time in New England. When forced into the lineup due to Tom Brady's suspension to start the 2016 season, Garoppolo amassed 225 DYAR on just 68 pass plays with a DVOA of 44.4%. There were some concerns about how he would perform outside the Belichick-McDaniels offensive cocoon, but the early returns had clearly been positive when he had seen the field for the Patriots.

Those concerns were quickly forgotten as Garoppolo completed both passes he attempted (one for a touchdown) in garbage time against the Seahawks and never looked back. San Francisco closed the season on a five-game winning streak, spearheaded by Garoppolo's play. His most impressive performance came against a Jacksonville defense that ranked first in DVOA against the pass by a country mile, where he accounted for 178 total DYAR on 30 passes and three runs. The streak featured wins against three eventual playoff teams in the Titans, Jaguars, and Rams, although that Rams win comes with an asterisk because Los Angeles was resting starters in preparation for its playoff game the following week.

As far as small sample breakouts go, Garoppolo's was one of the best for quarterbacks in their first significant playing time. Table 1 shows all quarterbacks dating back to 1986 who posted a passing DVOA of 20.0% or higher with 120 to 250 pass plays in their first significant playing time. The "first significant playing time" qualifier excludes veterans such as Josh McCown and an injured Dan Marino, as well as accounting for the 1987 strike.

Garoppolo wasn't the only quarterback to join this group in 2017, as rookie Deshaun Watson had a similarly excellent small-sample breakout for Houston. Interestingly enough, five out of the nine players on this list played for the 49ers, so it appears there might be something special in the water on the west side of the Bay Area. Garoppolo inflated his numbers a bit by blowing out the Rams backups in Week 17, but heading into the final week of the season, he still had a 37.7% passing DVOA.

What does this mean moving forward? Tim Rattay, Marc Bulger, Paul Justin, Elvis Grbac, Steve Bono, and John Fourcade combined to make four Pro Bowls between them, but none of them had much in the way of draft pedigree, with Bono going the earliest in the draft at 142nd overall (then the sixth round). Comparing them to Garoppolo and Watson may not be particularly instructive because they were not highly regarded as prospects entering the league. That leaves us with only one example: Kaepernick, who is currently out of the

2018 49ers Schedule

Week	Opp.	Week	Opp.	Week	Opp.
1	at MIN	7	LAR	13	at SEA
2	DET	8	at ARI	14	DEN
3	at KC	9	OAK (Thu.)	15	SEA
4	at LAC	10	NYG (Mon.)	16	CHI
5	ARI	11	BYE	17	at LAR
6	at GB (Mon.)	12	at TB		

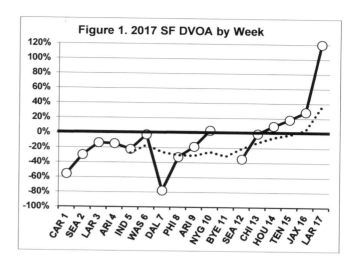

Figure 1. 2017 SF DVOA by Week

league for non-football reasons that have been discussed ad nauseam over the past two years. Otherwise, there just isn't much to use for historical comparison.

It may be too early to anoint Garoppolo as the league's next superstar simply because of how little he has played, but that has not stopped the 49ers from being considered a trendy early wild-card contender based on how strongly they finished. Thanks to Garoppolo's play, San Francisco's offense took off late in the season. They ranked ninth in weighted offensive DVOA entering the Week 17 game against the Rams before lighting up a Los Angeles unit that finished sixth in defensive DVOA but was resting most of its starters.

Our outlook for the 49ers is not quite as rosy because Garoppolo's small sample of excellent play makes it difficult to project them as a top tier offense in spite of their strong finish to the season. Garoppolo has looked every bit the franchise quarterback he is now being paid to be after signing what was then a record-setting contract with the team during the offseason. However, the 49ers offense currently projects as an average unit thanks to how poorly they started the season; even including the Rams blowout, San Francisco only finished 19th for the year in offensive DVOA despite their hot streak to close out the season.

Ignoring Watson and Garoppolo, every quarterback in Table 1 who held a starting role for most of the following season experienced a notable drop in passing DVOA from their breakout year. Kaepernick remained a top-10 quarterback in 2013, but he was not nearly as efficient as he had been in his breakout. Bulger made the Pro Bowl in 2003 despite throwing as many interceptions as touchdowns and finishing as an average starter by both DVOA and DYAR, and Rattay and Fourcade both cratered in their follow-up campaigns. Bono, Grbac, and

Justin held onto backup roles in their subsequent seasons, with two of these demotions making much more sense than the other one. Bono and Grbac had excelled filling in for some guy named Steve Young, so after their brief breakout seasons in his stead, they returned to clipboard-holding duties before departing for greener pastures. In both cases, that meant Kansas City, as Bono and Grbac both ended up starting for the Chiefs after leaving the 49ers, with each making the Pro Bowl there exactly once. On the other hand, Justin returned to the backup role behind, yes, Jim Harbaugh and was unable to beat him out for the starting job despite being significantly more efficient when given the opportunity to play in both 1996 and 1997.

It is tempting to predict that Garoppolo is destined for superstardom, but it would be unprecedented for him to match his level of play from 2017 across a full season this year. That does not mean that he will be "exposed" as average or worse and that his hot streak to end the season was just some fluke. After all, Kaepernick still finished eighth in passing DYAR and seventh in passing DVOA in 2013 and almost brought the 49ers back to the Super Bowl.

Even if Garoppolo can't equal his 2017 production moving forward, there are certainly non-quarterback reasons for optimism on the offensive side of the ball. Shanahan and his offensive creativity will not be leaving town anytime soon. Running back Matt Breida quietly finished 15th in rushing DYAR and fifth in rushing DVOA in a part-time role, and former Vi-

Table 1: Breakout! First-Time Quarterbacks with DVOA over 20.0% in 120 to 250 Passes, 1986-2017

Player	Team	Year	Age	Draft	DYAR	DVOA	Passes	Yards	TD	INT	Comp %	Y/A
Jimmy Garoppolo	SF	2017	26	2-62	598	39.1%	185	1502	7	5	68.2%	8.8
Deshaun Watson	HOU	2017	22	1-12	497	23.1%	221	1583	19	6	62.4%	8.3
Colin Kaepernick	SF	2012	25	2-36	555	25.8%	234	1687	10	3	62.7%	8.3
Tim Rattay	SF	2003	26	7-212	315	30.6%	125	802	7	2	61.9%	7.3
Marc Bulger	STL	2002	25	6-168	597	34.7%	222	1721	14	6	65.7%	8.5
Paul Justin	IND	1996	28	7-190	370	34.7%	134	781	2	0	58.3%	6.6
Elvis Grbac	SF	1995	25	8-219	600	38.3%	189	1433	8	5	70.2%	8.0
Steve Bono	SF	1991	29	6-142	556	23.9%	249	1502	11	4	60.0%	6.8
John Fourcade	NO	1989	29	NA	376	37.7%	120	834	7	4	57.0%	8.7

kings running back Jerick McKinnon will be joining him in the backfield after signing as a free agent. When McKinnon was in college at Georgia Southern, he had a variety of roles, spending time at running back, wide receiver, and quarterback in their triple-option offense. Minnesota used him primarily as a third-down back and as a receiving threat out of the backfield, with McKinnon exceeding 50 targets in both 2016 and 2017. It is easy to picture Shanahan turning McKinnon into a matchup nightmare lining up all over the formation, creating a similar dynamic to what he had in Atlanta with Devonta Freeman and Tevin Coleman.

The offensive line finished 18th in adjusted sack rate and added former Giants center Weston Richburg in free agency as well as the top offensive tackle prospect in the draft in Mike McGlinchey, hoping to turn that group into a top pass-protection unit to go along with its already strong run-blocking performance. The addition of Richburg echoes Atlanta signing center Alex Mack as a free agent prior to the 2016 season, and Mack received his fair share of credit for Atlanta's offensive improvement from 2015 to 2016. Add all that up and it makes sense why many are predicting that San Francisco will use its hot finish to the 2017 season as a springboard into playoff contention in 2018. However, all those changes are not guaranteed to have the desired impact, and the offense will need to be the driving force behind a potential playoff push. Any regression from that late-season offensive burst will lower San Francisco's ceiling, barring a massive step forward from a defense that had issues throughout 2017.

Garoppolo may have led an offensive resurgence once he arrived in San Francisco, but the defense continued to struggle, particularly against the pass. Despite using first-round picks on defensive linemen Armstead, Buckner, and Solomon Thomas in 2015, 2016, and 2017, respectively, the 49ers had a difficult time getting pressure on the quarterback and taking him down in the backfield, finishing 23rd in pressure rate and 29th in adjusted sack rate. Buckner and veteran Elvis Dumervil were bright spots for the San Francisco pass rush, but the team collectively had problems generating pressure even though the 49ers had the fortune of playing eight games against teams ranked in the bottom ten for adjusted sack rate.

That lack of pass rush played a big role in the team finishing 28th in defensive DVOA against the pass and 26th overall, representing a disappointing lack of progress in spite of all the recent high draft picks invested on the defensive side of the ball. San Francisco tried to improve its defense in the offseason, notably signing former Seahawks cornerback Richard Sherman as a free agent. If Sherman can fully return to health from the torn Achilles he suffered last season and come close to matching his previous level of play in the secondary, that would be a welcome change for a 49ers secondary that ranked 30th in DVOA against wide receivers lined up out wide. However, there is some uncertainty surrounding what version of Sherman the 49ers can reasonably expect coming back from that injury.

While adding Sherman should have a positive influence on the San Francisco pass defense, the 49ers are already missing a key defensive piece for the start of the 2018 season. 2017 first-round pick Reuben Foster made an impact at linebacker when on the field as a rookie, finishing 15th in run stop rate among linebackers, but he will be suspended for two games under the personal conduct policy because of multiple arrests during the offseason. The 49ers are hoping that Foster will take a step forward in his second season, but after missing six games in his rookie season due to injury and now suspended to start this year, any additional time lost to new injuries could hurt his development moving forward.

There is certainly a path toward improvement for the San Francisco defense in 2018, but a lot of that potential improvement depends on young defensive players taking that crucial next step forward in their development. Another year in defensive coordinator Robert Saleh's 4-3 system will likely help as the defense grows more familiar with their responsibilities. However, our projections have them near the bottom of the league in defensive DVOA, and if the defense struggles again, any hope of a playoff push will fall squarely on the shoulders of their well-compensated franchise quarterback.

It should come as no surprise if the 49ers do end up running a top offense out there in Year 2 under Kyle Shanahan, allowing them to take the next step into playoff contention after their hot finish to the 2017 campaign. Garoppolo was everything the 49ers could have asked for and more, given that he only joined the team halfway through the season. But considering last year's struggles on defense and the uncertainty involved in projecting Garoppolo's future performance, it looks like making the playoffs in 2018 will be a tough proposition for the 49ers in what is again shaping up to be a brutally difficult NFC.

Carl Yedor

2017 49ers Stats by Week

Wk	vs.	W-L	PF	PA	YDF	YDA	TO	Total	Off	Def	ST
1	CAR	L	3	23	217	287	0	-56%	-51%	5%	1%
2	at SEA	L	9	12	248	312	-1	-30%	-40%	2%	12%
3	LAR	L	39	41	421	418	0	-14%	6%	26%	6%
4	at ARI	L	15	18	305	368	0	-15%	-19%	5%	9%
5	at IND	L	23	26	402	447	+1	-22%	-16%	5%	-1%
6	at WAS	L	24	26	335	419	+1	-2%	9%	16%	4%
7	DAL	L	10	40	290	501	-3	-78%	-22%	51%	-5%
8	at PHI	L	10	33	238	304	-1	-32%	-39%	-6%	1%
9	ARI	L	10	20	329	368	0	-18%	-16%	3%	1%
10	NYG	W	31	21	474	374	-1	3%	37%	36%	3%
11	BYE										
12	SEA	L	13	24	280	318	0	-35%	-22%	10%	-3%
13	at CHI	W	15	14	388	147	-1	-1%	-2%	-14%	-13%
14	at HOU	W	26	16	416	311	0	10%	6%	0%	4%
15	TEN	W	25	23	414	328	+1	18%	22%	17%	14%
16	JAX	W	44	33	369	472	+2	29%	35%	12%	6%
17	at LAR	W	34	13	461	251	-1	120%	57%	-55%	8%

Trends and Splits

	Offense	Rank	Defense	Rank
Total DVOA	-3.0%	19	8.3%	26
Unadjusted VOA	-6.8%	21	7.0%	23
Weighted Trend	7.3%	9	6.7%	25
Variance	9.3%	22	5.3%	13
Average Opponent	-4.1%	1	-3.2%	27
Passing	8.8%	16	23.1%	28
Rushing	-5.0%	13	-7.8%	17
First Down	3.4%	14	6.4%	26
Second Down	-22.9%	32	2.3%	19
Third Down	12.2%	7	20.9%	30
First Half	-15.1%	26	5.4%	23
Second Half	8.8%	10	11.2%	27
Red Zone	-20.8%	26	13.4%	28
Late and Close	-2.2%	17	10.4%	28

Five-Year Performance

Year	W-L	Pyth W	Est W	PF	PA	TO	Total	Rk	Off	Rk	Def	Rk	ST	Rk	Off AGL	Rk	Def AGL	Rk	Off Age	Rk	Def Age	Rk	ST Age	Rk
2013	12-4	11.5	10.6	406	272	+12	17.4%	7	9.1%	8	-4.6%	13	3.7%	7	34.7	17	46.8	27	27.8	5	27.4	9	26.9	4
2014	8-8	7.0	9.0	306	340	+7	6.6%	11	-0.4%	16	-10.1%	5	-3.0%	24	30.0	15	71.8	31	27.6	6	26.8	16	26.4	8
2015	5-11	3.8	4.1	238	387	-5	-27.5%	32	-14.0%	28	9.9%	27	-3.6%	27	58.2	28	25.8	11	27.7	6	25.4	32	25.1	31
2016	2-14	3.9	4.6	309	247	-5	-19.6%	28	-7.2%	23	12.1%	28	-0.3%	17	39.0	21	58.5	26	27.7	6	25.4	22	26.1	17
2017	6-10	6.6	6.7	331	383	-3	-8.4%	20	-3.0%	19	8.3%	26	2.9%	11	24.7	8	66.8	32	27.3	9	25.4	29	25.8	18

2017 Performance Based on Most Common Personnel Groups

SF Offense					SF Offense vs. Opponents					SF Defense				SF Defense vs. Opponents			
Pers	Freq	Yds	DVOA	Run%	Pers	Freq	Yds	DVOA	Run%	Pers	Freq	Yds	DVOA	Pers	Freq	Yds	DVOA
11	48%	5.4	6.9%	20%	Base	50%	5.5	0.2%	49%	Base	36%	5.2	1.0%	11	63%	5.6	10.3%
21	31%	5.6	-0.8%	53%	Nickel	42%	5.2	5.4%	23%	Nickel	45%	5.5	11.4%	12	19%	6.4	14.3%
12	15%	5.5	-1.7%	45%	Dime+	6%	6.0	12.0%	6%	Dime+	15%	6.4	29.6%	13	7%	3.3	-26.0%
22	2%	5.8	21.9%	65%	Goal Line	1%	-0.6	-12.9%	100%	Goal Line	1%	-0.1	-75.1%	21	3%	4.2	-7.5%
13	2%	0.5	-90.3%	25%	Big	0%	1.2	32.9%	80%	Big	3%	5.4	-3.5%	22	2%	6.1	21.6%
20	1%	5.8	57.0%	38%										10	2%	4.7	71.5%

Strategic Tendencies

Run/Pass		Rk	Formation		Rk	Pass Rush		Rk	Secondary		Rk	Strategy		Rk
Runs, first half	37%	26	Form: Single Back	57%	32	Rush 3	3.6%	26	4 DB	36%	10	Play action	24%	7
Runs, first down	46%	23	Form: Empty Back	9%	12	Rush 4	74.0%	7	5 DB	45%	22	Avg Box (Off)	6.37	5
Runs, second-long	28%	24	Pers: 3+ WR	49%	28	Rush 5	17.0%	23	6+ DB	15%	10	Avg Box (Def)	6.35	8
Runs, power sit.	61%	11	Pers: 2+ TE/6+ OL	20%	30	Rush 6+	5.3%	19	CB by Sides	78%	17	Offensive Pace	29.31	5
Runs, behind 2H	29%	12	Pers: 6+ OL	3%	17	Int DL Sacks	25.0%	14	S/CB Cover Ratio	30%	12	Defensive Pace	29.79	6
Pass, ahead 2H	43%	24	Shotgun/Pistol	46%	29	Second Level Sacks	10.0%	27	DB Blitz	7%	19	Go for it on 4th	0.64	27

As you might expect, the replacement of Chip Kelly with Kyle Shanahan completely transformed San Francisco's strategic tendencies. They went from the most shotgun of all time, 99 percent of plays in 2016, to using shotgun or pistol on less than half of plays in 2017. Their run/pass ratios in nearly every situation moved towards passing even though the 49ers had more wins than the year before. They went from using single-back formations 92 percent of the time (second in 2016) to just 57 percent of the time (dead last in 2017). ☞ The 49ers used two or more running backs on a league-leading 54 percent of running back carries. However, they actually were slightly better from one-back sets, with 4.4 yards per carry and -6.5% DVOA compared to 4.0 yards per carry and -14.5% DVOA from two-back sets. ☞ The 49ers ranked second in dropped passes (41) and fourth in rate of dropped passes (6.5 percent). This was the third straight season San Francisco was among the seven worst teams in rate of dropped passes. ☞ San Francisco's "CB by Sides" number changed significantly at midseason. It was at 64 percent with Rashard Robinson and Dontae Johnson through Week 7, then leaped to 88 percent when Ahkello Witherspoon replaced Robinson in Week 8 and beyond. ☞ San Francisco was tied for 29th in penalties by opponents and benefited from a league-low 791 penalty yards. ☞ San Francisco opponents hit only 30 of 37 extra points.

Passing

Player	DYAR	DVOA	Plays	NtYds	Avg	YAC	C%	TD	Int
C.J.Beathard	-176	-23.1%	243	1286	5.3	5.2	55.6%	4	6
B.Hoyer*	-88	-17.4%	222	1112	5.0	4.4	58.8%	4	4
J.Garoppolo	598	39.1%	185	1502	8.1	6.0	68.2%	7	5

Rushing

Player	DYAR	DVOA	Plays	Yds	Avg	TD	Fum	Suc
C.Hyde*	12	-7.4%	239	940	3.9	8	2	44%
M.Breida	87	13.0%	104	471	4.5	2	1	47%
C.J.Beathard	73	44.6%	23	139	6.0	3	0	-
K.Juszczyk	12	21.3%	7	31	4.4	0	0	57%
J.Garoppolo	2	-8.8%	7	18	2.6	1	0	-
R.Mostert	-11	-49.6%	6	30	5.0	0	1	50%
B.Hoyer*	-29	-96.7%	5	-2	-0.4	1	2	-
J.McKinnon	-24	-12.7%	150	570	3.8	3	2	43%

Receiving

Player	DYAR	DVOA	Plays	Ctch	Yds	Y/C	YAC	TD	C%
M.Goodwin	155	5.9%	105	56	962	17.2	3.4	2	53%
P.Garcon	45	-3.8%	67	40	500	12.5	4.7	0	60%
T.Taylor	114	11.4%	60	43	430	10.0	4.3	2	72%
A.Robinson	-43	-24.5%	48	19	260	13.7	2.0	2	40%
K.Bourne	8	-9.7%	34	16	257	16.1	7.1	0	47%
L.Murphy*	4	-9.4%	17	8	121	15.1	4.9	1	47%
G.Kittle	55	5.6%	63	43	515	12.0	6.2	2	68%
G.Celek	89	31.5%	33	21	336	16.0	8.2	4	64%
C.Hyde*	-43	-22.4%	89	60	350	5.8	5.4	0	67%
K.Juszczyk	41	3.7%	42	33	317	9.6	6.3	1	79%
M.Breida	16	-4.8%	37	22	174	7.9	7.3	1	59%
J.McKinnon	48	-0.4%	68	51	421	8.3	9.0	2	75%

Offensive Line

Player	Pos	Age	GS	Snaps	Pen	Sk	Pass	Run	Player	Pos	Age	GS	Snaps	Pen	Sk	Pass	Run
Daniel Kilgore*	C	31	16/16	1100	7	4.0	10	12	Zane Beadles*	RT/LG	32	16/5	397	1	3.0	14	4
Brandon Fusco*	RG	29	16/16	1085	6	5.5	12	8	Erik Magnuson	OT	24	4/2	186	0	1.0	2	3
Laken Tomlinson	LG	26	15/15	1043	5	5.0	11	11	Jonathan Cooper	LG	28	13/13	838	6	0.5	13	7
Joe Staley	LT	34	15/15	985	3	3.5	19	5	Mike Person	C	30	12/4	317	1	1.0	3	1
Trenton Brown*	RT	25	10/10	668	7	1.5	7	7	Weston Richburg	C	27	4/4	239	1	0.0	4	0

Year	Yards	ALY	Rank	Power	Rank	Stuff	Rank	2nd Lev	Rank	Open Field	Rank	Sacks	ASR	Rank	Press	Rank	F-Start	Cont.
2015	3.51	3.44	32	67%	14	26%	31	1.05	22	0.57	26	53	9.1%	31	30.2%	28	16	35
2016	3.99	3.46	32	69%	11	22%	25	1.12	17	0.72	14	47	8.4%	30	28.6%	22	15	32
2017	4.13	4.20	10	62%	20	23%	25	1.24	7	0.76	14	43	6.8%	18	31.3%	17	22	28

2017 ALY by direction: Left End: 5.31 (6)   Left Tackle: 4.94 (5)   Mid/Guard: 4.11 (19)   Right Tackle: 4.11 (14)   Right End: 2.90 (26)

The 49ers finished in the top ten for adjusted line yards due in large part to their performance running off left tackle and left end, finishing fifth and sixth, respectively. Much of that can be credited to the play of veteran tackle Joe Staley, who blew only five run blocks in his 11th season. Staley's pass protection numbers were a different story, as he blew a pass block twice as frequently as he blew a run block. ☞ Slotting in next to Staley was Laken Tomlinson, originally a first-round pick of the Lions in 2015. After acquiring Tomlinson for a future fifth-round pick at the end of the preseason, the 49ers plugged him into the lineup in Week 2, and he held down the spot for the rest of 2017. The 49ers signed Tomlinson to a three-year extension in June, so they clearly see him in their future plans. ☞ Former 2016 first-round pick Joshua Garnett injured his knee in preseason and subsequently spent the whole season on injured reserve. Garnett split time with Mike Person at right guard in OTAs, and the 49ers are hoping he will be able to lock down that job with Brandon Fusco now in Atlanta. ☞ Trent Brown was the primary starter at right tackle in 2017, but the 49ers traded him to New England along with a 2018 fifth-round pick for a 2018 third-rounder. Replacing Brown at right tackle will be rookie first-rounder Mike McGlinchey from Notre Dame. McGlinchey projects as the long-term replacement for Staley at left tackle after being the first tackle selected at No. 9 overall. He may not be quite ready for prime time as a rookie, as he will need time to add strength and mass to his frame, but he possesses advanced technique for a college draftee and moves well for someone his size thanks to his background as a tight end and basketball player. ☞ Daniel Kilgore manned the center spot for the 49ers in 2017 and received a three-year contract extension in February, only to be traded to the Dolphins a month later once the team signed former Giants center Weston Richburg to a big free agent contract. Richburg missed most of the 2017 season recovering from a concussion, but when he was last healthy in 2016, he only allowed one sack and had just four blown blocks on passes.

Defensive Front Seven

Defensive Line	Age	Pos	G	Snaps	Plays	TmPct	Rk	Stop	Dfts	BTkl	Runs	St%	Rk	RuYd	Rk	Sack	Hit	Hur	Dsrpt
											vs. Run					Pass Rush			
DeForest Buckner	24	DT	16	866	66	7.9%	3	45	16	6	53	66%	77	2.7	70	3.0	19	29.0	6
Earl Mitchell	31	DT	16	624	36	4.3%	56	26	6	3	29	72%	62	2.4	58	1.0	2	10.0	3
Sheldon Day	24	DT	12	321	21	3.3%	77	14	5	2	17	59%	80	2.3	54	2.0	2	5.0	2

Edge Rushers	Age	Pos	G	Snaps	Plays	TmPct	Rk	Stop	Dfts	BTkl	Runs	St%	Rk	RuYd	Rk	Sack	Hit	Hur	Dsrpt
											vs. Run					Pass Rush			
Solomon Thomas	23	DE	14	702	39	5.3%	42	29	11	11	32	78%	37	1.7	26	3.0	10	17.0	0
Cassius Marsh	26	DE	15	457	26	3.5%	76	17	9	3	21	62%	84	3.7	90	3.0	5	20.0	0
Eli Harold	24	OLB	16	454	33	3.9%	66	17	7	5	23	48%	95	3.9	91	2.0	2	5.5	0
Elvis Dumervil*	34	DE	16	343	12	1.4%	--	12	10	2	4	100%	--	0.8	--	6.5	12	27.0	2
Tank Carradine*	28	DE	8	214	18	4.3%	--	12	2	1	16	63%	--	4.0	--	1.5	2	4.0	0

Linebackers	Age	Pos	G	Snaps	Plays	TmPct	Rk	Stop	Dfts	BTkl	Runs	St%	Rk	RuYd	Rk	Sack	Hit	Hur	Tgts	Suc%	Rk	AdjYd	Rk	PD	Int
											vs. Run					Pass Rush			vs. Pass						
Brock Coyle	28	MLB	16	649	63	7.5%	81	32	11	12	38	61%	52	3.9	57	0.5	2	6.0	25	48%	44	5.5	15	1	0
Reuben Foster	24	OLB	10	554	72	13.8%	29	44	11	7	48	73%	15	2.7	14	0.0	5	6.5	19	40%	64	7.6	53	1	0

Year	Yards	ALY	Rank	Power	Rank	Stuff	Rank	2nd Level	Rank	Open Field	Rank	Sacks	ASR	Rank	Press	Rank
2015	4.19	4.53	27	64%	15	17%	29	1.01	5	0.81	18	28	5.4%	29	25.7%	14
2016	4.97	4.68	29	71%	28	16%	27	1.27	23	1.29	32	33	5.8%	20	22.6%	31
2017	3.82	4.09	15	64%	17	22%	9	1.05	8	0.62	10	30	5.0%	29	29.4%	23

2017 ALY by direction:	Left End: 4.96 (28)	Left Tackle: 3.59 (11)	Mid/Guard: 4.31 (19)	Right Tackle: 3.84 (17)	Right End: 2.69 (5)

DeForest Buckner led the charge for the 49ers in his second year out of Oregon. Hot on Buckner's heels was veteran edge rusher Elvis Dumervil, who led the team with 6.5 sacks and nearly matched Buckner's hurry total while playing less than half the snaps. Dumervil remains unsigned, and the 49ers will have to replenish their pass-rushing depth from within since they didn't acquire anyone in free agency to do so. ☞ Getting Arik Armstead back after he missed most of 2017 recovering from a broken hand could help, but he will be playing more of a run-stopping role across from 2017 rookie Solomon Thomas. After being drafted No. 3 overall, Thomas started at defensive end in a relatively quiet rookie season. Thomas tied for the second-most defeats for the 49ers with 11 but had just as many broken tackles. Fellow 2017 first-round pick Reuben Foster was among the players tied with Thomas. Both Thomas and Foster should take a step forward in their sophomore seasons, but Foster will be suspended for the first two games due to off-field incidents. ☞ Brock Coyle made 10 starts at middle linebacker for the 49ers after three years as a Seattle backup and parlayed his play into a three-year extension following the season. Joining Coyle in the front seven will be another former Seattle defender in Cassius Marsh, who started 2017 in New England and signed with the 49ers after being cut midseason. ☞ Veteran defensive tackle Earl Mitchell signed a four-year deal heading into the 2017 season, but he could find himself looking for a new team next season at age 31, thanks to a $4.45 million cap hit on the books for 2019 and the young linemen competing with him for playing time already. San Francisco acquired 24-year-old Sheldon Day off waivers from Jacksonville in November 2017, and he could push Mitchell for a larger share of his snaps this year. ☞ Eli Harold will have the opportunity to keep his job at strongside linebacker opposite Malcolm Smith on the weak side, but Harold has struggled since the 49ers took him in the third round of the 2015 draft. Harold was more of an edge rusher in college, not a coverage linebacker, and the 49ers have changed his responsibilities as they have changed schemes. The 49ers want to use Harold in more of the LEO edge rusher role this season, so perhaps he'll get his mojo back. ☞ Smith missed all of 2017 with a torn pectoral after signing a five-year deal in free agency. ☞ If Harold and Smith do not step up, rookie third-round pick Fred Warner could take on a larger role, particularly in pass coverage. Warner played a hybrid linebacker/safety role at BYU, so he should definitely have a chance to make an impact on passing downs.

Defensive Secondary

Secondary	Age	Pos	G	Snaps	Plays	TmPct	Rk	Stop	Dfts	BTkl	Runs	St%	Rk	RuYd	Rk	Tgts	Tgt%	Rk	Dist	Suc%	Rk	AdjYd	Rk	PD	Int
Dontae Johnson*	27	CB	16	1027	83	9.9%	21	24	11	12	23	43%	41	4.3	12	84	18.4%	26	12.4	38%	79	9.5	77	10	1
Eric Reid*	27	SS	13	740	70	10.3%	34	35	12	8	31	55%	15	4.4	11	43	12.9%	61	7.4	65%	4	5.1	3	4	2
Ahkello Witherspoon	23	CB	12	662	39	6.2%	69	19	9	6	9	67%	11	2.6	3	55	18.5%	28	13.5	41%	78	9.4	75	7	2
K'Waun Williams	27	CB	14	635	59	8.1%	--	28	13	11	12	58%	--	3.3	--	40	14.0%	--	9.0	52%	--	6.0	--	5	1
Jaquiski Tartt	26	FS	9	595	57	12.1%	15	27	10	6	30	50%	21	4.7	15	20	7.6%	18	10.8	54%	28	7.1	24	3	1
Adrian Colbert	25	FS	14	536	37	5.1%	72	12	7	8	15	33%	58	9.6	61	21	8.8%	33	16.5	51%	42	7.3	26	5	0
Jimmie Ward	27	FS	7	429	33	9.0%	--	6	4	3	15	20%	--	12.2	--	12	6.0%	--	19.3	16%	--	16.9	--	0	0
Leon Hall*	34	CB	9	209	17	3.6%	--	5	2	6	8	38%	--	8.3	--	11	11.8%	--	10.8	49%	--	9.0	--	1	0
Richard Sherman	30	CB	9	572	42	9.0%	32	18	5	3	15	60%	15	5.4	25	42	17.5%	21	16.1	52%	36	6.9	30	7	2

Year	Pass D Rank	vs. #1 WR	Rk	vs. #2 WR	Rk	vs. Other WR	Rk	WR Wide	Rk	WR Slot	Rk	vs. TE	Rk	vs. RB	Rk
2015	30	2.9%	18	22.0%	28	10.2%	23	--	--	--	--	9.1%	22	11.7%	25
2016	28	19.1%	31	7.6%	24	-7.0%	9	-4.9%	13	16.1%	28	17.5%	27	17.1%	27
2017	28	21.1%	27	-1.6%	16	30.7%	32	17.3%	30	20.2%	27	-19.5%	5	13.2%	24

Even if Richard Sherman never returns to his previous heights post-injury, he should be an upgrade over Dontae Johnson (who has traded places with Sherman and gone to Seattle). At a glance, Johnson's 10 passes defensed and one interception may suggest that he was consistently making plays, but his adjusted success rate of 38 percent suggests that when he wasn't knocking passes away, he was getting roasted. The only qualifying cornerback with a worse success rate was Robert McClain in Tampa. ☞ Rookie cornerback Ahkello Witherspoon was impressive against the run in his first season out of Colorado, ranking 11th in stop rate and third in average depth of run tackle, but struggled in pass coverage with a success rate that barely topped the departed Johnson. ☞ K'Waun Williams handled nickel duties and did an excellent job limiting yards after the catch, finishing with the third-fewest average allowed (1.9 yards) among corners with at least 40 passes faced. ☞ Strong safety Jaquiski Tartt began the season as a backup to Eric Reid but stepped into the lineup after Reid suffered an injury early in the season. His play in Reid's stead earned him a two-year contract extension in the offseason. After returning to health, Reid briefly slotted into a weakside linebacker role before Tartt went on injured reserve. The change in role likely contributed to Reid improving his run stop rate from 31 percent in 2016 to 55 percent in 2017. ☞ Jimmie Ward initially struggled at free safety before breaking his forearm halfway through the season; his 16.9 adjusted yards per target allowed would have ranked only ahead of Pittsburgh's Mike Mitchell among safeties had Ward had enough targets to qualify for our rankings. ☞ To further bolster their secondary, the 49ers added third-round pick Tarvarius Moore out of Southern Mississippi. Moore is an explosive athlete, posting a 4.32-second 40-yard dash, 38.5-inch vertical jump, and 11-foot-1 broad jump at his pro day. He will be moving from safety in college to cornerback with the 49ers.

Special Teams

Year	DVOA	Rank	FG/XP	Rank	Net Kick	Rank	Kick Ret	Rank	Net Punt	Rank	Punt Ret	Rank	Hidden	Rank
2015	-3.6%	27	0.7	15	-4.3	27	-5.3	28	-4.6	22	-4.4	22	11.3	4
2016	-0.3%	17	3.9	8	-2.7	23	-6.7	29	5.1	9	-0.9	14	-1.2	19
2017	2.9%	11	14.2	2	3.0	10	-6.4	32	3.6	13	0.0	16	4.9	10

The names change, but the problem remains: the 49ers have been among the worst kick return teams in each of the last three years despite completely different returners in each season. Last year, it was the combination of running backs Matt Breida and Raheem Mostert and wide receiver Victor Bolden finishing dead last in kick return value. ☞ Enter second-round pick Dante Pettis, who set the NCAA record for career punt return touchdowns at Washington. Pettis is likely to play a major role on both kick and punt returns, though wide receiver Trent Taylor was a slight positive on punt returns as a rookie and could share the job. ☞ Bradley Pinion is entering the final year of his rookie contract and will hope to improve on his 2017 season, when he finished 28th among punters with -5.6 points of gross punt value. Strong coverage teams, led by Mostert, gave the 49ers an overall positive rating for net punts. Pinion did have slightly above-average gross value as a kickoff specialist, however. ☞ Robbie Gould returns for his second season in San Francisco after missing just two field goals in 2017. He was perfect on his four field goal attempts of 50-plus yards and went 17 for 18 from 40 to 49 yards out. Gould's extra point conversion rate (93.3 percent) was actually worse than his field goal percentage (95.1 percent).

Seattle Seahawks

2017 Record: 9-7	**Total DVOA:** -8.3% (14th)	**2018 Mean Projection:** 8.3 wins	**On the Clock (0-4):** 8%
Pythagorean Wins: 9.0 (13th)	**Offense:** 1.3% (14th)	**Postseason Odds:** 38.7%	**Mediocrity (5-7):** 30%
Snap-Weighted Age: 26.4 (17th)	**Defense:** -3.8% (13th)	**Super Bowl Odds:** 5.4%	**Playoff Contender (8-10):** 42%
Average Opponent: -0.9% (20th)	**Special Teams:** -2.0% (20th)	**Proj. Avg. Opponent:** 0.4% (12th)	**Super Bowl Contender (11+):** 20%

2017: Don't let the past remind us of what we are not now.

2018: Long may you run, although these changes have come.

Don't call it a rebuild! They've been here for years.

That's Seattle General Manager ~~LL Cool J~~ John Schneider's mantra for the 2018 Seahawks. He prefers the term "reset" to describe the turnover and transition the team has experienced this year. "It's a constant reset every single year," he told ESPN, "it doesn't stop." And so 2018 is business as usual.

Business as usual like … seeing Richard Sherman in 49ers' red and gold. Losing Michael Bennett, Sheldon Richardson, Jimmy Graham, Paul Richardson—that's nine Pro Bowls in Seattle uniforms out the door. Cliff Avril and Kam Chancellor are gone, with injuries cutting their All-Pro careers short. Earl Thomas is holding out, in a contract standoff which may result in him leaving Seattle as well. That's not to mention the losses of defensive coordinator Kris Richard, offensive coordinator Darrell Bevell, and assistant head coach/offensive line coach Tom Cable.

Alright, so not all losses are created equal. Still, downplaying the impact of this level of turnover is disingenuous. This isn't a standard year-over-year restocking; this is a substantial turning point in the history of the franchise. Call it a rebuild, a reset, a reorganization, or a revamp, the fact remains: the run of the Legion of Boom Seahawks is over.

Perhaps the best word to use in this case is *reboot*. Sometimes, it takes a little adversity for a franchise to recognize and address issues that have built up over time. Success can breed complacency—don't fix what ain't broken and so on and so forth. It becomes easy to ignore or accept a small problem here and there because the team is winning, but that often results in drifting further and further from the core principles that led to success in the first place. Sometimes it takes a *Batman & Robin* to get to a *Dark Knight*—hitting rock bottom can serve as a much-needed wakeup call.

The Seahawks did not hit rock bottom in 2017 by any measure. Flip the Week 11 34-31 loss to Atlanta, and Seattle would have been playoff-bound for the sixth straight year. If Blair Walsh connects on that 52-yard field goal at the end of regulation, or if the team had not opted to try a baffling fake field goal at the end of the first half, maybe we're not here. Sherman and Bennett were still under contract for 2018, and while the Seahawks were low on cap space, they could have made a more concerted effort to try to patch together as much of the old guard as possible for one more run.

Give credit where credit is due, then. Missing the playoffs gave Schneider and Pete Carroll an opportunity for their reset, and they've decided to embrace it. One of the hallmarks of well-run franchises is the ability to come up with a plan of action and commit to it, rather than trying to piece together a strategy on the fly. Seattle's brain trust realized that the team that had four straight first-place DVOA finishes—as well as a few less prestigious prizes, such as a Super Bowl ring—was no longer the powerhouse it once was. It's time to find the next generation of stars that will lead the team towards further success, and that means parting with beloved veterans in order to give that new generation a time to shine.

The goal is to fix the underlying issues that have sprung up without collapsing to the back of the pack. What exactly does that mean, in terms of 2018?

Defensively, the Seahawks' young talent pipeline sputtered out after the 2012 draft. Matching the success Schneider had in his first three drafts, which brought in Thomas, Chancellor, Sherman, K.J. Wright, and Bobby Wagner, was never in the cards. That's going to go down in history as one of the best drafting runs a franchise has ever had. In the five drafts since then, however, only Jarran Reed and Frank Clark have started more than 12 games for the Seahawks, and no one has had more than seven points of Approximate Value in a single season. (Approximate Value is Pro Football Reference's statistic that estimates the value of every player in the league; Cameron Jordan led all defenders with 17 AV last year.)

Some of that, of course, is due to the difference in opportunities. The first few years of the Carroll/Schneider era saw a lot of turnover as old veterans were traded away, opening up slots for the new draftees to slide into place. They have been holding down the fort ever since, which is a significant obstacle for young players. It's hard to beat out a member of the Legion of Boom!

Still, in 2012, 54.9 percent of Seattle's defensive snaps came from players on their rookie deals, most of them already playing at a near Pro Bowl level. In 2017, that was just 26.8 percent, and a significant chunk of that was Sheldon Richardson, rather than home-grown talent. There's not an inherent problem with filling out a roster with veterans from other teams, and middling players like Bradley McDougald or Michael Wilhoite can have their places on a good defense. It's just not how Seattle built up their defensive powerhouse. This is when the Legion of Boom

2018 Seahawks Schedule

Week	Opp.	Week	Opp.	Week	Opp.
1	at DEN	7	BYE	13	SF
2	at CHI (Mon.)	8	at DET	14	MIN (Mon.)
3	DAL	9	LAC	15	at SF
4	at ARI	10	at LAR	16	KC
5	LAR	11	GB (Thu.)	17	ARI
6	at OAK (U.K.)	12	at CAR		

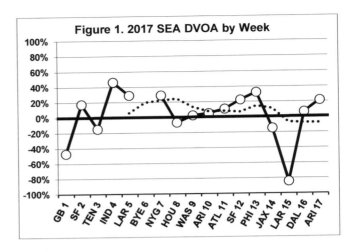

Figure 1. 2017 SEA DVOA by Week

Mark II should have been stepping up, providing cost-effective replacements that were built up and trained in house to replace expensive or injured veterans.

Just one problem: there *was* no Legion of Boom Mark II.

From 2013 to 2017, only two teams spent less draft capital on the defensive side of the ball than Seattle, according to Chase Stuart's draft value chart (Table 1). To be fair, one of the reasons Seattle didn't spend a lot of draft capital on defense is the fact that they were among the teams with the least amount of draft capital, period; when you make the playoffs every year, you're not exactly rolling in top 10 picks. Seattle also found themselves with less draft capital thanks to trades for offensive players like Percy Harvin and Jimmy Graham, as well as veteran reserve defensive pieces with low upside but more immediate impact. There was also less of an impetus to spend a lot of picks on defense when there were more pressing offensive issues to solve and a Super Bowl window to maximize. We're not proclaiming this as a good strategy or a bad strategy; it simply *was* the strategy, and it meant that the pipeline of young defensive talent wasn't flowing. Seattle is now reaping what it sowed.

It also doesn't help that when Seattle *did* splurge draft value on a player, they ended up with Malik McDowell, who may end up never playing a game in the NFL. Other mid-level picks like Jordan Hill and Cassius Marsh never really worked

Table 1: Least Draft Capital Spent on Defense, 2013-2017

Team	No. Picks	Def Draft Value	Pct of Total Value	Highest Valued Pick
LAR	16	70.7	27.3%	Aaron Donald (13, 2014)
TB	12	77.9	33.8%	Vernon Hargreaves (11, 2016)
SEA	**22**	**81.6**	**44.8%**	**Malik McDowell (35, 2017)**
DEN	16	83.5	46.7%	Shane Ray (23, 2015)
TEN	19	87.3	30.6%	Adoree' Jackson (18, 2017)
PHI	24	91.6	41.9%	Derek Barnett (14, 2017)
BUF	15	92.0	44.6%	Shaq Lawson (19, 2016)
KC	18	94.4	44.0%	Marcus Peters (18, 2015)
NE	21	94.6	57.2%	Dominique Easley (29, 2014)
CIN	19	95.2	42.0%	William Jackson (24, 2016)

No. Picks = Number of defensive players drafted.
Def Draft Value = Estimated value of draft picks spent on defensive players.
Pct of Total Value = Share of draft capital spent on defensive players.
Based on Pro Football Reference's Approximate Value metric and Chase Stuart's draft value chart: http://www.footballperspective.com/draft-value-chart/

out, either. That's just poor luck more than anything else, but it contributed to the talent drain. The 2013 and 2014 drafts were particularly rough; no one from either of those Seattle draft classes had even a single defensive snap in 2017.

The end result was a Seattle defense that looked old and slow, at least at times. That's pretty much the direct antithesis of what we had come to expect from Seattle's defenses. They had their worst rush defense DVOA since 2012. They were especially bad in short-yardage situations, ranking 30th on second-and-short and 25th on third- or fourth-and-short. They were dead last in DVOA in goal-to-go situations at 48.0%. Overall they were an average defense, but "average" isn't acceptable for a team with this defensive pedigree.

There's good news, though—reinforcements are on the way.

Seattle may be looking to develop half a new defense on the fly, but their last couple of drafts have been significantly better at finding potential quality talent. From the 2015 class, with Avril and Bennett out of the picture, Frank Clark looks to move up to being a 16-game starter for the first time in his career. He has already proven to be a productive pass-rusher and, crucially, kept up a high level of production even as his role has increased over the past two seasons. There are plenty of pass-rush specialists who flounder when asked to play a bigger part in a defense, but Clark hasn't missed a beat. It remains to be seen if he can handle being The Guy as an edge rusher, but the future looks bright for him.

2016 brought in Jarran Reed, who will be teaming up with 2017 pick Nazair Jones at defensive tackle now that Sheldon Richardson is gone. 2017 also brought in Shaquill Griffin, who quickly took over the second corner slot from Jeremy Lane as a rookie; he'll be replacing Richard Sherman as the top corner for the foreseeable future. 2018's class brings in some very promising players like Shaquem Griffen and Rasheem Green, each of whom have open paths to play significant roles right off the bat. That's an impressive collection of young talent and potential—and we have seen the ability of Carroll and company to coach up young defensive talent when they've had the chance.

Will they live up to the classes of 2010-12? Almost certainly not, if for no other reason than the number of defenses that can live up to that group can be counted on one hand with a couple fingers left over. It's also likely that not every player we've listed will continue to develop; every one of them needs to take a step forward in order to successfully fill the roles Seattle will be asking them to play in 2018, and the odds are that someone, somewhere will fail to live up to that challenge.

And those roles would be difficult to fill even if Seattle had a bevy of top-10 picks waiting in the wings. Chancellor was the only defensive back in football to rack up 400 solo tackles, 200 assists, and 10 interceptions in the 2010s, as his combination of ball skills, range, and ferocious hitting ability is unmatched in recent memory. Sherman, in his prime, essentially made half the field a no-throw zone as quarterbacks went out of their way to avoid targeting him. Avril is one of only two players in football to have at least five sacks in every year from 2008 to 2016. These aren't replaceable talents, and expecting the new defensive corps to live up to that standard is asking for disappointment.

All that being said, though, this is a very promising collection of young talent, most of whom have shown at least flashes of being top-level players at their respective positions. Group them with Bobby Wagner and K.J. Wright up the middle, the surprising resurgence of Dion Jordan, the immediate impact of Justin Coleman in the slot, and possibly Earl Thomas at safety (pending a nasty contact spat), and you have a promising defense. It may be more realistic to expect a resurgence in 2019 rather than this season, but there's plenty of reason for optimism here. Seahawks fans should be excited to see how this defense develops.

And then we turn to look at the offense, and that excitement and optimism drains away.

The collapse of Seattle's running game has been well established—only one touchdown produced all season that did not involve Russell Wilson, no running back gaining more than 240 yards on the ground, Wilson being just the fifth quarterback since 1960 to lead his team in rushing yards, and so on— but even that doesn't really get to the historical level of failure Seattle had on the ground.

The 2017 Seahawks had the second-worst red zone rushing DVOA we have ever recorded (Table 2). They had 43 carries inside the red zone, and managed just 46 yards. But wait, it gets worse—29 of those yards came from Wilson or Tyler Lockett, rather than running backs. So that's just 17 yards on 34 carries. But wait, it gets worse—20 of those 17 running back yards came from outside the 10-yard line. Seattle running backs carried the ball 20 times inside the 10, and managed *negative-three yards*

Seattle ranked eighth in red zone passing DVOA. Maybe next time they reach the goal line, they should try throwing a quick slant instead.

The Seahawks stand out among the teams in Table 2 because they weren't a bad offense in general—their offensive DVOA was 2.0%. The only other team on this list with a positive offensive DVOA was the 1992 Falcons. It's rare for an offense this competent to look this terrible in any split, and for it to be as crucial a split as red zone running makes it stand out all the more.

This is not something that can afford to continue. If the Seahawks want to return to the playoffs, it would help to be able to score when in scoring range. The good news is that it almost certainly *won't* continue. Red zone performance is one of those statistics which pretty heavily regresses towards the mean. Even ignoring the massive 1998-99 Raiders turnaround as an outlier, most of these offenses ended up merely being bad in the red zone the next season as opposed to historically terrible. Seattle could have done nothing this offseason, and they'd have every reason to expect more success running the ball at the goal line in 2018.

They most certainly did *not* do nothing, however. The Seahawks brain trust has a pretty clear philosophy on how to kickstart their offense. They're going all-in on pumping up their running game, with the working theory that returning to the sort of ground success they had from 2012 to 2015, where they ranked in the top 10 in rushing DVOA every year, will bring them success.

With that in mind, they drafted a running back in the first

Table 2: Worst Red Zone Rushing DVOA, 1987-2017

Year	Team	Red Pass DVOA	Rank	Red Rush DVOA	Rank	All Off DVOA	Rank	Red Rush DVOA Y+1	Rank	All Off DVOA Y+1	Rank
2007	STL	22.7%	13	-81.0%	32	-22.7%	31	-42.8%	31	-28.2%	32
2017	**SEA**	**38.1%**	**8**	**-78.0%**	**32**	**2.0%**	**14**	--	--	--	--
2000	ATL	-66.5%	29	-69.9%	31	-29.6%	31	-18.3%	26	-11.5%	25
2005	ARI	-36.9%	25	-61.2%	32	-9.5%	22	-10.9%	25	-9.4%	24
1995	NYJ	-17.7%	17	-60.6%	30	-30.7%	30	-2.3%	17	-11.7%	25
1987	KC	16.7%	13	-55.8%	28	-4.7%	19	-27.7%	27	-8.3%	22
2015	IND	13.1%	17	-55.5%	32	-15.6%	30	10.2%	14	3.7%	12
2008	CLE	-45.3%	29	-55.5%	32	-21.3%	29	-4.5%	16	-16.4%	24
1998	OAK	51.1%	3	-54.4%	30	-24.2%	29	19.1%	7	20.5%	2
2011	CLE	-8.7%	12	-54.2%	32	-11.2%	25	-4.8%	21	-15.2%	27
1992	ATL	60.2%	1	-52.9%	28	2.9%	13	-24.5%	25	-7.4%	19
1994	CIN	-17.9%	21	-50.4%	28	-16.2%	26	-4.6%	19	2.5%	14
1999	TB	8.5%	10	-49.8%	31	-10.2%	24	0.2%	19	4.7%	11
AVERAGE (w/o SEA)		-1.7%	15.8	-58.4%	30.5	-16.1%	25.8	-9.2%	20.6	-6.4%	19.8

round, Rashaad Penny. They brought in blocking tight ends Will Dissly and Ed Dickson to replace Jimmy Graham. They've handed the keys of the offense over to Brian Schottenheimer and returned to Mike Solari (who was with the franchise in 2008 and 2009) for a more straightforward blocking system on the offensive line. The goal, per Schottenheimer, is to "have the ability to run the football when people know you are going to run the football."

This offensive philosophy is definitely something of a throwback. Over the past few decades, NFL offenses have become more and more aerial focused, as the efficiency and effectiveness of the passing game have eclipsed that of the running game. Using a first-round pick on a running back is also the sort of personnel strategy that makes us analytics types go red in the face and start producing charts and tables talking about positional scarcity and the fungibility of running backs and salary cap models and so on and so forth. (Check out the Giants chapter for more of that sort of argument.) For the moment, let's put that aside and take a look at the running rebuild as it stands, to see how effective it's likely to be.

Penny had the fourth highest BackCAST score of the 2018 running back class at +81.0%—in other words, he's projected to gain 81 percent more yards than the average drafted running back. He has the second-highest adjusted yards per attempt in BackCAST's database at 7.37, and his 111.2 Speed Score shows that's he's really fast for a big guy. His projections get a knock because he wasn't able to beat out the likes of Donnel Pumphrey at San Diego State, and that *is* a red flag, but whenever he was able to get onto the field, he produced. Pair him with Chris Carson, who managed to claw his way from afterthought to starter last season before breaking his ankle, and the Seattle running back corps should be more talented in 2018.

Getting away from Tom Cable's blocking schemes is likely to help as well, if for no other reason than there's nowhere to go but up. Cable emphasized a zone-blocking scheme that focused heavily on timing and athleticism, while Solari's style is more of a power-first, scheme-second zone blocking style, emphasizing hitting the guy in front of you in the mouth rather than complicated schematic decisions. Theoretically, that should help some of the Seahawks' linemen who struggled implementing Cable's schemes. All five projected starters were either first- or second-round picks, so you'd expect them to have a level of talent that simply was not at all reflected by their performance last year; they were subpar in all aspects of the game even after Duane Brown came over from Houston.

Solari's ability to turn the line around is going to be absolutely critical. Yes, Seattle's running success from 2012 to 2015 had a lot to do with the talent of Marshawn Lynch, but what truly made them exceptional was their offensive line. Seattle finished in the top five in adjusted line yards, as well as the top 10 in power (short-yardage) success and stuff rate, in three out of those four seasons. Seattle's run game collapse corresponded not only with the loss of Lynch but with the losses of Russell Okung and J.R. Sweezy as well.

The most talented running backs in the league struggle when their offensive line can't get any push. The last two years, Seattle has ranked 26th and 31st in adjusted line yards, 27th twice in

power success, and 30th and 32nd in stuff rate. That's not to say the running back corps didn't need an upgrade—the Seahawks fell from 18th to 28th in second-level yards between 2016 and 2017, indicating that even when the backs had holes open last year, they couldn't do much with them—but the offensive line is the real villain here. A first-round back might bump Seattle's running attack back to 2016 levels, when they ranked 22nd in the league with a -11.3% DVOA, but to get anywhere near where they were in their glory days, they're going to need the offensive line to make a sudden 180.

Even if the running game is able to be more successful in 2018, there are multiple other reasons to be pessimistic about Seattle's run-focused offensive philosophy.

Firstly, the running game is far, far less important than the passing game in the modern NFL. Since 2000, 63 percent of the teams in the top 10 in passing DVOA have made the playoffs. Only 37 percent of teams in top 10 of rushing DVOA can say the same. The fact that nine of the ten teams with the most rushing yards made the playoffs last year is a classic example of the "teams run when they win, not win when they run" fallacy. Rush DVOA, rush success rate, and rush EPA/play all have roughly a 0.3 correlation with point differential; the corresponding passing metrics all have about a 0.7 correlation. During Seattle's 2012-15 run, they had a higher DVOA in the passing game than in the rushing game in three out of four seasons.

None of this is to say success on the ground is bad, or that the addition of Penny and the new offensive line philosophy won't help, or that by focusing on the running game, the Seahawks will be ignoring the passing game. It's just that passing is so much more valuable in today's NFL. If you had to choose between the two, you would rather be good at passing and bad at rushing than vice versa.

Speaking of vice versa, welcome new offensive coordinator Brian Schottenheimer.

Schottenheimer was previously offensive coordinator for the Jets from 2006 to 2011 and then for the Rams from 2012 to 2014. In those nine seasons, only one of his offenses finished in the top 15 offensive DVOA, the 2006 Jets. That also happened the be the only time his passing offenses finished in the top 12, as well, in his one season with a healthy Chad Pennington. Schottenheimer's offenses did have three top-11 rushing DVOA seasons in a row from 2008 to 2010, though those offenses never finished above 16th in offensive DVOA. He also was the coordinator in 2015 at Georgia, where they finished 14th in Rushing S&P+ but only 81st in Offensive S&P+.

Schottenheimer has been a Football Outsiders punching bag for years at this point. By the end of his Jets tenure, we described his offense as "more wrinkles than substance" and noted that he used modern, three-receiver sets as rarely as any offensive coordinator in the NFL in *Football Outsiders Almanac 2012*. He says that he'll keep about "70 percent" of Seattle's old offensive structure in place in 2018, which does track with what he did when he arrived in St. Louis in 2012—but, sure as can be, the Schottenheimer effect creeped in year after year, with three-receiver sets dropping every single season like clockwork even as the rest of the league was eagerly incorporating more and more three-wide sets into their systems. By his last season, more than 65 percent of the Rams' runs came out of two-back sets as if it were still the 1980s and pro formations were still all the cutting edge of offensive philosophy. He's the last coordinator in football to ever have that high of a ratio; only the 49ers were even over 50 percent last season.

And yes, Schottenheimer has brought in three fullbacks to the Seahawks roster. While we doubt Seattle will be using two-back sets as often as the 2014 Rams, Schottenheimer's history and current roster construction indicates that we should expect the use of 11 personnel (one running back, one tight end, three receivers) to drop and the frequency of loaded backfields to rise. This, despite the fact that Seattle's offensive DVOA in 11 personnel was 18.0% last year, eighth in the league, while their DVOA in all other sets was -11.0%, 24th in the league.

Schottenheimer's passing philosophy worships at the altar of the 4-yard curl, especially on third-and-5. Schottenheimer's teams in New York and St. Louis regularly ranked near the bottom of the league in the percentage of their passing yards gained through the air. They were, in general, happy to throw the ball short and were reliant on their receivers turning up-field and gaining yards after the catch. It wasn't super effective; Schottenheimer offenses never ranked in the top 20 of net yards per attempt after 2006. No, Sam Bradford and Chad Pennington were not known for having rocket arms, but Schottenheimer's conservative play calling had a lot to do with that as well.

And while there's some traditional offseason hyperbole there, "running when people know you are going to run" is just about the worst philosophy an offense can have. The best results for the running game come from running the ball when the other team *doesn't* think you're going to run; it's essentially the only time where rushing offense has a positive DVOA in the modern NFL. Table 3 shows the effectiveness of running back rushing attempts by number of defenders in the box.

Table 3: Don't Run Against Loaded Fronts!

Box	RB Runs	Avg	Off DVOA
4	63	7.5	40.2%
5	387	5.3	0.8%
6	4391	4.2	-8.3%
7	4792	3.9	-12.2%
8	1799	3.8	-16.8%
9	342	1.4	-11.8%

While there are times when you need to go power against power and gain a yard or 2, and there are times when you may want to run the ball just to keep an opposing defense honest, you generally want to do what the other team isn't set up to stop. This is why the run-pass option was all the rage last season; it allows teams to see how the defense lines up and take the path of least resistance, throwing against soft coverages and running against empty boxes. In the words of baseball's Wee Willie Keeler, "hit 'em where they ain't."

To be entirely fair, Schottenheimer's offense worked better in the mid-2000s for players like Pennington and Brett Favre, who each were strong at pre-snap reads and making quick decisions in the pocket. No offensive system is going

to work brilliantly with Shaun Hill and Austin Davis under center. Russell Wilson is the best quarterback Schottenheimer has ever gotten to coach, with the possible exception of a 39-year-old Favre. It's quite possible his skill will help paper over deficiencies in the scheme and open up opportunities Schottenheimer didn't have elsewhere. It could easily be the best offense Schottenheimer has ever put together, thanks in large part to the perennial MVP candidate.

Except it just seems like, more and more, Seattle's answer to offensive issues is to have Wilson's skill paper over deficiencies. Seattle hasn't had an offensive line finish even average in adjusted sack rate since 2010, usually finishing at or near the very bottom of the table. That's alright, though, because Wilson will find a way to Houdini out of sacks and keep plays alive. They lost 27 percent of their pass targets from last year with Jimmy Graham and Paul Richardson out of town, and Tyler Lockett's injuries mean he has been unable to put together a season like his 2015 breakout year. That's OK, though; Wilson's skill will help elevate newcomer Jaron Brown beyond what he was ever able to do in Arizona and help turn back the clock for Brandon Marshall.

The fact that this has worked so well up to this point is a credit to Wilson's skill. Only Aaron Rodgers comes close to matching his ability to turn nothing into something, and Wilson's chemistry with Doug Baldwin is exceptional. It's that connection, more than anything else, that gives Seattle an average offensive projection. They dragged Seattle to within a field goal of the playoffs a year ago; they may well be able to do so again, in spite of the team's offensive strategies.

The Seahawks reboot shows a clear plan of action on both sides of the ball. That already puts them ahead of a significant chunk of their rivals. And even with all the star power that's gone missing, there's only so low a team with players like Wilson, Baldwin, Wagner, and Wright could possibly fall. It's not hard to imagine the defense being a terror once again, the running game becoming merely remedial instead of disastrous, and a return to the playoffs in the cards. It's also not hard to imagine the young defense not being ready yet, new schemes not being enough to improve the offensive production, and the team falling to third or even fourth in the West on their way to a full and complete rebuild.

The Seahawks are betting against analytical wisdom with their offensive focus, drafting a running back in the first round and basing their philosophy around the ground game. Sometimes, zigging when the rest of the NFL zags is a great way to discover players and strategies the rest of the league has overlooked—just turn to the Philadelphia chapter to see an example of how this can work—but often, a consensus exists because it happens to be correct. Seattle's last dynasty was built on finding and exploiting gaps in the conventional wisdom, building their defense around tall cornerbacks and short quarterbacks that the rest of the league didn't value properly. In order for this reboot to work, they're going to need lightning to strike twice. Otherwise, we'll see another reboot in a year or two, and what could be more modern than that?

Bryan Knowles

2017 Seahawks Stats by Week

Wk	vs.	W-L	PF	PA	YDF	YDA	TO	Total	Off	Def	ST
1	at GB	L	9	17	225	370	0	-47%	-40%	15%	9%
2	SF	W	12	9	312	248	+1	17%	-11%	-39%	-10%
3	at TEN	L	27	33	433	420	0	-15%	23%	31%	-6%
4	IND	W	46	18	477	237	0	46%	35%	-13%	-1%
5	at LAR	W	16	10	241	375	+3	29%	-29%	-47%	11%
6	BYE										
7	at NYG	W	24	7	425	177	0	29%	0%	-25%	4%
8	HOU	W	41	38	479	509	+2	-7%	6%	19%	6%
9	WAS	L	14	17	437	244	-1	2%	10%	-11%	-18%
10	at ARI	W	22	16	287	290	+1	5%	12%	3%	-4%
11	ATL	L	31	34	360	279	-1	11%	3%	7%	14%
12	at SF	W	24	13	318	280	0	23%	7%	-23%	-7%
13	PHI	W	24	10	310	425	+2	32%	31%	1%	2%
14	at JAX	L	24	30	401	424	-2	-14%	43%	36%	-21%
15	LAR	L	7	42	149	352	-1	-84%	-62%	-4%	-26%
16	at DAL	W	21	12	136	282	+3	7%	-22%	-27%	1%
17	ARI	L	24	26	296	259	+1	22%	7%	2%	16%

Trends and Splits

	Offense	Rank	Defense	Rank
Total DVOA	2.0%	14	-3.8%	13
Unadjusted VOA	2.8%	13	-5.5%	10
Weighted Trend	3.9%	13	-2.9%	10
Variance	7.9%	18	5.7%	18
Average Opponent	-1.3%	10	-2.3%	25
Passing	21.1%	12	0.7%	13
Rushing	-12.1%	23	-9.0%	14
First Down	-10.4%	24	-9.0%	7
Second Down	23.3%	2	-2.0%	15
Third Down	-7.2%	22	3.8%	19
First Half	-22.6%	31	-6.7%	9
Second Half	25.7%	1	-0.7%	15
Red Zone	-11.6%	22	8.0%	22
Late and Close	17.4%	4	-8.8%	12

Five-Year Performance

Year	W-L	Pyth W	Est W	PF	PA	TO	Total	Rk	Off	Rk	Def	Rk	ST	Rk	Off AGL	Rk	Def AGL	Rk	Off Age	Rk	Def Age	Rk	ST Age	Rk
2013	13-3	12.8	13.0	417	231	+20	40.0%	1	9.4%	7	-25.9%	1	4.7%	5	43.8	22	16.2	7	25.7	32	26.0	27	26.1	14
2014	12-4	11.9	12.7	394	254	+10	31.9%	1	16.8%	5	-16.8%	1	-1.7%	19	39.5	24	35.3	13	25.3	31	26.3	23	25.8	24
2015	10-6	11.8	12.5	423	277	+7	38.1%	1	18.7%	1	-15.2%	4	4.2%	3	23.7	9	16.4	4	25.9	25	27.0	12	26.3	12
2016	10-5-1	9.8	9.1	354	292	+1	8.0%	11	-2.6%	16	-10.6%	5	-0.1%	15	23.8	6	17.3	4	25.7	29	27.2	7	26.4	8
2017	9-7	9.0	8.5	366	332	+8	3.8%	14	2.0%	14	-3.8%	13	-2.0%	20	45.5	23	42.7	22	26.1	29	27.0	8	25.8	20

2017 Performance Based on Most Common Personnel Groups

SEA Offense					SEA Offense vs. Opponents					SEA Defense					SEA Defense vs. Opponents			
Pers	Freq	Yds	DVOA	Run%	Pers	Freq	Yds	DVOA	Run%	Pers	Freq	Yds	DVOA	Pers	Freq	Yds	DVOA	
11	66%	5.8	18.0%	29%	Base	25%	4.7	-12.8%	49%	Base	29%	4.9	-2.6%	11	65%	5.1	-2.5%	
12	16%	5.0	5.1%	34%	Nickel	60%	5.7	21.0%	30%	Nickel	68%	5.1	-7.5%	12	14%	4.5	-23.4%	
13	5%	3.8	-40.7%	45%	Dime+	13%	5.7	8.7%	15%	Dime+	3%	5.4	50.6%	21	7%	5.3	6.9%	
21	4%	7.6	-24.3%	44%	Goal Line	1%	-0.1	-73.8%	50%	Goal Line	1%	0.9	54.7%	13	4%	4.1	-21.3%	
612	3%	4.3	-11.3%	93%										22	3%	5.2	-7.2%	

Strategic Tendencies

Run/Pass		Rk	Formation		Rk	Pass Rush		Rk	Secondary		Rk	Strategy		Rk
Runs, first half	34%	30	Form: Single Back	79%	14	Rush 3	4.5%	23	4 DB	29%	22	Play action	23%	9
Runs, first down	43%	30	Form: Empty Back	14%	2	Rush 4	76.8%	5	5 DB	68%	3	Avg Box (Off)	6.00	31
Runs, second-long	28%	23	Pers: 3+ WR	70%	8	Rush 5	15.2%	26	6+ DB	3%	21	Avg Box (Def)	6.19	22
Runs, power sit.	47%	26	Pers: 2+ TE/6+ OL	27%	21	Rush 6+	3.5%	24	CB by Sides	81%	14	Offensive Pace	30.02	12
Runs, behind 2H	24%	28	Pers: 6+ OL	1%	32	Int DL Sacks	14.1%	27	S/CB Cover Ratio	24%	26	Defensive Pace	29.58	3
Pass, ahead 2H	53%	3	Shotgun/Pistol	62%	15	Second Level Sacks	12.8%	25	DB Blitz	4%	31	Go for it on 4th	0.78	25

Seattle has been above-average in penalties for years, but nothing quite like last season, when the Seahawks led the NFL with 183 penalties including declined and offsetting. That was 20 more than any other team; in fact, Miami was the only other team within 30 penalties of Seattle. The Seahawks led the league in penalties on both offense and defense. Seattle opponents were also called for more penalties than average, but only by a small amount, roughly 5 percent. ☞ Seattle's offense was the worst in the league in the first quarter of games, average in the second and third quarters, and then the best in the league in the fourth quarter or overtime. ☞ Seattle's defense ranked in the top 10 for adjusted sack rate on both first and second down but ranked 30th on third and fourth downs. ☞ The Seattle defense had big problems with running backs out of two-back sets. They allowed just 3.5 yards per carry with -22.6% DVOA out of one-back sets, but 5.0 yards per carry and 8.0% DVOA out of two-back sets.

Passing

Player	DYAR	DVOA	Plays	NtYds	Avg	YAC	C%	TD	Int
R.Wilson	530	2.9%	598	3586	6.0	4.7	62.5%	34	11

Rushing

Player	DYAR	DVOA	Plays	Yds	Avg	TD	Fum	Suc
R.Wilson	154	28.9%	79	599	7.6	3	3	-
M.Davis	-38	-23.1%	69	240	3.5	0	0	29%
E.Lacy*	-81	-37.9%	69	179	2.6	0	0	29%
T.Rawls*	-83	-40.9%	58	157	2.7	0	1	33%
C.Carson	33	7.0%	49	208	4.2	0	0	43%
J.D.McKissic	31	8.2%	45	186	4.1	1	0	51%
C.J.Prosise	-5	-19.8%	11	23	2.1	0	0	36%
T.Lockett	36	29.2%	10	58	5.8	0	0	-

Receiving

Player	DYAR	DVOA	Plays	Ctch	Yds	Y/C	YAC	TD	C%
D.Baldwin	200	9.6%	118	77	983	12.8	3.3	8	65%
P.Richardson*	161	13.4%	80	44	703	16.0	2.8	6	55%
T.Lockett	48	-3.4%	71	45	555	12.3	4.2	2	63%
A.Darboh	-6	-19.1%	13	8	71	8.9	2.0	0	62%
T.McEvoy	8	-0.8%	9	5	116	23.2	4.4	0	56%
J.Brown*	6	-11.5%	69	31	477	15.4	2.8	4	45%
M.Johnson	-7	-22.4%	8	5	45	9.0	1.4	0	63%
J.Graham*	9	-6.0%	96	57	520	9.1	3.7	10	59%
L.Willson*	18	4.7%	22	15	153	10.2	6.0	4	68%
N.Vannett	36	31.0%	15	12	124	10.3	3.8	1	80%
E.Dickson	83	18.1%	48	30	437	14.6	6.7	1	63%
J.D.McKissic	49	3.9%	47	35	267	7.6	5.5	2	74%
M.Davis	26	15.2%	18	15	131	8.7	11.2	0	83%
T.Rawls*	28	26.8%	13	9	94	10.4	9.2	0	69%
C.J.Prosise	6	-4.2%	11	6	87	14.5	8.3	0	55%
C.Carson	26	34.9%	8	7	59	8.4	6.6	1	88%
E.Lacy*	24	64.5%	6	6	47	7.8	8.5	0	100%

Offensive Line

Player	Pos	Age	GS	Snaps	Pen	Sk	Pass	Run	Player	Pos	Age	GS	Snaps	Pen	Sk	Pass	Run
Germain Ifedi	RT	24	16/16	1068	20	5.0	27	11	Oday Aboushi*	RG	27	8/8	557	6	1.0	7	6
Justin Britt	C	27	16/16	1062	5	2.0	7	12	Rees Odhiambo	LT	26	7/7	484	1	3.0	12	9
Luke Joeckel*	LG	27	11/11	703	2	6.5	14	7	Mark Glowinski*	LG	26	10/2	198	1	1.0	5	1
Ethan Pocic	LG/RG	23	16/11	639	5	4.5	11	8	D.J. Fluker	RG	27	9/6	447	4	2.0	13	4
Duane Brown	LT	33	10/10	68	4	4.5	13	3									

Year	Yards	ALY	Rank	Power	Rank	Stuff	Rank	2nd Lev	Rank	Open Field	Rank	Sacks	ASR	Rank	Press	Rank	F-Start	Cont.
2015	4.44	4.56	4	71%	8	18%	5	1.20	15	0.81	12	46	9.0%	30	31.8%	30	21	30
2016	3.82	3.77	26	53%	27	23%	30	1.12	18	0.70	15	42	6.9%	25	33.7%	32	26	28
2017	3.30	3.18	31	55%	27	30%	32	0.97	28	0.54	21	43	8.1%	25	36.9%	30	20	29

2017 ALY by direction: Left End: 3.66 (21)   Left Tackle: 1.79 (32)   Mid/Guard: 3.85 (26)   Right Tackle: 3.17 (26)   Right End: 2.11 (31)

For years, the Seahawks were known for having a stellar run-blocking line, helping make their pass-blocking struggles more palatable. For the second year in a row, however, that was not the case; only Detroit managed worse than Seattle's 3.18 adjusted line yards. ☞ On paper, Duane Brown is a huge upgrade over Rees Odhiambo; he's a stronger, more agile, and generally more talented player. However, it was hard to find an actual impact last season when Brown entered the lineup. In the passing game, Brown had a slight advantage; he went 29.6 snaps per blown block while Odhiambo lasted only 25.7. Odhiambo blew a run block about four times more frequently than Brown did, but the Seahawks' adjusted line yards when running to the left didn't improve at all with Brown. The Seahawks will need to get more actual improvements from Brown's superior talent in 2018. ☞ Germain Ifedi led the league by drawing 20 penalty flags in 2017. His nine false starts also were the most in football. ☞ Ifedi, Odhiambo, Luke Joeckel, and Ethan Pocic all ranked in the bottom 10 at their respective positions in snaps per blown block. ☞ Pocic showed off some good technique as a rookie, but he had a tendency to get bowled over by power rushes. He has added 20 pounds during offseason weight training, which should help him to hold his own. It will also help him to be in a consistent role; he moved from college center to training camp tackle to left guard to right guard in the past 12 months. ☞ D.J.

Fluker comes over from the Giants to bolster the right guard position. He missed most of the second half of 2017 with a toe injury; when he was healthy, he ranked 100th out of 102 inside linemen in snaps per blown block. Those struggles were almost entirely in pass protection; his 43.3 run snaps per blown block was thoroughly average, and far better than any of Seattle's offensive linemen a year ago. ☙ Justin Britt remains Seattle's best offensive lineman, even with the addition of Brown. He had an off year in 2017, however, especially in the run game. Britt had some uncharacteristic difficulties dealing with some of the bigger nose tackles and other two-gappers throughout the league, which didn't mesh well with Seattle's strategy of slamming its backs up the middle. ☙ Fifth-round pick Jamarco Jones had a terrible combine, sending his draft stock plummeting—his athletic testing was described by one exec as "reject level." He looked better on the field at Ohio State, where he was first-team all-conference. Seattle hopes that he'll be their left tackle of the future (Brown's contract expires at the end of 2018), but he'll compete with Ifedi and George Fant for the right tackle spot this season.

Defensive Front Seven

Defensive Line	Age	Pos	G	Snaps	Plays	TmPct	Rk	Stop	Dfts	BTkl	Runs	St%	Rk	RuYd	Rk	Sack	Hit	Hur	Dsrpt
Sheldon Richardson*	28	DT	15	655	45	5.8%	28	32	8	6	38	71%	66	3.1	76	1.0	10	15.0	1
Jarran Reed	26	DT	15	617	46	5.9%	25	32	7	5	40	68%	75	2.9	73	1.5	7	18.0	2
Nazair Jones	24	DT	11	284	21	3.7%	--	17	7	2	14	79%	--	1.9	--	2.0	2	5.0	4
Tom Johnson	34	DT	16	675	32	4.3%	57	24	8	4	27	74%	59	2.2	50	2.0	11	22.0	1
Shamar Stephen	27	DT	15	384	28	4.0%	63	21	2	2	26	73%	61	2.8	72	1.0	2	7.0	0

Edge Rushers	Age	Pos	G	Snaps	Plays	TmPct	Rk	Stop	Dfts	BTkl	Runs	St%	Rk	RuYd	Rk	Sack	Hit	Hur	Dsrpt
Michael Bennett*	33	DE	16	934	41	4.9%	50	35	21	10	30	80%	31	1.3	16	8.5	17	38.5	2
Frank Clark	25	DE	16	742	33	4.0%	65	27	17	8	18	78%	38	1.1	12	9.0	13	28.5	3
Branden Jackson	26	DE	12	263	10	1.6%	--	8	3	2	8	75%	--	2.5	--	0.5	1	9.5	1
Barkevious Mingo	28	OLB	16	501	46	5.5%	38	28	9	9	28	64%	78	3.6	87	2.0	6	16.5	2

Linebackers	Age	Pos	G	Snaps	Plays	TmPct	Rk	Stop	Dfts	BTkl	Runs	St%	Rk	RuYd	Rk	Sack	Hit	Hur	Tgts	Suc%	Rk	AdjYd	Rk	PD	Int
Bobby Wagner	28	MLB	16	1026	139	16.7%	11	72	27	4	81	60%	53	3.6	40	1.5	12	14.5	45	45%	55	7.1	46	4	2
K.J. Wright	29	OLB	15	958	114	14.6%	25	63	19	9	68	65%	33	3.0	23	0.0	3	9.0	48	56%	20	6.4	32	5	1
Michael Wilhoite*	32	MLB	14	318	27	3.7%	--	20	4	2	20	70%	--	3.0	--	0.0	1	2.5	7	90%	--	4.6	--	1	1

Year	Yards	ALY	Rank	Power	Rank	Stuff	Rank	2nd Level	Rank	Open Field	Rank	Sacks	ASR	Rank	Press	Rank
2015	3.54	3.93	12	72%	26	21%	15	0.94	3	0.42	3	37	6.7%	14	29.3%	2
2016	3.42	3.81	8	58%	8	23%	7	0.97	6	0.40	3	42	6.7%	10	28.6%	10
2017	4.01	4.10	18	67%	22	18%	27	1.00	7	0.75	18	39	6.6%	15	30.9%	14

2017 ALY by direction:	Left End: 4.57 (23)	Left Tackle: 4.69 (27)	Mid/Guard: 3.75 (5)	Right Tackle: 4.78 (30)	Right End: 3.11 (7)

As a 2015 draft pick, Frank Clark is now the longest-tenured veteran on the Seahawks' defensive line. Some pass-rush specialists drop off when asked to play a full-time role, but Clark stepped up after Cliff Avril's injury without missing too much of a beat. Clark is one of only nine players to have at least nine sacks in each of the last two seasons, and he should only have more opportunities in 2018. ☙ Dion Jordan hadn't played a snap in two and a half years before Seattle activated him in November. With four sacks, five QB knockdowns, and three hurries in just 138 snaps, he far exceeded expectations. ☙ Succeeding Jordan in the "rehabilitate a draft bust" sweepstakes, Barkevious Mingo comes over from Indianapolis to compete with D.J. Alexander at strongside linebacker. Mingo had 16.5 hurries last season, which would put him fourth among current Seahawks, but he ranked in the bottom ten among edge rushers in average depth of run tackle. ☙ Third-round pick Rasheem Green (USC) needs to add mass—he only weighs 275 pounds and needs to bulk up to really hold his own as an every-down player. His quickness and athleticism are undeniable, however, and with the team thin at edge rusher, don't count him out as part of the rotation as a rookie. ☙ Seattle's high ranking in adjusted line yards up the middle had plenty to do with the departed Sheldon Richardson, but Jarran Reed more than held his own. Reed also displayed more of an interior pass rush than he had either as a rookie or at Alabama. ☙ Tom Johnson isn't going to dominate double-teams like Richardson could, but his quickness off the snap means that Seattle isn't going to lose much interior pass rush with the swap. ☙ Nazair Jones was already Johnson's equal as a run defender as a rookie. If he can develop an actual pass-rushing move as a sophomore, don't be surprised if he ends the year as the regular starter. ☙ Among his many other talents, Bobby Wagner is the best tackling linebacker in football. He has never allowed more than 13 broken tackles in a season, and his 4.3 percent broken tackle rate in 2017 was the best among inside linebackers. He also had the second-best YAC allowed for any linebacker. When he tackles you, you stay tackled. ☞ It's one thing to have one exceptional linebacker; having Wagner and K.J. Wright on the same team is almost unfair. Wright's 63 stops would have been the most by any player on 15 teams last season. He'll have one more year of being in Wagner's shadow before hitting free agency in 2019. ☞ Fifth-round pick Shaquem Griffin is more than just an inspirational story. He's a whirlwind on the field, a great pass-rusher with sideline-to-sideline range as a tackler. He needs to work on finishing—he missed 24 tackles over the past two seasons—and, yes, the lack of a left hand will always create physical limitations. As a high-energy dynamo, however, he'll have an immediate impact on special teams and could be the heir apparent for Wright at weakside linebacker.

Defensive Secondary

Secondary	Age	Pos	G	Snaps	Plays	Overall TmPct	Rk	Stop	Dfts	BTkl	Runs	vs. Run St%	Rk	RuYd	Rk	Tgts	vs. Pass Tgt%	Rk	Dist	Suc%	Rk	AdjYd	Rk	PD	Int
Earl Thomas	29	FS	14	925	95	13.0%	9	26	11	10	47	21%	70	8.2	55	27	6.9%	13	13.7	50%	45	9.0	47	7	2
Shaquill Griffin	23	CB	15	877	73	9.3%	28	34	16	5	14	57%	18	5.6	30	83	22.9%	60	12.1	57%	12	5.9	8	15	1
Bradley McDougald	28	SS	16	681	71	8.5%	59	37	16	8	38	63%	5	3.5	3	31	11.0%	50	8.4	62%	9	5.2	5	4	0
Justin Coleman	25	CB	16	657	44	5.3%	76	25	11	9	8	88%	4	5.1	21	53	19.3%	32	10.1	47%	65	7.2	32	8	2
Kam Chancellor	30	SS	9	598	50	10.7%	28	23	8	8	26	65%	4	4.1	8	21	8.5%	29	11.8	60%	16	6.6	18	2	0
Byron Maxwell	30	CB	9	584	53	12.2%	2	27	13	7	14	57%	18	5.9	38	56	22.8%	58	12.7	45%	77	9.4	74	7	1
Richard Sherman*	30	CB	9	572	42	9.0%	32	18	5	3	15	60%	15	5.4	25	42	17.5%	21	16.1	52%	36	6.9	30	7	2
Jeremy Lane*	28	CB	13	348	28	4.1%	--	6	1	0	9	22%	--	14.7	--	29	19.8%	--	11.9	40%	--	9.2	--	0	0
Dontae Johnson	27	CB	16	1027	83	9.9%	21	24	11	12	23	43%	41	4.3	12	84	18.4%	26	12.4	38%	79	9.5	77	10	1

Year	Pass D Rank	vs. #1 WR	Rk	vs. #2 WR	Rk	vs. Other WR	Rk	WR Wide	Rk	WR Slot	Rk	vs. TE	Rk	vs. RB	Rk
2015	3	-33.3%	1	-21.5%	5	-9.5%	10	--	--	--	--	20.0%	26	-17.8%	5
2016	13	1.3%	16	22.3%	31	-3.2%	11	-9.4%	9	15.8%	27	-1.3%	18	-20.3%	5
2017	13	0.9%	16	38.9%	31	-5.3%	14	20.2%	31	0.8%	13	-23.9%	3	-33.0%	2

At least Kam Chancellor went out with a bang, again appearing near the top of every run defense metric we have. Bradley McDougald will once more try to fill some very large shoes. McDougald was actually a more effective tackler than Chancellor was last season; he had a 16 percent broken tackle rate compared to Chancellor's 22 percent. He's not as good as Kam—very few players are—but he's a solid replacement. ☞ It was Earl Thomas' turn to be the subject of offseason trade rumors this year, as he enters the last year of his current deal. Due to injuries, he's not quite the player he once was—but that just means he's *one* of the best free safeties in the league, instead of *the* best. It is worth noting that his success rate in coverage for the past two years has hovered around 50 percent, rather than the 70-plus percent he put up before his broken leg. ☞ Shaquill Griffin becomes the man at corner now, with Richard Sherman looking very strange in red and gold. Griffin was playing Sherman's old left side during OTAs, and it will be interesting to see if the Seahawks continue to keep him there. When Sherman was healthy, Seattle kept their corners on one side of the field 88 percent of the time. That dropped to 71 percent after Sherman's injury, with Griffin on the right and Byron Maxwell on the left. ☞ Sometimes, there's no place like home. Maxwell definitely looked more comfortable back in Seattle than he did in either Miami or Philadelphia. His limited speed makes him a poor fit when asked to play off the line, but place him on the line of scrimmage and let him jam people, and he's in his comfort zone. ☞ Justin Coleman played more defensive snaps in 2017 than he did in his first two seasons combined and had immediate success. He was an immediate upgrade over Jeremy Lane in essentially every way, and he has the potential to move to the outside if Griffin or Maxwell stutter or get injured. ☞ Seattle is converting fifth-round pick Tre Flowers (Oklahoma State) from safety to corner. At 6-foot-3 and 200 pounds, with 35-inch arms, he has the size of the prototypical Seattle corner. He also has excellent straight-line speed, but there are questions about his agility and physicality going forward.

Special Teams

Year	DVOA	Rank	FG/XP	Rank	Net Kick	Rank	Kick Ret	Rank	Net Punt	Rank	Punt Ret	Rank	Hidden	Rank
2015	4.2%	3	6.6	4	0.8	13	7.6	4	-5.4	23	11.3	1	-8.9	29
2016	-0.1%	15	-4.0	22	6.2	4	3.1	8	-7.4	27	1.6	10	8.7	7
2017	-2.0%	20	-7.6	27	3.0	11	8.1	3	-13.4	31	0.1	15	-7.5	26

Seattle's special teams DVOA was their worst since 2001, including their third-worst FG/XP performance and second-worst punt performance since 1986. Significant changes were needed and have been made. ✒ In 2016, Steven Hauschka missed four field goals and six extra points, prompting Seattle to replace him with Blair Walsh. Walsh only missed one extra point, which is good! He also missed eight field goals, including one that would have sent the crucial Atlanta game into overtime, which is bad. This year's replacement is Sebastian Janikowski, who spent all of 2017 on injured reserve. His leg strength, even at age 40, is undeniable, but he hasn't had an above-average field goal season since 2014. ✒ Fifth-round pick Michael Dickson is a rarity—a punter who went pro early. Forty-two of his 84 punts last season ended up inside the 20; 33 of them were fair caught. If you ever want to see a punter single-handedly win a football game, watch the 2018 Texas Bowl, where eight of Dickson's 11 punts pinned Missouri inside the 10 and only one gave Missouri a drive start further downfield than its own 14. ✒ Tyler Lockett was much better on kick returns than punt returns in 2017. With Lockett moving back up to WR2, Seattle is expected to try to take some of the special teams load off of him this season. First-round pick Rashaad Penny ranked fifth in the FBS, averaging 30.7 yards per kickoff return, but only returned two punts—and would you really want your first-round pick on kick return duty? Another option may be J.D. McKissic; he served as the primary returner during last year's preseason when Lockett missed time.

Tampa Bay Buccaneers

2017 Record: 5-11	**Total DVOA:** -11.9% (23rd)	**2018 Mean Projection:** 7.0 wins	**On the Clock (0-4):** 16%
Pythagorean Wins: 6.7 (18th)	**Offense:** 5.3% (11th)	**Postseason Odds:** 22.3%	**Mediocrity (5-7):** 42%
Snap-Weighted Age: 26.5 (15th)	**Defense:** 11.7% (32nd)	**Super Bowl Odds:** 2.0%	**Playoff Contender (8-10):** 32%
Average Opponent: 2.8% (6th)	**Special Teams:** -5.5% (29th)	**Proj. Avg. Opponent:** 2.5% (3rd)	**Super Bowl Contender (11+):** 9%

2017: Their eyes were bigger than their stomachs when it came to eating the Ws.

2018: Find a D and you won't have to eat so many Ls.

The careers of Jameis Winston and Marcus Mariota were forever linked after they were made the first two picks of the 2015 NFL draft. Did Tampa Bay choose the right quarterback? The debate rages on, years after Winston and Mariota met in the first game of their careers. Both had impressive rookie seasons, although neither led his team to a winning record in 2015. Both improved to lead their teams to matching 9-7 records in 2016, but still came up short of the playoffs. With expectations higher last year, Tennessee snuck into the playoffs at 9-7 in a weaker AFC despite Mariota having his worst season yet. The Buccaneers disappointed and finished 5-11 in another lost season, the 10th in a row without a postseason in Tampa Bay.

This most recent letdown seems to have built a perception that Winston declined in 2017, but the reality in the numbers could not be more different. In 2017, Winston set career-bests in completion rate (63.8 percent), interception rate (2.5 percent), yards per attempt (7.9), passer rating (92.2), passing yards per game (269.5), passing DYAR (779), and passing DVOA (14.3%). He also led the league with the lowest rate of failed completions (17.7 percent) and strengthened his case as the league's most aggressive passer with the highest ALEX on all downs at +1.8. It was not a stellar third season for Winston, but it was better than what Mariota did.

So why the difference in perception? That's simple. People have vivid memories of Mariota leading a comeback win in Kansas City in his first playoff start. Winston was the guy who tried to "eat a W" before a game that saw him also try to instigate a fight from the sideline. Yes, the most memorable part of Tampa Bay's 2017 season was not the very end when Winston led a 95-yard touchdown drive to beat the Saints in Week 17. It was the first matchup in New Orleans in Week 9 when Winston was caught on camera giving a rousing pregame speech. He licked his fingers before forming a "W" and repeatedly asking if his teammates wanted to eat one. The Saints won 30-10 and Winston was sidelined early with a shoulder injury, but from the sideline he still managed to poke Marcus Lattimore from behind to start a little scuffle that led to him being fined over $12,000. The injury caused Winston to miss three games, the first games he has missed in his NFL career. (It probably did not help matters that the Buccaneers were 2-1 with Ryan Fitzpatrick starting in Winston's place, but that was partly the benefits of getting to play the Jets and Dolphins.)

It would be facetious to pretend only the on-field perfor-

mance matters here. There's also the way these quarterbacks have conducted themselves off the field. Mariota has been a quiet presence with the Titans, while Winston has brought baggage to Tampa Bay dating back to his Florida State days. His history includes less serious incidents such as shouting an obscenity from a student union table and stealing crab legs, but it also includes a rape allegation that was originally filed in December 2012. Winston was never charged in that case, but since turning pro he has been accused by an Uber driver of grabbing her crotch in March 2016. No criminal charges were filed, but the driver reported the incident to Uber. In November 2017 the NFL reportedly was investigating the claim, and on June 21, 2018, news broke that Winston was expected to serve a three-game suspension for violating the league's personal conduct policy.

Winston denies the allegation. Ronald Darby, a former college teammate and current Eagles cornerback, was with Winston that night in 2016, and he backs up Winston's statement that the two were in the backseat while a third passenger sat up front. However, former Vanderbilt player Brandon Banks alleges that he was the third man with Winston and Darby, and that the trio arrived to a party with a different Uber driver. Banks said that an intoxicated Winston left the party alone in the Uber driven by the accuser. Banks is now serving 15 years in prison for his role in a gang rape of a female student at Vanderbilt in 2013. Not exactly the smartest company for Winston to associate himself with, but decision-making has never been his strong suit.

In fact, while we downplayed the seriousness of Winston's other incidents, there may be a troubling pattern of behavior here. In 2017, Winston spoke to a group of elementary students and told the girls that they're "supposed to be silent, polite, and gentle." Would a man who thinks women should be silent, who feels entitled to steal things, and who objectifies women be someone who is capable of grabbing a female driver's crotch while sitting in a drive-thru at 2 a.m.? The NFL sure seems to think there is enough there (and more could be coming out after we've gone to press), hence the suspension. The Buccaneers, however, still picked up Winston's fifth-year option in April. For better or worse, Winston should resume his starting quarterback duties for Tampa Bay this season. Since this is a football preview book rather than a psychological profile, we now have to focus on the football side of things.

2018 Buccaneers Schedule

Week	Opp.	Week	Opp.	Week	Opp.
1	at NO	7	CLE	13	CAR
2	PHI	8	at CIN	14	NO
3	PIT (Mon.)	9	at CAR	15	at BAL
4	at CHI	10	WAS	16	at DAL
5	BYE	11	at NYG	17	ATL
6	at ATL	12	SF		

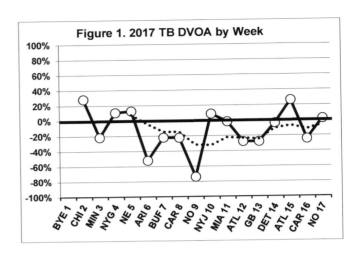

Figure 1. 2017 TB DVOA by Week

Winston, who is only entering his age-24 season, might be respected a bit more for his on-field accomplishments if he played in a different division. One of the biggest factors in Tampa Bay's decade-long playoff drought is that the NFC South has been so competitive thanks to consistency at head coach and quarterback that no other division recently has. Sean Payton and Drew Brees have been in New Orleans since 2006. Matt Ryan has had two head coaches, but he has been a game-changer for Atlanta since he was drafted in 2008. The Panthers hired Ron Rivera and drafted Cam Newton in 2011. Brees is a Super Bowl MVP and set to break the NFL record for passing yards this season. Newton and Ryan won MVP in 2015 and 2016, respectively, while leading their teams to Super Bowl appearances. All three of these teams made the playoffs last year.

Through no fault of his own, Winston starts the season at a disadvantage that no other quarterback in the NFL's 32-team era (since 2002) has had to face. The 2017 NFC South was the first division since 2002 to feature three starting quarterbacks that had won an MVP and/or Super Bowl in their career prior to that season. No other division even comes close. The Patriots and Tom Brady never have to deal with this; the only AFC East rival who would qualify was Brett Favre's one year in New York, and that was in 2008, the same season Brady tore his ACL in Week 1. The AFC North comes closest with Ben Roethlisberger and Joe Flacco combining to start 32 games in both 2013 and 2014, but Flacco has only declined since he won his Super Bowl MVP in 2012. All told, the NFC South has had 489 regular-season starts since 2002 by quarterbacks who have won an MVP and/or Super Bowl. That far outpaces the rest of the divisions: the AFC North (385), NFC North (290), AFC East (253), NFC East (253), AFC South (196), NFC West (185), and AFC West (142).

It's not easy being the fourth-best quarterback in your own division. Winston has often drawn comparisons to his division rival Newton, which is accurate. They both absorb a lot of contact by holding the ball longer than average in an effort to make plays down the field. Since 2015, both rank in the top three in average depth of target, with Winston the only quarterback to average more than 10.0 air yards per pass attempt. They also have a tendency to be erratic passers and benefit from having tall receivers. They have the two highest rates of off-target throws among active starters since 2015 according to ESPN Stats & Info. Newton provides more rushing value than Winston, but his passing has never dramatically improved like one would expect over his first seven seasons. In fact, Winston's 779 passing DYAR last year would be a career high for Newton, who peaked at 630 passing DYAR in his 2015 MVP season.

So how has Newton reached the playoffs four times in the last five years? The difference is simply that the Panthers have built a better team around Newton. That team can win games with marginal passing production thanks to the defense, special teams, and a commitment to running the ball. Those three things combine to give Newton a lighter workload and better starting field position to facilitate more scoring. Winston has yet to enjoy these advantages in Tampa Bay.

The Buccaneers provided Winston with a good running game in his rookie year when Doug Martin rushed for 1,402 yards at 4.9 yards per carry. In the last two seasons there has been a huge decline. Martin is the only player since 1940 to have multiple seasons where he averaged less than 3.0 yards per carry on at least 120 carries, and he just did it in consecutive seasons. Peyton Barber led the team in rushing instead, with just 423 yards in 2017. Without much help from the running game, Winston does press at times, which can lead to some ugly interceptions. However, he's really no more egregious in this area than Andrew Luck, who has a similar career interception rate (2.6 percent) to Winston's 2.8 percent.

There is one stat where Winston is quietly excellent: first downs per pass attempt. It's not a commonly quoted stat by any means, but moving the chains is hugely important, and it is a stat where the cream rises to the top. It's just that no one would expect to see Winston (38.5 percent) second behind only Peyton Manning (39.6 percent) among all quarterbacks since 2001, according to data from ESPN Stats & Info (Table 1). The top eight quarterbacks in this stat (along with Aaron Rodgers) also make the top nine when looking only at third down, where Winston is still an impressive fifth.

One has to wonder why Winston's offenses have not produced at a level similar to those of these other quarterbacks. The fact that first downs per pass does not account for sacks could be one factor, but Winston's career sack rate (5.8 percent) is respectable among his peers. His sack rate on third downs (7.5 percent) is actually lower than that of Roethlisberger (9.7 percent), Rodgers (9.4 percent), and Brady (7.8 percent). Really, Winston excels in this stat due to his affinity for attacking down the field. It's his greatest strength, but it also can be his greatest weakness at times. His playing style has led to a good amount of contact behind an offensive line that hasn't had any star talent in years. Winston led all quarterbacks with 123 knockdowns as a rookie, and finished third in 2016 with 120 knockdowns. He was down to 81 knockdowns in 13 games last year, but the accumulated punishment led to a shoulder injury against the Cardinals, an injury he tried to play through before the team shut him down for three games.

To his credit, Winston has been productive while under pressure. According to ESPN Stats & Info, Winston has the highest QBR under pressure (51.7) since 2015. His 76.7 QBR under pressure in 2016 is the highest season in ESPN's database (back to 2009), while DVOA ranked Winston third under pressure that year. However, Winston had a career-low -60.0% DVOA under pressure in 2017, which ranked 23rd in the league.

There is no denying that Winston can move the chains at the level of a franchise quarterback, but Tampa Bay was supposed to score a lot more points last season after adding DeSean Jackson and drafting tight end O.J. Howard in the first round. The Buccaneers finished seventh in yards per drive, but only 16th in points per drive. We saw a very similar pattern in Winston's rookie year when the Buccaneers were fifth in yards per drive, but 18th in points per drive. In both years the offense was below average in the red zone, finishing 24th last year in points per red zone trip and 24th in touchdowns per red zone opportunity. Winston could certainly afford to get better in the red zone, where he has been average at best, but this is another area where the running game has been a real letdown. In fact, we compiled Tampa Bay's DVOA splits for the run and pass over the last three years and found that the passing game has often been above average to great in areas such as first down, third down, and the red zone. The running game, though, has been feeble since 2016 (Table 2).

One of the solutions in the red zone could be to feature Howard more in his second season. He only caught 26 balls last year and had just six red zone targets, but showed some great athletic ability, or at least enough awareness to completely lose the defense for some of Winston's easiest touchdowns ever (see games against the Giants and Bills). The Buccaneers return the same top four wideouts and two tight ends from a year ago, so not much should change here except for more experience for Howard and Chris Godwin.

We already explained the deficiencies that have existed in the running game and offensive line. So what has general manager Jason Licht done to improve those areas this year? First, the Buccaneers said goodbye to Martin after six seasons at running back. While the so-so trio of Peyton Barber, Jacquizz Rodgers, and Charles Sims returns, the Buccaneers

Table 1. Most First Downs per Pass Attempt Since 2001

Rk	Player	1D/Att (All Downs)	Rk	Player	1D/Att (3rd Downs)
1	Peyton Manning	39.6%	1	Ben Roethlisberger	46.6%
2	Jameis Winston	38.5%	2	Peyton Manning	46.4%
3	Ben Roethlisberger	38.3%	3	Matt Ryan	45.6%
4	Philip Rivers	38.2%	4	Drew Brees	45.6%
5	Tony Romo	38.1%	5	Jameis Winston	45.5%
6	Tom Brady	37.3%	6	Aaron Rodgers	45.5%
7	Matt Ryan	37.2%	7	Tony Romo	45.1%
8	Drew Brees	37.0%	8	Philip Rivers	45.0%
9	Chad Pennington	37.0%	9	Tom Brady	44.0%
10	Matt Schaub	37.0%	10	Daunte Culpepper	43.7%

also added Ronald Jones II with the 38th pick in April. Jones averaged 5.9 yards on 261 carries as a junior at USC last year. He has drawn comparisons to Jamaal Charles and will likely take over as the leader of a committee.

The blocking up front will look similar except for Ali Marpet moving from center to left guard. The Buccaneers made Baltimore's Ryan Jensen the highest-paid center in the league with a four-year deal worth $42 million and $22 million guaranteed. That's an unexpected payday for a player with 25 career starts who only took over as a full-time starter last season, his fifth in the league after being drafted in the sixth round in 2013. To Jensen's credit, Baltimore's running game was one of the very few positives about its offense last year. However, this is not like adding a perennial All-Pro center. It's not as big as Atlanta adding Alex Mack in 2016.

Jensen can aid in the improvement of this line, but he alone won't move the needle in Tampa Bay. The initial blocking was actually passable for Tampa Bay last year, which wasn't the case in 2016 when the Buccaneers were 32nd in stuffed run rate and power situations. The 2017 line ranked 16th in adjusted line yards, but the running game was especially bad at second-level yards (ranked 31st) and open-field yards (ranked 30th). The running backs simply couldn't produce on their own after getting past their initial blocks. This may be a case where Jones living up to the Charles comparisons and breaking a few long runs makes the difference in 2018.

Defense has to be where Tampa Bay improves the most. This is defensive coordinator Mike Smith's third year on the job. He was fired from his previous job as head coach in Atlanta after the 2014 Falcons finished 29th and 32nd in defensive DVOA in consecutive seasons. He seemed to have the Buccaneers moving in the right direction after a No. 13 finish in 2016, but a bad spell of injuries—Tampa Bay ranked 28th

Table 2. Tampa Bay's Run/Pass Splits in DVOA, 2015-2017

Year	1st Pass	Rk	1st Rush	Rk	3rd/4th Pass	Rk	3rd/4th Run	Rk	Red Zone Pass	Rk	Red Zone Run	Rk	All Pass	Rk	All Run	Rk
2015	45.0%	3	-7.4%	14	-14.5%	23	10.7%	16	16.5%	14	6.8%	13	13.0%	17	-6.1%	11
2016	22.0%	15	-33.8%	32	24.5%	8	-31.9%	31	24.5%	9	-28.1%	30	20.3%	12	-22.8%	30
2017	44.7%	6	-21.9%	25	34.7%	3	10.3%	21	15.4%	12	-15.9%	25	28.3%	9	-14.4%	25

in adjusted games lost on defense—and a horrific pass rush led the Bucs into last place in 2017. For those keeping count at home, that means three of Smith's last four defenses have finished in the bottom four in DVOA.

Last season's biggest problem was that Tampa Bay had the worst pass rush in the league. They had the lowest pressure rate (26.0 percent) according to Sports Info Solutions, and the fewest sacks in the league with just 22. That sounds even worse when you consider that nine of them were charted as non-pressure sacks, which includes coverage sacks, plays where the quarterback tripped over his own feet, and failed scrambles where the quarterback ran but an open hole closed before he got to the line of scrimmage. Tampa Bay also loaded up with six sacks of the Jets' Josh McCown, who has the second-worst career sack rate (8.3 percent) among active quarterbacks.

Smith did not force the issue much by blitzing from his traditional 4-3 front. Tampa Bay only sent five or more pass rushers on 19 percent of plays, the sixth-lowest rate in 2017. Tyrod Taylor and Brett Hundley were the only quarterbacks the Buccaneers were able to pressure over 30 percent of the time, and little blitzing was necessary to do that since those are two quarterbacks that like to hold the ball. By comparison, the Super Bowl-winning Eagles pressured 11 of the 19 quarterbacks they faced over a third of the time. According to ESPN Stats & Info, Tampa Bay had the lowest pressure rate in both the first quarter and the fourth quarter/overtime last year. They were also in the bottom five in the two quarters in between, so the pass rush was *consistently* nonexistent, which put a lot of pressure on a flawed secondary.

Even on the rare occasions when the Buccaneers got pressure, they still had the worst DVOA (-17.5%) in the league last year. This speaks more to that problematic secondary, where there are concerns over whether or not cornerback Vernon Hargreaves is a bust, and that the aging Brent Grimes (35 this year) might fall off a cliff. Tampa Bay used a pair of second-round picks on cornerbacks Carlton Davis (Auburn) and M.J. Stewart (North Carolina), but neither is likely a Week 1 starter.

The linebackers, led by Lavonte David, are good, and the secondary has a lot of young, high draft picks to develop. Licht's plan to solve the pass rush was to shed contracts of underperforming veterans and to bring in great talent in free agency. Gerald McCoy is still the foundation at defensive tackle, but he'll now be joined in the trenches by veteran additions Jason Pierre-Paul (Giants) and Vinny Curry (Eagles), as well as first-round rookie Vita Vea (Washington).

The selection of Vea took some by surprise given the defensive backs still on the board, but revamping this defensive line was clearly the top priority for Licht. Vea flashes great ability at times, but there are red flags in his scouting reports related to not correcting mistakes and concerns about being a threat to rush the passer at the next level. With his size and the focus opponents will put on his teammates, Vea could find early success at stopping the run, but he'll have to show something in the pass-rushing department for this pick to be praised.

Pierre-Paul (40 hurries) and Curry (27.5 hurries) both had more hurries last year than anyone on the Buccaneers. Curry only had 22 sacks in six years with the Eagles, but he was never

a full-time starter until last year as part of that great rotation Philadelphia had. He may have only had 3.0 sacks last year, but that's still more than any of Tampa Bay's edge rushers had. Pierre-Paul is still only 29 and should be the best edge rusher this defense has had since it let Michael Bennett get away after 2012. You have to go back to the days of Simeon Rice, Warren Sapp, and Derrick Brooks since the Buccaneers had this much talent in the front seven. We'll see if Smith can get this collection of talent to produce on the field.

Even if the offense and defense both improve, will yet another kicker screw things up again for Tampa Bay? Buccaneers special teams have been poor the last three years, but nothing symbolizes that struggle more than the kicker position. The three years in the Winston era have been three of Tampa Bay's four worst seasons since 1986 in value added on field goals and extra points.

Roberto Aguayo would live in infamy as the worst second-round pick of the 2016 draft, if not for the grace of Christian Hackenberg. The Buccaneers had to cut Aguayo last August, with the film crew of *Hard Knocks* present, after more poor kicks last preseason. With kicker being such a mental position, it is hard not to think that the high draft pick used on Aguayo negatively affected him. The pick was rightfully bashed as soon as it was made, and Aguayo seemed to succumb to the criticism immediately.

Worse, the Buccaneers have struggled to replace Aguayo. Nick Folk infamously missed three field goals in a winnable game against the Patriots. He was replaced by Patrick Murray, who did a better job, but still missed a 54-yard field goal that would have taken the Falcons to overtime in Week 15. A week later, Murray missed a 51-yard field goal in Carolina that would have given the Buccaneers a 22-15 lead with 3:00 left; they instead lost 22-19 after allowing a last-second touchdown. Chandler Catanzaro is the latest candidate to try to make us forget that Tampa Bay used a second-round pick on a kicker who completely bombed. Many have probably forgotten that the Buccaneers let Matt Bryant go in 2009 in favor of Mike Nugent. Since then, Bryant has been one of the greatest clutch kickers ever … for the rival Falcons.

The schedule-makers really did Tampa Bay no favors in getting off to a good start. Week 1 puts the Buccaneers back at the scene of the uneaten W in New Orleans, which is followed by two weeks of hosting Pennsylvania teams with Super Bowl aspirations. Even if Winston was not suspended and started those games instead of Ryan Fitzpatrick, an 0-3 start would be tough for this team to avoid. The schedule should lighten up considerably after that point, but the revamped defense is going to be tested immediately, and the offense has to be on point in September. We'll know if Tampa Bay is for real if it survives that stretch, but things could get ugly fast. The revamped trenches should be stronger, the offensive weapons are still the team's strength, and they'll just have to hope that the aerial defenses aren't as easily penetrated this time around. It all adds up to a better squad this year, but one that still likely will have to ration how many Ws it eats.

Scott Kacsmar

2017 Buccaneers Stats by Week

Wk	vs.	W-L	PF	PA	YDF	YDA	TO	Total	Off	Def	ST
1	BYE										
2	CHI	W	29	7	311	310	+3	28%	8%	-13%	7%
3	at MIN	L	17	34	342	494	-3	-22%	10%	37%	6%
4	NYG	W	25	23	434	379	0	11%	34%	14%	-10%
5	NE	L	14	19	409	402	+2	13%	22%	-20%	-29%
6	at ARI	L	33	38	412	432	0	-52%	8%	65%	5%
7	at BUF	L	27	30	447	434	-2	-22%	16%	40%	2%
8	CAR	L	3	17	279	254	-2	-22%	-28%	-10%	-4%
9	at NO	L	10	30	200	407	+1	-74%	-41%	22%	-12%
10	NYJ	W	15	10	271	275	+1	9%	-14%	-15%	8%
11	at MIA	W	30	20	321	448	+5	-2%	-1%	-9%	-10%
12	at ATL	L	20	34	373	516	+1	-28%	24%	49%	-4%
13	at GB	L	20	26	395	276	0	-28%	-12%	8%	-8%
14	DET	L	21	24	400	434	-2	-4%	8%	14%	2%
15	ATL	L	21	24	373	410	-1	26%	37%	5%	-5%
16	at CAR	L	19	22	392	255	-2	-24%	-8%	-7%	-24%
17	NO	W	31	24	455	323	-2	2%	15%	0%	-13%

Trends and Splits

	Offense	Rank	Defense	Rank
Total DVOA	5.2%	11	11.7%	32
Unadjusted VOA	1.0%	14	12.1%	32
Weighted Trend	3.3%	14	11.5%	30
Variance	4.6%	7	6.4%	22
Average Opponent	-0.6%	16	1.6%	12
Passing	28.3%	9	26.4%	31
Rushing	-14.4%	25	-5.1%	19
First Down	7.6%	8	10.9%	29
Second Down	-6.0%	21	2.8%	20
Third Down	20.5%	3	26.5%	31
First Half	-7.0%	21	9.5%	29
Second Half	17.6%	6	13.9%	29
Red Zone	-3.7%	18	15.2%	30
Late and Close	8.3%	10	9.1%	25

Five-Year Performance

Year	W-L	Pyth W	Est W	PF	PA	TO	Total	Rk	Off	Rk	Def	Rk	ST	Rk	Off AGL	Rk	Def AGL	Rk	Off Age	Rk	Def Age	Rk	ST Age	Rk
2013	4-12	5.3	6.3	288	389	+10	-5.1%	19	-10.4%	24	-6.8%	8	-1.5%	22	75.6	31	9.6	2	27.0	16	25.0	32	26.2	11
2014	2-14	4.4	4.1	277	410	-8	-28.3%	30	-26.3%	32	1.1%	18	-0.8%	17	31.1	17	56.1	25	27.5	7	25.7	30	26.0	18
2015	6-10	6.0	6.7	342	417	-5	-9.1%	21	-1.1%	17	3.3%	18	-4.7%	30	42.2	21	32.8	20	25.9	27	25.9	28	26.2	16
2016	9-7	7.6	7.2	354	369	+2	-3.0%	22	-4.1%	19	-2.9%	13	-1.8%	20	59.6	28	17.9	6	25.7	28	26.2	21	25.8	22
2017	5-11	6.7	6.2	335	382	-1	-12.0%	23	5.2%	11	11.7%	32	-5.5%	29	26.3	9	52.3	28	26.2	27	27.0	7	25.9	12

2017 Performance Based on Most Common Personnel Groups

TB Offense					TB Offense vs. Opponents					TB Defense					TB Defense vs. Opponents			
Pers	Freq	Yds	DVOA	Run%	Pers	Freq	Yds	DVOA	Run%	Pers	Freq	Yds	DVOA		Pers	Freq	Yds	DVOA
11	62%	6.2	19.5%	21%	Base	29%	5.4	0.5%	56%	Base	36%	5.5	2.0%		11	56%	6.5	17.8%
12	22%	5.4	4.2%	49%	Nickel	60%	6.1	12.1%	25%	Nickel	62%	6.6	18.2%		12	18%	5.2	2.4%
13	7%	5.7	3.4%	66%	Dime+	9%	5.9	47.3%	7%	Dime+	0%	0.7	-39.1%		21	11%	7.4	32.6%
21	3%	3.7	-19.7%	41%	Goal Line	2%	0.6	17.9%	74%	Goal Line	1%	1.8	10.6%		13	3%	4.5	-42.7%
612	2%	4.3	16.3%	70%											22	3%	4.9	-22.1%
															10	3%	6.1	17.0%

Strategic Tendencies

Run/Pass		Rk	Formation		Rk	Pass Rush		Rk	Secondary		Rk	Strategy		Rk
Runs, first half	35%	29	Form: Single Back	77%	18	Rush 3	3.8%	25	4 DB	36%	11	Play action	21%	22
Runs, first down	45%	26	Form: Empty Back	8%	16	Rush 4	77.3%	4	5 DB	62%	11	Avg Box (Off)	6.22	21
Runs, second-long	22%	32	Pers: 3+ WR	63%	17	Rush 5	12.1%	29	6+ DB	0%	30	Avg Box (Def)	6.26	15
Runs, power sit.	52%	19	Pers: 2+ TE/6+ OL	34%	10	Rush 6+	6.9%	12	CB by Sides	91%	5	Offensive Pace	29.83	11
Runs, behind 2H	26%	22	Pers: 6+ OL	3%	20	Int DL Sacks	52.3%	1	S/CB Cover Ratio	24%	25	Defensive Pace	29.97	7
Pass, ahead 2H	52%	7	Shotgun/Pistol	49%	28	Second Level Sacks	9.1%	29	DB Blitz	5%	29	Go for it on 4th	1.03	14

The Bucs ran less often than the season before in most every situation, going from ninth to 29th in run/pass ratio in the first half of games and from fifth to 26th on first downs. ✎ Despite the drafting of O.J. Howard, the Bucs' usage of two-tight end sets actually went down slightly, from 37 percent to 34 percent. ✎ Tampa Bay continues to have problems gaining yards after the catch, finishing 29th with an average of 4.3 YAC after ranking dead last with 3.9 average YAC in 2016. ✎ The Bucs also finished tied for 31st with 84 broken tackles and dead last with a broken tackle on just 7.1 percent of their offensive plays. They had a league-low 50 broken tackles combined from all their running backs. Ronald Jones to the rescue? ✎ The Bucs rarely run the ball from shotgun formations. They had 40 running back carries from shotgun last season, ahead of only Arizona. ✎ Tampa Bay's defense did one thing well: they gave away a league-low 229 yards on penalties, when every other defense was at 296 yards or higher. It helped that Tampa Bay was called for only five defensive pass interference penalties, and only one above 10 yards.

Passing

Player	DYAR	DVOA	Plays	NtYds	Avg	YAC	C%	TD	Int
J.Winston	779	14.3%	474	3288	6.9	4.4	64.2%	19	11
R.Fitzpatrick	307	17.3%	170	1059	6.2	4.1	59.3%	7	3

Rushing

Player	DYAR	DVOA	Plays	Yds	Avg	TD	Fum	Suc
D.Martin*	-77	-22.5%	138	405	2.9	3	1	35%
P.Barber	63	4.4%	108	423	3.9	3	2	57%
J.Rodgers	2	-7.7%	64	244	3.8	1	0	41%
J.Winston	-14	-21.7%	27	132	4.9	1	2	-
C.Sims*	9	2.9%	21	95	4.5	0	0	33%
R.Fitzpatrick	17	17.5%	12	81	6.8	0	0	-

Receiving

Player	DYAR	DVOA	Plays	Ctch	Yds	Y/C	YAC	TD	C%
M.Evans	149	1.2%	136	71	1004	14.1	1.7	5	52%
D.Jackson	105	1.6%	90	50	668	13.4	3.8	3	56%
A.Humphries	112	5.1%	83	61	631	10.3	4.6	1	73%
C.Godwin	138	20.5%	55	34	525	15.4	5.0	1	62%
F.Martino	41	88.6%	6	5	96	19.2	7.0	0	83%
C.Brate	154	24.7%	77	48	591	12.3	3.0	6	62%
O.J.Howard	101	32.2%	39	26	433	16.7	5.8	6	67%
A.Cross	19	39.6%	6	5	58	11.6	6.0	0	83%
C.Sims*	1	-13.4%	47	35	252	7.2	6.4	1	74%
P.Barber	3	-11.1%	19	16	114	7.1	7.1	0	84%
D.Martin*	-18	-30.4%	18	9	84	9.3	6.7	0	50%
J.Rodgers	24	30.5%	11	9	74	8.2	9.8	0	82%

Offensive Line

Player	Pos	Age	GS	Snaps	Pen	Sk	Pass	Run	Player	Pos	Age	GS	Snaps	Pen	Sk	Pass	Run
Donovan Smith	LT	25	16/16	1064	9	7.5	33	9	Evan Smith	LG/C	32	15/6	688	5	3.5	14	3
J.R. Sweezy*	RG	28	14/14	903	6	2.5	8	15	Caleb Benenoch	RT	24	13/5	364	3	6.0	14	3
Kevin Pamphile*	LG	28	16/15	787	2	3.0	14	4	Joe Hawley*	C	30	4/2	208	2	0.0	1	0
Ali Marpet	C	25	11/11	723	4	1.5	9	8	*Ryan Jensen*	C	27	16/16	1086	3	2.0	7	7
Demar Dotson	RT	33	11/11	715	6	2.0	13	4									

Year	Yards	ALY	Rank	Power	Rank	Stuff	Rank	2nd Lev	Rank	Open Field	Rank	Sacks	ASR	Rank	Press	Rank	F-Start	Cont.
2015	4.86	4.36	9	71%	8	20%	13	1.20	13	1.40	1	27	5.8%	14	29.3%	26	19	25
2016	3.61	4.01	21	47%	32	24%	32	1.06	25	0.45	28	35	5.9%	16	29.9%	26	16	32
2017	3.53	4.06	16	65%	12	20%	17	0.93	31	0.41	30	40	6.5%	16	30.5%	14	18	34

2017 ALY by direction: Left End: 2.87 (27)   Left Tackle: 4.59 (10)   Mid/Guard: 4.15 (16)   Right Tackle: 4.66 (4)   Right End: 3.37 (25)

This has not been a unit of strength for quite some time, but the Buccaneers tried to do something flashy in free agency. Unfortunately, it's not a move that analytics will support. It's like they never say: "When you have someone who was only good enough to win a starting job once in five years for one of the worst offenses in the league, you just have to make him the highest-paid player at his position." At $10.5 million per season, the Buccaneers made Ryan Jensen the highest-paid center in the league after one season as a full-time starter. Jensen finished 10th in snaps per blown block with the Ravens in 2017. He may have held up well enough for Joe Flacco to throw 4-yard darts in under 2.5 seconds, but Jameis Winston is known for holding the ball longer to throw deep. ✎ The Jensen move will allow Ali Marpet to move to left guard after 2017's failed center experiment. Marpet believes that the transition from right guard to left guard is easier than moving from right guard to center, especially since he'll be playing between "good players" in Jensen and left tackle Donovan Smith. Marpet and Smith were the first two picks Tampa Bay made in 2015 after taking Winston first overall, but they have not delivered yet. Smith allowed a team-high 7.5 sacks in 2017. We'll see if a contract year can bring out his best, or if Tampa Bay should just move on in the offseason. ✎ Guard Evan Smith also struggled in pass protection last year. The team drafted Alex Cappa in the third round, but it's far from a given that he'll slide into the right guard job—particularly since he is trying to transition from Division II Humboldt State to the NFL. (Then again, Marpet went from Division III Hobart to 13 starts as a rookie.) General manager Jason Licht has said that Cappa could eventually play all five positions on the offensive line, which sounds like nice GM code for "we don't know how we'll develop this college kid." Tampa Bay released J.R. Sweezy in late June, leaving an open competition at right guard between Smith, Cappa, and 2016 fifth-round pick Caleb Benenoch. ☞ One success story for Tampa Bay has been right tackle Demar Dotson, signed by the Bucs as an undrafted free agent in 2009. He has charted out as the team's best offensive lineman in each of the last two seasons, ranking as high as 13th in snaps per blown block in 2017.

Defensive Front Seven

Defensive Line	Age	Pos	G	Snaps	Plays	Overall TmPct	Rk	Stop	Dfts	BTkl	Runs	vs. Run St%	Rk	RuYd	Rk	Pass Rush Sack	Hit	Hur	Dsrpt
Gerald McCoy	30	DT	15	810	48	6.2%	20	38	19	1	38	76%	50	1.4	15	6.0	21	26.5	3
Clinton McDonald*	31	DT	14	467	30	4.1%	61	20	8	3	19	53%	84	3.9	85	5.0	5	7.5	1
Chris Baker*	31	DT	15	457	34	4.4%	55	25	4	2	29	69%	73	2.4	62	0.5	4	7.5	3
Beau Allen	27	DT	15	422	20	2.8%	83	17	6	1	19	84%	18	1.4	13	1.0	2	9.0	0

Edge Rushers	Age	Pos	G	Snaps	Plays	Overall TmPct	Rk	Stop	Dfts	BTkl	Runs	vs. Run St%	Rk	RuYd	Rk	Pass Rush Sack	Hit	Hur	Dsrpt
Robert Ayers*	33	DE	12	589	31	5.0%	48	22	7	7	26	73%	54	2.4	51	2.0	18	26.5	1
Ryan Russell*	26	DE	14	459	16	2.2%	94	10	2	2	13	62%	86	2.5	57	2.0	4	17.5	0
William Gholston	27	DE	14	447	36	5.0%	49	25	5	2	36	69%	69	2.2	41	0.0	1	4.5	0
Will Clarke	27	DE	15	315	14	1.8%	--	10	3	3	9	67%	--	2.9	--	2.5	2	8.0	1
Jason Pierre-Paul	29	DE	16	1011	71	8.6%	7	53	20	5	52	71%	61	2.5	55	8.5	5	40.0	4
Vinny Curry	30	DE	16	578	42	5.5%	39	36	14	5	37	84%	20	1.1	14	3.0	20	27.5	2
Mitch Unrein	31	DE	12	389	31	5.1%	43	25	5	3	27	85%	12	2.0	37	1.5	3	4.5	0

Linebackers	Age	Pos	G	Snaps	Plays	Overall TmPct	Rk	Stop	Dfts	BTkl	Runs	vs. Run St%	Rk	RuYd	Rk	Pass Rush Sack	Hit	Hur	vs. Pass Tgts	Suc%	Rk	AdjYd	Rk	PD	Int
Kendell Beckwith	24	OLB	16	850	75	9.1%	69	46	16	6	45	64%	36	3.4	36	1.0	1	5.0	39	61%	7	5.0	11	2	0
Lavonte David	28	OLB	13	817	101	15.0%	20	68	23	10	61	80%	5	4.3	68	0.0	3	11.0	35	39%	66	7.7	58	1	0
Kwon Alexander	24	MLB	12	723	101	16.3%	13	62	19	24	55	75%	10	2.3	8	0.0	4	13.0	37	37%	69	10.5	75	3	3
Adarius Glanton	28	MLB	14	285	27	3.7%	--	16	6	6	17	65%	--	2.5	--	1.0	1	4.5	19	55%	--	4.9	--	1	0
Korey Toomer	30	MLB	15	266	50	6.5%	--	31	5	5	35	71%	--	4.2	--	1.0	1	1.0	14	72%	1	4.3	2	2	1

Year	Yards	ALY	Rank	Power	Rank	Stuff	Rank	2nd Level	Rank	Open Field	Rank	Sacks	ASR	Rank	Press	Rank
2015	3.55	4.06	15	69%	23	21%	16	1.07	13	0.29	1	38	7.6%	5	24.4%	23
2016	4.20	4.53	26	57%	5	19%	17	1.29	27	0.57	9	38	7.1%	6	24.7%	25
2017	4.18	4.16	20	62%	13	21%	14	1.19	21	0.84	24	22	4.3%	32	24.8%	32

2017 ALY by direction: Left End: 3.27 (10)   Left Tackle: 5.31 (32)   Mid/Guard: 4.11 (14)   Right Tackle: 3.82 (16)   Right End: 4.40 (22)

This was the worst defense at creating pressure last season, and the brunt of blame falls on the front seven. The odd part is this wasn't a unit lacking in talent or experience. Gerald McCoy and Robert Ayers each racked up 27 hurries, but only combined for 8.0 sacks. McCoy's 6.0 sacks were his fewest since 2012, though he will only be 30 this season and should bounce back. Ayers was one of 55 players with at least 25 hurries last season, but one of only four to have fewer than 3.0 sacks. The Buccaneers did not retain a trio of veterans along the defensive line as Ayers, Chris Baker, and Clinton McDonald are no longer with the team. ☞ McCoy has plenty of new help around him after the team acquired Jason Pierre-Paul, Vinny Curry, and first-round rookie Vita Vea to create a new defensive line. ☞ We are used to praising Lavonte David (The Stop Machine), but 2017 was his quietest season yet. David did not register a sack or an interception, and he only defensed one pass. He also missed three games in a season for the first time in his career. David still had a team-high 68 stops, but Kwon Alexander had a comparable season, and actually made the Pro Bowl as an alternate. ☞ Strongside linebacker Kendell Beckwith's rookie season was never a sure thing after he was recovering from a torn ACL he suffered at LSU. He ended up playing in every game for the Buccaneers and even started games at all three linebacker positions. His rookie season was respectable against both the pass and run. For the second year in a row Beckwith's health will be a topic going into training camp. He was involved in a car accident in April and required surgery for a fractured ankle.

Defensive Secondary

Secondary	Age	Pos	G	Snaps	Plays	TmPct	Rk	Stop	Dfts	BTkl	Runs	St%	Rk	RuYd	Rk	Tgts	Tgt%	Rk	Dist	Suc%	Rk	AdjYd	Rk	PD	Int
													Overall → vs. Run								**vs. Pass**				
Brent Grimes	35	CB	13	850	60	8.9%	35	26	10	6	14	43%	42	5.4	23	67	16.9%	18	12.6	55%	18	8.3	58	11	3
Chris Conte	29	SS	16	775	83	10.0%	38	26	6	13	34	41%	47	6.3	40	29	8.0%	25	11.3	50%	44	7.7	33	6	1
Justin Evans	23	FS	14	716	70	9.7%	46	20	9	11	26	27%	64	9.8	63	29	8.7%	32	15.0	45%	62	12.8	73	6	3
Robert McClain*	30	CB	14	695	51	7.0%	63	16	10	6	10	50%	32	5.7	32	50	15.2%	11	9.7	37%	80	8.3	59	4	3
Ryan Smith	25	CB	15	597	66	8.5%	39	18	6	7	19	26%	70	8.3	65	65	23.1%	62	14.1	47%	62	9.1	70	5	0
Vernon Hargreaves	23	CB	9	501	47	10.1%	17	17	4	7	14	64%	12	4.0	9	54	23.1%	61	14.4	45%	76	7.8	42	6	0
T.J. Ward*	32	SS	12	409	44	7.1%	--	16	5	4	25	40%	--	7.2	--	15	7.6%	--	12.3	35%	--	11.4	--	3	0

Year	Pass D Rank	vs. #1 WR	Rk	vs. #2 WR	Rk	vs. Other WR	Rk	WR Wide	Rk	WR Slot	Rk	vs. TE	Rk	vs. RB	Rk
2015	26	-1.4%	16	41.6%	32	34.0%	32	--	--	--	--	2.9%	18	-8.0%	10
2016	6	-5.5%	8	-2.1%	13	-18.5%	6	-12.5%	7	-4.7%	9	-22.4%	4	16.6%	26
2017	31	0.9%	15	8.4%	21	21.0%	27	2.5%	21	14.6%	22	6.1%	22	13.3%	25

He'll be 35 this season, but Brent Grimes is likely still the best cornerback in Tampa Bay. He re-signed a one-year deal that could be worth up to $10 million with incentives. ☞ We like to give highly-drafted cornerbacks a pass for bad rookie years, but Vernon Hargreaves isn't trending in the right direction. He has one pick in 25 games and his coverage success rate was almost identical from his rookie year (44.83 percent) to his second year (44.86 percent). That's a number that puts him 69th or lower in each of the last two years. Last year he was moved to the slot and missed seven games with an injury, so this is a big year for him to prove he was worth the 11th pick in the draft. ☞ Cornerback Ryan Smith's first attempt at starting did not go well either, so it's no surprise that Tampa Bay added corners Carlton Davis (Auburn) and M.J. Stewart (North Carolina) in the second round. Stewart has drawn comparisons to Micah Hyde and could easily fill a third safety spot if desired. Davis only had four interceptions in college, but he has been praised for playing press coverage against SEC athletes. These players should see plenty of action this year as Tampa Bay searches for answers at corner. ☞ Things are a bit clearer at safety. Chris Conte has never been great, but he wasn't a liability last season. Without the veteran presence of Grimes and Conte, this unit would really be a collection of young misfits. Keith Tandy has been with the team since 2012, but has never started more than five games in a season. Justin Evans, a 2017 second-round pick, should be in the mix to start again, but his rookie season was rough against both the run and pass.

Special Teams

Year	DVOA	Rank	FG/XP	Rank	Net Kick	Rank	Kick Ret	Rank	Net Punt	Rank	Punt Ret	Rank	Hidden	Rank
2015	-4.7%	30	-17.5	32	-3.1	23	0.2	12	1.1	17	-4.3	21	2.8	11
2016	-1.8%	20	-15.0	32	2.6	11	-8.9	32	13.6	2	-1.2	16	9.6	6
2017	-5.5%	29	-13.2	31	-14.4	32	-0.6	16	0.2	18	0.3	14	-1.2	14

Tampa Bay fielded below-average special teams for the sixth year in a row. ☞ The struggle to replace kicker Roberto Aguayo has been real. Patrick Murray did a better job than Nick Folk, but he also had the league's lowest touchback rate (23.7 percent) last year, which may not have been a terrible thing since the new rule moved touchbacks to the 25-yard line. However, Murray was the only kicker to have two kickoffs returned for touchdowns in 2017. The rest of the league allowed five combined. ☞ Chandler Catanzaro is the latest kicker to try reversing Tampa Bay's luck. He finished 10th in net points above average for the Jets last year. ☞ Punter Bryan Anger had the second-lowest gross punt value (-8.1 points) last year, but at least his coverage units were good on punt returns. ☞ Stop me if you've heard this one before: Tampa Bay's return units were nothing special and did not score a touchdown. The Buccaneers haven't had a kick or punt return touchdown since 2010, the longest active drought in the NFL. Backup running back Jacquizz Rodgers did a mediocre job on kick returns and could hold that job again. Adam Humphries may be the favorite to take over punt returns after he only had six returns last season.

Tennessee Titans

2017 Record: 9-7	Total DVOA: -5.6% (18th)	2018 Mean Projection: 8.0 wins	On the Clock (0-4): 9%
Pythagorean Wins: 7.4 (16th)	Offense: -2.1% (18th)	Postseason Odds: 37.8%	Mediocrity (5-7): 33%
Snap-Weighted Age: 26.7 (10th)	Defense: 5.1% (21st)	Super Bowl Odds: 4.6%	Playoff Contender (8-10): 41%
Average Opponent: -4.3% (30th)	Special Teams: 1.6% (13th)	Proj. Avg. Opponent: -1.7% (26th)	Super Bowl Contender (11+): 17%

2017: If nothing changes, nothing changes.

2018: I think a change (a change) would do you good.

You are what your record says you are.

It's the most *football* of football truisms. Winning cures everything. Better a playoff team by record than a DVOA darling stuck at home in January. It doesn't matter how you win, as long as you win. *Hello? You play. To win. The game.*

Our research paints a different, more nuanced picture. Wins are wins, for sure; but there is a notable difference between a winning season in the NFC South, one of the league's toughest divisions which sent three teams to the playoffs, and a winning season in the AFC South, in which two of your division opponents missed their franchise quarterbacks for more than half the year and the other never had one to begin with. Most of the time, such nuances are lost on franchise owners concerned solely with the bottom line. When news broke that much-maligned head coach Mike Mularkey had been offered an extension by the Titans, it appeared that Amy Adams Strunk was just one more such owner. It is to the credit of Strunk that, as news broke later the same day that Mularkey had rejected the conditions attached to the contract offer, her decision on the future of the franchise appears to have been affected by more than simply the win/loss columns.

In defense of Mularkey, the Titans are in a much better place now than they were when he took over from Ken Whisenhunt in November 2015. Then, the team was 1-6 en route to a second straight season of three or fewer wins. Many of the key components were in place for a successful team: quarterback Marcus Mariota was a rookie, but Delanie Walker, Taylor Lewan, and Jurrell Casey among others were established starters on a roster that was far superior to its record. Two years later, those four players are key components of a franchise which won as many games in Mularkey's two full seasons as it had in the previous four. Tennessee even picked up its first playoff win in 14 years—or to put it another way, since *Steve McNair* was the quarterback—with a come-from-behind victory in Kansas City. The Titans are not a bad team, and certainly not the type of bad team that usually gets the coach fired.

Instead, what the Titans were under Mularkey was a distinctly average team. A cursory glance at the roster and statistics across the first two seasons shows a team that was competent at everything, had no glaring weaknesses or roster holes, and was even quite good at its quaint staple diet of "run the ball and stop the run" (ranking eighth and seventh in DVOA in those respective categories). It also had no outstanding strengths—no elite pass rush, no shutdown secondary, no truly dominant run or pass offense, nor even a deadly return game. The Titans led the league in only one category: punting, where Brett Kern had both the highest gross and net average punt distance. Against one of the league's easiest schedules—third-easiest in 2016, second-easiest in 2017—Mularkey's Titans were just solid enough to get blown out by the first truly elite team they came up against, as evidenced not only by the 35-14 playoff defeat in New England but also the 40-17 regular-season shellacking in Pittsburgh and the 57-14 evisceration by the Deshaun Watson Texans.

Still, few NFL coaches get their first job taking over a team that was good enough to win a playoff game the previous year. Mike Vrabel inherits a solid, fundamentally sound roster. The few additions made by general manager Jon Robinson have specifically targeted areas in need of improvement: an edge rusher, a cover linebacker, a third cornerback, and injury cover on the offensive line. With some development from their young receiving corps, the Titans should have enough roster pieces to contend again for a wild-card berth, or even a division title if results break their way elsewhere. The difference—the critical, make-or-break difference—will be coaching.

The new coaching staff's first priority should be fixing the pass defense. Dick LeBeau was a pedigreed, acclaimed defensive coordinator and an innovator in his heyday, but the 80-year-old's more recent defenses have failed to replicate the success he enjoyed earlier in his career. In his three years in Tennessee, LeBeau never coached the pass defense to a DVOA rank higher than 24th. Including playoff games, the Titans allowed 35 or more points eight times in LeBeau's three seasons, fourth-most behind only the Saints (12), Jaguars (nine), and 49ers (nine). They ranked 26th in regular-season points allowed over that span, 29th in passing touchdowns, and 25th in field goal attempts against. They also ranked in the bottom quarter in interception rate and turnover rate—highly inconsistent metrics from year to year that tell a more persuasive story over a three-year period. (It was also a prominent criticism of LeBeau's final few seasons in Pittsburgh.) Though LeBeau had hoped to remain in Tennessee when Vrabel was hired, it was no surprise to see the team move on.

It was more of a surprise to see them hire another elder statesman. Dean Pees had announced his retirement after almost 40 years of coaching defense in the NCAA and then the

2018 Titans Schedule

Week	Opp.	Week	Opp.	Week	Opp.
1	at MIA	7	at LAC (U.K.)	13	NYJ
2	HOU	8	BYE	14	JAX (Thu.)
3	at JAX	9	at DAL (Mon.)	15	at NYG
4	PHI	10	NE	16	WAS
5	at BUF	11	at IND	17	IND
6	BAL	12	at HOU (Mon.)		

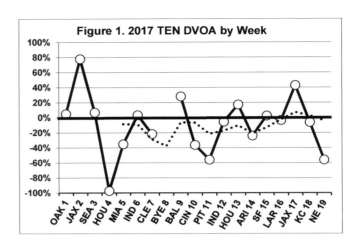

Figure 1. 2017 TEN DVOA by Week

NFL, but he was persuaded by a persistent Vrabel to join the staff of a player he coached during his time in New England. Pees had his critics in Baltimore, but the Ravens defense finished in the top half of the DVOA table five times in his six years as defensive coordinator, and the pass defense ranked second behind only the Jaguars in 2017. The only time the Ravens defense dropped out of the top half of the league was in 2015, when injuries annihilated the team's entire offense; Matt Schaub threw as many touchdowns to Ravens opponents as to Ravens teammates; and the defense lost its best player, Terrell Suggs, in Week 2 to a torn Achilles.

Where LeBeau built his reputation on a disguised pass rush so that the offensive line did not know who was rushing from where, Pees is more likely to switch up and conceal his coverages in an effort to deceive the quarterback. In Baltimore, the versatility of Eric Weddle and Lardarius Webb made the disguise all the more effective, and when the equally adroit Tony Jefferson was added to the mix last season the pass defense became one of the league's best. Tennessee's starting safety pair is not quite so adaptable: Kevin Byard is a deserved All-Pro who can certainly play multiple roles, but Johnathan Cyprien is much more of a run-stuffer than a coverage defender. This may mean more opportunities for Kendrick Lewis or Brynden Trawick, both of whom played under Pees in Baltimore, or it may signal the team's intentions for the development of fifth-round pick Dane Cruikshank. Alternatively, one of the team's deep pool of cornerbacks could be deployed as a situational safety.

Farther forward, Pees has stated his desire to run multiple fronts, basing his packages and schemes on the players available rather than a specific, ordained system. Pees did this during his time in both New England and Baltimore, so there is little reason to doubt that he will do something similar in Tennessee. The most common defensive line is likely to be a three-man look very similar to last season. Jurrell Casey will obviously man one spot, primarily as a 5-technique end in base defense. The other end spot will probably go to DaQuan Jones, whose 2017 season was ended by a torn biceps in early December. Jones can play either tackle or end in a 3-4, but he is more likely to be an end in base packages. That would leave classic two-gap plugger Bennie Logan as the most likely nose tackle, though Austin Johnson will compete for those snaps. David King projects as a rotational backup in this base alignment.

Those potential four-man configurations are more variable. We have seen star 3-4 defensive ends be effective when deployed as situational 3-technique tackles before—Calais Campbell needs no introduction to followers of the AFC South—and there is plenty of reason to believe that Casey could be effective in that role. King is not a dynamic edge rusher, but he is closer to a traditional 4-3 strong-side defensive end than a natural 5-technique. Though Jones appears to have found a home at 3-4 defensive end, he has extensive college experience as a 4-3 defensive tackle. Edge rushers Derrick Morgan and Brian Orakpo are equally comfortable standing up or with a hand in the dirt, and second-round rookie Harold Landry is a college defensive end transitioning to NFL outside linebacker who should be perfectly happy on a four-man defensive line. Off-ball linebacker was more of a question entering the offseason, but first-round pick Rashaan Evans should slot in neatly beside Wesley Woodyard in either system, with last year's emergent starter Jayon Brown on hand to bolster the rotation. If Pees can weave those pieces together into a cohesive tapestry, the Titans could be a less predictable defensive front even after moving on from the master of the zone blitz.

On the other side of the ball, the offense under new coordinator Matt LaFleur will be drastically different from what we saw throughout Mularkey's two-year reign. Gone is the power-based "exotic smashmouth" ground-and-pound, replaced by a heavy dose of Kubiak-Shanahan outside zone. When Mularkey was in charge, he was often criticized for effectively having two offenses: his preferred power running game for first and second downs, and a completely separate offense of shotgun-based pass plays for those times when the regular offense stuck them in a hole. Not so under LaFleur: the entire system is, in his words, "predicated on a marriage between the running game and the passing game." The entire offense is designed to flow around the staple diet of outside zone, with plays packaged together so that runs and passes start out looking like the exact same play. Expect a heavy dose of play-action: between Kyle Shanahan and Sean McVay, LaFleur's last two bosses have not finished lower than seventh over the past three seasons in the percentage of pass plays that incorporated a play-fake. The two teams that had winning records—the 2016 Falcons and 2017 Rams—ranked first and second in the league respectively. In comparison, the Titans ranked 14th in this category in 2016 and 11th in 2017.

Given LaFleur's background with Kyle Shanahan, much has been made of the athleticism of Marcus Mariota, occasionally with a wistful glance at what might have been for Robert Griffin in Washington. Kyle Shanahan is on record stating that roughly 70 percent of that offense was *also* based around outside zone, with other concepts mixed in to play off the additional threat presented by his exceptionally quick and agile quarterback. LaFleur was the quarterbacks coach for that Washington team, and will almost certainly have learned from that experience—both the good and the bad. He has expressed his excitement about working with the particular skill set possessed by Mariota, but he has also stated over and again that Mariota's health is absolutely key to the success of the offense. If Mariota's mobility is to be a key feature, a better comparison might be Jake Plummer for the mid-2000s Broncos: a heavy dose of bootlegs and boot actions, with moving pockets to disrupt the pass rush and stretch defenses horizontally at the line of scrimmage. It is a formula that worked well not only for Plummer (three straight top-ten seasons in DYAR), but also for the less mobile quintet of Jay Cutler, Kirk Cousins, Matt Ryan, Jared Goff, and Jimmy Garoppolo.

Indeed, if the 2016 Falcons offense is to be the template for this season's Titans, then it is easy to see how the pieces fit together in Nashville. Derrick Henry and Dion Lewis make a passable adumbration of Devonta Freeman and Tevin Coleman, while Taywan Taylor has been expected from Day 1 to fill the role of Taylor Gabriel. Julio Jones is his own special player, but LaFleur's enthusiasm for Corey Davis is already evident and there is a lot of similarity in the size and physique of the two. Davis battled injury throughout his rookie season, most notably a bad ankle that kept him out early in the summer and a finicky hamstring problem during the regular season. He finally caught his first two touchdown passes in the playoff defeat at New England and is expected to contribute much more with a full offseason under his belt.

Notably, Delanie Walker is a better receiving tight end than anybody the Falcons had in 2016. Typically, tight ends in this scheme account for around 20 to 25 percent of pass targets, or roughly 100 to 120 per year, but those Falcons only targeted Jacob Tamme, Tony Moeaki, Austin Hooper, and Levine Toilolo a total of 175 times over two seasons (15 percent of 1,147 attempts). Walker alone has accounted for a 22 percent share of the Titans passing game over the past two seasons. We may see that number fall slightly as Jonnu Smith is worked more into the passing game, but Walker does provide a threat from the one position the 2016 Falcons noticeably lacked.

This is, it must be said, an absolute best-case scenario that is unlikely to be realized immediately in 2018, if at all. Even that Falcons team, with a quarterback who would be a surefire Hall of Fame player if he played for one of a dozen other franchises and a star receiver who should achieve that goal regardless, finished a mere 23rd in offensive DVOA after hiring Kyle Shanahan as offensive coordinator in 2015. It took until the end of their second offseason for them to finally get their stuff together. The success of Sean McVay with Jared Goff and the immediate impact of Jimmy Garoppolo with Kyle Shanahan should not blind us to the larger picture: these things usually take some time.

Time, at least, the new coaching staff should have. Vrabel was hired on a reported five-year contract, though such long-term deals often come with an escape route somewhere along the line. LaFleur will have the security of being the rookie head coach's first pick as an assistant, a highly sought-after offensive coach who, unless he flops disastrously, is more likely to leave at his leisure for the head coaching vacancy of his choice than to be given his marching orders if things are not immediately spectacular.

All of which makes the Titans a much more interesting prospect in 2018 than they looked set to be in early January. Had the owner retained Mike Mularkey, this would have been one of the simplest teams to project in 2018. They did not, and they are substantially more intriguing for that. The head coach has never been a head coach in the NFL before. The young offensive coordinator has one year of experience in that role but has never been a playcaller before; Sean McVay retained those responsibilities in Los Angeles, and thus claims most of the credit for that Rams offense. Likewise, the 2016 Falcons offense is mostly credited to Kyle Shanahan. We have never seen LaFleur away from those mentors, but we know that he will change the Tennessee offense a lot next year strategically despite using mostly the same personnel. Ultimately, those 2017 Rams and 2016 Falcons might tell us more about how the 2018 Titans approach the game on offense than either the 2017 or 2016 Titans.

Defensively, Pees coached the league's second-best pass defense last year but still had his critics in Baltimore, in large part due to a perception that Pees' defense was at its worst when it was needed most, protecting a narrow lead late in the fourth quarter. He will not be short of talent, particularly in the secondary, and now has a deeper group of defensive linemen and a trio of enticing edge rushers who can each operate from either defensive end or outside linebacker spots.

Ultimately, under Mularkey, the concepts that helped make the Titans competitive also limited their ceiling. They were not particularly bad at anything but were not great at anything either. They parlayed an easy schedule into an eventual playoff berth but were never a threat to upset the established order in the AFC.

This year, the team's performance is likely to be much more variable. If everything gels together quickly during the course of the offseason, the Titans should be much better configured to win difficult games and be a genuine threat in a weak conference. If it does not, the transition period could mean fewer wins while they bind together the scheme and personnel. The owner appears to have one eye on the bigger picture, and the fans might be well-served to take the long view. To this outside observer, at least, this should be a very interesting football season in Nashville.

Andrew Potter

2017 Titans Stats by Week

Wk	vs.	W-L	PF	PA	YDF	YDA	TO	Total	Off	Def	ST
1	OAK	L	16	26	350	359	0	5%	21%	12%	-4%
2	at JAX	W	37	16	390	310	+2	78%	53%	-14%	12%
3	SEA	W	33	27	420	433	0	7%	35%	33%	5%
4	at HOU	L	14	57	195	445	-4	-97%	-56%	42%	1%
5	at MIA	L	10	16	188	178	0	-35%	-62%	-24%	2%
6	IND	W	36	22	473	297	0	3%	18%	14%	-1%
7	at CLE	W	12	9	269	284	+2	-22%	-38%	-16%	0%
8	BYE										
9	BAL	W	23	20	257	341	+1	28%	19%	-1%	9%
10	CIN	W	24	20	416	308	0	-36%	0%	27%	-9%
11	at PIT	L	17	40	316	349	-4	-56%	-36%	14%	-6%
12	at IND	W	20	16	276	254	-1	-5%	-6%	4%	5%
13	HOU	W	24	13	344	384	0	17%	29%	8%	-3%
14	at ARI	L	7	12	204	261	-2	-24%	-25%	-5%	-4%
15	at SF	L	23	25	328	414	-1	3%	14%	22%	10%
16	LAR	L	23	27	366	402	0	-3%	-2%	5%	3%
17	JAX	W	15	10	232	229	+3	43%	-13%	-49%	7%
18	at KC	W	22	21	397	325	-2	-6%	7%	16%	3%
19	at NE	L	14	35	267	438	0	-56%	-34%	19%	-4%

Trends and Splits

	Offense	Rank	Defense	Rank
Total DVOA	-2.2%	18	5.0%	21
Unadjusted VOA	-3.3%	19	2.3%	17
Weighted Trend	-6.1%	21	2.0%	18
Variance	11.0%	29	5.2%	12
Average Opponent	-1.0%	12	-5.4%	32
Passing	2.2%	19	18.9%	24
Rushing	1.0%	8	-15.6%	7
First Down	2.6%	15	3.4%	22
Second Down	-6.1%	22	10.6%	29
Third Down	-6.0%	21	-0.6%	14
First Half	-11.3%	23	1.8%	18
Second Half	7.1%	12	8.2%	24
Red Zone	11.1%	12	-9.6%	10
Late and Close	8.8%	9	-3.0%	16

Five-Year Performance

Year	W-L	Pyth W	Est W	PF	PA	TO	Total	Rk	Off	Rk	Def	Rk	ST	Rk	Off AGL	Rk	Def AGL	Rk	Off Age	Rk	Def Age	Rk	ST Age	Rk
2013	7-9	7.5	6.6	362	381	0	-6.1%	21	1.4%	16	4.2%	22	-3.2%	26	28.3	12	15.6	6	27.3	13	26.2	20	26.4	8
2014	2-14	3.3	4.0	254	438	-10	-29.3%	31	-16.4%	29	11.2%	29	-1.8%	20	38.8	22	40.9	19	27.0	14	27.0	10	26.7	2
2015	3-13	4.8	4.4	299	423	-14	-26.6%	31	-15.7%	32	7.1%	23	-3.8%	28	38.7	20	26.5	13	25.6	29	26.5	18	25.7	24
2016	9-7	8.1	8.7	381	378	0	3.5%	15	10.8%	9	6.4%	24	-1.0%	19	21.0	4	11.0	3	26.2	24	27.0	8	26.2	14
2017	9-7	7.4	7.6	334	356	-4	-5.7%	18	-2.2%	18	5.0%	21	1.6%	13	11.2	4	16.4	9	26.5	22	26.9	10	26.8	2

2017 Performance Based on Most Common Personnel Groups

TEN Offense

Pers	Freq	Yds	DVOA	Run%
11	45%	4.6	-19.6%	24%
12	21%	5.4	6.7%	52%
13	9%	5.4	3.8%	63%
21	9%	7.3	40.9%	51%
612	4%	8.2	67.6%	79%
22	4%	3.2	-11.3%	85%

TEN Offense vs. Opponents

Pers	Freq	Yds	DVOA	Run%
Base	48%	5.7	9.3%	59%
Nickel	42%	4.8	-10.8%	26%
Dime+	6%	4.7	-40.8%	5%
Goal Line	2%	1.1	44.8%	87%
Big	1%	14.8	134.0%	100%

TEN Defense

Pers	Freq	Yds	DVOA
Base	30%	4.3	-8.3%
Nickel	64%	5.3	7.2%
Dime+	5%	7.6	74.7%
Goal Line	0%	-1.5	-28.6%

TEN Defense vs. Opponents

Pers	Freq	Yds	DVOA
11	65%	5.5	10.0%
12	15%	4.6	-8.2%
21	9%	5.5	15.4%
13	3%	1.8	-40.2%
611	2%	4.1	-6.3%

Strategic Tendencies

Run/Pass		Rk	Formation		Rk	Pass Rush		Rk	Secondary		Rk	Strategy		Rk
Runs, first half	43%	2	Form: Single Back	72%	25	Rush 3	13.3%	7	4 DB	30%	19	Play action	23%	11
Runs, first down	48%	20	Form: Empty Back	7%	18	Rush 4	54.7%	29	5 DB	64%	8	Avg Box (Off)	6.40	4
Runs, second-long	46%	1	Pers: 3+ WR	49%	29	Rush 5	26.4%	6	6+ DB	5%	19	Avg Box (Def)	6.08	28
Runs, power sit.	64%	7	Pers: 2+ TE/6+ OL	43%	2	Rush 6+	5.6%	18	CB by Sides	83%	11	Offensive Pace	31.72	28
Runs, behind 2H	29%	10	Pers: 6+ OL	3%	15	Int DL Sacks	30.2%	11	S/CB Cover Ratio	23%	27	Defensive Pace	29.70	5
Pass, ahead 2H	44%	22	Shotgun/Pistol	56%	20	Second Level Sacks	24.4%	10	DB Blitz	12%	9	Go for it on 4th	0.76	26

For the second straight year, Tennessee was the only NFL team to run more often than it passed on second downs, with a 52/48 ratio. ☞ Tennessee's offense ranked sixth with the quarterback under center but 25th with the quarterback in shotgun. ☞ The Titans were fantastic when they used six offensive linemen, with 46.5% DVOA and 7.5 yards per play. Both figures were by far the best among the ten teams that used six or more linemen on at least 3.0 percent of plays. ☞ In the red zone, Tennessee ranked second running the ball but 25th passing the ball. ☞ The Tennessee offense ranked eighth in DVOA at home, but 26th on the road. ☞ Tennessee recovered only two of nine fumbles on offense. ☞ Tennessee's defense faced the league's lowest rate of outside runs at 11 percent. ☞ Tennessee had the league's worst DVOA against short passes but ranked third (behind only Jacksonville and Buffalo) against deep passes.

Passing

Player	DYAR	DVOA	Plays	NtYds	Avg	YAC	C%	TD	Int
M.Mariota	236	-3.3%	479	3059	6.4	4.5	62.2%	13	15
M.Cassel*	-257	-96.0%	50	125	2.5	1.8	59.5%	1	2
B.Gabbert	-189	-26.4%	194	944	4.9	4.3	55.9%	6	6

Rushing

Player	DYAR	DVOA	Plays	Yds	Avg	TD	Fum	Suc
D.Murray*	27	-5.0%	184	659	3.6	6	1	39%
D.Henry	56	-1.2%	176	744	4.2	5	1	48%
M.Mariota	114	35.6%	47	319	6.8	5	2	-
T.Taylor	30	62.9%	8	43	5.4	0	0	-
A.Jackson	25	120.7%	5	55	11.0	0	0	80%
D.Fluellen	6	35.0%	4	21	5.3	0	0	75%
D.Lewis	273	27.6%	180	896	5.0	6	0	56%
B.Gabbert	-21	-36.0%	18	82	4.6	0	2	-
M.Campanaro	29	57.7%	5	42	8.4	0	0	-

Receiving

Player	DYAR	DVOA	Plays	Ctch	Yds	Y/C	YAC	TD	C%
R.Matthews	173	13.6%	87	53	795	15.0	5.2	4	61%
E.Decker*	72	-1.6%	83	54	563	10.4	2.1	1	65%
C.Davis	-88	-30.2%	65	34	375	11.0	3.1	0	52%
T.Taylor	6	-9.7%	28	16	231	14.4	3.4	1	57%
M.Campanaro	34	3.4%	27	19	173	9.1	4.3	1	70%
D.Walker	-3	-7.6%	111	74	807	10.9	3.3	3	67%
J.Smith	-44	-30.7%	30	18	157	8.7	5.3	2	60%
P.Supernaw	7	8.8%	6	4	39	9.8	3.8	1	67%
D.Murray*	25	-3.3%	47	39	266	6.8	6.3	1	83%
D.Henry	31	23.6%	17	11	136	12.4	11.8	1	65%
D.Lewis	90	32.0%	35	32	214	6.7	7.0	3	91%

Offensive Line

Player	Pos	Age	GS	Snaps	Pen	Sk	Pass	Run	Player	Pos	Age	GS	Snaps	Pen	Sk	Pass	Run
Ben Jones	C	29	16/16	1024	6	0.0	1	7	Quinton Spain	LG	27	14/14	878	4	3.5	7	2
Josh Kline	RG	29	16/16	1023	2	1.0	7	14	Dennis Kelly	G/T	28	16/1	180	0	3.0	4	4
Jack Conklin	RT	24	16/16	1023	8	0.0	8	6	Xavier Su'a-Filo	LG	27	16/16	1082	4	8.5	19	8
Taylor Lewan	LT	27	16/16	937	10	5.5	8	9	Kevin Pamphile	LG	28	16/15	787	2	3.0	14	4

Year	Yards	ALY	Rank	Power	Rank	Stuff	Rank	2nd Lev	Rank	Open Field	Rank	Sacks	ASR	Rank	Press	Rank	F-Start	Cont.
2015	3.66	3.98	20	37%	32	22%	20	0.95	31	0.58	25	54	9.6%	32	28.1%	24	10	24
2016	4.39	4.63	5	68%	12	19%	13	1.27	9	0.72	13	28	5.7%	15	20.8%	4	15	33
2017	4.00	3.85	23	60%	23	23%	24	1.09	21	0.90	9	35	6.4%	14	24.5%	4	12	36

2017 ALY by direction: Left End: 6.40 (1)   Left Tackle: 3.22 (25)   Mid/Guard: 3.79 (28)   Right Tackle: 3.15 (27)   Right End: 2.41 (30)

Tennessee's offensive linemen played a combined 4,955 offensive snaps, but were only charged with 80 blown blocks. That's a rate of one blown block every 61.9 snaps, marginally ahead of the Saints (61.2) for the best rate in the league. Tennessee and New Orleans finished way ahead of the field; the next-best rate was Oakland at 54.0. ☞ The individual statistics reflect this: Jack Conklin, Quinton Spain, and Ben Jones all ranked second at their respective positions in snaps per blown block, and left tackle Taylor Lewan ranked fourth at his. Of the Titans starters, only right guard Josh Kline averaged more than one blown block for every 50 snaps; Kline ranked 15th at his position by this measure. ☞ This year, the Titans are expected to transition from being a primarily man-blocking offense to a much more zone-based scheme, but they will do so with mostly the same personnel they have used in the past two seasons. Former Buccaneers guard Kevin Pamphile and former Texans 2017 All-Keep Choppin' Wood left guard Xavier Su'a-Filo were signed in free agency, theoretically to compete with incumbent Spain. Spain, who joined the team in 2015 as an undrafted free agent, was re-signed on a one-year contract as a restricted free agent after an inconsistent 2017 season. ☞ If Spain retains his starting spot on the interior, Pamphile may instead find a temporary home at right tackle. Jack Conklin is still expected to begin the regular season on the Physically Unable to Perform list after tearing his ACL during the playoffs. This would keep Conklin, who has yet to miss a start as a professional, out for a minimum of six weeks. The other candidate at that spot as of early June is veteran backup Dennis Kelly, who replaced Conklin in the lineup against New England. ☞ Prior to that Conklin injury, Tennessee had enjoyed excellent injury luck last season. Only Spain missed any games, and the Titans had the second-healthiest line in the league by adjusted games lost behind only the Los Angeles Rams. ☞ At the time of writing, Lewan had informed the Titans that he would not attend the team's mandatory veteran minicamp while talks on a long-term deal are stalled. This is not expected to grow into a full-blown holdout, but Lewan's situation is worth monitoring over the summer.

Defensive Front Seven

Defensive Line	Age	Pos	G	Snaps	Plays	TmPct	Rk	Stop	Dfts	BTkl	Runs	St%	Rk	RuYd	Rk	Sack	Hit	Hur	Dsrpt
					Overall						vs. Run					Pass Rush			
Jurrell Casey	29	DT	16	867	59	7.2%	6	44	16	1	46	78%	40	2.1	41	6.0	16	29.0	3
DaQuan Jones	27	DE	12	437	31	5.1%	42	25	7	1	25	84%	21	1.9	32	3.5	2	9.0	0
Sylvester Williams*	30	DT	15	351	19	2.5%	--	17	3	0	19	89%	--	1.6	--	0.0	0	0.5	0
Karl Klug*	30	DE	15	324	18	2.4%	--	13	4	1	14	79%	--	1.7	--	1.5	1	6.0	0
Austin Johnson	24	DT	16	319	24	2.9%	--	18	2	2	20	75%	--	1.9	--	1.0	0	3.0	1
Bennie Logan	29	DT	15	574	53	6.9%	12	42	14	0	47	79%	37	1.3	11	1.5	1	7.5	1

Edge Rushers	Age	Pos	G	Snaps	Plays	TmPct	Rk	Stop	Dfts	BTkl	Runs	St%	Rk	RuYd	Rk	Sack	Hit	Hur	Dsrpt
					Overall						vs. Run					Pass Rush			
Brian Orakpo	32	OLB	16	836	46	5.6%	37	37	17	4	28	82%	25	2.6	62	7.0	13	36.0	1
Derrick Morgan	29	OLB	14	719	34	4.8%	53	23	15	3	16	56%	93	2.5	54	7.5	5	32.5	3
Erik Walden*	33	OLB	16	581	36	4.4%	55	22	9	5	26	65%	77	3.4	82	4.0	6	14.0	0

Linebackers	Age	Pos	G	Snaps	Plays	TmPct	Rk	Stop	Dfts	BTkl	Runs	St%	Rk	RuYd	Rk	Sack	Hit	Hur	Tgts	Suc%	Rk	AdjYd	Rk	PD	Int
					Overall						vs. Run					Pass Rush			vs. Pass						
Wesley Woodyard	32	ILB	16	1018	126	15.4%	16	71	26	13	69	67%	22	3.4	34	5.0	5	19.5	55	42%	61	6.8	39	4	0
Avery Williamson*	26	ILB	16	654	94	11.5%	49	48	9	6	70	57%	67	3.6	45	3.0	1	9.5	15	52%	30	5.9	23	0	0
Jayon Brown	23	ILB	16	490	55	6.7%	84	30	16	5	14	86%	3	2.9	19	1.5	1	7.0	43	57%	18	6.5	34	4	0
Will Compton	29	ILB	9	150	20	4.2%	--	14	2	0	15	73%	--	3.7	--	0.0	0	1.0	9	73%	--	6.2	--	2	1

Year	Yards	ALY	Rank	Power	Rank	Stuff	Rank	2nd Level	Rank	Open Field	Rank	Sacks	ASR	Rank	Press	Rank
2015	3.91	4.47	26	56%	6	18%	26	1.10	14	0.44	4	39	7.8%	3	25.2%	16
2016	3.80	3.97	12	45%	1	20%	15	0.96	5	0.60	12	40	6.2%	14	24.9%	23
2017	3.44	4.07	14	65%	20	20%	22	0.94	5	0.23	1	43	6.9%	12	31.4%	12

2017 ALY by direction: Left End: 3.10 (7)   Left Tackle: 5.21 (31)   Mid/Guard: 4.36 (24)   Right Tackle: 3.47 (14)   Right End: 0.49 (1)

Entering the offseason, the linebacker corps was generally considered the weakest unit on the Titans. The front office evidently agreed, as they spent both the team's first- and second-round picks on linebackers. ☞ First-round pick Rashaan Evans (Alabama) is a highly-rated cover linebacker who should immediately step into the starting spot vacated by departed free agent Avery Williamson. Evans should immediately upgrade the unit's pass coverage, which was Williamson's primary weakness. ☞ Evans' running mate at inside linebacker will be former Broncos veteran Wesley Woodyard, who played at a very high level during his tenth season as a professional. Woodyard ranked near the top of the inside linebacker tables in almost all of the individual statistics we track, including total defeats (fifth), pass defeats (fourth), run defeats (seventh), sacks (second), and pass deflections (11th). 2016 fifth-round pick Jayon Brown, a talented cover linebacker who ultimately contributed to Williamson's departure by taking a chunk of his playing time in 2017, will be the primary backup. ☞ Second-round pick Harold Landry (Boston College) was a college defensive end who will make the common professional move to 3-4 outside linebacker. He projects as a classic edge rusher who will compete immediately for snaps alongside veterans Brian Orakpo and Derrick Morgan. Landry may not start straight away, but he should be a part of the rotation from Day 1. ☞ If the top of the outside linebacker depth chart is set, the fourth, fifth, and sixth spots are anything but. The team retained six outside linebackers last year. Any three from 2016 second-round pick Kevin Dodd, past seventh-rounders Aaron Wallace and Josh Carraway, and 2018 undrafted free agent Sharif Finch (Temple) could make the final roster.

Defensive Secondary

Secondary	Age	Pos	G	Snaps	Plays	Overall TmPct	Rk	Stop	Dfts	BTkl	vs. Run Runs	St%	Rk	RuYd	Rk	vs. Pass Tgts	Tgt%	Rk	Dist	Suc%	Rk	AdjYd	Rk	PD	Int
Kevin Byard	25	FS	16	1087	103	12.6%	10	39	13	12	36	42%	46	7.8	50	52	13.2%	62	11.8	48%	50	9.2	50	14	8
Adoree' Jackson	23	CB	16	1022	86	10.5%	8	35	9	15	14	43%	42	6.4	49	107	28.8%	75	10.7	50%	46	5.9	7	17	0
Logan Ryan	27	CB	15	921	73	9.5%	24	29	12	7	20	35%	60	4.6	14	72	21.6%	49	10.6	50%	45	7.3	36	11	0
Johnathan Cyprien	28	SS	10	605	58	11.4%	19	26	7	8	33	67%	3	3.8	4	22	10.1%	44	5.8	34%	76	7.6	31	1	0
LeShaun Sims	25	CB	13	430	33	5.0%	--	10	4	7	2	50%	--	0.0	--	48	30.6%	--	11.0	38%	--	8.3	--	3	1
Brice McCain*	32	CB	16	414	13	1.6%	--	3	2	3	1	0%	--	6.0	--	31	20.7%	--	13.2	45%	--	7.7	--	3	0
Da'Norris Searcy*	30	SS	16	363	25	3.1%	--	7	4	7	12	25%	--	5.2	--	9	6.9%	--	14.1	59%	--	11.6	--	2	1
Malcolm Butler	28	CB	16	1040	71	8.9%	33	30	10	8	15	33%	61	7.2	59	90	18.7%	30	12.7	50%	44	9.1	69	15	2

Year	Pass D Rank	vs. #1 WR	Rk	vs. #2 WR	Rk	vs. Other WR	Rk	WR Wide	Rk	WR Slot	Rk	vs. TE	Rk	vs. RB	Rk
2015	24	12.2%	27	33.3%	31	14.3%	25	--	--	--	--	15.8%	24	-39.0%	1
2016	27	2.5%	18	21.7%	30	0.2%	16	2.7%	21	14.6%	25	-14.8%	8	36.3%	30
2017	24	-8.1%	11	29.2%	28	-0.3%	17	0.1%	18	9.5%	18	10.1%	24	28.0%	32

Between first-round pick Adoree' Jackson and highly-priced free agents Logan Ryan and Malcolm Butler, the Titans have a lot invested in their top three cornerbacks. It is not yet entirely clear how the team plans to deploy the trio, but the most likely configuration would see Jackson and Butler play the outside spots in a nickel base with Ryan in the slot. Against two-receiver sets, specific matchups will probably determine which cornerbacks stay on the field. ☞ Few teams' safeties had more clearly defined roles than those of the Titans. Kevin Byard led the league in interceptions; Johnathan Cyprien had the third-highest run stop rate among safeties. Byard had 70 percent more pass targets than run plays; Cyprien 50 percent more run plays than pass targets. Byard made his average run tackle 7.8 yards downfield; Cyprien made his at a linebacker depth of 3.8 yards. Backup Da'Norris Searcy, now in Carolina, split the difference across the board. ☞ Despite Byard's league-leading interception total, the Titans had a below-average interception rate. On average, NFL teams intercepted one of every 40.7 passes. The Titans intercepted one of every 50.4, which ranked 22nd. Tennessee was the only team in the league to have neither starting outside cornerback record an interception; Ryan failed to collect one for the first time in his five-year professional career. ☞ Fifth-round pick Dane Cruikshank (Arizona) was listed as a cornerback during the draft, but he is more likely to play safety in Tennessee. Cruikshank projects as a slot defender who has the physical attributes to match up against both tight ends and slot receivers in coverage, and he is a keen tackler in run support. He is not, however, considered trustworthy enough against wide receivers to man a cornerback spot full-time.

Special Teams

Year	DVOA	Rank	FG/XP	Rank	Net Kick	Rank	Kick Ret	Rank	Net Punt	Rank	Punt Ret	Rank	Hidden	Rank
2015	-3.8%	28	1.5	12	-1.2	19	-10.0	32	-6.7	26	-2.4	19	-5.9	23
2016	-1.0%	19	8.1	5	-2.7	22	-2.5	21	-6.4	26	-1.4	18	5.1	8
2017	1.6%	13	0.6	15	2.9	12	0.8	11	3.0	16	0.7	13	-5.8	22

Even on special teams, "slightly above average" was the story of the team's season. The Titans ranked between 11th and 16th in added value in each of the five special teams phases. They were the first team to finish within 3.0 points of average in all five areas of special teams since the 2007 Cowboys. ☞ Return specialist Adoree' Jackson had his ups and downs in his rookie season, but in yardage he finished middle-of-the-pack among qualifying punt returners (15th of 25) and kick returners (sixth of 12, both minimum 20 attempts). He is expected to retain those duties in 2018. ☞ Unusually, the Titans have very few rookies who are looking to special teams to help secure a roster spot. Dane Cruikshank, whose defensive attributes were mentioned above, has a chance to make a name for himself on kick and punt coverage. A quick and strong athlete who loves a tackle, he should quickly find a home as a punt gunner. Undrafted edge rusher Sharif Finch is the other rookie who is frequently mentioned as a likely special teams contributor, should he make the final roster. ☞ Brett Kern had the league's highest gross and net average punt distance. Despite this, the team's punt unit as a whole ranked 11th in our metrics. Kern had more yardage because he had more of the field to cover; Tennessee's average punt came from the 31.7-yard line, compared to the league average of 33.8. Tennessee also allowed too many returns on those long punts; 53 percent of Kern's punts had some kind of return compared to a league average of 44 percent.

Washington Redskins

2017 Record: 7-9	**Total DVOA:** -0.5% (16th)	**2018 Mean Projection:** 7.8 wins	**On the Clock (0-4):** 10%
Pythagorean Wins: 6.8 (17th)	**Offense:** -3.0% (20th)	**Postseason Odds:** 32.1%	**Mediocrity (5-7):** 35%
Snap-Weighted Age: 26.4 (18th)	**Defense:** -4.9% (11th)	**Super Bowl Odds:** 3.9%	**Playoff Contender (8-10):** 39%
Average Opponent: 4.5% (3rd)	**Special Teams:** -2.4% (22nd)	**Proj. Avg. Opponent:** 1.7% (8th)	**Super Bowl Contender (11+):** 16%

2017: What Do You Want Me to Say?

2018: Do the Standing Still

What, really, is left to say at this point? What can we tell you about Washington that we haven't already said a dozen times in the past? The Football Outsiders crew has been covering this team in assorted Almanacs and Prospecti for more than a decade now, and so much of what we have written before still applies to this team in 2018. Consider what Al Bogdan wrote in 2005: "This franchise makes one bad decision after another, changing long-term strategies at the drop of a hat." Or what Doug Farrar said in 2009: "The Redskins' blueprint for success hasn't worked to date, and it's not one that's been effective through NFL history." And then Aaron Schatz offered this in 2012: "Washington's stars-and-scrubs roster model makes even less sense when you realize that the scrubs aren't really joined by many stars." In 2014, Rivers McCown gave up on the whole idea of a traditional Washington chapter and wrote the rules for a Daniel Snyder roleplaying game instead. We won't be doing that again, but we're not above recycling some old ideas—this gimmick of recapping old Washington material in the intro was stolen from Farrar, who used it back in 2013.

For every step forward Washington has taken since Daniel Snyder bought the team in 1999, there has eventually been a backwards step of equal or greater magnitude. And now we have the loss of Kirk Cousins, which is less a backwards step and more of a Dick Fosbury-style reverse flying leap. We can argue all day about Cousins' precise level in the NFL's quarterback hierarchy, and how he'll fare in Minnesota this season, but the simple fact is this: no team in NFL history has let a player so young, so healthy, and so productive at the game's most important position walk out the door while getting nothing in return. Every club will lose a good player once in a while, but a setback like this requires a special level of roster mismanagement. At least, it would be special in most cities. In Washington, it's almost routine. (Mike Tanier, 2011: "Last year was a Redskins season like any other, only more so: a loud, expensive, muddled catastrophe, one which would set a typical franchise back three years but only kept the Redskins splaying mud in the rut they've called home since 2002.")

Really, Cousins' departure was a foregone conclusion, set in stone by decisions the team had made in years past. Using the franchise tag on him in 2016 was short-sighted; doing it again in 2017 was mind-bending. It almost guaranteed they would be looking for a new passer this offseason. (Tanier, 2017: "By applying the franchise tag to Cousins for two consecutive seasons, Washington has simultaneously paid top dollar for his services and alienated the most important player on the roster.") Cousins was good enough in 2015 and 2016 that some team was certain to offer him a massive deal as soon as he became available. In essence, Washington spent nearly $44 million in two years for the privilege of developing Minnesota's next quarterback and came away with zero playoff wins or long-term assets to show for it.

Just to make sure this entire experiment ended badly, even as Washington was going out of its way to boot one quarterback out the door, they ignored the need to develop a Plan B prospect along the way. Since Cousins was drafted in the fourth round in 2012, Washington has drafted just one quarterback: Nate Sudfeld, who was taken out of Indiana in the sixth round in 2016, cut a year later without ever taking the field, then won a Super Bowl ring with Philadelphia. It's unconscionable that Washington was so negligent as to spend two years toying around with Cousins while simultaneously doing nothing in that time to find and develop his replacement.

Regardless, Washington found themselves in need of a quarterback. And in an offseason with a ton of quarterback movement, they had plenty of options. They could have bundled a bunch of picks and traded up in the draft (though the last time Snyder and Bruce Allen made such a move—the Robert Griffin trade in 2012—it didn't work out so well). They could have picked up Teddy Bridgewater and hoped the former first-rounder could return to health. They could have gambled on a half-dozen different cheap, young veterans and hoped for lightning in a bottle. But before the 2017 season even officially ended, word broke that Washington had reached a deal to trade slot corner Kendall Fuller and a third-round pick to Kansas City in exchange for Alex Smith.

On the surface, the Cousins-to-Smith transition looks like a lateral move. Comparing Cousins' numbers in his three years as a starter to what Smith did in the same time in Kansas City yields fascinating results. Overall the two are pretty similar. Cousins was the more efficient passer in general, but Smith had better ball security and was the more effective runner. By QBR, this quarterback competition is a virtual dead heat (Table 1).

The puzzling part of the Smith acquisition is his age: the first overall draft pick way back in 2005, Smith turned 34 in May. He's four years older than Cousins, a huge difference at

2018 Redskins Schedule

Week	Opp.	Week	Opp.	Week	Opp.
1	at ARI	7	DAL	13	at PHI (Mon.)
2	IND	8	at NYG	14	NYG
3	GB	9	ATL	15	at JAX
4	BYE	10	at TB	16	at TEN
5	at NO (Mon.)	11	HOU	17	PHI
6	CAR	12	at DAL (Thu.)		

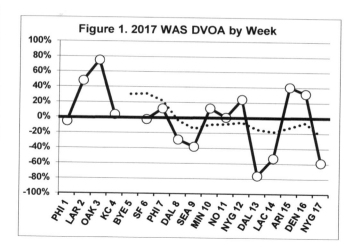

Figure 1. 2017 WAS DVOA by Week

this point in their respective careers. Despite what Tom Brady and Drew Brees and even Josh McCown did in 2017, the vast majority of NFL quarterbacks have declined sharply in their mid- to late thirties. As Cousins enters the peak of his career in Minneapolis, we can reasonably expect Smith's performance to slip in D.C. Allen and Snyder apparently disagree, because they doubled down by signing Smith to a four-year extension that lasts through 2022. Realistically, Washington can get out of the deal after 2020, but it's puzzling that they opted to guarantee $71 million to Smith, barely any less than the $80 million Cousins got from the Vikings.

Washington clearly expects Smith to be around for the long haul. "That's somebody you can build your team around and know he's going to be here, year in and year out," coach Jay Gruden said when Smith was introduced to D.C. media. "You're not always looking down the road: 'Oh, who's going to be our quarterback next year?'" Gruden also said he was excited to have a quarterback "for the next four, five, six years." Gruden was not around the last time Washington acquired a 34-year-old veteran quarterback—Donovan McNabb in 2010—but you'd think somebody in the team's brain trust would realize that old quarterbacks get worse, not better. (Tanier, 2015: "The Redskins used to make the same mistake every year. Now they spend three years prolonging the same mistake. It's a subtle difference.")

The too long-didn't read version of all this: after rebuilding around Robert Griffin in 2012 and Kirk Cousins in 2014 and Alex Smith in 2018, in two years Washington will likely be rebuilding again around, oh, let's say Jake Fromm. The Smith trade only makes sense for a team that is in win-now mode, and you can't use that term to describe a Washington franchise that hasn't won a playoff game in 13 seasons and hasn't won more than 10 games in a season since the Mark Rypien Super Bowl winners in 1991. The move was weird when it was announced, weird when it became official, and even weirder given months of hindsight. Consider that Cleveland would later trade for Tyrod Taylor, who is basically a poor man's Alex Smith as a passer but with better mobility. The Browns gave up a third-round pick for the quarterback, as Washington did

for Smith, but they didn't have to throw in a good defensive back as well. And at age 29, Taylor should still be a valuable player after Smith has retired.

If Washington does improve in 2018, it's less likely to be due to Smith, and more because he'll have some healthy blockers around him. Washington ranked 25th in offensive line continuity score last year, and 30th in adjusted games lost at the position. Those are both bad numbers, yet they underscore just how much carnage and devastation befell Washington's offensive line in the second half of 2017. Things were solid on the right side, where guard Brandon Scherff and tackle Morgan Moses played 86 and 95 percent of Washington's 1,016 offensive snaps, respectively. And through six games, the rest of the line looked solid too—left tackle Trent Williams, left guard Shawn Lauvao, and center Spencer Long played a total of 1,144 snaps and missed only 26. In the final ten games, however, that trio played only 399 combined snaps, but missed 1,479. To make matters worse, the backups were also often hurt. Tackle T.J. Clemmings and guard Tyler Catalina entered the starting lineup in Week 8; two weeks later, Catalina was cut, then Clemmings went on IR with an ankle injury, and Catalina was re-signed to fill Clemmings' roster spot. Center Chase Roullier missed three weeks in November and December. Arie Kouandjio and Tony Bergstrom were signed to the roster in late October and ended up starting nine games between them. Ty Nsekhe, who never really recovered from "core muscle surgery" early in the season, ended up starting at left tackle and left guard, and even played right tackle (badly) against Dallas on one of the rare occasions when Morgan left the field. Washington was the only team last year to get at least 100 offensive snaps out of 11 different offensive linemen, and they basically accomplished that in the last two-thirds of the season. (Schatz, 2007: "This

Table 1: Kirk Cousins vs. Alex Smith, 2015-2017

Player	Team	G/GS	Snaps	Att	Comp	C%	Yds	TD	INT/Adj	FUM	SakRate	NY/P	Rk	DVOA	Rk	DYAR	Rk	YAR	Runs	Yds	TD	DVOA	DYAR	QBR
Cousins	WAS	48/48	3101	1689	1132	67.0%	13176	81	36/49	30	5.1%	7.0	8.3	12.6%	9.7	2735	8.7	2640	109	323	13	-1.2%	48	62.4
Smith	KC	46/46	2872	1464	976	66.7%	11030	61	20/32	13	6.9%	6.7	15.0	10.4%	12.0	2182	12.0	1968	192	987	8	12.6%	198	61.2

All ranks listed are seasonal averages.

is what happens when a team with no depth gets hit by a rash of injuries.") As you can imagine, this all had a dramatically negative effect on Washington's offense, one that should be reversed in 2018 with just average health (Table 2).

Table 2: Washington Offense DVOA Before and After OL Injuries

Weeks	Pass	Rk	Run	Rk	Total	Rk
Weeks 1-7	36.4%	5	-11.6%	21	12.8%	8
Weeks 8-17	0.5%	22	-19.2%	29	-12.9%	28

But as we said, for every step forward, there must be a step backwards. And while Washington will benefit from the return of its offensive linemen, it will suffer the loss of two of its top three cornerbacks. Josh Norman was excellent for most of 2017, but he also had a tremendous supporting crew in veteran Bashaud Breeland and second-year man Kendall Fuller. Fuller, in particular, was exceptional, a big reason Washington ranked fourth in the NFL in coverage against slot receivers. But now both are gone. Breeland's contract expired after the season, and he remains unsigned due to an off-field foot injury, while Fuller was shipped off to Kansas City in the Smith trade. (This kind of trickle-down effect is another reason it's unhealthy to switch quarterbacks often. Inevitably, every new acquisition comes with a loss of valuable resources, be it cash, draft capital, or the loss of cheap, young talent—or in Washington's case, all three.) Norman's backup band now consists of Orlando Scandrick, who has nine years of experience on some very bad secondaries in Dallas; Fabian Moreau, Quinton Dunbar, and Josh Holsey, a trio of holdovers in their mid-twenties with little playing experience; and seventh-round rookie Greg Stroman out of Virginia Tech. This is the crew that will play four total games against the Giants and Eagles' receivers; top-shelf quarterbacks Aaron Rodgers, Matt Ryan, and Drew Brees; and superstar wideouts such as Mike Evans, DeAndre Hopkins, and T.Y. Hilton. There could be some long Sundays ahead.

The good news for Washington is that they have been a lot more prudent with their draft picks lately. It has been a while since they have traded away massive amounts of draft capital. (Bogdan, 2006: "Washington treats its early draft picks like a few extra Euros an American discovers in his pocket before boarding his flight back home from Amsterdam.") Indeed, their first two draft picks in 2018 directly addressed their two biggest weaknesses in 2017: rushing offense and rushing defense, where they were in the league's bottom five in both categories. Alabama's Da'Ron Payne, their first-round choice, is a 311-pounder who has been bench pressing 400 pounds

since he was in high school and can run a 40-yard dash in less than five seconds. His NFL.com draft profile called him "the premier run-stuffer in this draft" and said he was "built like a wall of granite with exceptional lean muscle mass." And in the second round they benefitted from the slide of LSU's Derrius Guice. Guice's health wasn't perfect in 2017, but he still led all SEC players with 2,638 rushing yards over the last two years. He plays with a violent, tackle-breaking style reminiscent of Marshawn Lynch, and should be able to create tough yards on his own. These two picks should go a long way in finally fixing problems that have vexed this team for a while now. (Sterling Xie, 2016: "Washington is as bad as any team in the league in terms of the run game, and did very little to fix either front.")

Manning this ship will be Jay Gruden, who is about to become the first head coach of the Dan Snyder era to get a fifth season at the helm. That alone makes him a strong hot-seat candidate this fall. And what has he accomplished to earn that extra season? One playoff game, in which his team jumped out to an 11-0 lead and still lost by 17 points? "We are not in here to build the team around [Smith], the team is built and he has to lead it like right now," Gruden said at OTAs, seemingly aware of his tenuous employment status. "This isn't a two- or three-year process. This is a one-year process and we have got to win right away."

If Washington has another mediocre season, it could be time for a new coaching search, and we know how much fun those can be for this team. (In 2008, Washington hired two coordinators before hiring a head coach, then promoted Jim Zorn to head coach because nobody else wanted the job. Bill Barnwell: "It's a marker of how much faith the Redskins have in Zorn—or the mess they've gotten themselves into.")

There are some reasons for optimism here. The front seven includes several good players. An improved ground attack and a low-risk quarterback should keep Washington in games into the fourth quarter. There's not a proven wide receiver to be found, but the position at least has depth and youth on its side. But there are holes on the roster too, and the schedule is brutal. Seven of Washington's opponents in 2018 made the playoffs last year, and if you count the Eagles twice, they won a combined 11 playoff games. The Smith era in D.C. seems destined to end up like the Cousins era: unremarkable, unsatisfying, and unlikely to last long before giving way to another regime.

It's Washington. Everything is always changing, which is why nothing ever really changes.

Vincent Verhei

2017 Redskins Stats by Week

Wk	vs.	W-L	PF	PA	YDF	YDA	TO	Total	Off	Def	ST
1	PHI	L	17	30	264	356	-2	-5%	-10%	-6%	-2%
2	at LAR	W	27	20	385	332	+2	48%	19%	-35%	-6%
3	OAK	W	27	10	472	128	+1	75%	14%	-67%	-6%
4	at KC	L	20	29	331	429	-1	4%	10%	12%	5%
5	BYE										
6	SF	W	26	24	419	335	-1	-3%	10%	7%	-5%
7	at PHI	L	24	34	344	371	0	12%	30%	13%	-5%
8	DAL	L	19	33	285	307	-2	-29%	-24%	-10%	-15%
9	at SEA	W	17	14	244	437	+1	-38%	-23%	7%	-8%
10	MIN	L	30	38	394	406	+1	12%	18%	12%	6%
11	at NO	L	31	34	456	535	+1	0%	36%	35%	0%
12	NYG	W	20	10	323	170	0	24%	-26%	-41%	8%
13	at DAL	L	14	38	280	275	-4	-76%	-45%	2%	-29%
14	at LAC	L	13	30	201	488	0	-53%	-33%	12%	-8%
15	ARI	W	20	15	218	286	+1	40%	10%	-27%	3%
16	DEN	W	27	11	386	330	+1	32%	13%	-8%	12%
17	at NYG	L	10	18	197	381	-2	-59%	-78%	-10%	10%

Trends and Splits

	Offense	Rank	Defense	Rank
Total DVOA	-3.1%	20	-4.9%	11
Unadjusted VOA	-4.8%	20	-1.1%	13
Weighted Trend	-7.8%	22	-1.3%	13
Variance	9.5%	24	6.5%	23
Average Opponent	-1.9%	8	3.3%	4
Passing	13.9%	14	-10.2%	6
Rushing	-16.2%	28	0.8%	29
First Down	-11.0%	25	1.3%	16
Second Down	9.6%	9	-4.5%	12
Third Down	-9.6%	23	-16.5%	7
First Half	0.1%	16	-7.0%	8
Second Half	-6.6%	22	-2.6%	12
Red Zone	-4.9%	19	-11.2%	9
Late and Close	-16.9%	25	-4.4%	14

Five-Year Performance

Year	W-L	Pyth W	Est W	PF	PA	TO	Total	Rk	Off	Rk	Def	Rk	ST	Rk	Off AGL	Rk	Def AGL	Rk	Off Age	Rk	Def Age	Rk	ST Age	Rk
2013	3-13	4.8	4.2	334	478	-8	-26.2%	29	-10.0%	23	4.2%	21	-12.0%	32	14.6	4	26.8	13	27.0	15	28.0	3	27.1	2
2014	4-12	4.5	4.4	301	438	-12	-27.0%	28	-11.8%	28	9.9%	27	-5.4%	29	21.9	7	67.6	29	27.1	13	26.9	14	25.9	21
2015	9-7	8.2	7.8	388	379	+5	-0.3%	15	1.9%	12	5.4%	21	3.2%	6	44.0	24	75.1	32	25.9	26	27.1	7	26.0	17
2016	8-7-1	8.3	9.7	396	383	0	9.5%	9	15.8%	5	6.8%	25	0.4%	13	27.6	10	68.9	31	27.1	8	27.4	4	26.1	15
2017	7-9	6.8	7.2	342	388	-4	-0.6%	16	-3.1%	20	-4.9%	11	-2.4%	22	70.6	31	50.4	27	27.1	15	26.3	16	25.3	26

2017 Performance Based on Most Common Personnel Groups

WAS Offense					WAS Offense vs. Opponents					WAS Defense					WAS Defense vs. Opponents			
Pers	Freq	Yds	DVOA	Run%	Pers	Freq	Yds	DVOA	Run%	Pers	Freq	Yds	DVOA		Pers	Freq	Yds	DVOA
11	66%	5.4	1.0%	28%	Base	31%	5.7	8.5%	54%	Base	34%	5.7	6.9%		11	61%	5.4	-12.3%
12	24%	6.3	8.3%	47%	Nickel	49%	5.4	5.0%	32%	Nickel	63%	5.5	-12.4%		12	22%	6.1	11.9%
13	8%	3.6	-15.9%	64%	Dime+	19%	5.0	-26.0%	16%	Dime+	2%	2.5	-73.5%		22	5%	4.4	-2.7%
622	1%	0.5	6.4%	83%	Goal Line	1%	1.4	-14.3%	79%	Goal Line	1%	0.3	15.9%		13	5%	5.6	-9.7%
612	1%	1.2	-103.0%	100%											21	3%	6.2	14.6%

Strategic Tendencies

Run/Pass		Rk	Formation		Rk	Pass Rush		Rk	Secondary		Rk	Strategy		Rk
Runs, first half	39%	18	Form: Single Back	89%	5	Rush 3	6.9%	16	4 DB	34%	13	Play action	21%	20
Runs, first down	56%	5	Form: Empty Back	4%	26	Rush 4	63.5%	16	5 DB	63%	10	Avg Box (Off)	6.30	10
Runs, second-long	23%	29	Pers: 3+ WR	66%	13	Rush 5	22.4%	12	6+ DB	2%	24	Avg Box (Def)	6.36	7
Runs, power sit.	52%	21	Pers: 2+ TE/6+ OL	34%	9	Rush 6+	7.2%	8	CB by Sides	89%	6	Offensive Pace	30.95	18
Runs, behind 2H	21%	31	Pers: 6+ OL	2%	28	Int DL Sacks	31.0%	9	S/CB Cover Ratio	26%	21	Defensive Pace	30.24	12
Pass, ahead 2H	52%	5	Shotgun/Pistol	58%	16	Second Level Sacks	9.5%	28	DB Blitz	5%	30	Go for it on 4th	0.96	19

In 2016, Washington was the best offense in the league running the ball on second-and-long, with 6.4 yards per carry and 20.5% DVOA. Last year, they dropped back towards the league average, with 4.5 yards per carry and -29.0% DVOA. ☛ New Washington quarterback Alex Smith was blitzed on just 18 percent of passes, the lowest figure of any quarterback in the league.

(Kirk Cousins was blitzed on 23 percent of passes, which ranked 24th.) ☞ Washington opponents dropped 39 passes, second in the league behind Cincinnati. ☞ Washington's top two safeties had the lowest gap between the location of their average play, suggesting that the Redskins used their safeties interchangeably. However, that's a bit of a mirage because Washington's third safety, Montae Nicholson, made his average play 14.3 yards downfield compared to D.J. Swearinger and Deshazor Everett both under 8 yards. ☞ Only four of Washington's 42 sacks were tagged as "coverage sack," "failed scramble," or "QB fault." That means 95 percent of Washington sacks were primarily attributed to pass pressure, the highest rate in the NFL. Notably, Washington was also at the top of this stat on offense, with 37 of 41 sacks primarily attributed to pass pressure.

Passing

Player	DYAR	DVOA	Plays	NtYds	Avg	YAC	C%	TD	Int
K.Cousins*	395	-0.6%	586	3709	6.3	6.1	64.6%	27	13
A.Smith	1026	18.3%	541	3840	7.1	5.7	67.7%	26	5
K.Hogan	-120	-32.4%	82	484	5.9	4.8	62.7%	4	5

Rushing

Player	DYAR	DVOA	Plays	Yds	Avg	TD	Fum	Suc
S.Perine	-85	-20.5%	174	599	3.4	1	2	43%
C.Thompson	9	-4.9%	64	296	4.6	2	1	42%
R.Kelley	15	-2.8%	62	194	3.1	3	0	48%
K.Cousins*	21	-2.3%	36	168	4.7	4	3	-
K.Bibbs	9	2.2%	21	79	3.8	0	0	38%
B.Marshall	-5	-22.8%	9	32	3.6	0	0	44%
M.Brown*	-9	-30.1%	8	29	3.6	0	0	38%
J.Crowder	17	1.0%	7	34	4.9	0	0	-
A.Smith	85	20.3%	50	366	7.3	1	0	-
K.Hogan	27	45.5%	10	71	7.1	0	0	-

Receiving

Player	DYAR	DVOA	Plays	Ctch	Yds	Y/C	YAC	TD	C%
J.Crowder	64	-4.5%	103	66	789	12.0	5.6	3	64%
J.Doctson	37	-7.1%	78	35	502	14.3	3.7	6	45%
R.Grant*	146	16.7%	65	45	573	12.7	5.2	4	69%
T.Pryor*	23	-5.3%	37	20	240	12.0	2.9	1	54%
B.Quick	29	33.7%	8	6	76	12.7	4.5	0	75%
M.Harris	18	24.3%	6	4	62	15.5	2.0	1	67%
P.Richardson*	161	13.4%	80	44	703	16.0	2.8	6	55%
V.Davis	61	6.7%	69	43	648	15.1	7.0	3	62%
J.Reed	-7	-10.1%	35	27	211	7.8	2.9	2	77%
N.Paul*	-16	-20.1%	19	13	94	7.2	2.4	0	68%
C.Thompson	223	67.3%	54	39	510	13.1	12.2	4	72%
S.Perine	84	42.6%	25	23	184	8.0	9.3	1	92%
K.Bibbs	36	32.7%	17	14	128	9.1	9.1	1	82%
B.Marshall	-27	-93.6%	8	6	36	6.0	8.5	0	75%
R.Kelley	-6	-23.8%	7	4	18	4.5	5.0	0	57%

Offensive Line

Player	Pos	Age	GS	Snaps	Pen	Sk	Pass	Run	Player	Pos	Age	GS	Snaps	Pen	Sk	Pass	Run
Morgan Moses	RT	27	16/16	962	5	4.8	26	7	Arie Kouandjio	LG	26	8/6	428	4	1.5	12	4
Brandon Scherff	RG	27	14/14	871	2	5.3	17	7	Spencer Long*	C	28	7/6	397	0	1.0	5	7
Trent Williams	LT	30	10/10	615	4	0.5	11	8	Ty Nsekhe	LT/LG	33	11/5	309	4	4.5	9	1
Shawn Lauvao	LG	31	9/9	531	1	2.3	12	2	Tony Bergstrom	OT	32	13/3	225	1	0.0	1	5
Chase Roullier	C	25	13/7	461	0	0.0	4	0	Tyler Catalina	RG	25	7/2	187	2	4.5	6	1

Year	Yards	ALY	Rank	Power	Rank	Stuff	Rank	2nd Lev	Rank	Open Field	Rank	Sacks	ASR	Rank	Press	Rank	F-Start	Cont.
2015	3.82	3.96	21	65%	18	22%	19	1.02	27	0.68	17	27	5.4%	10	20.4%	2	13	34
2016	4.67	4.57	6	72%	5	15%	3	1.15	14	1.06	6	23	3.9%	3	24.2%	11	25	28
2017	3.65	3.86	21	55%	27	20%	15	1.04	22	0.45	28	41	7.7%	24	34.9%	27	16	25

2017 ALY by direction: Left End: 4.05 (16) Left Tackle: 3.03 (28) Mid/Guard: 3.84 (27) Right Tackle: 4.26 (8) Right End: 3.88 (16)

Left tackle Trent Williams has struggled with injuries, missing 13 games over the past four seasons. Right tackle Morgan Moses has been more reliable, starting every game over the past three seasons, but he struggled last year. He ranked 28th among right tackles in snaps per blown block last season, after ranking seventh in the same category in 2016. Neither participated in OTAs—Williams sat out after December knee surgery, while Morgan was recuperating from ankle surgery. Both are expected to be full-go for Week 1. After the carnage of 2017, better safe than sorry. ☞ The other sure thing for 2018: right guard Brandon Scherff, the fifth overall pick of 2015 who made the Pro Bowl in each of the last two seasons. Washington picked up his fifth-year option for 2018, and he will get (and deserve) a hefty payout in 2019. ☞ That leaves center and left guard. A sixth-round rookie, Chase Roullier wasn't expected to do much last season, but he wound up starting seven games and finished fifth among centers in rate of snaps per blown block. That's a tiny sample size, but so far, so good. That's more than can be said for Shaun Lauvao, who has struggled to stay healthy, missing 22 games over the past three years. And he hasn't been great when he has played, failing to make the top 70 interior linemen in rate of snaps per blown block in either of the past two seasons. He was a free agent and wasn't expected to return, but Washington re-signed him after failing to find a quality replacement in the draft. They did select Louisville tackle Geron Christian in the third round, but Christian is an undersized prospect who will be strictly a depth player in his first season.

Defensive Front Seven

Defensive Line	Age	Pos	G	Snaps	Plays	TmPct	Rk	Stop	Dfts	BTkl	Runs	St%	Rk	RuYd	Rk	Sack	Hit	Hur	Dsrpt
						Overall						vs. Run				Pass Rush			
Matthew Ioannidis	24	DE	14	588	27	3.7%	69	19	8	1	19	58%	81	3.2	79	4.5	13	22.5	0
Ziggy Hood	31	DT	15	538	25	3.2%	80	13	1	2	23	52%	85	3.3	81	0.5	2	12.5	0
Stacy McGee	28	DE	16	431	45	5.3%	--	32	5	3	44	70%	--	2.5	--	0.0	4	13.5	1
Anthony Lanier	25	DE	11	342	20	3.4%	73	18	11	4	9	78%	42	3.1	77	5.0	5	8.5	7
Terrell McClain*	30	DE	12	327	20	3.2%	80	9	4	0	17	41%	86	4.8	86	2.0	1	6.0	0

Edge Rushers	Age	Pos	G	Snaps	Plays	TmPct	Rk	Stop	Dfts	BTkl	Runs	St%	Rk	RuYd	Rk	Sack	Hit	Hur	Dsrpt
						Overall						vs. Run				Pass Rush			
Ryan Kerrigan	30	OLB	16	822	46	5.5%	40	39	21	3	27	85%	16	1.9	30	14.0	4	35.0	1
Preston Smith	26	OLB	16	756	45	5.3%	41	33	16	1	27	70%	64	2.0	35	8.0	16	29.0	5
Junior Galette*	30	OLB	16	411	21	2.5%	--	17	6	4	15	73%	--	3.9	--	3.0	10	24.0	3
Pernell McPhee	29	OLB	13	386	24	3.6%	71	18	8	3	13	69%	70	4.1	92	4.0	7	14.0	3

Linebackers	Age	Pos	G	Snaps	Plays	TmPct	Rk	Stop	Dfts	BTkl	Runs	St%	Rk	RuYd	Rk	Sack	Hit	Hur	Tgts	Suc%	Rk	AdjYd	Rk	PD	Int
						Overall						vs. Run				Pass Rush				vs. Pass					
Zach Brown	29	ILB	13	834	127	18.5%	1	71	26	14	72	64%	39	3.1	24	2.5	2	12.5	44	50%	34	7.4	51	2	0
Martrell Spaight	25	ILB	15	414	70	8.8%	71	47	8	14	46	76%	8	3.4	32	0.0	1	3.0	30	46%	53	5.9	25	2	0
Zach Vigil	27	ILB	7	396	57	15.4%	17	29	7	4	39	49%	79	4.5	74	0.0	0	0.0	17	67%	--	4.5	--	2	0
Mason Foster	29	ILB	5	287	31	11.8%	45	20	3	7	19	79%	6	2.6	13	0.5	1	7.0	12	50%	--	13.0	--	1	1
Will Compton*	29	ILB	9	150	20	4.2%	--	14	2	0	15	73%	--	3.7	--	0.0	0	1.0	9	73%	--	6.2	--	2	1

Year	Yards	ALY	Rank	Power	Rank	Stuff	Rank	2nd Level	Rank	Open Field	Rank	Sacks	ASR	Rank	Press	Rank
2015	4.68	4.37	24	49%	1	19%	20	1.35	30	1.07	30	38	7.3%	9	22.6%	28
2016	4.52	4.54	27	69%	26	17%	25	1.37	29	0.76	19	38	6.9%	9	28.4%	12
2017	4.49	4.91	32	74%	27	15%	31	1.23	23	0.71	16	42	8.1%	4	36.7%	1

2017 ALY by direction: Left End: 4.18 (19)   Left Tackle: 4.15 (20)   Mid/Guard: 4.89 (31)   Right Tackle: 6.52 (32)   Right End: 4.44 (24)

If Washington is going to make a playoff run in 2018, this is the unit most likely to lead the way. That's due in part to the players listed in the table above, but also to a pair of Alabama linemen who don't appear there: Jonathan Allen, the 17th overall pick in 2017, and Da'Ron Payne, the 13th overall pick this year. Before going down with a foot injury, Allen started the first five games of his rookie season. Over those five games, Washington ranked 11th with a run defense DVOA of -15.4%; after Allen went down, they were 30th at 5.7%. There was also a decline in adjusted line yards, from 4.52 with Allen to 4.97 without him. Allen was a full participant in OTAs. Between Allen and Payne, Washington's interior defensive line is basically getting two first-round draft picks this year. ☞ Despite Washington's outstanding pass-rush numbers, they have more questions than you might expect at edge rusher. Ryan Kerrigan had elbow surgery after the season. Preston Smith, despite a size/speed combo that his teammates and coaches have repeatedly called "freakish," remains inconsistent. He had one sack in each of Washington's first four games, half a sack in their fifth, and then just half a sack total in their next eight. He's also going into the last year of his contract. Junior Galette, whose first two years in Washington were wiped out by injury, finally turned in a useful season, but his contract expired and he remained un-signed in June. Pernell McPhee collected 14.0 sacks and more than $23 million in three years in Chicago. He'll make about one-fourth as much in D.C., but for that price, a handful of sacks is a good return. ☞ After four years in Tennessee and one in Buffalo, Zach Brown had a monster season for Washington, while Martrell Spaight (27.6 snaps per game) only saw so much playing time because Zach Vigil (56.6) and Mason Foster (57.4) couldn't stay healthy. The contracts of Brown and Foster both expired after the year, but Washington re-signed Foster in January, and then re-acquired Brown a few days into free agency. ☞ You can't argue with those pass-rush numbers, but it's worth pointing out that Washington had to blitz to pressure the quarterback. With four pass-rushers, they got pressure 35 percent of the time and had a -0.4% DVOA. With five rushers, those numbers were 50 percent and -11.7%; with six, 52 percent and -17.1%. As a result of all that blitzing, Washington got pressure from everywhere—they were the NFL's only team with seven players who each had at least a dozen hurries, and Allen (who had ten in his abbreviated season) likely would have joined them if he had stayed healthy.

Defensive Secondary

Secondary	Age	Pos	G	Snaps	Plays	Overall TmPct	Rk	Stop	Dfts	BTkl	vs. Run Runs	St%	Rk	RuYd	Rk	vs. Pass Tgts	Tgt%	Rk	Dist	Suc%	Rk	AdjYd	Rk	PD	Int
D.J. Swearinger	27	SS/FS	16	1095	89	10.5%	31	36	16	15	51	43%	43	6.0	36	43	9.9%	40	13.4	59%	19	8.3	41	9	4
Josh Norman	31	CB	14	904	72	9.7%	22	27	8	4	33	48%	36	6.9	56	45	12.5%	4	13.3	47%	60	9.5	76	8	0
Bashaud Breeland*	26	CB	15	856	66	8.3%	42	35	11	14	16	31%	65	5.8	34	62	18.0%	25	12.0	56%	15	6.6	16	15	1
Kendall Fuller*	23	CB	16	725	64	7.6%	55	36	19	7	19	37%	56	7.0	57	54	18.5%	29	10.2	65%	2	6.8	27	10	4
Deshazor Everett	26	SS	14	591	57	7.7%	68	21	6	9	33	36%	55	6.5	42	23	9.8%	39	10.1	60%	13	5.9	14	5	0
Quinton Dunbar	26	CB	15	373	35	4.4%	--	15	5	1	7	14%	--	13.0	--	39	25.9%	--	14.4	54%	--	7.5	--	8	1
Montae Nicholson	23	FS	8	318	26	6.2%	--	6	2	3	13	23%	--	10.9	--	9	6.7%	--	23.2	46%	--	11.1	--	3	1
Orlando Scandrick	31	CB	11	614	39	7.0%	62	19	7	8	13	69%	8	3.6	6	45	18.4%	27	10.1	50%	47	8.7	64	4	0

Year	Pass D Rank	vs. #1 WR	Rk	vs. #2 WR	Rk	vs. Other WR	Rk	WR Wide	Rk	WR Slot	Rk	vs. TE	Rk	vs. RB	Rk
2015	20	13.2%	28	23.7%	30	-5.3%	13	--	--	--	--	8.0%	21	-17.8%	6
2016	24	4.4%	22	18.1%	29	10.5%	24	-0.5%	19	18.9%	30	13.0%	25	-16.4%	7
2017	6	-20.1%	5	31.2%	29	-23.0%	4	6.5%	25	-18.0%	4	-6.5%	10	-23.0%	4

Josh Norman's numbers show how coverage statistics can be complicated. He was mostly excellent, so teams rarely threw at him—but because teams rarely threw at him, a small number of big plays terribly skewed his numbers. He gave up two plays of 49 yards or more against Minnesota, and two more against the Chargers. Those four plays accounted for more than 40 percent of the yards he gave up on the year. Norman gave up 19.5 yards per pass and 136.5 yards per game to the Vikings and Chargers, but just 7.1 yards per pass and 20.7 yards per game otherwise. Even his poor success rate translates to less than two successful completions allowed per game. There may have been a dozen or so cornerbacks in the NFL better than Josh Norman in 2017, but certainly not 60 or 70. ☞ The other corners on the roster? Yuck. Orlando Scandrick is old and coming off two bad seasons following a torn ACL and MCL that knocked him out for all of 2015. Quinton Dunbar has all of eight starts in his first three seasons and has yet to hit a thousand defensive snaps in his career, and not once has he had enough playing time to qualify for our cornerback coverage tables. Fabian Moreau, a third-round rookie, played in all 16 games last year, but only had 59 snaps on defense. Bashaud Breeland remained available in June, but his foot injury could render him un-signable. ☞ D.J. Swearinger had the best year of his career in 2017, tying his career high in defeats and setting new personal bests in starts, tackles, interceptions, passes defensed, and total plays. He was a terror against Minnesota, with two of the seven interceptions Case Keenum threw all year, plus a tackle for loss on a running play. He'll play strong safety in 2018, with Montae Nicholson taking the free safety spot. Nicholson started six of his eight games as a rookie before a concussion ended his season.

Special Teams

Year	DVOA	Rank	FG/XP	Rank	Net Kick	Rank	Kick Ret	Rank	Net Punt	Rank	Punt Ret	Rank	Hidden	Rank
2015	3.2%	6	3.0	10	5.1	4	8.9	3	4.8	8	-5.8	27	2.5	13
2016	0.4%	13	-3.7	20	-1.5	18	0.6	13	-2.4	19	9.3	2	-0.2	18
2017	-2.4%	22	-1.6	18	6.9	3	-4.1	28	-7.8	25	-5.5	29	-7.3	25

Tress Way led the NFL in punting average as a rookie in 2014, but in three years since he has just been in the middle of the pack. And he doesn't make up for it by pinning opponents deep—he has ranked 29th, 29th, and 22nd in ratio of punts inside the 20 to touchbacks since 2015. ☞ Dustin Hopkins missed eight weeks during the season with a hip injury. The team signed 2016 UDFA Nick Rose to replace Hopkins, but then released him as soon as Hopkins was healthy. (Rose's last game for Washington was against the Chargers. Two weeks later, he was kicking for the Chargers.) Rose actually had the better numbers on both kickoffs and placekicks, but Washington stuck with Hopkins, who has been quite reliable on kickoffs in his career. He is one of five men with positive gross kickoff value in each of the past three years, ranking behind Justin Tucker and Graham Gano in total value over that span. ☞ Josh Doctson was very bad on punt returns in 2015, very good in 2016, and then very bad again last year, so he's due for a good season. (jk) ☞ Kickoff returns were a mess for Washington last year. Nine different players had at least one return. Six of those men are still on the roster. So are two rookies, Mr. Irrelevant Trey Quinn and UDFA Darvid Kidsey, who had some experience returning kickoffs in college. In other words, it's still a mess.

Quarterbacks

On the following pages, we provide the last three years of statistics for the top two quarterbacks on each team's depth chart, as well as a number of other quarterbacks who played significant time in 2017.

Each quarterback gets a projection from our KUBIAK fantasy football projection system, based on a complicated regression analysis that takes into account numerous variables including projected role, performance over the past two years, performance on third down vs. all downs, experience of the projected offensive line, historical comparables, collegiate stats, height, age, and strength of schedule.

It is difficult to accurately project statistics for a 162-game baseball season, but it is exponentially more difficult to accurately project statistics for a 16-game football season because of the small size of the data samples involved. With that in mind, we ask that you consider the listed projections not as a prediction of exact numbers, but the mean of a range of possible performances. What's important is not so much the exact number of yards and touchdowns we project, but whether or not we're projecting a given player to improve or decline. Along those same lines, rookie projections will not be as accurate as veteran projections due to lack of data.

Our quarterback projections look a bit different than our projections for the other skill positions. At running back and wide receiver, second-stringers see plenty of action, but, at quarterback, either a player starts or he does not start. We recognize that, when a starting quarterback gets injured in Week 8, you don't want to grab your *Football Outsiders Almanac* to find out if his backup is any good only to find that we've projected that the guy will throw 12 passes this year. Therefore, each year we project all quarterbacks to start all 16 games. If Russell Wilson goes down in November, you can look up Austin Davis, divide the stats by 16, and get an idea of what we think he will do in an average week (and then, if you are a Seattle fan, pass out). There are full-season projections for the top two quarterbacks on all 32 depth charts.

The first line of each quarterback table contains biographical data—the player's name, height, weight, college, draft position, birth date, and age. Height and weight are the best data we could find; weight, of course, can fluctuate during the offseason. **Age** is very simple: the number of years between the player's birth year and 2018, but birthdate is provided if you want to figure out exact age.

Draft position gives draft year and round, with the overall

pick number with which the player was taken in parentheses. In the sample table, it says that Kirk Cousins was chosen in the fourth round of the 2012 NFL draft, with the 102nd overall pick. Undrafted free agents are listed as "FA" with the year they came into the league, even if they were only in training camp or on a practice squad.

To the far right of the first line is the player's Risk variable for fantasy football in 2018, which measures the likelihood of the player hitting his projection. The default rating for each player is Green. As the risk of a player failing to hit his projection rises, he's given a rating of Yellow or, in the worst cases, Red. The Risk variable is not only based on age and injury probability, but how a player's projection compares to his recent performance as well as our confidence (or lack thereof) in his offensive teammates. A few players with the strongest chances of surpassing their projections are given a Blue rating. Most players marked Blue will be backups with low projections, but a handful are starters or situational players who can be considered slightly better breakout candidates.

Next, we give the last three years of player stats. The majority of these statistics are passing numbers, although the final five columns on the right are the quarterback's rushing statistics.

The first few columns after the year and team the player played for are standard numbers: games and games started (**G/GS**), offensive **Snaps**, pass attempts (**Att**), pass completions (**Cmp**), completion percentage (**C%**), passing yards (**Yds**), passing touchdowns (**TD**). These numbers are official NFL totals and therefore include plays we leave out of our own metrics, such as clock-stopping spikes, and omit plays we include in our metrics, such as sacks and aborted snaps. (Other differences between official stats and Football Outsiders stats are described in the "Statistical Toolbox" introduction at the front of the book.)

The column for interceptions contains two numbers, representing the official NFL total for interceptions (**Int**) as well as our own metric for adjusted interceptions (**Adj**). For example, if you look at our sample table, Kirk Cousins had 13 interceptions and 20 adjusted interceptions in 2017. Adjusted interceptions use game charting data to add dropped interceptions, plays where a defender most likely would have had an interception but couldn't hold onto the ball. Then we remove Hail Mary passes and interceptions thrown on fourth down when losing in the final two minutes of the game. We also remove "tipped interceptions," when a perfectly catchable ball

Kirk Cousins				Height: 6-3		Weight: 214		College: Michigan State			Draft: 2012/4 (102)			Born: 19-Aug-1988			Age: 30			Risk: Green
Year	Team	G/GS	Snaps	Att	Comp	C%	Yds	TD	INT/Adj	FUM	ASR	NY/P	Rk	DVOA	Rk	DYAR	Rk	YAR	Runs	Yds	TD	DVOA	DYAR	QBR
2015	WAS	16/16	1026	543	379	69.8%	4166	29	11/13	8	5.4%	7.0	6	16.9%	6	1023	7	1125	26	48	5	-3.1%	8	70.1
2016	WAS	16/16	1063	606	406	67.0%	4917	25	12/16	9	3.9%	7.6	3	20.9%	5	1317	3	1197	34	96	4	1.9%	18	71.7
2017	WAS	16/16	1012	540	347	64.3%	4093	27	13/20	13	7.7%	6.5	16	-0.6%	18	395	16	318	49	179	4	-2.3%	21	52.3
2018	MIN			541	356	65.8%	4055	27	13	8		6.7		12.0%					51	168	0	2.2%		
2016:	51% Short		29% Mid	12% Deep	8% Bomb		aDOT: 9.2 (9)		YAC: 4.8 (26)		ALEX: 2.3		2017:	57% Short		28% Mid	9% Deep		6% Bomb	aDOT: 8.1 (24)		YAC: 6.1 (3)	ALEX: 0.7

deflected off the receiver's hands or chest and into the arms of a defender.

Overall, adjusted interception rate is higher than standard interception rate, so most quarterbacks will have more adjusted interceptions than standard interceptions. On average, a quarterback will have one additional adjusted interception for every 120 pass attempts. Once this difference is accounted for, adjusted interceptions are a better predictor of next year's interception total than standard interceptions.

The next column is fumbles (**FUM**), which adds together all fumbles by this player, whether turned over to the defense or recovered by the offense (explained in the essay "Pregame Show"). Even though this fumble total is listed among the passing numbers, it includes all fumbles, including those on sacks, aborted snaps, and rushing attempts. By listing fumbles and interceptions next to one another, we're giving readers a general idea of how many total turnovers the player was responsible for.

Next comes Adjusted Sack Rate (**ASR**). This is the same statistic you'll find in the team chapters, only here it is specific to the individual quarterback. It represents sacks per pass play (total pass plays = pass attempts + sacks) adjusted based on down, distance, and strength of schedule. For reference, the NFL average was 6.4 percent in 2015, 6.1 percent in 2016, and 6.7 percent in 2017.

The next two columns are Net Yards per Pass (**NY/P**), a standard stat but a particularly good one, and the player's rank (**Rk**) in Net Yards per Pass for that season. Net Yards per Pass consists of passing yards minus yards lost on sacks, divided by total pass plays.

The five columns remaining in passing stats give our advanced metrics: **DVOA** (Defense-Adjusted Value Over Average), **DYAR** (Defense-Adjusted Yards Above Replacement), and **YAR** (Yards Above Replacement), along with the player's rank in both DVOA and DYAR. These metrics compare each quarterback's passing performance to league-average or replacement-level baselines based on the game situations that quarterback faced. DVOA and DYAR are also adjusted based on the opposing defense. The methods used to compute these numbers are described in detail in the "Statistical Toolbox" introduction at the front of the book. The important distinctions between them are:

- DVOA is a rate statistic, while DYAR is a cumulative statistic. Thus, a higher DVOA means more value per pass play, while a higher DYAR means more aggregate value over the entire season.
- Because DYAR is defense-adjusted and YAR is not, a player whose DYAR is higher than his YAR faced a harder-than-average schedule. A player whose DYAR is lower than his YAR faced an easier-than-average schedule.

To qualify for a ranking in Net Yards per Pass, passing DVOA, and passing DYAR in a given season, a quarterback must have had 200 pass plays in that season. 37 quarterbacks ranked for 2015, 34 for 2016, and 35 for 2017.

The final five columns contain rushing statistics, starting with **Runs**, rushing yards (**Yds**), and rushing touchdowns (**TD**). Once again, these are official NFL totals and include kneeldowns, which means you get to enjoy statistics such as Landry Jones rushing eight times for -10 yards. The final two columns give **DVOA** and **DYAR** for quarterback rushing, which are calculated separately from passing. Rankings for these statistics, as well as numbers that are not adjusted for defense (YAR and VOA) can be found on our website, FootballOutsiders.com.

The last number listed is the Total QBR metric from ESPN Stats & Information. Total QBR is based on the expected points added by the quarterback on each play, then adjusts the numbers to a scale of 0-100. There are five main differences between Total QBR and DVOA:

- Total QBR incorporates information from game charting, such as passes dropped or thrown away on purpose.
- Total QBR splits responsibility on plays between the quarterback, his receivers, and his blockers. Drops, for example, are more on the receiver, as are yards after the catch, and some sacks are more on the offensive line than others.
- Total QBR has a clutch factor which adds (or subtracts) value for quarterbacks who perform best (or worst) in high-leverage situations.
- Total QBR combines passing and rushing value into one number and differentiates between scrambles and planned runs.

The italicized row of statistics for the 2018 season is our 2018 KUBIAK projection, as detailed above. Again, in the interest of producing meaningful statistics, all quarterbacks are projected to start a full 16-game season, regardless of the likelihood of them actually doing so.

The final line below the KUBIAK projection represents data on how far the quarterback throws his passes. First, we break down charted passes based on distance: **Short** (5 yards or less), **Mid** (6-15 yards), **Deep** (16-25 yards), and **Bomb** (26 or more yards). These numbers are based on distance in the air only and include both complete and incomplete passes. Passes thrown away or tipped at the line are not included, nor are passes on which the quarterback's arm was hit by a defender while in motion. We also give average depth of target (**aDOT**) and average yards after catch (**YAC**) with the rank in parentheses for the 35 quarterbacks who qualify. The final number listed here is **ALEX**, which stands for Air Less EXpected, and measures the distance of each quarterback's average third-down throw compared to how many yards were needed for a first down. Aaron Rodgers' ALEX of 3.9 means his average third-down pass was thrown 3.9 yards deeper than the sticks, the highest in the league; Mitchell Trubisky had the lowest ALEX at -2.4.

A number of third- and fourth-string quarterbacks are briefly discussed at the end of the chapter in a section we call "Going Deep."

Top 20 QB by Passing DYAR (Total Value), 2017

Rank	Player	Team	DYAR
1	Tom Brady	NE	1,595
2	Philip Rivers	LAC	1,412
3	Drew Brees	NO	1,390
4	Case Keenum	MIN	1,293
5	Ben Roethlisberger	PIT	1,270
6	Jared Goff	LAR	1,125
7	Matt Ryan	ATL	1,084
8	Carson Wentz	PHI	1,047
9	Alex Smith	KC	1,026
10	Matthew Stafford	DET	1,004
11	Jameis Winston	TB	779
12	Derek Carr	OAK	709
13	Russell Wilson	SEA	530
14	Deshaun Watson	HOU	497
15	Blake Bortles	JAX	408
16	Kirk Cousins	WAS	395
17	Dak Prescott	DAL	375
18	Aaron Rodgers	GB	334
19	Marcus Mariota	TEN	236
20	Carson Palmer	ARI	145

Minimum 200 passes.

Top 20 QB by Passing DVOA (Value per Pass), 2016

Rank	Player	Team	DVOA
1	Case Keenum	MIN	28.1%
2	Tom Brady	NE	27.8%
3	Drew Brees	NO	27.4%
4	Philip Rivers	LAC	26.1%
5	Jared Goff	LAR	24.0%
6	Carson Wentz	PHI	23.8%
7	Deshaun Watson	HOU	23.1%
8	Ben Roethlisberger	PIT	21.8%
9	Matt Ryan	ATL	19.1%
10	Alex Smith	KC	18.3%
11	Matthew Stafford	DET	14.9%
12	Jameis Winston	TB	14.3%
13	Derek Carr	OAK	9.7%
14	Aaron Rodgers	GB	7.8%
15	Russell Wilson	SEA	2.9%
16	Blake Bortles	JAX	0.3%
17	Dak Prescott	DAL	-0.2%
18	Kirk Cousins	WAS	-0.6%
19	Carson Palmer	ARI	-3.2%
20	Marcus Mariota	TEN	-3.3%

Minimum 200 passes.

Josh Allen

Height: 6-5 Weight: 237 College: Wyoming Draft: 2018/1 (7) Born: 21-May-1996 Age: 22 Risk: Yellow

Year	Team	G/GS	Snaps	Att	Comp	C%	Yds	TD	INT/Adj	FUM	ASR	NY/P	Rk	DVOA	Rk	DYAR	Rk	YAR	Runs	Yds	TD	DVOA	DYAR	QBR
2018	BUF			481	255	53.0%	2987	16	15	10		5.1		-29.1%					63	290	2	8.8%		

A parody of an NFL quarterback prospect, Allen was abysmal in 2017 en route to not even making an all-Mountain West team. We don't want to say there's absolutely no chance he'll ever be good—he's got a deep ball, he's got some ability to make plays on the run and under pressure—but there is zero empirical evidence to support him becoming a reasonable NFL starting quarterback. And if you thought the excuses for his supporting cast were bad in Wyoming, wait till you see this Bills offense. Bills corner Tre'Davious White heaped praise on Allen in OTAs, saying that he was going to break a lot of guys' fingers this year. Jaguars corner Jalen Ramsey retweeted Allen's first OTA snaps and said that his throw was a pick waiting to happen. Allen is the battleground that old school scouts are going to die on, whether they're right about it or, as all evidence suggests, wrong about it.

Matt Barkley

Height: 6-2 Weight: 230 College: USC Draft: 2013/4 (98) Born: 8-Sep-1990 Age: 28 Risk: Green

Year	Team	G/GS	Snaps	Att	Comp	C%	Yds	TD	INT/Adj	FUM	ASR	NY/P	Rk	DVOA	Rk	DYAR	Rk	YAR	Runs	Yds	TD	DVOA	DYAR	QBR
2016	CHI	7/6	412	216	129	59.7%	1611	8	14/14	4	2.7%	7.1	7	-10.9%	26	4	26	127	7	2	0	-321.8%	-34	39.2
2018	CIN			520	308	59.3%	3626	21	21	9		6.0		-20.8%					37	-12	1	-25.0%		
2016:	33% Short	43% Mid	14% Deep	9% Bomb	aDOT: 10.8 (2)	YAC: 4.2 (32)	ALEX: 4.3

Mike Brown reportedly wanted to draft Colin Kaepernick back in 2011, but he bowed to Jay Gruden's desire for Andy Dalton. Cincy in theory could have closed the circle while ending the post-kneeling stupidity and brought in Kaepernick as Dalton's backup with the departure of AJ McCarron. But of course not. Brown and Co. opted instead for the retread's retread in Barkley, who was in Arizona last year. The Bengals will be Barkley's fifth team in sixth years, assuming he sticks; he could be pushed aside by low-round draftee Logan Woodside, which says as much about Barkley as it does Woodside.

C.J. Beathard

Height: 6-2 | Weight: 219 | College: Iowa | Draft: 2017/3 (104) | Born: 16-Nov-1993 | Age: 25 | Risk: Red

Year	Team	G/GS	Snaps	Att	Comp	C%	Yds	TD	INT/Adj	FUM	ASR	NY/P	Rk	DVOA	Rk	DYAR	Rk	YAR	Runs	Yds	TD	DVOA	DYAR	QBR
2017	SF	7/5	390	224	123	54.9%	1430	4	6/4	3	8.5%	5.3	32	-23.1%	31	-176	30	-271	26	136	3	44.6%	73	32.0
2018	SF			529	312	59.0%	3559	21	16	10		5.7		-17.0%					62	376	3	25.0%		

2017:	59% Short	28% Mid	8% Deep	5% Bomb	aDOT: 7.6 (31)	YAC: 5.2 (18)	ALEX: 1.3

Beathard profiled as a backup coming out of Iowa, and that is how he began as a rookie. After a poor start to the season by Brian Hoyer, Beathard took over the starting job in Week 7 against the Cowboys. Although Beathard was able to lead the team to its first win of the year over the Giants, he actually performed worse than Hoyer in both passing DYAR and DVOA. After San Francisco traded for Jimmy Garoppolo at midseason, Beathard stayed in the lineup while Garoppolo learned the playbook, then gave way to the former Patriots backup after an injury against the Seahawks. With Garoppolo firmly entrenched as the starter in San Francisco, Beathard will return to the backup role. His time on the field in 2017 may not have been pretty, but at least the 49ers know what they have with Beathard now.

Blake Bortles

Height: 6-4 | Weight: 232 | College: Central Florida | Draft: 2014/1 (3) | Born: 16-Dec-1991 | Age: 27 | Risk: Yellow

Year	Team	G/GS	Snaps	Att	Comp	C%	Yds	TD	INT/Adj	FUM	ASR	NY/P	Rk	DVOA	Rk	DYAR	Rk	YAR	Runs	Yds	TD	DVOA	DYAR	QBR
2015	JAX	16/16	1058	606	355	58.6%	4428	35	18/26	14	8.0%	6.3	18	-9.9%	25	54	25	100	52	310	2	24.5%	86	46.4
2016	JAX	16/16	1111	625	368	58.9%	3905	23	16/17	8	5.3%	5.6	30	-10.0%	24	52	23	3	58	359	3	23.3%	90	49.2
2017	JAX	16/16	1110	523	315	60.2%	3687	21	13/16	9	4.4%	6.7	13	0.3%	16	408	15	597	57	322	2	25.1%	84	55.6
2018	JAX			536	332	61.9%	3701	23	13	8		6.2		-2.2%					66	302	2	12.7%		

2016:	47% Short	34% Mid	14% Deep	6% Bomb	aDOT: 8.8 (17)	YAC: 5.1 (15)	ALEX: 1.7
2017:	56% Short	25% Mid	12% Deep	7% Bomb	aDOT: 8.3 (22)	YAC: 6.1 (4)	ALEX: 0.7

It sounds great to say that in 2017 Bortles set career highs in DVOA and DYAR and career lows in interception rate and adjusted sack rate, but as noted in the Jaguars chapter those marks were achieved mostly by protecting him from himself. Bortles threw fewer passes than he had in any full season since his rookie year, and fewer passes per game even than his debut season. This was not purely a function of winning, as he averaged slightly fewer pass attempts in defeats than victories. The Jaguars were at or near the top of the league in the percentage of runs called in almost any situation we can think of; only when trailing in the second half did they not call at least the fourth-highest percentage of run plays.

This was reflected very strongly in Bortles' passing splits. Though most research indicates that a strong play-action passing game does not require a strong running game, the Jaguars appear to have been an exception to the rule. Bortles' DVOA on play-action passes leapt from 6.6% to 53.2% in 2017. He had the highest DVOA of any regular starting quarterback (minimum four starts) when using play-action on first down, but his DVOA dropped to seventh on all play-action passes and 16th overall. Bortles had the numbers of an average starter in just about the most favorable circumstances the team could possibly manufacture, but he remains the weak point of the Jaguars offense as currently constructed.

Sam Bradford

Height: 6-4 | Weight: 236 | College: Oklahoma | Draft: 2010/1 (1) | Born: 8-Nov-1987 | Age: 31 | Risk: Red

Year	Team	G/GS	Snaps	Att	Comp	C%	Yds	TD	INT/Adj	FUM	ASR	NY/P	Rk	DVOA	Rk	DYAR	Rk	YAR	Runs	Yds	TD	DVOA	DYAR	QBR
2015	PHI	14/14	987	532	346	65.0%	3725	19	14/15	9	6.2%	6.3	16	-8.2%	24	107	24	221	26	39	0	-76.7%	-43	41.8
2016	MIN	15/15	978	552	395	71.6%	3877	20	5/9	10	6.3%	6.1	24	2.2%	17	510	16	571	20	53	0	54.3%	23	49.2
2017	MIN	2/2	91	43	32	74.4%	382	3	0/0	0	9.2%	7.1	--	44.2%	--	169	--	131	2	-3	0	--		72.4
2018	ARI			586	382	65.2%	4035	23	13	9		5.8		1.4%					32	35	1	-20.3%		

2016:	62% Short	24% Mid	10% Deep	5% Bomb	aDOT: 6.5 (34)	YAC: 5.0 (18)	ALEX: -1.2
2017:	55% Short	21% Mid	17% Deep	6% Bomb	aDOT: 8.2 (--)	YAC: 4.8 (--)	ALEX: -1.7

The story of Sam Bradford's career is one of untapped potential. That is a little odd to say about a quarterback entering his ninth season, but every time Bradford has seemed on the verge of a breakout year, the old injury bug has come back to bite him. After a 2016 season in which he set what was then the record for completion percentage (bolstered by a heavy diet of short passes) but only finished 16th in passing DYAR, Bradford missed all but two games in 2017 due to a knee injury. Bradford was activated late in the season, but by then, Case Keenum had an iron grip on both the Vikings' starting job and one of the season's feel-good stories. If Bradford can recreate his 2016 campaign—which he looked quite capable of doing after coming out on fire in the first two games of 2017—he should be able to hold off rookie Josh Rosen for at least this season in Arizona. As always, the question is whether the former No. 1 overall pick can stay healthy.

Tom Brady

Height: 6-4 Weight: 225 College: Michigan Draft: 2000/6 (199) Born: 3-Aug-1977 Age: 41 Risk: Yellow

Year	Team	G/GS	Snaps	Att	Comp	C%	Yds	TD	INT/Adj	FUM	ASR	NY/P	Rk	DVOA	Rk	DYAR	Rk	YAR	Runs	Yds	TD	DVOA	DYAR	QBR
2015	NE	16/16	1105	624	402	64.4%	4770	36	7/9	6	6.5%	6.9	7	19.5%	5	1312	2	1269	34	53	3	6.5%	25	64.4
2016	NE	12/12	819	432	291	67.4%	3554	28	2/3	5	4.2%	7.8	2	33.4%	2	1286	5	1361	28	64	0	-18.9%	-9	83.0
2017	NE	16/16	1118	581	385	66.3%	4577	32	8/13	7	6.4%	7.4	6	27.8%	2	1595	1	1621	25	28	0	-12.2%	0	67.4
2018	NE			570	385	67.6%	4481	32	12	8		7.0		20.6%					31	44	1	-3.6%		

| 2016: | 54% Short | 27% Mid | 11% Deep | 7% Bomb | aDOT: 8.1 (23) | YAC: 6.0 (2) | ALEX: 2.1 | 2017: | 51% Short | 29% Mid | 12% Deep | 8% Bomb | aDOT: 9.6 (8) | YAC: 5.0 (21) | ALEX: 2.9 |

It's pretty rare to see a 40-year-old quarterback change in a material way that has nothing to do with regression, but here's Tom Brady. New England's 2017 offense focused more on the deep ball than arguably any year Brady and Belichick had been together. Lacking much in the way of open-field tackle-breaking in the receiving corps outside of Rob Gronkowski, the Patriots had to have their quarterback lead their way down the field. The future Hall of Famer responded with a barrage of strikes and a few underthrown pass interference penalties, and threw for 500 yards in the Super Bowl against one of the best defenses in the NFL. All that's left for Brady at this point is setting the career achievements bar for the position for the near future—Drew Brees will have better counting stats, but you know the ring count will be more important in the eyes of the public. We're through predicting decline. He'll have to show it to us first.

Drew Brees

Height: 6-0 Weight: 209 College: Purdue Draft: 2001/2 (32) Born: 15-Jan-1979 Age: 39 Risk: Green

Year	Team	G/GS	Snaps	Att	Comp	C%	Yds	TD	INT/Adj	FUM	ASR	NY/P	Rk	DVOA	Rk	DYAR	Rk	YAR	Runs	Yds	TD	DVOA	DYAR	QBR
2015	NO	15/15	1089	627	428	68.3%	4870	32	11/13	5	5.3%	7.0	5	15.8%	7	1111	6	1184	24	14	1	32.1%	21	75.5
2016	NO	16/16	1151	673	471	70.0%	5208	37	15/14	5	4.5%	7.3	5	23.3%	4	1599	2	1473	23	20	2	17.2%	21	72.0
2017	NO	16/16	1034	536	386	72.0%	4334	23	8/12	5	4.0%	7.5	3	27.4%	3	1390	3	1402	33	12	2	-5.6%	6	59.0
2018	NO			558	392	70.2%	4388	28	10	6		7.1		23.5%					25	23	1	-10.9%		

| 2016: | 54% Short | 28% Mid | 11% Deep | 6% Bomb | aDOT: 7.7 (29) | YAC: 5.1 (12) | ALEX: 1.5 | 2017: | 62% Short | 22% Mid | 11% Deep | 6% Bomb | aDOT: 6.7 (35) | YAC: 6.1 (2) | ALEX: -0.2 |

Brees is 1,496 passing yards away from breaking Peyton Manning's record of 71,940. At his usual production, Brees should break that record in his fifth or sixth game this season. Based on the NFL schedule, odds are on Week 5 when he'll be at home in prime time against Washington, the team against which he led a dramatic comeback last year in a vintage performance. This record actually could stand for some time since Brees is two years younger than Tom Brady and leads him by 4,286 yards.

There is no indication that 2018 will be Brees' swan song, but 39 is rare territory. Warren Moon, Doug Flutie, Brett Favre, and Brady are the only quarterbacks to attempt at least 400 passes in their age-39 season in NFL history. Manning was limited to 331 attempts in 2015, his age-39 last hurrah in Denver, but was able to go out with a Super Bowl win. That would be nice to see for Brees, who ended last season with the 18th lost comeback (a game in which he led a go-ahead drive in the fourth quarter only to lose) of his career. That also is an NFL record that may stand for Brees for decades.

Teddy Bridgewater

Height: 6-2 Weight: 214 College: Louisville Draft: 2014/1 (32) Born: 10-Nov-1992 Age: 26 Risk: Red

Year	Team	G/GS	Snaps	Att	Comp	C%	Yds	TD	INT/Adj	FUM	ASR	NY/P	Rk	DVOA	Rk	DYAR	Rk	YAR	Runs	Yds	TD	DVOA	DYAR	QBR
2015	MIN	16/16	994	447	292	65.3%	3231	14	9/11	8	8.8%	6.0	29	-5.1%	22	187	21	93	44	192	3	5.3%	32	62.7
2017	MIN	1/0	9	2	0	0.0%	0	0	1/0	0	0.0%	0.0	--	-493.2%	--	-68	--	-66	3	-3	0	--	--	0.0
2018	NYJ			534	339	63.5%	3743	22	14	11		5.8		-13.4%					41	112	2	-3.3%		

| | | | | | | 2017: | 100% Short | 0% Mid | 0% Deep | 0% Bomb | aDOT: 3.5 (--) | YAC: 0.0 (--) | ALEX: -1 |

Minnesota's first-round pick in 2014, Bridgewater had two semi-successful years behind one of the worst offensive lines in the league, then suffered a devastating knee injury and didn't return to the field until late last season. If healthy, he's a bargain play with upside for the Jets, even if his deep ball floats a bit too much to be an elite quarterback. Jets fans would happily settle for Chad Pennington's shadow at this point. OTA news seemed to be positive, and it would be a feel-good story for Bridgewater to deliver on his early promise.

Jacoby Brissett Height: 6-4 Weight: 231 College: North Carolina State Draft: 2016/3 (91) Born: 11-Dec-1992 Age: 26 Risk: Green

Year	Team	G/GS	Snaps	Att	Comp	C%	Yds	TD	INT/Adj	FUM	ASR	NY/P	Rk	DVOA	Rk	DYAR	Rk	YAR	Runs	Yds	TD	DVOA	DYAR	QBR
2016	NE	3/2	156	55	34	61.8%	400	0	0/0	3	9.4%	5.9	—	-10.0%	—	4	—	-4	16	83	1	-24.4%	-8	44.8
2017	IND	16/15	989	469	276	58.8%	3098	13	7/11	8	9.8%	5.5	29	-14.4%	27	-105	28	-178	63	260	4	-13.7%	-4	39.6
2018	IND			511	303	59.2%	3430	17	12	11		5.7		-15.5%					61	255	3	15.0%		
2016:	63% Short	14% Mid	13% Deep	11% Bomb	aDOT: 7.5 (–)	YAC: 9.7 (–)	ALEX: 0.4	2017:	59% Short	29% Mid	8% Deep	5% Bomb	aDOT: 7.7 (30)	YAC: 5.7 (8)	ALEX: 0.3

Acquired in an unexpected preseason trade, Brissett was thrust into the lineup in Week 1 after Scott Tolzien looked overmatched, and held on to the job the rest of the season. It is diffcult to separate his play from the context of his offense. Behind a struggling offensive line, he struggled to process quickly enough and was sacked too often. In a vertically oriented scheme, he stuck with his deep read too long. When he finally got off it, or sometimes before that, he locked on to the tight end. The return of a healthy Luck should relegate Brissett to the bench for the two years left on his rookie deal. He showed enough in 2017 so the right team looking for their next quarterback might find him interesting, but not so much so that the Colts got an offer overwhelming enough to trade him with Luck still on the mend.

Derek Carr Height: 6-3 Weight: 220 College: Fresno St. Draft: 2014/2 (36) Born: 3/28/1991 Age: 27 Risk: Green

Year	Team	G/GS	Snaps	Att	Comp	C%	Yds	TD	INT/Adj	FUM	ASR	NY/P	Rk	DVOA	Rk	DYAR	Rk	YAR	Runs	Yds	TD	DVOA	DYAR	QBR
2015	OAK	16/16	1014	573	350	61.1%	3987	32	13/15	10	4.6%	6.2	22	4.1%	13	582	12	428	33	138	0	-25.3%	-13	49.2
2016	OAK	15/15	1048	560	357	63.8%	3937	28	6/12	5	3.3%	6.7	12	19.8%	6	1164	7	1038	39	70	0	-50.3%	-39	62.1
2017	OAK	15/15	937	515	323	62.7%	3496	22	13/19	8	4.3%	6.6	14	9.7%	13	709	12	721	23	66	0	-66.5%	-35	46.7
2018	OAK			548	350	63.8%	3972	26	12	6		6.6		13.7%					39	76	0	-11.0%		
2016:	51% Short	33% Mid	9% Deep	7% Bomb	aDOT: 8 (25)	YAC: 5.1 (13)	ALEX: 1.0	2017:	53% Short	29% Mid	10% Deep	9% Bomb	aDOT: 8.7 (17)	YAC: 5.0 (20)	ALEX: 1.4

Carr completed 67.9 percent of his passes for seven touchdowns and just two interceptions in his first four games last year. Then he suffered a back injury against the Broncos, and all of his numbers gradually sagged as the year went on, give or take a freaky Thursday night Chiefs game. Carr was down to a 58.1 percent completion rate and a 5:5 touchdown to interception ratio in his final five games, when it was clear that he wasn't comfortable holding on to the ball for too long and opponents had figured out Todd Dowling's quick-passing game.

The big offseason Carr question doesn't involve his back, but his relationship with Jon Gruden, who is known for his demanding, difficult relationships with actual quarterbacks (as opposed to rookie prospects smiling for the cameras on Gruden's ESPN shows). Successful Gruden quarterbacks like Brad Johnson and Rich Gannon were of a different generation; late-career Gruden expected Chris Simms to rub some dirt on a ruptured spleen and get back in the game. The good news for Carr is that there is no serious challenger on the roster. The bad news is that Gruden has never trusted a quarterback under 30, and Carr is still just 26.

Matt Cassel Height: 6-5 Weight: 230 College: USC Draft: 2005/7 (230) Born: 17-May-1982 Age: 36 Risk: Green

Year	Team	G/GS	Snaps	Att	Comp	C%	Yds	TD	INT/Adj	FUM	ASR	NY/P	Rk	DVOA	Rk	DYAR	Rk	YAR	Runs	Yds	TD	DVOA	DYAR	QBR
2015	2TM	9/8	415	204	119	58.3%	1276	5	7/7	4	6.6%	5.5	35	-23.7%	35	-172	34	-210	15	78	0	-29.3%	-10	33.7
2016	TEN	4/1	98	51	30	58.8%	284	2	2/2	1	9.4%	4.8	—	-23.1%	—	-38	—	-68	4	3	0	-107.8%	-7	71.7
2017	TEN	2/1	77	42	25	59.5%	162	1	2/2	2	16.9%	2.5	—	-96.0%	—	-257	—	-222	0	0	0	—	—	12.0
2018	DET			557	335	60.1%	3783	21	17	8		5.3		-9.5%					21	38	1	-4.4%		
2016:	45% Short	41% Mid	9% Deep	5% Bomb	aDOT: 8.1 (–)	YAC: 2.4 (–)	ALEX: 0.8	2017:	54% Short	35% Mid	7% Deep	4% Bomb	aDOT: 8.0 (–)	YAC: 1.8 (–)	ALEX: -0.5

Uh-oh. Could Matthew Stafford's ironman streak be in jeopardy after the Lions signed Matt Cassel in April? Cassel has a bit of Ryan Fitzpatrick in him in that he inexplicably keeps finding a way to start each season. Cassel has at least one start in each of the last 10 seasons, and he has taken over for past injured starters such as Tom Brady, Christian Ponder, Tony Romo, and Marcus Mariota last year with Tennessee. Cassel was atrocious in his only start last year, a loss to the lowly Dolphins, so Detroit fans better hope he doesn't find his way onto the field for anything more than a few handoffs or kneeldowns in a blowout win.

Kirk Cousins

| | | Height: 6-3 | | Weight: 214 | | College: Michigan State | | | Draft: 2012/4 (102) | | Born: 19-Aug-1988 | | Age: 30 | | Risk: Green | | | | | | |

Year	Team	G/GS	Snaps	Att	Comp	C%	Yds	TD	INT/Adj	FUM	ASR	NY/P	Rk	DVOA	Rk	DYAR	Rk	YAR	Runs	Yds	TD	DVOA	DYAR	QBR
2015	WAS	16/16	1026	543	379	69.8%	4166	29	11/13	8	5.4%	7.0	6	16.9%	6	1023	7	1125	26	48	5	-3.1%	8	70.1
2016	WAS	16/16	1063	606	406	67.0%	4917	25	12/16	9	3.9%	7.6	3	20.9%	5	1317	3	1197	34	96	4	1.9%	18	71.7
2017	WAS	16/16	1012	540	347	64.3%	4093	27	13/20	13	7.7%	6.5	16	-0.6%	18	395	16	318	49	179	4	-2.3%	21	52.3
2018	MIN			541	356	65.8%	4055	27	13	8		6.7		12.0%					51	168	0	2.2%		

| 2016: | 51% Short | 29% Mid | 12% Deep | 8% Bomb | aDOT: 9.2 (9) | YAC: 4.8 (26) | ALEX: 2.3 | 2017: | 57% Short | 28% Mid | 9% Deep | 6% Bomb | aDOT: 8.1 (24) | YAC: 6.1 (3) | ALEX: 0.7 |

When Cousins was in Washington, his team went 1-21 when his passer rating was under 85.0 (minimum 15 attempts), a rating that is a little below the league average (87.8) since his rookie year of 2012. Some of this is the era in which Cousins plays. If your passer rating was above 85.0 in 1975, then you were doing very well. But in Cousins' era, you would likely be having a mediocre day at best. Still, 1-21 is the worst record in NFL history for any quarterback with at least 16 such games in his career. Cousins didn't even finish the lone win (2014 Titans), as Colt McCoy had to lead a game-winning drive that day. Cousins really needed above-average statistical passing games to win in Washington, but those days are over for him.

In theory, adding a good quarterback in his prime to a Super Bowl contender should work well. As we showed in the Minnesota chapter, this just doesn't happen often in NFL history, but the Vikings have a fun experiment beginning in 2018. If everything around Cousins is going to be better, then it stands to reason that he should reap the benefits of that and have a career season.

Jay Cutler

| | | Height: 6-3 | | Weight: 220 | | College: Vanderbilt | | | Draft: 2006/1 (11) | | Born: 29-Apr-1983 | | Age: 35 | | Risk: N/A | | | | | | |

Year	Team	G/GS	Snaps	Att	Comp	C%	Yds	TD	INT/Adj	FUM	ASR	NY/P	Rk	DVOA	Rk	DYAR	Rk	YAR	Runs	Yds	TD	DVOA	DYAR	QBR
2015	CHI	15/15	992	483	311	64.4%	3659	21	11/14	8	5.2%	6.9	8	8.6%	9	659	10	556	38	201	1	43.7%	84	60.7
2016	CHI	5/5	275	137	81	59.1%	1059	4	5/8	6	10.8%	6.2	--	-18.5%	--	-69	--	-218	5	24	0	-0.1%	3	33.2
2017	MIA	14/14	764	429	266	62.0%	2666	19	14/17	6	4.8%	5.7	24	-9.9%	26	35	26	63	19	32	0	1.4%	5	39.8

| 2016: | 49% Short | 27% Mid | 14% Deep | 10% Bomb | aDOT: 9.2 (--) | YAC: 5.1 (--) | ALEX: 0.7 | 2017: | 54% Short | 28% Mid | 10% Deep | 8% Bomb | aDOT: 8.7 (16) | YAC: 4.6 (28) | ALEX: 0.1 |

$10 million was enough to get Cutler to postpone his retirement for a year. Helped by his relationship with former Bears offensive coordinator Adam Gase, Cutler was pushed into an underneath passing offense and still managed to throw a pick per start. It would have been best for both sides if last year never happened. The Dolphins could have made headway on a real backup plan for Ryan Tannehill, and Cutler would have a better broadcasting gig. Cutler finishes his career with 3,204 DYAR, 2,022 of which came in his first three years in Denver before the surprising trade to the Bears. This feels about like the middle-of-the-road result for a first-round quarterback.

Andy Dalton

| | | Height: 6-2 | | Weight: 215 | | College: TCU | | | Draft: 2011/2 (35) | | Born: 29-Oct-1987 | | Age: 31 | | Risk: Green | | | | | | |

Year	Team	G/GS	Snaps	Att	Comp	C%	Yds	TD	INT/Adj	FUM	ASR	NY/P	Rk	DVOA	Rk	DYAR	Rk	YAR	Runs	Yds	TD	DVOA	DYAR	QBR
2015	CIN	13/13	798	386	255	66.1%	3250	25	7/9	5	5.1%	7.7	3	31.7%	2	1135	4	1059	57	142	3	-8.1%	9	73.1
2016	CIN	16/16	1085	563	364	64.7%	4206	18	8/16	9	7.3%	6.6	15	7.6%	12	738	10	667	46	184	4	20.6%	60	58.3
2017	CIN	16/16	941	496	297	59.9%	3320	25	12/16	4	7.3%	5.8	23	-8.6%	24	87	24	75	38	99	0	11.3%	24	41.1
2018	CIN			520	322	62.0%	3638	22	11	6		5.9		0.0%					38	113	1	-0.3%		

| 2016: | 48% Short | 34% Mid | 12% Deep | 6% Bomb | aDOT: 8.1 (24) | YAC: 5.1 (16) | ALEX: 0.8 | 2017: | 53% Short | 31% Mid | 10% Deep | 7% Bomb | aDOT: 8.6 (20) | YAC: 5.8 (6) | ALEX: 2.2 |

Dalton had surprisingly not-terrible red zone numbers (8.6% DVOA), given the Bengals' overall offensive misery. That can only improve if Tyler Eifert, John Ross, and the other injury-prone Bengals can stay on the field and give Dalton a full complement of weaponry for the first time since 2015. So much for the good news. Most of Red's numbers fell in 2017, but most worrisome is the completion percentage, which fell below 60 percent for the first time since his rookie year. It's a warning sign that can't all be chalked up to the chaos on the offensive line and in the coaching booth. Much of it can be explained by the increase in his average depth of target and number of longer throws. Dalton has never been known for his deep-ball accuracy; the defining image of his career is an open A.J. Green fruitlessly chasing a Dalton long toss out of bounds. He remains an accurate underneath passer, which has allowed him to be a starter in the league, albeit one whose value continues to plummet as more and more teams find better quarterbacks. His team-friendly contract keeps Dalton from being in Joe Flacco territory for the moment, and with next year's draftable crop of passers looking far grimmer than those in recent years, Dalton's gig appears safe for the moment—which is good news for him, but not necessarily for anyone else.

Chase Daniel   Height: 6-0   Weight: 225   College: Missouri   Draft: 2009/FA   Born: 7-Oct-1986   Age: 32   Risk: Red

Year	Team	G/GS	Snaps	Att	Comp	C%	Yds	TD	INT/Adj	FUM	ASR	NY/P	Rk	DVOA	Rk	DYAR	Rk	YAR	Runs	Yds	TD	DVOA	DYAR	QBR
2015	KC	2/0	13	2	2	100.0%	4	0	0/0	0	0.0%	2.0	--	-32.7%	--	-3	--	-1	2	-2	0	--	--	98.5
2016	PHI	1/0	6	1	1	100.0%	16	0	0/0	0	0.0%	11.0	--	360.8%	--	16	--	13	0	0	0	--	--	99.5
2017	NO	1/0	5	0	0	0.0%	0	0	0/0	0	--	--	--	--	--	--	--	--	3	-2	0	--	--	--
2018	CHI			550	326	59.3%	3842	23	19	11		5.7		-19.6%					53	153	1	-12.5%		

2016:   100% Short   0% Mid   0% Deep   0% Bomb   aDOT: 5.0 (–)   YAC: 11.0 (–)   ALEX: 0.0

Daniel is the David Humm (look him up) of his era. Daniel can tie Humm's record of 10 consecutive seasons to start a quarterback's career without ever throwing more than 40 passes in a year. Daniel was undrafted in 2009, and never has there been another NFL quarterback about whom we knew so little after nine years. He has only thrown 78 passes in that time with two starts (both in Week 17 games). After already making more than $24 million in his NFL career, Daniel signed a two-year deal worth $10 million with the Bears. He's familiar with Matt Nagy from their time together in Kansas City, but unless Mitchell Trubisky is injured, we're still not going to know much about Daniel. It makes you a little jealous to think that someone can enjoy millions and the NFL experience without really demonstrating if they can play. Chase Daniel, a quarterback for the everyman.

Sam Darnold   Height: 6-3   Weight: 221   College: USC   Draft: 2018/1 (3)   Born: 5-Jun-1997   Age: 21   Risk: Red

Year	Team	G/GS	Snaps	Att	Comp	C%	Yds	TD	INT/Adj	FUM	ASR	NY/P	Rk	DVOA	Rk	DYAR	Rk	YAR	Runs	Yds	TD	DVOA	DYAR	QBR
2018	NYJ			510	308	60.3%	3768	19	19	11		6.2		-17.4%					51	76	2	-21.3%		

This was how we all predicted things would end up before the 2017 season, but it took a couple of twists. Darnold was the darling of the mock draft community, but suffered a dip in production at USC, missing a few too many easy throws and getting picked 13 times. Meanwhile, the Jets were supposed to be the worst team in the NFL, and instead wound up competent enough that they had to surrender three No. 2 picks to get into franchise quarterback selection territory. QBASE expects average production from Darnold, but he has the tantalizing combination of arm talent and throws on the run that get scouts drooling. Sounds a lot like what was said about Jameis Winston when he came out. It's unlikely that Teddy Bridgewater and Josh McCown will hold him off the field all season, but Darnold is definitely a quarterback whom a franchise would prefer to beat the bad habits out of before throwing him into the fire. And as we went over in the Jets chapter, there are quite a few of them.

Austin Davis   Height: 6-2   Weight: 221   College: Southern Mississippi   Draft: 2012/FA   Born: 2-Jun-1989   Age: 29   Risk: Yellow

Year	Team	G/GS	Snaps	Att	Comp	C%	Yds	TD	INT/Adj	FUM	ASR	NY/P	Rk	DVOA	Rk	DYAR	Rk	YAR	Runs	Yds	TD	DVOA	DYAR	QBR
2015	CLE	3/2	159	94	56	59.6%	547	1	3/5	2	11.5%	4.0	--	-52.9%	--	-269	--	-287	7	33	0	-24.5%	-5	22.1
2017	SEA	3/0	5	0	0	0.0%	0	0	0/0	0	--	--	--	--	--	--	--	--	1	-1	0	--	--	--
2018	SEA			507	306	60.4%	3382	17	14	11		5.4		-19.9%					43	154	1	-0.1%		

There was a time when Davis was hailed as potentially the next Kurt Warner; an undrafted free agent who had fought his way to NFL relevancy and looked halfway competent for a month ... until defenses figured out his tendencies and turned him into a turnover machine. Davis is a scrambler with a popgun for an arm. He's adequate, for a backup, when given time to throw, but he tends to panic when faced with pressure. That sounds like exactly what you want behind this Seattle offensive line.

Ryan Fitzpatrick   Height: 6-2   Weight: 221   College: Harvard   Draft: 2005/7 (250)   Born: 24-Nov-1982   Age: 36   Risk: Red

Year	Team	G/GS	Snaps	Att	Comp	C%	Yds	TD	INT/Adj	FUM	ASR	NY/P	Rk	DVOA	Rk	DYAR	Rk	YAR	Runs	Yds	TD	DVOA	DYAR	QBR
2015	NYJ	16/16	1046	562	335	59.6%	3905	31	15/23	5	3.9%	6.6	14	3.5%	14	542	13	670	60	270	2	18.0%	73	63.6
2016	NYJ	14/11	765	403	228	56.6%	2710	12	17/20	10	4.8%	6.2	23	-22.6%	32	-319	32	-329	33	130	0	-19.5%	-11	45.4
2017	TB	6/3	299	163	96	58.9%	1103	7	3/3	0	5.2%	6.3	--	17.3%	--	307	--	315	15	78	0	17.5%	17	54.4
2018	TB			576	338	58.8%	3993	21	22	5		5.9		-15.9%					48	202	1	6.1%		

2016:   42% Short   32% Mid   19% Deep   7% Bomb   aDOT: 9.7 (6)   YAC: 4.9 (23)   ALEX: 1.7   2017:   50% Short   31% Mid   11% Deep   8% Bomb   aDOT: 9.5 (–)   YAC: 4.1 (–)   ALEX: 1.0

We know Fitzpatrick went to Harvard, but did he major in Machiavellianism? Fitzpatrick has rarely been even a competent starter, but thanks to Jameis Winston's three-game suspension he is expected to make multiple starts for the 11th season in a row. Fitzpatrick survived last year's three-game stint in place of Winston, but good luck to him this year when he opens against the Saints, Eagles, and Steelers.

Joe Flacco

Height: 6-6 Weight: 236 College: Delaware Draft: 2008/1 (18) Born: 16-Jan-1985 Age: 33 Risk: Red

Year	Team	G/GS	Snaps	Att	Comp	C%	Yds	TD	INT/Adj	FUM	ASR	NY/P	Rk	DVOA	Rk	DYAR	Rk	YAR	Runs	Yds	TD	DVOA	DYAR	QBR
2015	BAL	10/10	717	413	266	64.4%	2791	14	12/14	5	4.2%	6.3	21	-10.5%	26	17	27	55	13	23	3	6.8%	15	40.9
2016	BAL	16/16	1111	672	436	64.9%	4317	20	15/19	5	5.4%	5.8	28	-14.6%	29	-155	30	-44	21	58	2	15.8%	21	58.4
2017	BAL	16/16	1027	549	352	64.1%	3141	18	13/17	6	4.5%	5.2	33	-19.3%	30	-301	32	-102	25	54	1	37.0%	24	43.0
2018	BAL			557	351	63.0%	3486	21	13	7		5.4		-13.9%					21	47	1	-3.5%		

| 2016: | 56% Short | 29% Mid | 9% Deep | 6% Bomb | aDOT: 7.7 (30) | YAC: 4.8 (27) | ALEX: 0.8 | 2017: | 60% Short | 27% Mid | 9% Deep | 5% Bomb | aDOT: 7.0 (34) | YAC: 4.1 (34) | ALEX: 0.5 |

Remember when debating Flacco's "elite" status was a thing? It's hard to conjure said memories, it's been so long. All he is these days is "execrable." Since Gary Kubiak left Baltimore after the 2014 season, Flacco has gone downhill like an 18-wheeler whose brakes have failed. There aren't any splits or schemes that could sugarcoat Flacco's 2017 season. Flacco was bad in the red zone, bad under center, worse in the shotgun. About the best thing Flacco can cling to is the fact that he closed the season on a relative high—four of his six best games by QBR came in the last five contests. Alas, the bummer of the bunch was the critical finale against the Bengals. Flacco seldom plays well against Cincinnati, but even a decent performance might have put that game out of reach.

As we've stated elsewhere in this and previous versions of the *Almanac*, Flacco is paid to be one quarterback, and performs like a different, far worse quarterback. It's an untenable position, which is why Lamar Jackson is in town and will, soon enough, be the starter.

Nick Foles

Height: 6-5 Weight: 243 College: Arizona Draft: 2012/3 (88) Born: 20-Jan-1989 Age: 29 Risk: Red

Year	Team	G/GS	Snaps	Att	Comp	C%	Yds	TD	INT/Adj	FUM	ASR	NY/P	Rk	DVOA	Rk	DYAR	Rk	YAR	Runs	Yds	TD	DVOA	DYAR	QBR
2015	STL	11/11	656	337	190	56.4%	2052	7	10/12	4	3.8%	5.6	34	-27.9%	37	-353	37	-428	17	20	1	32.0%	21	30.0
2016	KC	3/1	106	55	36	65.5%	410	3	0/1	0	7.1%	6.4	—	-9.9%	—	5	—	26	4	-4	0	—	—	35.3
2017	PHI	7/3	212	101	57	56.4%	537	5	2/2	6	5.4%	4.8	—	-28.5%	—	-114	—	-63	11	3	0	-123.1%	-19	28.0
2018	PHI			559	347	62.0%	3866	23	11	8		6.1		0.2%					35	104	0	-0.6%		

| 2016: | 56% Short | 27% Mid | 7% Deep | 9% Bomb | aDOT: 8.1 (–) | YAC: 5.5 (–) | ALEX: -1.0 | 2017: | 51% Short | 30% Mid | 14% Deep | 5% Bomb | aDOT: 8.7 (–) | YAC: 4.2 (–) | ALEX: 0.9 |

Add Foles' four playoff starts (three last year, one for the 2013 Eagles) to his regular-season stats, then subtract the Rams season from Foles' resume, and he has completed 743-of-1,198 passes (62.0 percent) for 8,866 yards (7.4 yards per attempt), 62 touchdowns, and 20 interceptions in 32 starts. Because 32 starts amount to two 16-game seasons, Foles' career to date suggests he could have 4,433-yard, 31-touchdown, 10-interception seasons in an offensive system untainted by Jeff Fisher. His teams have a 21-11 record in those non-Rams games if you are into that sort of thing, 17-6 since his rookie season with the pathetic 2012 Eagles. So Foles has starter credentials beyond the whole "Super Bowl MVP" thing.

Foles' career shape, if not his play style, is similar to Jeff Hostetler's arc in many ways. Hoss had a few solid years as a starter after his Super Bowl heroics but peaked as a guy who could help you squeak into the playoffs. That's Foles: at 29 years old and with minimal mobility, he probably maxed out in Super Bowl LII, and future buyers of his services should be wary of that. Still, it was a heck of a time and place to peak.

Blaine Gabbert

Height: 6-4 Weight: 234 College: Missouri Draft: 2011/1 (10) Born: 15-Oct-1989 Age: 29 Risk: Yellow

Year	Team	G/GS	Snaps	Att	Comp	C%	Yds	TD	INT/Adj	FUM	ASR	NY/P	Rk	DVOA	Rk	DYAR	Rk	YAR	Runs	Yds	TD	DVOA	DYAR	QBR
2015	SF	8/8	511	282	178	63.1%	2031	10	7/6	4	8.0%	6.1	27	-15.6%	31	-85	31	-118	32	185	1	16.2%	34	42.6
2016	SF	6/5	344	160	91	56.9%	925	5	6/8	0	5.5%	5.1	—	-25.4%	—	-158	—	-205	40	173	2	13.3%	52	60.3
2017	ARI	5/5	345	171	95	55.6%	1086	6	6/9	7	10.6%	5.1	—	-26.4%	—	-189	—	-304	22	82	0	-36.0%	-21	30.7
2018	TEN			504	301	59.7%	3206	16	17	6		5.4		-20.2%					43	106	0	-13.0%		

| 2016: | 48% Short | 35% Mid | 14% Deep | 4% Bomb | aDOT: 8.6 (–) | YAC: 4.0 (–) | ALEX: -1.2 | 2017: | 50% Short | 33% Mid | 12% Deep | 6% Bomb | aDOT: 9.8 (–) | YAC: 4.3 (–) | ALEX: 0.2 |

The highlight of Gabbert's professional career, when his last pass is finally thrown, will probably be Arizona's 27-24 victory last year against Jacksonville, the franchise that made him a first-round pick. In that game, he threw two touchdown passes and led a last-minute drive to set up the game-winning 57-yard field goal against the No. 1 DVOA pass defense. The rest of the season was not nearly so redemptive: Gabbert posted the third-worst DVOA of his career despite the best efforts and encouragement of head coach Bruce Arians.

Gabbert's days as a first-round reclamation project are probably, thankfully, done; he will stick around to hold clipboards and make the occasional start as an injury replacement, providing yet another example of just how difficult it is for a high draft pick at quarterback to play his way out of the league.

Jimmy Garoppolo Height: 6-2 Weight: 226 College: Eastern Illinois Draft: 2014/2 (62) Born: 11-Feb-1991 Age: 27 Risk: Yellow

Year	Team	G/GS	Snaps	Att	Comp	C%	Yds	TD	INT/Adj	FUM	ASR	NY/P	Rk	DVOA	Rk	DYAR	Rk	YAR	Runs	Yds	TD	DVOA	DYAR	QBR
2015	NE	5/0	13	4	1	25.0%	6	0	0/0	0	1.2%	1.5	—	-98.6%	—	-25	—	-21	5	-5	0	—	—	2.4
2016	NE	6/2	144	63	43	68.3%	502	4	0/0	2	3.6%	7.3	—	44.4%	—	225	—	182	10	6	0	-4.3%	1	89.9
2017	2TM	6/5	353	178	120	67.4%	1560	7	5/8	1	3.2%	8.2	—	39.1%	—	598	—	556	15	11	1	-8.8%	2	80.5
2018	SF			555	359	64.8%	4244	24	15	5		6.8		9.6%					45	103	1	-9.3%		

| 2016: | 48% Short | 37% Mid | 10% Deep | 6% Bomb | aDOT: 7.7 (–) | YAC: 5.8 (–) | ALEX: 1.8 | 2017: | 41% Short | 42% Mid | 14% Deep | 4% Bomb | aDOT: 9.2 (–) | YAC: 6.0 (–) | ALEX: 1.7 |

Heading into the 2017 season, Garoppolo was cozily ensconced in New England as the backup and likely successor to Tom Brady. As Brady continued to excel in 2017, Garoppolo became expendable, as there was no feasible way for New England to keep both on the roster the following season, and he was shipped to San Francisco mid-year. Handing a five-year, $137.5 million contract to someone who has started less than a full season is risky, but the 49ers can get out of the contract for minimal dead money after 2019 if Garoppolo does not perform. From his short stint as the starter, it does not look like that will be necessary. Had Garoppolo thrown enough passes to qualify, he would have ranked first in percentage of passes thrown to the intermediate level (6 to 15 yards past the line of scrimmage). The 2018 season will be a good test to see if he can keep living in that midrange area and shredding defenses.

Garrett Gilbert Height: 6-4 Weight: 220 College: Southern Methodist Draft: 2014/6 (214) Born: 19-Jul-1991 Age: 27 Risk: Yellow

Year	Team	G/GS	Snaps	Att	Comp	C%	Yds	TD	INT/Adj	FUM	ASR	NY/P	Rk	DVOA	Rk	DYAR	Rk	YAR	Runs	Yds	TD	DVOA	DYAR	QBR
2018	CAR			522	291	55.7%	3317	15	15	11		5.1		-25.0%					45	181	0	-0.8%		

Garrett Gilbert was drafted in the sixth round in 2014. Since then, he has bounced from practice squad to practice squad, and has yet to throw an NFL pass. Last season was the first time he was ever placed on an active roster. Now, with Derek Anderson out of town, he's the apparent backup quarterback in Carolina. Gilbert's draft bio praised his size and his NFL pedigree—his father, Gale, was an 11-year NFL backup—and not so much his arm, release point, or grace under pressure. The Panthers have gone from the team with the most experience at backup quarterback to one of the teams with the least, and hopefully, they'll never have to find out just how Gilbert will look when he finally gets a chance to line up behind center.

Mike Glennon Height: 6-6 Weight: 218 College: North Carolina State Draft: 2013/3 (73) Born: 12-Dec-1989 Age: 29 Risk: Red

Year	Team	G/GS	Snaps	Att	Comp	C%	Yds	TD	INT/Adj	FUM	ASR	NY/P	Rk	DVOA	Rk	DYAR	Rk	YAR	Runs	Yds	TD	DVOA	DYAR	QBR
2016	TB	2/0	15	11	10	90.9%	75	1	0/0	0	1.7%	6.8	—	65.8%	—	65	—	64	0	0	0	—	—	96.9
2017	CHI	4/4	264	140	93	66.4%	833	4	5/7	6	5.4%	5.0	—	-37.1%	—	-231	—	-151	4	4	0	-114.7%	-13	21.9
2018	ARI			579	367	63.4%	3543	17	15	10		5.2		-14.6%					33	26	1	-25.0%		

| 2016: | 82% Short | 18% Mid | 0% Deep | 0% Bomb | aDOT: 3.9 (–) | YAC: 3.7 (–) | ALEX: -2.0 | 2017: | 62% Short | 29% Mid | 7% Deep | 2% Bomb | aDOT: 6.5 (–) | YAC: 3.6 (–) | ALEX: -1.5 |

Going into 2017, Glennon had performed like a backup throughout his career, but that did not stop the Bears from shelling out $18.5 million to have him make four starts before turning over quarterback duties to rookie Mitchell Trubisky. The Bears then released Glennon once it became clear that Trubisky would be the quarterback moving forward, which was simultaneously the right decision and pretty embarrassing for the front office. How Glennon managed to garner such a large guarantee was mindboggling considering that he had not started a game since 2014 at that point, and the Bears certainly looked foolish when he racked up -231 DYAR in those four games, third-worst among quarterbacks with less than 200 passes. Glennon is slated to be third-string in Arizona this year, but given the injury history of both rookie Josh Rosen and starter Sam Bradford, it is entirely possible that Glennon sees the field at some point. Of course, in that case, something will have gone terribly wrong.

Jared Goff

Height: 6-4 Weight: 215 College: California Draft: 2016/1 (1) Born: 14-Oct-1994 Age: 24 Risk: Green

Year	Team	G/GS	Snaps	Att	Comp	C%	Yds	TD	INT/Adj	FUM	ASR	NY/P	Rk	DVOA	Rk	DYAR	Rk	YAR	Runs	Yds	TD	DVOA	DYAR	QBR
2016	LAR	7/7	393	205	112	54.6%	1089	5	7/8	5	11.1%	3.8	34	-74.8%	34	-881	34	-819	8	16	1	-22.8%	-3	22.2
2017	LAR	15/15	937	477	296	62.1%	3804	28	7/10	8	5.4%	7.4	4	24.0%	5	1125	6	1041	28	51	1	-20.6%	-6	52.0
2018	LAR			525	330	62.8%	3807	25	12	12		6.4		6.8%					33	84	2	0.7%		

2016: 54% Short 33% Mid 8% Deep 5% Bomb aDOT: 7.1 (32) YAC: 5.1 (14) ALEX: -2.5 2017: 52% Short 29% Mid 12% Deep 7% Bomb aDOT: 8.5 (21) YAC: 6.8 (1) ALEX: 0.2

After the greatest one-year turnaround we've ever seen for a quarterback, where does Goff go from here? The best news for Rams fans is that Goff isn't a finished project yet. He still struggled with pressure, ranking 33rd in the league as his passing DVOA dropped from 83.4% in a clean pocket to -56.8% under duress. He also holds on to the ball too long; according to NFL.com's Next Gen Stats, he averaged 2.93 seconds before the throw, the fifth-longest time in the league. That just means there are areas where Goff can improve, and we've seen what he can do with some competent coaching. Sean McVay rightfully gets lots of credit for simplifying Goff's reads and placing him in situations where he can succeed. At the end of the day, however, Goff had to make those throws—something 2016's Goff showed no ability to actually do. Goff needs to continue to make forward strides if he's going to be a player you build an offense around, but last season showed that he is capable of making those strides. That's a huge sigh of relief for Rams fans, who went from watching a historic bust to someone who looked right at home in a playoff-caliber team.

Robert Griffin

Height: 6-2 Weight: 223 College: Baylor Draft: 2012/1 (2) Born: 12-Feb-1990 Age: 28 Risk: Red

Year	Team	G/GS	Snaps	Att	Comp	C%	Yds	TD	INT/Adj	FUM	ASR	NY/P	Rk	DVOA	Rk	DYAR	Rk	YAR	Runs	Yds	TD	DVOA	DYAR	QBR
2016	CLE	5/5	302	147	87	59.2%	886	2	3/5	4	12.9%	4.4	–	-36.0%	–	-270	–	-331	31	190	2	17.0%	39	45.0
2018	BAL			513	311	60.6%	3258	14	15	12		5.5		-23.8%					82	339	3	-0.1%		

2016: 54% Short 31% Mid 5% Deep 10% Bomb aDOT: 8.4 (–) YAC: 5.0 (–) ALEX: -2.0

After a year in the wilderness, Griffin is back on an NFL roster, at least for the moment. The oddity is that Griffin went from "that's a weird signing" to "hey, he'll be a great mentor" the split-second Baltimore drafted a player who resembles the 2012 wonder version of Griffin. I'm sure RG3 does have some sound advice for Lamar Jackson, such as, "Don't play for a passive-aggressive coach who can't wait to chuck you overboard in favor of the white guy" and "Don't play on a bad knee when the field looks like a sand dune" and "Don't solicit wedding gifts from the public shortly after signing a multi-million dollar contract." Otherwise, something tells us Jackson will be just fine without Griffin's guidance on poor pocket presence and inaccurate throws.

Chad Henne

Height: 6-2 Weight: 230 College: Michigan Draft: 2008/2 (57) Born: 2-Jul-1985 Age: 33 Risk: Yellow

Year	Team	G/GS	Snaps	Att	Comp	C%	Yds	TD	INT/Adj	FUM	ASR	NY/P	Rk	DVOA	Rk	DYAR	Rk	YAR	Runs	Yds	TD	DVOA	DYAR	QBR
2016	JAX	1/0	1	0	0	0.0%	0	0	0/0	0	–	–	–	–	–	–	–	–	1	-2	0	–	–	–
2017	JAX	2/0	23	2	0	0.0%	0	0	0/1	0	0.0%	0.0	–	-87.5%	–	-10	–	-12	5	-5	0	–	–	3.0
2018	KC			531	324	60.9%	3591	17	14	6		5.4		-18.4%					35	144	0	2.1%		

2017: 100% Short 0% Mid 0% Deep 0% Bomb aDOT: 2.0 (–) YAC: 0.0 (–) ALEX: -7.0

Henne faded into the shadows after being benched for a rookie Blake Bortles in 2014. Since then, he has thrown just two regular season passes. Henne has started at least 10 games in three separate seasons in his career, two of them in Miami. In all three seasons, Henne failed to rank in the top 20 in quarterback DVOA. Henne also threw more interceptions than touchdowns all three times. Throughout his career, Henne has been best in small doses, either as a placeholder for a future quarterback or in relief of an injured starter. Henne has proven to be functional in those situations, but hopefully Kansas City will not require his services in an expanded role.

Kevin Hogan

Height: 6-3 Weight: 218 College: Stanford Draft: 2016/5 (162) Born: 20-Oct-1992 Age: 26 Risk: Yellow

Year	Team	G/GS	Snaps	Att	Comp	C%	Yds	TD	INT/Adj	FUM	ASR	NY/P	Rk	DVOA	Rk	DYAR	Rk	YAR	Runs	Yds	TD	DVOA	DYAR	QBR
2016	CLE	4/0	50	26	14	53.8%	104	0	2/2	0	7.8%	3.4	–	-86.2%	–	-131	–	-133	8	105	1	108.2%	45	70.3
2017	CLE	4/1	134	75	46	61.3%	517	4	5/7	1	9.2%	6.0	–	-32.4%	–	-120	–	-86	10	71	0	45.5%	27	35.8
2018	WAS			489	279	61.9%	3220	21	20	9		5.7		-17.0%					92	440	4	19.3%		

2016: 62% Short 33% Mid 5% Deep 0% Bomb aDOT: 5.6 (–) YAC: 3.8 (–) ALEX: 2.5 2017: 56% Short 23% Mid 11% Deep 10% Bomb aDOT: 9.4 (–) YAC: 4.8 (–) ALEX: 6.4

Hogan is a third-rate Bobby Douglass: he pairs (cough) deceptive speed with the kind of arm that should automatically disqualify him from throwing passes in the NFL. Hogan showed what he can do as a runner in his rookie year, when he ran for 104 yards in just three quarters against Cincinnati. That is all well and good, but when he got more playing time in 2017, he threw as many interceptions as his new teammate Alex Smith did in the same season despite throwing 430 fewer passes. Washington shipped the 188th pick in this year's draft to Cleveland in exchange for Hogan and the 205th pick. Even at that bargain-basement price, it was a surprising move that only makes sense if a) they are going to lean heavily on Smith's mobility this year and were desperate for a backup who could run the same game plan, or b) they have lost their minds.

Brian Hoyer   Height: 6-2   Weight: 215   College: Michigan State   Draft: 2009/FA   Born: 13-Oct-1985   Age: 33   Risk: Red

Year	Team	G/GS	Snaps	Att	Comp	C%	Yds	TD	INT/Adj	FUM	ASR	NY/P	Rk	DVOA	Rk	DYAR	Rk	YAR	Runs	Yds	TD	DVOA	DYAR	QBR
2015	HOU	11/9	674	369	224	60.7%	2606	19	7/6	6	7.5%	6.1	26	-3.0%	20	201	20	372	15	44	0	57.9%	26	59.6
2016	CHI	6/5	314	200	134	67.0%	1445	6	0/0	3	2.5%	7.1	6	19.4%	7	404	18	506	7	-2	0	-47.9%	-3	61.1
2017	2TM	11/6	381	211	123	58.3%	1287	4	4/8	3	7.7%	5.2	34	-16.7%	28	-80	27	-111	9	4	1	-96.7%	-29	31.9
2018	NE			545	347	63.8%	3666	21	10	9		6.0		-0.6%					48	67	0	-20.8%		
2016:		51% Short		30% Mid		15% Deep		5% Bomb		aDOT: 7.8 (27)		YAC: 5.2 (11)		ALEX: 1.3		2017:		57% Short		27% Mid		11% Deep	4% Bomb	aDOT: 8.1 (25) YAC: 4.6 (30) ALEX: 0.1

A punishment-absorbing starter when you have no real quarterback, Hoyer can soak up all the snaps you'd use to evaluate someone with a future and give you the kind of performance that fondly makes you think "meh." The questions about how he'd do in a high-stakes situation were answered firmly in Kansas City's 35-14 butt-whipping of the Texans, in Houston, in the 2015 divisional round. Hoyer threw four picks and had 3.03 net yards per attempt. Now in New England, where it all began, Hoyer can look forward to several offensive snaps dedicated to the pursuit of kneeling.

Brett Hundley   Height: 6-3   Weight: 226   College: UCLA   Draft: 2015/5 (147)   Born: 15-Jun-1993   Age: 25   Risk: Yellow

Year	Team	G/GS	Snaps	Att	Comp	C%	Yds	TD	INT/Adj	FUM	ASR	NY/P	Rk	DVOA	Rk	DYAR	Rk	YAR	Runs	Yds	TD	DVOA	DYAR	QBR
2016	GB	4/0	22	10	2	20.0%	17	0	1/0	1	0.0%	1.7	--	-109.2%	--	-80	--	-75	3	-2	0	--	--	6.3
2017	GB	11/9	622	316	192	60.8%	1836	9	12/12	4	9.1%	4.8	35	-28.3%	34	-396	34	-517	36	270	2	40.3%	100	41.2
2018	GB			523	322	61.5%	3221	20	16	10		5.5		-14.8%					70	298	3	13.9%		
2016:		30% Short		50% Mid		10% Deep		10% Bomb		aDOT: 9.3 (–)		YAC: 6.5 (–)		ALEX: 5.7		2017:		61% Short		23% Mid		9% Deep	7% Bomb	aDOT: 8.1 (23) YAC: 5.3 (17) ALEX: 2.0

Hundley once had some pre-draft buzz, but fell to the fifth round in 2015. We saw him in his first significant action last season after Aaron Rodgers broke his collarbone, and let's just say the draft slotting was justified. Hundley showed flashes of Rodgers' greatness at times in the way he would scramble out of trouble before finding a receiver, but he was just never going to be able to replicate what Rodgers can do for that long of a period. That doesn't mean he can't be backup material in this league, but the Packers traded for DeShone Kizer from Cleveland, who actually has a similar style to Hundley. Each had his best game last year against Pittsburgh. Hundley's comeback effort against the Browns also cost Kizer the elusive win he was hoping for in his rookie year. Now they can both sit behind Rodgers while the rest of us hope QB1's collarbone has been strengthened with adamantium.

Lamar Jackson   Height: 6-2   Weight: 216   College: Louisville   Draft: 2018/1 (32)   Born: 17-Jan-1997   Age: 21   Risk: Yellow

Year	Team	G/GS	Snaps	Att	Comp	C%	Yds	TD	INT/Adj	FUM	ASR	NY/P	Rk	DVOA	Rk	DYAR	Rk	YAR	Runs	Yds	TD	DVOA	DYAR	QBR
2018	BAL			474	286	60.4%	3207	17	15	9		6.0		-16.3%					99	340	4	-3.8%		

As we mentioned in the Ravens chapter, Jackson is a very good prospect merely as a passer, and there is every reason to expect him to push Joe Flacco for the starting role sooner rather than later. Ironically, his main flaw in 2017 was throwing on the move, and like many college quarterbacks his progressions and mechanics have room for improvement. But with good coaching he should be fine.

Then, of course, there are his wheels, which are exceptional. Jackson averaged more than 6 yards a carry for his career, and scored an even 50 touchdowns on the ground. The numbers don't quite convey the experience of watching him accelerate past defenders or seemingly evaporate just as he is about to be tackled, only to reform in the open space beyond—he had some runs that can only be called Barry Sanders-esque. While running as a stratagem isn't very viable long-term for NFL quarterbacks (and Jackson will need to beef up his spindly trunk in order to last), elusiveness in the pocket certainly is, and Jackson's sack rate was well down in 2017 despite a less talented offensive line. About the only credible criticism to make against Jackson's collegiate career was that he was spotty in big games, though calling bowl games "big" sometimes stretches the meaning of the word. On the basis that first-round quarterbacks seldom sit out the entire season anymore, plus the possibility of special packages built into weekly game plans for him, Jackson is worthy of a late-round flier in your fantasy draft.

Landry Jones

			Height: 6-4			Weight: 218		College: Oklahoma			Draft: 2013/4 (115)			Born: 4-Apr-1989			Age: 29			Risk: Red

Year	Team	G/GS	Snaps	Att	Comp	C%	Yds	TD	INT/Adj	FUM	ASR	NY/P	Rk	DVOA	Rk	DYAR	Rk	YAR	Runs	Yds	TD	DVOA	DYAR	QBR
2015	PIT	7/2	109	55	32	58.2%	513	3	4/4	1	3.1%	8.7	--	-1.5%	--	37	--	-12	5	-5	0	--	--	35.9
2016	PIT	8/2	161	86	53	61.6%	558	4	2/3	0	4.9%	5.9	--	-13.7%	--	-14	--	46	6	-4	0	--	--	46.6
2017	PIT	3/1	70	28	23	82.1%	239	1	1/1	1	10.5%	7.1	--	-36.5%	--	-52	--	-12	8	-10	0	--	--	43.3
2018	PIT			575	352	61.2%	3861	24	17	9		6.0		-3.9%					32	64	1	-3.9%		

2016: 47% Short 29% Mid 14% Deep 9% Bomb aDOT: 9.0 (–) YAC: 4.6 (–) ALEX: 1.9   2017: 61% Short 23% Mid 10% Deep 6% Bomb aDOT: 7.8 (–) YAC: 3.4 (–) ALEX: -0.1

Jones' biggest asset is his experience. He's locked in a battle for the backup slot with rookie Mason Rudolph and second-year player Joshua Dobbs, but Jones is the only one who has actually seen NFL action. Jones got his second straight Week 17 start against Cleveland last year, and looked … serviceable. He completed 23-of-28 passes, but had -44 DYAR as he sliced his way through a defense that in no way wanted to challenge any of his receivers. Jones is someone Pittsburgh trusts; they consider him an elite backup who can come in for a spot start here and there without causing disaster. While his days in Pittsburgh are numbered—this is the last year on his current deal—that experience and trust mean he's likely to be the guy Pittsburgh turns to if they need an emergency start to keep them in playoff contention.

Case Keenum

			Height: 6-2			Weight: 209		College: Houston			Draft: 2012/FA			Born: 17-Feb-1988			Age: 30			Risk: Green

Year	Team	G/GS	Snaps	Att	Comp	C%	Yds	TD	INT/Adj	FUM	ASR	NY/P	Rk	DVOA	Rk	DYAR	Rk	YAR	Runs	Yds	TD	DVOA	DYAR	QBR
2015	STL	6/5	297	125	76	60.8%	828	4	1/4	3	3.1%	6.2	--	-1.1%	--	83	--	144	12	5	0	-70.7%	-17	47.7
2016	LAR	10/9	596	322	196	60.9%	2201	9	11/10	5	6.3%	6.0	26	-19.5%	31	-183	31	-174	20	51	1	22.2%	25	43.4
2017	MIN	15/14	1017	481	325	67.6%	3547	22	7/10	1	4.0%	7.1	8	28.1%	1	1293	4	1307	40	160	1	58.3%	76	69.7
2018	DEN			560	348	62.2%	3893	23	15	7		6.1		1.2%					43	112	2	-5.3%		

2016: 53% Short 29% Mid 10% Deep 7% Bomb aDOT: 8.3 (19) YAC: 5.3 (8) ALEX: 0.7   2017: 57% Short 25% Mid 13% Deep 6% Bomb aDOT: 8.0 (26) YAC: 5.6 (11) ALEX: 0.4

Keenum threw 215 passes while his team was leading last season and just 154 when they were trailing (plus 111 when the game was tied). He threw just 16 passes with the Vikings trailing in the final four minutes and just 101 fourth-quarter passes overall, a telltale sign of how often the Vikings were protecting relatively safe leads. In other words, Keenum benefited from all of the little tilts that can make a decent quarterback on a great team look like an all-time great; see Dak Prescott in 2017 for an example of what can happen when conditions suddenly become less than ideal. Keenum's league-leading DVOA indicates that he made the most of the great circumstances that he was handed. He's a fine "game manager" in the non-insulting, non-euphemistic sense. The Broncos need, and seem to think they are getting, something more.

Cody Kessler

			Height: 6-1			Weight: 220		College: USC			Draft: 2016/3 (93)			Born: 11-Apr-1993			Age: 25			Risk: Red

Year	Team	G/GS	Snaps	Att	Comp	C%	Yds	TD	INT/Adj	FUM	ASR	NY/P	Rk	DVOA	Rk	DYAR	Rk	YAR	Runs	Yds	TD	DVOA	DYAR	QBR
2016	CLE	9/8	349	195	128	65.6%	1380	6	2/3	4	9.7%	5.8	29	-7.6%	22	50	24	80	11	18	0	-37.1%	-9	49.6
2017	CLE	3/0	48	23	11	47.8%	126	0	1/1	0	18.9%	2.7	--	-66.4%	--	-98	--	-73	1	-1	0	--	--	5.1
2018	JAX			529	330	62.4%	3540	18	15	11		5.7		-14.3%					40	111	1	-9.0%		

2016: 47% Short 36% Mid 12% Deep 6% Bomb aDOT: 8.1 (22) YAC: 5.0 (21) ALEX: -0.8   2017: 67% Short 8% Mid 8% Deep 17% Bomb aDOT: 10.7 (–) YAC: 6.4 (–) ALEX: -1.1

The Browns don't so much throw muck at a wall and see what sticks, as throw muck at a wall and powerscrub it before it has a chance to dry. As a third-round rookie thrown onto a terrible team in 2016, Kessler was never likely to be much of a success in Cleveland, but he did show flashes of the ability that made him a three-year starter at USC. Last year he appeared in only three games after the team drafted another quarterback, this time second-round pick DeShone Kizer. Naturally, both were traded away this offseason to make way for yet *another* highly drafted rookie.

Kessler is the kind of quarterback who could easily make a 15-year career of holding clipboards with the occasional injury replacement cameo. Smart and poised, but weak-armed and extremely conservative, he is a coach's dream backup: clever and competent enough to hold the fort until the starter returns, but not a convincing threat to take the job for himself. In his rookie campaign, he managed a 3:1 touchdown-to-interception ratio—but that still amounted to only six touchdowns in nine games. He ranked 31st out of 34 qualifiers in ALEX that season. Kessler will be fine as the backup to Blake Bortles, and might even steal a start or two if Bortles plays particularly poorly, but he is very unlikely to be the long-term answer to the Jaguars' questionable quarterback situation.

DeShone Kizer

Height: 6-4 Weight: 233 College: Notre Dame Draft: 2017/2 (52) Born: 3-Jan-1996 Age: 23 Risk: Red

Year	Team	G/GS	Snaps	Att	Comp	C%	Yds	TD	INT/Adj	FUM	ASR	NY/P	Rk	DVOA	Rk	DYAR	Rk	YAR	Runs	Yds	TD	DVOA	DYAR	QBR
2017	CLE	15/15	887	476	255	53.6%	2894	11	22/23	9	6.7%	5.4	31	-34.5%	35	-756	35	-889	77	419	5	-3.7%	32	29.4
2018	GB			528	309	58.5%	3352	19	18	12		5.6		-18.9%					84	418	4	19.5%		

2017: 56% Short 22% Mid 14% Deep 8% Bomb aDOT: 9.5 (9) YAC: 5.5 (14) ALEX: 1.2

"Young. I mean, young." That was the impression Green Bay coach Mike McCarthy had for Kizer, a quarterback the team traded for in March, after a few weeks of drills and OTA practices in May. Yes, Kizer is just 22, and last year he threw the second-most passes in NFL history by a quarterback in his age-21 season. He also threw 22 interceptions and fumbled nine times for the winless Browns in a generally terrible debut year. Kizer's six red zone interceptions were tied for the most by any quarterback in a season since 2001, and Cleveland had the fifth-lowest red zone passing DVOA since 1986. The receiver depth and offensive creativity has not been up to Green Bay's usual standards lately, so while Kizer should see an upgrade in his surroundings, he's really just Brett Hundley with a better college pedigree.

Kyle Lauletta

Height: 6-3 Weight: 222 College: Richmond Draft: 2018/4 (108) Born: 27-Oct-1995 Age: 23 Risk: Green

Year	Team	G/GS	Snaps	Att	Comp	C%	Yds	TD	INT/Adj	FUM	ASR	NY/P	Rk	DVOA	Rk	DYAR	Rk	YAR	Runs	Yds	TD	DVOA	DYAR	QBR
2018	NYG			528	298	56.5%	3241	14	18	9		5.1		-25.0%					32	66	2	-5.8%		

After the Giants just drafted Davis Webb in 2017, the selection of Lauletta came as something of a surprise. Lauletta is a former FCS standout and three-year starter from Richmond. He tore his right ACL in the final regular-season game of his junior year in 2016 and missed the Spiders' playoff run. Despite an 8-3 regular season record, including a win over the FBS Virginia Cavaliers, Richmond failed to make it out of the quarterfinals without Lauletta at the helm. When Lauletta returned in 2017, he reasserted himself as one of the best quarterbacks in the FCS through his mobility and quick throwing process. Lauletta not only processes the field well pre-snap, but he has a swift throwing motion that works in tandem with his processing ability to enable him to be effective in the quick game. With his mobility, Lauletta is able to execute sprint-outs, boot-action, and any number of option running or run-pass option concepts. Lauletta's lackluster arm strength may put a low ceiling on his potential, but in a well-constructed offense, Lauletta can be the one to help his team stay the course when the starter goes down.

Andrew Luck

Height: 6-4 Weight: 234 College: Stanford Draft: 2012/1 (1) Born: 12-Mar-1989 Age: 29 Risk: Red

Year	Team	G/GS	Snaps	Att	Comp	C%	Yds	TD	INT/Adj	FUM	ASR	NY/P	Rk	DVOA	Rk	DYAR	Rk	YAR	Runs	Yds	TD	DVOA	DYAR	QBR
2015	IND	7/7	508	293	162	55.3%	1881	15	12/16	3	5.4%	5.8	30	-17.5%	32	-126	33	-189	33	196	0	31.2%	59	47.6
2016	IND	15/15	1013	545	346	63.5%	4240	31	13/13	6	7.6%	6.8	10	7.3%	13	719	11	671	64	341	2	26.2%	93	71.2
2018	IND			541	332	61.3%	4082	29	13	5		6.6		11.5%					60	251	2	14.5%		

2016: 47% Short 32% Mid 14% Deep 7% Bomb aDOT: 8.9 (13) YAC: 4.9 (22) ALEX: 1.5

The projection you see assumes Luck will play all 16 games and be in reasonable health. Obviously, that sort of projection for a player who did not play last year deserves a Red risk sign, and only technological limitations mean the "Red" in this table is not blinking and accompanied by a warning siren. Hopefully you'll have a better idea of Luck's precise details by the time you do your fantasy draft, and the KUBIAK workbook we sell on our website will have a projection updated accordingly. The offensive scheme change and, yes, offensive line additions mean that a return to a sack rate more like 2015's seems reasonable, and you will probably not see quite as many deep throws, so Luck's yards per completion will probably fall closer to league average. One key for Luck will be consistent mechanics, as he has in the past shown an occasional tendency to be spotty on short throws.

Paxton Lynch

Height: 6-7 Weight: 244 College: Memphis Draft: 2016/1 (26) Born: 12-Feb-1994 Age: 24 Risk: Green

Year	Team	G/GS	Snaps	Att	Comp	C%	Yds	TD	INT/Adj	FUM	ASR	NY/P	Rk	DVOA	Rk	DYAR	Rk	YAR	Runs	Yds	TD	DVOA	DYAR	QBR
2016	DEN	3/2	176	83	49	59.0%	497	2	1/2	2	10.2%	5.0	--	-18.8%	--	-46	--	-57	11	25	0	-43.0%	-12	28.8
2017	DEN	2/2	98	45	30	66.7%	295	2	3/4	2	17.9%	4.5	--	-76.3%	--	-224	--	-191	5	30	0	16.5%	5	22.9
2018	DEN			566	340	59.9%	3484	15	17	11		4.7		-30.0%					46	193	1	0.8%		

| 2016: | 38% Short | 37% Mid | 12% Deep | 12% Bomb | aDOT: 11.2 (--) | YAC: 3.2 (--) | ALEX: 3.0 | 2017: | 53% Short | 30% Mid | 14% Deep | 4% Bomb | aDOT: 8.5 (--) | YAC: 4.0 (--) | ALEX: 2.9 |

The scuttlebutt on Lynch is that he enjoyed being a redshirt freshman a little too much in 2016, failing to assert himself as a potential starter the way first-round rookies are supposed to, then didn't respond well to the pressure of having to compete for the job with Trevor Siemian last year. We're not usually in the scuttlebutt business, but the story clicks with the reality: Lynch was comically overmatched before getting injured in his Week 11 start, and he surrendered two interceptions and a strip-sack touchdown against Chiefs backups in Week 17 relief duty. It's not a good sign when a handpicked-by-the-CEO first-round pick still looks like a street free agent making an emergency start after two full seasons with the team, but handpicked status has its privileges. Lynch faces little competition to be Case Keenum's backup in 2018. Look for him to settle into the role a little too comfortably.

Patrick Mahomes

Height: 6-2 Weight: 225 College: Texas Tech Draft: 2017/1 (10) Born: 17-Sep-1995 Age: 23 Risk: Yellow

Year	Team	G/GS	Snaps	Att	Comp	C%	Yds	TD	INT/Adj	FUM	ASR	NY/P	Rk	DVOA	Rk	DYAR	Rk	YAR	Runs	Yds	TD	DVOA	DYAR	QBR
2017	KC	1/1	63	35	22	62.9%	284	0	1/1	0	5.8%	7.3	--	11.7%	--	54	--	57	7	10	0	9.2%	4	64.8
2018	KC			541	335	61.9%	4078	26	17	8		6.7		-1.2%					66	271	2	8.5%		

| | | | | | | | | | 2017: | 61% Short | 24% Mid | 8% Deep | 8% Bomb | aDOT: 7.7 (--) | YAC: 7.9 (--) | ALEX: -0.6 |

Excitement over Mahomes has been pent up since the moment he was drafted. After four seasons of the consistent yet lackluster Alex Smith leading the way, the Chiefs organization is ready to steer in the other direction. Mahomes is a college Air Raid quarterback, coming from Kliff Kingsbury's Texas Tech system that blends the traditional Mike Leach Air Raid with modern NFL concepts. Mahomes was often chastised for running an "easy" offense, but given Kingsbury's influence from NFL playbooks and the autonomy Kingsbury gave Mahomes, "easy" was an unfit description. Mahomes was given a mountain of responsibilities and handled them well. In the rare event Texas Tech's offensive line held up, Mahomes showed great knowledge and execution of the offense, in addition to quality ball placement to every level of the field. As daring as he was, Mahomes seldom made poor decisions and often knew what was best for keeping the offense on pace. Mahomes did all of this while playing with unique footwork patterns and a flexible throwing motion, two traits that are rooted in his days as a baseball player and give Mahomes an edge over some of his more robotic peers playing quarterback. The Chiefs may not reap immediate rewards from Mahomes in 2018, but there is reason to believe the future is bright.

Eli Manning

Height: 6-4 Weight: 218 College: Mississippi Draft: 2004/1 (1) Born: 3-Jan-1981 Age: 38 Risk: Red

Year	Team	G/GS	Snaps	Att	Comp	C%	Yds	TD	INT/Adj	FUM	ASR	NY/P	Rk	DVOA	Rk	DYAR	Rk	YAR	Runs	Yds	TD	DVOA	DYAR	QBR
2015	NYG	16/16	1106	618	387	62.6%	4432	35	14/15	11	5.2%	6.6	13	-1.9%	19	404	18	535	20	61	0	-0.4%	5	60.5
2016	NYG	16/16	1061	598	377	63.0%	4027	26	16/26	7	3.8%	6.3	20	-6.5%	20	188	20	192	21	-9	0	-12.5%	0	51.8
2017	NYG	15/15	1018	571	352	61.6%	3468	19	13/17	11	5.6%	5.5	28	-8.2%	23	117	23	-1	12	26	1	-15.1%	-1	43.8
2018	NYG			570	352	61.7%	3860	23	13	6		6.1		-4.3%					22	37	0	-12.6%		

| 2016: | 52% Short | 31% Mid | 9% Deep | 8% Bomb | aDOT: 8.0 (26) | YAC: 5.3 (9) | ALEX: 2.9 | 2017: | 55% Short | 32% Mid | 7% Deep | 6% Bomb | aDOT: 7.4 (32) | YAC: 4.6 (27) | ALEX: 1.9 |

The Giants' offense quickly devolved into a nightmare situation for Manning. A slew of injuries at wide receiver ravaged the unit, leaving Manning with little to work with. Sprinkle a poor offensive line and a lack of dynamic running backs into the equation, and it becomes clear as to why the offense struggled. It would be foolish to argue any quarterback would have looked good in that offense. That being said, Manning himself did little to make up for the losses, and showed continued signs of decline. More damning than anything are Manning's down-by-down splits. On first and second down, Manning posted subpar DVOA ratings at -3.5% and -4.8%, respectively, but that could have been expected given the lack of surrounding talent. However, Manning plummeted to -17.9% DVOA on third and fourth downs, despite having one of the lowest average yards-to-go in the league at 6.7 yards. Manning was given enough opportunity to salvage drives on manageable third downs, but his ever-declining mobility and arm strength have rendered him ineffective. For now, Manning is still the man in New York, and he should be better equipped for success this season as the offense has reloaded and players return from injury, but it has become increasingly difficult to bank on Manning returning to Super Bowl form this late in his career.

Sean Mannion Height: 6-6   Weight: 229   College: Oregon State   Draft: 2015/3 (89)   Born: 23-Apr-1992   Age: 26   Risk: Yellow

Year	Team	G/GS	Snaps	Att	Comp	C%	Yds	TD	INT/Adj	FUM	ASR	NY/P	Rk	DVOA	Rk	DYAR	Rk	YAR	Runs	Yds	TD	DVOA	DYAR	QBR
2015	STL	1/0	7	7	6	85.7%	31	0	0/0	0	0.0%	4.4	--	4.3%	--	7	--	4	0	0	0	--	--	92.4
2016	LAR	1/0	16	6	3	50.0%	19	0	1/1	1	0.0%	3.2	--	-108.8%	--	-45	--	-53	1	-1	0	-373.2%	-20	0.4
2017	LAR	5/1	102	37	22	59.5%	185	0	0/0	2	8.3%	4.1	--	-66.6%	--	-141	--	-97	9	-2	0	-33.0%	-6	14.4
2018	LAR			483	291	60.3%	3327	18	15	11		5.6		-16.7%					21	35	1	-8.7%		

2016:   86% Short   0% Mid   14% Deep   0% Bomb   aDOT: 3.9 (–)   YAC: 4.7 (–)   ALEX: -6.0   2017:   70% Short   13% Mid   13% Deep   5% Bomb   aDOT: 7.0 (–)   YAC: 3.3 (–)   ALEX: -3.3

Mannion saw his first extended action in 2017, getting to start Week 17 against San Francisco with the rest of the backups. It was not particularly pretty, as he put up -141 passing DYAR and missed multiple easy throws. One would presume he would do better if given the opportunity to play with the Rams' starters, as he missed out on a few big plays thanks to drops. Mannion has the frame old-school quarterback coaches dream of; at 6-foot-6 with 33-inch arms, he looks like he just walked out of QB central casting. "Walked" is the operative term; he ran a 5.14-second 40-yard dash and is basically a stationary target in the backfield for opposing pass-rushers. He has the backup job sewn up for now, but he's a holdover from the Jeff Fisher regime. It would not be shocking if he's replaced sooner rather than later.

EJ Manuel Height: 6-5   Weight: 240   College: Florida State   Draft: 2013/1 (16)   Born: 19-Mar-1990   Age: 28   Risk: Yellow

Year	Team	G/GS	Snaps	Att	Comp	C%	Yds	TD	INT/Adj	FUM	ASR	NY/P	Rk	DVOA	Rk	DYAR	Rk	YAR	Runs	Yds	TD	DVOA	DYAR	QBR
2015	BUF	7/2	155	84	52	61.9%	561	3	3/5	2	8.1%	5.7	--	-16.0%	--	-26	--	-12	17	64	1	20.8%	34	37.0
2016	BUF	6/1	78	26	11	42.3%	131	0	0/1	2	10.8%	3.9	--	-47.2%	--	-58	--	-22	8	22	0	-55.2%	-17	29.3
2017	OAK	2/1	76	43	24	55.8%	265	1	1/2	0	8.3%	5.0	--	9.6%	--	56	--	17	2	15	0	44.1%	6	51.8
2018	OAK			544	327	60.1%	3736	19	21	10		5.8		-16.0%					41	124	1	0.0%		

2016:   26% Short   48% Mid   19% Deep   7% Bomb   aDOT: 11.5 (–)   YAC: 2.5 (–)   ALEX: 4.5   2017:   48% Short   32% Mid   16% Deep   5% Bomb   aDOT: 10.1 (–)   YAC: 3.5 (–)   ALEX: 2.5

Manuel is now 0-4 in spot starts over the last three years. Yeah, we know, we know: you don't come here for Quarterback Winz. Let's look at the games. Manuel led the Raiders to a 30-17 loss to the Ravens last year; he didn't play poorly, but the Ravens led 24-10 at halftime, which gives a general sense of how the game went. He led the Bills to a 30-10 loss to the Jets in Week 17 of 2016, with Cardale Jones mopping up the game. He led the 2015 Bills to a 34-21 loss to the Bengals that wasn't as close as the score, and to a 34-31 London loss to the Jaguars that was 27-10 midway through the second quarter thanks to both a pick-six and a strip-six. If the purpose of a veteran backup is to give his team a chance during random relief appearances, Manuel has proven he's not the man for the job, primarily because he's shockingly inaccurate on even simple throws and doesn't scramble as well as all that. Nonetheless, Manuel is locked in as Derek Carr's backup unless Connor Cook blossoms under Jon Gruden, which feels unlikely to happen.

Marcus Mariota Height: 6-4   Weight: 222   College: Oregon   Draft: 2015/1 (2)   Born: 30-Oct-1993   Age: 25   Risk: Green

Year	Team	G/GS	Snaps	Att	Comp	C%	Yds	TD	INT/Adj	FUM	ASR	NY/P	Rk	DVOA	Rk	DYAR	Rk	YAR	Runs	Yds	TD	DVOA	DYAR	QBR
2015	TEN	12/12	736	370	230	62.2%	2818	19	10/14	10	10.1%	6.3	17	-13.2%	29	-53	30	123	34	252	2	-0.6%	20	61.0
2016	TEN	15/15	963	451	276	61.2%	3426	26	9/11	8	5.4%	7.0	9	11.1%	10	681	13	719	60	349	2	9.5%	52	64.9
2017	TEN	15/15	945	453	281	62.0%	3232	13	15/17	2	5.3%	6.4	17	-3.3%	20	236	19	262	60	312	5	35.6%	114	54.9
2018	TEN			506	316	62.5%	3646	23	12	6		6.3		3.1%					67	388	3	27.0%		

2016:   37% Short   38% Mid   16% Deep   9% Bomb   aDOT: 10.0 (4)   YAC: 4.6 (29)   ALEX: 2.4   2017:   47% Short   32% Mid   16% Deep   5% Bomb   aDOT: 9.3 (10)   YAC: 4.5 (31)   ALEX: 2.3

Assuming Matt LaFleur implements a reasonably traditional brand of the Kubiak-Shanahan offense as expected, Mariota should be very excited about next season. Twenty-two teams had a higher DVOA last season when using play-action than when not, but only the Dolphins saw a bigger DVOA improvement than Mariota's Titans, and no team saw a greater increase in yards per play. The Titans pass offense ranked No. 27 in DVOA without play-action, but No. 8 with a play fake (both of those numbers include quarterback scrambles). Under Mike Mularkey, the team only used play-action on a roughly league-average 23 percent of pass plays, but the Rams team with LaFleur as its offensive coordinator had the second-highest rate in the league (29 percent) and the Falcons team he coached the previous year ranked No. 1. Anytime the game situation permits it, LaFleur is likely to have the Titans near the league lead in play-action percentage. That should be very good news for his quarterback.

Mariota did have one odd statistical outlier: last year, only five teams had a lower DVOA on passes marked deep in the NFL play-by-play (16-plus yards in the air) than on passes marked short. Tennessee's -21.9% difference was the biggest drop-off, and can be almost entirely accounted for by their -63.1% DVOA on passes to the deep left—by far the worst mark in the league, way behind Cincinnati's -27.9%. Mariota threw five of his 15 interceptions to that area of the field, and it was the only area to which he did not throw a touchdown in the regular season. Tennessee's DVOA there was 124.6% in 2016, and Mariota did throw a touchdown deep left to Corey Davis in the postseason, so this is more likely an odd piece of small-sample randomness than a significant issue.

Baker Mayfield

| | | Height: 6-1 | | Weight: 215 | | College: Oklahoma | | | | Draft: 2018/1 (1) | | Born: 14-Apr-1995 | | Age: 23 | | Risk: Red | |

Year	Team	G/GS	Snaps	Att	Comp	C%	Yds	TD	INT/Adj	FUM	ASR	NY/P	Rk	DVOA	Rk	DYAR	Rk	YAR	Runs	Yds	TD	DVOA	DYAR	QBR
2018	CLE			516	313	60.7%	3560	24	17	9		6.1		-13.0%					82	375	4	14.5%		

Sports Info Solutions' college charting shows just how dominant Mayfield's senior season was. Against man coverage, he was second in FBS in adjusted yards per attempt. Against zone coverage, he was first. Throwing inside the numbers, he was first. Throwing outside the numbers, he was second. He excelled at throwing comebacks and fades, and was the most accurate quarterback in FBS on "broken plays," a.k.a. scramble drills. The one place he struggled was on third down, where his stats were more middle-of-the-pack, but this seems to be a one-year blip. Look at 2016 as well, and out of the two-year span he had the best third-down conversion rate out of this year's top dozen quarterback prospects. And lest you worry about his leadership skills, let us remind you that Hue Jackson after the draft compared Mayfield to the Pied Piper when it came to getting teammates to follow him. Unless the Browns shock conventional wisdom by staying in wild-card contention all year, expect Mayfield to be starting by December. We're definitely believers and can't wait to see what he does in the NFL.

AJ McCarron

| | | Height: 6-3 | | Weight: 220 | | College: Alabama | | | | Draft: 2014/5 (164) | | Born: 13-Sep-1990 | | Age: 28 | | Risk: Red | |

Year	Team	G/GS	Snaps	Att	Comp	C%	Yds	TD	INT/Adj	FUM	ASR	NY/P	Rk	DVOA	Rk	DYAR	Rk	YAR	Runs	Yds	TD	DVOA	DYAR	QBR
2015	CIN	7/3	257	119	79	66.4%	854	6	2/2	1	8.5%	6.0	--	6.9%	--	151	--	138	14	31	0	-8.2%	2	64.4
2016	CIN	1/0	2	0	0	0.0%	0	0	0/0	0	--	--	--	--	--	--	--	--	0	0	0	--	--	--
2017	CIN	3/0	26	14	7	50.0%	66	0	0/0	0	5.5%	3.8	--	-11.1%	--	0	--	-11	0	0	0	--	--	21.3
2018	BUF			483	292	60.3%	3178	17	17	8		5.6		-19.0%					54	161	1	-12.4%		

| | | | | | | | | 2017: | 57% Short | 29% Mid | 7% Deep | 7% Bomb | aDOT: 7.6 (–) | YAC: 8.1 (–) | ALEX: -6.8 |

After winning his grievance to become a free agent, McCarron went from "hot property who could be worth two Day 2 picks from the Browns" to "the last available guy NFL teams would consider as a starting quarterback." McCarron doesn't have the cannon to even deke some team into a Mike Glennon contract. The Bengals screwed up royally by not dealing him, particularly if those offers were anything near the rumored second- and third-round picks they were getting from Cleveland before a deal was nixed at the deadline due to "late paperwork." Per McCarron, he thought he was a Brown at 4 p.m. EST, and learned it fell apart at 4:03. We hear Tyrod Taylor missed a few throws as Bills starting quarterback. McCarron will miss even more if he beats out Josh Allen to start.

Josh McCown

| | | Height: 6-4 | | Weight: 215 | | College: Sam Houston State | | | | Draft: 2002/3 (81) | | Born: 4-Jul-1979 | | Age: 39 | | Risk: Green | |

Year	Team	G/GS	Snaps	Att	Comp	C%	Yds	TD	INT/Adj	FUM	ASR	NY/P	Rk	DVOA	Rk	DYAR	Rk	YAR	Runs	Yds	TD	DVOA	DYAR	QBR
2015	CLE	8/8	509	292	186	63.7%	2109	12	4/5	9	7.1%	6.2	23	-5.8%	23	110	23	81	20	98	1	0.7%	12	53.9
2016	CLE	5/3	262	165	90	54.5%	1100	6	6/10	7	10.5%	5.3	--	-34.4%	--	-269	--	-276	7	21	0	-37.8%	-6	35.1
2017	NYJ	13/13	819	397	267	67.3%	2926	18	9/14	11	9.4%	6.2	19	-8.9%	25	62	25	133	37	124	5	24.3%	50	51.9
2018	NYJ			533	329	61.8%	3784	23	15	14		6.0		-6.2%					42	133	2	5.4%		

| 2016: | 43% Short | 36% Mid | 9% Deep | 13% Bomb | aDOT: 10.2 (–) | YAC: 5.2 (–) | ALEX: 2.8 | 2017: | 57% Short | 29% Mid | 8% Deep | 6% Bomb | aDOT: 7.9 (29) | YAC: 4.7 (24) | ALEX: 0.0 |

OK, the Jets got more out of McCown than anyone thought they would in 2018. That said, it was still below-average play, he still can't be relied on to stay healthy for more than six games at a time, and it didn't get them anywhere. Somewhere along the way, mainstream outlets started to value the steadily below-average again, and the Jets agreed in giving McCown $10 million to keep him away from the Bills. But what have the Jets learned from using Josh McCown other than that their offense can work a lot better with a real quarterback? Whatever black magic and charisma McCown has conjured up to make people think he's a worthwhile mentor, he should bottle it and sell it.

Colt McCoy

		Height: 6-1		Weight: 216		College: Texas				Draft: 2010/3 (85)		Born: 5-Sep-1986		Age: 32		Risk: Red

Year	Team	G/GS	Snaps	Att	Comp	C%	Yds	TD	INT/Adj	FUM	ASR	NY/P	Rk	DVOA	Rk	DYAR	Rk	YAR	Runs	Yds	TD	DVOA	DYAR	QBR
2015	WAS	2/0	44	11	7	63.6%	128	1	0/0	1	7.9%	9.5	--	20.9%	--	22	--	14	3	-3	0	--	--	36.8
2017	WAS	1/0	4	0	0	0.0%	0	0	0/0	0	--	--	--	--	--	--	--	--	0	0	0	--	--	--
2018	WAS			535	346	64.6%	3838	22	15	11		6.0		-6.8%					48	176	2	7.5%		

McCoy has started only four games and thrown just 157 passes in the last six seasons. At some point, a respectable franchise would have brought in a younger passer to challenge McCoy's backup position and perhaps take over for Kirk Cousins; the best Washington could do was to trade for Kevin Hogan. McCoy should easily fend off Hogan in training camp, then make $2.8 million to punch a clock and hold a clipboard.

Matt Moore

		Height: 6-3		Weight: 202		College: Oregon State				Draft: 2007/FA		Born: 9-Aug-1984		Age: 34		Risk: N/A

Year	Team	G/GS	Snaps	Att	Comp	C%	Yds	TD	INT/Adj	FUM	ASR	NY/P	Rk	DVOA	Rk	DYAR	Rk	YAR	Runs	Yds	TD	DVOA	DYAR	QBR
2015	MIA	1/0	7	1	1	100.0%	14	0	0/0	0	0.0%	14.0	--	340.2%	--	12	--	11	3	-2	0	--	--	98.1
2016	MIA	4/3	190	87	55	63.2%	721	8	3/5	1	2.0%	8.5	--	34.7%	--	259	--	285	1	-1	0	--	--	82.9
2017	MIA	4/2	203	127	78	61.4%	861	4	5/5	0	9.2%	5.8	--	-16.1%	--	-41	--	-30	3	9	0	-51.2%	-8	37.7

2016:	58% Short	22% Mid	11% Deep	9% Bomb	aDOT: 8.8 (–)	YAC: 6.6 (–)	ALEX: 3.3	2017:	58% Short	23% Mid	9% Deep	10% Bomb	aDOT: 8.8 (–)	YAC: 4.1 (–)	ALEX: 0.1

The last quarterback to start a playoff game for the Dolphins, Moore has been a halfway decent backup passer for the last decade. The only real blunder on his resume was a 2010 cameo with the Panthers after Jake Delhomme's career subsumed the season. He had a positive DYAR in every other year he had more than 10 attempts up until 2017. Surprisingly unemployed as of this writing, Moore should send out a press release letting everyone know he has never protested anything.

Cam Newton

		Height: 6-5		Weight: 248		College: Auburn				Draft: 2011/1 (1)		Born: 11-May-1989		Age: 29		Risk: Yellow

Year	Team	G/GS	Snaps	Att	Comp	C%	Yds	TD	INT/Adj	FUM	ASR	NY/P	Rk	DVOA	Rk	DYAR	Rk	YAR	Runs	Yds	TD	DVOA	DYAR	QBR
2015	CAR	16/16	1077	495	296	59.8%	3837	35	10/14	5	6.9%	6.8	11	7.6%	12	630	11	855	132	636	10	8.1%	142	66.0
2016	CAR	15/14	1023	510	270	52.9%	3509	19	14/22	3	6.8%	6.0	25	-13.0%	28	-64	28	-64	90	359	5	-12.5%	-2	53.1
2017	CAR	16/16	1063	492	291	59.1%	3302	22	16/16	9	7.2%	6.0	21	-6.9%	21	141	21	197	139	754	6	6.5%	120	47.7
2018	CAR			479	290	60.5%	3344	23	12	7		6.1		-3.9%					114	697	5	15.4%		

2016:	31% Short	47% Mid	12% Deep	10% Bomb	aDOT: 11.0 (1)	YAC: 4.9 (24)	ALEX: 3.5	2017:	53% Short	29% Mid	13% Deep	6% Bomb	aDOT: 8.9 (14)	YAC: 5.5 (13)	ALEX: 2.5

Blake Bortles. Blaine Gabbert. Cam Newton? It's an odd trio, for sure, but they do have one unfortunate statistic in common: a lower than expected completion percentage. Newton's passing plus-minus of -14.6 was third-worst in the league last year among qualified quarterbacks, and this is nothing new. He's at -64.9 for his career, the third lowest in the NFL since 2011 behind the two aforementioned gentlemen. With Bortles hitting a career high of -5.5 last season and Gabbert hopefully banished to the phantom zone, Newton has a real chance of passing both of them and taking the crown for himself.

Of course, one of the reasons Newton is in that position is because he does so many other things well, making him valuable above and beyond his passing statline. No, precision ball placement isn't his forte, but his athleticism allows him to do things few other quarterbacks in NFL history have been able to do. He also hasn't been blessed with the best receiving corps in his time in Carolina, meaning some of those incompletions aren't entirely his fault. New offensive coordinator Norv Turner says he is going to both feature Newton as a runner and improve his completion percentage to the mid- to high-60s. That's somewhat doubtful—Newton has never been above 61.7 percent—but if he can do that, few quarterbacks in the league would match Newton's value.

Brock Osweiler

Height: 6-7 Weight: 242 College: Arizona State Draft: 2012/2 (57) Born: 22-Nov-1990 Age: 28 Risk: Red

Year	Team	G/GS	Snaps	Att	Comp	C%	Yds	TD	INT/Adj	FUM	ASR	NY/P	Rk	DVOA	Rk	DYAR	Rk	YAR	Runs	Yds	TD	DVOA	DYAR	QBR
2015	DEN	8/7	515	275	170	61.8%	1967	10	6/10	4	7.2%	6.1	25	-3.2%	21	153	22	140	21	61	1	-6.1%	6	48.8
2016	HOU	15/14	977	510	301	59.0%	2957	15	16/21	5	5.4%	5.2	33	-26.8%	33	-558	33	-502	30	131	2	35.5%	54	55.3
2017	DEN	6/4	350	172	96	55.8%	1088	5	5/7	2	5.5%	5.7	--	-16.2%	--	-56	--	-90	14	64	1	-8.5%	2	46.4
2018	MIA			531	309	58.2%	3344	15	18	7		5.0		-26.2%					25	72	1	1.2%		

2016: 47% Short 35% Mid 11% Deep 7% Bomb aDOT: 8.9 (15) YAC: 3.9 (33) ALEX: 0.6 2017: 56% Short 29% Mid 9% Deep 6% Bomb aDOT: 7.8 (–) YAC: 5.3 (–) ALEX: -1.9

Osweiler has a quarterback's body and the mechanics of a startled chihuahua. However, he knows the right people (in this case, Adam Gase) and is behind a quarterback with a recent history of injuries, so it's likely that for the third year in a row, we'll see him get laughed off the field—that is, assuming he can beat out waiver claim Bryce Petty for the right to be the primary backup for Ryan Tannehill.

Carson Palmer

Height: 6-5 Weight: 230 College: USC Draft: 2003/1 (1) Born: 27-Dec-1979 Age: 39 Risk: N/A

Year	Team	G/GS	Snaps	Att	Comp	C%	Yds	TD	INT/Adj	FUM	ASR	NY/P	Rk	DVOA	Rk	DYAR	Rk	YAR	Runs	Yds	TD	DVOA	DYAR	QBR
2015	ARI	16/16	1039	537	342	63.7%	4671	35	11/18	6	4.9%	8.1	1	34.4%	1	1698	1	1755	25	24	1	-31.7%	-10	82.2
2016	ARI	15/15	1045	597	364	61.0%	4233	26	14/21	14	6.7%	6.2	22	-7.8%	23	137	21	283	14	38	0	59.0%	19	58.9
2017	ARI	7/7	459	267	164	61.4%	1978	9	7/14	2	8.6%	6.5	15	-3.2%	19	145	20	276	14	12	0	-45.0%	-18	46.3

2016: 41% Short 38% Mid 14% Deep 6% Bomb aDOT: 9.7 (5) YAC: 4.6 (30) ALEX: -0.1 2017: 45% Short 37% Mid 12% Deep 6% Bomb aDOT: 9.9 (5) YAC: 4.6 (29) ALEX: 0.3

Palmer intended to go out with a bang, but instead left with a whimper after suffering a season-ending injury halfway through the year. The former first overall pick may not have won a championship, but his career will certainly be worth remembering. His contemporaries may overshadow him, but his 2015 campaign was definitely MVP-worthy as he led the league in both passing DVOA and DYAR. While Palmer's 2017 was a slight step up over his 2016 in terms of efficiency, he was getting sacked at a frightening rate behind a porous offensive line before breaking his arm on a brutal hit by the Rams while standing in the pocket to deliver a deep ball. In former head coach Bruce Arians' offense, attacking downfield was the modus operandi, and few NFL quarterbacks threw it deep more aggressively than Palmer. It is unfortunate that the strategy that made late-career Palmer so effective ended up being what cut his final season short.

Nathan Peterman

Height: 6-2 Weight: 226 College: Pittsburgh Draft: 2017/5 (171) Born: 4-May-1994 Age: 24 Risk: Green

Year	Team	G/GS	Snaps	Att	Comp	C%	Yds	TD	INT/Adj	FUM	ASR	NY/P	Rk	DVOA	Rk	DYAR	Rk	YAR	Runs	Yds	TD	DVOA	DYAR	QBR
2017	BUF	4/2	97	49	24	49.0%	252	2	5/5	2	1.7%	4.9	--	-73.8%	--	-194	--	-195	7	23	0	-84.2%	-18	10.8
2018	BUF			470	260	55.4%	2878	14	18	11		5.1		-34.3%					66	222	2	-6.7%		

2017: 42% Short 42% Mid 13% Deep 4% Bomb aDOT: 9.2 (–) YAC: 2.9 (–) ALEX: 1.4

A recent BuzzFeed article titled "23 Honest Confessions From People Who Self-Harm" did not include "starting Nathan Peterman against the Chargers should have by all rights cost us our playoff spot." Just another example of our failing media. Peterman came out as a long-term project with some accuracy issues masked by playing in a screen-heavy Pitt offense, and was clearly not ready in Year 1. In Year 2, he will sit around and watch an offensive disaster that could have included him if he were more fortunate.

Bryce Petty

Height: 6-3 Weight: 230 College: Baylor Draft: 2015/4 (103) Born: 31-May-1991 Age: 27 Risk: Red

Year	Team	G/GS	Snaps	Att	Comp	C%	Yds	TD	INT/Adj	FUM	ASR	NY/P	Rk	DVOA	Rk	DYAR	Rk	YAR	Runs	Yds	TD	DVOA	DYAR	QBR
2016	NYJ	6/4	245	133	75	56.4%	809	3	7/8	1	9.2%	5.0	--	-57.5%	--	-414	--	-342	5	19	0	-11.8%	0	19.4
2017	NYJ	4/3	219	112	55	49.1%	544	1	3/2	1	5.8%	4.4	--	-26.8%	--	-122	--	-182	7	55	0	53.7%	20	26.7
2018	MIA			524	290	55.3%	3180	9	15	7		5.0		-29.4%					40	121	1	-4.3%		

2016: 54% Short 23% Mid 11% Deep 13% Bomb aDOT: 9.2 (–) YAC: 5.1 (–) ALEX: 1.3 2017: 53% Short 32% Mid 11% Deep 5% Bomb aDOT: 8.1 (–) YAC: 4.5 (–) ALEX: 1.6

Heading into the final year of his rookie deal, Petty has done enough damage in his appearances to single-handedly make the Jets come down with Josh McCown Stockholm Syndrome. The Jets have scored 13 or fewer points in five of Petty's seven career starts. They signed two quarterbacks and drafted Sam Darnold. Bryce Petty creates more jobs than most American corporations. He was claimed by the Dolphins on waivers. If history repeats itself, anyone hoping the Dolphins will make massive changes should be rooting for Petty to make an appearance.

Dak Prescott — Height: 6-2 — Weight: 226 — College: Mississippi State — Draft: 2016/4 (135) — Born: 29-Jul-1993 — Age: 25 — Risk: Green

Year	Team	G/GS	Snaps	Att	Comp	C%	Yds	TD	INT/Adj	FUM	ASR	NY/P	Rk	DVOA	Rk	DYAR	Rk	YAR	Runs	Yds	TD	DVOA	DYAR	QBR
2016	DAL	16/16	1013	459	311	67.8%	3667	23	4/7	9	5.3%	7.3	4	31.6%	3	1302	4	1220	57	282	6	43.6%	121	81.5
2017	DAL	16/16	1053	490	308	62.9%	3324	22	13/17	4	6.4%	6.3	18	-0.2%	17	375	17	322	57	357	6	46.9%	167	66.7
2018	DAL			500	327	65.5%	3619	22	11	8		6.6		9.2%					75	375	3	23.0%		

| 2016: | 41% Short | 41% Mid | 13% Deep | 5% Bomb | aDOT: 8.4 (18) | YAC: 5.0 (20) | ALEX: 1.1 | 2017: | 50% Short | 35% Mid | 9% Deep | 6% Bomb | aDOT: 8.7 (18) | YAC: 4.4 (33) | ALEX: 0.5 |

In the first eight games of 2017, Prescott had 16 touchdown passes, four interceptions, and ten sacks, averaging 6.61 net yards per pass. At that point, he ranked eighth among full-season qualifiers with a DVOA of 18.9%. In the second half of the year, he had six touchdowns, nine interceptions, and 22 sacks, averaging 5.38 net yards per pass. His DVOA in the last eight games was -21.1%, better than only DeShone Kizer (-23.5%), Brett Hundley (-28.5%), and Trevor Siemian (-43.7%). It would be easy to blame this decline on the absences of Ezekiel Elliott and Tyron Smith, and they certainly didn't help, but the film shows that Prescott was a completely different player in November and December. The young man whose first 24 games were marked by a precocious maturity suddenly looked panicky and indecisive, forcing balls into double coverage and air-mailing passes over the heads of open targets. It's important to remember that Prescott has played outstanding football for about three-quarters of his professional career, and in all likelihood this slump was just the result of a young player going through some growing pains and making the absolute worst of some very bad circumstances. Should he continue to struggle, though, the Cowboys will have to make some very difficult decisions concerning his contract after the season.

Philip Rivers — Height: 6-5 — Weight: 228 — College: North Carolina State — Draft: 2004/1 (4) — Born: 8-Dec-1981 — Age: 37 — Risk: Red

Year	Team	G/GS	Snaps	Att	Comp	C%	Yds	TD	INT/Adj	FUM	ASR	NY/P	Rk	DVOA	Rk	DYAR	Rk	YAR	Runs	Yds	TD	DVOA	DYAR	QBR
2015	SD	16/16	1153	661	437	66.1%	4792	29	13/16	4	5.5%	6.4	15	7.8%	11	847	8	780	17	28	0	-9.8%	1	59.4
2016	SD	16/16	1061	578	349	60.4%	4386	33	21/19	9	6.6%	6.8	11	1.4%	18	498	17	435	14	35	0	-9.3%	1	64.5
2017	LAC	16/16	1028	575	360	62.6%	4515	28	10/16	8	4.3%	7.5	2	26.1%	4	1412	2	1505	18	-2	0	-97.2%	-10	57.4
2018	LAC			581	364	62.7%	4432	29	12	6		7.0		16.6%					23	22	0	-12.6%		

| 2016: | 49% Short | 32% Mid | 14% Deep | 6% Bomb | aDOT: 8.9 (14) | YAC: 5.8 (3) | ALEX: 1.3 | 2017: | 52% Short | 29% Mid | 11% Deep | 8% Bomb | aDOT: 8.9 (13) | YAC: 5.9 (5) | ALEX: 0.9 |

Rivers' splits in the first quarters of games: 63-of-114 (55.3 percent), 786 yards (6.3 yards per attempt), one touchdown, two interceptions, and a quarterback rating of 72.5. Anthony Lynn was serious about his "establish the run" rhetoric in first quarters, especially early in the season, and both Rivers and the Chargers offense (they scored just 44 first quarter points) suffered. On the other hand, a more conservative approach may have contributed to the sharp reductions in Rivers' sack and interception rates. Rivers threw six interceptions against the Chiefs and four against the rest of the NFL, so he's happy to see Marcus Peters (who had three of those picks) in the NFC. The up-and-down pattern in Rivers' interception rate is worrying not so much because this is an "up" year, but because quarterbacks in their late thirties who lead the NFL in turnovers every other season are operating on razor-thin margins. Rivers' DVOA and DYAR last year were his best since 2013, but it wasn't an eye-popping season, and a little slippage could cause him to land in Eli Manning territory. It's the main reason the Chargers should be in "win now" mode instead of picking out upholstery for their move across the valley.

Aaron Rodgers — Height: 6-2 — Weight: 223 — College: California — Draft: 2005/1 (24) — Born: 2-Dec-1983 — Age: 35 — Risk: Yellow

Year	Team	G/GS	Snaps	Att	Comp	C%	Yds	TD	INT/Adj	FUM	ASR	NY/P	Rk	DVOA	Rk	DYAR	Rk	YAR	Runs	Yds	TD	DVOA	DYAR	QBR
2015	GB	16/16	1138	572	347	60.7%	3821	31	8/11	8	7.3%	5.7	32	-1.0%	17	406	17	258	58	344	1	37.1%	107	64.9
2016	GB	16/16	1066	610	401	65.7%	4428	40	7/11	8	5.6%	6.5	18	18.7%	8	1279	6	1299	67	369	4	22.4%	89	76.9
2017	GB	7/7	418	238	154	64.7%	1675	16	6/6	1	8.3%	6.0	22	7.8%	14	334	18	308	24	126	0	48.7%	55	62.6
2018	GB			552	365	66.1%	4138	33	11	4		6.7		21.9%					57	259	1	18.6%		

| 2016: | 46% Short | 32% Mid | 13% Deep | 8% Bomb | aDOT: 9.1 (11) | YAC: 5.1 (17) | ALEX: 3.8 | 2017: | 61% Short | 27% Mid | 6% Deep | 6% Bomb | aDOT: 7.2 (33) | YAC: 5.6 (12) | ALEX: 3.9 |

Among quarterbacks with at least 500 attempts since 2015, Aaron Rodgers ranks first in touchdown rate (6.1 percent), but 24th in yards per attempt (6.99). Such a dichotomy is unheard of in recent NFL history. We looked at the leader in touchdown pass percentage over each three-year period since 1988 and noted where that player ranked in yards per pass attempt (YPA) among his peers.

Rodgers: Dink-and-Dunking His Way to Touchdowns

Years	TD% Leader	TD%	YPA	Rk	Years	TD% Leader	TD%	YPA	Rk
1988-1990	Boomer Esiason	6.4%	8.13	1	2002-2004	Peyton Manning	6.3%	7.87	2
1989-1991	Jim Kelly	6.8%	8.09	2	2003-2005	Peyton Manning	7.0%	8.29	2
1990-1992	Jim Kelly	6.2%	7.90	2	2004-2006	Peyton Manning	7.2%	8.43	1
1991-1993	Steve Young	6.2%	8.75	1	2005-2007	Tony Romo	6.4%	8.30	1
1992-1994	Steve Young	6.7%	8.65	1	2006-2008	Tom Brady	6.7%	7.61	5
1993-1995	Steve Young	6.1%	8.17	1	2007-2009	Tom Brady	6.8%	8.04	1
1994-1996	Brett Favre	6.5%	7.19	9	2008-2010	Philip Rivers	6.1%	8.62	1
1995-1997	Brett Favre	6.9%	7.49	2	2009-2011	Aaron Rodgers	6.8%	8.56	1
1996-1998	Randall Cunningham	7.8%	8.20	1	2010-2012	Aaron Rodgers	7.3%	8.41	1
1997-1999	Kurt Warner	8.0%	8.61	1	2011-2013	Aaron Rodgers	7.5%	8.54	1
1998-2000	Kurt Warner	7.2%	9.13	1	2012-2014	Peyton Manning	7.1%	8.08	2
1999-2001	Kurt Warner	7.0%	9.06	1	2013-2015	Peyton Manning	6.5%	7.85	4
2000-2002	Kurt Warner	5.4%	8.71	1	2014-2016	Tony Romo	7.1%	8.25	1
2001-2003	Brett Favre	5.9%	7.14	8	**2015-2017**	**Aaron Rodgers**	**6.1%**	**6.99**	**24**

Minimum 500 pass attempts per period

Aside from Rodgers, every quarterback here ranked ninth or higher in YPA, including 17 finishes at No. 1 and six runner-ups at No. 2. Brett Favre (twice) was the only other player to rank out of the top five, but this isn't a Green Bay weather thing. If it was, how would one explain Rodgers having three of the highest YPA averages on this table from his early days? Rather than continue this weird split for a fourth season, Rodgers is more likely to see his YPA shoot back up to his normal range—or he'll start to throw touchdowns less efficiently than he has in recent years.

Ben Roethlisberger

Height: 6-5 Weight: 240 College: Miami (Ohio) Draft: 2004/1 (11) Born: 2-Mar-1982 Age: 36 Risk: Yellow

Year	Team	G/GS	Snaps	Att	Comp	C%	Yds	TD	INT/Adj	FUM	ASR	NY/P	Rk	DVOA	Rk	DYAR	Rk	YAR	Runs	Yds	TD	DVOA	DYAR	QBR
2015	PIT	12/11	794	469	319	68.0%	3938	21	16/18	1	4.3%	7.8	2	22.1%	4	1114	5	1056	15	29	0	-0.2%	4	76.9
2016	PIT	14/14	921	509	328	64.4%	3819	29	13/25	8	4.0%	7.0	8	12.1%	9	807	8	790	16	14	1	14.8%	7	66.3
2017	PIT	15/15	1038	561	360	64.2%	4251	28	14/18	3	3.6%	7.4	5	21.8%	8	1270	5	1247	28	47	0	-2.1%	6	63.2
2018	PIT			593	381	64.3%	4490	30	12	5		7.0		22.7%					24	41	0	-4.4%		

2016:	51% Short	25% Mid	14% Deep	10% Bomb	aDOT: 9.1 (10)	YAC: 5.2 (10)	ALEX: 4.2	2017:	50% Short	28% Mid	14% Deep	9% Bomb	aDOT: 9.6 (7)	YAC: 5.7 (9)	ALEX: 2.4

After leading the NFL in ALEX in both 2015 and 2016, Roethlisberger was downright conservative in 2017—at least, by his standards. Big Ben ranked just sixth in ALEX, and his ALEX on third-and-short dropped from 7.8 to a below-average 4.3. Clearly, Roethlisberger is morphing into Alex Smith before our very eyes.

All kidding aside, no quarterback this millennium has been better at converting on third down than Big Ben. Throughout his career, Roethlisberger has converted on 46.6 percent of his third-down pass attempts, more than anyone else in football. That's due in large part to his willingness to take risks and throw the ball deep downfield. Roethlisberger had 158 third-down passing attempts in 2017; 64.6 percent of them went past the first-down marker. That's 102 individual throws; no other quarterback in the league hit triple digits. In general, however, Roethlisberger was more prudent with the football in 2017 than he has been in years past; the drop in air yards came from better decisions rather than just forcing the ball downfield all willy-nilly. In 2016, Roethlisberger attempted 21 deep passes on third down with 5 or fewer yards to go; that number fell to nine in 2017. This paid off—Roethlisberger's conversion rate on those plays jumped from 54 percent to 63 percent, and his adjusted interceptions fell from 25 to 18.

Josh Rosen

Height: 6-4 Weight: 226 College: UCLA Draft: 2018/1 (10) Born: 10-Feb-1997 Age: 21 Risk: Yellow

Year	Team	G/GS	Snaps	Att	Comp	C%	Yds	TD	INT/Adj	FUM	ASR	NY/P	Rk	DVOA	Rk	DYAR	Rk	YAR	Runs	Yds	TD	DVOA	DYAR	QBR
2018	ARI			559	340	60.7%	3878	21	16	10		5.8		-11.7%					33	49	2	-12.1%		

Rosen arrived on campus at UCLA as the top quarterback recruit in the nation and burst onto the scene, winning the starting job as a true freshman and going on to win the award for Pac-12 Offensive Freshman of the Year. While he was never able to deliver a New Year's Six bowl appearance as he battled through injuries throughout his time in college, Rosen's potential still drew the attention of professional scouts, as some called him the best pure passer in his draft class. QBASE has him rated as an average first-round quarterback prospect, which in most cases would be nothing to sneeze at, but as has been the case for Rosen throughout high school and college, expectations are much higher. Arizona was thrilled to be able to draft him at No. 10, and with the added motivation from being the fourth quarterback selected in the draft, Rosen will be looking to prove plenty of people of wrong. It may not happen in 2018, but the man nicknamed "The Chosen One" will have every chance to be a long-term starter in the league.

Jake Rudock Height: 6-3 Weight: 208 College: Michigan Draft: 2016/6 (191) Born: 23-Jan-1993 Age: 25 Risk: Yellow

Year	Team	G/GS	Snaps	Att	Comp	C%	Yds	TD	INT/Adj	FUM	ASR	NY/P	Rk	DVOA	Rk	DYAR	Rk	YAR	Runs	Yds	TD	DVOA	DYAR	QBR
2017	DET	3/0	9	5	3	60.0%	24	0	1/1	0	0.0%	4.8	–	-136.7%	–	-43	–	-49	0	0	0	–	–	4.3
2018	DET			534	335	62.7%	3637	23	19	10		5.8		-13.7%					52	146	2	0.1%		

| | 2017: | 40% Short | 60% Mid | 0% Deep | 0% Bomb | aDOT: 3.6 (–) | YAC: 6.7 (–) | ALEX: -6.0 |

Rudock has tossed seven touchdowns to two interceptions in the last two preseasons for Detroit, but that kind of success doesn't always translate into the real games. Rudock won the job to back up Matthew Stafford, but he threw a pick in his only appearance against Baltimore in Week 13. Rudock will have to compete with Matt Cassel for that QB2 job this year. If it comes down to giving Rudock a chance or adding another million to Cassel's bank account, it doesn't feel cheap to stick with the kid.

Mason Rudolph Height: 6-5 Weight: 235 College: Oklahoma State Draft: 2018/3 (76) Born: 17-Jul-1995 Age: 23 Risk: Yellow

Year	Team	G/GS	Snaps	Att	Comp	C%	Yds	TD	INT/Adj	FUM	ASR	NY/P	Rk	DVOA	Rk	DYAR	Rk	YAR	Runs	Yds	TD	DVOA	DYAR	QBR
2018	PIT			549	325	59.2%	3663	22	15	12		5.5		-10.3%					27	40	1	-4.5%		

Ask a dozen people about Rudolph's pro prospects, and you'll get a dozen different answers. Detractors point to his history in a spread offense against weak Big 12 defenses. They say that he has never had to throw the ball into tight windows or worry about holding on to the ball for too long. Supporters will point out that his 65 percent completion rate was second amongst the top 2017 quarterback prospects, and that his 10.7 AYPA leaves the rest of the class in the dust. They'll note that he has a pretty deep ball and is a big-play machine, willing to take aggressive risks without being reckless. Both are correct, and Rudolph will need to work on his progressions and prove that he's not just a product of the Mike Gundy scheme at the next level. He may not have the arm strength or the speed of the guys drafted ahead of him, but his accuracy and toughness project very well going forward. QBASE gives him a mean projection of 343 DYAR in Years 3-5; that's higher than Josh Allen. He has a real chance to be a starting quarterback eventually.

Matt Ryan Height: 6-4 Weight: 228 College: Boston College Draft: 2008/1 (3) Born: 17-May-1985 Age: 33 Risk: Green

Year	Team	G/GS	Snaps	Att	Comp	C%	Yds	TD	INT/Adj	FUM	ASR	NY/P	Rk	DVOA	Rk	DYAR	Rk	YAR	Runs	Yds	TD	DVOA	DYAR	QBR
2015	ATL	16/16	1116	614	407	66.3%	4591	21	16/20	13	5.2%	6.8	10	-1.9%	18	389	19	669	36	63	0	-9.6%	3	61.8
2016	ATL	16/16	1021	534	373	69.9%	4944	38	7/10	4	6.6%	8.2	1	39.1%	1	1885	1	1765	35	117	0	12.7%	32	83.3
2017	ATL	16/16	1026	529	342	64.7%	4095	20	12/9	4	4.8%	7.2	7	19.1%	9	1084	7	1076	32	143	0	43.4%	54	63.7
2018	ATL			534	348	65.0%	4157	25	10	4		6.9		20.2%					38	147	0	9.9%		

| 2016: | 48% Short | 32% Mid | 12% Deep | 7% Bomb | aDOT: 9.0 (12) | YAC: 6.1 (1) | ALEX: -0.2 | 2017: | 51% Short | 30% Mid | 12% Deep | 6% Bomb | aDOT: 9.1 (12) | YAC: 5.4 (15) | ALEX: 1.2 |

The richest man in the NFL. Ryan made headlines by signing a five-year, $150 million contract a few weeks after the draft. The statistical drop-off for Ryan was significant last year, but that was to be expected given the colossal jump from 2015 to 2016. Those 2017 numbers are very in line with Ryan's whole career prior to 2015. Ryan was also the victim of some terrible turnover luck. He threw five interceptions on accurate throws that should have been caught by his own teammates, most by any player since 2010. If the Falcons receivers had just hung on to those throws, Ryan's stats would have been considerably better on the season. With an extremely talented group of skill players, a good offensive line, and another year with offensive coordinator Steve Sarkisian, Ryan could move up again in 2018.

Tom Savage

Height: 6-4 Weight: 228 College: Pittsburgh Draft: 2014/4 (135) Born: 26-Apr-1990 Age: 28 Risk: Yellow

Year	Team	G/GS	Snaps	Att	Comp	C%	Yds	TD	INT/Adj	FUM	ASR	NY/P	Rk	DVOA	Rk	DYAR	Rk	YAR	Runs	Yds	TD	DVOA	DYAR	QBR
2016	HOU	3/2	146	73	46	63.0%	461	0	0/1	1	6.9%	5.5	--	-5.4%	--	31	--	21	6	12	0	32.0%	8	63.1
2017	HOU	8/7	421	223	125	56.1%	1412	5	6/9	8	8.8%	5.4	30	-27.5%	33	-249	31	-252	4	2	0	-54.0%	-3	38.1
2018	NO			538	334	62.1%	3645	22	14	12		5.9		-9.0%					36	36	1	-21.6%		

2016: 41% Short 47% Mid 7% Deep 5% Bomb aDOT: 8.2 (–) YAC: 3.7 (–) ALEX: 0.0 2017: 46% Short 32% Mid 15% Deep 7% Bomb aDOT: 9.7 (6) YAC: 4.1 (35) ALEX: 2.2

It was a rough 2017 for Savage. He surprisingly won the starting job in Houston, but was benched at halftime in Week 1 for Deshaun Watson. He regained the job only after Watson tore his ACL, but Savage also saw his season end after a scary concussion against San Francisco that the team did not handle well. Savage was allowed to return to the game before leaving for good, and Houston was ultimately not disciplined for the incident. Savage signed a one-year deal for $1.5 million in March to back up Drew Brees in New Orleans. Savage is not particularly productive, accurate, durable, protective of the ball, or able to avoid sacks. At the very least, he'll be sure to stand tall for every national anthem.

Matt Schaub

Height: 6-5 Weight: 235 College: Virginia Draft: 2004/3 (90) Born: 25-Jun-1981 Age: 37 Risk: Red

Year	Team	G/GS	Snaps	Att	Comp	C%	Yds	TD	INT/Adj	FUM	ASR	NY/P	Rk	DVOA	Rk	DYAR	Rk	YAR	Runs	Yds	TD	DVOA	DYAR	QBR
2015	BAL	2/2	137	80	52	65.0%	540	3	4/4	0	4.8%	6.2	--	-38.4%	--	-146	--	-71	4	10	0	-76.1%	-17	34.3
2016	ATL	4/0	21	3	1	33.3%	16	0	0/0	0	0.0%	5.3	--	-15.0%	--	-1	--	3	2	-2	0	--	--	18.4
2018	ATL			539	345	63.9%	3644	18	16	6		6.0		-5.7%					47	116	0	-10.7%		

2016: 33% Short 67% Mid 0% Deep 0% Bomb aDOT: 6.0 (–) YAC: 5.0 (–) ALEX: -0.7

Yes, Schaub is still collecting NFL paychecks. Schaub is one of the most well-compensated backup quarterbacks in the league, racking in an average salary of $4.5 million per year. Schaub has thrown a whopping three passes since 2016, including a pristine zero pass attempts in 2017. Schaub's value to the organization likely comes from things off the field, since his on-field impact in Atlanta has been virtually nothing. Must be nice.

Trevor Siemian

Height: 6-3 Weight: 220 College: Northwestern Draft: 2015/7 (250) Born: 26-Dec-1991 Age: 27 Risk: Green

Year	Team	G/GS	Snaps	Att	Comp	C%	Yds	TD	INT/Adj	FUM	ASR	NY/P	Rk	DVOA	Rk	DYAR	Rk	YAR	Runs	Yds	TD	DVOA	DYAR	QBR
2015	DEN	1/0	1	0	0	0.0%	0	0	0/0	0	--	--	--	--	--	--	--	--	1	-1	0	--	--	--
2016	DEN	14/14	904	486	289	59.5%	3401	18	10/13	4	7.0%	6.2	21	-7.1%	21	137	22	214	28	57	0	-17.0%	-4	55.8
2017	DEN	11/10	677	349	206	59.0%	2285	12	14/20	5	9.5%	5.6	25	-24.6%	32	-327	33	-242	31	127	1	-11.4%	1	27.8
2018	MIN			540	333	61.7%	3496	24	17	7		5.7		-10.8%					64	218	2	-0.5%		

2016: 41% Short 41% Mid 10% Deep 8% Bomb aDOT: 9.3 (8) YAC: 4.9 (25) ALEX: 1.5 2017: 52% Short 31% Mid 12% Deep 5% Bomb aDOT: 9.2 (11) YAC: 4.9 (22) ALEX: 1.7

Some of Siemian's numbers were on par with his 2016 performance, but he turned into a sack and turnover machine, which is the easiest way to get benched for players such as Brock Osweiler and Paxton Lynch. Denver finally had enough of that trio and inked Case Keenum this offseason. Siemian is essentially switching places with Keenum from last year. Keenum will go from Sam Bradford's backup to Denver's starter, while Siemian is going from Denver's starter to Minnesota's backup (but this time to Kirk Cousins). Just don't expect Siemian to lead the league in passing DVOA or anything crazy like that.

Alex Smith

Height: 6-4 Weight: 212 College: Utah Draft: 2005/1 (1) Born: 7-May-1984 Age: 34 Risk: Yellow

Year	Team	G/GS	Snaps	Att	Comp	C%	Yds	TD	INT/Adj	FUM	ASR	NY/P	Rk	DVOA	Rk	DYAR	Rk	YAR	Runs	Yds	TD	DVOA	DYAR	QBR
2015	KC	16/16	989	470	307	65.3%	3486	20	7/11	4	8.6%	6.3	19	3.0%	15	468	15	359	84	498	2	11.5%	86	66.5
2016	KC	15/15	917	489	328	67.1%	3502	15	8/11	7	5.5%	6.5	17	9.4%	11	688	12	538	48	134	5	4.8%	26	66.1
2017	KC	15/15	966	505	341	67.5%	4042	26	5/10	2	6.8%	7.1	9	18.3%	10	1026	9	1071	60	355	1	20.3%	85	61.6
2018	WAS			542	356	65.6%	3996	26	9	4		6.4		10.3%					58	225	1	6.3%		

2016: 54% Short 32% Mid 9% Deep 5% Bomb aDOT: 6.9 (33) YAC: 5.5 (6) ALEX: 0.5 2017: 62% Short 21% Mid 8% Deep 8% Bomb aDOT: 8.0 (27) YAC: 5.7 (7) ALEX: 0.7

For the first half of his career, Smith was something of a mad bomber, always looking for the big play and often handing the ball to the other team as a result. Everything changed when he met Jim Harbaugh in 2011. Since then, Smith has the lowest interception rate of anyone with at least 1,000 passes, and hasn't thrown more than eight interceptions in a season. In that same timeframe, he has fumbled only 35 times in 102 games. (Washington's last two starting quarterbacks—Kirk Cousins and Robert Griffin—each topped 30 fumbles in a burgundy uniform in about half as many games apiece.) The tradeoff for that was a conservative approach that rarely tested opponents deep, but Smith seemed to put it all together last season. Eighteen percent of his passes in 2017 were deep balls, his highest rate since 2007, but his turnovers were lower than ever. He led the league in both interception rate and NFL passer rating. Yet for all that, when Kansas City got on offer of a slot corner and a third-round pick, they kicked Smith out the door as fast as they could. Smith has now had two seasons in which he finished in the top ten in either DVOA or DYAR. Despite his new contract in D.C., it's not likely to happen a third time.

Geno Smith — Height: 6-3 — Weight: 208 — College: West Virginia — Draft: 2013/2 (39) — Born: 10-Oct-1990 — Age: 28 — Risk: Red

Year	Team	G/GS	Snaps	Att	Comp	C%	Yds	TD	INT/Adj	FUM	ASR	NY/P	Rk	DVOA	Rk	DYAR	Rk	YAR	Runs	Yds	TD	DVOA	DYAR	QBR
2015	NYJ	1/0	65	42	27	64.3%	265	2	1/1	0	7.5%	5.5	--	11.0%	--	72	--	83	2	34	0	168.6%	14	66.2
2016	NYJ	2/1	33	14	8	57.1%	126	1	1/1	1	17.3%	6.2	--	-70.8%	--	-68	--	-83	2	9	0	39.6%	5	30.9
2017	NYG	2/1	66	36	21	58.3%	212	1	0/0	2	8.6%	5.3	--	-41.4%	--	-83	--	-44	4	12	0	6.4%	4	34.5
2018	LAC			524	311	59.3%	3469	22	20	12		5.6		-23.0%					64	278	3	12.3%		

2016: 50% Short — 43% Mid — 7% Deep — 0% Bomb — aDOT: 6.9 (--) — YAC: 10.4 (--) — ALEX: 1.5   2017: 64% Short — 28% Mid — 8% Deep — 0% Bomb — aDOT: 6.5 (--) — YAC: 5.1 (--) — ALEX: -1.0

Smith is a bad quarterback with miserable luck who was enjoying an image rehabilitation year in a quiet corner of the Giants locker room when Ben McAdoo blew a brain gasket and decided that humiliating Eli Manning by replacing him with Smith was the best way to salvage his coaching career. Smith can still run and throw, but whatever play recognition skills he ever had are now toast, so he's a sack or ill-advised scramble waiting to happen on every snap. He was a bad fit in McAdoo's offense but a worse one in Ken Whisenhunt's scheme, which is only suitable for licensed pocket-passing neurosurgeons. The way things go for Smith, he'll be forced into a spot start for Rivers, the Chargers will lose on three blocked field goals, and Cardale Jones will be forced to finish the game after Smith sprains an ankle while getting sacked.

Matthew Stafford — Height: 6-2 — Weight: 225 — College: Georgia — Draft: 2009/1 (1) — Born: 7-Feb-1988 — Age: 30 — Risk: Green

Year	Team	G/GS	Snaps	Att	Comp	C%	Yds	TD	INT/Adj	FUM	ASR	NY/P	Rk	DVOA	Rk	DYAR	Rk	YAR	Runs	Yds	TD	DVOA	DYAR	QBR
2015	DET	16/16	1033	592	398	67.2%	4262	32	13/14	4	7.3%	6.3	20	8.0%	10	804	9	637	44	159	1	11.4%	35	62.6
2016	DET	16/16	1037	594	388	65.3%	4327	24	10/16	3	6.1%	6.5	16	7.2%	14	761	9	768	37	207	2	29.3%	64	70.5
2017	DET	16/16	1035	565	371	65.7%	4446	29	10/18	11	7.6%	7.0	11	14.9%	11	1004	10	913	29	98	0	0.2%	11	61.7
2018	DET			570	373	65.5%	4268	27	14	4		6.5		13.0%					34	83	0	-1.0%		

2016: 52% Short — 31% Mid — 10% Deep — 7% Bomb — aDOT: 7.6 (31) — YAC: 5.8 (4) — ALEX: 1.7   2017: 57% Short — 26% Mid — 9% Deep — 8% Bomb — aDOT: 8.7 (19) — YAC: 5.7 (10) — ALEX: 2.1

Hard to believe, but 2018 will wrap up the first decade of Matthew Stafford's career. He has sure killed that "injury prone" narrative, starting every game since 2011 and rarely appearing on the injury report. Stafford has 34,749 passing yards in his career; he needs barely more than 1,000 yards this year to pass Joe Flacco and move into fourth place in NFL history in most yards through a player's first 10 seasons, trailing only Matt Ryan (41,796), Peyton Manning (41,626), and Dan Marino (39,502). He just needs 20 touchdown passes to rank fifth in that category through 10 years as well.

Stafford quietly had the highest yards per pass attempt of his career last season. Detroit had the highest DVOA (206.3%) on deep passes in 2017, which is some credit to Stafford, but also a credit to the way Marvin Jones and Kenny Golladay made some spectacular catches on go routes and other deep balls. Stafford never established a strong connection with tight end Eric Ebron, but 2018 could be a chance for him to set more career bests if Golladay makes a big leap in his second year and rookie running back Kerryon Johnson brings some balance to the offense.

Drew Stanton — Height: 6-3 — Weight: 230 — College: Michigan State — Draft: 2007/2 (43) — Born: 7-May-1984 — Age: 34 — Risk: Red

Year	Team	G/GS	Snaps	Att	Comp	C%	Yds	TD	INT/Adj	FUM	ASR	NY/P	Rk	DVOA	Rk	DYAR	Rk	YAR	Runs	Yds	TD	DVOA	DYAR	QBR
2015	ARI	7/0	65	25	11	44.0%	104	0	2/2	0	7.2%	3.6	--	-57.4%	--	-82	--	-99	13	-13	0	--	--	12.3
2016	ARI	5/1	106	48	19	39.6%	192	2	3/2	0	1.9%	3.8	--	-50.9%	--	-119	--	-84	3	-3	0	--	--	26.9
2017	ARI	5/4	320	159	79	49.7%	894	6	5/5	3	4.3%	5.3	--	-18.3%	--	-75	--	-62	9	7	0	-21.2%	-2	35.9
2018	CLE			525	294	56.1%	3428	16	19	11		5.7		-24.3%					38	66	0	-25.0%		

2016: 36% Short — 40% Mid — 11% Deep — 13% Bomb — aDOT: 11.4 (--) — YAC: 4.1 (--) — ALEX: 5.4   2017: 36% Short — 40% Mid — 14% Deep — 9% Bomb — aDOT: 11.1 (--) — YAC: 3.8 (--) — ALEX: 1.6

Forced into the lineup for four games late in the year, Stanton wasn't as bad as he was in limited 2015-16 playing time, but he wasn't particularly good either. There's no need to keep him on the roster in Cleveland behind Tyrod Taylor and Baker Mayfield, but he'll probably resurface sometime this season as the new veteran backup for whatever team has a starting quarterback injury.

Ryan Tannehill

Height: 6-4   Weight: 221   College: Texas A&M   Draft: 2012/1 (8)   Born: 27-Jul-1988   Age: 30   Risk: Yellow

Year	Team	G/GS	Snaps	Att	Comp	C%	Yds	TD	INT/Adj	FUM	ASR	NY/P	Rk	DVOA	Rk	DYAR	Rk	YAR	Runs	Yds	TD	DVOA	DYAR	QBR
2015	MIA	16/16	1026	586	363	61.9%	4208	24	12/15	10	7.6%	6.1	28	-10.6%	27	20	26	67	32	141	1	36.5%	49	43.2
2016	MIA	13/13	758	389	261	67.1%	2995	19	12/16	9	7.2%	6.7	14	-10.8%	25	10	25	92	39	164	1	-7.0%	8	54.6
2018	MIA			529	337	63.7%	3830	23	12	6		6.3		-4.4%					42	147	1	11.2%		
2016:	53% Short	30% Mid	8% Deep	9% Bomb	aDOT: 8.2 (20)	YAC: 5.5 (7)	ALEX: 1.2																	

The Dolphins stuck with Tannehill rather than chase any of the available free-agent quarterbacks. It's super weird from an outside, non-tape perspective that the Dolphins are treating a guy with a seasonal high DVOA of 4.1% like he's Matthew Stafford. That said, is he so much different than Joe Flacco without a playoff hot streak? And he did actually show some signs of promise in 2016. Tannehill doesn't have make-or-break seasons, he just has a make-or-break career. But if our projections are to be believed, the Dolphins will again be faced with the dilemma of the familiar or the large investment in someone new in 2019. At least he's not Jay Cutler.

Tyrod Taylor

Height: 6-1   Weight: 216   College: Virginia Tech   Draft: 2011/6 (180)   Born: 3-Aug-1989   Age: 29   Risk: Red

Year	Team	G/GS	Snaps	Att	Comp	C%	Yds	TD	INT/Adj	FUM	ASR	NY/P	Rk	DVOA	Rk	DYAR	Rk	YAR	Runs	Yds	TD	DVOA	DYAR	QBR
2015	BUF	14/14	923	380	242	63.7%	3035	20	6/11	8	8.5%	6.8	12	9.8%	8	536	14	486	104	568	4	19.8%	133	67.8
2016	BUF	15/15	969	436	269	61.7%	3023	17	6/6	4	9.2%	5.9	27	-2.1%	19	275	19	347	95	580	6	2.1%	65	68.2
2017	BUF	15/14	931	420	263	62.6%	2799	14	4/4	4	10.2%	5.6	26	-7.0%	22	121	22	263	84	427	4	20.8%	110	52.7
2018	CLE			522	320	61.3%	3523	21	8	7		5.8		-9.0%					100	558	4	20.7%		
2016:	43% Short	36% Mid	13% Deep	9% Bomb	aDOT: 9.6 (7)	YAC: 4.2 (31)	ALEX: 2.6	2017:	57% Short	27% Mid	8% Deep	8% Bomb	aDOT: 8.8 (15)	YAC: 4.8 (23)	ALEX: 1.2								

November 19, 2017—the day of Nate Peterman's five-pick Bills massacree—was an important date in football analytics history because it perfectly illustrated the value of league-average quarterback play over replacement-level play. The Bills-Chargers game provided strong evidence that the Bills were a wild-card team with Tyrod Taylor-level quarterbacking but a bottom-feeder with "replacement-level" Peterman, your basic mid-round rookie with moxie. It's important to learn the right lessons from it. The Peterman implosion did not prove Taylor was great or that Peterman had no NFL future. But it did demonstrate the incredibly wide value gap between a mid-range NFL starter and your typical backup, which is why even mid-range starters are so highly valued. The fact that the Bills lacked a DeAndre Hopkins to lean on—or even a particularly clever coordinator—makes the Bills-Chargers game an even more useful illustrator of the difference between average and NFL-minimum quarterback play. Discussions of Tyrod Taylor's sack rate or other deficiencies, while useful, must acknowledge the fact that his backup, in the same circumstances and despite the best efforts of his coaches, was completely incapable of even functioning. Evaluating Tyrod Taylor analytically starts with recognizing the high inherent value of a league-average starting quarterback with his strengths and weaknesses. Otherwise smart people, including the Bills last year, failed to do this.

DeShone Kizer wasn't Peterman bad last year, but he was the worst starting quarterback in the game. We're about to see that difference between average and NFL-minimum quarterback play demonstrated over the course of an entire season, or at least until the Browns brass decides it's time to see what Baker Mayfield can do. Taylor hits free agency after the 2018 season and may spend the next two or three years bouncing around the league as a veteran bridge quarterback keeping the seat warm for various rookie prospects. He'll be better than most quarterbacks who fill that role.

Mitchell Trubisky

Height: 6-2   Weight: 222   College: North Carolina   Draft: 2017/1 (2)   Born: 20-Aug-1994   Age: 24   Risk: Yellow

Year	Team	G/GS	Snaps	Att	Comp	C%	Yds	TD	INT/Adj	FUM	ASR	NY/P	Rk	DVOA	Rk	DYAR	Rk	YAR	Runs	Yds	TD	DVOA	DYAR	QBR
2017	CHI	12/12	726	330	196	59.4%	2193	7	7/8	10	8.7%	5.5	27	-16.8%	29	-119	29	-176	41	248	2	9.7%	32	29.2
2018	CHI			553	339	61.4%	3928	24	14	13		6.1		-2.4%					58	304	3	17.8%		
										2017:	57% Short	27% Mid	12% Deep	3% Bomb	aDOT: 7.9 (28)	YAC: 5.1 (19)	ALEX: -2.4							

Trubisky is one of the most difficult quarterbacks to project in 2018. Of course there's a strong likelihood he improves in his second season, though quarterbacks rarely make improvements like what we saw from Jared Goff and Carson Wentz in 2017. Trubisky has a new offensive system and a rookie head coach. The top wide receivers and tight ends that Trubisky targeted last year are likely to be a whole new group in 2018. This is a season of change, and one where Trubisky must show development. If he's still looking like the same guy from last year with all of these improvements, then we might as well label him Cade McNown 2.0.

Deshaun Watson　Height: 6-2　Weight: 221　College: Clemson　Draft: 2017/1 (12)　Born: 14-Sep-1995　Age: 23　Risk: Yellow

Year	Team	G/GS	Snaps	Att	Comp	C%	Yds	TD	INT/Adj	FUM	ASR	NY/P	Rk	DVOA	Rk	DYAR	Rk	YAR	Runs	Yds	TD	DVOA	DYAR	QBR
2017	HOU	7/6	464	204	126	61.8%	1699	19	8/8	3	8.5%	7.7	1	23.1%	7	497	14	529	36	269	2	29.3%	70	81.3
2018	HOU			533	329	61.7%	4164	27	16	10		6.8		3.6%					82	509	3	22.1%		

2017: 47% Short　30% Mid　13% Deep　10% Bomb　aDOT: 11.5 (1)　YAC: 5.3 (16)　ALEX: 2.1

Watson was practicing without a knee brace in June and is expected to be full go for the start of training camp. Health may be a continuing worry for the Texans after he has now torn his ACL in both knees. Bill O'Brien mentioned in June that Houston's offensive scheming was limited and that he intended to do more knowing Watson will be available and the starter from Week 1. One particular key for O'Brien should be on third downs, where Watson's DVOA was just -15.6%. That was due in part to sacks, as Watson's adjusted sack rate on third downs was the worst in the league among passers with at least 50 third-down plays, but even disregarding sacks Watson was no better than average. As much fun as he was last year, there are still several areas for Watson's overall game to grow, and that will determine whether his fate is to become one of the league's best quarterbacks or to remain a tier or two below that.

Davis Webb　Height: 6-5　Weight: 229　College: California　Draft: 2017/3 (87)　Born: 22-Jan-1995　Age: 23　Risk: Green

Year	Team	G/GS	Snaps	Att	Comp	C%	Yds	TD	INT/Adj	FUM	ASR	NY/P	Rk	DVOA	Rk	DYAR	Rk	YAR	Runs	Yds	TD	DVOA	DYAR	QBR
2018	NYG			529	297	56.2%	3415	16	15	9		5.3		-16.7%					23	85	1	11.6%		

Webb, the quarterback whom Patrick Mahomes Jr. dethroned at Texas Tech, left more to be desired as a college player. Despite playing in an Air Raid offense at both Texas Tech and Cal, Webb ended his career with 7.3 adjusted yards per attempt, cementing him as a painfully mediocre college quarterback. Webb did occasionally dazzle with arm strength and deep passing, but those traits stood out as oddities, not accents on an overall quality skill set. The drafting of Kyle Lauletta surely signals that Webb's job is already on the line.

Brandon Weeden　Height: 6-4　Weight: 221　College: Oklahoma State　Draft: 2012/1 (22)　Born: 14-Oct-1983　Age: 35　Risk: Yellow

Year	Team	G/GS	Snaps	Att	Comp	C%	Yds	TD	INT/Adj	FUM	ASR	NY/P	Rk	DVOA	Rk	DYAR	Rk	YAR	Runs	Yds	TD	DVOA	DYAR	QBR
2015	2TM	6/4	313	140	97	69.3%	1043	5	2/4	2	7.0%	6.5	—	3.8%	—	139	—	209	16	47	1	49.8%	27	66.2
2018	HOU			517	302	58.4%	3359	13	16	7		5.4		-20.4%					45	106	1	-8.7%		

Weeden played a key role in Houston's 2015 division title and hasn't had any snaps in the past two seasons to show he couldn't do the same once again if called upon to do so. After all, what's the chance a player who has been mediocre in 923 of his NFL pass attempts could fail to replicate what he did in the other 42? Plus, he's not Tom Savage or T.J. Yates. At least this year if Deshaun Watson misses extended time and the Texans get a top-five pick out of it, they'll be able to use it.

Carson Wentz　Height: 6-5　Weight: 237　College: North Dakota State　Draft: 2016/1 (2)　Born: 30-Dec-1992　Age: 26　Risk: Yellow

Year	Team	G/GS	Snaps	Att	Comp	C%	Yds	TD	INT/Adj	FUM	ASR	NY/P	Rk	DVOA	Rk	DYAR	Rk	YAR	Runs	Yds	TD	DVOA	DYAR	QBR
2016	PHI	16/16	1127	607	379	62.4%	3782	16	14/19	14	5.4%	5.6	31	-12.0%	27	-36	27	12	46	150	2	-3.6%	16	52.8
2017	PHI	13/13	879	440	265	60.2%	3296	33	7/13	9	6.1%	6.9	12	23.8%	6	1047	8	934	64	299	0	6.7%	52	75.9
2018	PHI			573	362	63.2%	4222	31	12	14		6.6		7.4%					63	303	2	4.9%		

2016: 51% Short　32% Mid　11% Deep　5% Bomb　aDOT: 7.8 (28)　YAC: 4.7 (28)　ALEX: 0.2　　2017: 47% Short　33% Mid　11% Deep　9% Bomb　aDOT: 10.4 (3)　YAC: 4.6 (26)　ALEX: 3.7

Wentz participated in 7-on-7 drills and a host of individual drills throughout Eagles minicamp, including activities that required him to cut and plant while dodging objects before throwing passes. At press time, it's safe to say that he is ahead of schedule in his recovery and will be the Eagles starting quarterback, if not on opening day, then close to it.

Wentz is an object lesson on the limitations of football analytics in their current state. There will never be enough data points for FCS quarterback prospects for analytics to say much more about them before the draft except "there aren't enough data points to responsibly analyze FCS quarterback prospects." Much of Wentz's improvement was the result of mechanical changes to his footwork, pocket mobility, launch platforms, and such. Wentz was a different quarterback after two years with Doug Pederson's staff than what was visible on North Dakota State film or at the Senior Bowl. Coaching quality differs widely across the league, and coaches move around so much and interact with individual players so briefly that there will probably never be a "John DiFilippo Index" or anything to measure coaching impact.

So as analytics types, we recommended caution on Wentz and questioned the decision to trade up for him, but "analytics" never advocated wiping him off any draft boards. The Air Yards/aDOT metric revealed a lot of fluff in the numbers during Wentz's rookie-year hot streak; we reported it, got creamed for it, then watched the Wentz Wagon derail in the second half of the 2016 season. We took note of Wentz's upgraded receiving corps and increased experience level last offseason. We also had boots on the ground in Philly throughout training camp, but you can't stick reports about how good Wentz looks in 7-in-7s on a spreadsheet, because that's not analytics. We advised cautious optimism. Wentz instead exploded into MVP status. That took part of the analytics community by surprise—and some in the analytics community were loathe to admit that Wentz really had improved significantly, because we sometimes lose sight of the fact that we cannot measure and predict as much as we would like to—but it was always a possibility based on the available data.

Now we must evaluate Wentz upon return from ACL surgery. Again: there aren't enough data points for a useful sample. We're still performing surgery with stone hammers in this business. Just remember that analytics are often more likely to say "I don't know" than "no" about any given player, prospect or situation, and that those two statements are not in any way synonymous.

Mike White

	Height: 6-5		Weight: 224		College: South Florida			Draft: 2018/5 (171)		Born: 25-Mar-1995		Age: 23		Risk: Green		
Year Team	G/GS	Snaps	Att	Comp	C%	Yds	TD	INT/Adj	FUM	ASR	NY/P	Rk	DVOA	Rk	DYAR	Rk	YAR	Runs	Yds	TD	DVOA	DYAR	QBR
2018 DAL			472	275	58.2%	3048	17	13	10		5.3		-16.5%					21	31	0	-10.8%		

White started as a freshman and sophomore at South Florida and struggled badly, completing 51.6 percent of his passes with 11 touchdowns and 16 interceptions. In dire need of a change of scenery, he transferred to Western Kentucky, where he turned his career around. In two years as the Hilltoppers' starter, he completed 66.4 percent of his passes with 63 touchdowns and 15 interceptions. His raw totals jump out at you—in the last two years of NCAA football, only Luke Falk had more completions or attempts; only Mason Rudolph and Baker Mayfield passed for more yards; and only six players passed for more touchdowns. His best year was in 2016, when he was second behind Mayfield with 10.5 yards per pass and in the nation's top ten in completion percentage as well. White will have to beat out Cooper Rush for the backup job behind Dak Prescott, but if the Cowboys didn't think he could do that, they wouldn't have drafted him in the fifth round.

Russell Wilson

	Height: 5-11		Weight: 204		College: Wisconsin			Draft: 2012/3 (75)		Born: 29-Nov-1988		Age: 30		Risk: Green		
Year Team	G/GS	Snaps	Att	Comp	C%	Yds	TD	INT/Adj	FUM	ASR	NY/P	Rk	DVOA	Rk	DYAR	Rk	YAR	Runs	Yds	TD	DVOA	DYAR	QBR
2015 SEA	16/16	1050	483	329	68.1%	4024	34	8/11	7	9.0%	7.1	4	24.3%	3	1190	3	1159	103	553	1	17.4%	123	74.9
2016 SEA	16/16	1008	546	353	64.7%	4219	21	11/15	7	7.0%	6.7	13	4.0%	15	569	14	599	72	259	1	-12.3%	-1	63.2
2017 SEA	16/16	1063	553	339	61.3%	3983	34	11/15	14	8.1%	6.1	20	2.9%	15	530	13	564	95	586	3	28.9%	154	58.3
2018 SEA			520	330	63.4%	3773	24	10	10		6.2		3.1%					81	449	3	20.6%		
2016:	49% Short	31% Mid	12% Deep	9% Bomb	aDOT: 8.8 (16)	YAC: 5.0 (19)	ALEX: 0.9	2017:	52% Short	27% Mid	11% Deep	9% Bomb	aDOT: 10.1 (4)	YAC: 4.7 (25)	ALEX: 1.5	

Wilson faced pressure on 262 plays in 2017, more than any other quarterback. He was hit 93 times, more than any other quarterback. He was sacked 46 times (including plays which ended up not counting statistically due to penalty, but still involved a 300-pound defender slamming into Seattle's franchise player), more than any other quarterback. Some of this is Wilson's fault; according to NFL.com's Next Gen Stats, he held on to the ball an average of 3.05 seconds before throwing it, the second-highest average in the league. Most of it, however, comes from playing behind a sieve of an offensive line and still finding some way to make plays happen. Twenty-eight percent of his passes came outside the pocket, more than any other quarterback, and he maintained a 25.7% DVOA when doing so. On top of everything else, he became one of only five quarterbacks to lead his team in rushing yards since the 1970 merger. There are so many things to admire about Wilson's game; his ability to create something out of nothing, his Houdini-like ability to get out of surefire sacks, his mobility in the open field. His single most impressive ability, however, seems pretty clear. Wilson has been in the top five in all of those pressure statistics in each of the past five seasons; no other quarterback has taken anywhere near the sort of pounding he's gone through. And yet, he has never missed a game. He is Iron Man.

Jameis Winston   Height: 6-4   Weight: 230   College: Florida State   Draft: 2015/1 (1)   Born: 6-Jan-1994   Age: 25   Risk: Red

Year	Team	G/GS	Snaps	Att	Comp	C%	Yds	TD	INT/Adj	FUM	ASR	NY/P	Rk	DVOA	Rk	DYAR	Rk	YAR	Runs	Yds	TD	DVOA	DYAR	QBR
2015	TB	16/16	1093	535	312	58.3%	4042	22	15/22	6	5.8%	6.8	9	2.1%	16	467	16	495	54	213	6	7.6%	42	58.6
2016	TB	16/16	1123	567	345	60.8%	4090	28	18/20	10	5.9%	6.4	19	3.6%	16	556	15	539	53	165	1	-23.8%	-19	64.7
2017	TB	13/13	795	442	282	63.8%	3504	19	11/19	15	7.0%	7.1	10	14.3%	12	779	11	684	33	135	1	-21.7%	-14	48.2
2018	TB			599	375	62.6%	4626	28	16	9		6.7		7.9%					48	193	2	8.0%		

2016:	33% Short	42% Mid	17% Deep	8% Bomb	aDOT: 10.6 (3)	YAC: 3.9 (34)	ALEX: 3.3	2017:	41% Short	38% Mid	14% Deep	8% Bomb	aDOT: 11.0 (2)	YAC: 4.4 (32)	ALEX: 3.2

One of the common boasts from Winston fans is that he holds NFL records for the most passing yards (11,636) and passing touchdowns (69) before a player's age-24 season. That is all true, but he also has a big advantage in pass attempts (1,544) over everyone not named Drew Bledsoe. Winston is still very young, but he's also come into the NFL at a time when it is more pass-happy than ever, and he only played two years at Florida State, which would have been unheard of even in Bledsoe's era just over 25 years ago. So Winston's youth can be cited as a positive for what he has been able to accomplish, but his numbers are more due to the opportunities Winston has had in today's NFL.

Winston won't be enjoying more opportunities to start the year. He will serve a three-game suspension to start 2018 for violating the league's personal conduct policy. That's where Winston's youth could also be a negative, in his numerous off-field incidents, some of which just speak to someone who needs to grow up so he can advance his career. Note that the KUBIAK projection here is for a 16-game season, not for the 13-game season Winston will actually play.

T.J. Yates   Height: 6-3   Weight: 195   College: North Carolina   Draft: 2011/5 (152)   Born: 28-May-1987   Age: 31   Risk: N/A

Year	Team	G/GS	Snaps	Att	Comp	C%	Yds	TD	INT/Adj	FUM	ASR	NY/P	Rk	DVOA	Rk	DYAR	Rk	YAR	Runs	Yds	TD	DVOA	DYAR	QBR
2015	HOU	4/2	132	57	28	49.1%	370	3	1/1	1	7.9%	5.4	--	-7.0%	--	17	--	-18	6	0	0	81.8%	3	55.7
2017	HOU	4/3	206	97	47	48.5%	523	4	3/3	5	10.8%	4.1	--	-45.0%	--	-235	--	-242	5	51	0	32.8%	12	29.6

2017:	51% Short	30% Mid	7% Deep	12% Bomb	aDOT: 10.5 (–)	YAC: 4.0 (–)	ALEX: 6.6

2017 marked the third time in seven seasons this popgun-armed quarterback with extensive clipboard-holding experience and West Coast offense familiarity has gone from third-string or not on the roster at the start of the year to multi-game starter, all in Houston despite sojourns in Atlanta, Buffalo, and Miami. Yates was unsigned in late June, but available and probably on speed dial for half a dozen teams should they need a quarterback on Tuesday who can back up on Sunday.

Going Deep

Derek Anderson, FA: Last season, 13 different quarterbacks suited up for their seventh consecutive season with the same franchise. Eleven of them are long-time starters: your Bradys, your Rodgerses, your Ryans, players around whom you build franchises. The 12th was Matt Moore, who was a one-year starter before being relegated to the bench. That just leaves Derek Anderson, the longest-tenured backup quarterback in football. Carolina valued him for his reliability and his knowledge of the system, and maybe less so for his actual performance. Since 2008, only Blaine Gabbert has a lower ANY/A figure among quarterbacks with at least 1,000 dropbacks. Anderson is currently unsigned and, at 35, may be out of chances.

Joe Callahan, PHI: Waiver-wire superstar who bounced between the Packers and Browns practice squads for two seasons. Callahan will now compete with Nate Sudfeld for the No. 3 job in Philly.

Kellen Clemens, FA: Now 35 years old and five seasons removed from his last significant playing time. Clemens' career is over unless some team really wants to push the Colin Kaepernick collusion case to Twilight Zone levels. Clemens once graced the cover of our publication as a hot prospect. We feel old. And, whoops.

Connor Cook, OAK: Oddly enough, the one thing Jon Gruden didn't purchase during his madcap free-agent shopping spree was a veteran challenger for the backup quarterback role. Cook lost the backup job to Matt McGloin as a rookie—receiving a disastrous playoff start in 2016 only after McGloin suffered a shoulder injury—then fell behind EJ Manuel last year. Cook got a long look in the 2017 preseason but completed just 50.7 percent of his passes. The bloom is off his prospect rose, but he'll do battle again with the reliably inaccurate Manuel for the right to back up Derek Carr.

Joshua Dobbs, PIT: When the Steelers drafted Dobbs in the fourth round last year, they raved about his intelligence and upside, and gave every indication he'd be their developmental project for the foreseeable future. That plan seems out the window now that Mason Rudolph is in town, and Dobbs will have to battle with Landry Jones to make the 53-man roster. Dobbs did not shine in 2017's preseason, rushing throws and throwing three interceptions while completing less than 60 percent of his passes. Still, his athleticism, height, and intelligence (he's an aerospace engineer!) will likely keep him hanging on somewhere in 2018.

Danny Etling, NE: A play-action specialist at LSU, Etling showed deep-ball promise but mixed with inconsistent feet placement and an inability to just give up on a dead play. Etling transferred from Purdue to LSU and threw just two interceptions in his senior season in the SEC before New England took him in the seventh round. There are reasons to believe he could develop into something more, but he will need the development to be playable.

David Fales, MIA: A small-bodied passer without much trajectory on his throws, Fales nonetheless was drafted in 2014 because he showed a lot of proficiency with the San Jose Spartans offense and excelled as a pre-snap reader. Given a start to show this last year, he nearly led a comeback from down 22-0 against the Bills. He's nobody's idea of a hot prospect, but this is the kind of player who gets lost in the shuffle when teams decide they need to employ Matt Cassel because he's tall.

Luke Falk, TEN: A sixth-round rookie, Falk threw 2,054 passes as a four-year starter at Washington State, the fourth-highest tally in college football history. A high-volume short passer, Falk completed 68.3 percent of those passes for more than 14,000 yards (7.1 yards per attempt) and 119 touchdowns but was also sacked 125 times in 42 games. Of the other nine players in the top ten for career attempts in college, only Case Keenum has thus far enjoyed significant success as a starter in the NFL.

Christian Hackenberg, FA: Going against Hackenberg when he was drafted were: the tape, the numbers, and the performances. Going for him: he's tall and can throw the ball really far. Two years in, with zero career starts on a Jets team with a horrific depth chart, it turns out that Hackenberg makes a better quarterback model than a quarterback.

Taylor Heinicke, CAR: Heinicke has a shot to win Carolina's backup quarterback role with Derek Anderson out of town. With one career pass attempt, he is actually the most experienced backup candidate on Carolina's roster. He also has some history with new offensive coordinator Norv Turner, having played for him in Minnesota.

Taysom Hill, NO: Hill had a productive preseason for the Packers last year but did not make the final cut. The Saints picked him up in September and did not find any use for him until December when he started making plays on special teams. He had a couple of tackles on kick returns and almost came up with a blocked punt against Carolina. It's a unique way to use a third-string quarterback, but it also could be the way that Hill stays on the team.

Cardale Jones, LAC: The Chargers traded for Jones on the eve of training camp last year and gave him the bulk of their preseason passes. Jones threw three interceptions and zero touchdowns in 61 preseason attempts, then spent the year as the deactivated third quarterback. Ken Whisenhunt's offense needs an Urban Meyer quarterback the way a school of fish needs a read-option playbook, but the Chargers doubled down on wild-armed, inconsistent collegiate scrambling stars by signing Geno Smith to compete with Jones. The name you want to remember when handicapping the Philip Rivers heir apparent race is Nic Shimonek, a UDFA rookie from Texas Tech.

Chad Kelly, DEN: Kelly is Jim Kelly's nephew, was Mr. Irrelevant in the 2017 draft, and remains the poster child for the difference between Internet tape scouting and holistic player evaluation. Kelly was throwing during OTAs and should be on track to compete for the Broncos backup job after missing last season with a wrist injury. He missed most of his final college season with an ACL tear, and his college career is generously sprinkled with arrests, dismissals, transfers and indications that he might be a wee bit entitled. John Elway drafted him on Uncle Jim's say-so, which … doesn't do much to dismiss the "entitled" concerns. Kelly does, in fact, look like an NFL quarterback on film when healthy and dialed-in. His competition to back up Case Keenum is Paxton Lynch, who could either crumble under the pressure or just Netflix and chill until Kelly gets hurt or in trouble. The Broncos backup quarterbacks are your college roommates, folks, and that's not a good thing.

Tanner Lee, JAX: Essentially forced to choose between turning professional after a poor season, transferring schools for the second straight offseason, or settling for a backup role in Nebraska's new offensive system, Lee chose to enter the NFL draft and Jacksonville selected him in the sixth round. Lee threw the most interceptions of any Power Five quarterback in 2017—16, including five pick-sixes—and never completed more than 57.5 percent of his passes in a college season. He has just enough size and arm strength to get a chance in the NFL, but his most likely destination after the offseason program is somebody's practice squad.

Ryan Mallett, FA: Once upon a time Mallett was the proto-Garoppolo, a Pats backup groomed to take over in New England. But Brady, and poor play, and recidivist oversleeping, and now Mallett is on the cusp of being out of the league.

Matt McGloin, KC: Minnesota Vikings offensive coordinator John DeFilippo can partially thank McGloin for his meteoric rise through the coaching ranks. In Oakland, McGloin was DeFilippo's first tangible success as a quarterback coach, when McGloin provided a surprisingly functional stretch of games in 2013. Since then, McGloin has started just one game and has yet to reach the heights to which DeFilippo once brought him.

Alex McGough, SEA: The Seahawks have drafted precisely two quarterbacks under Pete Carroll and John Schneider: first Russell Wilson, and now McGough in the seventh round. He was a four-year starter at Florida International, throwing 65 touchdowns to just 37 interceptions, and had a 65 percent completion rate as a senior. He has some mobility and can put zip on the ball when required, though his mechanics are still iffy. Seattle's pre-draft quarterbacks room consisted of just Wilson and a cantaloupe with a smiley face drawn on it, so McGough could find himself as the backup before all is said and done.

Cooper Rush, DAL: In four years at Central Michigan, Rush was among the top five passers in the country with 90 touchdowns, tied with Deshaun Watson and just behind Patrick Mahomes. Of course, he also threw 55 interceptions, eight more than anyone else. He went undrafted, then beat out Kellen Moore for the backup job in Dallas with a monster preseason: a 75 percent completion rate, six touchdowns, no interceptions, and a 135.9 passer rating, plus four rushes for 33 yards. The Cowboys drafted Mike White in the fifth round, putting Rush's roster spot in some jeopardy, but he'd likely get a second chance somewhere else in a hurry.

Mark Sanchez, FA: The latest stats on Sanchez include 73 drug tests in nine years (source: himself), and one positive test for a banned substance. That's more failed drug tests than touchdown passes in the last two years, and it's landed the free agent a four-game suspension to start 2018. The Butt Fumble legend has only thrown 109 passes in the last three regular seasons, including none last year for Chicago.

Kyle Sloter, MIN: Some felt that Sgt. Sloter had a say in the Vikings' quarterback future, but after the team brought in Kirk Cousins and Trevor Siemian, it is clear that he'll have to settle for the third-string job. Sloter had a strong first preseason for Denver with 413 yards, 9.6 yards per attempt, three touchdowns, and no interceptions. Now he could have to back up Siemian for a second franchise. But if you're looking for a future Tony Romo-type breakout candidate, keep an eye on Sloter.

Nate Sudfeld, PHI: Sudfeld completed 19-of-23 passes for 134 yards in the meaningless season finale against the Cowboys. It was like he was trolling fans of the empty completion percentage. He'll compete with Joe Callahan for the Eagles' third quarterback spot. Sudfeld's secret edge is that he looks like Carson Wentz facially; reporters can be fooled from a distance (Carson's giving 1-on-1's? Oh, it's just Nate.) and maybe coaches will get mixed up when making final cuts.

Scott Tolzien, FA: Tolzien started the season for the Colts. The idea he could be a decent starter while waiting and waiting for Andrew Luck's return died on his first pass, a short out route that itself died on the way to T.Y. Hilton and finished in Trumaine Johnson's hands in the end zone. Tolzien lasted about three quarters, enough to throw one more pick that counted and another that was wiped out on a penalty, and Chuck Pagano and company had seen enough for the season. Unsigned at press time.

Joe Webb, HOU: Webb was the rare quarterback with more rushes than passing attempts in 2017, at least if you consider him a "quarterback" as opposed to a special teamer who's good at throwing the ball. Buffalo got stuck playing him at quarterback for half of their blizzard game against Indianapolis after Nathan Peterman suffered a concussion. Webb signed with Houston in the offseason, and he's probably fourth on the depth chart, but he may again stick around to play special teams.

Logan Woodside, CIN: For a seventh-round draft pick, the Toledo Terror has plenty of fans. Woodside is extremely accurate and has some in-pocket wiggle. But his arm strength makes Andy Dalton look like John Elway. Practice squad and eventual elevation to backup would be a nice career path for Woodside. A DUI arrest in June didn't help his cause.

Running Backs

In the following section we provide the last three years of statistics, as well as a 2018 KUBIAK projection, for every running back who either played a significant role in 2017 or is expected to do so in 2018.

The first line contains biographical data—each player's name, height, weight, college, draft position, birth date, and age. Height and weight are the best data we could find; weight, of course, can fluctuate during the offseason. **Age** is very simple, the number of years between the player's birth year and 2018, but birthdate is provided if you want to figure out exact age.

Draft position gives draft year and round, with the overall pick number with which the player was taken in parentheses. In the sample table, it says that Alvin Kamara was chosen in the 2017 NFL draft in the third round with the 67th overall pick. Undrafted free agents are listed as "FA" with the year they came into the league, even if they were only in training camp or on a practice squad.

To the far right of the first line is the player's Risk for fantasy football in 2018. As explained in the quarterback section, the standard is for players to be marked Green. Players with higher than normal risk are marked Yellow, and players with the highest risk are marked Red. Players who are most likely to match or surpass our forecast—primarily second-stringers with low projections—are marked Blue. Risk is not only based on age and injury probability, but how a player's projection compares to his recent performance as well as our confidence (or lack thereof) in his offensive teammates.

Next we give the last three years of player stats. First come games played and games started (**G/GS**). Games played is the official NFL total and may include games in which a player appeared on special teams, but did not carry the ball or catch a pass. We also have a total of offensive **Snaps** for each season. The next four columns are familiar: **Runs**, rushing yards (**Yds**), yards per rush (**Yd/R**) and rushing touchdowns (**TD**).

The entry for fumbles (**FUM**) includes all fumbles by this running back, no matter whether they were recovered by the offense or defense. Holding onto the ball is an identifiable skill; fumbling it so that your own offense can recover it is not. (For more on this issue, see the essay "Pregame Show" in the front of the book.) This entry combines fumbles on both carries and receptions. Fumbles on special teams are not included.

The next five columns give our advanced metrics for rushing: **DVOA** (Defense-Adjusted Value Over Average), **DYAR** (Defense-Adjusted Yards Above Replacement), and **YAR** (Yards Above Replacement), along with the player's rank (**Rk**) in both **DVOA** and **DYAR**. These metrics compare ev-

ery carry by the running back to a league-average baseline based on the game situations in which that running back carried the ball. DVOA and DYAR are also adjusted based on the opposing defense. The methods used to compute these numbers are described in detail in the "Statistical Toolbox" introduction in the front of the book. The important distinctions between them are:

- DVOA is a rate statistic, while DYAR is a cumulative statistic. Thus, a higher DVOA means more value per play, while a higher DYAR means more aggregate value over the entire season.
- Because DYAR is defense-adjusted and YAR is not, a player whose DYAR is higher than his YAR faced a harder-than-average schedule. A player whose DYAR is lower than his YAR faced an easier-than-average schedule.

To qualify for ranking in rushing DVOA and DYAR, a running back must have had 100 carries in that season. Last year, 47 running backs qualified to be ranked in these stats, compared to 42 backs in 2016 and 44 backs in 2015.

Success Rate (**Suc%**), listed along with rank, represents running back consistency as measured by successful running plays divided by total running plays. (The definition for success is explained in the "Statistical Toolbox" introduction in the front of the book.) A player with high DVOA and a low Success Rate mixes long runs with plays on which he was stuffed at or behind the line of scrimmage. A player with low DVOA and a high Success Rate generally gets the yards needed, but rarely gets more. The league-average Success Rate in 2017 was 45 percent. Success Rate is not adjusted for the defenses a player faced.

We also give a total of broken tackles (**BTkl**) according to charting from Sports Info Solutions. This total includes broken tackles on both runs and receptions. Please note that last year SIS marked broken tackles roughly 8 percent more often than in 2016, and roughly 24 percent more often than in 2015. So most running backs with consistent playing time will be listed with more broken tackles in 2017 than in 2015; it doesn't necessarily mean they suddenly became more powerful or elusive.

The shaded columns to the right of broken tackles give data for each running back as a pass receiver. Receptions (**Rec**) counts passes caught, while Passes (**Pass**) counts total passes thrown to this player, complete or incomplete. The next four columns list receiving yards (**Yds**), receiving touchdowns (**TD**), catch rate (**C%**), yards per catch (**Yd/C**), and average yards after the catch (**YAC**).

Alvin Kamara		Height: 5-10		Weight: 214		College: Tennessee			Draft: 2017/3 (67)			Born: 25-May-1995	Age: 23				Risk: Yellow	

Year	Team	G/GS	Snaps	Runs	Yds	TD	Yd/R	FUM	DVOA	Rk	DYAR	Rk	YAR	Suc%	Rk	BTkl	Pass	Rec	Yds	TD	C%	Yd/C	YAC	DVOA	Rk	DYAR	Rk
2017	NO	16/3	464	120	728	8	6.1	1	44.5%	1	255	3	255	53%	6	66	100	81	826	5	81%	10.2	8.5	36.4%	6	278	1
2018	NO			175	874	8	5.0	4	12.6%								105	85	730	3	81%	8.6		26.7%			

Our research has shown that receivers bear some responsibility for incomplete passes, even though only their catches are tracked in official statistics. Catch rate represents receptions divided by all intended passes for this running back. The average NFL running back caught 74 percent of passes in 2017. Unfortunately, we don't have room to post the best and worst running backs in receiving plus-minus, but you'll find the top 10 and bottom 10 running backs in this metric listed in the statistical appendix.

Finally we have receiving DVOA and DYAR, which are entirely separate from rushing DVOA and DYAR. To qualify for ranking in receiving DVOA and DYAR, a running back must have 25 passes thrown to him in that season. There are 62 running backs ranked for 2017, 53 backs for 2016, and 58 backs for 2015. Numbers without opponent adjustment (YAR, and VOA) can be found on our website, FootballOutsiders.com.

The italicized row of statistics for the 2018 season is our 2018 KUBIAK projection based on a complicated regression analysis that takes into account numerous variables including projected role, performance over the past two years, projected team offense and defense, historical comparables, height, age, experience of the offensive line, and strength of schedule.

It is difficult to accurately project statistics for a 162-game baseball season, but it is exponentially more difficult to accurately project statistics for a 16-game football season. Consider the listed projections not as a prediction of exact numbers, but the mean of a range of possible performances. What's important is less the exact number of yards we project, and more which players are projected to improve or decline. Actual performance will vary from our projection less for veteran starters and more for rookies and third-stringers, for whom we must base our projections on much smaller career statistical samples. Touchdown numbers will vary more than yardage numbers.

For many rookie running backs, we'll also include a metric from our college football arsenal: **Highlight Yards**. Highlight Yards are those yards not included in adjusted line yards. So, for example, if a runner gains 12 yards on a given carry, and we attribute 7.0 of those yards to the line (the ALY formula gives the offensive line 100 percent credit for all yards gained between zero and four yards and 50 percent credit between five and 10), then the player's highlight yardage on the play is 5.0 yards. Highlight Yards are shown as an average per opportunity, which means Highlight Yards divided by the total number of carries that went over four yards.

Finally, in a section we call "Going Deep," we briefly discuss lower-round rookies, free-agent veterans, and practice-squad players who may play a role during the 2018 season or beyond.

Top 20 RB by Rushing DYAR (Total Value), 2017

Rank	Player	Team	DYAR
1	Dion Lewis	NE	273
2	Todd Gurley	LAR	268
3	Alvin Kamara	NO	255
4	Kareem Hunt	KC	222
5	Le'Veon Bell	PIT	214
6	Alex Collins	BAL	205
7	Ezekiel Elliott	DAL	205
8	Mark Ingram	NO	193
9	Marshawn Lynch	OAK	165
10	Jordan Howard	CHI	160
11	Leonard Fournette	JAX	115
12	Jamaal Williams	GB	108
13	Buck Allen	BAL	96
14	Devonta Freeman	ATL	89
15	Matt Breida	SF	87
16	Alfred Morris	DAL	79
17	Joe Mixon	CIN	68
18	Frank Gore	IND	66
19	Peyton Barber	TB	63
20	Latavius Murray	MIN	59

Minimum 100 carries.

Top 20 RB by Rushing DVOA (Value per Rush), 2017

Rank	Player	Team	DVOA
1	Alvin Kamara	NO	44.5%
2	Dion Lewis	NE	27.6%
3	Alex Collins	BAL	15.1%
4	Todd Gurley	LAR	13.9%
5	Matt Breida	SF	13.0%
6	Kareem Hunt	KC	11.9%
7	Mark Ingram	NO	11.2%
8	Ezekiel Elliott	DAL	11.1%
9	Marshawn Lynch	OAK	10.1%
10	Alfred Morris	DAL	8.4%
11	Le'Veon Bell	PIT	7.9%
12	Jamaal Williams	GB	7.4%
13	Buck Allen	BAL	6.2%
14	Jordan Howard	CHI	5.8%
15	Peyton Bernard	TB	4.4%
16	Giovani Bernard	CIN	3.4%
17	Leonard Fournette	JAX	2.1%
18	Devonta Freeman	ATL	1.5%
19	Joe Mixon	CIN	1.0%
20	Mike Gillislee	NE	-0.8%

Minimum 100 carries.

Top 10 RB by Receiving DYAR (Total Value), 2017

Rank	Player	Team	DYAR
1	Alvin Kamara	NO	278
2	Todd Gurley	LAR	236
3	Chris Thompson	WAS	223
4	Lamar Miller	HOU	134
5	Christian McCaffrey	CAR	128
6	Tevin Coleman	ATL	121
7	Duke Johnson	CLE	110
8	Rex Burkhead	NE	102
9	Kareem Hunt	KC	102
10	Devonta Freeman	ATL	102

Minimum 25 passes.

Top 10 RB by Receiving DVOA (Value per Pass), 2017

Rank	Player	Team	DVOA
1	Chris Thompson	WAS	67.3%
2	Lamar Miller	HOU	42.7%
3	Samaje Perine	WAS	42.6%
4	Tevin Coleman	ATL	41.2%
5	Benny Cunningham	CHI	39.6%
6	Alvin Kamara	NO	36.4%
7	Todd Gurley	LAR	35.9%
8	Rex Burkhead	NE	33.7%
9	Jalen Richard	OAK	33.3%
10	Dion Lewis	NE	32.0%

Minimum 25 passes.

Ameer Abdullah   Height: 5-9   Weight: 205   College: Nebraska   Draft: 2015/2 (54)   Born: 13-Jun-1993   Age: 25   Risk: Red

Year	Team	G/GS	Snaps	Runs	Yds	TD	Yd/R	FUM	DVOA	Rk	DYAR	Rk	YAR	Suc%	Rk	BTkl	Pass	Rec	Yds	TD	C%	Yd/C	YAC	DVOA	Rk	DYAR	Rk
2015	DET	16/9	355	143	597	2	4.2	4	-8.9%	37	-2	37	21	51%	7	16	38	25	183	1	66%	7.3	7.7	-11.3%	40	6	40
2016	DET	2/2	57	18	101	0	5.6	0	16.5%	--	18	--	32	61%	--	7	5	5	57	1	100%	11.4	10.8	87.2%	--	33	--
2017	DET	14/11	378	165	552	4	3.3	2	-10.0%	37	-9	36	-47	35%	47	26	35	25	162	1	71%	6.5	5.8	1.7%	30	-33	32
2018	DET			16	55	1	3.5	1	0.2%								19	15	117	0	79%	7.8		2.0%			

While it hasn't happened yet, expectations are for Detroit to cut ties with Abdullah after three unimpressive seasons. Abdullah couldn't stay healthy and doesn't really offer Detroit any upside it cannot get from the rest of the backfield. Theo Riddick catches the ball better, LeGarrette Blount runs downhill better, and rookie Kerryon Johnson has more potential. Look for Abdullah to be the odd man out barring some unfortunate August injuries.

Jay Ajayi   Height: 6-0   Weight: 221   College: Boise State   Draft: 2015/5 (149)   Born: 15-Jun-1993   Age: 25   Risk: Green

Year	Team	G/GS	Snaps	Runs	Yds	TD	Yd/R	FUM	DVOA	Rk	DYAR	Rk	YAR	Suc%	Rk	BTkl	Pass	Rec	Yds	TD	C%	Yd/C	YAC	DVOA	Rk	DYAR	Rk
2015	MIA	9/0	158	49	187	1	3.8	0	-17.7%	--	-17	--	-3	39%	--	17	11	7	90	0	64%	12.9	11.1	38.1%	--	28	--
2016	MIA	15/12	582	260	1272	8	4.9	4	9.3%	13	185	7	126	43%	32	59	35	27	151	0	77%	5.6	4.9	-20.7%	47	-14	46
2017	2TM	14/8	509	208	873	1	4.2	3	-5.1%	28	27	27	21	43%	30	59	34	24	158	1	71%	6.6	7.3	-23.6%	55	-18	53
2018	PHI			197	853	5	4.3	3	1.4%								34	26	196	1	76%	7.5		3.7%			

Twenty-three of Ajayi's 112 regular and postseason carries for the Eagles (20.5 percent) netted 8 or more yards. He also gained 8 or more yards on nine of his 16 completions. Ajayi thrived in the 10- to 15-touch role the Eagles crafted for him, and there were no traces of the alleged bad attitude that made him expendable in Miami. When an organization begins gift-wrapping and shipping talented players to contenders in an effort to "change the culture," it's a safe bet that the organization itself is more of a problem than the individual players.

LeGarrette Blount's absence should result in more touches for Ajayi, but the Eagles backfield is still pretty crowded, so don't expect him to suddenly become a 25-carry workhorse.

Buck Allen   Height: 6-0   Weight: 221   College: USC   Draft: 2015/4 (125)   Born: 27-Aug-1991   Age: 27   Risk: Green

Year	Team	G/GS	Snaps	Runs	Yds	TD	Yd/R	FUM	DVOA	Rk	DYAR	Rk	YAR	Suc%	Rk	BTkl	Pass	Rec	Yds	TD	C%	Yd/C	YAC	DVOA	Rk	DYAR	Rk
2015	BAL	16/6	393	137	514	1	3.8	2	-3.2%	29	31	30	0	47%	19	23	62	45	353	2	73%	7.8	6.7	-6.2%	33	27	29
2016	BAL	8/0	41	9	34	0	3.8	0	-18.0%	--	-3	--	2	56%	--	3	4	3	15	0	75%	5.0	7.3	-12.1%	--	0	--
2017	BAL	16/0	466	153	591	4	3.9	0	6.2%	13	96	13	67	47%	17	22	60	46	250	2	77%	5.4	4.7	-16.7%	49	-10	51
2018	BAL			71	281	1	3.9	2	-6.2%								33	27	160	0	82%	5.9		-8.6%			

The Ravens offense perked up once Allen ceded the role of RB1 to Alex Collins. A big part of the problem came close to the end zone. The Ravens gave Buck the ball nine times inside the 5, and he only cracked paydirt twice, well under the league average and a main reason why John Harbaugh often used a word that rhymed with Allen's nickname after those plays. That said, Allen wasn't awful inside the 20-yard line, and was quite effective as a third-down runner, posting a 21.8% DVOA on the money down. Allen is supposed to be the main receiving threat out of the backfield, but he was poor in that regard last year, opening the door for a challenge from Kenneth Dixon, who is back from injury.

C.J. Anderson Height: 5-8   Weight: 224   College: California   Draft: 2013/FA   Born: 2-Feb-1991   Age: 27   Risk: Yellow

Year	Team	G/GS	Snaps	Runs	Yds	TD	Yd/R	FUM	DVOA	Rk	DYAR	Rk	YAR	Suc%	Rk	BTkl	Pass	Rec	Yds	TD	C%	Yd/C	YAC	DVOA	Rk	DYAR	Rk
2015	DEN	15/6	500	152	720	5	4.7	2	-3.2%	27	34	28	70	41%	41	31	36	25	183	0	69%	7.3	6.0	-27.8%	53	-23	51
2016	DEN	7/7	314	110	437	4	4.0	0	-13.5%	36	-23	35	9	39%	41	17	24	16	128	1	67%	8.0	6.8	-15.4%	--	-2	--
2017	DEN	16/16	617	245	1007	3	4.1	1	-6.9%	34	16	30	74	42%	34	47	40	28	224	1	70%	8.0	7.7	-13.2%	44	1	44
2018	CAR			177	704	4	4.0	3	-2.7%								28	21	158	0	75%	7.5		-1.0%			

The Panthers are missing a little over 200 caries from last season with Jonathan Stewart out of town. Anderson is much more likely to pick up the lion's share than Christian McCaffrey or Cameron Artis-Payne. Anderson has averaged more than 4.0 yards per carry in each of his first five seasons, and topped 1,000 yards for the first time last year as well. He did that despite being essentially the sole focus of opposing defenses, considering Denver's many, many issues at the quarterback position in 2017. Anderson isn't going to fill up the highlight reel or earn a lot of Pro Bowl berths, but he's a reliable workhorse. He'll give Carolina more consistent production out of the backfield than Stewart has been able to put up in the last two or three years.

Cameron Artis-Payne Height: 5-10   Weight: 212   College: Auburn   Draft: 2015/5 (174)   Born: 23-Jun-1992   Age: 26   Risk: Green

Year	Team	G/GS	Snaps	Runs	Yds	TD	Yd/R	FUM	DVOA	Rk	DYAR	Rk	YAR	Suc%	Rk	BTkl	Pass	Rec	Yds	TD	C%	Yd/C	YAC	DVOA	Rk	DYAR	Rk
2015	CAR	7/0	113	45	183	1	4.1	0	-9.2%	--	-1	--	-10	38%	--	7	5	5	58	0	100%	11.6	12.2	90.1%	--	31	--
2016	CAR	3/3	84	36	144	2	4.0	0	-4.5%	--	6	--	21	50%	--	8	1	1	11	0	100%	11.0	15.0	128.6%	--	8	--
2017	CAR	13/0	37	18	95	1	5.3	0	4.1%	--	11	--	10	44%	--	3	1	1	2	0	100%	2.0	6.0	-77.2%	--	-4	--
2018	CAR			45	205	1	4.5	2	5.5%								4	3	23	0	75%	7.5		6.3%			

Artis-Payne will be in the mix to replace some of Jonathan Stewart's carries as the big back in Carolina's offense. So far, however, his career has been trending in the wrong direction, with fewer touches in each successive season since being drafted out of Auburn in 2015. Even when Stewart was averaging just 3.4 yards per carry, Artis-Payne only earned 18 carries, spending most of his time on special teams. He hasn't been terrible when given opportunities, with rushing DVOA slightly below average in each season (in small sample sizes). He has just never been able to really earn the trust of his coaching staff. A new offensive coordinator is a possible benefit for CAP, as is the fact that the Panthers didn't add a running back in the draft. The addition of C.J. Anderson is a negative, however, and Artis-Payne may have to settle for being one of the preseason's leading rushers four a fourth straight season.

Peyton Barber Height: 5-10   Weight: 228   College: Auburn   Draft: 2016/FA   Born: 27-Jun-1994   Age: 24   Risk: Green

Year	Team	G/GS	Snaps	Runs	Yds	TD	Yd/R	FUM	DVOA	Rk	DYAR	Rk	YAR	Suc%	Rk	BTkl	Pass	Rec	Yds	TD	C%	Yd/C	YAC	DVOA	Rk	DYAR	Rk
2016	TB	15/1	136	55	223	1	4.1	0	-17.2%	--	-19	--	11	47%	--	8	6	5	28	0	83%	5.6	2.8	-10.2%	--	1	--
2017	TB	16/4	254	108	423	3	3.9	2	4.4%	15	63	19	58	57%	3	16	19	16	114	0	84%	7.1	7.1	-11.1%	--	3	--
2018	TB			90	349	2	3.9	2	-3.1%								19	16	117	0	84%	7.3		3.1%			

Barber is fine for depth, but he ended up leading the Buccaneers in rushing last year. He had only 88 yards on 30 carries in the first 11 games of the year before collecting 102 yards on 23 carries against Green Bay in Week 13, but failed to gain more than 71 yards in a game after that. There's nothing in his skill set that screams workhorse back, so the Buccaneers needed to get better at the position. The answer looks to be second-round rookie Ronald Jones, who will likely push Barber down the depth chart again.

Saquon Barkley Height: 6-0   Weight: 233   College: Penn State   Draft: 2018/1 (2)   Born: 7-Feb-1997   Age: 21   Risk: Red

Year	Team	G/GS	Snaps	Runs	Yds	TD	Yd/R	FUM	DVOA	Rk	DYAR	Rk	YAR	Suc%	Rk	BTkl	Pass	Rec	Yds	TD	C%	Yd/C	YAC	DVOA	Rk	DYAR	Rk
2018	NYG			305	1326	7	4.3	4	3.6%								94	67	610	3	71%	9.1		1.7%			

Barkley was the annual "best running back prospect since Adrian Peterson" award winner for the 2018 draft class. Barkley clocked in at 4.40 seconds in the 40-yard dash at the NFL combine and has multiple college careers' worth of highlight tape, so it is no wonder the comparisons flooded in. On top of being an exciting runner, Barkley is the caliber of pass-catcher and pass-blocker required for today's NFL. If Pat Shurmur so pleases, Barkley is plenty talented enough be split out on occasion as a true wide receiver, a la Le'Veon Bell or David Johnson. The primary concern with Barkley entering the league boils down to whether his lapses in vision in college were self-inflicted or more a result of a relatively disastrous Penn State offensive line. In the NFL, consistent vision and efficiency become more important, and bad plays become more difficult to counterbalance. However, even if Barkley does put himself in poor situations from time to time via his creative nature, the same can be said of Buffalo's LeSean McCoy, who can be a bit of a rollercoaster but is ultimately a productive and threatening running back.

Le'Veon Bell
Height: 6-1   Weight: 230   College: Michigan State   Draft: 2013/2 (48)   Born: 18-Feb-1992   Age: 26   Risk: Yellow

Year	Team	G/GS	Snaps	Runs	Yds	TD	Yd/R	FUM	DVOA	Rk	DYAR	Rk	YAR	Suc%	Rk	BTkl	Pass	Rec	Yds	TD	C%	Yd/C	YAC	DVOA	Rk	DYAR	Rk
2015	PIT	6/6	301	113	556	3	4.9	0	28.1%	1	162	5	127	50%	10	19	26	24	136	0	92%	5.7	5.8	-21.3%	49	-10	48
2016	PIT	12/12	781	261	1268	7	4.9	4	17.3%	5	277	3	271	56%	3	61	94	75	616	2	80%	8.2	8.9	16.2%	12	165	2
2017	PIT	15/15	945	321	1291	9	4.0	3	7.9%	11	214	5	261	49%	11	79	106	85	655	2	80%	7.7	8.0	2.5%	29	101	11
2018	PIT			324	1458	12	4.5	3	9.3%								103	81	660	3	79%	8.1		15.2%			

Despite ranking third in the league in rushing yardage, Bell only averaged 4.02 yards per carry last season. That was below league average, his lowest mark since his rookie season, and a very hard feat to pull off while still having so much volume on the ground. No other player had hit the 1,200-yard mark with a lower yards per carry since Rashard Mendenhall did it back in 2010. The reason for that low YPC mark was a lack of deep highlight-reel runs. Bell's longest carry in 2017 went for just 27 yards; 71 players managed to have a run that topped that last season, including Darrius Heyward-Bey. This makes Bell's production that much more impressive, because after a certain point, yardage on long runs becomes more random than skill-based. The difference between a 30-yard carry and a 60-yard carry often depends on what yard line you started on and what scheme the opposition was playing. Bell managed at least a positive gain on 85 percent of his carries, the third-highest rate in the league. If you were to discard any rushing yards over 15 on any given play, Bell would have led the league with 1,259 yards, 106 more than second-place Todd Gurley. In other words, don't worry about that low average; Bell was just somewhat unlucky in 2017.

As a receiver, Bell is known for splitting out wide, but he's also a major security blanket from the backfield. He had 11 targets charted as "check & release" against the Packers (Week 12) and Ravens (Week 14) late in the season, and 20 total in 2017. No other running back had more than 11 such plays in the entire season.

Giovani Bernard
Height: 5-8   Weight: 202   College: North Carolina   Draft: 2013/2 (37)   Born: 22-Nov-1991   Age: 27   Risk: Yellow

Year	Team	G/GS	Snaps	Runs	Yds	TD	Yd/R	FUM	DVOA	Rk	DYAR	Rk	YAR	Suc%	Rk	BTkl	Pass	Rec	Yds	TD	C%	Yd/C	YAC	DVOA	Rk	DYAR	Rk
2015	CIN	16/1	580	154	730	2	4.7	1	11.8%	8	131	10	130	49%	13	37	66	49	472	0	74%	9.6	9.3	14.6%	16	97	12
2016	CIN	10/2	394	91	337	2	3.7	1	-2.1%	--	24	--	22	49%	--	17	51	39	336	1	76%	8.6	6.4	22.4%	7	101	10
2017	CIN	16/2	486	105	458	2	4.4	0	3.4%	16	48	24	43	40%	40	22	60	43	389	2	72%	9.0	10.0	-10.3%	41	11	40
2018	CIN			118	498	2	4.2	2	-0.1%								58	44	393	1	76%	8.9		10.6%			

The Cincinnati offense hummed much better when Bernard got the rock on first down. Joe Mixon had twice as many first-down attempts, but Bernard out-DVOA'd Mixon on those handoffs, 23.3% to -3.5%. Bernard was also notably better from shotgun looks (15.6% to 4.8% on essentially the same number of carries). Bernard is supposed to be a third-down specialist, and it appears enemy defenses realize this, too. He was much worse carrying the ball (-25.1%) on the money down, and his receiving efficiency was terrifyingly bad (-61.9%). Bernard has been an effective back in bursts, but Cincy has never really figured out how to use him best. He is more effective between the tackles than his size would indicate, but isn't quite the impossible mismatch in space the Bengals seem to believe he is. His catch rate remains high, however, which would seem to put the onus on scheme rather than player. The numbers are screaming for a fresh approach to Gio's usage.

LeGarrette Blount

Height: 6-0   Weight: 247   College: Oregon   Draft: 2010/FA   Born: 5-Dec-1986   Age: 32   Risk: Green

Year	Team	G/GS	Snaps	Runs	Yds	TD	Yd/R	FUM	DVOA	Rk	DYAR	Rk	YAR	Suc%	Rk	BTkl	Pass	Rec	Yds	TD	C%	Yd/C	YAC	DVOA	Rk	DYAR	Rk
2015	NE	12/6	308	165	703	6	4.3	1	0.2%	20	64	21	91	52%	6	23	7	6	43	1	86%	7.2	5.2	39.5%	--	21	--
2016	NE	16/8	527	299	1161	18	3.9	2	1.5%	18	131	14	84	44%	28	48	8	7	38	0	88%	5.4	6.1	-31.0%	--	-7	--
2017	PHI	16/11	353	173	766	2	4.4	1	-9.8%	36	-9	37	-5	43%	33	48	8	8	50	1	100%	6.3	5.9	41.4%	--	25	--
2018	DET			97	382	4	4.0	0	1.6%								6	5	37	0	83%	7.4		8.5%			

Blount has been the leading rusher for three of the last four Super Bowl winners. Since his first playoff appearance in 2013 with New England, his 600 postseason rushing yards are second only to Marshawn Lynch's 626, and he has run for 11 touchdowns in the playoffs, five more than anyone else. There aren't many opportunities for running backs in their age-32 season these days, but Blount should see his share of carries in Detroit's expected committee approach.

Alfred Blue

Height: 6-2   Weight: 223   College: Louisiana State   Draft: 2014/6 (181)   Born: 27-Apr-1991   Age: 27   Risk: Green

Year	Team	G/GS	Snaps	Runs	Yds	TD	Yd/R	FUM	DVOA	Rk	DYAR	Rk	YAR	Suc%	Rk	BTkl	Pass	Rec	Yds	TD	C%	Yd/C	YAC	DVOA	Rk	DYAR	Rk
2015	HOU	16/9	368	183	698	2	3.8	2	-0.2%	22	61	22	10	45%	29	20	16	15	109	1	94%	7.3	4.5	26.1%	--	31	--
2016	HOU	14/2	238	100	420	1	4.2	1	-7.2%	27	6	27	29	45%	24	10	16	12	40	0	75%	3.3	2.3	-59.7%	--	-42	--
2017	HOU	11/0	158	71	262	1	3.7	0	-4.0%	--	14	--	6	42%	--	9	9	7	54	0	78%	7.7	6.0	15.8%	--	15	--
2018	HOU			71	284	1	4.0	2	-5.7%								14	10	84	1	71%	8.4		3.3%			

Blue was a rarely-used third stringer until D'Onta Foreman tore his Achilles, and it was not until the final three games of the season that he had 10 carries in a game. In need of a grinder back, Houston re-signed him after failing to select one in the draft. Foreman's availability for the start of the season is in doubt, so the Texans' depth chart means Blue could be in line for big workloads with just one more injury. His history suggests that would mean a lot of 22-carry, 73-yard games.

Devontae Booker

Height: 5-11   Weight: 219   College: Utah   Draft: 2016/4 (136)   Born: 27-May-1992   Age: 26   Risk: Red

Year	Team	G/GS	Snaps	Runs	Yds	TD	Yd/R	FUM	DVOA	Rk	DYAR	Rk	YAR	Suc%	Rk	BTkl	Pass	Rec	Yds	TD	C%	Yd/C	YAC	DVOA	Rk	DYAR	Rk
2016	DEN	16/6	497	174	612	4	3.5	4	-21.1%	39	-95	41	-62	45%	27	24	45	31	265	1	69%	8.5	8.3	-31.4%	51	-41	50
2017	DEN	13/0	291	79	299	1	3.8	2	-9.2%	--	-2	--	25	47%	--	18	38	30	275	0	79%	9.2	7.8	7.7%	17	45	25
2018	DEN			171	699	4	4.1	2	-4.0%								60	41	362	1	68%	8.8		0.4%			

Booker broke a wrist in OTAs last year, erasing all of training camp. He was the No. 3 running back behind C.J. Anderson and Jamaal Charles when he returned to action in October, but he slowly worked his way up to a split-backfield role with Anderson. Booker didn't really do anything to earn the promotion, mind you: he's a John Elway Project, so after he rushed 14 times for 44 yards against the Bengals, newly-promoted offensive coordinator Bill Musgrave decreed that Booker had earned more playing time (he rushed 17 times for 41 yards in the next three games). Booker will battle Royce Freeman for the lead back role with Anderson gone; may the back who brings the CEO the tastiest coffee win.

Matt Breida

Height: 5-11   Weight: 190   College: Georgia Southern   Draft: 2017/FA   Born: 28-Feb-1995   Age: 23   Risk: Green

Year	Team	G/GS	Snaps	Runs	Yds	TD	Yd/R	FUM	DVOA	Rk	DYAR	Rk	YAR	Suc%	Rk	BTkl	Pass	Rec	Yds	TD	C%	Yd/C	YAC	DVOA	Rk	DYAR	Rk
2017	SF	16/0	310	105	465	2	4.4	1	13.0%	5	87	15	79	47%	16	12	37	21	180	1	59%	8.6	7.3	-4.8%	37	16	37
2018	SF			130	593	3	4.6	3	4.4%								30	22	173	0	73%	7.9		-6.7%			

The rookie undrafted free agent from Georgia Southern filled a multifaceted role as the backup to former starter Carlos Hyde. Breida was one of the most efficient running backs in the league. Hyde received more than twice as many carries but ranked 35th in DVOA, so it might have made more sense to split the workload more evenly. With Hyde off to Cleveland, that point is moot, and it is unlikely it would have made that much of a difference for the 49ers' overall outlook anyway. Breida should play a similar role this year, backing up Jerick McKinnon instead of Hyde.

Malcolm Brown

Height: 5-11   Weight: 224   College: Texas   Draft: 2015/FA   Born: 15-May-1993   Age: 25   Risk: Yellow

Year	Team	G/GS	Snaps	Runs	Yds	TD	Yd/R	FUM	DVOA	Rk	DYAR	Rk	YAR	Suc%	Rk	BTkl	Pass	Rec	Yds	TD	C%	Yd/C	YAC	DVOA	Rk	DYAR	Rk
2015	STL	1/0	9	4	17	0	4.3	0	-5.9%	--	0	--	2	50%	--	1	1	1	-2	0	100%	-2.0	3.0	-184.6%	--	-9	--
2016	LAR	16/0	65	18	39	0	2.2	1	-67.0%	--	-44	--	-43	22%	--	4	3	3	46	0	100%	15.3	14.0	166.9%	--	25	--
2017	LAR	11/1	150	63	246	1	3.9	1	-6.9%	--	4	--	-3	33%	--	13	11	9	53	0	82%	5.9	6.6	-24.6%	--	-7	--
2018	LAR			66	229	0	3.5	2	-14.3%								12	9	65	1	75%	7.2		-2.7%			

Brown ended up fighting off the injured Lance Dunbar to earn the Rams' backup running back job. Backup running back behind Todd Gurley is a pretty sweet gig; only two backs in football played a higher percentage of their team's snaps than Gurley did. Brown was mostly relegated to mop-up duty, with 55 of his 63 carries coming in either the meaningless Week 17 game or in blowouts with the Rams up by at least 24 points. Some of his poor DVOA can be chalked up to operating solely in poor situations, where the Rams were more concerned about chewing clock than efficiency, and the defense knew they would be pounding the rock every play. Brown will have to fight off rookie John Kelly to keep his spot in 2018, but his experience and reliability likely means he'll be the one the Rams turn to for the fourth quarter of those blowout victories.

Rex Burkhead

Height: 5-10   Weight: 214   College: Nebraska   Draft: 2013/6 (190)   Born: 2-Jul-1990   Age: 28   Risk: Red

Year	Team	G/GS	Snaps	Runs	Yds	TD	Yd/R	FUM	DVOA	Rk	DYAR	Rk	YAR	Suc%	Rk	BTkl	Pass	Rec	Yds	TD	C%	Yd/C	YAC	DVOA	Rk	DYAR	Rk
2015	CIN	16/0	73	4	4	0	1.0	1	-222.9%	--	-30	--	-31	0%	--	0	15	10	94	1	67%	9.4	2.5	0.9%	--	13	--
2016	CIN	16/1	238	74	344	2	4.6	1	42.0%	--	163	--	126	62%	--	24	20	17	145	0	85%	8.5	8.4	7.3%	--	22	--
2017	NE	10/3	196	64	264	5	4.1	1	10.5%	--	56	--	65	53%	--	14	36	30	254	3	83%	8.5	6.1	33.7%	8	102	8
2018	NE			121	557	5	4.6	3	17.0%								44	35	290	2	80%	8.3		17.1%			

Underutilized in Cincinnati behind Jeremy Hill and Gio Bernard, Burkhead showed his skill as both a rusher and a receiver for the Patriots, helping Tom Brady dust slow linebackers up and down the field. Somehow the league still didn't catch on, handing the free agent Burkhead back to the Pats for less than $10 million over three years. Sony Michel's selection complicates usage, but Burkhead has been useful whenever he's had a chance so far in his career. He should still be a big part of the New England offense moving forward.

Chris Carson

Height: 6-0   Weight: 218   College: Oklahoma State   Draft: 2017/7 (249)   Born: 16-Sep-1994   Age: 24   Risk: Red

Year	Team	G/GS	Snaps	Runs	Yds	TD	Yd/R	FUM	DVOA	Rk	DYAR	Rk	YAR	Suc%	Rk	BTkl	Pass	Rec	Yds	TD	C%	Yd/C	YAC	DVOA	Rk	DYAR	Rk
2017	SEA	4/3	152	49	208	0	4.2	0	7.0%	--	33	--	21	43%	--	21	8	7	59	1	88%	8.4	6.6	34.9%	--	26	--
2018	SEA			87	348	2	4.0	3	-4.8%								26	19	150	0	73%	7.9		-3.7%			

Carson clawed his way up the depth chart early last season, jumping from fifth to first as it became readily apparent he was the best running back Seattle had to offer. That's not just by default either; Carson's 208 rushing yards in his first four NFL games is the second-most in Seattle history, trailing only Curt Warner in 1983. That month of Carson looked very promising. He showed off tremendous vision and the ability find and slip through cutback lanes. Of course, that ended with a traumatic broken leg and ankle after just a month, and Seattle's running woes got worse from there. Coming back from that severe injury and with only 49 career carries to go on, it's understandable why Seattle wouldn't rely on Carson to carry the full rushing load in 2018. Carson's carries will probably be limited as you don't use a first-round pick on a running back (Rashaad Penny) with the intention of splitting the workload. Through OTAs, however, Carson again looked like the best running back Seattle had to offer.

Jamaal Charles

Height: 5-11   Weight: 200   College: Texas   Draft: 2008/3 (73)   Born: 27-Dec-1986   Age: 32   Risk: N/A

Year	Team	G/GS	Snaps	Runs	Yds	TD	Yd/R	FUM	DVOA	Rk	DYAR	Rk	YAR	Suc%	Rk	BTkl	Pass	Rec	Yds	TD	C%	Yd/C	YAC	DVOA	Rk	DYAR	Rk
2015	KC	5/5	264	71	364	4	5.1	3	24.8%	--	96	--	90	48%	--	16	30	21	177	1	70%	8.4	9.8	-12.1%	42	3	42
2016	KC	3/0	27	12	40	1	3.3	0	2.6%	--	6	--	8	42%	--	0	3	2	14	0	67%	7.0	8.5	-64.0%	--	-11	--
2017	DEN	14/0	205	69	296	1	4.3	2	-7.9%	--	2	--	37	51%	--	16	28	23	129	0	82%	5.6	6.9	-18.5%	51	-6	49

Unsigned at press time. Charles wasn't completely cooked last year, but his play had obviously declined to near-replacement level change-up back territory. The Broncos still thought he was some sort of dangerous playmaker early in the season, then slowly ramped his touches down from 10 per game to zero as they realized what little juice he had left. Charles was a great running back for the Chiefs; in Denver, he was just another example of the organization's pitiful self-scouting.

Nick Chubb Height: 5-11 Weight: 227 College: Georgia Draft: 2018/2 (35) Born: 27-Dec-1995 Age: 23 Risk: Green

Year	Team	G/GS	Snaps	Runs	Yds	TD	Yd/R	FUM	DVOA	Rk	DYAR	Rk	YAR	Suc%	Rk	BTkl	Pass	Rec	Yds	TD	C%	Yd/C	YAC	DVOA	Rk	DYAR	Rk
2018	CLE			116	482	4	4.1	3	-0.7%								15	11	86	0	73%	7.9		-8.1%			

Georgia teammate Sony Michel may have gone before Chubb on draft day, but Chubb shouldered a much larger share of the workload than Michel, and he came out with a higher BackCAST score. He's a between-the-tackles runner with good vision and the ability to explode through small holes. Once he gets to the second level, well, you're talking about a bowling ball that weighs 227 pounds and ran a 4.52-second 40. And Chubb is not afraid to physically finish his runs. He played almost no role in the Georgia passing game; Chubb had 18 receptions as a freshman but just 13 over the last three seasons combined. But hey, that's what Duke Johnson is for.

Corey Clement Height: 5-10 Weight: 220 College: Wisconsin Draft: 2017/FA Born: 2-Nov-1994 Age: 24 Risk: Yellow

Year	Team	G/GS	Snaps	Runs	Yds	TD	Yd/R	FUM	DVOA	Rk	DYAR	Rk	YAR	Suc%	Rk	BTkl	Pass	Rec	Yds	TD	C%	Yd/C	YAC	DVOA	Rk	DYAR	Rk
2017	PHI	16/0	256	74	321	4	4.3	0	14.5%	--	71	--	71	50%	--	11	15	10	123	2	67%	12.3	12.8	41.7%	--	50	--
2018	PHI			100	419	3	4.2	2	2.5%								34	26	221	0	76%	8.5		7.8%			

Clement became an unusual type of third-down specialist late in the year. He caught seven of eight targets on third or fourth down from Week 13 through the Super Bowl for 115 yards and five first downs (including his Super Bowl touchdown), adding late-season/playoff rushing conversions on third-and-6, third-and-3, and fourth-and-1. Clement doesn't look like a third-down receiver or a short-yardage bruiser, but he has a knack for catching swing passes and dragging tacklers past the sticks. Clement may cede much of his third-down role to Darren Sproles or Donnell Pumphrey, but will replace it with some of LeGarrette Blount's former carries. He's just good enough at everything to be the ideal low-cost committee running back.

Tarik Cohen Height: 5-6 Weight: 179 College: North Carolina A&T Draft: 2017/4 (119) Born: 26-Jul-1995 Age: 23 Risk: Yellow

Year	Team	G/GS	Snaps	Runs	Yds	TD	Yd/R	FUM	DVOA	Rk	DYAR	Rk	YAR	Suc%	Rk	BTkl	Pass	Rec	Yds	TD	C%	Yd/C	YAC	DVOA	Rk	DYAR	Rk
2017	CHI	16/4	360	87	370	2	4.3	2	-6.8%	--	6	--	4	46%	--	33	71	53	353	1	75%	6.7	5.9	-30.6%	58	-64	61
2018	CHI			75	318	1	4.2	2	-1.6%								82	62	488	1	76%	7.9		1.6%			

In his rookie season, Cohen had a 46-yard run, a 70-yard reception, a 61-yard punt return, and a 46-yard kickoff return. He can be an exciting player, but Cohen led the NFL with 35 failed receptions in 2017—a whopping 66 percent of his catches were not successful plays. We'll see if Matt Nagy can bring Andy Reid's success with backs in the passing game over to Chicago. Cohen has the talent, but he has to do better than -64 DYAR as a receiver. That was the second-worst total in the league.

Tevin Coleman Height: 5-11 Weight: 206 College: Indiana Draft: 2015/3 (73) Born: 16-Apr-1993 Age: 25 Risk: Yellow

Year	Team	G/GS	Snaps	Runs	Yds	TD	Yd/R	FUM	DVOA	Rk	DYAR	Rk	YAR	Suc%	Rk	BTkl	Pass	Rec	Yds	TD	C%	Yd/C	YAC	DVOA	Rk	DYAR	Rk
2015	ATL	12/3	226	87	392	1	4.5	3	-11.9%	--	-12	--	13	49%	--	3	11	2	14	0	18%	7.0	5.5	-99.5%	--	-46	--
2016	ATL	13/0	353	118	520	8	4.4	1	9.7%	12	86	18	90	45%	25	24	40	31	421	3	78%	13.6	12.1	48.8%	1	136	5
2017	ATL	15/3	425	156	628	5	4.0	1	-6.5%	31	14	32	9	40%	39	31	39	27	299	3	69%	11.1	8.1	41.2%	4	121	6
2018	ATL			155	668	5	4.3	3	3.9%								52	37	369	2	71%	10.0		15.4%			

A terribly dangerous weapon in the passing game, Coleman has ranked sixth or better among running backs in both receiving DYAR and DVOA in each of the last two seasons. Coleman can get lost in the shuffle a bit because Atlanta has so many prominent players on their offense, but he's arguably a more explosive player than Devonta Freeman. Coleman needs to be a more featured part of the passing offense in 2018, or Atlanta needs to find creative ways to get him the ball in space.

Alex Collins

Height: 5-10 Weight: 217 College: Arkansas Draft: 2016/5 (171) Born: 26-Aug-1994 Age: 24 Risk: Red

Year	Team	G/GS	Snaps	Runs	Yds	TD	Yd/R	FUM	DVOA	Rk	DYAR	Rk	YAR	Suc%	Rk	BTkl	Pass	Rec	Yds	TD	C%	Yd/C	YAC	DVOA	Rk	DYAR	Rk
2016	SEA	11/0	141	31	125	1	4.0	2	-13.0%	--	-6	--	-8	35%	--	7	11	11	84	0	100%	7.6	7.4	35.7%	--	37	--
2017	BAL	15/12	378	212	973	6	4.6	4	15.1%	3	205	6	181	51%	8	64	36	23	187	0	64%	8.1	8.4	-55.6%	62	-92	62
2018	BAL			237	1024	7	4.3	4	0.7%								39	29	197	1	74%	6.8		-8.6%			

Dumped by the Seahawks, the former Arkansas Razorbacks runner found a welcome home on a team with a semblance of run blocking. It wasn't merely the line, though—only five players broke more tackles than the 64 Collins wriggled free from in 2017, and the men in front of him (Kareem Hunt, Le'Veon Bell, Todd Gurley, Melvin Gordon, and Alvin Kamara) were all far more exalted as the best the league has to offer in the running back department. Collins showed excellent balance after contact, and a nose for reversing field and finding open spaces where none were scheduled. He was also strong in the red zone. Of backs with 20 or more red zone carries, only Jordan Howard, Dion Lewis, and Kamara were more effective than Collins' 39.8% DVOA on 27 carries.

So is he a one-hit wonder, or can Collins repeat and build upon his performance in 2018? Anyone who plays fantasy, or even cursorily follows the NFL, will know that history is littered with the wreckage of backs who rose above the tide for a year, only to be ruthlessly cut down by injury, or regression, or a teammate taking his turn to shine. Still, with a relatively low usage rate in 2017, Collins seems a reasonable bet to approach or surpass his raw totals next season.

James Conner

Height: 6-1 Weight: 233 College: Pittsburgh Draft: 2017/3 (105) Born: 5-May-1995 Age: 23 Risk: Green

Year	Team	G/GS	Snaps	Runs	Yds	TD	Yd/R	FUM	DVOA	Rk	DYAR	Rk	YAR	Suc%	Rk	BTkl	Pass	Rec	Yds	TD	C%	Yd/C	YAC	DVOA	Rk	DYAR	Rk
2017	PIT	14/0	68	32	144	0	4.5	0	10.2%	--	20	--	18	53%	--	4	1	0	0	0	0%	0.0	0.0	-130.7%	--	-7	--
2018	PIT			51	209	1	4.1	2	-2.3%								9	7	59	1	78%	8.4		12.3%			

Conner's rookie season was cut short with a torn MCL suffered in Week 15, though it's not like he had a strenuous workload up to that point. It wasn't Conner's first MCL injury (he suffered one in 2015 in college) so there have to be some questions about his long-term health. Connor has reportedly taken significant steps forward in pass protection and conditioning in his second offseason, and more reps will help—with Le'Veon Bell holding out, Conner is in line to get most of the first-team snaps throughout preseason. If his pass protection really does improve, he could be in line for more snaps going forward; Bell led the league in running back snaps last season, and an effective backup could let the Steelers get him some much-needed rest.

Dalvin Cook

Height: 5-10 Weight: 210 College: Florida State Draft: 2017/2 (41) Born: 10-Aug-1995 Age: 23 Risk: Red

Year	Team	G/GS	Snaps	Runs	Yds	TD	Yd/R	FUM	DVOA	Rk	DYAR	Rk	YAR	Suc%	Rk	BTkl	Pass	Rec	Yds	TD	C%	Yd/C	YAC	DVOA	Rk	DYAR	Rk
2017	MIN	4/4	169	74	354	2	4.8	1	7.4%	--	48	--	66	55%	--	23	16	11	90	0	69%	8.2	9.5	-19.0%	--	-5	--
2018	MIN			286	1347	9	4.7	4	8.7%								68	53	482	2	78%	9.1		17.0%			

Cook didn't even complete four games last year before he tore his ACL. In that brief time we saw a back who could carry the load (127 yards on 22 carries in his debut against the Saints; 97 yards on 27 carries against the Buccaneers) and offer value in the passing game (he also had 72 yards on five catches against Tampa Bay). He should rebound nicely this season, but the Vikings would probably still be wise to keep him fresh by using Latavius Murray as well.

Isaiah Crowell

Height: 5-11 Weight: 225 College: Alabama State Draft: 2014/FA Born: 8-Jan-1993 Age: 25 Risk: Yellow

Year	Team	G/GS	Snaps	Runs	Yds	TD	Yd/R	FUM	DVOA	Rk	DYAR	Rk	YAR	Suc%	Rk	BTkl	Pass	Rec	Yds	TD	C%	Yd/C	YAC	DVOA	Rk	DYAR	Rk
2015	CLE	16/9	476	185	706	4	3.8	0	-4.0%	30	36	27	-21	41%	40	25	22	19	182	1	86%	9.6	11.9	17.9%	--	37	--
2016	CLE	16/16	568	198	952	7	4.8	2	13.4%	8	169	11	94	39%	40	37	53	40	319	0	75%	8.0	8.4	-2.4%	28	33	28
2017	CLE	16/16	536	206	853	2	4.1	1	-2.9%	26	46	25	57	40%	38	32	43	28	182	0	67%	6.5	6.9	-35.9%	60	-52	59
2018	NYJ			181	749	6	4.1	2	-0.3%								40	31	239	1	78%	7.7		2.4%			

Crowell was the early-down part of a running back platoon in Cleveland that never actually committed to running the ball. Coming off a down year in a dysfunctional offense, he was a solid buy-low move for the Jets. Still only 26, Crowell can be the No. 1 back on a good offense. Behind a stagnant Jets offensive line though, the yards per carry will likely not reflect that this year. Crowell has shown some aptitude as a receiver, but Duke Johnson was such a good receiver out of the backfield that

Cleveland had no need to feature Crowell. If the Jets utilize Crowell over Bilal Powell and Elijah McGuire on third downs, he could be a sneaky fantasy football pick.

Benny Cunningham Height: 5-10   Weight: 217   College: Middle Tennessee State   Draft: 2013/FA   Born: 7-Jul-1990   Age: 28   Risk: Green

Year	Team	G/GS	Snaps	Runs	Yds	TD	Yd/R	FUM	DVOA	Rk	DYAR	Rk	YAR	Suc%	Rk	BTkl	Pass	Rec	Yds	TD	C%	Yd/C	YAC	DVOA	Rk	DYAR	Rk
2015	STL	16/1	282	37	140	0	3.8	1	-14.9%	--	-10	--	-29	38%	--	21	36	26	250	0	72%	9.6	9.2	28.3%	8	67	20
2016	LAR	11/0	179	21	101	0	4.8	1	-11.4%	--	-2	--	-14	48%	--	9	21	16	91	0	76%	5.7	5.0	-24.0%	--	-12	--
2017	CHI	14/0	175	9	29	0	3.2	1	-16.1%	--	-3	--	-6	22%	--	11	26	20	240	2	77%	12.0	12.4	39.6%	5	72	19
2018	CHI			8	33	0	4.0	0	-6.8%								15	12	92	0	80%	7.7		4.7%			

Cunningham is a capable receiving back who can complement what Jordan Howard and Tarik Cohen bring to the offense. Cohen will still probably get the first crack at the receiving role, but Cunningham could work his way onto the field more often in an offensive system that feeds on passes to backs à la the way Charcandrick West supported Kareem Hunt in Kansas City last year.

Orleans Darkwa   Height: 6-0   Weight: 215   College: Tulane   Draft: 2014/FA   Born: 28-Feb-1992   Age: 26   Risk: N/A

Year	Team	G/GS	Snaps	Runs	Yds	TD	Yd/R	FUM	DVOA	Rk	DYAR	Rk	YAR	Suc%	Rk	BTkl	Pass	Rec	Yds	TD	C%	Yd/C	YAC	DVOA	Rk	DYAR	Rk
2015	NYG	16/0	85	36	153	1	4.3	0	7.7%	--	27	--	17	46%	--	7	5	3	31	0	60%	10.3	8.7	6.6%	--	6	--
2016	NYG	10/2	63	30	111	2	3.7	0	6.9%	--	18	--	21	40%	--	2	4	2	12	0	50%	6.0	8.5	-48.2%	--	-8	--
2017	NYG	15/11	315	171	751	5	4.4	1	-1.3%	22	53	23	61	46%	19	18	28	19	116	0	68%	6.1	6.2	-7.3%	39	10	41

It is unlikely that the Giants expected Darkwa to be their leading rusher in 2017, but after a miserable start to the year from Paul Perkins, Darkwa had to step up. Darkwa, like the rest of the running backs on the team, was made to be more of a blunt force weapon than anything. Darkwa often trudged downhill and took what he could out of plays. That being said, Darkwa did show more creativity in the open field and explosivity than his counterpart, Wayne Gallman. Though it was not commonplace to be sprung free into the second level of the defense, Darkwa kept linebackers and safeties on their toes when given the chance and flashed the speed to threaten with long runs. Darkwa capped off the season with a 75-yard touchdown on the second play of the game versus Washington in Week 17, placing a neat bow on a pleasantly surprising season from a journeyman running back. It also may be the last season: Darkwa had offseason surgery to remove a plate inserted in the leg he fractured in 2016, and he hasn't drawn much interest in free agency.

Mike Davis   Height: 5-9   Weight: 217   College: South Carolina   Draft: 2015/4 (126)   Born: 19-Feb-1993   Age: 25   Risk: Green

Year	Team	G/GS	Snaps	Runs	Yds	TD	Yd/R	FUM	DVOA	Rk	DYAR	Rk	YAR	Suc%	Rk	BTkl	Pass	Rec	Yds	TD	C%	Yd/C	YAC	DVOA	Rk	DYAR	Rk
2015	SF	6/0	125	35	58	0	1.7	0	-17.3%	--	-13	--	-42	31%	--	6	13	7	38	0	54%	5.4	5.0	-62.7%	--	-41	--
2016	SF	8/1	66	19	50	1	2.6	1	-38.1%	--	-28	--	-25	47%	--	0	5	3	25	0	60%	8.3	5.0	-10.4%	--	1	--
2017	SEA	6/6	176	68	240	0	3.5	0	-23.1%	--	-38	--	-53	29%	--	25	18	15	131	0	83%	8.7	11.2	15.2%	--	26	--
2018	SEA			20	68	1	3.5	1	-9.0%								13	8	46	0	62%	5.7		-32.9%			

Davis' 240 rushing yards led all Seattle running backs last season. Since the NFL expanded to 16-game seasons in 1978, no team's leading running back had ever finished with less than 311 yards, so congratulations, Mike, you're in the history books! His 1.7 yards per carry in 2015 was the lowest for a rookie with at least 35 carries since 1946, but he has improved every year since then; his 3.5 average was higher than Seattle's non-Russell Wilson average. Davis only got a chance last year because the Seahawks' backfield was decimated with injuries, but he performed well enough when given the opportunity that he could hang around as the third back in 2018.

Kenneth Dixon   Height: 5-10   Weight: 215   College: Louisiana Tech   Draft: 2016/4 (134)   Born: 21-Jan-1994   Age: 24   Risk: Yellow

Year	Team	G/GS	Snaps	Runs	Yds	TD	Yd/R	FUM	DVOA	Rk	DYAR	Rk	YAR	Suc%	Rk	BTkl	Pass	Rec	Yds	TD	C%	Yd/C	YAC	DVOA	Rk	DYAR	Rk
2016	BAL	12/0	258	88	382	2	4.3	1	5.1%	--	54	--	54	55%	--	34	41	30	162	1	73%	5.4	6.2	-20.6%	46	-14	47
2018	BAL			94	413	1	4.4	3	4.4%								34	27	179	1	79%	6.6		-2.9%			

Football in a nutshell: Dixon played well in small bursts in 2016, and was being groomed to become the lead back. Instead, he got hit with a second PED suspension, then tore his meniscus and missed the entire season. While Dixon watched, Alex Collins seized the role, and doesn't figure to give it back—unless, you know, *football*. Collins isn't much of a receiver, so Dixon will be battling a third back, Buck Allen, for the swing pass role. Provided he stays clean in the lavatory, that is.

Kenyan Drake

Height: 6-1 Weight: 210 College: Alabama Draft: 2016/3 (73) Born: 26-Jan-1994 Age: 24 Risk: Yellow

Year	Team	G/GS	Snaps	Runs	Yds	TD	Yd/R	FUM	DVOA	Rk	DYAR	Rk	YAR	Suc%	Rk	BTkl	Pass	Rec	Yds	TD	C%	Yd/C	YAC	DVOA	Rk	DYAR	Rk
2016	MIA	16/1	109	33	179	2	5.4	0	38.1%	--	60	--	57	42%	--	3	10	9	46	0	90%	5.1	7.1	0.6%	--	8	--
2017	MIA	16/6	477	133	644	3	4.8	2	-11.3%	39	-14	38	30	44%	25	39	48	32	239	1	67%	7.5	6.7	-19.1%	52	-13	52
2018	MIA			194	877	5	4.5	4	0.5%								50	39	292	1	78%	7.5		0.0%			

While dealing Jay Ajayi was a bit of a head-scratcher, perhaps the Dolphins had seen enough of what Drake could do in practice to see that this was coming. Drake averaged at least 4.3 yards per carry in each of his last five starts, including 193 total yards in an upset of the Patriots. Drake went from -25.0% DVOA and 29 percent success rate before Week 13 to -5.1% DVOA and 52 percent success rate after Week 13. However, it wasn't quite as impressive as it looked; four of Miami's last five games came against the three teams with the worst defensive DVOA against the run (Kansas City, New England, and Buffalo twice).

Anyway, don't expect a David Johnson-esque boom, but if the Dolphins stick to anything near the offense they had the last time Ryan Tannehill was healthy, Drake should be in line for big numbers as an every-down back. So, of course, the talk of OTAs was that Drake would lose snaps to Frank Gore. If there's anything we learned from the 2017 Colts, it's that there just weren't nearly enough snaps of the 35-year-old Gore.

Austin Ekeler

Height: 5-10 Weight: 195 College: Western State Draft: 2017/FA Born: 17-May-1995 Age: 23 Risk: Green

Year	Team	G/GS	Snaps	Runs	Yds	TD	Yd/R	FUM	DVOA	Rk	DYAR	Rk	YAR	Suc%	Rk	BTkl	Pass	Rec	Yds	TD	C%	Yd/C	YAC	DVOA	Rk	DYAR	Rk
2017	LAC	16/0	197	47	260	2	5.5	2	22.7%	--	59	--	61	55%	--	23	35	27	279	3	77%	10.3	9.3	27.1%	12	84	16
2018	LAC			35	142	2	4.0	1	6.0%								31	24	197	0	77%	8.2		1.8%			

Ekeler made the Chargers roster as an undrafted rookie last year and took over as Melvin Gordon's change-up back when Branden Oliver suffered a hamstring injury. Ekeler generated some big plays as a rusher and receiver but also made some critical errors, including devastating fumbles in losses to the Jaguars and Chiefs. (Marcus Peters broke Ekeler's hand while stripping the ball, ending the rookie's season.) Ekeler is likely to retain his change-up role this year, because the Chargers love inexpensive players who break their hearts at the worst possible moments.

Andre Ellington

Height: 5-9 Weight: 199 College: Clemson Draft: 2013/6 (187) Born: 3-Feb-1989 Age: 29 Risk: N/A

Year	Team	G/GS	Snaps	Runs	Yds	TD	Yd/R	FUM	DVOA	Rk	DYAR	Rk	YAR	Suc%	Rk	BTkl	Pass	Rec	Yds	TD	C%	Yd/C	YAC	DVOA	Rk	DYAR	Rk
2015	ARI	10/2	213	45	289	3	6.4	1	24.4%	--	64	--	63	58%	--	7	24	15	148	0	63%	9.9	5.3	3.7%	--	27	--
2016	ARI	16/0	150	34	96	0	2.8	0	-26.8%	--	-25	--	-33	35%	--	5	19	12	85	0	63%	7.1	6.0	-4.3%	--	8	--
2017	2TM	12/2	315	20	55	1	2.8	0	-16.3%	--	-6	--	-5	40%	--	5	59	39	369	0	66%	9.5	6.1	5.3%	23	59	20

David Johnson's injury elevated Ellington from fourth-string to Arizona's primary passing-down back and earned him a significant role in the offense (50 targets in eight games). He fell out of favor as the year went on and was waived. He only found a role in Houston when Lamar Miller missed time, and was not re-signed. Still a free agent in July, he should remain on the call list for a team in need of a veteran passing-game back.

Ezekiel Elliott

Height: 6-0 Weight: 225 College: Ohio State Draft: 2016/1 (4) Born: 22-Jul-1995 Age: 23 Risk: Yellow

Year	Team	G/GS	Snaps	Runs	Yds	TD	Yd/R	FUM	DVOA	Rk	DYAR	Rk	YAR	Suc%	Rk	BTkl	Pass	Rec	Yds	TD	C%	Yd/C	YAC	DVOA	Rk	DYAR	Rk
2016	DAL	15/15	716	322	1631	15	5.1	5	15.9%	6	339	1	354	57%	2	69	40	32	363	1	80%	11.3	12.2	26.9%	5	82	11
2017	DAL	10/10	591	242	983	7	4.1	1	11.1%	8	205	7	198	57%	2	42	38	26	269	2	68%	10.3	10.0	-11.2%	43	5	43
2018	DAL			324	1488	11	4.6	4	8.0%								70	57	489	2	81%	8.6		20.3%			

Elliott has led the league in rushing yards per game in each of his first two seasons, with 104.6 yards per game in his career. Only two other non-strike players had a better average in their first two seasons: Eric Dickerson (122.3) and Clinton Portis (106.9). Others to go over the century mark include Chris Johnson, Adrian Peterson, Jim Brown, Edgerrin James, Earl Campbell, and George Rogers. All of these men were productive for at least another four or five years. So no, Elliott's production is not likely to come to a screeching halt in his third season. With his domestic violence suspension finally over and done with, Elliott is a reasonable bet to lead the league in rushing again, and could even be an MVP candidate if our projections are right about Dallas this year.

D'Onta Foreman | Height: 6-0 | Weight: 233 | College: Texas | Draft: 2017/3 (89) | Born: 24-Apr-1996 | Age: 22 | Risk: Yellow

Year	Team	G/GS	Snaps	Runs	Yds	TD	Yd/R	FUM	DVOA	Rk	DYAR	Rk	YAR	Suc%	Rk	BTkl	Pass	Rec	Yds	TD	C%	Yd/C	YAC	DVOA	Rk	DYAR	Rk
2017	HOU	10/1	147	78	327	2	4.2	2	-5.5%	--	10	--	-5	42%	--	14	8	6	83	0	75%	13.8	11.0	39.8%	--	25	--
2018	HOU			87	366	2	4.2	2	-0.9%								14	11	100	0	79%	9.1		16.1%			

Foreman's rookie season came to a premature end on a high note, as he tore his Achilles on maybe his best run of the year, a 34-yard touchdown against the Cardinals in Week 11. The Arizona game, where he had both the go-ahead score and that clinching run in the fourth quarter, was his best of the year, and the only one where he had a positive VOA on multiple carries. Offseason reports about his recovery were optimistic for an Achilles injury, not ruling out Week 1 availability and even citing a possible return during training camp. When ready, Foreman will supplant Alfred Blue as the grinder complement to Lamar Miller's more versatile game, but he still needs to show he is more of a step beyond Blue rather than a similar alternative.

Matt Forte | Height: 6-2 | Weight: 218 | College: Tulane | Draft: 2008/2 (44) | Born: 10-Dec-1985 | Age: 33 | Risk: N/A

Year	Team	G/GS	Snaps	Runs	Yds	TD	Yd/R	FUM	DVOA	Rk	DYAR	Rk	YAR	Suc%	Rk	BTkl	Pass	Rec	Yds	TD	C%	Yd/C	YAC	DVOA	Rk	DYAR	Rk
2015	CHI	13/13	600	218	898	4	4.1	2	12.0%	7	192	2	147	48%	17	37	58	44	389	3	76%	8.8	8.0	23.5%	11	112	7
2016	NYJ	14/13	488	218	813	7	3.7	1	-8.8%	30	-2	30	-5	41%	37	38	43	30	263	1	70%	8.8	9.2	-5.6%	33	21	32
2017	NYJ	12/4	363	103	381	2	3.7	1	-13.9%	41	-20	39	11	41%	36	28	45	37	293	1	82%	7.9	6.8	5.6%	22	44	26

Forte is a candidate for the 2010s version of those *Bill James Historical Abstract* awards for "Can I try this career over?" Stuck playing in putrid situations at Tulane, with Chicago, and with the Jets, Forte's only season in a top-5 DVOA offense was with the 2013 Bears, where he had 384 touches all by himself. The only starting quarterback Forte knew for most of his career was Jay Cutler, and his college quarterback in his 2,000-yard senior year was something called "Anthony Scelfo." In some timeline, Forte got to work his dynamic talents with a dominant offense. In this one, he made the Bears somewhat watchable.

Leonard Fournette | Height: 6-0 | Weight: 228 | College: Louisiana State | Draft: 2017/1 (4) | Born: 18-Jan-1995 | Age: 23 | Risk: Yellow

Year	Team	G/GS	Snaps	Runs	Yds	TD	Yd/R	FUM	DVOA	Rk	DYAR	Rk	YAR	Suc%	Rk	BTkl	Pass	Rec	Yds	TD	C%	Yd/C	YAC	DVOA	Rk	DYAR	Rk
2017	JAX	13/13	564	268	1040	9	3.9	2	2.1%	17	115	11	57	44%	26	55	48	36	302	1	75%	8.4	8.5	7.2%	18	58	21
2018	JAX			306	1319	9	4.3	4	1.4%								65	48	403	1	74%	8.4		4.5%			

The Jaguars drafted Fournette fourth overall to be a workhorse, and a workhorse he was: despite missing three full games and several in-game series through injury, Fournette finished seventh in total rushing attempts and fourth in attempts per game. He ranked sixth in total touches (rushes plus receptions), and eighth among running backs in total yards from scrimmage. He took a handoff on 48 percent of his offensive snaps, the second-highest rate for backs with at least 500 snaps on offense behind only Chicago's Jordan Howard. When you add in the team's above-average rate of play-action on both first and second down, coupled with his 48 pass targets, it's clear that the Jaguars have fully constructed their base offense around their highly-drafted running back.

Only further injury is likely to affect that in 2018, but that is a legitimate concern with Fournette. Ankle and foot woes hobbled him at various points last year, and he almost missed out on the AFC Championship Game after re-injuring his right ankle in the divisional round. Ankle injuries were also a feature of Fournette's senior year at LSU, so this could require careful management to avoid becoming a chronic issue. As long as he is healthy, however, Fournette will be the workhorse back in Jacksonville.

Devonta Freeman Height: 5-8 Weight: 206 College: Florida St. Draft: 2014/4 (103) Born: 15-Mar-1992 Age: 26 Risk: Yellow

Year	Team	G/GS	Snaps	Runs	Yds	TD	Yd/R	FUM	DVOA	Rk	DYAR	Rk	YAR	Suc%	Rk	BTkl	Pass	Rec	Yds	TD	C%	Yd/C	YAC	DVOA	Rk	DYAR	Rk
2015	ATL	15/13	768	265	1056	11	4.0	3	-0.5%	24	90	15	122	46%	23	54	97	73	578	3	75%	7.9	6.0	-1.2%	28	68	19
2016	ATL	16/16	604	227	1079	11	4.8	1	6.4%	14	148	13	179	50%	12	63	65	54	462	2	83%	8.6	7.7	24.9%	6	141	4
2017	ATL	14/14	552	196	865	7	4.4	4	1.5%	18	89	14	105	51%	9	59	47	36	317	1	77%	8.8	6.8	23.6%	13	102	10
2018	ATL			202	887	7	4.4	2	6.6%								60	44	374	2	73%	8.5		12.6%			

Freeman went from being a fourth-round pick in 2014 to being the second-highest paid running back in the league for the 2018 season. Freeman was an effective runner and receiver last season, continuing his status as one of the most well-rounded running backs in the league. Freeman isn't a physical freak, but his patience, footwork, and vision routinely allow him to find creases in the offensive line. Since breaking out during the 2015 season, Freeman has been a core piece of the Falcons offense and will look to improve his numbers in 2018.

Royce Freeman Height: 5-11 Weight: 229 College: Oregon Draft: 2018/3 (71) Born: 24-Feb-1996 Age: 22 Risk: Yellow

Year	Team	G/GS	Snaps	Runs	Yds	TD	Yd/R	FUM	DVOA	Rk	DYAR	Rk	YAR	Suc%	Rk	BTkl	Pass	Rec	Yds	TD	C%	Yd/C	YAC	DVOA	Rk	DYAR	Rk
2018	DEN			155	643	5	4.1	3	0.1%								38	27	200	0	71%	7.4		-17.4%			

The BACKCast system loves Freeman (rating: +88.1%) because of his measurables and his college production: 5,621 rushing yards spread across four seasons, an impressive 5.9 yards per rush. Freeman was a rock star early in his Ducks career, then suffered a series of nagging injuries and was briefly benched in 2016. He rebounded for a strong senior season after adjusting to a new offense. Freeman should be a high success rate all-purpose runner in the NFL, assuming he didn't leave his best work among his 1,026 collegiate touches. The only person standing between him and a featured role is Devontae Booker, who is only a threat because the Broncos are infatuated with giving old draft picks 500 chances.

Wayne Gallman Height: 6-0 Weight: 215 College: Clemson Draft: 2017/4 (140) Born: 1-Oct-1994 Age: 24 Risk: Green

Year	Team	G/GS	Snaps	Runs	Yds	TD	Yd/R	FUM	DVOA	Rk	DYAR	Rk	YAR	Suc%	Rk	BTkl	Pass	Rec	Yds	TD	C%	Yd/C	YAC	DVOA	Rk	DYAR	Rk
2017	NYG	13/1	325	111	476	0	4.3	3	-5.2%	29	15	31	21	50%	10	31	48	34	193	1	71%	5.7	5.9	-14.6%	48	-2	48
2018	NYG			56	244	1	4.4	2	2.4%								22	16	119	0	73%	7.5		-5.0%			

It may seem unfair for Gallman to not get a proper opportunity to start, but a relief role will continue to serve him well. Gallman is an efficient albeit uninspiring runner. As his high success rate shows, Gallman proved that his downhill, grind-it-out style of running had value behind an offensive line that had the sixth-best stuff rate and ranked 15th in adjusted line yards. The Giants' offensive line did well to provide the bare minimum on the ground, while Gallman succeeded in milking each run with his surprising slipperiness in tight quarters and his relentless motor through contact. That said, Gallman's inability to be counted on for big plays hurts his value. Per Bill Connelly, during Gallman's senior season at Clemson in 2016, he ran for just 4.0 highlight yards per opportunity, cementing him in below-average territory in terms of generating explosive runs. As a rookie in 2017, Gallman posted just two 20-plus-yard runs on 111 attempts and did not score a single rushing touchdown. Thankfully, Saquon Barkley will provide plenty of explosive plays and will receive the lion's share of carries, but Gallman should have a fair opportunity to beat out Jonathan Stewart for the backup spot.

Mike Gillislee Height: 5-11 Weight: 208 College: Florida Draft: 2013/5 (164) Born: 1-Nov-1990 Age: 28 Risk: Red

Year	Team	G/GS	Snaps	Runs	Yds	TD	Yd/R	FUM	DVOA	Rk	DYAR	Rk	YAR	Suc%	Rk	BTkl	Pass	Rec	Yds	TD	C%	Yd/C	YAC	DVOA	Rk	DYAR	Rk
2015	BUF	5/1	112	47	267	3	5.7	1	20.9%	--	54	--	20	36%	--	4	7	6	29	0	86%	4.8	5.2	-4.0%	--	4	--
2016	BUF	15/1	284	101	577	8	5.7	0	44.9%	1	256	4	236	66%	1	19	11	9	50	1	82%	5.6	5.1	-48.0%	--	-18	--
2017	NE	9/2	171	104	383	5	3.7	1	-0.8%	20	39	26	58	58%	1	10	1	1	15	0	100%	15.0	20.0	123.7%	--	8	--
2018	NE			63	246	2	3.9	3	-0.9%								9	7	39	1	78%	5.6		-15.7%			

One Jets appearance away from having the entire AFC East as his employer, Gillislee's LeGarrette Blount impersonation was found wanting, and he was mostly a healthy scratch after October. Coming into this year with a clean slate, the opportunity is certainly there for Gillislee to handle goal-line work. Dion Lewis isn't around to steal the show again. Sony Michel is a rookie. Jeremy Hill is just as enigmatic. Or Gillislee might just fail to make the roster—really, nothing should surprise us at this point.

Melvin Gordon   Height: 6-1   Weight: 215   College: Wisconsin   Draft: 2015/1 (15)   Born: 13-Apr-1993   Age: 25   Risk: Yellow

Year	Team	G/GS	Snaps	Runs	Yds	TD	Yd/R	FUM	DVOA	Rk	DYAR	Rk	YAR	Suc%	Rk	BTkl	Pass	Rec	Yds	TD	C%	Yd/C	YAC	DVOA	Rk	DYAR	Rk
2015	SD	14/12	395	184	641	0	3.5	6	-17.4%	43	-68	43	-94	43%	32	38	37	33	192	0	89%	5.8	7.8	-16.1%	46	-5	45
2016	SD	13/11	659	254	997	10	3.9	2	-8.4%	29	2	29	83	45%	26	52	57	41	419	2	72%	10.2	10.1	21.0%	9	105	9
2017	LAC	16/16	750	284	1105	8	3.9	1	-6.8%	33	21	29	30	40%	41	73	83	58	476	4	70%	8.2	8.5	3.0%	28	76	18
2018	LAC			293	1203	9	4.1	4	-2.1%								80	55	491	2	69%	8.9		1.4%			

Gordon on first downs last year: 174 carries, 576 yards, 3.3 yards per rush, three touchdowns. The Chargers really liked starting drives with a handoff to Gordon, and opponents knew it.

Gordon has now averaged just 3.8 yards per rush in three seasons as a primary running back. Since 1990, only 16 running backs have averaged less than 4.0 yards per carry over the first three seasons of their careers, with a minimum of 600 carries. The list is full of impressive, encouraging names: Marshall Faulk, Jerome Bettis, Curtis Martin, Eddie George, Warrick Dunn, Marshawn Lynch, Matt Forte, Willis McGahee, and Ricky Williams, as well as a few Trent Richardson and Errict Rhett clunkers. One reason to worry: all of the best names hovered in the 3.95-yard per carry range after three seasons except Faulk, who was a different back from a different era trapped in a weird early-career situation. Gordon has slowly grown more durable and become a better receiver over three seasons but needs to take another step forward to be more than a fantasy stat compiler on a team that nobody pays attention to. An interesting receiving note: Gordon led all players with 22 targets on swing passes last year—no one else had more than 10—but he only produced -6 DYAR on those plays.

Frank Gore   Height: 5-9   Weight: 215   College: Miami   Draft: 2005/3 (65)   Born: 14-May-1983   Age: 35   Risk: Red

Year	Team	G/GS	Snaps	Runs	Yds	TD	Yd/R	FUM	DVOA	Rk	DYAR	Rk	YAR	Suc%	Rk	BTkl	Pass	Rec	Yds	TD	C%	Yd/C	YAC	DVOA	Rk	DYAR	Rk
2015	IND	16/16	690	260	967	6	3.7	4	-8.6%	36	0	36	-65	40%	42	41	58	34	267	1	59%	7.9	8.0	-32.1%	56	-60	56
2016	IND	16/16	650	263	1025	4	3.9	2	5.6%	16	159	12	88	49%	19	32	48	38	277	4	81%	7.3	7.6	0.7%	25	40	23
2017	IND	16/16	555	261	961	3	3.7	3	-2.3%	23	66	18	46	44%	23	41	38	29	245	1	76%	8.4	9.5	4.1%	25	35	31
2018	MIA			125	475	2	3.8	2	-3.7%								28	21	142	1	75%	6.7		-7.7%			

A terrific running back and worthy Hall of Fame candidate, Gore defied the odds and Indianapolis defied common sense in featuring a 34-year-old running back. He became the first running back to have 100 or more carries in a season at 34 since Ricky Williams did it in a change-of-pace role with the Ravens in 2011. A great mentor for Kenyan Drake, Gore is one of the NFL's finest technicians at running back. He reads every crease well, he knows his blocks and sets, and he sees plays before they develop. After last season, though, we've seen all we've needed to see of Gore as a No. 1 option.

Corey Grant   Height: 5-11   Weight: 205   College: Auburn   Draft: 2015/FA   Born: 19-Dec-1991   Age: 27   Risk: Blue

Year	Team	G/GS	Snaps	Runs	Yds	TD	Yd/R	FUM	DVOA	Rk	DYAR	Rk	YAR	Suc%	Rk	BTkl	Pass	Rec	Yds	TD	C%	Yd/C	YAC	DVOA	Rk	DYAR	Rk
2015	JAX	6/0	17	6	2	0	0.3	1	-114.1%	--	-25	--	-27	33%	--	1	3	2	13	0	67%	6.5	7.5	7.1%	--	4	--
2016	JAX	11/1	99	32	164	1	5.1	0	-15.0%	--	-9	--	13	47%	--	3	7	4	35	1	57%	8.8	8.0	9.3%	--	8	--
2017	JAX	16/0	49	30	248	2	8.3	0	53.6%	--	79	--	75	63%	--	9	4	3	41	0	75%	13.7	13.3	18.1%	--	8	--
2018	JAX			38	179	0	4.7	2	5.5%								11	8	67	0	73%	8.4		1.5%			

A 2015 undrafted free agent with only 68 career regular-season carries, Grant was the Jaguars' secret weapon for the first half of the AFC Championship Game. His 59 receiving yards that day were a career high, but that game—like the preseason game against the same opponent in which he scored a 79-yard rushing touchdown—was a massive outlier. Grant has never caught more than two passes or gained more than 28 receiving yards in a regular-season game. He has only had more than five carries five times in his three-year career, and four of those were extended mop-up duty in 20-point blowout wins. His only game with more than 10 carries was the meaningless 2016 season finale, which was most notable for being the last time we saw Andrew Luck in live action. He did have 100 yards rushing that day, albeit against the worst run defense in the league.

Grant is the type of quick, elusive scatback the Patriots themselves seem to churn out by the dozen, and the Jaguars valued him enough to place a second-round tender on him in restricted free agency. Offensive coordinator Nathaniel Hackett has spoken of his desire to get Grant on the field more, but as long as both Leonard Fournette is healthy, Grant's opportunities are likely to stay relatively limited in the current incarnation of the Jaguars offense. He should, at least, continue to get opportunities as a kick returner—and on fake punts, which accounted for 114 of his 248 rushing yards last year.

Derrius Guice

Height: 5-10   Weight: 224   College: Louisiana State   Draft: 2018/2 (59)   Born: 21-Jun-1997   Age: 21   Risk: Red

Year	Team	G/GS	Snaps	Runs	Yds	TD	Yd/R	FUM	DVOA	Rk	DYAR	Rk	YAR	Suc%	Rk	BTkl	Pass	Rec	Yds	TD	C%	Yd/C	YAC	DVOA	Rk	DYAR	Rk
2018	WAS			230	1010	8	4.4	4	4.3%								34	28	206	1	82%	7.4		-3.9%			

In the end, we may never know why Guice slid out of the draft's first round. Guice claimed teams asked him inappropriate questions about his mother and his sexuality; the NFL denied this. Rumors circulated that Guice had been late to pre-draft meetings and even gotten in some sort of confrontation with Philadelphia management; Guice denied that. During the draft, NFL Network's Mike Mayock cited anonymous reports from general managers about "another investigation out there that could be potentially highly embarrassing to the kid and maybe to the team that selects him," but nothing of the sort ever materialized.

What we do know is this: Guice had a tremendous career at LSU and a fine combine performance, and as a result he ranked third among draftable running backs in BackCAST, and fourth in Speed Score. All reports out of Washington say that he has been a great teammate and very coachable. He raised more than $17,000 for Mary Bird Perkins Center, a Baton Rouge cancer treatment facility where a family friend had been cared for. Guice's size and angry running style should make him a productive starter from Day 1 and for a long time after that. His receiving ability is unproven—he caught only 32 balls in 35 games at LSU—but Washington has Chris Thompson to handle third-and-long detail anyway. All appearances in this case are that Washington will benefit from everyone else's mistake.

Todd Gurley

Height: 6-1   Weight: 222   College: Georgia   Draft: 2015/1 (10)   Born: 3-Aug-1994   Age: 24   Risk: Yellow

Year	Team	G/GS	Snaps	Runs	Yds	TD	Yd/R	FUM	DVOA	Rk	DYAR	Rk	YAR	Suc%	Rk	BTkl	Pass	Rec	Yds	TD	C%	Yd/C	YAC	DVOA	Rk	DYAR	Rk
2015	STL	13/12	456	229	1106	10	4.8	3	10.0%	9	170	4	124	43%	36	46	26	21	188	0	81%	9.0	9.6	2.1%	25	25	31
2016	LAR	16/16	742	278	885	6	3.2	2	-14.4%	37	-66	37	-75	41%	36	56	58	43	327	0	74%	7.6	8.2	-9.9%	39	13	35
2017	LAR	15/15	794	279	1305	13	4.7	5	13.9%	4	268	2	205	53%	5	79	87	64	788	6	74%	12.3	12.3	35.9%	7	236	2
2018	LAR			308	1431	11	4.6	3	11.2%								79	62	544	4	78%	8.8		30.9%			

Free from the death-grasp of Jeff Fisher, Gurley's rebound season got him much-deserved MVP consideration, as his combination of production, volume, and efficiency was unmatched. Most backs who end up with more than 2,000 yards from scrimmage—already a pretty exclusive group—do it by racking up monstrous amounts of touches, up to and over 400. Gurley became the eighth player in NFL history to hit the 2,000-yard mark with 350 touches or fewer. Jim Brown, O.J. Simpson, Roger Craig, Thurman Thomas, Garrison Hearst, Marshall Faulk, Ray Rice, Todd Gurley. Not a bad little club. Gurley nearly started his own little club last year, too. Entering Week 17, Gurley led all running backs in rushing yards, rushing touchdowns, receiving yards and receiving touchdowns, which has never been done before. He didn't quite complete the sweep due to the Rams prioritizing "playoff preparation" over "meaningless statistical novelties" and resting Gurley in the final game of the season, but it remains one of the most remarkable seasons in recent memory. And he doesn't even turn 24 until August.

Gurley was a monster on running back screens last year. Not only did he have the most screens (28), but his 127 DYAR on them nearly doubled the next closest player (Mark Ingram, 64 DYAR).

Derrick Henry

Height: 6-3   Weight: 247   College: Alabama   Draft: 2016/2 (45)   Born: 17-Jul-1994   Age: 24   Risk: Green

Year	Team	G/GS	Snaps	Runs	Yds	TD	Yd/R	FUM	DVOA	Rk	DYAR	Rk	YAR	Suc%	Rk	BTkl	Pass	Rec	Yds	TD	C%	Yd/C	YAC	DVOA	Rk	DYAR	Rk
2016	TEN	15/1	270	110	490	5	4.5	0	19.6%	4	131	15	139	55%	6	27	15	13	137	0	87%	10.5	9.5	46.9%	--	45	--
2017	TEN	16/2	411	176	744	5	4.2	1	-1.2%	21	56	22	37	48%	15	45	17	11	136	1	65%	12.4	11.8	23.6%	--	31	--
2018	TEN			209	953	5	4.6	3	3.6%								26	19	169	1	73%	8.9		8.7%			

Henry has not yet been the primary running back for the Titans, but he was drafted for that purpose and, with DeMarco Murray released, he should finally get the opportunity this season. Murray's roster replacement, seven-year veteran Dion Lewis, has only one season with more than 64 carries; although our projection for Henry is more conservative, it is not out of the question that he could almost double his career total of 286 carries in 2018 alone.

Efficiency is more of a question. Henry's carry and yardage totals increased in his second year, but his efficiency plummeted by just about every measure. A change of offense and blocking scheme could do him good: Henry is an experienced zone runner who by all accounts is ideally suited to the one-cut-and-go reads for which the Kubiak-Shanahan offense is famed. One of his biggest college highlights was a cutback on an outside zone run that he took for a 65-yard touchdown against Mississippi State, and nobody wants to be matched against a runner this size at the second level. Todd Gurley or Devonta Freeman may be an excessively ambitious comparison, but Matt LaFleur was involved in coaching the Washington offenses that made a consistent 1,000-yard rusher out of sixth-round draft pick Alfred Morris. Henry certainly has more raw talent than Morris; it is up to him to make the most of the opportunities he will undoubtedly be given.

Jeremy Hill   Height: 6-1   Weight: 233   College: Louisiana State   Draft: 2014/2 (55)   Born: 10/20/1992   Age: 26   Risk: Green

Year	Team	G/GS	Snaps	Runs	Yds	TD	Yd/R	FUM	DVOA	Rk	DYAR	Rk	YAR	Suc%	Rk	BTkl	Pass	Rec	Yds	TD	C%	Yd/C	YAC	DVOA	Rk	DYAR	Rk
2015	CIN	16/15	458	223	794	11	3.6	3	0.1%	21	85	16	64	49%	12	23	19	15	79	1	79%	5.3	5.8	-13.4%	--	0	--
2016	CIN	15/13	443	222	839	9	3.8	0	-5.0%	24	34	25	36	44%	29	32	27	21	174	0	78%	8.3	7.8	3.1%	23	27	30
2017	CIN	7/7	77	37	116	0	3.1	1	-14.2%	--	-9	--	-19	41%	--	5	4	4	16	0	100%	4.0	7.5	-30.0%	--	-3	--
2018	NE			67	275	3	4.1	3	4.1%								8	7	53	1	88%	7.5		13.2%			

2014 sure was a long time ago, huh? Three seasons after he averaged 5.1 yards per carry as a rookie, Hill is now a goal-line pounder with no upside as a receiving back, and he needs good blocking to be effective. He'll push Mike Gillislee for Pats goal-line duties, so he could randomly become the reason you lose in fantasy sometime this year. Jonas Gray had a 200-yard game once, remember? Other than that, Hill is just trying to cling to an NFL roster as a non-special teams factor with no receiving game.

Nyheim Hines   Height: 5-8   Weight: 198   College: North Carolina State   Draft: 2018/4 (104)   Born: 12-Nov-1996   Age: 22   Risk: Yellow

Year	Team	G/GS	Snaps	Runs	Yds	TD	Yd/R	FUM	DVOA	Rk	DYAR	Rk	YAR	Suc%	Rk	BTkl	Pass	Rec	Yds	TD	C%	Yd/C	YAC	DVOA	Rk	DYAR	Rk
2018	IND			132	535	3	4.1	2	0.4%								46	35	360	1	76%	10.3		11.0%			

Frank Reich has not yet declared Hines to be an "offensive weapon" rather than just a running back, but it seems only a matter of time after the North Carolina State rookie spent plenty of his first NFL OTAs lining up both in the backfield and elsewhere on offense. His 39 percent college success rate, well behind that of other drafted rookies, further suggests his NFL future is less as a runner than as a versatile player who can run if needed, but whose best use will come in helping Reich and Andrew Luck stretch defenses horizontally and forcing them to declare coverages by how they defend him. The Colts have plenty of questions at receiver and in the backfield, so there is opportunity here.

Jordan Howard   Height: 6-0   Weight: 230   College: Indiana   Draft: 2016/5 (150)   Born: 2-Nov-1994   Age: 24   Risk: Red

Year	Team	G/GS	Snaps	Runs	Yds	TD	Yd/R	FUM	DVOA	Rk	DYAR	Rk	YAR	Suc%	Rk	BTkl	Pass	Rec	Yds	TD	C%	Yd/C	YAC	DVOA	Rk	DYAR	Rk
2016	CHI	15/13	654	252	1313	6	5.2	2	12.3%	9	219	5	246	49%	17	51	50	29	298	1	58%	10.3	10.3	-7.5%	36	17	33
2017	CHI	16/16	578	276	1122	9	4.1	1	5.8%	14	160	10	122	42%	35	42	32	23	125	0	72%	5.4	6.7	-53.3%	61	-60	60
2018	CHI			256	1038	5	4.1	4	-5.8%								48	32	255	1	67%	8.0		-11.9%			

Howard is the third-leading rusher in the NFL since 2016 with 2,435 yards. That's pretty strong value for a fifth-round pick. Howard is a volume runner, though all eight times he has had at least 23 carries in a game, he did go over 100 rushing yards. The Bears are actually 0-21 when Howard has fewer than 20 carries, the only winless back in the league in the last two years (minimum 15 games). When Howard had fewer than 15 carries, the Bears were 0-10 and never scored more than 17 points. Andy Reid has been notorious for abandoning the run in games, so we'll have to see if Matt Nagy carries over that approach when Howard has been the foundation of this offense the last two years. He could end up maximizing Howard's carries, but Howard is still a back who will be at his best when he sees the ball often. Tarik Cohen and Benny Cunningham will still have to carry the receiving load.

Kareem Hunt | Height: 5-10 | Weight: 216 | College: Toledo | Draft: 2017/3 (86) | Born: 6-Aug-1995 | Age: 23 | Risk: Yellow

Year	Team	G/GS	Snaps	Runs	Yds	TD	Yd/R	FUM	DVOA	Rk	DYAR	Rk	YAR	Suc%	Rk	BTkl	Pass	Rec	Yds	TD	C%	Yd/C	YAC	DVOA	Rk	DYAR	Rk
2017	KC	16/16	670	272	1327	8	4.9	1	11.9%	6	222	4	248	47%	18	89	63	53	455	3	84%	8.6	7.8	15.6%	14	102	9
2018	KC			270	1238	7	4.6	3	5.4%								80	58	470	2	73%	8.1		4.5%			

Hunt boasted a fairly impressive profile as a prospect out of Toledo, but his immediate rise to stardom came as a bit of a shock to even his most staunch supporters. What sent Hunt over the top as a rookie was an unexpected jump in explosive ability. According to Bill Connelly, Hunt averaged 4.3 yards per highlight opportunity (a measure of a running back's ability to produce explosive plays) during his final college season, firmly entrenched near the bottom of the 2017 draft class in that regard. However, Hunt erupted as a rookie and ripped off 12 20-plus-yard runs, tying LeSean McCoy for most in the league. Hunt also converted three of those runs into 40-plus-yard trips, only falling short of Bilal Powell's four such runs. Hunt's rare sense of balance and ability to maintain speed through contact propelled him to the season he had on the ground. Additionally, like any feature Andy Reid running back, Hunt is a fantastic pass-catcher, be it as a checkdown option or when flying down the seam for a touchdown versus the New England Patriots in Week 1. A slew of injuries to the offensive line put a bit of a damper on Hunt's otherwise incredible rookie season, but he should have no problem producing with a healthy unit leading the way in 2018.

Carlos Hyde | Height: 6-0 | Weight: 230 | College: Ohio St. | Draft: 2014/2 (57) | Born: 9/20/1991 | Age: 27 | Risk: Green

Year	Team	G/GS	Snaps	Runs	Yds	TD	Yd/R	FUM	DVOA	Rk	DYAR	Rk	YAR	Suc%	Rk	BTkl	Pass	Rec	Yds	TD	C%	Yd/C	YAC	DVOA	Rk	DYAR	Rk
2015	SF	7/7	295	115	470	3	4.1	1	3.9%	14	60	23	27	49%	14	24	15	11	53	0	73%	4.8	5.5	-33.9%	—	-18	—
2016	SF	13/13	535	217	988	6	4.6	5	15.3%	7	204	6	98	48%	21	51	34	27	163	3	82%	6.0	5.4	6.2%	19	38	25
2017	SF	16/16	783	240	938	8	3.9	2	-7.4%	35	12	33	14	44%	27	52	89	59	350	0	67%	5.9	5.4	-22.4%	53	-43	58
2018	CLE			138	562	5	4.1	2	-1.9%								30	24	153	0	80%	6.4		-7.3%			

The Browns gave Hyde $5 million guaranteed as part of a three-year, $15 million contract … and then rendered him superfluous by drafting Nick Chubb at the top of the second round. Hyde probably has the edge over Chubb for more of the workload this year, but is he even going to see the rest of that contract? Even if Hyde is the starter, two things are likely to change for him. First, he isn't going to have the same kind of opportunity to score touchdowns. Last year, Hyde carried the ball 17 times inside the 5; only Todd Gurley had more carries that close to the goal line. Second, he's not going to get as many receptions. Last year's 59 catches were more than his first three years combined, and were generally forced by the lack of receiving options in San Francisco. That's not the case in Cleveland, especially with Duke Johnson around for passing downs. It's a good thing, too, because Hyde was awful as a receiver last year; he led all running backs with 8 drops (no other back had more than 6) and had -1.3 YAC+.

Mark Ingram | Height: 5-11 | Weight: 215 | College: Alabama | Draft: 2011/1 (28) | Born: 21-Dec-1989 | Age: 29 | Risk: Yellow

Year	Team	G/GS	Snaps	Runs	Yds	TD	Yd/R	FUM	DVOA	Rk	DYAR	Rk	YAR	Suc%	Rk	BTkl	Pass	Rec	Yds	TD	C%	Yd/C	YAC	DVOA	Rk	DYAR	Rk
2015	NO	12/10	534	166	769	6	4.6	2	6.6%	12	108	14	120	45%	30	34	60	50	405	0	83%	8.1	9.2	4.0%	21	59	21
2016	NO	16/14	530	205	1043	6	5.1	2	11.3%	11	175	10	223	56%	5	46	58	46	319	4	79%	6.9	7.1	10.6%	16	81	12
2017	NO	16/12	571	230	1124	12	4.9	3	11.2%	7	193	8	210	49%	12	56	71	58	416	0	82%	7.2	8.7	-10.7%	42	13	39
2018	NO			153	724	7	4.7	3	10.5%								55	41	323	1	75%	7.9		0.3%			

At one point last season Ingram was receiving buzz for the first-team All-Pro selection at running back, but his production slowed down while the hype for rookie teammate Alvin Kamara only increased. We already know Ingram's 2018 won't live up to last year after he got hit with a four-game suspension for violating the league's substance abuse policy. If it helps keep Ingram fresher later in the season, that may not be such a bad thing. Ingram only rushed 19 times for 47 yards in the postseason and did not score a touchdown after having a career-high 12 of them in the regular season.

Chris Ivory Height: 6-0 Weight: 222 College: Tiffin Draft: 2010/FA Born: 22-Mar-1988 Age: 30 Risk: Green

Year	Team	G/GS	Snaps	Runs	Yds	TD	Yd/R	FUM	DVOA	Rk	DYAR	Rk	YAR	Suc%	Rk	BTkl	Pass	Rec	Yds	TD	C%	Yd/C	YAC	DVOA	Rk	DYAR	Rk
2015	NYJ	15/14	537	247	1070	7	4.3	4	-11.5%	39	-31	40	23	43%	35	45	37	30	217	1	81%	7.2	9.2	-4.3%	32	21	32
2016	JAX	11/1	311	117	439	3	3.8	5	-34.3%	42	-125	42	-93	45%	22	22	28	20	186	0	71%	9.3	9.5	-12.0%	42	3	42
2017	JAX	14/3	299	112	382	1	3.4	2	-17.0%	44	-38	42	-50	38%	44	27	28	21	175	1	75%	8.3	9.0	4.4%	24	27	33
2018	BUF			86	317	3	3.7	2	-6.9%								23	15	110	0	65%	7.4		-18.4%			

A back capable of surprising you in his prime, Ivory has uncommon burst and can bowl over defenders when he gets low. He didn't show that in his first year with the Jaguars, and was relegated to Leonard Fournette injury change-up last season. A cap casualty in Jacksonville ... wait did we just type that? Somebody was a cap casualty in Jacksonville? We're getting old. So is Ivory, who takes his talents to back up LeSean McCoy in Buffalo. At 30, with a bad offensive line in front of him, we're not expecting much.

Justin Jackson Height: 6-0 Weight: 199 College: Northwestern Draft: 2018/7 (251) Born: 22-Apr-1995 Age: 23 Risk: Yellow

Year	Team	G/GS	Snaps	Runs	Yds	TD	Yd/R	FUM	DVOA	Rk	DYAR	Rk	YAR	Suc%	Rk	BTkl	Pass	Rec	Yds	TD	C%	Yd/C	YAC	DVOA	Rk	DYAR	Rk
2018	LAC			45	198	1	4.4	1	3.0%								24	20	140	1	83%	7.0		-9.8%			

Jackson rushed for 5,440 career yards at Northwestern, adding 122 career receptions. He has a slender frame and lacks a fourth gear, but he's determined and slippery. Jackson should push for Austin Ekeler's role as Melvin Gordon's change-up. He could be a sleeper, but he could also be just athletic enough to succeed in the Big Ten but spend his NFL career on the back end of the depth chart.

David Johnson Height: 6-1 Weight: 224 College: Northern Iowa Draft: 2015/3 (86) Born: 16-Dec-1991 Age: 27 Risk: Red

Year	Team	G/GS	Snaps	Runs	Yds	TD	Yd/R	FUM	DVOA	Rk	DYAR	Rk	YAR	Suc%	Rk	BTkl	Pass	Rec	Yds	TD	C%	Yd/C	YAC	DVOA	Rk	DYAR	Rk
2015	ARI	16/5	412	125	581	8	4.6	3	15.7%	4	133	8	149	56%	3	27	57	36	457	4	63%	12.7	9.6	22.1%	12	120	6
2016	ARI	16/16	964	293	1239	16	4.2	5	5.1%	17	177	9	139	50%	13	80	121	80	879	4	67%	11.0	8.0	27.7%	4	274	1
2017	ARI	1/1	46	11	23	0	2.1	2	-100.3%	--	-40	--	-34	18%	--	5	9	6	67	0	67%	11.2	7.7	-33.0%	--	-9	--
2018	ARI			285	1226	11	4.3	4	2.3%								106	77	705	2	73%	9.2		11.6%			

After leading the league in yards from scrimmage in 2016, expectations for Johnson in 2017 were sky-high. If Arizona was going to return to the playoffs in Carson Palmer's last hurrah, it was going to be thanks to their workhorse back. Needless to say, things did not go according to plan. Johnson got off to a rough start in Week 1 against the Lions, posting a single-game rushing DVOA of -100.3% on 11 carries, but it was the broken wrist he suffered during the game that had a larger impact on the Cardinals' season. As he enters the final year of his rookie contract, Johnson will be the feature back once again, and another big season would go a long way towards securing a lucrative long-term deal moving forward. While running back contracts have declined in total value in recent years, Johnson's versatility in the passing game could help him secure a bigger payhaul if Arizona does not use the franchise tag on him after the season.

Duke Johnson Height: 5-9 Weight: 207 College: Miami Draft: 2015/3 (77) Born: 23-Sep-1993 Age: 25 Risk: Green

Year	Team	G/GS	Snaps	Runs	Yds	TD	Yd/R	FUM	DVOA	Rk	DYAR	Rk	YAR	Suc%	Rk	BTkl	Pass	Rec	Yds	TD	C%	Yd/C	YAC	DVOA	Rk	DYAR	Rk
2015	CLE	16/7	561	104	379	0	3.6	1	-1.4%	25	30	31	9	45%	26	47	74	61	534	2	82%	8.8	8.0	2.3%	23	68	18
2016	CLE	16/1	457	73	358	1	4.9	2	11.2%	--	54	--	45	45%	--	35	74	53	514	0	72%	9.7	8.0	19.2%	11	134	6
2017	CLE	16/0	565	82	348	4	4.2	3	15.7%	--	90	--	92	53%	--	51	94	74	693	3	80%	9.4	8.6	6.7%	19	110	7
2018	CLE			62	263	1	4.3	1	0.7%								82	58	470	2	71%	8.1		6.8%			

We wondered what kind of role was waiting for Johnson after the Browns drafted Nick Chubb to go with Carlos Hyde. The answer was "a bigger one than you think," because the Browns handed Johnson a three-year, $15.6 million extension with $7.7 guaranteed in early June. Johnson may be around to catch passes more than take handoffs, but he's not a third-down specialist by any means. His targets were split almost evenly between first, second, and third down, and first down is where he had the most success, with 8.7 yards per pass and 48.3% receiving DVOA.

Kerryon Johnson

Height: 5-11   Weight: 213   College: Auburn   Draft: 2018/2 (43)   Born: 30-Jun-1997   Age: 21   Risk: Red

Year	Team	G/GS	Snaps	Runs	Yds	TD	Yd/R	FUM	DVOA	Rk	DYAR	Rk	YAR	Suc%	Rk	BTkl	Pass	Rec	Yds	TD	C%	Yd/C	YAC	DVOA	Rk	DYAR	Rk
2018	DET		150	619	7	4.1	3	2.5%								47	34	341	2	72%	10.0		5.4%			

Ever since Barry Sanders retired, the bar for running back performance in Detroit has barely been picked up off the floor. Reggie Bush in 2013 is the only player in the Matthew Stafford era (since 2009) to rush for at least 1,000 yards. Johnson, last year's SEC rushing leader, can make an impression rather easily if he just stays healthy and produces. He'll likely have to split time with LeGarrette Blount and Theo Riddick, but My Wayward Son could be the franchise back Detroit has repeatedly tried to draft with no success. One thing Johnson will have to adjust to is a much pass-happier offense. Auburn did not even throw 400 passes in his junior season when he had 285 carries for 1,391 yards.

Aaron Jones

Height: 5-9   Weight: 208   College: Texas-El Paso   Draft: 2017/5 (182)   Born: 2-Dec-1994   Age: 24   Risk: Yellow

Year	Team	G/GS	Snaps	Runs	Yds	TD	Yd/R	FUM	DVOA	Rk	DYAR	Rk	YAR	Suc%	Rk	BTkl	Pass	Rec	Yds	TD	C%	Yd/C	YAC	DVOA	Rk	DYAR	Rk
2017	GB	12/4	236	81	448	4	5.5	0	31.3%	--	143	--	134	53%	--	15	18	9	22	0	50%	2.4	3.3	-75.4%	--	-60	--
2018	GB			111	507	2	4.6	2	8.2%								23	18	132	1	77%	7.5		6.1%			

Jones seized some opportunities last year when Ty Montgomery and Jamaal Williams were injured. He had two games with at least 125 rushing yards, and the longest Green Bay run of the season (a 46-yard touchdown vs. New Orleans), but had a very minimal impact in the other 10 games he played. Jones will have to develop much more as a blocker and receiver if he is to get more snaps this season. Jones only gained 22 yards on his 18 pass targets, though most of those were thrown by Brett Hundley rather than Aaron Rodgers. Jones has been suspended for the first two games of the year after a positive PED test.

Ronald Jones

Height: 6-0   Weight: 200   College: USC   Draft: 2018/2 (38)   Born: 2-Aug-1997   Age: 21   Risk: Yellow

Year	Team	G/GS	Snaps	Runs	Yds	TD	Yd/R	FUM	DVOA	Rk	DYAR	Rk	YAR	Suc%	Rk	BTkl	Pass	Rec	Yds	TD	C%	Yd/C	YAC	DVOA	Rk	DYAR	Rk
2018	TB			228	946	5	4.1	3	0.1%								34	27	220	1	79%	8.1		-2.8%			

Second-round rookie Ronald Jones fully embraces the comparisons to Jamaal Charles. He wore No. 25 and grew dreadlocks to honor Charles. Now we'll see if he can come anywhere close to Charles' gaudy yards per carry average and ability to hit home runs in the pros. Jones likely won't see a huge workload right away, but for what it's worth, he accounted for 52 percent of USC's carries as a junior. The average drafted running back only accounts for 37 percent of his team's carries as a junior. Jones' BackCAST score of +60% ranked him sixth among this year's backs, behind four backs who were drafted before him plus Royce Freeman.

Kyle Juszczyk

Height: 6-1   Weight: 248   College: Harvard   Draft: 2013/4 (130)   Born: 23-Apr-1991   Age: 27   Risk: Red

Year	Team	G/GS	Snaps	Runs	Yds	TD	Yd/R	FUM	DVOA	Rk	DYAR	Rk	YAR	Suc%	Rk	BTkl	Pass	Rec	Yds	TD	C%	Yd/C	YAC	DVOA	Rk	DYAR	Rk
2015	BAL	16/11	383	2	3	0	1.5	0	-20.3%	--	-1	--	-4	0%	--	10	56	41	321	4	73%	7.8	6.6	7.0%	18	72	17
2016	BAL	16/7	463	5	22	1	4.4	0	72.5%	--	19	--	19	60%	--	7	49	37	266	0	76%	7.2	5.9	-11.9%	41	6	41
2017	SF	14/10	397	7	31	0	4.4	2	21.3%	--	12	--	7	57%	--	6	42	33	315	1	79%	9.5	6.3	3.7%	27	41	28
2018	SF			10	43	0	4.4	0	9.5%								48	39	326	1	81%	8.4		18.7%			

The 49ers have a thing for overpaying for running backs in free agency, as demonstrated by both Juszczyk and new addition Jerick McKinnon. The total value of Juszczyk's deal is nearly three times larger than the next largest fullback contract. Juszczyk was used more as a receiver out of the backfield than as a runner, but he failed to make the top 20 in receiving DVOA and DYAR among running backs in 2017. Having Jimmy Garoppolo around for a full season should improve his numbers, but the 49ers are not getting a ton of surplus value from Juszczyk when you consider that his average salary per year is $5.25 million.

Alvin Kamara   Height: 5-10   Weight: 214   College: Tennessee   Draft: 2017/3 (67)   Born: 25-Jul-1995   Age: 23   Risk: Yellow

Year	Team	G/GS	Snaps	Runs	Yds	TD	Yd/R	FUM	DVOA	Rk	DYAR	Rk	YAR	Suc%	Rk	BTkl	Pass	Rec	Yds	TD	C%	Yd/C	YAC	DVOA	Rk	DYAR	Rk
2017	NO	16/3	464	120	728	8	6.1	1	44.5%	1	255	3	255	53%	6	66	100	81	826	5	81%	10.2	8.5	36.4%	6	278	1
2018	NO			175	874	8	5.0	4	12.6%								105	85	730	3	81%	8.6		26.7%			

Kamara's rookie season was so impressive that we are just left questioning if he'll ever be able to do the things he did again. Joe Perry is the only back to ever surpass 6.0 yards per carry in multiple seasons (minimum 100 rushes), though Lenny Moore did it three times in seasons where he had 82 to 92 carries. Kamara has one of 12 seasons in NFL history by a running back with at least 80 catches and better than 10 yards per reception; Marshall Faulk (three times) is the only player who was able to do that more than once. Kamara was targeted 25 times from the slot to lead all running backs, and his receiving DVOA in the slot (48.0%) and out wide (55.7%) was even better than it was in a traditional backfield role (33.7%). Kamara had just as much DYAR (34) on eight wide receiver screens as he had on 26 running back screens.

The four-game suspension to Mark Ingram just means that we should get an early look at Kamara in a bigger role, but it is still likely that the Saints won't use him on 20-plus carries a game. He can stick to 10 to 15 carries while still being a major threat in the passing game.

Rob Kelley   Height: 6-0   Weight: 228   College: Tulane   Draft: 2016/FA   Born: 3-Oct-1992   Age: 26   Risk: Green

Year	Team	G/GS	Snaps	Runs	Yds	TD	Yd/R	FUM	DVOA	Rk	DYAR	Rk	YAR	Suc%	Rk	BTkl	Pass	Rec	Yds	TD	C%	Yd/C	YAC	DVOA	Rk	DYAR	Rk
2016	WAS	15/9	343	168	704	6	4.2	0	5.8%	15	102	17	62	48%	20	43	18	12	82	1	67%	6.8	6.5	-4.8%	--	10	--
2017	WAS	7/7	136	62	194	3	3.1	0	-2.8%	--	15	--	9	48%	--	10	7	4	18	0	57%	4.5	5.0	-23.8%	--	-6	--
2018	WAS			25	104	1	4.2	1	3.9%								8	6	37	0	75%	6.2		-11.9%			

The top ten list of great fat people and things goes something like this: 1. Fatburger; 2. "Fat Bottomed Girls" by Queen; 3. Fats Domino; 4. Fat Albert; 5. Fat Joe; 6. Charles the Fat, descendant of Charlemagne and emperor of the Carolingian Dynasty in the ninth century; 7. Fatty Arbuckle; 8. Fat Lever; 9. Chow Yun Fat; 10. "Fat" by "Weird Al" Yankovic. We could add dozens of names to this list before we got to Fat Rob, who was even worse for most of 2017 than his overall numbers would indicate. Take away Kelley's 12 carries for 78 yards against the Rams in Week 2 and you're left with 2.3 yards per carry and a -12.7% DVOA over his other six games. Kelley's season ended due to sprains of his ankle and MCL. His roster spot is not guaranteed, but he could be a red zone vulture. Nine of his ten career touchdowns have come inside the 10; half (including all three in 2017) came from exactly 1 yard out.

Eddie Lacy   Height: 5-11   Weight: 240   College: Alabama   Draft: 2013/2 (61)   Born: 1-Jan-1990   Age: 29   Risk: N/A

Year	Team	G/GS	Snaps	Runs	Yds	TD	Yd/R	FUM	DVOA	Rk	DYAR	Rk	YAR	Suc%	Rk	BTkl	Pass	Rec	Yds	TD	C%	Yd/C	YAC	DVOA	Rk	DYAR	Rk
2015	GB	15/12	471	187	758	3	4.1	4	-8.3%	35	3	35	42	49%	15	29	28	20	188	2	71%	9.4	10.7	-0.6%	26	20	33
2016	GB	5/5	166	71	360	0	5.1	0	20.4%	--	84	--	61	49%	--	26	7	4	28	0	57%	7.0	10.0	-45.4%	--	-12	--
2017	SEA	9/3	137	69	179	0	2.6	0	-37.9%	--	-81	--	-71	29%	--	13	6	6	47	0	100%	7.8	8.5	64.5%	--	24	--

Lacy didn't qualify for our running back leaders table, because his performance was so poor that he became a healthy scratch by the end of the season, despite Seattle's historic lack of production. Lacy's -37.9% DVOA would have been the worst in the league by a wide margin, had he qualified. In fact, if you lower the threshold from 100 carries to 60, it's the fifth-worst rushing DVOA we've seen in the past 10 years. With essentially no ability to bounce the ball outside, and very limited tackle-breaking ability, Lacy thudded into loaded boxes on snap after snap. His 2.59 yards per attempt were the fewest of anyone with at least 50 carries last season, and his success rate of 29 percent was no great shakes, either. As of press time, Lacy is still a free agent. It is not difficult to see why.

Dion Lewis   Height: 5-7   Weight: 195   College: Pittsburgh   Draft: 2011/5 (149)   Born: 27-Sep-1990   Age: 28   Risk: Red

Year	Team	G/GS	Snaps	Runs	Yds	TD	Yd/R	FUM	DVOA	Rk	DYAR	Rk	YAR	Suc%	Rk	BTkl	Pass	Rec	Yds	TD	C%	Yd/C	YAC	DVOA	Rk	DYAR	Rk
2015	NE	7/6	298	49	234	2	4.8	2	28.1%	--	77	--	83	55%	--	25	50	36	388	2	72%	10.8	9.6	14.7%	15	78	14
2016	NE	7/5	163	64	283	0	4.4	1	21.0%	--	74	--	52	59%	--	20	24	17	94	0	71%	5.5	4.9	-31.9%	--	-25	--
2017	NE	16/8	404	180	896	6	5.0	0	27.6%	2	273	1	280	56%	4	60	35	32	214	3	91%	6.7	7.0	32.0%	10	90	12
2018	TEN			153	737	3	4.8	2	12.7%								46	36	274	0	78%	7.6		2.7%			

For the first time in his seven-year professional career, Lewis played all 16 games in 2017. That was enough to elevate him from his usual position as a talented runner with too few carries to qualify into the No. 1 spot in DYAR. A versatile scatback in the mold of every versatile Patriots scatback of the past 15 years, Lewis more than doubled his career rush attempts and yardage totals over the past 16 games. If he can continue to stay healthy, he brings speed and elusiveness as well as exceptional receiving ability to the Titans backfield. It's all cliché by now, but Lewis is the speed to Derrick Henry's strength, the (sigh) lightning to his thunder, the [repeat running back tandem clichés ad infinitum].

The trick will be keeping him healthy. Lewis missed the entire 2013 season with a broken leg, half of 2015 with a torn ACL, then the first half of 2016 after requiring follow-up surgery on his injured knee. Last year was only the second time he appeared in more than nine games, and the first since his rookie season in 2011. The Patriots handled him conservatively, with frequent reports suggesting that they were specifically being cautious with his workload (as they evidently were with receiver Danny Amendola). The Titans might do well to emulate that cautious approach; Lewis should be a very effective back in Matt LaFleur's scheme, provided the Titans can keep him on the field.

Marshawn Lynch

Height: 5-11   Weight: 215   College: California   Draft: 2007/1 (12)   Born: 22-Apr-1986   Age: 32   Risk: Yellow

Year	Team	G/GS	Snaps	Runs	Yds	TD	Yd/R	FUM	DVOA	Rk	DYAR	Rk	YAR	Suc%	Rk	BTkl	Pass	Rec	Yds	TD	C%	Yd/C	YAC	DVOA	Rk	DYAR	Rk
2015	SEA	7/6	310	111	417	3	3.8	0	1.2%	19	47	25	54	50%	11	24	21	13	80	0	62%	6.2	6.7	-34.6%	--	-24	--
2017	OAK	15/15	462	207	891	7	4.3	1	10.1%	9	165	9	131	49%	13	60	31	20	151	0	65%	7.6	8.2	-27.2%	56	-23	54
2018	OAK			201	874	8	4.3	1	9.8%								24	18	140	0	75%	7.8		0.1%			

Lynch rushed for 434 yards in five December games, averaging 5.2 yards per carry, after spending the first three months of the season as a committee back with an ill-defined role. He took a modest pay cut to stay with the Raiders this year and reportedly had some private offseason meetings with Jon Gruden, the transcripts of which we would pay a large sum of money to see. Lynch can still Beast Mode through tackles, which makes Doug Martin's arrival curious. Gruden may be justifiably unsold on Beast Mode's ability to stay healthy and on our plane of existence for 16 games, but doesn't want to be the Grinch Who Stole Marshawn without a backup plan if something goes wrong. In a fair battle for carries, Lynch will win. If the new staff goes looking for reasons to be rubbed the wrong way, well, Lynch will be sure to give them some easy ones.

Marlon Mack

Height: 5-11   Weight: 213   College: South Florida   Draft: 2017/4 (143)   Born: 7-Mar-1996   Age: 22   Risk: Green

Year	Team	G/GS	Snaps	Runs	Yds	TD	Yd/R	FUM	DVOA	Rk	DYAR	Rk	YAR	Suc%	Rk	BTkl	Pass	Rec	Yds	TD	C%	Yd/C	YAC	DVOA	Rk	DYAR	Rk
2017	IND	14/0	310	93	358	3	3.8	1	-6.9%	--	6	--	11	41%	--	23	33	21	225	1	64%	10.7	13.5	9.2%	16	38	29
2018	IND			143	606	2	4.2	2	-1.8%								43	27	212	1	63%	7.8		-15.6%			

Did Chuck Pagano and Rob Chudzinski hate Mack's occasional inconsistency, love Frank Gore that much, or were they simply at a loss for how to handle a player of Mack's type? Or was it the torn labrum he played through that general manager Chris Ballard revealed after the draft? Either way, Frank Reich offers a new slate. Pity, then, that Mack missed the offseason rehabbing the injury. Mack should be ready for training camp, and an offense that looks to use the running backs in the passing game and asks them to attack the perimeter more and between the tackles less could be a great fit for his skill set as long as he develops more consistency. If not, Indianapolis drafted two backs and still has Robert Turbin as a reliable veteran, so Mack could be on the outside looking in.

Doug Martin

Height: 5-9   Weight: 210   College: Boise State   Draft: 2012/1 (31)   Born: 13-Jan-1989   Age: 29   Risk: Green

Year	Team	G/GS	Snaps	Runs	Yds	TD	Yd/R	FUM	DVOA	Rk	DYAR	Rk	YAR	Suc%	Rk	BTkl	Pass	Rec	Yds	TD	C%	Yd/C	YAC	DVOA	Rk	DYAR	Rk
2015	TB	16/16	622	288	1402	6	4.9	5	-1.6%	26	81	18	150	48%	16	63	44	33	271	1	75%	8.2	7.0	-8.9%	38	11	36
2016	TB	8/8	322	144	421	3	2.9	1	-22.0%	40	-82	39	-76	42%	34	33	16	14	134	0	88%	9.6	7.6	24.7%	--	30	--
2017	TB	11/8	289	138	406	3	2.9	1	-22.5%	47	-77	45	-83	35%	46	12	18	9	84	0	50%	9.3	6.7	-30.4%	--	-18	--
2018	OAK			101	389	2	3.9	1	-2.8%								17	12	86	0	71%	7.2		-8.8%			

In between a drug-policy suspension, a benching for violating team rules, and a concussion, Martin produced some stunning stat lines last season in Tampa: eight carries for 7 yards in the first Saints game, six carries for 7 yards against the Panthers, three carries for a loss of 3 in the second Saints game. His one-year Raiders contract is modest, and in a sane universe Martin would be a high-probability September cut because he duplicates the services of the older, flightier, yet somehow more productive Marshawn Lynch. The Raiders do not appear to operate in a sane universe at present, so Martin will probably get multiple chances to duplicate the success of 2015, if only because he's more likely than Lynch to tell the coaching staff exactly what they want to hear.

Christian McCaffrey Height: 5-11　Weight: 202　College: Stanford　Draft: 2017/1 (8)　Born: 7-Jun-1996　Age: 22　Risk: Green

Year	Team	G/GS	Snaps	Runs	Yds	TD	Yd/R	FUM	DVOA	Rk	DYAR	Rk	YAR	Suc%	Rk	BTkl	Pass	Rec	Yds	TD	C%	Yd/C	YAC	DVOA	Rk	DYAR	Rk
2017	CAR	16/10	757	117	435	2	3.7	1	-6.2%	30	11	34	14	45%	22	47	113	80	651	5	71%	8.1	7.4	5.7%	21	128	5
2018	CAR			145	609	3	4.2	4	-4.0%								103	78	699	3	76%	9.0		17.6%			

McCaffrey was drafted for his versatility, more of a hybrid back/receiver than a pure running back. We talked about the issues the Panthers had utilizing his receiving ability in the Carolina chapter, but it's worth looking at how he performed on the ground, especially as Carolina scrambles to replace Jonathan Stewart's carries. McCaffrey had just 435 rushing yards, the lowest total for a first-round rookie running back since David Wilson in 2012, and the lowest for a top-ten rookie since C.J. Spiller in 2010. For all his explosiveness with the ball in his hands, he managed just one carry of 20 yards or more. McCaffrey improved over the second half of the season, jumping from 2.4 yards per carry in Weeks 1-8 to 4.7 the rest of the way. Some of that is becoming more comfortable in the NFL, but some of it also appears to be play selection. Early on in the year, Carolina tried to get McCaffrey in space using misdirection, running him on a bunch of counters that averaged just 3.5 yards per carry. In the second half, they decided to try pitching him the ball and letting his speed and athleticism create extra space; he averaged 5.9 yards per carry on those plays. Hopefully, Norv Turner was taking notes.

LeSean McCoy Height: 5-11　Weight: 198　College: Pittsburgh　Draft: 2009/2 (53)　Born: 12-Jul-1988　Age: 30　Risk: Red

Year	Team	G/GS	Snaps	Runs	Yds	TD	Yd/R	FUM	DVOA	Rk	DYAR	Rk	YAR	Suc%	Rk	BTkl	Pass	Rec	Yds	TD	C%	Yd/C	YAC	DVOA	Rk	DYAR	Rk
2015	BUF	12/12	598	203	895	3	4.4	2	8.8%	11	139	7	110	47%	21	39	50	32	292	2	64%	9.1	9.0	-2.0%	29	30	26
2016	BUF	15/15	645	234	1267	13	5.4	3	28.3%	2	338	2	244	51%	10	65	58	50	356	1	88%	7.1	7.6	21.2%	8	117	7
2017	BUF	16/16	722	287	1138	6	4.0	3	-10.8%	38	-26	41	-7	43%	32	61	78	59	448	2	77%	7.6	6.9	-1.8%	33	48	24
2018	BUF			279	1210	6	4.3	3	1.6%								68	51	402	1	75%	7.9		-1.0%			

Ignore all the statistics. Bundle them in a carpet, throw the carpet off a cliff, and drive away. Anybody who reaches the counting stats McCoy did last year when the passing game keyed off Zay Jones and Deonte Thompson deserves some benefit of the doubt. Unfortunately, the difficulty only goes up for McCoy this offseason. New coordinator, same bad receivers, no Richie Incognito or Eric Wood, and an unsettled quarterback situation. Going into Year 4 of a five-year deal, it's worth wondering if the Bills and McCoy might both be better off parting before 2018 starts.

Just before we went to press, McCoy was accused of domestic violence in a complicated situation connected to a home invasion where his ex-girlfriend was living in Milton, Georgia. The police are calling this an "open and active investigation," and a statement from the Bills said "we will continue to gather information." As of now, we have no idea how this will affect McCoy's season.

Elijah McGuire Height: 5-10　Weight: 214　College: Louisiana-Lafayette　Draft: 2017/6 (188)　Born: 1-Jun-1994　Age: 24　Risk: Yellow

Year	Team	G/GS	Snaps	Runs	Yds	TD	Yd/R	FUM	DVOA	Rk	DYAR	Rk	YAR	Suc%	Rk	BTkl	Pass	Rec	Yds	TD	C%	Yd/C	YAC	DVOA	Rk	DYAR	Rk
2017	NYJ	16/2	267	88	315	1	3.6	1	-25.8%	--	-56	--	-38	34%	--	22	26	17	177	1	65%	10.4	8.4	-1.4%	32	18	36
2018	NYJ			77	345	2	4.5	2	3.9%								41	30	293	1	73%	9.8		15.0%			

McGuire is a bit of an odd duck. He's got a scatback body without much success as a receiver, and he doesn't do anything particularly well but doesn't have a major weakness. He's durable, and has no real fumble problems. But without the one key skill that opens the door to playing time, he's likely looking at an uphill battle to get into a committee. He begins the offseason looking up at Isaiah Crowell and Bilal Powell, at the very least. Special teams is his ticket to staying on this roster all season.

Jerick McKinnon

Height: 5-9 Weight: 209 College: Georgia Southern Draft: 2014/3 (96) Born: 5-Mar-1992 Age: 26 Risk: Red

Year	Team	G/GS	Snaps	Runs	Yds	TD	Yd/R	FUM	DVOA	Rk	DYAR	Rk	YAR	Suc%	Rk	BTkl	Pass	Rec	Yds	TD	C%	Yd/C	YAC	DVOA	Rk	DYAR	Rk
2015	MIN	16/0	160	52	271	2	5.2	0	15.3%	--	50	--	61	50%	--	17	29	21	173	1	72%	8.2	8.4	2.4%	22	27	28
2016	MIN	15/7	510	159	539	2	3.4	0	-11.0%	34	-15	33	-56	42%	35	32	53	43	255	2	81%	5.9	6.3	-10.7%	40	10	36
2017	MIN	16/1	528	150	570	3	3.8	2	-12.7%	40	-24	40	-25	43%	28	43	68	51	421	2	75%	8.3	9.0	-0.4%	31	48	23
2018	SF			184	767	4	4.2	2	-1.3%								80	63	574	2	79%	9.1		22.7%			

McKinnon spent four seasons in Minnesota primarily as a backup with a role in the passing game as well. Even in a limited sample size, he did not put up the type of efficiency numbers that would justify making him a hot free-agent commodity. McKinnon definitely brings versatility to an offense, but the deal he signed made him the fifth-highest paid running back in the league by annual average. In head coach Kyle Shanahan's offense, McKinnon could be a matchup nightmare by lining up all over the formation; with that said, the 49ers likely did not need to pay him that much to add that element to their offense. Few will be complaining if it works out, but the 49ers sure paid a pretty penny in the hopes that they would strike it rich with McKinnon.

J.D. McKissic

Height: 5-11 Weight: 193 College: Arkansas State Draft: 2016/FA Born: 15-Aug-1993 Age: 25 Risk: Yellow

Year	Team	G/GS	Snaps	Runs	Yds	TD	Yd/R	FUM	DVOA	Rk	DYAR	Rk	YAR	Suc%	Rk	BTkl	Pass	Rec	Yds	TD	C%	Yd/C	YAC	DVOA	Rk	DYAR	Rk
2016	2TM	1/0	7	1	2	0	2.0	0	-67.7%	--	-2	--	-1	0%	--	0	2	2	16	0	100%	8.0	6.5	10.4%	--	2	--
2017	SEA	13/1	296	46	187	1	4.1	0	8.2%	--	31	--	26	51%	--	8	47	34	266	2	74%	7.8	5.5	3.9%	26	49	22
2018	SEA			25	110	1	4.3	1	9.4%								29	22	163	0	76%	7.4		-6.8%			

Seattle's backfield chaos meant that no Seahawks running back qualified for the rushing DVOA rankings last season; no one lasted long enough for a decent sample size to really evaluate them. That being said, of the five Seattle backs with at least 45 carries last season, McKissic had the highest DVOA, both in the passing game and the running game. It's his receiving ability that could earn him a role on the 2018 Seahawks; if he can beat out C.J. Prosise, he could be the guy Seattle turns to in passing situations. McKissic also has value as an emergency wide receiver; 49 percent of his passing targets came when line up outside the backfield, and his 16 targets lined up out wide led all running backs. So did his average depth of target, 4.4 yards.

Sony Michel

Height: 5-11 Weight: 214 College: Georgia Draft: 2018/1 (31) Born: 17-Feb-1995 Age: 23 Risk: Green

Year	Team	G/GS	Snaps	Runs	Yds	TD	Yd/R	FUM	DVOA	Rk	DYAR	Rk	YAR	Suc%	Rk	BTkl	Pass	Rec	Yds	TD	C%	Yd/C	YAC	DVOA	Rk	DYAR	Rk
2018	NE			161	745	7	4.6	3	11.6%								31	26	193	1	84%	7.4		-0.9%			

This was as stacked a running back class as we've seen in a while, yet the Patriots still felt compelled to go with Michel in the first round. In theory, there's no reason he can't be an every-down back in the NFL. He's a terrific blocker. While he may not quite be a receiver on the level of a James White, he's certainly not overmatched in that area. The only real ding for him coming out of college was a high fumble rate, something that has gotten backs in the Belichick doghouse before. If he can hold on to the ball and the lead job, though, perhaps Michel can be the first real threat for an every-down workload for New England since Corey Dillon.

Lamar Miller

Height: 5-11 Weight: 212 College: Miami Draft: 2012/4 (97) Born: 25-Apr-1991 Age: 27 Risk: Yellow

Year	Team	G/GS	Snaps	Runs	Yds	TD	Yd/R	FUM	DVOA	Rk	DYAR	Rk	YAR	Suc%	Rk	BTkl	Pass	Rec	Yds	TD	C%	Yd/C	YAC	DVOA	Rk	DYAR	Rk
2015	MIA	16/16	631	194	872	8	4.5	1	1.7%	18	81	19	105	43%	34	26	57	47	397	2	82%	8.4	9.0	-3.6%	31	32	25
2016	HOU	14/14	623	268	1073	5	4.0	2	-10.5%	32	-21	34	29	45%	23	37	39	31	188	1	79%	6.1	6.0	-14.4%	44	-1	44
2017	HOU	16/13	757	238	888	3	3.7	1	-2.8%	25	57	21	42	45%	21	34	45	36	327	3	80%	9.1	8.2	42.7%	2	134	4
2018	HOU			237	946	5	4.0	2	-0.9%								37	29	226	2	78%	7.8		10.5%			

That second-place rank in receiving DVOA comes courtesy of Deshaun Watson, with whom Miller posted 98 DYAR and 79.7% DVOA on 20 targets. By now, the Texans should be over the idea that Miller was a secret superduperstar hidden by poor coaching in Miami, and accept him for who he is—not the best between-the-tackles runner, better in a committee role, but as those Watson numbers show, potentially an extremely good player in the right situation. Maybe D'Onta Foreman comes back healthy and makes the jump to really let Miller thrive in a specialized role. Probably not, so expect another season of pretty good passing-game work and too many carries that feel like they'd be better given to somebody else, if only there was somebody else.

Joe Mixon Height: 6-1 Weight: 228 College: Oklahoma Draft: 2017/2 (48) Born: 24-Jul-1996 Age: 22 Risk: Green

Year	Team	G/GS	Snaps	Runs	Yds	TD	Yd/R	FUM	DVOA	Rk	DYAR	Rk	YAR	Suc%	Rk	BTkl	Pass	Rec	Yds	TD	C%	Yd/C	YAC	DVOA	Rk	DYAR	Rk
2017	CIN	14/7	385	178	626	4	3.5	3	1.0%	19	68	17	-1	41%	37	22	35	30	287	0	89%	9.6	10.9	-6.8%	38	13	38
2018	CIN			206	802	5	3.9	3	-7.6%								37	31	237	1	84%	7.7		9.9%			

None of Mixon's rushing stats were particularly good in his rookie year, but few backs were so up against it in terms of scheme and usage. He spent most of the season eluding defenders in the backfield. The coaching staff was unwilling to quit the plodding Jeremy Hill until late in the year. The offensive line was shambolic. Mixon was, as expected, better in shotgun sets (68-281-4.1) than when Andy Dalton was under center (110-345-3.1), by a full yard per carry, yet he was not used in those sets nearly enough.

If you looked carefully, Mixon did display the spellbinding combination of power and speed that made him a second-round pick—while, it should be noted, not causing any distraction or reason for the Bengals to be sorry for drafting him after his terrible assault of a woman while at Oklahoma. There were plenty of issues with the Cincinnati offense in 2017, but Mixon wasn't one of them, and offensive coordinator Bill Lazor has anointed him the "bellcow back" for the coming season.

Ty Montgomery Height: 6-0 Weight: 221 College: Stanford Draft: 2015/3 (94) Born: 22-Jan-1993 Age: 25 Risk: Green

Year	Team	G/GS	Snaps	Runs	Yds	TD	Yd/R	FUM	DVOA	Rk	DYAR	Rk	YAR	Suc%	Rk	BTkl	Pass	Rec	Yds	TD	C%	Yd/C	YAC	DVOA	Rk	DYAR	Rk
2015	GB	6/3	242	3	14	0	4.7	0	-28.6%	--	2	--	4	--	--	4	19	15	136	2	79%	9.1	6.1	32.3%	--	74	--
2016	GB	15/6	392	77	457	3	5.9	2	17.6%	--	86	--	105	55%	--	25	56	44	348	0	79%	7.9	7.3	-4.2%	32	33	27
2017	GB	8/5	274	71	273	3	3.8	0	2.8%	--	37	--	41	49%	--	12	31	23	173	1	74%	7.5	9.3	-3.7%	35	19	35
2018	GB			83	349	2	4.2	2	0.3%								49	39	307	1	80%	7.9		10.3%			

The Packers only began to tap into the potential of Montgomery at running back after he converted from wide receiver during the 2016 season. He was very elusive in this new role, but his durability failed him in 2017 and he missed half the season. When he did play, his yards per carry dropped from 5.9 to 3.8. There have been some whispers of moving Montgomery back to wide receiver if only because of the lack of depth there, but he should still be in the mix with Jamaal Williams and Aaron Jones for the lead role at running back.

Alfred Morris Height: 5-10 Weight: 219 College: Florida Atlantic Draft: 2012/6 (173) Born: 12-Dec-1988 Age: 30 Risk: N/A

Year	Team	G/GS	Snaps	Runs	Yds	TD	Yd/R	FUM	DVOA	Rk	DYAR	Rk	YAR	Suc%	Rk	BTkl	Pass	Rec	Yds	TD	C%	Yd/C	YAC	DVOA	Rk	DYAR	Rk
2015	WAS	16/16	385	202	751	1	3.7	0	-15.0%	41	-52	42	9	39%	44	12	13	10	55	0	77%	5.5	3.8	-27.6%	--	-10	--
2016	DAL	14/0	130	69	243	2	3.5	0	-7.7%	--	3	--	11	52%	--	13	6	3	11	0	50%	3.7	3.7	-53.4%	--	-13	--
2017	DAL	14/5	204	115	547	1	4.8	0	8.4%	10	79	16	99	51%	7	30	9	7	45	0	78%	6.4	6.3	-18.4%	--	-2	--

Last year was the first time in Morris' six NFL seasons that his rushing yardage actually increased from the prior season, ending a run of several years of perpetual disappointment. That's mainly due to Ezekiel Elliott's suspension—Morris averaged 67.8 yards in his five starts, compared to 18.9 yards coming off the bench—but hey, facts is facts. Morris only had two carries in the two games after Elliott's suspension ended. His contract expired after the season, and he remained available as of press time.

DeMarco Murray Height: 6-0 Weight: 213 College: Oklahoma Draft: 2011/3 (71) Born: 12-Feb-1988 Age: 30 Risk: N/A

Year	Team	G/GS	Snaps	Runs	Yds	TD	Yd/R	FUM	DVOA	Rk	DYAR	Rk	YAR	Suc%	Rk	BTkl	Pass	Rec	Yds	TD	C%	Yd/C	YAC	DVOA	Rk	DYAR	Rk
2015	PHI	15/8	482	193	702	6	3.6	2	-12.1%	40	-29	39	19	45%	31	33	55	44	322	1	80%	7.3	8.7	-9.3%	39	13	35
2016	TEN	16/16	861	293	1287	9	4.4	4	-5.3%	25	42	24	140	50%	11	49	67	53	377	3	79%	7.1	6.5	-3.2%	30	40	24
2017	TEN	15/15	647	184	659	6	3.6	1	-5.0%	27	27	28	-1	39%	43	40	47	39	266	1	83%	6.8	6.3	-3.3%	34	25	34

Murray was released by the Titans as a cost-saving measure after a career-worst season in yards and yards per attempt, and a third straight season of negative DVOA. His 1,200-yard season for the Titans in 2016 was more a function of volume than effectiveness, and he has never quite replicated his 2014 form since leaving Dallas. Rather than trying to hook on with a new team, Murray announced his retirement in July.

Latavius Murray Height: 6-2 Weight: 223 College: UCF Draft: 2013/6 (181) Born: 21-Feb-1991 Age: 27 Risk: Green

Year	Team	G/GS	Snaps	Runs	Yds	TD	Yd/R	FUM	DVOA	Rk	DYAR	Rk	YAR	Suc%	Rk	BTkl	Pass	Rec	Yds	TD	C%	Yd/C	YAC	DVOA	Rk	DYAR	Rk
2015	OAK	16/16	680	266	1066	6	4.0	4	-5.6%	32	32	29	27	39%	43	39	53	41	232	0	77%	5.7	6.0	-30.6%	55	-47	54
2016	OAK	14/12	525	195	788	12	4.0	2	-3.4%	23	46	23	100	49%	16	36	43	33	264	0	77%	8.0	8.5	-9.4%	38	10	37
2017	MIN	16/11	421	216	842	8	3.9	1	-2.3%	24	59	20	58	44%	23	34	17	15	103	0	88%	6.9	8.3	-11.6%	--	2	--
2018	MIN			108	410	5	3.8	1	2.1%								19	15	115	1	79%	7.7		4.0%			

No one expected Murray to leave Oakland and lead the Vikings in rushing, but injuries happen. Murray and Jerick McKinnon were good at replacing Dalvin Cook after he tore his ACL just four games into the season. Now with Cook back, Murray should see a big drop in his usage. Murray only had 14 carries in the first four games combined last year, but exceeded that number almost every week the rest of the season. It would still be a good idea for the Vikings to spell Cook with Murray, but in fantasy football, at best, Murray is just a handcuff draft pick this year.

Elijhaa Penny Height: 6-2 Weight: 234 College: Idaho Draft: 2016/FA Born: 17-Aug-1993 Age: 25 Risk: Green

Year	Team	G/GS	Snaps	Runs	Yds	TD	Yd/R	FUM	DVOA	Rk	DYAR	Rk	YAR	Suc%	Rk	BTkl	Pass	Rec	Yds	TD	C%	Yd/C	YAC	DVOA	Rk	DYAR	Rk
2017	ARI	16/0	96	31	124	2	4.0	0	15.8%	--	33	--	44	61%	--	6	6	4	38	0	67%	9.5	10.3	6.3%	--	6	--
2018	ARI			17	68	0	3.9	1	-2.0%								8	7	42	0	88%	6.0		-1.3%			

After going undrafted out of Idaho in 2016, Penny signed with the Cardinals as an undrafted free agent but did not see any game action until 2017. In the absence of David Johnson, Penny got 31 carries for a seriously hamstrung Arizona rushing attack and managed to be a somewhat positive force in his limited time. Penny will again be a backup in the desert, and if he sees any extended playing time, something will have gone horribly wrong (again) for the Cardinals. For now, but probably not much longer, Penny can take solace in the fact that he still has more career rushing yards than his younger brother Rashaad, drafted in the first round by the Seahawks this year.

Rashaad Penny Height: 5-11 Weight: 220 College: San Diego State Draft: 2018/1 (27) Born: 2-Feb-1996 Age: 22 Risk: Yellow

Year	Team	G/GS	Snaps	Runs	Yds	TD	Yd/R	FUM	DVOA	Rk	DYAR	Rk	YAR	Suc%	Rk	BTkl	Pass	Rec	Yds	TD	C%	Yd/C	YAC	DVOA	Rk	DYAR	Rk
2018	SEA			214	901	7	4.2	3	3.5%								44	35	301	1	80%	8.6		3.7%			

Forget Marshawn Lynch for a moment—the Seahawk Penny will most immediately be tasked with replacing is Jimmy Graham. Graham hauled in seven touchdowns inside the 5-yard line last season, third-most in the league. That leaves some pretty big shoes to fill when the Seahawks get close to the end zone, where they absolutely could not run the ball a year ago. This has not typically been Penny's forte, if for no other reason than his normal experience in the red zone is running through it to finish a long score. Penny led the NCAA with 31 plays from scrimmage of 20 or more yards in 2017, and his 7.37 adjusted yards per carry is the second-highest in our BackCAST database. Don't mistake him for someone who can only exceed in the open field, however; Penny was also among college football's leaders in broken tackles.

Samaje Perine Height: 5-11 Weight: 233 College: Oklahoma Draft: 2017/4 (114) Born: 16-Sep-1995 Age: 23 Risk: Green

Year	Team	G/GS	Snaps	Runs	Yds	TD	Yd/R	FUM	DVOA	Rk	DYAR	Rk	YAR	Suc%	Rk	BTkl	Pass	Rec	Yds	TD	C%	Yd/C	YAC	DVOA	Rk	DYAR	Rk
2017	WAS	16/8	360	175	603	1	3.4	2	-20.5%	45	-85	47	-63	43%	31	34	25	22	182	1	92%	8.3	9.3	42.6%	3	84	15
2018	WAS			56	203	1	3.6	1	-9.4%								14	11	64	0	79%	5.8		-11.5%			

Perine started each of Washington's last seven games after Rob Kelley went down with an injury. His first two starts were excellent—47 carries for 217 yards and a touchdown against the Saints and Giants—but he only managed 176 yards on 62 carries (a 2.8-yard average) after that. He had the worst third-down DVOA of any runner with at least 100 carries last year, with five carries that went for no gain or a loss (including a fumble) and only two first downs. His receptions come in small doses—he never had more than four catches or 31 yards in a game. Perine is strictly a depth player behind Derrius Guice and Chris Thompson this season.

Adrian Peterson Height: 6-2   Weight: 217   College: Oklahoma   Draft: 2007/1 (7)   Born: 21-Mar-1985   Age: 33   Risk: N/A

Year	Team	G/GS	Snaps	Runs	Yds	TD	Yd/R	FUM	DVOA	Rk	DYAR	Rk	YAR	Suc%	Rk	BTkl	Pass	Rec	Yds	TD	C%	Yd/C	YAC	DVOA	Rk	DYAR	Rk
2015	MIN	16/16	665	327	1485	11	4.5	7	2.2%	17	143	6	133	45%	25	51	36	30	222	0	83%	7.4	8.6	-16.3%	47	-5	47
2016	MIN	3/3	84	37	72	0	1.9	1	-49.1%	--	-57	--	-63	38%	--	2	6	3	8	0	50%	2.7	3.7	-109.4%	--	-30	--
2017	2TM	10/7	300	156	529	2	3.4	3	-21.9%	46	-85	46	-79	40%	42	32	19	11	70	0	58%	6.4	5.0	-35.7%	--	-23	--

Peterson started the year in a crowded running back room in New Orleans, competing for time with Mark Ingram and Alvin Kamara, but he was traded to Arizona in short order after David Johnson got hurt. At first, it looked like Peterson might still have some gas in the tank, but he ended up struggling for a poor Arizona offense, finishing with the second-worst rushing DYAR and DVOA totals in the league among backs with at least 100 carries. While Peterson has shown interest in several potential landing spots, he is still without a team for 2018, and it does not look like he will be getting signed any time soon. A team desperate for some help might snatch him up early in the season in case of injury, but Peterson has not been an above-average running back since 2015. If 2017 was the last gasp for Peterson, it was a rather underwhelming end to what was frequently a breathtaking career.

Bilal Powell Height: 5-10   Weight: 205   College: Louisville   Draft: 2011/4 (126)   Born: 27-Oct-1988   Age: 30   Risk: Yellow

Year	Team	G/GS	Snaps	Runs	Yds	TD	Yd/R	FUM	DVOA	Rk	DYAR	Rk	YAR	Suc%	Rk	BTkl	Pass	Rec	Yds	TD	C%	Yd/C	YAC	DVOA	Rk	DYAR	Rk
2015	NYJ	11/2	367	70	313	1	4.5	2	1.0%	--	25	--	48	46%	--	20	63	47	388	2	75%	8.3	8.9	-3.3%	30	36	24
2016	NYJ	16/4	531	131	722	3	5.5	1	23.1%	3	182	8	197	56%	4	49	75	58	388	2	79%	6.7	7.2	-1.9%	27	49	20
2017	NYJ	15/10	401	178	772	5	4.3	1	-14.8%	42	-43	43	5	35%	45	36	33	23	170	0	70%	7.4	7.0	-30.4%	57	-30	56
2018	NYJ			97	450	2	4.6	2	8.4%								24	17	147	0	71%	8.6		1.1%			

Powell has been a Jet since 2011, meaning he has seen one winning season and zero playoff games. Powell's a capable third-down back with enough burst to be a fill-in when injuries struck. He's not the player you want to start 10 games for you. The Jets agreed, which is why you'll see his carries decrease massively with Isaiah Crowell in the fold. Powell will turn 30 in October, and the optimistic way to look at his future is a series of year-to-year deals while the Jets try to get a replacement set up.

C.J. Prosise Height: 6-0   Weight: 220   College: Notre Dame   Draft: 2016/3 (90)   Born: 20-May-1994   Age: 24   Risk: Red

Year	Team	G/GS	Snaps	Runs	Yds	TD	Yd/R	FUM	DVOA	Rk	DYAR	Rk	YAR	Suc%	Rk	BTkl	Pass	Rec	Yds	TD	C%	Yd/C	YAC	DVOA	Rk	DYAR	Rk
2016	SEA	6/2	147	30	172	1	5.7	0	19.6%	--	38	--	18	52%	--	6	19	17	208	0	89%	12.2	6.9	55.2%	--	62	--
2017	SEA	5/0	75	11	23	0	2.1	0	-19.8%	--	-5	--	-11	36%	--	6	11	6	87	0	55%	14.5	8.3	-4.2%	--	6	--
2018	SEA			23	105	1	4.6	1	12.1%								25	18	181	0	72%	10.0		14.5%			

After putting up some very impressive numbers in limited action in 2016, 2017 was supposed to be Prosise's year to really burst onto the scene and claim a larger role, especially in the passing game. That was not to be, as the one consistent thing about Prosise to this point in his career has been his inability to stay healthy. In his first two seasons, Prosise has missed time with a hip flexor, a hamstring strain, a broken bone in his hand, a fractured scapula, a strained groin, and three separate sprained ankles. His numbers were down last season, though considering he was being held together by athletic tape and hope, that may not be particularly surprising. Prosise has missed 21 of his first 32 games, and while his potential is enough to keep him in the mix at running back, his lack of availability may ultimately doom him.

Donnel Pumphrey Height: 5-8   Weight: 176   College: San Diego State   Draft: 2017/4 (132)   Born: 6-Dec-1994   Age: 24   Risk: Blue

Year	Team	G/GS	Snaps	Runs	Yds	TD	Yd/R	FUM	DVOA	Rk	DYAR	Rk	YAR	Suc%	Rk	BTkl	Pass	Rec	Yds	TD	C%	Yd/C	YAC	DVOA	Rk	DYAR	Rk
2018	PHI			11	50	0	4.6	0	8.0%								7	5	35	0	71%	7.0		-14.4%			

Pumphrey looked tentative and out of his depth in Eagles OTAs last summer, then ordinary at best in the preseason. The Eagles used a hamstring injury as an excuse to stash the diminutive scatback on injured reserve. Pumphrey is part of a crowded Eagles third-down landscape populated by Darren Sproles, Corey Clement, and others. He was exciting to watch in college and remains fun to root for, but he may not make the roster.

Thomas Rawls

Height: 5-9 | Weight: 215 | College: Central Michigan | Draft: 2015/FA | Born: 8-Aug-1993 | Age: 25 | Risk: Red

Year	Team	G/GS	Snaps	Runs	Yds	TD	Yd/R	FUM	DVOA	Rk	DYAR	Rk	YAR	Suc%	Rk	BTkl	Pass	Rec	Yds	TD	C%	Yd/C	YAC	DVOA	Rk	DYAR	Rk
2015	SEA	13/7	289	147	830	4	5.6	1	26.4%	2	216	1	224	62%	1	27	11	9	76	1	82%	8.4	8.4	5.8%	--	13	--
2016	SEA	9/7	303	109	349	3	3.2	0	-9.0%	31	-2	31	-26	41%	38	20	17	13	96	0	76%	7.4	6.3	10.9%	--	22	--
2017	SEA	12/3	219	58	157	0	2.7	1	-40.9%	--	-83	--	-86	33%	--	9	13	9	94	0	69%	10.4	9.2	26.8%	--	28	--
2018	NYJ			45	177	1	3.9	1	-3.4%								10	7	44	0	70%	6.3		-17.4			

Rawls looked like a future star for the 2015 Seahawks, then spent the last two years averaging 3.0 yards per carry behind the worst offensive lines Tom Cable could create. The Jets had success importing Jermaine Kearse from Seattle, so they opted to see what Rawls could do with … well, OK, probably only marginally better linemen in front of him. Still only 25, Rawls could write a second act if his style plays better away from Cable and the putrid Hawks line. It's worth noting that pretty much everyone beside Chris Carson was garbage behind the Seattle line the last two years, so it's hardly all about Rawls. Alex Collins showed him the blueprint.

Jalen Richard

Height: 5-8 | Weight: 207 | College: Southern Mississippi | Draft: 2016/FA | Born: 15-Oct-1993 | Age: 25 | Risk: Green

Year	Team	G/GS	Snaps	Runs	Yds	TD	Yd/R	FUM	DVOA	Rk	DYAR	Rk	YAR	Suc%	Rk	BTkl	Pass	Rec	Yds	TD	C%	Yd/C	YAC	DVOA	Rk	DYAR	Rk
2016	OAK	16/0	237	83	491	1	5.9	0	16.7%	--	76	--	97	49%	--	23	39	29	194	2	74%	6.7	4.9	-8.8%	37	9	39
2017	OAK	16/1	219	56	275	1	4.9	1	-1.4%	--	15	--	15	38%	--	10	36	27	256	1	75%	9.5	9.0	33.3%	9	86	14
2018	OAK			38	180	0	4.8	2	7.2%								39	30	269	1	77%	9.0		17.3			

Your basic replacement-level third down back, Richard had his moments last season when Marshawn Lynch was suspended or DeAndre Washington was limited. Richard's role was reduced when the others were healthy and dialed in late in the season, and a lost fumble in the Christmas loss to the Eagles were no doubt noticed by the color commentator in the broadcast booth. In fact Richard had a mind-boggling nine fumbles last year, but eight of them were on special teams: two muffed kickoffs, four muffed punts, and another two fumbles during punt returns.

Theo Riddick

Height: 5-10 | Weight: 201 | College: Notre Dame | Draft: 2013/6 (199) | Born: 4-May-1991 | Age: 27 | Risk: Yellow

Year	Team	G/GS	Snaps	Runs	Yds	TD	Yd/R	FUM	DVOA	Rk	DYAR	Rk	YAR	Suc%	Rk	BTkl	Pass	Rec	Yds	TD	C%	Yd/C	YAC	DVOA	Rk	DYAR	Rk
2015	DET	16/1	470	43	133	0	3.1	1	-24.5%	--	-29	--	-19	42%	--	40	99	80	697	3	81%	8.7	8.2	24.6%	10	201	2
2016	DET	10/8	423	92	357	1	3.9	0	-9.8%	--	-5	--	-1	42%	--	33	67	53	371	5	79%	7.0	7.3	3.9%	21	67	15
2017	DET	16/5	472	84	286	3	3.4	1	-9.5%	--	-3	--	-8	39%	--	31	71	53	444	2	75%	8.4	8.2	-4.6%	36	37	30
2018	DET			77	294	4	3.8	2	0.1%								74	56	459	2	76%	8.2		5.3%			

Riddick has been a reliable safety valve for Matthew Stafford. He has 220 receptions in the last four seasons, more than any other running back except Le'Veon Bell (267). He has had back-to-back seasons with 53 receptions while the Lions almost always keep him to single-digit carries each week. The additions of LeGarrette Blount and Kerryon Johnson shouldn't have any real impact on Riddick's role this season.

Jacquizz Rodgers

Height: 5-6 | Weight: 196 | College: Oregon State | Draft: 2011/5 (145) | Born: 6-Feb-1990 | Age: 28 | Risk: Yellow

Year	Team	G/GS	Snaps	Runs	Yds	TD	Yd/R	FUM	DVOA	Rk	DYAR	Rk	YAR	Suc%	Rk	BTkl	Pass	Rec	Yds	TD	C%	Yd/C	YAC	DVOA	Rk	DYAR	Rk
2015	CHI	5/0	41	14	41	0	2.9	0	2.1%	--	7	--	-1	36%	--	2	3	1	10	0	33%	10.0	14.0	-85.8%	--	-13	--
2016	TB	10/5	341	129	560	2	4.3	0	0.2%	19	47	22	64	49%	18	22	16	13	98	0	81%	7.5	6.9	9.3%	--	19	--
2017	TB	16/4	168	64	244	1	3.8	0	-7.7%	--	2	--	15	41%	--	15	11	9	74	0	82%	8.2	9.8	30.5%	--	24	--
2018	TB			25	100	0	4.0	1	-1.8%								12	9	80	0	75%	8.9		10.8%			

Rodgers had at least 52 catches in back-to-back seasons for Atlanta in 2012 and 2013, but he has 52 receptions total since 2014. He's good for a committee and can start in a pitch, but the Buccaneers kept kicking the tires on Doug Martin last season. Rodgers had 40 carries in the season's first three games, but just 24 carries in the final 12 games.

Charles Sims Height: 6-0 Weight: 214 College: West Virginia Draft: 2014/3 (69) Born: 9/19/1990 Age: 28 Risk: Red

Year	Team	G/GS	Snaps	Runs	Yds	TD	Yd/R	FUM	DVOA	Rk	DYAR	Rk	YAR	Suc%	Rk	BTkl	Pass	Rec	Yds	TD	C%	Yd/C	YAC	DVOA	Rk	DYAR	Rk
2015	TB	16/0	457	107	529	0	4.9	2	2.6%	16	50	24	71	57%	2	36	70	51	561	4	73%	11.0	9.5	29.2%	7	150	3
2016	TB	7/2	238	51	149	1	2.9	1	-33.6%	--	-52	--	-56	39%	--	17	32	24	190	1	75%	7.9	7.3	3.5%	22	32	29
2017	TB	16/0	383	21	95	0	4.5	1	2.9%	--	9	--	12	33%	--	7	47	35	249	1	74%	7.1	6.4	-13.4%	45	1	45
2018	TB			25	102	1	4.1	1	3.9%								53	42	344	1	79%	8.2		9.0%			

Here's a wild one. Since 2000, only two running backs have come into the league and had multiple seasons with less than 3.0 yards per carry (minimum 50 rushes): Sims in 2014 and 2016, and his former Tampa Bay teammate Doug Martin the last two years. This says a ton about the blocking in Tampa Bay, but the backs have not been good either. Sims is more of a receiver, but he could be losing touches to rookie Ronald Jones in that area too.

Wendell Smallwood Height: 5-10 Weight: 208 College: West Virginia Draft: 2016/5 (153) Born: 29-Jan-1994 Age: 24 Risk: Green

Year	Team	G/GS	Snaps	Runs	Yds	TD	Yd/R	FUM	DVOA	Rk	DYAR	Rk	YAR	Suc%	Rk	BTkl	Pass	Rec	Yds	TD	C%	Yd/C	YAC	DVOA	Rk	DYAR	Rk
2016	PHI	13/3	164	77	312	1	4.1	1	-3.4%	--	17	--	9	49%	--	12	13	6	55	0	46%	9.2	8.3	-27.6%	--	-9	--
2017	PHI	8/3	172	47	174	1	3.7	0	-19.5%	--	-20	--	-3	36%	--	11	18	13	103	0	72%	7.9	6.7	14.2%	--	30	--
2018	PHI			25	96	0	3.8	1	-5.2%								12	9	69	0	75%	7.6		-1.9%			

Smallwood played a major offensive role in the Week 3 Giants victory (12 carries for 71 yards) and the Week 4 Chargers win (10 carries for 34 yards and a touchdown, four catches for 45 yards). He was then limited by a knee injury and became a weekly healthy scratch when Jay Ajayi arrived. Smallwood and Corey Clement fill similar niches in the running back ecosystem. One of them is a Super Bowl Hero, a Local Boy Made Good, and a fine player to boot. The other is Wendell Smallwood. Guess which one is unlikely to play for the Eagles this season.

Rod Smith Height: 6-3 Weight: 226 College: Ohio State Draft: 2015/FA Born: 10-Jan-1992 Age: 26 Risk: Blue

Year	Team	G/GS	Snaps	Runs	Yds	TD	Yd/R	FUM	DVOA	Rk	DYAR	Rk	YAR	Suc%	Rk	BTkl	Pass	Rec	Yds	TD	C%	Yd/C	YAC	DVOA	Rk	DYAR	Rk
2015	2TM	11/0	26	2	5	0	2.5	0	-12.1%	--	0	--	0	50%	--	1	2	1	6	0	50%	6.0	5.0	40.3%	--	5	--
2016	DAL	7/0	4	0	0	0	0.0	--	--	--	--	--	--	--	--	--	1	1	4	0	100%	4.0	7.0	-85.5%	--	-4	--
2017	DAL	15/1	230	55	232	4	4.2	0	23.9%	--	81	--	82	60%	--	10	23	19	202	1	83%	10.6	9.3	26.9%	--	50	--
2018	DAL			32	128	1	4.0	1	0.7%								15	11	82	1	73%	7.4		-5.3%			

In his third NFL season, Smith finally saw significant action, mixing in some big rushing days (eight carries for 61 yards against San Francisco, six for 47 against the Giants) with some real stinkers (8-11 against Philadelphia, 10-27 against Washington, 7-13 against Oakland). He had established himself as a valuable receiver by the end of the year. In a three-week period against the Giants, Raiders, and Seahawks, he caught each of the 11 passes thrown his way for 157 yards, with an 81-yard touchdown on a simple circle route over the middle in New York. He might get more playing time as a receiving back in 2018, but then Ezekiel Elliott has shown he can be a dangerous receiver in his own right, so Smith's opportunities will still be limited.

Darren Sproles Height: 5-6 Weight: 181 College: Kansas State Draft: 2005/4 (130) Born: 20-Jun-1983 Age: 35 Risk: Red

Year	Team	G/GS	Snaps	Runs	Yds	TD	Yd/R	FUM	DVOA	Rk	DYAR	Rk	YAR	Suc%	Rk	BTkl	Pass	Rec	Yds	TD	C%	Yd/C	YAC	DVOA	Rk	DYAR	Rk
2015	PHI	16/4	393	83	317	3	3.8	1	14.8%	--	80	--	64	49%	--	14	83	55	388	1	66%	7.1	6.5	-24.9%	51	-50	55
2016	PHI	15/5	511	94	438	2	4.7	0	17.6%	--	99	--	83	52%	--	36	71	52	427	2	73%	8.2	7.9	3.0%	24	65	16
2017	PHI	3/0	88	15	61	0	4.1	0	-5.5%	--	2	--	14	40%	--	4	12	7	73	0	58%	10.4	11.9	12.7%	--	16	--
2018	PHI			69	325	1	4.7	1	12.3%								74	51	489	2	69%	9.6		10.0%			

Sproles still had a significant role in the Eagles offense before tearing an ACL in Week 3 against the Giants, catching five passes in the opener against Washington and rushing 10 times in the Week 2 Chiefs loss. The Eagles re-signed him to a one-year deal in the offseason, but penciling in a major role for a 35-year-old, 5-foot-6 all-purpose back coming back from a knee injury is madness. Sproles ranks eighth in NFL history with 19,155 all-purpose yards. He's unlikely to make it to 20,000.

Jonathan Stewart

Height: 5-10   Weight: 235   College: Oregon   Draft: 2008/1 (13)   Born: 21-Mar-1987   Age: 31   Risk: Yellow

Year	Team	G/GS	Snaps	Runs	Yds	TD	Yd/R	FUM	DVOA	Rk	DYAR	Rk	YAR	Suc%	Rk	BTkl	Pass	Rec	Yds	TD	C%	Yd/C	YAC	DVOA	Rk	DYAR	Rk
2015	CAR	13/13	607	242	989	6	4.1	3	-6.2%	34	23	33	78	43%	33	49	21	16	99	1	76%	6.2	7.3	-5.4%	--	10	--
2016	CAR	13/13	565	218	824	9	3.8	3	-11.8%	35	-29	36	9	44%	31	46	21	8	60	0	38%	7.5	9.3	-70.1%	--	-67	--
2017	CAR	15/10	407	198	680	6	3.4	3	-14.8%	43	-54	44	-34	45%	20	34	15	8	52	1	53%	6.5	8.6	-38.8%	--	-20	--
2018	NYG			58	211	2	3.6	2	-3.2%								10	6	36	0	60%	6.0		-32.1%			

There was a time when Stewart was a power runner with surprising speed and agility, when necessary. Stewart could rely on his typical bruising nature to carry him, while also making work of linebackers in space at the second level. Those days of well-rounded athleticism have long passed, yet Stewart still tries to run the same way. Now, Stewart is the heavy, plodding runner whose attempts to get creative in the open field too often fall flat. Only three running backs finished with a worse DYAR in 2017. Dave Gettleman brought Stewart from Carolina to New York as part of his attempt to mold the Giants into a downhill, run-oriented offensive style. However, Wayne Gallman will contest Stewart for the secondary carries behind Saquon Barkley, and Stewart does not provide much of anything as a runner that Gallman does not.

Chris Thompson

Height: 5-8   Weight: 187   College: Florida State   Draft: 2013/5 (154)   Born: 20-Oct-1990   Age: 28   Risk: Red

Year	Team	G/GS	Snaps	Runs	Yds	TD	Yd/R	FUM	DVOA	Rk	DYAR	Rk	YAR	Suc%	Rk	BTkl	Pass	Rec	Yds	TD	C%	Yd/C	YAC	DVOA	Rk	DYAR	Rk
2015	WAS	13/0	274	35	216	0	6.2	2	8.0%	--	22	--	25	43%	--	8	48	35	240	2	73%	6.9	4.7	-15.6%	45	-5	46
2016	WAS	16/0	489	68	356	3	5.2	2	33.9%	--	111	--	99	53%	--	30	62	49	349	2	79%	7.1	5.1	10.6%	17	77	13
2017	WAS	10/1	338	64	294	2	4.6	1	-4.9%	--	9	--	8	42%	--	29	54	39	510	4	72%	13.1	12.2	67.3%	1	223	3
2018	WAS			55	251	1	4.6	2	3.0%								71	52	414	1	73%	8.0		8.7%			

Thompson's 804 yards from scrimmage were just 19 yards short of the team lead even though he missed the final third of the season with a broken leg. He was very much a boom-or-bust runner—of the 72 runners with at least 60 carries, he was in the bottom 15 in stuff rate, but the top 10 in open-field yards. It's as a receiver, though, where he really shined. He averaged 11.1 yards after the catch out of the backfield, fifth-best among qualifying backs. Washington only threw him eight passes when he was wide or in the slot, but he caught five of them for 124 yards. In just ten games, he had nine catches of 20 or more yards, more than any running back except Todd Gurley (12) and Alvin Kamara (11). He also had ten catches for third-down conversions; only four running backs had more. Add it all up, and Thompson had the best receiving DVOA of any qualifying running back since 2008, and the best we've ever measured for any runner with at least 50 targets.

Top Receiving DVOA by Running Backs, 1986-2017

Year	Player	Team	DYAR	Rank	DVOA	Rank	Rec	Passes	Yards	TD	C%	Rec Fum
2008	Darren Sproles	SD	167	4	70.7%	1	29	34	348	5	85%	1
2004	Larry Johnson	KC	141	5	70.0%	1	22	28	278	2	79%	0
2003	Tony Fisher	GB	96	10	68.7%	1	21	25	206	2	84%	0
1996	Jerris McPhail	MIA	118	6	67.3%	1	20	29	282	0	69%	0
2017	**Chris Thompson**	**WAS**	**223**	**3**	**67.3%**	**1**	**39**	**54**	**510**	**4**	**72%**	**0**
1990	Barry Sanders	DET	186	2	67.0%	1	36	49	480	3	73%	0
1997	Jamal Anderson	ATL	141	4	66.5%	1	29	37	284	3	78%	1
1999	Marshall Faulk	STL	419	1	64.8%	1	87	104	1048	5	84%	0
2011	Charles Clay	MIA	119	6	62.5%	1	16	25	233	3	64%	0
1997	Larry Bowie	WAS	174	3	61.8%	2	34	40	388	2	85%	1

Minimum 25 passes.

Thompson is unlikely to be that effective in 2018 (or ever again, honestly), but he should remain one of the NFL's premier third-down backs.

Mike Tolbert   Height: 5-9   Weight: 243   College: Coastal Carolina   Draft: 2008/FA   Born: 23-Nov-1985   Age: 33   Risk: N/A

Year	Team	G/GS	Snaps	Runs	Yds	TD	Yd/R	FUM	DVOA	Rk	DYAR	Rk	YAR	Suc%	Rk	BTkl	Pass	Rec	Yds	TD	C%	Yd/C	YAC	DVOA	Rk	DYAR	Rk
2015	CAR	16/3	422	62	256	1	4.1	0	9.8%	--	54	--	53	56%	--	12	23	18	154	3	78%	8.6	7.6	25.3%	--	56	--
2016	CAR	16/2	324	35	114	0	3.3	0	-18.6%	--	-14	--	-7	37%	--	11	15	10	72	1	67%	7.2	8.7	0.2%	--	11	--
2017	BUF	12/0	203	66	247	1	3.7	2	-12.1%	--	-9	--	-31	39%	--	15	17	14	78	0	82%	5.6	3.4	-44.2%	--	-24	--

The only running backs with more carries and a lower rushing DVOA than Tolbert last season were Mike Davis, Elijah McGuire, and Eddie Lacy. Tolbert was also a part of Rick Dennison's beloved fullback outlet pass. He and Patrick DiMarco combined to catch 21 of 27 targets thrown to them, for -47 DYAR. Wow, it's surprising this hasn't caught on elsewhere! A free agent as of press time, Tolbert was a beloved player for a long time, but teams are increasingly reluctant to carry fullbacks or fullback-only special-teamers.

Robert Turbin   Height: 5-10   Weight: 222   College: Utah State   Draft: 2012/4 (106)   Born: 2-Dec-1989   Age: 29   Risk: Green

Year	Team	G/GS	Snaps	Runs	Yds	TD	Yd/R	FUM	DVOA	Rk	DYAR	Rk	YAR	Suc%	Rk	BTkl	Pass	Rec	Yds	TD	C%	Yd/C	YAC	DVOA	Rk	DYAR	Rk
2015	2TM	10/0	150	50	199	1	4.0	0	13.5%	--	45	--	32	48%	--	9	10	7	23	0	70%	3.3	3.7	-89.2%	--	-31	--
2016	IND	15/0	300	47	164	7	3.5	0	32.2%	--	96	--	83	61%	--	17	35	26	179	1	74%	6.9	8.4	-14.2%	43	-1	43
2017	IND	6/1	124	23	53	1	2.3	0	-2.4%	--	7	--	0	52%	--	5	11	9	56	0	82%	6.2	7.7	-16.9%	--	-1	--
2018	IND			24	82	0	3.4	1	-10.9%								8	6	49	1	75%	8.1		6.1%			

Turbin was working as the starter in May and June, and Frank Reich indicated he could be in line for an important role. Turbin's career, including a 2017 season truncated by an arm injury, indicates he might just be a "you must be at least this good to play" placeholder for the trio of young backs, and his starter status was partly the result of Marlon Mack's injury absence. But protecting Andrew Luck will be a priority, and Turbin's veteran status may give him an edge as a backfield player on pass downs for that reason. First he'll have to get through a four-game suspension for a positive PED test.

Shane Vereen   Height: 5-10   Weight: 205   College: California   Draft: 2011/2 (56)   Born: 2-Mar-1989   Age: 29   Risk: N/A

Year	Team	G/GS	Snaps	Runs	Yds	TD	Yd/R	FUM	DVOA	Rk	DYAR	Rk	YAR	Suc%	Rk	BTkl	Pass	Rec	Yds	TD	C%	Yd/C	YAC	DVOA	Rk	DYAR	Rk
2015	NYG	16/0	431	61	260	0	4.3	1	-4.8%	--	9	--	20	41%	--	15	81	59	494	4	73%	8.4	7.2	8.4%	17	103	9
2016	NYG	5/1	117	33	158	1	4.8	2	-7.8%	--	1	--	14	45%	--	13	19	11	94	0	58%	8.5	8.0	-33.6%	--	-19	--
2017	NYG	16/0	325	45	164	0	3.6	0	-22.6%	--	-22	--	-13	42%	--	10	53	44	253	0	83%	5.8	5.6	-22.7%	54	-26	55

Following a fairly productive 2014 season in New England as a situational back and pass-catcher, Vereen appeared to be primed for a stable career as a rotational player. Over the past three seasons with the New York Giants, Vereen has not done much to fulfill that reality. Vereen had his least efficient season as both a runner and a passer in 2017. Once a back with great balance and power, as well as a sneaky knack for catching balls down the field, Vereen devolved into a lumbering battering ram for the Giants. Even as a pass-catcher, Vereen was demoted almost exclusively to checkdown duty, no different than the handful of other running backs on the team. In a crowded backfield with no clear top back, Vereen had a chance last season to emerge as the bellcow in New York, but it never came together for him. Currently unsigned.

Spencer Ware   Height: 5-10   Weight: 228   College: Louisiana State   Draft: 2013/6 (194)   Born: 23-Nov-1991   Age: 27   Risk: Green

Year	Team	G/GS	Snaps	Runs	Yds	TD	Yd/R	FUM	DVOA	Rk	DYAR	Rk	YAR	Suc%	Rk	BTkl	Pass	Rec	Yds	TD	C%	Yd/C	YAC	DVOA	Rk	DYAR	Rk
2015	KC	11/2	159	72	403	6	5.6	0	25.8%	--	106	--	144	58%	--	12	6	6	5	0	100%	0.8	2.0	-167.8%	--	-42	--
2016	KC	14/14	546	214	921	3	4.3	4	-2.7%	22	54	20	72	53%	7	55	42	33	447	2	79%	13.5	11.4	32.7%	2	115	8
2018	KC			51	236	1	4.6	1	5.5%								11	9	71	1	82%	7.8		14.7%			

Ware had the spotlight before Kareem Hunt strolled along to steal it. Primed to be the starting running back heading into 2017, Ware tore the PCL in his right knee in Week 3 of the preseason. Though not an explosive runner, Ware is efficient and consistent. Ware plays a tough, grounded style of football that enables him to squeeze the most out of typical running plays and fall forward for a couple yards here and there, as seen in his 2016 success rate. Ware also possesses surprising skills as a pass-catcher given his short, stocky build and bulldozer style of running. Ware can catch out of the backfield effectively and make quick work of smaller defensive backs trying to give him a run for his money on the perimeter. Hunt's the established starter now, but if he's healthy, Ware will serve as one of the best secondary running backs in the league.

DeAndre Washington Height: 5-8   Weight: 204   College: Texas Tech   Draft: 2016/5 (143)   Born: 22-Feb-1993   Age: 25   Risk: Green

Year	Team	G/GS	Snaps	Runs	Yds	TD	Yd/R	FUM	DVOA	Rk	DYAR	Rk	YAR	Suc%	Rk	BTkl	Pass	Rec	Yds	TD	C%	Yd/C	YAC	DVOA	Rk	DYAR	Rk
2016	OAK	14/2	241	87	467	2	5.4	1	7.0%	--	55	--	78	47%	--	14	23	17	115	0	74%	6.8	6.8	-12.9%	--	1	--
2017	OAK	15/0	223	57	153	2	2.7	2	-33.1%	--	-55	--	-34	40%	--	23	45	34	197	1	76%	5.8	4.9	-13.6%	46	1	46
2018	OAK			25	97	0	3.9	1	-5.1%								22	16	114	1	73%	7.1		-6.7%			

Raiders offensive coordinator Todd Dowling never quite figured out how to assign roles in his committee backfield last year. Washington was the Guy Who Gets Carries Because We Don't Want to Overwork Marshawn Lynch crossed with the Maybe Third-Down Back. He was ineffective at both tasks, so by December he was getting two or three random touches per game. Washington and Jalen Richard are similar backs and may compete for the No. 3 job behind Lynch and Doug Martin. Then again, Jon Gruden may sour on both of them and try to sign Jamaal Charles or something.

Charcandrick West Height: 5-10   Weight: 205   College: Abilene Christian   Draft: 2014/FA   Born: 2-Jun-1991   Age: 27   Risk: Red

Year	Team	G/GS	Snaps	Runs	Yds	TD	Yd/R	FUM	DVOA	Rk	DYAR	Rk	YAR	Suc%	Rk	BTkl	Pass	Rec	Yds	TD	C%	Yd/C	YAC	DVOA	Rk	DYAR	Rk
2015	KC	15/9	497	160	634	4	4.0	1	2.8%	15	77	20	74	45%	27	29	34	20	214	1	59%	10.7	11.9	-20.4%	48	-13	50
2016	KC	15/2	358	88	293	1	3.3	0	-25.5%	--	-60	--	-56	36%	--	19	34	28	188	2	82%	6.7	6.5	-3.0%	29	21	31
2017	KC	13/0	224	18	72	2	4.0	1	-11.4%	--	-2	--	10	33%	--	10	34	27	150	2	79%	5.6	4.9	-31.6%	59	-31	57
2018	KC			17	59	0	3.4	1	-11.2%								18	13	91	0	72%	7.0		-11.9%			

It feels like just yesterday West was a league-winning midseason fantasy pickup in the wake of Jamaal Charles' injury in 2015. The journey for West since that time has been interesting. Over the past two seasons, West has seen his workload in the run game diminished, but has remained stable as a pass-catching option out of the backfield. West is somewhat of a nuisance to deal with in the open field, making him a viable pass-catcher, but he lacks the balance and decisiveness as a runner to conduct a reliable ground game. Andy Reid opted to stress Kareem Hunt with nearly 300 carries in 2017 instead of looking to West for relief, and there is not much reason to expect that to change moving forward, especially with Spencer Ware's return from injury.

Terrance West Height: 5-9   Weight: 225   College: Towson   Draft: 2014/3 (94)   Born: 1/28/1991   Age: 27   Risk: N/A

Year	Team	G/GS	Snaps	Runs	Yds	TD	Yd/R	FUM	DVOA	Rk	DYAR	Rk	YAR	Suc%	Rk	BTkl	Pass	Rec	Yds	TD	C%	Yd/C	YAC	DVOA	Rk	DYAR	Rk
2015	2TM	8/0	125	62	231	0	3.7	2	-17.2%	--	-22	--	-35	42%	--	8	5	4	21	0	80%	5.3	4.5	-40.7%	--	-7	--
2016	BAL	16/13	443	193	774	5	4.0	2	-8.2%	28	3	28	-10	42%	33	49	45	34	236	1	76%	6.9	7.0	4.9%	20	50	19
2017	BAL	5/4	66	39	138	2	3.5	1	0.2%	--	14	--	18	51%	--	7	4	2	23	0	50%	11.5	10.5	0.7%	--	4	--

It seemed like a storybook ending. After a rocky start to his career, West, a Baltimore native and Towson grad, came home to the Ravens and won the starting job heading into last season. But then Alex Collins went and pissed on the campfire. West hurt his calf, sank to fourth string as a healthy scratch, was cut loose at season's end, and is now without a team. You really can't go home again.

James White Height: 5-9   Weight: 204   College: Wisconsin   Draft: 2014/4 (130)   Born: 3-Feb-1992   Age: 26   Risk: Yellow

Year	Team	G/GS	Snaps	Runs	Yds	TD	Yd/R	FUM	DVOA	Rk	DYAR	Rk	YAR	Suc%	Rk	BTkl	Pass	Rec	Yds	TD	C%	Yd/C	YAC	DVOA	Rk	DYAR	Rk
2015	NE	14/1	290	22	56	2	2.5	0	-22.1%	--	-12	--	-13	32%	--	9	54	40	410	4	74%	10.3	8.7	33.3%	5	140	4
2016	NE	16/4	426	39	166	0	4.3	0	7.8%	--	24	--	24	51%	--	16	86	60	551	5	70%	9.2	8.8	20.1%	10	163	3
2017	NE	14/4	384	43	171	0	4.0	0	-9.3%	--	-1	--	8	51%	--	10	72	56	429	3	78%	7.7	6.1	6.4%	20	86	13
2018	NE			64	254	1	4.0	2	-3.1%								71	57	496	3	80%	8.7		20.8%			

The offseason for White was all about talking up how Shane Vereen mentored him as a rookie and how he's willing to do that if a rookie shows up in New England. Surprise, one did! White has been a reliable receiving-down back who also happened to rush for a winning touchdown in Super Bowl LI. With no signs of a downturn, White will probably stick around as a steady hand through the end of his contract (after 2020).

Jordan Wilkins   Height: 6-1   Weight: 216   College: Mississippi   Draft: 2018/5 (169)   Born: 18-Jul-1994   Age: 24   Risk: Green

Year	Team	G/GS	Snaps	Runs	Yds	TD	Yd/R	FUM	DVOA	Rk	DYAR	Rk	YAR	Suc%	Rk	BTkl	Pass	Rec	Yds	TD	C%	Yd/C	YAC	DVOA	Rk	DYAR	Rk
2018	IND		70	312	1	4.4	1	3.8%									14	11	84	0	79%	7.6		-4.3%			

In a different situation, Wilkins might be an intriguing deep fantasy play, a fifth-round pick with 1,011 yards in his one year as a starter at Ole Miss and some all-around ability highlighted by an above-average 53 percent success rate on receptions. In Indianapolis, though, he'll likely remain in a murky committee, behind Marlon Mack and fourth-round pick Nyheim Hines in the role for passing-game duties and possibly behind Robert Turbin for grinder work.

Damien Williams   Height: 5-11   Weight: 221   College: Oklahoma   Draft: 2014/FA   Born: 3-Apr-1992   Age: 26   Risk: Red

Year	Team	G/GS	Snaps	Runs	Yds	TD	Yd/R	FUM	DVOA	Rk	DYAR	Rk	YAR	Suc%	Rk	BTkl	Pass	Rec	Yds	TD	C%	Yd/C	YAC	DVOA	Rk	DYAR	Rk
2015	MIA	16/0	159	16	59	0	3.7	1	-49.1%	--	-28	--	-27	31%	--	7	28	21	142	1	75%	6.8	4.2	-7.4%	35	10	37
2016	MIA	15/0	160	35	115	3	3.3	1	6.3%	--	22	--	9	37%	--	14	31	23	249	3	74%	10.8	9.0	12.5%	14	45	21
2017	MIA	11/4	195	46	181	0	3.9	0	-22.7%	--	-25	--	-28	28%	--	20	28	20	155	1	71%	7.8	7.7	12.2%	15	44	27
2018	KC		20	93	0	4.6	1	6.3%									17	12	88	0	71%	7.3		-7.7%			

In Andy Reid's mind, there is no such thing as a shortage of running backs who can catch out of the backfield. Being a quality runner is not even a requirement for such players, despite "running" literally being part of the title. Williams is of that exact mold: a running back who is not a valuable runner, but can be a nice piece in the passing game. Williams has reliable hands and a decent sense for how to play in space, as well as the flexibility to be play out of the slot on occasion. With a loaded running back room in Kansas City, it is unlikely that Williams sees many touches, but good on Reid for seeking out his archetype and securing an insurance plan in the case of injury.

Jamaal Williams   Height: 6-0   Weight: 212   College: BYU   Draft: 2017/4 (134)   Born: 3-Apr-1995   Age: 23   Risk: Green

Year	Team	G/GS	Snaps	Runs	Yds	TD	Yd/R	FUM	DVOA	Rk	DYAR	Rk	YAR	Suc%	Rk	BTkl	Pass	Rec	Yds	TD	C%	Yd/C	YAC	DVOA	Rk	DYAR	Rk
2017	GB	16/7	443	153	556	4	3.6	0	7.4%	12	108	12	86	48%	14	23	34	25	262	2	74%	10.5	10.2	29.9%	11	84	17
2018	GB		139	606	5	4.4	1	4.4%									37	29	226	1	78%	7.8		6.9%			

Williams was the first of three running backs drafted by Green Bay in 2017. After injuries to Ty Montgomery and fellow rookie Aaron Jones, Williams led the team in carries and rushing yards. Jones was actually more effective on a per-run basis, but Williams was much better as a receiver than Jones. This trio is going to give the Packers many options, but Williams' pass protection could give him an edge in winning the RB1 job.

Kerwynn Williams   Height: 5-8   Weight: 195   College: Utah State   Draft: 2013/7 (230)   Born: 9-Jun-1991   Age: 27   Risk: Green

Year	Team	G/GS	Snaps	Runs	Yds	TD	Yd/R	FUM	DVOA	Rk	DYAR	Rk	YAR	Suc%	Rk	BTkl	Pass	Rec	Yds	TD	C%	Yd/C	YAC	DVOA	Rk	DYAR	Rk
2015	ARI	6/0	51	27	142	1	5.3	1	-27.1%	--	-19	--	-9	37%	--	3	2	2	16	0	100%	8.0	3.5	60.8%	--	8	--
2016	ARI	10/0	51	18	157	2	8.7	0	78.7%	--	69	--	62	56%	--	4	2	1	6	0	50%	6.0	7.0	-6.6%	--	1	--
2017	ARI	16/6	241	120	426	1	3.6	0	-6.6%	32	10	35	17	43%	28	20	15	10	93	0	67%	9.3	4.6	11.6%	--	21	--
2018	KC		17	59	0	3.4	0	-11.2%									9	6	42	0	67%	7.0		-11.9%			

Williams' role gradually got larger over the course of the season. Initially, Arizona tried to replace David Johnson with Chris Johnson and Adrian Peterson, but it was 2017 and not 2009, leading to some disastrous results for the Arizona offense. Williams was not particularly efficient himself, and his lack of production led to the former Utah State product signing only a one-year contract with the Chiefs to compete for a backup role behind Kareem Hunt. It would not be surprising if Williams is looking for another new team in a few months considering the other players present in the Kansas City backfield.

T.J. Yeldon · Height: 6-1 · Weight: 226 · College: Alabama · Draft: 2015/2 (36) · Born: 2-Oct-1993 · Age: 25 · Risk: Green

Year	Team	G/GS	Snaps	Runs	Yds	TD	Yd/R	FUM	DVOA	Rk	DYAR	Rk	YAR	Suc%	Rk	BTkl	Pass	Rec	Yds	TD	C%	Yd/C	YAC	DVOA	Rk	DYAR	Rk
2015	JAX	12/12	620	182	740	2	4.1	0	-3.2%	28	39	26	31	42%	38	38	46	36	279	1	78%	7.8	8.3	5.7%	20	52	23
2016	JAX	15/13	576	130	465	1	3.6	2	-24.8%	41	-81	38	-57	38%	42	42	68	50	312	1	74%	6.2	7.1	-27.9%	49	-52	53
2017	JAX	10/0	230	49	253	2	5.2	2	-6.7%	--	4	--	-3	43%	--	13	41	30	224	0	73%	7.5	6.3	-9.9%	40	8	42
2018	JAX			81	381	2	4.7	3	1.1%								49	37	284	1	76%	7.7		-0.6%			

The departure of Chris Ivory promotes Yeldon from the murkier depths of the running back chart to Leonard Fournette's immediate backup. That is less alluring than it sounds: the 2015 second-round pick has been in Jacksonville for three seasons now and never had a positive DVOA. Yeldon has been praised repeatedly by the coaching staff, but his carry total has gone down every year thus far and he fumbled twice last season in only 49 carries. He fared little better as a receiver, posting the only negative DVOA of the team's top four running backs.

Going Deep

Kalen Ballage, MIA: A fourth-round rookie out of Arizona State, Ballage has an enticing fantasy profile in that he's blazing fast and has feature-back size. What he does not have quite so much of is the nuanced and layered techniques it takes to run at the NFL level. He's going to return kicks and be a solid outlet receiver on third down either way, but how much he can learn as a runner is going to dictate a lot about his future.

Kenjon Barner, CAR: Kenjon comes home! Barner was a 2013 draft pick for the Panthers, later traded to Philadelphia to reunite him with college coach Chip Kelly. Now he's back, as Fozzy Whittaker's torn ACL opened up a roster slot. Barner isn't going to be a factor on offense, but he has kick return and special teams experience, and might be able to take some of the return load off of Christian McCaffrey.

Kapri Bibbs, WAS: After bouncing on and off Denver's roster for three years, Bibbs was traded to San Francisco during the 2017 draft, but then failed to make the 49ers roster. Washington signed him in November and he showed some surprising ability as a receiver, with 14 catches for 128 yards and a touchdown in three games. That might have been enough to win him another job in 2018, though it may not be in Washington, where the backfield is quite crowded.

Brandon Bolden, NE: What used to happen is the Patriots would get some backs dinged up and let special teams demon Bolden take a few carries, often with surprisingly decent results. The Pats wised up and started signing more backs, and Bolden has 14 carries in the last two seasons.

Mack Brown, MIN: The only notable play of Brown's brief career was his 61-yard touchdown run for Washington against Chicago in 2016. It was one of those plays where Brown could have gone down at any point after 4 yards and the game would have ended with Washington already up 34-21 with just over a minute remaining. To be fair, Brown also broke a 60-yard touchdown run in the preseason that year, albeit in a game loaded with backups. He's only going to see the field this year if Dalvin Cook or Latavius Murray is injured.

Travaris Cadet, BUF: Over the past three seasons, Cadet has 38 carries and 95 pass targets. Nobody is fooled here, so he's more of a change-up against teams who are too stubborn to realize that Cadet is a receiver playing running back. In Buffalo, that goes double. Any time LeSean McCoy is off the field for Cadet, defenses should see a neon sign that says "we will not run the ball" and act accordingly. Buffalo's offensive staff is sorry, sorry, they're trying to delete it.

Trenton Cannon, NYJ: The 204th pick in the draft out of Virginia State, Cannon blew up his pro day, with a 4.40-second 40-yard dash and a 1.49-second 10-yard split. Cannon is a slight back without much of a history of receiving prowess, and nobody really picked up on the CIAA offensive player of the year as an easy NFL fit. But he's a lotto ticket for the Jets. In all likelihood, he either returns kicks and gets a handful of carries, or is never written about in this book again.

Matthew Dayes, CLE: Dayes was a seventh-round pick last year because he only ran a 4.66-second 40 at his pro day. He was the third running back for a team that now has three other good running backs, so his best shot at a roster spot is to keep the kick return job.

Lance Dunbar, FA: The most interesting thing to happen to Dunbar this past season was getting cut—five days before he was scheduled to be a free agent anyway. He missed most of 2017 with the latest in a series of knee injuries, ending up with just 11 carries and three pass targets for the Rams. When healthy, Dunbar is a solid third-down back, though that "when" is looming larger with each passing year. As of press time, Dunbar remains unsigned.

Chase Edmonds, ARI: After a decorated career at FCS Fordham, Edmonds was a fourth-round pick in April's draft. He was named a first-team FCS All-American in 2016 before an ankle injury in his senior season hampered his production. Edmonds was the first Fordham player drafted since former Cardinals quarterback John Skelton in 2010. Arizona will certainly be hoping things work out better this time.

Trey Edmunds, NO: Edmunds was removed as the Saints' kick returner after just three returns early last season. He only carried the ball in one game, against Buffalo, but had a 41-yard touchdown run. He could be in the mix for some early-season touches thanks to Mark Ingram's four-game suspension. Edmunds comes from a football family where each member played a different position. Father Ferrell was a tight end drafted by Miami in 1988. Trey's brothers Terrell (safety for Pittsburgh) and Tremaine (linebacker for Buffalo) were drafted this year.

Tyler Ervin, HOU: Squint hard enough and you can talk yourself into Ervin a little bit as a useful satellite back for the 2018 Texans. He has held the return jobs when healthy, had a couple touches a game, positional depth is limited, and general manager Brian Gaine said he expected a similar role for Ervin next year. All that is pending successful return from an October patellar tendon injury, which is a huge question mark.

Josh Ferguson, IND: Ferguson went from 35 touches on offense as a rookie to four in his second season, and any opportunity created by the departure of Frank Gore was more than dashed by the selection of two backs in the draft. At this point, he's depth in case one of the four backs ahead of him gets hurt.

David Fluellen, TEN: Though officially listed as a running back, Fluellen contributes almost exclusively on special teams for the Titans. He played 66 percent of special teams snaps, primarily as a blocker on kick and punt returns. After four years in the league, Fluellen only has four career carries—all of them in the first four games of last season—and one career kick return to his name.

D.J. Foster, ARI: In his second year after going undrafted out of Arizona State, Foster carved out a small role as a pass-catching back in the Cardinals' piecemeal attempt to fill the hole left after David Johnson was injured. The hometown kid will likely not have much of a role now that Johnson is healthy again, but at least he got to play in front of his family as a professional.

De'Angelo Henderson, DEN: A 5-foot-7 fireplug of a seventh-round pick who shined in training camp and the preseason last year, Henderson received just nine regular season touches in 2017, one of them a 29-yard touchdown catch in the meaningless season finale. He'll compete for carries with Royce Freeman, who appears poised to take over C.J. Anderson's role; and Devontae Booker, who has at least one year remaining on his guaranteed scholarship.

Brian Hill, CIN: Hill was picked in the fifth round in 2017 by the Falcons, then placed on the practice squad, where he was swiped by Cincy. Somehow both teams missed the fact that Hill was playing with a serious hand injury that required offseason surgery. "Football was fun with 1 hand!" Hill tweeted after the procedure. He has a nice blend of size and burst, though he may need a rash of injuries (not his own) to ever fully prove what he can do.

Akeem Hunt, KC: Hunt is the spokesman for ideal depth running backs. Hunt ran a 4.4-second 40-yard dash at his pro day at Purdue and posted impressive marks throughout the rest of his athletic testing. He has the explosive ability to make plays on occasion, both as a runner and as a pass catcher out of the backfield. Hunt also averaged 24.4 yards per kickoff return, ranking among the best in the league for full-time kick returners. It is hard to ask for more than that from a third- or fourth-string running back.

Chris Johnson, FA: Johnson's third season in Arizona was an abbreviated one to forget. After David Johnson's injury, the artist formerly known as CJ2K was unable to sufficiently fill that massive hole, posting -19 rushing DYAR on 45 carries, so the Cardinals traded for Adrian Peterson. In 2009, a tandem of Chris Johnson and Peterson would have been the envy of the league, but the pairing was never meant to be, as Peterson ended up taking Johnson's roster spot.

Matt Jones, PHI: A 2015 third-round selection by Washington with three 100-yard games to his credit, Jones has five touches in the last season and a half, four of them on the final plays of the Colts' 28-point loss to the Seahawks. Cut loose by Indianapolis after they drafted two running backs, his path to touches is no clearer in Philadelphia.

John Kelly, LAR: In the run game, this sixth-round rookie was more than a little boom-or-bust. A full 27 percent of his carries at Tennessee went for no gain or negative yards, resulting in just a 36 percent success rate. When he does get past the line of scrimmage, however, he's a stout and tough tackle-breaker who's hard to bring down. He also has soft hands and is a very good receiver out of the backfield and has above-average pass protection skills for a rookie. That gives him a good shot at sticking as a third-down back and giving Todd Gurley some much-needed rest. "Chief of Staff" would be an awesome running back nickname.

T.J. Logan, ARI: A fifth-round pick in 2017, Logan missed the entire season thanks to a wrist injury suffered during the preseason. Logan will be competing for a role as both a backup running back and a kick returner. During his college career at North Carolina, Logan returned five kickoffs for touchdowns, which was both a school record and two shy of the all-time NCAA record.

Byron Marshall, WAS: Washington signed Marshall off of Philadelphia's practice squad after Chris Thompson was lost for the year, but he lasted only three games before suffering his own season-ending leg injury. Marshall went undrafted out of Oregon and has only 267 all-purpose yards in his first two NFL seasons. He might not get to 268.

Devante Mays, GB: Mays' first NFL touch was a 4-yard loss and lost fumble. He fumbled on his second carry as well, and he ended his season with a reception for minus-2 yards on a fourth-and-9. His seven touches in 2017 netted a single yard, and he had zero successful plays. After averaging 2.7 yards per carry in the preseason too, there's little hope to believe that Mays will ever have value for Green Bay.

Raheem Mostert, SF: Since entering the league as an undrafted free agent in 2015, Mostert has played for five different teams, primarily as a kick returner. In his freshman year at Purdue, Mostert set a school record with an average of 33.5 yards per return for the season. Unfortunately for him, he has not had much of an opportunity to make his mark in the return game as a pro.

Marcus Murphy, BUF: America was forced to learn about Murphy last January when the playoffs hit and LeSean McCoy's status was questionable, and Murphy improbably was his backup. A veteran of four different practice squads and a decent returner, Murphy plays up to a spot on an NFL roster. That spot is not "starting running back in a playoff game."

Branden Oliver, FA: Oliver was ineffective after returning from an Achilles injury at the start of last season, averaging just 2.4 yards per carry before the Chargers shut him down for most of the second half of the season with a hamstring injury. Oliver was unsigned at press time. The bloom is long off the "fantasy sleeper" rose.

Paul Perkins, FA: This time last year, Perkins was primed to be the Week 1 starter for the New York Giants. After a decent rookie year in 2016, Perkins looked like someone who could become a staple back, but instead suffered a rib injury early in the season and never regained his starting spot upon return. Perkins was extremely ineffective prior to injury, with -30 DYAR and a 2.2-yard average on 41 rushing attempts that cemented him firmly behind teammate Orleans Darkwa. Perkins was released by the Giants this offseason following a non-football pectoral injury.

Senorise Perry, MIA: Four years after entering the league, Perry got the first eight carries of his career in two games against Denver and Buffalo as Miami played out the string. He's a solid special-teamer.

Stevan Ridley, PIT: Ridley was a late-season addition in Pittsburgh, joining the team after James Conner went down. He ended up with 35 DYAR in Week 17 as the Steelers rested Le'Veon Bell, which earned him at least another look in training camp. Ridley has only had 65 carries since he tore his ACL and MCL in 2014.

Jaylen Samuels, PIT: A fifth-round pick out of North Carolina State, Samuels does not fit neatly into standard NFL positional brackets. On draft day, he was listed as a fullback, but that's not quite right—most fullbacks don't end up as the all-time leader in receptions at their college. At the combine, he was listed as a tight end, but that's not quite right either—a 6-foot-0, 225-pound tight end would have been both the shortest and lightest player at that position in 2017. The Steelers list him as a running back, but that's not quite right—he wasn't asked to run between the tackles much and isn't going to be replacing Le'Veon Bell anytime soon. Samuels can do a little bit of everything, from lining up in the slot and separating from linebackers to breaking tackles on the goal line to being an asset returning kicks. There's plenty of potential for use as a general offensive weapon with a clever offensive coordinator. To stick around long-term, Samuels will have to find at least one thing he does *very* well, as opposed to fifty things he does *fairly* well, but there's plenty of potential here.

Bo Scarbrough, DAL: Scarbrough rushed for 1,408 yards in his last two years at Alabama, third on the team behind Damien Harris and quarterback Jalen Hurts. Rather than spend another season in his teammates' shadows, he declared for the draft early, and Dallas grabbed him in the seventh round. With carries so hard to come by in Tuscaloosa, it's not surprising that Scarbrough's BackCAST projection was a poor -20.9%, but Speed Score pegged him as one of the top five backs at the combine. He ran for 20 touchdowns for the Crimson Tide and could vulture some scores away from Ezekiel Elliott this year.

Boston Scott, NO: Let the Darren Sproles comparisons begin, because Scott is just 5-foot-6 like Sproles, and it is believed that he will be in the mix for punt return duties. However, Scott never returned a punt at Louisiana Tech and was marginal as a kick returner, with zero touchdowns. He also had just 32 receptions in college but did have his first 1,000-yard rushing season in 2017. The Saints have done a great job with unheralded backs, but don't count on Scott to be the next Sproles or Pierre Thomas.

Ito Smith, ATL: Since hiring Dan Quinn, the Falcons have drafted a player who attended the Senior Bowl every year, including Grady Jarrett, Deion Jones, and Duke Riley. They continued that trend this year with the selection of Southern Mississippi running back Ito Smith in the fourth round. The selection of Smith came as a bit of a surprise, but Atlanta is going to have a tough decision to make about Tevin Coleman as his contract expires this offseason; Smith could wind up being insurance for Coleman.

Fitzgerald Toussaint, PIT: Toussaint lost his spot on the 53-man roster to rookie James Conner last season, spending half the year on the practice squad. He'll be battling Stevan Ridley for the third running back slot and will be counting on his special teams value—he has returned kickoffs and spent plenty of time on kick coverage units—to put him over the top.

Mark Walton, CIN: Walton was something of a surprise choice out of Miami in the fourth round, as he isn't likely to take snaps from Joe Mixon or Gio Bernard in the immediate future. But he profiles as Gio insurance (Geico for Gio?), sporting a similar skill set of lateral burst, elusiveness, and good hands, assuming he is fully recovered from the ankle injury that ended his season at The U. Maybe the Bengals will figure out a way to use Walton better than they have Bernard.

Dwayne Washington, DET: Washington is the first running back since Rodney Culver (1992-93) to average less than 3.0 yards per carry in each of his first two seasons (minimum 20 carries). The backfield is too crowded for the Lions to keep Washington around.

Fozzy Whittaker, CAR: A third-down back and sometimes return man, Whittaker tore his right ACL during OTAs and will not play in 2018.

David Williams, DEN: Williams is a big, upright-running back who transferred to Arkansas in 2017 after getting lost in the crowd at South Carolina. The Broncos signed him as an undrafted free agent and likely camp body.

Joe Williams, SF: Williams was a fourth-round pick in 2017 but spent his entire rookie season on injured reserve due to an ankle injury he suffered in September. He briefly retired from football in 2016 before returning midseason and subsequently running for 332 yards in his second game back with Utah. Williams will need to overcome Matt Breida to win the role as primary backup to offseason acquisition Jerick McKinnon.

Jonathan Williams, NO: The Bills drafted Williams in the fifth round in 2016 when they needed to get another LeSean McCoy backup, but he did not make the final roster cut in 2017. The Saints never activated him last year and he'll have a lot of competition to back up the duo of Mark Ingram and Alvin Kamara this year.

Zach Zenner, DET: It's well known that Detroit's run blocking was poor last season, but Zenner averaged a team-low 1.9 yards per carry on 14 runs. He did not catch a pass, with Theo Riddick a much more attractive option there. There's little reason to keep Zenner around after the Lions added LeGarrette Blount and Kerryon Johnson.

Wide Receivers

In the following two sections we provide the last three years of statistics, as well as a 2018 KUBIAK projection, for every wide receiver and tight end who either played a significant role in 2017 or is expected to do so in 2018.

The first line contains biographical data—each player's name, height, weight, college, draft position, birth date, and age. Height and weight are the best data we could find; weight, of course, can fluctuate during the off-season. **Age** is very simple, the number of years between the player's birth year and 2018, but birth date is provided if you want to figure out exact age.

Draft position gives draft year and round, with the overall pick number with which the player was taken in parentheses. In the sample table, it says that DeAndre Hopkins was chosen in the 2013 NFL draft with the 27th overall pick in the first round. Undrafted free agents are listed as "FA" with the year they came into the league, even if they were only in training camp or on a practice squad.

To the far right of the first line is the player's Risk for fantasy football in 2018. As explained in the quarterback section, the standard is for players to be marked Green. Players with higher than normal risk are marked Yellow, and players with the highest risk are marked Red. Players who are most likely to match or surpass our forecast—primarily second-stringers with low projections—are marked Blue. Risk is not only based on age and injury probability, but how a player's projection compares to his recent performance as well as our confidence (or lack thereof) in his offensive teammates.

Next we give the last three years of player stats. Note that rushing stats are not included for receivers, but that any receiver with at least five carries last year will have his 2017 rushing stats appear in his team's chapter.

Next we give the last three years of player stats. First come games played and games started (**G/GS**). Games played represents the official NFL total and may include games in which a player appeared on special teams but did not play wide receiver or tight end. We also have a total of offensive **Snaps** for each season. Receptions (**Rec**) counts passes caught, while Passes (**Pass**) counts passes thrown to this player, complete or incomplete. Receiving yards (**Yds**) and touchdowns (**TD**) are the official NFL totals for each player.

Catch rate (**C%**) includes all passes listed in the official play-by-play with the given player as the intended receiver, even if those passes were listed as "Thrown Away," "Tipped at Line," or "Quarterback Hit in Motion." The average NFL wide receiver has caught between 58 and 60 percent of passes over the last three seasons; tight ends caught between 64 and 65 percent of passes over the last three seasons.

Plus/minus (+/-) is a metric that we introduced in *Football Outsiders Almanac 2010*. It estimates how many passes a receiver caught compared to what an average receiver would have caught, given the location of those passes. Unlike simple catch rate, plus/minus does not consider passes listed as "Thrown Away," "Tipped at Line," or "Quarterback Hit in Motion." Player performance is compared to a historical baseline of how often a pass is caught based on the pass distance, the distance required for a first down, and whether it is on the left, middle, or right side of the field. Note that plus/minus is not scaled to a player's target total.

Drops (**Drop**) list the number of dropped passes according to charting from Sports Info Solutions. Our totals may differ from the drop totals kept by other organizations. Yards per catch (**Yd/C**) is a standard statistic.

We have added a new column this year, listing each player's average depth of target (**aDOT**). This is the average distance beyond the line of scrimmage on all throws to this player, not counting passes listed as "Thrown Away," "Tipped at Line," or "Quarterback Hit in Motion." Long-ball specialists will rank high in this category (Arizona's J.J. Nelson had an 18.4 aDOT, most of any qualifying wide receiver) while players who see a lot of passes on slots and screens will rank low (Green Bay's Randall Cobb was lowest at 5.8 aDOT).

Next we list yards after catch (**YAC**), rank (**Rk**) in yards after catch, and **YAC+**. YAC+ is similar to plus/minus; it estimates how much YAC a receiver gained compared to what we would have expected from an average receiver catching passes of similar length in similar down-and-distance situations. This is imperfect—we don't specifically mark what route a player runs, and obviously a go route will have more YAC than a comeback—but it does a fairly good job of telling you if this receiver gets more or less YAC than other receivers with similar usage patterns. We also give a total of broken tackles (**BTkl**) according to Sports Info Solutions charting.

The next five columns include our main advanced metrics for receiving: **DVOA** (Defense-Adjusted Value Over Average), **DYAR** (Defense-Adjusted Yards Above Replacement), and **YAR** (Yards Above Replacement), along with the player's rank in both DVOA and DYAR. These metrics compare every pass intended for a receiver and the results of that pass to a league-average baseline based on the game situations in

DeAndre Hopkins				Height: 6-1		Weight: 214		College: Clemson				Draft: 2013/1 (27)		Born: 6-Jun-1992			Age: 26		Risk: Green	
Year	Team	G/GS	Snaps	Pass	Rec	Yds	TD	C%	+/-	Drop	Yd/C	aDOT	Rk	YAC	Rk	YAC+	BTkl	DVOA	Rk	DYAR	Rk	YAR	Use	Rk	Slot
2015	HOU	16/16	1150	192	111	1521	11	58%	+4.5	3	13.7	14.3	20	2.0	87	-1.7	5	4.8%	41	268	13	307	31.7%	4	--
2016	HOU	16/16	1086	151	78	954	4	52%	-6.1	4	12.2	11.9	44	3.3	74	-0.6	6	-9.3%	70	43	66	27	27.0%	8	35%
2017	HOU	15/15	1027	174	96	1378	13	55%	-1.7	5	14.4	13.2	31	3.7	49	-0.2	9	13.3%	22	367	4	340	37.0%	1	20%
2018	HOU			160	92	1286	10	58%			14.0							5.6%							

which passes were thrown to that receiver. DVOA and DYAR are also adjusted based on the opposing defense and include Defensive Pass Interference yards on passes intended for that receiver. The methods used to compute these numbers are described in detail in the "Statistical Toolbox" introduction in the front of the book. The important distinctions between them are:

- DVOA is a rate statistic, while DYAR is a cumulative statistic. Thus, a higher DVOA means more value per pass play, while a higher DYAR means more aggregate value over the entire season.
- Because DYAR is defense-adjusted and YAR is not, a player whose DYAR is higher than his YAR faced a harder-than-average schedule. A player whose DYAR is lower than his YAR faced an easier-than-average schedule.

To qualify for ranking in YAC, receiving DVOA, or receiving DYAR, a wide receiver must have had 50 passes thrown to him in that season. We ranked 86 wideouts in 2017, 93 in 2016, and 87 in 2015. Tight ends qualify with 25 targets in a given season; we ranked 51 tight ends in 2017, 46 in 2016, and 51 in 2015.

The final columns are also new for 2018 and attempt to measure each player's role in his offense. Usage rate (**Use**) measures each player's share of his team's targets, adjusted for games played. Jacksonville's Dede Westbrook was targeted on just 9.7 percent of his team's targets, but he also missed nine games. Adjusting for those missing games gives Westbrook a usage rate of 22.2 percent, a more accurate assessment of his workload. The final column shows the percentage of each player's targets came when he lined up in the **Slot** (or at tight end). New England's Danny Amendola saw 97 percent of his targets from the slot, the highest rate in the league; the Giants' Roger Lewis had the lowest rate of slot targets at 14 percent. Tight ends have an additional column listing how frequently they were split **Wide**, from a high of 27 percent (Seattle's Jimmy Graham) to a low of zero percent (lots of guys).

"Slot" and "Wide" here are defined based on where the players are lined up in relation to the field, not based on where they are lined up in relation to other receivers. For example, if three wide receivers are in a trips bunch that is tight to the formation, all three receivers are marked as "slot" even if no other receiver is further out wide on that same side of the formation. Note that we have slot/wide splits only for 2016 and 2017, so those columns are empty for 2015.

The italicized row of statistics for the 2018 season is our 2018 KUBIAK projection based on a complicated regression analysis that takes into account numerous variables including projected role, performance over the past two years, projected team offense and defense, projected quarterback statistics, historical comparables, height, age, and strength of schedule.

It is difficult to accurately project statistics for a 162-game baseball season, but it is exponentially more difficult to accurately project statistics for a 16-game football season. Consider the listed projections not as a prediction of exact numbers, but as the mean of a range of possible performances. What's important is less the exact number of yards we project, and more which players are projected to improve or decline. Actual performance will vary from our projection less for veteran starters and more for rookies and third-stringers, for whom we must base our projections on much smaller career statistical samples. Touchdown numbers will vary more than yardage numbers. Players facing suspension or recovering from injury have those missed games taken into account.

Note that the receiving totals for each team will add up to higher numbers than the projection for that team's starting quarterback, because we have done KUBIAK projections for more receivers than will actually make the final roster.

A few low-round rookies, guys listed at seventh on the depth chart, and players who are listed as wide receivers but really only play special teams are briefly discussed at the end of the chapter in a section we call "Going Deep."

Two notes regarding our advanced metrics: We cannot yet fully separate the performance of a receiver from the performance of his quarterback. Be aware that one will affect the other. In addition, these statistics measure only passes thrown to a receiver, not performance on plays when he is not thrown the ball, such as blocking and drawing double teams.

Top 20 WR by DYAR (Total Value), 2017

Rank	Player	Team	DVOA
1	Antonio Brown	PIT	430
2	Marvin Jones	DET	395
3	Keenan Allen	LAC	378
4	DeAndre Hopkins	HOU	367
5	Michael Thomas	NO	330
6	JuJu Smith-Schuster	PIT	317
7	Julio Jones	ATL	313
8	Tyreek Hill	KC	304
9	Stefon Diggs	MIN	295
10	Cooper Kupp	LAR	272
11	Adam Thielen	MIN	261
12	Ted Ginn	NO	259
13	Brandin Cooks	NE	258
14	Sammy Watkins	LAR	216
15	Davante Adams	GB	215
16	Golden Tate	DET	204
17	Doug Baldwin	SEA	200
18	Mohamed Sanu	ATL	179
19	Rishard Matthews	TEN	173
20	Robert Woods	LAR	172

Minimum 50 passes.

Top 20 WR by DVOA (Value per Pass), 2017

Rank	Player	Team	DVOA
1	JuJu Smith-Schuster	PIT	37.3%
2	Ted Ginn	NO	34.8%
3	Marvin Jones	DET	33.8%
4	Cooper Kupp	LAR	24.8%
5	Stefon Diggs	MIN	24.7%
6	Sammy Watkins	LAR	24.1%
7	Tyreek Hill	KC	23.6%
8	Albert Wilson	KC	21.4%
9	Allen Hurns	JAX	20.6%
10	Chris Godwin	TB	20.5%
11	Antonio Brown	PIT	20.1%
12	Will Fuller	HOU	17.6%
13	Ryan Grant	WAS	16.7%
14	Keenan Allen	LAC	16.5%
15	Tyrell Williams	LAC	15.4%
16	Michael Thomas	NO	15.0%
17	Brandin Cooks	NE	14.9%
18	Julius Jones	ATL	13.7%
19	Rishard Matthews	TEN	13.6%
20	Paul Richardson	SEA	13.4%

Minimum 50 passes.

Davante Adams

Height: 6-1 Weight: 212 College: Fresno St. Draft: 2014/2 (53) Born: 12/24/1992 Age: 26 Risk: Green

Year	Team	G/GS	Snaps	Pass	Rec	Yds	TD	C%	+/-	Drop	Yd/C	aDOT	Rk	YAC	Rk	YAC+	BTkl	DVOA	Rk	DYAR	Rk	YAR	Use	Rk	Slot
2015	GB	13/12	763	94	50	483	1	53%	-7.1	6	9.7	10.2	62	3.0	78	-1.7	6	-27.8%	84	-109	86	-131	20.0%	35	--
2016	GB	16/15	915	121	75	997	12	62%	+1.8	9	13.3	11.9	43	5.2	23	+0.6	14	11.3%	21	230	14	216	19.8%	39	28%
2017	GB	14/14	776	117	74	885	10	63%	+4.7	6	12.0	10.1	59	4.5	35	+0.1	23	10.3%	25	215	15	205	23.8%	13	32%
2018	GB			120	75	1005	10	63%			13.4							14.3%							

Adams still doesn't have a 1,000-yard season, but his 22 touchdown catches since 2016 lead the NFL. That may even continue this year after Jordy Nelson, who ranks third with 20 scores since 2016, left for Oakland. Adams became the team's red zone preference last year with 10 more targets than the next closest receiver (Nelson). Adams even caught five touchdowns from Brett Hundley during the most productive stretch of his 2017 season, so his success wasn't entirely due to Rodgers. Now he's expected to face the biggest workload of his career, but he appears to be ready for the opportunity.

Nelson Agholor

Height: 6-0 Weight: 198 College: USC Draft: 2015/1 (20) Born: 24-May-1993 Age: 25 Risk: Yellow

Year	Team	G/GS	Snaps	Pass	Rec	Yds	TD	C%	+/-	Drop	Yd/C	aDOT	Rk	YAC	Rk	YAC+	BTkl	DVOA	Rk	DYAR	Rk	YAR	Use	Rk	Slot
2015	PHI	13/12	670	44	23	283	1	52%	-3.0	2	12.3	11.1	--	4.0	--	-0.9	4	-21.3%	--	-31	--	-16	9.0%	--	--
2016	PHI	15/14	883	70	36	365	2	53%	-4.9	6	10.1	11.0	52	3.3	73	-1.6	7	-23.3%	86	-60	88	-60	12.7%	81	48%
2017	PHI	16/10	813	95	62	768	8	65%	+2.1	8	12.4	10.6	54	4.9	24	-0.2	12	6.7%	33	141	32	130	16.8%	54	92%
2018	PHI			102	65	751	5	64%			11.6							2.0%							

Agholor went 29-310-2 in five December games as the Eagles gradually expanded his slot role late in the season, adding 15-167-0 (plus a critical 21-yard end-around against the Falcons) in three playoff games. The real story of Agholor's career resurrection began in 2017 OTAs, however, not late in the season. Agholor was visibly more confident and comfortable last offseason, as if that proverbial light bulb flickered on after a year away from Chip Kelly's malpractice. Agholor left USC as a top slot prospect with reliable hands and a knack for middle-of-the-field YAC. Now that he's back on track and the Eagles know what he's capable of, Agholor could have Anquan Boldin-level impact.

Keenan Allen Height: 6-2 Weight: 206 College: California Draft: 2013/3 (76) Born: 27-Apr-1992 Age: 26 Risk: Green

Year	Team	G/GS	Snaps	Pass	Rec	Yds	TD	C%	+/-	Drop	Yd/C	aDOT	Rk	YAC	Rk	YAC+	BTkl	DVOA	Rk	DYAR	Rk	YAR	Use	Rk	Slot
2015	SD	8/8	540	89	67	725	4	75%	+8.0	2	10.8	7.7	79	3.5	67	-0.8	6	11.9%	22	173	24	181	27.2%	11	--
2016	SD	1/1	27	7	6	63	0	86%	+1.4	0	10.5	7.1	--	3.0	--	-0.5	0	36.8%	--	33	--	29	22.3%	--	38%
2017	LAC	16/15	897	159	102	1393	6	64%	+8.3	8	13.7	9.8	65	4.9	25	+0.7	16	16.5%	14	378	3	378	28.3%	6	54%
2018	LAC			165	105	1430	7	64%			13.6							6.3%							

Allen caught 62 passes for 845 yards and five touchdowns in his final eight games after going just 40-548-1 in the first eight games. He was slowed at the start of the year by a minor shoulder injury, timing issues with Philip Rivers after a year in ACL rehab, and tough secondaries. By mid-November, Allen was running wild against opponents like the Bills, Cowboys, and Browns. Allen may be the NFL's best pure route-runner, prolific on out routes (league-high 106 DYAR), curl routes (league-high 94 DYAR), and dig routes.(second in NFL, 61 DYAR). With Aqib Talib and Marcus Peters out of the AFC West picture, he's a strong candidate to lead the NFL in receptions and/or yards.

Geronimo Allison Height: 6-3 Weight: 202 College: Illinois Draft: 2016/FA Born: 18-Jan-1994 Age: 24 Risk: Red

Year	Team	G/GS	Snaps	Pass	Rec	Yds	TD	C%	+/-	Drop	Yd/C	aDOT	Rk	YAC	Rk	YAC+	BTkl	DVOA	Rk	DYAR	Rk	YAR	Use	Rk	Slot
2016	GB	10/2	185	22	12	202	2	55%	-0.1	3	16.8	13.7	--	4.2	--	+0.3	1	15.2%	--	47	--	51	5.7%	--	68%
2017	GB	15/2	343	39	23	253	0	59%	-1.6	4	11.0	7.9	--	5.2	--	+0.3	3	-15.0%	--	-8	--	-12	7.7%	--	44%
2018	GB			58	36	455	3	62%			12.6							5.0%							

Allison caught Aaron Rodgers' longest completion since 2015 when he went for 72 yards against the Bengals last year to set up a win in overtime. Aside from that, there wasn't much to say about the fourth receiver's second season on the active roster. Even though the loss of Jordy Nelson strengthens Allison's case for a roster spot, he'll have to compete for playing time with a trio of rookies the Packers just drafted. "Equanimeous" may be the new fancy first name in Green Bay.

Danny Amendola Height: 5-11 Weight: 186 College: Texas Tech Draft: 2008/FA Born: 2-Nov-1985 Age: 33 Risk: Red

Year	Team	G/GS	Snaps	Pass	Rec	Yds	TD	C%	+/-	Drop	Yd/C	aDOT	Rk	YAC	Rk	YAC+	BTkl	DVOA	Rk	DYAR	Rk	YAR	Use	Rk	Slot
2015	NE	14/7	576	87	65	648	3	75%	+8.2	2	10.0	7.0	82	4.1	54	-0.8	12	8.6%	33	139	30	132	15.7%	58	--
2016	NE	12/4	267	29	23	243	4	79%	+4.2	0	10.6	8.8	--	3.2	--	-1.8	0	27.0%	--	85	--	96	7.0%	--	90%
2017	NE	15/8	569	86	61	659	2	71%	+6.9	3	10.8	8.2	76	3.4	62	-0.9	6	8.4%	29	138	34	150	15.4%	61	97%
2018	MIA			67	43	432	2	64%			10.1							-7.3%							

Signed to be the next Wes Welker, Amendola escaped Jeff Fisher's Rams in his prime and … did for the Patriots about what he had done for Fisher's Rams. He's a sure-handed slot target who gets dinged up a bit too often and, turning 33 in November, isn't likely to suddenly discover a new dimension. Puzzlingly signed by the Dolphins for a quarter of Ndamukong Suh's cap hit, Amendola will provide about a tenth of Suh's value. But at least he's giving the Dolphins some good OTA material—you never hear anything positive about Dolphins players in OTAs.

Robby Anderson Height: 6-3 Weight: 190 College: Temple Draft: 2016/FA Born: 9-May-1993 Age: 25 Risk: Green

Year	Team	G/GS	Snaps	Pass	Rec	Yds	TD	C%	+/-	Drop	Yd/C	aDOT	Rk	YAC	Rk	YAC+	BTkl	DVOA	Rk	DYAR	Rk	YAR	Use	Rk	Slot
2016	NYJ	16/8	717	78	42	587	2	54%	+0.6	6	14.0	16.9	3	2.8	84	-1.6	2	-17.9%	81	-31	80	-24	14.1%	71	18%
2017	NYJ	16/15	812	116	63	941	7	56%	-3.4	7	14.9	12.9	34	4.4	38	-0.3	7	-0.1%	47	113	41	99	23.1%	15	33%
2018	NYJ			109	59	825	6	54%			14.0							-3.1%							

Anderson has been involved in separate off-field incidents in each of the last two offseasons. Each was a felony, though this year's chargers were dropped due to "insufficient evidence." On the field, Anderson blossomed into one of the premiere deep-ball catchers in the NFL, and one of the best examples that general manager Mike Maccagnan has some skill in the undrafted free agent game. Of Anderson's 113 DYAR, 109 came on go routes. A quarterback change to Sam Darnold could mean better-thrown deep balls for Anderson to go get if the two create good chemistry. A Teddy Bridgewater season could force Anderson out of his comfort zone. It's all up in the air!

Tavon Austin Height: 5-8   Weight: 174   College: West Virgina   Draft: 2013/1 (8)   Born: 15-Mar-1991   Age: 27   Risk: Green

Year	Team	G/GS	Snaps	Pass	Rec	Yds	TD	C%	+/-	Drop	Yd/C	aDOT	Rk	YAC	Rk	YAC+	BTkl	DVOA	Rk	DYAR	Rk	YAR	Use	Rk	Slot
2015	STL	16/15	742	88	52	473	5	60%	-6.1	2	9.1	7.5	81	6.8	3	-0.6	34	-30.6%	86	-122	87	-122	18.5%	43	--
2016	LAR	15/15	732	106	58	509	3	55%	-12.5	10	8.8	7.5	85	4.7	37	-1.6	20	-39.1%	94	-219	94	-199	21.4%	29	75%
2017	LAR	16/9	228	24	13	47	0	63%	-3.2	0	3.6	2.7	--	6.4	--	-2.8	17	-68.2%	--	-99	--	-98	4.6%	--	67%
2018	DAL			26	17	160	0	65%			9.4							-8.6%		(Also: 43 runs, 251 RuYd, 1.3 RuTD)					

Through five seasons Austin has amassed a total of -452 receiving DYAR, the worst total of any wideout since 1986. His average DVOA, weighted by number of targets each season, is -30.4%, worst of any wide receiver with at least 200 targets. Since he was drafted in 2013, Austin is the only player in the league at any position with 100 targets, a catch rate south of 60 percent, and less than 10.0 yards per catch.

Austin has had mixed results as a punt returner. He is one of 70 players with at least three punt return touchdowns since the merger with the AFL in 1970, but only two of those men—Reggie Bush (7.78) and Antwaan Randle El (8.22)—have averaged fewer yards per return than Austin's 8.38. Austin has a league-high 17 fumbles on punt returns in the past five years, five more than anyone else. (Add in his four fumbles on receptions and you get 21 total fumbles, most of any non-quarterback in the NFL—Adrian Peterson is a distant second with 16.) By our numbers, Austin has been almost exactly average in punt return value in his career, but the Rams disagree—they took him off punt returns in October in favor of Pharoh Cooper, and he finished with a 4.4-yard average on just 12 returns, all in the first five games of the year.

Where Austin shines is running the football. His 183 runs for 1,231 yards and 646 DYAR are all the best marks for any wide receiver in our database. He is the only non-quarterback in league history with at least a thousand career rushing yards and better than 6.0 yards per carry.

The Cowboys have told different stories about how they will use Austin, referring to him as a "web back," which is … whatever. The best role for Austin will be to put him in the backfield to give Ezekiel Elliott a breather, especially on second-and-long when they need a big play; let him return punts when trailing, but have a Plan B when they're protecting the lead; and for God's sake, never throw him a pass.

Doug Baldwin Height: 5-11   Weight: 189   College: Stanford   Draft: 2011/FA   Born: 21-Sep-1988   Age: 30   Risk: Green

Year	Team	G/GS	Snaps	Pass	Rec	Yds	TD	C%	+/-	Drop	Yd/C	aDOT	Rk	YAC	Rk	YAC+	BTkl	DVOA	Rk	DYAR	Rk	YAR	Use	Rk	Slot
2015	SEA	16/16	798	103	78	1069	14	76%	+13.3	1	13.7	9.5	68	5.6	14	+1.0	15	39.6%	1	414	2	391	21.7%	29	--
2016	SEA	16/15	896	128	94	1128	7	76%	+12.9	5	12.0	9.0	73	4.9	30	-0.4	12	13.0%	16	263	9	287	23.3%	21	86%
2017	SEA	16/16	855	118	75	991	8	65%	+7.7	3	13.2	13.0	33	3.3	64	-1.5	15	9.6%	28	200	17	218	22.5%	17	80%
2018	SEA			114	76	984	7	67%			12.9							12.5%							

Baldwin's 2017 campaign was a tale of two stats. Baldwin ranked ninth in receiving plus-minus, catching 7.7 more passes than an average receiver would have in the same situations. Russell Wilson only finished with a +10.9 plus-minus, so Baldwin provided a significant chunk of Wilson's value as a passer; Baldwin's hands and ability to make catches in contested situations are comparable to anyone else in the league. At the same time, Baldwin's -1.5 YAC+ ranked 70th out of 82 qualified receivers, the lowest total of his career. All of Seattle's receivers finished fairly low in that stat, but Baldwin finished below both Tyler Lockett and Paul Richardson. Seattle led the league in broken plays, so a lot of that low YAC is a result of receivers scrambling to get open as Wilson was running around in the backfield. Baldwin was Wilson's most trusted safety valve, and when you're dashing around trying to keep plays alive, you're not putting yourself in the best situation to turn the ball upfield. Baldwin remains one of, if not the, best slot receivers in the game, but the state of Seattle's offense limits the raw production he can put up. As the only proven receiver on the team in 2018, Baldwin's ability to make contested catches is going to be more vital than ever before.

Cole Beasley Height: 5-8   Weight: 177   College: Southern Methodist   Draft: 2012/FA   Born: 26-Apr-1989   Age: 29   Risk: Yellow

Year	Team	G/GS	Snaps	Pass	Rec	Yds	TD	C%	+/-	Drop	Yd/C	aDOT	Rk	YAC	Rk	YAC+	BTkl	DVOA	Rk	DYAR	Rk	YAR	Use	Rk	Slot
2015	DAL	16/3	563	75	52	536	5	69%	+1.2	4	10.3	4.7	86	6.2	7	+1.4	7	-1.9%	53	64	58	73	14.3%	66	--
2016	DAL	16/6	604	99	75	833	5	77%	+9.5	4	11.1	6.4	91	5.3	19	+0.7	11	31.0%	5	341	5	342	20.8%	32	86%
2017	DAL	15/4	576	63	36	314	4	57%	-1.3	2	8.7	7.9	79	3.4	60	-0.4	1	-16.9%	74	-22	73	-8	14.0%	69	88%
2018	DAL			83	56	563	3	67%			10.1							-0.4%							

Last summer, Beasley revealed that he had played the last third of the 2016 season with a nagging hamstring injury, an injury that lingered into 2017 and no doubt played a part in what would be his worst NFL season. This was especially true on third downs—his DVOA on the money down slipped from 10.1% in 2015 and 50.2% in 2016 to -34.5% last season. A healthy Beasley should be a bounce-back candidate this fall, but don't expect many deep balls. Among qualifying wide receivers, Beasley has had the lowest rate of targets coming more than 15 yards downfield in each of the past three seasons.

Odell Beckham Height: 5-11   Weight: 198   College: Louisiana State   Draft: 2014/1 (12)   Born: 5-Nov-1992   Age: 26   Risk: Yellow

Year	Team	G/GS	Snaps	Pass	Rec	Yds	TD	C%	+/-	Drop	Yd/C	aDOT	Rk	YAC	Rk	YAC+	BTkl	DVOA	Rk	DYAR	Rk	YAR	Use	Rk	Slot
2015	NYG	15/15	998	158	96	1450	13	61%	+4.6	4	15.1	12.1	40	6.2	8	+2.0	12	10.3%	27	304	10	345	27.9%	10	--
2016	NYG	16/16	1002	169	101	1367	10	60%	+0.3	10	13.5	10.9	54	5.2	24	+0.8	32	-1.1%	52	161	29	177	28.8%	4	27%
2017	NYG	4/2	212	41	25	302	3	61%	+0.3	6	12.1	12.9	--	2.6	--	-1.5	4	3.5%	--	57	--	64	28.3%	--	9%
2018	NYG			156	96	1242	9	62%			12.9							4.7%							

Through four years of playing in Ben McAdoo's isolation-centric offense, Beckham asserted himself as one of the most productive young receivers the sport has seen. From giving Richard Sherman the work as a rookie in 2014 to his infamous one-handed reception versus the Dallas Cowboys in 2015, there have been no shortage of moments where Beckham has proven himself to be one of the league's best. Beckham's blend of acceleration, stop-start explosion, and body control make him a dangerous route-runner to all levels of the field. Be it a quick slant or a deep go route, Beckham can consistently get open versus top cornerbacks. Beckham's athletic tools are equally as impressive once the ball is in his hands, as he has the potential to turn any routine catch into six points. Beckham's versatility and game-breaking ability make him one of the few true No.1 wide receivers left in the NFL. While it may be true that Beckham's catch rate is consistently around the middle of the pack, he provides so much value to the offense that the drops are easy to live with.

Josh Bellamy Height: 6-0   Weight: 206   College: Louisville   Draft: 2012/FA   Born: 18-May-1989   Age: 29   Risk: Green

Year	Team	G/GS	Snaps	Pass	Rec	Yds	TD	C%	+/-	Drop	Yd/C	aDOT	Rk	YAC	Rk	YAC+	BTkl	DVOA	Rk	DYAR	Rk	YAR	Use	Rk	Slot
2015	CHI	16/3	437	34	19	224	2	56%	-2.1	2	11.8	10.6	--	3.6	--	-1.9	2	-16.8%	--	-11	--	-12	6.4%	--	--
2016	CHI	16/2	304	38	19	282	1	50%	-2.9	5	14.8	15.9	--	2.7	--	-1.1	4	-11.2%	--	4	--	14	6.8%	--	55%
2017	CHI	15/7	438	46	24	376	1	52%	-1.5	5	15.7	12.9	--	4.8	--	+0.5	2	-6.8%	--	20	--	35	10.4%	--	44%
2018	CHI			22	12	137	1	55%			11.4							-13.8%							

Almost half of Bellamy's targets were curls and digs last year, and he had very meager production on those 20 plays (14 catches, 153 yards, 17 DYAR, -1.5% DVOA). At his best, Bellamy was never more than a third or fourth receiver on some bad Bears teams. With all the new additions in Chicago, Bellamy is again just competing for a WR4 role at best this season.

Kelvin Benjamin Height: 6-5   Weight: 240   College: Florida St.   Draft: 2014/1 (28)   Born: 5-Feb-1991   Age: 27   Risk: Yellow

Year	Team	G/GS	Snaps	Pass	Rec	Yds	TD	C%	+/-	Drop	Yd/C	aDOT	Rk	YAC	Rk	YAC+	BTkl	DVOA	Rk	DYAR	Rk	YAR	Use	Rk	Slot
2016	CAR	16/13	801	118	63	941	7	53%	-5.1	8	14.9	12.4	34	3.7	64	+0.1	14	3.0%	46	145	33	128	21.2%	30	37%
2017	2TM	14/14	597	78	48	692	3	62%	+1.5	5	14.4	11.5	46	2.9	71	-0.8	3	8.1%	30	125	36	129	18.5%	41	24%
2018	BUF			112	62	887	6	55%			14.3							-0.6%							

Benjamin's 4.6-second 40-yard speed appeared to be left either on the operating table after his 2015 ACL tear or in the kitchen after he repeatedly showed up to OTAs/training camp in poor shape, and he was dealt away by the Panthers at midseason in an attempt to "fix their spacing." He struggled with a torn meniscus after joining the Bills, and barely seemed like he was part of their offense at all. Benjamin is One Of Their Guys for Brandon Beane and Sean McDermott, but his career is on life support as he enters his fifth-year option season. A healthy year as a red zone beast is necessary to erase some doubts.

Travis Benjamin

Height: 5-10 Weight: 172 College: Miami Draft: 2012/4 (100) Born: 29-Dec-1989 Age: 29 Risk: Green

Year	Team	G/GS	Snaps	Pass	Rec	Yds	TD	C%	+/-	Drop	Yd/C	aDOT	Rk	YAC	Rk	YAC+	BTkl	DVOA	Rk	DYAR	Rk	YAR	Use	Rk	Slot
2015	CLE	16/15	851	125	68	966	5	54%	-4.1	4	14.2	12.7	34	4.8	34	-0.4	8	-8.7%	69	38	65	37	20.9%	31	--
2016	SD	14/8	548	75	47	677	4	63%	+3.3	6	14.4	13.3	26	5.2	21	+0.6	4	12.1%	19	144	35	110	15.2%	67	59%
2017	LAC	16/3	566	66	34	567	4	53%	-1.8	6	16.7	16.1	6	6.6	7	+1.1	6	0.5%	43	65	54	76	11.4%	78	54%
2018	LAC			62	35	552	3	56%			15.8							5.6%							(Also: 9 runs, 62 RuYd, 0.3 RuTD)

Benjamin is a useful score-from-anywhere type who mixes huge games (a receiving and a punt return touchdown to beat the Broncos in Week 7) with invisible ones (three zero-catch games last year). Benjamin is also the guy who ran backwards into the end zone for a punt return safety against the Patriots. Benjamin will eat up $7 million in cap space this year to be excitingly erratic on returns while subsisting on fourth-receiver carries and jet sweeps. If you are thinking that makes him a likely cap casualty, you have never taken a long look at the Chargers' cap management strategy.

Tyler Boyd

Height: 6-1 Weight: 197 College: Pittsburgh Draft: 2016/2 (55) Born: 15-Nov-1994 Age: 24 Risk: Green

Year	Team	G/GS	Snaps	Pass	Rec	Yds	TD	C%	+/-	Drop	Yd/C	aDOT	Rk	YAC	Rk	YAC+	BTkl	DVOA	Rk	DYAR	Rk	YAR	Use	Rk	Slot
2016	CIN	16/2	739	81	54	603	1	67%	+3.4	2	11.2	9.2	71	3.7	60	-0.9	3	2.4%	47	96	53	85	14.9%	68	85%
2017	CIN	10/1	307	32	22	225	2	69%	+1.2	2	10.2	6.9	--	4.1	--	-0.5	1	19.5%	--	76	--	71	10.3%	--	97%
2018	CIN			59	38	404	2	64%			10.6							3.2%							

Boyd was in the coaching doghouse for much of the season, with his blocking, route-running, and overall discipline called into question. But when he hit the field his numbers were rather good, and of course he turned in the play of the season in Baltimore, catching a game-winning, playoff-hopes-destroying, fourth-and-long bomb. Boyd is somewhat forgotten in the Cincy receiving carousel, but if he can iron out the details he could become the reliable slot man he was drafted to be.

Kenny Britt

Height: 6-3 Weight: 218 College: Rutgers Draft: 2009/1 (30) Born: 19-Sep-1988 Age: 30 Risk: Red

Year	Team	G/GS	Snaps	Pass	Rec	Yds	TD	C%	+/-	Drop	Yd/C	aDOT	Rk	YAC	Rk	YAC+	BTkl	DVOA	Rk	DYAR	Rk	YAR	Use	Rk	Slot
2015	STL	16/14	650	72	36	681	3	50%	-1.4	3	18.9	16.0	6	3.3	73	-1.4	5	11.0%	26	139	31	141	15.8%	57	--
2016	LAR	15/15	789	111	68	1002	5	61%	+3.1	5	14.7	12.3	37	4.4	43	+0.3	13	6.4%	37	166	28	177	22.6%	26	33%
2017	2TM	12/4	392	43	20	256	2	47%	-3.5	0	12.8	6.6	--	4.4	--	-0.1	6	-19.0%	--	-20	--	-23	10.1%	--	19%
2018	NE			28	15	203	3	54%			13.5							-4.5%							

Britt treated his stay in Cleveland with all the attention to detail of a bored teenager on Instagram. The Patriots snatched him up both as a potential solution to next year's problems and as a salve to the troubling lack of Rutgers players on the roster. He may enter 2018 as the backup plan or backup backup plan depending on how training camp and OTAs go. The talent has never been the issue with Britt—if the Patriots can coax an interested year out of him, it would be stealing.

Antonio Brown

Height: 5-10 Weight: 186 College: Central Mighican Draft: 2010/6 (195) Born: 10-Jul-1988 Age: 30 Risk: Green

Year	Team	G/GS	Snaps	Pass	Rec	Yds	TD	C%	+/-	Drop	Yd/C	aDOT	Rk	YAC	Rk	YAC+	BTkl	DVOA	Rk	DYAR	Rk	YAR	Use	Rk	Slot
2015	PIT	16/16	1029	193	136	1834	10	70%	+18.2	4	13.5	11.7	46	4.4	45	-0.5	18	19.7%	9	517	1	490	33.3%	1	--
2016	PIT	15/15	975	154	106	1284	12	69%	+8.1	4	12.1	10.5	59	3.8	56	-1.0	13	11.1%	22	295	7	306	28.3%	6	26%
2017	PIT	14/14	888	163	101	1533	9	62%	+12.0	6	15.2	14.3	17	4.8	27	+0.1	29	20.1%	11	430	1	389	32.3%	2	21%
2018	PIT			164	108	1460	10	66%			13.5							13.5%							

For the third time in the past four years, Brown topped the wide receivers DYAR table, bouncing back from a down year in 2016 where he "only" finished seventh. His DVOA was his highest in three years. He has now averaged 100 receiving yards per game over his past five seasons, a feat that only Julio Jones and Lance Alworth have ever matched. Despite the wide array of weapons the Steelers have to choose from, Brown had 34 percent of Pittsburgh's receiving yards, the third-highest amount in the league. His numbers would look even better if Pittsburgh would stop trying to throw him screen passes. Brown's the crispest route-runner in football. He had DVOA above 35.0% on slants, posts, and go routes: long-developing routes where he can use his speed and precision to beat defenders. On wide receiver screens, Brown had -58.0% DVOA and -36 DYAR. It's not a one-year phenomenon, either; Brown has always been well below average on screens. It's like using a Lamborghini to go off-roading. Hopefully, a change at offensive coordinator will put an end to it.

Jaron Brown Height: 6-2   Weight: 205   College: Clemson   Draft: 2013/FA   Born: 8-Jan-1990   Age: 28   Risk: Red

Year	Team	G/GS	Snaps	Pass	Rec	Yds	TD	C%	+/-	Drop	Yd/C	aDOT	Rk	YAC	Rk	YAC+	BTkl	DVOA	Rk	DYAR	Rk	YAR	Use	Rk	Slot
2015	ARI	16/0	272	23	11	144	1	48%	-1.7	1	13.1	13.5	--	2.0	--	-2.1	1	-16.1%	--	-7	--	-5	4.2%	--	--
2016	ARI	7/2	190	22	11	187	1	50%	-2.4	0	17.0	12.7	--	5.3	--	+0.3	1	-8.5%	--	7	--	12	7.7%	--	23%
2017	ARI	16/8	822	69	31	477	4	45%	-4.4	2	15.4	15.6	8	2.8	74	-0.8	1	-11.5%	71	6	71	33	11.9%	77	46%
2018	SEA			39	20	276	3	51%			13.8							-7.8%							

Brown saw his first extended action in 2017, passing 300 offensive snaps for the first time in his career as he recovered from a 2016 ACL tear. Taking advantage of a slew of injuries behind Larry Fitzgerald, Brown set career highs in receptions, yards, and touchdowns. He was sort of Arizona's second receiver by default. He would be a much more effective third or fourth wideout, where he could face easier matchups in the secondary. Seattle would be well advised to consider using Brown in the slot more often. Arizona split his snaps roughly 60-40 between wide and slot positions, but he was much more effective inside, with a -2.9% DVOA in the slot compared to -27.3% lined up out wide.

John Brown Height: 5-10   Weight: 179   College: Pittsburg St. (KS)   Draft: 2014/3 (91)   Born: 4-Mar-1990   Age: 28   Risk: Red

Year	Team	G/GS	Snaps	Pass	Rec	Yds	TD	C%	+/-	Drop	Yd/C	aDOT	Rk	YAC	Rk	YAC+	BTkl	DVOA	Rk	DYAR	Rk	YAR	Use	Rk	Slot
2015	ARI	15/11	826	101	65	1003	7	64%	+6.6	5	15.4	15.6	10	4.8	32	+0.0	7	29.9%	4	352	5	345	19.9%	37	--
2016	ARI	15/6	595	73	39	517	2	53%	-0.6	1	13.3	13.8	19	2.7	88	-1.5	1	-1.9%	57	61	61	69	12.3%	83	39%
2017	ARI	10/5	491	55	21	299	3	38%	-6.4	2	14.2	17.0	3	2.8	73	-0.8	1	-24.4%	83	-51	83	-29	15.3%	62	39%
2018	BAL			102	53	726	5	52%			13.7							-9.9%							

The man nicknamed "Smoke" evaporated into the ether in 2017, when injuries and mediocre play spelled the end of his time in Arizona. In 2015, Brown was a desert version of DeSean Jackson, but the last two years have seen sickle-cell problems and a spinal cyst turn him into a shadow of his old self. Compared to the speed on the Baltimore perimeter in recent years, Brown will look like Jesse Owens, so if healthy he will play the deep threat complement to Michael Crabtree's possession receiver.

Dez Bryant Height: 6-2   Weight: 225   College: Oklahoma State   Draft: 2010/1 (24)   Born: 4-Nov-1988   Age: 30   Risk: N/A

Year	Team	G/GS	Snaps	Pass	Rec	Yds	TD	C%	+/-	Drop	Yd/C	aDOT	Rk	YAC	Rk	YAC+	BTkl	DVOA	Rk	DYAR	Rk	YAR	Use	Rk	Slot
2015	DAL	9/9	444	72	31	401	3	43%	-8.5	6	12.9	12.8	33	4.2	49	+0.1	6	-26.8%	83	-86	85	-88	25.7%	14	--
2016	DAL	13/13	688	96	50	796	8	52%	-2.0	4	15.9	15.0	6	2.9	82	-0.9	6	7.5%	32	153	31	154	24.8%	15	30%
2017	DAL	16/16	894	132	69	838	6	52%	-7.4	10	12.1	11.8	42	3.9	45	-0.5	21	-13.5%	72	-9	72	-8	27.5%	8	32%

Over and over the Cowboys kept giving Bryant chances, and over and over they were rewarded with minimal production. Bryant did not make the NFL's top 20 in receptions, yards, or touchdowns, but he was tied for the league lead in drops. There were 34 wide receivers last year with an adjusted use rate of 20 percent or more. Only three finished with negative receiving DYAR: Dede Westbrook and Emmanuel Sanders, who played with questionable quarterbacks in Jacksonville and Denver, and Bryant, who didn't.

Bryant hasn't gone over 100 yards in any of his last 23 games. He couldn't get open downfield last year, he wasn't good at catching passes in traffic, and he was nothing special with the ball in his hands. His days as a No. 1 wide receiver are done but he still has some value, using his size to wall defenders off intermediate routes. On slants, digs, and curls, he caught 38 of 62 passes for 501 yards and a 2.6% DVOA; on all other routes, those numbers were 31-70-337 and -26.1%. NFL Network's Ian Rapoport reported this summer that Bryant had turned down a contract offer from Baltimore, and was willing to wait until training camps opened to get the deal he wanted from a quality team. It's not clear if he'll get that deal even then.

Martavis Bryant

Height: 6-4 Weight: 211 College: Clemson Draft: 2014/4 (118) Born: 20-Dec-1991 Age: 27 Risk: Red

Year	Team	G/GS	Snaps	Pass	Rec	Yds	TD	C%	+/-	Drop	Yd/C	aDOT	Rk	YAC	Rk	YAC+	BTkl	DVOA	Rk	DYAR	Rk	YAR	Use	Rk	Slot
2015	PIT	11/5	511	92	50	765	6	54%	-3.7	6	15.3	14.3	18	7.0	2	+1.7	14	-2.4%	54	75	56	47	22.8%	26	--
2017	PIT	15/8	685	84	50	603	3	60%	+1.7	3	12.1	15.1	14	3.4	61	-1.5	6	4.9%	38	118	39	107	15.9%	57	26%
2018	OAK			90	53	710	5	59%			13.4							3.4%							

For a coach who claims to be an old-school no-nonsense guy who wants to turn back the clock to 1998, Jon Gruden assumed an awful lot of character/suspension risk in his offseason acquisitions. Bryant missed all of 2016 with a substance abuse suspension and never quite found a role when he returned in 2017. Bryant still has big-play potential, and of course there is nothing wrong with giving players another chance or digging for value among talented weapons in need of a change of scenery. The problem is that it takes a combination of planning and organizational patience to build a team out of Bryant, Doug Martin, Marshawn Lynch, Arden Key and the like; a coach who is 20 years behind the curve on analytics probably isn't forward-thinking when it comes to marijuana, and someone who cuts a punter for being too cocky on Twitter may not be the best coach for a locker room that may need a little 21st-century management. Gruden could smell incense burning, have a hissy fit, and cut half the roster, is what we're saying.

Brice Butler

Height: 6-3 Weight: 205 College: San Diego State Draft: 2013/7 (209) Born: 29-Jan-1990 Age: 28 Risk: Red

Year	Team	G/GS	Snaps	Pass	Rec	Yds	TD	C%	+/-	Drop	Yd/C	aDOT	Rk	YAC	Rk	YAC+	BTkl	DVOA	Rk	DYAR	Rk	YAR	Use	Rk	Slot
2015	DAL	7/2	261	26	12	258	0	46%	-0.9	2	21.5	13.0	--	8.0	--	+3.5	2	0.3%	--	28	--	30	11.8%	--	--
2016	DAL	16/3	429	32	16	219	3	50%	-2.4	2	13.7	14.2	--	1.2	--	-2.0	1	-10.4%	--	6	--	21	6.6%	--	34%
2017	DAL	13/0	263	23	15	317	3	65%	+3.2	3	21.1	18.9	--	1.9	--	-2.4	3	61.6%	--	135	--	133	6.0%	--	25%
2018	ARI			81	47	677	5	58%			14.4							7.9%							

Butler joins the Cardinals after five mostly quiet seasons in Oakland and Dallas, where he never received more than 35 targets in a year. Butler was used primarily as a deep threat for the Cowboys this past season, and despite the fact that the aggressive Bruce Arians is no longer at the helm in Arizona, he will the opportunity to make some big plays down the field as the No. 3 receiver. Butler has the talent to make 2018 his biggest season on a short-term deal, but he could also easily end up as the forgotten fifth receiver competing for targets with the likes of J.J. Nelson and Chad Williams.

DJ Chark

Height: 6-4 Weight: 198 College: Louisiana State Draft: 2018/2 (61) Born: 23-Sep-1996 Age: 22 Risk: Yellow

Year	Team	G/GS	Snaps	Pass	Rec	Yds	TD	C%	+/-	Drop	Yd/C	aDOT	Rk	YAC	Rk	YAC+	BTkl	DVOA	Rk	DYAR	Rk	YAR	Use	Rk	Slot
2018	JAX			27	14	256	1	52%			18.3							5.4%							

Despite losing previous starting tandem Allen Robinson and Allen Hurns to free agency this past offseason, most Jaguars observers do not expect Chark to step immediately into the starting lineup. Chark is tall, very fast, and has a massive catch radius, but he is not a refined receiver and often relied on pure athletic ability to get open in the SEC. His 874 yards and 21.9 yards per reception were belied by a 59 percent catch rate, which will have to improve for him to ever become a No. 1 receiver in Jacksonville. Chark has been working with special teams coach Joe DeCamillis and may see opportunities as a kick and punt returner, where his limited experience does include two touchdowns on 18 returns in college. On offense, absent an injury crisis or an unexpectedly rapid ascent, this is widely expected to be something of a redshirt year.

Randall Cobb

Height: 5-11 Weight: 190 College: Kentucky Draft: 2011/2 (64) Born: 22-Aug-1990 Age: 28 Risk: Green

Year	Team	G/GS	Snaps	Pass	Rec	Yds	TD	C%	+/-	Drop	Yd/C	aDOT	Rk	YAC	Rk	YAC+	BTkl	DVOA	Rk	DYAR	Rk	YAR	Use	Rk	Slot
2015	GB	16/15	1050	129	79	829	6	61%	-2.3	6	10.5	7.9	77	5.5	18	+0.2	16	-5.1%	60	77	53	54	23.0%	25	--
2016	GB	13/10	681	84	60	610	4	71%	+3.4	1	10.2	6.6	90	6.0	10	+0.6	15	6.6%	35	133	39	131	16.8%	57	81%
2017	GB	15/14	742	93	66	653	4	72%	+4.1	1	9.9	5.8	86	6.2	8	+0.4	9	-6.0%	62	48	61	41	17.7%	47	76%
2018	GB			112	74	823	4	66%			11.1							2.0%		(Also: 6 runs, 32 RuYd, 0.2 RuTD)						

In 2015, Cobb signed a four-year deal for $40 million that seemed fair and logical at the time. He was coming off his best season yet with 1,287 receiving yards and 12 touchdowns. Since signing that deal, Cobb has fewer receiving yards (2,092) than

37 other players, including Travis Benjamin (2,210) and even Ted Ginn (2,278). Cobb has not surpassed 95 receiving yards in his last 24 regular-season games. So expectations aren't necessarily high at a time when the Packers have never needed Cobb more following Jordy Nelson's departure. This is the thinnest the receiving corps has been in the Aaron Rodgers era, so in another contract year, it will be interesting to see if Cobb suddenly finds his game again.

Keelan Cole   Height: 6-1   Weight: 194   College: Kentucky Wesleyan   Draft: 2017/FA   Born: 20-Apr-1993   Age: 25   Risk: Green

Year	Team	G/GS	Snaps	Pass	Rec	Yds	TD	C%	+/-	Drop	Yd/C	aDOT	Rk	YAC	Rk	YAC+	BTkl	DVOA	Rk	DYAR	Rk	YAR	Use	Rk	Slot
2017	JAX	16/6	755	83	42	748	3	51%	-1.9	6	17.8	13.3	30	7.0	3	+2.5	6	-7.4%	66	35	65	57	16.0%	55	54%
2018	JAX			22	13	165	2	59%			12.7							0.0%							

Our numbers overwhelmingly support the statement that Cole is an archetypal slot receiver. Only three wide receivers had a larger DVOA difference in favor of their targets in the slot over targets split wide. Cole's 44 slot targets resulted in 523 yards (11.9 yards per target) and a DVOA of 21.5%; his 37 targets split wide resulted in only 243 yards (6.6 yards per target) and a DVOA of -34.9%. We could infer from the narrow split in targets that the Jaguars staff were still learning about their young receiver in his debut season. One would hope that they will keep Cole in his most effective role if he has to play significant time this year—which he probably won't because of the signing of Donte Moncrief and drafting of DJ Chark.

Corey Coleman   Height: 5-11   Weight: 194   College: Baylor   Draft: 2016/1 (15)   Born: 6-Jul-1994   Age: 24   Risk: Green

Year	Team	G/GS	Snaps	Pass	Rec	Yds	TD	C%	+/-	Drop	Yd/C	aDOT	Rk	YAC	Rk	YAC+	BTkl	DVOA	Rk	DYAR	Rk	YAR	Use	Rk	Slot
2016	CLE	10/10	533	73	33	413	3	45%	-3.6	4	12.5	14.3	14	2.9	81	-1.6	10	-22.9%	85	-57	87	-84	20.9%	31	24%
2017	CLE	9/8	450	58	23	305	2	40%	-6.0	4	13.3	14.7	15	1.1	86	-2.9	2	-21.5%	80	-41	80	-60	18.4%	42	17%
2018	CLE			49	24	321	3	49%			13.4							-16.4%							

Does breaking your hand twice render you "injury-prone"? It doesn't seem like the kind of injury that becomes repetitive, as opposed to hamstring problems or back issues. Coleman has now missed half of each of his first two seasons to hand fractures. But the problem is less the injuries and more the fact that when he's on the field, Coleman hasn't yet lived up to either his first-round status or his excellent Playmaker Score (best of the class of 2016). There have been problems with dropped passes, especially a fourth-and-2 near the end of Week 17, when the Browns were driving in a desperate attempt to win their final game of the season and avoid 0-16. No longer a nominal starter, Coleman should still be set to line up on the outside in three-receiver sets, but there's a lot of talk in Browns media about Cleveland trying to trade Coleman away to make room for fourth-round rookie Antonio Callaway.

Chris Conley   Height: 6-2   Weight: 213   College: Georgia   Draft: 2015/3 (76)   Born: 25-Oct-1992   Age: 26   Risk: Yellow

Year	Team	G/GS	Snaps	Pass	Rec	Yds	TD	C%	+/-	Drop	Yd/C	aDOT	Rk	YAC	Rk	YAC+	BTkl	DVOA	Rk	DYAR	Rk	YAR	Use	Rk	Slot
2015	KC	16/5	369	31	17	199	1	55%	-1.1	3	11.7	12.3	--	4.1	--	-0.1	3	2.7%	--	39	--	39	6.9%	--	--
2016	KC	16/11	818	69	44	530	0	64%	+1.6	3	12.0	10.0	63	3.4	69	-0.4	3	1.1%	49	74	56	57	12.8%	79	28%
2017	KC	5/5	293	16	11	175	0	69%	+1.8	0	15.9	14.4	--	4.1	--	-0.1	0	27.2%	--	50	--	49	9.6%	--	13%
2018	KC			48	26	323	2	54%			12.4							-12.3%							

Prior to suffering an Achilles injury in Week 5, Conley looked to have blossomed into a secondary deep threat for the Chiefs in 2017. Though Conley only saw 16 targets on the year, six of those targets were more than 15 yards downfield, and three of them were caught. Between Conley and Tyreek Hill, defenses could not lapse for even a second or else one of those two would torch them over the top. In turn, the loss of Conley was quietly one of the shifting factors in the drop-off that the Chiefs offense experienced after dominationg the first five weeks of the season. Conley was obviously not the team's star pass-catcher, but his injury resulted in his workload being passed on to Demarcus Robinson, who does not provide the same potential for big plays down the field. The addition of Sammy Watkins may mitigate some of the need for Conley to be a deep threat, but Conley will most certainly still have an important, albeit under-the-radar role in the Chiefs offense.

Brandin Cooks   Height: 5-10   Weight: 189   College: Oregon St.   Draft: 2014/1 (20)   Born: 25-Sep-1993   Age: 25   Risk: Green

Year	Team	G/GS	Snaps	Pass	Rec	Yds	TD	C%	+/-	Drop	Yd/C	aDOT	Rk	YAC	Rk	YAC+	BTkl	DVOA	Rk	DYAR	Rk	YAR	Use	Rk	Slot
2015	NO	16/12	959	130	84	1138	9	65%	+5.8	3	13.5	12.5	36	4.6	41	-0.8	4	7.1%	40	192	21	186	19.7%	38	--
2016	NO	16/12	880	118	78	1173	8	67%	+8.7	6	15.0	13.4	24	4.9	31	+0.1	4	11.6%	20	226	16	212	17.8%	48	66%
2017	NE	16/15	1058	114	65	1082	7	57%	+2.1	8	16.6	16.5	4	3.5	57	-1.3	8	14.9%	17	258	13	266	20.0%	34	29%
2018	LAR			113	62	934	7	55%			15.1							4.8%							

Is Cooks just a like-for-like replacement for Sammy Watkins? That's the general idea; both are (theoretically) explosive play-makers with speed to run under deep balls, and they finished fourth and ninth in average depth of target last season. There are some subtle differences, however. While Cooks is an upgrade and will likely easily pass Watkins' 593 yards from last season, they're two different players and should be used, well, differently. For example, Watkins is the better option in the red zone; his 87.2% DVOA there crushed Cooks' 18.8%. Watkins led the league with 101 DYAR on slants and had a 88.0% DVOA; Cooks had a -16.8% DVOA on slants. Where Cooks really excels is on the go route—just run straight forward and beat everyone down the field. He had 123 DYAR and 97.2% DVOA on go/fly routes last season, both among the top numbers in the league. Watkins had -17 DYAR and a -44.3% DVOA, and never really provided that same level of fear from the deep safeties. Expect the deep ball to be much more of a thing in Los Angeles this season, as Cooks is one of the top two or three best in the game on those plays.

Amari Cooper   Height: 6-1   Weight: 211   College: Alabama   Draft: 2015/1 (4)   Born: 18-Jun-1994   Age: 24   Risk: Yellow

Year	Team	G/GS	Snaps	Pass	Rec	Yds	TD	C%	+/-	Drop	Yd/C	aDOT	Rk	YAC	Rk	YAC+	BTkl	DVOA	Rk	DYAR	Rk	YAR	Use	Rk	Slot
2015	OAK	16/15	900	130	72	1070	6	55%	-6.6	10	14.9	11.1	50	5.2	23	+0.0	11	-1.0%	50	122	37	130	21.8%	28	--
2016	OAK	16/14	997	132	83	1153	5	63%	+0.8	4	13.9	10.0	64	5.3	18	+0.0	12	8.8%	28	231	13	185	22.9%	24	32%
2017	OAK	14/12	710	95	48	680	7	51%	-7.6	9	14.2	12.2	38	6.0	11	+1.6	6	-9.1%	68	27	67	20	19.8%	36	42%
2018	OAK			137	82	1135	8	60%			13.8							6.1%							

Cooper went 11-210-2 in a bonkers Thursday night shootout with the Chiefs, but 18-146-1 in the six games before that and 19-324-4 in seven games after. Chalk the bad year up mostly to injuries—Cooper suffered a concussion and an ankle sprain late in the year and missed practices with a knee issue earlier—and to Todd Downing's complete lack of offensive creativity. Jon Gruden has called Cooper the "main vein" of the Raiders offense, and it would be the smartest thing Gruden said all offseason if he didn't somehow mix up a urination metaphor with a compliment for his top offensive weapon.

Keke Coutee   Height: 5-10   Weight: 181   College: Texas Tech   Draft: 2018/4 (103)   Born: 14-Jan-1997   Age: 21   Risk: Red

Year	Team	G/GS	Snaps	Pass	Rec	Yds	TD	C%	+/-	Drop	Yd/C	aDOT	Rk	YAC	Rk	YAC+	BTkl	DVOA	Rk	DYAR	Rk	YAR	Use	Rk	Slot
2018	HOU			61	37	524	3	61%			14.2							3.7%							

The Red Raiders' top target as a slot receiver in 2017, Coutee flashed yards after catch talent that made him a favorite of many draftniks. His frame and difficulty against physical coverage likely limit him to a pure slot role in the NFL. If he can use his quickness and stop-start ability to separate anywhere near as easily from NFL defenders as he could from Big 12 ones, he should push Braxton Miller off the roster immediately and could displace Bruce Ellington as the third option at receiver as early as this season.

Michael Crabtree   Height: 6-2   Weight: 215   College: Texas Tech   Draft: 2009/1 (10)   Born: 14-Sep-1987   Age: 31   Risk: Yellow

Year	Team	G/GS	Snaps	Pass	Rec	Yds	TD	C%	+/-	Drop	Yd/C	aDOT	Rk	YAC	Rk	YAC+	BTkl	DVOA	Rk	DYAR	Rk	YAR	Use	Rk	Slot
2015	OAK	16/15	809	146	85	922	9	58%	-6.7	6	10.8	10.1	63	3.1	75	-1.4	14	-13.0%	76	-4	77	3	24.1%	21	--
2016	OAK	16/16	835	145	89	1003	8	61%	+0.1	11	11.3	11.1	49	2.8	83	-1.4	12	5.3%	40	212	18	171	24.8%	14	49%
2017	OAK	14/14	603	101	58	618	8	57%	-2.7	7	10.7	11.2	49	3.3	65	-0.8	10	-6.5%	64	52	59	54	21.2%	26	33%
2018	BAL			120	76	807	7	63%			10.6							-7.4%							

Back in 2012, Crabtree, then with the San Francisco 49ers, went out for a pass in the end zone. Baltimore's Jimmy Smith was all over him. Crabtree will tell you it was interference. The refs disagreed. The Niners thus lost the Super Bowl to the Ravens. And now, Crabtree has joined Smith and the other lads in purple after being dumped by the Raiders. Irony can be pretty ironic sometimes.

Crabtree signed with the Ravens after a meh season in Oakland, where he led the team in targets but didn't do much with them. Crabtree has a rep as a red zone threat, but over the last three seasons he has just 46 percent catch rate with -7.7% DVOA in the red zone. Now 30 and on his third team, Crabtree will be catching passes (for the time being, anyway) from a quarterback on a major downward trend. Is Crabtree the sort of wideout who can help arrest that slide? Maybe as a third option, but in Baltimore he will be asked to be WR1. That seems beyond his capabilities at this stage of his career.

Jamison Crowder — Height: 5-8 — Weight: 185 — College: Duke — Draft: 2015/4 (105) — Born: 17-Jun-1993 — Age: 25 — Risk: Green

Year	Team	G/GS	Snaps	Pass	Rec	Yds	TD	C%	+/-	Drop	Yd/C	aDOT	Rk	YAC	Rk	YAC+	BTkl	DVOA	Rk	DYAR	Rk	YAR	Use	Rk	Slot
2015	WAS	16/6	734	78	59	604	2	76%	+5.1	2	10.2	6.0	85	5.7	12	+0.1	4	-4.4%	59	52	62	49	14.1%	68	--
2016	WAS	16/9	784	99	67	847	7	68%	+2.8	3	12.6	8.1	80	5.6	13	+0.8	11	4.6%	44	129	42	127	16.7%	58	97%
2017	WAS	15/6	674	103	66	789	3	64%	+1.4	8	12.0	7.5	80	5.6	12	+0.6	5	-4.5%	57	64	55	50	20.3%	30	89%
2018	WAS			100	64	768	5	64%			12.0							4.8%							

It's not exactly common, but NFL history is littered with late-round or undrafted wide receivers who failed to go over a thousand yards in any of their first three seasons, then developed into stars down the line. Cris Carter and Andre Reed did it in the '80s; Tony Martin and Terance Mathis did it in the '90s; and Donald Driver, Wes Welker, and T.J. Houshmandzadeh all did it this century. So yes, there is still time for Crowder to break out.

Crowder got off to a very slow start in 2017. Through five games he was averaging just 7.1 yards per catch (including one catch for -7 yards against Kansas City) with a DVOA of -41.7%. His average catch after that nearly doubled at 13.6 yards, and his DVOA jumped to 3.4%. The big difference schematically was throwing Crowder fewer quick outs and slants and more digs and curls. He was better at getting open in the middle of the field on midrange routes than catching passes underneath the defense and trying to make plays with the ball in his hands. Hopefully, in his fourth year in Jay Gruden's system, Crowder will be used to his full potential.

Corey Davis — Height: 6-3 — Weight: 209 — College: Western Michigan — Draft: 2017/1 (5) — Born: 11-Jan-1995 — Age: 23 — Risk: Red

Year	Team	G/GS	Snaps	Pass	Rec	Yds	TD	C%	+/-	Drop	Yd/C	aDOT	Rk	YAC	Rk	YAC+	BTkl	DVOA	Rk	DYAR	Rk	YAR	Use	Rk	Slot
2017	TEN	11/9	516	65	34	375	0	52%	-4.8	2	11.0	11.7	43	3.1	67	-1.4	10	-30.2%	85	-88	85	-97	19.4%	38	28%
2018	TEN			108	64	911	7	59%			14.2							5.7%							

Titans general manager Jon Robinson understandably bemoaned the injuries that cost his player chunks of the offseason, preseason, and regular season, but by any measure Davis' debut campaign was a disappointment. Only Zay Jones finished lower in either DVOA and DYAR, and Davis was closer to Jones' DVOA than that of third-from-the-bottom Bruce Ellington. It is possible to recover from a year like that—Steve Smith and Larry Fitzgerald have both recorded worse seasons, albeit with far worse quarterbacks—and Davis has spoken publicly about the learning experience he believes will benefit him in the near future.

Davis can point to his two playoff touchdowns against the Patriots as evidence that better things are in store for his second year, and we agree with that assessment. (As do his teammates: Taylor Lewan chose Davis as his player most likely to break out next year.) Matt LaFleur intends to simplify the route combinations for his receivers, which should be of greatest benefit to the younger players in the group. Davis also was not late to camp as his contract was worked out this year, and he will hope for better luck with health. If offseason reports are to be believed, he has bedded in comfortably as the No. 1 receiver in LaFleur's new offense, giving him a great chance to fulfil some of the potential that made him a fifth overall draft pick.

Eric Decker — Height: 6-3 — Weight: 217 — College: Minnesota — Draft: 2010/3 (87) — Born: 15-Mar-1987 — Age: 31 — Risk: N/A

Year	Team	G/GS	Snaps	Pass	Rec	Yds	TD	C%	+/-	Drop	Yd/C	aDOT	Rk	YAC	Rk	YAC+	BTkl	DVOA	Rk	DYAR	Rk	YAR	Use	Rk	Slot
2015	NYJ	15/13	906	132	80	1027	12	61%	+4.2	5	12.8	12.1	41	2.7	82	-1.1	1	13.6%	17	278	12	290	23.7%	23	--
2016	NYJ	3/3	211	21	9	194	2	43%	-2.2	0	21.6	15.9	--	3.3	--	-0.5	0	17.3%	--	48	--	43	20.2%	--	81%
2017	TEN	16/8	736	83	54	563	1	65%	+1.0	5	10.4	10.2	58	2.1	83	-1.7	3	-1.6%	51	72	51	80	17.5%	49	68%

Last year, Decker had both his lowest DVOA and his worst DYAR in a healthy season since Tim Tebow was his starting quarterback in Denver. His 9.8% red zone DVOA was better than his -5.5% overall figure, but Tennessee's investment in younger players ultimately made him expendable. He was not retained by the Titans, and is still unsigned as of late June. Decker could probably still do a solid job for a team in need of an emergency starter, but his best days as a receiver are behind him.

Stefon Diggs

Height: 6-0 Weight: 195 College: Maryland Draft: 2015/5 (146) Born: 29-Nov-1993 Age: 25 Risk: Yellow

Year	Team	G/GS	Snaps	Pass	Rec	Yds	TD	C%	+/-	Drop	Yd/C	aDOT	Rk	YAC	Rk	YAC+	BTkl	DVOA	Rk	DYAR	Rk	YAR	Use	Rk	Slot
2015	MIN	13/9	654	84	52	720	4	62%	+4.0	2	13.8	11.1	49	5.6	15	+0.8	14	3.8%	43	108	44	85	23.6%	24	--
2016	MIN	13/11	693	111	84	903	3	76%	+11.3	5	10.8	8.6	77	3.8	57	-0.8	9	8.2%	29	186	24	218	23.4%	20	69%
2017	MIN	14/14	781	95	64	849	8	67%	+6.8	5	13.3	11.9	41	4.7	30	+0.3	9	24.7%	5	295	9	308	21.4%	25	40%
2018	MIN			111	74	956	6	67%			12.9							13.2%							

Diggs has a highlight for life with The Minneapolis Miracle, the first walk-off fourth-quarter touchdown in NFL postseason history. Diggs is more than a guy with one big catch in a playoff game, but surprisingly he has never had a 1,000-yard receiving season in his three tries, partly because he's always missed two or three games each season. Kirk Cousins is no stranger to throwing the ball often to his wideouts, so Diggs could be in for a career year. We don't know exactly how the Vikings will use Diggs and Adam Thielen this year. Diggs was primarily used in the slot in 2016, while Thielen took on that responsibility in 2017. With Kendall Wright in town, perhaps the Vikings will keep Diggs and Thielen out wide more. For what it's worth, Cousins' top receiver in Washington last year was Jamison Crowder, who worked almost exclusively from the slot. Diggs can get open from anywhere, but there may be some touchdown regression. He had eight scores last year after just seven in his first two seasons combined. If there was a knock on Cousins, it was in the red zone, where he just didn't connect on as many touchdowns as expected, especially to his wide receivers.

Josh Doctson

Height: 6-2 Weight: 202 College: TCU Draft: 2016/1 (22) Born: 3-Dec-1992 Age: 26 Risk: Green

Year	Team	G/GS	Snaps	Pass	Rec	Yds	TD	C%	+/-	Drop	Yd/C	aDOT	Rk	YAC	Rk	YAC+	BTkl	DVOA	Rk	DYAR	Rk	YAR	Use	Rk	Slot
2016	WAS	2/0	31	6	2	66	0	33%	-0.8	0	33.0	14.4	--	7.5	--	+1.5	0	-9.3%	--	2	--	-3	8.0%	--	0%
2017	WAS	16/14	756	78	35	502	6	45%	-6.7	6	14.3	14.3	18	3.7	48	-0.7	3	-7.1%	65	37	64	22	15.2%	64	30%
2018	WAS			86	49	730	6	57%			14.9							5.5%							

After missing most of his rookie year with an Achilles injury, Doctson wasn't used much early in 2017. He had only nine targets in Washington's first five games, and never played much more than half the offense's snaps in any of those games. He played 80 percent of the snaps in every game after that, as the team gave up on Terrelle Pryor and let the youngster play instead.

Doctson's catch rate really fell off a cliff in the last two games of the year, when he caught only six passes in 23 targets. His first seven targets against Denver were all incomplete, and the eighth was intercepted. Only two players with at least 80 targets over the last two years have a worse catch rate than Doctson: Breshad Perriman and Corey Coleman. All three were first-round draft picks, which goes to show that you never know how prospects are going to turn out.

Julian Edelman

Height: 6-0 Weight: 198 College: Kent State Draft: 2009/7 (232) Born: 22-May-1986 Age: 32 Risk: Yellow

Year	Team	G/GS	Snaps	Pass	Rec	Yds	TD	C%	+/-	Drop	Yd/C	aDOT	Rk	YAC	Rk	YAC+	BTkl	DVOA	Rk	DYAR	Rk	YAR	Use	Rk	Slot
2015	NE	9/9	525	88	61	692	7	69%	+2.6	6	11.3	8.0	76	5.1	25	+0.5	15	8.1%	35	144	28	159	25.0%	17	--
2016	NE	16/13	875	159	98	1106	3	62%	-4.0	10	11.3	9.1	72	5.0	29	+0.2	12	-9.2%	68	43	65	38	28.9%	3	80%
2018	NE			97	68	756	5	71%			11.1							13.6%							

After missing last year with a torn ACL, Edelman returns to a Patriots team counting on him once again. Brandin Cooks is in Los Angeles with the Rams, and the New England short game suffered greatly in Edelman's absence. Is he still up for the challenge at 32, or will he leave something on the operating table? A lot of New England's offensive blueprint will depend on the answer to this question. Edelman was a limited participant in OTAs, but should still be on track for a training camp return. Word broke in June that Edelman was facing a four-game suspension for PED use; he can still be plenty valuable in fantasy football, but make sure you have a strong bench receiver to sit in for him in September.

Bruce Ellington

Height: 5-9 Weight: 197 College: South Carolina Draft: 2014/4 (106) Born: 22-Aug-1991 Age: 27 Risk: Red

Year	Team	G/GS	Snaps	Pass	Rec	Yds	TD	C%	+/-	Drop	Yd/C	aDOT	Rk	YAC	Rk	YAC+	BTkl	DVOA	Rk	DYAR	Rk	YAR	Use	Rk	Slot
2015	SF	13/0	143	19	13	153	0	68%	+0.1	1	11.8	8.8	--	8.5	--	-0.1	2	-32.7%	--	-27	--	-34	4.4%	--	--
2017	HOU	11/6	591	57	29	330	2	51%	-4.2	3	11.4	9.2	70	4.7	29	-0.2	5	-24.5%	84	-53	84	-61	15.8%	58	93%
2018	HOU			58	33	404	2	57%			12.2							-7.2%							

With Deshaun Watson: 23 targets, 3.3% DVOA, 28 DYAR. Without: 35 targets, -43.0% DVOA, -81 DYAR. Ellington lost the early season to a concussion and dealt with a hamstring injury late. Overall, the August addition played more than expected; it was a varied role, from the third option with Will Fuller available to a more prominent one when Fuller missed time. Ellington did enough that the Texans brought him back on a one-year deal. The selection of Keke Coutee should limit his snaps some, but Houston's depth on the outside remains thin.

Quincy Enunwa Height: 6-2 Weight: 225 College: Nebraska Draft: 2014/6 (209) Born: 31-May-1992 Age: 26 Risk: Red

Year	Team	G/GS	Snaps	Pass	Rec	Yds	TD	C%	+/-	Drop	Yd/C	aDOT	Rk	YAC	Rk	YAC+	BTkl	DVOA	Rk	DYAR	Rk	YAR	Use	Rk	Slot
2015	NYJ	12/6	522	46	22	315	0	48%	-6.9	5	14.3	10.5	--	6.7	--	+1.9	7	-27.0%	--	-48	--	-40	10.1%	--	--
2016	NYJ	16/13	873	105	58	857	4	55%	-9.0	7	14.8	9.4	69	6.1	7	+1.1	13	-4.5%	63	69	58	72	19.3%	41	82%
2018	NYJ			82	48	655	5	59%			13.6							2.6%							

Shelved early with a bulging disk, Enunwa's absence wasn't an altogether bad thing for the Jets, as it allowed them some time to examine the multitude of other young receivers on the roster. Enunwa is their best tackle-breaker in the open field, though, so he gives the offense a dimension it lacked in 2017. Tendered at a second-round level, Enunwa is playing for a new contract this year. If he has any setbacks, he might have a hard time getting back on the field, because the Jets have merely 800 other receivers on the depth chart aching for a chance.

Mike Evans Height: 6-5 Weight: 231 College: Texas A&M Draft: 2014/1 (7) Born: 21-Aug-1993 Age: 25 Risk: Yellow

Year	Team	G/GS	Snaps	Pass	Rec	Yds	TD	C%	+/-	Drop	Yd/C	aDOT	Rk	YAC	Rk	YAC+	BTkl	DVOA	Rk	DYAR	Rk	YAR	Use	Rk	Slot
2015	TB	15/14	857	148	74	1206	3	50%	-6.2	10	16.3	15.5	12	3.3	74	-0.9	4	2.8%	44	187	22	153	30.7%	5	--
2016	TB	16/16	950	173	96	1321	12	55%	+2.3	8	13.8	14.6	9	1.8	94	-1.9	2	10.0%	26	309	6	312	30.2%	1	43%
2017	TB	15/15	884	136	71	1001	5	52%	-2.6	7	14.1	14.2	19	1.7	85	-2.0	4	1.2%	42	149	27	145	24.6%	12	39%
2018	TB			147	80	1185	9	54%			14.8							-0.2%							

With three catches on the final drive of the season, Mike Evans eclipsed the thousand-yard barrier with 3 feet to spare. He joins Randy Moss (1998-2001) and A.J. Green (2011-2014) as the only players in NFL history to start their career with four straight 1,000-yard receiving seasons. Last year was not the best we've seen from Evans. It even included a one-game suspension after he pushed Marshon Lattimore from behind during a scuffle in New Orleans. By now we know Evans for his large catch radius and lack of YAC. His importance to the passing game in snagging some off-target throws by Jameis Winston cannot be understated. Roughly 61 percent of Winston's career passing DYAR is from just his targets to Evans.

Larry Fitzgerald Height: 6-3 Weight: 225 College: Pittsburgh Draft: 2004/1 (3) Born: 31-Aug-1983 Age: 35 Risk: Yellow

Year	Team	G/GS	Snaps	Pass	Rec	Yds	TD	C%	+/-	Drop	Yd/C	aDOT	Rk	YAC	Rk	YAC+	BTkl	DVOA	Rk	DYAR	Rk	YAR	Use	Rk	Slot
2015	ARI	16/16	984	146	109	1215	9	75%	+14.7	2	11.1	8.6	71	4.2	48	-0.6	8	18.9%	10	363	4	356	26.5%	12	--
2016	ARI	16/16	1052	152	107	1023	6	72%	+7.3	4	9.6	7.1	88	3.4	68	-1.1	16	-6.8%	65	71	57	119	23.7%	19	79%
2017	ARI	16/16	1074	161	109	1156	6	68%	+7.1	5	10.6	8.6	75	3.7	47	-1.1	8	-1.3%	50	147	28	182	27.2%	10	81%
2018	ARI			154	106	1101	6	69%			10.4							-0.4%							

Fitzgerald is destined for Canton, and he managed to stave off Father Time for one more season, finishing with more than 1,000 receiving yards for the ninth time in his 14-year career despite catching passes from the shell of Carson Palmer, career backup Drew Stanton, and just-plain-bad Blaine Gabbert. While his efficiency numbers are no longer at the lofty levels he posted as recently as 2015, Fitzgerald has still been a useful player in his advanced age, as Cardinals quarterbacks targeted him 161 times in 2017, good for the fourth-highest total of his career. Part of that was because with the loss of running back David Johnson there were no other strong options in the Arizona receiving corps. Part of it was that Fitzgerald was getting a lot of the "bubble screens to keep his games with a catch streak alive" treatment that Bruce Arians once gave Hines Ward in his twilight years in Pittsburgh. No player had more WR screens than Fitzgerald's 28 last season, but he also had a league-low -68 DYAR on those plays with only five of them producing a first down.

Back for what could be his last hurrah in 2018, Fitzgerald should at worst provide a veteran security blanket for either Sam Bradford or Josh Rosen, and it would not be surprising to see him go out with another 1,000-yard year.

Bennie Fowler | Height: 6-1 | Weight: 212 | College: Michigan State | Draft: 2014/FA | Born: 10-Jun-1991 | Age: 27 | Risk: Green

Year	Team	G/GS	Snaps	Pass	Rec	Yds	TD	C%	+/-	Drop	Yd/C	aDOT	Rk	YAC	Rk	YAC+	BTkl	DVOA	Rk	DYAR	Rk	YAR	Use	Rk	Slot
2015	DEN	16/1	264	25	16	203	0	64%	-0.5	0	12.7	7.8	—	6.1	—	+1.4	8	-3.4%	—	20	—	24	4.4%	—	—
2016	DEN	13/0	242	24	11	145	2	46%	-3.0	1	13.2	11.1	—	5.8	—	+2.0	0	-22.2%	—	-16	—	-16	5.2%	—	83%
2017	DEN	16/4	575	56	29	350	3	52%	-5.3	4	12.1	10.2	57	3.7	50	-0.1	3	-9.8%	69	12	70	14	10.0%	82	77%
2018	CHI			25	13	146	1	52%			11.2							-18.5%							

Fowler was more active for Denver last season, but his legacy is still going to be "caught the last completion in Peyton Manning's career." Actually, his 76-yard touchdown against the Chiefs in 2016 was pretty good too, though it's also the only game in Fowler's career where he broke 60 receiving yards, and that was on one play. In Chicago he'll have to compete with Josh Bellamy, Demarcus Ayers, and others for a reserve role.

Will Fuller | Height: 6-0 | Weight: 186 | College: Notre Dame | Draft: 2016/1 (21) | Born: 16-Apr-1994 | Age: 24 | Risk: Green

Year	Team	G/GS	Snaps	Pass	Rec	Yds	TD	C%	+/-	Drop	Yd/C	aDOT	Rk	YAC	Rk	YAC+	BTkl	DVOA	Rk	DYAR	Rk	YAR	Use	Rk	Slot
2016	HOU	14/13	829	92	47	635	2	51%	-2.4	6	13.5	15.7	4	4.7	35	-0.2	7	-14.8%	77	-15	78	-15	18.0%	45	43%
2017	HOU	10/10	530	50	28	423	7	56%	+1.7	2	15.1	17.4	2	3.5	56	-0.7	0	17.6%	12	126	35	134	15.6%	59	42%
2018	HOU			95	53	788	6	56%			14.9							7.5%							

With Deshaun Watson: 24 targets, 68.2% DVOA, 156 DYAR. Without: 28 targets, -25.9% DVOA, -30 DYAR. What happens when a deep-ball specialist receiver finally has a good deep-ball passer? Fuller showed with Watson he could be amazingly productive. His role was best expressed in one stat: his average target with Watson came more than 23 yards downfield (without Watson, it came just 11 yards downfield). His productivity … well, seven touchdowns on 13 catches in four games speaks for itself. That rate is unsustainable, but a young Mike Wallace did lead all receivers in DYAR in 2010 catching a bunch of bombs from Ben Roethlisberger. Health will be a key, as Fuller was banged up all year, with a broken collarbone early, a rib injury midseason, and a late knee injury that required surgery.

Devin Funchess | Height: 6-4 | Weight: 232 | College: Michigan | Draft: 2015/2 (41) | Born: 21-May-1994 | Age: 24 | Risk: Yellow

Year	Team	G/GS	Snaps	Pass	Rec	Yds	TD	C%	+/-	Drop	Yd/C	aDOT	Rk	YAC	Rk	YAC+	BTkl	DVOA	Rk	DYAR	Rk	YAR	Use	Rk	Slot
2015	CAR	16/5	493	63	31	473	5	49%	-5.1	3	15.3	13.4	26	3.6	63	-0.4	3	-10.7%	73	9	73	32	12.7%	71	—
2016	CAR	15/7	494	58	23	371	4	40%	-8.9	5	16.1	14.1	16	4.5	42	+1.0	2	-7.4%	66	26	68	28	11.8%	86	39%
2017	CAR	16/16	853	112	63	840	8	56%	-2.0	4	13.3	13.4	26	4.5	36	+0.2	3	6.8%	32	168	21	157	22.8%	16	38%
2018	CAR			120	64	900	8	53%			14.1							-1.7%							

After a couple of very poor seasons to open his career, the light came on for Funchess last season. A 56 percent catch rate isn't exactly Canton worthy, but considering his average depth of target, and the fact that he was dead last in catch rate among qualified receivers in 2016, it's a tremendous step forward. His route-running took steps forward as well. There were 45 players with at least eight dig routes in 2017; none had a better DVOA on those routes than Funchess' 58.4%. In an ideal world, Funchess is probably still a very good second receiver as opposed to being the guy around whom you build an offense, but before last season, he looked more like a failed draft pick than anything else. If he continues to improve in the fine details of playing the position, he could take another significant step forward in 2018.

Taylor Gabriel | Height: 5-8 | Weight: 167 | College: Abilene Christian | Draft: 2014/FA | Born: 17-Feb-1991 | Age: 27 | Risk: Yellow

Year	Team	G/GS	Snaps	Pass	Rec	Yds	TD	C%	+/-	Drop	Yd/C	aDOT	Rk	YAC	Rk	YAC+	BTkl	DVOA	Rk	DYAR	Rk	YAR	Use	Rk	Slot
2015	CLE	13/4	401	48	28	241	0	58%	-4.4	4	8.6	7.6	—	3.9	—	-2.3	2	-31.8%	—	-74	—	-95	9.8%	—	—
2016	ATL	13/3	349	51	35	579	6	71%	+4.4	0	16.5	11.0	51	7.7	1	+1.9	7	33.7%	1	181	25	185	11.8%	85	71%
2017	ATL	16/4	540	51	33	378	1	65%	+0.2	2	11.5	10.3	56	6.6	6	+0.8	7	-8.0%	67	18	68	19	9.9%	84	48%
2018	CHI			57	32	388	1	56%			12.1							-10.4%							

Some of Gabriel's best highlights in Atlanta were on screen passes. This makes sense—not many of those plays pop for big gains, so we certainly remember the ones that do. But Gabriel had some success with them in 2016 when he had 31 DYAR on

10 screens. He got 10 screens again last year, with 16 DYAR. That's still pretty respectable seeing as how most receivers have negative DYAR on screens. Gabriel had his most DYAR on slants (39) and digs (25) last year, so hopefully he'll be more than a gadget receiver for Matt Nagy and the Bears.

Michael Gallup   Height: 6-1   Weight: 205   College: Colorado State   Draft: 2018/3 (81)   Born: 4-Mar-1996   Age: 22   Risk: Red

Year	Team	G/GS	Snaps	Pass	Rec	Yds	TD	C%	+/-	Drop	Yd/C	aDOT	Rk	YAC	Rk	YAC+	BTkl	DVOA	Rk	DYAR	Rk	YAR	Use	Rk	Slot
2018	DAL			35	21	276	2	60%			13.2							-0.4%							

Jerry Jones said during the draft that Gallup would be a contributor in Week 1, and Jon Machota of the *Dallas Morning News* said the rookie could finish as the Cowboys' leading receiver, but that all says as much about the scarcity of quality weapons in the Dallas passing game as it does about Gallup. That said, Gallup does know something about big-time production. He had 2,690 yards, 15.3 yards per catch, and 21 touchdowns in two seasons at Colorado State, with three 200-yard games.

Pierre Garcon   Height: 6-0   Weight: 210   College: Mount Union   Draft: 2008/6 (205)   Born: 8-Aug-1986   Age: 32   Risk: Yellow

Year	Team	G/GS	Snaps	Pass	Rec	Yds	TD	C%	+/-	Drop	Yd/C	aDOT	Rk	YAC	Rk	YAC+	BTkl	DVOA	Rk	DYAR	Rk	YAR	Use	Rk	Slot
2015	WAS	16/16	811	111	72	777	6	65%	+3.9	2	10.8	10.9	52	2.3	86	-2.1	3	2.4%	45	128	33	129	20.0%	36	--
2016	WAS	16/16	808	114	79	1041	3	69%	+8.8	2	13.2	10.3	60	4.3	45	-0.1	13	16.3%	14	262	10	256	19.2%	42	27%
2017	SF	8/8	430	67	40	500	0	60%	-2.9	0	12.5	10.0	62	4.7	31	-0.2	3	-3.8%	55	45	63	41	22.5%	18	54%
2018	SF			117	70	898	8	60%			12.8							4.1%							

In his first season with the team after coming over from Washington as a free agent, Garcon provided a steady veteran presence in the San Francisco wide receiver room. At the halfway point of the season, Garcon was the team's leading receiver with an even 500 yards, but a neck injury suffered in the Week 8 tilt against Philadelphia ended his year. San Francisco paid a premium for his services before the 2017 season, and he will hope to spark a connection with Jimmy Garoppolo this fall after catching passes from Brian Hoyer and C.J. Beathard last year. Garcon's starting job is safe for now, though as he progresses into the more expensive years of his contract, he could see his role diminished with young receivers Trent Taylor and Dante Pettis taking on more responsibilities in the San Francisco offense.

Ted Ginn   Height: 5-11   Weight: 178   College: Ohio State   Draft: 2007/1 (9)   Born: 12-Apr-1985   Age: 33   Risk: Green

Year	Team	G/GS	Snaps	Pass	Rec	Yds	TD	C%	+/-	Drop	Yd/C	aDOT	Rk	YAC	Rk	YAC+	BTkl	DVOA	Rk	DYAR	Rk	YAR	Use	Rk	Slot
2015	CAR	15/13	670	96	44	739	10	46%	-6.4	7	16.8	16.6	3	5.5	19	+1.4	2	-2.5%	55	77	52	106	20.8%	34	--
2016	CAR	16/8	687	95	54	752	4	57%	-2.9	6	13.9	13.2	29	3.4	70	-1.6	5	-10.8%	72	13	72	15	16.9%	56	37%
2017	NO	15/10	617	70	53	787	4	76%	+10.0	2	14.8	12.6	36	5.4	14	+0.1	9	34.8%	2	259	12	266	14.0%	68	59%
2018	NO			69	46	626	3	67%			13.6							13.0%		*(Also: 9 runs, 51 RuYd, 0.3 RuTD)*						

How much can a quarterback help a receiver? In his 11th season, the notoriously inconsistent Ginn finished second in DVOA, a stat in which he had never ranked higher than 47th. Ginn had 24 receiving DYAR in his first 10 seasons (193 DYAR in his five best seasons combined), but shot up to 259 DYAR in his first year with Drew Brees in New Orleans. Ginn caught 52 percent of his targets in his first decade, but was at 76 percent last year. His success mostly came on early downs. Ginn had 49.6% DVOA and caught 85 percent of his targets on first and second down, but was down to 6.6% DVOA and a 58 percent catch rate on third and fourth down. He'll have to compete with Cameron Meredith this year, so he's far from a lock to repeat last year's success.

Chris Godwin   Height: 6-1   Weight: 209   College: Penn State   Draft: 2017/3 (84)   Born: 27-Feb-1996   Age: 22   Risk: Green

Year	Team	G/GS	Snaps	Pass	Rec	Yds	TD	C%	+/-	Drop	Yd/C	aDOT	Rk	YAC	Rk	YAC+	BTkl	DVOA	Rk	DYAR	Rk	YAR	Use	Rk	Slot
2017	TB	16/2	449	55	34	525	1	62%	+2.4	2	15.4	13.4	27	5.0	23	+0.8	7	20.5%	10	138	33	130	9.1%	86	44%
2018	TB			74	41	588	4	55%			14.4							-2.9%							

Godwin had just 83 receiving yards halfway through his rookie season, but he finished strong with 442 yards over his last eight games. He picked a good time to score his first touchdown, the 39-yard game winner against the Saints in Week 17. That also capped off Godwin's first 100-yard receiving game. He has a lot of competition for targets in Tampa Bay, but Godwin showed a diverse route tree last year to deserve more opportunities. He just has to be trusted more to produce on money downs. He only had nine targets on third/fourth down last year with a -15.7% DVOA, as opposed to early downs where he was at 27.6% DVOA.

Kenny Golladay

Height: 6-4 Weight: 218 College: Northern Illinois Draft: 2017/3 (96) Born: 3-Nov-1993 Age: 25 Risk: Red

Year	Team	G/GS	Snaps	Pass	Rec	Yds	TD	C%	+/-	Drop	Yd/C	aDOT	Rk	YAC	Rk	YAC+	BTkl	DVOA	Rk	DYAR	Rk	YAR	Use	Rk	Slot
2017	DET	11/5	477	48	28	477	3	58%	+0.7	1	17.0	14.9	--	6.5	--	+1.5	2	21.9%	--	130	--	126	12.4%	--	33%
2018	DET			93	55	859	6	59%			15.6							10.0%							

In his NFL debut against Arizona, Golladay caught a game-winning touchdown in the fourth quarter and followed it up with a beautiful, diving effort for another 45-yard score. It was such a nice debut with 69 yards for Golladay, but we didn't see him surpass that total or score another touchdown until the season finale, when he had 80 yards and a score against Green Bay. Golladay's most common route was the go route, where he had ten targets for a 66.1% DVOA and 55 DYAR, which ranked eighth in the league. If he can stay healthy and progress this season, then his size and deep-threat ability could be a way for Detroit's offense to move up a tier.

Marquise Goodwin

Height: 5-9 Weight: 183 College: Texas Draft: 2013/3 (78) Born: 19-Nov-1990 Age: 28 Risk: Green

Year	Team	G/GS	Snaps	Pass	Rec	Yds	TD	C%	+/-	Drop	Yd/C	aDOT	Rk	YAC	Rk	YAC+	BTkl	DVOA	Rk	DYAR	Rk	YAR	Use	Rk	Slot
2015	BUF	2/0	28	2	2	24	0	100%	+0.7	0	12.0	11.0	--	1.0	--	-2.2	0	69.3%	--	13	--	15	3.4%	--	--
2016	BUF	15/9	638	68	29	431	3	43%	-7.1	3	14.9	15.2	5	2.8	86	-0.9	1	-23.8%	87	-56	86	-50	15.6%	64	26%
2017	SF	16/16	769	105	56	962	2	53%	-0.3	7	17.2	15.3	11	3.4	58	-0.8	7	5.9%	34	155	24	149	17.5%	48	57%
2018	SF			75	39	650	4	52%			16.7							3.1%							

The former Bills receiver and Olympic long jumper provided solid value in his first season as a starter in San Francisco. While his catch rate was not particularly impressive, he still was a useful contributor as a deep threat, with 36 percent of his targets coming 16 or more yards down the field. Goodwin's play in 2017 earned him a three-year contract extension just prior to the official start of free agency. The contract contains almost no guaranteed money, meaning Goodwin needs to continue to produce, but at the age of 28, he should still have a few more good years in him. His role will likely be limited again to that of the deep threat, but opposing teams will always need to be aware when a receiver like Goodwin can take the top off the defense.

Josh Gordon

Height: 6-4 Weight: 220 College: Baylor Draft: 2012/2 (SUP) Born: 12-Apr-1991 Age: 27 Risk: Red

Year	Team	G/GS	Snaps	Pass	Rec	Yds	TD	C%	+/-	Drop	Yd/C	aDOT	Rk	YAC	Rk	YAC+	BTkl	DVOA	Rk	DYAR	Rk	YAR	Use	Rk	Slot
2017	CLE	5/5	259	42	18	335	1	43%	-2.5	1	18.6	17.2	--	6.8	--	+2.2	4	-7.8%	--	16	--	13	23.1%	--	38%
2018	CLE			119	58	1003	7	49%			17.3							-1.0%							

Gordon led the NFL with 1,646 receiving yards in 2013 despite playing only 14 games—and, he later admitted, drinking or getting high before every game. Those addiction problems cost Gordon most of the 2014 season and all of 2015 and 2016 before he came back last December ... and immediately put up 85 yards in his first game back, mostly against Pro Bowl cornerback Casey Hayward. Anybody who loves good football is hoping that Gordon can keep clean and show off his talents for an entire season. He has freakish physical abilities, an astonishing combination of size and speed, and excels at picking the ball out of the air over cornerbacks. Once he catches the ball, he's difficult to take down in the open field. It's hard to imagine a bigger risk-reward in fantasy football this year. But if he hits that upside, man, is it going to be fun to watch every week.

Ryan Grant

Height: 6-0 Weight: 199 College: Tulane Draft: 2014/5 (142) Born: 19-Dec-1990 Age: 28 Risk: Yellow

Year	Team	G/GS	Snaps	Pass	Rec	Yds	TD	C%	+/-	Drop	Yd/C	aDOT	Rk	YAC	Rk	YAC+	BTkl	DVOA	Rk	DYAR	Rk	YAR	Use	Rk	Slot
2015	WAS	16/5	456	42	23	268	2	55%	-0.4	2	11.7	9.4	--	4.3	--	-0.1	2	-1.1%	--	40	--	31	7.7%	--	--
2016	WAS	16/1	271	19	9	76	0	47%	-2.9	1	8.4	8.7	--	2.8	--	-1.7	0	-34.9%	--	-35	--	-38	3.2%	--	63%
2017	WAS	16/7	616	65	45	573	4	69%	+4.1	4	12.7	9.7	68	5.2	18	+0.7	7	16.7%	13	146	31	152	12.0%	76	58%
2018	IND			93	56	762	4	60%			13.6							3.6%							

Grant's most notable move this offseason was for the Ravens to have apparent buyer's remorse on the free-agent contract they gave him, flunking him on a physical after the Raiders released Michael Crabtree. He found his way to a less lucrative (one year, $5 million vs. four years, $29 million) offer in Indianapolis' benighted depth chart. On the field, his precision and route-running kept earning him snaps over more heralded players in Washington. With question marks aplenty after T.Y. Hilton and a new staff putting all players on an even footing, it would not be a surprise to see Grant earn a regular role in 2018, if only until the rookies get up to speed.

A.J. Green

Height: 6-4　　Weight: 207　　College: Georgia　　Draft: 2011/1 (4)　　Born: 31-Jul-1988　　Age: 30　　Risk: Green

Year	Team	G/GS	Snaps	Pass	Rec	Yds	TD	C%	+/-	Drop	Yd/C	aDOT	Rk	YAC	Rk	YAC+	BTkl	DVOA	Rk	DYAR	Rk	YAR	Use	Rk	Slot
2015	CIN	16/16	932	132	86	1297	10	65%	+13.2	3	15.1	13.1	31	3.9	57	-0.3	6	26.5%	7	414	3	403	26.4%	13	--
2016	CIN	10/10	554	100	66	964	4	66%	+6.8	3	14.6	12.4	35	3.9	54	-1.1	9	19.1%	9	250	11	232	29.9%	2	24%
2017	CIN	16/16	857	143	75	1078	8	52%	-1.3	6	14.4	13.9	23	4.0	44	+0.2	11	-6.4%	63	73	49	88	29.7%	3	25%
2018	CIN			141	79	1111	7	56%			14.1							-2.0%							

2017 was, by Adriel Jeremiah's lofty standards, a terrible year. Sure, he got to 1,000 yards for the sixth time in seven seasons (only in 2016, when Green missed six games, has he fallen shy of a grand), but had to be force-fed targets to do so—a full 30 percent of the Bengals' passes went to Green, tied for most in the league. As such, his efficiency went into the toilet. There were some extenuating circumstances; Ken Zampese essentially forgot Green existed during the first two games, so replacement Bill Lazor made up for it by tilting a bit too far in the other direction. Since Cincy was devoid of other receivers, and the offensive line couldn't run block, tossing one in A.J.'s direction and hoping for the best—ordinarily a sound stratagem—became the Bengals' Plans A, B and C. Green responded with an unusually high number of drops, which fed into a career low catch rate. 2018 is his age-30 season, and a sudden drop from the top tier of wideouts would be disastrous for an offense already challenged in several areas. The Bengals don't function if Green isn't playing at an All-Pro level.

Justin Hardy

Height: 5-10　　Weight: 192　　College: East Carolina　　Draft: 2015/4 (107)　　Born: 18-Dec-1991　　Age: 27　　Risk: Green

Year	Team	G/GS	Snaps	Pass	Rec	Yds	TD	C%	+/-	Drop	Yd/C	aDOT	Rk	YAC	Rk	YAC+	BTkl	DVOA	Rk	DYAR	Rk	YAR	Use	Rk	Slot
2015	ATL	9/1	337	36	21	194	0	58%	-1.6	2	9.2	8.0	--	3.1	--	-1.0	0	-24.8%	--	-32	--	-20	10.3%	--	--
2016	ATL	16/3	290	31	21	203	4	68%	+2.2	0	9.7	8.7	--	2.3	--	-1.5	1	14.8%	--	70	--	73	5.7%	--	39%
2017	ATL	16/1	383	29	20	221	3	69%	+1.0	2	11.1	8.4	--	3.8	--	-0.3	1	12.5%	--	59	--	62	5.7%	--	67%
2018	ATL			26	15	169	1	58%			11.2							-12.1%							

Hardy has been a reliable receiver for the Falcons when he receives targets, but he has been unable to break into the starting rotation throughout his four-year career. He completely disappeared from Atlanta's playbook at times. He didn't even get a target in consecutive games gainst Tampa Bay, Minnesota, and New Orleans despite playing 58 offensive snaps in those three contests. With addition of Calvin Ridley, Hardy once again looks wedged into the fourth wide receiver spot on the depth chart.

Carlos Henderson

Height: 5-11　　Weight: 199　　College: Louisiana Tech　　Draft: 2017/3 (82)　　Born: 19-Dec-1994　　Age: 24　　Risk: Yellow

Year	Team	Snaps	Pass	Rec	Yds	TD	C%	+/-	Drop	Yd/C	aDOT	Rk	YAC	Rk	YAC+	BTkl	DVOA	Rk	DYAR	Rk	YAR	Use	Rk	Slot
2018	DEN		33	20	290	2	61%			14.5							2.8%							

Henderson, the Broncos' third-round pick last year, missed the entire season with a thumb injury. He was also arrested on a DUI in January and may face a suspension. Henderson has potential as an elusive slot receiver, but the Broncos haven't been able to do anything with players like him over the last three years except stick them on the bench and cross their fingers that something good will happen.

Rashard Higgins

Height: 6-1 | Weight: 196 | College: Colorado State | Draft: 2016/5 (172) | Born: 7-Oct-1994 | Age: 24 | Risk: Red

Year	Team	G/GS	Snaps	Pass	Rec	Yds	TD	C%	+/-	Drop	Yd/C	aDOT	Rk	YAC	Rk	YAC+	BTkl	DVOA	Rk	DYAR	Rk	YAR	Use	Rk	Slot
2016	CLE	16/0	183	12	6	77	0	50%	-0.9	1	12.8	11.7	--	5.2	--	+1.4	1	-26.4%	--	-14	--	-11	2.1%	--	33%
2017	CLE	15/4	664	51	27	312	2	55%	-1.5	2	11.6	9.6	69	5.3	16	+0.7	9	-23.1%	82	-41	81	-50	9.4%	85	92%
2018	CLE			27	14	153	0	52%			11.0							-24.0%							

"Hollywood" Higgins—it's a nickname left over from a pee-wee coach—was almost exclusively a slot receiver last year, so the Jarvis Landry trade renders him superfluous unless the Browns decide to use Landry a lot more on the outside. Otherwise you start to wonder if Higgins will make the roster, since he has limited upside compared to competition such as Corey Coleman, Antonio Callaway, and even Ricardo Louis.

Tyreek Hill

Height: 5-9 | Weight: 185 | College: West Alabama | Draft: 2016/5 (165) | Born: 1-Mar-1994 | Age: 24 | Risk: Green

Year	Team	G/GS	Snaps	Pass	Rec	Yds	TD	C%	+/-	Drop	Yd/C	aDOT	Rk	YAC	Rk	YAC+	BTkl	DVOA	Rk	DYAR	Rk	YAR	Use	Rk	Slot
2016	KC	16/1	418	83	61	593	6	73%	+3.9	6	9.7	8.0	82	4.5	41	-1.1	26	0.8%	50	87	55	67	15.4%	66	53%
2017	KC	15/13	779	106	75	1183	7	72%	+10.0	3	15.8	11.7	44	6.1	9	+0.4	19	23.6%	7	304	8	303	21.4%	24	42%
2018	KC			107	71	1065	7	66%			15.0							16.6%		(Also: 18 runs, 120 RuYd, 0.6 RuTD)						

Hill is not the most versatile wide receiver in the league, but he is an absolute terror of a deep threat. Similar to a prime DeSean Jackson, Hill forces defenses to account for his speed, thus allowing for routes from other players underneath and over the middle to have more breathing room. Of course, a deep threat as devastating as Hill will find ways to still get open despite the attention. Hill managed to catch 15 passes on 28 deep targets in 2017. Furthermore, Hill converted those receptions into 40-plus-yard plays a league-best nine times. Given his speed, Hill also makes for a great screen receiver, end-around option, and underneath yards-after-catch generator. His twitch and agility are difficult to corral in tight quarters. The criticism of Hill will always be that he can not handle the most strenuous route tree, but given how effective he can be on just a handful of key patterns, there is no necessity to expand his role. Andy Reid knows better than to force a square peg into a round hole.

T.Y. Hilton

Height: 5-10 | Weight: 183 | College: Florida International | Draft: 2012/3 (92) | Born: 14-Nov-1989 | Age: 29 | Risk: Yellow

Year	Team	G/GS	Snaps	Pass	Rec	Yds	TD	C%	+/-	Drop	Yd/C	aDOT	Rk	YAC	Rk	YAC+	BTkl	DVOA	Rk	DYAR	Rk	YAR	Use	Rk	Slot
2015	IND	16/15	925	134	69	1124	5	51%	-7.8	1	16.3	13.1	32	5.5	17	+0.9	8	-7.7%	64	52	61	77	22.1%	27	--
2016	IND	16/16	947	155	91	1448	6	59%	+6.3	10	15.9	13.2	28	3.8	58	-0.4	6	17.3%	12	360	4	333	26.8%	9	76%
2017	IND	16/16	926	109	57	966	4	52%	-0.9	5	16.9	13.4	28	5.3	15	+0.7	3	-3.8%	56	75	48	60	23.2%	14	68%
2018	IND			128	73	1182	7	57%			16.2							8.7%							

Hilton's 2018 usage will be fascinating to watch. As bad a fit as the vertically-oriented scheme was for other players, it seemed to play perfectly to Hilton's strengths as a deep receiver who could successfully use his downfield speed to win in more ways than just vertically. The new scheme built more around shorter passes setting up big gains will be a bit of a change for him. He'll still get some downfield targets, but may be asked to do more after the catch on shorter throws. Minus the carries, though, Hilton should be able to excel in a combined role that might be along similar lines as what the similarly sized Tyreek Hill did with the Chiefs last year.

Chris Hogan

Height: 6-1 | Weight: 220 | College: Monmouth | Draft: 2012/FA | Born: 24-Oct-1988 | Age: 30 | Risk: Red

Year	Team	G/GS	Snaps	Pass	Rec	Yds	TD	C%	+/-	Drop	Yd/C	aDOT	Rk	YAC	Rk	YAC+	BTkl	DVOA	Rk	DYAR	Rk	YAR	Use	Rk	Slot
2015	BUF	16/4	612	59	36	450	2	61%	+1.3	5	12.5	13.4	22	2.8	81	-1.8	5	-12.4%	75	1	75	15	12.7%	70	--
2016	NE	15/14	830	58	38	680	4	66%	+5.3	4	17.9	14.0	18	6.3	6	+1.4	2	18.0%	11	145	34	158	11.4%	87	56%
2017	NE	9/7	591	59	34	439	5	58%	-1.5	2	12.9	13.3	29	5.0	22	+0.9	2	2.5%	40	71	52	84	17.9%	44	73%
2018	NE			89	55	812	7	62%			14.8							15.4%							

Hogan sat most of the second half of the season with a shoulder injury, which is too bad because he was on pace to shatter his career bests in receiving yardage and catches. Hogan is Actually Fast, as he showed in 2016 by leading the NFL in yards per reception, and he's got the size to deal with contact and still go pluck the ball. With Brandin Cooks moving on, Hogan becomes the third option in the Pats offense. A thousand yards isn't out of the question with a healthy season, particularly if Julian Edelman comes back at something less than his old form after his four-game September suspension.

Mack Hollins Height: 6-4 Weight: 221 College: North Carolina Draft: 2017/4 (118) Born: 16-Sep-1993 Age: 25 Risk: Yellow

Year	Team	G/GS	Snaps	Pass	Rec	Yds	TD	C%	+/-	Drop	Yd/C	aDOT	Rk	YAC	Rk	YAC+	BTkl	DVOA	Rk	DYAR	Rk	YAR	Use	Rk	Slot
2017	PHI	16/0	287	22	16	226	1	73%	+3.2	2	14.1	13.3	--	2.7	--	-1.8	0	25.0%	--	59	--	61	3.9%	--	73%
2018	PHI			22	13	166	1	59%			12.8							-1.2%							

Hollins' 16 catches were scattered across the season: he caught three passes in the Week 2 loss to the Chiefs, fell out of the game plan for three weeks, then caught one or two passes per game (including a highlight-reel 64-yard touchdown against Washington) until Nick Foles entered the lineup and the Eagles started using fewer four-receiver sets. Hollins was a backup receiver and high-effort special teamer in college and filled that role well for the Eagles last year, so it's hard to project him to be much more. But Hollins is 6-foot-4 with 4.4 speed, so there still may be a superstar lurking in him, waiting for a big break.

Andre Holmes Height: 6-5 Weight: 206 College: Hillsdale Draft: 2011/FA Born: 16-Jun-1988 Age: 30 Risk: Green

Year	Team	G/GS	Snaps	Pass	Rec	Yds	TD	C%	+/-	Drop	Yd/C	aDOT	Rk	YAC	Rk	YAC+	BTkl	DVOA	Rk	DYAR	Rk	YAR	Use	Rk	Slot
2015	OAK	16/1	346	33	14	201	4	42%	-2.7	2	14.4	15.0	--	3.1	--	-0.3	1	-15.9%	--	-8	--	-7	5.4%	--	--
2016	OAK	16/2	261	25	14	126	3	56%	-1.0	1	9.0	8.0	--	1.9	--	-1.8	2	-9.9%	--	6	--	0	4.3%	--	62%
2017	BUF	14/2	340	23	13	120	3	57%	-0.4	1	9.2	13.9	--	0.8	--	-2.0	0	9.8%	--	43	--	50	5.8%	--	33%
2018	BUF			17	8	96	0	47%			12.0							-23.8%							

Holmes is sort of the Josh Allen of wide receivers: he's so impressive physically, and looks so good in pads, that wideout-desperate teams keep giving him chances to prove that he can't win contested balls. He still can't! He's a good special-teamer though, and he'll probably have a roster spot as long as those matter. And he's in Buffalo, so there's nobody to clearly keep him from playing wideout. Rumor has it that if Allen throws to Holmes, the ball will just suddenly levitate out of the stadium rather than waste anyone's time.

DeAndre Hopkins Height: 6-1 Weight: 214 College: Clemson Draft: 2013/1 (27) Born: 6-Jun-1992 Age: 26 Risk: Green

Year	Team	G/GS	Snaps	Pass	Rec	Yds	TD	C%	+/-	Drop	Yd/C	aDOT	Rk	YAC	Rk	YAC+	BTkl	DVOA	Rk	DYAR	Rk	YAR	Use	Rk	Slot
2015	HOU	16/16	1150	192	111	1521	11	58%	+4.5	3	13.7	14.3	20	2.0	87	-1.7	5	4.8%	41	268	13	307	31.7%	4	--
2016	HOU	16/16	1086	151	78	954	4	52%	-6.1	4	12.2	11.9	44	3.3	74	-0.6	6	-9.3%	70	43	66	27	27.0%	8	35%
2017	HOU	15/15	1027	174	96	1378	13	55%	-1.7	5	14.4	13.2	31	3.7	49	-0.2	9	13.3%	22	367	4	340	37.0%	1	20%
2018	HOU			160	92	1286	10	58%			14.0							5.6%							

With Deshaun Watson: 76 targets, 27.2% DVOA, 234 DYAR. Without: 109 targets, 3.4% DVOA, 133 DYAR. The latter numbers represent a veritable miracle akin to Hopkins' 2015 season, showcasing rare ball-winning ability even on just vaguely accurate passes. The lower slot percentage relative to 2016 also points to slight but important change in Hopkins' usage. In an attempt to cadge decent play out of Brock Osweiler, the Texans in 2016 asked Hopkins to win on more in-breaking routes like digs. Watson's arrival let Hopkins return to winning on the outside with more fade routes and comebacks—and like in 2015, he did, repeatedly, on ludicrously large volume. Thirty-seven of his 2017 targets were fades or comebacks; the next closest player was Dez Bryant (28).

Adam Humphries Height: 5-11 Weight: 195 College: Clemson Draft: 2015/FA Born: 24-Jun-1993 Age: 25 Risk: Green

Year	Team	G/GS	Snaps	Pass	Rec	Yds	TD	C%	+/-	Drop	Yd/C	aDOT	Rk	YAC	Rk	YAC+	BTkl	DVOA	Rk	DYAR	Rk	YAR	Use	Rk	Slot
2015	TB	13/0	437	40	27	260	1	68%	-0.8	2	9.6	6.8	--	4.6	--	-0.7	4	-4.1%	--	26	--	24	9.3%	--	--
2016	TB	15/4	650	83	55	622	2	66%	-0.1	4	11.3	6.3	92	6.9	2	+1.6	4	-1.9%	56	68	59	77	15.6%	65	74%
2017	TB	16/3	684	83	61	631	1	73%	+4.7	2	10.3	7.1	81	4.6	33	-0.6	8	5.1%	36	112	42	99	13.8%	70	83%
2018	TB			76	52	580	2	68%			11.2							1.6%							

Humphries may be the least heralded of Tampa Bay's primary receivers, but he was the most consistent from 2016 to 2017 in his slot role. He had the same number of targets, catching just six more passes for 9 more yards. Almost half of Humphries' targets were screens (18), curls (13), and out (9) routes. Half of Humphries' screens were on first down, which was a struggle for him last year (-33.7% DVOA). Humphries was charted with 11 different route types on first down and had negative DYAR on all but one of them (19 DYAR on three deep crosses). Humphries' DVOA was much higher on second (28.7%) and third/fourth downs (23.1%).

Allen Hurns

Height: 6-3 Weight: 195 College: Miami Draft: 2014/FA Born: 12-Nov-1991 Age: 27 Risk: Red

Year	Team	G/GS	Snaps	Pass	Rec	Yds	TD	C%	+/-	Drop	Yd/C	aDOT	Rk	YAC	Rk	YAC+	BTkl	DVOA	Rk	DYAR	Rk	YAR	Use	Rk	Slot
2015	JAX	15/15	865	105	64	1031	10	61%	+5.2	1	16.1	12.0	44	5.4	20	+1.2	5	16.1%	12	236	16	243	18.7%	41	--
2016	JAX	11/11	635	76	35	477	3	46%	-7.8	6	13.6	10.3	61	6.0	9	+1.1	4	-24.0%	88	-71	89	-63	17.9%	46	86%
2017	JAX	10/8	537	56	39	484	2	70%	+5.5	1	12.4	10.1	60	4.5	34	+0.5	7	20.6%	9	149	26	154	17.3%	50	82%
2018	DAL			113	69	907	6	61%			13.2							5.8%							

After his breakout year in 2015, Hurns signed a four-year extension with Jacksonville with $20 million guaranteed. Hurns then regressed and was the Jaguars' third receiver at best, and was cut just two years later. The Cowboys inked him to a two-year deal with only $6.5 million guaranteed. Hurns was primarily a slot receiver for the Jaguars, but Cole Beasley has that role nailed down in Dallas, so expect to see Hurns lining up out wide more unless the Cowboys break out some four-receiver sets. His fantasy football numbers should surprise, because he's probably the Cowboys' No. 1 receiver by default and they still have a very good quarterback and offensive line.

Dontrelle Inman

Height: 6-3 Weight: 205 College: Virginia Draft: 2011/FA Born: 31-Jan-1989 Age: 29 Risk: N/A

Year	Team	G/GS	Snaps	Pass	Rec	Yds	TD	C%	+/-	Drop	Yd/C	aDOT	Rk	YAC	Rk	YAC+	BTkl	DVOA	Rk	DYAR	Rk	YAR	Use	Rk	Slot
2015	SD	14/7	691	63	35	486	3	56%	-0.5	3	13.9	12.6	35	5.1	26	+1.0	4	-6.2%	61	32	67	35	11.1%	81	--
2016	SD	16/16	958	97	58	810	4	60%	+2.2	6	14.0	11.5	47	3.7	62	-0.7	5	5.5%	38	140	37	134	17.8%	47	64%
2017	2TM	12/7	457	44	25	343	1	57%	-0.4	5	13.7	13.0	--	1.2	--	-2.5	0	3.6%	--	54	--	60	11.4%	--	27%

Inman is a solid role player, but he became expendable with the Chargers after undergoing core muscle surgery last May. He was traded to Chicago during the season, where he had a couple of productive games, but was mostly just taking advantage of opportunities in a receiving corps riddled by injury. Inman met with the Colts and Cowboys in March for workouts, but remains unsigned in July. He'll likely catch on somewhere this season.

DeSean Jackson

Height: 5-9 Weight: 169 College: California Draft: 2008/2 (49) Born: 1-Dec-1986 Age: 32 Risk: Yellow

Year	Team	G/GS	Snaps	Pass	Rec	Yds	TD	C%	+/-	Drop	Yd/C	aDOT	Rk	YAC	Rk	YAC+	BTkl	DVOA	Rk	DYAR	Rk	YAR	Use	Rk	Slot
2015	WAS	9/9	359	49	30	528	4	61%	+5.3	0	17.6	16.3	4	5.3	22	-0.6	4	12.7%	20	97	47	99	16.2%	56	--
2016	WAS	15/15	707	100	56	1005	4	56%	+4.3	6	17.9	17.6	1	5.1	28	+0.3	4	16.4%	13	241	12	233	18.7%	44	58%
2017	TB	14/13	610	90	50	668	3	56%	+2.2	2	13.4	16.4	5	3.8	46	-0.3	1	1.6%	41	105	45	99	17.8%	45	43%
2018	TB			94	49	803	4	52%			16.4							-0.5%							

Some receivers, such as Terrell Owens and Brandon Marshall, could seemingly go to a different team each year and put up 1,000 yards with any quarterback. DeSean Jackson tried to do that when moving to in Tampa Bay, but his debut was arguably the worst season of his career. He set a career low in receiving yards per game (47.7), and his 13.4 yards per reception was well below his averages in Philadelphia (17.2) and Washington (19.0).

The Bucs seemed like a natural fit for Jackson with his speed down the field and Jameis Winston's love of the deep ball. The two connected on their first go route for a 25-yard touchdown in Week 3. However, for the rest of the season Jackson caught 0-of-8 go routes, picking up a defensive pass interference flag on a ninth attempt. He was rarely ever a factor on third down or in the red zone. Tampa Bay has a lot of weapons now, and we'll have to see how much Jackson may lose snaps to Chris Godwin.

Alshon Jeffery Height: 6-3 Weight: 216 College: South Carolina Draft: 2012/2 (45) Born: 14-Feb-1990 Age: 28 Risk: Yellow

Year	Team	G/GS	Snaps	Pass	Rec	Yds	TD	C%	+/-	Drop	Yd/C	aDOT	Rk	YAC	Rk	YAC+	BTkl	DVOA	Rk	DYAR	Rk	YAR	Use	Rk	Slot
2015	CHI	9/8	506	94	54	807	4	57%	+1.8	1	14.9	14.8	15	3.3	71	-1.1	3	4.1%	42	126	35	134	32.0%	3	--
2016	CHI	12/12	692	94	52	821	2	55%	+2.3	5	15.8	13.4	23	3.7	63	-0.7	6	5.0%	42	132	40	140	22.9%	23	27%
2017	PHI	16/16	927	120	57	789	9	48%	-7.6	4	13.8	14.2	21	3.4	59	-0.4	3	-1.2%	49	108	43	115	21.8%	22	36%
2018	PHI			104	56	794	9	54%			14.2							2.1%							

The Jeffery signing was a mild disappointment from the fantasy and DVOA viewpoints but a huge success from the "help team win Super Bowl" viewpoint, which is the only one the Eagles give a damn about. Jeffery went 12-219-3 in the postseason; converted 19 regular-season third and fourth downs; caught seven red zone touchdowns; and became a favorite target on RPOs, using his mammoth hands to catch slants in traffic after play-fakes. Jeffery spent OTAs with his arm in a sling after rotator cuff surgery, but he is expected to be ready for the start of the preseason and was a constant injury worry in last year's training camp as well. Now under contract for the Eagles through 2021, Jeffery is a nominal No. 1 wide receiver for a team that would rather throw into the slot and to its tight ends. His numbers will never be spectacular, but he's on the field for the tough catches, not the bulk yardage.

Julio Jones Height: 6-3 Weight: 220 College: Alabama Draft: 2011/1 (6) Born: 3-Feb-1989 Age: 29 Risk: Yellow

Year	Team	G/GS	Snaps	Pass	Rec	Yds	TD	C%	+/-	Drop	Yd/C	aDOT	Rk	YAC	Rk	YAC+	BTkl	DVOA	Rk	DYAR	Rk	YAR	Use	Rk	Slot
2015	ATL	16/16	970	203	136	1871	8	67%	+10.6	7	13.8	10.7	53	4.7	38	-0.1	21	8.5%	34	343	6	409	33.1%	2	--
2016	ATL	14/14	705	129	83	1409	6	64%	+7.9	5	17.0	14.5	11	4.7	36	+0.2	9	31.7%	2	458	1	469	28.5%	5	50%
2017	ATL	16/16	766	148	88	1444	3	59%	+3.1	8	16.4	14.2	20	5.5	13	+1.1	17	13.7%	18	313	7	326	28.7%	4	51%
2018	ATL			152	89	1451	7	59%			16.3							8.4%							

Jones is the NFL's all-time leader with 95.3 receiving yards per game. He has tied Marvin Harrison's record streak with a fourth-consecutive 1,400-yard receiving season, and can become the first player ever to do that five years in a row this year. There should also be some positive touchdown regression for Jones in 2018. Out of 185 seasons in NFL history with at least 1,300 receiving yards, Jones is the only player to catch fewer than four touchdowns. Perhaps it was fitting that Atlanta's season ended with Jones unable to snag a touchdown from Matt Ryan on fourth down in Philadelphia. Jones only has one double-digit touchdown season, and that was back in 2012. This has been the one downside to an otherwise dominant career that has Jones well on his way to Canton.

Marvin Jones Height: 6-2 Weight: 199 College: California Draft: 2012/5 (166) Born: 12-Mar-1990 Age: 28 Risk: Yellow

Year	Team	G/GS	Snaps	Pass	Rec	Yds	TD	C%	+/-	Drop	Yd/C	aDOT	Rk	YAC	Rk	YAC+	BTkl	DVOA	Rk	DYAR	Rk	YAR	Use	Rk	Slot
2015	CIN	16/13	901	104	65	816	4	63%	+5.3	3	12.6	13.4	24	4.6	40	-0.6	11	7.6%	37	171	25	149	21.6%	30	--
2016	DET	15/15	879	103	55	930	4	53%	-3.5	9	16.9	14.1	15	4.3	47	+0.0	7	10.9%	23	202	21	200	19.8%	38	9%
2017	DET	16/16	1005	107	61	1101	9	57%	+2.8	1	18.0	16.0	7	3.2	66	-1.2	11	33.8%	3	395	2	385	19.9%	35	21%
2018	DET			111	63	1013	7	57%			16.1							14.4%							

Jones is coming off the best season of his career, where he had a personal best 1,101 receiving yards and leading the NFL with 18.0 yards per reception. While his 2016 Detroit debut was marred by inconsistency, Jones finished last year on a hot stretch. After being held under 55 yards in the first five games of the season, Jones had at least 80 yards in eight of the final 11 games. He's a great option for Matthew Stafford on 50/50 balls—he led the NFL with 149 DYAR on go/fly routes (DVOA: 130.4%) and 59 DYAR on broken plays (DVOA: 110.2%).

T.J. Jones Height: 5-11 Weight: 188 College: Notre Dame Draft: 2014/6 (189) Born: 19-Jul-1992 Age: 26 Risk: Yellow

Year	Team	G/GS	Snaps	Pass	Rec	Yds	TD	C%	+/-	Drop	Yd/C	aDOT	Rk	YAC	Rk	YAC+	BTkl	DVOA	Rk	DYAR	Rk	YAR	Use	Rk	Slot
2015	DET	10/0	159	18	10	132	1	56%	-1.8	1	13.2	10.8	--	4.1	--	-0.9	1	-7.8%	--	7	--	-5	4.6%	--	--
2016	DET	3/0	52	14	5	93	0	36%	-3.2	1	18.6	12.3	--	6.0	--	-1.3	1	-33.6%	--	-20	--	-18	12.6%	--	21%
2017	DET	14/6	400	49	30	399	1	61%	+3.6	2	13.3	11.4	48	2.6	78	-1.5	1	6.9%	31	73	50	68	10.0%	83	44%
2018	DET			47	28	343	1	60%			12.3							-3.6%							

Detroit's rarely used WR4 had a career season in 2017, starting games for the first time in his career and setting career-highs in, well, everything. That's largely due to the injury to rookie Kenny Golladay. Jones then suffered his own injury, a shoulder ailment that ended his season and required surgery in January. It was somewhat surprising that Detroit re-signed Jones, but he provides solid depth as he enters his fifth season with the team. You just won't notice him in fantasy football.

Zay Jones

Height: 6-2 Weight: 201 College: East Carolina Draft: 2017/2 (37) Born: 30-Mar-1995 Age: 23 Risk: Green

Year	Team	G/GS	Snaps	Pass	Rec	Yds	TD	C%	+/-	Drop	Yd/C	aDOT	Rk	YAC	Rk	YAC+	BTkl	DVOA	Rk	DYAR	Rk	YAR	Use	Rk	Slot
2017	BUF	15/10	793	74	27	316	2	36%	-11.8	3	11.7	13.1	32	2.3	81	-1.4	1	-35.2%	86	-131	86	-119	16.8%	53	32%
2018	BUF			75	34	443	3	45%			13.0							-21.2%							

Jones spent his winter being featured on TMZ for a felony arrest in which he allegedly kicked open a 30th floor window and had to be restrained from jumping, which makes it hard to be snarky in his player comment. He had a horrendous rookie season, with the worst catch rate in the NFL among qualifying receivers. The league is still reportedly looking into added discipline for his arrest. There have been better first years for a second-round receiver, is what we're saying. However, there's also nobody in Jones' way for snaps, as last year proved.

Jermaine Kearse

Height: 6-1 Weight: 209 College: Washington Draft: 2012/FA Born: 6-Feb-1990 Age: 28 Risk: Green

Year	Team	G/GS	Snaps	Pass	Rec	Yds	TD	C%	+/-	Drop	Yd/C	aDOT	Rk	YAC	Rk	YAC+	BTkl	DVOA	Rk	DYAR	Rk	YAR	Use	Rk	Slot
2015	SEA	16/16	771	68	49	685	5	72%	+7.5	3	14.0	12.0	43	4.8	37	+0.4	6	29.8%	5	227	19	217	14.6%	65	--
2016	SEA	16/15	828	89	41	510	1	46%	-5.3	3	12.4	11.9	40	3.4	71	-1.4	7	-28.7%	91	-114	92	-90	16.0%	62	44%
2017	NYJ	16/14	880	102	65	810	5	64%	+3.8	5	12.5	9.1	71	4.4	40	+0.0	6	5.2%	35	146	30	133	20.7%	28	69%
2018	NYJ			86	50	589	3	58%			11.8							-7.4%							

Demonized as part of the problem in Seattle after a 46 percent catch rate and countless pass interference penalties, Kearse turned into a nice buy-low opportunity for the Jets, and set a career high in receiving yards while giving Josh McCown a nice, big target. The Jets used him effectively on slants, creating 54 DYAR on 17 slant targets. Offseason scuttle had him as a possible release, but Kearse remains a solid lower-rung target in a passing game that can isolate him against smaller defensive backs. In theory, that should make him even more effective this season, now that Quincy Enunwa has returned and the Jets can mix and match personnel better.

Jeremy Kerley

Height: 5-9 Weight: 188 College: TCU Draft: 2011/5 (153) Born: 8-Nov-1988 Age: 30 Risk: Green

Year	Team	G/GS	Snaps	Pass	Rec	Yds	TD	C%	+/-	Drop	Yd/C	aDOT	Rk	YAC	Rk	YAC+	BTkl	DVOA	Rk	DYAR	Rk	YAR	Use	Rk	Slot
2015	NYJ	16/1	223	26	16	152	2	62%	-2.2	1	9.5	5.3	--	5.9	--	+1.0	3	-5.3%	--	14	--	10	4.3%	--	--
2016	SF	16/13	790	115	64	667	3	56%	-9.0	3	10.4	8.6	76	3.3	72	-1.4	4	-26.4%	90	-124	93	-94	23.7%	18	95%
2017	NYJ	8/2	277	27	22	217	1	81%	+4.9	0	9.9	9.0	--	3.0	--	-1.9	2	19.0%	--	64	--	72	10.7%	--	89%
2018	BUF			60	37	393	1	62%			10.6							-9.1%							

Your favorite journeyman's favorite journeyman, Kerley has made a career out of finding bad wide receiver depth charts, catching 20 to 50 balls, then doing it again. Coming off a four-game PED suspension that forced a release from the Jets, he succeeded in finding a one-year pact with the Buffalo Bills. Their desolate depth chart leaves him a spot as the regualr slot receiver.

Christian Kirk

Height: 5-10 Weight: 201 College: Texas A&M Draft: 2018/2 (47) Born: 18-Nov-1996 Age: 22 Risk: Red

Year	Team	G/GS	Snaps	Pass	Rec	Yds	TD	C%	+/-	Drop	Yd/C	aDOT	Rk	YAC	Rk	YAC+	BTkl	DVOA	Rk	DYAR	Rk	YAR	Use	Rk	Slot
2018	ARI			100	65	751	5	65%			11.6							0.6%							

Selected in the second round out of Texas A&M in April, Kirk will have plenty of opportunities to make an impact as a rookie for the Cardinals in a fairly thin receiving corps. While running back David Johnson will certainly play a large role in the passing game after returning from injury, Kirk has a strong chance to produce alongside veteran Larry Fitzgerald. Kirk physically profiles as a slot receiver, but with Fitzgerald still in the fold, Kirk will need to work on the outside as well to accommodate the future Hall of Famer. On top of averaging nearly 13 yards per reception as the Aggies' No. 1 receiver as a senior, Kirk added seven total return touchdowns (six punts, one kickoff), which could be a boon for an Arizona special teams unit that has struggled for years.

Cooper Kupp Height: 6-2 Weight: 204 College: Eastern Washington Draft: 2017/3 (69) Born: 15-Jun-1993 Age: 25 Risk: Yellow

Year	Team	G/GS	Snaps	Pass	Rec	Yds	TD	C%	+/-	Drop	Yd/C	aDOT	Rk	YAC	Rk	YAC+	BTkl	DVOA	Rk	DYAR	Rk	YAR	Use	Rk	Slot
2017	LAR	15/6	740	92	62	869	5	65%	+3.3	7	14.0	9.8	66	6.0	10	+1.7	15	24.8%	4	272	10	266	19.4%	39	94%
2018	LAR			116	71	918	6	61%			12.9							4.9%							

Kupp was supposed to be a possession receiver, getting open in short areas and serving as a safety valve for Jared Goff. To be fair, he did all those things as a rookie, but he also led the team with 155 DYAR and an 84.7% DVOA on deep passes. That was supposed to be Sammy Watkins' role, but Watkins only had one more deep ball thrown his way than Kupp did. This isn't going to continue in 2018—you don't bring in Brandin Cooks and *not* have him be your primary deep threat—but it's good to know that Kupp has the ability to make those big plays when called upon. If there's one thing he needs to work on going forward, it's holding on to the football. Kupp's seven drops are what really kept him from being among the very best slot receivers as a rookie. It's not that he was horrible—his adjusted catch rate was above average—but his hands were the weakest part of his game. If he can improve there and bump his catch rate from 65 percent up into the 70 percent range, he'll be right up there with the best of the best.

Brandon LaFell Height: 6-3 Weight: 211 College: Louisiana State Draft: 2010/3 (78) Born: 4-Nov-1986 Age: 32 Risk: Yellow

Year	Team	G/GS	Snaps	Pass	Rec	Yds	TD	C%	+/-	Drop	Yd/C	aDOT	Rk	YAC	Rk	YAC+	BTkl	DVOA	Rk	DYAR	Rk	YAR	Use	Rk	Slot
2015	NE	11/7	659	74	37	515	0	50%	-8.9	6	13.9	13.4	25	6.1	9	-0.2	1	-20.1%	82	-43	82	-52	17.2%	49	--
2016	CIN	16/14	1010	107	64	862	6	60%	-2.0	3	13.5	9.7	66	5.5	15	+0.6	5	10.8%	24	202	22	180	20.3%	36	32%
2017	CIN	16/15	863	89	52	548	3	58%	-5.9	4	10.5	8.7	74	4.6	32	-0.3	3	-16.9%	73	-30	75	-35	18.6%	40	62%
2018	CIN			85	51	611	3	60%			12.0							-5.2%							

LaFell was best on third downs, with a DVOA (15.4%) and yards per target far higher than on other downs. He was also noticeably better when lined up in the slot, which makes sense given his limited athleticism at this point in his career. LaFell in general doesn't do anything particularly well, except be the "veteran pro" so valued by the coaching staff. Whatever that special sauce consists of, it hasn't seemed to rub off on the younger Bengals wideouts thus far.

Jarvis Landry Height: 5-11 Weight: 205 College: Louisiana State Draft: 2014/2 (63) Born: 11/28/1992 Age: 26 Risk: Green

Year	Team	G/GS	Snaps	Pass	Rec	Yds	TD	C%	+/-	Drop	Yd/C	aDOT	Rk	YAC	Rk	YAC+	BTkl	DVOA	Rk	DYAR	Rk	YAR	Use	Rk	Slot
2015	MIA	16/14	868	167	110	1157	4	66%	+2.3	6	10.5	7.5	80	4.8	33	-1.1	33	-7.1%	63	72	57	55	28.5%	9	--
2016	MIA	16/16	892	131	94	1136	4	72%	+6.2	5	12.1	6.6	89	6.6	4	+1.2	30	4.8%	43	174	26	190	27.8%	7	79%
2017	MIA	16/16	932	161	112	987	9	70%	+1.8	7	8.8	6.4	83	4.4	37	-0.7	15	-4.9%	59	98	46	75	27.3%	9	76%
2018	CLE			125	84	821	4	67%			9.8							-7.3%							

Football Outsiders is famous for our criticisms of Jarvis Landry, but now that he's in Cleveland, we may finally learn whether the problem is Landry himself or rather how Miami chose to use him. The dilemma is just that too many of Landry's catches don't gain enough yards to be considered successful plays. He led the NFL with 112 catches last season, but also led the league with 31 "failed completions." A year ago, we did a study showing that in Landry's first three seasons, the Dolphins pass offense actually rated worse the more often they threw to Landry. But Landry never asked to only be used on the shortest of short routes. The Browns had Landry running more downfield routes in OTAs, so perhaps this year all of Landry's talent will actually contribute to scoring more points. It better, if the Browns want him to be worth anything close to the $47 million guaranteed they handed him in a five-year, $75.5 million extension.

Cody Latimer

Height: 6-2   Weight: 215   College: Indiana   Draft: 2014/2 (56)   Born: 10-Oct-1992   Age: 26   Risk: Yellow

Year	Team	G/GS	Snaps	Pass	Rec	Yds	TD	C%	+/-	Drop	Yd/C	aDOT	Rk	YAC	Rk	YAC+	BTkl	DVOA	Rk	DYAR	Rk	YAR	Use	Rk	Slot
2015	DEN	14/1	191	11	6	59	1	55%	-0.7	1	9.8	12.5	--	5.3	--	+1.4	1	7.5%	--	18	--	21	2.2%	--	--
2016	DEN	12/1	217	15	8	76	0	53%	-0.6	0	9.5	13.1	--	3.0	--	-1.5	0	-10.9%	--	2	--	0	3.8%	--	31%
2017	DEN	11/1	376	31	19	287	2	61%	+2.4	1	15.1	11.6	--	3.4	--	-0.7	1	21.9%	--	88	--	88	8.1%	--	61%
2018	NYG			42	22	284	2	52%			12.9							-6.3%							

A second-round pick in 2014, Latimer did not crack double-digit receptions until last season. Latimer is one of many tall, strong, vertical receivers to attract the NFL's attention, but ultimately disappoint by not being able to piece it all together. In OTAs, Latimer had generally moved ahead of Roger Lewis on the depth chart and was lining up opposite Odell Beckham Jr. with Sterling Shepard in the slot. It helps his cause that Latimer a) is an excellent special teams gunner and b) spent the last four years in Denver with new Giants wide receivers coach Tyke Tolbert. However, with so little to show from his previous stint, Latimer should not be counted on to produce on offense.

Marqise Lee

Height: 6-0   Weight: 192   College: USC   Draft: 2014/2 (39)   Born: 11/25/1991   Age: 27   Risk: Yellow

Year	Team	G/GS	Snaps	Pass	Rec	Yds	TD	C%	+/-	Drop	Yd/C	aDOT	Rk	YAC	Rk	YAC+	BTkl	DVOA	Rk	DYAR	Rk	YAR	Use	Rk	Slot
2015	JAX	10/1	240	32	15	191	1	47%	-3.4	2	12.7	12.8	--	6.1	--	+0.9	5	-13.4%	--	-2	--	9	8.7%	--	--
2016	JAX	16/6	817	105	63	851	3	60%	-0.7	5	13.5	12.3	36	5.5	14	+1.0	10	12.2%	18	211	19	192	17.0%	55	40%
2017	JAX	14/14	738	96	56	702	3	58%	+0.8	9	12.5	11.6	45	5.2	20	+0.8	14	3.0%	39	119	38	115	21.5%	23	48%
2018	JAX			113	68	881	4	60%			13.0							0.1%							

When Allen Robinson was lost for the year in the opening quarter of last season, Lee became the unquestioned No. 1 receiver in Jacksonville. He responded by leading the team in targets, posting a second consecutive season over 100 DYAR, and again finishing a close second on the team in receiving yards—this time behind Keelan Cole instead of Robinson. His former rivals on the outside—Robinson and Allen Hurns—now play elsewhere, and Donte Moncrief poses little threat to Lee's position atop the wide receiver pecking order. Another season of 700 yards and 100-plus DYAR should be the absolute minimum the former USC product is aiming for.

Jacksonville was a big fan of using drag routes with its wide receivers last year, but Lee (league-high 67 DYAR) was far better at them than teammates Cole (-19 DYAR) and Dede Westbrook (-33 DYAR) were.

Roger Lewis

Height: 6-0   Weight: 196   College: Bowling Green   Draft: 2016/FA   Born: 27-Nov-1993   Age: 25   Risk: Green

Year	Team	G/GS	Snaps	Pass	Rec	Yds	TD	C%	+/-	Drop	Yd/C	aDOT	Rk	YAC	Rk	YAC+	BTkl	DVOA	Rk	DYAR	Rk	YAR	Use	Rk	Slot
2016	NYG	13/1	207	19	7	97	2	37%	-2.1	2	13.9	18.4	--	0.6	--	-1.8	0	-31.5%	--	-29	--	-27	3.9%	--	26%
2017	NYG	15/8	695	72	36	416	2	50%	-6.8	3	11.6	10.5	55	2.1	82	-2.0	2	-18.7%	77	-35	77	-39	12.8%	72	14%
2018	NYG			23	12	158	0	52%			13.2							-12.6%							

Lewis picked up many of the targets that Odell Beckham left behind when he went down with an injury in Week 5. However, Lewis was disastrously inefficient, posting a negative DVOA on first, second, and third downs. Lewis also recorded a catch rate lower than 60 percent on all three downs. When Lewis is asked to be an all-around receiver like he was in 2017, the results are bound to not be pretty. However, if a healthier wide receiver unit in 2018 can funnel Lewis' targets to primarily deep passes, he may reignite some of the vertical prowess he showed in college.

Tyler Lockett

Height: 5-10   Weight: 182   College: Kansas State   Draft: 2015/3 (69)   Born: 28-Sep-1992   Age: 26   Risk: Green

Year	Team	G/GS	Snaps	Pass	Rec	Yds	TD	C%	+/-	Drop	Yd/C	aDOT	Rk	YAC	Rk	YAC+	BTkl	DVOA	Rk	DYAR	Rk	YAR	Use	Rk	Slot
2015	SEA	16/8	664	69	51	664	6	74%	+8.1	2	13.0	13.3	29	5.0	28	-0.4	7	35.1%	3	249	15	242	14.6%	64	--
2016	SEA	15/9	558	68	41	597	1	63%	-0.1	2	14.6	10.8	55	5.7	12	-0.2	3	5.5%	39	99	52	105	13.3%	74	44%
2017	SEA	16/8	692	71	45	555	2	63%	+2.5	1	12.3	12.7	35	4.2	42	-1.0	8	-3.4%	54	48	60	68	13.2%	71	68%
2018	SEA			78	49	643	3	63%			13.1							2.6%		(Also: 9 runs, 55 RuYd, 0.3 RuTD)						

How was Lockett's 2017? It depends on where your expectations were. Compared to his 2016 season, last year was very successful for Lockett—not quite a bounce-back to his all-world rookie season, but a year in which showed improvements in his route-running and catching abilities, important steps forward in his development as an all-around receiver as opposed to just a big-play threat. Compared to his 2017 preseason hype, when he was supposed to cement himself as Seattle's second receiver, it was disappointing. Paul Richardson grabbed that two spot, and Lockett found himself splitting time in the slot. His DVOA dropped last season, but that may be due to a combination of lingering injuries and the result of playing out of position. While Lockett actually had a higher DVOA in the slot last season, he performed better when split out wide in previous years. The departure of both Richardson and Jimmy Graham (who lined up wide more often than any other tight end) should move Lockett back out wide, which should be beneficial.

Ricardo Louis   Height: 6-2   Weight: 215   College: Auburn   Draft: 2016/4 (114)   Born: 23-Mar-1994   Age: 24   Risk: Red

Year	Team	G/GS	Snaps	Pass	Rec	Yds	TD	C%	+/-	Drop	Yd/C	aDOT	Rk	YAC	Rk	YAC+	BTkl	DVOA	Rk	DYAR	Rk	YAR	Use	Rk	Slot
2016	CLE	16/3	316	36	18	205	0	50%	-2.5	4	11.4	9.9	–	5.1	–	+0.1	4	-42.6%	–	-82	–	-73	6.4%	–	50%
2017	CLE	16/9	572	61	27	357	0	44%	-3.4	6	13.2	13.6	25	3.0	69	-1.5	3	-23.0%	81	-50	82	-57	10.7%	80	22%
2018	CLE			19	10	112	0	53%			11.2							-21.3%							

Louis was considered an athletic project when drafted, but the Browns have had two years to work on the project and now they're running out of workspace. Louis had just one reception after Week 11, thanks to the returns of Corey Coleman (Week 11) and then Josh Gordon (Week 13). Unless Coleman is traded, Louis is probably competing with Rashard Higgins and Damion Ratley for one roster spot, though he's more talented than Higgins and further along in development than Ratley. One area for improvement: Louis caught just 4-of-18 passes on third down (-60.7% DVOA).

Jeremy Maclin   Height: 6-0   Weight: 198   College: Missouri   Draft: 2009/1 (19)   Born: 11-May-1988   Age: 30   Risk: N/A

Year	Team	G/GS	Snaps	Pass	Rec	Yds	TD	C%	+/-	Drop	Yd/C	aDOT	Rk	YAC	Rk	YAC+	BTkl	DVOA	Rk	DYAR	Rk	YAR	Use	Rk	Slot
2015	KC	15/15	828	124	87	1088	8	70%	+9.6	3	12.5	10.6	55	3.8	59	-0.7	3	11.3%	24	234	18	217	28.6%	8	–
2016	KC	12/12	629	76	44	536	2	58%	-2.1	4	12.2	10.9	53	3.1	77	-1.5	4	-4.3%	62	50	62	29	19.1%	43	48%
2017	BAL	12/12	512	72	40	440	3	56%	-5.4	4	11.0	9.9	64	2.7	76	-2.0	2	-19.1%	78	-36	78	-17	17.2%	52	74%

Maclin scored a touchdown on opening day, but it was mostly downhill from there. Tellingly, even the receiver-desperate Ravens don't have a use for a player only two years removed from back-to-back 1,000-yard seasons, as injuries and creeping age have stolen Maclin's burst. He may wind up on a roster of a team even more in need of pass-catchers than Baltimore, but his days as a difference-maker are long gone.

Brandon Marshall   Height: 6-4   Weight: 229   College: UCF   Draft: 2006/4 (119)   Born: 23-Mar-1984   Age: 34   Risk: Yellow

Year	Team	G/GS	Snaps	Pass	Rec	Yds	TD	C%	+/-	Drop	Yd/C	aDOT	Rk	YAC	Rk	YAC+	BTkl	DVOA	Rk	DYAR	Rk	YAR	Use	Rk	Slot
2015	NYJ	16/16	1059	173	109	1502	14	63%	+7.0	8	13.8	12.5	37	4.0	56	+0.0	15	9.3%	31	303	11	343	28.8%	7	–
2016	NYJ	15/15	901	127	59	788	3	46%	-14.0	10	13.4	13.3	25	3.0	80	-1.0	6	-16.1%	79	-35	82	-29	25.2%	12	26%
2017	NYG	5/5	254	33	18	154	0	55%	-1.9	2	8.6	10.7	–	2.2	–	-1.9	3	-24.9%	–	-33	–	-37	17.4%	–	9%
2018	SEA			69	43	449	3	62%			10.4							-6.0%							

Marshall has enjoyed a fruitful, decade-plus-long career, but the end is nigh. Marshall played through 2016 with a badly sprained knee, but it was not until 2017 that he truly hit a wall. Marshall produced one of the worst catch rates of his career as well as a career-low 8.6 yards per reception. Marshall was slow through his routes and less capable of bodying defenders at the catch point than at any time previously in his career. Even in the red zone, Marshall did not have the value he used to. Marshall was targeted in the red zone just twice in five games. Though he caught both targets, neither resulted in scores. The hope for Seattle is that Marshall can at least regain some of his red zone dominance and have value in short-yardage situations, which will be much needed with the departure of tight end Jimmy Graham.

Jordan Matthews

Height: 6-3   Weight: 212   College: Vanderbilt   Draft: 2014/2 (42)   Born: 7/16/1992   Age: 26   Risk: Yellow

Year	Team	G/GS	Snaps	Pass	Rec	Yds	TD	C%	+/-	Drop	Yd/C	aDOT	Rk	YAC	Rk	YAC+	BTkl	DVOA	Rk	DYAR	Rk	YAR	Use	Rk	Slot
2015	PHI	16/12	919	128	85	997	8	66%	+2.2	5	11.7	8.7	69	4.9	31	+0.4	10	-1.8%	52	112	41	120	20.9%	32	--
2016	PHI	14/13	844	117	73	804	3	62%	+0.8	10	11.0	10.1	62	3.2	75	-1.8	5	-13.2%	76	-4	76	2	22.1%	27	75%
2017	BUF	10/7	509	36	25	282	1	69%	+1.6	2	11.3	7.3	--	5.0	--	+1.1	3	-0.6%	--	33	--	32	12.1%	--	92%
2018	NE			28	19	223	1	68%			11.7							9.2%							

Traded to Buffalo in the Ronald Darby deal, Matthews is a great window into how the NFL works on offense these days. Put in a slot role with a team that knows how to manipulate him, Matthews was a consistent 800-yard receiver with fantasy football touchdown upside. Joining up with the Rick Dennison Bills, Matthews was an afterthought in a fullback-heavy offense, then went to IR with a leg injury. Signed to a one-year deal by the Patriots, he's suddenly in a situation more like Philadelphia again, but with only $170,000 guaranteed, it's best to see how camp shakes out for him before getting too excited. The Julian Edelman suspension at least means he's likely to get a shot at playing time early in the year.

Rishard Matthews

Height: 6-0   Weight: 217   College: Nevada   Draft: 2012/7 (227)   Born: 12-Oct-1989   Age: 29   Risk: Green

Year	Team	G/GS	Snaps	Pass	Rec	Yds	TD	C%	+/-	Drop	Yd/C	aDOT	Rk	YAC	Rk	YAC+	BTkl	DVOA	Rk	DYAR	Rk	YAR	Use	Rk	Slot
2015	MIA	11/11	520	61	43	662	4	70%	+6.3	4	15.4	11.6	47	5.7	13	+1.4	2	36.4%	2	235	17	237	15.6%	60	--
2016	TEN	16/10	782	108	65	945	9	60%	+3.2	3	14.5	13.5	21	3.1	76	-0.5	6	14.4%	15	229	15	218	21.5%	28	58%
2017	TEN	14/11	746	87	53	795	4	61%	+3.2	2	15.0	12.0	40	5.2	17	+0.8	13	13.6%	19	173	19	183	20.4%	29	52%
2018	TEN			105	62	843	6	59%			13.6							11.5%							

Matthews led Titans wide receivers in targets again, was by far their most effective receiver, and recorded his third straight year in the top 20 wideouts in DYAR (the first of those came in Miami). Matthews is the only Titans player who has surpassed Delanie Walker in targets in any of the past four seasons, and appears firmly entrenched as the starter opposite Corey Davis. Still only 28, and entering the final year of his three-year contract, Matthews has every incentive to keep his level of performance high next year.

Cameron Meredith

Height: 6-3   Weight: 207   College: Illinois State   Draft: 2015/FA   Born: 21-Sep-1992   Age: 26   Risk: Green

Year	Team	G/GS	Snaps	Pass	Rec	Yds	TD	C%	+/-	Drop	Yd/C	aDOT	Rk	YAC	Rk	YAC+	BTkl	DVOA	Rk	DYAR	Rk	YAR	Use	Rk	Slot
2015	CHI	11/0	136	16	11	120	0	69%	+0.6	0	10.9	11.1	--	3.4	--	-2.1	2	-6.3%	--	7	--	4	4.4%	--	--
2016	CHI	14/10	703	98	66	888	4	68%	+2.8	7	13.5	9.6	68	4.5	40	-0.3	14	4.1%	45	128	43	158	20.4%	34	67%
2018	NO			65	40	539	3	62%			13.5							3.4%							

Meredith was one of the few bright spots for Chicago's offense in 2016. His ascension to the No. 1 wide receiver role never happened after a torn ACL ended his 2017 in the preseason. The Bears hoped to bring him back, but after the Saints signed Meredith to an offer sheet, Chicago declined to match with other options now in town. New Orleans is an excellent landing spot for any wide receiver thanks to Drew Brees, so it would not be a surprise to see Meredith as the Saints' second-leading receiver this year behind only Michael Thomas.

Anthony Miller

Height: 5-11   Weight: 201   College: Memphis   Draft: 2018/2 (51)   Born: 9-Oct-1994   Age: 24   Risk: Red

Year	Team	G/GS	Snaps	Pass	Rec	Yds	TD	C%	+/-	Drop	Yd/C	aDOT	Rk	YAC	Rk	YAC+	BTkl	DVOA	Rk	DYAR	Rk	YAR	Use	Rk	Slot
2018	CHI			79	48	669	4	61%			13.9							2.9%							

Miller is not related to the San Diego and Denver wide receiver who had four 1,000-yard seasons from 1992 to 1995. If this Miller can produce anything like that one, then the Bears will be very happy with their selection in the second round. Miller can play outside and in the slot, but it is a wonder why he stayed on for a senior season at Memphis. Most top-tier receiving prospects leave school early these days, but Miller still had the fifth-best projection by Playmaker Score for this draft class This is a building block piece for the future of Mitchell Trubisky in Matt Nagy's offense, but Miller may get a lot of playing time early. Only four rookie wideouts drafted in the second round since the merger have eclipsed 1,000 receiving yards, but as Cooper Kupp showed last year in Los Angeles, rookies in the slot can still be very productive in the right system.

Braxton Miller   Height: 6-1   Weight: 201   College: Ohio State   Draft: 2016/3 (85)   Born: 30-Nov-1992   Age: 26   Risk: Green

Year	Team	G/GS	Snaps	Pass	Rec	Yds	TD	C%	+/-	Drop	Yd/C	aDOT	Rk	YAC	Rk	YAC+	BTkl	DVOA	Rk	DYAR	Rk	YAR	Use	Rk	Slot
2016	HOU	10/6	379	28	15	99	1	54%	-3.0	5	6.6	5.7	--	3.5	--	-1.9	3	-48.3%	--	-79	--	-74	7.9%	--	83%
2017	HOU	11/3	427	29	19	162	1	66%	-0.6	0	8.5	7.9	--	3.7	--	-2.1	0	-26.9%	--	-31	--	-36	7.9%	--	69%
2018	HOU			23	13	150	0	57%			11.6							-10.7%							

Deshaun Watson's arrival meant even the snarkiest Twitter user could no longer claim Miller would be Houston's best quarterback, if only they used him there, not that Bill O'Brien did much with him on that type of gadget play anyway. The selection of Keke Coutee was a direct threat to Miller's slot receiver job and probably even roster spot, as Miller has yet to break through at his new position even when Watson threw him the ball (-48.2% DVOA, albeit on just 10 targets). Receivers coach John Perry praised how he responded to the challenge, but that was in June, and Miller's NFL fate will be determined in August.

Malcolm Mitchell   Height: 6-0   Weight: 198   College: Georgia   Draft: 2016/4 (112)   Born: 20-Jul-1993   Age: 25   Risk: Red

Year	Team	G/GS	Snaps	Pass	Rec	Yds	TD	C%	+/-	Drop	Yd/C	aDOT	Rk	YAC	Rk	YAC+	BTkl	DVOA	Rk	DYAR	Rk	YAR	Use	Rk	Slot
2016	NE	14/6	538	48	32	401	4	67%	+2.4	4	12.5	11.5	46	5.2	22	+1.2	6	19.6%	7	132	41	143	10.3%	89	22%
2018	NE			47	29	387	2	62%			13.4							6.6%							

Mitchell had phenomenal tape coming out of Georgia, and yet the Patriots keep putting roadblocks in front of him. First it was Chris Hogan and Brandin Cooks, now it's Kenny Britt and Jordan Matthews. Mitchell has prototypical outside receiver size and has shown flashes of his enormous talent when he has been a featured receiver. However, he missed all of last year with a knee problem and his comeback has been going slowly. He'd be a surefire FO top prospect if he had fewer snaps. Is this the year the Patriots trust him and he gets healthy? Or is it just one more year that proves the flashes will stay flashes?

Donte Moncrief   Height: 6-2   Weight: 221   College: Mississippi   Draft: 2014/3 (90)   Born: 8-Jun-1993   Age: 25   Risk: Yellow

Year	Team	G/GS	Snaps	Pass	Rec	Yds	TD	C%	+/-	Drop	Yd/C	aDOT	Rk	YAC	Rk	YAC+	BTkl	DVOA	Rk	DYAR	Rk	YAR	Use	Rk	Slot
2015	IND	16/10	836	105	64	733	6	61%	-0.3	2	11.5	10.3	59	4.2	51	-0.3	7	1.1%	49	110	43	121	17.2%	50	--
2016	IND	9/7	468	56	30	307	7	54%	-2.9	3	10.2	10.6	58	2.6	89	-1.1	4	-1.9%	58	50	63	49	17.4%	53	58%
2017	IND	12/8	614	47	26	391	2	55%	+3.0	4	15.0	14.6	--	3.0	--	-0.7	3	11.4%	--	94	--	88	13.5%	--	19%
2018	JAX			89	50	657	4	56%			13.1							-3.8%							

Two summers ago, Moncrief was coming off a 700-yard, six-touchdown, 110-DYAR season as Andrew Luck's second-favorite target. He has fewer targets, receptions, and yards in the two seasons since than he did in that one career year, has failed to reach 450 yards in three of his four professional seasons, and the Colts let him leave in free agency without much fanfare. Lost amid that, however, is that Moncrief's advanced statistics were quite solid in 2017: with just five more targets (to qualify for our rankings), his 11.4% DVOA would have tied Trent Taylor at 23rd, and his 94 DYAR would have ranked 48th, right above teammate T.Y. Hilton. His health has been an issue over the past two years: he variously missed time with a shoulder sprain, a hamstring strain, and a sprained ankle. A four-year veteran who will still only be 25 years old on opening day, Moncrief is actually younger than Keelan Cole, so he still has plenty of time to make a career for himself if he can recapture his 2015 form.

Chris Moore   Height: 6-1   Weight: 206   College: Cincinnati   Draft: 2016/4 (107)   Born: 16-Jun-1993   Age: 25   Risk: Green

Year	Team	G/GS	Snaps	Pass	Rec	Yds	TD	C%	+/-	Drop	Yd/C	aDOT	Rk	YAC	Rk	YAC+	BTkl	DVOA	Rk	DYAR	Rk	YAR	Use	Rk	Slot
2016	BAL	15/0	162	16	7	46	0	44%	-3.8	3	6.6	8.6	--	2.7	--	-2.1	0	-66.1%	--	-68	--	-63	2.5%	--	88%
2017	BAL	13/4	375	38	18	248	3	47%	-1.5	4	13.8	13.2	--	2.3	--	-0.9	3	-14.1%	--	-4	--	-5	8.3%	--	34%
2018	BAL			38	18	196	0	47%			10.9							-30.6%							

Moore has tremendous speed, which translated well to kickoff returns, but his splits suggest a classic chains-mover, a savvy-over-sprinting type. He had a 19.9% DVOA on third down, while he was deep into the negatives on the first two. With all the new receivers in Baltimore, targets may be hard to come by, so further developing that third-down specialty seems like a wise move.

D.J. Moore

Height: 6-0 | Weight: 210 | College: Maryland | Draft: 2018/1 (24) | Born: 14-Apr-1997 | Age: 21 | Risk: Yellow

Year	Team	G/GS	Snaps	Pass	Rec	Yds	TD	C%	+/-	Drop	Yd/C	aDOT	Rk	YAC	Rk	YAC+	BTkl	DVOA	Rk	DYAR	Rk	YAR	Use	Rk	Slot
2018	CAR			73	40	526	3	55%			13.2							-10.1%							

While Calvin Ridley topped most of the mock drafts around the league, our Playmaker Score had Moore as the best of the wide receivers in the 2018 class. His statistics don't jump off the page at you—just 80 receptions for 1,033 yards and eight touchdowns as a junior—but Maryland almost *never* threw the ball last season. Moore had 45 percent of Maryland's receptions and nearly 55 percent of their yards; he *was* their receiving offense. Moore's place atop our Playmaker projections is more about a weak receiver class than anything else—it's the lowest score to top a year in our current version of the system—and he has size questions, but his short-area quickness and his skills after the catch could lead him to being a valuable slot receiver and returner immediately.

J.J. Nelson

Height: 5-10 | Weight: 156 | College: Alabama-Birmingham | Draft: 2015/5 (159) | Born: 24-Apr-1992 | Age: 26 | Risk: Green

Year	Team	G/GS	Snaps	Pass	Rec	Yds	TD	C%	+/-	Drop	Yd/C	aDOT	Rk	YAC	Rk	YAC+	BTkl	DVOA	Rk	DYAR	Rk	YAR	Use	Rk	Slot
2015	ARI	11/2	148	27	11	299	2	41%	+0.0	0	27.2	22.9	--	5.1	--	+0.4	2	25.7%	--	84	--	82	7.7%	--	--
2016	ARI	15/6	471	74	34	568	6	46%	-5.5	7	16.7	17.5	2	5.1	27	+1.2	5	-2.3%	59	62	60	70	12.3%	82	29%
2017	ARI	16/5	539	61	29	508	2	48%	-1.1	6	17.5	18.4	1	2.0	84	-1.8	1	-1.9%	52	48	62	44	10.2%	81	31%
2018	ARI			39	21	335	2	54%			15.9							1.4%							

Nelson may never be a go-to receiver in the league, but there is one thing he can do decently and that is go long. Over the past three seasons, the speedster from Alabama-Birmingham has served as a deep threat in Bruce Arians' offense in the desert, making full use of his 4.28 40 time to stretch defenses to their breaking points. After coming in second in average depth of target to DeSean Jackson in 2016, Nelson claimed the top spot in 2017. Improvement at the quarterback position for the Cardinals would go a long way toward helping Nelson secure a lucrative second contract, as the only time in his career that he had positive receiving DVOA was as a rookie during Carson Palmer's MVP-caliber season. Entering the final year of his rookie contract, Nelson has a lot to prove, but if he can get on the end of enough bombs from Arizona passers, it should be enough to give him a reasonable market come 2019.

Jordy Nelson

Height: 6-2 | Weight: 217 | College: Kansas State | Draft: 2008/2 (36) | Born: 31-May-1985 | Age: 33 | Risk: Red

Year	Team	G/GS	Snaps	Pass	Rec	Yds	TD	C%	+/-	Drop	Yd/C	aDOT	Rk	YAC	Rk	YAC+	BTkl	DVOA	Rk	DYAR	Rk	YAR	Use	Rk	Slot
2016	GB	16/16	1015	152	97	1257	14	64%	+7.6	9	13.0	12.6	32	3.7	61	+0.1	3	19.2%	8	382	3	366	24.6%	16	44%
2017	GB	15/15	806	89	53	482	6	60%	+1.5	3	9.1	11.5	47	2.4	80	-1.5	3	-5.0%	60	58	57	49	17.3%	51	47%
2018	OAK			91	58	652	6	64%			11.2							3.9%							

Was Nelson's decline last season due to injury, age, or Brent Hundley? If you answer "all of the above," you may be correct, but it doesn't really help project Nelson's 2018 production. Nelson went 17-206-5 with Rodgers in four September games last season, which suggests that he can still deliver in the right situation. Then again, he missed all but seven snaps of the Week 2 Falcons game with a quad injury and was only targeted 10 times once all season (in the Vikings game where Rodgers was hurt). Davante Adams, Randall Cobb, and sometimes even Geronimo Allison out-targeted Nelson late in the year, even during Rodgers' brief return. However you parse out the causes of Nelson's miserable 2017 season, he's 33 years old and changing quarterbacks, schemes, and likely roles. If he duplicates Michael Crabtree's 58-618-8 line from last year, it will be a modest uptick, a pleasant surprise, and a wasted opportunity for the Raiders to get younger and cheaper at wide receiver.

DeVante Parker

Height: 6-3 | Weight: 209 | College: Louisville | Draft: 2015/1 (14) | Born: 20-Jan-1993 | Age: 25 | Risk: Red

Year	Team	G/GS	Snaps	Pass	Rec	Yds	TD	C%	+/-	Drop	Yd/C	aDOT	Rk	YAC	Rk	YAC+	BTkl	DVOA	Rk	DYAR	Rk	YAR	Use	Rk	Slot
2015	MIA	14/4	468	50	26	494	3	52%	+1.3	3	19.0	14.7	16	3.8	61	-0.7	6	11.4%	23	93	48	90	9.9%	85	--
2016	MIA	15/8	736	88	56	744	4	64%	+4.6	3	13.3	12.5	33	4.2	50	-0.2	6	7.8%	31	141	36	141	20.4%	35	14%
2017	MIA	13/12	678	96	57	670	1	59%	+0.4	3	11.8	12.5	37	3.7	51	-1.0	3	-11.0%	70	12	69	6	20.0%	32	14%
2018	MIA			106	64	842	5	60%			13.2							2.5%							

What is Parker at this point? It was thought that the move to Jay Cutler would open him up as a vertical receiver, but it was clear that Adam Gase didn't really trust Cutler to do that, and that Kenny Stills was trusted more on deep balls anyway. On 18 curl routes, Parker generated -37 DYAR. Parker is wildly athletic, but three years in he still seems to have no idea what to do with his skills. The Dolphins are notorious for talking up their players during the offseason, so get ready for another round of how Parker could be a 1,000-yard receiver. Realistically, he could, but it would take a healthy year from Ryan Tannehill and a major step forward from each of them. At this point, it doesn't seem terribly likely. The Dolphins picked up his fifth-year option, but the direction we're going in is more Kelvin Benjamin than Odell Beckham.

Cordarrelle Patterson   Height: 6-2   Weight: 216   College: Tennessee   Draft: 2013/1 (29)   Born: 17-Mar-1991   Age: 27   Risk: Blue

Year	Team	G/GS	Snaps	Pass	Rec	Yds	TD	C%	+/-	Drop	Yd/C	aDOT	Rk	YAC	Rk	YAC+	BTkl	DVOA	Rk	DYAR	Rk	YAR	Use	Rk	Slot
2015	MIN	16/1	58	2	2	10	0	100%	+0.4	0	5.0	3.0	--	2.0	--	-4.9	1	13.1%	--	3	--	2	0.4%	--	--
2016	MIN	16/8	531	70	52	453	2	74%	+3.5	2	8.7	4.7	94	6.4	5	+0.4	19	-9.5%	71	17	71	28	12.0%	84	49%
2017	OAK	16/2	431	42	31	309	0	74%	+1.5	1	10.0	5.5	--	6.3	--	+0.6	14	-7.4%	--	17	--	5	7.7%	--	42%
2018	NE			13	9	74	1	69%			8.2							-10.0%		(Also: 8 runs, 67 RuYd, 0.3 RuTD)					

The receiver who has never learned how to run routes goes to New England. (Reads up on Patterson's special teams contributions.) Ohhh ... ohhh ... OK, we get it. Patterson might get some run as a screens and 9-routes specialist, and actually has shown some success as a runner in the backfield. He brings some interesting elements to the New England offense, and knows how to block. But otherwise, expect his impact to be mostly away from the offense. At least as the focal point, anyway.

Breshad Perriman   Height: 6-2   Weight: 212   College: UCF   Draft: 2015/1 (26)   Born: 10-Sep-1993   Age: 25   Risk: Red

Year	Team	G/GS	Snaps	Pass	Rec	Yds	TD	C%	+/-	Drop	Yd/C	aDOT	Rk	YAC	Rk	YAC+	BTkl	DVOA	Rk	DYAR	Rk	YAR	Use	Rk	Slot
2016	BAL	16/1	484	66	33	499	3	50%	-5.9	5	15.1	14.3	12	5.2	25	+0.6	2	-8.7%	67	21	70	20	10.3%	90	25%
2017	BAL	11/3	387	35	10	77	0	29%	-7.8	3	7.7	14.4	--	0.5	--	-4.0	0	-71.8%	--	-158	--	-150	9.0%	--	22%
2018	BAL			28	14	168	1	50%			12.0							-19.6%							

Perriman has been godawful since the Ravens used a first-round pick on him in 2015, and unlike previous seasons he didn't even have an injury excuse last year. The Ravens brought in three, count 'em, three proven vets at wideout to play in front of Perriman. He needs to make something happen in whatever chances he does get, though it's possible he is cut before those come.

Dante Pettis   Height: 6-0   Weight: 186   College: Washington   Draft: 2018/2 (44)   Born: 23-Oct-1995   Age: 23   Risk: Blue

Year	Team	G/GS	Snaps	Pass	Rec	Yds	TD	C%	+/-	Drop	Yd/C	aDOT	Rk	YAC	Rk	YAC+	BTkl	DVOA	Rk	DYAR	Rk	YAR	Use	Rk	Slot
2018	SF			25	14	209	1	56%			14.9							-7.5%							

After spending the 2016 season as the No. 2 target behind future first-round pick John Ross, Pettis stepped into the leading role in 2017, averaging 13.4 yards per reception with a 64 percent catch rate. A versatile player, the rookie second-round pick out of Washington set the NCAA record for career punt return touchdowns with nine scores over the course of his time in college. He was also used as a passer on trick plays, averaging an even 25 yards per attempt on five passes in his junior and senior seasons. The 49ers may not need any help throwing the ball given that they have a guy named Garoppolo running the show, but an added trick play dimension could make head coach Kyle Shanahan's offense even more difficult to prepare for, as was the case with Pettis's Washington teams under Chris Petersen. The 49ers will certainly be hoping that Pettis goes on to have a more successful career than his cousin Austin did with the Rams and Chargers.

Terrelle Pryor   Height: 6-4   Weight: 233   College: Ohio State   Draft: 2011/3 (SUP)   Born: 20-Jun-1989   Age: 29   Risk: Red

Year	Team	G/GS	Snaps	Pass	Rec	Yds	TD	C%	+/-	Drop	Yd/C	aDOT	Rk	YAC	Rk	YAC+	BTkl	DVOA	Rk	DYAR	Rk	YAR	Use	Rk	Slot
2015	CLE	3/2	91	8	1	42	0	13%	-2.8	1	42.0	15.7	--	5.0	--	-2.3	1	-67.7%	--	-34	--	-32	7.1%	--	--
2016	CLE	16/15	899	140	77	1007	4	55%	-1.8	7	13.1	14.3	13	2.8	85	-1.4	6	-2.5%	60	112	49	115	25.4%	11	23%
2017	WAS	9/2	378	37	20	240	1	54%	-1.6	3	12.0	11.3	--	2.9	--	-0.8	1	-5.3%	--	23	--	21	12.5%	--	13%
2018	NYJ			77	44	580	5	57%			13.2							-5.0%							

Washington signed Pryor to a one-year prove-it deal and essentially gave him no chance to do so. He was targeted just 37 times all season after Josh Doctson squeezed him out of the offense. Pryor's next prove-it deal comes from the Jets, where he is the monetary favorite to beat out every Day 2 and 3 receiver draft pick of the past three seasons to be their fourth wideout. Absent at OTAs after apparently suffering another ankle injury during the offseason, Pryor didn't leave a good opening impression on the Jets.

Josh Reynolds

Height: 6-3   Weight: 194   College: Texas A&M   Draft: 2017/4 (117)   Born: 16-Feb-1995   Age: 23   Risk: Blue

Year	Team	G/GS	Snaps	Pass	Rec	Yds	TD	C%	+/-	Drop	Yd/C	aDOT	Rk	YAC	Rk	YAC+	BTkl	DVOA	Rk	DYAR	Rk	YAR	Use	Rk	Slot
2017	LAR	16/1	280	24	11	104	1	46%	-3.9	0	9.5	7.4	–	3.1	–	-0.4	1	-31.0%	–	-35	–	-43	4.6%	–	79%
2018	LAR			19	10	130	1	53%			13.0							-9.5%							

Reynolds was mostly an injury replacement for Robert Woods and showed a fair bit of promise. It's not that he was good, per se; more that the elements of a good player could be seen in his game. He's big and athletic, makes a good option for jump balls in the end zone, shows promising catching and blocking abilities for a rookie, and so on and so forth. There was a brief window this offseason when it looked like Reynolds would have a chance for a breakout season. Sammy Watkins' departure opened up a spot on the outside, and maybe Reynolds would work on developing that full route tree and becoming a solid second receiver in 2018. Then the Brandin Cooks trade happened, and it was revealed that Reynolds is recovering from a torn labrum, and that was just about that. Reynolds will be the fourth receiver once again, where he can continue his development outside of the spotlight.

Paul Richardson

Height: 6-0   Weight: 175   College: Colorado   Draft: 2014/2 (45)   Born: 4/13/1992   Age: 26   Risk: Yellow

Year	Team	G/GS	Snaps	Pass	Rec	Yds	TD	C%	+/-	Drop	Yd/C	aDOT	Rk	YAC	Rk	YAC+	BTkl	DVOA	Rk	DYAR	Rk	YAR	Use	Rk	Slot
2015	SEA	1/0	6	1	1	40	0	100%	+0.7	0	40.0	28.0	–	12.0	–	+3.4	0	253.5%	–	21	–	21	3.4%	–	–
2016	SEA	15/0	338	36	21	288	1	58%	+2.9	0	13.7	13.3	–	4.6	–	+0.3	1	7.9%	–	56	–	61	6.8%	–	36%
2017	SEA	16/13	816	80	44	703	6	55%	-2.3	6	16.0	15.4	10	2.8	72	-1.4	5	13.4%	20	161	23	183	15.4%	60	35%
2018	WAS			83	47	720	4	57%			15.3							4.6%							

Richardson's season peaked in a three-game stretch against the Giants, Houston, and Washington in the middle of the year, when he caught 11-of-12 passes for 207 yards and three touchdowns. And then he disappeared—in the eight games after that, he had 19 receptions for 288 yards and one touchdown, with a catch rate south of 50 percent. In Washington, he'll join Jamison Crowder and Josh Doctson to form a trio of highly drafted, underperforming wideouts. Richardson figures to be the primary deep threat. He had 11 catches on deep passes last year, as many as Crowder (five) and Doctson (six) combined.

Calvin Ridley

Height: 6-0   Weight: 189   College: Alabama   Draft: 2018/1 (26)   Born: 20-Dec-1994   Age: 24   Risk: Red

Year	Team	G/GS	Snaps	Pass	Rec	Yds	TD	C%	+/-	Drop	Yd/C	aDOT	Rk	YAC	Rk	YAC+	BTkl	DVOA	Rk	DYAR	Rk	YAR	Use	Rk	Slot
2018	ATL			86	54	768	5	63%			14.2							5.5%							

Ridley is an interesting case because he clearly has the talent to be a top-tier receiver, but his production in college was subpar largely due to inconsistent (that's putting it kindly) quarterback play and a run-heavy scheme. Moving from Jalen Hurts to Matt Ryan is a *massive* upgrade at quarterback for Ridley. Ridley's opportunity to make plays might be a bit dampened this year because Atlanta's offense has a lot of mouths to feed. Still, he'll see plenty of single coverage throughout his rookie year and has the potential to put up an effective, efficient season even if the target total isn't high.

Seth Roberts

Height: 6-2   Weight: 195   College: West Alabama   Draft: 2014/FA   Born: 22-Feb-1991   Age: 27   Risk: Green

Year	Team	G/GS	Snaps	Pass	Rec	Yds	TD	C%	+/-	Drop	Yd/C	aDOT	Rk	YAC	Rk	YAC+	BTkl	DVOA	Rk	DYAR	Rk	YAR	Use	Rk	Slot
2015	OAK	16/5	565	55	32	480	5	58%	-0.8	4	15.0	10.0	64	4.2	50	-0.2	2	13.3%	19	114	38	127	9.4%	86	–
2016	OAK	16/6	749	77	38	397	5	49%	-12.3	9	10.4	8.5	78	5.3	20	+0.4	14	-18.6%	83	-37	84	-54	13.0%	76	85%
2017	OAK	15/7	752	65	43	455	1	66%	+1.2	5	10.6	10.0	61	2.5	79	-2.0	2	-5.8%	61	34	66	33	12.5%	74	92%
2018	OAK			32	20	239	1	63%			11.9							-0.6%							

Roberts is a standard-issue, budget-friendly slot receiver. He managed to hold onto his role in the offense last year, when the organization would much rather have developed Cordarrelle Patterson into an all-purpose slot weapon instead. Roberts is exactly the kind of useful, non-flashy role player who gets squeezed out when a new coach arrives and decides that he needs room on the bench for Dwayne Harris and Griff Whalen.

Aldrick Robinson Height: 5-10 Weight: 182 College: Southern Methodist Draft: 2011/6 (178) Born: 11-Apr-1988 Age: 30 Risk: Green

Year	Team	G/GS	Snaps	Pass	Rec	Yds	TD	C%	+/-	Drop	Yd/C	aDOT	Rk	YAC	Rk	YAC+	BTkl	DVOA	Rk	DYAR	Rk	YAR	Use	Rk	Slot
2016	ATL	16/1	315	32	20	323	2	63%	+1.5	1	16.2	12.5	--	3.8	--	+0.3	1	24.5%	--	91	--	90	5.9%	--	63%
2016	ATL	16/1	315	32	20	323	2	63%	+1.5	1	16.2	12.5	--	3.8	--	+0.3	1	24.5%	--	91	--	90	5.9%	--	63%
2017	SF	16/1	438	48	19	260	2	40%	-8.1	4	13.7	12.3	--	2.0	--	-1.9	4	-24.5%	--	-43	--	-59	7.9%	--	44%
2018	SF			20	11	154	0	55%			14.0							-12.1%							

Robinson has bounced around the league, as he is now on his fourth team since being drafted by Washington in 2011. He reunited with his former offensive coordinator Kyle Shanahan in 2017, following him over from Atlanta after initially playing for him in Washington, but that familiarity did not generate much in the way of results. Robinson is entering the final year of a two-year contract, making it easy for the 49ers to cut him should he not perform well enough to justify keeping him on the roster.

Allen Robinson Height: 6-2 Weight: 220 College: Penn St. Draft: 2014/2 (61) Born: 8/24/1993 Age: 25 Risk: Yellow

Year	Team	G/GS	Snaps	Pass	Rec	Yds	TD	C%	+/-	Drop	Yd/C	aDOT	Rk	YAC	Rk	YAC+	BTkl	DVOA	Rk	DYAR	Rk	YAR	Use	Rk	Slot
2015	JAX	16/16	983	151	80	1400	14	53%	+1.4	5	17.5	15.5	11	4.5	43	+0.2	8	14.0%	16	318	8	343	25.1%	16	--
2016	JAX	16/16	1047	151	73	883	6	48%	-10.4	10	12.1	13.5	20	2.8	87	-1.2	5	-12.0%	74	8	73	-16	24.9%	13	33%
2017	JAX	1/1	3	1	1	17	0	100%	+0.6	0	17.0	15.0	--	2.0	--	-2.2	0	123.1%	--	12	--	12	3.0%	--	0%
2018	CHI			114	67	968	9	59%			14.4							9.0%							

Sometimes a young receiver needs to leave town to reinvigorate his game. After he tore his ACL in Week 1 last year, we're still not sure if Robinson is the star who had 1,400 yards and 14 touchdowns in 2015, or the inconsistent player with 10 drops and poor YAC in 2016. The Bears didn't go full Al Davis and give Robinson the Javon Walker deal, but signing Robinson was a gamble that needs to pay instant dividends. Robinson should have plenty of opportunities to shine given Kevin White's injury history and the fact that Chicago's other receivers are better suited for the slot.

Demarcus Robinson Height: 6-1 Weight: 203 College: Florida Draft: 2016/4 (126) Born: 21-Sep-1994 Age: 24 Risk: Green

Year	Team	G/GS	Snaps	Pass	Rec	Yds	TD	C%	+/-	Drop	Yd/C	aDOT	Rk	YAC	Rk	YAC+	BTkl	DVOA	Rk	DYAR	Rk	YAR	Use	Rk	Slot
2016	KC	16/0	6	0	0	0	0	--	--	--	--	--	--	--	--	--	--	--	--	--	--	--	--	--	--
2017	KC	16/8	586	39	21	212	0	54%	-1.8	3	10.1	11.0	--	2.0	--	-2.0	0	-16.9%	--	-14	--	-12	7.7%	--	51%
2018	KC			23	12	154	0	52%			12.8							-14.6%							

When the Chiefs drafted Robinson in 2016, there was an understanding that he would be a project. Robinson was a talented yet inconsistent receiving threat at Florida, making him the stereotypical Andy Reid selection. Not a single target went Robinson's way as a rookie in 2016, but Robinson found the field more frequently in 2017. Robinson's role in the offense is quite ambiguous—he bounces between playing out wide and in the slot, as well as running a wide variety of routes. Robinson does not have a clear strength. He is not a fantastic route-runner, nor is he a consistent deep threat or yards-after-catch monster. Rather, Robinson is a passable short-to-intermediate possession receiver who can serve as a valuable role player behind two or three star receiving threats, which Kansas City will have in 2018.

Chester Rogers Height: 6-1 Weight: 180 College: Grambling State Draft: 2016/FA Born: 12-Jan-1994 Age: 24 Risk: Yellow

Year	Team	G/GS	Snaps	Pass	Rec	Yds	TD	C%	+/-	Drop	Yd/C	aDOT	Rk	YAC	Rk	YAC+	BTkl	DVOA	Rk	DYAR	Rk	YAR	Use	Rk	Slot
2016	IND	14/2	434	34	19	273	0	56%	-0.6	3	14.4	12.3	--	2.8	--	-0.8	2	5.4%	--	51	--	41	7.1%	--	25%
2017	IND	11/4	445	37	23	284	1	62%	+0.4	2	12.3	9.4	--	4.5	--	-0.5	4	-3.1%	--	28	--	15	11.4%	--	56%
2018	IND			48	28	415	3	58%			14.8							5.4%							

Somebody has to be the No. 2 receiver on the Colts. If the hamstring that has cost him time in both of his NFL seasons and whatever kept him out of minicamp this offseason heal up, it could easily be Rogers due to Andrew Luck having gotten to play him before. Offseason reports had Rogers as part of a clear top three at receiver, with the rookies well behind. He also has punt return experience. As the rookies improve, though, Rogers' lack of a selling point may be more important unless he develops one.

Eli Rogers

Height: 5-10　Weight: 187　College: Louisville　Draft: 2015/FA　Born: 23-Dec-1992　Age: 26　Risk: N/A

Year	Team	G/GS	Snaps	Pass	Rec	Yds	TD	C%	+/-	Drop	Yd/C	aDOT	Rk	YAC	Rk	YAC+	BTkl	DVOA	Rk	DYAR	Rk	YAR	Use	Rk	Slot
2016	PIT	13/8	550	66	48	594	3	73%	+4.3	2	12.4	9.6	67	4.3	48	-0.6	4	18.3%	10	150	32	150	13.6%	72	89%
2017	PIT	14/4	386	36	18	149	1	50%	-4.3	5	8.3	8.1	--	4.5	--	-0.8	2	-22.3%	--	-28	--	-23	7.3%	--	92%

It seems doubtful Rogers will have much of an impact on 2018. After he served as Pittsburgh's primary slot receiver as a rookie two years ago, the arrival of JuJu Smith-Schuster relegated him to fourth receiver duties last season. The departure of Martavis Bryant opens up a more prominent spot, but that's almost assuredly going to go to James Washington—and that's even without considering the fact that Rogers is recovering from a torn ACL suffered in January and is technically still a free agent. He's expected to re-sign with the team when fully healthy, but he would just be depth at that point.

John Ross

Height: 5-11　Weight: 188　College: Washington　Draft: 2017/1 (9)　Born: 27-Nov-1994　Age: 24　Risk: Yellow

Year	Team	G/GS	Snaps	Pass	Rec	Yds	TD	C%	+/-	Drop	Yd/C	aDOT	Rk	YAC	Rk	YAC+	BTkl	DVOA	Rk	DYAR	Rk	YAR	Use	Rk	Slot
2017	CIN	3/1	17	2	0	0	0	0%	-0.9	0	0.0	23.0	--	0.0	--	+0.0	0	-105.6%	--	-14	--	-13	2.1%	--	50%
2018	CIN			31	19	302	2	61%			15.9							9.0%							

The Bengals desperately sought Speed, with a capital "s," entering the 2017 draft. Unfortunately, instead of Keanu Reeves, they wound up with Jason Patric. Ross memorably shattered the NFL combine record when he blazed out a 4.24-second 40-yard dash, and his college tape showed a complete receiver, not just a track star. But he also brought with him a worrisome injury history, and he never got healthy in Cincinnati. Marvin Lewis seemed not to trust him, which proved at least somewhat justified when Ross was shown to be hiding a shoulder injury near season's end.

First-round wideouts who are invisible in their rookie seasons do not have a promising track record. If Ross can live up to his top-ten draft billing, the Bengals will have a weapon to at last free coverage from rolling over toward A.J. Green. There is still time for that to happen, but 2018 is a crucial crossroads in his career.

Curtis Samuel

Height: 5-11　Weight: 196　College: Ohio State　Draft: 2017/2 (40)　Born: 11-Aug-1996　Age: 22　Risk: Green

Year	Team	G/GS	Snaps	Pass	Rec	Yds	TD	C%	+/-	Drop	Yd/C	aDOT	Rk	YAC	Rk	YAC+	BTkl	DVOA	Rk	DYAR	Rk	YAR	Use	Rk	Slot
2017	CAR	9/4	226	26	15	115	0	58%	-2.1	2	7.7	11.0	--	3.4	--	-2.3	4	-18.3%	--	-12	--	-10	9.9%	--	71%
2018	CAR			27	14	149	0	52%			10.6							-24.5%							

Samuel was not ready for prime time as a rookie. The converted running back was not prepared to run a full route tree, and was essentially asked to only run curls and outs. His hands weren't anything to write home about either; a 58 percent catch rate when your average depth of target is only 11.0 yards is definitely in the lower half of the league. His season ended prematurely with an ankle fracture, which is not good for anyone but particularly bad for someone who needs practice and reps switching to a new position. He was still not at 100 percent through OTAs and minicamp, further hampering his development. Samuel might have to spend another year as a glorified gadget player, if he produces anything in 2018 at all.

Emmanuel Sanders

Height: 5-11　Weight: 186　College: Southern Methodist　Draft: 2010/3 (82)　Born: 17-Mar-1987　Age: 31　Risk: Yellow

Year	Team	G/GS	Snaps	Pass	Rec	Yds	TD	C%	+/-	Drop	Yd/C	aDOT	Rk	YAC	Rk	YAC+	BTkl	DVOA	Rk	DYAR	Rk	YAR	Use	Rk	Slot
2015	DEN	15/15	859	137	76	1135	6	55%	-0.7	6	14.9	14.7	17	4.8	36	+0.0	5	-4.1%	58	90	49	110	23.9%	22	--
2016	DEN	16/16	869	137	79	1032	5	58%	+2.4	3	13.1	13.3	27	3.0	79	-0.9	12	-3.3%	61	103	51	82	24.3%	17	41%
2017	DEN	12/11	635	91	47	555	2	51%	-7.1	6	11.8	11.0	50	3.6	54	-0.6	7	-18.2%	75	-40	79	-36	22.0%	21	39%
2018	DEN			118	70	895	5	59%			12.8							-1.9%							

Sanders is 31 and coming off a poor year caused by an ankle injury and poor Broncos quarterbacks. It's hard to separate any decline on Sanders' part from the injury and the fact that no Broncos quarterback could successfully reach a receiver more than 10 yards downfield; the smart money is on a return to 2015-16 form, but not to his mammoth 2014 production (1,404 yards, 9 touchdowns). From a fantasy standpoint, the important thing to remember about both Sanders and Demaryius Thomas is that the Broncos don't have much behind them or at tight end or running back; Case Keenum will be looking for them a lot, even if neither is the playmaker he was three years ago.

Mohamed Sanu Height: 6-2   Weight: 211   College: Rutgers   Draft: 2012/3 (83)   Born: 22-Aug-1989   Age: 29   Risk: Green

Year	Team	G/GS	Snaps	Pass	Rec	Yds	TD	C%	+/-	Drop	Yd/C	aDOT	Rk	YAC	Rk	YAC+	BTkl	DVOA	Rk	DYAR	Rk	YAR	Use	Rk	Slot
2015	CIN	16/4	643	49	33	394	0	67%	-0.2	0	11.9	7.0	–	6.2	–	+1.0	7	-8.3%	–	16	–	14	9.7%	–	–
2016	ATL	15/15	744	81	59	653	4	73%	+5.7	2	11.1	8.1	81	4.9	32	+0.2	10	6.5%	36	123	44	135	16.2%	61	87%
2017	ATL	15/15	756	96	67	703	5	70%	+4.3	6	10.5	8.0	77	3.7	53	-0.6	8	10.7%	24	179	18	180	20.0%	33	78%
2018	ATL			84	57	677	4	68%			11.9							7.5%							

Many Falcons fans were upset when Sanu signed a five-year contract worth up to $32.5 million prior to the 2016 season. Since then, Sanu has grown into a fan favorite and the perfect No. 2 receiver to have across from Julio Jones. Sanu is signed through 2020, but due to age and salary cap implications he is unlikely to see the end of his contract. This upcoming season might be his last with the team, but he has more than proven he was worth the money.

Sterling Shepard Height: 5-10   Weight: 194   College: Oklahoma   Draft: 2016/2 (40)   Born: 10-Feb-1994   Age: 24   Risk: Green

Year	Team	G/GS	Snaps	Pass	Rec	Yds	TD	C%	+/-	Drop	Yd/C	aDOT	Rk	YAC	Rk	YAC+	BTkl	DVOA	Rk	DYAR	Rk	YAR	Use	Rk	Slot
2016	NYG	16/16	1005	105	65	683	8	62%	-3.3	5	10.5	9.2	70	4.0	53	-0.6	9	-1.8%	55	91	54	101	17.5%	50	89%
2017	NYG	11/10	688	84	59	731	2	70%	+4.5	6	12.4	8.8	72	5.0	21	+0.6	6	4.9%	37	120	37	122	20.1%	31	89%
2018	NYG			96	62	726	4	65%			11.7							1.3%							

The overall defunct state of the New York Giants led to a seemingly milquetoast year from Shepard. As a rookie in 2016, Shepard dominated the red zone with a 77 percent catch rate, 6.5 yards per target, and six touchdowns on just 13 throws. However, in 2017, Shepard's red zone performance dropped. On 11 targets, Shepard had a 45 percent catch rate, a measly 1.5 yards per target, and zero touchdowns. With other wide receivers out with injury, it became easy for defenses to target and shut down Shepard in the red zone. Despite a dip in red zone production, Shepard still found success elsewhere, primarily out of the slot as a possession receiver. He had 18 catches on 22 targets on slant routes. Though not a wonderful athlete, Shepard plays with crispness and calculation rarely seen from young route-runners, enabling him to finish off plays with his strong hands. That combination of skills made Shepard particularly good on quick slant routes. With more stability regarding the Giants offense heading into 2018, Shepard will have a clean opportunity to regain his red zone prowess and maintain his effectiveness out of the slot.

JuJu Smith-Schuster Height: 6-1   Weight: 215   College: USC   Draft: 2017/2 (62)   Born: 22-Nov-1996   Age: 22   Risk: Green

Year	Team	G/GS	Snaps	Pass	Rec	Yds	TD	C%	+/-	Drop	Yd/C	aDOT	Rk	YAC	Rk	YAC+	BTkl	DVOA	Rk	DYAR	Rk	YAR	Use	Rk	Slot
2017	PIT	14/7	707	79	58	917	7	73%	+8.1	2	15.8	9.9	63	6.7	5	+2.2	8	37.3%	1	317	6	321	15.3%	63	59%
2018	PIT			111	68	951	6	61%			14.0							5.6%							

Smith-Schuster was arguably the most efficient receiver in football last season. He was dinged for a lack of speed coming out of USC, but that didn't actually manifest itself in any way on the field. Among receivers, he ranked first in DVOA, sixth in DYAR, seventh in plus-minus and third in YAC+. That last stat might be the most interesting. Smith-Schuster won't be winning any medals on the track anytime soon, but he doesn't need to. He has more than enough speed with the ball in his hands, and his combination of precise route-running and a willingness and ability to go over the middle and work through traffic means he can put himself into positions where he can take off and run after the catch. Take drag routes for instance—Smith-Schuster had a 54.0% DVOA and was second in the league with 54 DYAR on drag routes, and his 10.6 YAC was third-most among players with at least 10 of those routes. The Steelers got a major component in their office for years to come.

Torrey Smith   Height: 6-1   Weight: 204   College: Maryland   Draft: 2011/2 (58)   Born: 26-Jan-1989   Age: 29   Risk: Green

Year	Team	G/GS	Snaps	Pass	Rec	Yds	TD	C%	+/-	Drop	Yd/C	aDOT	Rk	YAC	Rk	YAC+	BTkl	DVOA	Rk	DYAR	Rk	YAR	Use	Rk	Slot
2015	SF	16/12	775	62	33	663	4	53%	+0.3	4	20.1	14.8	14	6.6	5	+1.1	1	14.3%	14	134	32	112	12.1%	77	--
2016	SF	12/12	643	49	20	267	3	41%	-7.4	5	13.4	13.5	22	3.1	78	-1.2	2	-33.0%	93	-78	90	-69	13.5%	73	36%
2017	PHI	16/14	735	69	36	430	2	54%	-3.9	8	11.9	13.8	24	3.3	63	-1.3	1	-18.2%	76	-29	74	-26	12.7%	73	36%
2018	CAR			54	29	376	3	54%			13.0							-7.7%							

Torrey Smith was a non-factor last season, just as he was the year before. He was near the bottom in receiving plus-minus, catching just 36 of his 69 targets. He wasn't even the downfield weapon that he was billed as coming in to Philadelphia; the once-productive deep threat had just six receptions that traveled further than 15 yards down the field last year. He doesn't block very well, his hands are questionable, and he was losing snaps to Mack Hollins by the time the season was through. The Eagles were almost certainly going to cut him, but the Panthers swooped in and actually traded a player away for him in one of the more baffling moves of the offseason. Some say that he might fill the Ted Ginn role in 2018. Well, Ginn made $1.1 million when he came to Carolina in 2013, and cost the Panthers nothing in return. Smith cost $5 million and a 23-year-old corner with starting experience on a rookie contract.

Tre'Quan Smith   Height: 6-1   Weight: 205   College: Central Florida   Draft: 2018/3 (91)   Born: 7-Jan-1996   Age: 22   Risk: Green

Year	Team	G/GS	Snaps	Pass	Rec	Yds	TD	C%	+/-	Drop	Yd/C	aDOT	Rk	YAC	Rk	YAC+	BTkl	DVOA	Rk	DYAR	Rk	YAR	Use	Rk	Slot
2018	NO			25	18	253	2	72%			14.0							19.4%							

Smith was the Knights' leading receiver in all three of his seasons at Central Florida, but some scouts saw Smith as a low-ceiling prospect that may only compete for a WR4/WR5 role. Playmaker Score was more optimistic, giving Smith the sixth-highest projection in this draft class. By going to New Orleans, he can only expect to be WR4 this year behind a depth chart of Michael Thomas, Cameron Meredith, and Ted Ginn.

Willie Snead   Height: 5-11   Weight: 195   College: Ball State   Draft: 2014/FA   Born: 17-Oct-1992   Age: 26   Risk: Red

Year	Team	G/GS	Snaps	Pass	Rec	Yds	TD	C%	+/-	Drop	Yd/C	aDOT	Rk	YAC	Rk	YAC+	BTkl	DVOA	Rk	DYAR	Rk	YAR	Use	Rk	Slot
2015	NO	15/8	780	101	69	984	3	68%	+8.8	2	14.3	10.4	56	5.0	28	+0.5	9	10.1%	28	175	23	198	16.2%	55	--
2016	NO	15/4	740	104	72	895	4	69%	+2.5	4	12.4	7.4	87	5.4	17	+0.8	12	12.5%	17	206	20	195	16.6%	59	90%
2017	NO	11/7	259	16	8	92	0	50%	-1.1	1	11.5	7.6	--	4.0	--	-1.2	1	-31.0%	--	-23	--	-22	4.4%	--	81%
2018	BAL			89	49	579	3	55%			11.8							-14.0%							

Snead was the pride of the Saints' personnel department, who plucked the undrafted free agent from obscurity and watched him catch 141 passes in two seasons. Then came last year, when a night of partying resulted in a three-game suspension for a DWI arrest, and a hamstring injury further stymied Snead. He did little with the 16 targets that came his way. All that, plus the signing of Cameron Meredith, spelled *sayonara*, as New Orleans didn't match the Ravens' offer sheet. Now removed from the comfortable bosom of Drew Brees, Snead becomes Joe Flacco's slot receiver. Both wideout and quarterback have something to prove in this combination. If healthy, and sober, Snead figures to hold up his end of the bargain.

Kenny Stills   Height: 6-0   Weight: 194   College: Oklahoma   Draft: 2013/5 (144)   Born: 22-Apr-1992   Age: 26   Risk: Yellow

Year	Team	G/GS	Snaps	Pass	Rec	Yds	TD	C%	+/-	Drop	Yd/C	aDOT	Rk	YAC	Rk	YAC+	BTkl	DVOA	Rk	DYAR	Rk	YAR	Use	Rk	Slot
2015	MIA	16/8	594	63	27	440	3	43%	-5.9	4	16.3	16.2	5	3.8	60	-1.3	0	-17.2%	80	-22	80	-26	10.7%	83	--
2016	MIA	16/16	795	81	42	726	9	52%	-2.7	3	17.3	14.8	8	4.6	38	+0.5	4	6.8%	34	121	45	144	17.4%	52	56%
2017	MIA	16/16	942	105	58	847	6	55%	+1.0	4	14.6	15.2	12	2.7	75	-1.4	4	0.4%	44	107	44	91	18.0%	43	54%
2018	MIA			99	54	849	6	55%			15.7							4.8%							

The agenda for Kenny Stills: torch you deep and make you worried enough about getting torched to allow the curls and comebacks. Another player who should theoretically benefit from a healthy Ryan Tannehill, Stills is overpaid at a $9.75 million cap figure, but he's a solid outside receiver who would comfortably start for most teams. It's worth pointing out that almost a quarter of his seasonal yardage came in one game against the Bucs in Week 11. Still, he's Miami's clear best receiver now that

Jarvis Landry is gone, and it shouldn't shock anyone if he finds career highs across the board if Tannehill plays 16 games. Just don't expect the kind of efficiency he had in New Orleans, because that isn't ever coming back.

Courtland Sutton Height: 6-3   Weight: 218   College: Southern Methodist   Draft: 2018/2 (40)   Born: 10-Oct-1995   Age: 23   Risk: Yellow

Year	Team	G/GS	Snaps	Pass	Rec	Yds	TD	C%	+/-	Drop	Yd/C	aDOT	Rk	YAC	Rk	YAC+	BTkl	DVOA	Rk	DYAR	Rk	YAR	Use	Rk	Slot
2018	DEN			62	38	494	3	61%			13.0							-1.4%							

Sutton looked like Randy Moss at times against mid-major cornerbacks in college but was much quieter against better opponents like TCU (who held him catchless last season) and Central Florida (five catches for 46 yards). It's the profile of a size-speed prospect with little separation quickness and rudimentary route-running chops. Luckily, the Broncos have a great track record developing raw pros.

Aw heck, we can't even type those words sarcastically. Moss fantasies aside, Sutton's upside is 2013-14 Demaryius Thomas, but he's more likely to max out as 2017 Thomas, the guy who catches a few jump balls and lots of little hitches against off coverage. The Broncos don't really need two of this kind of receiver, but try telling them that.

Golden Tate Height: 5-10   Weight: 199   College: Notre Dame   Draft: 2010/2 (60)   Born: 2-Aug-1988   Age: 30   Risk: Green

Year	Team	G/GS	Snaps	Pass	Rec	Yds	TD	C%	+/-	Drop	Yd/C	aDOT	Rk	YAC	Rk	YAC+	BTkl	DVOA	Rk	DYAR	Rk	YAR	Use	Rk	Slot
2015	DET	16/16	926	128	90	813	6	70%	+1.7	5	9.0	6.2	83	5.9	10	+0.1	27	-1.7%	51	113	39	74	20.9%	33	--
2016	DET	16/16	866	135	91	1077	4	67%	+3.0	9	11.8	7.8	84	6.8	3	+0.9	27	-1.8%	54	114	48	111	22.9%	22	43%
2017	DET	16/12	791	120	92	1003	5	77%	+8.6	3	10.9	6.0	85	6.8	4	+1.2	23	9.7%	27	204	16	205	20.9%	27	80%
2018	DET			135	93	1004	5	69%			10.8							3.9%							

If Jarvis Landry was better at his job, he'd be Golden Tate. Since coming to Detroit in 2014, Tate has had four straight seasons with at least 90 receptions. Antonio Brown is the only other receiver to have done that the last four years. Tate catches a lot of short passes as opposed to his more vertical days with Seattle, but he's a fine fit in Detroit, where he had the most targets (23) and DYAR (68) on dig routes in the NFL last year. Unfortunately, his more memorable plays last year were some of the key breaking points to Detroit's non-playoff season. Tate was ruled to be down short of the goal line against Atlanta, wiping out a go-ahead touchdown in the final seconds. He also had an odd fumble in the fourth quarter against Pittsburgh. At 30 years old, Tate is still virtually a lock for 1,000 yards and a handful of touchdowns.

Taywan Taylor Height: 5-11   Weight: 203   College: Western Kentucky   Draft: 2017/3 (72)   Born: 2-Mar-1995   Age: 23   Risk: Red

Year	Team	G/GS	Snaps	Pass	Rec	Yds	TD	C%	+/-	Drop	Yd/C	aDOT	Rk	YAC	Rk	YAC+	BTkl	DVOA	Rk	DYAR	Rk	YAR	Use	Rk	Slot
2017	TEN	16/4	246	28	16	231	1	57%	+0.7	0	14.4	13.5	--	3.4	--	-2.7	4	-9.7%	--	6	--	18	6.0%	--	66%
2018	TEN			72	42	515	3	58%			12.3							-5.9%							

Taylor has already been penciled in for the Taylor Gabriel role in Matt LaFleur's attempt at replicating the 2016 Falcons. It is easy to see why: a slot-and-screen receiver with sharp acceleration, 4.40 top-end speed, and a reputation for making would-be tacklers look silly, Taylor has all of the physical attributes to live up to those favorable comparisons. He needs to be more consistent at the catch point, and he did not live up to his potential in his rookie year in Tennessee, but Taylor is another player who could benefit greatly from the Titans' change of offensive system.

Trent Taylor Height: 5-8   Weight: 181   College: Louisiana Tech   Draft: 2017/5 (177)   Born: 30-Apr-1994   Age: 24   Risk: Green

Year	Team	G/GS	Snaps	Pass	Rec	Yds	TD	C%	+/-	Drop	Yd/C	aDOT	Rk	YAC	Rk	YAC+	BTkl	DVOA	Rk	DYAR	Rk	YAR	Use	Rk	Slot
2017	SF	15/1	491	60	43	430	2	72%	+1.8	4	10.0	6.9	82	4.3	41	+0.0	7	11.4%	23	114	40	92	10.8%	79	84%
2018	SF			60	40	438	2	67%			10.9							-2.6%							

A rookie fifth-round pick out of Louisiana Tech, Taylor carved out a role as the slot receiver and exceeded expectations from the get-go. Taylor did the majority of his damage in the midrange, with 52 percent of his targets coming 6 to 15 yards downfield. Coincidentally, that was quarterback Jimmy Garoppolo's preferred depth to target, so Taylor could be in line for even more targets moving forward. Even if Taylor does not manage to keep up his per-play efficiency on a higher frequency of targets, he is well on his way to making the San Francisco front office look smart by outperforming the normal expectation for a fifth-round pick. His role on punt returns will likely decline with the addition of rookie wide receiver Dante Pettis, but that could be a good thing for his receiving numbers with more time to devote to offense.

Adam Thielen

Height: 6-2 Weight: 195 College: Minnesota State Draft: 2013/FA Born: 22-Aug-1990 Age: 28 Risk: Yellow

Year	Team	G/GS	Snaps	Pass	Rec	Yds	TD	C%	+/-	Drop	Yd/C	aDOT	Rk	YAC	Rk	YAC+	BTkl	DVOA	Rk	DYAR	Rk	YAR	Use	Rk	Slot
2015	MIN	16/2	218	18	12	144	0	67%	+1.4	0	12.0	10.1	--	3.9	--	+0.0	3	-8.4%	--	6	--	-5	4.0%	--	--
2016	MIN	16/10	786	92	69	967	5	75%	+12.2	2	14.0	11.2	48	4.3	44	-0.3	9	26.2%	6	270	8	299	15.8%	63	49%
2017	MIN	16/16	1034	142	91	1276	4	64%	+8.1	6	14.0	10.9	52	4.9	26	+0.1	11	10.1%	26	261	11	269	27.5%	7	60%
2018	MIN			132	86	1222	8	65%			14.2							15.3%							

Thielen did not sustain his high catch rate from 2016, but he more than proved he was not a one-year wonder. His 1,276 receiving yards ranked fifth in the NFL as the preferred target in Minnesota over Stefon Diggs. There are some interesting splits in the data that suggest Minnesota might not be using Thielen to his full potential. Thielen had 83 targets when lined up in the slot and 59 targets when lined up out wide last season. That made Thielen one of 17 wide receivers last year with at least 40 targets in both the slot and out wide. Thielen's DVOA on wide targets was 27.1%, but only -2.1% on slot targets. That drop of 29.2 percentage points in DVOA was the largest among those 17 wideouts. A similar, smaller split existed in 2016 when Thielen's usage was split 50-50, but he had 20.1% DVOA in the slot and 30.2% DVOA out wide. He has simply been more effective out wide where he still has the skills to beat cornerbacks in man coverage. No matter where he primarily lines up, Thielen should be in for another big season.

Demaryius Thomas

Height: 6-3 Weight: 224 College: Georgia Tech Draft: 2010/1 (22) Born: 25-Dec-1987 Age: 31 Risk: Yellow

Year	Team	G/GS	Snaps	Pass	Rec	Yds	TD	C%	+/-	Drop	Yd/C	aDOT	Rk	YAC	Rk	YAC+	BTkl	DVOA	Rk	DYAR	Rk	YAR	Use	Rk	Slot
2015	DEN	16/16	937	177	105	1304	6	59%	-3.3	9	12.4	10.7	54	4.7	39	+0.0	15	-8.7%	70	56	60	80	29.6%	6	--
2016	DEN	16/16	890	144	90	1083	5	63%	+1.6	10	12.0	11.1	50	3.6	65	-0.6	11	2.1%	48	172	27	149	26.6%	10	29%
2017	DEN	16/16	886	140	83	949	5	59%	-1.8	10	11.4	10.9	51	3.6	55	-0.7	10	0.2%	46	146	29	151	26.2%	11	34%
2018	DEN			138	86	1075	7	62%			12.5							2.9%							

The Broncos exercised a $4 million offseason roster bonus on Thomas, who is now 30 and has seen all phases of his production slip for four consecutive years. Bad quarterback play is a big part of his decline—Trevor Siemian's sideline passes took seven seconds to reach their targets, Paxton Lynch threw Thomas nothing but receiver screens, and we don't get paid enough to rewatch Brock Osweiler tape—but Thomas rarely gets separation on his own anymore and dropped too many contested catches. Thomas would be a cap casualty on a team that knew whether it was rebuilding or not; the Broncos will probably give him another 140 targets to show what he used to be able to do.

Michael Thomas

Height: 6-3 Weight: 212 College: Ohio State Draft: 2016/2 (47) Born: 3-Mar-1994 Age: 24 Risk: Green

Year	Team	G/GS	Snaps	Pass	Rec	Yds	TD	C%	+/-	Drop	Yd/C	aDOT	Rk	YAC	Rk	YAC+	BTkl	DVOA	Rk	DYAR	Rk	YAR	Use	Rk	Slot
2016	NO	15/12	865	121	92	1137	9	76%	+11.4	4	12.4	8.3	79	5.1	26	+1.1	17	31.6%	3	431	2	408	19.6%	40	31%
2017	NO	16/14	851	149	104	1245	5	70%	+14.9	3	12.0	9.8	67	4.1	43	-0.5	14	15.0%	16	330	5	335	28.3%	5	52%
2018	NO			150	102	1252	9	68%			12.3							10.9%							

It has been a stellar start to Thomas' career in New Orleans. He has had at least 40 receiving yards in 30 of his first 31 regular-season games. The previous record through a receiver's first 31 games was 27 by a trio of Houston Oilers: Ernest Givins, Bill Groman, and Charley Hennigan. Beyond volume, Thomas is a very efficient target too. Thomas is the NFL's only wide receiver since 2011 to gain a first down on 50 percent of his targets. Thomas led all wide receivers in receiving plus-minus in 2017, and he caught two touchdowns in his first postseason. Thomas won't always have Drew Brees as his quarterback, but he may be the most talented wide receiver the quarterback has ever played with. For now, the two should continue to be a highly efficient and productive duo.

Deonte Thompson Height: 6-0 Weight: 204 College: Florida Draft: 2012/FA Born: 14-Feb-1989 Age: 29 Risk: Red

Year	Team	G/GS	Snaps	Pass	Rec	Yds	TD	C%	+/-	Drop	Yd/C	aDOT	Rk	YAC	Rk	YAC+	BTkl	DVOA	Rk	DYAR	Rk	YAR	Use	Rk	Slot
2015	CHI	7/0	44	3	2	81	0	67%	+1.1	0	40.5	34.3	--	1.5	--	-6.3	0	123.0%	--	31	--	33	1.3%	--	--
2016	CHI	16/6	320	36	22	249	2	61%	+1.4	1	11.3	14.5	--	2.0	--	-2.1	4	10.0%	--	65	--	79	6.6%	--	22%
2017	2TM	16/10	662	69	38	555	2	55%	-0.2	2	14.6	15.1	13	2.7	77	-1.9	2	-0.9%	48	64	56	85	14.7%	66	40%
2018	DAL			39	23	303	1	59%			13.2							0.0%							

Thompson amassed 22 receptions in five years with the Ravens, Bills, and Bears, then started three of Chicago's first five games last season. The Bears then released him, the Bills immediately snapped him up, and he played every game for Buffalo from Week 7 on. With Buffalo, Thompson had 27 catches for 430 yards and a touchdown, with a 1.3% DVOA and a team-high 56 DYAR. He had 148 more yards than any of his teammates in that time frame, and 211 more than any other Bills wideout. The team opted not to re-sign him, because they hate useful football players in Buffalo, and Dallas inked him to a one-year, $2.5 million deal. Dallas' wide receiver corps is hardly any better than Buffalo's, and Thompson will get every chance to improve on his 2017 numbers this fall.

Laquon Treadwell Height: 6-2 Weight: 221 College: Mississippi Draft: 2016/1 (23) Born: 14-Jun-1995 Age: 23 Risk: Red

Year	Team	G/GS	Snaps	Pass	Rec	Yds	TD	C%	+/-	Drop	Yd/C	aDOT	Rk	YAC	Rk	YAC+	BTkl	DVOA	Rk	DYAR	Rk	YAR	Use	Rk	Slot
2016	MIN	9/1	80	3	1	15	0	33%	+0.2	0	15.0	17.3	--	0.0	--	-4.6	0	-38.8%	--	-8	--	-5	1.2%	--	0%
2017	MIN	16/7	502	35	20	200	0	57%	+0.9	2	10.0	13.2	--	2.9	--	-1.9	0	-18.2%	--	-15	--	-12	6.9%	--	11%
2018	MIN			28	17	175	0	61%			10.3							-10.1%							

At least Treadwell improved on his one-catch rookie season with 20 grabs for 200 yards, but he was less effective than even Jarius Wright. He still hasn't scored a touchdown or broken a tackle in the NFL. Treadwell only had four targets from the slot last season, so he's not of much use there either. With the Vikings signing Kendall Wright, who can play the slot well, there's not much use for Treadwell in 2018 unless one of Minnesota's two studs gets hurt. Third-year breakout wide receivers are not uncommon, but Treadwell feels like a longshot to get his fifth-year option with the Vikings.

Mike Wallace Height: 6-0 Weight: 199 College: Mississippi Draft: 2009/3 (84) Born: 1-Aug-1986 Age: 32 Risk: Green

Year	Team	G/GS	Snaps	Pass	Rec	Yds	TD	C%	+/-	Drop	Yd/C	aDOT	Rk	YAC	Rk	YAC+	BTkl	DVOA	Rk	DYAR	Rk	YAR	Use	Rk	Slot
2015	MIN	16/12	751	72	39	473	2	54%	-2.7	4	12.1	11.5	48	4.3	47	-0.5	4	-6.4%	62	36	66	16	16.7%	54	--
2016	BAL	16/16	872	116	72	1017	4	62%	+3.8	8	14.1	12.6	31	5.8	11	+1.3	14	0.0%	51	114	47	122	17.4%	51	28%
2017	BAL	15/14	714	92	52	748	4	57%	-1.0	5	14.4	13.9	22	2.9	70	-1.4	7	0.4%	45	96	47	123	17.7%	46	32%
2018	PHI			76	42	582	4	55%			13.9							-1.8%							

Wallace replaces Torrey Smith as the Eagles' speedy, unreliable deep threat. Wallace was 13-of-35 for 410 yards and four 40-plus-yard gains on passes labeled "deep" in the play-by-play, passes thrown 16 or more yards downfield. Smith had a reputation for making huge plays in critical situations; Wallace is known for disappearing the moment he's covered too tightly. The Eagles hope there's no substance to that reputation.

James Washington Height: 5-11 Weight: 213 College: Oklahoma State Draft: 2018/2 (60) Born: 2-Apr-1996 Age: 22 Risk: Red

Year	Team	G/GS	Snaps	Pass	Rec	Yds	TD	C%	+/-	Drop	Yd/C	aDOT	Rk	YAC	Rk	YAC+	BTkl	DVOA	Rk	DYAR	Rk	YAR	Use	Rk	Slot
2018	PIT			75	44	653	4	59%			14.8							1.8%							

Can Pittsburgh hit gold on second-round receivers two years in a row? The Steelers are counting on Washington to replace Martavis Bryant. He was a big-play machine at Oklahoma State, where he averaged more than 20 yards per reception over the past three seasons. If he is given a clean release at the line, he will absolutely blow by opposing cornerbacks—he didn't run particularly well at the combine, but that's he's because he's one of those guys who builds up more and more speed as the routes get longer and longer. His route-running still needs plenty of work, and he has a bad habit of body-catching and generally not having the softest hands in the world. His Playmaker Score rating was only 69.9%, hampered by a somewhat low touchdown rate for a top prospect and the fact that he stayed in college through his senior year, which top prospects historically do not do. Still, he was the best deep-ball threat available in this year's draft.

Sammy Watkins

| | Height: 6-1 | | Weight: 211 | | | College: Clemson | | | | Draft: 2014/1 (4) | | | Born: 14-Jun-1993 | | | Age: 25 | | Risk: Yellow |

Year	Team	G/GS	Snaps	Pass	Rec	Yds	TD	C%	+/-	Drop	Yd/C	aDOT	Rk	YAC	Rk	YAC+	BTkl	DVOA	Rk	DYAR	Rk	YAR	Use	Rk	Slot
2015	BUF	13/13	714	96	60	1047	9	63%	+9.6	2	17.5	17.3	2	3.0	77	-1.2	2	28.9%	6	312	9	312	25.7%	15	--
2016	BUF	8/8	382	52	28	430	2	54%	+0.6	3	15.4	14.1	17	1.9	93	-1.8	2	-1.3%	53	48	64	56	22.8%	25	43%
2017	LAR	15/14	776	70	39	593	8	56%	+3.4	3	15.2	15.5	9	4.7	28	+0.8	2	24.1%	6	216	14	206	15.0%	65	47%
2018	KC			96	54	826	7	56%			15.3							5.1%							

The perception that Watkins underperformed last season because he only caught 39 passes is an incomplete assessment. Part of the issue came down to Watkins' connection with quarterback Jared Goff. Watkins thrives on vertical routes, but Goff does not throw them particularly well. Watkins was targeted on 23 deep passes, but was only able to haul in five of them, with 11 attempts registering as overthrows and another two resulting in defensive pass interference. Thankfully for Watkins, his new home in Kansas City comes along with an aggressive and capable deep passer in Patrick Mahomes. In tandem with Tyreek Hill, Watkins will punish teams down the field with speed and finally receive the deep targets he deserves—something he has not gotten since his 2015 season in Buffalo with Tyrod Taylor. Furthermore, a healthy Watkins has traditionally done his best work out wide. Despite that, Watkins saw near equal targets from the slot versus out wide, receiving 39 targets when lined up out wide and 33 targets when playing from the slot. With the likes of wide receiver Chris Conley and a flex tight end in Travis Kelce on the roster, Watkins' slot usage should go down in Kansas City and allow him to return to a more comfortable role.

Dede Westbrook

| | Height: 6-0 | | Weight: 178 | | | College: Oklahoma | | | | Draft: 2017/4 (110) | | | Born: 21-Nov-1993 | | | Age: 25 | | Risk: Red |

Year	Team	G/GS	Snaps	Pass	Rec	Yds	TD	C%	+/-	Drop	Yd/C	aDOT	Rk	YAC	Rk	YAC+	BTkl	DVOA	Rk	DYAR	Rk	YAR	Use	Rk	Slot
2017	JAX	7/5	386	51	27	339	1	53%	-2.0	2	12.6	12.0	39	3.7	52	-1.2	3	-21.5%	79	-35	76	-24	22.2%	20	39%
2018	JAX			81	45	580	4	56%			12.9							-5.4%							

Westbrook was the yin to Keelan Cole's yang; no receiver had a larger DVOA difference in favor of being targeted out wide. Westbrook's 20 targets from the slot accounted for just 90 yards, a paltry 4.5 yards per target, and a league-worst -57.1% DVOA. Out wide, his 31 targets gained 249 yards (8.0 yards per target), and his DVOA was 2.1%. Like Cole, Westbook's usage in each role was probably closer than his DVOA splits merited. Unlike Cole, however, even Westbrook's better split was mediocre. The addition of Donte Moncrief dashed Westbrook's hopes of moving up the receiving order.

Kevin White

| | Height: 6-3 | | Weight: 215 | | | College: West Virginia | | | | Draft: 2015/1 (7) | | | Born: 25-Jun-1992 | | | Age: 26 | | Risk: Yellow |

Year	Team	G/GS	Snaps	Pass	Rec	Yds	TD	C%	+/-	Drop	Yd/C	aDOT	Rk	YAC	Rk	YAC+	BTkl	DVOA	Rk	DYAR	Rk	YAR	Use	Rk	Slot
2016	CHI	4/4	191	36	19	187	0	53%	-2.0	2	9.8	12.1	--	2.8	--	-2.1	3	-35.6%	--	-64	--	-70	25.8%	--	47%
2017	CHI	1/1	47	4	2	6	0	50%	-1.2	1	3.0	3.0	--	1.0	--	-5.3	1	-104.9%	--	-24	--	-23	13.6%	--	25%
2018	CHI			31	16	224	2	52%			14.0							-6.9%							

There have been 54 wide receivers drafted in the top 10 since the 1970 merger. So far, 47 of those players gained at least 1,000 receiving yards in their career. The debuts last year for Corey Davis (375), Mike Williams (95), and John Ross (0) were rough, but we'll give them each a mulligan for now. That leaves Kevin White (193), Charles Rogers (440), David Verser (454), and Larry Burton (804) as the biggest underachievers. White's biggest problem has been his health—a litany of injuries has limited him to five games in three years. And as his numbers show, on the rare instances he has been available, his performance has underwhelmed. We may never know what White could have been in this league. With the amount of talent the Bears added this offseason, it's not paramount for him to produce this season. It's really not even expected at this point, so anything he shows Chicago is a positive.

Chad Williams

| | Height: 6-0 | | Weight: 207 | | | College: Grambling State | | | | Draft: 2017/3 (98) | | | Born: 19-Oct-1994 | | | Age: 24 | | Risk: Green |

Year	Team	G/GS	Snaps	Pass	Rec	Yds	TD	C%	+/-	Drop	Yd/C	aDOT	Rk	YAC	Rk	YAC+	BTkl	DVOA	Rk	DYAR	Rk	YAR	Use	Rk	Slot
2017	ARI	6/1	100	7	3	31	0	43%	+0.2	0	10.3	17.7	--	2.0	--	-1.9	0	-0.4%	--	7	--	1	3.5%	--	0%
2018	ARI			29	19	235	2	66%			12.3							4.1%							

Williams only suited up for six games in his rookie season after being drafted in the third round and barely made an impact when he did see the field. Arizona drafting Christian Kirk in the second round suggests that the new coaching staff does not see him as the eventual successor to Larry Fitzgerald, but assuming Williams can beat out J.J. Nelson and Brice Butler, he will have a chance to carve out a role as a No. 3 receiver in his second campaign. Outside of Fitzgerald, the Cardinals' receiver room is mostly unproven, so a major step forward from Williams would be a massive help for Arizona's offensive outlook.

Mike Williams

Height: 6-4　　Weight: 218　　College: Clemson　　Draft: 2017/1 (7)　　Born: 4-Oct-1994　　Age: 24　　Risk: Red

Year	Team	G/GS	Snaps	Pass	Rec	Yds	TD	C%	+/-	Drop	Yd/C	aDOT	Rk	YAC	Rk	YAC+	BTkl	DVOA	Rk	DYAR	Rk	YAR	Use	Rk	Slot
2017	LAC	10/1	234	23	11	95	0	48%	-2.8	2	8.6	9.7	--	1.0	--	-3.0	0	-18.0%	--	-10	--	-24	6.8%	--	20%
2018	LAC			82	54	620	7	66%			11.5							7.9%							

Williams suffered a herniated disc in his back on the first day of rookie camp last year, missed all of training camp, then saw some limited midseason action before getting carted off the field in the Thanksgiving victory over the Cowboys. The serious-looking injury turned out be a bone bruise, and Williams returned for a few late-season snaps. Williams missed nearly all of Clemson's 2015 season with a neck injury, so while he declared himself fully healthy this offseason, two medical redshirts in three years are a legitimate cause for concern. Williams has the skill set to be an excellent big-target complement to Keenan Allen, and after the injury to Hunter Henry, the Chargers badly need Williams to fulfill his potential as a red zone target.

Terrance Williams

Height: 6-2　　Weight: 208　　College: Baylor　　Draft: 2013/3 (74)　　Born: 18-Sep-1989　　Age: 29　　Risk: Green

Year	Team	G/GS	Snaps	Pass	Rec	Yds	TD	C%	+/-	Drop	Yd/C	aDOT	Rk	YAC	Rk	YAC+	BTkl	DVOA	Rk	DYAR	Rk	YAR	Use	Rk	Slot
2015	DAL	16/13	789	93	52	840	3	56%	-0.7	4	16.2	13.3	27	5.3	21	+0.8	5	7.4%	38	140	29	147	17.9%	44	--
2016	DAL	16/15	745	61	44	594	4	72%	+6.8	2	13.5	12.2	39	3.8	59	-0.3	6	31.1%	4	214	17	218	13.0%	77	43%
2017	DAL	16/14	692	78	53	568	0	68%	+3.5	3	10.7	8.8	73	4.4	39	-0.7	10	-1.9%	53	67	53	75	16.0%	56	30%
2018	DAL			72	47	552	2	65%			11.7							3.4%							

Williams set a personal high in catches last year, but his yards per catch plummeted, he only topped 50 yards in a game three times, and he failed to score a touchdown for the first time in his career. Then he broke his foot while working out in March, and then he was arrested for public intoxication and leaving the scene of an accident after his Lamborghini crashed into a light pole near Cowboys headquarters. Police video showed Williams telling police that he hadn't even been in the car and that ex-Baylor teammate Kendall Wright had been driving, but then Williams released a statement saying he had driven onto the curb to avoid a car that had stopped in front of him. So that's weird. Regardless, Williams is facing misdemeanor charges that wouldn't be a big deal for most players, but won't do any favors for a 29-year-old with a bad wheel coming off a down year.

Tyrell Williams

Height: 6-3　　Weight: 204　　College: Western Oregon　　Draft: 2015/FA　　Born: 12-Feb-1992　　Age: 26　　Risk: Green

Year	Team	G/GS	Snaps	Pass	Rec	Yds	TD	C%	+/-	Drop	Yd/C	aDOT	Rk	YAC	Rk	YAC+	BTkl	DVOA	Rk	DYAR	Rk	YAR	Use	Rk	Slot
2015	SD	7/0	30	6	2	90	1	33%	-0.7	0	45.0	26.8	--	25.5	--	+18.8	0	21.9%	--	15	--	10	2.0%	--	--
2016	SD	16/12	891	118	69	1059	7	58%	+0.4	9	15.3	11.9	42	6.0	8	+1.7	8	9.0%	27	201	23	174	20.6%	33	50%
2017	LAC	16/15	852	69	43	728	4	62%	+2.2	4	16.9	14.3	16	7.7	1	+2.6	6	15.4%	15	150	25	142	12.0%	75	56%
2018	LAC			76	43	662	4	57%			15.4							5.0%							

Williams is a quintessential Chargers role player. He's a talented, budget-priced small-program discovery who lights up the highlight reel but crushes your soul at the worst possible moments. Williams dropped deep touchdown passes in losses to the Jaguars and Chiefs losses; he also had a costly drop and stepped out of bounds to negate a deep reception against the Patriots. Williams signed a $2.9 million one-year tender to remain with the Chargers as a third or fourth receiver. He'll be a situational mismatch nightmare, but if Philip Rivers loses confidence in him (Williams disappeared for long stretches last year), he'll be reduced to glorified decoy duty.

Albert Wilson

Height: 5-9 **Weight:** 200 **College:** Georgia State **Draft:** 2014/FA **Born:** 12-Jul-1992 **Age:** 26 **Risk:** Red

Year	Team	G/GS	Snaps	Pass	Rec	Yds	TD	C%	+/-	Drop	Yd/C	aDOT	Rk	YAC	Rk	YAC+	BTkl	DVOA	Rk	DYAR	Rk	YAR	Use	Rk	Slot
2015	KC	14/12	654	57	35	451	2	61%	-1.0	2	12.9	10.3	58	6.3	6	+1.0	10	1.5%	48	61	59	59	14.2%	67	--
2016	KC	16/5	466	51	31	279	2	61%	-4.4	5	9.0	7.4	86	4.8	34	-0.8	7	-22.1%	84	-37	83	-48	9.5%	92	73%
2017	KC	13/7	538	62	42	554	3	68%	+0.5	7	13.2	6.3	84	7.5	2	+1.5	13	21.4%	8	167	22	157	14.5%	67	71%
2018	MIA			82	53	603	3	65%			11.4							1.3%							

Wilson's health strongly correlated with the Chiefs' offensive success. Wilson didn't draw more than three targets in a game from October 8 to November 26, a period of time in which many Chiefs fans were puzzled as to why their offense was not replicating September over and over again. The Dolphins believed that correlation equaled causation, and inked Wilson to a three-year deal with nearly $15 million in guarantees. While Wilson is a nice receiver to have around, this deal looked like a stretch the instant it was signed. Jarvis Landry does need replacing, and Danny Amendola is more like Danny Amen-old-a. So, perhaps Wilson can make us eat these words in *FOA 2019*.

Wilson led all players with 51 DYAR on 12 WR screens last season. Considering that Jarvis Landry was next to last with -58 DYAR on 25 WR screens, this might be a fine trade-off for the Dolphins.

Robert Woods

Height: 6-0 **Weight:** 201 **College:** USC **Draft:** 2013/2 (41) **Born:** 10-Apr-1992 **Age:** 26 **Risk:** Green

Year	Team	G/GS	Snaps	Pass	Rec	Yds	TD	C%	+/-	Drop	Yd/C	aDOT	Rk	YAC	Rk	YAC+	BTkl	DVOA	Rk	DYAR	Rk	YAR	Use	Rk	Slot
2015	BUF	14/9	774	80	47	552	3	59%	-2.8	2	11.7	10.4	57	3.3	72	-0.7	3	-14.6%	78	-12	79	-3	19.7%	39	--
2016	BUF	13/10	633	75	51	613	1	67%	+7.2	2	12.0	11.6	45	2.5	90	-1.6	3	7.9%	30	117	46	123	20.1%	37	67%
2017	LAR	12/11	649	85	56	781	5	66%	+4.4	4	13.9	10.6	53	5.2	19	+0.3	6	13.4%	21	172	20	178	22.4%	19	84%
2018	LAR			101	65	770	3	64%			11.8							1.3%							

Raise your hand if you saw Woods' 2017 season coming. Alright, Coach McVay, put your hand down, but allow the rest of us to be surprised. Woods never surpassed 700 receiving yards in Buffalo; he was a blocking-first player who had somewhat disappointed as a former second-round pick. In retrospect, there were some signs that he was trending positive after a 2016 season saw him set a career high in catch rate, but the move to Los Angeles really did great things for Woods' production. Despite missing a quarter of the season, Woods set career highs in DVOA, DYAR, and receiving yards as he was a perfect fit for McVay's offense.

Jarius Wright

Height: 5-10 **Weight:** 182 **College:** Arkansas **Draft:** 2012/4 (118) **Born:** 25-Nov-1989 **Age:** 29 **Risk:** Green

Year	Team	G/GS	Snaps	Pass	Rec	Yds	TD	C%	+/-	Drop	Yd/C	aDOT	Rk	YAC	Rk	YAC+	BTkl	DVOA	Rk	DYAR	Rk	YAR	Use	Rk	Slot
2015	MIN	16/3	431	50	34	442	0	68%	+5.2	2	13.0	9.5	67	5.1	24	+0.2	3	7.6%	36	78	51	68	11.1%	80	--
2016	MIN	8/1	119	14	11	67	1	79%	+0.6	0	6.1	4.0	--	3.8	--	-1.2	1	-1.8%	--	12	--	12	4.7%	--	79%
2017	MIN	16/0	256	25	18	198	2	72%	+2.0	0	11.0	8.2	--	4.9	--	-0.3	1	29.0%	--	84	--	86	4.9%	--	96%
2018	CAR			20	11	127	0	55%			11.5							-14.1%							

When a new coordinator comes to town, they like bringing with them familiar faces from old places. That's the case with Wright, who spent three years with Norv Turner in Minnesota and now comes to join him in Carolina. Wright's a bottom-of-the-roster receiver, usually used in four-wide sets in Minnesota last season before sliding in as the Vikings' third receiver down the stretch. Wright will be in a competition with D.J. Moore and Curtis Samuel for slot duties in Carolina, with unremarkable reliability being his primary asset. There are worse things in which to specialize.

Kendall Wright

Height: 5-10 **Weight:** 196 **College:** Baylor **Draft:** 2012/1 (20) **Born:** 12-Nov-1989 **Age:** 29 **Risk:** Green

Year	Team	G/GS	Snaps	Pass	Rec	Yds	TD	C%	+/-	Drop	Yd/C	aDOT	Rk	YAC	Rk	YAC+	BTkl	DVOA	Rk	DYAR	Rk	YAR	Use	Rk	Slot
2015	TEN	10/9	412	60	36	408	3	60%	+0.3	3	11.3	12.0	42	4.0	55	-0.9	8	-8.1%	66	21	70	17	17.6%	45	--
2016	TEN	11/4	309	43	29	416	3	67%	+2.9	1	14.3	10.8	--	4.3	--	+0.2	3	21.9%	--	119	--	115	12.7%	--	91%
2017	CHI	16/4	580	91	59	614	1	65%	+2.8	3	10.4	8.0	78	3.1	68	-1.8	7	-4.8%	58	53	58	53	19.5%	37	88%
2018	MIN			48	29	314	2	60%			10.8							-3.1%							

Wright can be a useful slot receiver for an offense that used Adam Thielen a lot in that role last year even though Thielen actually had a much better DVOA when he lined up out wide. With Thielen and Stefon Diggs on the outside, Wright can play from the slot and help Kirk Cousins with the slants and screens expected of that position. He'll likely have to keep Laquon Treadwell off the field as the first-rounder tries to prove his worth in Year 3.

Going Deep

Kamar Aiken, FA: In line for a big role after the preseason trade of Philip Dorsett, Aiken showed absolutely no rapport with Jacoby Brissett and finished the season with just 15 catches on 44 targets and -144 DYAR, second-worst among all wide receivers. Unsigned at press time, his 75-catch 2015 season is at least as amazing in hindsight as it was at the time.

Marcell Ateman, OAK: Big (6-foot-4), high-effort, high-character possession receiver who served as Mason Rudolph's safety valve and James Washington's complement at Oklahoma State. Attelman has no separation ability or long speed. The Oakland seventh-rounder could play a role once Jordy Nelson is injured and Martavis Bryant is in Jon Gruden's doghouse.

Braxton Berrios, NE: At 5-foot-9 with 28-inch arms, Berrios was drafted in the seventh round by the Patriots, an organization with zero easy recent comparisons. After all, which former Patriots would remind you of a small, scrappy, high-efficiency slot receiver who returned punts? We certainly can't think of any.

Brenton Bersin, FA: The Panthers are making a habit of firing Brenton Bersin. The wideout has been waived five times by Carolina in his four-year career, only to keep coming back each time. He even ended up as Carolina's fourth receiver by the end of 2017 out of necessity, with 8 catches for 128 yards and 5.6% DVOA. Bersin is currently without a contract, but if and when injuries pile up, you know the Panthers still have him on speed dial.

Kendrick Bourne, SF: The former Eastern Washington receiver will be fighting to maintain a backup job in 2018 after appearing in 11 games as an undrafted rookie. He caught 16 of 34 passes for 257 yards with -9.7% DVOA. Bourne might have had a little more buzz coming out of college if not for the fact that he was playing second fiddle to future third-round pick Cooper Kupp. Now, Bourne will have to fend off 2018 second-round pick Dante Pettis and others in order to keep his role.

Noah Brown, DAL: At 225 pounds, Brown is the biggest wide receiver on the Dallas roster heading into training camp. He averaged 18 offensive snaps over the Cowboys' last five games in 2017, and that value as a blocker and possible red zone threat could earn him a roster spot again in 2018. He only caught four passes as a rookie last year, but that's four more than most of the team's tight ends, so he could contribute as a middle-of-the-field receiver too.

Damiere Byrd, CAR: Byrd has been fighting for a roster spot for the Panthers for his entire career. An undersized track star, he saw his first regular-season opportunities last year. On the positive side, his speed helped him set a franchise record for longest kick return, the first Panthers kickoff return touchdown since 2011. On the minus side, his slim frame meant he ended up on injured reserve twice. He'll be on the roster bubble yet again in 2018.

Deon Cain, IND: Cain inherited the top receiver job at Clemson from Mike Williams but was hamstrung by quarterback play and drops and only had 734 receiving yards. The drops and past drug issues helped him fall to the sixth round, but he has the talent to be one of the steals of the draft as a big receiver with good speed. The Colts don't have much clarity at receiver past T.Y. Hilton, so it's not hard to see Cain contributing as a rookie.

Antonio Callaway, CLE: The Browns hope they have found their Tyreek Hill, in terms of story if not playing style. Callaway led the Florida Gators in receiving yards as both a freshman and sophomore, then missed his entire junior year after being suspended for involvement in a credit card fraud. There has also been a sexual assault allegation after his freshman year (he was cleared) and a positive test for marijuana at the combine (he apologized). Callaway is explosive at the line of scrimmage and shined in college beating press and man coverage. This is the kind of player you can throw a fourth-round dart at when you have the most draft capital in two decades.

Michael Campanaro, TEN: The Ravens selected Campanaro, a diminutive receiver out of Wake Forest, in the seventh round of the 2014 draft, but thanks largely to a series of injuries he never really made the breakthrough in Baltimore. Campanaro missed most of his rookie campaign with a hamstring injury; his 2015 season was ended by a herniated disc in his back; he was healthy but kept on the practice squad for most of 2016; then he began the 2017 season with a nagging toe injury. Fourty-three targets in four years tells its own story, though he did appear in more games last year than in his previous three seasons combined and ended up with 19 catches for 173 yards (3.4% DVOA). If he can stay healthy, the Titans have acquired a shifty slot receiver and possible replacement for Adoree Jackson as a punt returner. Campanaro's history suggests that's a substantial "if."

Dylan Cantrell, LAC: A sixth-round rookie, Cantrell is one of those big spread-offense receivers who put up big numbers (139-1,491-15 in his final two seasons at Texas Tech) in a pinball conference by running to a spot in the field and catching short tosses in front of 5-foot-9 defensive backs. Cantrell also missed the 2015 season with a back injury, because if there's one thing the Chargers receiving corps needs, it's more of an injury risk. There will be wide-open competition for the fifth and sixth receiver spots in Carson, California, but the top three guys are the only ones likely to see significant targets.

Austin Carr, NO: The Patriots were the first team to give the undrafted Carr a shot last year, but he's not from the Wes Welker assembly line. Carr is a bigger slot receiver at 6-foot-1. Despite a productive preseason and injuries to Julian Edelman and Malcolm Mitchell, Carr did not make the cut in New England. The Saints snatched him up, but he'll face a lot of competition to make the roster again.

Leonte Carroo, MIA: The Dolphins clearly soured on their former third-round pick, who was beaten out by Jakeem Grant for the majority of backup snaps. Danny Amendola and Albert Wilson are in town to make it even more unlikely Carroo will do more than play in the fourth preseason game. Vegas refuses to give odds on Carroo, a former Rutgers receiver, surfacing with the Patriots.

Jehu Chesson, KC: Chesson housed a 76-yard punt return in the final week of the 2017 preseason, but hardly got the chance to recreate that magic during the regular season. Tyreek Hill, Akeem Hunt, and De'Anthony Thomas primarily handled return duties, leaving Chesson buried on the wide receiver and returner depth chart. A tall, athletic player, Chesson was a nice gamble in the fourth round of the 2017 draft as someone who could develop as a solid post/dig/go route type of wide receiver.

Michael Clark, GB: Clark didn't get to debut until Week 16, when the injury-ravaged Packers gave the 6-foot-6 former basketball player a shot. He had 36 yards against the Vikings' tough defense. Learning the playbook was an issue last year, but Clark's rare size at the position gives him an advantage that should be considered when roster cuts come around.

Kaelin Clay, BUF: You won't believe this, but a former Panthers player appealed to the Bills so much that they traded for him! Then, the Bills waived him at midseason and let the Panthers claim him but re-signed him in March. There's no telling which of the two teams will have him again in August! Oh, and he returns punts. Clay caught just 6 of 20 passes last year for 85 yards with -43.5% DVOA.

Sammie Coates, HOU: The 2015 third-round pick came out of Auburn with major issues catching the ball, and Pittsburgh finally gave up on him after two years. Coates struggled to carve out a role on Cleveland's depth chart last season while also missing time with ankle and hamstring injuries, and had only six catches on 11 targets in 12 games. Houston claimed him off waivers in March. He has a chance as a backup to Will Fuller as the deep threat, plus special teams value.

Brandon Coleman, NO: Since 2015, Coleman averages the lowest YAC per catch (4.2 yards) of all Saints wide receivers, but he has been used as a deep threat at times. He's reliable enough to be a WR3 for some teams, but he only has to be WR4 (or even WR5) for New Orleans. Coleman had 23 catches for 364 yards and three touchdowns last year (6.0% DVOA) and the Saints hope he has less this year.

Stacy Coley, MIN: Coley had the second-most catches ever for the Miami Hurricanes, but he didn't see a target last year as a seventh-round rookie with the Vikings. He had one kick return for 19 yards, but 2017 was basically a redshirt season. Minnesota could be looking for 15 to 20 catches from Coley this year, which would put his production through two years right on line with former first-round pick Laquon Treadwell. However, that's more of a criticism of Treadwell than anything else.

Pharoh Cooper, LAR: By FO metrics, Cooper was worth a combined 17.8 points of estimated field position on kickoff and punt returns last season. But he's also got a bit of a fumbling issue, with three fumbles during the regular season and both a muffed kickoff and a muffed punt in the playoff loss to Atlanta. Cooper's 11 catches turned into 84 yards but a miserable -49.2% DVOA.

Amara Darboh, SEA: Darboh was buried on the depth chart as a rookie, but the departures of Paul Richardson and Jimmy Graham have opened a void in Seattle's passing game that should give Darboh an opportunity. He will battle for the third receiver slot with Jaron Brown and Brandon Marshall, and his big weakness there is his lack of experience. Darboh was targeted just 13 times last season (8 catches for 71 yards) and showed some of the same body-catching tendencies he had at Michigan. His size is one of his best attributes, but he's actually smaller than both Brown and Marshall. Darboh probably needs another year to develop before really playing a major role.

Trevor Davis, GB: Special teams is the way for Davis to continue making the roster. He was Green Bay's return specialist last season. His kick returns were nothing special, but he had the third-highest added value on punt returns in 2017, including a long return of 65 yards. Davis remains a favorite to keep those return jobs in 2018.

Phillip Dorsett, NE: Putting Dorsett in a section called "Going Deep" is a little on the nose. He caught 12 of 18 passes for 194 yards (21.6% DVOA).

Alex Erickson, CIN: After a very good 2016 returning kicks, Erickson was terrible at both kickoff and punt returns in 2017. At the same time, he got an opportunity to play wideout with John Ross out, and mostly caught the balls thrown his way (12-of-16, 180 yards, 1 TD, 31.1% DVOA). He's on the roster bubble, but Erickson has been there before and proven hard to displace.

Michael Floyd, FA: Floyd's career has gone off the rails since he was released by the Cardinals following a DUI arrest in 2016. Once a deep threat, Floyd was miscast as a possession receiver in the Minnesota offense, catching 10 balls for just 78 yards. He's a free agent still south of 30 years old, but he's probably not worth the trouble for most teams.

Daurice Fountain, IND: An outstanding leaper who was a state hurdles and long jump champion, fifth-rounder Fountain has a big transition from Northern Iowa to the NFL. General manager Chris Ballard suggested after the draft that Fountain will need time, but he can contribute as a rookie at least as a jump-ball specialist with the potential to be more.

Russell Gage, ATL: Gage was the second receiver the Falcons added in the draft. He was a special teams ace at LSU and a jack of all trades for their offense. Gage finished his senior season with 28 rushing attempts, 21 receptions, 517 yards from scrimmage, and four touchdowns. He began his time at LSU as a defensive back and will spend some time there as the Falcons tinker with their roster throughout the summer. As intriguing as sixth-round picks go, Gage has a unique profile and could make some noise during training camp and the preseason.

Shelton Gibson, PHI: Gibson averaged 22.6 yards per catch as West Virginia's big-play guy and entered Eagles camp as a competitor to Torrey Smith for the deep-threat role. He then dropped everything in sight: footballs, beats, car keys. It was ugly and got worse as OTAs and training camps wore on: a clear case of the rookie yips, one which did not respond to normal treatments. The Eagles shut Gibson down until their meaningless Week 17 game last year to get his hands and mind right. OTA reports on Gibson this year were cautiously positive, and the deep-threat role could be up for grabs with Mike Wallace penciled in as Smith's replacement. If Gibson can catch, he can play.

Brittan Golden, FA: Golden has primarily added value through special teams after going undrafted in 2012, never catching more than eight passes in a season. After spending the past five years with Arizona, Golden is currently unsigned. If a team needs a veteran special teamer and emergency wide receiver, he could certainly fit that bill.

Jakeem Grant, MIA: A shifty returner without the size (5-foot-7, 168 pounds) to hang as an NFL slot receiver. An enterprising head coach could use Grant as a screen-and-go routes type—Grant had 43 DYAR on seven WR screens last year. But the Dolphins paid a lot of money to other receivers to not have to do any thinking about Grant's role beyond returner.

Rashad Greene, JAX: A fifth-round pick in 2015, Greene had his high-profile moments in his rookie campaign, catching 19 passes and scoring three touchdowns (one on a punt return). Since then, he has been relegated almost exclusively to punt return duties—he had almost as many fumbles (four, two of which were lost) as receptions (five) in 2016. He missed 2017 with an undisclosed injury and is now battling for his spot on a crowded wide receiver depth chart.

Marvin Hall, ATL: The shining moment of Hall's season was a 40-yard touchdown catch against the Miami Dolphins. Outside of that play, he only had eight other targets in eight games played last season, and only one other catch. With Julio Jones, Mohamed Sanu, Taylor Gabriel, and Justin Hardy ahead of him on the depth chart, there was no real way for him to get playing time in a loaded group. Gabriel has moved on, but with the additions of Calvin Ridley and Russell Gage, Hall faces an upward battle to make the final 53-man roster.

DaeSean Hamilton, DEN: Hamilton was Christian Hackenberg's favorite target at Penn State when Hamilton was a freshman and Hackenberg a senior. Hackenberg left, the Nittany Lions offense became Saquon Barkley-focused, and Hamilton had a pair of down years as he pressed too hard to make the most of fewer touches. He bounced back for a solid senior year and great offseason performances at all-star games and his pro day. Hamilton has slot experience and is a big receiver with some crafty route-running skills. Courtland Sutton is currently penciled into the No. 3 role, but he's raw and duplicates too many of Demaryius Thomas' traits, so Hamilton could get surprising playing time. Hamilton has sleeper/keeper fantasy value, and he could quickly become the Broncos' first competent slot receiver since Wes Welker.

Chad Hansen, NYJ: Hansen's pedigree coming out of Cal was worth getting excited about, and his rookie season wasn't half-bad either, as he played his way into some of the share of Quincy Enunwa's vacated targets (8-of-17, 94 yards, -26.3% DVOA). Unfortunately, on this crowded depth chart, it's hard to believe he's going to get a chance to play a big role at the start of the season. He might have the most long-term upside of any receiver the Jets have. Maybe they'll find that out by Week 13 again.

Maurice Harris, WAS: Washington activated Harris off the practice squad in November, and one day later he played a career-high 41 offensive snaps against Minnesota, scoring a 36-yard touchdown in the first quarter. It was a spectacular play, as he burned Trae Waynes down the right sideline and made a one-handed grab, barely getting an elbow down in bounds. He had only two more catches the rest of the year. Washington's depth at receiver isn't the best, but Harris will have to earn a third season in D.C. this summer.

Darrius Heyward-Bey, PIT: At this point, calling Heyward-Bey a receiver is basically just muscle memory. He has just over 500 yards receiving in the four years he has been in Pittsburgh and had a career-low two receptions in 2017. However, he has quietly developed into one of the top gunners in the league, using the speed that once made him a first-round draft pick to keep plays inside and force fair catches. That may not be how he envisioned his career arc going, but it's likely enough to keep a roster slot.

Johnny Holton, OAK: Holton caught a 64-yard touchdown against the Broncos and a 44-yard touchdown against the Dolphins, added a 47-yard pass in the second Broncos game, and punched Patriots cornerback Jonathan Jones after a possible touchdown bomb sailed over Holton's head (there was a lot of contact when the ball was in the air). You would think Holton earned more than 18 targets last season, but the Raiders were committed to injured Amari Cooper, fading Michael Crabtree, disappointment savant Cordarrelle Patterson, and the most predictable offense west of Atlanta. Holton will likely be squeezed out by one of the 4,000 veterans Jon Gruden brought in; Martavis Bryant offers similar one-bomb-per-month potential, but at higher cost and with more headaches.

Justin Hunter, PIT: Although he had just four receptions in 2017, Hunter was in line to move up to the third receiver role when Martavis Bryant was traded on draft day … or, at least, he was until the Steelers picked up James Washington in the second round. His 4.4-second 40-yard dash speed still makes him a useful fourth receiver, at least until Eli Rogers can recover from his ACL tear.

Richie James, SF: A rookie seventh-round pick from Middle Tennessee State, James had a monstrous season in 2016, racking up 1,641 yards. He is coming off an injury-shortened final season in college, playing only five games and amassing just 290 receiving yards, but he still managed to set Middle Tennessee State's school record for receiving yards and receiving touchdowns in a career.

Jeff Janis, CLE: Janis is the Timmy Smith of the divisional round. He basically had his entire receiving career with 145 yards and two touchdowns against Arizona in January 2016. Last year he caught just two passes, one for 12 yards and one for zero. At this point he's primarily a special teams player and will be a good gunner addition for Cleveland.

Charles Johnson, NYJ: Remember that year when Johnson finished the season as the best receiver on the Vikings roster? Yeah, that was a long time ago. Any storm in a port worked for Johnson before though, so he had the good sense to wash up with the Jets for one of his last chances.

Marcus Johnson, SEA: Johnson has just five career catches in two seasons, so he wasn't brought in for his on-field track record. Rather, he was brought in for his record on the track—Johnson ran a 4.39-second 40-yard dash coming out of college, and his vertical speed gave him a few deep ball opportunities in Philadelphia. Johnson's best chance at making the team is in a Ricardo Lockette-type special teams coverage role.

Tavarres King, MIN: King has moved around a lot since Denver drafted him in the fifth round in 2013. He finally got some opportunities to shine for the Giants last year after literally every other main receiver in that offense was injured. King scored two touchdowns against the Eagles in Week 15, and finished the year with 18 catches, 240 yards and -7.5% DVOA. There may not be enough balls to go around in Minnesota, but he can certainly produce on par with the likes of Laquon Treadwell or what Jarius Wright did for the team last year.

Jordan Lasley, BAL: Fifth-round rookie Lasley comes to Baltimore straight outta Compton, with a stopover in Westwood. He's got the blazing speed of Ice Cube (in his younger days, anyway), drops 'em like Dr. Dre (21 drops over the past two season), and gets in trouble with the law like Eazy-E (multiple suspensions at UCLA). The Ravens need outside speed desperately, so they would live with the bad stuff if Lasley provides a couple of top-ten hits along the way.

Tommylee Lewis, NO: Tommylee Lewis? Was he a cast member of *In Living Color* or in a naughty tape with Pamela Anderson? Neither? Oh, this Lewis has been a marginal return man for the Saints the last two years. Last year he spelled Alvin Kamara on kickoffs and Ted Ginn on punt returns. The Saints would probably be better off with those players handling more of these returns, but it's not the worst idea to give a non-starter some of those opportunities for the sake of health preservation.

Josh Malone, CIN: Malone's physical traits earned him a roster spot as a low-drafted rookie. Now comes the time for him to keep it with better play. Cincy dialed up multiple nine routes for Malone, as though he could simply replicate what the team drafted John Ross to be, and Malone almost never came down with them. Some of that is on Andy Dalton, but 22 percent catch rates on third down don't scream "blame the quarterback!"

Freddie Martino, TB: Martino has way more roster transactions (33 according to Pro Football Reference) than he does catches (13) since 2014. Perhaps he can step in after a rash of injuries, but the Buccaneers have at least four better options at wide receiver going into the season.

Tre McBride, NYJ: Two teams and two years after coming out as a major sleeper, McBride still hasn't gotten much of an NFL shake. With the Jets he'll have to beat out three other Matt Waldman RSP favorites and a 3D-printed robot made out of PDFs of the Rookie Scouting Portfolio just to make the roster.

Ray-Ray McCloud, BUF: An interesting little gadget RB/WR at Clemson, McCloud is undersized but explosive, and if nothing else should contribute as a potential kick returner. Think of this sixth-round pick as a lesser version of Dexter McCluster: a satellite back who's a bit of an oddball fit for the NFL.

Tanner McEvoy, SEA: McEvoy is one of those players who looks much greater on highlight reels than the football field. As a rookie in 2016, he had a blocked punt, a trick play completion, and nine receptions, all for first downs or touchdowns. He struggled more in 2017, eventually finishing the year as a healthy scratch. He's still got that big-play potential and a massive frame, but he needs to show more consistency to make the 53-man roster for a third time.

Isaiah McKenzie, DEN: We don't usually write capsules for pure return men but think about McKenzie for a moment. The Broncos drafted McKenzie—who is 5-foot-7, lists at 173 pounds, and was strictly a returner/gadget guy in college—in the fifth round in 2017. So John Elway was so freakin' confident in how stacked his roster was last April that he figured he could splurge on a middle school-sized return man. A sane organization would cut losses on McKenzie and let one of the other receiver projects on the depth chart return punts. We'll bet you a dollar McKenzie is still on the Broncos roster, and averaging 8.7 yards per punt return, in 2020.

Jaydon Mickens, JAX: After being promoted to the active roster for the Jaguars last October, Mickens established himself as the team's top punt returner, twice earning AFC Special Teams Player of the Week honors. Despite his two receiving touchdowns, he is not a factor in the team's passing game; his only multiple-reception game came late in the year against a depleted Texans roster, and he had no targets in nine of the 12 games for which he was active. Absent a rash of injuries farther up the depth chart, that is unlikely to change in 2018.

J'Mon Moore, GB: Moore is your classic "physical tools are there, but a raw project" type of draft pick. His Playmaker Score rating (51.6%) had him projected for the fourth round, which is where Green Bay picked him. At the very least he'll have Aaron Rodgers' accurate throws to help him acclimate to the pro game.

Louis Murphy, FA: Originally drafted by the Raiders, Murphy has bounced around the league, playing for five teams over the past seven seasons. Murphy made seven starts for the 49ers last season and holds the distinction of catching Jimmy Garoppolo's first touchdown pass with the team. However, that catch was one of only eight on the season, and he's still looking for a new team for 2018.

JoJo Natson, NYJ: Another practice-squad refugee, this time from the Colts, Natson returned six punts for touchdowns in college between Utah State and Akron. He will need to break one soon in the NFL if he hopes to stay on a roster.

DeVier Posey, BAL: All hail the Grey Cup MVP! Posey made history in the snow last season with the Toronto Argonauts, hauling in a 100-yard touchdown pass (remember, they do it different in the north) to set a record in the Tim Horton's Super Bowl. The coach of the Argos is none other than former Ravens offensive coordinator Marc Trestman, who recommended his wideout to the club that canned him. Posey last caught a pass on this side of the border in 2014, one of 22 NFL grabs. He isn't likely to make much of an impact in Baltimore, but at least he has one heck of a story to tell in those draggy team meetings.

Austin Proehl, BUF: That's right, it's Ricky Proehl's son and you're getting old. Another undersized, quick, possession receiver, Proehl showed a lot of burst as a returner, and he and Ray-Ray McCloud will likely fight each other for the same snaps. As a receiver, Proehl is better than McCloud, but did a bit too much body-catching at North Carolina.

Brian Quick, WAS: Yes, he's still in the league. Quick hasn't scored a touchdown since Week 4 of 2016, and he hasn't gone over 100 yards in a game since … well, ever, unless you go back to his time at Applachian State. Quick has earned more than $8 million since the Rams drafted him in the second round in 2012, catching 111 passes in that time frame. (You'll recall that Jarvis Landry had 112 receptions in 2017 alone.) Quick caught only six passes last season for Washington, but then he re-signed with the team in March. Apparently, the team feels he'll finally live up to his draft status at age 29.

Trey Quinn, WAS: Mr. Irrelevant 2018, Quinn caught only 22 passes in two seasons at LSU. Then he transferred to Southern Methodist, where he led the nation with 114 catches in 2017, gaining 1,236 yards and scoring 13 touchdowns. Quinn's NFL profile matches what he was in college: a big possession receiver out of the slot with good hands, but little in the way of tackle-breaking ability or deep speed. ("No second gear" were Lance Zierlein's exact words at NFL.com.)

Damion Ratley, CLE: This sixth-round pick is a pure deep threat, with 23.1 yards per reception as Texas A&M's No. 3 target last season. Tall (6-foot-3), fast (4.45-second 40 at his pro day), and raw like sushi.

Travis Rudolph, NYG: Rudolph tested below the 15th percentile in the 40-yard dash, vertical jump, broad jump, and 20-yard shuttle at the 2017 combine. A middle-of-the-pack 3-cone time was Rudolph's only glimmer of hope to be an NFL-quality athlete. While at Florida State, Rudolph produced 2,331 yards over three seasons, but did so in part because of an uncharacteristically poor Seminoles wide receiver corps over that span. The Giants signed him as a UDFA and after all the injuries above him on the depth chart, he had 8 catches for 101 yards (-43.2% DVOA). Though he has some value in the quick game, Rudolph does not do anything that will push him over the top and into more playing time.

Jaleel Scott, BAL: The Ravens' fourth-rounder from New Mexico State has great height (6-foot-6) and strong hands, making him a red zone threat, but like many receivers with his size, he isn't particularly explosive. Will need to show special teams value to make the roster.

Tajae Sharpe, TEN: A 2016 fifth-round pick, Sharpe missed the entire 2017 season with a foot injury and now faces stiff competition to return to a significant role in the Titans offense. He started ten games as a rookie, posting 500 yards and two touchdowns, so the potential is there; that was before the team drafted Corey Davis, however. Sharpe will have to climb at least two spots higher in the current depth chart to have a serious shot at replicating those numbers.

Hunter Sharp, NYG: Sharp was the last player to catch a touchdown pass for the New York Giants last season. If the team's final touchdown being caught by a second-year undrafted free agent who began his season on a different team (Denver) does not perfectly summarize the Giants' problems on offense last season, then nothing does. With Brandon Marshall and Tavarres King officially gone, Sharp should be able to retain a spot as the fifth or sixth wide receiver on the team.

Russell Shepard, NYG: There may be a receiver in the league with worse hands than Russell Shepard, though it's hard to fathom. Only Eli Rogers had both a lower catch rate and a shorter average depth of target than Shepard last season. After refusing to take a pay cut in Carolina, Shepard signed with the Giants, where his best hope of making the roster is his special teams skill.

Equanimeous St. Brown, GB: St. Brown has quite the name and size (6-foot-5) but slipped to the sixth round after a so-so junior season at Notre Dame. Granted, the Irish didn't even throw the ball 400 times, but a lot of the hope here is that St. Brown can be the player he was in 2016, when he had 961 yards and nine touchdowns. That was in an offense quarterbacked by De-Shone Kizer, who will be his new teammate (but hopefully not the starter) in Green Bay. St. Brown had the best Playmaker Score rating (75.2%) among the three wideouts drafted by the Packers this year.

ArDarius Stewart, NYJ: Stewart's raw talent led him to mostly be a change-of-pace receiver for the Jets, but he'll need to get more technically proficient to be a mainstay. The 5-foot-11 Alabama product did show some skill in the preseason, now all he has to do is improve and win the Jets Wideout Playing Time Lottery.

Jaelen Strong, FA: Houston's 2015 third-round pick—whom the Texans traded up to select—scored touchdowns on each of his first two catches as professional, including a 42-yard Hail Mary against the Colts. Since then, Strong has been suspended one game for violating the league's substance abuse policy; ended two of his three seasons on injured reserve, most recently with a torn ACL; and was cut by both the Texans and the Jaguars. His ongoing ACL recovery will probably keep him unsigned through the rest of the offseason. It will be his often-questioned mentality that determines how long he remains unsigned after that.

Ryan Switzer, OAK: Tough, tiny, stereotypical (white!) slot guy. Switzer returned a punt for a touchdown for the Cowboys last year but was useless on offense (4.5 yards per touch on screens and reverses, with a fumble), and the Cowboys deemed him expendable when they realized that they needed real receivers, not fun little project players. Enter the Raiders, who acquired Switzer in a draft-day trade for some reason.

Auden Tate, CIN: Picture Kelvin Benjamin, then take away whatever deep speed and separation he has, and you are left with Tate. The cat is slooooooow. But he is big, and possesses pretty good aerial combat skills, so there could be some red zone value. Likely with a different team, though—despite costing Cincinnati a seventh-round pick, he's a long shot to make the Bengals roster.

Brandon Tate, FA: A long-time Bengals return specialist, Tate spent the last two years with the Bills and was good enough to add 14 catches, 198 yards, and a touchdown to his return work over the course of the two seasons combined. He turns 31 this October and is currently unsigned, so his career may be done.

Jordan Taylor, DEN: Taylor earned increased playing time and a pair of late-season starts when Emmanuel Sanders was shelved, catching eight passes in four December games and returning a few punts. He's a third-year undrafted free agent who sticks around because the Broncos are bad at drafting. Taylor missed OTAs after undergoing hip surgery, but it takes more than major surgery to keep a rando wide receiver out of the Broncos' long-term plans.

De'Anthony Thomas, KC: After a two-year lull, Thomas had a minor resurgence in 2017, serving as one of Kansas City's many gadget players. From end-arounds to simple shifts and motions, Thomas was typically used as a distraction to open up room for others because Thomas' speed could be devastating if he were to actually get the ball. As the Chiefs bring along a new quarterback in Patrick Mahomes, it is possible that Thomas retains a role as a gadget player who can take pressure of the quarterback.

Mike Thomas, LAR: After serving a four-game PED suspension to start the year, Thomas was used primarily as a special teams player in 2017. Sixty of his 100 offensive snaps came in Week 17's Backup Appreciation Day. The coaching staff was high enough on Thomas to take the unusual step of carrying seven receivers after he returned from suspension, however, and he routinely gets high praise in OTAs. He'll be scrapping for one of Los Angeles' last roster slots.

Chris Thompson, HOU: The undrafted free agent out of Florida was primarily a special teams player after being signed from the practice squad early in the season. Like almost every Houston returner ever, he was below average on both punts and kick-offs. He'll compete for a similar role in 2018.

Bryce Treggs, PHI: Back with the Eagles on a futures contract after an uneventful stint with the Browns in 2017. An annual training camp All-Star who maxes out as a fifth receiver.

Marquez Valdes-Scantling, GB: The Packers drafted three wideouts in the later rounds, and South Florida's Valdes-Scantling was the middle selection, going in the fifth. He has a great 40 time (4.37 seconds), but Playmaker Rating (23.2%) saw him as a seventh-round pick. He's a potential deep threat for Aaron Rodgers.

Justin Watson, TB: Watson blew scouts away at his pro day after dominating lesser competition in the Ivy League for Penn. He's too big for any Wes Welker comparison, but he has compared himself to Jordy Nelson. He went to the Bucs in the fifth round. Watson will likely watch a lot of teammate Adam Humphries this year before he makes any impact in Tampa Bay.

Markus Wheaton, PHI: A former third-round pick by the Steelers, Wheaton is now four full years removed from his one pretty good year. Persistent minor injuries derailed his development, but old scouting reports never die, and Wheaton has developed just enough special teams value over the years to keep getting opportunities as a fourth/fifth wideout.

Kasen Williams, IND: Williams had 119 yards in the first preseason game in 2017 but did not make the Seahawks roster and ended up on the Browns practice squad notwithstanding back-to-back four-catch games. Like most May signings, he'll "improve the competitiveness" of the position group while not having a realistic shot at making the team.

Cedrick Wilson, DAL: At 6-foot-2 and 197 pounds, Wilson is something of a beanpole receiver, but that didn't limit his production at Boise State. His 139 catches, 2,640 yards, 18 touchdowns, and 19.0-yard average reception each rank in the top 20 in the nation over the past two years (minimum 50 catches). Wilson was also a trick-play demon for the Broncos, completing 4-of-5 passes for 130 yards and a touchdown. The Cowboys are desperate for a playmaker, and the sixth-round pick will get every chance to show what he can do at the next level.

Javon Wims, CHI: The former Georgia Bulldog doesn't fit the speedy receiver type that Matt Nagy enjoyed in Kansas City the last couple of years. He could struggle to get separation but has a shot to make the team as a fifth or sixth receiver. If there's an advantage for Wims over most of his competition, it's that he was a draft pick, taken in the seventh round.

DeAngelo Yancey, GB: Yancey was a big-play receiver at Purdue who caught 10 touchdowns in 2016. He spent his rookie season on Green Bay's practice squad and will have to beat out a trio of rookie draft picks to make the team again.

Tight Ends

Top 20 TE by DYAR (Total Value), 2017

Rank	Player	Team	DYAR
1	Rob Gronkowski	NE	339
2	Travis Kelce	KC	197
3	Hunter Henry	LAC	165
4	Zach Ertz	PHI	154
5	Cameron Brate	TB	154
6	Coby Fleener	NO	107
7	O.J. Howard	TB	101
8	Garrett Celek	SF	89
9	Kyle Rudolph	MIN	88
10	Trey Burton	PHI	85
11	Ed Dickson	CAR	83
12	Nick O'Leary	BUF	73
13	Austin Hooper	ATL	71
14	Vernon Davis	WAS	61
15	Rhett Ellison	NYG	56
16	George Kittle	SF	55
17	Jared Cook	OAK	53
18	Eric Ebron	DET	50
19	Darren Fells	DET	48
20	Jason Witten	DAL	40

Minimum 25 passes.

Top 20 TE by DVOA (Value per Play), 2017

Rank	Player	Team	DVOA
1	Coby Fleener	NO	50.1%
2	Rob Gronkowski	NE	40.4%
3	Trey Burton	PHI	35.0%
4	Hunter Henry	LAC	32.3%
5	O.J. Howard	TB	32.2%
6	Garrett Celek	SF	31.5%
7	Nick O'Leary	BUF	29.9%
8	Cameron Brate	TB	24.7%
9	Darren Fells	DET	21.9%
10	Ed Dickson	CAR	18.1%
11	Rhett Ellison	NYG	17.7%
12	Travis Kelce	KC	17.0%
13	Zach Ertz	PHI	14.2%
14	Austin Hooper	ATL	9.4%
15	Kyle Rudolph	MIN	8.8%
16	Vernon Davis	WAS	6.7%
17	George Kittle	SF	5.6%
18	Zach Miller	CHI	4.4%
19	Jared Cook	OAK	2.1%
20	Eric Ebron	DET	2.0%

Minimum 25 passes.

Stephen Anderson
Height: 6-2   Weight: 230   College: California   Draft: 2016/FA   Born: 30-Jan-1993   Age: 25   Risk: Yellow

Year	Team	G/GS	Snaps	Pass	Rec	Yds	TD	C%	+/-	Drop	Yd/C	aDOT	Rk	YAC	Rk	YAC+	BTkl	DVOA	Rk	DYAR	Rk	YAR	Use	Rk	Slot	Wide
2016	HOU	13/0	129	16	11	93	1	69%	+0.2	1	8.5	6.6	--	3.5	--	-0.3	0	8.0%	--	17	--	24	3.6%	--	71%	6%
2017	HOU	15/5	441	52	25	342	1	48%	-6.8	6	13.7	9.6	13	3.8	38	-0.3	2	-14.0%	40	-22	42	-10	10.8%	28	26%	0%
2018	HOU			49	30	368	2	61%			12.3							0.5%								

With Deshaun Watson: 15 targets, 12.2% DVOA, 19 DYAR. Without: 39 targets, -24.6% DVOA, -41 DYAR. Houston's tight end depth chart is a mess after the concussion-induced retirement of C.J. Fiedorowicz. An injury to Ryan Griffin elevated Anderson to starter late in the season. Anderson is a modern tight end, a sort of blocking-optional oversized slot receiver. The Texans spent a third-round pick on another one of those, Jordan Akins. It is difficult to give significant snaps to more than one of those at a time, so Anderson getting playing time may depend on his ability to develop into a passable blocker.

Mark Andrews
Height: 6-5   Weight: 256   College: Oklahoma   Draft: 2018/3 (86)   Born: 6-Sep-1996   Age: 22   Risk: Red

Year	Team	G/GS	Snaps	Pass	Rec	Yds	TD	C%	+/-	Drop	Yd/C	aDOT	Rk	YAC	Rk	YAC+	BTkl	DVOA	Rk	DYAR	Rk	YAR	Use	Rk	Slot	Wide
2018	BAL			52	36	358	3	69%			10.0							-1.0%								

Andrews' collegiate numbers were considerably better than the tight end drafted by the Ravens two rounds earlier, Hayden Hurst, especially in yards per target and success rate. Some of that is having caught passes from a significantly better quarterback, of course, but there is no doubting Andrews' ability to get up the field, turn, and latch onto balls. Just how he is used, and how often, is the mystery, but it wouldn't surprise anyone if three years from now Andrews is considered the better pick.

Martellus Bennett

Height: 6-6 | Weight: 259 | College: Texas A&M | Draft: 2008/2 (61) | Born: 10-Mar-1987 | Age: 31 | Risk: N/A

Year	Team	G/GS	Snaps	Pass	Rec	Yds	TD	C%	+/-	Drop	Yd/C	aDOT	Rk	YAC	Rk	YAC+	BTkl	DVOA	Rk	DYAR	Rk	YAR	Use	Rk	Slot	Wide
2015	CHI	11/11	728	80	53	439	3	66%	-0.9	3	8.3	6.9	36	4.3	31	-1.0	9	-10.7%	35	-18	38	-30	23.1%	4	--	4%
2016	NE	16/12	868	73	55	701	7	75%	+3.9	3	12.7	5.3	45	7.6	3	+2.3	14	33.4%	4	197	3	164	13.5%	22	28%	17%
2017	2TM	9/7	411	44	30	286	0	68%	+0.3	4	9.5	6.0	46	5.6	14	+0.0	2	-7.5%	30	-1	29	-12	14.4%	17	51%	7%

Often labeled as an outcast by NFL teams that had to put up with someone who had his own point of view. Bennett's last season was marred by accusations of a phantom injury. He'll play next year for the Imagination Agency, the multimedia firm he founded to produce children's entertainment. On the field, Bennett will go down as one of the best second-contract signings ever after spending his first four years buried behind Jason Witten in Dallas. Bennett finished those years with -20 DYAR. Over the next five years with the Bears, Giants, and Patriots, he produced 417 DYAR.

Nick Boyle

Height: 6-4 | Weight: 268 | College: Delaware | Draft: 2015/5 (171) | Born: 17-Feb-1993 | Age: 25 | Risk: Green

Year	Team	G/GS	Snaps	Pass	Rec	Yds	TD	C%	+/-	Drop	Yd/C	aDOT	Rk	YAC	Rk	YAC+	BTkl	DVOA	Rk	DYAR	Rk	YAR	Use	Rk	Slot	Wide
2015	BAL	11/2	295	23	18	153	0	78%	+2.5	0	8.5	4.7	--	5.6	--	+0.3	4	-3.6%	--	6	--	9	5.0%	--	--	0%
2016	BAL	6/0	114	6	6	44	0	100%	+1.4	0	7.3	3.8	--	3.5	--	-1.1	0	-7.7%	--	0	--	2	2.4%	--	83%	0%
2017	BAL	15/11	696	37	28	203	0	76%	+0.5	0	7.3	2.2	51	5.5	15	-0.5	4	-19.3%	45	-32	45	-37	7.0%	42	19%	11%
2018	BAL			28	19	178	1	68%			9.4							-8.1%								

Boyle is a good blocking tight end (just seven blown blocks in 348 snaps), but doesn't help Joe Flacco in any other way, which is why the Ravens drafted a pair of tight ends who can catch the ball. Hopefully that gives the Ravens another place to throw on second down other than to Boyle, who had horrendous splits (-46.0% DVOA) on those targets.

Cameron Brate

Height: 6-5 | Weight: 235 | College: Harvard | Draft: 2014/FA | Born: 13-Jul-1991 | Age: 27 | Risk: Green

Year	Team	G/GS	Snaps	Pass	Rec	Yds	TD	C%	+/-	Drop	Yd/C	aDOT	Rk	YAC	Rk	YAC+	BTkl	DVOA	Rk	DYAR	Rk	YAR	Use	Rk	Slot	Wide
2015	TB	14/4	341	30	23	288	3	77%	+3.8	0	12.5	10.1	6	2.2	51	-2.0	1	33.6%	4	81	15	85	6.5%	41	--	7%
2016	TB	15/10	709	81	57	660	8	70%	+6.9	4	11.6	9.8	8	2.4	45	-1.4	3	20.4%	8	149	4	146	15.0%	18	65%	7%
2017	TB	16/5	586	77	48	591	6	62%	+2.4	4	12.3	9.5	15	3.0	45	-1.2	3	24.7%	8	154	5	114	12.8%	19	60%	8%
2018	TB			63	40	499	4	63%			12.5							4.5%								

Just when you thought first-round pick O.J. Howard may have made Brate expendable, the Buccaneers locked him up in March to a six-year extension worth $41 million. It looks like a two-tight end offense is here to stay. He's not the kind of athletic specimen that Howard is, but Brate is a very reliable part of the offense, and his numbers were in line with what he did in his 2016 breakout year. For the second year in a row, Brate was Tampa Bay's most effective receiver on third down.

Trey Burton

Height: 6-3 | Weight: 235 | College: Florida | Draft: 2014/FA | Born: 29-Oct-1991 | Age: 27 | Risk: Green

Year	Team	G/GS	Snaps	Pass	Rec	Yds	TD	C%	+/-	Drop	Yd/C	aDOT	Rk	YAC	Rk	YAC+	BTkl	DVOA	Rk	DYAR	Rk	YAR	Use	Rk	Slot	Wide
2015	PHI	16/0	63	4	3	54	0	75%	+0.0	0	18.0	6.8	--	10.3	--	+6.2	1	40.2%	--	12	--	15	0.6%	0	--	0%
2016	PHI	15/4	331	60	37	327	1	62%	-2.2	5	8.8	7.8	23	3.6	33	-1.3	3	-27.9%	44	-83	44	-70	10.5%	31	60%	7%
2017	PHI	15/1	300	31	23	248	5	74%	+4.3	1	10.8	9.5	16	1.5	51	-2.0	0	35.0%	3	85	10	86	5.9%	47	68%	6%
2018	CHI			64	39	442	4	61%			11.3							-0.9%								

Burton will look to spread his wings after playing third wheel to the Eagles' tight end nest of Zach Ertz and Brent Celek. Burton had his best game against the Rams with 71 yards and a pair of touchdowns. HE only had one reception for 12 yards in Philadelphia's entire Super Bowl run, but he did throw a pretty unforgettable 1-yard touchdown pass to Nick Foles before halftime of Super Bowl LII. He's going to be a step down for Matt Nagy, who got to use Travis Kelce in Kansas City, but Burton is one of the more intriguing breakout prospects heading into 2018.

Jake Butt Height: 6-5 Weight: 246 College: Michigan Draft: 2017/5 (145) Born: 11-Jul-1995 Age: 23 Risk: Green

Year	Team	G/GS	Snaps	Pass	Rec	Yds	TD	C%	+/-	Drop	Yd/C	aDOT	Rk	YAC	Rk	YAC+	BTkl	DVOA	Rk	DYAR	Rk	YAR	Use	Rk	Slot	Wide
2018	DEN			45	29	306	3	64%			10.5							-11.1%								

There were rumblings throughout last offseason and into October that Butt might return to the field in 2017, but the team wisely shelved him when they knew they had nothing to play for, making last season a medical redshirt year for their talented fifth-round pick. Butt suffered an ACL tear in the 2016 Orange Bowl and an early one in 2014, so projecting him to be 100 percent healthy with no worries takes a degree of optimism. Butt projects as a Heath Miller-type blocker/receiver if healthy. The rest of the Broncos depth chart at tight end is pretty barren (as usual), so there's a lot riding on Butt's knee ligaments.

Garrett Celek Height: 6-5 Weight: 252 College: Michigan State Draft: 2012/FA Born: 29-May-1988 Age: 30 Risk: Green

Year	Team	G/GS	Snaps	Pass	Rec	Yds	TD	C%	+/-	Drop	Yd/C	aDOT	Rk	YAC	Rk	YAC+	BTkl	DVOA	Rk	DYAR	Rk	YAR	Use	Rk	Slot	Wide
2015	SF	11/8	399	28	19	186	3	68%	+1.1	0	9.8	6.4	41	5.2	17	+0.5	1	5.4%	21	25	29	29	7.7%	37	--	0%
2016	SF	16/6	605	50	29	350	3	58%	-1.5	6	12.1	9.4	11	4.2	21	+0.3	2	-9.0%	30	-6	31	-23	10.1%	33	16%	2%
2017	SF	16/13	561	33	21	336	4	64%	+2.3	1	16.0	8.4	26	8.2	1	+4.2	5	31.5%	6	89	8	82	5.5%	48	30%	6%
2018	SF			33	23	282	2	70%			12.3							8.6%								

Celek has never been known as a star tight end, but he managed to finish eighth in DYAR and sixth in DVOA among tight ends, ahead of better-known players such as Kyle Rudolph, Vernon Davis, Jason Witten, and Jimmy Graham. Celek will be competing with second-year player George Kittle for time and targets, but if he can replicate his production from last year, he should be able to hang on to the starting job for 2018. Celek is on a modest contract that would make him a free agent after 2019, so even if he cedes ground to Kittle, the veteran should still be around San Francisco for two more seasons.

Charles Clay Height: 6-3 Weight: 239 College: Tulsa Draft: 2011/6 (174) Born: 13-Feb-1989 Age: 29 Risk: Green

Year	Team	G/GS	Snaps	Pass	Rec	Yds	TD	C%	+/-	Drop	Yd/C	aDOT	Rk	YAC	Rk	YAC+	BTkl	DVOA	Rk	DYAR	Rk	YAR	Use	Rk	Slot	Wide
2015	BUF	13/13	764	77	51	528	3	66%	-1.5	5	10.4	7.6	30	4.6	22	-0.9	11	-6.0%	32	6	32	-2	20.4%	8	--	3%
2016	BUF	15/15	871	87	57	552	4	66%	-2.3	7	9.7	8.1	21	3.4	37	-1.2	10	-6.5%	27	4	27	6	20.2%	5	30%	5%
2017	BUF	13/13	577	74	49	558	2	66%	-1.4	5	11.4	7.2	38	5.3	19	+0.2	6	-2.8%	25	22	25	37	19.4%	7	24%	4%
2018	BUF			84	51	574	2	61%			11.3							-6.9%								

The Bills spent heavily to get Clay, thinking they were harming the Dolphins in the process. But Clay's five-year deal with $24.5 million in guarantees has essentially wound up as an overpay for a league-average receiving tight end. Clay's swift return from a midseason knee scope is to be commended, but it's time to stop believing he'll be a fantasy TE1, no matter how bad the rest of the Buffalo receivers are.

Jared Cook Height: 6-6 Weight: 246 College: South Carolina Draft: 2009/3 (89) Born: 7-Apr-1987 Age: 31 Risk: Green

Year	Team	G/GS	Snaps	Pass	Rec	Yds	TD	C%	+/-	Drop	Yd/C	aDOT	Rk	YAC	Rk	YAC+	BTkl	DVOA	Rk	DYAR	Rk	YAR	Use	Rk	Slot	Wide
2015	STL	16/12	673	75	39	481	0	52%	-6.6	3	12.3	9.9	7	5.1	18	-0.1	3	-23.5%	44	-76	51	-71	16.2%	18	--	7%
2016	GB	10/5	329	51	30	377	1	59%	-1.7	2	12.6	10.5	4	4.9	13	+0.2	3	-11.5%	33	-15	32	-7	13.4%	23	62%	17%
2017	OAK	16/16	796	86	54	688	2	63%	+0.0	5	12.7	9.6	12	3.9	37	-0.6	5	2.1%	19	53	17	76	15.7%	13	59%	14%
2018	OAK			90	59	729	4	66%			12.4							4.3%								

Cook posted career highs in receptions and yards for the Raiders. He also fumbled early in the Ravens loss last year, with Jimmy Smith scooping the loose ball up and scoring. Cook is good for at least one devastating fumble after a reception per year and often disappears when he's most needed, but he is now in his tenth season as a bounce-around starter because of his size and athleticism. Jon Gruden did not sign Cook, but he would have if Cook were not already on the Raiders roster.

Vernon Davis

Height: 6-3		Weight: 250			College: Maryland				Draft: 2006/1 (6)				Born: 31-Jan-1984				Age: 34			Risk: Green				

Year	Team	G/GS	Snaps	Pass	Rec	Yds	TD	C%	+/-	Drop	Yd/C	aDOT	Rk	YAC	Rk	YAC+	BTkl	DVOA	Rk	DYAR	Rk	YAR	Use	Rk	Slot	Wide
2015	2TM	15/9	621	58	38	395	0	66%	+2.5	3	10.4	9.9	8	3.8	39	-0.9	4	-8.8%	34	-6	34	1	10.7%	28	--	7%
2016	WAS	16/14	673	59	44	583	2	75%	+4.7	4	13.3	9.0	14	5.4	8	+0.7	11	16.8%	11	96	14	100	9.8%	36	42%	5%
2017	WAS	16/16	803	69	43	648	3	62%	+2.1	4	15.1	10.9	5	7.0	4	+1.8	16	6.7%	16	61	14	37	12.8%	20	29%	7%
2018	WAS			63	40	485	4	63%			12.1							5.6%								

In this golden age of tight ends, we tend to overlook what Davis has accomplished. He is one of eight tight ends with 60 touchdown catches; with a big year, he can pass Shannon Sharpe (62) and Jason Witten (68) on that list. That's not very likely—he has just 16 red zone targets in two seasons in Washington—but it's certainly plausible if circumstances fall the right way. Davis often lines up tight but then runs patterns to the outside; his most common pass routes last year were flats, outs, and corners, plays that can get him the ball on the perimeter and let him use his still-formidable YAC ability. Davis could still start for several teams, but he'll once again play second banana to Jordan Reed this fall.

A.J. Derby

Height: 6-4		Weight: 255			College: Arkansas				Draft: 2015/6 (202)				Born: 20-Sep-1991				Age: 27			Risk: Green				

Year	Team	G/GS	Snaps	Pass	Rec	Yds	TD	C%	+/-	Drop	Yd/C	aDOT	Rk	YAC	Rk	YAC+	BTkl	DVOA	Rk	DYAR	Rk	YAR	Use	Rk	Slot	Wide
2016	2TM	10/3	226	20	16	160	0	80%	+2.6	1	10.0	7.1	--	3.2	--	-1.3	1	-6.7%	--	1	--	1	5.6%	--	20%	0%
2017	2TM	11/1	337	40	21	244	2	53%	-3.4	2	11.6	9.2	18	4.4	31	+0.3	5	-27.3%	50	-53	50	-49	10.4%	30	53%	8%
2018	MIA			34	24	268	2	71%			11.2							5.4%								

A former FO top prospect, Derby was claimed off waivers from the Broncos by Miami in November. He's a solid No. 2 tight end who can contribute on special teams and be some team's fourth or fifth receiving option, à la Mychal Rivera. Set up to fail by a broken Broncos offense, Derby should get a second chance in Miami, though Mike Gesicki is set up to be the real No. 1 option.

Seth DeValve

Height: 6-4		Weight: 244			College: Princeton				Draft: 2016/4 (138)				Born: 29-Jan-1993				Age: 25			Risk: Yellow				

Year	Team	G/GS	Snaps	Pass	Rec	Yds	TD	C%	+/-	Drop	Yd/C	aDOT	Rk	YAC	Rk	YAC+	BTkl	DVOA	Rk	DYAR	Rk	YAR	Use	Rk	Slot	Wide
2016	CLE	12/2	94	12	10	127	2	83%	+1.9	0	12.7	8.4	--	4.4	--	+1.0	4	57.5%	--	52	--	55	2.8%	--	42%	8%
2017	CLE	16/4	531	58	33	395	1	57%	-2.1	3	12.0	8.3	27	5.2	20	+0.8	4	-11.5%	38	-15	40	-5	10.2%	31	39%	7%
2018	CLE			39	23	267	1	59%			11.6							-7.6%								

DeValve might be better used as a more traditional tight end: he had -28.1% receiving DVOA on 27 passes from wide receiver positions (mostly the slot) but 2.5% on 29 passes lining up tight to the line. It's hard to tell how much playing time there's going to be for DeValve compared to last year. David Njoku is headed for a breakout year as a receiver and the Browns brought Darren Fells in to be the blocking tight end.

Ed Dickson

Height: 6-4		Weight: 249			College: Oregon				Draft: 2010/3 (70)				Born: 25-Jul-1987				Age: 31			Risk: Yellow				

Year	Team	G/GS	Snaps	Pass	Rec	Yds	TD	C%	+/-	Drop	Yd/C	aDOT	Rk	YAC	Rk	YAC+	BTkl	DVOA	Rk	DYAR	Rk	YAR	Use	Rk	Slot	Wide
2015	CAR	16/11	598	26	17	121	2	65%	-0.6	2	7.1	6.1	43	3.1	47	-1.4	0	-26.3%	46	-35	41	-15	5.2%	49	--	4%
2016	CAR	16/8	479	19	10	134	1	53%	-1.7	3	13.4	9.2	--	6.9	--	+2.5	3	-2.6%	--	6	--	7	3.4%	--	37%	5%
2017	CAR	16/12	875	48	30	437	1	63%	+2.9	2	14.6	9.8	10	6.7	7	+2.0	3	18.1%	10	83	11	78	9.8%	32	40%	6%
2018	SEA			38	26	293	2	68%			11.3							4.2%								

Injuries to Greg Olsen gave Dickson his first chance to see significant action in the passing game since he left Baltimore; his 48 targets were the second-most in his career, and just 14 fewer than he had in his first three years in Carolina combined. An 11th-place finish in DYAR and a 10th-place finish in DVOA sounds really promising at first glance, but 62 of his 84 DYAR came in Week 5 against the Lions, when he caught all five of his targets for 175 yards. Take out that one game, and Dickson's DVOA would have been -0.2%, 23rd in the league. While he has a reputation in some circles as being miscast as a blocking tight end, the numbers show that you can expect at least a solid level of competence. Dickson was asked to block on more than half of his snaps, and ranked third among tight ends in snaps per blown block. He may not be a people-mover like a Rob Gronkowski, but plays don't usually fail because Dickson missed his assignment.

Jack Doyle　　Height: 6-6　　Weight: 258　　College: Western Kentucky　　Draft: 2013/FA　　Born: 5-May-1990　　Age: 28　　Risk: Red

Year	Team	G/GS	Snaps	Pass	Rec	Yds	TD	C%	+/-	Drop	Yd/C	aDOT	Rk	YAC	Rk	YAC+	BTkl	DVOA	Rk	DYAR	Rk	YAR	Use	Rk	Slot	Wide
2015	IND	16/2	332	14	12	72	1	86%	+1.1	0	6.0	1.6	--	4.7	--	-1.0	2	-7.9%	--	-1	--	-1	2.3%	--	--	0%
2016	IND	16/14	750	75	59	584	5	79%	+6.2	4	9.9	6.3	41	4.2	23	-0.2	7	18.7%	10	131	9	96	13.0%	25	43%	0%
2017	IND	15/15	909	108	80	690	4	74%	+4.0	3	8.6	5.0	50	4.2	33	-0.7	9	-7.5%	29	-2	31	31	24.3%	2	44%	4%
2018	IND			90	64	662	6	71%			10.3							4.6%								

After a season as Jacoby Brissett's security blanket, Doyle's passing game role seems likely to shrink with the arrival of Frank Reich and the return of Andrew Luck. If Eric Ebron is to be what Zach Ertz was with the Eagles, Doyle is more along the lines of Trey Burton or Brent Celek. He'll be a valuable blocker, whether in-line or as an H-back, and a mostly short receiver who can be valuable in the right role, but not a mismatch player and not the sure position group leader in receptions.

Eric Ebron　　Height: 6-4　　Weight: 250　　College: North Carolina　　Draft: 2014/1 (10)　　Born: 10-Apr-1993　　Age: 25　　Risk: Yellow

Year	Team	G/GS	Snaps	Pass	Rec	Yds	TD	C%	+/-	Drop	Yd/C	aDOT	Rk	YAC	Rk	YAC+	BTkl	DVOA	Rk	DYAR	Rk	YAR	Use	Rk	Slot	Wide
2015	DET	14/8	613	70	47	537	5	67%	-2.4	7	11.4	5.9	48	6.2	8	+1.3	3	6.5%	18	64	18	81	12.7%	24	--	0%
2016	DET	13/13	708	85	61	711	1	72%	+3.1	7	11.7	8.0	22	4.6	14	+0.3	3	20.1%	9	149	5	141	18.1%	12	53%	11%
2017	DET	16/9	552	86	53	574	4	62%	-1.7	6	10.8	7.8	32	4.9	25	+0.3	9	2.0%	20	50	18	24	15.0%	15	47%	10%
2018	IND			66	42	486	4	64%			11.6							0.2%								

A disappointment as a top-ten pick in Detroit who was released before his fifth-year option would be guaranteed, Ebron quickly found a home in Indianapolis on a good contract that suggested he would be more than an afterthought. Frank Reich reinforced that impression, calling him an elite tight end. Ebron seems likely to be in Indianapolis along the lines of what Zach Ertz was in Philadelphia, a mismatch tight end who can line up in-line, in the slot, or out wide. He was a key target and efficient performer on third downs for Matt Stafford the past two seasons and reportedly thrived in the new role in offseason work.

Tyler Eifert　　Height: 6-6　　Weight: 251　　College: Notre Dame　　Draft: 2013/1 (21)　　Born: 8-Sep-1990　　Age: 28　　Risk: Red

Year	Team	G/GS	Snaps	Pass	Rec	Yds	TD	C%	+/-	Drop	Yd/C	aDOT	Rk	YAC	Rk	YAC+	BTkl	DVOA	Rk	DYAR	Rk	YAR	Use	Rk	Slot	Wide
2015	CIN	13/12	751	74	52	615	13	70%	+7.2	5	11.8	8.1	24	4.5	28	+0.4	5	42.0%	1	247	1	230	18.3%	13	--	0%
2016	CIN	8/2	428	47	29	394	5	62%	+3.5	1	13.6	8.6	18	5.0	10	+1.0	0	9.6%	15	57	18	79	17.4%	14	50%	6%
2017	CIN	2/1	104	5	4	46	0	80%	+0.8	0	11.5	9.4	--	2.8	--	-4.3	0	11.6%	--	6	--	12	8.0%	--	60%	0%
2018	CIN			94	66	780	6	70%			11.8							9.9%								

Eifert has appeared in just 39 of 80 possible games since he became a pro in 2013, a number that actually flatters his health by including several games he either left early or played at a clearly diminished capability. Relying on him for a full season seems foolishly optimistic, yet visions of Eifert's mismatch dominance when he is right (and the specter of him defecting to Pittsburgh or Cleveland and playing well) forced the Bengals into re-signing him to a one-year, $8 million deal this offseason. All in all, a reasonable bargain for both sides. The team didn't draft a replacement, but his fellow Tyler, Kroft, showed he was more than competent in the starting role should Eifert follow form and miss sizable chunks of 2018. The pressure is on Eifert to stay on the field.

Rhett Ellison　　Height: 6-4　　Weight: 251　　College: USC　　Draft: 2012/FA　　Born: 3-Oct-1988　　Age: 30　　Risk: Yellow

Year	Team	G/GS	Snaps	Pass	Rec	Yds	TD	C%	+/-	Drop	Yd/C	aDOT	Rk	YAC	Rk	YAC+	BTkl	DVOA	Rk	DYAR	Rk	YAR	Use	Rk	Slot	Wide
2015	MIN	15/9	471	19	11	124	1	58%	-1.2	1	11.3	0.5	--	11.5	--	+4.2	3	-8.6%	--	-2	--	-9	4.5%	--	--	0%
2016	MIN	15/6	258	14	9	57	0	64%	-0.1	0	6.3	3.8	--	3.8	--	-2.3	0	-51.9%	--	-41	--	-53	2.5%	--	7%	0%
2017	NYG	16/14	538	32	24	235	2	75%	+3.2	1	9.8	5.0	49	5.5	16	+1.1	6	17.7%	11	56	15	57	5.3%	49	3%	3%
2018	NYG			34	21	163	1	62%			7.8							-17.1%								

Ellison is New York's blander, yet more consistent tight end. A free-agent signing a year ago, Ellison provides the Giants with a security blanket in the quick game and a viable blocking option, either from an in-line tight end alignment or out of the backfield as a fullback. The average depth of Ellison's targets was 5.1 yards, illustrating his use as a means to safely pick up yards on quick hitches, drag routes, and releases following chip blocks. Ellison is not going to be a productive tight end in the traditional sense, but with Evan Engram doing some of the lifting elsewhere, Ellison can continue to provide a safety valve for Eli Manning.

Evan Engram

Height: 6-3 Weight: 234 College: Mississippi Draft: 2017/2 (23) Born: 2-Sep-1994 Age: 24 Risk: Yellow

Year	Team	G/GS	Snaps	Pass	Rec	Yds	TD	C%	+/-	Drop	Yd/C	aDOT	Rk	YAC	Rk	YAC+	BTkl	DVOA	Rk	DYAR	Rk	YAR	Use	Rk	Slot	Wide
2017	NYG	15/11	777	115	64	722	6	56%	-7.1	7	11.3	8.5	25	4.7	27	+0.5	7	-8.0%	33	-5	33	-20	20.2%	6	25%	15%
2018	NYG			114	71	802	6	62%			11.3							-0.5%								

Despite a bad case of the dropsies, Engram racked up the fourth-most yards ever by a rookie tight end—which oddly still ranks second by a rookie in franchise history behind Jeremy Shockey's 894 yards in 2002. Out of Ole Miss, Engram was criticized as being ill-equipped to play tight end in the NFL, and someone who needed to move permanently to wide receiver, à la Devin Funchess. Engram's rookie target distribution says differently, crediting him with 68 targets from a tight end position as compared to a combined 46 from the slot or out wide. In addition to playing a variety of alignments, Engram showed the depth to handle a myriad of different routes, ranging from the curl route he was so often asked to run to the deep crossers and seam routes that earned him his explosive reputation. If Engram can iron out his hands, he has the tools to skyrocket into the league's top tier of tight ends.

Zach Ertz

Height: 6-5 Weight: 249 College: Stanford Draft: 2013/2 (35) Born: 10-Nov-1990 Age: 28 Risk: Green

Year	Team	G/GS	Snaps	Pass	Rec	Yds	TD	C%	+/-	Drop	Yd/C	aDOT	Rk	YAC	Rk	YAC+	BTkl	DVOA	Rk	DYAR	Rk	YAR	Use	Rk	Slot	Wide
2015	PHI	15/7	788	112	75	853	2	67%	+4.9	4	11.4	8.4	18	4.0	36	-0.5	4	0.2%	27	56	19	55	19.3%	11	--	0%
2016	PHI	14/12	851	106	78	816	4	74%	+11.4	3	10.5	8.1	20	3.4	39	-1.1	2	3.4%	22	75	17	106	20.0%	6	62%	4%
2017	PHI	14/13	778	110	74	824	8	67%	+4.0	8	11.1	8.0	29	3.4	43	-0.8	4	14.2%	13	154	4	129	22.3%	4	48%	4%
2018	PHI			112	76	853	6	68%			11.2							5.9%								

Ertz caught 12 of 18 red zone targets last year for eight touchdowns. He was 6-of-14 for three touchdowns in 2016, 3-of-9 for one touchdown in 2015. Red zone targets are all about opportunity: Ertz's role in the Eagles offense hasn't changed much (see the similar-looking stat lines above), but a better offense means more trips to the red zone, which can cause touchdown spikes despite the huge amount of randomness in these tiny sample sizes. The Eagles offense will still be very good in 2018, and so will Ertz.

Gerald Everett

Height: 6-3 Weight: 239 College: South Alabama Draft: 2017/2 (44) Born: 25-Jun-1994 Age: 24 Risk: Yellow

Year	Team	G/GS	Snaps	Pass	Rec	Yds	TD	C%	+/-	Drop	Yd/C	aDOT	Rk	YAC	Rk	YAC+	BTkl	DVOA	Rk	DYAR	Rk	YAR	Use	Rk	Slot	Wide
2017	LAR	16/2	299	32	16	244	2	50%	-3.3	3	15.3	9.5	14	6.8	6	+1.6	1	-17.0%	44	-20	41	-36	6.2%	45	41%	9%
2018	LAR			56	39	482	4	70%			12.4							10.5%								

To quote last year's almanac: "Lance Kendricks had a catch rate of 57 percent in 2016 to go with eight dropped passes, so Los Angeles will be hoping for a more reliable set of hands from [Everett]." Well, not so much. As a rookie, Everett's catch rate was just 50 percent, with three drops on 32 targets. That will have to improve going forward. On a more positive note, when he *did* manage to catch the ball, he did quite well with it. He averaged 6.8 yards after the catch, sixth-most among qualifiers at the position, and his +1.6 YAC+ ranked seventh, placing him above both of last year's first-round tight ends. If he can get his hands on the same level as his legs, he could be yet another weapon for the Rams going forward.

Coby Fleener

Height: 6-6 Weight: 247 College: Stanford Draft: 2012/2 (34) Born: 20-Sep-1988 Age: 30 Risk: N/A

Year	Team	G/GS	Snaps	Pass	Rec	Yds	TD	C%	+/-	Drop	Yd/C	aDOT	Rk	YAC	Rk	YAC+	BTkl	DVOA	Rk	DYAR	Rk	YAR	Use	Rk	Slot	Wide
2015	IND	16/11	732	84	54	491	3	64%	-0.3	3	9.1	8.2	22	3.3	42	-1.4	2	-15.9%	40	-49	46	-38	14.1%	21	--	4%
2016	NO	16/8	663	82	50	631	3	61%	-1.9	4	12.6	9.4	10	4.2	22	+0.0	0	-4.5%	25	16	24	18	12.4%	27	51%	5%
2017	NO	11/1	269	30	22	295	2	73%	+1.6	1	13.4	7.5	34	5.0	21	+1.0	1	50.1%	1	107	6	99	8.2%	37	77%	0%

Fleener had a reputation for some really bad drops when he was in Indianapolis. He never became an integral part of the Saints' passing game, and things only declined in his second season with the team. He had two games where he didn't catch a pass, and a third where his only reception lost a yard. A concussion put Fleener on injured reserve, and the Saints released him in May. He remains unclaimed at the time of publication.

Antonio Gates		Height: 6-4		Weight: 260		College: Kent State			Draft: 2003/FA			Born: 18-Jun-1980			Age: 38		Risk: N/A	
Year	Team	G/GS	Snaps	Pass	Rec	Yds	TD	C%	+/-	Drop	Yd/C	aDOT	Rk	YAC	Rk	YAC+	BTkl	DVOA	Rk	DYAR	Rk	YAR	Use	Rk	Slot	Wide
2015	SD	11/4	496	85	56	630	5	66%	+3.2	3	11.3	8.3	20	4.3	32	+0.0	4	13.1%	11	113	7	91	18.7%	12	--	1%
2016	SD	14/9	585	93	53	548	7	57%	-5.2	8	10.3	8.7	17	3.5	35	-0.2	4	-6.6%	28	4	28	6	18.9%	9	72%	6%
2017	LAC	16/4	500	52	30	316	3	58%	+0.1	1	10.5	8.9	20	2.2	49	-1.6	1	-3.2%	26	13	26	5	8.8%	35	80%	0%

The Chargers released Gates in early May; after five straight years of declining numbers, he's expected to retire. Jason Witten also retired in early May, and their careers line up in many ways. Both began their careers in 2003; both played for franchises that hovered in the playoff picture but never broke through as true Super Bowl contenders; both had long, slow decline phases. Witten ends his career fourth on the all-time reception list, Gates 20th (they rank second and third among tight ends). Witten was the better blocker, but Gates blows him away in yards per catch (12.4 to 10.8) and touchdowns (124 to 68). Both are Hall of Famers, but Witten will get in first because he's Mr. Personality and will stay in the public consciousness as a broadcaster, while Gates spent the latter half of his career playing for a team that went out of its way to alienate its own fans.

Mike Gesicki		Height: 6-5		Weight: 247		College: Penn State			Draft: 2018/2 (42)			Born: 3-Oct-1995			Age: 23		Risk: Red	
Year	Team	G/GS	Snaps	Pass	Rec	Yds	TD	C%	+/-	Drop	Yd/C	aDOT	Rk	YAC	Rk	YAC+	BTkl	DVOA	Rk	DYAR	Rk	YAR	Use	Rk	Slot	Wide
2018	MIA			47	32	350	2	68%			10.9							-1.4%								

It's always weird when someone gets drafted and they go immediately to basketball and volleyball highlights, even if it is to showcase that player's ridiculous athleticism. Gesicki is a freak athlete who blew up the combine. The only thing he didn't do particularly well was the bench press, which is to be expected out of a lighter move tight end. He doesn't quite live up to his combine speed on tape, but Gesicki can go get it in the post, and that bodes well for his chances of contributing sooner rather than later. Well, that and the rest of the Dolphins depth chart at tight end.

Dallas Goedert		Height: 6-5		Weight: 256		College: South Dakota State			Draft: 2018/2 (49)			Born: 3-Jan-1995			Age: 24		Risk: Yellow	
Year	Team	G/GS	Snaps	Pass	Rec	Yds	TD	C%	+/-	Drop	Yd/C	aDOT	Rk	YAC	Rk	YAC+	BTkl	DVOA	Rk	DYAR	Rk	YAR	Use	Rk	Slot	Wide
2018	PHI			43	25	318	2	58%			12.7							0.4%								

Your basic small-program super-athlete with gaudy numbers (164 catches and 18 touchdowns in his final two seasons) and a fun backstory (comes from a tiny South Dakota town, juggles and rides a unicycle in parades). In the fantasy short term, Goedert will get the touches Trey Burton had behind Zach Ertz, though with fewer overall targets (Goedert is very raw) and a little more big-play ability. In the long term, Goedert draws Ertz comparisons, and the Eagles could build the most dangerous two-tight end offense in the NFL.

Jimmy Graham		Height: 6-6		Weight: 260		College: Miami			Draft: 2010/3 (95)			Born: 24-Nov-1986			Age: 32		Risk: Red	
Year	Team	G/GS	Snaps	Pass	Rec	Yds	TD	C%	+/-	Drop	Yd/C	aDOT	Rk	YAC	Rk	YAC+	BTkl	DVOA	Rk	DYAR	Rk	YAR	Use	Rk	Slot	Wide
2015	SEA	11/11	571	74	48	605	2	65%	+2.3	2	12.6	9.3	11	4.6	27	-0.3	4	14.8%	10	110	8	72	23.0%	5	--	3%
2016	SEA	16/15	790	96	65	923	6	69%	+3.7	5	14.2	9.7	9	5.0	12	+0.3	9	25.1%	6	204	2	194	17.4%	13	38%	4%
2017	SEA	16/13	730	96	57	520	10	59%	-3.8	7	9.1	7.9	30	3.7	39	-0.4	6	-6.0%	28	9	27	-4	18.0%	10	43%	27%
2018	GB			85	60	721	8	71%			12.0							18.7%								

Aaron Rodgers has never posted huge numbers with his tight ends, but a healthy Jimmy Graham—and a lack of Jordy Nelson—could be his best opportunity to do so. Graham still had 10 touchdowns last year in an injury-plagued season, but he also averaged a career-low 9.1 yards per catch and turns 32 in November. Still, it's hard to imagine this signing could go any worse than that of Martellus Bennett did a year ago. Graham provides instant credibility in the red zone, where he has 55 touchdowns since 2010, tied with Rob Gronkowski for the league lead.

Virgil Green Height: 6-5 Weight: 240 College: Nevada Draft: 2011/7 (204) Born: 3-Aug-1988 Age: 30 Risk: Yellow

Year	Team	G/GS	Snaps	Pass	Rec	Yds	TD	C%	+/-	Drop	Yd/C	aDOT	Rk	YAC	Rk	YAC+	BTkl	DVOA	Rk	DYAR	Rk	YAR	Use	Rk	Slot	Wide
2015	DEN	16/5	383	15	12	173	1	80%	+1.8	0	14.4	4.4	--	10.1	--	+5.9	3	51.3%	--	66	--	62	2.5%	--	--	0%
2016	DEN	12/11	494	37	22	237	1	59%	-2.0	3	10.8	7.3	28	4.6	16	-0.4	4	-14.8%	37	-19	35	-11	8.7%	39	11%	0%
2017	DEN	16/16	534	22	14	191	1	64%	-0.8	3	13.6	8.0	--	6.6	--	+1.8	1	0.8%	--	12	--	20	3.9%	--	14%	0%
2018	LAC			50	34	385	4	68%			11.3							6.4%								

Green spent a full seven seasons in Denver as the talented tight end prospect who was going to break big any day now. He officially started all 16 games last year for the Broncos, though Vance Joseph and his coordinators often gave Jeff Heuerman, Austin Taylor, and A.J. Derby more snaps after satisfying John Elway that his longtime pet project was indeed a "starter." Green was set to backup Hunter Henry in L.A., but Henry's torn ACL will make Green a starter for real this time.

Jermaine Gresham Height: 6-5 Weight: 261 College: Oklahoma Draft: 2010/1 (21) Born: 16-Jun-1988 Age: 30 Risk: Yellow

Year	Team	G/GS	Snaps	Pass	Rec	Yds	TD	C%	+/-	Drop	Yd/C	aDOT	Rk	YAC	Rk	YAC+	BTkl	DVOA	Rk	DYAR	Rk	YAR	Use	Rk	Slot	Wide
2015	ARI	15/12	596	32	18	223	1	56%	-0.1	1	12.4	8.1	25	4.1	33	-0.8	0	-14.0%	38	-16	36	-11	6.4%	42	--	3%
2016	ARI	16/14	835	61	37	391	2	61%	-1.3	7	10.6	7.8	25	3.7	29	-0.7	9	-18.7%	38	-48	38	-40	9.5%	37	16%	0%
2017	ARI	14/14	750	46	33	322	2	72%	+0.9	4	9.8	6.5	44	4.1	34	-0.9	9	-0.1%	23	22	24	15	8.9%	34	15%	2%
2018	ARI			38	21	207	1	55%			9.8							-14.2%								

Gresham is entering his ninth season in the league this year, and the Cardinals have to be disappointed from the level of production they got in 2017 after signing him to a four-year, $28 million deal last year. While Gresham has not been bad in Arizona, you would expect more from a tight end making an average of $7 million annually, as he finished in the middle of the pack among qualifying tight ends in both DVOA and DYAR. Gresham is recovering from a torn Achilles tendon; combined with his advancing age, that might limit his effectiveness upon his return. He may be the nominal starter, but Ricky Seals-Jones is likely to play a larger role in the passing game.

Ryan Griffin Height: 6-6 Weight: 247 College: Connecticut Draft: 2013/6 (201) Born: 11-Jan-1990 Age: 28 Risk: Green

Year	Team	G/GS	Snaps	Pass	Rec	Yds	TD	C%	+/-	Drop	Yd/C	aDOT	Rk	YAC	Rk	YAC+	BTkl	DVOA	Rk	DYAR	Rk	YAR	Use	Rk	Slot	Wide
2015	HOU	9/4	351	34	20	251	2	59%	-2.2	2	12.6	8.6	16	5.0	19	+0.1	2	11.5%	14	42	22	39	10.0%	31	--	6%
2016	HOU	16/5	507	74	50	442	2	68%	+0.1	6	8.8	6.7	36	3.4	42	-1.1	4	-22.9%	43	-77	43	-62	12.7%	26	31%	3%
2017	HOU	7/6	349	26	13	158	1	50%	-2.5	1	12.2	10.3	9	5.6	13	+1.4	1	-11.0%	37	-6	34	-9	11.1%	26	8%	0%
2018	HOU			54	33	378	2	61%			11.5							-3.6%								

All but one of Griffin's targets came from Deshaun Watson, as a concussion ended his season not long after Watson's ACL ended his. At times a passable blocker, Griffin is the best at that skill among Texans tight ends and seems likely to earn regular snaps because of it. More targets, though, may be directed elsewhere.

Rob Gronkowski Height: 6-6 Weight: 264 College: Arizona Draft: 2010/2 (42) Born: 14-May-1989 Age: 29 Risk: Yellow

Year	Team	G/GS	Snaps	Pass	Rec	Yds	TD	C%	+/-	Drop	Yd/C	aDOT	Rk	YAC	Rk	YAC+	BTkl	DVOA	Rk	DYAR	Rk	YAR	Use	Rk	Slot	Wide
2015	NE	15/15	939	120	72	1176	11	60%	-0.1	1	16.3	10.4	5	7.7	2	+3.3	14	21.0%	7	235	2	211	20.4%	9	--	6%
2016	NE	8/6	354	38	25	540	3	66%	+4.5	1	21.6	14.2	1	9.1	1	+5.0	7	44.5%	2	136	7	142	14.1%	21	38%	23%
2017	NE	14/14	905	105	69	1084	8	66%	+7.9	3	15.7	12.2	1	5.0	22	+1.0	12	40.4%	2	339	1	347	21.1%	5	41%	15%
2018	NE			117	77	1158	8	66%			15.0							20.5%								

Your favorite party animal tight end had a sobering season. In between his signature spikes and the dominant on-field play, he was concussed in the AFC Championship Game, lowered his helmet into Bills corner Tre'Davious White after a play in a dirty fashion, and contemplated retirement early in the offseason. He also continued his downfield dominance by leading all receivers in both targets (16) and DYAR (81) on seam routes. There's no reason for Gronkowski to hang it up based on his on-field performance. As long as his body can keep going, Gronk is a superstar. And whenever he actually follows through on the retirement threats, we'll still always have *A Gronking To Remember.*

Hunter Henry

Height: 6-5		Weight: 250		College: Arkansas			Draft: 2016/2 (35)			Born: 7-Dec-1994			Age: 24			Risk: N/A										

Year	Team	G/GS	Snaps	Pass	Rec	Yds	TD	C%	+/-	Drop	Yd/C	aDOT	Rk	YAC	Rk	YAC+	BTkl	DVOA	Rk	DYAR	Rk	YAR	Use	Rk	Slot	Wide
2016	SD	15/10	573	53	36	478	8	68%	+3.6	2	13.3	9.0	13	5.4	6	+2.2	5	33.4%	3	148	6	140	9.9%	35	43%	8%
2017	LAC	14/13	598	62	45	579	4	73%	+5.8	3	12.9	9.2	19	4.2	32	+0.3	1	32.3%	4	165	3	183	12.4%	23	50%	3%

Henry sometimes went untargeted early in the season, despite playing 30 or 40 snaps in rotation with Antonio Gates. Anthony Lynn and Ken Whisenhunt slowly accepted that Henry was a better option than the Chargers legend, and Henry went 19-235-2 in his final four games, despite a lingering calf injury, before a lacerated kidney ended his season. A huge leap in production seemed likely, but then a torn ACL suffered on the first day of OTAs ended Henry's 2018 season months before it even began.

Tyler Higbee

Height: 6-6		Weight: 249		College: Western Kentucky			Draft: 2016/4 (110)			Born: 1-Jan-1993			Age: 26			Risk: Green										

Year	Team	G/GS	Snaps	Pass	Rec	Yds	TD	C%	+/-	Drop	Yd/C	aDOT	Rk	YAC	Rk	YAC+	BTkl	DVOA	Rk	DYAR	Rk	YAR	Use	Rk	Slot	Wide
2016	LAR	16/6	405	29	11	85	1	38%	-7.2	4	7.7	6.9	32	2.4	46	-2.5	1	-68.5%	46	-109	46	-111	5.4%	45	14%	7%
2017	LAR	16/16	733	45	25	295	1	56%	-2.6	2	11.8	10.8	6	3.4	42	-0.9	6	-10.4%	36	-9	36	-19	8.7%	36	24%	7%
2018	LAR			51	29	260	2	57%			9.0							-16.6%								

While much of the preseason hype was on second-round pick Gerald Everett, it was Higbee who ended up with 70 percent of the tight end snaps last season. The big difference between the two, and Higbee's major advantage? Blocking. While Higbee's blown block rate was nothing to write home about (one per 29.3 snaps, among the lowest for qualified tight ends), he was clearly the more proficient of the two, especially when it came to opening holes for Todd Gurley. Higbee ranked 40th out of 48 tight ends in YAC+, so he didn't do much with the ball in his hands. Sean McVay frequently employs two-tight end sets, but Higbee will likely see his snaps decrease somewhat as Everett gets more accustomed to NFL-level play.

Austin Hooper

Height: 6-4		Weight: 254		College: Stanford			Draft: 2016/3 (81)			Born: 4-Nov-1994			Age: 24			Risk: Yellow										

Year	Team	G/GS	Snaps	Pass	Rec	Yds	TD	C%	+/-	Drop	Yd/C	aDOT	Rk	YAC	Rk	YAC+	BTkl	DVOA	Rk	DYAR	Rk	YAR	Use	Rk	Slot	Wide
2016	ATL	14/3	405	27	19	271	3	70%	+2.8	2	14.3	10.3	5	3.8	27	-0.4	1	46.8%	1	106	11	95	5.9%	43	25%	4%
2017	ATL	16/8	787	65	49	526	3	75%	+5.8	4	10.7	6.8	40	5.3	17	+0.4	10	9.4%	14	71	13	47	12.4%	21	43%	0%
2018	ATL			57	41	411	4	72%			10.5							7.2%								

Atlanta didn't just bolster their defense in the 2016 draft, they also found a potential long-term starter at tight end. Atlanta's fan base has been very critical of Hooper's untimely drops in 2017, but that doesn't mean he isn't an exciting prospect for the future. As a rookie, Hooper finished second in DVOA among all tight ends, only behind Rob Gronkowski. As expected, his efficiency dropped in 2017 as his targets increased. Hooper will probably never reach the elite ranks with guys like Travis Kelce and Rob Gronkowski, but he doesn't have to. He's a good, young tight end who has a bright future for the team. That's a fine return on a third-round pick.

O.J. Howard

Height: 6-6		Weight: 251		College: Alabama			Draft: 2017/1 (19)			Born: 19-Nov-1994			Age: 24			Risk: Green										

Year	Team	G/GS	Snaps	Pass	Rec	Yds	TD	C%	+/-	Drop	Yd/C	aDOT	Rk	YAC	Rk	YAC+	BTkl	DVOA	Rk	DYAR	Rk	YAR	Use	Rk	Slot	Wide
2017	TB	14/14	608	39	26	432	6	67%	+4.0	1	16.6	11.9	2	5.8	12	+1.5	1	32.2%	5	101	7	91	7.4%	39	21%	3%
2018	TB			57	38	519	5	67%			13.7							12.2%								

Howard seems to have this ability to play a Madden Card where defenses completely lose track of him on the field. He did it in college, and he scored touchdowns against the Bills and Giants last year in similar fashion. Howard is in some historic company with his rookie season. He's only the third rookie tight end, following legends Mike Ditka (1961) and John Mackey

(1963), to have at least 25 catches, six touchdowns, and average 16.6 yards per catch. He still has to contend with Cameron Brate and wide receivers that go four deep, but Howard should be more involved in his second season.

Hayden Hurst

Height: 6-4   Weight: 250   College: South Carolina   Draft: 2018/1 (25)   Born: 24-Aug-1993   Age: 25   Risk: Red

Year	Team	G/GS	Snaps	Pass	Rec	Yds	TD	C%	+/-	Drop	Yd/C	aDOT	Rk	YAC	Rk	YAC+	BTkl	DVOA	Rk	DYAR	Rk	YAR	Use	Rk	Slot	Wide
2018	BAL			40	28	308	3	70%			11.0							8.0%								

Hurst only sported a 48 percent receiving success rate with the South Carolina Gamecocks, and none of his numbers leap off the page, save perhaps his 70 percent catch rate. He figures to see early action in target-deprived Baltimore, though he will a) have to learn the offense, b) have to fight off a challenge from similarly skilled rookie Mark Andrews, and c) have to consistently collect passes from Joe Flacco. If he's worthy of the first-round selection, Hurst should accomplish all three.

Jesse James

Height: 6-7   Weight: 261   College: Penn State   Draft: 2015/5 (160)   Born: 4-Jun-1994   Age: 24   Risk: Green

Year	Team	G/GS	Snaps	Pass	Rec	Yds	TD	C%	+/-	Drop	Yd/C	aDOT	Rk	YAC	Rk	YAC+	BTkl	DVOA	Rk	DYAR	Rk	YAR	Use	Rk	Slot	Wide
2015	PIT	8/2	181	11	8	56	1	73%	+1.1	0	7.0	7.4	--	2.5	--	-1.6	0	-13.3%	--	-5	--	0	3.7%	--	--	0%
2016	PIT	16/13	855	60	39	338	3	65%	-3.9	5	8.7	6.8	33	3.2	43	-0.9	1	-13.7%	34	-26	37	-21	10.0%	34	38%	3%
2017	PIT	16/14	907	63	43	372	3	68%	+0.2	2	8.7	6.1	45	4.5	30	-0.5	4	-12.8%	39	-23	43	2	10.5%	29	22%	2%
2018	PIT			36	25	236	2	69%			9.4							-4.2%								

It turns out, James played more than one snap last season. He was a regular contributor in the blocking game and he was capable of sneaking out and hauling in a few passes if defenses spent too much time covering one of the Steelers' 17 other skill position threats. When everyone was healthy, he played second-fiddle to Vance McDonald in the passing game, but as a role player, you could do far worse than having James around. Of course, the only thing people are going to remember from James' 2017 is the overturned touchdown at the end of the Patriots game—a play that would have given the Steelers home-field advantage and let them avoid the divisional round game against Jacksonville. Under the new rules implemented this offseason, James' play was probably a catch. Under the old rules used in 2017 … James' play was probably a catch.

Blake Jarwin

Height: 6-5   Weight: 246   College: Oklahoma State   Draft: 2017/FA   Born: 16-Jul-1994   Age: 24   Risk: Green

Year	Team	G/GS	Snaps	Pass	Rec	Yds	TD	C%	+/-	Drop	Yd/C	aDOT	Rk	YAC	Rk	YAC+	BTkl	DVOA	Rk	DYAR	Rk	YAR	Use	Rk	Slot	Wide
2018	DAL			50	36	364	2	72%			10.1							-0.8%								

Jarwin's rise to the Cowboys' first string was a mild upset in OTAs. As a rookie, Jarwin was promoted to the active roster in October to prevent the Eagles from signing him away. He appeared in just one game and played 12 snaps, nine of them on special teams. His experience and collegiate production (just 19 catches in 12 games in his senior year with Mason Rudolph and the Oklahoma State Cowboys) are both limited, but the Cowboys are enamored with his blocking ability.

Travis Kelce

Height: 6-5   Weight: 255   College: Cincinnati   Draft: 2013/3 (63)   Born: 5-Oct-1989   Age: 29   Risk: Yellow

Year	Team	G/GS	Snaps	Pass	Rec	Yds	TD	C%	+/-	Drop	Yd/C	aDOT	Rk	YAC	Rk	YAC+	BTkl	DVOA	Rk	DYAR	Rk	YAR	Use	Rk	Slot	Wide
2015	KC	16/16	923	103	72	875	5	70%	+0.2	5	12.2	5.7	50	7.3	4	+1.8	14	9.3%	16	110	9	108	22.1%	6	--	0%
2016	KC	16/15	888	117	85	1125	4	73%	+4.8	8	13.2	6.8	34	7.4	4	+2.5	12	26.0%	5	261	1	222	21.7%	4	59%	14%
2017	KC	15/15	875	122	83	1038	8	68%	+7.4	7	12.5	9.6	11	4.9	24	+0.2	18	17.0%	12	197	2	206	24.4%	1	56%	16%
2018	KC			127	84	1043	5	66%			12.4							8.5%								

Kelce is the only tight end in the league who can rival Rob Gronkowski. What makes Kelce so effective is how smooth and explosive he is with a 6-foot-5, 260-pound frame. Kelce's fluidity in and out of route breaks rivals top-tier wide receivers despite his size, making it nearly impossible for defenders to find a comfortable position to keep up with him. Once the ball is in his hands, Kelce becomes the most threatening yards-after-catch tight end in the league. Kelce's dominance is more nuanced than just creating explosive plays, though. For one, Kelce is fantastic at clearing room for his teammates, as put on display in Week 1 when the Chiefs ran option concepts with Kelce as a lead blocker. Kelce is also plenty effective on short routes because he can stop on a dime and quickly box out defenders. With a more aggressive quarterback at the helm in Kansas City, Kelce will again find himself near the top of tight end rankings.

George Kittle Height: 6-4 Weight: 247 College: Iowa Draft: 2017/5 (146) Born: 9-Oct-1993 Age: 25 Risk: Green

Year	Team	G/GS	Snaps	Pass	Rec	Yds	TD	C%	+/-	Drop	Yd/C	aDOT	Rk	YAC	Rk	YAC+	BTkl	DVOA	Rk	DYAR	Rk	YAR	Use	Rk	Slot	Wide
2017	SF	15/7	591	63	43	515	2	68%	-0.1	7	12.0	7.4	35	6.2	10	+1.6	6	5.6%	17	55	16	59	11.3%	25	44%	2%
2018	SF			81	53	678	4	65%			12.8							4.5%								

Kittle originally made a name for himself through his outstanding athletic testing at the combine. He spent most of his rookie year backing up Garrett Celek, but was a steady presence in the lineup with at least two targets in every game he played. His best game of the year came against the Rams' backups in Week 17 with an even 100 receiving yards. If he can develop a stronger connection with Jimmy Garoppolo moving forward, the 49ers could have themselves another useful piece for Kyle Shanahan's offensive chessboard. Celek is still around to compete for playing time, but Kittle will have every opportunity to make the starting job his to keep.

Tyler Kroft Height: 6-5 Weight: 246 College: Rutgers Draft: 2015/3 (85) Born: 15-Oct-1992 Age: 26 Risk: Green

Year	Team	G/GS	Snaps	Pass	Rec	Yds	TD	C%	+/-	Drop	Yd/C	aDOT	Rk	YAC	Rk	YAC+	BTkl	DVOA	Rk	DYAR	Rk	YAR	Use	Rk	Slot	Wide
2015	CIN	16/6	347	15	11	129	1	73%	+1.5	1	11.7	6.5	—	6.2	—	+0.4	1	24.9%	—	27	—	24	3.0%	—	—	0%
2016	CIN	14/11	374	12	10	92	0	83%	+1.5	1	9.2	7.7	—	3.1	—	-1.7	0	0.0%	—	5	—	5	2.5%	—	33%	8%
2017	CIN	16/16	829	62	42	404	7	68%	+1.0	4	9.6	6.6	42	4.6	28	+0.5	6	1.3%	21	35	21	45	12.4%	22	45%	5%
2018	CIN			25	16	153	2	64%			9.5							-6.9%								

Kroft proved that Diet Tyler, when consumed in moderation, can be quite refreshing and not at all bad for you. Forced into the starting role with Tyler Eifert on injured reserve, Kroft provided a nice target in the red zone. He's not the mismatch nightmare Eifert is, but Kroft will make enough plays to cause Cincy to consider more two-tight end sets than they might have otherwise.

Coming out of Rutgers, Kroft was thought to be a good in-line tight end as well, but Sports Info Solutions charting had 25 other tight ends with fewer blown blocks per snap. Maybe all the extra action downfield got him too distracted from the ruck and maul at the line of scrimmage. How you gonna keep 'em down in the trenches once they've seen paydirt?

Jordan Leggett Height: 6-5 Weight: 258 College: Clemson Draft: 2017/5 (150) Born: 31-Jan-1995 Age: 23 Risk: Green

Year	Team	G/GS	Snaps	Pass	Rec	Yds	TD	C%	+/-	Drop	Yd/C	aDOT	Rk	YAC	Rk	YAC+	BTkl	DVOA	Rk	DYAR	Rk	YAR	Use	Rk	Slot	Wide
2018	NYJ			37	23	232	2	62%			10.1							-17.0%								

"Lazy Leggett" was an alleged nickname for Jordan on campus at Clemson, and though he has a clear path to playing time, both his OTA work and his offseason work have been thoroughly criticized to this point. He didn't play as a rookie because of a knee injury that eventually landed him on injured reserve. In a best-case scenario, Leggett could have a Charles Clay career as a move H-back. But with little special teams experience, he better impress the staff in a hurry. He opened OTAs as one of the co-favorites to win the tight end job, so that's a start at least.

Marcedes Lewis Height: 6-6 Weight: 255 College: UCLA Draft: 2006/1 (28) Born: 19-May-1984 Age: 34 Risk: Green

Year	Team	G/GS	Snaps	Pass	Rec	Yds	TD	C%	+/-	Drop	Yd/C	aDOT	Rk	YAC	Rk	YAC+	BTkl	DVOA	Rk	DYAR	Rk	YAR	Use	Rk	Slot	Wide
2015	JAX	16/16	670	37	16	226	0	43%	-7.2	1	14.1	7.0	35	10.1	1	+3.2	3	-37.0%	51	-76	50	-63	6.1%	44	—	3%
2016	JAX	10/10	280	30	20	169	1	67%	-1.9	0	8.5	4.7	46	5.3	9	-0.2	4	-14.8%	36	-16	33	-23	7.5%	42	17%	3%
2017	JAX	16/16	895	48	24	318	5	50%	-5.9	3	13.3	8.8	21	6.8	5	+2.5	5	1.0%	22	27	22	42	9.3%	33	22%	6%
2018	GB			28	17	184	3	61%			10.8							1.6%								

The only player to play on both the Jaguars' 2007 and 2017 playoff teams, Lewis turned 34 in May and was not re-signed. He joined the Green Bay Packers late in free agency, specifically as a veteran at a position in which young players typically struggle, but his best days as a receiver are well behind him. If he is to carve out a role in Green Bay, it is likely to be primarily as a blocker.

Vance McDonald

	Height: 6-4		Weight: 267		College: Rice				Draft: 2013/2 (55)			Born: 13-Jun-1990			Age: 28		Risk: Yellow	

Year	Team	G/GS	Snaps	Pass	Rec	Yds	TD	C%	+/-	Drop	Yd/C	aDOT	Rk	YAC	Rk	YAC+	BTkl	DVOA	Rk	DYAR	Rk	YAR	Use	Rk	Slot	Wide
2015	SF	14/11	473	46	30	326	3	65%	-0.5	5	10.9	8.4	19	6.1	9	+1.2	4	-19.2%	43	-34	40	-29	9.9%	32	--	7%
2016	SF	11/11	442	45	24	391	4	53%	-4.6	3	16.3	10.3	6	8.6	2	+4.3	2	6.7%	18	41	19	22	13.3%	24	13%	0%
2017	PIT	10/7	270	24	14	188	1	58%	-1.4	3	13.4	8.7	--	6.3	--	+1.9	3	-2.4%	--	7	--	25	6.4%	--	21%	0%
2018	PIT			63	39	483	4	62%			12.4							3.0%								

McDonald never really clicked in San Francisco. He developed a reputation for hands of stone, and the new regime was happy to get rid of him, despite the five-year contract extension the previous general manager had signed him to the year before. Pittsburgh presumably hoped that McDonald would have been on the field for more than 10 games, as a variety of injuries limited his availability last season. They also presumably would have hoped for more than 188 yards from the 16th-highest paid tight end in football. McDonald's potential and athleticism are clear to see, and his 10-reception, 112-yard game in the playoffs shows what he's capable of. He has just never put it all together consistently enough.

David Njoku

	Height: 6-4		Weight: 246		College: Miami				Draft: 2017/1 (29)			Born: 10-Jul-1996			Age: 22		Risk: Yellow	

Year	Team	G/GS	Snaps	Pass	Rec	Yds	TD	C%	+/-	Drop	Yd/C	aDOT	Rk	YAC	Rk	YAC+	BTkl	DVOA	Rk	DYAR	Rk	YAR	Use	Rk	Slot	Wide
2017	CLE	16/5	501	60	32	386	4	53%	-4.1	4	12.1	10.4	8	4.7	26	-0.3	3	-9.7%	34	-10	37	-2	10.8%	27	23%	16%
2018	CLE			80	50	614	6	63%			12.3							3.9%								

One of the less commented-on details about the Sashi Brown administration in Cleveland is the way they went after young players specifically. Last year's top four draft picks all played their rookie years at age 21, giving them more potential for growth than older players with similar skill sets. Twenty-two tight ends in NFL history caught at least one pass in their age-21 season, and Njoku's 386 receiving yards as a rookie rank him third in that group. He trails only the 2010 New England duo of Rob Gronkowski and Aaron Hernandez. Njoku is a muscular, athletic tight end in the best Miami Hurricanes tradition and is poised for a breakout season if the Browns get the improved quarterback play we're all expecting.

Nick O'Leary

	Height: 6-3		Weight: 252		College: Florida State				Draft: 2015/6 (194)			Born: 31-Aug-1992			Age: 26		Risk: Green	

Year	Team	G/GS	Snaps	Pass	Rec	Yds	TD	C%	+/-	Drop	Yd/C	aDOT	Rk	YAC	Rk	YAC+	BTkl	DVOA	Rk	DYAR	Rk	YAR	Use	Rk	Slot	Wide
2015	BUF	4/0	41	3	1	37	0	33%	-1.1	0	37.0	6.7	--	37.0	--	+31.0	1	38.9%	--	8	--	5	2.6%	0	--	0%
2016	BUF	16/7	375	14	9	114	0	64%	-0.4	1	12.7	8.9	--	4.8	--	-0.3	2	-1.2%	--	5	--	7	3.0%	--	14%	0%
2017	BUF	15/5	549	32	22	322	2	69%	+3.2	1	14.6	11.1	4	5.8	11	+1.4	0	29.9%	7	73	12	77	7.2%	40	16%	3%
2018	BUF			29	19	221	2	66%			11.7							0.9%								

A sure-handed, unspectacular athlete. O'Leary was Jameis Winston's favorite underneath player at Florida State, but offers little feel as a route-runner and is not much of a blocker. Jack Nicklaus' grandson, O'Leary is proof that the truth can be more on point than fiction ever could be, because nobody could ever design a player more custom-built to be loved by Chris Berman.

Greg Olsen

	Height: 6-6		Weight: 254		College: Miami				Draft: 2007/1 (31)			Born: 11-Mar-1985			Age: 33		Risk: Green	

Year	Team	G/GS	Snaps	Pass	Rec	Yds	TD	C%	+/-	Drop	Yd/C	aDOT	Rk	YAC	Rk	YAC+	BTkl	DVOA	Rk	DYAR	Rk	YAR	Use	Rk	Slot	Wide
2015	CAR	16/16	1057	124	77	1104	7	62%	+3.3	2	14.3	11.0	1	4.5	29	+0.3	1	8.9%	17	132	6	184	25.4%	2	--	9%
2016	CAR	16/16	1033	129	80	1073	3	62%	+2.5	3	13.4	11.3	3	4.4	17	+0.2	2	8.3%	17	134	8	123	23.4%	1	72%	4%
2017	CAR	7/7	367	38	17	191	1	45%	-4.0	0	11.2	10.6	7	2.8	47	-1.0	0	-24.5%	49	-44	49	-39	18.2%	9	63%	3%
2018	CAR			98	63	767	5	64%			12.2							6.4%								

Over the past few seasons, Olsen seemed to defy aging. One of the very few players to see his numbers improve as he entered his thirties, he was consistently good and available year in and year out. That came to crashing to an end in 2017, as Olsen missed his first games since his rookie year in 2007. A broken foot cost him all but seven games, and he wasn't the same player even when he was able to get back into the lineup. When he's healthy, there are few tight ends in the league with pass-catching credentials this solid, something the Panthers desperately need. Olsen appears healthy now, and there's no reason to believe he won't return to his 2014-16 form, but age does make injuries more and more likely.

Jordan Reed | Height: 6-2 | Weight: 236 | College: Florida | Draft: 2013/3 (85) | Born: 3-Jul-1990 | Age: 28 | Risk: Red

Year	Team	G/GS	Snaps	Pass	Rec	Yds	TD	C%	+/-	Drop	Yd/C	aDOT	Rk	YAC	Rk	YAC+	BTkl	DVOA	Rk	DYAR	Rk	YAR	Use	Rk	Slot	Wide
2015	WAS	14/8	704	114	87	952	11	76%	+9.6	2	10.9	6.5	40	5.4	15	+0.9	19	20.1%	8	206	4	213	23.2%	3	--	1%
2016	WAS	12/8	568	89	66	686	6	74%	+6.9	1	10.4	7.5	26	4.0	25	-0.2	12	9.9%	14	102	13	130	19.8%	7	54%	15%
2017	WAS	6/5	233	35	27	211	2	77%	+3.8	0	7.8	6.6	43	2.9	46	-1.6	3	-10.1%	35	-7	35	-18	17.3%	12	60%	17%
2018	WAS			98	71	720	6	72%			10.1							6.9%								

Reed's 2017 campaign was ruined by toe, shoulder, and chest injuries. He didn't play after Halloween, and a hamstring ailment finally put him on IR in December. That's nothing new for Reed, who has missed two to ten games in each of his five NFL seasons. A healthy Reed would be a good fantasy starter—only five tight ends have averaged more yards per game since he was drafted in 2013—but at this point we're not likely to ever see that. Washington has tried to protect him by frequently playing him off the line of scrimmage. Reed was second behind Antonio Gates in percentage of targets from the slot or split wide last season, and he was in the top 10 in 2016 as well. His DVOA on targets from a tight end position has been south of -10.0% in both seasons, so there's really no benefit to using him as anything other than on oversized slot receiver.

Kyle Rudolph | Height: 6-6 | Weight: 265 | College: Notre Dame | Draft: 2011/2 (43) | Born: 9-Nov-1989 | Age: 29 | Risk: Red

Year	Team	G/GS	Snaps	Pass	Rec	Yds	TD	C%	+/-	Drop	Yd/C	aDOT	Rk	YAC	Rk	YAC+	BTkl	DVOA	Rk	DYAR	Rk	YAR	Use	Rk	Slot	Wide
2015	MIN	16/16	847	73	49	495	5	67%	+6.0	3	10.1	8.0	26	3.9	37	-0.4	7	-6.3%	33	5	33	12	16.3%	17	--	3%
2016	MIN	16/16	969	132	83	840	7	63%	-1.9	7	10.1	6.7	37	4.3	19	-0.2	5	-9.1%	31	-17	34	3	22.5%	2	35%	3%
2017	MIN	16/16	924	81	57	532	8	70%	+5.3	2	9.3	7.6	33	4.0	36	-0.2	6	8.8%	15	88	9	91	15.1%	14	28%	3%
2018	MIN			99	66	640	6	67%			9.7							1.9%								

Rudolph has never been a dynamic receiver or dominant blocker in Minnesota. In 2017, Rudolph surpassed 500 receiving yards for the second time in his career, and his eight touchdowns were also the second-highest total he's had in a season. After seven years, Rudolph has likely shown us his ceiling, but Kirk Cousins was fond of throwing to tight ends in Washington. Rudolph remains the likely candidate to be Minnesota's third-leading receiver.

Ricky Seals-Jones | Height: 6-5 | Weight: 243 | College: Texas A&M | Draft: 2017/FA | Born: 15-Mar-1995 | Age: 23 | Risk: Green

Year	Team	G/GS	Snaps	Pass	Rec	Yds	TD	C%	+/-	Drop	Yd/C	aDOT	Rk	YAC	Rk	YAC+	BTkl	DVOA	Rk	DYAR	Rk	YAR	Use	Rk	Slot	Wide
2017	ARI	10/1	132	28	12	201	3	43%	-4.8	3	16.8	11.4	3	6.2	9	+2.4	2	-4.6%	27	5	28	13	7.4%	38	21%	11%
2018	ARI			63	39	387	2	62%			9.9							-9.4%								

2017 starter Jermaine Gresham tore an Achilles tendon in the season finale, which will open up more opportunities for Seals-Jones in his second season. He only managed 12 catches as a rookie while backing up Gresham, but the combination of Gresham's injury and advancing age will give Seals-Jones the chance to make his presence felt. Seals-Jones turned one quarter of his catches into touchdowns in 2017; while it's unlikely he'll be able to maintain that rate, he should still see an uptick in his total production as he receives more targets. All of that should make Hall of Fame running back Eric Dickerson happy since the two are cousins.

Austin Seferian-Jenkins | Height: 6-5 | Weight: 262 | College: Washington | Draft: 2014/2 (38) | Born: 9/29/1992 | Age: 26 | Risk: Red

Year	Team	G/GS	Snaps	Pass	Rec	Yds	TD	C%	+/-	Drop	Yd/C	aDOT	Rk	YAC	Rk	YAC+	BTkl	DVOA	Rk	DYAR	Rk	YAR	Use	Rk	Slot	Wide
2015	TB	7/3	218	39	21	338	4	54%	-2.9	1	16.1	11.0	2	4.6	26	+1.2	3	5.0%	23	33	25	62	16.8%	15	--	3%
2016	2TM	9/2	190	20	13	154	1	65%	-0.5	3	11.8	10.2	--	2.2	--	-1.2	1	15.4%	--	32	--	37	6.7%	--	33%	29%
2017	NYJ	13/10	655	74	50	357	3	68%	+0.9	4	7.1	6.9	39	2.3	48	-2.5	6	-23.4%	48	-83	51	-83	18.7%	8	51%	7%
2018	JAX			70	47	534	4	67%			11.4							4.3%								

Seferian-Jenkins is often discussed as a receiving target, but the early free-agency signing was probably targeted more for his blocking by the Jaguars. Seferian-Jenkins ranked eighth among tight ends in snaps per blown block last year, and No. 11 when limited to run blocking. Conversely, despite career highs of 357 yards and 50 receptions, the 78 targets it took to get him those figures gave him the worst receiving DYAR and fourth-worst DVOA of any qualifying tight end. And no, that overturned receiving touchdown against the Patriots would not have made a huge difference to his rank; he trailed second-worst A.J. Derby by 30 DYAR, which is almost the same value as the difference between that would-be touchdown and the lost fumble.

Seferian-Jenkins has signed a two-year deal in Jacksonville, marking his third stop already in the five years since Tampa Bay made him a second-round draft pick in 2014. Most of that nomadism is due to struggles with substance abuse: he was released by the Buccaneers after being arrested on a charge of DUI, and was suspended for the first two games of last season for violating the NFL Policy and Program for Substances of Abuse. The Jaguars coaches have (naturally) spoken openly about their excitement at his offseason performance, and his talent is seldom questioned. His temperament, thus far at least, has been a different story.

Adam Shaheen

Height: 6-6 **Weight:** 278 **College:** Ashland **Draft:** 2017/2 (45) **Born:** 24-Oct-1993 **Age:** 25 **Risk:** Green

Year	Team	G/GS	Snaps	Pass	Rec	Yds	TD	C%	+/-	Drop	Yd/C	aDOT	Rk	YAC	Rk	YAC+	BTkl	DVOA	Rk	DYAR	Rk	YAR	Use	Rk	Slot	Wide
2017	CHI	13/7	239	14	12	127	3	86%	+2.7	0	10.6	6.5	--	4.1	--	+1.1	0	26.0%	--	40	--	52	3.9%	--	0%	0%
2018	CHI			25	16	185	2	64%			11.6							-0.5%								

Don't get greedy with those Trey Burton shares without remembering that the Bears spent the 45th pick in the 2017 draft on Shaheen, who led the Bears with three receiving touchdowns. He peaked in his last game of the season, catching four passes in five targets for 44 yards and a touchdown against the Bengals in Week 14 before missing the rest of the season with a chest injury. He's not going to turn into Rob Gronkowski overnight, but Shaheen should see a boost in his second season.

Jonnu Smith

Height: 6-3 **Weight:** 248 **College:** Florida International **Draft:** 2017/3 (100) **Born:** 22-Aug-1995 **Age:** 23 **Risk:** Green

Year	Team	G/GS	Snaps	Pass	Rec	Yds	TD	C%	+/-	Drop	Yd/C	aDOT	Rk	YAC	Rk	YAC+	BTkl	DVOA	Rk	DYAR	Rk	YAR	Use	Rk	Slot	Wide
2017	TEN	16/13	556	30	18	157	2	60%	-1.8	1	8.7	7.2	37	5.3	18	-0.1	4	-30.7%	51	-44	48	-37	6.2%	46	10%	10%
2018	TEN			37	25	232	2	68%			9.3							-5.7%								

We have noted in various spots that it usually takes a young tight end at least a year to acclimatize to the NFL, and Smith's rookie year was exceptionally illustrative of the point. At least his rate of one blown block every 32.9 run-blocking snaps was merely below average; his -30.7% receiving DVOA was the worst of any tight end with enough targets to qualify for our receiving leaderboard. Smith ate into veteran Delanie Walker's playing time, particularly as a run blocker, and Walker has sung the praises of his young counterpart, but Walker remains the more effective player and Matt LaFleur's Rams offense used by far the lowest percentage of multiple-tight end sets last year. That almost certainly means Smith will have to do much better with his future opportunities if he hopes to take over as the team's primary option at the position.

Julius Thomas

Height: 6-5 **Weight:** 251 **College:** Portland State **Draft:** 2011/4 (129) **Born:** 27-Jun-1988 **Age:** 30 **Risk:** N/A

Year	Team	G/GS	Snaps	Pass	Rec	Yds	TD	C%	+/-	Drop	Yd/C	aDOT	Rk	YAC	Rk	YAC+	BTkl	DVOA	Rk	DYAR	Rk	YAR	Use	Rk	Slot	Wide
2015	JAX	12/10	541	80	46	455	5	58%	-4.3	5	9.9	8.6	17	3.2	44	-0.8	3	-17.7%	41	-57	49	-42	17.7%	14	--	1%
2016	JAX	9/6	449	51	30	281	4	59%	-3.5	1	9.4	7.5	27	3.4	40	-0.8	0	-13.8%	35	-23	36	-39	14.4%	20	40%	4%
2017	MIA	14/12	640	62	41	388	3	66%	+0.5	3	9.5	7.9	31	3.6	40	-0.7	5	-14.6%	42	-30	44	-28	11.9%	24	29%	26%

Released by the Dolphins after a pedestrian season, Thomas caught 24 touchdowns in two years with Peyton Manning and 12 over the next three years without him. At this point, Thomas is a former basketball player who can box out smaller players over the middle of the field, but there's little other reason to recommend him for any team's starting tight end role. He's big, but not much of a blocker. He did make $21.2 million under the terms of his old Jaguars contract, so at least he's got that to fall back on even if nobody calls.

Nick Vannett

Height: 6-6 **Weight:** 257 **College:** Ohio State **Draft:** 2016/3 (94) **Born:** 6-Mar-1993 **Age:** 25 **Risk:** Yellow

Year	Team	G/GS	Snaps	Pass	Rec	Yds	TD	C%	+/-	Drop	Yd/C	aDOT	Rk	YAC	Rk	YAC+	BTkl	DVOA	Rk	DYAR	Rk	YAR	Use	Rk	Slot	Wide
2016	SEA	9/2	84	4	3	32	0	75%	+0.1	1	10.7	6.5	--	4.0	--	-1.2	0	-17.1%	--	-2	--	-2	1.3%	--	0%	0%
2017	SEA	15/4	278	15	12	124	1	80%	+1.5	2	10.3	7.2	--	3.8	--	-0.7	0	31.0%	--	36	--	30	3.0%	--	27%	0%
2018	SEA			60	37	401	3	62%			10.8							-3.5%								

Vannett is in line for a huge jump in snaps in 2018, with both Jimmy Graham and Luke Willson out of town. The 2016 third-round pick has spent most of his career buried on the depth chart, playing in jumbo packages or when games had already been mostly decided. Vannett's size and athleticism are what made him an early draft pick to begin with, and his catch rate of 79 percent in a very, *very* limited sample size is a positive. You do have to wonder why he was never able to pass Willson on the depth chart. Expect him to be the Seahawks' receiving tight end, with Ed Dickson getting most of the blocking assignments in 2018.

Delanie Walker   Height: 6-1   Weight: 241   College: Central Missouri   Draft: 2006/6 (175)   Born: 12-Aug-1984   Age: 34   Risk: Yellow

Year	Team	G/GS	Snaps	Pass	Rec	Yds	TD	C%	+/-	Drop	Yd/C	aDOT	Rk	YAC	Rk	YAC+	BTkl	DVOA	Rk	DYAR	Rk	YAR	Use	Rk	Slot	Wide
2015	TEN	15/10	688	133	94	1088	6	71%	+9.9	5	11.6	9.0	14	4.1	34	-0.3	11	13.0%	12	174	5	164	25.8%	1	--	4%
2016	TEN	15/10	707	103	65	800	7	64%	+3.2	6	12.3	9.9	7	4.3	20	-0.4	11	8.4%	16	102	12	102	22.1%	3	67%	6%
2017	TEN	16/11	744	111	74	807	3	67%	+6.7	2	10.9	9.3	17	3.3	44	-1.4	5	-7.6%	32	-3	32	33	22.8%	3	51%	3%
2018	TEN			101	68	770	5	67%			11.3							6.4%								

For the fourth straight season, Walker had more than 100 pass targets and led the Titans in receptions; his share of targets again accounted for more than 20 percent of the Titans passing game. He had his lowest receiving DVOA since moving to Tennessee, but that was partly a result of his -23.0% DVOA on targets from Matt Cassel. On passes from only Marcus Mariota, Walker's DVOA was -5.5%. His two fumbles were also a factor: Mariota's own DVOA when targeting Walker, which is not affected by those fumbles, was 9.6%. Though Walker's efficiency did drop from its 2016 level in just about any way you can slice it, he remained the team's most effective receiving tight end: Jonnu Smith, last year's third-round rookie who is touted as a long-term replacement for Walker, managed only a -30.7% DVOA in his rookie season.

Walker is also one of the league's premier run-blocking tight ends. In more than 200 snaps as a run blocker, Walker was charted with only two blown blocks—the sixth-best rate in the league. He did cede snaps to Smith, particularly on those running downs—Smith had 296 run-blocking snaps to Walker's 202—but still played more than 70 percent of snaps on offense. Though his target share may drop under his new offensive coordinator, and he has already begun to lose playing time to his younger counterpart, Walker's experience and versatility should mean that he continues to be a major part of the Titans offense at least for this coming season.

Benjamin Watson   Height: 6-3   Weight: 255   College: Duke   Draft: 2004/1 (32)   Born: 18-Dec-1980   Age: 38   Risk: Red

Year	Team	G/GS	Snaps	Pass	Rec	Yds	TD	C%	+/-	Drop	Yd/C	aDOT	Rk	YAC	Rk	YAC+	BTkl	DVOA	Rk	DYAR	Rk	YAR	Use	Rk	Slot	Wide
2015	NO	16/16	984	110	74	825	6	67%	+5.1	5	11.1	9.3	10	3.3	43	-1.0	3	4.9%	24	87	13	102	16.5%	16	--	6%
2017	BAL	16/12	699	79	61	522	4	77%	+4.4	4	8.6	5.4	47	4.1	35	-0.8	4	-7.5%	31	-1	30	20	14.0%	18	34%	0%
2018	NO			61	44	434	4	72%			9.9							4.5%								

It was just in 2015 when Watson set career highs in New Orleans with 74 receptions for 825 yards. Then he lost the 2016 season with a torn Achilles. He was still solid last year for Baltimore given the dismal offense, but Watson will be 38 in December. Only three players in NFL history have surpassed 200 receiving yards at age 38 or older: Jerry Rice (five times), Charlie Joiner (twice), and Irving Fryar. Even Tony Gonzalez was done after his age-37 season, so Watson is in rarified air here, but the Saints need him after Coby Fleener did not work out.

Luke Willson   Height: 6-5   Weight: 250   College: Rice   Draft: 2013/5 (158)   Born: 15-Jan-1990   Age: 28   Risk: Red

Year	Team	G/GS	Snaps	Pass	Rec	Yds	TD	C%	+/-	Drop	Yd/C	aDOT	Rk	YAC	Rk	YAC+	BTkl	DVOA	Rk	DYAR	Rk	YAR	Use	Rk	Slot	Wide
2015	SEA	14/7	451	26	17	213	1	65%	+0.4	1	12.5	8.0	27	5.5	14	+0.6	4	10.5%	15	30	27	32	6.3%	43	--	4%
2016	SEA	11/6	350	21	15	129	2	71%	+0.9	2	8.6	6.9	--	5.0	--	-0.3	0	2.5%	--	13	--	19	5.4%	--	29%	5%
2017	SEA	16/7	377	22	15	153	4	68%	+0.8	2	10.2	8.0	--	6.0	--	+0.4	1	4.7%	--	18	--	19	4.1%	--	38%	5%
2018	DET			63	43	421	4	68%			9.8							0.1%								

Willson actually got less for a one-year deal from Detroit ($2.5 million) than he received from Seattle a year ago ($3 million) to back up Jimmy Graham. With 1,129 receiving yards in five seasons, Willson isn't coming to fully replace Eric Ebron, but he has reliable hands, is a willing blocker, and can make the occasional big play. The opportunity presents Willson with a chance for a career year, but it really depends on how much second-year player Michael Roberts develops.

Jason Witten Height: 6-6   Weight: 265   College: Tennessee   Draft: 2003/3 (69)   Born: 6-May-1982   Age: 36   Risk: N/A

Year	Team	G/GS	Snaps	Pass	Rec	Yds	TD	C%	+/-	Drop	Yd/C	aDOT	Rk	YAC	Rk	YAC+	BTkl	DVOA	Rk	DYAR	Rk	YAR	Use	Rk	Slot	Wide
2015	DAL	16/16	1019	104	77	713	3	74%	+7.9	0	9.3	7.3	31	3.0	48	-1.3	3	-1.9%	28	36	24	37	19.8%	10	--	2%
2016	DAL	16/16	1018	95	69	673	3	73%	+4.7	3	9.8	6.8	35	3.7	32	-0.6	10	-7.2%	29	0	29	25	19.5%	8	52%	1%
2017	DAL	16/16	1050	87	63	560	5	72%	+6.5	1	8.9	7.4	36	1.7	50	-2.1	1	-0.4%	24	40	20	37	17.8%	11	65%	1%

On October 12, 2003, the Dallas Cowboys got a late field goal from Billy Cundiff to beat the Philadelphia Eagles 23-21. We bring this up because it is the only game the Cowboys have played in the past 15 years without Jason Witten in the lineup. Witten has appeared in 235 straight games since then, and he hasn't missed a start since 2006. He is the team's all-time leader in catches and receiving yards; in NFL history, he ranks fourth with 1,152 receptions, 21st with 12,448 receiving yards, and 46th with 68 touchdowns. He holds all-time tight end records for catches in a season (110 in 2012) and in a single game (18 against the Giants that same year). Witten played in the same era as some of the great tight ends the game has ever seen, and so his season totals seem mundane in some respects. He never scored double-digit touchdowns or averaged 12 yards per catch, and "only" went over a thousand yards four times. But he still averaged 77 catches for 830 yards and four or five touchdowns for a decade and a half. Not a bad return for the investment of a third-round pick.

Witten retires with 2,073 receiving DYAR. That's fourth among tight ends since 1986, behind Tony Gonzalez (3,250), Antonio Gates (2,663), and Shannon Sharpe (2,090). Rob Gronkowski (2,023) will probably pass him by October, but then there will be a big drop-off from Witten to sixth-place Mark Bavaro (1,139). Witten never finished first among tight ends in DYAR, but he was in the top five ten times, tied with Sharpe behind the 13 of Gonzalez. He was not as efficient as the other greats though—he was in the top five in DVOA just once, when he finished second in 2005.

We haven't yet mentioned blocking, where Witten is regularly considered to among the upper tier of all tight ends. He was 15th out of 46 qualifying tight ends in rate of snaps per blown block in 2017. His retirement announcement during the draft caught the team off guard, but it's not his fault the team failed to prepare for the departure of a 36-year-old whose production had been slipping for half a decade now. Witten is clearly one of the great Cowboys of all-time and a surefire future Hall of Famer.

Going Deep

Jerell Adams, NYG: With a slew of injuries at wide receiver last season, rookie tight end Evan Engram was forced to line up wide at times, allowing Adams to sneak in for some snaps at tight end. Adams has the athletic profile to be productive, but lacks the requisite feel for zone coverages, as well as the ability to make tough catches the way a tight end should. As a third tight end, Adams is fine, but he will not be finding catches anytime soon unless Engram or Rhett Ellison become injured.

Jordan Akins, HOU: Akins is an exemplar of the current breed of collegiate tight ends and the way they have morphed into blocking-optional slot receivers. He'll be a 26-year-old rookie, as he went to Central Florida after four years in minor league baseball. Spending a third-round pick on him says that Houston expects him to play a role in 2018. Assuming Deshaun Watson is healthy, Akins' 16.1 yards per catch average says he could be a useful seam-stretcher, as long as he beats out Stephen Anderson for that role.

Dwayne Allen, NE: Thought to be an underused part of the Indianapolis game plan for years, Allen was poached by the Patriots and hyped up as their next big find. Then, New England discovered they aren't going to use him as a receiver very much either. He caught just 10 passes for 86 yards and a touchdown (-42.6% DVOA). Allen is still a plus blocker, but we probably don't need to worry about any fantasy football upside anymore. Allen has yet to really show any rapport with the New England offense.

Braedon Bowman, LAC: Bowman once starred for the Fighting Artichokes of Scottsdale Community College, then backed up Gerald Everett at South Alabama. He has spent time in training camps with the Jaguars, Jets, and Saints, then last year on the Chargers practice squad. This is what passes for a No. 2 tight end in Los Angeles after Hunter Henry's injury, or at least what will pass until the Chargers sign one of the veteran free agents still floating around.

Daniel Brown, CHI: The Bears have kept Brown around since 2016, and he has been good for about 15 catches and 125 yards per season as a backup. He's facing stiffer competition this time to make the roster after the Bears added Trey Burton from Philadelphia, and they still have Dion Sims and 2017 second-round pick Adam Shaheen.

Derek Carrier, OAK: The journeyman comes home! Carrier was originally an undrafted free agent for Oakland in 2012, but never appeared in a game for the team. Six years and four teams later, he's back in the silver and black. Primarily a blocker, Carrier's most productive season came with Washington in 2015, with 17 receptions for 141 yards and 17 DYAR. Perhaps his old coach Jay Gruden got in touch with brother Jon to put in a few good words.

Brent Celek, FA: Celek retires ranked fourth on the Eagles' all-time receptions list (398), eighth in receiving yards (4,998), and 11th in receiving touchdowns. He played 11 seasons for the team and appeared in nine playoff games. Yet Football Outsiders' Mike Tanier, a career Eagles fan who has interviewed Celek on several occasions and written his name hundreds of times, never got straight whether his first name was "Brett" or "Brent" and had to look it up every time. Maybe he'll get it straight when Celek appears at the Super Bowl Tenth Anniversary celebration.

Tyler Conklin, MIN: Minnesota traded up 10 spots in the fifth round to get this former basketball player. Conklin had the second-best vertical jump (38 inches) at the combine among tight ends. He was a productive receiver at Central Michigan with 504 receiving yards in eight games in 2017. Minnesota hasn't had a second tight end break 125 receiving yards behind Kyle Rudolph in any of the last three years. But Kirk Cousins is used to playing in offenses that use multiple tight ends, so Conklin could be a factor in due time for Minnesota.

Anthony Fasano, FA: Fasano is nearing the end of the line on the field, but he's already doing some commendable things off of it. He opened up an all-male treatment center called "Next Chapter Addiction" in response to a family member hitting rock bottom. Fasano hasn't signed yet as we go to press, though that's not uncommon for players this old and with this skill set. If he wants to play, he can be someone's No. 2 tight end easily, even at this age.

Darren Fells, CLE: Fells originally entered the NFL as a basketball player project; he played at UC Irvine, which doesn't even have football. But for a basketball player project, he has turned into quite the talented blocker, and that's the main reason Cleveland signed him in free agency. He did catch 17-of-26 passes for 177 yards and 21.9% DVOA with the Lions last year, though.

Troy Fumagalli, DEN: Denver's fifth-round pick out of Wisconsin: your basic college tight end who runs and catches smoothly and blocks just well enough to get in a defender's way on a screen pass. Fumagalli is missing his left index finger, but it does not hamper his receiving skills, and he had a strong showing at Senior Bowl week. Fumagalli would be competing for a bottom-of-the-roster job on most teams, but the Broncos are so thin at tight end that he's one Jake Butt health setback away from getting regular touches in the offense.

Rico Gathers, DAL: The Cowboys drafted Gathers, a basketball player at Baylor, in the sixth round of 2016 even though he had not played football since middle school. He spent his rookie season on the practice squad and missed his sophomore year with a concussion. In between, though, he showed some big-play potential, with 25- and 26-yard touchdown catches in the preseason last year. Gathers is 6-foot-6 and 285 pounds and still only 24 years old, but early reports said he wasn't getting many chances in OTAs.

MarQueis Gray, MIA: "Hello and welcome to the Mike Tannenbaum School of Roster Management. I'm Mike Tannenbaum. Our first lesson for today is how to create an offseason tight end depth chart topped by a career special teamer. You start by making sure the entire scope of the depth chart is lousy, then, add in free agency! Voila, you've created a need to spend two draft picks on! Next week: How to use Mike Wallace to launder money."

Demetrius Harris, KC: Harris has quietly turned into a valuable second tight end for the Kansas City Chiefs. Since catching just three passes as a rookie in 2014, Harris has increased his production each season, scaling up to 18 receptions for 224 yards and a touchdown last year (-23.3% DVOA). Though his hands may be generally unreliable, Harris is a good athlete who dazzles once or twice with a fantastic play, only to return back to the shadows.

Christopher Herndon, NYJ: New York's fourth-round pick out of Miami. A torn MCL kept Herndon out of the pre-draft process, but he shows some proto H-back skills, plays special teams, and has shown to be a good blocker. There's upside here if he gets a little more polished as a route-runner, and even if he doesn't, Herndon should be able to fill in as a back-end guy on profile alone. A preseason DWI won't help him win the starting job.

Jeff Heuerman, DEN: Heuerman tore an ACL in rookie minicamp in 2015, redshirted for a year, missed a chunk of 2016 with ankle and hamstring issues, then spent most of 2017 healthy but failed to unseat tenured perma-prospect Virgil Green, managing only to upgrade his stat line from 9-141-0 all the way up to 9-142-2. Heuerman is the subject of regular John Elway edicts about needing to "step up" but could easily remain in the tight end rotation if anything happens to Jake Butt, another medical redshirt freshman. Heuerman's frequent injuries and imperceptible development wouldn't be a big problem if the Broncos didn't have about a dozen players on their roster just like him.

Ryan Hewitt, CIN: An H-back with good hands and anvils for blocking shoulders, once upon a time Hewitt would have been an extremely valuable chess piece. But in shotgun spread formations there is just no good place to use him. An offensive wizard might be able to pry some use out of Hewitt; it remains to be seen if Bill Lazor is that adept with the schematic wand.

Josh Hill, NO: Hill is already going into his sixth season as an undrafted free agent with the Saints. He has never been asked to take on much of a receiving burden, as the Saints have preferred for him to block while they throw to Jimmy Graham, Benjamin Watson, or Coby Fleener. Watson is back, which should again relegate Hill to his normal role even though he stepped up in the playoffs with 103 yards and a touchdown. Specifically, Hill had 49 yards in the wild-card round against Carolina, and then 54 a week later against Minnesota. He has only hit that mark twice in his 71 regular-season games, so it was an out-of-character stretch for Hill.

Jacob Hollister, NE: Hollister was handed a guaranteed $90,000 by the Patriots as an undrafted free agent, and he made an immediate impact on special teams. Although Hollister did not come into the league as a great blocker, he showed promise as a deep threat working with Josh Allen at Wyoming. This is the kind of guy who could suddenly make a non-Gronkowski tight end replaceable with a good training camp.

Lance Kendricks, GB: Kendricks had a career-low 203 receiving yards in his Green Bay debut last year, but isn't the surprising news that he has had more than 200 yards in all seven of his seasons? Kendricks spent most of his career stuck on bad offenses for the Rams, but his hopes of playing a full season with Aaron Rodgers were dashed last year thanks to the quarterback's collarbone injury. Now with Jimmy Graham in town, Kendricks will continue to be a TE2 at best, but he could be fantasy-viable if something goes awry with Graham. Kendricks also ranked first in snaps per blown block among tight ends last year.

Chris Manhertz, CAR: Manhertz has played 23 NFL games. He has just three receptions. Pretty much the platonic ideal of a blocking tight end, Manhertz will likely see an increase in snaps with Ed Dickson out of town. However, a left foot injury suffered in minicamp means he's going to miss some time during training camp, which will give some of the other tight ends on the roster the chance to pass him.

David Morgan, MIN: Morgan is sparingly used as a blocking tight end but did log more than 40 snaps in each of the season's final three games after Kyle Rudolph was not 100 percent. He could see some of his playing time challenged by rookie tight end Tyler Conklin, who is much more of a receiving threat than Morgan. It's not like Morgan is unapproachable as a blocker—he ranked next to last in snaps per blown block in 2017.

Troy Niklas, NE: Niklas seemed to have a lot of positive attributes coming out of Notre Dame as a big, agile, converted front-seven defender. But it's hard to believe in anybody who couldn't seize the starting role in Arizona. Injuries definitely played a part in Niklas' stagnation and were a big reason the Cardinals gave up on him. Now with the Patriots, he'll be depth. As Bruce Matthews' nephew, he's perhaps the least successful Matthews relative of the past 10 years outside of Casey. He also didn't get the Matthews blocking genetics, ranking dead last among tight ends in snaps per blown block (minimum 200 blocking snaps).

James O'Shaughnessy, JAX: O'Shaughnessy started three of the Jaguars' final four games last season, including two of the three playoff contests. Even then, he only had two catches across the four games—the same number as fellow backup tight end Ben Koyack. O'Shaughnessy and Koyack will likely fall further down the pecking order with the arrival of Niles Paul and Austin Seferian-Jenkins, leaving them fighting over the same playing-time scraps.

Niles Paul, JAX: A seven-year veteran who was drafted as a wide receiver, Paul converted to tight end ahead of his sophomore professional season then spent most of his Washington career sitting third on a crowded depth chart. In 2014, with Fred Davis retired and Jordan Reed missing time due to a persistent hamstring injury, Paul started seven games and posted a 24.4% DVOA, hauling in 75 percent of a career-high 52 targets for 507 yards and one touchdown. He then dislocated his ankle and missed the entire 2015 season. Paul only has 29 receptions on 49 targets across his other six seasons but was a special teams captain in Washington. He should be perfectly adequate for the Jaguars as a backup receiving tight end and a stalwart on special teams.

Logan Paulsen, ATL: Paulsen was targeted only times last season despite playing in 14 games for the 49ers. Since 2014, Paulsen has yet to receive more than 16 targets in a season even though he played all 16 games in 2014 and 2016. Paulsen was brought in to be a run blocker (where he actually is effective) and to be a special teams player.

Michael Roberts, DET: A fourth-round pick in 2017, Roberts caught four passes in his preseason debut, but only contributed four catches in the whole regular season. More opportunities should be there in 2018 since the team let starter Eric Ebron go, but Roberts will have to compete with Luke Willson and Levine Toilolo for snaps.

Richard Rodgers, PHI: Rodgers' role evaporated into a series of one-catch, 3- to 8-yard stat lines last year, when both Martellus Bennett (when healthy) and Lance Kendricks played larger roles in the Packers offense. Rodgers' 2015 season (510 yards, 8 TD) looks more like a fluke each year. Now in Philly, Rodgers will compete with rookie Dallas Goedert for a backup role behind Zach Ertz. The Eagles have roles for three tight ends. Expect Rodgers to be the third one.

Eric Saubert, ATL: One of the team's three fifth-round picks in 2017, Eric Saubert only saw 30 offensive snaps throughout the entire season. Austin Hooper and Levine Toilolo were entrenched as the top two tight ends, so there wasn't really an opportunity for him to get offensive snaps. If you've seen his performance in the East-West Shrine Game, you'd probably agree a quasi-redshirt season was what he needed. Now he'll have a chance to battle for the No. 2 tight end spot with Logan Paulsen. Saubert has the potential to be a much, much more dynamic receiver than Paulsen, so he might have the edge there if he can provide competent blocking.

Dalton Schultz, DAL: Schultz was drafted 137th overall this year, meaning he went off the board 80 picks earlier than any other Cowboys tight end did in their respective draft classes. At Stanford, Schultz's primary duty was to clear space for Christian McCaffrey and Bryce Love, but he still managed to catch 55 passes for 555 yards and five touchdowns (seriously) for the Cardinal. He has the highest ceiling of any tight end in Dallas and could be starting sooner rather than later.

Dion Sims, CHI: Sims is the league's milquetoast tight end. He's good enough to start games, but he has never been able to impress enough to take a bigger role in any offense. He peaked with 284 receiving yards in 2014 with Miami. Sims is now in his second season with Chicago, where the Bears have big hopes for free-agent acquisition Trey Burton from Philadelphia. Look for Sims to keep up his usual job of starting games, sometimes catching passes, sometimes blocking, and rarely leaving an impression.

Lee Smith, OAK: Jon Gruden mostly ignored the Raiders tight end depth chart when he realized that it was already loaded with 30-plus-year-old knockaround journeymen and therefore could not be improved upon. At least Smith is the right kind of tight end knockaround journeyman: a blocking specialist, who ranked fourth in snaps per blown block last year.

Durham Smythe, MIA: A fourth-round pick more lauded for his blocking than his receiving—there aren't a lot of tight ends like this coming out of college these days—Smythe lands in a spot where he basically continues the Anthony Fasano chain if all goes right. He'll be the blocking tight end from Notre Dame with the skill to get open and fall down after a 7-yard dig.

Jeremy Sprinkle, WAS: On a team that has Jordan Reed and Vernon Davis, there just wasn't much playing time for a fifth-round rookie, and so Sprinkle's rookie production was limited to just two catches (though he did score a touchdown against the Saints in Week 11). Reed and Davis are both still in D.C., so the Arkansas alumnus will likely struggle to get on the field again in 2018.

Neal Sterling, NYJ: The Jaguars drafted Sterling out of Monmouth and converted him to tight end. The Jets thought enough of him to give him the RFA $1.9 million contract after, you guessed it, plucking him off the Chiefs practice squad. The Jets tight end depth chart is definitely a place where you can envision just about anybody getting snaps, so there's that.

Geoff Swaim, DAL: The top news story on Swaim's Rotoworld page in June examined Dallas' committee of tight ends heading into training camp; the next three stories covered the surgeries Swaim has had on his knee, foot, and pectorals over the years. There's not much else to say about a tight end who has nine catches in three seasons, but Swaim is the grizzled vet of the crew. He's useful as a blocker, but a lack of receiving ability appears to have cost him the starting job in favor of Blake Jarwin.

Erik Swoope, IND: 2017 could have been the breakout season for basketball convert Swoope, but a training camp knee injury ended up sidelining him for the season. The addition of Eric Ebron limits him to a TE3 role barring injury.

Ian Thomas, CAR: Drafted at the top of the fourth round, Thomas is a long-term project at tight end. He has the strength, hands, and raw talent position coaches would love to mold, but lacks the experience and polish necessary to contribute right away. He jumped from junior college to Indiana, although injuries limited his production as a senior. With Ed Dickson out of town, there is a spot open in Carolina, but Thomas may not be quite ready to step in as a rookie.

Logan Thomas, BUF: Hey look, it's what would have happened to Tim Tebow if he had continued to play football! We'll always have those early mock drafts where Thomas was No. 1 overall after his freshman season.

Levine Toilolo, DET: Toilolo averaged 9.2 receiving yards per game in five seasons with Atlanta, so in the words of Marshawn Lynch, y'all know why he's here in Detroit. Toilolo will look to take over the blocking role that Darren Fells had last year.

Eric Tomlinson, NYJ: "Hello and welcome to the Mike Maccagnan School of Roster Management, I'm Mike Maccagnan, the only person on the planet who knows who Eric Tomlinson is or why he's near the top of an NFL depth chart. I brought you this UTEP blocker who looks like a metal singer to expand your horizons. Tune in next time, when we talk about how to roster 17 different No. 3 receivers!"

Austin Traylor, DEN: A former undrafted rookie from Wisconsin, Traylor cycled through four different camps and practice squads before landing in Denver, where no tight end is too obscure to end up with three starts and eight receptions.

C.J. Uzomah, CIN: Unlike Tyler Kroft, Uzomah didn't make much hay while Tyler Eifert was out. Uzomah is gifted athletically but still very raw after three seasons. He's in a battle with Mason Schreck and special teams ace Cethan Carter to be the third tight end, though Eifert's frailty gives Uzomah a fighting chance for a roster spot.

Clive Walford, NYJ: Walford was a physically impressive prospect whom the Raiders never seemed to find a fit to feature. An ATV crash in 2016 lost Walford time, and Oakland then decided Jared Cook was better for some reason. Perhaps he's this year's Austin Seferian-Jenkins? It's not like anyone in front of him on the depth chart is intimidating. The real question will be how much of Walford's college skill set survived the ATV crash.

Brandon Williams, FA: A basketball convert who has made his bones as a depth tight end and special teams player, the 30-year-old Williams' 13 catches in 2017 more than doubled his career total. Unsigned as of publication.

Maxx Williams, BAL: Seems like just yesterday that Double-X was the hot rookie drafted to be the deep-seam mismatch tight end in the passing game. Then he tore up his knee so badly the team couldn't even describe it, simply calling it "rare" and "something no other player has had." We still don't really know much about it, and it happened in 2016. Pro football has taught us all so much about the myriad ways the human body can be rent asunder that when something new comes along, the shock factor is real. Williams played last year but his special traits were gone; hence, the club drafted a pair of guys to replace him. Whether Williams is on the Ravens roster, on a different team, or even in football by September is open for debate.

2018 Kicker Projections

isted below are the 2018 KUBIAK projections for kickers. Because of the inconsistency of field goal percentage from year to year, kickers are projected almost entirely based on team forecasts, although a handful of individual factors do come into play:

- More experience leads to a slightly higher field goal percentage in general, with the biggest jump between a kicker's rookie and sophomore seasons.
- Kickers with a better career field goal percentage tend to get more attempts, although they are not necessarily more accurate.
- Field goal percentage on kicks over 40 yards tends to

regress to the mean.

Kickers are listed with their total fantasy points based on two different scoring systems. For **Pts1**, all field goals are worth three points. For **Pts2**, all field goals up to 39 yards are worth three points, field goals of 40-49 yards are worth four points, and field goals over 50 yards are worth five points. Kickers are also listed with a Risk of Green, Yellow, or Red, as explained in the introduction to the section on quarterbacks.

Note that field goal totals below are rounded, but "fantasy points" are based on the actual projections, so the total may not exactly equal (FG * 3 + XP).

Fantasy Kicker Projections, 2018

Kicker	Team	FG	Pct	XP	Pts1	Pts2	Risk	Kicker	Team	FG	Pct	XP	Pts1	Pts2	Risk
Greg Zuerlein	LAR	35-38	92%	37	141	159	Yellow	Steven Hauschka	BUF	29-34	85%	26	113	125	Green
Stephen Gostkowski	NE	31-36	86%	46	140	155	Green	Jason Sanders	MIA	26-33	79%	34	112	124	Yellow
Justin Tucker	BAL	34-38	89%	32	135	156	Green	Randy Bullock	CIN	27-32	84%	30	112	123	Yellow
Adam Vinatieri	IND	31-36	86%	40	132	150	Green	Cody Parkey	CHI	27-31	87%	32	112	125	Yellow
Matt Bryant	ATL	31-35	89%	38	131	149	Yellow	Giorgio Tavecchio	OAK	24-32	75%	37	110	121	Green
Chris Boswell	PIT	30-33	91%	40	129	142	Red	Graham Gano	CAR	24-27	89%	36	109	121	Green
Jake Elliott	PHI	29-35	83%	39	127	143	Red	Daniel Carlson	MIN	23-28	82%	40	109	119	Green
Matt Prater	DET	29-35	83%	38	126	144	Red	Brandon McManus	DEN	25-33	76%	32	108	119	Green
Robbie Gould	SF	31-34	91%	33	126	140	Yellow	Chandler Catanzaro	TB	23-29	79%	35	104	115	Green
Dan Bailey	DAL	29-35	83%	39	126	139	Yellow	Dustin Hopkins	WAS	22-29	76%	37	104	113	Red
Mason Crosby	GB	28-35	80%	41	126	137	Green	Zane Gonzalez	CLE	22-29	76%	37	102	113	Green
Phil Dawson	ARI	29-35	83%	37	124	137	Green	Cairo Santos	NYJ	22-32	69%	33	100	108	Red
Ryan Succop	TEN	29-35	83%	36	122	135	Green	Aldrick Rosas	NYG	20-27	74%	33	93	103	Red
Sebastian Janikowski	SEA	27-34	79%	38	120	132	Yellow								

Other kickers who may win jobs:

Kicker	Team	FG	Pct	XP	Pts1	Pts2	Risk
Caleb Sturgis (LAC)							

Kicker	Team	FG	Pct	XP	Pts1	Pts2	Risk
Greg Joseph	MIA	26-33	79%	34	112	124	Yellow
Kai Forbath	MIN	27-31	87%	39	119	132	Yellow
Eddy Pineiro	OAK	25-31	81%	35	109	121	Red
Jason Myers	SEA	24-32	75%	39	110	121	Yellow

Kicker	Team	FG	Pct	XP	Pts1	Pts2	Risk
Caleb Sturgis	LAC	26-30	87%	39	118	130	Yellow
Ka'imi Fairbairn	HOU	26-32	81%	40	118	130	Green
Josh Lambo	JAX	28-32	88%	34	118	132	Red
Wil Lutz	NO	25-30	83%	41	116	128	Green
Harrison Butker	KC	27-32	84%	34	116	129	Red

2018 Fantasy Defense Projections

Listed below are the 2018 KUBIAK projections for fantasy team defense. The projection method is discussed in an essay in *Pro Football Prospectus 2006*, the key conclusions of which were:

- Schedule strength is very important for projecting fantasy defense.
- Categories used for scoring in fantasy defense have no consistency from year-to-year whatsoever, with the exception of sacks and interceptions.

Fumble recoveries and defensive touchdowns are forecast solely based on the projected sacks and interceptions, rather than the team's totals in these categories from a year ago. This is why the 2018 projections may look very different from the fantasy defense values from the 2017 season. Safeties and shutouts are not common enough to have a significant effect on the projections. Team defenses are also projected with Risk factor of Green, Yellow, or Red; this is based on the team's projection compared to performance in recent seasons.

In addition to projection of separate categories, we also give an overall total based on our generic fantasy scoring formula: one point for a sack, two points for a fumble recovery or interception, and six points for a touchdown. Remember that certain teams (for example, the Rams) will score better if your league also gives points for limiting opponents' scoring or yardage. Special teams touchdowns are listed separately and are not included in the fantasy scoring total listed.

Fantasy Team Defense Projections, 2018

Team	Fant Pts	Sack	Int	Fum Rec	Def TD	Risk	ST TD	Team	Fant Pts	Sack	Int	Fum Rec	Def TD	Risk	ST TD
MIN	113	40.6	15.9	10.5	3.2	Red	0.4	CIN	96	35.9	13.2	9.6	2.4	Red	0.5
LAR	109	43.5	16.5	8.9	2.5	Yellow	0.5	ATL	94	33.9	13.6	8.8	2.5	Yellow	0.6
PIT	107	44.2	16.5	8.6	2.0	Red	0.7	LAC	93	34.4	13.7	9.3	2.2	Green	0.5
JAX	103	38.9	13.3	8.9	3.3	Green	0.9	DET	93	33.8	13.4	9.3	2.3	Red	1.0
NO	102	36.9	15.8	9.8	2.4	Red	0.6	DEN	93	38.1	12.9	9.0	1.8	Yellow	0.5
PHI	100	38.5	15.3	9.1	2.2	Green	0.8	NYJ	93	32.2	13.2	7.6	3.1	Red	0.5
GB	100	38.8	14.9	8.8	2.3	Yellow	0.6	BAL	92	36.8	14.6	8.4	1.5	Green	0.5
NE	100	41.6	14.8	9.7	1.6	Red	0.5	OAK	91	36.2	12.3	8.8	2.0	Red	0.5
CLE	100	39.2	13.1	9.9	2.5	Red	0.5	IND	91	33.6	13.2	9.5	1.9	Red	0.7
SEA	100	35.1	14.3	8.8	3.1	Yellow	0.7	BUF	90	31.3	14.8	8.2	2.1	Yellow	0.6
TEN	99	38.3	14.1	8.9	2.5	Red	0.6	SF	88	35.0	12.7	7.9	2.0	Red	0.6
HOU	99	38.8	14.1	8.8	2.3	Red	0.3	CHI	87	34.6	12.2	7.5	2.2	Yellow	0.8
CAR	98	41.0	13.1	10.1	1.8	Yellow	0.6	KC	86	32.9	12.6	7.2	2.3	Green	0.7
WAS	98	36.6	13.9	8.1	2.9	Yellow	0.5	MIA	85	32.1	12.5	8.5	1.8	Green	0.4
ARI	98	34.9	14.2	9.7	2.6	Yellow	0.5	NYG	83	31.2	12.2	7.1	2.2	Green	0.5
DAL	98	35.2	14.7	8.9	2.5	Red	0.7	TB	81	29.9	12.0	8.0	1.8	Green	0.5

Projected Defensive Leaders, 2018

Solo Tackles			Total Tackles			Sacks			Interceptions		
Player	Team	Tkl	Player	Team	Tkl	Player	Team	Sacks	Player	Team	Int
K.Alexander	TB	93	B.Wagner	SEA	138	J.Bosa	LAC	12.6	M.Peters	LAR	3.4
S.Lee	DAL	92	S.Lee	DAL	135	K.Mack	OAK	12.3	A.Bethea	ARI	3.3
T.Smith	JAX	91	L.Kuechly	CAR	135	C.Jones	ARI	11.7	T.White	BUF	3.2
B.Wagner	SEA	90	T.Edmunds	BUF	132	T.Suggs	BAL	11.0	M.Hooker	IND	3.2
D.Jones	ATL	90	D.Jones	ATL	132	D.Lawrence	DAL	10.9	H.Smith	MIN	3.1
R.Jones	MIA	87	C.Kirksey	CLE	131	V.Beasley	ATL	10.7	X.Howard	MIA	3.1
L.David	TB	86	C.J.Mosley	BAL	130	D.Hunter	MIN	10.6	M.Williams	NO	3.1
M.Barron	LAR	85	Z.Brown	WAS	127	M.Garrett	CLE	10.5	E.Weddle	BAL	3.1
B.Martinez	GB	85	K.Alexander	TB	125	V.Miller	DEN	10.5	D.Slay	DET	3.0
L.Kuechly	CAR	85	L.David	TB	122	R.Kerrigan	WAS	10.4	J.Evans	TB	2.9
C.J.Mosley	BAL	84	B.Martinez	GB	121	C.Jordan	NO	10.1	K.Byard	TEN	2.9
Z.Brown	WAS	84	B.McKinney	HOU	121	J.J.Watt	HOU	10.1	R.McLeod	PHI	2.8

College Football Introduction and Statistical Toolbox

Nick Saban's Alabama Crimson Tide began and ended the 2017 college football season at No. 1. They won the College Football Playoff with wins over annual CFP foe Clemson and SEC rival Georgia. It was their fifth title in the last nine seasons, an almost unprecedented run of dominance even in a sport long controlled by blue bloods.

Everything about the above paragraph is true. But it doesn't quite feel right. Alabama is indeed on an unprecedented run at the moment, but the Tide needed a little bit of magic in 2017, both to get into the CFP and to win it when they got there. They lost to Auburn to end the regular season, missing out on a spot in the SEC title game. They needed Ohio State to beat undefeated Wisconsin in the Big Ten Championship just to secure the No. 4 seed in the CFP. And once there, though they vanquished Clemson with ease, they found themselves down 13-0 and desperate at halftime against Georgia.

The title was saved with youth. Freshman quarterback Tua Tagovailoa entered the game in the third quarter and cut Georgia's lead to 13-7 with a touchdown pass to freshman Henry Ruggs III. Freshman Najee Harris's 35-yard run set up a field goal to cut the lead to 20-13 early in the fourth, and after a second Tagovailoa touchdown pass sent the game to overtime, his second-and-long bomb to freshman DeVonta Smith won the game, 26-23.

There are two ways to look at how the 2017 season ended. Either it was the beginning of the end of the Tide dynasty … or the beginning of a new one.

Beginning of the end?

It only took Georgia head coach Kirby Smart two seasons to take the Dawgs to the precipice. The former Saban defensive coordinator nearly took down the Tide on the field, and about a month after the national title game, he polished off a different kind of win, as Georgia became the first non-Bama team in years to finish No. 1 in the recruiting rankings. Urban Meyer's Ohio State finished second, and Alabama, No. 1 every year this decade, finished only sixth per the 247Sports Composite.

Georgia is only going to grow more loaded in the coming seasons, even if the Dawgs take a brief step backwards this year following the loss of top draft picks like linebacker Roquan Smith (the eighth pick to the Bears), offensive tackle Isaiah Wynn (23rd, Patriots), running backs Sony Michel (31st, Patriots) and Nick Chubb (35th, Browns), and linebacker Lorenzo Carter (66th, Giants). Meanwhile, Ohio State has maybe its most purely talented team ever, and Clemson returns almost everyone from last season's ACC champ and CFP semifinalist.

Saban is falling victim to a lot of the things that can catch up to even the most successful coaches. He's on his fifth offensive coordinator in six years, and now that defensive coordinator Jeremy Pruitt—who succeeded Smart in 2016—has become Tennessee's head coach, he's on his third DC in four years, too. When you win a lot, you lose a lot of assistants to other jobs, and eventually iffy hires or a lack of continuity drag you down. Just ask former Florida State great Bobby Bowden.

Same story, new cast?

Of course, all that turnover *did* catch up to Alabama somewhat last year. And the Tide went out and won anyway. And now, all of those blue-chip freshmen who saved Saban's bacon last year are sophomores. Tagovailoa is a Heisman favorite. The receiving corps looks loaded. And while the defense has to deal with quite a bit of turnover, the last time Bama *didn't* have an elite defense was 2007, Saban's first year.

Oh yeah, and at press time, Alabama has the No. 1 recruiting class for 2019.

When Saban's dynasty ends, it'll look like 2017—desperation on the field and a new king in recruits' living rooms. But the old *The Wire* principle could still be at play here: if you come at the king, you best not miss. Georgia missed. And Alabama is still the king until otherwise noted.

Welcome to the college football portion of *Football Outsiders Almanac 2018* and our deep dive into the numbers that will shape the 2018 season. Since 2003, Brian Fremeau has been developing and enhancing the drive-based Fremeau Efficiency Index (FEI) and its companion statistics; for the last ten years, Bill Connelly has explored play-by-play and drive data to refine his system, the S&P+ ratings. Both systems are opponent-adjusted and effective in evaluating team strengths and weaknesses.

The College Statistical Toolbox section that follows this introduction explains the methodology of FEI, S&P+, F/+, and other stats you will encounter in the college chapters of this book. There are similarities to Football Outsiders' NFL-based DVOA ratings in the combined approach, but college football presents a unique set of challenges different from the NFL. All football stats must be adjusted according to context, but how? If Team A and Team B do not play one another and don't share any common opponents, how can their stats be effectively compared? Should a team from the SEC or Big 12 be measured against that of an average team in its own conference, or an average team across all conferences?

Our mission is to continue to drill deeper into the statistical measures that fuel success on the field for each and every FBS team, though this book is particularly focused on the playoff and conference contenders for the year ahead. Each of the 50 team capsules provides a snapshot of the team's projection for 2018 and the statistical factors that went into the projection. The capsules also included a game-by-game graphic highlighting our projected win likelihoods for the year ahead. Supplementing the stat work, college football staff writers Chad Peltier and Ian Boyd explore player and coaching personnel changes, offensive and defensive advantages and deficiencies, and schedule highlights and pitfalls in a thorough summary of each team's keys to the upcoming season.

For each of the 130 FBS teams, we project the likelihood of every possible regular-season record, conference and non-conference alike. We've included division, overall conference, and College Football Playoff projections for every team as well.

By taking two different statistical approaches to reach one exciting series of answers to college football's most important questions, we're confident we have the tools to answer key questions and spark new insights to the game we love.

College Statistics Toolbox: Regular readers of FootballOutsiders.com may be familiar with the FEI and S&P+ stats published throughout the year. Others may be learning about our advanced approach to college football stats analysis for the first time by reading this book. In either case, this College Statistics Toolbox section is highly recommended reading before getting into the conference chapters. The stats that form the building blocks for F/+, FEI, and S&P+ are constantly being updated and refined.

Each team profile begins with a statistical snapshot. The projected overall and conference records—rounded from the team's projected Mean Wins—are listed alongside the team name in the header. Other stats and rankings provided in the team snapshot and highlighted in the team capsules are explained below.

Drive-by-Drive Data

Fremeau Efficiency Index: The Fremeau Efficiency Index (FEI) is based on opponent-adjusted drive efficiency. Approximately 20,000 possessions are contested annual in FBS vs. FBS games. First-half clock-kills and end-of-game garbage drives are filtered out. Unadjusted game efficiency is a measure of net success on non-garbage possessions, the success of the offensive, defensive, and special teams units in terms of maximizing the team's own scoring opportunities and minimizing those of its opponent. FEI opponent adjustments are calculated with an emphasis placed on quality performances against good teams, win or lose.

Offensive and Defensive FEI: Maximizing success on offensive possessions and minimizing success on opponent possessions begins with an understanding of the value of field position. An average offense facing an average defense may expect to score 2.1 points on average at the conclusion of the drive. If that drive begins at the offense's own 15-yard line, the average scoring value is only 1.5 points. If it begins at the opponent's 15-yard line, the average scoring value is 4.9 points. Offensive and defensive efficiency is in part a function of the variable value of starting field position.

Likewise, drive-ending field position is an important component as well. Touchdowns represent the ultimate goal of an offensive possession, but drives that fall short of the end zone can add scoring value as well. National field goal success rates correlate strongly with proximity to the end zone, and an offense that drives deep into opponent territory to set up a chip shot field goal generates more scoring value than one that ends a drive at the edge of or outside field goal range.

The basic value generated by an offense on a given possession is the difference between the drive-ending value and the value of field position at the start of the drive. Offensive efficiency is the average per-possession value generated or lost by the offense. Defensive efficiency is the average per-possession value generated or lost by the defense. Offensive FEI and Defensive FEI are the opponent-adjusted per-possession values generated or lost by these units.

Play-by-Play Data

In January 2014, Bill Connelly introduced a new set of concepts for analysis and debate within the realm of college football stats. At Football Study Hall, a college football stats

No. 1 Alabama Crimson Tide

2018 Projections			Projection Factors		
F/+	52.7 (1)		2017 F/+	53.4 (1)	
FEI	.279 (1)		2017 FEI	.305 (2)	
S&P+	26.9 (2)		2017 S&P+	20.0 (2)	
Total Wins	10.7		5-Year F/+	65.2 (1)	
Conf Wins	6.8		5-Year FEI	.303 (1)	
SOS	.073 (35)		5-Year S&P+	25.8 (1)	
Conf SOS	.097 (26)		2-Yr/5-Yr Recruiting	4/1	
Div Champ	63%		Ret. Offense	62% (83)	
Conf Champ	32%		Ret. Defense	53% (102)	
CFP Berth	37%		Ret. Total	58% (102)	

Projected Win Likelihood by Game

Date	Opponent (Proj Rank)	PWL	Projected Loss / Projected Win
Sep 1	vs Louisville (28)	87%	
Sep 8	vs Arkansas St. (70)	99%	
Sep 15	at Ole Miss (31)	84%	
Sep 22	vs Texas A&M (25)	88%	
Sep 29	vs UL-Lafayette (116)	99%	
Oct 6	at Arkansas (51)	95%	
Oct 13	vs Missouri (40)	95%	
Oct 20	at Tennessee (72)	99%	
Nov 3	at LSU (19)	71%	
Nov 10	vs Mississippi St. (14)	78%	
Nov 17	vs Citadel (FCS)	100%	
Nov 24	vs Auburn (5)	71%	

site within the SB Nation network, he wrote the following: "Over time, I've come to realize that the sport comes down to five basic things, four of which you can mostly control. You make more big plays than your opponent, you stay on schedule, you tilt the field, you finish drives, and you fall on the ball. *Explosiveness, efficiency, field position, finishing drives, and turnovers are the five factors to winning football games.*"

Unlike the Four Factors used by ESPN's Dean Oliver for discussion of basketball, these factors are heavily related to each other. But looking at these factors individually can allow you to quickly home in on a given team's strengths and weaknesses in a way that looking at total yardage or even yards per play cannot.

Success Rates: Efficiency is by far the most predictive and vital of the factors. Without it, you find yourself in unfavorable downs and distances (which can lead to either turnovers or unfavorable downs and distances for your offense or a lack thereof for your defense), and your offense can't stay on the field long enough to generate big plays.

The most effective tool for efficiency measurement is success rate. More than one million plays over the last ten years in college football have been collected and evaluated to determine baselines for success for every situational down in a game. Similar to DVOA, basic success rates are determined by national standards. The distinction for college football is in defining the standards of success. We use the following determination of a "successful" play:

- First down success = 50 percent of necessary yardage
- Second down success = 70 percent of necessary yardage
- Third/Fourth down success = 100 percent of necessary yardage

On a per play basis, these form the standards of efficiency for every offense in college football. Defensive success rates are based on preventing the same standards of achievement.

Equivalent Points and Isolated Points per Play (IsoPPP): All yards are not created equal. A 10-yard gain from a team's own 15-yard line does not have the same value as a 10-yard gain that goes from the opponent's 10-yard line into the end zone. Based on expected scoring rates by field position, we calculate a point value for each play in a drive. Equivalent Points (EqPts) are calculated by subtracting the value of the resulting yard line from the initial yard line of a given play. This assigns credit to the yards that are most associated with scoring points, the end goal in any possession.

With EqPts, the game can be broken down and built back up again in a number of ways. Average EqPts per play (PPP) measures consistency and IsoPPP measures EqPts per play on successful plays only as a way to isolate of explosiveness. For the S&P+ formula, IsoPPP is used, which allows us to ask two specific questions:

1. How frequently successful are you (consistency)?
2. When you're successful, *how* successful are you (magnitude)?

A boom-or-bust running back may have an excellent per carry average and IsoPPP, but his low Success Rate will lower his S&P. A consistent running back that gains between four and six yards every play, on the other hand, will have a strong Success Rate but low IsoPPP. The best offenses in the country can maximize both efficiency and explosiveness on a down-by-down basis. Reciprocally, the best defenses can limit both.

S&P+: Along with applying extra weight for plays inside the opponent's 40, plus a selection of other field position and turnover factors, success rate and IsoPPP make up the meat of the S&P+ formula.

As with the FEI stats discussed above, context matters in college football. Adjustments are made to the S&P unadjusted data with a formula that takes into account a team's production, the quality of the opponent, and the quality of the opponent's opponent. To eliminate the noise of less-informative blowout stats, we filtered the play-by-play data to include only those that took place when the game was "close." This excludes plays where the score margin is larger than 28 points in the first quarter, 24 points in the second quarter, 21 points in the third quarter, or 16 points in the fourth quarter.

The combination of the play-by-play and drive data gives us S&P+, a comprehensive measure that represents a team's efficiency and explosiveness as compared to all other teams in college football. S&P+ values are calibrated around adjusted scoring averages. Taking a team's percentile ratings and applying it to a normal distribution of points scored in a given season, can give us an interesting, descriptive look at a team's performance in a given season.

Highlight Yards: Highlight yards represent the yards gained by a runner outside of those credited to the offensive line through adjusted line yards. The ALY formula, much like the same stat in the NFL, gives 100 percent credit to all yards gained between zero and four yards and 50 percent strength to yards between five and 10. If a runner gains 12 yards in a given carry, and we attribute 7.0 of those yards to the line, and the player's highlight yardage on the play is 5.0 yards. Beginning in 2013, we began calculating highlight yardage averages in a slightly different manner: Instead of dividing total highlight yardage by a player's overall number of carries, we divide it only by the number of carries that gain more than four yards; if a line is given all credit for gains smaller than that, then it makes sense to look at highlight averages only for the carries on which a runner got a chance to create a highlight.

Opportunity Rate: Opportunity Rate represents the percentage of a runner's carries that gained at least five yards. This gives us a look at a runner's (and his line's) consistency and efficiency to go along with the explosiveness measured by Highlight Yards.

Havoc Rate: Havoc rate is a quick glance at defensive disruption. It is the sum total of tackles for loss, passes defensed (intercepted or broken up), and forced fumbles divided by total plays. We produce Havoc rate for total defense as well as split into front seven and defensive backfield. These rankings can be found during the season at FootballOutsiders.com.

Combination Data

F/+: Introduced in *Football Outsiders Almanac 2009*, the F/+ measure combines FEI and S&P+. There is a clear distinction between the two individual approaches, and merging the two diminishes certain outliers caused by the quirks of each method. The resulting metric is both powerfully predictive and sensibly evaluative.

Projected F/+: Relative to the pros, college football teams are much more consistent in year-to-year performance. Breakout seasons and catastrophic collapses certainly occur, but generally speaking, teams can be expected to play within a reasonable range of their baseline program expectations. The idea of a Football Outsiders program rating began with the introduction of Program FEI in *Pro Football Prospectus 2008* as a way to represent those individual baseline expectations.

As the strength of the F/+ system has been fortified with more seasons of full drive-by-drive and play-by-play data, the Program F/+ measure has emerged. Program F/+ is calculated from five years of FEI and S&P+ data. The result not only represents the status of each team's program power but provides the first step in projecting future success. For each team statistical profile, we provide each team's five-year ratings profile and other projection factors that are included in the formula for the Projected FEI, Projected S&P+, and Projected F/+ ratings.

Recruiting success rates are based on a blend of Rivals.com and 247Sports.com recruiting ratings. The percentile rating for each team's two-year recruiting success and five-year recruiting success reflect the potential impact for both recent star-studded classes and the depth of talent for each team. Our returning experience data represents the percentage of production that returns to the roster this fall rather than a simple count of players labeled as starters. Program F/+ ratings are a function of program ratings and these recruiting and returning production transition factors.

Strength of Schedule: Unlike other rating systems, our Strength of Schedule (SOS) calculation is not a simple average of the Projected F/+ data of each team's opponents. Instead, it represents the likelihood that an elite team (typical top-five team) would win every game on the given schedule. The distinction is valid. For any elite team, playing No. 1 Alabama and No. 130 Alabama-Birmingham in a two-game stretch is certainly more difficult than playing No. 65 Syracuse and No. 66 Temple. An average rating might judge these schedules to be equal.

The likelihood of an undefeated season is calculated as the product of individual game projected win likelihoods. Generally speaking, an elite team may have a 75 percent chance of defeating a team ranked No. 10, an 85 percent chance of defeating a team ranked No. 20, and a 95 percent chance of defeating a team ranked No. 40. Combined, the elite team has a 61 percent likelihood of defeating all three (0.75 x 0.85 x 0.95 = 0.606).

A lower SOS rating represents a lower likelihood of an elite team running the table, and thus a stronger schedule. For our calculations of FBS versus FCS games, with all due apologies to North Dakota State et al., the likelihood of victory is 100 percent in the formula.

Mean Wins and Win Probabilities: To project records for each team, we use Projected F/+ and win likelihood formulas to estimate the likelihood of victory for a given team in its individual games. The probabilities for winning each game are added together to represent the average number of wins the team is expected to tally over the course of its scheduled games. Potential conference championship games and bowl games are not included.

The projected records listed next to each team name in the conference chapters are rounded from the mean wins data listed in the team capsule. Mean Wins are not intended to represent projected outcomes of specific matchups; rather they are our most accurate forecast for the team's season as a whole. The correlation of mean projected wins to actual wins is 0.69 for all games, 0.61 for conference games.

Win likelihoods are also used to produce the likelihood of each team winning a division or championship. Our College Football Playoff appearance likelihoods are a function of each team's likelihood to go undefeated or finish the season with one loss as well as the strength of the team's conference and overall schedule, factors that the CFP selection committee considers in their process.

The Win Probability tables that appear in each conference chapter are also based on the game-by-game win likelihood data for each team. The likelihood for each record is rounded to the nearest whole percent.

Brian Fremeau and Bill Connelly

NCAA Top 50

1. Alabama Crimson Tide (11-1, 7-1)

2018 Projections

F/+	52.7 (1)
FEI	.279 (1)
S&P+	26.9 (2)
Total Wins	10.7
Conf Wins	6.8
SOS	.073 (35)
Conf SOS	.097 (26)
Div Champ	63%
Conf Champ	32%
CFP Berth	37%

Projection Factors

2017 F/+	53.4 (1)
2017 FEI	.305 (2)
2017 S&P+	20.0 (2)
5-Year F/+	65.2 (1)
5-Year FEI	.303 (1)
5-Year S&P+	25.8 (1)
2-Yr/5-Yr Recruiting	4/1
Ret. Offense	62% (83)
Ret. Defense	53% (102)
Ret. Total	58% (102)

Projected Win Likelihood by Game

Date	Opponent (Proj Rank)	PWL
Sep 1	vs Louisville (28)	87%
Sep 8	vs Arkansas St. (70)	99%
Sep 15	at Ole Miss (31)	84%
Sep 22	vs Texas A&M (25)	88%
Sep 29	vs UL-Lafayette (116)	99%
Oct 6	at Arkansas (51)	95%
Oct 13	vs Missouri (40)	95%
Oct 20	at Tennessee (72)	99%
Nov 3	at LSU (19)	71%
Nov 10	vs Mississippi St. (14)	78%
Nov 17	vs Citadel (FCS)	100%
Nov 24	vs Auburn (5)	71%

Another season, another Crimson Tide national championship. And another preseason where Alabama sits on top of the F/+ preseason projections. It's not just Football Outsiders, either: Athlon, CBS Sports, and Yahoo Sports (among others) have Alabama on top of their preseason forecasts as well.

But Alabama's place among the preseason top teams was never in doubt. The focus through spring practice has instead revolved around two big questions: did Tua Tagovailoa's national championship-winning touchdown throw cement him as the favorite at quarterback over Jalen Hurts? And how are the Crimson Tide going to replace all six defensive backs from their dime package, including all-everything Minkah Fitzpatrick?

Everyone knows the Jalen vs. Tua storyline by now. Hurts was benched at halftime in the National Championship Game after completing just three of eight passes for 21 yards. Alabama was shut out at the half 13-0, and so Nick Saban turned to his true freshman to give the offense a spark. And Tagovailoa did, improbably completing a comeback win in overtime. Spring workouts didn't change very much, despite rumors flying around about Hurts possibly transferring, because Tua broke a bone in his throwing hand on the first day of practice. Given the quarterback depth behind Hurts and Tagovailoa, Nick Saban has tried to keep the battle going for as long as possible. We may not know who the starter is until he jogs onto the field for the opening snap of the season.

While Alabama is one of the top playoff contenders regardless of who wins that battle, the competition is extremely interesting nevertheless. There's a perception that Hurts has a limited ceiling as a passer, and elite defenses can effectively confuse his reads and take away his rushing ability (Hurts was second on the team in rushing last season and averaged 5.5 yards per carry with a 51.5 percent opportunity rate). In a lot of ways he mirrors Ohio State's recently graduated quarterback, J.T. Barrett, who faced similar concerns about his passing ability against elite defenses. While there's relatively limited film on Tua, the general

consensus is that he offers a higher ceiling for the passing game, and therefore the offense as a whole.

But let's be clear here. Last year's offense was already 23rd overall in offensive S&P+. They were 12th overall in rushing S&P+ and return one of the best running back duos in the country in Damien Harris and Najee Harris. They should take the load off of whoever ends up starting at quarterback.

Essentially, while the quarterback race is interesting, it's not a cause for concern. Instead, if you're looking for reasons why the Tide might take a step back (and you really do have to look hard), the offensive questions are at receiver and coordinator. Few offenses relied on a single player as much as Alabama relied on Calvin Ridley last season. Ridley accounted for 30.9 percent of targets and 35.7 percent of total receiving yards last year. And returning receiving production is strongly correlated with changes in offensive S&P+. But the next in the line of elite Alabama receivers is likely Jerry Jeudy, a sophomore and former five-star recruit.

Just as big a concern is the new offensive coordinator, Mike Locksley. With Brian Daboll returning to the NFL, Locksley, the former New Mexico head coach, is Alabama's fourth offensive coordinator in three years (including Steve Sarkisian's brief stint in the role). Locksley's hire was mostly praised, but it is another question mark for the Tide this season.

The bigger concerns are instead on the defense, with six defensive backs leaving the program. That's on top of losing Rashaan Evans, Da'Ron Payne, Shaun Dion-Hamilton, and Da'Shawn Hand from the front seven too. Oh, and defensive coordinator Jeremy Pruitt left to be Tennessee's head coach. But still, this is the Alabama defense we're talking about—probably the surest thing in all of college football. Over the past three seasons, the Tide have finished second, first, and first in defensive FEI.

Until the Auburn game, there's little beyond a transcendent quarterback performance from someone like Jordan Ta'amu or Drew Lock to think the Tide won't be undefeated.

2. Clemson Tigers (10-2, 7-1)

2018 Projections

F/+	52.5 (2)
FEI	.274 (2)
S&P+	25.4 (3)
Total Wins	10.4
Conf Wins	6.8
SOS	.114 (56)
Conf SOS	.200 (57)
Div Champ	68%
Conf Champ	34%
CFP Berth	32%

Projection Factors

2017 F/+	51.4 (4)
2017 FEI	.289 (3)
2017 S&P+	15.4 (8)
5-Year F/+	49.8 (3)
5-Year FEI	.268 (2)
5-Year S&P+	19.8 (3)
2-Yr/5-Yr Recruiting	12/9
Ret. Offense	73% (47)
Ret. Defense	75% (30)
Ret. Total	74% (25)

Projected Win Likelihood by Game

Date	Opponent (Proj Rank)	PWL
Sep 1	vs Furman (FCS)	100%
Sep 8	at Texas A&M (25)	69%
Sep 15	vs Ga. Southern (89)	99%
Sep 22	at Georgia Tech (50)	90%
Sep 29	vs Syracuse (73)	99%
Oct 6	at Wake Forest (36)	82%
Oct 20	vs NC State (34)	90%
Oct 27	at Florida St. (16)	59%
Nov 3	vs Louisville (28)	86%
Nov 10	at Boston College (42)	84%
Nov 17	vs Duke (32)	89%
Nov 24	vs South Carolina (33)	90%

Clemson, at first glance, is in a similar situation as Alabama, the team they've traded wins with in the playoff for the last three years: an older, incumbent quarterback with a potentially lower ceiling as a passer trying to fend off an elite younger quarterback. Incumbent quarterback Kelly Bryant was in the unenviable position of following Deshaun Watson last season, and this season he has to face off with the top overall recruit in the 247 Composite rankings: Trevor Lawrence.

Bryant was more than solid as a passer last season, even if his numbers don't fly off the page—25th in passing S&P+, 65.8 percent completion rate, and only eight interceptions. But he only averaged 7.0 yards per pass, and the Tigers were 40th in passing downs S&P+ (after ranking 12th the season before) and 124th in passing IsoPPP last year. The Tigers had not been all that much more explosive under Watson, but Watson was insanely efficient, ranking fourth overall in passing success rate and averaging about a yard more per attempt.

The drop to 36th in passing success rate and 40th on passing downs was felt the most against Alabama, where Bryant threw two interceptions and averaged just 2.2 yards per attempt. The Clemson offense became one-dimensional, overly reliant on the quarterback run game—much like Alabama in the first half of the National Championship Game and Ohio State under J.T. Barrett. Bryant had 14 carries for 53 yards, while the Clemson running back trio combined for 13 carries for 46 yards. Bryant was a fine option as a ballcarrier (much like Hurts and Barrett), but the offense had just a 17 percent success rate on passing downs (although who could be blame

them against the country's top overall defense?).

To summarize, Clemson had a great offense last season, but it just wasn't effective enough against elite defenses, particularly in must-pass situations. Lawrence, despite being a true freshman, offers a potentially higher ceiling for the passing game. In the spring game, Lawrence went 11-for-16 for 122 yards, including an effortlessly thrown sideline deep ball from midfield.

The Clemson offense must also replace two of its top three receivers after Deon Cain and Ray-Ray McCloud left for the NFL. Hunter Renfrow returns as a reliable option (77 percent catch rate), and sophomore Tee Higgins looks like the next deep threat after averaging 20.3 yards per catch as a freshman. But it can also build on running back Travis Etienne, who was the Tigers' best option as a freshman, averaging 7.2 yards per carry and an explosive 7.5 highlight yards per opportunity, and gaining 5 yards or more on 5.5 percent more carries than either Adam Choice or Tavien Feaster.

While improvements on offense could take the Tigers to the next level, the defense is the foundation of the team. Ranked second in defensive S&P+ last season, the defense returns 75 percent of its 2017 production, including a monstrous defensive line led by Dexter Lawrence, Clelin Ferrell, Austin Bryant, and Christian Wilkins. And that's not even counting Xavier Thomas and K.J. Henry, two of the country's five-star defensive linemen in the 2018 recruiting class. The defensive line generated a ton of havoc last year—seventh overall—and led the country in adjusted sack rate. Clemson's run at another playoff appearance will be built on their elite play.

3. Ohio State Buckeyes (10-2, 8-1)

2018 Projections

F/+	52.5 (3)
FEI	.254 (3)
S&P+	27.0 (1)
Total Wins	10.2
Conf Wins	7.6
SOS	.078 (39)
Conf SOS	.116 (40)
Div Champ	39%
Conf Champ	20%
CFP Berth	19%

Projection Factors

2017 F/+	52.5 (3)
2017 FEI	.248 (6)
2017 S&P+	20.8 (1)
5-Year F/+	56.4 (2)
5-Year FEI	.251 (4)
5-Year S&P+	22.4 (2)
2-Yr/5-Yr Recruiting	1/2
Ret. Offense	72% (50)
Ret. Defense	51% (112)
Ret. Total	62% (87)

Projected Win Likelihood by Game

Date	Opponent (Proj Rank)	PWL
Sep 1	vs Oregon St. (107)	99%
Sep 8	vs Rutgers (93)	99%
Sep 15	vs TCU (20)	71%
Sep 22	vs Tulane (90)	99%
Sep 29	at Penn St. (10)	51%
Oct 6	vs Indiana (66)	98%
Oct 13	vs Minnesota (62)	98%
Oct 20	at Purdue (61)	95%
Nov 3	vs Nebraska (60)	98%
Nov 10	at Michigan St. (9)	50%
Nov 17	at Maryland (80)	99%
Nov 24	vs Michigan (11)	67%

The team that finished at the top of the S&P+ rankings last year wasn't one of the two teams playing in the National Championship Game. In fact, they didn't even make the playoff.

Ohio State finished seventh in offensive S&P+, eighth in defensive S&P+, and sixth in FEI last season. They topped the overall S&P+ rankings and were left to wonder what could have been if they hadn't been left out of the playoff for Alabama.

Of course, it could have been a repeat of 2016, when Clemson infamously shut the Buckeyes out in the playoff semifinals. While the passing game undoubtedly improved in 2017—fourth in passing S&P+, up from 64th a year before—there were still lingering doubts about whether the offense was in good enough shape to beat top defenses, and whether pro-style teams could find success against the defense. After all, Oklahoma's defense somehow managed to hold the Buckeyes to 16 points, while Iowa scored 55 (!) points on Ohio State.

The Buckeyes will look slightly different in 2018. Instead of the consistent J.T. Barrett, who led the Buckeyes to two playoff appearances, Dwayne Haskins will take the reins for the Ohio State offense as a redshirt sophomore. Haskins is a different style of quarterback than Barrett, Braxton Miller, or even Terrelle Pryor before him. Superficially he resembles Cardale Jones—both are tall, big-armed quarterbacks who have some mobility, but they are far more pass-first than typical Ohio State or Urban Meyer quarterbacks. Haskins not only has the arm to open up the intermediate and deep passing game, but more importantly he has the confidence to do so as well. Taken together, it's possible that the Buckeyes offense becomes even more reliant on the passing game and is able to generate more explosive passing downfield (Ohio State relied on shorter mesh routes and receivers getting yards after the catch to create explosive passing plays last year), and that Haskins leans more on the pass side of run-pass options.

Just as importantly, center Billy Price left for the NFL after winning yet another Rimington Trophy for the school, and co-offensive coordinator Ryan Day looks to assume more play-calling duties. Day, a Chip Kelly disciple, received a raise in the offseason, with rumors of increased game day responsibilities relative to offensive coordinator Kevin Wilson. Look for increased variety in the passing game, especially with the most veteran group of receivers that Ohio State has had since 2014. Senior Brady Taylor, who hasn't seen much in-game action in his career, emerged from the spring with the starting quarterback job, but former five-star redshirt freshman Josh Myers is on his heels.

At least Ohio State fans can feel optimistic about the insane talent returning at running back. The Buckeyes have two 1,000-yard backs returning in sophomore J.K. Dobbins and Mike Weber. These two have the potential to be as productive as Nick Chubb and Sony Michel were for Georgia last year. Dobbins has Heisman-like potential depending on his workload, while Weber offers between-the-tackles power and incredible straight-line speed. Besides that pair, Parris Campbell and Austin Mack should lead the team in receiving, while Demario McCall is a name to watch at slot receiver.

Defensively, Ohio State is dealing with annual turnover in the secondary as well as the loss of three defensive ends from last year's loaded group. There's no need to stress much for Ohio State's defensive line—if anything, the group will almost assuredly get even better now that Nick Bosa, Chase Young, Jonathan Cooper, and Jashon Cornell are the top four ends. In fact, with Dre'Mont Jones healthy in the middle of the line, growing depth from junior college transfer Antwuan Jackson Jr., and top-rated tackles Tommy Togiai and Taron Vincent, the Buckeyes' defensive line will rival those at Clemson and Michigan as the best in the country.

The biggest concern is instead in the secondary, where the group lost senior Damon Webb and fourth overall NFL draft pick Denzel Ward. Ward will be difficult to replace. While Kendall Sheffield started to come into his own by the end of the season, it's still a question whether he and Damon Arnette, along with former top-rated corners Jeffrey Okudah and Shaun Wade, can continue the Buckeyes secondary's legacy. An even bigger question is who will take over at safety opposite Jordan Fuller. Malik Hooker had seven interceptions two seasons ago, a big reason why Ohio State was fourth in the country in interceptions. But the Buckeyes dropped to 45th in 2017, unable to generate as many game-shifting big plays. Isaiah Pryor seemed to be the front runner heading in to the spring, but he didn't seize the job like many hoped he would.

It's possible true freshman Josh Proctor or sophmore Amir Riep wins the job instead. All are talented, athletic players, but it's still a question mark, and a position that will definitely be manned by a young starter.

There's little question that Ohio State is one of the top three, probably two most talented teams in the country. But they also have clear question marks on both sides of the ball and a pretty brutal schedule that includes TCU out of conference, plus Penn State, Michigan State, Scott Frost's Nebraska, and, of course, Michigan.

4. Georgia Bulldogs (10-2, 7-1)

2018 Projections

F/+	51.7 (4)
FEI	.249 (4)
S&P+	22.1 (6)
Total Wins	10.5
Conf Wins	6.6
SOS	.138 (59)
Conf SOS	.149 (47)
Div Champ	75%
Conf Champ	38%
CFP Berth	35%

Projection Factors

2017 F/+	52.7 (2)
2017 FEI	.312 (1)
2017 S&P+	17.5 (3)
5-Year F/+	33.7 (12)
5-Year FEI	.252 (3)
5-Year S&P+	12.3 (15)
2-Yr/5-Yr Recruiting	2/3
Ret. Offense	65% (74)
Ret. Defense	54% (95)
Ret. Total	60% (95)

Projected Win Likelihood by Game

Date	Opponent (Proj Rank)	PWL
Sep 1	vs Austin Peay (FCS)	100%
Sep 8	at South Carolina (33)	79%
Sep 15	vs Middle Tenn. (84)	99%
Sep 22	at Missouri (40)	83%
Sep 29	vs Tennessee (72)	99%
Oct 6	vs Vanderbilt (83)	99%
Oct 13	at LSU (19)	60%
Oct 27	vs Florida (30)	81%
Nov 3	at Kentucky (63)	96%
Nov 10	vs Auburn (5)	59%
Nov 17	vs Massachusetts (101)	99%
Nov 24	vs Georgia Tech (50)	95%

The Bulldogs were only a few plays away from their senior-heavy team getting an improbable national championship win over Alabama. But instead, Tua Tagovailoa and DeVonta Smith ended the game with a wide-open deep ball on second-and-26. And Georgia has had to live with coming so close, but still short, all offseason.

A recruiting championship in February suggested that it won't be Kirby Smart's last trip to the playoff as Georgia's head coach, but it did little to make fans, or the team, feel better. The good news is that there's a model to emulate for Georgia. Just two years before, Clemson lost in heartbreaking fashion to Alabama too, only to come back a year later and get revenge.

But Georgia lost a significant percentage of its 2017 production to the NFL and graduation, highlighted by the majority of its linebacker corps, including Butkus winner Roquan Smith; several members of the secondary, including long-time starters Aaron Davis and Dominick Sanders; first-round NFL offensive lineman Isaiah Wynn; and the elite running back duo of Nick Chubb and Sony Michel. All in all, Georgia ranks 95th in total returning production.

What the Bulldogs lack in returning production or senior leadership, they more than make up for in young talent. Not only did they sign the top recruiting class in the country in February—dethroning Alabama by signing seven five-star recruits: quarterback Justin Fields, two of the top three running backs, and four blue-chip offensive linemen—but that historically good class followed their third-ranked 2017 class. Only Ohio State has a better two-year recruiting average.

Many of those young players will assume important roles in 2018. Richard LeCounte III, a hard-hitting safety with a high ceiling, is expected to take one of the open spots in the secondary. Andrew Thomas will take over Isaiah Wynn's spot at left tackle, while five-star 2017 offensive tackle prospect Isaiah Wilson has the edge at right tackle over early enrollee and five-star 2018 prospect Cade Mays. Incoming five-star corner Tyson Campbell could snag a starting job too. Outside linebackers Brenton Cox and Robert Beal are expected to fill pass-rushing roles at the least.

And that doesn't even consider D'Andre Swift and Jake Fromm, two sophomores who played huge roles in their freshman seasons. Fromm showed everything you'd want to see out of a freshman quarterback, averaging an excellent 9.0 yards per attempt (tied for sixth in the country!) and only throwing seven interceptions. Fromm was accurate, and capable of throwing a solid deep ball, so there's every reason to think he'll build off a solid season despite losing top receiver Javon Wims and playing in front of all-world freshman Justin Fields. Much was made of the Fromm-Fields "competition" in the spring, but Fromm's consistent, great play last season offers little evidence of a true quarterback debate.

Swift had about as good of a freshman season as you could hope for, especially considering that he was third on the depth chart behind two running backs taken in the first two rounds of the NFL draft. Swift averaged 7.5 yards per carry with a 42.7 percent opportunity rate—slightly lower than Nick Chubb's, and six percent lower than Sony Michel's. But while Swift will need to be a little more consistent to keep up Georgia's sixth-ranked rushing S&P+ offense from last season, he also averaged almost a full highlight yard more than even Michel. And he'll have plenty of help behind him. Elijah Holyfield looks to have made strides during the offseason, projecting as a strong volume runner who can thrive in between the tackles to close out games. And the aforementioned top 2018 running back recruits include top overall back Zamir White as well as James Cook, Dalvin Cook's younger brother.

The bigger question than who will replace Chubb or Michel's production is likely whether Andrew Thomas can successfully take over for Wynn and whether Isaiah Wilson or Cade Mays can lock down the right side for Thomas. The line's play, led by Sam Pittman, was probably the single biggest difference between the 2017 and 2018 teams. Georgia was 12th in adjusted line yards after ranking 101st in Kirby Smart's first season. Continuing that level of excellent line play will be critical for making a second playoff run.

Potentially more important is finding replacements in the linebacker corps and secondary. All signs point to Natrez Patrick returning in a middle linebacker spot, but watching Georgia's defense from last season it's almost hard to imagine how the Bulldogs handle not having Roquan Smith. He had a knack for tracking the ballcarrier and coming up big in critical moments, like late in the Rose Bowl. The spring game suggested that Monty Rice could have a ball-hawking future at the position, but it's nevertheless a huge question mark.

Likewise, Georgia must replace both outside linebackers. Talent won't be a question—the Bulldogs have loaded up on insanely athletic linebackers. But Lorenzo Carter and Davin Bellamy effectively set the edge and allowed Smith to clean up in the middle last season, so a rotation of players will have to build on their consistency, and potentially raise Georgia's pass rush, too, which ranked just 71st in adjusted sack rate.

On the back end of the defense, the Bulldogs lose a ton of experience—Dominick Sanders, Malkom Parrish, and Aaron Davis had been there for what felt like a decade—but they'll actually get talent upgrades in the process. The big concern, of course, is that returning production seems to matter the most in the secondary.

The good news for all of Georgia's new starters is that the schedule isn't brutal. South Carolina could be tricky, LSU got its quarterback in graduate transfer Joe Burrow, and Auburn will be a near-even fight, but Georgia should be favored in most, if not all, of its regular season games.

5. Auburn Tigers (9-3, 5-3)

2018 Projections			Projection Factors		
F/+	51.4 (5)		2017 F/+	50.2 (9)	
FEI	.229 (5)		2017 FEI	.265 (5)	
S&P+	22.4 (5)		2017 S&P+	14.3 (10)	
Total Wins	9.0		5-Year F/+	41.4 (5)	
Conf Wins	5.5		5-Year FEI	.227 (6)	
SOS	.010 (1)		5-Year S&P+	17.3 (4)	
Conf SOS	.021 (1)		2-Yr/5-Yr Recruiting	11/7	
Div Champ	17%		Ret. Offense	78% (29)	
Conf Champ	8%		Ret. Defense	61% (76)	
CFP Berth	6%		Ret. Total	69% (45)	

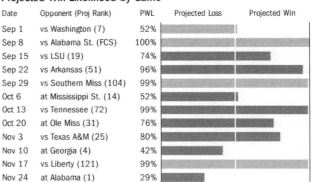

Projected Win Likelihood by Game

Date	Opponent (Proj Rank)	PWL	Projected Loss	Projected Win
Sep 1	vs Washington (7)	52%		
Sep 8	vs Alabama St. (FCS)	100%		
Sep 15	vs LSU (19)	74%		
Sep 22	vs Arkansas (51)	96%		
Sep 29	vs Southern Miss (104)	99%		
Oct 6	at Mississippi St. (14)	52%		
Oct 13	vs Tennessee (72)	99%		
Oct 20	at Ole Miss (31)	76%		
Nov 3	vs Texas A&M (25)	80%		
Nov 10	at Georgia (4)	42%		
Nov 17	vs Liberty (121)	99%		
Nov 24	at Alabama (1)	29%		

Heading into the SEC Championship Game, the Tigers were in a sweet place for a two-loss team. Not only were they coming off an Iron Bowl win over Alabama, but a second win over Georgia would have given Auburn an outside chance at the playoff. But then Auburn would lose by three touchdowns to Georgia and also drop its bowl game against Central Florida. And while non-playoff bowl results are often meaningless and Auburn clearly didn't look like it was interested in being there, it still, you know, lost.

The good news for the Plainsmen is that they return a ton of production on offense. Despite losing Kerryon Johnson and Kamryn Pettway to the NFL, Auburn returns 78 percent of its offensive production from a year ago, including quarterback Jarrett Stidham and receivers Ryan Davis, Darius Slayton, and Nate Craig-Myers. Those four (along with Will Hastings and Eli Stove, both of whom tore their ACLs in spring practice) formed the tenth-ranked passing S&P+ offense last season, and should be the core of the 2018 offense—particularly with the departures of Pettway and Johnson at running back. Stidham had an excellent first year as a Tiger, throwing for more

than 3,100 yards while averaging 8.5 yards per attempt, and with just six interceptions. Stidham was really only slowed in his losses to Clemson, LSU, and Georgia, which all had top-20 passing S&P+ defenses.

The main concern on offense is the offensive line, which must replace four starters and its position coach. Despite ranking 16th in rushing S&P+ overall last year, only 38.8 percent of Auburn's rushes went for 5 or more yards, which was 64th best in the country. The Tigers were also 94th in adjusted sack rate. So potentially it will be addition by subtraction, but that's still a lot of uncertainty.

A second question is whether the Tigers have an every-down running back or if they will take a committee approach similar to 2015, when Peyton Barber, Jovon Robinson and Roc Thomas shared the load. Kam Martin is the top returning back (6.0 yards per carry, 7.0 highlight yards per opportunity, and 38.7 percent opportunity rate), but as those stats show, he's more suited to big plays than shouldering a heavy workload. Incoming four-star freshman Asa Martin could be the guy to take some of the burden from the other Martin.

Defensively Auburn returns just 61 percent of its production from last season, but its line will likely help the Tigers remain one of the best groups in college football. After ranking fourth overall in defensive FEI last season, Auburn returns Derrick Brown, Dontavius Russell, and Andrew Williams. The major need is someone to fill Jeff Holland's shoes as a pass-rush specialist. Holland had ten sacks and 11 run stuffs last year (11th in the country), while no one else had more than 3.5.

6. Notre Dame Fighting Irish (10-2)

2018 Projections

F/+	50.6 (6)
FEI	.207 (6)
S&P+	21.3 (7)
Total Wins	9.8
Conf Wins	-
SOS	.061 (27)
Conf SOS	-
Div Champ	-
Conf Champ	-
CFP Berth	10%

Projection Factors

2017 F/+	45.8 (11)
2017 FEI	.217 (10)
2017 S&P+	11.3 (13)
5-Year F/+	31.3 (13)
5-Year FEI	.184 (8)
5-Year S&P+	12.2 (16)
2-Yr/5-Yr Recruiting	10/8
Ret. Offense	54% (99)
Ret. Defense	96% (1)
Ret. Total	75% (18)

Projected Win Likelihood by Game

Date	Opponent (Proj Rank)	PWL
Sep 1	vs Michigan (11)	64%
Sep 8	vs Ball St. (112)	99%
Sep 15	vs Vanderbilt (83)	99%
Sep 22	at Wake Forest (36)	80%
Sep 29	vs Stanford (17)	71%
Oct 6	at Virginia Tech (22)	65%
Oct 13	vs Pittsburgh (48)	95%
Oct 27	vs Navy (74)	99%
Nov 3	at Northwestern (41)	82%
Nov 10	vs Florida St. (16)	70%
Nov 17	vs Syracuse (73)	99%
Nov 24	at USC (15)	55%

It appeared as though the 2017 Fighting Irish were having a breakthrough season under new coordinators Chip Long (offense) and Mike Elko (defense) when they rolled to an 8-1 start, with the only defeat a one-point loss to the eventual national runner-up Georgia Bulldogs. Then they took on the Miami Hurricanes late in the year under the renewed "Catholics vs Convicts" rivalry and took a crushing 41-8 defeat. They took another loss, an 18-point thumping to Stanford, to close the regular season, and then starting quarterback Brandon Wimbush was benched during the bowl game against LSU in favor of sophomore Ian Book, who sparked a victory.

The 2018 Irish have to sort through the fallout of the Wimbush-Book quarterback battle while replacing multiple NFL draft picks from their pounding offensive attack that ranked fifth nationally in rushing S&P+. The left guard/left tackle tandem of Mike McGlinchey and Quenton Nelson was drafted sixth and ninth overall respectively, while the fourth round took tight end Durham Smythe and the sixth got wide receiver Equanimeous St. Brown. Lead running back Josh Adams also left early for the NFL after a 1,430-yard rushing season and ended up signing with the Eagles as an undrafted free agent.

The defense had a strong year as well and did not take the same kind of grievous losses from graduation and the draft. They did lose Elko to a $1.8 annual contract from Texas A&M. The Irish are bringing back linebackers Te'Von Coney (16 run stuffs) and Drue Tranquill (11 run stuffs) behind a young line that returns defensive end Daelin Hayes (6.5 tackles for loss) and defensive tackle Jerry Tillery (a 6-foot-6 athletic freak who led the team with 4.5 sacks). The Irish have four starters back in the secondary as well but seem likely to move players around to make room for rising talents like junior cornerback Troy Pride Jr.

Overall it looks like the defense could make yet another leap off a top-30 S&P+ season, even without Elko at the helm, thanks to their returning veterans and a focus on continuity in scheme under promoted linebackers coach Clark Lea. The big questions for this team center around how well they "reload" on offense.

The prospective starting lineup for the Irish offense includes blue-chip recruits like right guard Tommy Kraemer and the new left guard/left tackle tandem of Alex Bars (who started at right guard in 2017) and Liam Eichenberg. Notre Dame's approach figures to evolve in Year 2 under offensive coordinator Chip Long given the loss of the team's top playmakers and Long's own preference for using run/pass options on offense rather than the quarterback option/power game that Notre Dame utilized in 2017.

If Wimbush can pick up the evolutions in the offense, the Irish could adjust enough to overcome the departure of absurdly talented run-game personnel. There's a lot of speed and talent in Notre Dame's returning cast of skill players, and they can put three big targets on the field at once with tight end Alize Mack and receivers Chase Claypool and Miles Boykin, all of whom are at least 6-foot-4 and 225 pounds or more. If the passing game can't pick up the slack, then despite their overall talent level, it'll be hard to finish in the top 10 with a schedule that pits them against Michigan, Stanford, Virginia Tech, Florida State, and USC.

7. Washington Huskies (10-2, 8-1)

2018 Projections

F/+	50.6 (7)
FEI	.192 (8)
S&P+	23.9 (4)
Total Wins	10.1
Conf Wins	7.6
SOS	.090 (47)
Conf SOS	.194 (56)
Div Champ	65%
Conf Champ	33%
CFP Berth	27%

Projection Factors

2017 F/+	49.3 (10)
2017 FEI	.199 (11)
2017 S&P+	16.8 (5)
5-Year F/+	33.8 (11)
5-Year FEI	.179 (9)
5-Year S&P+	13.5 (12)
2-Yr/5-Yr Recruiting	17/24
Ret. Offense	70% (58)
Ret. Defense	81% (19)
Ret. Total	75% (20)

Projected Win Likelihood by Game

Date	Opponent (Proj Rank)	PWL	Projected Loss / Projected Win
Sep 1	vs Auburn (5)	49%	
Sep 8	vs North Dakota (FCS)	100%	
Sep 15	at Utah (29)	73%	
Sep 22	vs Arizona St. (44)	93%	
Sep 29	vs BYU (67)	98%	
Oct 6	at UCLA (38)	81%	
Oct 13	at Oregon (23)	66%	
Oct 20	vs Colorado (92)	99%	
Oct 27	at California (58)	93%	
Nov 3	vs Stanford (17)	71%	
Nov 17	vs Oregon St. (107)	99%	
Nov 23	at Washington St. (49)	88%	

The Huskies were a popular pick to repeat as playoff contenders in 2017 despite losing first-round draft pick and star wide receiver John Ross along with their top three coverage defenders in Kevin King, Budda Baker, and Sidney Jones (all taken in the second round of the draft). The assumption was that Chris Petersen's program was off and running and could now contend annually for titles by reloading, and this assumption proved mostly true. Washington put together a 10-3 season and narrowly missed playing for its second consecutive Pac-12 title after losing to Stanford late in the year.

The missing pieces for the team proved to be the explosiveness that John Ross offered (his primary replacement, Chico McClatcher, went down in Game 4) and the ball-hawking from that veteran secondary. The 2016 starting Huskies secondary picked off 10 passes, while the younger 2017 unit snagged six. The Huskies still played good defense because of superior play at defensive tackle (Vita Vea would be drafted 12th overall in 2018), but they didn't have the same overwhelming strength in the secondary.

The strong points of the 2017 team included Jake Browning starting for his third consecutive year at quarterback, and he returns for a final run as a senior in 2018 along with running back Myles Gaskin and a well-seasoned offensive line that has a total of 96 starts between its returning members. The 2017 season also saw the Huskies work to develop their tight end position, which now returns star sophomore Hunter Bryant along with fifth-year senior Drew Sample and third-year sophomore Jacob Kizer. This team is going to be loaded with experience and versatility in the trenches and the backfield while getting much closer to having some game-changing speed outside with McClatcher healthy and joined by returning starter Aaron Fuller.

The offensive philosophy of this team is shaped by Petersen, who gained fame for the way his Boise State offenses of the 2000s would carefully carve opponents up with run/pass balance and the occasional trick play. The more experience and versatility they have, the more dangerous they become.

On defense, the Huskies have all five starters back from their young secondary, which is now a veteran unit and likely to once again define the team. At linebacker they return lead tackler Ben Burr-Kirven and are sliding outside linebacker Tevis Bartlett into the weak inside linebacker position to join him in the middle. Up front this team returns only one of their two monster defensive tackles (the 320-pound senior Greg Gaines) but versatile swing man Ryan Bowman is back after leading the team with five sacks, while Bartlett may find better angles in the pass-rush (four sacks in 2017) from his new position inside.

The preferred philosophy with defensive coordinator Pete Kwiatkowski is to bring creative pressures that only involve four or occasionally five pass-rushers while playing pattern-matching coverages on the back end with a deep safety over the top, much like the local Seattle Seahawks. This is a team with a lot of experience, a clear identity on both sides of the ball, and a philosophy for winning games that builds off experience and precision. With all of these returning players and emerging young playmakers, they will likely prove the class of the Pac-12 and a contender for the playoffs. We'll find out early in the year what their ceiling might be when they open the season in Atlanta against the Auburn Tigers.

8. Oklahoma Sooners (10-2, 7-2)

2018 Projections		Projection Factors	
F/+	49.9 (8)	2017 F/+	51.0 (6)
FEI	.203 (7)	2017 FEI	.281 (4)
S&P+	19.5 (9)	2017 S&P+	15.0 (9)
Total Wins	10.3	5-Year F/+	42.0 (4)
Conf Wins	7.5	5-Year FEI	.240 (5)
SOS	.142 (60)	5-Year S&P+	16.4 (6)
Conf SOS	.176 (53)	2-Yr/5-Yr Recruiting	6/11
Div Champ	-	Ret. Offense	55% (98)
Conf Champ	51%	Ret. Defense	52% (108)
CFP Berth	34%	Ret. Total	53% (110)

Projected Win Likelihood by Game

Date	Opponent (Proj Rank)	PWL	Projected Loss	Projected Win
Sep 1	vs Florida Atlantic (39)	90%		
Sep 8	vs UCLA (38)	90%		
Sep 15	at Iowa St. (43)	83%		
Sep 22	vs Army (86)	99%		
Sep 29	vs Baylor (37)	89%		
Oct 6	vs Texas (24)	72%		
Oct 20	at TCU (20)	61%		
Oct 27	vs Kansas St. (46)	94%		
Nov 3	at Texas Tech (53)	89%		
Nov 10	vs Oklahoma St. (21)	77%		
Nov 17	vs Kansas (102)	99%		
Nov 23	at West Virginia (45)	84%		

Year 1 for Lincoln Riley as the head coach replacing Bob Stoops went almost as smoothly as Oklahoma could have hoped for. With third-year starting quarterback Baker Mayfield at the helm and an offensive line with five returning starters, the Sooners produced a historically great offense, ranking no. 1 in offensive S&P+ and nearly winning a title via shootouts. Bob Stoops left Riley in charge at the perfect time to give his successor a strong boost, allowing him to claim much of the credit for an offensive season that was three years in the making under Riley's own coordination of Mayfield and the offense the previous two seasons.

However, Stoops also left his younger brother Mike Stoops behind and in charge of the defense. The Sooners defense has struggled since Mike Stoops returned in 2012, and longtime defensive coordinator Brent Venables was edged out only to have major success at Clemson. In 2017 they fell apart, finishing 101st in S&P+ and giving up 317 rushing yards to Georgia in a 54-48 overtime defeat in the playoffs. Now things could get worse, as the 2018 Sooners have to replace star pass-rusher Obo Okoronkwo (17 sacks in two years), both starting safeties, leading tackler Emmanuel Beal, and premier athletes such as cornerback Jordan Thomas and defensive tackle Du'Vonta Lampkin.

The Sooners' attempt to rebuild their defense in 2018 is likely to be both essential and difficult. Oklahoma's next generation of defenders is headlined by sophomore linebacker Kenneth Murray, sophomore cornerback Tre Norwood, freshman defensive back Brendan Radley-Hiles, and then some older players who haven't put it all together yet such as junior linebacker Caleb Kelly. If they can simply clean up their play to be able to avoid busts and missed assignments of the sort that regularly gifted points to opponents in 2017 (79th in IsoPPP+) that alone would make a big difference.

On offense there's a good deal of intrigue around the replacement of Mayfield, but the floor for this unit is fairly high thanks to the return of three starters on offensive line and a deep group of running backs headlined by Rodney Anderson (1,161 rushing yards and 13 rushing touchdowns in 2017). Mayfield is likely to be replaced by former high school phenomenon and Texas A&M transfer Kyler Murray, but Murray has already signed a deal worth nearly $5 million to play baseball for the Oakland Athletics after this season concludes. Murray hasn't proven to be a savvy field general or passer, but he's a plus athlete at the position, hence the interest from Major League Baseball.

The 2017 Sooners changed the game on offense with a 21-personnel "spread" package that used fullback Dmitri Flowers primarily as a blocker and used tight end Mark Andrews like an NFL team would, flexing him out wide to create matchup problems in the passing game. That blend of pro-style spread tactics (creating matchups with a flex tight end) and college spread tactics (spreading out an opponent only to throw two-back run plays at them) was devastating. They'll have new figures stepping into those roles in 2018, but the blueprint has been established now and outside receivers Marquise Brown (1,ß095 receiving yards in 2017) and CeeDee Lamb (807 receiving yards) are back and should be ready to play even larger roles.

This team has as high a beta as most any in the country with the potential to be devastating on offense again while also fielding a competent defense. Or they could struggle without Mayfield's leadership and diverse skill set while the defense continues to wander in the wilderness.

9. Michigan State Spartans (10-2, 7-2)

2018 Projections

F/+	47.9 (9)
FEI	.173 (9)
S&P+	18.0 (11)
Total Wins	10.1
Conf Wins	7.2
SOS	.103 (53)
Conf SOS	.124 (43)
Div Champ	29%
Conf Champ	14%
CFP Berth	13%

Projection Factors

2017 F/+	32.5 (23)
2017 FEI	.095 (30)
2017 S&P+	9.0 (21)
5-Year F/+	30.2 (16)
5-Year FEI	.120 (22)
5-Year S&P+	11.2 (19)
2-Yr/5-Yr Recruiting	33/23
Ret. Offense	92% (3)
Ret. Defense	91% (5)
Ret. Total	92% (1)

Projected Win Likelihood by Game

Date	Opponent (Proj Rank)	PWL
Aug 31	vs Utah St. (78)	99%
Sep 8	at Arizona St. (44)	83%
Sep 22	at Indiana (66)	95%
Sep 29	vs C. Michigan (117)	99%
Oct 6	vs Northwestern (41)	89%
Oct 13	at Penn St. (10)	44%
Oct 20	vs Michigan (11)	60%
Oct 27	vs Purdue (61)	97%
Nov 3	at Maryland (80)	99%
Nov 10	vs Ohio St. (3)	50%
Nov 17	at Nebraska (60)	92%
Nov 24	vs Rutgers (93)	99%

The Michigan State Spartans are probably the most under-inked team in college football for 2018, with a case as a major contender obscured by a series of horrifying scandals in the athletics department. In 2017, the Spartans rebounded from a miserable 3-9 season thanks to a turnaround on defense, going from 41st to fourth in S&P+, and finding a quarterback in sophomore Brian Lewerke. They finished 10-3 and have a chance to do more in 2018.

The formula for the playoff Michigan State team back in 2015 was to play good defense and rely on senior quarterback Connor Cook to make plays in the passing game to extend drives. The formula for last year's comeback was exactly the same. Lewerke proved capable both as a passer, where he threw 20 touchdowns to seven interceptions, and in the run game, where he added 559 rushing yards and five more scores. As a junior he'll be playing behind four or five returning starters on the offensive line (pending how camp battles shake out) while being reunited with all four of his top targets in the passing game and backfield mates L.J. Scott and Madre London.

The Spartans ranked only 92nd in offensive S&P+ in 2017 but were ninth on passing downs and now return all of the key components that made that possible. They stand to improve with so much continuity across their lineup, and that improvement can be even larger if their run game can produce more explosive plays.

The defense came alive in large part due to the emergence of sophomore defensive end (and former walk-on) Kenny Willekes, who led the team in tackles for loss (14.5) and sacks (seven) while finishing second in run stuffs (14). Middle linebacker Joe Bachie added 15 more run stuffs. The Spartans also upgraded their athleticism at the safety and star linebacker positions, who have to operate in space, with the Dowell twins (Andrew and David) and safety Khari Willis. All of these players return in 2018, while the cornerback tandem of Josiah Scott and Justine Layne comes back with a chance to build on a season with 18 combined pass break-ups and three interceptions.

The Spartans defensive structure asks a lot of the cornerbacks, and Scott and Layne held up well despite being in their freshman and sophomore years, respectively. Now as returning starters flanked by other experienced and proven defenders, they could have a big year. The other trouble spot is generally the interplay between star linebacker and free safety, but the Dowell twins navigated those waters masterfully in 2017 and avoided the big plays from spread attacks that have often plagued this defense.

The schedule worked out favorably for the Spartans as well. They get Big Ten East frontrunners Ohio State and Michigan at home in Lansing while taking on rebuilding Penn State in State College. So the biggest challenges to this team may be distractions or ramifications from the fallout over the various scandals that have plagued the athletics department. The Spartans have veteran units on both sides of the ball with some key playmakers returning after breakout 2017 campaigns.

10. Penn State Nittany Lions (10-2, 7-2)

2018 Projections		Projection Factors	
F/+	47.1 (10)	2017 F/+	51.2 (5)
FEI	.148 (16)	2017 FEI	.238 (7)
S&P+	20.2 (8)	2017 S&P+	17.3 (4)
Total Wins	9.6	5-Year F/+	24.7 (21)
Conf Wins	6.8	5-Year FEI	.170 (11)
SOS	.066 (28)	5-Year S&P+	11.2 (18)
Conf SOS	.078 (16)	2-Yr/5-Yr Recruiting	8/16
Div Champ	18%	Ret. Offense	51% (105)
Conf Champ	9%	Ret. Defense	53% (101)
CFP Berth	8%	Ret. Total	52% (115)

Projected Win Likelihood by Game

Date	Opponent (Proj Rank)	PWL	Projected Loss	Projected Win
Sep 1	vs Appalachian St. (65)	98%		
Sep 8	at Pittsburgh (48)	85%		
Sep 15	vs Kent St. (122)	99%		
Sep 21	at Illinois (103)	99%		
Sep 29	vs Ohio St. (3)	49%		
Oct 13	vs Michigan St. (9)	57%		
Oct 20	at Indiana (66)	95%		
Oct 27	vs Iowa (27)	81%		
Nov 3	at Michigan (11)	43%		
Nov 10	vs Wisconsin (12)	59%		
Nov 17	at Rutgers (93)	99%		
Nov 24	vs Maryland (80)	99%		

The story of the Penn State offense should be one of the more interesting stories in 2018. This unit exploded after hiring offensive coordinator Joe Moorhead in 2016 and installing Trace McSorley at quarterback. The 2018 team will still have McSorley, back for his third year behind a line with four returning starters, but they'll be without Moorhead, who filled the head coaching vacancy at Mississippi State. They'll also have to replace running back Saquon Barkley, who was the second overall pick in the draft, and tight end Mike Gesicki, who went in the second round.

Head coach James Franklin looked to maintain continuity on offense by promoting Ricky Rahne to coordinator. Rahne has been with him since 2006 at Kansas State, with only a two-year interruption in their working relationship. Rahne learned the Moorhead system as a tight end coach over the last two years and will now take over the spread system and look to plug in new stars from the ranks of blue-chip skill players that Franklin has been recruiting to State College.

No. 2 receiver Juwan Johnson is back to work with Trace McSorley but running back, tight end, and the other receiving positions will feature new faces. Former five-star running back recruit Miles Stevens will likely be a big part of the reload process, and senior wideout DeAndre Thompkins is next in line to get more targets from McSorley. Where Rahne will have a chance to make a name for himself as a coordinator is with back-up quarterback Tommy Stevens. The 6-foot-4, 230-pound athletic junior got some work in a new hybrid position they created last season named "Lion" and finished the year with nine total touchdowns between his passing, running, and receiving.

Rahne may expand the dual-quarterback formations they explored in 2017 in order to keep McSorley's heir apparent involved while making use of his unique athleticism.

Things are more straightforward on defense, where Brent Fry remains the coordinator and five starters return from a unit that finished 12th in S&P+ in 2017. There are some obstacles, though, with the departures of both defensive tackles, both inside linebackers, and both starting safeties up the middle of the unit. Defensive tackle appears to be in good hands with explosive fourth-year junior Keith Givens stepping up alongside fellow fourth-year junior Robert Windsor. The Nittany Lions also have some talented players that have seen several years of development within the program to plug in at safety.

Linebacker is the key spot, as this is "Linebacker U" and the defense is designed to feature the position. The Nittany Lions have recruited some major talent to play here, but much of it is still young. Koa Farmer returns after a strong 2017 season with nine run stuffs. He figures to move to weakside linebacker from his strongside hybrid position. That spot will probably be filled by 6-foot-5, 222-pound junior Cam Brown, who brings major disruption and athleticism to the field but little experience. The middle remains to be settled between redshirt freshman Ellis Brooks and former walk-on Jan Johnson, who also joined the wrestling team and may prove a better athlete than his recruiting ranking would have suggested.

There's no doubt Penn State will be talented in 2018, but lots of first-time starters will need to be ready to go in order to allow the Lions to keep pace playing in the same division as Ohio State, Michigan, and Michigan State.

11. Michigan Wolverines (9-3, 7-2)

2018 Projections

F/+	46.7 (11)
FEI	.152 (14)
S&P+	18.3 (10)
Total Wins	8.9
Conf Wins	6.6
SOS	.021 (4)
Conf SOS	.052 (11)
Div Champ	14%
Conf Champ	7%
CFP Berth	5%

Projection Factors

2017 F/+	29.6 (30)
2017 FEI	.088 (33)
2017 S&P+	7.9 (27)
5-Year F/+	30.3 (15)
5-Year FEI	.109 (23)
5-Year S&P+	13.6 (11)
2-Yr/5-Yr Recruiting	15/22
Ret. Offense	74% (43)
Ret. Defense	83% (14)
Ret. Total	78% (13)

Projected Win Likelihood by Game

Date	Opponent (Proj Rank)	PWL
Sep 1	at Notre Dame (6)	36%
Sep 8	vs W. Michigan (81)	99%
Sep 15	vs SMU (82)	99%
Sep 22	vs Nebraska (60)	96%
Sep 29	at Northwestern (41)	78%
Oct 6	vs Maryland (80)	99%
Oct 13	vs Wisconsin (12)	59%
Oct 20	at Michigan St. (9)	40%
Nov 3	vs Penn St. (10)	57%
Nov 10	at Rutgers (93)	99%
Nov 17	vs Indiana (66)	98%
Nov 24	at Ohio St. (3)	33%

This is potentially the season for Michigan fans. Jim Harbaugh has been back in Ann Arbor for three years, but the Wolverines have yet to finish better than third in their own division during his tenure. Last season was seen as a big disappointment for many fans as the team fell to 8-5 (with 7-6 Purdue as their only win over a team with a winning record) and 30th in the final F/+ rankings—but it shouldn't have. 2017 was always going to be the rebuilding year for the team, while 2018 was always going to be the year where Michigan could really challenge Ohio State and Penn State (and/or Michigan State!) for the Big Ten East title.

That goal got even more realistic with the immediate eligibility of Ole Miss transfer quarterback Shea Patterson, the former top passer in his recruiting class, who along with a high-ceiling group of receivers might just give the Wolverines the offensive firepower they've been lacking during Harbaugh's time in Ann Arbor. The last three years, Michigan's offense has ranked 31st, 41st, and then 86th in offensive S&P+ last season. Michigan had three quarterbacks receive significant snaps last year, and none threw for even 1,000 yards, completed 55 percent of his passes, or averaged more than 7.2 yards per attempt. John O'Korn has graduated and Wilton Speight is now with Chip Kelly at UCLA, but Brandon Peters has returned to battle Patterson and redshirt freshman Dylan McCaffrey (the fifth-ranked pro-style quarterback in his recruiting class) for the starting job. The entire depth chart is an upgrade for Jim Harbaugh's offense.

Most are assuming that Patterson wins the job. After all, he has starting quarterback experience at Ole Miss and was the highest rated recruit of the three. But there are still some question marks with Patterson. After his injury last season, Jordan Ta'amu was actually even more efficient for the Ole Miss offense, with a lower interception rate, completing almost 3 percent more of his passes, and averaging a full yard per attempt more than Patterson. Of course, that may say more about Ta'amu, the Ole Miss receivers, or the offensive system as a whole than it does about Patterson, but it's worth noting for some who pencil Michigan on top of the Big Ten East with Patterson's eligibility announcement.

The receiving corps looks solid for whoever wins the job. Donovan Peoples-Jones was the top wide receiver in his class and finished with the most targets of any receiver on the team last year (although he only had a 42 percent catch rate). Fellow freshman Tarik Black looked even better before he was lost for the season with an injury. And Nico Collins could be another strong option.

The offensive line is probably the biggest concern for the offense. At 117th in adjusted sack rate last year, they remain the passing game's biggest liability. And while the rushing offense was explosive—Karan Higdon and Chris Evans, who both return, averaged nearly 7.0 highlight yards per opportunity last year—the offensive line didn't manage too many big holes, as the Wolverines gained 5 yards on only 36.6 percent of rushes (90th).

However, if last year's team, with an offense that ranked in the low 80s, was essentially good enough to be an eight- or nine-win team (if you go by second-order wins), then that says more about the extremely high floor that Don Brown's defense gives Michigan. That's why it's fair to be so high on Michigan: because the defense gives the Wolverines an eight-win floor, any offensive improvement on offense could be huge.

Michigan was tenth overall in defensive S&P+ last season and best in the country in overall defensive success rate. And 83 percent of last year's defensive production returns for 2018, 15th most in the country. They're led by a nasty defensive line including Chase Winovich and Rashan Gary, as well as Devin Bush at linebacker and Khaleke Hudson as a hybrid safety/linebacker "viper." Led by those four last year, no defense was as disruptive—Michigan topped the country in overall havoc rate—and few are likely to be in 2018, either.

12. Wisconsin Badgers (10-2, 7-2)

2018 Projections

F/+	46.5 (12)
FEI	.152 (13)
S&P+	17.8 (12)
Total Wins	10.1
Conf Wins	7.1
SOS	.109 (54)
Conf SOS	.114 (39)
Div Champ	60%
Conf Champ	30%
CFP Berth	23%

Projection Factors

2017 F/+	50.9 (7)
2017 FEI	.237 (8)
2017 S&P+	16.6 (6)
5-Year F/+	35.9 (10)
5-Year FEI	.201 (7)
5-Year S&P+	14.5 (8)
2-Yr/5-Yr Recruiting	36/35
Ret. Offense	84% (15)
Ret. Defense	42% (124)
Ret. Total	63% (81)

Projected Win Likelihood by Game

Date	Opponent (Proj Rank)	PWL
Aug 31	vs W. Kentucky (87)	99%
Sep 8	vs New Mexico (114)	99%
Sep 15	vs BYU (67)	98%
Sep 22	at Iowa (27)	67%
Oct 6	vs Nebraska (60)	96%
Oct 13	at Michigan (11)	42%
Oct 20	vs Illinois (103)	99%
Oct 27	at Northwestern (41)	78%
Nov 3	vs Rutgers (93)	99%
Nov 10	at Penn St. (10)	41%
Nov 17	at Purdue (61)	91%
Nov 24	vs Minnesota (62)	97%

Yes, this is the fifth Big Ten team in our top dozen, and the first one from the Big Ten West (which goes to show you how tough a schedule the Big Ten East champ will have). This may be the best version of the Badgers we've seen in years—and that's saying something.

A good way to think about Wisconsin is as the western version of Michigan, but with a better passing game and without as much defensive production returning in 2018. Seriously: Michigan was 10th in defensive S&P+, first in defensive havoc rating, 86th in offensive S&P+, and 87th in passing S&P+. Wisconsin was third in defensive S&P+, second in defensive havoc rating, 41st in offensive S&P+, and seventh in passing S&P+. Wisconsin didn't play the most brutal schedule in the Big Ten West, but they cleared every test they had except in the Big Ten Championship Game, where they lost to Ohio State by just six points.

Wisconsin should look similar in 2018, but rely more on their offense, and play a tougher schedule. While 79 percent of their offensive production returns in 2018, including quarterback Alex Hornibrook and star running back Jonathan Taylor, only 42 percent of their defensive production returns. But the schedule should also be a little trickier this year, with Western Kentucky, a Scott Frost-led Nebraska, Michigan with presumably a better offense, Penn State, and, likely, the Big Ten East champion.

While Wisconsin has a low percentage of defensive production returning, they have a star linebacker corps built around Ryan Connelly, T.J. Edwards, and Andrew Van Ginkel, who combined for 32 tackles for loss. They'll have to keep up the pressure, because the defensive line lost some major contributors in Alec James (eight tackles for loss, 6.5 sacks) and Conor Sheehy (5.5 tackles for loss). There are high expectations for Isaiahh Loudermilk and Garrett Rand in their places.

Led by Hornibrook and Taylor, and an experienced offensive line, the offense should be great to elite in 2018. Hornibrook led a top-ten S&P+ passing offense as a sophomore last season. Although the Badgers were about as conventional as can be from a run/pass perspective—running on 74.4 percent of standard downs and passing on 70.6 percent of passing downs—Hornibrook still was efficient and led the top third-down offense by S&P+. Even more, Hornibrook's top four wide receiver targets all return in 2018. The only major loss is his top overall target, tight end Troy Fumagalli.

If Wisconsin can answer questions about its defensive line and navigate a few slightly more difficult games than last season, then the Badgers are looking at a Big Ten Championship appearance at least.

13. Miami Hurricanes (10-2, 7-1)

2018 Projections

F/+	46.0 (13)
FEI	.148 (15)
S&P+	17.4 (13)
Total Wins	10.0
Conf Wins	6.5
SOS	.144 (61)
Conf SOS	.250 (64)
Div Champ	66%
Conf Champ	33%
CFP Berth	26%

Projection Factors

2017 F/+	38.8 (15)
2017 FEI	.151 (17)
2017 S&P+	9.2 (17)
5-Year F/+	24.4 (24)
5-Year FEI	.124 (21)
5-Year S&P+	10.6 (21)
2-Yr/5-Yr Recruiting	9/17
Ret. Offense	68% (64)
Ret. Defense	70% (40)
Ret. Total	69% (46)

Projected Win Likelihood by Game

Date	Opponent (Proj Rank)	PWL	Projected Loss	Projected Win
Sep 2	vs LSU (19)	99%		
Sep 8	vs Savannah St. (FCS)	100%		
Sep 15	at Toledo (55)	87%		
Sep 22	vs Fl. International (119)	99%		
Sep 27	vs North Carolina (52)	94%		
Oct 6	vs Florida St. (16)	64%		
Oct 13	at Virginia (75)	99%		
Oct 26	at Boston College (42)	78%		
Nov 3	vs Duke (32)	84%		
Nov 10	at Georgia Tech (50)	85%		
Nov 17	at Virginia Tech (22)	58%		
Nov 24	vs Pittsburgh (48)	93%		

After ten games, Miami was undefeated and intent on challenging Clemson for a likely playoff bid. But Mark Richt's Hurricanes had gone relatively unchallenged. Besides a dominant win over Notre Dame in November and a win over Virginia Tech, Toledo was the highest-rated S&P+ team that Miami had faced all season. Pitt's 24-14 upset over the Hurricanes started an end-of-season slide that also saw losses to Clemson and Wisconsin, which were understandable.

The main thing these latter three teams did was expose the offense. Against the Panthers, quarterback Malik Rosier completed just 44 percent of his passes for 187 yards, while running back Travis Homer averaged 1.7 yards per carry without a single run of 5 or more yards. Similar stories against Clemson and Wisconsin: 48 percent completion rate with two interceptions and a 38 percent rushing opportunity rate against the Tigers, and a 42 percent completion rate and three interceptions against the Badgers. While the run game was hampered by Mark Walton's injury (he averaged 7.6 yards per carry and a 48.2 percent opportunity rate), the passing game was inconsistent all season. Rosier averaged just a 54 percent completion rate and a 39 percent passing success rate on the year.

2018 might be determined by whether Rosier progresses as a passer. His top two targets are gone in Braxton Berrios and Chris Herndon IV, but a trio of receivers behind them ensures that there's significant experience in the receivers room. Ahmmon Richards is the likely leader after 447 yards and 17.9 yards per catch in an injury-filled sophomore season. Richards missed games against Clemson and Wisconsin due to a torn MCL, but ankle and hamstring problems also hurt his year.

Richards had nearly 1,000 receiving yards as a freshman in 2016.

And even though Walton is off to the NFL following his own injuries, freshman Lorenzo Lingard could form an elite tandem with Travis Homer. The second-ranked running back in the 2018 recruiting class, the five-star enrolled early and also ran track for Miami. Along with sophomore Deejay Dallas, Miami could have an elite run game in 2018.

The defense returns 70 percent of its production from a year ago, but loses some key players along the defensive line, which was fourth in havoc rate last season. Chad Thomas, Trent Harris, and RJ McIntosh combined for 35.5 tackles for loss and 16.5 sacks. Maybe worse, defensive line coach Craig Kuligowski also left for the Crimson Tide (as if Alabama needed more defensive line talent). But Demetrius Jackson and Joe Jackson should still be formidable ends, while Joe Garvin could be a breakout star as a sophomore edge rusher. True freshman Nesta Silvera, the second-ranked defensive tackle, could make an immediate impact too. The problem here isn't the top-end talent, which is excellent—it's depth, which forced Scott Patchan to move from tight end over to defensive end.

Miami avoids Clemson (until a potential ACC title game) but has an interesting Week 1 matchup against LSU. That's an intriguing game that could set the course of the season for both teams. A win for the Hurricanes would be a confidence-inducing SEC victory that would end their three-game slide from last season, while a loss would be deflating, even if it doesn't impact the ACC standings.

14. Mississippi State Bulldogs (9-3, 5-3)

2018 Projections

F/+	45.6 (14)
FEI	.157 (11)
S&P+	15.7 (14)
Total Wins	9.1
Conf Wins	5.3
SOS	.033 (13)
Conf SOS	.040 (8)
Div Champ	12%
Conf Champ	6%
CFP Berth	5%

Projection Factors

2017 F/+	35.9 (16)
2017 FEI	.145 (18)
2017 S&P+	7.9 (28)
5-Year F/+	27.8 (19)
5-Year FEI	.128 (19)
5-Year S&P+	11.7 (17)
2-Yr/5-Yr Recruiting	26/27
Ret. Offense	82% (17)
Ret. Defense	80% (22)
Ret. Total	81% (8)

Projected Win Likelihood by Game

Date	Opponent (Proj Rank)	PWL	Projected Loss / Projected Win
Sep 1	vs SF Austin (FCS)	100%	
Sep 8	at Kansas St. (46)	82%	
Sep 15	vs UL-Lafayette (116)	99%	
Sep 22	at Kentucky (63)	93%	
Sep 29	vs Florida (30)	82%	
Oct 6	vs Auburn (5)	48%	
Oct 20	at LSU (19)	51%	
Oct 27	vs Texas A&M (25)	74%	
Nov 3	vs Louisiana Tech (69)	98%	
Nov 10	at Alabama (1)	22%	
Nov 17	vs Arkansas (51)	94%	
Nov 22	at Ole Miss (31)	69%	

Joe Moorhead enters an ideal situation for a first-year head coach at the Power 5 level. The Bulldogs, who finished 9-4 with a bowl win over Louisville and 16th in the final F/+ rankings last season, return more production from last season than almost anyone else in the country. They rank fourth among Power 5 teams in returning production, with 81 percent overall, behind just Michigan State, Kansas, and Baylor.

The offense will be senior-led, with dynamic runners Nick Fitzgerald and Aeris Williams leading the way. Dan Mullen's offense was defined by efficiency and running the ball. Ranking 21st in success rate and 17th in rushing S&P+ but 125th in IsoPPP, and running the ball on nearly 70 percent of standard downs (21st-most), the Bulldogs ran often, and were efficient doing it. They picked up 5 yards on 44.8 percent of carries (sixth overall) as both Williams and Fitzgerald crossed the 1,000-yard mark. And that's even with their backups, Kylin Hill and Keytaon Thompson, receiving a fair number of snaps themselves. Expect both running backs, Hill and Williams, to become more involved in the passing game—as Saquon Barkley was last season for Penn State.

There has been some offseason talk about how Moorhead's offensive system would work at Mississippi State with Fitzgerald, who averaged just 6.2 yards per attempt and completed only 55.6 percent of his passes as a junior. Moorhead and Trace McSorley, his quarterback at Penn State, were known for effective shots downfield over the last two seasons—something that

Fitzgerald, ranking 122nd in passing IsoPPP last year, was not. But that's a little misleading. Penn State's 2017 offense was far more efficiency-minded that 2016's, and Moorhead usually designs and calls for "shot plays" only when they have a relatively high chance of success; it's not a deep pass-only offense. And if Moorhead is good at anything, it's adapting his scheme to fit personnel, which is something everyone preaches but few coordinators practice. Expect Moorhead to only improve the Bulldogs' offensive output.

The Bulldogs defense mirrored its offense with an efficiency focus, ranking 13th in success rate and 120th in IsoPPP, meaning that Mississippi State rarely gave up big plays, but they tended to be total breakdowns when they happened. The Bulldogs tied for fourth in the country in plays allowed of 10-plus yards, but they were 77th in plays of 30-plus yards and 118th in plays of 40-plus yards allowed, giving up 22. Nearly everyone returns for the defense in 2018, including Montez Sweat and Jeffery Simmons, who combined for 27.5 tackles for loss last season. Top defensive backs Mark McLaurin and Jonathan Abrams also return. The biggest change is at defensive coordinator, where the aggressive Todd Grantham is out for Bob Shoop, who came from Tennessee. While his Volunteers units weren't impressive, it's highly possible that that was more due to Tennessee than his own coaching ability, as Shoop led a couple of highly successful Penn State defenses before his time with the Volunteers.

15. USC Trojans (9-3, 7-2)

2018 Projections

F/+	43.3 (15)
FEI	.143 (17)
S&P+	14.0 (15)
Total Wins	9.3
Conf Wins	7.3
SOS	.077 (38)
Conf SOS	.209 (59)
Div Champ	74%
Conf Champ	37%
CFP Berth	23%

Projection Factors

2017 F/+	35.1 (19)
2017 FEI	.132 (20)
2017 S&P+	8.1 (26)
5-Year F/+	36.3 (9)
5-Year FEI	.146 (15)
5-Year S&P+	14.2 (10)
2-Yr/5-Yr Recruiting	3/5
Ret. Offense	40% (122)
Ret. Defense	65% (61)
Ret. Total	52% (114)

Projected Win Likelihood by Game

Date	Opponent (Proj Rank)	PWL	Projected Loss / Projected Win
Sep 1	vs UNLV (105)	99%	
Sep 8	at Stanford (17)	44%	
Sep 15	at Texas (24)	56%	
Sep 21	vs Washington St. (49)	91%	
Sep 29	at Arizona (35)	71%	
Oct 13	vs Colorado (92)	99%	
Oct 20	at Utah (29)	64%	
Oct 27	vs Arizona St. (44)	89%	
Nov 3	at Oregon St. (107)	99%	
Nov 10	vs California (58)	95%	
Nov 17	at UCLA (38)	73%	
Nov 24	vs Notre Dame (6)	46%	

The Trojans had the ignominious distinction of being the lowest-rated 11-win team in S&P+ last season, finishing 26th following their loss to Ohio State in the postseason. 2018, Clay Helton's third season, is a little bit of a reset year personnel-wise. Quarterback Sam Darnold is off to the NFL, but more than Darnold and his 4,143 passing yards and leadership of the 11th-ranked passing S&P+ offense have left. The entire team is 115th in returning production, returning just 40 percent on offense and 65 percent on defense. That's a lot to replace, even with USC's elite talent.

But it's hard to overlook just how talented the Trojans are. They ranked third behind Alabama and Ohio State in the 247 Team Talent Composite last season, then brought in the fourth-ranked recruiting class in February. That class could hold the answer to some of USC's biggest holes, especially at quarterback.

Matt Fink attempted all of nine passes last season and was a three-star prospect coming in. But thanks to his reclassification to graduate early, five-star J.T. Daniels could be the early heir for Darnold. Daniels is considered an elite quarterback prospect and rated similarly to Trevor Lawrence and Justin Fields in 2018.

The USC offense also loses a lot of skill talent. Wide receivers Deontay Burnett (27.9 percent target rate, 13 yards per catch) and Steven Mitchell Jr. (third in targets, 15.7 yards per catch) are both gone, but sophomore Tyler Vaughns and incoming freshman and 11th overall prospect Amon-Ra St. Brown should be a pretty fearsome duo at receiver. Similarly, while Ronald Jones II left for the NFL, true freshman Stephen Carr got valuable experience and equaled Jones' efficiency despite foot injuries. Maybe even better, the offensive line returns two all-conference linemen in Chris Brown and Toa

Lobendahn. The line could stand to improve though, ranking 38th in adjusted line yards and 31st in adjusted sack rate. With the offense likely led by a true freshman, an improving offensive line could be the most critical element for the offense's overall success.

The biggest things for the offense will be avoiding negative plays and finishing drives in the red zone. The Trojans scored touchdowns on just 57.6 percent of their red zone trips (86th) and averaged 4.2 points per trip inside the 40 (92nd). They had runs stopped at or behind the line on 19.5 percent of carries, and the two issues are probably related. That's not to mention turnovers, where USC was 91st in interceptions with 13 (and 121st in total turnovers).

The defense as a whole was pretty mediocre in 2017, ranking 55th in defensive S&P+. The problems were primarily against the run, where the Trojans were 47th, allowing 5-yard carries on 41.1 percent of opponents' runs (102nd) and only making tackles at or behind the line on 15.3 percent of plays (113th). The defense loses some big names, including Uchenna Nwosu, Rasheem Green, and Josh Fatu, but the return of star Porter Gustin and Cameron Smith should help shore up the run and the pass rush, while Christian Rector should have a big season at end. Top overall inside linebacker recruit Palaie Gaoteote could crack an already stacked rotation too. In the secondary, the Trojans will miss Chris Hawkins and Jack Jones, but they have a number of former blue-chippers ready to fill the gaps.

Overall, USC's season likely depends on how quickly the Trojans can get a quarterback ready for elite play and whether elite talent can be maximized with increased playing time. Overall team talent is as high as it ever has been—the only thing lacking is experience. The Trojans should fight Washington for the Pac-12 title.

16. Florida State Seminoles (8-4, 5-3)

2018 Projections

F/+	42.5 (16)
FEI	.155 (12)
S&P+	12.2 (19)
Total Wins	8.5
Conf Wins	5.4
SOS	.031 (9)
Conf SOS	.092 (22)
Div Champ	18%
Conf Champ	9%
CFP Berth	5%

Projection Factors

2017 F/+	25.6 (35)
2017 FEI	.107 (27)
2017 S&P+	4.9 (43)
5-Year F/+	41.0 (6)
5-Year FEI	.146 (14)
5-Year S&P+	17.0 (5)
2-Yr/5-Yr Recruiting	5/4
Ret. Offense	73% (45)
Ret. Defense	46% (119)
Ret. Total	59% (96)

Projected Win Likelihood by Game

Date	Opponent (Proj Rank)	PWL
Sep 3	vs Virginia Tech (22)	68%
Sep 8	vs Samford (FCS)	100%
Sep 15	at Syracuse (73)	96%
Sep 22	vs Northern Illinois (68)	97%
Sep 29	at Louisville (28)	62%
Oct 6	at Miami-FL (13)	36%
Oct 20	vs Wake Forest (36)	83%
Oct 27	vs Clemson (2)	42%
Nov 3	at NC State (34)	70%
Nov 10	at Notre Dame (6)	30%
Nov 17	vs Boston College (42)	86%
Nov 24	vs Florida (30)	78%

While the roster may be stockpiled with talent from years of top-10 recruiting by former head coach Jimbo Fisher, 2018 figures to be a transition year for the Florida State Seminoles. When Texas A&M lured Fisher away with a $75 million contract, the Seminoles moved fairly quickly to snatch up Willie Taggart from Oregon. Taggart had just parlayed a very successful run at South Florida into the Oregon gig and then went 7-5 with the Ducks before coming back to the Sunshine State to take over in Tallahassee.

Taggart will bring a style of offense to Florida State that is going to be markedly different than what the Seminoles were known for under Fisher. Taggart coined the term "Gulf Coast offense" for the spread system he created at South Florida when trying to adapt the power run game concepts he had taught alongside Jim Harbaugh at Stanford with dual-threat quarterback Quinton Flowers. It was a run/pass option-heavy system that turned Flowers into a primary run game option and often gave him quick pass options if opponents tried to keep defenders in the box. That approach evolved at Oregon with pocket passer Justin Herbert at the helm, but the main thrust of the system was consistent. The philosophy is about using pass options on the perimeter to create favorable numbers and angles for the run game.

Fisher preferred a straight, pro-style approach and would vacillate between emphasizing the I-formation run game or a three-receiver spread set and dropback passing based on where his star talent was clustered in a given year. Adjust-ing these players to the simple but radically different world of RPO spread offense could take some time.

Fortunately for Taggart, the Florida State roster includes four returning starters on the offensive line, returning starting quarterback James Blackman, and potential star running back Cam Akers. If they can get their quarterbacks up to speed in the option system, it should be relatively simple to create favorable numbers and angles for Akers in the run game.

The transition on the defense is going to be similar. Florida State is moving from an elaborate, Nick Saban-inspired approach to the uber-simple over-quarters structure favored by new defensive coordinator Harlon Barnett, formerly of Michigan State. Instead of having a variety of pattern-matching coverages, fronts, and sub-packages, the Seminoles will now focus on mastering press-man coverage outside and teaching their linemen, linebackers, and safeties to work in careful concert to sniff out and snuff out opposing offenses from a few base defenses. Much like on offense, it's a style that emphasizes execution of simple concepts over pro-style versatility and comprehensive playbooks.

This is a style that should translate very cleanly to a talented Florida State roster and a program that is well positioned to regularly recruit some of the best athletes in the country. Taggart should find big success relatively early in his tenure, but Year 1 will feature enough changes that 2019 is the more likely season for a big breakthrough to occur.

17. Stanford Cardinal (9-3, 6-3)

2018 Projections

F/+	42.4 (17)
FEI	.158 (10)
S&P+	11.9 (20)
Total Wins	8.7
Conf Wins	6.4
SOS	.036 (15)
Conf SOS	.090 (20)
Div Champ	19%
Conf Champ	9%
CFP Berth	6%

Projection Factors

2017 F/+	35.3 (18)
2017 FEI	.156 (16)
2017 S&P+	7.1 (32)
5-Year F/+	38.8 (7)
5-Year FEI	.173 (10)
5-Year S&P+	14.4 (9)
2-Yr/5-Yr Recruiting	27/21
Ret. Offense	81% (22)
Ret. Defense	51% (113)
Ret. Total	66% (61)

Projected Win Likelihood by Game

Date	Opponent (Proj Rank)	PWL
Aug 31	vs San Diego St. (59)	95%
Sep 8	vs USC (15)	56%
Sep 15	vs UC Davis (FCS)	100%
Sep 22	at Oregon (23)	54%
Sep 29	at Notre Dame (6)	30%
Oct 6	vs Utah (29)	77%
Oct 18	at Arizona St. (44)	77%
Oct 27	vs Washington St. (49)	91%
Nov 3	at Washington (7)	30%
Nov 10	vs Oregon St. (107)	99%
Nov 17	at California (58)	87%
Nov 24	at UCLA (38)	72%

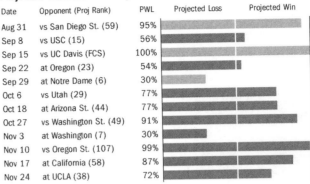

The Cardinal came very close to producing a Heisman winner in 2017 when running back Bryce Love replaced Christian McCaffrey and ran for 1,973 yards behind a mauling Stanford offensive line. The Cardinal finished 29th in offensive S&P+ thanks largely to an explosive ground attack with Love that produced regular explosive runs of 50 yards or more. They also did some real damage through the air, particularly down the stretch when redshirt freshman K.J. Costello found a rhythm at quarterback.

Riding that wave, Stanford rolled to the Pac-12 Championship Game, where they narrowly lost to USC 31-28 when Costello couldn't match the production of Trojans quarterback Sam Darnold. It's hard to imagine the Stanford running game being so effective again, but then Love and most of the offensive line returns. And opponents who want to game-plan to shut down Love will likely face serious complications from an improving passing attack. Costello will return at quarterback and has all of his major targets back, most notably tight end Kaden Smith. The truly scary dimension to this offense is in the fact that Costello, left tackle Walker Little, left guard Nate Herbig, and Smith all stand to improve substantially as young players coming into the 2018 season after confidence-building 2017 campaigns.

Stanford's defense has to improve to give them a shot to translate offensive growth into a Pac-12 title or playoff berth. That could be tricky given that the unit finished only 59th in defensive S&P+ in 2017 and now must replace star defensive lineman Harrison Phillips (23 run stuffs, seven sacks) and top defensive backs Justin Reid (leading tackler, five interceptions) and Quenton Meeks (eight pass break-ups). The defensive line in particular is now bereft of an established playmaker after enjoying the play of Solomon Thomas in 2016 and Phillips in 2017.

The Cardinal have been at the forefront of the same kind of single-high pattern matching coverages paired with a 2-4-5 defensive package that has helped put the Washington Huskies defense on the map. Without impact defensive lineman up front attacking gaps and commanding the attention of offensive linemen while linebackers shoot through unguarded gaps, the scheme doesn't work out the same. Stanford's ceiling in 2018 will be set by whether one of their up-and-coming defensive linemen—such as sophomores Jovan Swann and Michael Williams or junior Dylan Jackson—are ready to carry the day.

18. Central Florida Knights (11-1, 8-0)

2018 Projections

F/+	41.0 (18)
FEI	.120 (18)
S&P+	13.9 (17)
Total Wins	11.1
Conf Wins	7.6
SOS	.586 (115)
Conf SOS	.771 (87)
Div Champ	95%
Conf Champ	47%
CFP Berth	3%

Projection Factors

2017 F/+	50.3 (8)
2017 FEI	.237 (9)
2017 S&P+	15.5 (7)
5-Year F/+	3.9 (60)
5-Year FEI	.136 (16)
5-Year S&P+	0.9 (65)
2-Yr/5-Yr Recruiting	66/67
Ret. Offense	71% (52)
Ret. Defense	76% (28)
Ret. Total	74% (24)

Projected Win Likelihood by Game

Date	Opponent (Proj Rank)	PWL
Aug 30	at Connecticut (123)	99%
Sep 8	vs S. Carolina St. (FCS)	100%
Sep 15	at North Carolina (52)	82%
Sep 21	vs Florida Atlantic (39)	83%
Sep 29	vs Pittsburgh (48)	90%
Oct 6	vs SMU (82)	99%
Oct 13	at Memphis (47)	78%
Oct 20	at East Carolina (124)	99%
Nov 1	vs Temple (71)	97%
Nov 10	vs Navy (74)	98%
Nov 17	vs Cincinnati (91)	99%
Nov 23	at South Florida (64)	90%

The Central Florida Knights had a legendary 2017 season, finishing 13-0 with an American Athletic Conference title earned via shootout victories over South Florida (49-42) and then Memphis in the championship game (62-55) before punctuating the season with a victory over near-playoff team Auburn in the Peach Bowl. Since then the program has been celebrating a claimed national championship and trolling Alabama on social media while faced with the daunting task of replacing head coach Scott Frost, who departed for his alma mater, Nebraska.

Frost's replacement is Josh Heupel, the one-time national championship quarterback for the Oklahoma Sooners who has since molded himself into an offensive coach who utilizes the vertically oriented, spread-RPO system popularized by the Baylor Bears under Art Briles. Heupel got a first-hand look at that scheme while coaching the Oklahoma offense in the early 2010s before being fired after the Sooners went "only" 8-5 in 2014 despite producing a 2,000-yard rusher in freshman running back Samaje Perine. From there he took his offense to Missouri, where quarterback Drew Lock threw for 3,964 yards and 44 touchdowns in 2017. It's an explosive and cutting-edge offensive system, but it's also one that depends on the quarterback firing passes down the field from the pocket, which is more or less the antithesis of how Central Florida played last year with then-sophomore quarterback Milton McKenzie.

McKenzie's strong point was running around and distributing the ball on options under the direction of Frost, a former championship-winning, triple-option practitioner himself. McKenzie threw for 4,037 yards and ran for another 683 while scoring 45 total touchdowns in the Frost offense. Nearly all of his fellow starters on offense are also back, as Frost went with a youth movement early. The obvious move would be to carry on with the existing offense, but Heupel has made hires within the Baylor style, so there may be an adjustment in Orlando that makes for a less explosive offense than expected.

Heupel made a home-run hire on defense by landing longtime Florida coach Randy Shannon. Shannon will bring the classic wide-9, 4-3 over Miami defense and quarters coverage along with a well-established acumen for recruiting top players out of the state. The adjustment here should be less jarring since most of the impact players on the 2017 Knights defense, such as fifth-round pick linebacker Shaquem Griffin, are now gone. Additionally, while Shannon prefers a different front than the previous staff, he played the same quarters coverages, so the returning starters in the secondary may be able to anchor the unit through the transition.

There will be a lot of eyes on Central Florida after their 13-0 season and national title claims, but the road from here on out in the tumultuous American could be rougher than expected.

19. LSU Tigers (8-4, 4-4)

2018 Projections

F/+	40.5 (19)
FEI	.115 (20)
S&P+	14.0 (16)
Total Wins	7.5
Conf Wins	4.2
SOS	.012 (2)
Conf SOS	.022 (2)
Div Champ	4%
Conf Champ	2%
CFP Berth	1%

Projection Factors

2017 F/+	33.5 (21)
2017 FEI	.102 (28)
2017 S&P+	9.1 (19)
5-Year F/+	38.4 (8)
5-Year FEI	.135 (17)
5-Year S&P+	16.0 (7)
2-Yr/5-Yr Recruiting	7/6
Ret. Offense	39% (123)
Ret. Defense	57% (87)
Ret. Total	48% (121)

Projected Win Likelihood by Game

Date	Opponent (Proj Rank)	PWL
Sep 2	vs Miami-FL (13)	41%
Sep 8	vs SE Louisiana (FCS)	100%
Sep 15	at Auburn (5)	26%
Sep 22	vs Louisiana Tech (69)	97%
Sep 29	vs Ole Miss (31)	76%
Oct 6	at Florida (30)	62%
Oct 13	vs Georgia (4)	40%
Oct 20	vs Mississippi St. (14)	49%
Nov 3	vs Alabama (1)	29%
Nov 10	at Arkansas (51)	81%
Nov 17	vs Rice (127)	99%
Nov 24	at Texas A&M (25)	52%

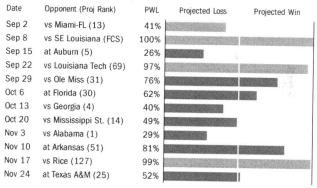

One and a half years in and the Ed Orgeron era at LSU has been pretty up and down. After he served as the interim coach for much of 2016, part of Orgeron's plan to secure the head coaching job was taking a reduced salary that would leave money on the table to pay defensive coordinator Dave Aranda to stick around, then secure one of the top offensive coordinators on the market. LSU signed Matt Canada from Pittsburgh, fresh off a season where his offense outscored the eventual champions at Clemson 43-42. However, Canada didn't work well with the LSU staff, and they negotiated a buyout before the bowl. Orgeron then turned back to the man who had coordinated the Tigers offense during his interim season, Steve Ensminger.

This could lead to a significant change for the offense.

Canada's system is geared around running traditional downhill schemes like inside zone or power, but always attaching jet sweeps to control opponents' edge players. As soon as an opponent would get aggressive with their edge players, the Tigers would hand off on the sweep for big yardage around the end. Ensminger plans to bring more of a multiple system with an extensive passing game to make the most of LSU's deep wide receiver roster and to overcome the lack of a proven, game-changing running back.

To help secure an effective transition, the Tigers recruited Ohio State grad transfer quarterback Joe Burrow, who narrowly lost the spring competition with Dwayne Haskins. He'll now join forces with Texas Tech wide receiver transfer Jonathan Giles (1,158 yards and 13 touchdowns in 2017) to take charge of an offense that's finally transitioning away from the downhill style preferred by Les Miles.

Things continue on a positive trajectory for the defense, which returns star linebacker Devin White (19 run stuffs in 2017), starting safeties John Battle and Grant Delpit, and freshman phenom cornerback Andrea "Greedy" Williams (11 pass break-ups, six interceptions). Like on offense, the Tigers are supplementing their defensive line that is getting hit with graduations by welcoming another Texas Tech transfer, Breiden Fehoko.

The defensive line will have some new faces, but Fehoko, sophomore pass-rusher K'Lavon Chaisson, and White should give Aranda some good options when he's drawing up his blitz packages, which are often designed to create one-on-ones with a blitzing linebacker against a running back. Meanwhile, the secondary could be poised for a major improvement thanks to stability at safety, a year of growth from sophomore strong safety Grant Delpit, and improved depth that should allow Aranda to get into his "peso" 2-4-5 nickel package more often.

In 2017, the Tigers played more base 3-4 personnel with senior linebacker Corey Thompson playing to the wide edge rather than a defensive back, which helped LSU finish 24th in rushing S&P+ but might have been a hindrance to their pass defense, which ranked 55th on passing downs. This team could put together a special season if Burrow is ready to run the show, but the schedule won't be forgiving if he isn't, with Miami, Auburn, Florida, Georgia, and Alabama all looming on the docket.

20. TCU Horned Frogs (9-3, 6-3)

2018 Projections

F/+	38.0 (20)
FEI	.116 (19)
S&P+	11.4 (22)
Total Wins	8.7
Conf Wins	6.4
SOS	.072 (33)
Conf SOS	.160 (50)
Div Champ	-
Conf Champ	20%
CFP Berth	9%

Projection Factors

2017 F/+	43.3 (13)
2017 FEI	.177 (13)
2017 S&P+	11.0 (14)
5-Year F/+	27.9 (17)
5-Year FEI	.161 (12)
5-Year S&P+	10.9 (20)
2-Yr/5-Yr Recruiting	31/33
Ret. Offense	44% (116)
Ret. Defense	61% (73)
Ret. Total	52% (113)

Projected Win Likelihood by Game

Date	Opponent (Proj Rank)	PWL
Sep 1	vs Southern (FCS)	100%
Sep 7	at SMU (82)	97%
Sep 15	vs Ohio St. (3)	29%
Sep 22	at Texas (24)	48%
Sep 29	vs Iowa St. (43)	83%
Oct 11	vs Texas Tech (53)	90%
Oct 20	vs Oklahoma (8)	39%
Oct 27	at Kansas (102)	99%
Nov 3	vs Kansas St. (46)	86%
Nov 10	at West Virginia (45)	73%
Nov 17	at Baylor (37)	66%
Nov 24	vs Oklahoma St. (21)	61%

The 2017 TCU Horned Frogs were coming off a very disappointing 6-7 season in which their offense took a big dip without quarterback Trevone Boykin or wide receiver Josh Doctson, while their defense struggled to get back on track. Head coach Gary Patterson figured out the defensive side of things (his area of expertise) and unleashed one of his best units yet while the offense leaned on a senior-laden line and a cautious, senior game manager at quarterback in Kenny Hill to grind out wins. They went 11-3 but couldn't beat Oklahoma either in the regular season or the Big 12 Championship Game.

TCU's next team is going to look very different and require a different formula. The keys to the offense are now likely to be turned over to sophomore quarterback Shawn Robinson, a dynamic runner who is still raw as a passer, and sophomore receiver Jalen Reagor (576 receiving yards, eight touchdowns in 2017). Whereas the 2017 TCU offense was occasionally plodding and cautious, the 2018 offense will put a lot of explosive playmakers on the field without much in the way of experience at quarterback or offensive line.

How well the offensive line gels will be a major determinant of the upcoming season. The Horned Frogs got a lot of mileage out of keeping seniors Matt Pryor and Austin Schlottman paired together either at right tackle and right guard, respectively, or at right guard and center when fellow senior and starting center Patrick Morris was injured. Replacing their reliable push up front is a major concern for this upcoming season.

On defense the Horned Frogs are losing defensive end Mat Boesen (11.5 sacks), linebacker Travin Howard (the school's leading tackler for three consecutive seasons), safety Nick Orr (three interceptions, third-leading tackler), and cornerback Ranthony Texada (14 pass break-ups). Their defensive breakthrough in 2017 was due in part to the final effort of these veterans and in part to emerging stars like defensive tackle Ross Blacklock (10 run stuffs), defensive end Ben Banogu (8.5 sacks), linebacker Ty Summers (16 run stuffs), and safeties Innis Gaines and Ridwan Issahaku (12 combined tackles for loss, four combined sacks).

The Horned Frogs were truly strong and deep at every position, and their ability to play two defensive ends with passrushing ability and linebacker speed was a game-changer in dealing with the spread offenses in the Big 12. The 2018 defense should be very effective, and with Blacklock and Summers returning they have the big, tough guys up front to once again lean towards playing speed at every other position. But they are replacing a lot of skilled athletes who had played a lot of Big 12 football. If the 2017 season was about winning with grit and experience, the 2018 TCU season is going to be about growing pains with exciting young athletes.

21. Oklahoma State Cowboys (9-3, 6-3)

2018 Projections

F/+	36.6 (21)
FEI	.091 (27)
S&P+	12.9 (18)
Total Wins	8.7
Conf Wins	6.1
SOS	.088 (45)
Conf SOS	.112 (38)
Div Champ	-
Conf Champ	13%
CFP Berth	6%

Projection Factors

2017 F/+	45.8 (12)
2017 FEI	.179 (12)
2017 S&P+	13.2 (12)
5-Year F/+	25.6 (20)
5-Year FEI	.150 (13)
5-Year S&P+	9.6 (25)
2-Yr/5-Yr Recruiting	35/36
Ret. Offense	52% (103)
Ret. Defense	54% (97)
Ret. Total	53% (112)

Projected Win Likelihood by Game

Date	Opponent (Proj Rank)	PWL
Aug 30	vs Missouri St. (FCS)	100%
Sep 8	vs South Alabama (110)	99%
Sep 15	vs Boise St. (26)	63%
Sep 22	vs Texas Tech (53)	89%
Sep 29	at Kansas (102)	99%
Oct 6	vs Iowa St. (43)	82%
Oct 13	at Kansas St. (46)	73%
Oct 27	vs Texas (24)	61%
Nov 3	at Baylor (37)	64%
Nov 10	at Oklahoma (8)	23%
Nov 17	vs West Virginia (45)	83%
Nov 24	at TCU (20)	40%

It has been a few years since Oklahoma State wasn't led by the duo of Mason Rudolph (third last season in quarterback rating and yards per attempt, first in overall passing yards) and James Washington (1,544 yards and 20.9 yards per catch). The pair have torn up the Big 12 for three straight years, but now both have gone to the Pittsburgh Steelers, leaving the Cowboys with only 44 percent of their offensive production returning in 2018 (115th). The departures also include Marcell Ateman, who was second on the team with 1,156 receiving yards (an also-insane 19.6 yards per catch), and two all-conference linemen in Zach Crabtree and Brad Lundblade. It's a huge blow to an elite offense, and a little scary. Under Rudolph, the Cowboys were no worse than 19th in offensive S&P+, during his first season as a starter. But they were 78th in offensive S&P+ in 2014 when Daxx Garman was quarterback.

There's a wide-open race for Rudolph's replacement between senior Taylor Cornelius, sophomore Keondrew Wudtree, Hawaii grad transfer Dru Brown, redshirt junior John Kolar, and four-star freshman Spencer Sanders. Cornelius, Rudolph's primary backup last season, seems to be the front-runner, but he only attempted ten passes last season. At receiver, Jalen McCleskey, Dillon Stoner, and Tyron Johnson look like the most likely top targets, but the first two averaged 7 yards per catch less than either Washington or Ateman. In a passing offense that ranked eighth in passing IsoPPP last season through Rudolph's insanely good RPO reads, the hope is that someone—maybe Johnson—can become an explosive receiving option.

The good news is that at least the new quarterback will have running back Justice Hill to shoulder some of the load. Few backs got more touches than Hill last season (11th in the country overall in carries). So Hill is a workhorse back, but his 1,467 yards were relatively inefficient, as was the entire run game. Hill gained 5 or more rushing yards on just 36.9 percent of his carries (the offense was 89th overall in opportunity rate), getting stuffed at or behind the line on more than a fifth of rushes (84th). Losing two top offensive linemen doesn't help here.

The Cowboys defense was mediocre overall (70th in S&P+), but did a good job creating havoc up front (27th in defensive line havoc rate). The main problem was on third downs, where they ranked 96th in defensive S&P+ and 68th in opponent third-down conversion percentage. The concern is at the back end of the defense, which loses Tre Flowers and Ramon Richards, although some younger guys got into the rotation. But that's nevertheless the biggest concern. For a defense that already was liable to give up big plays—81st in 20-plus-yard plays allowed and 92nd IsoPPP, meaning that they both gave up a lot of big plays, and those big plays were usually pretty big—new starters in the secondary can be concerning.

Nevertheless, Oklahoma State has few games on their schedule when they aren't likely to be favorites. Their most difficult game is their rivalry against the Sooners. TCU, Boise State, and West Virginia will all be challenges, but Mike Gundy has created a stable, efficient team over the last three seasons.

22. Virginia Tech Hokies (9-3, 5-3)

2018 Projections

F/+	36.1 (22)
FEI	.099 (22)
S&P+	11.5 (21)
Total Wins	8.8
Conf Wins	5.5
SOS	.100 (52)
Conf SOS	.179 (55)
Div Champ	26%
Conf Champ	13%
CFP Berth	8%

Projection Factors

2017 F/+	29.8 (28)
2017 FEI	.094 (31)
2017 S&P+	7.6 (30)
5-Year F/+	23.1 (25)
5-Year FEI	.098 (25)
5-Year S&P+	8.4 (30)
2-Yr/5-Yr Recruiting	24/29
Ret. Offense	68% (66)
Ret. Defense	64% (63)
Ret. Total	66% (63)

Projected Win Likelihood by Game

Date	Opponent (Proj Rank)	PWL	Projected Loss	Projected Win
Sep 3	at Florida St. (16)	32%		
Sep 8	vs William & Mary (FCS)	100%		
Sep 15	vs East Carolina (124)	99%		
Sep 22	at Old Dominion (115)	99%		
Sep 29	at Duke (32)	59%		
Oct 6	vs Notre Dame (6)	35%		
Oct 13	at North Carolina (52)	77%		
Oct 25	vs Georgia Tech (50)	87%		
Nov 3	vs Boston College (42)	80%		
Nov 10	at Pittsburgh (48)	75%		
Nov 17	vs Miami-FL (13)	42%		
Nov 23	vs Virginia (75)	97%		

Justin Fuente's Hokies are entering a possible rebuild season. June wasn't a kind month to Virginia Tech, leaving question marks in the secondary. Compounding those personnel losses is an unforgiving schedule, with an opening game against Florida State.

Quarterback Josh Jackson had a solid first season where he passed for nearly 3,000 yards at 7.6 yards per attempt and led the 45th-ranked passing S&P+ offense, which was similar to Jerod Evans' year before him. After rumors of academic ineligibility, new reports in late June indicate that his status is resolved and that he is still with the team. As only a redshirt sophomore, Jackson is expected to build on a solid first season and help lead a team that would likely need the offense to compensate for losses on the defensive side of the ball.

The options to backup Jackson include Ryan Willis, a redshirt junior transfer from Kansas who had a solid showing in the spring game; Hendon Hooker, a redshirt freshman who was a higher-rated recruit than Willis but appears to be behind him on the depth chart; and true freshman Quincy Patterson, who comes with high expectations but no experience.

Fuente must also replace receiver Cam Phillips, who had more receiving yards than the next three most-targeted receivers combined. The receiver trio of Sean Savoy, Eric Kumah, and Henri Murphy are solid, but none equaled Phillips' combination of solid catch rate and yards per catch.

The other big concern is in the defensive secondary. The Hokies already lost a lot of production from last season's havoc-creating defense. Brothers Tremaine and Terrell Edmunds combined for 16.5 tackles for loss and 29 run stuffs, defensive tackle Tim Settle contributed 12.5 tackles for loss of his own, linebacker Andrew Motuapuaka was fourth on the team with 11.5 tackles for loss, and corner Greg Stroman led the team in interceptions and pass breakups. On top of those losses, the Hokies lost two more likely starting defensive backs with Adonis Alexander entering the NFL supplemental draft and JUCO transfer Jeremy Webb lost with an Achilles injury. That's an insane amount of talent to replace, creating a very young team on both sides of the ball. The losses weren't just to the NFL or injury—safeties coach Galen Scott resigned suddenly during the offseason, with Texas A&M analyst Tyrone Nix set to replace him.

The good news is that Bud Foster is still a Hokie (as he has been since time immemorial and always will be) and that there is plenty of talent along the defensive line. But the defense is probably going to take a step back from last year's ninth-ranked unit simply due to personnel losses.

23. Oregon Ducks (9-3, 6-3)

2018 Projections

F/+	35.3 (23)
FEI	.096 (24)
S&P+	11.3 (23)
Total Wins	9.1
Conf Wins	6.1
SOS	.148 (63)
Conf SOS	.151 (48)
Div Champ	15%
Conf Champ	8%
CFP Berth	5%

Projection Factors

2017 F/+	12.4 (50)
2017 FEI	.018 (55)
2017 S&P+	4.7 (47)
5-Year F/+	24.6 (22)
5-Year FEI	.074 (32)
5-Year S&P+	9.7 (24)
2-Yr/5-Yr Recruiting	18/19
Ret. Offense	72% (51)
Ret. Defense	63% (68)
Ret. Total	67% (56)

Projected Win Likelihood by Game

Date	Opponent (Proj Rank)	PWL
Sep 1	vs Bowling Green (94)	99%
Sep 8	vs Portland St. (FCS)	100%
Sep 15	vs San Jose St. (129)	99%
Sep 22	vs Stanford (17)	46%
Sep 29	at California (58)	82%
Oct 13	vs Washington (7)	35%
Oct 20	at Washington St. (49)	74%
Oct 27	at Arizona (35)	61%
Nov 3	vs UCLA (38)	77%
Nov 10	at Utah (29)	53%
Nov 17	vs Arizona St. (44)	82%
Nov 23	at Oregon St. (107)	99%

The Ducks move on to their third coach in as many years with Mario Cristobal getting a promotion to replace the Florida State-bound Willie Taggart. The consistency that Cristobal brings, along with a healthy Justin Herbert, could mean a return to form for the Ducks. They have languished since their 2014 playoff championship appearance, finishing 23rd, then 78th, and then 50th last season in the F/+ final rankings. But now, with one more hit of the reset button, the Ducks should develop some stability.

That stability hinges on Herbert's health. When healthy, he was one of the best quarterbacks in the country. He completed 67.5 percent of his passes while averaging 8.9 net yards per attempt (including sacks), which was tenth-best in the country. Oregon only lost two games when Herbert actually played—against Arizona State (by two points) and the meaningless bowl game against Boise State. And nearly all of Herbert's targets return, including Dillon Mitchell and Johnny Johnson III, while a number of new receivers arrive, including at least two blue-chip freshmen (which could be three: Oregon's second-highest rated recruit, receiver Jalen Hall, left after one practice but is still officially on the roster). Nearly as important, nearly everyone returns on a veteran offensive line that ranked 20th in adjusted line yards last season. Left tackle Tyrell Crosby's loss hurts, but there is decent depth and a huge crop of freshmen, most of whom are a step up in talent by 247's rankings. The line also adds Alabama grad transfer Dallas Warmack too. This is likely to be the most pass-heavy offense that Oregon has seen since Marcus Mariota's Heisman season.

If the offense has any questions, they are depth at quarterback—where then-freshman Braxton Burmeister averaged just 4.3 yards per attempt and a 7.8 percent interception rate—and at running back. Royce Freeman, who finally left for the NFL after setting Oregon's career rushing yards record, leaves only Tony Brooks-James and Darrian Felix as running backs with any experience. Brooks-James is on the smaller side but was less explosive than either Freeman or Kani Benoit. The Ducks will need at least one other back to emerge as a viable playmaking threat.

Taggart's lasting legacy at Oregon may be his hire of defensive coordinator Jim Leavitt. The former Colorado coach brought an aggressive defensive style to Eugene that finally took the Ducks defense from terrible to average (and occasionally good). In the three years after Oregon's championship game appearance (where they weren't exactly a defensive powerhouse either), the Ducks have ranked 84th, dead last, and 41st in defensive FEI.

Aggressive play is the key for Leavitt's defense. Last season the Ducks effectively applied pressure—ranking 19th in overall havoc rating—and were therefore content to give up occasional big plays (ranking 104th in IsoPPP) to be efficient overall (26th in success rate). While only 63 percent of Oregon's defensive production returns in 2018, the Ducks do have some star power, including defensive end Jalen Jelks (15 tackles for loss), linebacker Troy Dye (13.5 tackles for loss), and Justin Hollins (11.5 tackles for loss).

The major questions are depth on the line and in the secondary. The secondary is going to miss Arrion Springs and his 18 pass breakups and Tyree Robinson, but a number of young players got experience last season, including cornerback Deommodore Lenoir and safeties Brady Breeze and Nick Pickett.

The schedule sets up well, too. Washington is obviously the biggest challenge, but Stanford, Arizona, Washington State, and Utah are all more or less toss-up games. Take two out of those four and Oregon should have a relatively successful season.

24. Texas Longhorns (8-4, 6-3)

2018 Projections

F/+	35.0 (24)
FEI	.108 (21)
S&P+	9.6 (27)
Total Wins	8.4
Conf Wins	6.0
SOS	.093 (50)
Conf SOS	.138 (46)
Div Champ	-
Conf Champ	13%
CFP Berth	5%

Projection Factors

2017 F/+	20.0 (41)
2017 FEI	.085 (35)
2017 S&P+	3.7 (50)
5-Year F/+	9.5 (45)
5-Year FEI	.061 (37)
5-Year S&P+	5.5 (43)
2-Yr/5-Yr Recruiting	16/14
Ret. Offense	77% (31)
Ret. Defense	57% (88)
Ret. Total	67% (59)

Projected Win Likelihood by Game

Date	Opponent (Proj Rank)	PWL	Projected Loss / Projected Win
Sep 1	vs Maryland (80)	96%	
Sep 8	vs Tulsa (99)	99%	
Sep 15	vs USC (15)	44%	
Sep 22	vs TCU (20)	53%	
Sep 29	at Kansas St. (46)	71%	
Oct 6	vs Oklahoma (8)	28%	
Oct 13	vs Baylor (37)	76%	
Oct 27	at Oklahoma St. (21)	39%	
Nov 3	vs West Virginia (45)	82%	
Nov 10	at Texas Tech (53)	77%	
Nov 17	vs Iowa St. (43)	80%	
Nov 23	at Kansas (102)	99%	

Tom Herman's first year as Longhorns head coach wasn't exactly the kind of dream-season, immediate-turnaround year that Texas fans were hoping for. Finishing 7-6 and 41st in the F/+, the Longhorns generally lost the games they were supposed to (Oklahoma, Oklahoma State, TCU, USC), and then threw in a few unexpected losses for good measure (Maryland, Texas Tech).

The offense was the problem once again. Herman and offensive coordinator Tim Beck juggled between Shane Buechele and Sam Ehlinger all season due to injuries and relatively even play between them. Buechele, the incumbent sophomore who had previously elicited Colt McCoy comparisons, was frequently injured, causing the freshman Ehlinger to step in. The two remain in a quarterback battle going in to summer workouts. Last season Buechele completed 64.3 percent of passes to Ehlinger's 57.5 percent, but Ehlinger averaged 6.3 yards per play to Buechele's 5.4, and Ehlinger also took far fewer sacks, at a rate of 3.8 percent to 9.7 percent.

While neither quarterback had impressive numbers, they're not necessarily the offense's primary concern. Instead, that is either the offensive line or the skills positions. There are reasons to be optimistic about the line, which may have been the offense's biggest hindrance last season, ranking 90th in both adjusted sack rate and adjusted line yards. The Longhorns shuffled their starting line every game last season. While the inconsistency was bad for unit cohesion (and therefore, you know, blocking), the unit does benefit from a number of returning players with experience. Texas also has Rice graduate transfer Calvin Anderson, JUCO transfer Mikey Grandy, two four-star sophomores in Patrick Hudson and J.P. Urquidez, and three additional blue-chip freshmen coming in for new offensive line coach Herb Hand. It's easy to imagine the line, and therefore the entire offense, improving significantly with that mix of experience and young talent.

The skill players are another question mark, in part because the line didn't do the offense too many favors last year. Kyle Porter, Daniel Young, and Toneil Carter all played some, but no one had an opportunity rate above 36 percent, and Ehlinger actually led the team in rushing yards. One of those three could emerge with a more consistent line, but Texas also added Cal transfer Tre Watson, who at the very least gives the Longhorns another weapon (though it's not clear from his rushing numbers that he's a no-brainer upgrade at the position either). At receiver, both Collin Johnson and Lil'Jordan Humphrey return, while an incoming freshman like Brennan Eagles, Joshua Moore, or Al'vonte Woodard could crack the rotation as well. There's no defined superstar yet, but the hope is that a more consistent line, less quarterback run-centric play calling, and a second year in Herman's system can give the offense the boost necessary to compete in the Big 12.

For all of the offense's issues, the Longhorns defense was the only unit to consistently slow the elite offenses they saw each week in conference play. They held Oklahoma to 29, USC to 27, Oklahoma State to 13. Missouri and West Virginia didn't crack 20. They were the nation's best at third-down defense and created a fair bit of havoc, especially from the defensive backfield. The only issue is that the Longhorns lose a star at each level of the defense: Poona Ford on the line, linebacker Malik Jefferson, and DeShon Elliott in the defensive backfield. That's 26.5 tackles for loss, 39 run stuffs, and six interceptions lost between the three of them. Overall Texas only returns 57 percent of their defensive production from a year ago (90th), so there are opportunities for new stars to emerge. Todd Orlando has deserved a good amount of trust, however, and the Longhorns are bringing in a historically elite defensive back recruiting class to mitigate those losses. You never want to be in a situation where you're forced to rely on freshmen for key roles, but they are bringing in two of the top three safeties in the country as well as four other blue-chip defensive backs. If Orlando can strike the right balance of elite young talent and veteran players, and the offense can take a few steps forward, then Texas might be competitive in the Big 12 race once again.

25. Texas A&M Aggies (7-5, 4-4)

2018 Projections

F/+	34.8 (25)
FEI	.093 (26)
S&P+	11.0 (24)
Total Wins	7.4
Conf Wins	4.1
SOS	.012 (3)
Conf SOS	.023 (3)
Div Champ	2%
Conf Champ	1%
CFP Berth	1%

Projection Factors

2017 F/+	5.2 (59)
2017 FEI	.015 (58)
2017 S&P+	2.0 (61)
5-Year F/+	19.3 (29)
5-Year FEI	.049 (41)
5-Year S&P+	9.9 (23)
2-Yr/5-Yr Recruiting	14/10
Ret. Offense	66% (72)
Ret. Defense	78% (26)
Ret. Total	72% (33)

Projected Win Likelihood by Game

Date	Opponent (Proj Rank)	PWL
Aug 30	vs Northwestern St. (FCS)	100%
Sep 8	vs Clemson (2)	31%
Sep 15	vs UL-Monroe (106)	99%
Sep 22	at Alabama (1)	12%
Sep 29	vs Arkansas (51)	81%
Oct 6	vs Kentucky (63)	93%
Oct 13	at South Carolina (33)	59%
Oct 27	at Mississippi St. (14)	26%
Nov 3	at Auburn (5)	20%
Nov 10	vs Ole Miss (31)	69%
Nov 17	vs UAB (95)	99%
Nov 24	vs LSU (19)	48%

The Aggies welcome the richest man in Texas (don't quote us on that), Jimbo Fisher, to College Station after getting fed up with Kevin Sumlin's inability to bring (best player in program history) Johnny Manziel back for another year of eligibility. To be fair, 7-6 and 59th in the F/+ isn't really what fans have in mind for the program. But many of the program's recent troubles can be traced to quarterback play, as both Kyle Allen and Kyler Murray left the program, then Nick Starkel got injured against UCLA.

As a result of injuries, Starkel and Kellen Mond (a significantly higher-rated quarterback coming out of high school) split time. Starkel averaged 2.6 yards per attempt more and had an 8.5 percent higher completion rate than Mond, but Starkel also had the benefit of both a redshirt year and arguably easier competition—Mond made the starts against Alabama and Florida. Fisher has said that the competition will extend into fall camp, but Starkel made a statement by throwing for 499 yards in the bowl game against Wake Forest (some context, though: Wake Forest's Mike Elko-less defense was only ranked 87th in passing S&P+ last season). Mond does bring some rushing ability, averaging 6.7 yards per carry and 5 yards on a team-high of 47.1 percent of his rushes. Starkel finished with -2 rushing yards on just four carries. Either quarterback will have to deal with the loss of stalwart receivers Christian Kirk and Damion Ratley, although sophomore Jhamon Ausbon had an impressive freshman season (50-571-3).

Besides quarterback, what the Aggies really need on offense is an offensive line—that is apparent from comparing now-junior running back Trayveon Williams' freshman and sophomore seasons. As a freshman, Williams averaged 6.8 yards per carry, 8.0 highlight yards per opportunity, and a 41 percent opportunity rate for the 26th overall rushing S&P+ offense. As a sophomore, his numbers slumped to 4.6 yards per carry, 6.5 highlight yards per opportunity, and a completely inefficient 26.6 percent opportunity rate. The line was at least decent in pass protection, ranking 38th in adjusted sack rate, but 19.5 percent of rushes were stopped at or behind the line of scrimmage (65th). As Williams showed as a freshman, he's more than capable of being a feature back and one of the best in the SEC. And since the line's 2017 problems had to do primarily with injuries and lack of continuity, there's a chance that a more experienced, stable starting lineup could bring the run game back in to form.

Of course, both of those questions are dependent on the adaptation to a more "pro-style" offense under Fisher. Fisher's Florida State teams ran out of multiple sets and with the quarterback under center, and the Aggies are set to use a fullback reportedly about 70 percent of the time.

Most of the Aggies' questions are on the offensive side of the ball. While the defense was rated relatively worse than the offense, it benefits from 78 percent of last season's production returning (27th), including a number of freshmen who established major roles for themselves early on.

26. Boise State Broncos (11-1, 8-0)

2018 Projections

F/+	33.7 (26)
FEI	.094 (25)
S&P+	10.0 (25)
Total Wins	10.9
Conf Wins	7.7
SOS	.537 (107)
Conf SOS	.882 (102)
Div Champ	93%
Conf Champ	56%
CFP Berth	3%

Projection Factors

2017 F/+	34.1 (20)
2017 FEI	.121 (22)
2017 S&P+	8.2 (25)
5-Year F/+	24.5 (23)
5-Year FEI	.107 (24)
5-Year S&P+	9.0 (27)
2-Yr/5-Yr Recruiting	65/65
Ret. Offense	54% (100)
Ret. Defense	88% (9)
Ret. Total	71% (39)

Projected Win Likelihood by Game

Date	Opponent (Proj Rank)	PWL
Sep 1	at Troy (79)	94%
Sep 8	vs Connecticut (123)	99%
Sep 15	at Oklahoma St. (21)	37%
Sep 29	at Wyoming (77)	93%
Oct 6	vs San Diego St. (59)	90%
Oct 13	at Nevada (97)	99%
Oct 19	vs Colorado St. (98)	99%
Oct 27	at Air Force (108)	99%
Nov 3	vs BYU (67)	94%
Nov 9	vs Fresno St. (57)	89%
Nov 16	at New Mexico (114)	99%
Nov 24	vs Utah St. (78)	97%

2017 was a pretty ho-hum year for Boise State, winning another Mountain West Championship and then blasting Oregon in the Las Vegas Bowl. What was most interesting about this season was that it included a lot of impressive performances by young players who are returning for 2018.

The Broncos are bringing back three-year starting quarterback Brett Rypien, lead rusher Alexander Mattison, and the left side of their line on offense. They'll have to replace lead receiver Cedrick Wilson after a brilliant 1,531-receiving yard season but are plugging in a pair of sophomores in Octavius Evans and C.T. Thomas whose development has been a major focus of the offseason. The Broncos are at their very best when they can run the ball to help set up play-action and the rest of their passing game. After a slow start, they found their groove in conference play when Mattison assumed the role of lead back.

On defense the Broncos welcomed surprisingly great play from junior linebacker Leighton Vander Esch (19 run stuffs), sophomore pass-rusher Curtis Weaver (11 sacks), and sophomore nickelback Kekaula Kaniho (four pass break-ups). Vander Esch cashed in for the NFL and was selected 19th overall by the Dallas Cowboys, but the other 10 starters from a defense that ranked 30th nationally are returning. While Vander Esch was their best player, the Broncos are still poised to improve on defense and play at a nationally elite level in 2018.

The schedule pits them against fellow mid-major powers Troy and BYU while also including a trip to Stillwater to play Oklahoma State in a big-time Week 3 matchup. The Broncos will also play a San Diego State team that has beaten Stanford and Houston in recent years and will play Stanford again this season. If Boise State can finish undefeated, it could be an even bigger playoff selection controversy than last year's Central Florida situation.

27. Iowa Hawkeyes (9-3, 6-3)

2018 Projections

F/+	29.9 (27)
FEI	.096 (23)
S&P+	7.2 (36)
Total Wins	9.1
Conf Wins	6.5
SOS	.198 (67)
Conf SOS	.220 (61)
Div Champ	34%
Conf Champ	17%
CFP Berth	10%

Projection Factors

2017 F/+	29.1 (31)
2017 FEI	.169 (14)
2017 S&P+	3.8 (49)
5-Year F/+	17.1 (31)
5-Year FEI	.127 (20)
5-Year S&P+	6.2 (37)
2-Yr/5-Yr Recruiting	39/46
Ret. Offense	67% (70)
Ret. Defense	54% (94)
Ret. Total	61% (93)

Projected Win Likelihood by Game

Date	Opponent (Proj Rank)	PWL
Sep 1	vs Northern Illinois (68)	92%
Sep 8	vs Iowa St. (43)	74%
Sep 15	vs Northern Iowa (FCS)	100%
Sep 22	vs Wisconsin (12)	33%
Oct 6	at Minnesota (62)	79%
Oct 13	at Indiana (66)	82%
Oct 20	vs Maryland (80)	96%
Oct 27	at Penn St. (10)	19%
Nov 3	at Purdue (61)	78%
Nov 10	vs Northwestern (41)	72%
Nov 17	at Illinois (103)	99%
Nov 23	vs Nebraska (60)	88%

Other than their shocking, 55-14 beatdown of Ohio State and an exciting 21-19 loss to Penn State, 2017 was fairly quiet for Iowa. They finished 8-5 on the year and only third in the Big Ten West division behind Wisconsin and Northwestern. The inconsistency can be easily attributed to an offense that lit up the Ohio State defense but also finished only 105th in S&P+ on the year and was held below 20 points in six Big Ten games.

The offense could be significantly better in 2018 with young quarterback Nate Stanley returning and now a junior. The offensive line returns three starters and regularly produces NFL prospects out of Iowa natives. Stanley will have his two promising tight ends Noah Fant (494 receiving yards, 11 touchdowns) and T.J. Hockensen (337 receiving yards, three touchdowns) back along with leading receiver Nick Easley (530 receiving yards). They'll have to replace senior running back Akrum Wadley, but the Hawkeyes are well known for being a plug-and-play running team thanks to their consistent development of good linemen.

Iowa was really carried by their defense in 2017, and the unit finished 15th in S&P+ a year ago thanks to a trio of senior linebackers who finished the year first, second, and third on the team in tackles and run stuffs. Middle linebacker Josey Jewell was a star who had 18 run stuffs and 4.5 sacks and knew the Iowa defense backwards and forwards (and could call it from the field). He's gone, but the Hawkeyes have a good defensive end tandem back in senior Parker Hesse (four sacks) and junior Anthony Nelson (7.5 sacks) and are returning all four starters in the secondary.

They'll have to start over at linebacker, though, and hold up well enough in the transition to avoid standing pat at 8-5 again.

28. Louisville Cardinals (8-4, 5-3)

2018 Projections

F/+	29.8 (28)
FEI	.074 (30)
S&P+	9.3 (29)
Total Wins	8.1
Conf Wins	5.0
SOS	.053 (21)
Conf SOS	.158 (49)
Div Champ	9%
Conf Champ	5%
CFP Berth	2%

Projection Factors

2017 F/+	35.9 (17)
2017 FEI	.119 (23)
2017 S&P+	9.4 (16)
5-Year F/+	30.4 (14)
5-Year FEI	.131 (18)
5-Year S&P+	12.8 (13)
2-Yr/5-Yr Recruiting	28/34
Ret. Offense	54% (102)
Ret. Defense	38% (127)
Ret. Total	46% (124)

Projected Win Likelihood by Game

Date	Opponent (Proj Rank)	PWL
Sep 1	vs Alabama (1)	13%
Sep 8	vs Indiana St. (FCS)	100%
Sep 15	vs W. Kentucky (87)	98%
Sep 22	at Virginia (75)	89%
Sep 29	vs Florida St. (16)	38%
Oct 5	vs Georgia Tech (50)	81%
Oct 13	at Boston College (42)	59%
Oct 27	vs Wake Forest (36)	69%
Nov 3	at Clemson (2)	14%
Nov 9	at Syracuse (73)	88%
Nov 17	vs NC State (34)	67%
Nov 24	vs Kentucky (63)	90%

After producing more than 9,000 passing yards, more than 4,000 rushing yards, and 119 total touchdowns, former Heisman Trophy winner Lamar Jackson will no longer be at Louisville. Head coach Bobby Petrino had a reputation for developing good quarterbacks long before Jackson, but the dynamic player is still going to leave a huge vacuum and a lot of questions behind. Jackson's 2017 season was comparable to his Heisman-winning season, but it gained less attention due to the defense, which fell precipitously from 19th in S&P+ to 84th.

The Cardinals were replacing multiple impact players on defense as well as coordinator Todd Grantham (now at Florida) and they've already hired their second post-Grantham coordinator for 2018 in former Notre Dame coach Brian Van Gorder (fired from the Irish during the 2016 season). Their prospects in 2018 aren't great, with most of the impact players gone and fewer incoming transfers to help out than in previous years. What's more, Van Gorder will try to oversee a shift towards a 4-3 defense that will be a departure from the style the Cardinals have been teaching and recruiting towards.

On offense, the line was much better in 2017, and the receivers took a step forward and largely return this season. Jawon Pass, a 6-foot-4, 231-pound sophomore with a slower gait than Jackson but a stronger arm, is now taking over the offense. With a more traditional skill set behind center, the Petrino offense figures to get back to the more pro-style tactics of his previous teams. They'll need running back Dae Williams to be healthy and ready to carry the load for this new style to find balance, but with all three top receivers back, if Pass can become the next great Petrino quarterback, then this team shouldn't dip too far.

29. Utah Utes (8-4, 5-4)

2018 Projections

F/+	29.1 (29)
FEI	.069 (33)
S&P+	9.4 (28)
Total Wins	7.5
Conf Wins	4.8
SOS	.083 (42)
Conf SOS	.087 (19)
Div Champ	7%
Conf Champ	4%
CFP Berth	2%

Projection Factors

2017 F/+	22.5 (37)
2017 FEI	.052 (45)
2017 S&P+	6.9 (33)
5-Year F/+	22.2 (26)
5-Year FEI	.081 (30)
5-Year S&P+	8.6 (29)
2-Yr/5-Yr Recruiting	32/41
Ret. Offense	58% (91)
Ret. Defense	64% (62)
Ret. Total	61% (90)

Projected Win Likelihood by Game

Date	Opponent (Proj Rank)	PWL
Aug 30	vs Weber St. (FCS)	100%
Sep 8	at Northern Illinois (68)	83%
Sep 15	vs Washington (7)	27%
Sep 29	at Washington St. (49)	67%
Oct 6	at Stanford (17)	23%
Oct 12	vs Arizona (35)	67%
Oct 20	vs USC (15)	36%
Oct 26	at UCLA (38)	55%
Nov 3	at Arizona St. (44)	61%
Nov 10	vs Oregon (23)	47%
Nov 17	at Colorado (92)	96%
Nov 24	vs BYU (67)	91%

The Utes made a big transition in 2017 after hiring Eastern Washington offensive coordinator Troy Taylor to install an Air Raid-style offense at Utah to complement head coach Kyle Whittingham's always feisty defense. Early returns were mixed as the team went 7-6 while ranking 34th nationally in defense and 55th in offense per S&P+.

There were glimpses of potential breakthrough on offense that could make the 2018 season pretty interesting. Sophomore quarterback Tyler Huntley ran for 720 yards at 5.2 yards per carry (removing sack yardage) with six touchdowns and utilized the zone read concept to great effect. This helped free up sophomore running back Zach Moss to run for 1,170 yards at 5.4 yards per carry with 10 touchdowns. Both now return as experienced upperclassmen behind an offensive line that will feature four returning starters.

The passing game came along much more slowly, with Huntley owning a sack rate of 8.8 percent, throwing 10 interceptions, and averaging only 6.5 yards per attempt. Complicating matters here is the fact that top target Darren Car-

rington II is moving on while No. 2 target Raelon Singleton is transferring to Houston. Nevertheless, the passing game should make a leap in Year 2 of the system, and the run game could be legitimately strong.

Whittingham's defenses are always tough, and their two most disruptive pass-rushers—defensive end Bradley Anae (seven sacks) and linebacker Cody Barton (four sacks)—return to anchor the zone blitz-heavy defensive scheme. Utah is also moving longtime strong safety Chase Hansen down to linebacker where the big, heady, 230-pounder is fitting in very nicely after years of delivering big hits from safety.

In 2017, the Utes had to play a lot of young defensive backs who will now return as savvier and more proficient upperclassmen. If they can play tighter coverage and get after the passer like they're accustomed to doing up front, this could be one of the better-looking Whittingham defenses. Utah is also always phenomenal on special teams and return star punter Mitch Wishnowsky, who pinned 19 punts inside the 20 a year ago.

30. Florida Gators (8-4, 5-4)

2018 Projections

F/+	27.8 (30)
FEI	.072 (31)
S&P+	8.2 (32)
Total Wins	7.9
Conf Wins	4.7
SOS	.070 (32)
Conf SOS	.128 (44)
Div Champ	11%
Conf Champ	5%
CFP Berth	3%

Projection Factors

2017 F/+	-15.9 (85)
2017 FEI	-.050 (83)
2017 S&P+	-2.2 (86)
5-Year F/+	15.0 (35)
5-Year FEI	.009 (60)
5-Year S&P+	8.9 (28)
2-Yr/5-Yr Recruiting	13/13
Ret. Offense	77% (33)
Ret. Defense	74% (33)
Ret. Total	75% (19)

Projected Win Likelihood by Game

Date	Opponent (Proj Rank)	PWL
Sep 1	vs Charleston So. (FCS)	100%
Sep 8	vs Kentucky (63)	89%
Sep 15	vs Colorado St. (98)	99%
Sep 22	at Tennessee (72)	85%
Sep 29	at Mississippi St. (14)	18%
Oct 6	vs LSU (19)	38%
Oct 13	at Vanderbilt (83)	92%
Oct 27	vs Georgia (4)	19%
Nov 3	vs Missouri (40)	69%
Nov 10	vs South Carolina (33)	63%
Nov 17	vs Idaho (FCS)	100%
Nov 24	at Florida St. (16)	22%

Florida fell apart down the stretch in 2017 after firing head coach Jim McElwain in the midst of a bizarre situation in

which the coach claimed his family received death threats that they were then unable to substantiate. The Gators then brought back Urban Meyer-era offensive coordinator Dan Mullen, fresh off another solid season at Mississippi State.

This should be a fascinating season because while McElwain left behind more talent at Florida than Mullen ever had at Mississippi State, it doesn't exactly fit his offense like a glove. The Mullen Bulldogs figured out how to win a lot of games by using quarterbacks who could run like fullbacks (Dak Prescott, Nick Fitzgerald) and then using the passing game or option runs to set up short-yardage situations where the quarterback run game was nearly unstoppable. The Florida Gators have a big, veteran offensive line and some skill players like wide receivers Kadarius Toney (272 total yards) and Tyrie Cleveland (410 receiving yards) who should translate very easily to the spread offense. However, starting quarterback Feleipe Franks is more of a big pocket passer than an option runner.

How Mullen adjusts his offense to make the most of a talented group will be the story of the year in Gainesville.

On defense, new coordinator Todd Grantham is inheriting an embarrassment of riches starting with "rush end" Cece Jefferson (15 run stuffs in 2017) and middle linebacker David Reese (20 run stuffs). The Gators were young but solid up the middle of their defense in 2017, and now they're older but in need of an improved pass rush. As it happens, teaching pattern-matching coverage and creating pressure packages are strengths of Grantham, and he should find this group even easier to unleash than the effective units he has had in recent years at Mississippi State and Louisville. There's a good chance that different coaching and tactics combined with a roster that's getting older and more experienced lead to a major leap from the Gators in Year 1 under Mullen.

31. Ole Miss Rebels (7-5, 3-5)

2018 Projections

F/+	27.7 (31)
FEI	.059 (37)
S&P+	9.6 (26)
Total Wins	7.2
Conf Wins	3.5
SOS	.040 (17)
Conf SOS	.044 (9)
Div Champ	1%
Conf Champ	1%
CFP Berth	0%

Projection Factors

2017 F/+	4.3 (60)
2017 FEI	-.036 (76)
2017 S&P+	5.1 (42)
5-Year F/+	27.9 (18)
5-Year FEI	.045 (44)
5-Year S&P+	12.4 (14)
2-Yr/5-Yr Recruiting	30/20
Ret. Offense	64% (78)
Ret. Defense	62% (69)
Ret. Total	63% (77)

Projected Win Likelihood by Game

Date	Opponent (Proj Rank)	PWL	Projected Loss / Projected Win
Sep 1	vs Texas Tech (53)	75%	
Sep 8	vs S. Illinois (FCS)	100%	
Sep 15	vs Alabama (1)	16%	
Sep 22	vs Kent St. (122)	99%	
Sep 29	at LSU (19)	24%	
Oct 6	vs UL-Monroe (106)	99%	
Oct 13	at Arkansas (51)	68%	
Oct 20	vs Auburn (5)	24%	
Nov 3	vs South Carolina (33)	63%	
Nov 10	at Texas A&M (25)	31%	
Nov 17	at Vanderbilt (83)	92%	
Nov 22	vs Mississippi St. (14)	31%	

The Rebels' 2018 season is defined by life under NCAA sanctions, including a bowl ban, critical player transfers, and scholarship reductions. The transfers were notable: five-star quarterback Shea Patterson was the biggest, but former top safety recruit Deontay Anderson, receiver Tre Nixon, defensive back Breon Dixon, and receiver Van Jefferson were all former top recruits who transferred out as well.

But it's not all bad news for the Rebels, who made a somewhat surprising 6-6 run last season. Matt Luke, after serving as interim head coach last season, was named as permanent head coach in December and now can begin a foundation-building process. While the passing game is undoubtedly hurt by Patterson's and Jefferson's departures, Ole Miss still has one of the top receiver groups in the country, led by A.J. Alexander, DaMarkus Lodge, and D.K. Metcalf, the top three targets from last season. And just as important, Patterson's backup last season, Jordan Ta'amu, looked just as good, if not better than Patterson statistically. While Ta'amu missed Auburn and Alabama, he was still impressive during his starting run at the end of the season.

But with the departure of Jordan Wilkins (who had a solid, 1,000-yard 2017 campaign), the Rebels will need a replacement at running back, and all of last season's backup options were statistically a step down from Wilkins.

Ole Miss' primary concern is, again, the defense, which ranked 113th in the country last season. It had few bright spots, but it did have a fearsome pass rush, ranking ninth in adjusted sack rate. The only problem is that the Rebels' top two pass-rushers—Marquis Haynes and Breeland Speaks—are both in the NFL after combining for 14.5 sacks last season. So there's potential for the pass rush to regress, putting more strain on both the run defense, which ranked 76th last season, as well as the offense, which could be forced to win a lot of shootouts.

This also means that Ole Miss might be the most Big 12-ish of all SEC teams—potentially electric passing game, uncertain run game, and leaky, sporadically explosive defense that should be extremely entertaining to watch. Despite certain weaknesses and other glaring question marks, the Rebels have a lot of potential to surprise a team or three this season.

32. Duke Blue Devils (7-5, 4-4)

2018 Projections

F/+	25.8 (32)
FEI	.085 (29)
S&P+	5.8 (40)
Total Wins	7.2
Conf Wins	4.3
SOS	.059 (26)
Conf SOS	.093 (24)
Div Champ	4%
Conf Champ	2%
CFP Berth	1%

Projection Factors

2017 F/+	11.2 (52)
2017 FEI	.067 (41)
2017 S&P+	1.2 (65)
5-Year F/+	4.6 (57)
5-Year FEI	.061 (36)
5-Year S&P+	1.7 (61)
2-Yr/5-Yr Recruiting	51/47
Ret. Offense	82% (18)
Ret. Defense	78% (24)
Ret. Total	80% (9)

Projected Win Likelihood by Game

Date	Opponent (Proj Rank)	PWL	Projected Loss / Projected Win
Aug 31	vs Army (86)	97%	
Sep 8	at Northwestern (41)	51%	
Sep 15	at Baylor (37)	48%	
Sep 22	vs NC Central (FCS)	100%	
Sep 29	vs Virginia Tech (22)	41%	
Oct 13	at Georgia Tech (50)	63%	
Oct 20	vs Virginia (75)	94%	
Oct 27	at Pittsburgh (48)	62%	
Nov 3	at Miami-FL (13)	16%	
Nov 10	vs North Carolina (52)	79%	
Nov 17	at Clemson (2)	11%	
Nov 24	vs Wake Forest (36)	63%	

Almost no team returns as much production (80 percent, 11th) as Duke. And that's good, because there's a lot of potential from last season's streaky 7-6 team. The Blue Devils won their first four and their last three, dropping an incredible six games in a row in the middle of the season.

Daniel Jones is entering his third year as starting quarterback and has his top three receiving targets returning. There's a lot of optimism about the top tight ends as well, including Daniel Helm and Davis Koppenhaver, who were among Jones' most reliable targets last season. Based on the spring, they could force the Blue Devils into playing more two-tight end sets.

The only offensive concerns are the search for explosive playmakers and finding depth at running back. Duke was 108th in IsoPPP and 121st in the percentage of 20-plus-yard plays run last season (only 5 percent; 105th in 10-plus-yard plays). Jones averaged just 5.9 yards per attempt and no receiver averaged more than 13.7 yards per catch. The offense has lacked an explosive

pass game for years, though, and this is the most experienced combination of receivers and quarterback since at least 2014.

Running back may be a little less concerning. While starter Shaun Wilson graduated, he only averaged 5.0 yards per carry and a 36.4 percent opportunity rate, while backup and likely starter Brittain Brown had better averages in nearly every category. Daniel Jones will also chip in to the running game, as he was second on the team in rushing yards behind Wilson and by far the most consistent runner last season.

But besides an experienced offense, the Blue Devils' team DNA will likely be based on an equally experienced defense. Ranking 34th and 22nd in rushing and passing S&P+ last season, Duke's defensive performance far outstripped their recruiting talent and loses few impact players from 2017. Linebackers Ben Humphreys and Joe Giles-Harris, along with defensive end Tre Hornbuckle, return and should form the core of Duke's defense.

33. South Carolina Gamecocks (7-5, 5-3)

2018 Projections

F/+	24.6 (33)
FEI	.062 (36)
S&P+	7.2 (35)
Total Wins	7.5
Conf Wins	4.6
SOS	.072 (34)
Conf SOS	.201 (58)
Div Champ	9%
Conf Champ	5%
CFP Berth	2%

Projection Factors

2017 F/+	6.9 (57)
2017 FEI	.024 (54)
2017 S&P+	2.1 (60)
5-Year F/+	8.8 (48)
5-Year FEI	.041 (45)
5-Year S&P+	4.0 (50)
2-Yr/5-Yr Recruiting	20/18
Ret. Offense	84% (13)
Ret. Defense	44% (121)
Ret. Total	64% (71)

Projected Win Likelihood by Game

Date	Opponent (Proj Rank)	PWL	Projected Loss / Projected Win
Sep 1	vs Coastal Carolina (113)	99%	
Sep 8	vs Georgia (4)	21%	
Sep 15	vs Marshall (56)	81%	
Sep 22	at Vanderbilt (83)	89%	
Sep 29	at Kentucky (63)	76%	
Oct 6	vs Missouri (40)	64%	
Oct 13	vs Texas A&M (25)	41%	
Oct 27	vs Tennessee (72)	92%	
Nov 3	at Ole Miss (31)	37%	
Nov 10	at Florida (30)	37%	
Nov 17	vs Chattanooga (FCS)	100%	
Nov 24	at Clemson (2)	10%	

The Gamecocks have a lot of optimism heading in to 2018. There's a sense that Will Muschamp has found his footing as a head coach, guiding South Carolina to a pleasantly surprising 9-4 season. That is certainly an impressive record, particularly

for a team that was fourth in the SEC East in team total talent according to the 247 Composite. But the Gamecocks were still merely average, at 57th in the F/+ rankings last season.

Much of the Gamecocks' optimism centers around junior

quarterback Jake Bentley, who passed for nearly 2,800 yards and 7.1 yards per attempt last season. Since 2011, only Dylan Thompson's single season bettered Bentley's sophomore numbers. And besides tight end Hayden Hurst, who was an invaluable receiving target (second on the team, with the highest catch rate among Bentley's primary targets), nearly everyone on offense returns. Last season's 88th-ranked S&P+ offense returns 84 percent of their production (15th in the country), including leading rusher A.J. Turner, Rico Dowdle, and Ty'Son Williams. Even more importantly, every major wide receiver returns in 2018, including playmaker Deebo Samuel, who was lost to injury during the Kentucky game at the beginning of last season. Samuel, who averaged 16.7 yards per catch in his limited three games last year, has the potential to give the Gamecocks an explosive dimension to their passing game, which was just 102nd in passing IsoPPP.

Besides Hayden Hurst, the only big name that doesn't return from 2017 is offensive coordinator Kurt Roper. In his place, former Georgia stalwart coach Bryan McClendon was promoted to the position after an offer from new Tennessee coach Jeremy Pruitt. Opinions are mixed; while McClendon has a stellar reputation and was in high demand, he also has never called plays.

The biggest concern for the Gamecocks is the defense, which loses a considerable amount of production from last season's 37th-ranked S&P+ unit. Only 47 percent of 2017's production returns, placing South Carolina near the bottom of the FBS in returning defensive production. Big names like Skai Moore, Chris Lammons, and JaMarcus King have departed, putting increased pressure on the fewer upperclassmen leaders like cornerback Rashad Fenton and young talent like defensive back Jamyest Williams.

34. North Carolina State Wolfpack (8-4, 4-4)

2018 Projections

F/+	24.0 (34)
FEI	.058 (38)
S&P+	7.2 (37)
Total Wins	7.7
Conf Wins	4.4
SOS	.113 (55)
Conf SOS	.134 (45)
Div Champ	4%
Conf Champ	2%
CFP Berth	1%

Projection Factors

2017 F/+	31.9 (24)
2017 FEI	.144 (19)
2017 S&P+	5.9 (38)
5-Year F/+	11.0 (42)
5-Year FEI	.092 (27)
5-Year S&P+	5.7 (41)
2-Yr/5-Yr Recruiting	40/38
Ret. Offense	70% (56)
Ret. Defense	35% (129)
Ret. Total	53% (111)

Projected Win Likelihood by Game

Date	Opponent (Proj Rank)	PWL	Projected Loss / Projected Win
Sep 1	vs James Madison (FCS)	100%	
Sep 8	vs Georgia St. (118)	99%	
Sep 15	vs West Virginia (45)	69%	
Sep 22	at Marshall (56)	67%	
Sep 29	vs Virginia (75)	93%	
Oct 6	vs Boston College (42)	65%	
Oct 20	at Clemson (2)	10%	
Oct 27	at Syracuse (73)	83%	
Nov 3	vs Florida St. (16)	30%	
Nov 8	vs Wake Forest (36)	60%	
Nov 17	at Louisville (28)	33%	
Nov 24	at North Carolina (52)	63%	

North Carolina State had one of the best defensive lines in the country last season, led by NFL first rounder Bradley Chubb, who finished with 25 tackles for loss on the sixth-rated havoc-creating line. But the problem is that such a small percentage of that production returns for the Wolfpack defense in 2018—just 35 percent, which is next to last in the country. Sure, losing a player with 25 tackles for loss is going to be an almost irreplaceable hole by itself, but the defense lost more than just Chubb. Among North Carolina State's top ten tacklers last season, seven were seniors. Eight players had five or more tackles for loss last season; only two return. That puts a lot of pressure to fill the gaps on the young talent, including defensive end Darian Roseboro, safety Jarius Morehead, linebacker Germaine Pratt, and corner Nick McCloud. The good news is that these players are extremely solid, giving the defense at least some senior leadership despite how decimated the team was by graduation.

Although the defensive line received a lot of attention, the defense as a whole was statistically mediocre (63rd in the S&P+) and outplayed by the offense (21st). The real revelation was quarterback Ryan Finley, who has played well for years but still flown mostly under the radar. That's unlikely in 2018. The

6-foot-4 senior threw for 3,518 yards last season, only six interceptions, and 7.3 yards per attempt, and could work his way into the first round of the NFL draft with a comparable 2018 season. He'll return his top three receivers Kelvin Harmon, Stephen Louis, and Jakobi Meyers, but lose Will Richardson and Tony Adams on the offensive line. The stage is almost completely set for a high-powered passing offense again in 2018, assuming Richardson can be suitably replaced at tackle.

The major question on offense is who will step up at running back. Nyheim Hines and Jaylen Samuels (who was also third on the team in receiving yards) were both drafted in the middle rounds, leaving senior Reggie Gallaspy II as the only back with significant experience. Gallaspy II was a step back from both graduated backs, but the Wolfpack have incoming freshman Ricky Person, a four-star all-purpose running back, coming in. Person showed solid receiving skills in high school and should share carries almost immediately.

Assuming that the defense can survive the loss of star power, and that Person and Gallaspy II can replace Hines and Samuels effectively, Ryan Finley and the returning receivers should power an offense capable of keeping North Carolina State in the top-25 mix.

35. Arizona Wildcats (8-4, 6-3)

2018 Projections			Projection Factors	
F/+	23.6 (35)		2017 F/+	14.2 (47)
FEI	.051 (40)		2017 FEI	.040 (48)
S&P+	7.7 (33)		2017 S&P+	4.0 (48)
Total Wins	8.0		5-Year F/+	6.8 (53)
Conf Wins	5.5		5-Year FEI	.032 (52)
SOS	.211 (69)		5-Year S&P+	3.2 (55)
Conf SOS	.240 (63)		2-Yr/5-Yr Recruiting	45/43
Div Champ	16%		Ret. Offense	70% (60)
Conf Champ	8%		Ret. Defense	79% (23)
CFP Berth	4%		Ret. Total	75% (22)

Projected Win Likelihood by Game

Date	Opponent (Proj Rank)	PWL
Sep 1	vs BYU (67)	88%
Sep 8	at Houston (54)	63%
Sep 15	vs Southern Utah (FCS)	100%
Sep 22	at Oregon St. (107)	99%
Sep 29	vs USC (15)	29%
Oct 6	vs California (58)	82%
Oct 12	at Utah (29)	33%
Oct 20	at UCLA (38)	46%
Oct 27	vs Oregon (23)	39%
Nov 2	vs Colorado (92)	97%
Nov 17	at Washington St. (49)	59%
Nov 24	vs Arizona St. (44)	68%

The Arizona Wildcats are one of the most interesting, exciting teams in college football for 2018. Quarterback Khalil Tate was arguably the most exciting player in the country in 2017. The addition of Kevin Sumlin as head coach only raises the Wildcats' potential ceiling in a wide-open Pac-12 South.

Tate had one of the most insane seasons in recent memory. After taking over for Brandon Dawkins in October, Tate rushed for 1,492 non-sack yards at 13.2 highlight yards per opportunity and a mind-boggling 51.4 percent opportunity rate. Only a single quarterback had more rushing yards than Tate—Army's Ahmed Bradshaw, who had the benefit of starting a full season and with about 90 more rushing attempts. Tate was no slouch in the passing game either, leading the 29th-ranked passing S&P+ offense and averaging 8.9 yards per attempt (on admittedly just an average of 16.3 attempts per game). Tate was brought down to Earth later in the season, especially as a passer (against Oregon: 18-of-35 for 159 yards, two interceptions, 12 carries for 48 rushing yards), but there's no doubt that he is a top Heisman contender heading in to the new season.

Tate will also have top running back J.J. Taylor (5.8 yards per carry), his top three receivers (Tony Ellison, Shun Brown, and Shawn Poindexter), and the line's left tackle and center. Maybe the offense's main question is how new offensive coordinator Noel Mazzone fits in. Mazzone has seemingly been the offensive coordinator for half of the FBS in the last decade (actual resume since 2010: Arizona State, UCLA, Texas A&M, and now Arizona).

Similarly, the defense's main question is the retention of defensive coordinator Marcel Yates. Last season's Wildcats defense was very, very bad. Arizona was 115th in defensive S&P+ last season, lacking just about any statistical area on which to hang their hat. Maybe the most positive thing to say looking ahead to 2018 is that the defense was incredibly young—Arizona's top three tacklers and their sack leader were all freshmen—and the vast majority of that talent returns in 2018 (79 percent, 23rd in the country). So maybe you can chalk up the Wildcats' defensive failings to youth and inexperience, which would at least suggest some improvement for 2018.

36. Wake Forest Demon Deacons (7-5, 4-4)

2018 Projections			Projection Factors	
F/+	22.9 (36)		2017 F/+	29.7 (29)
FEI	.051 (41)		2017 FEI	.118 (25)
S&P+	7.4 (34)		2017 S&P+	6.1 (37)
Total Wins	6.8		5-Year F/+	-4.4 (73)
Conf Wins	3.7		5-Year FEI	.048 (42)
SOS	.059 (25)		5-Year S&P+	-1.5 (76)
Conf SOS	.107 (34)		2-Yr/5-Yr Recruiting	67/62
Div Champ	1%		Ret. Offense	74% (44)
Conf Champ	1%		Ret. Defense	69% (45)
CFP Berth	0%		Ret. Total	72% (34)

Projected Win Likelihood by Game

Date	Opponent (Proj Rank)	PWL
Aug 30	at Tulane (90)	92%
Sep 8	vs Towson (FCS)	100%
Sep 13	vs Boston College (42)	63%
Sep 22	vs Notre Dame (6)	20%
Sep 29	vs Rice (127)	99%
Oct 6	vs Clemson (2)	19%
Oct 20	at Florida St. (16)	17%
Oct 27	at Louisville (28)	31%
Nov 3	vs Syracuse (73)	91%
Nov 8	at NC State (34)	40%
Nov 17	vs Pittsburgh (48)	73%
Nov 24	at Duke (32)	37%

Wake Forest was one of the most fun offenses to watch in 2017 as senior quarterback Matt Wolford was operating their

creative spread offense at a really high level. He finished with 3,192 passing yards and 769 rushing yards (removing sack yardage) with 39 total touchdowns. That helped Wake Forest overcome the loss of defensive coordinator Mike Elko and their slide to 65th in defensive S&P+.

They'll have to move on from Wolford now, but his back-up, sophomore Kendall Hinton, threw for 399 yards and ran for 215 in spot duty and should be ready to take the helm if off-field troubles that garnered him a three-game suspension are resolved. He'll have lots of help from the skill talent that returns 6-foot-5 outside receiver Scotty Washington (45 catches, 15.8 yards per reception) and last year's top target, sophomore Greg Dortch (53 catches in just 8 games, 13.6 yards per reception). In the run game, the Demon Deacons will have another year from senior running back Matt Colburn II after a 904-rushing yard season in 2017. All five of the starting offensive linemen from Wake Forest's 55-52 Belk Bowl

victory over Texas A&M are also back, so this could be a huge year for the Demon Deacons offense.

On defense, the Demon Deacons are losing good run defenders like linebackers Grant Dawson and Jaboree Williams (35 combined run stuffs) and defensive linemen Duke Ejiofor and Wendell Dunn (29 combined run stuffs). They do have their entire secondary returning intact, a group that had a mixed season, finishing 86th in passing S&P+ but 29th in defending passing downs.

They'll have to deal with Florida State and Clemson in the fearsome Atlantic division of the ACC, where they finished in a three-way tie for third place last year while benefiting from Florida State's collapse and Louisville's defensive struggles. They'll need to improve on an impressive 2017 just to tread water in 2018.

37. Baylor Bears (7-5, 4-5)

2018 Projections

F/+	22.5 (37)
FEI	.085 (28)
S&P+	3.9 (50)
Total Wins	6.9
Conf Wins	4.4
SOS	.083 (41)
Conf SOS	.096 (25)
Div Champ	-
Conf Champ	2%
CFP Berth	1%

Projection Factors

2017 F/+	-27.8 (97)
2017 FEI	-.069 (88)
2017 S&P+	-6.5 (105)
5-Year F/+	21.4 (27)
5-Year FEI	.023 (54)
5-Year S&P+	9.9 (22)
2-Yr/5-Yr Recruiting	34/31
Ret. Offense	93% (2)
Ret. Defense	82% (16)
Ret. Total	88% (4)

Projected Win Likelihood by Game

Date	Opponent (Proj Rank)	PWL	Projected Loss	Projected Win
Sep 1	vs Ab. Christian (FCS)	100%		
Sep 8	at UTSA (109)	99%		
Sep 15	vs Duke (32)	52%		
Sep 22	vs Kansas (102)	98%		
Sep 29	at Oklahoma (8)	11%		
Oct 6	vs Kansas St. (46)	69%		
Oct 13	at Texas (24)	24%		
Oct 25	at West Virginia (45)	52%		
Nov 3	vs Oklahoma St. (21)	36%		
Nov 10	at Iowa St. (43)	49%		
Nov 17	vs TCU (20)	34%		
Nov 24	vs Texas Tech (53)	68%		

Matt Rhule rebooted the Baylor Bears in 2017, turning over the better part of the depth chart while overhauling the playbook on both sides of the ball and completely changing the culture. Whereas under Art Briles the Bears tended to rest in the summer and avoid hitting in practice, Rhule instituted physical practices with live tackling. The Bears struggled to adjust to the systemic overhaul, finishing 1-11 on the year with a humiliating early defeat to Liberty.

However, Rhule found some good players to build around in the midst of this struggle, particularly from a freshman class which could produce as many as six starters in 2018. Freshman quarterback Charlie Brewer stood out in a major way, throwing 11 touchdowns to four interceptions and running for 273 yards while trying to survive behind a rebuilt line. That offensive line should be much stronger in 2018 with more experience and maturity and welcomes Clemson trans-

fer and former starting tackle on a championship team, Jake Fuhrmorgen.

The bigger hope is found in the young skill talent Baylor has on its roster, particularly junior wide receiver Denzel Mims (1,087 receiving yards and 10 touchdowns). He'll be joined by Tennessee transfer and converted running back Jalen Hurd out wide and a deep running back room.

Rhule made his name at Temple with defense, and he won the 2016 American title in a conference loaded with unique and explosive offenses. Baylor's defense seems at least another year away, particularly due to the lack of impact playmaking up front along the defensive line. While Temple won a title with a defensive end tandem that combined for 18 sacks, the Bears got just 2.5 sacks from their entire defensive end depth chart in 2017 and are still in search of playmakers there to realize the vision for this defense.

38. UCLA Bruins (6-6, 4-5)

2018 Projections		Projection Factors		Projected Win Likelihood by Game				
				Date	Opponent (Proj Rank)	PWL	Projected Loss	Projected Win
F/+	21.6 (38)	2017 F/+	-3.8 (73)	Sep 1	vs Cincinnati (91)	97%		
FEI	.056 (39)	2017 FEI	-.010 (67)	Sep 8	at Oklahoma (8)	10%		
S&P+	6.0 (39)	2017 S&P+	0.1 (77)	Sep 15	vs Fresno St. (57)	79%		
Total Wins	5.9	5-Year F/+	20.1 (28)	Sep 28	at Colorado (92)	92%		
Conf Wins	4.0	5-Year FEI	.040 (47)	Oct 6	vs Washington (7)	19%		
SOS	.041 (18)	5-Year S&P+	9.4 (26)	Oct 13	at California (58)	67%		
Conf SOS	.102 (30)	2-Yr/5-Yr Recruiting	19/15	Oct 20	vs Arizona (35)	55%		
Div Champ	2%	Ret. Offense	45% (112)	Oct 26	vs Utah (29)	45%		
Conf Champ	1%	Ret. Defense	72% (37)	Nov 3	at Oregon (23)	23%		
CFP Berth	1%	Ret. Total	59% (98)	Nov 10	at Arizona St. (44)	50%		
				Nov 17	vs USC (15)	27%		
				Nov 24	vs Stanford (17)	28%		

UCLA made a big splash in the offseason by winning the Chip Kelly sweepstakes against Florida and bringing the highly influential coach back to the college game. 2017 was the sad conclusion of the Jim Mora era, which Mora tied to quarterback Josh Rosen. The Bruins fired spread offensive coordinator Noel Mazzone in order to get Rosen into a more "pro-style system" which resulted in consecutive losing seasons.

So Kelly is in Los Angeles now to bring back the spread offense. Interestingly, one of his first moves to was to welcome in former starting Michigan quarterback Wilton Speight, a pro-style passer with the Wolverines, as a grad transfer. Speight had a solid 2016 season but struggled in 2017 amidst the departure of his top receivers and eventually suffered a back injury that ended his season. His inclusion at UCLA suggests that Kelly will continue to go down the path he was headed in the NFL, evolving his offense for pocket passers rather than dual-threat quarterbacks.

There are some useful weapons for Kelly and Speight to work with, including running back Soso Jamabo (446 rushing yards in 2017) and tight end Caleb Wilson, who torched Texas A&M in the opener and had 490 receiving yards before his season was shortened by injury after five games.

The offensive and defensive lines are going to need to be rebuilt after losing most of the starters on either side of the ball. Mora came to UCLA as a defensive minded coach, and his early units played strong defense before faltering in recent seasons. Defense has never been a particularly strong suit for Kelly either, but he'll be looking to bring a style of 3-4 defense he preferred at both Oregon and in the NFL that could translate cleanly to what Mora recruited towards.

39. Florida Atlantic Owls (9-3, 7-1)

2018 Projections		Projection Factors		Projected Win Likelihood by Game				
				Date	Opponent (Proj Rank)	PWL	Projected Loss	Projected Win
F/+	21.3 (39)	2017 F/+	41.5 (14)	Sep 1	at Oklahoma (8)	10%		
FEI	.030 (46)	2017 FEI	.125 (21)	Sep 8	vs Air Force (108)	99%		
S&P+	8.7 (31)	2017 S&P+	13.4 (11)	Sep 15	vs B. Cookman (FCS)	100%		
Total Wins	9.5	5-Year F/+	-9.9 (81)	Sep 21	at Central Florida (18)	17%		
Conf Wins	7.2	5-Year FEI	.037 (48)	Sep 29	at Middle Tennessee (84)	88%		
SOS	.201 (68)	5-Year S&P+	-3.9 (91)	Oct 6	vs Old Dominion (115)	99%		
Conf SOS	.844 (100)	2-Yr/5-Yr Recruiting	77/79	Oct 20	at Marshall (56)	63%		
Div Champ	61%	Ret. Offense	56% (97)	Oct 26	vs Louisiana Tech (69)	87%		
Conf Champ	45%	Ret. Defense	90% (6)	Nov 3	at Fl. International (119)	99%		
CFP Berth	2%	Ret. Total	73% (29)	Nov 10	vs W. Kentucky (87)	96%		
				Nov 15	at North Texas (96)	94%		
				Nov 24	vs Charlotte (125)	99%		

Florida Atlantic has quickly become known as "Last Strike U" for its collection of coaches and players with troubled pasts, led by head coach Lane Kiffin. Younger brother Chris coached the defense after getting a "show clause" for his part in the Ole Miss recruiting violations and Kendall Briles of Baylor infamy coordinated the 2017 offense. Both have now moved on to bigger opportunities while Kiffin has hired Charlie Weis' son, Charlie Weis Jr. and poached Southern Miss defensive coordinator Tony Pecoraro.

These coaches will now take over an 11-3 football team that returns most of the key pieces from Year 1 under Kiffin. Kiffin started to embrace the RPO spread offense at Alabama, then went full-bore into that system when he hired Briles. The result was lots of space for sophomore running back Devin Singletary in a 1,920-yard, 32-touchdown season. The Owls will have to replace the guards who helped pave the way for Singletary. Quarterback Jason Driskel left the team but Florida Atlantic is plugging in transfer De'Andre Johnson from Florida State. Lead receiver Willie Wright is back, as are promising talents Harrison Bryant and DeAndre McNeal (fourth and fifth in receptions a year ago) and another infusion of incoming transfers.

The Florida Atlantic defense finished a very respectable 52nd nationally in S&P+ last year and now returns 10 starters and all of its impact performers on that side of the ball. Linebackers Azeez Al-Shaair and Rashad Smith led the way with a combined 8.5 sacks and 20 run stuffs. Pecoraro will bring a more aggressive and disguised style this veteran defense should be well-equipped to learn and deploy. The Owls open the year against Oklahoma in Norman in what could be a fascinating and enlightening season opener.

40. Missouri Tigers (7-5, 4-4)

2018 Projections

F/+	20.9 (40)
FEI	.027 (49)
S&P+	8.9 (30)
Total Wins	7.5
Conf Wins	4.2
SOS	.068 (29)
Conf SOS	.078 (15)
Div Champ	5%
Conf Champ	2%
CFP Berth	1%

Projection Factors

2017 F/+	7.8 (56)
2017 FEI	-.034 (74)
2017 S&P+	6.5 (35)
5-Year F/+	14.8 (36)
5-Year FEI	.013 (57)
5-Year S&P+	6.8 (32)
2-Yr/5-Yr Recruiting	44/40
Ret. Offense	71% (55)
Ret. Defense	60% (81)
Ret. Total	65% (66)

Projected Win Likelihood by Game

Date	Opponent (Proj Rank)	PWL
Sep 1	vs Tenn. Martin (FCS)	100%
Sep 8	vs Wyoming (77)	92%
Sep 15	at Purdue (61)	68%
Sep 22	vs Georgia (4)	18%
Oct 6	at South Carolina (33)	36%
Oct 13	at Alabama (1)	5%
Oct 20	vs Memphis (47)	67%
Oct 27	vs Kentucky (63)	84%
Nov 3	at Florida (30)	31%
Nov 10	vs Vanderbilt (83)	94%
Nov 17	at Tennessee (72)	79%
Nov 24	vs Arkansas (51)	73%

Missouri is seeing a little bit of an overhaul after a mixed 6-7 season that included quarterback Drew Lock throwing 44 touchdown passes, but the Tigers ending the year winless against teams with a record better than .500. Then-offensive coordinator Josh Heupel left for the head coaching vacancy at Central Florida, and Missouri head coach Barry Odom hired Derek Dooley to replace him. Evidently Dooley is going to bring a pro-style system that is completely different than the aggressive system they played a year ago while scoring at least 45 points every week during a six-game winning streak.

On the surface this could make for an interesting fit and a team concept that better aids Barry Odom in building a stronger defense. The 2017 Tigers weren't remotely interested in ball control and would throw it deep whenever they had opportunities to do so, leading to long, fast-paced, high-possession games with scores in the 40s. They'll return most of the offensive line, a strong backup running back in sophomore Larry Rountree III (703 rushing yards in 2017), and freshman phenomenon tight end Albert Okwuegbunam (415 receiving yards and 11 touchdowns). With Lock also back, they have all the pieces to play a more ball control-oriented style of offense, but it's hard to look away from the fact that they're turning away from a style that was exceptionally explosive a year ago.

The defense only ranked 90th in S&P+ in 2017 due to a penchant for giving up big plays (115th in IsoPPP+) and a struggle to get a good pass rush. But starting linebackers Cale Garrett and Terez Hall led the team in tackles and combined for 43 run stuffs. The defensive line brings back star tackle Terry Beckner Jr. (seven sacks) while also plugging in Texas transfer Jordan Elliott. This could be the most gifted defensive tackle tandem in the SEC, and the Tigers could make a surprising leap forward if they can clean up their play in the secondary.

41. Northwestern Wildcats (7-5, 5-4)

2018 Projections

F/+	20.6 (41)
FEI	.046 (42)
S&P+	6.5 (38)
Total Wins	6.6
Conf Wins	4.9
SOS	.054 (23)
Conf SOS	.111 (36)
Div Champ	5%
Conf Champ	3%
CFP Berth	1%

Projection Factors

2017 F/+	19.1 (42)
2017 FEI	.060 (43)
2017 S&P+	4.8 (45)
5-Year F/+	7.6 (52)
5-Year FEI	.060 (38)
5-Year S&P+	2.9 (58)
2-Yr/5-Yr Recruiting	54/53
Ret. Offense	67% (68)
Ret. Defense	61% (75)
Ret. Total	64% (70)

Projected Win Likelihood by Game

Date	Opponent (Proj Rank)	PWL
Aug 30	at Purdue (61)	67%
Sep 8	vs Duke (32)	49%
Sep 15	vs Akron (120)	99%
Sep 29	vs Michigan (11)	22%
Oct 6	at Michigan St. (9)	11%
Oct 13	vs Nebraska (60)	80%
Oct 20	at Rutgers (93)	92%
Oct 27	vs Wisconsin (12)	22%
Nov 3	vs Notre Dame (6)	18%
Nov 10	at Iowa (27)	28%
Nov 17	at Minnesota (62)	69%
Nov 24	vs Illinois (103)	98%

The Wildcats 2018 hopes hinge on the arm of quarterback Clayton Thorson. After passing for 2,844 yards last season and 3,182 as a sophomore, expectations for the senior (and early NFL draft favorite) are sky high. You have to go back to 2009 to find a Northwestern quarterback throw for more yards (Mike Kafka).

Although Thorson has prototypical NFL quarterback size (6-foot-4, 225 pounds), he didn't necessarily lead the most efficient passing offense. Averaging 6.6 yards per attempt with a 60.4 percent completion rate and 12 interceptions, he led a passing game that ranked just 62nd in the S&P+ and was one of the worst in the country in IsoPPP. Part of that lack of explosiveness can be due to his receivers, the best of whom averaged just 14.3 yards per catch. But Thorson's top two targets (senior Flynn Nagel and junior Ben Skowronek) return in 2018, along with a number of freshmen who managed to make an impact in this pass-heavy offense (93rd in standard-downs run rate).

Although Northwestern passed nearly as often as they ran the ball on standard downs, few players in the country carried the ball as much as departed senior Justin Jackson. He ranked eighth in total carries (just 14 behind the national leader) after ranking sixth and third the previous two seasons. While you hate to lose a workhorse like Jackson, Northwestern might get an upgrade in Jeremy Larkin, who had an excellent redshirt freshman season, bettering nearly all of Jackson's averages (i.e., 42.9 percent opportunity rate to Jackson's 34.5).

Defensively, it's a mixed bag. The Wildcats lose some major pieces—defensive backs Godwin Igwebuike and Kyle Queiro, linebacker Brett Walsh—but some of their best performers were also freshmen last season. Linebacker Paddy Fisher was the Big Ten defensive freshman of the year and the team's tackle leader, while defensive lineman Samdup Miller was second on the team in sacks. Linebacker Nate Hall (the team's tackles for loss leader) and lineman Joe Gaziano (the sack leader) also return, indicating that Northwestern could improve defensively again in 2018.

42. Boston College Eagles (6-6, 3-5)

2018 Projections

F/+	19.6 (42)
FEI	.066 (34)
S&P+	4.0 (49)
Total Wins	6.2
Conf Wins	2.7
SOS	.056 (24)
Conf SOS	.062 (14)
Div Champ	0%
Conf Champ	0%
CFP Berth	0%

Projection Factors

2017 F/+	17.3 (43)
2017 FEI	.118 (24)
2017 S&P+	1.0 (66)
5-Year F/+	3.0 (62)
5-Year FEI	.070 (35)
5-Year S&P+	1.8 (60)
2-Yr/5-Yr Recruiting	68/66
Ret. Offense	81% (23)
Ret. Defense	65% (58)
Ret. Total	73% (28)

Projected Win Likelihood by Game

Date	Opponent (Proj Rank)	PWL
Sep 1	vs Massachusetts (101)	98%
Sep 8	vs Holy Cross (FCS)	100%
Sep 13	at Wake Forest (36)	37%
Sep 22	at Purdue (61)	66%
Sep 29	vs Temple (71)	87%
Oct 6	at NC State (34)	35%
Oct 13	vs Louisville (28)	41%
Oct 26	vs Miami-FL (13)	22%
Nov 3	at Virginia Tech (22)	20%
Nov 10	vs Clemson (2)	16%
Nov 17	at Florida St. (16)	14%
Nov 24	vs Syracuse (73)	89%

Boston College, in Year 5 of Steve Adazio's tenure, was one of the most average teams in the country. The Eagles finished 7-6 after a one-score loss to Iowa in their bowl game, and 43rd in the final F/+ rankings. The Eagles looked a lot like what we've come to expect from an Adazio team: great rushing offense, solid defense, and poor passing game.

The most exciting part of the Eagles is sophomore running back A.J. Dillon. The freshman was third in the country in rushing attempts (one carry behind Devin Singletary and Phillip Lindsay) and ran for 1,589 yards with a 37.3 percent opportunity rate. That's extremely high volume, occasionally explosive, but with often mediocre blocking (team opportunity rate was 82nd in the country and stuff rate was 60th). The Eagles should improve in that respect in 2018, with seven players bringing at least ten starts into 2018, according to Coach Adazio. With a more experienced line, Dillon could challenge Andre Williams, who ran for a nation-best 2,177 yards in 2013.

More efficient quarterback play would help. Freshman Anthony Brown suffered a leg injury against North Carolina State and was knocked out for the rest of the season in early November. Brown rehabbed during spring practice, but he should be ready for 2018. As a starter he looked like most young quarterbacks—too many interceptions (nine), too low in yards per attempt (5.3), and too low a completion rate (51.9 percent). But these numbers should improve with another year under center and the return of pretty much every receiving target Brown had, including top receiver Kobay White and senior tight end Tommy Sweeney.

Last season's defense was 36th in the defensive S&P+, which was far higher than expected given Boston College's recruiting and Don Brown already gone to Michigan. The Eagles have a fairly solid mix of talent and experience returning in 2018, led by senior defensive end Zach Allen. They will have to replace second-round defensive end Harold Landry, as well as defensive backs Issac Yiadom and Kamrin Moore, but enough younger players got experience in 2017 that the defense should keep up relatively well.

43. Iowa State Cyclones (6-6, 4-5)

2018 Projections

F/+	18.8 (43)
FEI	.044 (43)
S&P+	5.6 (41)
Total Wins	6.4
Conf Wins	4.2
SOS	.077 (37)
Conf SOS	.108 (35)
Div Champ	-
Conf Champ	1%
CFP Berth	0%

Projection Factors

2017 F/+	30.8 (26)
2017 FEI	.163 (15)
2017 S&P+	4.7 (46)
5-Year F/+	-2.7 (71)
5-Year FEI	.075 (31)
5-Year S&P+	-0.9 (74)
2-Yr/5-Yr Recruiting	49/55
Ret. Offense	65% (75)
Ret. Defense	62% (70)
Ret. Total	64% (74)

Projected Win Likelihood by Game

Date	Opponent (Proj Rank)	PWL	Projected Loss / Projected Win
Sep 1	vs S. Dakota St. (FCS)	100%	
Sep 8	at Iowa (27)	26%	
Sep 15	vs Oklahoma (8)	17%	
Sep 22	vs Akron (120)	99%	
Sep 29	at TCU (20)	17%	
Oct 6	at Oklahoma St. (21)	19%	
Oct 13	vs West Virginia (45)	61%	
Oct 27	vs Texas Tech (53)	71%	
Nov 3	at Kansas (102)	96%	
Nov 10	vs Baylor (37)	52%	
Nov 17	at Texas (24)	20%	
Nov 24	vs Kansas St. (46)	64%	

The Cyclones had just about as successful a 2017 season as they could have hoped for: 8-5 with four one-score losses; wins over Oklahoma, TCU, and Memphis; and all of the national recognition that those upsets generated. Finishing 26th in F/+ with the 56th-most talented roster according to the 247 Sports Composite is an insane accomplishment. For context, Iowa State went 3-9 and 70th in F/+ in 2016 and 3-9 and 79th in F/+ in 2015. So how can the Cyclones follow that season up?

Well, it's going to be difficult. Iowa State was built on excellent run defense—22nd in rushing S&P+—that stopped opponents at or behind the line of scrimmage on 23.7 percent of runs (16th) while only allowing 5-plus yards on 32.2 percent of runs (10th). That translated to excellent play on first and second down (16th in first and second downs S&P+), but the pass defense couldn't keep up, ranking 65th and failing to get much of a pass rush (72nd in adjusted sack rate) despite creating a lot of run stuffs. Two key cogs in the run defense are gone in 2018—linebacker Joel Lanning and senior J.D. Waggoner, who combined for 24.5 tackles for loss and 10.5 sacks. There is still decent depth in the front seven, though. Marcel Spears Jr. and Willie Harvey will provide senior leadership at linebacker, while junior defensive end JaQuan Bailey was already the team leader in sacks. There's enough playmaking ability to think that the front seven should remain solid, while the defensive backs rotated enough to think that there won't be too much of a drop-off despite losing three defensive backs to graduation.

The Cyclones offense will count on the steady leadership of quarterback Kyle Kempt, who was granted another year of eligibility by the NCAA, as well as high-volume running back David Montgomery, who will enter his junior year. Montgomery was 15th in the country in attempts last season, but he wasn't the most efficient or explosive back, with just one-third of his runs going for 5 or more yards and 12.8 percent going for 10-plus yards (averaging 4.4 yards per carry overall). The offensive line was the main holdup, ranking 113th and 119th in adjusted line yards and opportunity rate. The good news is that the Cyclones have a number of promising-looking younger linemen who could lift the unit's performance.

Kempt took over at quarterback from Jacob Park (who has since transferred) and was solid if unspectacular. Averaging 7.4 yards per attempt and only three interceptions, he appears to have a relatively high floor. But he also loses three of his top four targets, including Allen Lazard. The good news is that

6-foot-6 redshirt junior Hakeem Butler might have already been the best receiver on the roster, averaging a team-high 17.0 yards per catch. There's enough talent on the roster that the passing game should be relatively stable.

The big question is whether the Cyclones can score more

big upsets on a schedule that's just as difficult as last season's. Iowa, Oklahoma, Oklahoma State, West Virginia, and Texas are all games we would have considered as sure losses before last season. But with Matt Campbell as head coach, the Cyclones might be able to pull out a win or two (or three) from that list.

44. Arizona State Sun Devils (5-7, 4-5)

2018 Projections

F/+	17.1 (44)
FEI	.069 (32)
S&P+	2.4 (57)
Total Wins	5.4
Conf Wins	3.7
SOS	.033 (12)
Conf SOS	.058 (13)
Div Champ	1%
Conf Champ	0%
CFP Berth	0%

Projection Factors

2017 F/+	4.2 (61)
2017 FEI	.063 (42)
2017 S&P+	-1.3 (81)
5-Year F/+	13.8 (39)
5-Year FEI	.072 (33)
5-Year S&P+	5.9 (38)
2-Yr/5-Yr Recruiting	38/28
Ret. Offense	79% (26)
Ret. Defense	48% (116)
Ret. Total	63% (76)

Projected Win Likelihood by Game

Date	Opponent (Proj Rank)	PWL
Sep 1	vs UTSA (109)	98%
Sep 8	vs Michigan St. (9)	18%
Sep 15	at San Diego St. (59)	61%
Sep 22	at Washington (7)	7%
Sep 29	vs Oregon St. (107)	98%
Oct 6	at Colorado (92)	89%
Oct 18	vs Stanford (17)	23%
Oct 27	at USC (15)	11%
Nov 3	vs Utah (29)	39%
Nov 10	vs UCLA (38)	50%
Nov 17	at Oregon (23)	18%
Nov 24	at Arizona (35)	32%

Arizona State made one of the most interesting coaching hires of the 2017 season, picking up Herm Edwards from ESPN. It has been a decade since Edwards coached football, and you have to look way back in his resume—back to 1989—for college coaching experience. But the Sun Devils seem to be looking for a new "CEO model" approach after averaging 38th in the S&P+ between 2013 and 2017 under Todd Graham. Sure, 7-6 with losses to San Diego State and Texas Tech last year is below expectations, but there's every reason to think that 2018 will see improvements, at least on offense.

Quarterback Manny Wilkins is back for his senior season, and he, along with a full stock of receivers, are the team's best hope for an exciting 2018 season. Wilkins led the 49th-ranked passing S&P+ offense last season, and all but one receiver who totaled more than 100 receiving yards returns (the one of the five who doesn't return, Jalen Harvey, moved to safety this offseason). N'Keal Harry, Wilkins' top target; Kyle Williams, who had a 76 percent catch rate; and extremely fast sophomore Frank Darby, who averaged 26 yards per catch last season, should be the core of an exciting passing game.

Of course, that depends on three factors. First, former receivers coach Rob Likens, now the offensive coordinator, should be a pass-heavy playcaller based on his Sonny Dykes Air Raid experience, but that's certainly not Edwards' tendency as a coach. So we'll see how much Herm really will delegate to

his coordinators here. Second, the running backs room loses both top backs, Demario Richard and Kalen Ballage, meaning sophomore former four-star recruit Eno Benjamin should take over. Benjamin looks like a great foundation, but there's unproven depth behind him, and even he only had 23 carries as a freshman last season. Finally, and most importantly, the offensive line couldn't keep Wilkins protected much last season. He was sacked 40 times, or 8.9 percent, which was 115th in adjusted sack rate. On passing downs, that adjusted sack rate jumped to 11.4 percent.

The defense loses more production than almost anyone in the country, returning only 48 percent (115th). In some ways that could be good, since the defense ranked 106th in the country last season. New defensive coordinator Danny Gonzales brings a 3-3-5 from San Diego State, where they have ranked in the top 40 of the defensive S&P+ for the last three seasons, so there's some reason for optimism defensively.

But no matter how the Edwards coaching experiment goes, the first year could be a little rough. Along with the defensive turnover and new coordinators, a tough schedule really doesn't do the Sun Devils any favors. Michigan State, San Diego State, and Washington in September should be a difficult run, and then the schedule picks up again in mid-October with six straight games where the S&P+ projects the Sun Devils as underdogs.

45. West Virginia Mountaineers (6-6, 4-5)

2018 Projections		Projection Factors	
F/+	16.9 (45)	2017 F/+	3.6 (62)
FEI	.040 (44)	2017 FEI	.011 (61)
S&P+	5.0 (44)	2017 S&P+	1.7 (63)
Total Wins	5.9	5-Year F/+	9.5 (44)
Conf Wins	3.8	5-Year FEI	.036 (49)
SOS	.086 (44)	5-Year S&P+	4.3 (49)
Conf SOS	.111 (37)	2-Yr/5-Yr Recruiting	42/39
Div Champ	-	Ret. Offense	72% (49)
Conf Champ	0%	Ret. Defense	57% (86)
CFP Berth	0%	Ret. Total	65% (68)

Projected Win Likelihood by Game

Date	Opponent (Proj Rank)	PWL
Sep 1	vs Tennessee (72)	81%
Sep 8	vs Youngstown St. (FCS)	100%
Sep 15	at NC State (34)	31%
Sep 22	vs Kansas St. (46)	61%
Sep 29	at Texas Tech (53)	53%
Oct 6	vs Kansas (102)	98%
Oct 13	at Iowa St. (43)	39%
Oct 25	vs Baylor (37)	48%
Nov 3	at Texas (24)	18%
Nov 10	vs TCU (20)	27%
Nov 17	at Oklahoma St. (21)	17%
Nov 23	vs Oklahoma (8)	16%

Expectations are surging for the Mountaineers with the return of quarterback Will Grier, who has 20/1 odds as a Heisman favorite following spring practice. Both Athlon Sports and USA Today have the Mountaineers in their post-spring top-25 lists, mostly due to their offensive star power and expectations of an improved defense.

First, the good. Despite getting injured in mid-November, Will Grier still finished eighth in the country in passing yards per game, averaging 9.0 yards per attempt. The Mountaineers lost all three games played without Grier and averaged roughly a yard per play less in that time span. He also returns four of his top five receiving targets, including 1,000 yard-receiver Gary Jennings, who had a 73 percent catch rate; converted 6-foot-4 quarterback David Sills V, who averaged 16.3 yards per catch; and Marcus Simms, who averaged 18.9. And most of the offensive line returns too, including both all-conference tackles and two other starters, as well as new JUCO transfers.

Dana Holgorsen went hard after transfers, picking up big-time players on defense as well. Former five-star USC defensive lineman Kenny Bigelow and Clemson's Jabril Robinson provide an immediate upgrade on the line, which was necessary due to personnel losses and a unit that was just 106th in defensive line havoc rate last season. One of the top freshmen defensive linemen in the country, Dante Stills, should also make an immediate impact. Linebacker David Long Jr., who led the team in tackles for loss last season (15.5), should again be the top playmaker. The Mountaineers also have young talent with experience at safety and a trio of players (including two more transfers) to fill an open cornerback spot, so they should be solid in the secondary. Last season was Tony Gibson's worst as defensive coordinator in Morgantown, but there are plenty of (transferred-in) reasons to be optimistic.

The only problem is that even assuming a return to a mid-40s defense and a top-end offense, the back end of the schedule is brutal. Even if the Mountaineers are a top-30ish team on paper, they still have Texas, TCU, Oklahoma State, and Oklahoma to close out the year, and North Carolina State and Tennessee as early out-of-conference matchups.

46. Kansas State Wildcats (6-6, 3-6)

2018 Projections		Projection Factors	
F/+	15.3 (46)	2017 F/+	14.1 (48)
FEI	.064 (35)	2017 FEI	.086 (34)
S&P+	1.9 (61)	2017 S&P+	1.3 (64)
Total Wins	5.6	5-Year F/+	15.5 (34)
Conf Wins	3.5	5-Year FEI	.094 (26)
SOS	.053 (22)	5-Year S&P+	5.6 (42)
Conf SOS	.082 (18)	2-Yr/5-Yr Recruiting	64/61
Div Champ	-	Ret. Offense	77% (35)
Conf Champ	0%	Ret. Defense	54% (98)
CFP Berth	0%	Ret. Total	65% (65)

Projected Win Likelihood by Game

Date	Opponent (Proj Rank)	PWL
Sep 1	vs South Dakota (FCS)	100%
Sep 8	vs Mississippi St. (14)	18%
Sep 15	vs UTSA (109)	98%
Sep 22	at West Virginia (45)	39%
Sep 29	vs Texas (24)	29%
Oct 6	at Baylor (37)	31%
Oct 13	vs Oklahoma St. (21)	27%
Oct 27	at Oklahoma (8)	7%
Nov 3	at TCU (20)	14%
Nov 10	vs Kansas (102)	97%
Nov 17	vs Texas Tech (53)	66%
Nov 24	at Iowa St. (43)	36%

Bill Snyder just keeps on keeping on in the "Little Apple" of Manhattan, Kansas. The Wildcats lost longtime defensive coordinator Tom Hayes to retirement while offensive coordinator Dana Dimel left for the head coaching job at UTEP, taking his son, starting fullback Winston, with him. Snyder just promoted a group of promising young assistants comprised of his own former players like receiver-turned-playcaller Andre Coleman, quarterback-turned-co-offensive coordinator Collin Klein, and defensive end-turned-defensive coordinator Blake Seiler.

This actually appears to be one of the stronger teams that Kansas State has had in recent seasons. The Wildcats originally seemed poised for a breakthrough in 2017, thanks to starting quarterback and thousand-yard rusher Jesse Ertz, but the oft-injured signal-caller missed more than half the season with a knee injury. In his stead the Wildcats tried redshirt sophomore Alex Delton (533 rushing yards in 2017) and redshirt freshman Skylar Thompson (689 passing yards) and are still sorting out the competition between them. They'll be replacing star receiver Byron Pringle but return all five starters on the offensive line and lead running back Alex Barnes (819 rushing yards). This should be a productive offense regardless

of the choice at quarterback, as this team buried UCLA in the bowl game after inserting Delton for Thompson and watching him run 20 times for 158 yards and three touchdowns.

Defense has been the biggest question mark for Kansas State since their 2012 Big 12 title win. The 2018 team looks like it'll be one of their faster units, with rising linebackers Elijah Sullivan and Da'Quan Patton emerging inside. The secondary will return starting safeties Denzel Goolsby (third-leading tackler) and Kendall Adams (fourth-leading tackler) along with cornerback Duke Shelley (13 passes defended). Up front, the defensive line returns tackle Trey Dishon but needs to find a pass rush from a defensive end rotation that produced only eight sacks between five players in 2017. If they can be more disruptive up front thanks to improvement from younger defensive linemen, the defensive backfield looks quicker and harder to attack than those of previous Wildcat defenses. Between that and an answer at quarterback, Kansas State could contend for the Big 12 title.

47. Memphis Tigers (10-2, 6-2)

2018 Projections

F/+	15.0 (47)
FEI	.029 (48)
S&P+	5.1 (43)
Total Wins	9.6
Conf Wins	6.3
SOS	.511 (104)
Conf SOS	.644 (76)
Div Champ	49%
Conf Champ	24%
CFP Berth	1%

Projection Factors

2017 F/+	33.3 (22)
2017 FEI	.101 (29)
2017 S&P+	9.1 (20)
5-Year F/+	14.2 (38)
5-Year FEI	.085 (29)
5-Year S&P+	5.2 (44)
2-Yr/5-Yr Recruiting	71/75
Ret. Offense	44% (114)
Ret. Defense	64% (64)
Ret. Total	54% (109)

Projected Win Likelihood by Game

Date	Opponent (Proj Rank)	PWL	Projected Loss	Projected Win
Sep 1	vs Mercer (FCS)	100%		
Sep 8	at Navy (74)	76%		
Sep 14	vs Georgia St. (118)	99%		
Sep 22	vs South Alabama (110)	98%		
Sep 28	at Tulane (90)	87%		
Oct 6	vs Connecticut (123)	99%		
Oct 13	vs Central Florida (18)	22%		
Oct 20	at Missouri (40)	33%		
Nov 3	at East Carolina (124)	99%		
Nov 10	vs Tulsa (99)	97%		
Nov 16	at SMU (82)	81%		
Nov 23	vs Houston (54)	66%		

For the last two years, Memphis has been largely fueled by the connection between quarterback Riley Ferguson and wide receiver Anthony Miller. Ferguson threw for 7,955 yards with 70 touchdowns over those two seasons, while Miller caught 191 balls for 2,896 yards and 32 touchdowns. Both are now moving on, but there may not be much respite for AAC defenses.

The Tigers added a brilliant run game to their offensive formula last season with a sophomore tandem of Patrick Taylor Jr. and Darrell Henderson combining for 2,020 rushing yards and 22 touchdowns. Head coach and offensive mastermind Mike Norvell combined run/pass option spread tactics with old school, downhill run schemes and multiple-tight end sets. Now they have to find a new triggerman at quarterback and a new primary perimeter option at receiver, but there's a lot in place here to suggest they can reload without losing too much steam. The offensive line returns four starters and the passing

game will be able to work off a very effective run game.

Memphis has been an offensively oriented team for several years now, essentially ever since Barry Odom left for Missouri, and that will probably continue in 2018. Linebacker Genard Avery was their main playmaker a year ago. He had 22 tackles for loss, 21 run stuffs, and 8.5 sacks as a 3-4 outside linebacker. That's a lot to replace. However, the Tigers have a lot of players coming back in the secondary, including leading tackler junior Austin Hall (12 run stuffs and three interceptions in 2017) and also sophomore Terrell Carter (five interceptions).

With all of their returning experience and entering into Year 2 of this defensive system, the defense could be a stouter overall unit and a better complement to the offense. Memphis vs. Houston should be a fun race with their head-to-head contest likely determining the American West division.

48. Pittsburgh Panthers (5-7, 4-4)

2018 Projections

F/+	13.1 (48)
FEI	.022 (51)
S&P+	4.8 (46)
Total Wins	4.9
Conf Wins	3.6
SOS	.032 (10)
Conf SOS	.216 (60)
Div Champ	2%
Conf Champ	1%
CFP Berth	0%

Projection Factors

2017 F/+	-10.7 (79)
2017 FEI	-.028 (71)
2017 S&P+	-1.5 (82)
5-Year F/+	11.1 (41)
5-Year FEI	.007 (62)
5-Year S&P+	6.4 (36)
2-Yr/5-Yr Recruiting	37/42
Ret. Offense	61% (85)
Ret. Defense	75% (31)
Ret. Total	68% (52)

Projected Win Likelihood by Game

Date	Opponent (Proj Rank)	PWL
Sep 1	vs Albany (FCS)	100%
Sep 8	vs Penn St. (10)	15%
Sep 15	vs Georgia Tech (50)	59%
Sep 22	at North Carolina (52)	46%
Sep 29	at Central Florida (18)	10%
Oct 6	vs Syracuse (73)	84%
Oct 13	at Notre Dame (6)	5%
Oct 27	vs Duke (32)	38%
Nov 2	at Virginia (75)	74%
Nov 10	vs Virginia Tech (22)	25%
Nov 17	at Wake Forest (36)	28%
Nov 24	at Miami-FL (13)	7%

The Pat Narduzzi era in Pittsburgh has not gone very well. The 2017 season was a definite step back, as Pitt went 5-7 after losing multiple key offensive players and offensive coordinator Matt Canada. It wasn't unexpected that the offense would take a step back after losing Canada and star quarterback Nathan Peterman. The bigger issue was the third consecutive decline on the defense in the S&P+ rankings.

After coordinating the famous "no-fly zone" defenses at Michigan State, Narduzzi took charge of a defense at Pitt that had just finished 67th in defensive S&P+. In Year 1 they rose to 50th; in Year 2 dropped back down to 62nd, and then last year finished 75th. The transformation of Pitt into a smashmouth offensive team that plays great defense has never occurred. The 2017 defense didn't have much in the way of play-making along the defensive line, with their lead pass-rusher coming from the linebacker corps (Oluwaseun Idowu with five sacks) and their second leading guy coming from the secondary (Avonte Maddox with four sacks).

To get Narduzzi's over/press quarters defense rolling, Pitt needs defensive linemen who can take advantage of the aggressive coverages and linebacker play and make plays in the backfield.

The offense evolved in 2017 from Canada's unique system of combining downhill runs with jet sweeps and options to new offensive coordinator Shawn Watson's pro-style, West Coast offense. They were excellent on standard downs thanks to a 19th-ranked rushing S&P+ unit; they weren't terribly explosive, but they kept the offense on track. Watson is very excited about sophomore quarterback Kenny Pickett, who led the upset win over Miami a year ago. If he can grow into the starting job, this offense could become even more efficient. They're adding transfer tight end Will Gragg from Arkansas to help him.

Still, it's hard to see the Narduzzi era taking off until Pitt is able to put a defense on the field anywhere close to the units he coached back in Lansing, Michigan.

49. Washington State Cougars (7-5, 4-5)

2018 Projections

F/+	12.9 (49)
FEI	.015 (55)
S&P+	5.4 (42)
Total Wins	6.5
Conf Wins	3.8
SOS	.091 (48)
Conf SOS	.093 (23)
Div Champ	1%
Conf Champ	0%
CFP Berth	0%

Projection Factors

2017 F/+	16.5 (45)
2017 FEI	.034 (50)
2017 S&P+	5.4 (39)
5-Year F/+	8.2 (51)
5-Year FEI	.041 (46)
5-Year S&P+	3.0 (57)
2-Yr/5-Yr Recruiting	46/52
Ret. Offense	49% (107)
Ret. Defense	61% (77)
Ret. Total	55% (106)

Projected Win Likelihood by Game

Date	Opponent (Proj Rank)	PWL
Sep 1	at Wyoming (77)	76%
Sep 8	vs San Jose St. (129)	99%
Sep 15	vs E. Washington (FCS)	100%
Sep 21	at USC (15)	9%
Sep 29	vs Utah (29)	33%
Oct 6	at Oregon St. (107)	94%
Oct 20	vs Oregon (23)	26%
Oct 27	at Stanford (17)	9%
Nov 3	vs California (58)	69%
Nov 10	at Colorado (92)	86%
Nov 17	vs Arizona (35)	41%
Nov 23	vs Washington (7)	12%

The Cougars had a really good 2017, but then a really tough offseason to follow it up. Defensive coordinator Alex Grinch's unit was devastating in Year 2 while utilizing a speedy,

aggressive backfield playing behind unique, 252-pound defensive tackle Hercules Mata'afa. The wrecking-ball tackle had 22.5 tackles for loss, 10.5 sacks, and 18 run stuffs, but now is off to the NFL. Grinch also left to become an assistant coach at Ohio State, with an obvious shot at a promotion if (and when) their defensive coordinator Greg Schiano leaves for a head coaching job.

Then the Cougars took a tragic hit when they lost quarterback Tyler Hilinski to suicide. They'll be bringing in Eastern Washington transfer Gardner Minshew but may struggle to overcome both the emotional hit and the loss of their prospective next man up. Leading receivers Isaiah Johnson-Mack and Tavares Martin also left on bad terms with head coach Mike Leach. Normally this style of offense has a "plug and play" aspect to it, but that doesn't hold as true if the team is experiencing heavy roster turnover from non-senior classes. They do return sixth-year senior Robert Lewis and started to develop

new targets in the passing game for their bowl game.

Leach almost left the program for the Tennessee job, but then had to return and rebuild the Washington State staff after they lost multiple assistants. They did add former Minnesota head coach Tracy Claeys as defensive coordinator. Things look somewhat better here as they lose Grinch and Mata'afa but also return speedy freshman linebacker Jahad Woods (19 run stuffs in 2017) and several experienced defensive backs. Claeys coaches a different style of defense than Grinch but has a knack for producing sound, physical units. The Cougars leaned on two freshmen and a sophomore in their defensive backfield in 2017, including Woods, and have some pieces to work with as Claeys looks to construct a unit with a new identity.

50. Georgia Tech Yellow Jackets (5-7, 3-5)

2018 Projections

F/+	12.4 (50)
FEI	.030 (47)
S&P+	3.6 (53)
Total Wins	5.2
Conf Wins	2.6
SOS	.039 (16)
Conf SOS	.106 (33)
Div Champ	1%
Conf Champ	0%
CFP Berth	0%

Projection Factors

2017 F/+	0.8 (67)
2017 FEI	.012 (60)
2017 S&P+	0.5 (73)
5-Year F/+	15.9 (33)
5-Year FEI	.052 (39)
5-Year S&P+	6.5 (33)
2-Yr/5-Yr Recruiting	48/49
Ret. Offense	66% (73)
Ret. Defense	52% (110)
Ret. Total	59% (99)

Projected Win Likelihood by Game

Date	Opponent (Proj Rank)	PWL
Sep 1	vs Alcorn St. (FCS)	100%
Sep 8	at South Florida (64)	61%
Sep 15	at Pittsburgh (48)	41%
Sep 22	vs Clemson (2)	10%
Sep 29	vs Bowling Green (94)	94%
Oct 5	at Louisville (28)	19%
Oct 13	vs Duke (32)	37%
Oct 25	at Virginia Tech (22)	13%
Nov 3	at North Carolina (52)	45%
Nov 10	vs Miami-FL (13)	15%
Nov 17	vs Virginia (75)	85%
Nov 24	at Georgia (4)	5%

Georgia Tech was set up for a very interesting 2017. On offense they faced the need to replace three-year starting quarterback Justin Thomas and lead running back Dedrick Mills after his dismissal from the team. The back-up quarterback poised to take over the team, Matthew Jordan, had proven a solid game manager but not a very explosive runner. On defense the team lost most of their starters, including all five starting defensive backs. The triple-option flexbone offense of head coach Paul Johnson hasn't always coincided with great defense, likely in part because the team's practice formats don't give their defenders very many quality snaps against the kinds of offenses they face from week to week in ACC play.

The Yellow Jackets ended up having another pretty solid offensive season thanks to the emergence of young quarterback Taquon Marshall, who ran for 1,255 yards and 17 touchdowns. Sophomore "B-back" KirVonte Benson took over for Mills and ran for another 1,053 yards and six scores. The offense generally held up their end of the bargain over

the course of the season with 28.1 points per game and just a few quiet games that came against elite defenses from playoff teams Clemson and Georgia. Beyond their two-headed run game, the Yellow Jackets never established a major passing threat with Marshall throwing for only 927 yards on the year. On the bright side, Marshall and Benson return to build on a strong inaugural campaign together.

The defense got off to a promising start but finished the year 66th in defensive S&P+ and had trouble with the big play, finishing only 84th in IsoPPP+. Their secondary now has to replace four of five starters, and the defensive line loses key pass-rusher Antonio Simmons (5.5 sacks). The 2018 defense looks to be led by the returning linebacker tandem of Victor Alexander and Brant Mitchell, both entering their senior seasons, but the two combined for only 3.5 tackles for loss and six run stuffs in 2017. The 2018 Yellow Jackets look like another middle-of-the-road ACC team whose ceiling is set by how many of the teams on their schedule are option-resistant.

NCAA Win Projections

Projected Win Probabilities For ACC Teams

ACC Atlantic	Overall Wins													Conference Wins								
	12-0	11-1	10-2	9-3	8-4	7-5	6-6	5-7	4-8	3-9	2-10	1-11	0-12	8-0	7-1	6-2	5-3	4-4	3-5	2-6	1-7	0-8
Boston College	-	-	-	1	4	10	25	31	21	7	1	-	-	-	-	2	5	16	30	32	13	2
Clemson	14	37	30	15	3	1	-	-	-	-	-	-	-	26	42	23	7	2	-	-	-	-
Florida State	1	5	17	29	27	14	5	2	-	-	-	-	-	2	16	30	29	17	5	1	-	-
Louisville	-	1	12	25	30	22	8	1	1	-	-	-	-	1	10	25	36	19	8	1	-	-
NC State	-	2	8	19	28	26	12	4	1	-	-	-	-	-	3	14	28	31	17	6	1	-
Syracuse	-	-	-	-	-	-	2	11	30	38	18	1	-	-	-	-	-	-	6	21	41	32
Wake Forest	-	-	2	10	18	31	25	12	2	-	-	-	-	-	1	6	20	28	28	15	2	-
ACC Coastal	12-0	11-1	10-2	9-3	8-4	7-5	6-6	5-7	4-8	3-9	2-10	1-11	0-12	8-0	7-1	6-2	5-3	4-4	3-5	2-6	1-7	0-8
Duke	-	1	5	14	27	26	19	7	1	-	-	-	-	-	2	11	32	30	19	6	-	-
Georgia Tech	-	-	-	1	4	12	24	29	21	8	1	-	-	-	-	1	5	17	33	29	14	1
Miami-FL	9	28	33	20	9	1	-	-	-	-	-	-	-	18	38	29	12	3	-	-	-	-
North Carolina	-	-	1	3	12	23	29	20	10	2	-	-	-	-	-	2	13	30	32	16	6	1
Pittsburgh	-	-	-	-	2	9	20	30	25	12	2	-	-	-	1	4	17	29	31	15	3	-
Virginia	-	-	-	-	-	1	6	20	31	31	10	1	-	-	-	-	-	-	5	23	39	33
Virginia Tech	1	8	20	30	28	10	3	-	-	-	-	-	-	2	19	32	28	14	4	1	-	-

Projected Win Probabilities For American Teams

American East	Overall Wins													Conference Wins								
	12-0	11-1	10-2	9-3	8-4	7-5	6-6	5-7	4-8	3-9	2-10	1-11	0-12	8-0	7-1	6-2	5-3	4-4	3-5	2-6	1-7	0-8
Central Florida	38	41	16	4	1	-	-	-	-	-	-	-	-	63	33	4	-	-	-	-	-	-
Cincinnati	-	-	-	1	4	12	23	28	21	9	2	-	-	-	1	2	12	32	33	16	4	-
Connecticut	-	-	-	-	-	-	1	5	13	33	34	14	-	-	-	-	-	2	7	24	42	25
East Carolina	-	-	-	-	-	-	-	1	9	34	38	18	-	-	-	-	-	-	3	17	52	28
South Florida	-	2	15	30	29	18	5	1	-	-	-	-	-	2	8	33	35	18	4	-	-	-
Temple	-	-	2	12	28	30	20	6	2	-	-	-	-	-	3	19	39	29	9	1	-	-
American West	12-0	11-1	10-2	9-3	8-4	7-5	6-6	5-7	4-8	3-9	2-10	1-11	0-12	8-0	7-1	6-2	5-3	4-4	3-5	2-6	1-7	0-8
Houston	-	2	7	24	32	25	9	1	-	-	-	-	-	10	33	34	16	6	1	-	-	-
Memphis	3	17	36	29	13	2	-	-	-	-	-	-	-	7	37	35	17	4	-	-	-	-
Navy*	-	-	-	1	11	23	29	22	10	3	1	-	-	-	1	6	17	32	28	13	3	-
SMU	-	-	-	1	4	13	26	28	21	6	1	-	-	-	-	6	17	32	26	15	4	-
Tulane	-	-	-	-	2	7	16	29	29	14	3	-	-	-	-	1	11	23	32	24	8	1
Tulsa	-	-	-	-	-	-	1	2	13	28	34	20	2	-	-	-	1	8	26	36	24	5

*Navy will play 13 regular season games; for projected overall records, 12-0 means 13-0, 11-1 means 12-1, etc.

Projected Win Probabilities For Big 12 Teams

Big 12	\<overall\> 12-0	11-1	10-2	9-3	8-4	7-5	6-6	5-7	4-8	3-9	2-10	1-11	0-12	\<conf\> 9-0	8-1	7-2	6-3	5-4	4-5	3-6	2-7	1-8	0-9
Baylor	-	-	3	9	20	26	24	12	5	1	-	-	-	-	1	5	14	26	30	18	5	1	-
Iowa State	-	-	-	1	4	16	25	28	19	6	1	-	-	-	1	3	11	24	31	21	8	1	-
Kansas	-	-	-	-	-	-	-	1	5	30	45	19	-	-	-	-	-	-	-	-	1	16	83
Kansas State	-	-	-	1	8	16	27	31	13	4	-	-	-	-	-	1	5	14	27	31	19	3	-
Oklahoma	12	34	31	17	5	1	-	-	-	-	-	-	-	16	35	30	14	4	1	-	-	-	-
Oklahoma State	-	1	8	24	28	22	12	4	1	-	-	-	-	1	10	29	31	20	8	1	-	-	-
TCU	1	7	19	27	25	13	7	1	-	-	-	-	-	3	17	30	29	16	4	1	-	-	-
Texas	1	6	14	26	27	18	6	2	-	-	-	-	-	2	11	27	29	20	9	2	-	-	-
Texas Tech	-	-	-	-	2	7	18	29	29	12	3	-	-	-	-	-	1	8	20	32	30	8	1
West Virginia	-	-	-	2	10	19	29	25	12	3	-	-	-	-	-	2	6	19	29	28	13	3	-

Projected Win Probabilities For Big Ten Teams

Big Ten East	\<overall\> 12-0	11-1	10-2	9-3	8-4	7-5	6-6	5-7	4-8	3-9	2-10	1-11	0-12	\<conf\> 9-0	8-1	7-2	6-3	5-4	4-5	3-6	2-7	1-8	0-9
Indiana	-	-	-	-	2	11	26	34	20	6	1	-	-	-	-	-	-	2	18	35	30	14	1
Maryland	-	-	-	-	-	3	14	29	31	18	4	1	-	-	-	-	-	1	8	27	45	17	2
Michigan	-	10	22	33	25	9	1	-	-	-	-	-	-	2	19	30	33	13	3	-	-	-	-
Michigan State	9	26	36	22	6	1	-	-	-	-	-	-	-	11	32	35	18	4	-	-	-	-	-
Ohio State	10	30	36	19	4	1	-	-	-	-	-	-	-	16	40	31	11	2	-	-	-	-	-
Penn State	4	20	31	31	12	2	-	-	-	-	-	-	-	6	22	35	24	11	2	-	-	-	-
Rutgers	-	-	-	-	-	3	14	29	33	17	4	-	-	-	-	-	-	-	1	8	33	46	12

Big Ten West	\<overall\> 12-0	11-1	10-2	9-3	8-4	7-5	6-6	5-7	4-8	3-9	2-10	1-11	0-12	\<conf\> 9-0	8-1	7-2	6-3	5-4	4-5	3-6	2-7	1-8	0-9
Illinois	-	-	-	-	-	-	-	3	16	37	36	8	-	-	-	-	-	-	-	2	18	39	41
Iowa	-	2	10	28	30	21	7	2	-	-	-	-	-	3	15	34	31	14	3	-	-	-	-
Minnesota	-	-	1	2	9	22	29	23	12	2	-	-	-	-	-	1	6	17	32	27	13	3	1
Nebraska	-	-	-	-	2	11	30	32	18	6	1	-	-	-	-	-	-	2	16	37	35	9	1
Northwestern	-	-	1	5	18	28	27	16	4	1	-	-	-	-	1	7	18	34	28	11	1	-	-
Purdue	-	-	-	-	2	7	15	27	27	14	6	2	-	-	-	-	2	9	24	31	26	8	-
Wisconsin	7	28	38	20	6	1	-	-	-	-	-	-	-	7	28	37	22	6	-	-	-	-	-

Projected Win Probabilities For Conference USA Teams

Conf USA East	\<overall\> 12-0	11-1	10-2	9-3	8-4	7-5	6-6	5-7	4-8	3-9	2-10	1-11	0-12	\<conf\> 8-0	7-1	6-2	5-3	4-4	3-5	2-6	1-7	0-8
Charlotte	-	-	-	-	-	-	3	10	23	34	24	6	-	-	-	-	-	5	22	36	28	9
Florida Atlantic	1	10	40	37	11	1	-	-	-	-	-	-	-	40	43	14	2	1	-	-	-	-
Florida International	-	-	-	-	-	1	6	19	29	29	14	2	-	-	-	-	1	10	26	35	23	5
Marshall	-	1	8	26	35	22	7	1	-	-	-	-	-	21	48	24	6	1	-	-	-	-
Middle Tennessee	-	-	-	1	5	16	30	28	15	4	1	-	-	-	5	25	37	24	8	1	-	-
Old Dominion	-	-	-	-	1	5	16	28	27	17	5	1	-	-	-	-	4	16	28	32	17	3
Western Kentucky	-	-	-	1	8	22	34	25	9	1	-	-	-	-	1	8	28	40	19	4	-	-

Conf USA West	\<overall\> 12-0	11-1	10-2	9-3	8-4	7-5	6-6	5-7	4-8	3-9	2-10	1-11	0-12	\<conf\> 8-0	7-1	6-2	5-3	4-4	3-5	2-6	1-7	0-8
Louisiana Tech	-	-	6	33	34	19	6	2	-	-	-	-	-	3	37	40	14	5	1	-	-	-
North Texas	-	-	1	5	17	27	25	17	6	2	-	-	-	-	2	13	26	32	20	6	1	-
Rice*	-	-	-	-	-	-	2	9	21	29	26	11	2	-	-	-	5	14	31	30	16	4
Southern Miss	-	-	-	1	4	14	23	31	20	6	1	-	-	-	1	5	18	29	29	14	3	1
UAB	-	-	3	12	24	27	19	10	4	1	-	-	-	1	7	23	31	25	9	4	-	-
UTEP	-	-	-	-	-	-	1	3	9	23	30	26	8	-	-	-	-	5	12	31	34	18
UTSA	-	-	-	1	3	12	23	33	20	7	1	-	-	-	1	4	15	26	29	21	4	-

*Rice will play 13 regular season games; for projected overall records, 12-0 means 13-0, 11-1 means 12-1, etc.

Projected Win Probabilities For Independent Teams

Independents	Overall Wins												
	12-0	11-1	10-2	9-3	8-4	7-5	6-6	5-7	4-8	3-9	2-10	1-11	0-12
Army	-	-	-	4	15	30	28	18	4	1	-	-	-
BYU	-	-	-	1	6	20	37	25	9	2	-	-	-
Liberty	-	-	-	-	-	1	6	16	28	28	17	4	-
Massachusetts	-	-	-	1	4	13	27	30	17	7	1	-	-
Notre Dame	6	22	29	27	11	4	1	-	-	-	-	-	-
New Mexico State	-	-	-	-	1	6	14	26	27	17	8	1	-

Projected Win Probabilities For MAC Teams

MAC East	Overall Wins													Conference Wins								
	12-0	11-1	10-2	9-3	8-4	7-5	6-6	5-7	4-8	3-9	2-10	1-11	0-12	8-0	7-1	6-2	5-3	4-4	3-5	2-6	1-7	0-8
Akron	-	-	-	-	-	1	2	10	24	32	24	7	-	-	-	-	3	7	24	34	25	7
Bowling Green	-	-	-	1	4	16	25	28	20	5	1	-	-	-	2	8	24	30	24	10	2	-
Buffalo	-	-	2	9	22	25	23	13	5	1	-	-	-	-	3	18	33	28	14	3	1	-
Kent State	-	-	-	-	-	-	1	8	21	33	29	8	-	-	-	-	2	5	19	31	33	10
Miami-OH	-	1	3	10	20	26	22	12	5	1	-	-	-	-	4	16	30	27	17	5	1	-
Ohio	1	7	18	28	24	14	7	1	-	-	-	-	-	3	19	31	31	13	3	-	-	-
MAC West	12-0	11-1	10-2	9-3	8-4	7-5	6-6	5-7	4-8	3-9	2-10	1-11	0-12	8-0	7-1	6-2	5-3	4-4	3-5	2-6	1-7	0-8
Ball State	-	-	-	-	-	1	5	15	30	32	14	3	-	-	-	-	2	9	24	37	23	5
Central Michigan	-	-	-	-	-	1	5	16	28	29	17	4	-	-	-	-	2	9	22	34	25	8
Eastern Michigan	-	-	-	-	-	2	10	22	30	24	10	2	-	-	2	4	15	30	30	15	4	-
Northern Illinois	-	1	6	19	31	28	12	3	-	-	-	-	-	9	28	34	20	8	1	-	-	-
Toledo	2	17	36	30	12	3	-	-	-	-	-	-	-	30	43	21	6	-	-	-	-	-
Western Michigan	-	-	2	13	24	26	21	10	4	-	-	-	-	1	7	21	30	27	11	3	-	-

Projected Win Probabilities For MWC Teams

MWC Mountain	Overall Wins													Conference Wins								
	12-0	11-1	10-2	9-3	8-4	7-5	6-6	5-7	4-8	3-9	2-10	1-11	0-12	8-0	7-1	6-2	5-3	4-4	3-5	2-6	1-7	0-8
Air Force	-	-	-	-	-	2	8	19	30	27	12	2	-	-	-	-	3	14	31	31	17	4
Boise State	23	47	23	6	1	-	-	-	-	-	-	-	-	67	29	4	-	-	-	-	-	-
Colorado State	-	-	-	1	3	14	26	30	18	7	1	-	-	-	1	7	22	31	26	11	2	-
New Mexico	-	-	-	-	-	3	13	28	34	19	3	-	-	-	-	-	-	2	8	28	41	21
Utah State	-	-	3	22	34	27	11	3	-	-	-	-	-	-	15	38	33	11	3	-	-	-
Wyoming	-	-	2	8	26	33	21	9	1	-	-	-	-	1	7	28	36	22	5	1	-	-
MWC West	12-0	11-1	10-2	9-3	8-4	7-5	6-6	5-7	4-8	3-9	2-10	1-11	0-12	8-0	7-1	6-2	5-3	4-4	3-5	2-6	1-7	0-8
Fresno State	-	3	13	32	29	18	4	1	-	-	-	-	-	3	37	39	17	3	1	-	-	-
Hawaii*	-	-	-	-	-	1	3	11	28	33	19	5	-	-	-	-	1	4	12	31	35	17
Nevada	-	-	-	1	4	15	27	29	17	6	1	-	-	-	-	4	14	30	30	17	5	-
San Diego State	-	2	14	36	37	10	1	-	-	-	-	-	-	2	31	50	15	2	-	-	-	-
San Jose State	-	-	-	-	-	1	4	20	33	29	13	-	-	-	-	-	-	2	12	33	37	16
UNLV	-	-	-	-	3	13	27	29	19	8	1	-	-	-	-	3	12	28	32	19	5	1

*Hawaii will play 13 regular season games; for projected overall records, 12-0 means 13-0, 11-1 means 12-1, etc.

Projected Win Probabilities For Pac-12 Teams

	Overall Wins													Conference Wins									
Pac 12 North	12-0	11-1	10-2	9-3	8-4	7-5	6-6	5-7	4-8	3-9	2-10	1-11	0-12	9-0	8-1	7-2	6-3	5-4	4-5	3-6	2-7	1-8	0-9
California	-	-	-	-	2	10	23	31	22	11	1	-	-	-	-	1	1	7	23	36	28	4	-
Oregon	2	12	27	26	22	9	2	-	-	-	-	-	-	2	12	26	31	19	9	1	-	-	-
Oregon State	-	-	-	-	-	-	-	-	2	18	42	38	-	-	-	-	-	-	-	-	6	34	60
Stanford	-	2	8	19	30	23	14	4	-	-	-	-	-	3	15	29	31	16	5	1	-	-	-
Washington	9	27	33	23	7	1	-	-	-	-	-	-	-	22	38	28	9	3	-	-	-	-	-
Washington State	-	-	-	5	16	29	30	16	4	-	-	-	-	-	-	1	6	19	34	28	10	2	-
Pac 12 South	12-0	11-1	10-2	9-3	8-4	7-5	6-6	5-7	4-8	3-9	2-10	1-11	0-12	9-0	8-1	7-2	6-3	5-4	4-5	3-6	2-7	1-8	0-9
Arizona	-	3	13	23	27	22	9	2	1	-	-	-	-	1	6	15	28	28	16	5	1	-	-
Arizona State	-	-	-	1	5	15	25	30	17	6	1	-	-	-	-	1	6	18	31	30	13	1	-
Colorado	-	-	-	-	-	1	7	22	40	26	4	-	-	-	-	-	-	-	1	5	29	52	13
UCLA	-	-	-	2	9	20	27	26	11	4	1	-	-	-	-	3	10	23	31	23	9	1	-
USC	2	14	28	30	17	7	2	-	-	-	-	-	-	11	32	33	18	4	2	-	-	-	-
Utah	-	2	5	17	26	25	16	8	1	-	-	-	-	-	2	7	19	27	26	15	3	1	-

Projected Win Probabilities For SEC Teams

	Overall Wins													Conference Wins								
SEC East	12-0	11-1	10-2	9-3	8-4	7-5	6-6	5-7	4-8	3-9	2-10	1-11	0-12	8-0	7-1	6-2	5-3	4-4	3-5	2-6	1-7	0-8
Florida	-	-	1	7	22	35	24	9	2	-	-	-	-	1	4	21	35	28	9	2	-	-
Georgia	19	36	31	12	2	-	-	-	-	-	-	-	-	17	38	31	11	3	-	-	-	-
Kentucky	-	-	-	-	-	6	20	37	27	10	-	-	-	-	-	-	2	6	21	42	25	4
Missouri	-	-	6	18	29	26	14	6	1	-	-	-	-	-	1	10	27	36	20	6	-	-
South Carolina	-	1	4	16	30	26	16	6	1	-	-	-	-	1	4	16	32	28	15	4	-	-
Tennessee	-	-	-	-	-	3	14	34	33	15	1	-	-	-	-	-	-	2	12	34	35	17
Vanderbilt	-	-	-	-	-	1	3	14	30	34	15	3	-	-	-	-	-	1	6	24	43	26
SEC West	12-0	11-1	10-2	9-3	8-4	7-5	6-6	5-7	4-8	3-9	2-10	1-11	0-12	8-0	7-1	6-2	5-3	4-4	3-5	2-6	1-7	0-8
Alabama	18	38	28	12	3	1	-	-	-	-	-	-	-	26	39	26	8	1	-	-	-	-
Arkansas	-	-	-	1	5	19	34	30	10	1	-	-	-	-	-	-	1	5	21	41	29	3
Auburn	2	8	23	30	24	11	2	-	-	-	-	-	-	2	15	33	30	15	4	1	-	-
LSU	-	1	6	17	26	28	16	5	1	-	-	-	-	-	3	13	23	32	18	9	2	-
Mississippi State	1	11	26	31	21	8	2	-	-	-	-	-	-	1	13	29	34	17	5	1	-	-
Ole Miss	-	1	4	13	24	29	19	9	1	-	-	-	-	-	1	4	14	31	30	16	4	-
Texas A&M	-	1	4	13	29	32	16	4	1	-	-	-	-	-	2	11	24	33	22	7	1	-

Projected Win Probabilities For Sun Belt Teams

	Overall Wins													Conference Wins								
Sun Belt East	12-0	11-1	10-2	9-3	8-4	7-5	6-6	5-7	4-8	3-9	2-10	1-11	0-12	8-0	7-1	6-2	5-3	4-4	3-5	2-6	1-7	0-8
Appalachian State	-	17	40	29	11	3	-	-	-	-	-	-	-	20	38	30	10	2	-	-	-	-
Coastal Carolina	-	-	-	-	1	4	11	21	27	21	12	3	-	-	-	-	4	13	26	33	20	4
Georgia Southern	-	-	4	13	24	27	19	10	3	-	-	-	-	1	7	17	34	24	12	4	1	-
Georgia State	-	-	-	-	-	2	6	21	29	28	12	2	-	-	-	-	4	17	31	29	15	4
Troy	-	2	10	23	31	24	8	2	-	-	-	-	-	5	26	38	23	6	2	-	-	-
Sun Belt West	12-0	11-1	10-2	9-3	8-4	7-5	6-6	5-7	4-8	3-9	2-10	1-11	0-12	8-0	7-1	6-2	5-3	4-4	3-5	2-6	1-7	0-8
Arkansas State	-	12	31	31	18	6	2	-	-	-	-	-	-	18	39	29	12	2	-	-	-	-
South Alabama	-	-	-	-	-	4	13	24	33	20	5	1	-	-	-	1	11	24	32	23	8	1
Texas State	-	-	-	-	-	1	4	15	27	30	19	4	-	-	-	-	1	4	15	35	34	11
UL-Lafayette	-	-	-	-	-	4	12	25	29	22	7	1	-	-	-	1	5	18	31	31	12	2
UL-Monroe	-	-	-	-	-	1	3	10	22	27	24	10	3	-	2	6	20	28	28	13	3	-

NCAA F/+ Projections

NCAA Teams, No. 1 to No. 130

Rk	Team	Rec	Conf	F/+	MW	CW	SOS	Rk	CSOS	Rk	Div	Conf	CFP
1	Alabama	11-1	7-1	52.7%	10.7	6.8	0.073	35	0.097	26	63.4%	31.7%	36.5%
2	Clemson	10-2	7-1	52.5%	10.4	6.8	0.114	56	0.200	57	67.8%	33.9%	31.7%
3	Ohio State	10-2	8-1	52.5%	10.2	7.6	0.078	39	0.116	40	39.3%	19.7%	18.6%
4	Georgia	10-2	7-1	51.7%	10.5	6.6	0.138	59	0.149	47	75.4%	37.7%	35.0%
5	Auburn	9-3	5-3	51.4%	9.0	5.5	0.010	1	0.021	1	16.7%	8.3%	5.7%
6	Notre Dame	10-2	-	50.6%	9.8	0.0	0.061	27	-	-	-	-	10.4%
7	Washington	10-2	8-1	50.6%	10.1	7.6	0.090	47	0.194	56	65.3%	32.7%	27.1%
8	Oklahoma	10-2	7-2	49.9%	10.3	7.5	0.142	60	0.176	53	-	51.3%	33.7%
9	Michigan State	10-2	7-2	47.9%	10.1	7.2	0.103	53	0.124	43	28.7%	14.3%	12.9%
10	Penn State	10-2	7-2	47.1%	9.6	6.8	0.066	28	0.078	16	18.0%	9.0%	7.7%
11	Michigan	9-3	7-2	46.7%	8.9	6.6	0.021	4	0.052	11	14.0%	7.0%	4.8%
12	Wisconsin	10-2	7-2	46.5%	10.1	7.1	0.109	54	0.114	39	59.9%	30.0%	22.7%
13	Miami-FL	10-2	7-1	46.0%	10.0	6.5	0.144	61	0.250	64	66.3%	33.1%	25.8%
14	Mississippi State	9-3	5-3	45.6%	9.1	5.3	0.033	13	0.040	8	12.3%	6.1%	4.5%
15	USC	9-3	7-2	43.3%	9.3	7.3	0.077	38	0.209	59	73.6%	36.8%	22.6%
16	Florida State	8-4	5-3	42.5%	8.5	5.4	0.031	9	0.092	22	17.5%	8.7%	5.3%
17	Stanford	9-3	6-3	42.4%	8.7	6.4	0.036	15	0.090	20	18.8%	9.4%	5.8%
18	Central Florida	11-1	8-0	41.0%	11.1	7.6	0.586	115	0.771	87	94.8%	47.4%	3.0%
19	LSU	8-4	4-4	40.5%	7.5	4.2	0.012	2	0.022	2	3.9%	1.9%	1.1%
20	TCU	9-3	6-3	38.0%	8.7	6.4	0.072	33	0.160	50	-	20.1%	8.6%
21	Oklahoma State	9-3	6-3	36.6%	8.7	6.1	0.088	45	0.112	38	-	12.6%	5.7%
22	Virginia Tech	9-3	5-3	36.1%	8.8	5.5	0.100	52	0.179	55	26.3%	13.1%	7.8%
23	Oregon	9-3	6-3	35.5%	9.1	6.1	0.148	63	0.151	48	15.1%	7.6%	5.3%
24	Texas	8-4	6-3	35.0%	8.4	6.0	0.093	50	0.138	46	-	12.8%	5.4%
25	Texas A&M	7-5	4-4	34.8%	7.4	4.1	0.012	3	0.023	3	2.4%	1.2%	0.6%
26	Boise State	11-1	8-0	33.7%	10.9	7.7	0.537	107	0.882	102	92.6%	55.6%	3.1%
27	Iowa	9-3	6-3	29.9%	9.1	6.5	0.198	67	0.220	61	34.0%	17.0%	9.7%
28	Louisville	8-4	5-3	29.8%	8.1	5.0	0.053	21	0.158	49	9.3%	4.7%	2.4%
29	Utah	8-4	5-4	29.1%	7.5	4.8	0.083	42	0.087	19	7.1%	3.5%	1.9%
30	Florida	8-4	5-3	27.8%	7.9	4.7	0.070	32	0.128	44	10.7%	5.4%	2.7%
31	Ole Miss	7-5	3-5	27.7%	7.2	3.5	0.040	17	0.044	9	1.3%	0.7%	0.4%
32	Duke	7-5	4-4	25.8%	7.2	4.3	0.059	26	0.093	24	4.3%	2.2%	1.1%
33	South Carolina	7-5	5-3	24.6%	7.5	4.6	0.072	34	0.201	58	8.9%	4.5%	2.2%
34	NC State	8-4	4-4	24.0%	7.7	4.4	0.113	55	0.134	45	3.8%	1.9%	1.0%
35	Arizona	8-4	6-3	23.6%	8.0	5.5	0.211	69	0.240	63	16.4%	8.2%	4.3%
36	Wake Forest	7-5	4-4	22.9%	6.8	3.7	0.059	25	0.107	34	1.4%	0.7%	0.4%
37	Baylor	7-5	4-5	22.5%	6.9	4.4	0.083	41	0.096	25	-	1.5%	0.5%
38	UCLA	6-6	4-5	21.6%	5.9	4.0	0.041	18	0.102	30	2.3%	1.1%	0.5%
39	Florida Atlantic	9-3	7-1	21.3%	9.5	7.2	0.201	68	0.844	100	60.6%	45.4%	2.0%
40	Missouri	7-5	4-4	20.9%	7.5	4.2	0.068	29	0.078	15	4.7%	2.4%	1.1%
41	Northwestern	7-5	5-4	20.6%	6.6	4.9	0.054	23	0.111	36	4.9%	2.5%	1.1%
42	Boston College	6-6	3-5	19.6%	6.2	2.7	0.056	24	0.062	14	0.2%	0.1%	0.1%
43	Iowa State	6-6	4-5	18.8%	6.4	4.2	0.077	37	0.108	35	-	1.1%	0.4%
44	Arizona State	5-7	4-5	17.1%	5.4	3.7	0.033	12	0.058	13	0.7%	0.3%	0.1%
45	West Virginia	6-6	4-5	16.9%	5.9	3.8	0.086	44	0.111	37	-	0.4%	0.2%
46	Kansas State	6-6	3-6	15.3%	5.6	3.5	0.053	22	0.082	18	-	0.2%	0.1%
47	Memphis	10-2	6-2	15.0%	9.6	6.3	0.511	104	0.644	76	48.5%	24.3%	1.1%
48	Pittsburgh	5-7	4-4	13.1%	4.9	3.6	0.032	10	0.216	60	1.7%	0.8%	0.4%
49	Washington State	7-5	4-5	12.9%	6.5	3.8	0.091	48	0.093	23	0.6%	0.3%	0.1%
50	Georgia Tech	5-7	3-5	12.4%	5.2	2.6	0.039	16	0.106	33	0.5%	0.2%	0.1%

Rk	Team	Rec	Conf	F/+	MW	CW	SOS	Rk	CSOS	Rk	Div	Conf	CFP
51	Arkansas	6-6	2-6	11.0%	5.8	2.0	0.028	6	0.029	5	0.0%	0.0%	0.0%
52	North Carolina	6-6	3-5	10.9%	6.1	3.4	0.147	62	0.224	62	1.0%	0.5%	0.2%
53	Texas Tech	5-7	3-6	10.4%	4.8	2.9	0.075	36	0.098	27	-	0.1%	0.0%
54	Houston	9-3	6-2	10.2%	9.0	6.2	0.620	117	0.789	89	46.0%	23.0%	1.0%
55	Toledo	10-2	7-1	9.5%	9.6	7.0	0.530	106	0.903	112	66.0%	33.0%	1.5%
56	Marshall	9-3	7-1	7.7%	9.1	6.8	0.570	112	0.841	98	36.4%	27.3%	1.2%
57	Fresno State	8-4	6-2	6.6%	8.4	6.2	0.445	100	0.613	73	51.4%	20.6%	0.9%
58	California	5-7	3-6	5.5%	5.1	3.0	0.093	49	0.101	29	0.2%	0.1%	0.0%
59	San Diego State	9-3	6-2	5.4%	8.5	6.2	0.293	79	0.582	70	46.3%	18.5%	0.8%
60	Nebraska	5-7	3-6	4.3%	5.3	2.6	0.028	7	0.029	6	0.0%	0.0%	0.0%
61	Purdue	5-7	3-6	4.3%	4.6	3.0	0.081	40	0.100	28	0.2%	0.1%	0.0%
62	Minnesota	6-6	4-5	2.7%	6.0	3.7	0.115	57	0.121	42	1.0%	0.5%	0.2%
63	Kentucky	5-7	2-6	1.1%	4.9	2.0	0.085	43	0.121	41	0.1%	0.1%	0.0%
64	South Florida	8-4	5-3	0.5%	8.3	5.2	0.558	111	0.600	72	4.1%	2.0%	0.1%
65	Appalachian State	10-2	7-1	-0.1%	9.6	6.7	0.424	96	0.918	124	61.7%	30.8%	1.3%
66	Indiana	5-7	3-6	-0.6%	5.2	2.7	0.051	20	0.053	12	0.0%	0.0%	0.0%
67	BYU	6-6	-	-1.4%	5.8	0.0	0.069	31	-	-	-	-	0.0%
68	Northern Illinois	7-5	6-2	-1.7%	6.7	6.1	0.286	76	0.893	110	26.4%	13.2%	0.6%
69	Louisiana Tech	8-4	6-2	-2.4%	8.1	6.2	0.213	70	0.752	85	68.6%	17.1%	0.7%
70	Arkansas State	9-3	7-1	-4.9%	9.3	6.6	0.244	72	0.913	121	92.4%	46.2%	2.0%
71	Temple	7-5	5-3	-5.0%	7.2	4.8	0.383	90	0.476	65	1.1%	0.6%	0.0%
72	Tennessee	5-7	1-7	-6.3%	4.6	1.5	0.032	11	0.037	7	0.0%	0.0%	0.0%
73	Syracuse	3-9	1-7	-7.5%	3.5	1.0	0.051	19	0.106	32	0.0%	0.0%	0.0%
74	Navy	7-6	4-4	-8.9%	7.0	3.7	0.229	71	0.483	66	2.8%	1.4%	0.1%
75	Virginia	4-8	1-7	-9.2%	3.8	1.0	0.153	64	0.163	51	0.0%	0.0%	0.0%
76	Ohio	8-4	6-2	-9.3%	8.5	5.6	0.876	128	0.903	114	51.9%	26.0%	1.1%
77	Wyoming	7-5	5-3	-11.0%	7.1	5.0	0.526	105	0.694	78	2.9%	1.7%	0.1%
78	Utah State	8-4	6-2	-11.5%	7.7	5.6	0.274	75	0.626	74	4.1%	2.5%	0.1%
79	Troy	8-4	6-2	-12.3%	8.0	5.9	0.663	119	0.895	111	29.1%	14.5%	0.6%
80	Maryland	3-9	2-7	-12.3%	3.3	2.2	0.034	14	0.049	10	0.0%	0.0%	0.0%
81	Western Michigan	7-5	5-3	-12.8%	7.0	4.7	0.415	95	0.886	103	6.5%	3.3%	0.1%
82	SMU	5-7	4-4	-14.3%	5.3	3.6	0.173	66	0.486	67	2.3%	1.2%	0.1%
83	Vanderbilt	3-9	1-7	-14.9%	3.5	1.1	0.069	30	0.171	52	0.1%	0.0%	0.0%
84	Middle Tennessee	7-5	5-3	-15.7%	6.6	5.0	0.287	77	0.776	88	2.2%	1.7%	0.1%
85	Miami-OH	6-6	5-3	-19.2%	5.9	4.5	0.805	125	0.903	113	18.5%	9.3%	0.4%
86	Army	7-5	-	-19.3%	7.4	0.0	0.297	80	-	-	-	-	0.0%
87	Western Kentucky	6-6	4-4	-19.8%	5.9	4.2	0.246	73	0.718	83	0.8%	0.6%	0.0%
88	Buffalo	7-5	5-3	-20.3%	6.8	4.6	0.811	126	0.840	96	19.0%	9.5%	0.4%
89	Georgia Southern	7-5	5-3	-20.3%	7.2	4.7	0.337	84	0.908	118	9.1%	4.5%	0.2%
90	Tulane	5-7	3-5	-21.0%	4.7	3.1	0.256	74	0.763	86	0.3%	0.2%	0.0%
91	Cincinnati	5-7	3-5	-21.3%	5.2	3.4	0.412	94	0.523	68	0.1%	0.0%	0.0%
92	Colorado	3-9	1-8	-21.8%	3.0	1.3	0.097	51	0.105	31	0.0%	0.0%	0.0%
93	Rutgers	3-9	1-8	-22.3%	3.4	1.4	0.028	5	0.029	4	0.0%	0.0%	0.0%
94	Bowling Green	5-7	4-4	-24.2%	5.4	3.9	0.474	102	0.840	97	9.6%	4.8%	0.2%
95	UAB	7-5	5-3	-24.9%	7.0	4.8	0.583	114	0.906	116	16.2%	4.0%	0.2%
96	North Texas	6-6	4-4	-25.6%	6.4	4.3	0.728	122	0.835	95	8.5%	2.1%	0.1%
97	Nevada	5-7	3-5	-28.0%	5.4	3.4	0.630	118	0.714	80	1.3%	0.5%	0.0%
98	Colorado State	5-7	4-4	-28.5%	5.4	3.9	0.437	97	0.626	75	0.4%	0.2%	0.0%
99	Tulsa	3-9	2-6	-30.0%	3.4	2.1	0.409	93	0.714	82	0.1%	0.1%	0.0%
100	Eastern Michigan	5-7	3-5	-30.2%	5.0	3.5	0.760	124	0.886	104	1.0%	0.5%	0.0%
101	Massachusetts	5-7	-	-31.2%	5.3	0.0	0.288	78	-	-	-	-	0.0%
102	Kansas	2-10	0-9	-31.3%	2.2	0.2	0.089	46	0.091	21	-	0.0%	0.0%
103	Illinois	3-9	1-8	-32.2%	2.7	0.8	0.171	65	0.178	54	0.0%	0.0%	0.0%
104	Southern Miss	5-7	4-4	-33.4%	5.2	3.6	0.335	83	0.891	108	3.4%	0.9%	0.0%
105	UNLV	5-7	3-5	-34.0%	5.2	3.3	0.440	98	0.844	101	0.9%	0.4%	0.0%
106	UL-Monroe	5-7	4-4	-34.2%	5.1	3.7	0.442	99	0.918	123	4.3%	2.1%	0.1%

Rk	Team	Rec	Conf	F/+	MW	CW	SOS	Rk	CSOS	Rk	Div	Conf	CFP
107	Oregon State	2-10	0-9	-34.2%	1.8	0.5	0.031	8	0.082	17	0.0%	0.0%	0.0%
108	Air Force	4-8	2-6	-34.3%	3.8	2.4	0.553	109	0.699	79	0.0%	0.0%	0.0%
109	UTSA	4-8	3-5	-34.9%	4.2	3.4	0.541	108	0.844	99	3.1%	0.8%	0.0%
110	South Alabama	4-8	3-5	-35.5%	4.3	3.1	0.476	103	0.890	105	2.0%	1.0%	0.0%
111	New Mexico State	5-7	-	-37.3%	5.3	0.0	0.834	127	-	-	-	-	0.0%
112	Ball State	4-8	2-6	-39.2%	3.5	2.2	0.325	82	0.833	94	0.0%	0.0%	0.0%
113	Coastal Carolina	4-8	2-6	-39.7%	4.0	2.4	0.689	121	0.908	120	0.1%	0.1%	0.0%
114	New Mexico	3-9	1-7	-40.2%	3.4	1.3	0.337	85	0.714	81	0.0%	0.0%	0.0%
115	Old Dominion	4-8	2-6	-40.5%	4.5	2.5	0.555	110	0.732	84	0.0%	0.0%	0.0%
116	UL-Lafayette	4-8	3-5	-41.6%	4.2	2.7	0.119	58	0.890	106	1.1%	0.5%	0.0%
117	Central Michigan	4-8	2-6	-41.7%	3.5	2.1	0.355	87	0.822	93	0.0%	0.0%	0.0%
118	Georgia State	4-8	3-5	-41.9%	3.7	2.5	0.591	116	0.890	107	0.1%	0.0%	0.0%
119	Florida International	4-8	2-6	-43.0%	3.7	2.2	0.389	91	0.819	92	0.0%	0.0%	0.0%
120	Akron	3-9	2-6	-43.1%	3.1	2.1	0.575	113	0.915	122	0.7%	0.4%	0.0%
121	Liberty	4-8	-	-44.7%	4.5	0.0	0.362	88	-	-	-	-	0.0%
122	Kent State	3-9	2-6	-45.0%	3.0	1.8	0.309	81	0.893	109	0.2%	0.1%	0.0%
123	Connecticut	3-9	1-7	-45.8%	2.6	1.2	0.366	89	0.557	69	0.0%	0.0%	0.0%
124	East Carolina	2-10	1-7	-45.9%	2.4	0.9	0.353	86	0.586	71	0.0%	0.0%	0.0%
125	Charlotte	3-9	2-6	-46.2%	3.2	1.9	0.665	120	0.693	77	0.0%	0.0%	0.0%
126	Texas State	3-9	2-6	-47.4%	3.5	1.7	0.881	130	0.908	119	0.2%	0.1%	0.0%
127	Rice	4-9	2-6	-47.8%	3.9	2.5	0.391	92	0.906	115	0.2%	0.1%	0.0%
128	Hawaii	3-10	2-6	-48.1%	3.3	1.5	0.754	123	0.804	90	0.0%	0.0%	0.0%
129	San Jose State	3-9	2-6	-50.0%	2.7	1.5	0.451	101	0.804	91	0.0%	0.0%	0.0%
130	UTEP	3-9	2-6	-51.4%	3.1	1.5	0.878	129	0.906	117	0.1%	0.0%	0.0%

Grounding the Run Game: A Pass-First Manifesto

Why do teams run the ball so often? The average pass play gained 6.2 yards in 2017, compared to 4.1 yards for the average rush play. And yet, on first-and-10, teams ran the ball 53 percent of the time. On these first-and-10 runs, 44 percent of rushes and 52 percent of passes were successful by Football Outsiders' baseline for success.

In order for rushing so frequently to be rational, rushes would need to carry some tangible future benefit to offset their cost. In other words, there must be some inherent value to a rush attempt that is not captured in the yardage it gains. However, as I will show in this piece (and in keeping with a long tradition of work that Football Outsiders has done), the commonly posited benefits of rushing do not stand up to scrutiny.

Let's run through some of the arguments that people use in order to defend high rates of rushing. When you take a closer look at these arguments, you'll find that (a) they are made without supporting evidence and (b) the evidence that we do have suggests that they are unfounded.

1. "Teams have to commit to running the ball first to open up play-action."

As Football Outsiders has long documented, play-action passing is more effective than non-play-action passing: in 2017, for example, play-action dropbacks gained 7.3 yards per play, compared to 6.0 yards per play for non-play-action dropbacks. Do teams need to run the ball in order to take advantage of play-action?

When play-action is based on a committed rushing attack, the argument goes, pass-rushers have to slow down and linebackers have to respect the threat of the run, pulling them towards the line of scrimmage and away from their coverage responsibilities. Examples of this argument abound: The Ringer's Robert Mays recently wrote that "as much as our understanding of the sport has shifted in recent years, the belief that a play-action game's effectiveness is linked to a strong, high-usage running offense has remained steadfast." (Mays, 2017). Former NFL lineman Geoff Schwartz tweeted that "teams have to commit to running the ball first to open up [play-action]." (Schwartz, 2018).

Earlier this year, in a piece on Football Outsiders, I investigated whether the purported relationship between rushing and play-action passing holds up (Baldwin, 2018a). First, I looked at whether rushing frequency or success rate is associated with a team's play-action effectiveness over the course of a season (Figure 1). In the upper left figure, the R^2 of 0.02 means that only 2 percent of the variation in a team's play-action effectiveness (as measured by yards per play-action dropback) in a given season can be explained by the number of rushes in that season.

The three plots above show that whether looking at total number of rushes, the proportion of plays that are rushes, or the proportion of rushes that are successes, no R^2 exceeds 0.03. In other words, knowing a team's rushing frequency or effectiveness in a given season tells one almost nothing about how effective that team was at play-action passing.

Second, I looked at whether a team's rushing frequency or success at a given point in a game was predictive of how successful that team would be at play-action passing (Figure 2). Regardless of which of the six measures of rushing one chooses, there is no meaningful relationship between the effectiveness of play-action passing and a team's rushing attack in the game to that point. Aside from a couple extreme cases with very small sample sizes (zero rushes or eight rushes in

Figure 1. Play-Action Passing vs. Measures of Rushing

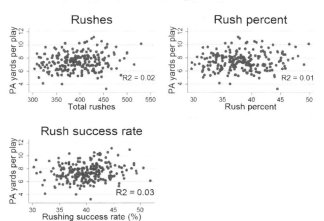

Figure 2. Yards Per Play-Action Dropback

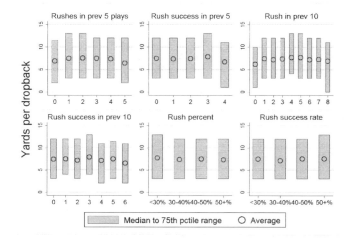

436

the previous 10 plays), there is no relationship in the data between the median, mean, or 75th percentile of yards gained and a team's previous rush attempts.

Putting this all together, I could not find any support for the success of play-action passing being related in any meaningful way to a team's rushing statistics, whether measured by frequency or effectiveness. Given this, one wonders why teams do not use play-action passing more often.

2. "Teams need to run the ball to open up the entire passing game."

If rushing doesn't benefit play-action passing, it is hard to believe that it would affect non-play-action passing.

This is supported by a study from Nathan Ernst of Hawkblogger (Ernst, 2017). Motivated by how the team with a higher QBR (ESPN's quarterback statistic based on expected points added) usually wins the game, he investigated whether QBR is influenced by the volume or effectiveness of rushing. He concluded the following:

> After removing [fourth]-quarter runs, the total number of rushes only explains [2 percent] of the variance in QBR. That's very small, and means there's effectively no relationship between how often a team runs and their QBR. So what does this mean? First, [quarterback] play is extremely important to winning games [..] And if running doesn't help you pass, then running does very little to help you win.

In a 2017 piece on Football Perspective, I looked at whether QBs who were asked to throw the ball more often saw a decrease in their efficiency (Baldwin, 2017). A common argument is that the efficiency of players like Dak Prescott and Russell Wilson early in their careers was not impressive because they were not asked to throw the ball at high volume. Once they are asked to throw more often, the argument goes, we can expect their efficiency to fall off. What I found was that a simple look at the data in a scatterplot showed no evidence that increased passing volume for a quarterback is associated with a decrease in efficiency (Figure 3).

Figure 3. Yards Per Attempt vs. Attempts

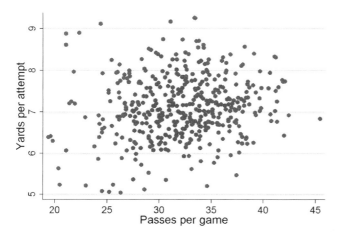

3. "These 5-, 6-, 5-, 7-yard runs early in the game turn into 8-, 10-, 12-, 15-plus later in the game."

This is a variant of the fabled "establish the run" argument, where rushing early in the game is needed to wear out the defense and make rushing more effective later in the game. For example, Geoff Schwartz tweeted during the Chiefs-Chargers game in December: "These [5-, 6-, 5-, 7-yard] runs early in the game turn into [8-, 10-, 12-, 15-plus] later in the game. Good start for the Chiefs [offensive line]." (Schwartz, 2017). And indeed, Kareem Hunt would go on to rush for 155 yards in the game.

Another strain of this belief is demonstrated by former Nebraska head coach Tom Osborne, who once stated that "we believed that a rushing yard was more valuable than a passing yard when it came to winning football games." (Kelly, 2015). Do early runs really lead to rushing effectiveness later in the game? Are rushes more valuable than passes?

Field Gulls writer Sean Clement looked at the extent to which teams with more rush attempts improved their rushing efficiency as the game went on (Clement, 2018). He found that the distribution of yards gained on rushes is remarkably similar throughout the game, regardless of how many times a team has previously rushed the ball. In other words, there is no evidence that shorter runs early in the game turn into longer runs later in the game.

In addition, Clement also found that there is no evidence that compiling rush attempts helps the passing game, writing "there seems to be little evidence that earlier running attempts increase the yardage obtained on passing plays."

4. "Passing too frequently puts your defense on the field and tires it out."

Another frequently stated belief is that by running the ball and chewing up clock, a team can keep its defense off the field and rested for the next drive, thereby allowing it to perform at its highest level. I recently investigated this for Football Outsiders (Baldwin, 2018b).

Anecdotes supporting the idea that rested defenses are more effective come to mind quickly. In Super Bowl LII, the Brandon Graham strip-sack—the only sack of the game—came after a 15-play drive (counting the attempted two-point conversion) that chewed up more than seven minutes of game time. In the AFC Championship Game, the Jaguars' defense finally showed cracks after a series of three-and-outs by the offense, with the game-deciding New England touchdown following a Jacksonville three-and-out that used less than a minute of game clock. And of course, in Super Bowl LI, Atlanta's defense looked gassed in the second half on the way to spending 93 snaps on the field.

Do we remember specific defensive performance following exceptionally long or short drives because of confirmation bias? Or is a given defense's time to rest actually predictive of how it will perform?

Figure 4 shows actual points per drive minus expected points per drive, where expected points per drive is based on starting field position. If rushing carried inherent value relative to passing in improving defensive performance, we would expect time of possession (the graphs on the right of the figure) to be more important than plays run (the graphs on the left) because the clock is more likely to continue running after a rushing play. In reality, neither matters, and we can cross off another purported benefit of rushing. This is consistent with earlier work on Football Outsiders that used information at the team-season level (Lawver, 2011).

The main—and perhaps only—channel through which an offense can help a defense on a per-drive basis is through field position. Turnovers and quick three-and-outs make a team more likely to give up points on the following drive, but this appears to have everything to do with field position and nothing to do with defensive rest time. In other words, whether it's one minute or eight minutes, knowing how long a defense has had to rest tells one nothing about how the defense will perform given its starting field position.

In a follow-up piece on Football Outsiders, I investigated whether long drives tend to have more rush attempts (Baldwin, 2018c). I found no evidence that this was the case either (Figure 5). Thus, even if it were the case that long drives helped a defense (it's not), rushing still wouldn't offer any advantages in producing these drives.

5. "You're just some nobody on the Internet. Do you really think you know more than NFL coaches and former players? They must have a reason for doing what they do."

The purported infallibility of NFL coaches doesn't pass the smell test, given that recent research from Derrick Yam and Michael Lopez shows that teams cost themselves wins by being too conservative on fourth downs (Yam & Lopez, 2018). If they are also costing themselves wins by rushing too often, it wouldn't come as much of a surprise.

It is also helpful to draw a parallel with the three-point shot in the NBA. The arguments in favor of the run game can't help but remind one of Charles Barkley, who famously stated in 2015 (Leung, 2015):

I don't like jump-shooting teams. I don't think you can win the championship beating good teams shooting jumpers [..], Klay (Thompson) and Steph (Curry) are great

players, and they've got a great home court, but I'm just saying…in a seven-game series, I don't think they can make enough jumpers…No disrespect to the Golden State Warriors. I like teams that are built inside-out.

In the time since Barkley's comments, Curry has won two MVP awards and the Warriors have won three championships while racking up more wins in a three-year span than any team in NBA history (ESPN, 2017). The team that gave them their biggest challenge in the past two seasons—the Houston Rockets—shattered the record for three-point attempts in a season.

Barkley's emphasis on building from the "inside out" can't help but remind one of the belief that NFL teams need to be built on a physical identity and rushing the football. And like passing in the NFL, the more efficient three-point shot has increased in frequency over time in the NBA: over the last six years alone, the league's three-point rate has increased by an astounding 49 percent (Kram, 2017). In the NFL, we have also seen an increase in pass frequency over time. In the 30 years since 1977, the percent of NFL plays that are pass attempts has risen by 40 percent (from 40 percent to 56 percent). For those who do not believe that NFL teams are currently rushing too often, this trend is very difficult—if not impossible—to explain.

Conclusion

It is possible that teams are still rushing frequently for good reason. However, the commonly stated reasons carry no supporting evidence. If there is a reason for running so often, we haven't found it yet. And while the optimal rushing frequency is not zero, it is probably less than what teams are currently doing.

In Q&A on Field Gulls prior to the 2017 season, Aaron Schatz recommended the following to NFL teams based on lessons learned from DVOA: "Go for it on fourth down more. Run more often on third-and-short and *pass more often the rest of the time* [emphasis added]" (Arthur, 2017). Given the historic struggles that Seattle's run game would face in 2017, maybe they should have heeded his advice.

Ben Baldwin

Figure 4. Actual Minus Expected Points Per Drive

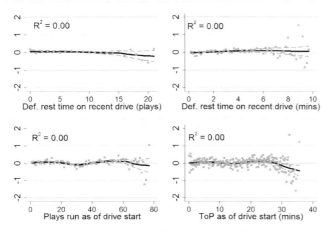

Figure 5. Rush Ratio by Drive Length

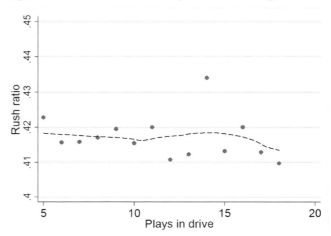

References

Arthur, Kenneth (2017). "5 Qs & 5 As about the Seahawks with Football Outsiders." *Field Gulls* (https://tinyurl.com/yc6nrecl).

Baldwin, Ben (2017). "Passing Volume vs. Passing Efficiency." *Football Perspective* (https://tinyurl.com/y8eonxwe).

Baldwin, Ben (2018a). "Rushing Success and Play-Action Passing." *Football Outsiders* (https://tinyurl.com/y9mgao9p).

Baldwin, Ben (2018b). "Defense and Rest Time." *Football Outsiders* (https://tinyurl.com/y8vaqxqe).

Baldwin, Ben (2018c). "Long Drives and the Running Game." *Football Outsiders* (https://tinyurl.com/y9q2qk5r).

Clement, Sean (2018). "Seahawks Couldn't 'Establish the Run' Because There's no Such Thing." *Field Gulls* (https://tinyurl.com/ya3bes3e).

Ernst, Nathan (2017). "The Relationship Between Passing and Rushing." *Hawkblogger* (https://tinyurl.com/y8vy2243).

ESPN Stats & Info (2017). *Tweet* (https://tinyurl.com/y9lw2p4m).

Kelly, Danny (2015). "The Real Value of Rushing Yards in the NFL." *SB Nation* (https://tinyurl.com/yaunlbnt).

Kram, Zach (2017). "Can You Take 3s Higher?" *The Ringer* (https://tinyurl.com/ya3y99wj).

Lavwer, Daniel (2011). "Keeping the Defense off the Field." *Football Outsiders* (https://tinyurl.com/ybnv8pvz).

Leung, Diamond (2015). "Draymond Green on Charles Barkley saying Warriors not a top-three team in West: 'That's funny.'" *Inside the Warriors.*

Mays, Robert (2017). "Harnessing the Power of Play-Action." *The Ringer* (https://tinyurl.com/ybh2lys3).

Schwartz, Geoff (2017). *Tweet* (https://tinyurl.com/y7ujp5q3).

Schwartz, Geoff (2018). *Tweet* (https://tinyurl.com/yc2caewy).

Yam, Derrick; and Michael Lopez (2018). "Quantifying the Causal Effects of Conservative Fourth Down Decision Making in the National Football League." *Working paper* (https://tinyurl.com/y8h9drlk).

FO Rookie Projections

Over the years, Football Outsiders has developed a number of methods for forecasting the NFL success of highly-drafted players at various positions Here is a rundown of those methods and what they say about players drafted in 2018.

Quarterbacks: QBASE

The QBASE (QuarterBack Adjusted Stats and Experience) system analyzes the last 20 years of rookie quarterbacks chosen among the top 100 picks of the NFL draft, and uses regression analysis to determine which factors helped predict their total passing DYAR in Years 3-5 of their careers. (We use these years to account for the fact that many highly drafted quarterbacks may not play regularly until their second or even third seasons.)

The primary factor in QBASE is the quarterback's college performance, analyzed with three metrics: completion rate, yards per attempt adjusted based on touchdowns and interceptions, and team passing S&P+ from Football Outsiders' college stats. We then adjust based on strength of schedule and strength of teammates. The latter element gives credit based on the draft-pick value of offensive linemen and receivers drafted in the quarterback's draft year as well as the projected draft position of younger teammates in 2019.

The measurement of past performance is then combined with two other factors: college experience and draft position. The latter factor accounts for what scouts will see but a statistical projection system will not, including personality, leadership, and projection of physical attributes to the next level.

QBASE also looks at the past performance of quarterbacks compared to their projection and using 50,000 simulations, produces a range of potential outcomes for each prospect: Elite quarterback (over 2,500 DYAR in Years 3-5), Upper Tier quarterback (1,500 to 2,500 DYAR), Adequate Starter (500 to 1,500 DYAR), or Bust (less than 500 DYAR in Years 3-5).

Here are QBASE projections for quarterbacks chosen in the top 100 picks of the 2018 NFL draft:

Player	College	Tm	Rd	Pick	QBASE	Elite	Upper Tier	Adequate	Bust
B.Mayfield	OKLA	CLE	1	1	1549	29%	19%	23%	29%
S.Darnold	USC	NYJ	1	3	398	4%	13%	29%	54%
J.Allen	WYO	BUF	1	7	-90	5%	10%	20%	65%
J.Rosen	UCLA	ARI	1	10	425	7%	16%	25%	51%
L.Jackson	LOU	BAL	1	32	621	9%	20%	27%	44%
M.Rudolph	OKST	PIT	3	76	363	6%	17%	26%	51%

Regular FO readers will notice that the projection listed for Josh Rosen is a bit lower than the one we listed on our website in March. This was due to a mistake in computing Rosen's college experience, counting a full sophomore year instead of the half-season he actually played.

Running Backs: BackCAST

BackCAST is Football Outsiders' metric for projecting the likelihood of success for running back prospects in the NFL draft. Historically, a college running back attack is more likely to succeed at the NFL level if he has a good size/speed combination, gained a high average yards per carry, and represented a large percentage of his college team's running attack. Criteria measured include:

- Weight and 40-yard dash time at the NFL combine. BackCAST uses pro day measurements for prospects who did not run at the combine.
- Average yards per rush attempt, with an adjustment for running backs who had fewer career carries than an average drafted running back.
- A measurement of how much each prospect's team used him in the running game during his career relative to an average drafted running back in the same year of eligibility.
- Prospect's receiving yards per game in his college career.

BackCAST considers these factors and projects the degree to which the running back will exceed the NFL production of an "average" drafted running back during his first five years in the NFL. For example, a running back with a 50% BackCAST is projected to gain 50 percent more yards than the "average" drafted running back. BackCAST also lists each running back's "RecIndex," measuring whether the player is likely to be a ground-and-pound two-down back, more of a receiving back, or something in between.

Here are the BackCAST numbers for running backs taken in the first three rounds of the 2018 draft, along with two later-round picks (and one UDFA) who had an above-average BackCAST Rating and one later-round pick with a particularly high RecIndex.

Player	College	Team	Rd	Pick	BackCAST	RecIndex
Saquon Barkley	PSU	NYG	1	2	181.9%	0.61
Rashaad Penny	SDSU	SEA	1	27	81.0%	-0.16
Sony Michel	UGA	NE	1	31	16.8%	0.05
Nick Chubb	UGA	CLE	2	35	76.2%	-0.30
Ronald Jones	USC	TB	2	38	60.0%	-0.09
Kerryon Johnson	AUB	DET	2	43	-29.0%	0.06
Derrius Guice	LSU	WAS	2	59	86.8%	-0.30
Royce Freeman	ORE	DEN	3	71	88.1%	0.02
Ryan Nall	ORST	CHI	UDFA		54.2%	0.10
Justin Jackson	NW	LAC	7	251	15.1%	0.40
Jordan Wilkins	MISS	IND	5	169	7.2%	-0.16
Nyheim Hines	NCST	IND	4	104	-20.7%	0.67

Edge Rushers: SackSEER

SackSEER is a method that projects sacks for edge rushers, including both 3-4 outside linebackers and 4-3 defensive ends, using the following criteria:

- An "explosion index" that measures the prospect's scores in the forty-yard dash, the vertical jump, and the broad jump in pre-draft workouts.
- Sacks per game, adjusted for factors such as early entry in the NFL Draft and position switches during college.
- Passes defensed per game.
- Missed games of NCAA eligibility due to academic problems, injuries, benchings, suspensions, or attendance at junior college.

SackSEER outputs two numbers. The first, SackSEER Rating, solely measures how high the prospect scores compared to players of the past. The second, SackSEER Projection, represents a forecast of sacks for the player's first five years in the NFL. It synthesizes metrics with conventional wisdom by adjusting based on the player's expected draft position (interestingly, not his actual draft position) based on pre-draft analysis at the site NFLDraftScout.com.

Here are the SackSEER numbers for edge rushers selected in the first three rounds of the 2018 draft, along with three later-round picks who had a high SackSEER Rating.

Wide Receivers: Playmaker Score

Playmaker Score projects success for NFL wide receivers using the following criteria:

- The wide receiver's peak season for receiving yards per team attempt and receiving touchdowns per team attempt.
- Differences between this prospect's peak season and most recent season, to adjust for players who declined in their final college year.
- College career yards per reception.
- Rushing attempts per game.
- Vertical jump from pre-draft workouts.
- A binary variable that rewards players who enter the draft as underclassmen.

Like SackSEER, Playmaker Score outputs two numbers. The first, Playmaker Rating, solely measures how high the prospect scores compared to players of the past. The second, Playmaker Projection, represents a forecast of average receiving yards per year in the player's first five seasons, synthesizing metrics with conventional wisdom by adjusting based on the player's expected draft position.

Here are the Playmaker Score numbers for players drafted in the first three rounds of the 2018 draft, along with three later-round picks (and two UDFAs) with a high Playmaker Rating.

Name	College	Team	Rnd	Pick	SackSEER Projection	SackSEER Rating
Bradley Chubb	NCST	DEN	1	5	24.6	81.5%
Marcus Davenport	UTSA	NO	1	14	25.9	84.9%
Harold Landry	BC	TEN	2	41	26.0	83.9%
Breeland Speaks	MISS	KC	2	46	4.1	30.7%
Uchenna Nwosu	USC	LAC	2	48	20.1	67.8%
Kemoko Turay	RUTG	IND	2	52	11.1	47.1%
Tyquan Lewis	OSU	IND	2	64	12.2	75.4%
Lorenzo Carter	UGA	NYG	3	66	18.3	55.4%
Chad Thomas	MIA	CLE	3	67	7.0	23.2%
Sam Hubbard	OSU	CIN	3	77	18.9	60.2%
Rasheem Green	USC	SEA	3	79	20.4	86.3%
Arden Key	LSU	OAK	3	87	14.5	33.9%
Josh Sweat	FSU	PHI	4	130	15.9	89.5%
Kylie Fitts	UTAH	CHI	6	181	13.2	75.4%
Ogbonnia Okoronkwo	OKLA	LAR	5	160	16.1	71.2%

Name	College	Team	Rnd	Pick	Playmaker Projection	Playmaker Rating
D.J. Moore	UMD	CAR	1	24	634	92.5%
Calvin Ridley	BAMA	ATL	1	26	525	69.3%
Courland Sutton	SMU	DEN	2	40	471	83.7%
Dante Pettis	WASH	SF	2	44	299	43.7%
Christian Kirk	TA&M	ARI	2	47	485	77.4%
Anthony Miller	MEM	CHI	2	51	462	77.6%
James Washington	OKST	PIT	2	60	366	69.9%
DJ Chark	LSU	JAX	2	61	410	67.9%
Michael Gallup	CSU	DAL	3	81	336	70.5%
Tre'Quan Smith	UCF	NO	3	91	428	92.7%
Richie James	MTSU	SF	7	240	284	92.5%
Byron Pringle	KSU	KC	UDFA		245	83.5%
Korey Robertson	USM	MIN	UDFA		288	78.0%
Jordan Lasley	UCLA	BAL	5	162	205	76.8%
Equanimeous St. Brown	ND	GB	6	207	413	75.2%

Top 25 Prospects

Every year, Football Outsiders takes it upon ourselves to put together a list of the NFL's best and brightest that have barely played. Eighty percent of the draft-day discussion is about first-round picks, and 10 percent is about the players that should have been first-round picks, but instead went in the second round.

This list is about the others.

Everybody knows that Saquon Barkley and Josh Rosen are good. There's a cottage industry around the idea of hyping every draft's No. 1 quarterback as a potential superstar. But players don't stop being promising just because they don't make waves in their rookie seasons. This is a list of players who have a strong chance to make an impact in the NFL despite their lack of draft stock and the fact that they weren't immediate NFL starters. Previous instances of the list have hyped players such as Geno Atkins, Grady Jarrett, Malcolm Butler, and Jamaal Charles before they blew up. Rotoworld has referred to this list as "an all-star team of waiver pickups" after we hit on players such as Arian Foster and Miles Austin. Last year's list included Tyreek Hill, Javon Hargrave, Justin Simmons, and Michael Pierce.

This is the 12th anniversary of the list. We're still relying on the same things we always do: scouting, statistics, measurables, context, ceiling, expected role, and what we hear from other sources. The goal is to bring your attention to players who are still developing in their second and third seasons, even after the draftniks have forgotten them.

Here's our full criteria:

• Drafted in the third round or later, or signed as an undrafted free agent.
• Entered the NFL between 2015 and 2017.
• Fewer than 500 career offensive or defensive snaps (except running backs, who are allowed just 300 offensive snaps).
• Have not signed a contract extension (players who have bounced around the league looking for the right spot, however, still qualify for the list).
• Age 26 or younger in 2018.

Most of these lists are heavily dependent on the depth of incoming draft classes. For instance, this year's list doesn't have a quarterback, because it has been a down few years for quarterback depth in the draft. However, it's quite wide receiver-heavy, and there are a few other wideouts who would normally be list-eligible who got pushed on to Honorable Mentions.

Our No. 1 prospect was not hard this year, as he also led the midseason list we publish on ESPN...

1 DE Carl Lawson, Cincinnati Bengals
492 defensive snaps, age 23, fourth-round pick 2017

It's kind of mind-boggling how the NFL let Lawson fall to the fourth round, as he was rumored to be a first-round prospect for years before he actually declared for the draft. A torn ACL and an injured hip in the years before 2016 likely had him red-flagged by some teams on medicals, despite Lawson tearing up the SEC with 13.5 tackles for loss and nine sacks.

Drafted by the Bengals, Lawson has been an immediate hit. Sports Info Solutions charting ranked Lawson in the NFL top 30 for hurries despite his low snap count, and he also picked up 8.5 sacks. The Bengals have a knack for hitting big on their middle-round picks by taking some risks, and Lawson may very well be the latest in the trend that started with Geno Atkins. While Lawson didn't exactly tear up our SackSEER system (with a SackSEER rating of just 27.5%), he also lost most of his last three years in college to injuries, so that makes some sense.

Lawson showed up to OTAs ripped and prepared for a bigger role this year. Watch out, AFC North quarterbacks.

2 WR Kenny Golladay, Detroit Lions
477 offensive snaps, age 25, third-round pick 2017

Golladay was a bit of a surprise pick in the third round, a player who was pegged as a Day 3 guy by most public analysts and publications. But Golladay profiles as a perfect outside receiver for the Lions—6-foot-4 and 218 pounds will play anywhere—and he cut into veteran snap counts early after an explosive training camp and a preseason that put him squarely on the fantasy radar.

Hamstring troubles kept him out of the full-time lineup, but Golladay was a big contributor for the Lions down the stretch. He finished with 130 DYAR, the second-most of any receiver targeted fewer than 50 times, and raised his catch rate from 50 percent after Week 9 to 58 percent at season's end. Golladay's combination of size and speed is fairly uncommon, and he has no trouble winning catches in traffic.

The Lions still have Marvin Jones and Golden Tate, but by removing Eric Ebron, some additional targets should open up for Golladay. It would not be a surprise to see him take a major step forward in his sophomore year, assuming he can stay healthy this time around.

3 CB Rasul Douglas, Philadelphia Eagles
420 defensive snaps, age 23, third-round pick 2017

A junior college guy who had the light turn on for him, Douglas was heavily recruited but chose West Virginia to stay closer to his home in New Jersey. He led the NCAA with eight interceptions in 2016, and his stellar size (6-foot-2, 209 pounds) and play made him a pretty safe third-round pick.

With rookie corners playing outside, all you're hoping for is respectability. Douglas was oft-targeted when he played, but his 57 percent success rate was in the top 30 among all qualifying cornerbacks. He broke up a ton of balls on his targets, finishing with two picks and 11 deflections in just 53 targets. Yes, that number is buttressed by the fact that Philadelphia's front seven has been excellent. Still, it was an admirable rookie year.

Douglas will have to play less hot-and-cold in 2018 to take the next leap in his skill level. He also isn't guaranteed a steady role, as the Eagles will break in second-rounder Sidney Jones off injury and return Jalen Mills and Ronald Darby. But he flashed heavily in his early snaps and has earned more playing time.

4 RB Aaron Jones, Green Bay Packers
236 offensive snaps, age 24, sixth-round pick 2017

While the backfield situation in Green Bay appears to be fluid at the moment, Jones has definitely been the runner with the most production on the field so far. A 31.3% DVOA and 143 DYAR in 81 runs was impressive—he had the most DYAR of any back with fewer than 100 rushes. An MCL sprain put him on the shelf in November and made it hard for him to find his way back into the rotation.

Jamaal Williams (who had too many snaps to be on the list) seems to be regarded as the favorite to lead the Packers in rushing this year. Williams is certainly a technically savvy back who offers a lot in pass protection and as a receiver. But Jones is far more explosive, testing in the top 84th percentile of all running backs since 2000 in the broad jump, vertical jump, and 3-cone drill at the combine. He's no slouch in the passing game either, and his style would seem to fit more with the quick-strike elements the Packers seem to favor under Mike McCarthy.

This isn't to say Williams or Ty Montgomery are bad backs or overrated in any way. We just think highly enough of Jones to say he has a chance to seize the job outright.

5 DE Derek Rivers, New England Patriots
0 defensive snaps, age 24, third-round pick 2017

A true athletic freak coming out of college, Rivers recorded a 4.61 40-yard dash and a 6.94 3-cone drill time at 248 pounds. The list of college edge rushers who have done that in the last 10 seasons who were actually well regarded as prospects is short, but it includes people you may have heard of such as Von Miller and Vic Beasley. The easy comparison here is Connor Barwin, another small-school, all-tools edge rusher who went in the second round. Rivers played at Youngstown State, which likely kept him from being popped earlier in the draft. He managed 36 sacks there over his last three seasons.

Rivers was a complete non-factor in his rookie season because of a torn ACL during training camp. Had he played, he probably would have seen enough action to make his way off this list given how dire things became for the Patriots at edge rusher last season. They were giving signed practice-squad players huge roles up front.

Rivers profiles as at least a Derrick Morgan-esque pass rusher, with the upside to be one of the 32 best pass-rushing ends in the game. It would be more than a mild surprise if he wasn't involved heavily in New England's defensive schemes this season. Only our total lack of NFL data prevents us from putting him higher.

6 WR Chris Godwin, Tampa Bay Buccaneers
449 offensive snaps, age 22, third-round pick 2017

A technically sound draftnik favorite coming out of Penn State in 2017, Godwin plays the ball well in the air, has the size to go get it, and was an instant contributor for the Nittany Lions. While velocity is not necessarily his best trait, his size (6-foot-1, 209 pounds) matched with 4.40-timed speed made him a bit of a problem for defenses without jumbo-sized cornerbacks. His only real weakness was a lack of open-field vision and change of direction.

Godwin's first start came in Week 9, and he became more of a contributor to Tampa's offense in December, playing the majority of the snaps over Adam Humphries. He ended the season with back-to-back 90-plus-yard efforts against Carolina and New Orleans, teasing what he could provide in 2018.

The Bucs have some post-hype sleeper feel to them this year, and their pass offense was actually pretty good last year even if everyone stopped watching. Godwin and Jameis Winston are a great match of player who can catch anything and quarterback who will throw anywhere. Don't be surprised if Godwin not only plays 80 percent of the snaps in 2018, but also makes DeSean Jackson sort of an afterthought.

7 DL Larry Ogunjobi, Cleveland Browns
303 defensive snaps, age 24, third-round pick 2017

A draft faller almost exclusively because of his average size (6-foot-3, 305 pounds), Ogunjobi was dinged for being too short even though he started from Day 1 at UNC-Charlotte and racked up 11 or more tackles for loss in each of his last three seasons. At the combine, he tested in the top 79th percentile of defensive tackles since 2000 in the 40-yard dash, vertical jump, and broad jump. That explosion helps him win off the snap.

In his rookie season, Ogunjobi was mostly a change-of-pace interior lineman, starting only when Danny Shelton was out. He managed 4.5 pressures and 1.0 sack but has the ability for more production if he can get off blocks a little better than he did in his rookie season.

With Shelton gone to New England, a starting role looks to be in the cards for Ogunjobi. At the very least, his run defense in his rookie season opened the door to dealing Shelton. And if he taps into his natural explosion, he could be a long-term difference-maker for the Browns up front.

8 DE Jordan Willis, Cincinnati Bengals
361 defensive snaps, age 23, third-round pick 2017

This starts with a ridiculously high SackSEER score coming out of college (93.3%). Willis posted Myles Garrett-like numbers at the combine, running the 40-yard dash in a blistering 4.53 seconds while recording a vertical leap of 39 inches and a broad jump of 10 feet, 5 inches. He combined that with 20.5 sacks in his last two years at Kansas State to have the second-highest rating in the class after Garrett.

But the college and combine results are draped with an inimitable downside: Willis didn't pass the eye test as a college rusher. He didn't bend the edge much in college and looked a little stiff after beating his man initially. He managed just 12.5 hurries and one sack in his rookie season. The college profile provides reason for optimism, and his run defense will make him a starter regardless, but Willis needs to take the next step in his pass-rush development to be more than solid.

A Bengals coach under the cover of anonymity told ESPN's Katherine Terrell that Willis should have seen the field more last year. The Bengals could have a radically different pass rush in 2018 with Lawson and Willis playing a larger role.

9 LB Alex Anzalone, New Orleans Saints
158 defensive snaps, age 23, third-round pick 2017

A Week 1 starter for the Saints, Anzalone was placed on IR with a shoulder injury after leaving New Orleans' fourth game against the Dolphins in the first quarter. Anzalone missed just one tackle before the injury. It was, unfortunately, the same shoulder that gave him so much trouble at Florida. He played just 18 total games over four years at Florida, despite being trusted enough to play as a true freshman, because of his shoulder and a broken arm in his senior season.

The reason Anzalone was valued as highly as he was despite the injuries is that he has true three-down linebacker skill. He ran a 4.63-second 40-yard dash at 6-foot-3, 241 pounds. So unlike most of the players who make it to the third round, where scouts had doubts about their bodies in the NFL, Anzalone likely profiled as an easy first- or second-round pick if he had played more in college. He has great instincts, covers well, and is a heady player. Scouts left the Senior Bowl raving about him.

Anzalone is a really hard player to rate on a list. Do you value his upside? He might have a top-five ceiling of anyone on this list. But health is a skill, and the NFL isn't going to do him any favors in that regard. We tried to split the difference between the two with this ranking. New Orleans retained some extra veteran depth in Craig Robertson in case Anzalone breaks again, but Anzalone looks to have every chance to start at weakside linebacker.

10 DE Trey Hendrickson, New Orleans Saints
282 defensive snaps, age 23, third-round pick 2017

A lesser-talked about part of the defensive resurgence in New Orleans, as Marshon Lattimore got and deserved the bulk of the attention, Hendrickson flashed in the edge rusher rotation before an ankle injury forced him out of the lineup in November. He did return as a bit player in December and the playoffs. Hendrickson finished with 13 hurries and 2.0 sacks in his paltry amount of snaps.

Coming out, Hendrickson definitely had the profile Sack-SEER likes, achieving a 90.0 percent rating and being projected for 15.7 sacks in his first five seasons despite a consensus fourth-round projection. Hendrickson is yet another example of a small-school sleeper come to life, and while the dings coming out were about his competition, he hasn't had any trouble adjusting yet.

His biggest problem might be playing time: With the addition of Marcus Davenport, the Saints suddenly have a deep rotation on the edge with Cameron Jordan and Alex Okafor also likely to draw a lot of snaps.

11 WR Dede Westbrook, Jacksonville Jaguars
386 offensive snaps, age 24, fourth-round pick 2017

Westbrook fell to the fourth round on account of domestic violence allegations, kind of like Tyreek Hill. Westbrook also had an, uh, interesting pre-draft process. He got kicked out of a combine interview, and an anonymous scout told NFL Network's Albert Breer that Westbrook was a "degenerate." Also, kind of like Tyreek Hill, Westbrook's suddenness and pure speed made him a big-play threat at Oklahoma. Our Playmaker Score projections loved Westbrook, giving him the seventh-highest score in the class despite a fourth-round projection.

Westbrook missed most of his early season with a core muscle injury that put him on PUP, then followed that up by being targeted so often in his later games that he actually qualified for FO's full-season ranking list. Granted, he had -35 DYAR. However, he was also playing with Blake Bortles, and hadn't really worked with anyone in the offense before.

Long-term, Westbrook profiles as a gadget receiver with burn-you speed. With Jacksonville purging their receiver corps by letting Allens Hurns and Robinson walk, Westbrook should find himself with plenty of playing time again. With some creative coordinating, he could be the field-stretcher that Bortles immediately overthrows by 10 yards.

12 LB Dylan Cole, Houston Texans
205 defensive snaps, age 24, undrafted 2017

Not invited to the combine out of tiny Missouri State, Cole came on the draft radar after putting up some eye-popping numbers at his pro day, when he ran a 4.52-second 40-yard dash and tacked on a 39-inch vertical leap for good measure. His college production? He led FCS in tackles in his senior year, with 142. His college career saw him rack up 40.5 tackles for loss.

Cole already showed off his ridiculous athleticism, picking two balls for the Texans early in the season, one that saw him run all the way down field from his linebacker spot to undercut a corner route. A Grade II hamstring strain limited his snaps, but he was definitely the pick of the litter next to Bernardrick McKinney early in the year, and then fought his way back on to the field after the injury.

Cole profiles as either a passing-down linebacker or a three-down linebacker in the pros, depending on if he can get his broken tackle rate (five in limited snaps) down without sacrificing the speed. He's stuck behind Zach Cunningham and McKinney for the time being, but could resurface later.

13 RB Chris Carson, Seattle Seahawks
152 offensive snaps, age 24, seventh-round pick 2017

Out of nowhere came Chris Carson. A relative unknown as the backup tailback for Oklahoma State, Carson was an afterthought in the general draft community when the Seahawks took him in the last round in 2017. He was stacked behind Eddie Lacy, Thomas Rawls, and C.J. Prosise on the Seattle depth chart, and measured against players such as Troymaine Pope who had their own supporters.

Carson simply came out in training camp and played better than all of them. For the games he was healthy before fracturing his ankle, he was the only player Seattle had that led to a functional running game. Behind a terrible offensive line, Carson had 33 rushing DYAR this year. All other Seattle backs combined for -171 rushing DYAR. He broke an insane

21 tackles in just 56 touches. And Carson showed off in the passing game as well.

Seattle decided to draft Rashaad Penny in the first round, which is why Carson is where he is on this list. But Penny might see less of the field than most observers expect if Carson returns fully healthy. Carson flashed true three-down ability in his first taste of the NFL and was the toast of OTAs.

14 CB Fabian Moreau, Washington
59 defensive snaps, age 24, third-round pick 2017

It's not very often you see Mike Mayock's favorite corners in the draft available for our list. Most of the time those guys are starting by Week 4. Moreau slipped out of the first two rounds after tearing his quad at his pro day. Before that, he put on a show at the combine, with a 4.35-second 40-yard dash at 206 pounds—that's prototype size and speed. He also demonstrated nuanced technique of the position at the Shrine Game. About the only real criticisms teams could pin on him were his lack of interceptions (three in four seasons) and general questions about his instincts.

Moreau made a token appearance for Washington last season, getting run early against the Chiefs and 49ers in October before disappearing back to special teams duty. The small sample size yielded a 50 percent success rate and an average of 12.8 passing yards in 12 passes. He was mostly playing inside.

Moreau definitely profiles more as an outside corner, though Washington is hurting for slot help after trading former FO top prospect Kendall Fuller to Kansas City in the Alex Smith trade. Competition is assured in camp but going against what's left of Orlando Scandrick and steady contributors like Quinton Dunbar, we expect Moreau to see plenty of time on the field this year.

15 OT Julie'n Davenport, Houston Texans
241 offensive snaps, age 23, fourth-round pick 2017

Davenport is an agile tackle with great size, a 6-foot-7, 318-pound block of clay. The 40-yard dash (5.15 seconds) and bench press (18 reps) were pretty bad, but the rest of his combine was impressive. Coming out of tiny Bucknell, he dominated against weak competition and hadn't really learned most of the technical attributes of playing tackle. He was a blank slate.

Early on, it showed. Davenport was a frequent push-back target in his first real action against the Bengals. His only experience as a full-time starter came in Houston's worthless end-of-season games, where he was the starting left tackle against Pittsburgh and Indianapolis. But Davenport acquitted himself fairly well in those games, at least compared to the rest of the offensive line.

The Texans didn't really add any other potential left tackles in the draft or free agency. Third-round pick Martinas Rankin was seen as more of a right tackle by scouts, and Seantrel Henderson is too iffy to rely on. It seems likely Davenport will get the first crack there, and he has the tools to make it work. The question will be: How much has he learned since last year?

16 DT Andrew Billings, Cincinnati Bengals
336 defensive snaps, age 22, fourth-round pick 2016

A player we expected to be a starter right away for the Bengals instead saw his role reduced by veteran Pat Sims. We still remain high on Billings' tools, though. He showed elite strength and nimble feet at Baylor, where he was the co-Big 12 Defensive Player of the Year at 20 years old. He racked up 26.5 tackles for loss in his last two years of college. And, over the second half of the season, he steadily became a starting tackle in Cincinnati.

Will he ever be more than a run-stuffing nose tackle? That remains to be seen. He may still be working the creaks out of his surgically repaired knee at this point. But the snap count is so low that we're banking more on his college performance.

The Bengals brought in ex-Bucs and Washington nose Chris Baker this offseason, so we'll know pretty quickly whether they've moved on from Billings. The talent is worth fighting for, but it's hard to blame them for being cautious two years in. Billings will be off the Top Prospects list one way (plays well) or another (non-factor) next year—we said the same thing about Saints corner P.J. Williams last year, and that worked out OK for New Orleans.

17 TE Jake Butt, Denver Broncos
0 offensive snaps, age 22, fifth-round pick 2017

Another argument against meaningless college bowl games, Butt tore his ACL in the Citrus Bowl, sending his draft stock tumbling from a likely Day 2 pick to the fifth round. He was not able to show anything timed pre-draft. Butt's college production was pretty solid considering the state of Michigan's passing game, but he didn't have a ton of burst off the snap. Butt won't stretch the field, but he can provide reliable, effective receiving ability within 20 yards of the line of scrimmage.

A non-factor in Denver in his rookie year following the injury, Butt was IR'ed before the season began. Had he been healthy, the Broncos hadn't placed much in the way of him playing early. Virgil Green and Jeff Heuerman were the main Broncos tight ends last season.

Heuerman is again the only real obstacle in front of Butt this year. The Broncos did little to address the position in free agency. Broncos coach Vance Joseph told reporters at OTAs that Butt will "do everything he has to do to be a great player. If I'm betting on Jake, I'm betting it's going to happen." Butt doesn't project as a high-ceiling, Gronkowski-esque tight end, but could be a long-term fixture and is one of the safest players on this list assuming he fully recovers from the ACL tear.

18 WR Mack Hollins, Philadelphia Eagles
287 offensive snaps, age 24, fourth-round pick 2017

Hollins had 20 touchdown receptions on just 81 catches in college for North Carolina. A hulking, 6-foot-4, 221-pound frame that comes at you like a freight train with 4.50-second 40-yard dash speed, Hollins checked a lot of boxes as a physical downfield receiver who could also contribute on special teams right away.

In his rookie season, he was a go-to for the Eagles on their shot plays. Hollins led all Eagles receivers in DVOA at 24.2%.

(Only Nelson Agholor also finished with an above-average DVOA). He did this despite only one long touchdown catch. Generally, receivers with this sort of DVOA in a small sample are boosted by a few big catches; Hollins was not.

The offseason saw Torrey Smith replaced by Mike Wallace, but Hollins could still force his way on to the field with a good training camp. He has got all the requisite physical attributes, and Philadelphia loved to chuck it down the field last season with Carson Wentz. All it would take is one injury for Hollins to have massive fantasy football appeal.

19 DL Chris Wormley, Baltimore Ravens
190 defensive snaps, age 24, third-round pick 2017

Wormley was a run-stuffer extraordinaire early at Michigan. Later in his career, he also developed some pass-rushing moves. Wormley finished with nine tackles for loss and 6.0 sacks, and he was a first-team All-Big 10 selection. He tacked on an impressive 7.08-second 3-Cone drill time at 298 pounds in Indianapolis. So, to no one's surprise, he was a second-day NFL pick.

Wormley had no sacks but four hurries early in his NFL career. He has basically replaced Michael Pierce as "promising young defensive line prospect" on both the Baltimore roster and on our list. The Ravens have a pretty decent defensive line, so there's not a lot of impetus for Wormley to get snaps early. However, his ceiling as an inside player with some pass-rush moves might be intriguing enough for him to see the field on pass-rushing downs. Outside of Pierce and Wormley, the Ravens only have oft-injured Carl Davis as an interior lineman with any kind of pass-rush promise.

20 S Damontae Kazee, Atlanta Falcons
164 defensive snaps, age 25, fifth-round pick 2017

A playmaker in the secondary, Kazee snatched 15 interceptions in his last two seasons at San Diego State, along with 43 passes defensed over his last three seasons. His combine was fairly pedestrian though, and that along with his size (5-foot-10, 184 pounds) had him last all the way until the fifth round, where Atlanta snatched him up.

In Kazee's first season, he flipped from cornerback to safety, coming in as a backup and playing large chunks of games against Buffalo in Week 4, Tampa Bay in Week 12, and Minnesota in Week 13. He forced two fumbles and continued to showcase those instincts, and the move to safety kept his recovery speed from being as big of an issue as it could have been for an NFL cornerback.

Heading into 2018 his role is almost fully dependent on Ricardo Allen. Allen has yet to sign his RFA tender in the hopes of getting a new long-term deal, while the Atlanta braintrust might be looking at Kazee, remembering how they created Allen as a UDFA, and making the thinking face emoji. Kazee's instincts make him a problem for opposing quarterbacks in the middle of the field.

21 RB D'onta Foreman, Houston Texans
147 offensive snaps, age 22, third-round pick 2017

Foreman is a size-speed nightmare for defenses who was dinged coming out of Texas for his fumbling and his tendency to flirt with cuts a bit much. But he was the workhorse back and entire offense for the Longhorns, and his talent was evident in his rookie season. Every time the Texans played without Deshaun Watson, Lamar Miller trudged in mud while Foreman's fresh legs provided more burst. Per DVOA, they were about even, with Miller picking up 57 DYAR to Foreman's 10 in about 170 more carries.

Unfortunately, Foreman tore his Achilles on a long touchdown run against Arizona, putting his status into a little more question. As we went to press, the Texans could only say that they hoped he'd be available for training camp. He hadn't taken the field yet in OTAs, and he's a likely PUP list candidate when he's there.

However, the talent box is checked, and the opportunity is wide open in the Houston backfield. Miller has been a disappointment who hasn't been able to do better than "steady," and the other backs on the roster are filler. So if Foreman gets healthy, he has got a lot of upside in front of him.

22 WR Josh Reynolds, Los Angeles Rams
280 offensive snaps, age 23, fourth-round pick 2017

Another player who the draftniks liked more than the scouts, primarily due to size. Reynolds is 6-foot-3, but only 194 pounds, and he was seen as skinny and frail by the body-obsessed scouts. Reynolds had a lackluster combine—not bad, but with nothing that really stood out. Reynolds caught 30 touchdowns in three SEC seasons at Texas A&M, but in a broad-picture view, was merely a good all-around prospect by the numbers. He had a good-not-great 83.9% Playmaker Score. Reynolds' college tape, however, was excellent. He was noted for his deep-ball prowess, with enough acrobatic ability to make twisting catches, and he showed great work on slant routes as well.

In his rookie season, buried behind Sammy Watkins, Cooper Kupp, and Robert Woods, Reynolds didn't play all that much. A low catch rate anchored him to a -31.0% DVOA in a small sample size.

Letting Watkins walk in free agency would seem to have opened up a job for Reynolds, but instead the team traded for Brandin Cooks, throwing Reynolds back into the No. 4 receiver role. The good news is that Tavon Austin's snaps are gone, which should at least enable Reynolds to showcase his talent if someone gets hurt. The sky is the limit here, but there are question marks.

23 LB Duke Riley, Atlanta Falcons
223 defensive snaps, age 23, third-round pick 2017

It comes in a Telvin Smith package—will it play like Telvin Smith? Riley was buried on the depth chart at LSU, only getting a real chance in his senior season. He's 6-foot-0, 232 pounds, and his play strength was questioned for the entire draft process. He didn't help himself there at the combine, performing only 18 bench reps. However, his change-of-direction metrics were strong, and he ran a 4.58-second 40-yard dash. So the Falcons, a team that already had the player who kept Riley off the field in his junior year—Deion Jones—sprung for him in the third round.

Riley had started seeing the field early before an October meniscus tear wiped him out of the lineup, and he was a non-factor when he returned in November. As you may have surmised, they weren't necessarily great reps. Riley missed 10 tackles in limited snaps and looked like a rookie in pass coverage as well.

However, the physical talent is still there, and the Falcons haven't cleanly blocked him from playing at all. The skill set to be a three-down linebacker is still here. But Riley hasn't earned much benefit of the doubt yet, and a bad year could make him an afterthought in Atlanta.

24 RB Kenneth Dixon, Baltimore Ravens
258 offensive snaps, age 24, fourth-round pick 2016

We just can't quit Dixon. At least not yet.

It's hard to understand how Dixon made it to the fifth round. Wildly productive, he held the career FBS touchdown record for a few days at the end of his senior season, before Keenan Reynolds snagged it back. He was first-team All-Conference—as a *freshman* at Louisiana Tech. He's a great receiver out of the backfield. He doesn't go down on first conta. He gets the most out of every run. He's not a premium athlete, but he showed plenty of burst at the NFL combine with his jump metrics. He had an extremely similar combine profile to Kareem Hunt.

Dixon's NFL career has been derailed by injuries and suspensions. A four-game suspension for PEDs became a six-game suspension when he ran afoul of the substance abuse policy. He ended up serving that suspension on injured reserve when he tore his meniscus before the 2017 season began, and his 2016 season was also cut into by a sprained MCL.

Still only 24, Dixon is looking up at Alex Collins' terrific season and will also have to prove himself over Buck Allen. He still has the talent to be the best back the Ravens have this season. But time is running out for him to show that. As you might expect, he's not exactly the most popular name in John Harbaugh's mind right now.

25 WR Carlos Henderson, Denver Broncos
0 offensive snaps, age 23, third-round pick 2017

Much like Derek Rivers, Henderson was a pre-draft favorite of many in the draftnik community who did absolutely noth-ing in his freshman NFL season due to injury. However, un-like Rivers, Henderson likely could have come back earlier if the Broncos wanted him to be on the field. He was placed on IR with a thumb injury that was likely a stash move, as his first training camp did not go well.

Henderson led the nation with 19 touchdown catches at Louisiana Tech in 2016, and as Conference USA's special teams player of the year he had star upside in the kicking game as well. There were some dings on Henderson's tape. He's physical, agile, and explosive, but put up poor combine times in the short-area quickness measurements: 7.18 3-cone drill, 4.35 20-yard shuttle, and an 11.79 60-yard shuttle. He also rarely had to face press coverage at Louisiana Tech, and has some work to do in the more technical aspects of route-running. Regardless, our Playmaker Score loved him, giving him a 97.4% rating.

Scuttlebutt out of Denver had the third receiver job behind Demaryius Thomas and Emmanuel Sanders as wide open in OTAs. Henderson is facing a bit of an uphill battle as Court-land Sutton was drafted in the second round this year and may have an edge. The Broncos also drafted DaeSean Hamilton in the fourth round. It could just be that all these players are meant to replace the aging Thomas and Sanders. Or, it could be that the Broncos are already not counting on further devel-opment from Henderson.

Honorable Mentions

RB James Conner, Pittsburgh Steelers
G Parker Ehinger, Kansas City Chiefs
TE Rico Gathers, Dallas Cowboys
DE Daeshon Hall, Carolina Panthers
DT Jaleel Johnson, Minnesota Vikings
QB Chad Kelly, Denver Broncos
S Montae Nicholson, Washington
G Nico Siragusa, Baltimore Ravens
WR ArDarius Stewart, New York Jets
WR Taywan Taylor, Tennessee Titans

Rivers McCown

Fantasy Projections

Here are the top 275 players according to the KUBIAK projection system, ranked by projected fantasy value (**FANT**) in 2018. We've used the following generic scoring system:

- 1 point for each 10 yards rushing, 10 yards receiving, or 20 yards passing
- 6 points for each rushing or receiving TD, 4 points for each passing TD
- -2 points for each interception or fumble lost
- Kickers: 1 point for each extra point, 3 points for each field goal
- Team defense: 2 points for a fumble recovery, interception, or safety, 1 point for a sack, and 6 points for a touchdown.

These totals are then adjusted based on each player's listed **Risk** for 2018:

- Green: Standard risk, no change
- Yellow: Higher than normal risk, value dropped by five percent
- Red: Highest risk, value dropped by 10 percent
- Blue: Significantly lower than normal risk, value increased by five percent

Note that fantasy totals may not exactly equal these calculations, because each touchdown projection is not necessarily a round number. (For example, a quarterback listed with 2 rushing touchdowns may actually be projected with 2.4 rushing touchdowns, which will add 14 fantasy points to the player's total rather than 12.) Fantasy value does not include adjustments for week-to-week consistency,

Players are ranked in order based on marginal value of each player, the idea that you draft based on how many more points a player will score compared to the worst starting player at that position, not how many points a player scores overall. We've ranked players in five league configurations:

- Flex Rk: 12 teams, starts 1 QB, 2 RB, 2 WR, 1 FLEX (RB/WR), 1 TE, 1 K, and 1 D.
- 3WR Rk: 12 teams, starts 1 QB, 2 RB, 3 WR, 1 TE, 1 K, and 1 D.
- PPR Rk: 12 teams, starts 1 QB, 2 RB, 2 WR, 1 FLEX (RB/WR), 1 TE, 1 K, and 1 D. Also adds one point per reception to scoring.
- 10-3WR Rk: same as 3WR, but with only 10 teams.
- 10-PPR Rk: same as PPR, but with only 10 teams.

The rankings also include half value for the first running back on the bench, and reduce the value of kickers and defenses to reflect the general drafting habits of fantasy football players. We urge you to draft using common sense, not a strict reading of these rankings.

A customizable spreadsheet featuring these projections is also available at FootballOutsiders.com for a $20 fee. This spreadsheet is updated based on injuries and changing forecasts of playing time during the preseason, and also has a version which includes individual defensive players.

The projections for Julian Edelman, Mark Ingram, and Jameis Winston incorporate four weeks of "replacement-level" value (three for Winston), accounting for the fact that a fantasy team that drafts one of these players will still get points from a bench player during the weeks he is suspended.

Player	Team	Bye	Pos	Age	PaYd	PaTD	INT	Ru	RuYd	RuTD	Rec	RcYd	RcTD	FL	Fant	Risk	Flex Rk	3WR Rk	PPR Rk	10-3WR Rk	10-PPR Rk
Le'Veon Bell	PIT	7	RB	26	0	0	0	324	1458	12	81	660	3	2	277	Yellow	1	1	1	1	1
Todd Gurley	LAR	12	RB	24	0	0	0	308	1431	11	62	544	4	1	269	Yellow	2	2	2	2	2
Ezekiel Elliott	DAL	8	RB	23	0	0	0	324	1488	11	57	489	2	2	237	Red	4	4	5	4	5
David Johnson	ARI	9	RB	27	0	0	0	285	1226	11	77	705	2	2	221	Red	5	5	9	6	9
Saquon Barkley	NYG	9	RB	21	0	0	0	305	1326	7	67	610	3	2	216	Yellow	6	6	11	7	11
Melvin Gordon	LAC	8	RB	25	0	0	0	293	1203	9	55	491	2	2	218	Red	7	7	12	8	12
Dalvin Cook	MIN	10	RB	23	0	0	0	286	1347	9	55	503	1	2	217	Yellow	8	8	15	9	15
Leonard Fournette	JAX	9	RB	23	0	0	0	306	1319	9	48	403	1	2	205	Yellow	9	10	7	11	7
Alvin Kamara	NO	6	RB	23	0	0	0	175	874	8	85	730	3	2	208	Yellow	10	11	14	12	14
Kareem Hunt	KC	12	RB	23	0	0	0	270	1238	7	58	470	2	1	207	Green	11	9	3	5	3
Antonio Brown	PIT	7	WR	30	0	0	0	2	13	0	108	1460	10	0	192	Green	12	12	8	10	8
DeAndre Hopkins	HOU	10	WR	26	0	0	0	2	13	0	92	1286	10	0	186	Green	13	13	6	13	6
Keenan Allen	LAC	8	WR	26	0	0	0	2	11	0	105	1430	7	0	181	Yellow	14	14	13	14	13
Julio Jones	ATL	8	WR	29	0	0	0	0	0	0	89	1451	7	0	176	Red	15	16	27	21	27
LeSean McCoy	BUF	11	RB	30	0	0	0	279	1210	6	51	402	1	1	178	Green	16	15	10	15	10
Michael Thomas	NO	6	WR	24	0	0	0	2	13	0	102	1252	9	0	157	Yellow	17	17	22	16	17
Rob Gronkowski	NE	11	TE	29	0	0	0	0	0	0	77	1158	8	0	168	Yellow	18	22	34	26	35
Devonta Freeman	ATL	8	RB	26	0	0	0	202	887	7	44	374	2	1	167	Yellow	19	18	16	17	16
Odell Beckham	NYG	9	WR	26	0	0	0	2	10	0	96	1242	9	0	165	Yellow	20	24	32	27	32
Mark Ingram (adj.)	NO	6	RB	29	0	0	0	181	844	7	52	415	1	2	165	Yellow	21	19	20	18	21
Davante Adams	GB	7	WR	26	0	0	0	2	10	0	75	1005	10	0	165	Green	22	27	19	30	20
Christian McCaffrey	CAR	4	RB	22	0	0	0	145	609	3	77	699	3	2	161	Green					

Player	Team	Bye	Pos	Age	PaYd	PaTD	INT	Ru	RuYd	RuTD	Rec	RcYd	RcTD	FL	Fant	Risk	Flex Rk	3WR Rk	PPR Rk	10-3WR Rk	10-PPR Rk
Mike Evans	TB	5	WR	25	0	0	0	0	0	0	80	1185	9	0	162	Yellow	23	20	21	19	22
Tyreek Hill	KC	12	WR	24	0	0	0	18	120	1	71	1065	7	0	161	Green	24	21	24	20	24
Adam Thielen	MIN	10	WR	28	0	0	0	0	0	0	86	1222	8	0	158	Yellow	25	23	17	22	18
Rashaad Penny	SEA	7	RB	22	0	0	0	214	901	7	35	301	1	1	156	Yellow	26	29	48	39	53
A.J. Green	CIN	9	WR	30	0	0	0	0	0	0	79	1111	7	0	154	Green	27	25	23	23	23
Amari Cooper	OAK	7	WR	24	0	0	0	2	12	0	82	1135	8	0	154	Yellow	28	26	25	24	25
T.Y. Hilton	IND	9	WR	29	0	0	0	2	12	0	73	1182	7	0	153	Yellow	29	28	29	25	30
Derrius Guice	WAS	4	RB	21	0	0	0	230	1010	8	28	206	1	2	149	Red	30	31	64	45	70
Jerick McKinnon	SF	11	RB	26	0	0	0	184	767	4	63	574	2	1	154	Red	31	35	35	48	36
Aaron Rodgers	GB	7	QB	35	4138	33	11	57	259	1	0	0	0	2	325	Yellow	32	30	38	28	37
Lamar Miller	HOU	10	RB	27	0	0	0	237	946	5	29	226	2	1	148	Yellow	33	38	66	50	73
Alex Collins	BAL	10	RB	24	0	0	0	237	1024	7	29	197	1	2	151	Red	34	39	68	51	76
Deshaun Watson	HOU	10	QB	23	4164	27	16	82	509	3	0	0	0	5	322	Yellow	35	34	42	32	39
Travis Kelce	KC	12	TE	29	0	0	0	0	0	0	84	1043	5	0	129	Yellow	36	33	31	29	28
Marshawn Lynch	OAK	7	RB	32	0	0	0	201	874	8	18	140	0	1	140	Yellow	37	47	100	60	116
Carson Wentz	PHI	9	QB	26	4222	31	12	63	303	2	0	0	0	7	315	Yellow	38	41	46	37	42
Doug Baldwin	SEA	7	WR	30	0	0	0	2	11	0	76	984	7	0	142	Green	39	32	30	31	31
Derrick Henry	TEN	8	RB	24	0	0	0	209	953	5	19	169	1	2	142	Green	40	50	98	64	112
Demaryius Thomas	DEN	10	WR	31	0	0	0	0	0	0	86	1075	7	0	141	Yellow	41	36	28	33	29
Allen Robinson	CHI	5	WR	25	0	0	0	2	11	0	67	968	9	0	141	Yellow	42	37	37	34	38
Jordan Howard	CHI	5	RB	24	0	0	0	256	1038	5	32	255	1	2	140	Red	43	53	80	66	90
Ronald Jones	TB	5	RB	21	0	0	0	228	946	5	27	220	1	2	142	Yellow	44	54	85	67	97
Jay Ajayi	PHI	9	RB	25	0	0	0	197	853	5	26	196	1	2	138	Green	45	55	86	68	98
Zach Ertz	PHI	9	TE	28	0	0	0	0	0	0	76	853	6	0	125	Green	46	44	36	36	33
Larry Fitzgerald	ARI	9	WR	35	0	0	0	0	0	0	106	1101	6	0	139	Yellow	47	40	18	35	19
Russell Wilson	SEA	7	QB	30	3773	24	10	81	449	3	0	0	0	5	314	Green	48	45	50	41	45
Tom Brady	NE	11	QB	41	4481	32	12	31	44	1	0	0	0	4	313	Yellow	49	46	51	42	46
Drew Brees	NO	6	QB	39	4388	28	10	25	23	1	0	0	0	3	313	Green	50	49	52	44	49
Brandin Cooks	LAR	12	WR	25	0	0	0	5	28	0	62	934	7	0	138	Green	51	42	39	38	40
Kenyan Drake	MIA	11	RB	24	0	0	0	194	877	5	39	292	1	2	130	Yellow	52	67	71	71	81
Marvin Jones	DET	6	WR	28	0	0	0	0	0	0	63	1013	7	0	138	Yellow	53	43	43	40	44
Sony Michel	NE	11	RB	23	0	0	0	161	745	7	26	193	1	2	137	Green	54	68	97	72	110
Cam Newton	CAR	4	QB	29	3344	23	12	114	697	5	0	0	0	3	311	Yellow	55	52	54	47	51
Joe Mixon	CIN	9	RB	22	0	0	0	206	802	5	31	237	1	2	136	Green	56	69	91	74	101
Julian Edelman (adj.)	NE	11	WR	32	0	0	0	6	42	0	84	962	7	0	132	Yellow	57	48	33	43	34
Golden Tate	DET	6	WR	30	0	0	0	5	22	0	93	1004	5	0	133	Green	58	51	26	46	26
Tevin Coleman	ATL	8	RB	25	0	0	0	155	668	5	37	369	2	1	130	Yellow	59	73	87	79	99
JuJu Smith-Schuster	PIT	7	WR	22	0	0	0	2	12	0	68	951	6	0	130	Green	60	56	40	49	41
Devin Funchess	CAR	4	WR	24	0	0	0	2	9	0	64	900	8	0	129	Yellow	61	57	49	52	54
Stefon Diggs	MIN	10	WR	25	0	0	0	2	12	0	74	956	6	0	127	Yellow	62	58	41	53	43
Pierre Garcon	SF	11	WR	32	0	0	0	0	0	0	70	898	8	0	128	Yellow	63	59	44	54	47
Josh Gordon	CLE	11	WR	27	0	0	0	2	12	0	58	1003	7	0	129	Red	64	60	57	55	60
Kerryon Johnson	DET	6	RB	21	0	0	0	150	619	7	34	341	2	1	125	Red	65	79	107	86	126
Evan Engram	NYG	9	TE	24	0	0	0	0	0	0	71	802	6	0	109	Yellow	66	62	55	56	50
Ben Roethlisberger	PIT	7	QB	36	4490	30	12	24	41	0	0	0	0	3	300	Yellow	67	65	65	63	57
Jimmy Graham	GB	7	TE	32	0	0	0	0	0	0	60	721	8	0	107	Red	68	64	77	58	66
Greg Olsen	CAR	4	TE	33	0	0	0	0	0	0	63	767	5	0	108	Green	69	66	61	61	56
Alshon Jeffery	PHI	9	WR	28	0	0	0	0	0	0	56	794	9	0	125	Yellow	70	61	62	57	68
Isaiah Crowell	NYJ	11	RB	25	0	0	0	181	749	6	31	239	1	1	125	Yellow	71	84	122	95	136
Marcus Mariota	TEN	8	QB	25	3646	23	12	67	388	3	0	0	0	3	298	Green	72	71	72	70	64
Matthew Stafford	DET	6	QB	30	4268	27	14	34	83	0	0	0	0	2	300	Green	73	72	74	73	67
Cooper Kupp	LAR	12	WR	25	0	0	0	2	11	0	71	918	6	0	123	Yellow	74	63	47	62	52
Matt Ryan	ATL	8	QB	33	4157	25	10	38	147	0	0	0	0	2	296	Green	75	77	75	78	72
Devontae Booker	DEN	10	RB	26	0	0	0	171	699	4	41	362	1	1	121	Red	76	91	109	101	132
Dak Prescott	DAL	8	QB	25	3619	22	11	75	375	3	0	0	0	4	292	Green	77	82	78	85	78
Robby Anderson	NYJ	11	WR	25	0	0	0	2	10	0	59	825	6	0	119	Green	78	70	60	69	65
Kirk Cousins	MIN	10	QB	30	4055	27	13	51	168	0	0	0	0	4	294	Green	79	89	81	90	82
Greg Zuerlein	LAR	12	K	31	0	0	0	0	0	0	0	0	0	0	156	Green	80	83	88	59	62
Delanie Walker	TEN	8	TE	34	0	0	0	0	0	0	68	770	5	0	100	Yellow	81	87	73	81	74
Tyler Eifert	CIN	9	TE	28	0	0	0	0	0	0	66	780	6	0	99	Red	82	88	83	82	74
Rishard Matthews	TEN	8	WR	29	0	0	0	0	0	0	62	843	6	0	117	Green	83	74	59	75	63
Corey Davis	TEN	8	WR	23	0	0	0	0	0	0	64	911	7	0	117	Red	84	75	70	76	80
Sammy Watkins	KC	12	WR	25	0	0	0	0	0	0	54	826	7	0	118	Yellow	85	76	79	77	89
Kelvin Benjamin	BUF	11	WR	27	0	0	0	0	0	0	62	887	6	0	117	Yellow	86	78	67	80	75
Alex Smith	WAS	4	QB	34	3996	26	9	58	225	1	0	0	0	2	296	Yellow	87	93	89	99	85

Player	Team	Bye	Pos	Age	PaYd	PaTD	INT	Ru	RuYd	RuTD	Rec	RcYd	RcTD	FL	Fant	Risk	Flex Rk	3WR Rk	PPR Rk	10-3WR Rk	10-PPR Rk
Andrew Luck	IND	9	QB	29	4082	29	13	60	251	2	0	0	0	2	291	Red	88	94	90	100	86
Stephen Gostkowski	NE	11	K	34	0	0	0	0	0	0	0	0	0	0	153	Green	89	92	95	65	71
Allen Hurns	DAL	8	WR	27	0	0	0	2	9	0	69	907	6	0	115	Red	90	80	63	83	69
Will Fuller	HOU	10	WR	24	0	0	0	3	17	0	53	788	6	0	116	Green	91	81	82	84	94
Jamaal Williams	GB	7	RB	23	0	0	0	139	606	5	29	226	1	1	116	Green	92	95	144	107	147
Michael Crabtree	BAL	10	WR	31	0	0	0	0	0	0	76	807	7	0	113	Yellow	93	85	53	87	55
Emmanuel Sanders	DEN	10	WR	31	0	0	0	0	0	0	70	895	5	0	115	Yellow	94	86	56	88	58
Jameis Winston (adj.)	TB	5	QB	24	4492	27	16	50	205	2	0	0	0	4	287	Red	95	99	94	106	93
Kenny Stills	MIA	11	WR	26	0	0	0	2	10	0	54	849	6	0	113	Yellow	96	90	93	93	105
Jordan Reed	WAS	4	TE	28	0	0	0	0	0	0	71	720	6	0	93	Red	97	98	84	98	77
Rex Burkhead	NE	11	RB	28	0	0	0	121	557	5	35	290	2	2	112	Red	98	100	149	114	149
Jared Cook	OAK	7	TE	31	0	0	0	0	0	0	59	729	4	0	95	Green	99	106	101	105	96
Jamison Crowder	WAS	4	WR	25	0	0	0	5	33	0	64	768	5	0	111	Green	100	96	69	102	79
Jaguars D	JAX	9	D	--	0	0	0	0	0	0	0	0	0	0	107	Green	101	107	108	89	84
Patrick Mahomes	KC	12	QB	23	4078	26	17	66	271	2	0	0	0	4	283	Yellow	102	111	102	119	103
Jarvis Landry	CLE	11	WR	26	0	0	0	4	24	0	84	821	4	0	110	Green	103	97	45	103	48
Nyheim Hines	IND	9	RB	22	0	0	0	132	535	3	35	360	1	1	109	Yellow	104	103	154	117	151
Adam Vinatieri	IND	9	K	46	0	0	0	0	0	0	0	0	0	0	146	Green	105	112	114	91	87
Matt Bryant	ATL	8	K	43	0	0	0	0	0	0	0	0	0	0	146	Green	106	113	115	92	88
Kenny Golladay	DET	6	WR	25	0	0	0	2	12	0	55	859	6	0	110	Red	107	101	104	108	123
Chris Hogan	NE	11	WR	30	0	0	0	2	11	0	55	812	7	0	106	Red	108	102	105	109	124
Dion Lewis	TEN	8	RB	28	0	0	0	153	737	3	36	274	0	1	108	Red	109	108	159	120	157
Rams D	LAR	12	D	--	0	0	0	0	0	0	0	0	0	0	110	Yellow	110	114	116	96	92
Jack Doyle	IND	9	TE	28	0	0	0	0	0	0	64	662	6	0	91	Red	111	117	113	116	106
Justin Tucker	BAL	10	K	29	0	0	0	0	0	0	0	0	0	0	146	Yellow	112	118	118	94	91
Marqise Lee	JAX	9	WR	27	0	0	0	3	17	0	68	881	4	0	107	Yellow	113	104	76	110	83
Josh Doctson	WAS	4	WR	26	0	0	0	0	0	0	49	730	6	0	108	Green	114	105	112	111	133
Royce Freeman	DEN	10	RB	22	0	0	0	155	643	5	27	200	0	1	107	Yellow	115	109	168	121	171
Eagles D	PHI	9	D	--	0	0	0	0	0	0	0	0	0	0	108	Green	116	119	119	97	95
Kyle Rudolph	MIN	10	TE	29	0	0	0	0	0	0	66	640	6	0	91	Red	117	123	110	118	102
Mitchell Trubisky	CHI	5	QB	24	3928	24	14	58	304	3	0	0	0	7	282	Yellow	118	126	111	132	111
Randall Cobb	GB	7	WR	28	0	0	0	6	32	0	74	823	4	0	107	Green	119	110	58	115	61
David Njoku	CLE	11	TE	22	0	0	0	0	0	0	50	614	6	0	87	Yellow	120	125	150	125	139
Tyrod Taylor	CLE	11	QB	29	3523	21	8	100	558	4	0	0	0	4	282	Red	121	130	117	140	114
Vikings D	MIN	10	D	--	0	0	0	0	0	0	0	0	0	0	104	Red	122	127	123	104	100
George Kittle	SF	11	TE	25	0	0	0	0	0	0	53	678	4	0	86	Green	123	129	130	126	134
DeVante Parker	MIA	11	WR	25	0	0	0	0	0	0	64	842	5	0	104	Red	124	115	96	122	109
DeSean Jackson	TB	5	WR	32	0	0	0	2	10	0	49	803	4	0	105	Green	125	116	121	123	135
Derek Carr	OAK	7	QB	27	3972	26	12	39	76	0	0	0	0	3	276	Green	126	134	120	143	122
Philip Rivers	LAC	8	QB	37	4432	29	12	23	22	0	0	0	0	3	277	Red	127	135	124	145	131
Nelson Agholor	PHI	9	WR	25	0	0	0	2	11	0	65	751	5	0	103	Yellow	128	124	92	129	104
Robbie Gould	SF	11	K	36	0	0	0	0	0	0	0	0	0	0	140	Green	129	136	112	112	107
Jake Elliott	PHI	9	K	23	0	0	0	0	0	0	0	0	0	0	138	Green	130	137	128	113	108
Marlon Mack	IND	9	RB	22	0	0	0	143	606	2	27	212	1	1	101	Green	131	120	174	134	183
Carlos Hyde	CLE	11	RB	27	0	0	0	138	562	5	24	153	0	1	101	Green	132	121	180	135	194
C.J. Anderson	CAR	4	RB	27	0	0	0	177	704	4	21	158	0	1	101	Yellow	133	122	186	136	204
Steelers D	PIT	7	D	--	0	0	0	0	0	0	0	0	0	0	98	Red	134	141	131	124	113
Christian Kirk	ARI	9	WR	22	0	0	0	7	44	0	65	751	5	0	95	Red	135	132	106	141	125
Packers D	GB	7	D	--	0	0	0	0	0	0	0	0	0	0	101	Yellow	136	146	134	130	120
Seahawks D	SEA	7	D	--	0	0	0	0	0	0	0	0	0	0	98	Yellow	137	147	135	131	121
Mason Crosby	GB	7	K	34	0	0	0	0	0	0	0	0	0	0	135	Green	138	151	138	127	118
Phil Dawson	ARI	9	K	43	0	0	0	0	0	0	0	0	0	0	135	Green	139	152	139	128	119
Sterling Shepard	NYG	9	WR	24	0	0	0	2	12	0	62	726	4	0	97	Green	140	138	103	146	117
Ryan Grant	IND	9	WR	28	0	0	0	2	10	0	56	762	4	0	97	Yellow	141	139	125	147	137
Theo Riddick	DET	6	RB	27	0	0	0	77	294	4	56	459	2	1	97	Yellow	142	128	126	142	138
Ravens D	BAL	10	D	--	0	0	0	0	0	0	0	0	0	0	98	Green	143	153	140	137	128
Panthers D	CAR	4	D	--	0	0	0	0	0	0	0	0	0	0	97	Yellow	144	154	141	138	129
Chargers D	LAC	8	D	--	0	0	0	0	0	0	0	0	0	0	96	Green	145	155	142	139	130
Ryan Succop	TEN	8	K	32	0	0	0	0	0	0	0	0	0	0	134	Green	146	156	145	133	127
Cardinals D	ARI	9	D	--	0	0	0	0	0	0	0	0	0	0	95	Yellow	147	157	146	187	162
Case Keenum	DEN	10	QB	30	3893	23	15	43	112	2	0	0	0	3	274	Green	148	168	136	163	140
Jared Goff	LAR	12	QB	24	3807	25	12	33	84	2	0	0	0	6	270	Green	149	169	137	164	141
Matt Prater	DET	6	K	34	0	0	0	0	0	0	0	0	0	0	134	Yellow	150	161	151	185	160
Chris Boswell	PIT	7	K	27	0	0	0	0	0	0	0	0	0	0	132	Yellow	151	162	152	186	161
Robert Woods	LAR	12	WR	26	0	0	0	2	12	0	65	770	3	0	96	Green	152	145	99	149	115

Player	Team	Bye	Pos	Age	PaYd	PaTD	INT	Ru	RuYd	RuTD	Rec	RcYd	RcTD	FL	Fant	Risk	Flex Rk	3WR Rk	PPR Rk	10-3WR Rk	10-PPR Rk
Giovani Bernard	CIN	9	RB	27	0	0	0	118	498	2	44	393	1	1	96	Yellow	153	131	163	144	164
Browns D	CLE	11	D		0	0	0	0	0	0	0	0	0	0	99	Red	154	163	153	196	167
O.J. Howard	TB	5	TE	24	0	0	0	0	0	0	38	519	5	0	79	Green	155	167	183	155	178
Blake Bortles	JAX	9	QB	27	3701	23	13	66	302	2	0	0	0	4	271	Yellow	156	175	143	168	142
Calvin Ridley	ATL	8	WR	24	0	0	0	4	26	0	54	768	5	0	94	Red	157	148	148	151	148
Jimmy Garoppolo	SF	11	QB	27	4244	24	15	45	103	1	0	0	0	3	272	Yellow	158	176	147	169	143
Matt Breida	SF	11	RB	23	0	0	0	130	593	3	22	173	0	2	94	Green	159	133	200	148	223
Martavis Bryant	OAK	7	WR	27	0	0	0	3	14	0	53	710	5	0	93	Red	160	158	157	156	155
Tyrell Williams	LAC	8	WR	26	0	0	0	0	0	0	43	662	4	0	92	Green	161	159	166	157	166
Mike Williams	LAC	8	WR	24	0	0	0	0	0	0	54	620	7	0	90	Red	162	164	158	160	156
Paul Richardson	WAS	4	WR	26	0	0	0	0	0	0	47	720	4	0	92	Yellow	163	165	165	161	165
Marquise Goodwin	SF	11	WR	28	0	0	0	3	15	0	39	650	4	0	92	Green	164	166	171	162	179
Mohamed Sanu	ATL	8	WR	29	0	0	0	0	0	0	57	677	4	0	91	Green	165	170	132	165	145
John Brown	BAL	10	WR	28	0	0	0	2	11	0	53	726	5	0	88	Red	166	171	162	166	159
Duke Johnson	CLE	11	RB	25	0	0	0	62	263	1	58	470	2	1	90	Green	167	140	129	150	144
Cameron Brate	TB	5	TE	27	0	0	0	0	0	0	40	499	4	0	73	Green	168	186	189	177	188
Jordy Nelson	OAK	7	WR	33	0	0	0	0	0	0	58	652	6	0	89	Red	169	177	156	170	154
Tyler Lockett	SEA	7	WR	26	0	0	0	9	55	0	49	643	3	0	88	Green	170	178	161	171	158
Ted Ginn	NO	6	WR	33	0	0	0	9	51	0	46	626	3	0	88	Green	171	179	167	172	170
Tarik Cohen	CHI	5	RB	23	0	0	0	75	318	1	62	488	1	1	88	Yellow	172	142	133	152	146
Charles Clay	BUF	11	TE	29	0	0	0	0	0	0	51	574	2	0	71	Green	173	188	173	178	163
Vernon Davis	WAS	4	TE	34	0	0	0	0	0	0	40	485	4	0	69	Green	174	189	192	179	190
Josh McCown	NYJ	11	QB	39	3784	23	15	42	133	2	0	0	0	7	264	Green	175	192	160	194	150
Brice Butler	ARI	9	WR	28	0	0	0	0	0	0	47	677	5	0	85	Red	176	180	172	176	180
James White	NE	11	RB	26	0	0	0	64	254	1	57	496	3	1	89	Yellow	177	143	155	153	152
Darren Sproles	PHI	9	RB	35	0	0	0	69	325	1	51	489	2	0	86	Red	178	144	169	154	172
Austin Seferian-Jenkins	JAX	9	TE	26	0	0	0	0	0	0	47	534	4	0	69	Red	179	195	193	182	191
Eric Ebron	IND	9	TE	25	0	0	0	0	0	0	42	486	4	0	69	Yellow	180	196	198	183	196
Vance McDonald	PIT	7	TE	28	0	0	0	0	0	0	39	483	4	0	71	Yellow	181	197	202	184	207
Ryan Tannehill	MIA	11	QB	30	3830	23	12	42	147	1	0	0	0	3	255	Yellow	182	202	164	204	153
Gerald Everett	LAR	12	TE	24	0	0	0	0	0	0	39	482	4	0	68	Yellow	183	201	206	189	209
Quincy Enunwa	NYJ	11	WR	26	0	0	0	2	9	0	48	655	5	0	84	Red	184	187	176	181	185
Ty Montgomery	GB	7	RB	25	0	0	0	83	349	2	39	307	1	1	85	Green	185	149	182	158	199
Donte Moncrief	JAX	9	WR	25	0	0	0	2	12	0	50	657	4	0	83	Yellow	186	190	170	188	175
Latavius Murray	MIN	10	RB	27	0	0	0	108	410	5	15	115	1	1	83	Green	187	150	235	159	245
Trey Burton	CHI	5	TE	27	0	0	0	0	0	0	39	442	4	0	67	Green	188	208	207	202	210
Anthony Miller	CHI	5	WR	24	0	0	0	4	23	0	48	669	4	0	81	Red	189	193	177	195	189
Austin Hooper	ATL	8	TE	24	0	0	0	0	0	0	41	431	4	0	65	Yellow	190	211	210	206	213
Mike Wallace	PHI	9	WR	32	0	0	0	0	0	0	42	582	4	0	82	Green	191	198	181	199	198
Chris Godwin	TB	5	WR	22	0	0	0	2	11	0	41	588	4	0	81	Green	192	199	185	200	203
Travis Benjamin	LAC	8	WR	29	0	0	0	9	62	0	35	552	3	0	81	Green	193	200	196	201	219
Terrelle Pryor	NYJ	11	WR	29	0	0	0	3	14	0	44	580	5	0	79	Red	194	203	188	205	211
James Washington	PIT	7	WR	22	0	0	0	3	19	0	44	653	4	0	76	Red	195	206	191	209	215
T.J. Yeldon	JAX	9	RB	25	0	0	0	81	381	2	37	284	1	1	78	Green	196	160	197	167	220
Andy Dalton	CIN	9	QB	31	3638	22	11	38	113	1	0	0	0	3	257	Green	197	221	175	232	174
Aaron Jones	GB	7	RB	24	0	0	0	111	507	2	18	132	1	1	74	Yellow	198	172	248	173	250
Benjamin Watson	NO	6	TE	38	0	0	0	0	0	0	44	434	4	0	60	Red	199	225	220	224	226
Jermaine Kearse	NYJ	11	WR	28	0	0	0	0	0	0	50	589	3	0	75	Green	200	215	178	219	192
Corey Clement	PHI	9	RB	24	0	0	0	100	419	3	26	221	0	1	74	Yellow	201	173	231	174	243
Nick Chubb	CLE	11	RB	23	0	0	0	116	482	4	11	86	0	1	74	Green	202	174	253	175	254
Luke Willson	DET	6	TE	28	0	0	0	0	0	0	43	421	4	0	57	Red	203	230	223	228	231
Brandon LaFell	CIN	9	WR	32	0	0	0	0	0	0	51	611	3	0	75	Yellow	204	219	184	223	202
Nick Vannett	SEA	7	TE	25	0	0	0	0	0	0	37	401	3	0	57	Yellow	205	233	232	235	237
Virgil Green	LAC	8	TE	30	0	0	0	0	0	0	34	385	4	0	57	Yellow	206	236	244	238	240
Cole Beasley	DAL	8	WR	29	0	0	0	2	12	0	56	563	3	0	72	Yellow	207	222	179	233	193
Dede Westbrook	JAX	9	WR	25	0	0	0	2	10	0	45	580	4	0	71	Red	208	223	204	234	229
Redskins D	WAS	4	D		0	0	0	0	0	0	0	0	0	0	97	Yellow	209	237	194	197	168
Saints D	NO	6	D		0	0	0	0	0	0	0	0	0	0	95	Red	210	238	195	198	169
Albert Wilson	MIA	11	WR	26	0	0	0	3	14	0	53	603	3	0	70	Red	211	226	190	237	214
Cameron Meredith	NO	6	WR	26	0	0	0	2	12	0	40	539	3	0	70	Green	212	231	213	240	233
Elijah McGuire	NYJ	11	RB	24	0	0	0	77	345	2	30	293	1	1	71	Yellow	213	181	236	180	246
Patriots D	NE	11	D		0	0	0	0	0	0	0	0	0	0	92	Red	214	241	201	208	173
D.J. Moore	CAR	4	WR	21	0	0	0	4	22	0	40	526	3	0	69	Yellow	215	234	218	245	236
Ricky Seals-Jones	ARI	9	TE	23	0	0	0	0	0	0	39	387	2	0	52	Green	216	244	237	254	238
Adam Humphries	TB	5	WR	25	0	0	0	3	16	0	52	580	2	0	68	Green	217	239	187	249	208

Player	Team	Bye	Pos	Age	PaYd	PaTD	INT	Ru	RuYd	RuTD	Rec	RcYd	RcTD	FL	Fant	Risk	Flex Rk	3WR Rk	PPR Rk	10-3WR Rk	10-PPR Rk
Terrance Williams	DAL	8	WR	29	0	0	0	2	12	0	47	552	2	0	68	Green	218	240	199	250	222
Broncos D	DEN	10	D	--	0	0	0	0	0	0	0	0	0	0	92	Yellow	219	245	203	213	177
Blake Jarwin	DAL	8	TE	24	0	0	0	0	0	0	36	364	2	0	51	Green	220	249	247	259	241
Frank Gore	MIA	11	RB	35	0	0	0	125	475	2	21	142	1	1	65	Red	221	182	254	190	255
Bilal Powell	NYJ	11	RB	30	0	0	0	97	450	2	17	147	0	1	67	Yellow	222	183	256	191	256
Dan Bailey	DAL	8	K	30	0	0	0	0	0	0	0	0	0	0	129	Yellow	223	250	209	212	176
Titans D	TEN	8	D	--	0	0	0	0	0	0	0	0	0	0	93	Red	224	251	211	217	181
Texans D	HOU	10	D	--	0	0	0	0	0	0	0	0	0	0	90	Red	225	252	212	218	182
Willie Snead	BAL	10	WR	26	0	0	0	0	0	0	49	579	3	0	63	Red	226	242	214	257	234
Taywan Taylor	TEN	8	WR	23	0	0	0	4	22	0	42	515	3	0	65	Red	227	243	225	258	239
Chris Thompson	WAS	4	RB	28	0	0	0	55	251	1	52	414	1	1	66	Red	228	184	205	192	230
LeGarrette Blount	DET	6	RB	32	0	0	0	97	382	4	5	37	0	0	67	Green	229	185	263	193	263
Courtland Sutton	DEN	10	WR	23	0	0	0	3	20	0	38	494	3	0	64	Yellow	230	246	230	260	242
Ryan Griffin	HOU	10	TE	28	0	0	0	0	0	0	33	378	2	0	47	Green	231	255	252	265	249
Stephen Anderson	HOU	10	TE	25	0	0	0	0	0	0	30	368	2	0	47	Yellow	232	256	255	266	251
Falcons D	ATL	8	D	--	0	0	0	0	0	0	0	0	0	0	91	Yellow	233	253	215	226	186
Cowboys D	DAL	8	D	--	0	0	0	0	0	0	0	0	0	0	91	Red	234	254	216	227	187
Zay Jones	BUF	11	WR	23	0	0	0	0	0	0	34	443	3	0	63	Green	235	247	239	263	247
Keke Coutee	HOU	10	WR	21	0	0	0	5	28	0	37	524	3	0	63	Red	236	248	240	264	248
Sam Bradford	ARI	9	QB	31	4035	23	13	32	35	1	0	0	0	4	237	Red	237	260	208	274	218
Ka'imi Fairbairn	HOU	10	K	24	0	0	0	0	0	0	0	0	0	0	128	Green	238	257	217	225	184
Chiefs D	KC	12	D	--	0	0	0	0	0	0	0	0	0	0	91	Green	239	258	219	236	195
Kenneth Dixon	BAL	10	RB	24	0	0	0	94	413	1	27	179	1	2	62	Yellow	240	191	250	203	252
Bengals D	CIN	9	D	--	0	0	0	0	0	0	0	0	0	0	89	Red	241	261	221	243	200
Dolphins D	MIA	11	D	--	0	0	0	0	0	0	0	0	0	0	85	Green	242	262	222	244	201
Peyton Barber	TB	5	RB	24	0	0	0	90	349	2	16	117	0	1	58	Green	243	194	259	207	259
Harrison Butker	KC	12	K	23	0	0	0	0	0	0	0	0	0	0	126	Green	244	263	224	242	197
Lions D	DET	6	D	--	0	0	0	0	0	0	0	0	0	0	90	Red	245	264	226	252	205
Bills D	BUF	11	D	--	0	0	0	0	0	0	0	0	0	0	86	Yellow	246	265	227	253	206
Brandon Marshall	SEA	7	WR	34	0	0	0	0	0	0	43	449	3	0	56	Green	247	259	234	273	244
Chris Ivory	BUF	11	RB	30	0	0	0	86	317	3	15	110	0	1	56	Green	248	204	261	210	261
Jets D	NYJ	11	D	--	0	0	0	0	0	0	0	0	0	0	88	Red	249	266	229	256	212
Doug Martin	OAK	7	RB	29	0	0	0	101	389	2	12	86	0	1	54	Green	250	205	265	211	265
Chris Carson	SEA	7	RB	24	0	0	0	87	348	2	19	150	0	1	54	Red	251	207	262	214	262
Bears D	CHI	5	D	--	0	0	0	0	0	0	0	0	0	0	86	Yellow	252	267	233	262	217
Eli Manning	NYG	9	QB	37	3860	23	13	22	37	0	0	0	0	3	230	Red	253	271	228	275	235
Jeremy Hill	NE	11	RB	26	0	0	0	67	275	3	7	53	1	1	53	Green	254	209	268	215	268
Steven Hauschka	BUF	11	K	33	0	0	0	0	0	0	0	0	0	0	123	Green	255	268	238	261	216
Raiders D	OAK	7	D	--	0	0	0	0	0	0	0	0	0	0	85	Red	256	269	241	268	224
Colts D	IND	9	D	--	0	0	0	0	0	0	0	0	0	0	85	Red	257	270	242	269	225
D'Onta Foreman	HOU	10	RB	22	0	0	0	87	366	2	11	100	0	1	51	Yellow	258	210	266	216	266
Jalen Richard	OAK	7	RB	25	0	0	0	38	180	0	30	269	1	1	49	Green	259	212	257	220	257
Sebastian Janikowski	SEA	7	K	40	0	0	0	0	0	0	0	0	0	0	122	Yellow	260	272	243	267	221
Bucs D	TB	5	D	--	0	0	0	0	0	0	0	0	0	0	84	Green	261	273	245	270	227
Giants D	NYG	9	D	--	0	0	0	0	0	0	0	0	0	0	82	Green	262	274	246	271	228
Charles Sims	TB	5	RB	28	0	0	0	25	102	1	42	344	1	0	48	Red	263	213	251	221	253
Buck Allen	BAL	10	RB	27	0	0	0	71	281	1	27	160	0	1	50	Green	264	214	258	222	258
Austin Ekeler	LAC	8	RB	23	0	0	0	35	142	2	24	197	0	1	45	Green	265	216	264	229	264
Jordan Wilkins	IND	9	RB	24	0	0	0	70	312	1	11	84	0	1	46	Green	266	217	270	230	270
Wil Lutz	NO	6	K	24	0	0	0	0	0	0	0	0	0	0	120	Yellow	267	275	249	272	232
Wayne Gallman	NYG	9	RB	24	0	0	0	56	244	1	16	119	0	0	45	Green	268	218	267	231	267
Alfred Blue	HOU	10	RB	27	0	0	0	71	284	1	10	84	1	1	42	Green	269	220	273	239	273
Kyle Juszczyk	SF	11	RB	27	0	0	0	10	43	0	39	326	1	0	39	Red	270	224	260	241	260
Justin Jackson	LAC	8	RB	23	0	0	0	45	198	1	20	140	1	1	38	Yellow	271	227	271	246	271
Spencer Ware	KC	12	RB	27	0	0	0	51	236	1	9	71	1	1	38	Green	272	228	274	247	274
Mike Gillislee	NE	11	RB	28	0	0	0	63	246	2	7	39	1	1	39	Red	273	229	275	248	275
Jaylen Samuels	PIT	7	RB	22	0	0	0	24	107	0	22	189	1	0	37	Green	274	232	269	251	269
J.D. McKissic	SEA	7	RB	25	0	0	0	25	110	1	22	163	0	1	33	Yellow	275	235	272	255	272

Statistical Appendix

Broken Tackles by Team, Offense

Rk	Team	Plays	Plays w/ BTkl	Pct	Total BTkl
1	NO	957	136	14.2%	161
2	KC	937	125	13.3%	166
3	ATL	947	120	12.7%	144
4	OAK	918	115	12.5%	138
5	JAX	1037	126	12.2%	150
6	TEN	925	111	12.0%	134
7	MIA	953	111	11.6%	136
8	MIN	1005	117	11.6%	137
9	PHI	1018	117	11.5%	142
10	LAR	951	109	11.5%	142
11	CLE	954	109	11.4%	137
12	WAS	932	106	11.4%	128
13	DET	924	105	11.4%	115
14	LAC	983	110	11.2%	135
15	CAR	971	108	11.1%	128
16	SEA	946	105	11.1%	134
17	DAL	964	106	11.0%	131
18	NE	1020	109	10.7%	129
19	PIT	1002	107	10.7%	141
20	CHI	889	94	10.6%	110
21	DEN	1012	105	10.4%	124
22	NYJ	918	95	10.3%	117
23	BAL	1008	103	10.2%	121
24	GB	938	95	10.1%	111
25	IND	925	91	9.8%	104
26	BUF	947	91	9.6%	112
27	SF	1002	89	8.9%	105
28	NYG	995	85	8.5%	97
29	ARI	992	83	8.4%	94
30	HOU	967	75	7.8%	84
31	CIN	868	64	7.4%	75
32	TB	985	70	7.1%	84

Play total includes Defensive Pass Interference.

Broken Tackles by Team, Defense

Rk	Team	Plays	Plays w/ BTkl	Pct	Total BTkl
1	NO	952	72	7.6%	81
2	MIN	908	78	8.6%	85
3	OAK	948	82	8.6%	94
4	NE	966	86	8.9%	100
5	DEN	904	81	9.0%	93
6	TEN	990	89	9.0%	106
7	BAL	992	92	9.3%	104
8	SEA	991	92	9.3%	107
9	IND	985	94	9.5%	107
10	NYJ	1016	97	9.5%	116
11	DAL	949	92	9.7%	110
12	CIN	1040	101	9.7%	114
13	MIA	938	92	9.8%	105
14	GB	963	95	9.9%	110
15	ARI	961	95	9.9%	110
16	HOU	918	92	10.0%	115
17	CHI	944	95	10.1%	108
18	WAS	988	100	10.1%	119
19	CAR	888	90	10.1%	103
20	JAX	923	94	10.2%	111
21	LAR	963	99	10.3%	120
22	NYG	1004	110	11.0%	124
23	PHI	932	104	11.2%	128
24	DET	988	111	11.2%	130
25	ATL	937	106	11.3%	123
26	KC	1001	115	11.5%	138
27	TB	974	112	11.5%	127
28	SF	1015	119	11.7%	138
29	BUF	1015	120	11.8%	144
30	CLE	972	115	11.8%	144
31	LAC	950	126	13.3%	147
32	PIT	874	122	14.0%	149

Play total includes Defensive Pass Interference.

Most Broken Tackles, Defenders

Rk	Player	Team	BTkl	Rk	Player	Team	BTkl	Rk	Player	Team	BTkl
1	J.Schobert	CLE	26	8	K.Fuller	CHI	18	14	E.Kendricks	MIN	16
2	K.Alexander	TB	24	8	R.Parker	KC	18	14	C.Kirksey	CLE	16
3	R.Shazier	PIT	23	8	D.Sorensen	KC	18	14	B.Marshall	DEN	16
4	S.Davis	PIT	21	11	N.Bowman	2TM	17	14	B.Martinez	GB	16
5	J.Davis	DET	20	11	N.Bradham	PHI	17	14	L.Timmons	MIA	16
6	L.Alexander	BUF	19	11	T.Whitehead	DET	17	20	9 tied with		15
6	A.Ogletree	LAR	19	14	D.Johnson	KC	16				

453

Top 20 Defenders, Broken Tackle Rate

Rk	Player	Team	BTkl	Tkl	Rate
1	B.Logan	KC	0	43	0.0%
2	P.Amukamara	CHI	1	46	2.1%
3	J.Casey	TEN	1	40	2.4%
4	B.Wagner	SEA	4	89	4.3%
5	T.Mitchell	KC	2	44	4.3%
6	M.Lattimore	NO	2	43	4.4%
7	P.Posluszny	JAX	2	41	4.7%
8	J.McCourty	CLE	3	54	5.3%
9	S.Gilmore	NE	3	44	6.4%
10	M.Te'o	NO	3	42	6.7%
11	D.Dennard	CIN	4	55	6.8%
12	M.Burnett	GB	3	41	6.8%
13	D.McCourty	NE	6	73	7.6%
14	V.Miller	DEN	4	47	7.8%
15	C.J.Mosley	BAL	8	92	8.0%
16	A.Barr	MIN	4	45	8.2%
17	J.Norman	WAS	4	43	8.5%
18	A.J.Bouye	JAX	5	53	8.6%
19	J.Bostic	IND	5	52	8.8%
19	C.Jones	CHI	5	52	8.8%

Broken Tackles divided by Broken Tackles + Solo Tackles.
Special teams not included; min. 40 Solo Tackles

Bottom 20 Defenders, Broken Tackle Rate

Rk	Player	Team	BTkl	Tkl	Rate
1	K.Alexander	TB	24	56	30.0%
2	R.Shazier	PIT	23	56	29.1%
3	J.Schobert	CLE	26	68	27.7%
3	D.Johnson	KC	16	45	26.2%
5	M.Hilton	PIT	14	41	25.5%
6	A.Ogletree	LAR	19	57	25.0%
7	R.Parker	KC	18	54	25.0%
8	D.Thompson	NYG	15	45	25.0%
9	S.Davis	PIT	21	64	24.7%
10	J.Davis	DET	20	61	24.7%
11	K.Fuller	CHI	18	56	24.3%
12	L.Timmons	MIA	16	52	23.5%
12	D.Sorensen	KC	18	60	23.1%
14	N.Bradham	PHI	17	57	23.0%
15	T.Boston	LAC	13	44	22.8%
16	J.Addae	LAC	15	53	22.1%
17	M.Peters	KC	11	40	21.6%
17	N.Vigil	CIN	11	40	21.6%
19	D.J.Swearinger	WAS	15	55	21.4%
20	J.Taylor	CLE	12	44	21.4%

Broken Tackles divided by Broken Tackles + Solo Tackles.
Special teams not included; min. 40 Solo Tackles

Most Broken Tackles, Running Backs

Rk	Player	Team	BTkl
1	K.Hunt	KC	89
2	L.Bell	PIT	79
2	T.Gurley	LAR	79
4	M.Gordon	LAC	73
5	A.Kamara	NO	66
6	A.Collins	BAL	64
7	L.McCoy	BUF	61
8	D.Lewis	NE	60
8	M.Lynch	OAK	60
10	J.Ajayi	PHI	59
10	D.Freeman	ATL	59
12	M.Ingram	NO	56
13	L.Fournette	JAX	55
14	C.Hyde	SF	52
15	D.Johnson	CLE	51
16	L.Blount	PHI	48
17	C.J.Anderson	DEN	47
17	C.McCaffrey	CAR	47
19	D.Henry	TEN	45
20	J.McKinnon	MIN	43

Most Broken Tackles, WR/TE

Rk	Player	Team	BTkl
1	A.Brown	PIT	29
2	D.Adams	GB	23
2	G.Tate	DET	23
4	D.Bryant	DAL	21
5	T.Hill	KC	19
6	T.Kelce	KC	18
7	T.Austin	LAR	17
7	J.Jones	ATL	17
9	K.Allen	LAC	16
9	V.Davis	WAS	16
11	D.Baldwin	SEA	15
11	C.Kupp	LAR	15
11	J.Landry	MIA	15
14	M.Lee	JAX	14
14	C.Patterson	OAK	14
14	M.Thomas	NO	14
17	R.Matthews	TEN	13
17	A.Wilson	KC	13
19	N.Agholor	PHI	12
19	R.Gronkowski	NE	12

Most Broken Tackles, Quarterbacks

Rk	Player	Team	Behind LOS	Beyond LOS	BTkl		Rk	Player	Team	Behind LOS	Beyond LOS	BTkl
1	C.Newton	CAR	11	24	35		6	R.Wilson	SEA	8	15	23
2	A.Smith	KC	19	10	29		8	M.Stafford	DET	22	0	22
2	C.Wentz	PHI	14	15	29		9	B.Hundley	GB	10	10	20
4	B.Bortles	JAX	21	6	27		10	D.Prescott	DAL	9	10	19
5	D.Kizer	CLE	9	15	24		10	P.Rivers	LAC	19	0	19
6	T.Taylor	BUF	11	12	23							

Best Broken Tackle Rate, Offensive Players (min. 80 touches)

Rk	Player	Team	BTkl	Touch	Rate		Rk	Player	Team	BTkl	Touch	Rate
1	A.Kamara	NO	66	201	32.8%		11	M.Lynch	OAK	60	227	26.4%
2	D.Johnson	CLE	51	156	32.7%		12	J.Ajayi	PHI	59	232	25.4%
3	M.Davis	SEA	25	83	30.1%		12	D.Freeman	ATL	59	232	25.4%
4	A.Brown	PIT	29	101	28.7%		14	D.Washington	OAK	23	91	25.3%
5	D.Lewis	NE	60	212	28.3%		15	A.Morris	DAL	30	122	24.6%
6	C.Thompson	WAS	29	103	28.2%		16	D.Henry	TEN	45	187	24.1%
7	K.Hunt	KC	89	325	27.4%		17	C.McCaffrey	CAR	47	197	23.9%
8	A.Collins	BAL	64	235	27.2%		18	G.Tate	DET	23	97	23.7%
9	D.Cook	MIN	23	85	27.1%		19	K.Drake	MIA	39	165	23.6%
10	L.Blount	PHI	48	181	26.5%		20	T.Cohen	CHI	33	140	23.6%

Top 20 Defenders, Passes Defended

Rk	Player	Team	PD
1	D.Slay	DET	26
2	C.Hayward	LAC	25
3	K.Fuller	CHI	22
4	A.J.Bouye	JAX	20
5	R.Alford	ATL	19
5	T.Mitchell	KC	19
5	P.Robinson	PHI	19
8	K.Crawley	NO	18
8	T.White	BUF	18
10	A.Jackson	TEN	17
10	M.Lattimore	NO	17
10	J.Ramsey	JAX	17
10	B.Roby	DEN	17
14	B.Breeland	WAS	15
14	M.Butler	NE	15
14	S.Griffin	SEA	15
14	W.Jackson	CIN	15
18	K.Byard	TEN	14
18	J.McCourty	CLE	14
18	R.Melvin	IND	14
18	J.Mills	PHI	14
18	T.Williams	LAC	14

Note: Based on the definition given in the Statistical Toolbox, not NFL totals.

Top 20 Defenders, Defeats

Rk	Player	Team	Dfts
1	C.Jones	ARI	33
2	C.Campbell	JAX	32
3	J.Clowney	HOU	31
3	C.Kirksey	CLE	31
5	L.Kuechly	CAR	30
6	D.Jones	ATL	28
6	R.Shazier	PIT	28
8	T.Smith	JAX	27
8	B.Wagner	SEA	27
10	Z.Brown	WAS	26
10	W.Woodyard	TEN	26
12	D.Davis	NYJ	25
12	E.Kendricks	MIN	25
12	V.Miller	DEN	25
12	C.J.Mosley	BAL	25
16	B.Graham	PHI	24
16	B.Martinez	GB	24
18	L.David	TB	23
18	C.Heyward	PIT	23
18	B.Irvin	OAK	23
18	C.Jordan	NO	23
18	D.Lawrence	DAL	23
18	J.Ramsey	JAX	23

Top 20 Defenders, Run Tackles for Loss

Rk	Player	Team	TFL
1	J.Clowney	HOU	15
2	J.Hughes	BUF	13
2	S.Lee	DAL	13
4	J.Burgess	CLE	12
4	C.Jones	ARI	12
4	L.Kuechly	CAR	12
7	Z.Brown	WAS	11
7	A.Hitchens	DAL	11
7	D.Kindred	CLE	11
7	T.Smith	JAX	11
7	B.Wagner	SEA	11
12	M.Bennett	SEA	10
12	V.Curry	PHI	10
12	B.Graham	PHI	10
12	G.Jarrett	ATL	10
16	12 tied with	PHI	9

Top 20 Defenders, Quarterback Hits

Rk	Player	Team	Hits
1	L.Williams	NYJ	23
2	A.Donald	LAR	21
2	C.Jones	ARI	21
2	G.McCoy	TB	21
5	V.Curry	PHI	20
6	D.Buckner	SF	19
7	R.Ayers	TB	18
7	C.Dunlap	CIN	18
7	T.Flowers	NE	18
7	C.Jordan	NO	18
11	M.Bennett	SEA	17
11	Y.Ngakoue	JAX	17
13	C.Campbell	JAX	16
13	J.Casey	TEN	16
13	P.Smith	WAS	16
13	C.Wake	MIA	16
17	S.Acho	CHI	15
17	E.Griffen	MIN	15
17	C.Long	PHI	15
20	5 tied with		14

Top 20 Defenders, QB Knockdowns (Sacks + Hits)

Rk	Defender	Team	KD
1	C.Jones	ARI	38
2	C.Campbell	JAX	33
3	A.Donald	LAR	32
4	C.Jordan	NO	31
5	M.Bennett	SEA	28
5	E.Griffen	MIN	28
5	D.Lawrence	DAL	28
5	C.Wake	MIA	28
9	M.Ingram	LAC	27
9	G.McCoy	TB	27
11	Y.Ngakoue	JAX	26
11	L.Williams	NYJ	26
13	D.Buckner	SF	25
13	C.Dunlap	CIN	25
13	T.Flowers	NE	25
16	J.Bosa	LAC	24
16	J.Clowney	HOU	24
16	V.Curry	PHI	24
16	K.Mack	OAK	24
16	V.Miller	DEN	24

Full credit for whole and half sacks; includes sacks cancelled by penalty. Does not include strip sacks.

Top 20 Defenders, Hurries

Rk	Defender	Team	Hur
1	D.Lawrence	DAL	55.0
2	V.Miller	DEN	53.0
3	K.Mack	OAK	52.0
4	M.Ingram	LAC	50.5
4	J.Sheard	IND	50.5
6	C.Dunlap	CIN	49.5
7	C.Jordan	NO	49.0
8	A.Donald	LAR	48.5
9	T.Suggs	BAL	47.5
10	J.Clowney	HOU	45.0
11	T.Flowers	NE	42.5
12	J.Bosa	LAC	42.0
13	J.Pierre-Paul	NYG	40.0
14	D.Hunter	MIN	39.5
15	M.Bennett	SEA	38.5
15	J.Houston	KC	38.5
17	C.Campbell	JAX	37.0
18	E.Griffen	MIN	36.5
18	C.Jones	ARI	36.5
20	B.Orakpo	TEN	36.0

Top 20 Quarterbacks, QB Hits

Rk	Player	Team	Hits
1	R.Wilson	SEA	93
2	D.Kizer	CLE	80
3	M.Ryan	ATL	74
4	C.Keenum	MIN	68
5	B.Bortles	JAX	64
5	J.Brissett	IND	64
7	K.Cousins	WAS	62
7	P.Rivers	LAC	62
9	D.Prescott	DAL	60
9	C.Wentz	PHI	60
11	T.Brady	NE	59
12	J.McCown	NYJ	52
13	J.Goff	LAR	51
13	M.Stafford	DET	51
15	A.Smith	KC	48
15	J.Winston	TB	48
17	B.Roethlisberger	PIT	46
18	D.Brees	NO	45
18	E.Manning	NYG	45
20	T.Taylor	BUF	44

Top 20 Quarterbacks, QB Knockdowns (Sacks + Hits)

Rk	Player	Team	KD
1	R.Wilson	SEA	139
2	D.Kizer	CLE	118
3	J.Brissett	IND	116
4	K.Cousins	WAS	104
5	M.Ryan	ATL	100
6	T.Brady	NE	94
6	M.Stafford	DET	94
8	J.McCown	NYJ	92
9	D.Prescott	DAL	91
9	C.Wentz	PHI	91
11	C.Keenum	MIN	90
12	T.Taylor	BUF	86
13	A.Smith	KC	85
14	B.Bortles	JAX	84
15	J.Winston	TB	81
16	C.Newton	CAR	76
17	J.Goff	LAR	74
17	E.Manning	NYG	74
17	P.Rivers	LAC	74
20	B.Hundley	GB	73

Includes sacks cancelled by penalties
Does not include strip sacks or "self sacks" with no defender listed.

Top 10 Quarterbacks, Knockdowns per Pass

Rk	Player	Team	KD	Pct
1	C.J.Beathard	SF	60	23.9%
2	T.Savage	HOU	57	21.5%
3	R.Wilson	SEA	139	21.5%
4	J.Brissett	IND	116	21.4%
5	D.Kizer	CLE	118	21.3%
6	C.Palmer	ARI	66	21.3%
7	J.McCown	NYJ	92	20.0%
8	B.Hundley	GB	73	19.9%
9	C.Wentz	PHI	91	18.3%
10	D.Watson	HOU	43	17.8%

Min. 200 passes; includes passes cancelled by penalty

Bottom 10 Quarterbacks in Knockdowns per Pass

Rk	Player	Team	KD	Pct
1	D.Carr	OAK	47	8.2%
2	J.Cutler	MIA	49	10.4%
3	J.Flacco	BAL	65	10.9%
4	B.Roethlisberger	PIT	68	11.0%
5	D.Brees	NO	65	11.2%
6	E.Manning	NYG	74	11.6%
7	A.Dalton	CIN	66	11.7%
8	P.Rivers	LAC	74	11.7%
9	M.Mariota	TEN	67	13.1%
10	C.Newton	CAR	76	13.7%

Min. 200 passes; includes passes cancelled by penalty

Top 10 Most Passes Tipped at Line, Quarterbacks

Rk	Player	Team	Total
1	M.Stafford	DET	19
2	B.Bortles	JAX	15
2	K.Cousins	WAS	15
4	P.Rivers	LAC	12
4	B.Roethlisberger	PIT	12
4	T.Taylor	BUF	12
7	C.Wentz	PHI	11
8	J.Cutler	MIA	10
8	A.Dalton	CIN	10
10	5 tied with		9

Top 10 Tipped at the Line, Defenders

Rk	Player	Team	Total
1	K.Ealy	NYJ	9
1	C.Jordan	NO	9
3	D.Autry	OAK	6
3	C.Dunlap	CIN	6
3	A.Lanier	WAS	6
3	E.Ogbah	CLE	6
7	D.Buckner	SF	5
7	W.Henry	BAL	5
7	D.Irving	DAL	5
7	A.Jones	JAX	5
7	A.Okafor	NO	5
7	A.Robinson	DET	5

2017 Quarterbacks with and without Pass Pressure

Rank	Player	Team	Plays	Pct Pressure	DVOA with Pressure	Yds with Pressure	DVOA w/o Pressure	Yds w/o Pressure	DVOA Dif	Rank
1	D.Brees	NO	562	21.5%	-65.8%	4.1	65.2%	8.4	-131.1%	28
2	B.Roethlisberger	PIT	602	22.9%	-40.5%	5.1	62.2%	8.2	-102.7%	19
3	D.Carr	OAK	554	24.0%	-78.3%	3.8	49.4%	7.5	-127.7%	26
4	M.Mariota	TEN	503	24.1%	-41.0%	3.3	30.4%	7.4	-71.4%	6
5	E.Manning	NYG	611	24.9%	-53.7%	4.0	27.1%	6.0	-80.9%	8
6	J.Flacco	BAL	584	26.5%	-74.9%	2.7	19.7%	6.1	-94.6%	16
7	T.Siemian	DEN	414	28.5%	-112.4%	2.2	26.8%	7.0	-139.2%	32
8	T.Brady	NE	634	28.5%	7.7%	6.1	62.0%	7.7	-54.3%	2
9	A.Dalton	CIN	556	29.3%	-59.9%	2.9	30.4%	7.1	-90.2%	13
10	J.Cutler	MIA	460	29.6%	-41.9%	4.1	23.1%	6.5	-65.0%	3
11	B.Hoyer	2TM	232	30.2%	-60.6%	2.3	14.9%	6.4	-75.5%	7
12	C.Newton	CAR	564	30.3%	-46.1%	3.7	36.5%	7.1	-82.6%	10
13	A.Smith	KC	577	30.3%	-30.4%	4.5	69.6%	8.4	-100.0%	18
14	J.Goff	LAR	518	30.7%	-56.8%	3.5	83.4%	9.2	-140.2%	33
15	C.J.Beathard	SF	256	30.9%	-92.5%	1.4	35.7%	7.2	-128.2%	27
16	J.McCown	NYJ	453	31.1%	-95.0%	2.5	56.6%	8.0	-151.6%	35
17	J.Winston	TB	502	31.5%	-60.0%	3.7	74.3%	8.6	-134.3%	29
18	M.Stafford	DET	638	31.7%	-56.4%	3.7	62.0%	8.4	-118.4%	25
19	M.Ryan	ATL	573	32.3%	-35.8%	4.7	61.4%	8.5	-97.2%	17
20	P.Rivers	LAC	610	32.3%	-23.4%	5.4	80.2%	8.6	-103.6%	21
21	M.Trubisky	CHI	386	33.2%	-99.9%	2.1	46.9%	7.8	-146.8%	34
22	D.Prescott	DAL	562	33.3%	-35.3%	4.5	34.3%	7.2	-69.5%	5
23	A.Rodgers	GB	281	33.8%	-42.8%	3.9	60.0%	7.2	-102.8%	20
24	B.Bortles	JAX	580	34.0%	-47.0%	4.2	45.2%	8.0	-92.2%	15
25	D.Kizer	CLE	568	34.5%	-80.7%	3.1	10.7%	6.8	-91.5%	14
26	C.Wentz	PHI	507	35.3%	-8.1%	5.1	78.4%	7.8	-86.5%	12
27	K.Cousins	WAS	613	35.6%	-55.8%	3.5	60.0%	8.1	-115.8%	23
28	T.Taylor	BUF	512	35.7%	-33.3%	4.8	32.4%	6.3	-65.7%	4
29	C.Palmer	ARI	297	36.0%	-69.7%	3.9	36.6%	7.9	-106.3%	22
30	J.Brissett	IND	560	37.7%	-56.6%	3.3	25.2%	6.9	-81.9%	9
31	B.Hundley	GB	372	38.2%	-83.1%	2.0	32.7%	7.0	-115.8%	24
32	T.Savage	HOU	252	38.5%	-105.4%	2.6	31.2%	7.1	-136.5%	31
33	C.Keenum	MIN	536	39.0%	6.8%	5.6	59.0%	8.1	-52.2%	1
34	R.Wilson	SEA	659	39.8%	-21.0%	4.5	64.6%	7.6	-85.6%	11
35	D.Watson	HOU	248	41.9%	-36.0%	5.6	99.3%	9.5	-135.3%	30

Includes scrambles and Defensive Pass Interference. Does not include aborted snaps.
Minimum: 200 passes.

WR: Highest Slot/Wide Ratio of Targets

Rk	Player	Team	Slot	Wide	Slot%
1	D.Amendola	NE	83	2	98%
2	R.Higgins	CLE	47	3	94%
3	C.Kupp	LAR	88	6	94%
4	B.Ellington	HOU	52	4	93%
5	N.Agholor	PHI	87	7	93%
6	S.Roberts	OAK	61	5	92%
7	C.Beasley	DAL	57	6	90%
8	J.Crowder	WAS	92	11	89%
9	S.Shepard	NYG	74	9	89%
10	K.Wright	CHI	79	10	89%
11	R.Cobb	GB	69	11	86%
12	T.Taylor	SF	51	9	85%
13	A.Humphries	TB	69	13	84%
14	A.Hurns	JAX	47	9	84%
15	R.Woods	LAR	73	14	84%
16	L.Fitzgerald	ARI	133	32	81%
17	D.Baldwin	SEA	97	24	80%
18	G.Tate	DET	95	24	80%
19	M.Sanu	ATL	76	20	79%
20	B.Fowler	DEN	43	13	77%

Min. 50 passes. Slot includes lined up tight.

WR: Highest Wide/Slot Ratio of Targets

Rk	Player	Team	Slot	Wide	Wide%
1	R.Lewis	NYG	10	63	86%
2	D.Parker	MIA	14	83	86%
3	C.Coleman	CLE	10	48	83%
4	D.Hopkins	HOU	36	146	80%
5	A.Brown	PIT	35	134	79%
6	M.Jones	DET	24	90	79%
7	R.Louis	CLE	13	46	78%
8	K.Benjamin	2TM	19	60	76%
9	A.J.Green	CIN	37	109	75%
10	M.Bryant	PIT	23	66	74%
11	C.Davis	TEN	18	47	72%
12	B.Cooks	NE	34	85	71%
13	T.Williams	DAL	24	55	70%
14	J.Doctson	WAS	25	57	70%
15	J.Nelson	ARI	19	43	69%
16	D.Bryant	DAL	43	93	68%
17	M.Wallace	BAL	30	64	68%
18	Z.Jones	BUF	23	49	68%
19	D.Adams	GB	38	79	68%
20	M.Crabtree	OAK	34	70	67%

Min. 50 passes. Slot includes lined up tight.

Top 10 WR Better Lined Up Wide

Rk	Player	Team	Slot	Wide	Slot	Wide	Dif
1	D.Westbrook	JAX	20	31	-57.1%	2.1%	59.2%
2	P.Garcon	SF	37	31	-21.1%	17.2%	38.4%
3	C.Godwin	TB	24	31	-0.3%	38.0%	38.2%
4	A.Thielen	MIN	88	59	-1.1%	27.1%	28.2%
5	T.Hill	KC	45	60	8.8%	36.8%	27.9%
6	D.Thompson	2TM	28	42	-15.8%	8.7%	24.4%
7	T.Ginn	NO	41	28	27.8%	51.5%	23.7%
8	S.Watkins	LAR	34	39	11.5%	34.7%	23.2%
9	T.Williams	DAL	24	55	-17.4%	5.1%	22.6%
10	D.Bryant	DAL	43	93	-28.7%	-6.7%	22.0%

Min. 20 targets from each position

Top 10 WR Better Lined Up in Slot/Tight

Rk	Player	Team	Slot	Wide	Slot	Wide	Dif
1	M.Wallace	BAL	30	64	37.5%	-17.2%	54.8%
2	K.Cole	JAX	45	37	18.4%	-34.9%	53.3%
3	J.Smith-Schuster	PIT	47	33	59.3%	6.5%	52.7%
4	L.Fitzgerald	ARI	133	32	6.8%	-36.4%	43.2%
5	M.Sanu	ATL	76	20	19.8%	-20.2%	40.0%
6	K.Stills	MIA	58	49	18.4%	-21.6%	40.0%
7	E.Sanders	DEN	36	56	5.9%	-33.9%	39.9%
8	R.Matthews	TEN	45	41	32.5%	-2.7%	35.2%
9	J.Brown	ARI	22	35	-1.4%	-36.5%	35.0%
10	J.Kearse	NYJ	72	33	16.1%	-18.8%	34.9%

Min. 20 targets from each position

Top 10 TE Highest Rate of Targets from WR Positions (Slot/Wide)

Rk	Player	Team	Tight	Slot	Wide	Back	WR%
1	A.Gates	LAC	10	41	0	0	80%
2	J.Reed	WAS	8	21	6	0	77%
3	C.Fleener	NO	7	23	0	0	77%
4	T.Burton	PHI	8	21	2	0	74%
5	J.Cook	OAK	24	52	12	0	73%
6	T.Kelce	KC	31	68	20	3	72%
7	J.Graham	SEA	29	41	26	0	70%
8	C.Brate	TB	24	46	6	1	68%
9	J.Witten	DAL	28	57	1	2	66%
10	Z.Miller	CHI	12	22	1	0	66%

Min. 25 passes

Top 10 TE Lowest Rate of Targets from WR Positions (Slot/Wide)

Rk	Player	Team	Tight	Slot	Wide	Back	WR%
1	R.Ellison	NYG	30	1	1	0	6%
2	R.Griffin	HOU	20	2	0	3	8%
3	J.Gresham	ARI	39	7	1	0	17%
4	N.O'Leary	BUF	26	5	1	0	19%
5	J.Smith	TEN	20	3	3	4	20%
6	B.Celek	PHI	20	5	0	0	20%
7	O.J.Howard	TB	30	8	1	0	23%
8	J.James	PIT	48	14	1	0	24%
9	S.Anderson	HOU	40	14	0	0	26%
10	C.Clay	BUF	54	18	3	0	28%

Min. 25 passes

Top 10 RB Highest Rate of Targets from WR Positions (Slot/Wide)

Rk	Player	Team	Back	Slot	Wide	Tight	WR%
1	T.Cohen	CHI	33	23	11	1	50%
2	J.D.McKissic	SEA	23	6	16	0	49%
3	D.J.Foster	ARI	13	8	5	1	48%
4	D.Woodhead	BAL	22	14	2	1	41%
5	C.Sims	TB	30	4	13	0	36%
6	A.Kamara	NO	64	25	9	0	35%
7	C.McCaffrey	CAR	72	24	14	2	34%
8	A.Ekeler	LAC	25	4	7	0	31%
9	R.Burkhead	NE	26	2	9	0	30%
10	T.Coleman	ATL	27	4	7	0	29%

Min. 25 passes

Top 10 Teams, Pct Passes Dropped

Rk	Team	Passes	Drops	Pct
1	NO	529	18	3.4%
2	DET	612	21	3.4%
3	HOU	589	21	3.6%
4	TEN	522	19	3.6%
5	TB	655	27	4.1%
6	NE	612	26	4.2%
7	PIT	608	26	4.3%
8	MIN	556	24	4.3%
9	MIA	615	27	4.4%
10	CAR	543	24	4.4%

Bottom 10 Teams, Pct Passes Dropped

Rk	Team	Passes	Drops	Pct
23	ARI	646	36	5.6%
24	LAC	576	33	5.7%
25	IND	537	32	6.0%
26	ATL	544	34	6.3%
27	PHI	604	38	6.3%
28	JAX	535	34	6.4%
29	SF	632	41	6.5%
30	OAK	576	38	6.6%
31	CHI	507	34	6.7%
32	NYG	628	46	7.3%

Top 20 Players, Passes Dropped

Rk	Player	Team	Total
1	D.Bryant	DAL	10
1	D.Thomas	DEN	10
3	A.Cooper	OAK	9
3	M.Lee	JAX	9
5	N.Agholor	PHI	8
5	K.Allen	LAC	8
5	B.Cooks	NE	8
5	J.Crowder	WAS	8
5	Z.Ertz	PHI	8
5	C.Hyde	SF	8
5	J.Jones	ATL	8
5	T.Smith	PHI	8
13	R.Anderson	NYJ	7
13	M.Crabtree	OAK	7
13	E.Engram	NYG	7
13	M.Evans	TB	7
13	M.Goodwin	SF	7
13	J.Graham	SEA	7
13	D.Harris	KC	7
13	T.Kelce	KC	7
13	G.Kittle	SF	7
13	C.Kupp	LAR	7
13	J.Landry	MIA	7
13	A.Wilson	KC	7

Top 20 Players, Pct. Passes Dropped

Rk	Player	Team	Drops	Passes	Pct
1	D.Martin	TB	4	18	22.2%
2	A.Peterson	2TM	4	19	21.1%
3	D.Harris	KC	7	35	20.0%
4	O.Darkwa	NYG	5	28	17.9%
5	M.Breida	SF	6	37	16.2%
6	M.Lynch	OAK	5	31	16.1%
7	J.Howard	CHI	5	32	15.6%
8	J.Ajayi	2TM	5	34	14.7%
9	O.Beckham	NYG	6	41	14.6%
10	E.Rogers	PIT	5	36	13.9%
11	K.Aiken	IND	6	44	13.6%
12	T.Coleman	ATL	5	39	12.8%
13	R.Shepard	CAR	4	32	12.5%
14	M.Mack	IND	4	33	12.1%
15	J.Williams	GB	4	34	11.8%
16	K.Britt	2TM	5	43	11.6%
17	T.Smith	PHI	8	69	11.6%
18	S.Anderson	HOU	6	52	11.5%
19	L.Kendricks	GB	4	35	11.4%
20	D.Inman	2TM	5	44	11.4%

Min. four drops

Top 20 Yards Lost to Drops by Quarterbacks

Rk	Player	Team	Drops	Yds
1	M.Ryan	ATL	34	317
2	D.Kizer	CLE	29	303
3	B.Bortles	JAX	34	297
4	D.Carr	OAK	36	290
5	K.Cousins	WAS	32	284
6	R.Wilson	SEA	29	251
7	J.Goff	LAR	22	250
8	J.Brissett	IND	32	249
9	J.Flacco	BAL	29	237
9	P.Rivers	LAC	33	237
11	B.Roethlisberger	PIT	24	227
12	D.Prescott	DAL	24	226
13	T.Brady	NE	26	218
14	T.Taylor	BUF	25	212
15	A.Smith	KC	29	205
16	E.Manning	NYG	44	198
17	C.Wentz	PHI	28	193
18	C.Newton	CAR	23	187
19	M.Trubisky	CHI	23	186
20	J.Cutler	MIA	22	184

Based on yardage in the air, no possible YAC included.

Top 20 Intended Receivers on Interceptions

Rk	Player	Team	Total
1	D.Thomas	DEN	9
2	A.J.Green	CIN	7
3	A.Brown	PIT	6
3	D.Hopkins	HOU	6
3	R.Matthews	TEN	6
3	J.Nelson	GB	6
3	D.Parker	MIA	6
8	R.Anderson	NYJ	5
8	D.Bryant	DAL	5
8	A.Cooper	OAK	5
8	B.Fowler	DEN	5
8	R.Higgins	CLE	5
8	R.Lewis	NYG	5
8	J.Nelson	ARI	5
8	K.Stills	MIA	5
16	15 tied with		4

Top 10 Plus/Minus for Running Backs

Rk	Player	Team	Pass	+/-
1	A.Kamara	NO	96	+6.5
2	D.Woodhead	BAL	36	+5.3
3	K.Hunt	KC	61	+4.3
4	D.Johnson	CLE	90	+4.2
5	D.Lewis	NE	34	+4.2
6	M.Ingram	NO	65	+4.0
7	D.Freeman	ATL	41	+3.8
8	L.Miller	HOU	41	+3.7
9	L.McCoy	BUF	72	+3.5
10	K.Juszczyk	SF	39	+3.2

Min. 25 passes; plus/minus adjusted for passes tipped/thrown away.

Bottom 10 Plus/Minus for Running Backs

Rk	Player	Team	Pass	+/-
1	C.Hyde	SF	84	-6.5
2	M.Breida	SF	34	-5.6
3	M.Mack	IND	30	-5.1
4	M.Lynch	OAK	29	-4.0
5	W.Gallman	NYG	46	-3.8
6	A.Collins	BAL	33	-3.8
7	M.Gordon	LAC	74	-3.6
8	I.Crowell	CLE	40	-3.6
9	J.Ajayi	2TM	33	-3.6
10	T.Riddick	DET	70	-3.0

Min. 25 passes; plus/minus adjusted for passes tipped/thrown away.

Top 10 Plus/Minus for Wide Receivers

Rk	Player	Team	Pass	+/-
1	M.Thomas	NO	139	+14.9
2	A.Brown	PIT	152	+12.0
3	T.Ginn	NO	68	+10.0
4	T.Hill	KC	103	+10.0
5	G.Tate	DET	116	+8.6
6	K.Allen	LAC	146	+8.3
7	J.Smith-Schuster	PIT	77	+8.1
8	A.Thielen	MIN	133	+8.1
9	D.Baldwin	SEA	114	+7.7
10	L.Fitzgerald	ARI	153	+7.1

Min. 50 passes; plus/minus adjusted for passes tipped/thrown away.

Bottom 10 Plus/Minus for Wide Receivers

Rk	Player	Team	Pass	+/-
1	Z.Jones	BUF	67	-11.8
2	A.Jeffery	PHI	112	-7.6
3	A.Cooper	OAK	90	-7.6
4	D.Bryant	DAL	126	-7.4
5	E.Sanders	DEN	87	-7.1
6	R.Lewis	NYG	69	-6.8
7	J.Doctson	WAS	72	-6.7
8	J.Brown	ARI	51	-6.4
9	C.Coleman	CLE	52	-6.0
10	B.LaFell	CIN	86	-5.9

Min. 50 passes; plus/minus adjusted for passes tipped/thrown away.

Top 10 Plus/Minus for Tight Ends

Rk	Player	Team	Pass	+/-
1	R.Gronkowski	NE	100	+7.9
2	T.Kelce	KC	116	+7.4
3	D.Walker	TEN	103	+6.7
4	J.Witten	DAL	82	+6.5
5	H.Henry	LAC	61	+5.8
5	A.Hooper	ATL	61	+5.8
7	K.Rudolph	MIN	77	+5.3
8	B.Watson	BAL	78	+4.4
9	T.Burton	PHI	29	+4.3
10	Z.Ertz	PHI	103	+4.0
10	J.Doyle	IND	103	+4.0

Min. 25 passes; plus/minus adjusted for passes tipped/thrown away.

Bottom 10 Plus/Minus for Tight Ends

Rk	Player	Team	Pass	+/-
1	E.Engram	NYG	108	-7.1
2	S.Anderson	HOU	50	-6.8
3	M.Lewis	JAX	45	-5.9
4	R.Seals-Jones	ARI	28	-4.8
5	D.Njoku	CLE	57	-4.1
6	G.Olsen	CAR	34	-4.0
7	D.Harris	KC	33	-4.0
8	J.Graham	SEA	91	-3.8
9	A.Derby	MIA	38	-3.5
10	G.Everett	LAR	30	-3.3

Min. 25 passes; plus/minus adjusted for passes tipped/thrown away.

Top 10 Quarterbacks, Yards Gained on Defensive Pass Interference

Rk	Player	Team	Pen	Yds
1	B.Roethlisberger	PIT	14	299
2	T.Brady	NE	12	287
3	C.Keenum	MIN	14	284
4	P.Rivers	LAC	16	231
5	D.Carr	OAK	10	213
6	D.Prescott	DAL	10	193
6	M.Stafford	DET	9	193
8	C.Wentz	PHI	7	181
9	D.Watson	HOU	8	173
10	J.Goff	LAR	8	161

Top 10 Receivers, Yards Gained on Defensive Pass Interference

Rk	Player	Team	Pen	Yds
1	M.Jones	DET	7	159
2	A.Brown	PIT	6	155
2	D.Hopkins	HOU	11	155
4	B.Cooks	NE	5	141
5	R.Gronkowski	NE	5	126
6	K.Allen	LAC	8	116
7	A.Thielen	MIN	5	115
8	D.Thomas	DEN	6	111
9	S.Diggs	MIN	5	105
10	M.Bryant	PIT	5	101

Top 10 Defenders, Yards Allowed on Defensive Pass Interference

Rk	Player	Team	Pen	Yds
1	D.Kirkpatrick	CIN	6	150
2	D.Johnson	SF	7	92
3	A.Burns	PIT	5	91
4	P.Amukamara	CHI	4	84
5	J.Hawkins	GB	3	81
5	J.Jenkins	NYG	5	81
7	K.Johnson	HOU	4	80
8	R.Cockrell	NYG	3	79
9	E.Apple	NYG	2	77
9	J.Mills	PHI	4	77

Top 20 First Downs/Touchdowns Allowed, Coverage

Rk	Player	Team	1D/TD	Rk	Player	Team	1D/TD
1	A.Jackson	TEN	42	13	A.Brown	DAL	31
2	J.Bradberry	CAR	39	13	K.Fuller	CHI	31
2	T.Mitchell	KC	39	13	B.Skrine	NYJ	31
4	D.Johnson	SF	38	16	K.Alonso	MIA	30
4	T.Johnson	LAR	38	16	R.Smith	TB	30
4	D.Slay	DET	38	16	J.Taylor	CLE	30
7	R.Alford	ATL	37	19	K.Jackson	HOU	29
8	T.Waynes	MIN	36	20	M.Claiborne	NYJ	28
9	M.Butler	NE	35	20	S.Griffin	SEA	28
10	J.Mills	PHI	34	20	D.Kirkpatrick	CIN	28
11	B.Carr	BAL	32	20	X.Rhodes	MIN	28
11	T.J.Carrie	OAK	32				

Includes Defensive Pass Interference.

Top 20 Passing Yards Allowed, Coverage

Rk	Player	Team	Yards	Rk	Player	Team	Yards
1	T.Mitchell	KC	880	11	K.Jackson	HOU	662
2	D.Johnson	SF	843	12	A.Jackson	TEN	659
3	J.Bradberry	CAR	842	13	R.Smith	TB	653
4	T.Waynes	MIN	808	14	J.Joseph	HOU	651
5	M.Butler	NE	804	15	K.Fuller	CHI	645
6	B.Carr	BAL	778	16	R.Alford	ATL	641
7	T.Johnson	LAR	771	17	T.White	BUF	615
8	J.Mills	PHI	759	18	X.Rhodes	MIN	612
9	J.Taylor	CLE	746	19	A.Brown	DAL	597
10	D.Slay	DET	673	20	D.Kirkpatrick	CIN	596

Includes Defensive Pass Interference.

Fewest Yards After Catch Allowed, Coverage by Cornerbacks

Rk	Player	Team	YAC
1	D.Johnson	SF	1.7
2	X.Howard	MIA	1.9
3	J.Ramsey	JAX	1.9
4	A.J.Bouye	JAX	2.0
5	E.Gaines	BUF	2.0
6	V.Hargreaves	TB	2.2
7	C.Tankersley	MIA	2.2
8	B.Skrine	NYJ	2.2
9	B.Roby	DEN	2.2
10	K.Webster	LAR	2.3
11	P.Amukamara	CHI	2.4
12	B.Poole	ATL	2.4
13	K.Jackson	HOU	2.4
14	D.Slay	DET	2.5
15	R.Alford	ATL	2.5
16	S.Griffin	SEA	2.5
17	D.McDonald	OAK	2.5
18	T.Waynes	MIN	2.6
19	D.Roberts	NYJ	2.6
20	M.Peters	KC	2.6

Min. 50 passes or 8 games started.

Most Yards After Catch Allowed, Coverage by Cornerbacks

Rk	Player	Team	YAC
1	J.Joseph	HOU	7.2
2	P.Robinson	PHI	6.7
3	J.Taylor	CLE	6.2
4	C.Harris	DEN	6.0
5	Q.Diggs	DET	5.7
6	J.Norman	WAS	5.2
7	D.Worley	CAR	5.1
8	R.Douglas	PHI	5.1
9	L.Johnson	BUF	5.0
10	R.Robinson	2TM	4.9
11	M.Butler	NE	4.8
12	O.Scandrick	DAL	4.8
13	J.Haden	PIT	4.8
14	D.Dennard	CIN	4.7
15	C.Hayward	LAC	4.6
16	J.Jenkins	NYG	4.5
17	N.Robey	LAR	4.4
17	J.Coleman	SEA	4.4
19	T.Johnson	LAR	4.3
20	L.Ryan	TEN	4.2

Min. 50 passes or 8 games started.

Most Dropped Interceptions, 2015-2017

Rk	Player	Team	2017	2016	2015	Total
1	T.Johnson	STL/LAR	4	1	2	7
1	J.Norman	CAR/WAS	3	3	1	7
3	M.Peters	KC	3	0	3	6
3	E.Weddle	SD/BAL	2	3	1	6
5	K.Alexander	TB	0	1	3	4
5	L.Collins	NYG	1	1	2	4
5	J.Joseph	HOU	3	1	0	4
5	A.Hal	HOU	1	1	2	4
5	D.Rodgers-Cromartie	NYG	0	0	4	4
5	J.Smith	BAL	1	1	2	4

Fewest Avg Yards on Run Tackle, Defensive Line or Edge Rusher

Rk	Player	Team	Tkl	Avg
1	B.Dupree	PIT	26	0.5
2	L.Ogunjobi	CLE	29	0.8
3	J.Hughes	BUF	38	0.8
4	V.Curry	PHI	37	1.1
5	K.Short	CAR	40	1.1
6	G.Jarrett	ATL	42	1.1
7	A.Donald	LAR	29	1.2
8	M.Bennett	SEA	30	1.3
9	M.Hunt	IND	26	1.3
10	V.Miller	DEN	42	1.3
11	C.Jones	ARI	37	1.3
12	B.Logan	KC	47	1.3
13	J.Hankins	IND	40	1.4
14	S.McLendon	NYJ	41	1.4
15	G.McCoy	TB	38	1.4
16	B.Williams	BAL	30	1.5
17	T.Suggs	BAL	32	1.5
18	A.Hicks	CHI	45	1.5
19	A.Okafor	NO	31	1.5
20	F.Rucker	ARI	25	1.5

Min. 25 run tackles

Fewest Avg Yards on Run Tackle, LB

Rk	Player	Team	Tkl	Avg
1	Z.Cunningham	HOU	46	1.9
2	C.James	OAK	29	2.0
3	S.Thompson	CAR	31	2.1
4	J.Burgess	CLE	39	2.2
5	M.Kendricks	PHI	38	2.3
6	K.Alexander	TB	55	2.3
7	C.Munson	NYG	33	2.5
8	S.Lee	DAL	51	2.5
9	M.Milano	BUF	26	2.5
10	R.Foster	SF	48	2.7
10	C.Robertson	NO	43	2.7
10	M.Te'o	NO	43	2.7
13	D.Lee	NYJ	53	2.8
14	T.Smith	JAX	62	2.8
15	C.Allen	MIA	28	2.9
16	N.Bradham	PHI	44	3.0
17	J.Bostic	IND	64	3.0
18	A.Hitchens	DAL	50	3.0
19	K.J.Wright	SEA	68	3.0
20	Z.Brown	WAS	72	3.1

Min. 25 run tackles

Fewest Avg Yards on Run Tackle, DB

Rk	Player	Team	Tkl	Avg
1	D.Kindred	CLE	31	3.5
2	B.McDougald	SEA	38	3.5
3	J.Cyprien	TEN	33	3.8
4	D.King	LAC	25	3.8
5	B.Baker	ARI	22	3.8
6	K.Vaccaro	NO	27	4.0
7	T.Gipson	JAX	36	4.0
8	K.Jackson	HOU	22	4.0
9	K.Chancellor	SEA	26	4.1
10	T.Green	IND	30	4.1
11	J.Addae	LAC	46	4.2
12	D.Johnson	SF	23	4.3
13	J.Adams	NYJ	50	4.3
14	E.Reid	SF	31	4.4
15	H.Smith	MIN	35	4.4
16	S.Williams	CIN	30	4.5
17	P.Chung	NE	28	4.5
18	L.Ryan	TEN	20	4.6
19	T.Waynes	MIN	21	4.6
20	J.Tartt	SF	30	4.7

Min. 20 run tackles

Top 20 Offensive Tackles, Blown Blocks

Rk	Player	Pos	Team	Sacks	All Pass	All Run	Total
1	B.Giacomini	RT	HOU	8.0	33	14	47
2	D.Smith	LT	TB	7.5	33	9	42
3	R.Reiff	LT	MIN	3.5	22	18	40
4	S.Drango	LT	CLE	8.5	33	6	39
5	G.Ifedi	RT	SEA	5.0	27	11	38
5	C.Robinson	LT	JAX	4.0	21	17	38
5	J.Wetzel	RT/LT	ARI	8.0	33	5	38
8	S.Coleman	RT	CLE	6.5	26	10	36
9	A.Villanueva	LT	PIT	6.5	25	10	35
10	G.Bolles	LT	DEN	7.0	28	6	34
10	L.Collins	RT	DAL	4.0	26	8	34
10	R.Okung	LT	LAC	2.0	19	15	34
13	M.Moses	RT	WAS	4.8	26	7	33
14	E.Flowers	LT	NYG	6.0	21	10	31
15	R.Hill	RT	MIN	2.0	16	14	30
15	J.Parnell	RT	JAX	1.0	18	12	30
15	H.Vaitai	LT	PHI	8.5	25	5	30
18	J.Haeg	RT	IND	8.0	19	10	29
18	M.Kalil	LT	CAR	4.5	23	6	29
18	J.Matthews	LT	ATL	2.3	20	9	29
18	N.Solder	LT	NE	5.0	24	5	29

Top 20 Offensive Tackles in Snaps per Blown Block

Rk	Player	Pos	Team	Sacks	All Pass	All Run	Total	Snaps	Snaps per BB
1	J.Thomas	LT	CLE	1.0	1	1	2	445	222.5
2	J.James	RT	MIA	1.0	5	0	5	463	92.6
3	J.Conklin	RT	TEN	0.0	8	6	14	972	69.4
4	D.Bakhtiari	LT	GB	3.5	9	2	11	709	64.5
5	A.Howard	RT	BAL	4.3	16	1	17	1020	60.0
6	R.Stanley	LT	BAL	2.3	11	5	16	952	59.5
7	R.Ramczyk	RT	NO	2.0	8	8	17	927	54.5
8	M.Newhouse	RT	OAK	4.0	9	6	15	784	52.3
9	T.Lewan	LT	TEN	5.5	8	9	17	888	52.2
10	K.Beachum	LT	NYJ	4.5	10	9	19	986	51.9
11	D.Penn	LT	OAK	2.5	8	7	15	769	51.3
12	R.Schraeder	RT	ATL	2.0	6	10	16	782	48.9
13	R.Wagner	RT	DET	4.5	8	7	15	733	48.9
14	L.Tunsil	LT	MIA	5.5	14	4	18	876	48.7
15	C.Leno	LT	CHI	4.3	14	6	20	922	46.1
16	T.Brown	RT	SF	1.5	7	7	14	635	45.4
17	D.Williams	RT	CAR	4.0	20	2	22	989	45.0
18	T.Armstead	LT	NO	3.0	9	2	11	484	44.0
19	M.Remmers	RT	MIN	1.0	8	7	15	630	42.0
20	J.Pugh	RT/LG	NYG	2.0	6	4	10	414	41.4

Minimum: 400 snaps

Top 20 Interior Linemen, Blown Blocks

Rk	Player	Pos	Team	Sacks	All Pass	All Run	Total
1	A.Boone	LG	ARI	4.5	17	19	36
2	J.Vujnovich	LG	IND	4.5	16	18	34
3	K.Wiggins	RG	LAC	3.0	20	13	33
4	A.J.Cann	RG	JAX	1.0	15	17	32
4	P.Elflein	C	MIN	3.0	15	17	32
4	S.Pulley	C	LAC	1.0	14	18	32
7	P.Omameh	LG	JAX	4.0	12	16	28
7	B.Winters	RG	NYJ	2.5	10	18	28
9	X.Su'a-Filo	LG	HOU	8.5	19	8	27
10	W.Johnson	C	NYJ	5.0	14	12	26
11	J.Bitonio	LG	CLE	4.0	15	10	25
11	D.Feeney	LG	LAC	1.0	15	10	25
11	W.Schweitzer	RG	ATL	4.0	10	15	25
11	A.Q.Shipley	C	ARI	5.0	9	16	25
15	N.Easton	LG	MIN	0.0	12	12	24
15	M.Paradis	C	DEN	1.0	10	14	24
15	B.Scherff	RG	WAS	5.3	17	7	24
15	K.Zeitler	RG	CLE	3.5	16	8	24
19	V.Ducasse	RG	BUF	2.5	11	12	23
19	M.Garcia	LG	DEN	3.0	13	10	23
19	J.Sweezy	RG	TB	2.5	8	15	23
19	S.Wisniewski	LG	PHI	1.0	16	7	23

Top 20 Interior Linemen in Snaps per Blown Block

Rk	Player	Pos	Team	Sacks	All Pass	All Run	Total	Snaps	Snaps per BB
1	T.J.Lang	RG	DET	1.0	1	3	4	754	188.5
2	R.Hudson	C	OAK	0.5	2	5	7	944	134.9
3	B.Brooks	RG	PHI	0.0	3	5	8	1001	125.1
4	B.Jones	C	TEN	0.0	1	7	8	973	121.6
5	T.Larsen	C	CAR	0.5	3	3	6	673	112.2
6	A.Norwell	LG	CAR	0.5	7	2	9	989	109.9
7	Z.Fulton	C/G	KC	1.5	3	4	7	743	106.1
8	C.Roullier	C	WAS	0.0	4	0	4	424	106.0
9	R.Leary	RG	DEN	2.5	5	2	7	685	97.9
10	Q.Spain	LG	TEN	3.5	7	2	9	836	92.9
11	A.Mack	C	ATL	1.0	5	6	11	963	87.5
12	L.Duvernay-Tardif	RG	KC	1.0	4	3	7	594	84.9
13	M.Unger	C	NO	2.5	6	5	11	927	84.3
14	J.Kelce	C	PHI	0.5	8	4	12	1007	83.9
15	G.Jackson	RG	OAK	0.0	2	8	10	833	83.3
16	B.Witzmann	LG	KC	1.0	4	6	10	824	82.4
17	R.Bodine	C	CIN	0.0	3	8	11	885	80.5
18	L.Warford	RG	NO	1.0	6	4	10	743	74.3
19	R.Jensen	C	BAL	2.0	7	7	14	1024	73.1
20	J.Sullivan	C	LAR	1.0	6	5	11	796	72.4

Minimum: 400 snaps

Top 20 Tight Ends, Blown Blocks

Rk	Player	Team	Sacks	All Pass	All Run	Total
1	J.Gresham	ARI	1.5	7	10	17
1	T.Niklas	ARI	0.5	5	12	17
1	K.Rudolph	MIN	0.0	5	12	17
4	V.Davis	WAS	0.5	5	11	16
4	J.James	PIT	1.0	2	14	16
6	J.Doyle	IND	2.0	3	12	15
7	T.Higbee	LAR	1.0	4	10	14
7	D.Morgan	MIN	1.0	3	11	14
9	A.Hooper	ATL	0.0	4	9	13
10	R.Ellison	NYG	0.0	0	10	10
10	M.Lewis	JAX	1.0	3	7	10
10	D.Sims	CHI	1.0	2	8	10
13	Z.Ertz	PHI	0.5	1	8	9
13	A.Fasano	MIA	0.0	1	8	9
13	T.Kroft	CIN	2.0	4	5	9
13	N.O'Leary	BUF	1.5	3	6	9
13	J.Smith	TEN	0.0	0	9	9
18	6 tied with					8

Most Penalties, Offense

Rk	Player	Team	Pen	Yds
1	G.Ifedi	SEA	20	120
2	G.Bolles	DEN	15	106
3	S.Coleman	CLE	14	90
4	C.Leno	CHI	13	88
5	C.Robinson	JAX	12	60
5	L.Tunsil	MIA	12	78
7	J.Gresham	ARI	11	80
7	M.Kalil	CAR	11	75
9	L.Johnson	PHI	10	68
9	T.Lewan	TEN	10	60
9	N.Solder	NE	10	80
12	J.Allen	HOU	9	55
12	C.Clark	HOU	9	35
12	E.Flowers	NYG	9	54
12	B.Giacomini	HOU	9	32
12	M.Pouncey	MIA	9	70
12	P.Rivers	LAC	9	81
12	D.Smith	TB	9	70
12	C.Whitehair	CHI	9	70
12	B.Winters	NYJ	9	65
12	B.Witzmann	KC	9	55

Includes declined and offsetting, but not special teams or penalties on turnover returns.

Most False Starts, Offense

Rk	Player	Team	Pen
1	65-G.Ifedi	SEA	9
2	67-L.Tunsil	MIA	8
3	77-T.Brown	SF	6
3	72-C.Leno	CHI	6
3	74-C.Robinson	JAX	6
6	65-L.Johnson	PHI	5
6	84-J.Gresham	ARI	5
6	72-J.Barksdale	LAC	5
6	71-A.Smith	CIN	5
6	79-J.Allen	HOU	5
11	11 tied with		4

Most Penalties, Defense

Rk	Player	Team	Pen	Yds	Rk	Player	Team	Pen	Yds
1	M.Bennett	SEA	14	70	8	X.Howard	MIA	10	98
1	V.Miller	DEN	14	60	11	J.Bosa	LAC	9	79
3	B.Breeland	WAS	13	71	11	A.Brown	DAL	9	69
3	J.Clowney	HOU	13	82	11	B.Carr	BAL	9	76
3	B.Skrine	NYJ	13	105	11	M.Claiborne	NYJ	9	66
3	N.Suh	MIA	13	61	11	D.Fowler	JAX	9	43
7	D.Johnson	SF	12	112	11	T.Johnson	LAR	9	83
8	K.Crawley	NO	10	76	11	K.Vaccaro	NO	9	71
8	D.Godchaux	MIA	10	55	18	13 tied with		8	

Includes declined and offsetting, but not special teams or penalties on turnover returns.

Top 10 Kickers, Gross Kickoff Value over Average

Rk	Player	Team	Kick Pts+	Net Pts+	Kicks
1	H.Butker	KC	+4.1	+5.6	77
2	J.Tucker	BAL	+3.4	+6.6	86
3	C.Catanzaro	NYJ	+2.5	+3.4	63
4	G.Gano	CAR	+2.4	+2.2	81
5	N.Rose	2TM	+2.4	+3.9	45
6	R.Succop	TEN	+1.8	+2.9	79
7	B.Pinion	SF	+1.6	+3.0	77
8	C.Boswell	PIT	+1.5	+5.2	87
9	Z.Gonzalez	CLE	+1.2	-6.1	49
10	D.Hopkins	WAS	+1.2	+3.7	40

Min. 20 kickoffs; squibs and onside not included

Bottom 10 Kickers, Gross Kickoff Value over Average

Rk	Player	Team	Kick Pts+	Net Pts+	Kicks
1	P.Dawson	ARI	-3.5	-5.9	71
2	B.McManus	DEN	-2.7	-9.5	63
3	A.Rosas	NYG	-2.3	-0.8	60
4	K.Forbath	MIN	-2.1	-4.7	85
5	J.Lambo	JAX	-2.1	-0.8	51
6	D.Bailey	DAL	-1.9	+2.1	56
7	P.Murray	TB	-1.7	-14.6	54
8	N.Novak	LAC	-1.3	-4.0	31
9	K.Fairbairn	HOU	-1.2	+0.3	72
10	J.Locke	DET	-1.1	-+1.8	23

Min. 20 kickoffs; squibs and onside not included

Top 10 Punters, Gross Punt Value over Average

Rk	Player	Team	Punt Pts+	Net Pts+	Punts
1	S.Lechler	HOU	+15.8	-10.7	92
2	J.Hekker	LAR	+8.5	+10.3	65
3	T.Morstead	NO	+8.4	+6.5	60
4	B.Kern	TEN	+6.4	+3.0	75
5	A.Lee	ARI	+5.3	-10.0	88
6	B.Colquitt	CLE	+5.2	-10.2	81
7	P.O'Donnell	CHI	+3.4	-12.3	87
8	C.Jones	DAL	+3.3	+16.9	66
9	J.Berry	PIT	+3.2	+3.3	64
10	L.Edwards	NYJ	+3.2	-6.0	94

Min. 20 punts

Bottom 10 Punters, Gross Punt Value over Average

Rk	Player	Team	Punt Pts+	Net Pts+	Punts
1	B.Wing	NYG	-15.6	-16.5	97
2	B.Anger	TB	-8.1	0.2	66
3	B.Nortman	JAX	-7.5	-4.4	88
4	R.Dixon	DEN	-7.5	-9.4	75
5	S.Martin	DET	-6.3	-1.6	41
6	B.Pinion	SF	-5.6	3.6	75
7	D.Jones	PHI	-2.8	+3.4	68
8	C.Schmidt	BUF	-2.7	+4.3	79
9	M.Palardy	CAR	-2.6	+7.8	72
10	M.Haack	MIA	-2.2	+6.6	83

Min. 20 punts

Top 10 Kick Returners, Value over Average

Rk	Player	Team	Pts+	Returns
1	T.Lockett	SEA	+8.4	37
2	A.Kamara	NO	+8.3	10
3	P.Cooper	LAR	+8.3	34
4	D.Lewis	NE	+6.7	22
5	J.Smith-Schuster	PIT	+6.7	8
6	B.Rainey	BAL	+6.5	11
6	C.Moore	BAL	+4.1	12
8	M.Dayes	CLE	+2.4	18
8	C.Patterson	OAK	+2.2	17
10	A.Hunt	KC	+2.2	24

Min. eight returns

Bottom 10 Kick Returners, Value over Average

Rk	Player	Team	Pts+	Returns
1	A.Erickson	CIN	-5.3	32
2	B.Tate	BUF	-4.6	28
3	A.Roberts	ATL	-3.9	38
4	V.Bolden	SF	-3.4	19
5	C.Thompson	HOU	-3.4	16
6	J.Agnew	DET	-3.0	11
7	K.Williams	ARI	-2.7	16
8	J.Natson	NYJ	-2.7	16
9	J.McKinnon	MIN	-2.6	12
10	M.Bryant	PIT	-2.5	9

Min. eight returns

Top 10 Punt Returners, Value over Average

Rk	Player	Team	Pts+	Returns
1	J.Agnew	DET	+17.3	29
2	P.Cooper	LAR	+9.5	32
3	T.Davis	GB	+6.1	24
4	T.Hill	KC	+6.0	25
5	R.Switzer	DAL	+5.9	29
6	J.Mickens	JAX	+5.1	26
7	T.Cohen	CHI	+4.9	29
8	W.Fuller	HOU	+3.9	9
9	M.Campanaro	BAL	+3.6	27
10	B.Tate	BUF	+3.3	20

Min. eight returns

Bottom 10 Punt Returners, Value over Average

Rk	Player	Team	Pts+	Returns
1	J.Richard	OAK	-8.3	26
2	K.Raymond	2TM	-6.2	18
3	J.Natson	NYJ	-5.6	16
4	T.Austin	LAR	-5.4	12
5	J.Crowder	WAS	-5.2	27
6	J.Peppers	CLE	-4.1	30
7	J.Kerley	NYJ	-4.0	16
7	I.McKenzie	DEN	-3.7	21
9	T.Ginn	NO	-3.3	19
10	A.Roberts	ATL	-3.1	27

Min. eight returns

Top 20 Special Teams Plays

Rk	Player	Team	Plays	Rk	Player	Team	Plays
1	N.Dzubnar	LAC	21	8	D.Payne	JAX	12
2	A.Ekeler	LAC	17	8	C.Uzomah	CIN	12
3	B.Baker	ARI	16	13	B.Cunningham	CHI	11
4	R.Miles	NYJ	15	13	K.Grugier-Hill	PHI	11
5	D.Coleman	ATL	14	13	C.Ham	MIN	11
5	M.Davis	LAC	14	13	S.Longa	DET	11
5	C.Fejedelem	CIN	14	13	S.McManis	CHI	11
8	B.Gedeon	MIN	12	13	E.Penny	ARI	11
8	J.Martin	NYJ	12	13	M.Thomas	MIA	11
8	T.Matakevich	PIT	12	13	B.Trawick	TEN	11

Plays = tackles + assists; does not include onside or end-half squib kicks.

Top 10 Offenses, 3-and-out per drive

Rk	Team	Pct
1	PIT	15.6%
2	LAC	16.8%
3	NO	17.6%
4	ATL	17.8%
5	NE	18.7%
6	MIN	19.7%
7	TB	20.3%
8	SF	21.0%
9	DAL	21.1%
10	KC	21.5%

Top 10 Defenses, 3-and-out per drive

Rk	Team	Pct
1	ARI	32.0%
2	DEN	31.2%
3	MIN	29.3%
4	PHI	28.6%
5	JAX	28.4%
6	NYJ	27.4%
7	PIT	26.2%
8	CIN	25.7%
9	BAL	25.4%
10	TEN	25.1%

Top 10 Offenses, Yards per drive

Rk	Team	Yds/Dr
1	NE	39.23
2	ATL	36.87
3	NO	36.19
4	PIT	35.62
5	LAC	35.40
6	KC	34.71
7	TB	33.48
8	MIN	32.73
9	DAL	32.35
10	LAR	32.33

Top 10 Defenses, Yards per drive

Rk	Team	Yds/Dr
1	JAX	22.91
2	DEN	25.00
3	ARI	25.46
4	MIN	25.91
5	PHI	27.48
6	BAL	27.56
7	PIT	28.45
8	SEA	28.48
9	LAR	28.60
10	WAS	28.72

Bottom 10 Offenses, 3-and-out per drive

Rk	Team	Pct
23	CIN	26.1%
24	CAR	26.3%
25	BAL	26.5%
26	HOU	27.7%
27	IND	28.9%
28	NYG	29.3%
29	SEA	29.4%
30	NYJ	29.5%
31	CLE	29.5%
32	CHI	29.7%

Bottom 10 Defenses, 3-and-out per drive

Rk	Team	Pct
23	OAK	22.3%
24	ATL	22.2%
25	GB	21.6%
26	NO	21.1%
27	NE	21.0%
28	KC	20.8%
29	TB	19.2%
30	LAR	18.9%
31	IND	18.9%
32	BUF	18.3%

Bottom 10 Offenses, Yards per drive

Rk	Team	Yds/Dr
23	DEN	27.32
24	BAL	27.14
25	CLE	26.93
26	ARI	26.69
27	MIA	26.47
28	IND	26.30
29	NYG	26.09
30	NYJ	25.98
31	CIN	25.81
32	CHI	25.64

Bottom 10 Defenses, Yards per drive

Rk	Team	Yds/Dr
23	NYG	31.25
24	SF	31.69
25	DAL	32.28
26	BUF	32.47
27	OAK	33.43
28	GB	33.82
29	KC	34.34
30	IND	34.54
31	TB	35.10
32	NE	35.27

Top 10 Offenses, avg LOS to start drive

Rk	Team	LOS
1	BAL	32.3
2	LAR	32.2
3	DAL	30.3
4	DET	29.7
5	PHI	29.6
6	CAR	29.3
7	MIN	29.3
8	KC	29.2
9	ARI	29.1
10	WAS	28.9

Top 10 Defenses, avg LOS to start drive

Rk	Team	LOS
1	NE	24.6
2	DAL	25.3
3	KC	25.5
4	NO	25.6
5	PIT	26.1
6	BAL	26.3
7	IND	27.0
8	LAC	27.0
9	MIN	27.2
10	LAR	27.4

Top 10 Offenses, Points per drive

Rk	Team	Pts/Dr
1	NE	2.69
2	NO	2.44
3	LAR	2.40
4	PHI	2.31
5	PIT	2.27
6	KC	2.26
7	ATL	2.17
8	MIN	2.11
9	DAL	2.08
10	DET	2.03

Top 10 Defenses, Points per drive

Rk	Team	Pts/Dr
1	JAX	1.26
2	MIN	1.39
3	LAC	1.50
4	PHI	1.52
5	BAL	1.56
6	NE	1.65
7	LAR	1.69
8	ARI	1.70
9	SEA	1.71
10	CHI	1.72

Bottom 10 Offenses, avg LOS to start drive

Rk	Team	LOS
23	SF	27.3
24	CIN	27.2
25	CHI	27.1
26	DEN	26.7
27	NYG	26.6
28	CLE	26.6
29	GB	26.2
30	LAC	26.1
31	ATL	26.0
32	HOU	25.2

Bottom 10 Defenses, avg LOS to start drive

Rk	Team	LOS
23	SF	29.0
24	ATL	29.2
25	CIN	29.2
26	HOU	29.5
27	BUF	29.5
28	WAS	30.1
29	CLE	30.2
30	NYG	30.2
31	GB	30.4
32	DEN	32.8

Bottom 10 Offenses, Points per drive

Rk	Team	Pts/Dr
23	HOU	1.63
24	NYJ	1.57
25	CIN	1.54
26	IND	1.47
27	ARI	1.46
28	MIA	1.42
29	DEN	1.40
30	CHI	1.34
31	CLE	1.24
32	NYG	1.24

Bottom 10 Defenses, Points per drive

Rk	Team	Pts/Dr
23	BUF	1.99
24	NYG	2.00
25	CLE	2.06
26	SF	2.07
27	MIA	2.08
28	IND	2.12
29	OAK	2.13
30	TB	2.14
31	HOU	2.18
32	GB	2.22

Top 10 Offenses, Better DVOA with Shotgun

Rk	Team	% Plays Shotgun	DVOA Shot	DVOA Not	Yd/Play Shot	Yd/Play Not	DVOA Dif
1	SEA	62%	25.4%	-29.7%	5.8	4.7	55.1%
2	LAC	67%	25.3%	-15.5%	6.7	4.8	40.8%
3	KC	74%	24.8%	-7.4%	6.4	5.3	32.2%
4	OAK	70%	15.3%	-16.0%	6.3	4.3	31.4%
5	PIT	71%	26.9%	-3.1%	6.6	4.9	29.9%
6	PHI	71%	19.3%	-9.8%	6.1	4.5	29.2%
7	TB	49%	17.1%	-3.9%	6.2	5.3	21.1%
8	NO	49%	33.2%	12.2%	7.2	5.7	21.0%
9	NE	51%	38.3%	17.4%	6.8	5.6	20.9%
10	IND	57%	-9.8%	-26.8%	5.2	4.0	17.0%

Top 10 Offenses, Better DVOA with Play-Action

Rk	Team	% PA	DVOA PA	DVOA No PA	Yd/Play PA	Yd/Play No PA	DVOA Dif
1	MIA	23%	45.6%	-13.7%	7.5	5.2	59.4%
2	TEN	23%	44.2%	-8.0%	8.9	5.2	52.2%
3	JAX	23%	50.9%	1.7%	8.7	6.0	49.2%
4	WAS	21%	55.1%	6.3%	8.3	6.0	48.7%
5	HOU	22%	38.8%	-7.4%	7.7	5.8	46.2%
6	DET	20%	60.6%	15.6%	9.4	6.3	45.0%
7	MIN	30%	69.0%	24.8%	8.8	6.4	44.2%
8	CHI	20%	12.0%	-15.0%	6.0	5.6	27.0%
9	CIN	27%	18.7%	-3.1%	7.5	5.2	21.8%
10	SF	24%	27.5%	6.1%	7.0	5.8	21.4%

Bottom 10 Offenses, Better DVOA with Shotgun

Rk	Team	% Plays Shotgun	DVOA Shot	DVOA Not	Yd/Play Shot	Yd/Play Not	DVOA Dif
23	DEN	65%	-17.9%	-20.7%	5.2	4.5	2.9%
24	LAR	43%	11.0%	11.2%	5.9	6.1	-0.2%
25	CLE	73%	-20.5%	-19.2%	5.2	4.5	-1.3%
26	GB	66%	-0.4%	1.5%	5.2	4.7	-1.9%
27	DAL	53%	4.7%	8.5%	5.7	5.2	-3.7%
28	MIA	70%	-14.7%	-9.6%	5.2	5.0	-5.1%
29	JAX	57%	-4.4%	4.3%	5.7	5.4	-8.7%
30	CHI	53%	-21.6%	-9.5%	5.1	4.8	-12.1%
31	BAL	50%	-11.8%	1.5%	4.5	5.0	-13.3%
32	TEN	56%	-9.7%	5.6%	5.1	5.4	-15.2%

Bottom 10 Offenses, Better DVOA with Play-Action

Rk	Team	% PA	DVOA PA	DVOA No PA	Yd/Play PA	Yd/Play No PA	DVOA Dif
23	BAL	25%	-6.3%	-2.6%	6.4	4.7	-3.7%
24	LAC	18%	40.5%	45.5%	8.4	7.3	-5.0%
25	NYJ	14%	1.3%	6.6%	5.9	5.9	-5.3%
26	PIT	11%	31.5%	37.8%	6.6	7.6	-6.2%
27	NE	28%	39.1%	50.5%	8.1	7.0	-11.4%
28	SEA	23%	22.5%	34.1%	7.6	6.0	-11.6%
29	ARI	17%	-20.0%	-2.4%	6.3	5.7	-17.6%
30	PHI	27%	15.0%	45.5%	6.3	6.5	-30.6%
31	NO	20%	11.8%	42.9%	7.0	7.6	-31.1%
32	OAK	14%	-7.7%	26.3%	5.9	6.6	-34.0%

Top 10 Defenses, Better DVOA vs. Shotgun

Rk	Team	% Plays Shotgun	DVOA Shot	DVOA Not	Yd/Play Shot	Yd/Play Not	DVOA Dif
1	BAL	67%	-24.8%	5.3%	5.0	5.4	-30.0%
2	JAX	58%	-27.6%	-2.6%	4.3	5.3	-25.0%
3	WAS	57%	-9.4%	0.2%	5.6	5.2	-9.6%
4	MIN	61%	-17.6%	-9.1%	4.9	4.6	-8.5%
5	HOU	55%	3.9%	7.4%	5.9	6.1	-3.4%
6	BUF	56%	0.4%	2.9%	5.8	5.1	-2.6%
7	PIT	63%	-6.9%	-5.8%	5.4	5.3	-1.1%
8	DET	59%	4.7%	3.1%	5.9	5.5	1.6%
9	CHI	61%	-0.7%	-2.6%	5.6	4.9	1.9%
10	SEA	57%	-2.7%	-5.0%	5.5	4.6	2.3%

Top 10 Defenses, Better DVOA vs. Play-Action

Rk	Team	% PA	DVOA PA	DVOA No PA	Yd/Play PA	Yd/Play No PA	DVOA Dif
1	CAR	20%	-42.7%	8.3%	4.9	6.6	-51.0%
2	TB	22%	9.4%	33.7%	7.5	7.3	-24.3%
3	CIN	21%	-1.4%	15.1%	5.4	6.0	-16.4%
4	NYG	27%	4.6%	19.1%	7.1	7.2	-14.5%
5	OAK	23%	16.5%	30.0%	8.0	6.6	-13.5%
6	SF	23%	14.0%	26.3%	7.1	6.5	-12.3%
7	DET	21%	5.9%	11.9%	6.6	6.7	-6.0%
8	NO	20%	-8.2%	-5.4%	6.5	6.3	-2.8%
9	MIN	22%	-14.1%	-11.6%	5.7	5.3	-2.5%
10	TEN	19%	20.3%	18.5%	6.9	5.8	1.8%

Bottom 10 Defenses, Better DVOA vs. Shotgun

Rk	Team	% Plays Shotgun	DVOA Shot	DVOA Not	Yd/Play Shot	Yd/Play Not	DVOA Dif
23	DAL	61%	14.1%	-5.7%	5.8	4.5	19.8%
24	OAK	61%	18.9%	-1.4%	6.0	5.4	20.4%
25	CLE	58%	11.8%	-9.9%	5.9	4.5	21.7%
26	PHI	67%	-3.0%	-28.5%	5.7	4.1	25.5%
27	IND	51%	22.7%	-4.1%	6.3	5.4	26.8%
28	SF	53%	21.7%	-5.2%	6.0	4.9	26.9%
29	GB	56%	18.1%	-9.7%	6.2	4.9	27.7%
30	CAR	57%	4.2%	-24.0%	6.1	4.6	28.2%
31	NYJ	57%	17.2%	-11.4%	6.3	4.4	28.5%
32	DEN	66%	7.2%	-26.6%	5.7	3.8	33.7%

Bottom 10 Defenses, Better DVOA vs. Play-Action

Rk	Team	% PA	DVOA PA	DVOA No PA	Yd/Play PA	Yd/Play No PA	DVOA Dif
23	JAX	17%	-5.0%	-29.2%	6.9	4.5	24.2%
24	MIA	22%	44.9%	18.8%	7.8	6.2	26.1%
25	CLE	26%	44.5%	16.6%	8.0	6.5	27.9%
26	LAC	24%	19.2%	-12.6%	6.9	5.4	31.8%
27	CHI	19%	32.1%	-1.1%	7.4	5.8	33.1%
28	PIT	22%	33.3%	-16.8%	9.1	5.1	50.1%
29	DEN	18%	51.4%	-1.2%	8.1	5.7	52.7%
30	HOU	22%	61.1%	5.8%	10.3	6.5	55.3%
31	BAL	20%	31.0%	-25.5%	7.2	5.4	56.5%
32	ARI	23%	40.4%	-18.8%	8.7	5.0	59.2%

2017 Defenses with and without Pass Pressure

Rank	Team	Plays	Pct Pressure	DVOA with Pressure	Yds with Pressure	DVOA w/o Pressure	Yds w/o Pressure	DVOA Dif	Rank
1	WAS	609	38.3%	-74.3%	3.8	36.0%	7.5	-110.3%	25
2	DAL	632	36.1%	-36.1%	4.2	42.1%	6.9	-78.1%	10
3	JAX	593	35.2%	-98.8%	2.4	14.3%	6.3	-113.1%	26
4	CIN	646	34.8%	-67.8%	2.3	53.0%	7.8	-120.7%	30
5	PIT	580	34.8%	-75.4%	2.7	34.0%	7.7	-109.3%	24
6	CAR	637	34.5%	-60.9%	3.8	26.4%	7.6	-87.3%	14
7	DEN	553	33.6%	-31.7%	4.2	29.4%	7.2	-61.1%	2
8	PHI	671	33.5%	-82.5%	3.0	37.8%	7.4	-120.4%	29
9	IND	563	33.0%	-20.6%	5.1	52.8%	8.7	-73.4%	8
10	NO	633	32.5%	-67.3%	3.9	24.4%	7.6	-91.7%	16
11	LAR	635	32.4%	-69.2%	3.2	16.7%	7.2	-85.9%	12
12	TEN	672	32.1%	-47.0%	2.8	47.9%	7.5	-95.0%	18
13	SEA	626	31.9%	-60.7%	3.6	32.5%	6.8	-93.1%	17
14	MIN	613	31.8%	-86.1%	2.3	20.4%	6.8	-106.4%	23
15	CLE	589	31.6%	-17.9%	5.5	44.1%	7.5	-62.0%	3
16	NYJ	613	31.3%	-27.9%	5.0	39.2%	7.5	-67.1%	6
17	KC	639	31.3%	-39.1%	4.6	47.9%	8.0	-87.0%	13
18	LAC	599	31.1%	-72.2%	3.6	25.8%	6.7	-98.0%	20
19	ATL	622	30.7%	-52.9%	3.6	49.1%	7.2	-102.0%	22
20	ARI	626	30.7%	-71.8%	2.9	25.3%	7.2	-97.1%	19
21	BAL	640	30.6%	-100.2%	2.5	24.7%	7.3	-124.9%	32
22	CHI	598	30.6%	-42.3%	4.3	27.0%	6.9	-69.2%	7
23	SF	609	30.5%	-22.4%	4.9	43.2%	7.5	-65.6%	5
24	HOU	566	29.9%	-25.5%	5.9	39.1%	7.9	-64.6%	4
25	NYG	620	29.8%	-48.5%	4.1	42.6%	8.5	-91.1%	15
26	GB	575	29.7%	-62.1%	3.3	59.5%	8.6	-121.6%	31
27	DET	631	29.0%	-76.1%	3.4	43.2%	8.0	-119.3%	28
28	NE	659	28.8%	-36.3%	4.7	40.7%	7.4	-77.1%	9
29	OAK	587	28.4%	-55.4%	3.8	59.4%	8.2	-114.8%	27
30	MIA	581	28.4%	-46.4%	3.4	52.8%	7.9	-99.2%	21
31	BUF	627	27.9%	-57.3%	3.9	23.5%	7.1	-80.8%	11
32	TB	600	26.0%	-17.5%	6.1	43.3%	7.8	-60.7%	1
	NFL AVERAGE	614	31.6%	-55.5%	3.8	37.5%	7.5	-93.0%	

Includes scrambles and Defensive Pass Interference. Does not include aborted snaps.

Author Bios

Editor-in-Chief and NFL Statistician

Aaron Schatz is the creator of FootballOutsiders.com and the proprietary NFL statistics within *Football Outsiders Almanac*, including DVOA, DYAR, adjusted line yards. He is responsible each year for both the Football Outsiders NFL team projections and the KUBIAK fantasy football projections. He writes regularly for ESPN Insider and *ESPN The Magazine*, and he has done custom research for a number of NFL teams. *The New York Times Magazine* referred to him as "the Bill James of football." Readers should feel free to blame everything in this book on the fact that he went to high school six miles from Gillette Stadium before detouring through Brown University and eventually landing in Natick, Massachusetts, where the road by the movie theater really is named Flutie Pass. He promises that someday Bill Belichick will retire, the Patriots will be awful, and he will write very mean and nasty things about them.

Layout and Design

Vincent Verhei has been a writer and editor for Football Outsiders since 2007. In addition to writing for *Football Outsiders Almanac 2018*, he did all layout and design on the book. During the season, he writes the "Quick Reads" column covering the best and worst players of each week according to Football Outsiders metrics. His writings have also appeared in *ESPN The Magazine* and in Maple Street Press publications, and he has done layout on a number of other books for Football Outsiders and Prospectus Entertainment Ventures. His other night job is as a writer and podcast host for pro wrestling/MMA website Figurefouronline.com. He is a graduate of Western Washington University.

College Football Statisticians

Bill Connelly has contributed college football play-by-play stats to Football Outsiders for the past decade. He's also the College Sports Editor and Analytics Director for SB Nation, where he runs the college football blog Football Study Hall. His most recent book, *The 50 Best* College Football Teams of All-Time*, was released in 2017. He grew up a numbers and sports nerd in western Oklahoma, but now lives in Missouri with his wife, pets, and young daughter.

Brian Fremeau has been analyzing college football drive stats for Football Outsiders since 2006. A lifelong Fighting Irish fan, Brian can be found every home football Saturday in Notre Dame Stadium. He can be found there every day, in fact, due to his campus facility operations responsibilities. He lives in South Bend, Indiana with his wife and two daughters.

Contributors

An economist by trade, **Ben Baldwin** uses large datasets to try to learn about human behavior. He also covers the Seahawks for The Athletic Seattle.

Ian Boyd is a history major graduate from the University of Texas, now based in southeast Michigan, who loves studying the trends and stories of college football. You can also find his work at the websites Inside Texas and Football Study Hall.

Tom Gower joined the FO writing staff in 2009. He has degrees from Georgetown University and the University of Chicago, whose football programs have combined for an Orange Bowl appearance and seven Big Ten Titles but are still trying to find success after Pearl Harbor. His work has also appeared at NBCSports.com, NBC Sports World, ESPN.com, and in *ESPN The Magazine*. He roots for the Tennessee Titans from the Chicago suburbs.

Scott Kacsmar has covered the NFL as a full-time analyst since 2011. He joined Football Outsiders as an Assistant Editor in 2013. Some of his unique contributions include the first standardized database of fourth-quarter comebacks and game-winning drives, quantifying catch radius and ALEX. He will not stop writing about the value of drive stats, the dominance of the quarterback sneak, and he continues to help the NFL fix the most mundane of statistical errors, such as Tony Graziani's 1998 rushing totals. His work has appeared on SI.com, Bleacher Report, ESPN Insider, FiveThirtyEight.com, and NFL Network. Scott lives near Pittsburgh and has an Industrial Engineering degree from the University of Pittsburgh.

Derrik Klassen is from the Central Valley of California, though he grew up near Tampa Bay, Florida. Covering the NFL draft gave him his start but studying the NFL itself has taken precedent. He has been published at SB Nation and Bleacher Report, and has worked for Optimum Scouting, doing charting and scouting reports for their NFL Draft Guide.

Bryan Knowles grew up watching Joe Montana and Steve Young ply their trade at quarterback, so he has somewhat overly-inflated expectations of how quarterbacks should perform. This has certainly done him no favors over the past decade or so of watching the San Francisco 49ers. A graduate of UC Davis and San Jose State University, he has opted to eschew all the useful advice those august institutions have supplied him with and become a sportswriter instead. He's also written for Bleacher Report and Fansided, and currently lives in Chicago with a wife who for some reason puts up with him.

Rivers McCown has written for ESPN.com, Bleacher Report, *USA Today*, and Deadspin, among other places. He's edited for Football Outsiders, *Rookie Scouting Portfolio*, and *Pre-Snap Reads Quarterback Catalogue*. He lives in Houston, Texas with his wife, under the control of two cats and two birds. He wants more jobs, and if you don't give them to him, he'll be forced to keep speedrunning video games and helping design randomizer hacks for them.

Charles McDonald covers the NFL for the Football Outsiders Film Room. He is also an NFL reporter for Bleacher Report and hosts the *Setting The Edge* podcast. He currently lives in Baltimore.

Chad Peltier was raised to be an Ohio State fan, but four years of "Run the damn ball, Bobo!" at the University of Georgia and living in Athens have made him a Bulldawg fan as well. In addition to writing two columns on college football at Football Outsiders, Chad also contributes to the SB Nation blogs Land Grant Holy Land and Football Study Hall. He currently lives in New Haven, Connecticut, working in aerospace and defense, but misses SEC country.

Anglo-Scot (so, Briton) **Andrew Potter** blames Mega Drive classics John Madden Football and Joe Montana Sports Talk Football for his Transatlantic love of the gridiron game. He joined Football Outsiders in 2013 to help with the infamous Twitter Audibles experiment, and still compiles Audibles at the Line to this day. He also authors the weekly Injury Aftermath report and co-authors Scramble for the Ball with Bryan Knowles. Though outwardly a fan of the New Orleans Saints, inwardly the Angus resident still yearns for his first gridiron love: NFL Europe's Scottish Claymores.

Mike Tanier has been writing for Football Outsiders publications for 14 years and is now entering his fifth season as an NFL lead columnist for Bleacher Report. He previously wrote for *The New York Times*, Sports on Earth, Fox Sports and gobs of other magazines and websites. He's the father of two black belts, husband of a Teacher of the Year award winner, and lifelong fan of the reigning Super Bowl champions.

Robert Weintraub is the author of the *New York Times* bestseller *No Better Friend: One Man, One Dog, and their Extraordinary Story of Courage and Survival in WWII*, as well as *The Victory Season* and *The House That Ruth Built*. He has also been a regular contributor to Sports on Earth, Slate, Grantland, *Columbia Journalism Review*, and *The New York Times*.

Carl Yedor was born and raised in Seattle, Washington, and his first vivid football memory was "We want the ball, and we're going to score." As an undergrad at Georgetown University, he worked with the varsity football team to implement football research into their strategy and game planning, drawing on his coursework in statistics and his high school experience as an undersized offensive guard and inside linebacker. He lives in Arlington, Virginia.

Acknowledgements

We want to thank all the Football Outsiders readers, all the people in the media who have helped to spread the word about our website and books, and all the people in the NFL who have shown interest in our work. This is our 14th annual book as part of the *Pro Football Prospectus* or *Football Outsiders Almanac* series. We couldn't do this if we were just one guy, or without the help and/or support from all these people:

- FootballOutsiders.com Technical Director Dave Bernreuther.
- Cale Clinton, the intern responsible for compiling both The Week in Quotes on our website and The Year in Quotes in this book.
- Mike Harris for help with the season simulation.
- Premium programmer Sean McCall, Excel macro master John Argentiero, and drive stats guru Jim Armstrong.
- Our offensive line guru Ben Muth and injury guru Zach Binney.
- Nathan Forster, creator of SackSEER and BackCAST, who is also responsible for improvements on Playmaker Score (originally created by Vincent Verhei).
- Jason McKinley, creator of Offensive Line Continuity Score.
- Jeremy Snyder, our incredibly prolific transcriber of old play-by-play gamebooks.
- Roland Beech, formerly of TwoMinuteWarning.com, who came up with the original ideas behind our individual defensive stats.
- Sharon Farnell, for this year's cover art.
- Our editors at ESPN.com and *ESPN The Magazine*, in particular Tim Kavanagh.
- Our friends at Sports Info Solutions who have really expanded what we can do with game charting, particularly Dan Foehrenbach and Matt Manocherian.
- Bill Simmons, for constantly promoting us on his podcast, and Peter King, for lots of promotion on The MMQB.
- Michael Katzenoff at the NFL, for responding to our endless questions about specific items in the official play-by-play.
- All the friends we've made on coaching staffs and in front offices across the National Football League, who generally don't want to be mentioned by name. You know who you are.
- Our comrades in the revolution: Doug Drinen (creator of the indispensable Pro Football Reference), Bill Barnwell (our long lost brother), Brian Burke and the guys from ESPN Stats & Information, Neil Paine, Robert Mays, Danny Kelly, Kevin Clark, and K.C. Joyner,

plus the kids at Numberfire, the football guys from footballguys.com, and our friends at Prospectus Entertainment Ventures.

- Also, our scouting buddies, including Andy Benoit, Chris Brown, Greg Cosell, Doug Farrar, Russ Lande, and Matt Waldman.
- Joe Alread, Justin Patel, and William Schautz, who handle the special Football Outsiders cards in Madden Ultimate Team, and the other folks at EA Sports who make FO a part of the Madden universe.
- Interns who helped prepare data over the past year or for this book specifically, including Ted Baas, Dan Kohan, Evan LeBlanc, and Mike Valverde.

As always, thanks to our family and friends for putting up with this nonsense.

And a very special thank you to our new partners at EdjSports. We look forward to growing Football Outsiders in the future together.

—Aaron Schatz

Follow Football Outsiders on Twitter

Follow the official account announcing new Football Outsiders articles at @fboutsiders. You can follow other FO and *FOA 2018* writers at these Twitter addresses:

Ben Baldwin: @BenBBaldwin
Zachary Binney: @zbinney_NFLinj
Ian Boyd: @Ian_A_Boyd
Bill Connelly: @SBN_BillC
Brian Fremeau: @bcfremeau
Tom Gower: @ThomasGower
Scott Kacsmar: @FO_ScottKacsmar
Derrik Klassen: @QBKlass
Bryan Knowles: @BryKno
Rivers McCown: @RiversMcCown
Charles McDonald: @FourVerts
Ben Muth: @FO_WordofMuth
Chad Peltier: @cgpeltier
Andrew Potter: @bighairyandy
Aaron Schatz: @FO_ASchatz
Mike Tanier: @MikeTanier
Vince Verhei: @FO_VVerhei
Robert Weintraub: @robwein
Carl Yedor: @CarlYedor61

Follow Football Outsiders on Facebook

https://www.facebook.com/footballoutsiders

About Sports Info Solutions

The mission of Sports Info Solutions (SIS) is to provide the most accurate, in-depth, timely professional sports data, including cutting-edge research and analysis, striving to educate professional teams and the public about sports analytics. SIS is thrilled to work with nearly every Major League Baseball team and a growing number of National Football League teams in service of that goal.

SIS opened its doors back in 2002 and has been on the leading edge of the advanced statistical study of sports ever since. The early years were dedicated to pioneering the analytical landscape in baseball, where SIS successfully played a large role in the growth of trends such as defensive shifting. More recently, SIS recognized the growing need for football analytics and launched a new operation to mirror its industry-leading baseball data collection operation.

That operation began with a partnership with Football Outsiders in 2015, one that continues to propel the industry forward by linking the most comprehensive, objective data provider with the most reputable source for football analysis.

SIS has built its success thanks to its staff of expert scouts and an army of highly trained video scouts who chart thousands of NFL, FBS, MLB, and MiLB games annually. SIS collects valuable data that cannot be found any place else, and each game is reviewed multiple times to ensure that the data is as accurate as possible. The company records everything from basic box score data to advanced defensive coverages and route information. The company's analysts and programmers dissect the data, producing a variety of predictive studies and analytics that are used by high-profile clients throughout the sports industry.

Sports Info Solutions was founded by John Dewan, who has been a leader in baseball analytics for more than 25 years. From his first partnership with Bill James as the Executive Director of Project Scoresheet to co-founding STATS, Inc. and his 15-year tenure as CEO, companies under John's leadership have continually broken new ground in sports data and analytics.

41 South 2nd Street   Coplay, PA 18037   610.261.2370   FAX 610.261.2307   www.SportsInfoSolutions.com

28645976R00286

Printed in Poland
by Amazon Fulfillment
Poland Sp. z o.o., Wrocław